FIELDING'S
WORLDWIDE
CRUISES
1997

The Buzz About Fielding...

Fielding Worldwide

"The new Fielding guidebook style mirrors the style of the company's new publisher: irreverent, urbane, adventuresome and in search of the unique travel experience."
—*San Diego Union Tribune*

"Sharp, energetic and savvy."
—*Des Moines Register*

"Individualistic, entertaining, comprehensive."
—*Consumers Digest*

"Guidebooks straight from the hip."
—*Cincinnati Enquirer*

"Guidebooks with attitude."
—*Dallas Morning News*

"Full of author's tips and asides, the books seem more personal and more credible than many similarly encyclopedic tomes."
—*Los Angeles Times*

"At Fielding Worldwide, adventurous might well be the order of the day."
—*Des Moines Register*

"Biting travel guides give readers a fresh look."
—*Houston Chronicle*

"For over 30 years Fielding guides have been the standard of modern travel books."
—*Observer Times*

"These guidebooks have attitude."
—*Tampa Tribune*

"Guidebooks not afraid to show honesty."
—*Desert News, Salt Lake City*

"The Fielding travel book empire seems to be thriving. Handsome, freshly revised guides are appearing under the imprint almost monthly and, in the best Fielding tradition, they are detailed, opinionated and authoritative."
—*Los Angeles Times*

Fielding's Las Vegas Agenda

"A concise but detailed look at the capital of glitter and gambling."
—*Atlanta Journal Constitution*

Fielding's Los Angeles Agenda

"...contains much more than the standard travel guide. The lists of theatres, sports arenas and attractions are worth the book's price by itself."
—*Baton Rouge Advocate*

Fielding's New York Agenda

"Loaded with advice...puts the whole of the Big Apple in hand."
—*Bon Appetit*

"It's a little like having a sassy lifelong friend in Manhattan take charge."
—*New York Times*

Fielding's Guide to Worldwide Cruises

" ...Lots of tips and inside information on each ship ... valuable beginner's information on the cruise life and choosing a cruise. Very detailed."
—*Los Angeles Times*

" ... Whereas the term 'expert' is thrown about with abandon when it comes to travel writing, these two are the real deal. Harry and Shirley are cruise *experts*.'"
—*Salt Lake City Tribune*

"... a fresh sea breeze blowing in cruise guidebooks ... a witty, pithy departure from the norm ..."
—*Vacations Magazine*

" ... insightful, always independent, frequently witty and occasionally irreverent personal reviews..."
—*Cruise and Vacation Views*

"You can trust them [Fielding] to tell the truth. It's fun—and very informative."
—*New Orleans Times-Picayune*

" ... If you have space for only one cruise guidebook in your library, it should be this one."
—*Cruise Travel Magazine*

Cruise Insider

"One of the best, most compact, yet interesting books about cruising today is the fact-filled *Cruise Insider*."
—*John Clayton's Travel With a Difference*

Fielding's The World's Most Dangerous Places

"Rarely does a travel guide turn out to be as irresistible as a John Grisham novel. But *The World's Most Dangerous Places*, a 1000-page tome for the truly adventurous traveler, manages to do just that."
—*Arkansas Democrat-Gazette*

"A travel guide that could be a real lifesaver. Practical tips for those seeking the road less traveled."

—Time Magazine

"The greatest derring do of this year's memoirs."

—Publishers Weekly

"Reads like a first-run adventure movie."

—Travel Books Worldwide

"One of the oddest and most fascinating travel books to appear in a long time."

—New York Times

"...publishing terra incognito...a primer on how to get in and out of potentially lethal places."

—U.S. News and World Report

"Tired of the same old beach vacation?...this book may be just the antidote."

—USA Today

"Guide to hot spots will keep travelers glued to their armchairs."

—The Vancouver Sun

Fielding's Borneo

"One of a kind...a guide that reads like an adventure story."

—San Diego Union

Fielding's Budget Europe

"This is a guide to great times, great buys and discovery in 18 countries."

—Monroe News-Star

"...meticulous detail...incisive commentary."

—Travel Europe

Fielding's Caribbean

"If you have trouble deciding which regional guidebook to reach for, you can't go wrong with *Fielding's Caribbean*."

—Washington Times

"Opinionated, clearly written and probably the only guide that any visitor to the Caribbean really needs."

—New York Times

Fielding's Europe

"Synonymous with the dissemination of travel information for five decades."

—Traveller's Bookcase

"The definitive Europe... shame on you if you don't read it before you leave."

—Travel Europe

Fielding's Far East

"This well-respected guide is thoroughly updated and checked out."

—The Reader Review

Fielding's France

"Winner of the annual 'Award of Excellence' [with Michelin and Dorling Kindersley]."

—FrancePresse

Fielding's Freewheelin' USA

"...an informative, thorough and entertaining 400-page guide to the sometimes maligned world of recreational vehicle travel."

—Travel Weekly

"...very comprehensive... lots more fun than most guides of this sort..."

—Los Angeles Times

Fielding's Italy

"A good investment...contains excellent tips on driving, touring, cities, etc."

—Travel Savvy

Fielding's Mexico

"Among the very best."

—Library Journal

Fielding's Spain and Portugal

"Our best sources of information were fellow tour-goers and *Fielding's Spain and Portugal*."

—New York Times

Vacation Places Rated

"...can best be described as a thinking person's guide if used to its fullest."

—Chicago Tribune

"Tells how 13,500 veteran vacationers rate destinations for satisfaction and how well a destination delivers on what is promised."

—USA Today

Fielding's Vietnam

"Fielding has the answer to every conceivable question."

—Destination Vietnam

"An important book about an important country."

—NPR Business Radio

"Informative, up to date, irreverent. Get it before you go."

—Automobile

"Excellent, the guide to consult before you go."

—Reader's Review

Fielding Titles

FIELDING'S WORLDWIDE CRUISES 1997

Shirley Slater
and
Harry Basch

Fielding Worldwide, Inc.
308 South Catalina Avenue
Redondo Beach, California 90277 U.S.A.

Fielding's Worldwide Cruises 1996

Published by Fielding Worldwide, Inc.

Text Copyright ©1996 FWI

Icons & Illustrations Copyright ©1996 FWI

Photo Copyrights ©1996 to Individual Photographers

FIELDING WORLDWIDE INC.

PUBLISHER AND CEO **Robert Young Pelton**
GENERAL MANAGER **John Guillebeaux**
MARKETING DIRECTOR **Paul T. Snapp**
OPERATIONS DIRECTOR **George Posanke**
ELECTRONIC PUBLISHING DIRECTOR **Larry E. Hart**
PUBLIC RELATIONS DIRECTOR **Beverly Riess**
ACCOUNT SERVICES MANAGER **Christy Harp**
PROJECT MANAGER **Chris Snyder**

EDITORS

Kathy Knoles   **Linda Charlton**
Laurel Ornitz

PRODUCTION

Martin Mancha   **Ramses Reynoso**
Alfredo Mercado   **Craig South**
COVER DESIGNED BY **Digital Artists, Inc.**
COVER PHOTOGRAPHERS—Front cover **Royal Caribbean Cruises, Ltd.**
Back cover **Windstar Cruises**
INSIDE PHOTOS **Harry Basch, Shirley Slater**
AUTHORS' PHOTO **Colin Bessonette**

Inquiries should be addressed to: Fielding Worldwide, Inc., 308 South Catalina Ave., Redondo Beach, California 90277 U.S.A., Telephone *(310) 372-4474*, Facsimile *(310) 376-8064*, 8:30 a.m.–5:30 p.m. Pacific Standard Time.
Web site: http://www.fieldingtravel.com
e-mail: fielding@fielding.com

ISBN 1-56952-115-8

Printed in the United States of America

DEDICATION

To Edwin Self, founder of *San Diego Magazine*, a gentleman and a scholar, who published our first cruise story in 1979.

And Jerry Hulse, former travel editor of the *Los Angeles Times*, who, when he ordered our column "Cruise Views" in 1983, said, "Do you think you guys can find enough to write about for a year?"

And to the memory of two great cruise lines that have sailed into the night—Royal Viking Line (b. 1971–d. 1994) and Royal Cruise Line (b. 1971–d. 1996).

"Lots of tips and inside information on each ship ... valuable beginner's information on the cruise life and choosing a cruise. Very detailed."

—Los Angeles Times

"Whereas the term 'expert' is thrown about with abandon, when it comes to travel writing, these two are the real deal. Harry and Shirley are cruise experts."

—Salt Lake City Tribune

"Slater and Basch ... probably are the top consumer writers about passenger ships.... You can trust them to tell the truth... .It's fun and very informative."

—New Orleans Times-Picayune

"... a fresh sea breeze blowing in cruise guidebooks ... a witty, pithy departure from the norm ..."

—Vacations Magazine

"... insightful, always independent, frequently witty and occasionally irreverent personal reviews..."

—Cruise and Vacation Views

"This entertaining and useful guide will make even the most hardened land-lubber want to set sail. Slater and Basch have redefined cruise guide books."

—Paul Lasley & Elizabeth Harriman, ON TRAVEL RADIO

"This year the bookstores are being flooded with guides to cruising. One of the best is Fielding's Guide to Worldwide Cruises, *simply because the authors, Shirley Slater and Harry Basch, have sailed on more than 200 vessels and know the inside scoop on what makes ships and lines different."*

—Boston Globe

"If you have space for only one cruise guidebook in your library, it should be this one."

—Cruise Travel Magazine

"... a very fresh approach to the subject ... much more colorful, lively and interesting than cruise guides from the past ..."

—Lawrence J. Frommer, travel agent consultant and cruise specialist

"Shirley Slater and Harry Basch are 'the travel agent's travel agent,' as far as cruise information is concerned ... they are frank and upfront as to what the public wants to hear."

—Duke Butler, president, Spur of the Moment Cruises

"If a useful, accurate and entertaining cruise guide can be compiled— and I have never been convinced it could—Shirley Slater and Harry Basch have brought it off for Fielding. Five star plus is no more, replaced by a point of view, a fresh layout and, yes, some wit. Bravo!"

—John Maxtone-Graham, marine historian and
author of *The Only Way to Cross* and *Liners to the Sun*

Letter from the Publisher

In 1946, Temple Fielding began the first of what would be a remarkable new series of well-written, highly personalized guidebooks for independent travelers. Temple's opinionated, witty and oft-imitated books have now guided travelers for almost a half-century. More important to some was Fielding's humorous and direct method of steering travelers away from the dull and the insipid. Today, Fielding travel guides are still written by experienced travelers for experienced travelers. Our authors carry on Fielding's reputation for delivering travel experiences with a sense of discovery and style.

Authors Harry Basch and Shirley Slater have personally been aboard all 160 ships reviewed in *Fielding's Worldwide Cruises* and have taken more than 200 cruises during the past 15 years. Their vast cruise experience will provide you with valuable insider information, enabling you to choose the perfect cruise.

Today the concept of independent travel has never been bigger. Our policy of *brutal honesty* and a highly personal point of view has never changed; it just seems the travel world has caught up with us.

Enjoy your cruise adventures with Harry, Shirley and Fielding.

R Y P

Robert Young Pelton
Publisher and CEO
Fielding Worldwide, Inc.

ABOUT THE
AUTHORS

Shirley Slater and Harry Basch

Called by the *Chicago Sun-Times* "America's premier cruise specialists," Shirley Slater and Harry Basch are an award-winning husband-and-wife travel writing and photography team whose work has been published internationally since 1976. For more than a decade, they have been the world's most widely read cruise experts.

They are editors of Fielding's *Cruise Insider*, a quarterly news-and-reviews journal about the cruise industry, as well as authors of Fielding's *Freewheelin' USA* and the monthly newsletter *Shirley and Harry's RV Adventures*.

As contributing editors for the trade magazine *Cruise & Vacation Views*, their monthly ship reviews are read throughout the travel agent community. They have also written ship reviews for trade publications *Travel Weekly*, *TravelAge* and *ASTA Agency Management* magazine.

Their syndicated column "Cruise Views" has appeared regularly in the *Los Angeles Times* and other major newspapers for 15 years. They have also contributed to magazines such as *Bon Appétit, Vogue, Modern Maturity, Travel & Leisure, Islands, Travel Holiday,* as well as various auto club and inflight publications.

For the two million subscribers to Prodigy Computer Services, they have created five editions of an annual North American Ski Guide, two Cruise Guides and a Caribbean Ports of Call Guide. Slater is also the author of *The Passport Guide to Switzerland.*

At the 60th World Travel Congress in Hamburg, Germany, in 1990 the couple was awarded the prestigious Melva C. Pederson Award from the American Society of Travel Agents for "extraordinary journalistic achievement in the field of travel," the third time the award was given and the first time it was awarded to freelance writers.

They also received the 1995 award for distinguished RV writing for their *Fielding's Freewheelin' USA.*

FOREWORD

When we were very young (if that were ever possible), we lived in Europe for several years, traveling on the cheap but always willing to splurge whenever we could afford it on the best of something. Our guidebook and bible, text and verse, was Temple Fielding's *Europe* guide, because it was the only guidebook that made us laugh, gave us a sense of fun and was absolutely honest—we literally couldn't afford to make any wrong choices.

In this cruise guide, we go back to the basics, to Temple Fielding and his philosophy of always telling the reader honestly but with style, verve and an occasional grumpy touch, about the best and worst of travel.

If we also occasionally sound a little curmudgeonly, it's only because we've been doing this for the last 20 years all over the world as full-time professional travel writers and photographers, tallying up along the way 175 countries and more than 200 cruises aboard virtually everything that floats.

This is the book we've always wanted to write. We hope you like it.

—**Shirley Slater and Harry Basch**

Fielding Rating Icons

The Fielding Rating Icons are highly personal and awarded to help the besieged traveler choose from among the dizzying array of activities, attractions, hotels, restaurants and sights. The awarding of an icon denotes unusual or exceptional qualities in the relevant category.

RATINGS: Fielding Award, Author Selection, Money Saver, Expensive, Quality, Warning, Danger, Inexpensive, Mild Disapproval, Spacious, Cramped

CULTURAL: Museum/Art, Interesting Architecture, History, Book Reference, Artistically Important, Musically Interesting, Cultural Archaeology, Crafts, Theatre

SIGHTS: Picturesque, Great Scenery, Market, Beaches/Resorts, Cultural, Fortress, Castles, Church

WHERE TO STAY: Simple, Luxurious, Cottage, Bed & Breakfast, Scenic, Business, Honeymoon, Chateau

TRAVEL TIPS: Arrival/Departure, By Air, By Water, By Train, By Car, Bus/Local Transit, Barge, Riverboat, Calendar, Itinerary, Compass, Kids

ACTIVITIES: Downhill Skiing, X-country Skiing, General Sports, Watersports, Sailing, Scuba Diving, Snorkeling/Diving, Deep-sea Fishing, Freshwater Fishing, Swimming, Hiking, Walking, Relaxing, Golf, Tennis, Horseback Riding, Cycling, Workout

SPECIAL INTEREST: Mystery, Singles, Romantic, Nude Beaches, Lecture, Spectacular Cuisine, Wine Tasting, Shopping, Nightlife, Cafe Stops, Gardening, Pro Sports

TABLE OF CONTENTS

LIST OF MAPS

SHIPS BY ALPHABETICAL LISTING

The Ratings

When the *Fielding Worldwide Guide to Cruises* first began in 1981, the late Antoinette DeLand initiated the rating system of stars that has always been associated with this guide. As new authors for the guide, we have decided to simplify the system somewhat by eliminating all the pluses but adding an extra star.

The present authors have been aboard all the ships rated with black stars and anchors in the following pages, and the **black star ratings** reflect our personal opinion of the ship and the cruise experience it offers.

White stars represent ships that are in transition from one company to another, which we have been aboard in the vessel's earlier life, or new vessels that are sister ships to existing, already inspected vessels due to come on line in 1997.

Anchor ratings were created by the publishers to reflect a cruise experience that was enriching and rewarding aboard an adventure, expedition, river or coastal vessel where the pleasure of the journey far exceeds the physical quality of the cruise vessel. A few ocean-going ships that offer expedition and educational sailings will carry both star and anchor ratings.

Unrated ships are those the authors have not been aboard in the ship's present incarnation, most of them new ships not yet on line.

★★★★★★	The ultimate cruise experience
★★★★★	A very special cruise experience
★★★★	A high quality cruise experience
★★★	An average cruise experience
★★	If you're on a budget and not fussy
★	A sinking ship

Ship	Rating	Page
Aegean I	**Unrated**	*612*
Amazing Grace	**Unrated**	*774*
Ambasador I	★★, ⚓⚓⚓⚓	*499*
American Queen	⚓⚓⚓⚓⚓	*325*
Americana	★★★	*448*
Amerikanis	★★	*404*
Ausonia	★★★	*382*
Azur	★★★	*386*
Bali Sea Dancer	★★★, ⚓⚓⚓⚓	*372*
Black Prince	★★★	*390*

Ship	Rating	Page
Black Watch	☆☆☆☆	394
Bolero	★★★	397
Bremen	★★★★★, ⚓⚓⚓⚓⚓	409
Caledonian Star	★★★, ⚓⚓⚓⚓⚓	375
Canadian Empress	⚓⚓⚓⚓	723
Canberra	★★	514
Caribbean Prince	⚓⚓⚓	120
Carnival Destiny	☆☆☆☆☆	155
Carnival Triumph	**Unrated**	155
Celebration	★★★	159
Century	★★★★★	184
Club Med 1	★★★	216
Club Med 2	★★★	216
Costa Allegra	★★★★	234
Costa Classica	★★★★★	240
Costa Marina	★★★★	234
Costa Playa	**Unrated**	246
Costa Riviera	★★	248
Costa Romantica	★★★★★	240
Costa Victoria	**Unrated**	252
Crown Princess	★★★★★	547
Crystal Harmony	★★★★★★	270
Crystal Symphony	★★★★★★	270
Cunard Countess	★★	290
Cunard Dynasty	★★★★	294
Daphne	★★★	254
Dawn Princess	☆☆☆☆☆	578
Delta Queen	⚓⚓⚓⚓⚓	330
Dolphin IV	★★	146
Dreamward	★★★★★	468
Ecstasy	★★★★★	165
Enchanted Isle	★★	224
Eugenio Costa	★★	258
Explorer	★★, ⚓⚓⚓⚓⚓	84
Fantasy	★★★★★	165
Fantome	⚓⚓⚓⚓	777
Fascination	★★★★★	165
Flying Cloud	⚓⚓⚓⚓	777
Funchal	★★	400
Galaxy	**Unrated**	184
Golden Princess	★★★	553
Grandeur of the Seas	☆☆☆☆☆	626
Hanseatic	★★★★★, ⚓⚓⚓⚓⚓	587

Ship	Rating	Page
Holiday	★★★	159
Horizon	★★★★★	190
Imagination	★★★★★	165
Independence	★★★	132
Inspiration	★★★★★	165
Island Princess	★★★	557
IslandBreeze	★★	342
Jubilee	★★★	159
Kazakhstan II	★★★★	314
Leeward	★★★★	474
Legend of the Seas	★★★★★	626
Maasdam	★★★★★	422
Majesty of the Seas	★★★★	631
Mandalay	⚓⚓⚓	777
Marco Polo	★★★★	506
Mayan Prince	⚓⚓⚓	120
MegaStar Aries	★★★★	738
MegaStar Taurus	★★★★	738
Meridian	★★★★	195
Mermoz	★★★	262
Minerva	**Unrated**	202
Mississippi Queen	⚓⚓⚓⚓	334
Monarch of the Seas	★★★★	631
Nantucket Clipper	⚓⚓⚓⚓	208
Niagara Prince	⚓⚓⚓	120
Nieuw Amsterdam	★★★★	428
Noordam	★★★★	428
Nordic Empress	★★★★	637
Norway	★★★★	478
Norwegian Crown	★★★★	484
OceanBreeze	★★★	345
Oceanic Grace	★★★★	495
Odysseus	★★★	752
Olympic	★★	358
Oriana	★★★★★	518
Orpheus	★★	362
Pacific Princess	★★★	557
Polaris	★★★, ⚓⚓⚓⚓	712
Polynesia	⚓⚓⚓	777
Queen of the West	⚓⚓⚓	142
Queen Elizabeth 2	★★★★★/★★★★	284
Radisson Diamond	★★★★★★	591
Regal Empress	★★	604

Ship	Rating	Page
Stella Oceanis	★★★	756
Stella Solaris	★★★★	760
Sun Princess	★★★★★	578
Sun Viking	★★	654
SuperStar Gemini	★★★★	745
Triton	★★	366
Tropicale	★★★	173
Universe Explorer	**Unrated**	797
Veendam	★★★★★	422
Victoria	★★★★	522
Viking Serenade	★★★★	658
Vistafjord	★★★★★	307
Westerdam	★★★★	440
Wind Song	★★★★★	790
Wind Spirit	★★★★★	790
Wind Star	★★★★★	790
Windward	★★★★★	468
World Discoverer	★★★, ⚓⚓⚓⚓⚓	703
Yankee Clipper	⚓⚓⚓⚓	777
Yorktown Clipper	⚓⚓⚓⚓⚓	208
Zenith	★★★★★	190

SHIPS BY RATING

The Ratings

When the *Fielding Worldwide Guide to Cruises* first began in 1981, the late Antoinette DeLand initiated the rating system of stars that has always been associated with this guide. As new authors for the guide, we have decided to simplify the system somewhat by eliminating all the pluses but adding an extra star.

The present authors have been aboard all the ships rated with black stars and anchors in the following pages, and the **black star ratings** reflect our personal opinion of the ship and the cruise experience it offers.

White stars represent ships that are in transition from one company to another, which we have been aboard in the vessel's earlier life, or new vessels that are sister ships to existing, already inspected vessels due to come on line in 1997.

Anchor ratings were created by the publishers to reflect a cruise experience that was enriching and rewarding aboard an adventure, expedition, river or coastal vessel where the pleasure of the journey far exceeds the physical quality of the cruise vessel. A few ocean-going ships that offer expedition and educational sailings will carry both star and anchor ratings.

Unrated ships are those the authors have not been aboard in the ship's present incarnation, most of them new ships not yet on line.

★★★★★★	The ultimate cruise experience
★★★★★	A very special cruise experience
★★★★	A high quality cruise experience
★★★	An average cruise experience
★★	If you're on a budget and not fussy
★	A sinking ship

Rating	Ship	Page
★★★★★★	*Crystal Harmony*	270
★★★★★★	*Crystal Symphony*	270
★★★★★★	*Radisson Diamond*	591
★★★★★★	*Royal Viking Sun*	298
★★★★★★	*Sea Goddess I*	303
★★★★★★	*Sea Goddess II*	303
★★★★★★	*Seabourn Legend*	670
★★★★★★	*Seabourn Pride*	670
★★★★★★	*Seabourn Spirit*	670
★★★★★	*Silver Cloud*	692

Rating	Ship	Page
★★★★★★	Silver Wind	692
★★★★★★	Song of Flower	596
★★★★★, ⚓⚓⚓⚓⚓	Bremen	409
☆☆☆☆☆	Carnival Destiny	155
★★★★★	Century	184
★★★★	CostaClassica	240
★★★★	CostaRomantica	240
★★★★	Crown Princess	547
☆☆☆☆☆	Dawn Princess	578
★★★★	Dreamward	468
★★★★★	Ecstasy	165
★★★★★	Fantasy	165
★★★★★	Fascination	165
☆☆☆☆☆	Grandeur of the Seas	626
★★★★★, ⚓⚓⚓⚓⚓	Hanseatic	587
★★★★★	Horizon	190
★★★★★	Imagination	165
★★★★★	Inspiration	165
★★★★★	Legend of the Seas	626
★★★★★	Maasdam	422
★★★★★	Oriana	518
★★★★★/★★★★	Queen Elizabeth 2	284
★★★★★	Regal Princess	547
★★★★★	Rotterdam	434
★★★★	Royal Princess	561
★★★★★	Ryndam	422
★★★★★	Sensation	165
★★★★	Splendour of the Seas	626
★★★★★	Statendam	422
★★★★★	Sun Princess	578
★★★★★	Veendam	422
★★★★★	Vistafjord	307
★★★★★	Wind Song	790
★★★★★	Wind Spirit	790
★★★★	Wind Star	790
★★★★★	Windward	468
★★★★★	Zenith	190
☆☆☆☆	Black Watch	394
★★★★	CostaAllegra	234
★★★★	CostaMarina	234
★★★★	Cunard Dynasty	294
★★★★	Kazakhstan II	314
★★★★	Leeward	474

Rating	Ship	Page
★★★★	*Majesty of the Seas*	631
★★★★	*Marco Polo*	506
★★★★	*MegaStar Aries*	738
★★★★	*MegaStar Taurus*	738
★★★★	*Meridian*	195
★★★★	*Monarch of the Seas*	631
★★★★	*Nieuw Amsterdam*	428
★★★★	*Noordam*	428
★★★★	*Nordic Empress*	637
★★★★	*Norway*	478
★★★★	*Norwegian Crown*	484
★★★★	*Oceanic Grace*	495
★★★★	*Renaissance I–IV*	614
★★★★	*Renaissance V–VIII*	614
★★★★	*Royal Majesty*	456
★★★★	*Seawind Crown*	684
★★★★, ⚓⚓⚓⚓⚓	*Sea Cloud*	675
★★★★	*Sky Princess*	567
★★★★	*Sovereign of the Seas*	650
★★★★	*Star Clipper*	730
★★★★	*Star Flyer*	730
★★★★	*Star Princess*	573
★★★★	*Stella Solaris*	760
★★★★	*SuperStar Gemini*	745
★★★★	*Victoria*	522
★★★★	*Viking Serenade*	658
★★★★	*Westerdam*	440
★★★	*Americana*	448
★★★	*Ausonia*	382
★★★	*Azur*	386
★★★, ⚓⚓⚓⚓	*Bali Sea Dancer*	372
★★★	*Black Prince*	390
★★★	*Bolero*	397
★★★, ⚓⚓⚓⚓⚓	*Caledonian Star*	375
★★★	*Celebration*	159
★★★	*Club Med 1*	216
★★★	*Club Med 2*	216
★★★	*Daphne*	254
★★★	*Golden Princess*	553
★★★	*Holiday*	159
★★★	*Independence*	132
★★★	*Island Princess*	557
★★★	*Jubilee*	159

Rating	Ship	Page
★★★	Mermoz	262
★★★	OceanBreeze	345
★★★	Odysseus	752
★★★	Pacific Princess	557
★★★, ⚓⚓⚓⚓⚓	Polaris	712
★★★	SeaBreeze	349
★★★	Seaward	488
★★★	Song of America	642
★★★	Star Aquarius	742
★★★	Star Pisces	742
★★★	Star/Ship Atlantic	532
★★★	Star/Ship Oceanic	536
★★★	Stella Oceanis	756
★★★	Tropicale	173
★★★, ⚓⚓⚓⚓⚓	World Discoverer	703
★★	Amerikanis	404
★★	Canberra	514
★★	CostaRiviera	248
★★	Cunard Countess	290
★★	Dolphin IV	146
★★	Enchanted Isle	224
★★	EugenioCosta	258
★★	Funchal	400
★★	IslandBreeze	342
★★	Olympic	358
★★	Orpheus	362
★★	Regal Empress	604
★★	Song of Norway	646
★★	Sun Viking	654
★★	Triton	366
★★, ⚓⚓⚓⚓⚓	Explorer	84
★★, ⚓⚓⚓⚓	Ambasador I	499
★★, ⚓⚓⚓⚓	Sea Bird	716
★★, ⚓⚓⚓⚓	Sea Lion	716
⚓⚓⚓⚓⚓	American Queen	325
⚓⚓⚓⚓⚓, ★★★★★	Bremen	409
⚓⚓⚓⚓⚓, ★★★	Caledonian Star	375
⚓⚓⚓⚓⚓	Delta Queen	330
⚓⚓⚓⚓⚓, ★★	Explorer	84
⚓⚓⚓⚓⚓, ★★★★★	Hanseatic	587
⚓⚓⚓⚓⚓	Mississippi Queen	334
⚓⚓⚓⚓⚓	Nantucket Clipper	208
⚓⚓⚓⚓⚓, ★★★	Polaris	712

Rating	Ship	Page
⚓⚓⚓⚓⚓, ★★★★	Sea Cloud	675
⚓⚓⚓⚓⚓	Spirit of '98	110
⚓⚓⚓⚓⚓, ★★★	World Discoverer	703
⚓⚓⚓⚓⚓	Yorktown Clipper	208
⚓⚓⚓⚓, ★★	Ambasador I	499
⚓⚓⚓⚓, ★★★	Bali Sea Dancer	372
⚓⚓⚓⚓	Canadian Empress	723
⚓⚓⚓⚓	Fantome	777
⚓⚓⚓⚓	Flying Cloud	777
⚓⚓⚓⚓	Mandalay	777
⚓⚓⚓⚓	Mayan Prince	120
⚓⚓⚓⚓	Niagara Prince	120
⚓⚓⚓⚓	Polynesia	777
⚓⚓⚓⚓	Queen of the West	142
⚓⚓⚓⚓, ★★	Sea Bird	716
⚓⚓⚓⚓, ★★	Sea Lion	716
⚓⚓⚓⚓	Sir Francis Drake	767
⚓⚓⚓⚓	Spirit of Alaska	95
⚓⚓⚓⚓	Spirit of Columbia	95
⚓⚓⚓⚓	Spirit of Discovery	100
⚓⚓⚓⚓	Yankee Clipper	777
⚓⚓⚓	Caribbean Prince	120
⚓⚓⚓	Spirit of Glacier Bay	106
Unrated	Aegean I	612
Unrated	Amazing Grace	774
Unrated	Carnival Triumph	155
Unrated	CostaPlaya	246
Unrated	CostaVictoria	252
Unrated	Galaxy	184
Unrated	Minerva	202
Unrated	Spirit of Endeavor	104
Unrated	Universe Explorer	797

CRUISE LINE CONTACTS

Company	Phone	Website
Abercrombie & Kent	*(800) 323-7308*	
Airtours (U.K.)	*(01706) 260000*	
Alaska Sightseeing/Cruise West	*(800) 426-7702*	
American Canadian Caribbean Line	*(800) 556-7450*	
American Hawaii Cruises	*(800) 765-7000*	http://www.cruisehawaii.com
American West Steamboat Company	*(800) 434-1232*	
Bergen Line	*(800) 323-7436*	
Canaveral Cruise Line Inc.	*(904) 427-6892*	
Carnival Cruise Line	*(800) 327-9501*	
Celebrity Cruises	*(800) 437-3111*	http://celebrity-cruises.com
Classical Cruises	*(800) 252-7745*	
Clipper Cruise Line	*(800) 325-0010*	
Club Med Cruises	*(800) 453-7447*	http://clubmed.com
Commodore Cruise Line	*(800) 832-1122*	
Costa Cruises	*(800) 462-6782*	
Crystal Cruises	*(800) 446-6620*	
Cunard Line	*(800) 221-4770*	
Delta Queen Steamboat Company	*(800) 543-1949*	
Dolphin Cruise Line	*(800) 222-1003*	http://dolphincruises.com
Epirotiki Cruise Line	*(800) 872-6400*	
Esplanade Tours	*(800) 426-5492*	
EuroCruises	*(800) 661-1119*	
EuropAmerica Cruises	*(800) 348-8287*	
Fantasy Cruises	*(800) 423-2100*	
Galapagos Cruise Line	*(800) 221-3254*	

Company	Phone	Website
Holland America Line	(800) 426-0327	
Ivaran Cruise Line	(800) 451-1639	
Majesty Cruise Line	(800) 645-8111	http://www.majestycruises.com
Marine Expeditions	(800) 263-9147	
Mediterranean Shipping Cruises	(800) 666-9333	
Norwegian Cruise Line	(800) 327-7030	http://www.ncl.com/ncl
Oceanic Cruises	(800) 545-5778	
OdessAmerica Cruise Co.	(800) 221-3254	
Orient Lines	(800) 333-7300	
P & O Cruises	(800) LOVEBOAT	
Premier Cruise Lines	(800) 327-7113	http://www.bigredboat.com
Princess Cruises	(800) LOVEBOAT	
Quark Expeditions	(800) 356-5699	
Radisson Seven Seas Cruises	(800) 333-3333	http://www.ten-io.com/clia/radisson/index.html
Regal Cruises	(800) 270-SAIL	
Renaissance Cruises	(800) 525-5350	
Royal Caribbean Cruises Ltd.	(800) 327-6700	http://www.royalcaribbean.com/main.html
Royal Seas Cruise Line	(800) 290-6222	
St. Lawrence Cruise Lines	(800) 267-7868	
Seabourn Cruise Line	(800) 929-4747	
Sea Cloud Cruises	(800) 683-6767	
Seawind Cruise Line	(800) 223-1877	
Silversea Cruises	(800) 722-6655	
Society Expeditions	(800) 548-8669	
Special Expeditions	(800) 348-2358	
Star Clippers	(800) 442-0556	
Star Cruise (Singapore)	(65) 733-6988	
Sun Line Cruises	(800) 872-6400	
Swan Hellenic Cruises	(800) 426-5492	
Tall Ship Adventures	(800) 662-0090	
Windjammer Cruises	(800) 327-2602	
Windstar Cruises	(800) 258-7245	http://www.windstarcruises.com
World Explorer Cruises	(800) 854-3835	

A NOTE ABOUT THE STARS

The first thing you will probably notice as you leaf through *Fielding's Worldwide Cruises 1997* is a change in the rating system. The famous Five-Stars-Plus has been retired, and the pluses as well phased out of the ship ratings, a victim of their own built-in waffling.

When the system was originally initiated, ships were simpler and the top-ranked vessels somewhat less sophisticated in food, service and cabin amenities. As ships improved, the star ratings started pushing the envelope, everyone crowding the top and hardly anyone back at the average or beginning.

Now you'll find a **One-to-Six** Star rating system reflecting a much wider range of cruise offerings in the marketplace than ever before in history. Herewith, we proudly introduce the **Six-Star cruise ships for 1997, the dazzling dozen,** offering the best cruise ship experiences in the world.

THE BEST OF 1997

The Six-Star Ships

The Five-Star Ships

Fascination	**Carnival Cruise Lines**	*page 165*
Horizon	**Celebrity Cruises**	*page 190*
Imagination	**Carnival Cruise Lines**	*page 165*
Inspiration	**Carnival Cruise Lines**	*page 165*
Legend of the Seas	**Royal Caribbean Cruise Ltd.**	*page 626*
Maasdam	**Holland America Line**	*page 422*
Queen Elizabeth 2	**Cunard Line**	*page 284*
Regal Princess	**Princess Cruises**	*page 547*
Royal Princess	**Princess Cruises**	*page 561*
Rotterdam	**Holland America Line**	*page 434*
Ryndam	**Holland America Line**	*page 422*
Sensation	**Carnival Cruise Lines**	*page 165*
Splendour of the Seas	**Royal Caribbean Cruise Ltd.**	*page 626*
Statendam	**Holland America Line**	*page 422*
Veendam	**Holland America Line**	*page 422*
Vistafjord	**Cunard Line**	*page 307*
Wind Song	**Windstar Cruises**	*page 790*
Wind Spirit	**Windstar Cruises**	*page 790*
Wind Star	**Windstar Cruises**	*page 790*
Windward	**Norwegian Cruise Line**	*page 468*
Zenith	**Celebrity Cruises**	*page 190*

Ten Best Buys at Sea

Delta Queen Steamboat Company	*American Queen*	A warm and richly rewarding experience in Americana in **a floating Victorian bed-and-breakfast**.
Carnival	*Fleet*	Providing a big, splashy **Las Vegas/Theme Park experience for the whole family** at affordable prices.
Celebrity	*Fleet*	Offering the finest cruise ship food and service in handsome, tasteful surroundings at an excellent value, **the best large-ship buy afloat**.
Norwegian Cruise Line	*Dreamward Windward*	Well-designed ships with a feeling of **intimate spaces in sophisticated surroundings** for young to middle-aged couples and singles.

Holland America Line	*Fleet*	**The most beautiful traditional cruise ships at sea**, a solid value for the money with tasty, imaginatively served food and warm friendly service, classy and classic.
Orient Lines	*Marco Polo*	A vintage vessel with **great itineraries, excellent food**, a chic, art deco style—and the price is right.
Royal Caribbean Cruise Ltd.	*Nordic Empress*	An **outstanding short-cruise experience** for first-time cruisers because of a tactful and caring staff that make you feel at ease.
Silverseas	*Fleet*	Looks expensive until you **see what you get for your money**, with airfare, all beverages and tips included.
Radisson Seven Seas Cruises	*Song of Flower*	Everybody's favorite little luxury ship with everything included in a base fare, **the best small-ship buy afloat.**
Alaska Sightseeing/ Cruise West	*Spirit of '98*	A replica turn-of-the-century coastal steamer with **an all-American staff and home-cooked cuisine**, giving a great close-up look at Alaska and the Northwest.

Six Best Ships for Families with Kids

1, 2	**Premier Cruise Lines**	*Both Big Red Boats*	Bugs Bunny is aboard with a full gamut of fun and games for all ages.
3	**Majesty Cruise Line**	*Royal Majesty*	Cruising with Fred Flintstone; special kids' menus and shore excursions.
4	**Carnival's**	*Holiday*	Offers a $1 million "virtual reality" entertainment complex, great for teens and preteens.
5	**Princess Cruises**	*Sky Princess*	Big, comfortable playroom, kiddy pool and well-trained counselors.
6	**P&O Cruises**	*Oriana*	The biggest and most complete kid's area at sea.

Going to Extremes: Top Adventure Vessels

Esplanade Tours Spice Islands Cruises	*Bali Sea Dancer*	Familiar to expeditioners as the *Illiria*, a small comfortable vessel sailing from Bali to Komodo these days.
Golden Bear Travel	*Bremen*	The former *Frontier Spirit*, a purpose-built new expedition ship that goes from the Arctic to the Antarctic and points in between.

Esplanade Tours	*Caledonian Star*	A comfortable, homey ship carrying mostly British passengers to exotic spots from Kuwait City to Tanna Island.
Abercrombie & Kent	*Explorer*	The original expedition cruise ship that pioneered China and the Antarctic and made the first passenger transit of the Northwest Passage.
Radisson Seven Seas Cruises	*Hanseatic*	Newest and most elegant of the expeditioners with music at teatime and the probable speed record for the Northwest Passage transit.
Quark Expeditions	*Kapitans Dranitsyn, Khlebnikov et al*	Russian icebreakers that crunch their way around the Antarctic or up to the North Pole.
Special Expeditions	*Polaris*	A sturdy, comfortable, unpretentious vessel that sails from Costa Rica to the British Isles and Spitsbergen.
Society Expeditions	*World Discoverer*	Another expedition champion that has garnered a lot of records on its worldwide wandering.

Ten Most Romantic Ships at Sea

Cunard	*Sea Goddess I* *Sea Goddess II*	Unfettered, laissez-faire cruise with a few like-minded romantics looking to **rekindle romance or launch a new love affair**. Take your lover along with you, however, since the ship rarely carries single passengers; recommended for couples only.
Silversea	*Silver Cloud* *Silver Wind*	Larger than Sea Goddess, so there's more anonymity if you really want to hide out. It also offers **those lovely private balconies** the Sea Goddess ships don't have. Couples are best, but there have been a few unattached males and females on both sailings we've made.
Windstar Cruises	*Wind Star,* *Wind Song* *Wind Spirit*	Attract a lot of handsome couples of all ages, but the **romance here comes from the sails**, from sitting alone together on the big gray-and-yellow cushions on the stern deck in the dark in the balmy tropical breezes.

Holland America Line	*Rotterdam*	Offers a different kind of romance, the romance of an ocean liner with polished woods and parquetry floors and two-level nightclubs; senior singles might find romance on a personal level, but also **young couples who could get caught up in the lushly romantic art deco atmosphere. Hurry, it's going out of service in September, 1997.**
Sea Cloud Cruises	*Sea Cloud*	Romantic in every sense of the word, particularly if you've booked one of the two owner's suites, where cereal heiress Marjorie Merriweather Post and her husband E.F. Hutton sequestered themselves (separately) in lavish 1930s splendor. If you're stuck in one of the newer, cheaper, smaller cabins, spend your free time **cuddled together on the big, blue-cushioned "blue lagoon" on the fantail.**
Costa Cruises	*CostaRomantica*	The name doesn't hurt but the spare and elegant suites with private verandas that are named after operas are among the most romantic digs at sea. Burled brierwood furniture and cabinetry, gauzy white bedroom, **an electronically-operated floor to ceiling window shade for total privacy, plus a large whirlpool tub, discreet butler service,** terrycloth robes and reclining deck chairs on the veranda. Yes!

Outer Space: The Sweetest Suites at Sea

Cunard	*Vistafjord*	Offers a pair of dazzling, duplex penthouses complete with private sauna, outdoor hot tub on private veranda, two marble bathrooms with Jacuzzi tubs, wet bar and treadmill for a morning workout.
Crystal	*Crystal Symphony*	Two Crystal Penthouses, separate living rooms, dining area, large private veranda, big walk-in closets, extra guest half-bath, wet bar, Jacuzzi tub, lovely cabinetry.
Royal Caribbean Cruise Ltd.	*Legend of the Seas Splendour of the Seas*	The Royal Suite has a huge white piano dominating one corner of a spacious living room, green marble compartmented bathroom, wet bar, long private veranda, full entertainment center—drop-dead gorgeous.

Holland America	Maasdam Ryndam Statendam Veendam	A single huge owner's suite on each ship has a wide private veranda, separate living room, dining room and bedroom, huge walk-in closet, compartmented bath, butler pantry to have meals prepared in suite.
Princess Cruises	Royal Princess	The Royal and the Princess Suites have big elegant marble bathrooms, wide veranda, light, bright and airy, handsomely furnished.

Splashy Ships for Watersports

American Canadian Caribbean Line		These ships have bow-landing capacity that lets swimmers and snorkelers disembark on a tropical island anywhere by walking down the steps.
Fred. Olson Line	Black Prince	Its Marina Park extends from the stern of the ship at anchor with teak decks, enclosed swimming pool and watersports galore.
Club Med	Club Med 1 and 2	Has a similar watersports platform sans pool.
Norwegian Cruise Line		Offers a super Dive-In Program.
Seabourn Cruises		Watersports platform with pool.
Sea Goddess Cruises		Watersports platform sans pool.
Windstar Cruises		Watersports platform.

Best Ships for Singles

Under 30	Windjammer Barefoot Cruises	Try the special Singles Sailings that promise equality between the sexes.
Females Under 30	Carnival Cruise Lines	These ships attract a lot of single guys under 30.
30-50	Royal Caribbean Cruise Line	A good mainstream place to meet.
Males 30-50	Majesty's Royal Majesty	Lots of great-looking thirtysomething women on board.
Women 50-up	Cunard Line	Dancing hosts, dress-up evenings and live music almost around the clock.
Men 50-up	Cunard Line	Try being a dancing host. See Everything You Ever Wanted to Know About Social Hosts, page 52.
Over 70	Ivaran's Americana	Inexpensive single cabins and no upper age limits.

Three Most Off-the-Wall Onboard Events

Costa Cruises	**Toga Night**	Virtually everyone on board dons a custom-made toga (with or without street clothes under them) and makes like Messalina and Claudius.
Tall Ship Adventures' *Sir Francis Drake*	**BLT night**	Everyone dons buccaneer, lingerie or toga, including the captain.
Carnival	**Men's Knobby Knees Contests**	Men model their best knee revealing outfits, or roll up their pants legs.

The Best Cruise Lines For Buffets

1	**Holland America Line**	Consistently the best day-in, day-out Lido food service.
2	**Celebrity Cruises**	The prettiest arrangements and most convenient layouts, plus wine by the glass on a rolling cart.
3	**Crystal Cruises**	Outstanding special theme buffets and great deck grills.
4	**Majesty Cruise Line**	Piazza San Marco deck bar is terrific.
5	**Cunard's** *Sea Goddess*	Imaginative deck food.
6	**American Hawaii Cruises**	Its deli counter, shoreside bag lunch for all-day sightseers, and regular food court options are crowd pleasers.

Three Best Theme Buffets at Sea

1	**Crystal**	**All Ships**	Italian deck buffet
2	**Cunard's**	*Royal Viking Sun*	Norwegian seafood buffet
3	**Cunard's**	*Sagafjord* **and** *Vistafjord*	The Bavarian Brunch

Best Spas at Sea

Celebrity	*Century*	The most innovative health, beauty and fitness center afloat.
Carnival	*Megaships*	**Nautica Spas** offer 12,000 square feet of space, with a huge glass-walled gym and fulltime instructor, aerobics room, beauty services, spas with skylights overhead.
NCL	*Norway*	**The Roman Spa and health and fitness centers** with lavish indoor pools like a Roman bath.

Cunard	*QE2*	The **Spa and Health and Fitness Center**, two decks of complete beauty and spa treatments, including a full thalassotherepy center.
Norwegian Caribbean Cruise Ltd.	*Legend of the Seas and Splendour of the Seas*	**The Solariums**, with a glass canopy-covered pool, water jets, Roman marble everywhere.

Best Alternative Restaurants

An alternative restaurant is an option to dine occasionally somewhere other than the ship's regular dining rooms, where you usually have assigned seating.

Radisson Seven Seas Cruises	*Radisson Diamond*	**An Evening at Don Vito's** where they serve up a delicious (and fun) all-Italian evening in a casual atmosphere.
Crystal Cruises	*Crystal Symphony*	**Prego Restaurant**, also Italian and very elegant.
Cunard	*Vistafjord*	**Tivoli Restaurant**, an intimate and romantic little Italian restaurant with candlelight.
Crystal Cruises	*Crystal Harmony*	**Kyoto Restaurant**, austere and Oriental, with spare decor and clean but simple dishes.

Best Cruise Entertainment at Sea

Carnival	*Fascination*	**Their production of "Hollywood"** is one of the most spectacular shows we've ever seen at sea, dazzling with its company of 18 singers and dancers and flawlessly professional.
Princess Cruises		**The new "Mystique,"** a sensational production set under the sea with 23 performers, including nine acrobats, has scenery that "grows" in front of your eyes. It's a knockout.
Crystal Cruises	*Crystal Symphony*	**Elegantly costumed "Cole"** sets a new high for class acts.
Norwegian Cruise Line		Offers well-performed Broadway shows like "Will Rogers Follies," "Dreamgirls," "Grease," "George M" and "Pirates of Penzance" on the stages of its ships; the classic *Norway* has a particularly fine theater with balcony and orchestra seating.

Maximizing Mini-Cruises

For the Kids

Premier	*Big Red Boats*	Port Canaveral to the Bahamas.
Majesty	*Royal Majesty*	Miami to the Bahamas and to Mexico's Caribbean.
Carnival	*Holiday*	Los Angeles to Ensenada.
Carnival	*Fantasy*	Port Canaveral to the Bahamas.

For Singles

Carnival	*Ecstasy*	Miami to the Bahamas.
NCL	*Leeward*	Miami to the Bahamas and to Mexico's Caribbean.
Regal Cruises	*Regal Empress*	Sailing from New York on party cruises in summer, from St. Petersburg on four-, five- and six-day sailings in winter.

For Couples

RCCL	*Viking Serenade*	From Los Angeles to Ensenada.
RCCL	*Nordic Empress*	From Miami to the Bahamas.
Radisson Seven Seas	*Radisson Diamond*	Special short sailings in March and April in the Caribbean aboard a super-luxury ship.

For Seniors

Dolphin	*OceanBreeze*	Miami to the Bahamas.
Regal Cruises	*Regal Empress*	Sailing from New York on party cruises in summer, from St. Petersburg on four-, five- and six-day sailings in winter.

Six Best Floating Dining Rooms

Besides serving the finest food at sea, each of the following ship dining rooms has additional special qualities.

Radisson Seven Seas	*Radisson Diamond*	The prettiest: The Grand Dining Room
Radisson Seven Seas	*Song of Flower*	Best service
Cunard	*Sea Goddess I* and *Sea Goddess II*	Most convivial: The Dining Salon
Seabourn	*Seabourn Legend, Seabourn Pride, Seabourn Spirit*	The most formal service
Cunard	*Royal Viking Sun*	Most spacious dining room
Celebrity	*Century*	Grandest entrance

Good Ships for First-Timers and Why

Budget

Dolphin Cruise Line — *OceanBreeze and SeaBreeze* — Clean, comfortable, affordable vintage vessels

Moderate

Seawind Cruise Line — *Seawind Crown* — Offers a good Southern Caribbean itinerary on a classic and comfortable ship that also carries some free land stays to extend your vacation.

RCCL — *Nordic Empress* — Offers top-drawer surroundings, excellent entertainment and good food and service with tactful attention to first-timers.

Norwegian Cruise Line — Dive-in and onboard sports programs, themed dinners and costume evenings on all ships add energy and direction to the overall experience.

Splurge

Radisson Seven Seas — *Radisson Diamond* — This twin-hulled ship is funny-looking to traditionalists, but it's great for first-time cruisers who want a top-drawer luxury sailing with space (sizable cabins, wide hallways) and stability (no seasickness on here!)

Special Experiences at Sea

American Hawaii Cruises — Tells you everything you ever wanted to know about Hawaiian culture, tradition and legends—and teaches you to hula, make leis and play the ukulele besides.

Classical Cruises — Takes you on focused expedition and lecture programs all around the world using travel as a learning experience.

Sun Line/ Royal Olympic Cruises — Takes you around the Mediterranean on Greek Culture and Mythology 101 cruises that will have you reeling from the tragedies of the House of Atreus before you make a dent in your sunblock.

Swan Hellenic/ Classical Cruises — Carries some of the most erudite and entertaining lecturers in the world. You can hobnob with them at mealtimes and cocktails.

World Explorer Cruises — Tells you more about Alaska than you could ever have imagined, with videos, films, lecturers, shore excursions and lots of ports of call in the 14 day cruise, plus a scholarly library that serves them on their winter Semesters at Sea for college credit as well.

Inaccessible Vessels for Wheelchair Passengers

Abercrombie & Kent	*Explorer*
ACCL	*Caribbean Prince, Mayan Prince, Niagara Prince*
American West Steamboat Company	*Queen of the West*
Clipper Cruises	*Nantucket and Yorktown Clipper*
Club Med Cruises	*Club Med 1 & 2*
Esplanade Tours	*Bali Sea Dancer*
	Caledonian Star
EuroCruises	*Ausonia, Funchal*
Ivaran Lines	*Americana*
Marine Expeditions Fleet	*All ships*
Quark Expeditions Fleet	*All ships*
Regal Cruises	*Regal Empress*
St. Lawrence Cruise	*Canadian Empress*
Sea Cloud Cruises	*Sea Cloud*
Society Expeditions	*World Discoverer*
Special Expeditions	*Polaris, Sea Bird, Sea Lion*
Star Clippers	*Star Clipper and Star Flyer*
Tall Ship Adventures	*Sir Francis Drake*
Windjammer Fleet	All sailing ships

INTRODUCTION: LOOK WHO'S AFLOAT

At twilight aboard the Rotterdam, this romantic couple at the rail might be shipboard companions of Noel Coward.

"Why do the wrong people travel, travel, travel
And the right people stay at home?"

Noel Coward song lyrics

Even the late Noel Coward, the most urbane and unflappable cruise passenger one can imagine, probably would have been rendered speechless at who and what's afloat these days.

On the decks he frequented, there were no earphone-wearing joggers or aerobics classes, just stately promenaders (the kind who nod only after being properly introduced) or dozing readers wrapped in steamer rugs. Certainly nobody ever requested a no-smoking table or a low-calorie lunch.

Coward definitely would have raised an eyebrow at cruise-ship dress codes allowing gentlemen to appear at dinner not only without black tie but without any tie or jacket at all. And he hardly could have imagined couples stealing away after dinner to screen a video in their cabin instead of dancing cheek to cheek to the ship's orchestra.

Suddenly four million Americans a year were going down to the sea in ships. And they weren't all wealthy retirees and they weren't all looking for love and attention. They were all ages, from all economic groups, singles, honeymoon couples, working couples on a budget, families with small children, grandparents with grandchildren.

We've been on cruises with—

- Amanda at 2 and Amy at 86
- High rollers and bingo buffs
- A fitness nut who found out she could cruise on a spa ship cheaper than going to a famous spa for a week
- Surfers, divers and joggers who run their daily mileage on deck from Bora Bora to Bequia
- A septuagenarian learning to operate a computer
- A purple-haired teen-aged punk rocker who spent more time on the deck than in the disco
- Bird watchers, whale watchers and girl watchers
- Women competing to see who could stuff the most ping pong balls into their bikinis
- A tycoon who has a long stretch limousine waiting to take him sightseeing in every port
- An accountant who celebrated his 50th birthday by cruising to both the Arctic and Antarctic within the same year
- Best-selling novelists and supermarket checkers, retired teachers and circus owners, movie stars and mechanics—and none of them have ever been boring—or bored.

To Cruise or Not To Cruise

A girl never really looks as well as she does on board a steamship, or even a yacht.

Anita Loos, Gentlemen Prefer Blondes, 1925

Life aboard cruise ships used to be thought of as a sedentary vacation for the very old and very rich, who reclined on wooden deck chairs reading books and sipping bouillon when they weren't wearing tuxedos and eating caviar.

Then along came the slick TV version, based on the premise that all a lovelorn individual had to do was get on board the "Love Boat" and the captain and his meddlesome staff would make everything smooth sailing. All problems would be settled, true love would triumph and, since the ship never seemed to move anyhow, no one's hairdo would even get mussed.

The real world of cruising today is volatile, ephemeral, constantly changing as lines are acquired, new ships come into service and old ships are retired or sold down the river into ignominious retirement as hotels or casinos.

Cruise lines are selling you a dream. And anyone old enough to remember the days of radio knows that the images the aural programs created in the mind were stronger, more dramatic and more compelling than the pallid stuff that came along later on TV. The power of your dream, your imagination, creates a challenge that the cruise industry is trying to meet. Sometimes they do, sometimes they don't.

Getting Real

TV commercials and brochures about cruises all promise the glamour life.

TV commercials and glossy color brochures about cruises all promise the same thing—an unexcelled excursion into the glamour life, with romantic evenings, a perfect tan, six or eight gourmet meals a day, and intermittent forays into picturesque and exotic ports of call where the sun always shines, the shopping is splendid and the natives friendly and photogenic.

Oddly enough, more often than not, it works out that way.

But based on some of the complaints we've had from readers over the years, several of them signed up for a cruise that should have been advertised more like this:

"You'll have fun aboard the friendly, 30-year-old *SS Rustbottom*, which failed her last five sanitation inspections in spite of heavily spiking the drinking water with chlorine...Our bottom-of-the-line cabins are so small you have to take turns getting dressed inside, and our menus are created by a Miami-based computer programmed to give you the maximum number of calories for the lowest possible cost... Our inexperienced and incompetent staff could not care less about your comfort or pleasure, and the residents of our popular ports of call make their livelihoods by harassing you in the streets to purchase their overpriced souvenirs."

What are some of the things that make passengers angry?

First and foremost seem to be promises the passenger felt were implied in the brochure or claimed were actually made by the travel agent prior to the trip. Ambiguous terms like "first class," "deluxe," "elegance"—and, of course, the ever-popular "five-star-plus," the monster created by this very guide—typical hyperbole churned out by ad agency copywriters who may never have been aboard the ship—are echoed bitterly by disappointed letter-writers who expected something grander than they received.

Some expectations appear unrealistic to more experienced cruisers—24-hour room service does not necessarily mean hot four-course meals are served in the cabin at 3 a.m., for instance, and no cruise-savvy travel agent would promise clients they could spend the entire disembarkation and turn-around day aboard the ship in their cabin until time to catch their evening flight home.

One of our favorite reader complaint letters was from a female attorney celebrating her 40th birthday on her first cruise. The ship was one of the former Royal Viking Line vessels, always top of the line in food and service, but the attorney was suing to have the price of her cruise refunded because at breakfast every morning the waiters persisted in offering her a silver tray of pastries despite the fact that she had told them she was on a diet.

Hey lady, get a life!

Take a Vacation from Vacations

The real pleasure of a cruise is not having to do anything you don't want to do.

At some point in every traveler's life, there comes a moment, bittersweet as the end of a love affair, when the vacation is over, the workaday world is looming and there's nothing you need worse than a vacation to recover from your vacation.

Next time, maybe you should take a cruise.

Cruise lines spend a lot of time and money telling us about the unending procession of meals and the nonstop fun and games, when the real pleasure of a cruise is not having to do anything you don't want to do—except attend the obligatory lifeboat drill at the beginning of the cruise.

No packing and unpacking to move from one hotel to another, no cars to rent or trains to catch, no lunchtime arguments about which restaurant or picnic spot looks more appealing, no bungled hotel reservations on a weary midnight arrival in Budapest because a convention of Bulgarians came to town.

Coming back to your ship after a day ashore is like coming home. Your waiter knows how you like your breakfast eggs, your steward knows what time you go to dinner so he can turn your bed down and put a chocolate on your pillow.

A travel agency that specializes in cruises can help you select the ship and itinerary that's best for you, as long as you make your wishes and your budget considerations clear to them. Don't just ask for a Caribbean cruise and take whichever one is mentioned first. Ships and ports of call vary tremendously, and everybody loses if you don't enjoy yourself.

Take the right cruise, and you'll come home rested and happy. Of course, you will be expecting to be served breakfast in bed the first few days home, and you'll miss finding that good-night chocolate on your pillow.

DID YOU KNOW?

"I rather wished that I had gone first class," Evelyn Waugh wrote about sailing from Port Said aboard P&O's Ranchi *in 1929. "It's not that my fellow passengers were not every bit as nice as the Port Said residents had told me they would be, but that there were so many of them."*

Future Trends

Passengers on today's cruise ships are far from sedentary, with deck games, gyms, spas and aerobics classes always available.

If we can believe present trends, passengers of the future are going to be healthy, wealthy and wise.

Healthy, because virtually every ship menu afloat is offering low-calorie, low-fat and vegetarian options; because more and more cruise lines are banning smoking in their dining rooms and show lounges; and because well-equipped fitness centers and aerobics classes are as common as casinos. We're also seeing more stringent inspections of water and air conditioning systems and tougher restrictions on food handlers.

Wealthy, (well, at least less poor), because money-saving early booking discounts that let you cut costs from the published brochure rate are in effect closer and closer to sailing time; no matter how late you book, have your travel agent check to see if you qualify. Frequent cruisers can qualify for free cruises with accrued cruise days from Cunard, and Seabourn passengers in the line's WorldFare program may purchase blocks of 45 to 120 cruise days at a reduced price and use them on any cruises over a period of three years.

Wise in the ways of the world, because there is more of it to see by ship than at any time in recent history.

Fear of Cruising

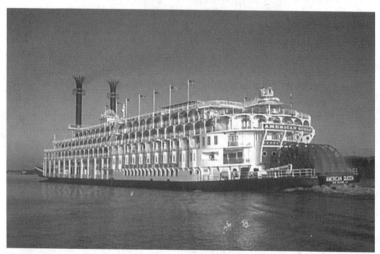

Paddlewheel cruises on the Mississippi River as on the **American Queen** *from* **Delta Queen Steamboat** *always keep you within sight of land.*

A lot of people who think nothing of buying a package coach tour to a foreign country, driving the car across the continent or booking a week at a resort hotel on the recommendation of a casual friend over lunch, shy away from the idea of taking a cruise. Why?

Here's what they tell the pollsters:

Six Common Excuses

1. "Stuck in the middle of an ocean somewhere? I might get bored or feel trapped."
2. "I'm scared I'd get seasick."
3. "I can't plan my vacations that far in advance."
4. "I'd feel uncomfortable—I wouldn't know what to wear or how much to tip or which cabins were good."
5. "I'm afraid of gaining weight with all that food around."
6. "What if I don't like the ship? Then I've wasted my whole vacation."

Six Quick Answers

1. Forget about the ocean if you don't want to go out on one. Alaska cruises that depart from Vancouver travel the Inside Passage through some of the most spectacular scenery on earth and never out of sight of land. The same is true aboard paddlewheelers on the Mississippi River, yachtlike luxury ships in the Intracoastal Waterway or friendly, low-key vessels on the St. Lawrence, along the Columbia or in the San Juan Islands. As for boredom, most first-time cruisers claim they need a vacation when they get home from a cruise because they're exhausted from the nonstop activity.

2. If your previous seagoing experience is limited to sailboats, fishing boats or a hitch in the Navy, modern cruise ships equipped with stabilizers that eliminate much of the rolling motion may surprise you. Fewer than five per cent of the passengers on any cruise complain of motion sickness; medications are readily available on board if you're bothered by *mal de mer*. (See Scoping Out Seasickness and Sidestepping Seasickness, page 1064.)

3. If there's one thing there's plenty of, baby, it's cruise ship cabins in 1997. A good travel agent can book you on almost any ship for any destination on short notice—sometimes with a deep discount.

4. If you're bugged by the unfamiliar, a cruise is the least complicated vacation you'll ever have to deal with; it all comes in one neat prepaid package. You don't need a special wardrobe for cruises; chances are, everything you need is already in your closet. (See Eleven Tips to Lighten Your Luggage, page 1055.) Tipping suggestions are spelled out on board toward the end of the sailing (also, see Tipping, page 1069) and there's a checklist on what to look for in a cabin (see Choosing A Cabin on page 40.)

5. Every ship offers a variety of seafoods, salads, fruits and vegetables, along with low-calorie, low-fat dishes. Some offer full spa menus. Even on small ships you'll find exercise classes and a full array of gym facilities. You could come back home in better shape than when you left. As for temptation, repeat after us—"Just because I paid for it doesn't mean I have to eat it all." (See How to Avoid Pigging Out at Sea, page 45.)

6. Selecting the right ship is the biggest single decision you'll have to make. Don't let anyone tell you all cruises are alike—they're not—or that Brand X Cruise Line is "the best" because there's not one single "best." The best cruise for you is the one you'll enjoy the most. See Choosing A Cruise, page 39 and How To Read A Brochure, page 35, below.

DID YOU KNOW?

Nearly 15 years ago when we first began writing our cruise column, a brusque California businessman planning his first cruise called us. He said he'd asked three travel agents which was the best cruise line–the first said Princess, the second said Carnival, the third said Sitmar (now defunct). So he called us to find out which of those three was the best. When we tried to counter by finding out something about him and what kind of cruise experience he was seeking, he screamed angrily into the phone, "I knew it! You don't know any more about it than those travel agents!" And he hung up.

The New Cruisers

More and more young singles and couples are discovering cruises as a fun and affordable mini-vacation.

A funny thing happened to ocean liners on the way to the 21st century—they got democratized.

The great and famous ships that carried royalty, heads of state, the Astors and the Glorias (Swanson and Vanderbilt) in first-class luxury, relegating to second and third class all other passengers from potato-famine Irish immigrants to '50s college students, have turned into one-class cruise ships where everyone on board is equal, more or less.

Meanwhile, the transatlantic jumbo jets that hastened the demise of ocean liners have become almost a parody of the old class system themselves, fawning over first-class passengers with sofa-sized seats and leg rests, personal video monitors and champagne and caviar, and cramming everyone else into steerage, where bodies are jackknifed into tortuous positions, babies cry all night and unidentifiable foods in plastic compartments are slapped down at intervals on wobbly trays.

Even a decade ago, the change was apparent, as cruise lines began to notice the huge numbers of first-timer cruisers aboard. Carnival's president, Bob Dickinson, then vice president of sales and marketing, pointed out in 1985 that 70 to 75 percent of all his line's passengers were first-time cruisers. "We don't think we're in the cruise business; we're in the vacation business." He went on to predict—correctly—that Carnival would have a 10-ship fleet by 1995.

The mini-cruise market, offering short, affordable getaways, was booming with Eastern Cruise Line's *Emerald Seas* (now the *Sapphire Seas*) sailing from Miami to the Bahamas and Western Cruise Line's *Azure Seas* (now Dolphin's *OceanBreeze*) cruising down to Ensenada from Los Angeles.

A lucrative and previously untapped new market was discovered— couples and singles from the world of young, upwardly-mobile professionals; baby boomers with income and leisure time for longer vacations; blue-collar and clerical workers who appreciated one up-front, all-inclusive ticket price for a vacation as luxurious as any they could find at a land-based resort and often less expensive.

In contrast to the retired and/or wealthy passengers who make up the rosters on around-the-world cruises, the new cruise passengers are looking for mini-vacations at sea, comparing a weekend cruise to a weekend spent in Nassau, Palm Springs, Las Vegas or Atlantic City.

You'll get the picture the minute you step aboard a cruise ship these days. Hardly a ship leaves dock without announcing a party for singles within a day or two of sailing, and guest hosts are on board many vessels expressly to dance, play bridge and socialize with unattached women.

If you're one of the new cruise passengers, you can count on more and more variety in the world of cruises. The day is not far off when you'll be able to cruise anywhere you wish for the length of time you prefer at a price you can afford, not once in a lifetime but once or twice a year.

Short Sails, Big Sales

The burgeoning mini-cruise market is the fastest-growing segment of cruising today as more and more first-timers decide to try the waters. They like the idea of sampling the experience for a few days before booking a longer sailing.

Short cruises seem to fit today's lifestyles, too, with people opting for several small vacations throughout the year rather than one big one. The newest wrinkle is family reunion cruises aboard mini-cruises where nobody has to host, cook or clean—and you can get a group discount as well. For every 15 or so people, there's usually a free or discounted escort or organizer's ticket.

The four major mini-cruise home ports are Miami, Port Canaveral, Ft. Lauderdale and Los Angeles.

DID YOU KNOW?

David Gevanthor, former president of now-defunct SeaQuest Cruises, once said about first-time cruisers starting out on modest ships or sailings, "That's like saying you start off buying a Ford and gradually work up to a Mercedes, and that ignores a guy that buys a Mercedes for his first car. Price is not a determiner; it's the lifestyle and desires of the client that determine what kind of cruise they take."

Anatomy of a Cruise Ship: A Curmudgeon's Guide

The funnel or stack is where the cruise line displays its logo and sends out its combustion gases; never sit downwind of the funnel without checking for soot.

The Basics

- The **FUNNEL** or **STACK** is where the cruise line displays its logo, such as Princess Cruises' sea witch with flowing hair or Costa Cruises' blue-and-yellow C or Celebrity's big white X, Greek for Chi or C. The stack also carries away the ship's combustion gases and occasional bursts of black smoke. When wearing white pants, **never sit in a deck chair downwind of the funnel** without checking first for soot.

- The **GANGWAY** is the external stairway or ramp leading to the ship from the shore. It is also the place where the ship's photographers take pictures of passengers embarking or disembarking in every port, thereby creating a traffic jam in both directions.

- The **LIFEBOATS** are the orange and white vessels that hang outside your cabin window blocking your view if your travel agent doesn't know how to read a deck plan. Some lines like Crystal and Princess point out in their brochures where a cabin view is partly or entirely obstructed and reduce the price accordingly. Some lines, however, sketch the boats in on the deck plan but fail to point out or reduce the price on partially obstructed views. And still other lines fail to indicate the lifeboats at all, leading to *Titanic*-tinged visions.

Deck Areas

- The **SWIMMING POOL** on some ships may be mistaken for a footbath or an ornamental fountain. Fancy pool areas with swim-up bars, waterfalls and other pool novelties tend to get clogged up with passengers under 16.

- Many of the newer ships have a **JOGGING TRACK** on a sports deck high atop the ship. Some of these are so short that it takes 13 (on *Radisson Diamond*) or 14 (on Seabourn) laps to make a mile. **Never, under any circumstances, book a cabin under the jogging track**.

- Some ships have a **CHILDREN'S WADING POOL** which can be identified by its singular lack of children, who prefer to spend their time belly-whopping into the adult pool.

Shuffleboard can reach fever pitch on a classic liner like the **Rotterdam.**

- **SHUFFLEBOARD** is a popular deck game that can reach fever pitch on a classic liner like the *Rotterdam*. On other ships, some passengers mistake it for hopscotch.

- The **Promenade** is the deck that goes all the way around the ship, giving passengers a chance for a brisk, breezy walk. Six or seven times around usually equals a mile. **Do not attempt to exchange pleasantries with a grim-faced walker counting laps.**

Lounges and Public Rooms

- The **SHOW LOUNGE** in the daytime is the setting for line dancing lessons, bingo games and port information lectures, but in the evening becomes Broadway and Las Vegas with musical extravaganzas or, all too often, the last refuge of magicians, jugglers, puppeteers and ventriloquists last seen on the Ed Sullivan Show.

- The **CINEMA** is where recent movies are screened; on some ships it is also considered an ideal spot to nap after lunch. On the Big Red Boats, passengers under 12 vie with each other for the record number of times they can come and go opening the entry doors wide enough to wipe out the image on the screen.

The disco is the place to meet junior officers in white uniforms late at night. Never book a cabin over, under or beside the disco.

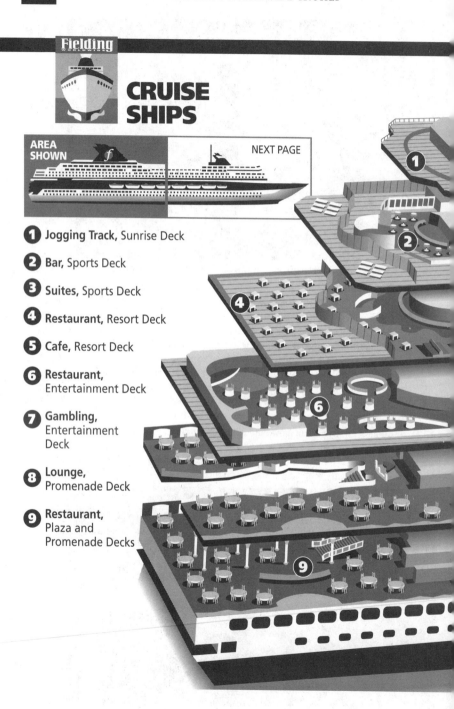

Fielding
CRUISE SHIPS

AREA SHOWN

NEXT PAGE

1 **Jogging Track,** Sunrise Deck

2 **Bar,** Sports Deck

3 **Suites,** Sports Deck

4 **Restaurant,** Resort Deck

5 **Cafe,** Resort Deck

6 **Restaurant,** Entertainment Deck

7 **Gambling,** Entertainment Deck

8 **Lounge,** Promenade Deck

9 **Restaurant,** Plaza and Promenade Decks

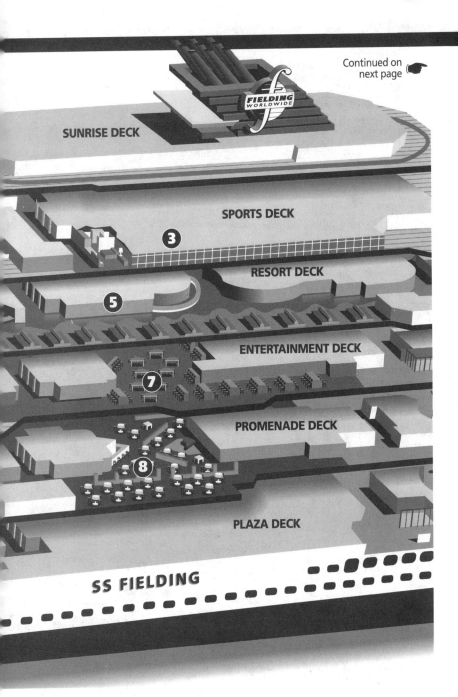

Continued on next page ☞

FIELDING
WORLDWIDE

SUNRISE DECK

SPORTS DECK

③

RESORT DECK

⑤

ENTERTAINMENT DECK

⑦

PROMENADE DECK

⑧

PLAZA DECK

SS FIELDING

CRUISE SHIPS

PREVIOUS PAGE

AREA SHOWN

CABINS

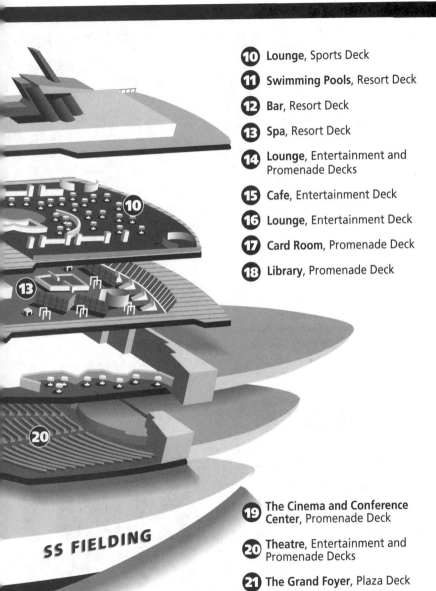

10 **Lounge**, Sports Deck

11 **Swimming Pools**, Resort Deck

12 **Bar**, Resort Deck

13 **Spa**, Resort Deck

14 **Lounge**, Entertainment and Promenade Decks

15 **Cafe**, Entertainment Deck

16 **Lounge**, Entertainment Deck

17 **Card Room**, Promenade Deck

18 **Library**, Promenade Deck

19 **The Cinema and Conference Center**, Promenade Deck

20 **Theatre**, Entertainment and Promenade Decks

21 **The Grand Foyer**, Plaza Deck

22 **Guest Relations and Lobby**, Plaza Deck

SS FIELDING

- The **DISCO** is the place to meet junior officers in white uniforms late at night. On older ships like the *Dolphin IV*, *OceanBreeze* and *SeaBreeze* it's located deep in the bowels of the vessel and in the daytime looks like a place where Dracula would sleep. On Carnival ships it flashes with neon and rock videos and throbs with amplified sound. **Never book a cabin over, under or beside the disco.**

- The **PHOTO GALLERY** is where the ship's photographers mount the pictures of passengers they've snapped at odd moments throughout the cruise. It's always crowded with people buying photos they want to keep and others buying photos they don't want anyone else to see.

- The **TEEN CENTER** is a euphemism for a video games arcade that is frequently filled with males far past their teens. A modern refinement introduced by Carnival's *Holiday* lets the kids use their own ship ID card to access the games in lieu of dogging dad for more quarters; the charge goes right into the billing computers along with dad's bar bills and mom's shipboard shopping.

- The **DUTY-FREE SHOPS** are the places to buy Lladro porcelain, Rolex watches, sequinned garments and other useless items. Essentials like toothpaste, aspirin and sunblock are harder to find since the profit margin is considerably smaller.

- The **SHIP'S CASINO** is a philosophical proving ground where optimists arrive and pessimists depart. A real gambler heads for the roulette table, taking a chance on whether the sea motion is in his favor or against it.

- The **LIBRARY** on most ships is the place to find books to read. It is also populated by competitive trivia quiz aficionados looking up answers in order to win still another bookmark or key chain. **You can tell how much your cruise line trusts you by noting whether the glass cases are locked or unlocked.**

- The **CARD ROOM** is the refuge of avid bridge players whose conversation beyond bids is limited to port of call observations such as, "It's only Hong Kong, shut up and deal." **Only a masochist should let himself be roped into being a fourth for bridge after lunch.**

Elevators come in all shapes and sizes, including this neon-lit glass elevator on Carnival's Fantasy.

- **ELEVATORS** on ships should be avoided at all costs, since the exercise of going up and down stairs is a major defense against weight gain. Elevators should only be used in an emergency except, of course, they do not operate during emergencies.

- The **BEAUTY SALON** is where all the women on board gather between 5 and 7 p.m. on formal nights. Naughty hairdressers direct them back to their cabins via the deck, where the wind destroys the comb-out and everything has to be done all over again.

All About Cabins

- **CABINS** come in all shapes and sizes, mostly small. As a rule, the higher the deck location, the higher the price, but **the smoothest ride is amidships (in the middle) on a lower deck.**

- If you go into your cabin and see a square or rectangular panel of glass with light coming through, you have an **OUTSIDE CABIN** with a window. If the glass is round, it is a **PORTHOLE**. If you fling the curtains open and find yourself facing a blank wall, you have an **INSIDE CABIN**.

- Windows and portholes in the cabin cannot be opened, except on very ancient vessels such as the Mayflower. Occupants of premium-priced **OUTSIDE CABINS ON PROMENADE DECK** are always admired by passers-by who look into the windows as they stroll by. On some ships the glass is covered with a special tinted film so outsiders see their own reflections during the daytime. But after dark, the situation is reversed, with the cabin occupants starring in their own X-rated TV shows for the passersby outside.

- Each cabin has a private bathroom with tub or shower, wash basin and **VACUUM MARINE TOILET**, which flushes with a loud "whooooosh." The best-designed have the flushing device situated where it cannot be activated until the top of the toilet is closed, an essential safety feature for absent-minded passengers.

- Before plugging a hair dryer or other **ELECTRICAL APPLIANCE** into a wall socket, **check whether the ship's electrical system is 110 volts and AC (alternating current) or 220 volts and DC (direct current)**. Plugging one of the former into one of the latter may blow more than the hairdo. Many ships carry voltage converters that will solve the problem; check with the purser's desk.

- Each cabin also has an individual **TEMPERATURE CONTROL KNOB**. When your choices are limited from cold to colder or hot to hotter, call Housekeeping to send up a repairman.

- **CABIN WALLS** on all but the newest ships can be very thin, and an entertaining alternative to a TV set or radio. The disembodied voice that gives greetings or commands from the cabin walls is usually the cruise director on the public address system, unless he's droning on about sea temperatures and windspeeds and nautical miles, in which case it's the captain. A panel of knobs located near the bed can tune in shipboard music programmed by overworked staffers at the reception desk who play "The Sound of Music" for three days in a row.

- Shipboard **CLOSETS** are designed to remind passengers that they should have left behind half the clothes they brought.

- Somewhere within the closet or under the beds are the **LIFE JACKETS**, which appear humorous at first glance but are extremely important should there be a problem at sea. **Always attend the life boat drill and never leave without learning to don the jacket properly, check for the whistle and light, and find which life boat is yours.**

- None of the many **PAPERS** which arrive under the cabin door is junk mail. Each has some message to impart, whether it is the full schedule of activities for the next day with the suggested dress code for the evening or a 20 per cent discount on perfume or gold chains in the gift shop. **Read all papers shoved under the door, no matter how boring they appear. One might be an invitation to dine at the captain's table**.

Service Areas

- The **PURSER'S DESK** is usually located in the lobby. It's the desk with the long line of people waiting to register a complaint, break a $100 bill into singles or buy postage stamps.

- The **SHORE EXCURSIONS DESK** is where you go to buy overpriced bus tours of minor Mexican cities which always stop at the cathedral, the cliff-divers and then an hour-long shopping opportunity at the gift shop of the guide's cousin.

- The **RADIO ROOM** is where you arrange to pay $15 a minute to send a fax to your office or make a call home to your answering machine and find out bad news that ruins your vacation.

The dining room — this one is aboard RCCL's Viking Serenade *— is a favorite shipboard gathering spot.*

The Dining Room

- **TABLES** rarely come with only two chairs but most often in fours, sixes, eights or even tens. **Couples who worry about being bored (or boring) are safer at tables of six or more**. After dining together throughout the cruise, passengers always wind up sending Christmas cards to each other.

- **MEAL SEATINGS** are the arbitrary times the cruise line has decided its passengers will eat. **MAIN** or **FIRST SEATING** offers lunch at noon and dinner at 6 or 6:30, but breakfast is at 7 a.m. **SECOND** or **LATE SEATING** passengers dine fashionably at 8 or 8:30, breakfast at a comfortable 8:30 or 9 in the morning, but can't have lunch until 1:30. This is why three-hour deck buffet breakfasts and lunches were invented.

- **SECOND SEATING** is preferred by really dedicated gourmands, who can fit in early riser's coffee and a few samples from the buffet breakfast before reporting for the regular dining room breakfast. Then morning bouillon at 11 settles any remaining hunger pangs until time for a hot dog or hamburger from the deck grill as an appetizer for the buffet lunch. Lingering over the 1:30 lunch fills the empty moments until teatime, with cocktail hour, dinner and midnight buffet left to round out the day—and the figure.

- Passengers who demand **SPECIAL DIET MENUS**—low in fats, calories or salt—at the beginning of a seven-day cruise usually throw abandon to the winds about Wednesday, then wonder why their shipboard diet plan didn't work.

- Ships that serve **MIDNIGHT BUFFET** at 10:30 p.m. rank high on the senior circuit. Swinging singles should seek vessels like Carnival's with midnight buffet at midnight, followed by the night owl buffet at 2 a.m.

The Only Ten Nautical Terms You Ever Need to Know

1. **Port**: the left side of the ship when you're facing the pointy end.

2. **Starboard**: the right side of the ship when you're facing the pointy end.

3. **Forward**: toward the front, or pointy end.

4. **Aft**: toward the back, or blunt end.

5. **Bow**: the pointy end.

6. **Stern**: the blunt end.

7. **Tender**: a boat carried aboard the ship that can ferry you ashore if the ship is not tied up at the dock; to use the boat to ferry passengers ashore.

8. **Gangway**: the detachable outside stairway from the ship's deck down to the dock or tender.

9. **Embark**: to get on a ship.

10. **Disembark**: to get off a ship.

Ten Questions to Ask Yourself Before Calling a Travel Agent

Before you sail away into the sunset, you need to know what you want and be able to communicate that information to a travel agent, since virtually all cruise lines prefer or require bookings to be made through agents. Read these questions and know the answers to them before you call the travel agent. It will make her job much easier and ensure that you'll get the right cruise for you.

1. **What are you looking for—sunny island beaches, duty-free shopping, a stress-free, do-nothing getaway, a razzle-dazzle good time with plenty of entertainment?**

You can get them all on a cruise, but not necessarily on the same ship. Try to be specific as to what you want. A working couple with young children might opt for a family cruise combined with a Disney World package, giving them quality time with the kids and still the chance to be alone together while the youngsters join in special shipboard youth programs. On the other hand, a grade-school teacher seeking a break from workaday reality would probably want to set sail in exactly the opposite direction from ships that carry hundreds of romping children.

2. **How long can you be away?**

Cruises can be three-day weekend sailings, seven-day cruises, 14-day sailings, even 100-plus day world cruises. First-timers usually opt for three to seven days, frequent cruisers for a longer period of time.

3. Where do you want to go?

Weekend or mini-cruises usually set out from Florida for the Bahamas or from Los Angeles to Catalina Island and Baja California. Seven-day cruises with air/sea packages let you sail around the Hawaiian Islands, the Caribbean, Mexican Riviera, Alaska, the South Pacific or Europe. It usually takes ten days for a Panama Canal cruise with a full transit, although several ships offer a cruise into part of the canal during a seven-day itinerary.

4. Are you traveling as a single, one of a pair, or part of a group of family and friends?

Others may have different needs or desires, so confer with them before making any decisions. A ship good for singles may not work so well with family groups.

5. What do you want in the way of shipboard lifestyle?

Decide what you think are the most important elements of a good vacation, jot them down and have them handy when you make your initial call to a travel agent. While many stressed-out travelers picture a cruise ship as a place to lounge quietly by the pool with a good book, they may be ready after a couple of days for livelier activities. Virtually all cruise ships today offer gym equipment, aerobics, lectures, shoreside golf and tennis, dancing, bridge or crafts classes and even shopping.

6. Do you want a large, medium-sized or small ship?

Big ships have more entertainment, bigger casinos and spas and longer lines; medium-sized ships have scaled-down versions of the same. Small ships are more apt to be free of regimentation and rigid dress codes, but you may be on your own for entertainment. Small to mid-sized vessels usually provide a more relaxed ambiance, while glittering megaliners throb with music and bright lights most of the night. But there's not a vessel afloat that doesn't have a sunny, secluded corner for reading or a lively spot around the bar for socializing.

7. Do you want a classic (read older) or contemporary (read newer) ship?

Most new ships will remind you of a chain resort hotel like Hyatt or Marriott, complete with atrium, glass elevators and identical modular cabins, while ships built 20 or more years ago have ocean liner looks, odd-sized cabins and nostalgic promenade decks.

8. Do you want frequent opportunities to wear your nicest party clothes, or would you prefer to stay casual day and night?

Super-deluxe small ships are quite dressy, expedition and sailing ships casual, and big ships usually have two dress-up evenings a week. Sometimes people who work in an office that requires business attire every day welcome the indulgence of casual sailing or adventure cruising where the only dress code may request "no bathing suits or bare feet at dinner."

9. Do you want to go island-hopping on a ship that stops at a lot of ports or spend your time relaxing aboard ship?

If relaxing is more important, look for itineraries that designate one or two days at sea during a seven-day cruise. You'll still have ports to visit but can get some rest in between.

10. What do you want to learn about the places you'll visit?

If the history, culture, flora and fauna is important, look to expedition ships that emphasize natural history lectures and birdwatching boatrides. Adventure and expedition cruises always seem to attract a lot of doctors, lawyers, teachers and other professionals who diligently attend all the lectures, then happily splash ashore in rubber landing craft to go on nature hikes. If you prefer to know where to pick up brand names like Rolex, Lladro or Colombian emeralds, any big mainstream cruise ship will fill the bill with its "guaranteed shopping" programs subsidized by the very merchants being recommended.

INSIDER TIP

Don't let price be the major factor when you choose your first cruise, especially if you assume all ships and cruises are alike. They're not, and the difference of $20 a day could mean a huge improvement in the quality of your shipboard experience. Once you've taken a couple of cruises, then you can afford to experiment, but a first-time cruise experience that doesn't meet your expectations could turn you away from cruising for good. A smart travel agent will try to steer you toward the most positive cruise experience for you and your family; that means future repeat business for the agent.

How to Read a Brochure

Whenever a new flock of brightly plumaged cruise brochures arrive, we find ourselves leafing through them and visualizing, not the romantic days at sea they portray, but an overworked copywriter in a tiny cubicle high atop a metropolitan office building.

Our fantasy copywriter, thesaurus at the ready, stares through a dirt-streaked window at a rainy sky between bouts of turning out hyperbolic sentences about "hibiscus-scented nights" and "elegant lounges where the decor is luxurious and plush."

Sometimes we wish cruise lines would spend a little less on the four-color pages and take the poor copywriter out on a cruise someday. It would certainly help clear up the vague and overblown prose.

In the meantime, however, the safest path for a potential cruise passenger is to skim the prose lightly and **CONCENTRATE ON THE PICTURES AND CHARTS—** you'd be surprised how much information you can glean from them—and then turn immediately to **READ THE "FINE PRINT"** on the inside back pages for the real nitty-gritty.

First, take a careful look at all the color photos. Don't get lost in reverie, imagining yourself standing on the deck with that Technicolor tropical drink in your hand—that's the intention of most successful advertising photography.

Instead, first **STUDY THE MODELS**, those beaming, bronzed beauties in each shot, then notice the slightly out-of-focus "real people" in some, but not all, of the backgrounds. The models represent the line's idealized version of their perfect prototype passengers, while the people in the background are real passengers on board during the photo shoot. If the ship seems suspiciously empty, the real passengers were all chased away so they could photograph the models alone. If the background people and the foreground people look as if they would be invited to the same party, you have a cruise line that is marketing realistically.

Next, flip quickly through the entire brochure to **GET AN OVERVIEW**. Where is the emphasis? If you see lots of nightlife and casino shots, the company is trying to tell you they're proud of the ship's after-dark entertainment. Where you see smiling waiters and cabin attendants, the line is telling you you'll get special treatment from their staff. If you see smiling children and their happy parents, the line is tipping you off that they welcome families on board. And if you see lots of food pictures, they're telling you, Miss Scarlett, you'll never be hungry again!

The **ITINERARY TABLES** are also valuable sources of information. If the copywriter extols a particular Caribbean island where you'll get a breathtaking view from atop a volcanic mountain in the island's center, and the itinerary says you dock at 9 a.m. and sail at noon, there's no way you'll see that view. And if your Greek Islands cruise arrives in Hydra at 9 p.m. and departs at 10:30 that same evening, you won't have many slides to show the folks back home.

Watch out for the little **ASTERISKS THAT DENOTE "CRUISE BY"** for some ports or islands. While you may get a look at them through binoculars or telephoto lenses, you won't set foot ashore.

If the itinerary has two cities shown, one of them in parentheses —say, Civitavecchia (for Rome) or Livorno (for Florence)—you can expect a long bus ride from the port town to the destination city. A nine-to-five stop in Civitavecchia would allow you only a couple of hours in Rome by the time the ship clears immigration and the bus makes its way through heavy traffic.

Be sure, too, to note the **DAY OF THE WEEK** you're scheduled to arrive in each port. If there's a special museum you want to visit, check to be sure it's open on the day you're there. If you're counting on some serious shopping in St. Thomas, remember that stores are closed on Sundays, except for a few that open for a quick couple of hours in the morning when a ship is in port.

DECK PLANS are helpful in spotting extra niceties on board that aren't always promoted—the library, card room, sauna and spa, beauty and barber shop, hospital, covered decks and enclosed galleries.

DINING ROOM DIAGRAMS can tip you off as to how close together the tables are and if there are many tables for two available. Note that on older ships the dining room is usually on a lower deck, where your only view is of closed draperies backlit with fluorescent tubing to give the illusion of daylight.

What **ABOUT THE FOOD** on board? A discerning gourmet can usually tell from the photographs. Don't waste too much time studying the overwrought, gelatin-encased gala buffet; it's as standard on mass market seven-day Caribbean ships as the deck chairs and about as tasty.

In today's more health-conscious world, salmon has supplanted beef as the food photo of choice in cruise brochures, and more space is given to appetizers and small plate dishes than main courses or gala buffets, suggesting to the nervous first-timer that he won't necessarily gain weight on this ship.

You can usually tell from the pictures whether the cruise line will go out of its way to offer an interesting excursion ashore or simply **sell you a three-hour bus tour**.

CABIN SIZE is better determined from deck plans than photographs. In the latter, the photographer is usually shooting with a wide-angle lens while braced in the doorway or crouching in the shower. These lenses can distort a standard-sized berth into a bed fit for Magic Johnson.

And watch out for the brochure that shows **ONLY PICTURES OF DESTINATIONS AND CLOSE-UPS OF ATTRACTIVE MODELS DRINKING CHAMPAGNE**. Unless the ship was still under construction or undergoing extensive refitting when the photos were made, you suspect, maybe rightly, that they're trying to hide something from you.

After practicing a while with the pictures and diagrams, you should be in fine shape to tackle the prose and read between the lines. For additional assistance, check out **The Brochure Says** and **Translation** segments for each ship in the ship review section.

EAVESDROPPING

"I expected something Noel Cowardish on my first cruise, but instead there were all these people in polyester acting like every night was New Year's Eve, the deck chairs were all jammed up together and the man next to me was listening to Mexican rock-and-roll on his radio. Later I learned ways of finding quiet, remote hiding places for reading, and some of the people turned out to be very nice." A female passenger who chose the wrong cruise line for her first cruise.

CHOOSING A CRUISE

Sometimes equating a ship with a hotel can help a first-time cruiser visualize it better; this soaring atrium lobby from Royal Caribbean's **Nordic Empress** *may remind you of your favorite Marriott.*

Pick a Ship, Any Ship

OK, you say, a cruise sounds great. Where do I sign up?

That's like saying a hotel is a hotel, book me a room. If you're a Ritz-Carlton regular, you might not be happy at the Motel 6. We feel a lot of otherwise experienced travelers might be more comfortable with cruising if they could equate a cruise line with a hotel company, so we've taken a bit of poetic license to give you a chance to relate your favorite type of land accommodations to the possibilities at sea. Bear in mind, however, that although ships are looking more and more like land hotels, the cruise ship experience is often superior, especially in service and entertainment, to its shoreside equivalent.

Bed-and-breakfasts	**Alaska Sightseeing**	*page 89*
	American Canadian Caribbean Line	*page 117*
	American Hawaii	*page 127*
	Clipper Cruises	*page 205*
	Delta Queen Steamboat	*page 319*
	St. Lawrence Cruise Lines	*page 721*
Club Med	**Club Med Cruises**	*page 213*
	Star Clippers	*page 727*
	Windjammer Barefoot Cruises	*page 771*
Four Seasons	**Silversea Cruises**	*page 689*
Holiday Inn	**Premier Cruises**	*page 527*
	Sun Line	*page 749*
Howard Johnson	**Commodore**	*page 221*
	Dolphin	*page 339*
	Regal Cruises	*page 601*
Hyatt Regency	**Costa Cruises**	*page 229*
	Princess Cruises	*page 541*
Inter-Continental	**Celebrity Cruises**	*page 179*
Marriott	**Norwegian Cruise Line**	*page 463*
	Royal Caribbean Cruise Ltd.	*page 621*
MGM Grand	**Carnival Cruises**	*page 149*
Relais & Chateaux	**Sea Goddess**	*page 303*
	Radisson Seven Seas	*page 583*
	Windstar Cruises	*page 787*
Ritz-Carlton	**Crystal Cruises**	*page 267*
	Cunard Royal Viking Sun	*page 298*
	Seabourn	*page 665*
	Vistafjord	*page 307*
Small Luxury Hotels	**Renaissance Cruises' Small Ships**	*page 609*
Westin	**Holland America Line**	*page 415*
Summer camp	**World Explorer**	*page 795*

Choosing a Cabin

Prices for the cruise are determined by the **cabin category**, which in turn is based on **deck location**, **amenities**, whether the cabin is **outside** (with a porthole or windows) or **inside** (with no daylight), and sometimes, but not always, on cabin **size**.

Don't expect to snap up the bottom-priced loss leader (the one advertised in big print in the ads) because some cruise ships may have only four or six of these, long since allotted or sometimes assigned to cruise staff or entertainers.

Standard cabin amenities always include a **bed** or berth for each passenger, closet and **storage** space, some sort of table or **dresser, private bathroom facilities** (except on P&O's *Canberra* and some sailing ships) with toilet, sink, tub or shower. Most have **individual temperature controls, telephone and radio and/or TV**.

Grand suites like the Royal Suite aboard RCCL's Majesty of the Seas have many pleasurable extras such as separate living and sleeping areas and entertainment centers.

Pleasurable extras in upper price categories may include **private verandas**, suites with **separate living room** and bedroom, **mini-refrigerators**, sitting areas and **picture windows**.

Families with children or several people traveling together will save money by booking cabins with third and fourth upper berths, pull-down bunks that go for much less money (sometimes free) than the first two beds in a cabin.

Disabled travelers will find most vessels have one or more cabins that are specially configured to take care of wheelchairs with **wider doors, turning space, low or flat sills and grab rails in the bathroom**.

Dining Room Know-How

Your cruise ship dining room will operate in one of three ways:

1. **Totally open seatings**, usually on small or ultra-luxury vessels, in which the passenger arrives within a given time frame and sits where and with whom he pleases.

2. **Single meal seatings**, in which the passenger arrives within a given time frame and occupies an assigned table for the duration of the cruise.

3. **Two meal seatings**, in which passengers are assigned to dine at a particular table at a specified time, usually 6 p.m. or 8:30 p.m. for dinner, with breakfast and lunch comparably early or late as well.

The two-seating arrangement is the most common. You'll probably be asked at the time of booking which you prefer, but there's no guarantee you'll get it. If you don't get **a card with a specified dining time and table number** in advance or find it in your cabin when you arrive on board, go immediately to the maitre d'hotel in the dining room or another designated area and arrange your seating.

Some ships offer in addition to the regular dining room an alternative restaurant available at no extra charge but by reservation only, like An Evening at Don Vito's aboard Radisson Seven Seas' Radisson Diamond.

Second seating times are the most in demand on Caribbean and Mediterranean cruises, first seating times in Alaska. Don't be upset if you don't get your first choice on a cruise, particularly if the ship is full, but if it means a lot, **chat quietly with the maitre d'hotel, expressing your desire while tactfully holding a $20 bill** and you may be able to negotiate a change.

You can request first or second seating, a smoking (on those ships that still allow smoking in the dining room) or nonsmoking table and the table size you wish. Most first-time cruisers request tables for two, which are relatively rare, but find they enjoy being seated at a larger table for six or eight. The most potentially problematic table size is for four. If you can't stand your tablemates and want to move, be decisive—**make your move at the end of the very first dinner**. Don't wait a couple of days to see if they get more charming. They won't.

Some ships offer alternative restaurant dining by reservation; there is no charge except sometimes a request to tip at point of service. This enables passengers seated at a large table in the regular dining room to have a private dinner for two or an opportunity to dine with new acquaintances.

Cruise Line Cuisine

It seems to us that TV's "The Love Boat" was on the wrong track. Episode after episode, the passengers seemed to spend an inordinate amount of time falling in and out of love. You hardly ever saw anybody agonizing about what to order for dinner.

But if you took a poll of real-life cruise passengers, you'd find more of them looking forward to encountering a lobster thermidor than a shipboard romance, and to lighting into a dish of cherries jubilee instead of starting a flame in someone's heart.

Italian buffet night brings a dessert display aboard Majesty's **Royal Majesty.**

Cruise ship brochures entice us with full-color photographs of voluptuous midnight buffets, centerfolds of sensuous bananas flambe, lush melons and wicked croissants on a bedside tray. Is it any wonder we bound up the gangway anticipating a tryst with a tournedos of tenderloin Rossini?

But all too often our hopes are cruelly dashed, like the heartsick swain on a recent trans-Pacific cruise who spent six fruitless days and nights searching for the grand buffet of his dreams. "It was right there on page 8 in the brochure," he sighed, "but I couldn't find it anywhere on the ship."

In the fantasy world of cruise-ship advertising, every meal is a gourmet feast fit for a king, or even a restaurant critic. But in the real world on board, that's not always the case.

Think for a minute about your favorite little gourmet restaurant, the place you go once or twice a year to celebrate a special occasion. Does it serve two full dinner seatings an evening to between 500 and 1000 people, plus offering breakfast and lunch?

Does it operate a cafeteria on the side, along with a tearoom, half-a-dozen bars with snacks and hot hors d'oeuvres, a specialty pizzeria or ice cream parlor, and a catering service that produces beach picnics, deck barbecues and delivers meals to your door?

Is it atop a remote mountain peak or on an island in the middle of the ocean, hundreds of miles from a reliable source of food supplies?

No? Then don't try to compare most cruise ship cooking to a three-star *Michelin Guide* restaurant. Of course, there are a few exceptions (see Six Best Floating Dining Rooms, page 11).

Small ships, on the other hand, usually turn out tastier food because they don't have to deal with as much volume, but on the down side, their menus are usually more restrictive.

Five Food Fanatic Tips About Ships

1. Most large ships serve high-quality **hotel banquet food**, most often capably prepared and attractively served. You'll encounter a few truly memorable dishes, some mediocre ones and, at least once during your cruise will be served something unidentifiable that you're sure you didn't order until the waiter affirms that it is indeed the chef's version of gazpacho or pecan pie.

2. Before you sign on the dotted line with your friendly neighborhood travel agent, ask to **see some menus** from the ship you're considering—not prototype menus like some publish in their brochures, but actual menus that have the date printed on them from a recent cruise, preferably one the agent picked up during her cruise. (Because you fussy eaters are not going to accept an agent's recommendation unless she's been aboard that ship, at least for lunch, are you?)

3. Most mass market, mini-cruise and seven-day Caribbean lines have **rotation menu plans** that are not repeated during a single cruise but rather follow each other every seven or 14 or 21 days. Theme evenings are popular—French night with onion soup and *escargots* and *coq au vin*, Italian nights with antipasto, pasta and veal scaloppine, American nights with shrimp cocktail, corn on the cob and roast turkey with cranberry sauce. **In this book, such cuisine is referred to as Themed**.

4. Once on board, **shop around early in the cruise** for the location of the breakfasts, lunches and snacks that really sing out to you, and once you've found a winner, stick with it. Menus are usually posted ahead of time, so you can do your window-shopping in advance.

5. **Talk to your waiter**, and if he's good, learn to trust him. He's there to make you happy; his tip depends on it. Let him know what you like and dislike early in the cruise, and he'll always lead you through the menu. We treasure a memory of one of our first cruises, a Sitmar waiter named Tony who delivered the luncheon dish we'd ordered but materialized a few minutes later with another dish we hadn't ordered, murmuring, "I thought you might like to taste this one, too." Our choice was wrong; his was right.

DID YOU KNOW?

Cruise line food has improved tremendously in the 15 years we've been covering the scene. We remember a Dutch chef on the Rotterdam world cruise in 1985 who was going to retire at the end of that 100-day journey, and went to bizarre extremes not to repeat a single dish during the entire cruise. By the time we got on for the last leg, he was down to truly terrible combinations.

Five Tips on Reading a Shipboard Menu

1. See if it gives you **a variety of lunch options** from brunch-type dishes if you missed breakfast (omelets, for instance) to lighter fare (sandwiches and main-dish salads) to something hearty if you're hungry.

2. Check the **light or low-calorie recommendation**. We saw a ship once listing the day's diet special as Cobb Salad, that high-fat, high-calorie concoction of chopped bacon, blue cheese, avocado, and eggs with a gloppy-thick dressing. You'd never lose weight on that diet.

3. See how much **fresh food versus canned** or prepepared dishes they offer. Fresh catch of the day may be prefrozen, but that's to be expected unless you're cruising in Alaska. Watch out for that long list of seven appetizers, most of them tinned juices.

4. See if they're pulling out all their stops on the dessert menu. A lot of lines cut food costs by **stuffing passengers with sugary sweets** and stodgy starches—you'll note the macaroni salads and jello on the buffets—spending about $1.98 a day per passenger on raw materials.

5. Eye the dish descriptions carefully to make sure the line isn't **blanding out all the dishes** with cream-based sauces instead of fresh herbs, garlic or imaginative seasoning.

INSIDER TIP

Check the nationality of the ship's officers, chef or dining room staff. Princess ships have British and Italian officers but an Italian dining room and galley staff, so you can expect continental cuisine with a definite Italian accent. Greek ships are going to serve continental dishes plus Greek salads and appetizers and at least one Greek menu a cruise. The Norwegians like to put out lavish seafood smorgasbords somewhere along the way.

How to Avoid Pigging Out at Sea

Take advantage of the exercise classes and spa aboard the ship; you've paid for them just as you have all that food you feel compelled to eat. Here, wanna-be Antarctic explorers work out aboard the World Discoverer.

1. Shop around, reading posted menus in advance and **checking out the entire buffet display** before plowing in.

2. **Don't stuff yourself.** Help save the whales by not being one; let the fishes finish your food.

3. Unless your metabolism is fantastic, **skip a meal every now and then**, substituting teatime for lunch or scheduling an hour in the disco before judiciously checking out the late buffet.

4. **Beware of Greeks** (or Italians or Jamaicans or Austrians) **bearing dishes**; a soulful-eyed waiter usually has his tip rather than your figure in mind when he coaxes you into ordering an appetizer, soup, salad, fish, meat and two desserts.

5. **Steer clear of piña coladas** and any other drink you can't see through or that has an umbrella in it. Opt instead for mineral water or diet soda, a glass of wine or light beer.

6. Take advantage of **the exercise classes and spa**; you've paid for them just as much as you have all that food you feel compelled to eat.

7. You'll find **vegetarian and low-fat** or low-calorie dishes on practically every menu these days, as well as a wider range of fish and poultry and less red meat.

8. If we want a vegetarian dinner, we sometimes order a plate of all the **side vegetable dishes** on the menu rather than the same old boring steamed cauliflower, broccoli and carrots.

9. Try ordering **dishes without the sauce**. Contrary to the famous Jack Nicholson "whole wheat toast" scene from *Five Easy Pieces*, most waiters will be happy to bring you sauce on the side or lemon wedges instead of salad dressing.

10. When you lunch on deck, plan to wear your bathing suit or shorts, and **check out the row of slender young sylphs and Adonises by the pool** (or for that matter, the not-so-slender ones) for positive reinforcement before you fill your plate.

Ship Sanitation Inspections

The way food is handled from its very arrival aboard the ship to its storage, as here in the food storage lockers on Cunard's **Vistafjord**, *and its final holding and preparation can affect the ship sanitation score.*

A great deal of attention is being paid these days to the "green sheet" ship sanitation inspection scores from U.S. Public Health's Center for Disease Control that are issued every two weeks.

It's laudable that the Center for Disease Control is carrying out the program because it keeps the cruise lines on their toes, making them train and carefully observe the galley employees, who may speak a dozen different languages.

But by **the time the score has been published, it's history**, and the infraction has been corrected long ago. As a rule, ships are inspected every six months, but may go a year or even longer without a reinspection unless the cruise line requests one. Many cruise lines employ a trained sanitation expert to establish and monitor their own sanitation practices.

The only real value of the scores for a potential passenger is as a longtime study of a specific ship over a couple of years. If the vessel is a consistent failure, then chances are its galley and sanitation practices are sloppy.

A single 30-point infraction causes the ship to fail automatically, since 86 out of a possible 100 is the passing grade. Improper methods of handling food are responsible for most major point losses, with temperature violations in food holding, preparation and serving areas the most critical.

Unannounced inspections are carried out at regular intervals on foreign-flag ships that call even occasionally in U.S. ports. When a ship fails, it can (and almost always does) request a reinspection as soon as possible to show the problem has been cleared up.

We went through all the "green sheets" for a one-year period and found an interesting pattern. Some of the cleanest and most highly-regarded ships were occasionally among the failures. The super-deluxe *Seabourn Pride*, which scored a 74 on February 19, 1995, but was retested March 21 and scored a 94; the spic-and-span *Rotterdam*, which scored a 78 on April 18, 1995, but bounced back with a 93 on May 24; and the stately *Sagafjord*, which failed with an 81 on April 23, 1995, but rescored a 96 on June 12. On the other hand, some vintage budget ships—notably the *Regal Empress* from Regal Cruises—held a score of a 95 during most of the time period, dropped to an 86, still passing, during a later period, and scored a 97 on the June 24, 1995, inspection. This despite the fact that before its first scheduled sailing from New York, officials went down to the dock and handed out flyers pointing out sanitation levels so low passengers might not wish to sail with her. In the first quarter of 1996, the *Crystal Symphony* and Celebrity's *Century* both scored a rare 100.

Ships most commonly fail on the last inspection before they're sold or transferred, probably because the crew is less motivated. Brand-new ships or new cruise lines (the latter the case with Regal Cruises) are usually given a couple of preliminary inspections with notes before getting a published score. "It's not unusual for a new ship to fail, because generally you have a lot of new people with new equipment," one of the inspectors told us.

The CDC inspectors have improved the quality of ship sanitation tremendously over the years, as well as carrying on an education program for kitchen workers who may come from a culture with different sanitation standards. Very few land-based restaurants could score an 86 or better under the CDC standards, according to former program head Tom Hunt, who had previously been a restaurant inspector. Unless a ship consistently fails over a period of time, there's no real way of determining whether a passenger might suffer a gastrointestinal illness aboard.

In fact, we were inadvertently once the cause of a ship sanitation rating failure when photographing the dining room for a food magazine. The chef had stuck a bouquet of fresh flowers in the walk-in refrigerator to keep them fresh until the shoot, and the CDC inspectors on the surprise inspection seized them as a major infraction—non-food items stored with food items.

Six Questions About Ship Sanitation Scores

1. Does anyone ever score a perfect score?

Yes, the first ship to make 100 on the numerical listings, which were initiated in 1989, was Carnival's *Fantasy* on April 30, 1990, followed by Windstar's *Wind Spirit* which scored 100 on August 27, 1990. More recently, *Crown Dynasty*, now *Cunard Dynasty*, scored 100 on February 8, 1994, and the *Crystal Symphony* and Celebrity's *Century* made it in early 1996.

2. What's the lowest score ever recorded?

The lowest one we've found was a 23 for Epirotiki's *Oceanos* back in 1989; that ship sank off the coast of South Africa in 1991.

3. Can the CDC keep a ship from sailing because of poor sanitation?

Cooperation is voluntary on the part of the ship being inspected. The vessel sanitation program cannot forbid a ship with extreme sanitation problems to sail until its problems are corrected; it can only recommend that it not sail.

4. Who pays for these inspections?

The cruise lines themselves.

5. Are all cruise ships inspected?

The CDC's jurisdiction covers all ships carrying 13 or more passengers that sail in international waters. It does not include U.S.-flag vessels sailing in U.S. waters like those of American Hawaii, Delta Queen Steamboat, Alaska Sightseeing/Cruise West, or American Queen. Those ships are the responsibility of the Food and Drug Administration and the state health departments within their cruising areas.

6. How can I get a copy of the latest scores?

Via Internet, FTP.CDC.GOV//PUB/SHIP_INSPECTIONS/SHIP-SCORE.TXT, or by calling ☎ *(404) 332-4565* and requesting Document No. 510051.

Safety of Life at Sea

Commonly called SOLAS, Safety of Life at Sea regulations govern cruise ships that call at U.S. ports. Whenever a new ship comes into service, or enters a U.S. port for its first call, it must undergo a rigorous set of inspections by the U.S. Coast Guard covering fire safety drills, use of emergency equipment, crew drills and detailed examinations of the condition and safety of the vessel's hull and its machinery. After the initial series of inspections, the ships are reinspected quarterly. Unlike the CDC inspectors described above, the Coast Guard has the power to detain a ship from sailing if it is deemed unsafe for its passengers.

The Coast Guard's Traveling Inspectors team boards ships with emergencies to investigate causes, such as those numerous incidents in the summer of 1995—ships running aground, engine room fires, main engines down and sweltering passengers aboard ships with no electricity, air conditioning or hot food. There were few injuries and no loss of life reported in any of the incidents, but in some of the vessels the backup equipment went out as well, which is unusual on modern ships.

Still, stringent new SOLAS regulations being implemented beginning in 1997 seriously affect the cruise industry, because they require detailed (and costly) amendments and additions to older vessels, from sprinkler systems to freon-free air conditioning systems and low-level lighting systems.

> **INSIDER TIP**
>
> *Many of the older ships are being sold to operators abroad to sail exclusively from non-U.S. ports, and so do not come under U.S. Coast Guard inspections and SOLAS regulations. Be cautious about buying a bargain cruise on a ship that sails only from Mediterranean or Asian ports if you're concerned about ship safety.*

Where in the World Do You Want to Go?

The Caribbean, Alaska, Mexican Riviera, New England and Canada, Panama Canal, the Mediterranean, Northern Europe, South Pacific and Asia are all familiar, at least in concept, and easily accessible.

But with the magic of overland excursions, riverboats and canal barges, you can also consider as ports of call the Taj Mahal, Kenya's game parks, the city of St. Louis, the Burgundy wine country or the Pyramids.

No poll, rating system or expert travel agent can tell all potential cruise passengers that any one experience is "best." A well-worn truism says neophyte cruisers care most about ports of call, veteran cruisers about which ship. In either case, you'll want to concern yourself about more than where you're going and how much it's going to cost.

To check out the dream ports you're planning to visit, read "Cruising to the World's Top Ports," page 823.

Five Hints for a Hassle-Free Cruise

1. The shorter the cruise, the younger and more casual the group on board is likely to be. For most first-time cruisers, the **introduction to cruising is aboard a three- or four-day mini-cruise** from Florida or California. See Short Sails, Big Sales, page 23.

2. If you want a smooth, trouble-free sailing, **avoid any shakedown, inaugural, maiden voyage or first sailing on the heels of major renovations**. Although some ships have sailed through these with flying colors, this is when the vessel is most vulnerable to plumbing, heating, air conditioning and water pressure problems.

3. If you are considering booking a ship that never sails from a U.S. port and your travel agent has no firsthand knowledge of it, take some time to **check it out before putting down a deposit no matter how tempting the price**. Some lesser-known vessels or very low-priced sailings may feature discounted cabins left over from a group or charter, or a cruise marketed primarily in another country, and you could find yourself odd man out. Also, these vessels are no longer inspected regularly by the U.S. Coast Guard and could represent a safety hazard.

4. When dealing **with waiters and stewards** to whom English is a second or third language, speak slowly and distinctly and **be ready with an alternative word** when they don't understand your initial request. That way you'll be spared the problem one infuriated passenger had with her Scandinavian stewardess who did not know what a "cantaloupe" was; if the passenger had switched to the word "melon," she would have gotten a serving of breakfast fruit instead of the envelope that was delivered by the bewildered Norwegian.

With waiters and stewards to whom English is a second language, like this Greek bartender, speak slowly and distinctly when ordering something.

5. **Read the fine print** at the end of the company brochure and on the back of your ticket/contract, and you'll find **the line is not responsible for missed ports of call**, changed itineraries or liabilities in connection with independent contractors such as airlines and ground tour operators.

Seven Ways to Protect Yourself from Travel Scams

1. **Be skeptical**. If an offer seems too good to be true, it probably is. Unsolicited "prizes" you get through the mail or over the phone promising a free cruise usually involve your calling in and giving someone your credit card number or paying a "service fee" for a trip that never materializes.

2. **Follow up**. If you book through a discount agency's 800 number, don't send them checks or money orders. Use a credit card, but only after ascertaining that the cruise line rather than the agency will process the charge. Verify the reservation by demanding the vendor's confirmation number.

3. **Never give out your credit card number on the phone to someone who called you.**

4. **Don't buy a cruise from a toll-free 800 telephone number if you haven't checked them out**; it's better to visit the office in person and **talk face-to-face with a travel agent**. Several major cruise travel agencies with 800 numbers, some of them in business for years and regarded as reliable, went bankrupt suddenly in the last year or two, leaving clients high and dry and cruise-less.

5. Check any agency you're dealing with to see if they're **members of professional travel organizations** such as ASTA (American Society of Travel Agents), ARTA (Association of Retail Travel Agents), CLIA (Cruise Line International Association) or NACOA (North American Cruise-Only Agencies).

6. **Double-check with the cruise line** itself to confirm bookings and all payments.

7. When in doubt, **call the National Consumer's League Hotline**, ☎ *(800) 876-7060.*

Grand staircase, *American Queen*

Holland America's *MS Statendam* in Monte Carlo

SPECIAL CASES

Many ships sail with a number of gentlemen hosts aboard to dance with unattached ladies; here a dance class is in progress.

Singles

Anyone browsing through a cruise brochure notices sooner or later that ubiquitous term "per person, double occupancy" in conjunction with prices.

But what happens to passengers, as many as 25 per cent of all potential travelers, who travel alone?

Generally, when one person occupies a double cabin, a surcharge that runs from 125 to 200 per cent of the per person double occupancy rate is charged.

There are only two sure-fire ways to avoid the singles surcharge:

Opt for a **"guaranteed share"** from lines that offer it, which means the line will attempt to find another passenger of the same sex, general age range and smoking preference to match up with you or let you have the double cabin to yourself at the per person double occupancy rate.

Find a ship, usually an older vessel, that has **designated single cabins** and pay the listed fare, which often works out to be nearly as much as a double cabin surcharge. Single cabins are available aboard Cunard's *Vistafjord* and *QE2*, American Hawaii, World Explorer, Norwegian Cruise Line's *Norway*, Holland America's *Rotterdam*, and Ivaran's *Americana*, which often prices single cabins at the same or lower price as the per person double occupancy rates.

For 20-to-40 year-olds, Windjammer Barefoot Cruises offers a half-dozen "singles cruises" throughout the year on designated dates, with half the passengers male and half female, they promise. (They cite five marriages from previous singles sailings.)

Over-50 travelers might want to opt for something a little less casual. Single women with social dancing and bridge-playing on their minds will find ships that carry social hosts (see below) have a definite appeal.

Everything You Ever Wanted to Know About Social Hosts

1. What lines carry them?

Cunard Line, Silversea Cruises, Delta Queen Steamboat Company, Crystal Cruises, Holland America (on longer cruises), American Hawaii (on selected Big Band sailings).

2. Who are they?

Usually retired businessmen or military men, single, divorced or widowed, and upwards of 50 years old.

3. Can I count on romance?

No, just socializing, dancing, bridge playing and companionship at mealtimes and on shore excursions. Anything else, including spending too much time with one passenger, is forbidden. However, some social hosts have met ladies aboard and continued to see them on land without having to follow the cruise line's rules. Several marriages are said to have come out of meetings between social hosts and passengers.

4. How many hosts are usually on board?

Anywhere from two to ten or more, depending on the size of the ship and how many single female passengers are booked for that sailing.

5. How can someone get a job as a social host?

The leading (and perhaps only) agent for social hosts is Lauretta Blake of **The Working Vacation**, *4277 Lake Santa Clara Drive, Santa Clara, CA 95054,* ☎ *(408) 727-9665.* She screens and books hosts for several cruise lines for $150 fee per week at sea, paid by the host.

The cruise lines themselves do not charge a fee for placing hosts; you could send a letter, picture and resume directly to the cruise line's personnel department or director of entertainment. Most hold regular "auditions."

The hosts usually receive no payment beyond the free cruise, economy class airfare to and from the ship, and a modest allowance for onboard expenditures such as wine and bar bills. Cruise lines usually require their hosts take two or three cruises back to back, and sleep two to a cabin.

Five Tips for Cruising with Kids

Children love diving into the plastic balls aboard Majesty's **Royal Majesty.**

1. Book a ship that is likely to have other young children aboard. Whether a kid is six or 16, he's happy if he can find someone near his own age. Otherwise he can get bored and fidgety. (See "Five Best Ships for Families," page 5).

2. Don't expect free 24-hour baby-sitting. The youth counselors are there to enrich your child's vacation, not take him off your hands. A few lines offer babysitting in the evenings in the youth center, usually with a surcharge.

3. Don't take the kids on a cruise line that doesn't offer a children's program, discounts on their fare and counselors on staff—that's a tipoff the ship and its regular passengers would be happier without children on board.

4. Check with the cruise line if your child is under two; many lines have minimum age limits.

5. Look for the 'toons—The Big Red Boats of Premier have a contract with Warner Brothers' Looney Tunes, which means Bugs Bunny and Tweety Bird on deck; Dolphin and Majesty sail with Hanna Barbera's Fred Flintstone and Yogi Bear aboard.

INSIDER TIP

In case you're wondering who's inside the furry suit animating Yogi Bear or Andy Panda, it's usually a member of the ship's crew—perhaps a dishwasher or night cleaning person—who's paid extra to portray the cartoon character. Look at it this way—he's in show biz.

Ten Cruise Tips for Seniors

Pick and choose among the many meals and snacks offered every day, perhaps enjoying teatime treats, like passengers aboard Cunard's Royal Viking Sun.

1. A ship's size and itinerary have a direct relationship with how quickly sophisticated medical care can be obtained in an emergency; large ships have more medical staff and facilities on board, and more importantly, some have a landing pad for a helicopter to land and evacuate a seriously ill passenger.

2. Have your doctor write the details of any ongoing medical condition, as well as any prescription drugs or serious allergies, on an index card and give it to the ship's doctor when you board.

3. Study the deck plan of the vessel you're considering for elevators if you use a wheelchair or tire easily climbing stairs.

4. Check to make sure the cabin category you're booking provides two lower beds rather than an upper and a lower, which can make getting in and out of bed more difficult.

5. Check itineraries to determine where the ship will dock as opposed to where it anchors and tenders; going down a gangway on the side of the ship and transferring to a bobbing launch calls for steady footing.

6. Exercise care and moderation in food and drink; avoid any major changes in your normal eating pattern.

7. Pick and choose; sample the six or eight meals a day a few at a time, skipping lunch, perhaps, in favor of a big breakfast and afternoon tea, or have a light dinner to save room for the midnight buffet.

8. Don't overtax yourself in every port of call; take a half-day tour instead of a full-day tour, or take an early morning stroll around the port town, come back to the ship for a midday break and then go back in late afternoon for a second look if you wish.

9. Remember that comfort is more important than fashion in tropical areas; wear broken-in walking shoes and loose-fitting clothing.

10. Mix and mingle; don't seclude yourself or limit your choice of companions to others your own age.

Getting Married Aboard

While the popularity of honeymoons at sea has been increasing steadily for the past five years, some cruise lines now offer the additional option of getting married aboard ship. Then the bride and groom can sail away on their honeymoon cruise with—or without—other members of the wedding party.

Couples on a budget like the convenience and romance of a shipboard wedding, where they can have a smaller ceremony with only a few guests. By marrying on a ship instead of celebrating a big wedding ashore, they might even save enough to pay for the honeymoon cruise.

Contrary to popular belief, a ship's captain is not empowered to conduct a wedding ceremony, "at least not one that will last longer than the cruise," one captain jokes.

But couples booked on the sailing may get married in port, using either an officiate provided by the cruise line, or a minister, rabbi or priest they bring themselves.

Packages vary from basic (under $300 for a notary and witnesses, cake and champagne for the newlyweds) to elaborate (a two-hour reception with open bar, hot and cold buffet and champagne toasts for around $75 a person). Many are coordinated for the cruise line by private wedding consultant companies.

Most common ports where weddings can be arranged include Miami and Los Angeles, several Hawaii ports including Honolulu, Hilo and Kona, St. Thomas in the U.S. Virgin Islands, Tortola in the British Virgin Islands, Vancouver, BC, and Juneau, Alaska.

Cruise lines that offer wedding packages include American Hawaii, Carnival, Celebrity, Dolphin, Holland America, Majesty, Norwegian Cruise Line, Princess, Royal Caribbean and Windjammer Barefoot Cruises.

EAVESDROPPING

"Twenty-five years ago if you took a honeymoon cruise, your name was Rockefeller. Now it's Smith or Jones," says Bob Dickinson, president of Carnival Cruise Lines.

Five Tips for Honeymooners at Sea

1. Check when booking if you want a double or king-sized bed; some vintage vessels have twin beds that cannot be pushed together.

2. Tables for two are not always guaranteed; some cruise lines put couples at tables of six or eight. Your travel agent can request a table for two or arrange for you to be seated with other honeymooners at a large table.

3. If you want to be singled out for congratulations, special onboard parties for newlyweds and the like, let your agent know. But if you want anonymity, say so in advance or you may be serenaded by the waiters in the dining room when you'd rather be left alone.

4. Check to see which lines offer complimentary champagne, souvenir photos or special receptions with other honeymooners. Others can provide extra goodies with add-on packages adoring friends or relatives might like to donate.

5. Since most cruise lines limit the number of onboard weddings per sailing, it's a good idea to make plans and reservations as far in advance as possible.

Cruising for the Physically Challenged

While going ashore by tender is normally difficult or impossible for wheelchair travelers, the large tender from NCL's Norway handles them with ease.

More and more of the estimated 36 million physically challenged Americans are booking cruise vacations, either with groups or as independent travelers. Most experience the same pleasurable holiday other cruise passengers do, but a few report everything from minor inconveniences to major problems.

The problem for some independent physically-challenged is the requirement or request from virtually every cruise line that they be accompanied by an "able-bodied" companion. One way around this would be to book a special group tour that would have its own escorts and personnel aboard to take the extra responsibility away from the ship's staff for alerting deaf or sightless travelers in case of an emergency.

Cruising is one of the very best vacations for wheelchair travelers so long as the ship has elevators, wide corridors, and cabins specially configured to take care of wheelchairs with wider doors, turning space, an absence of high sills, and grab rails and a pulldown shower seat in the bathroom. Often, but not always, these cabins may also have a lower hanging rack and storage shelves placed conveniently low. But sometimes cabins are designated accessible and their bathrooms don't comply. Even if there is no sill to negotiate and the door is 25 inches rather than the standard 22 inches wide—both adequate for wheelchairs—should the door open in and to the right, for instance, and the toilet is behind it, there's no way a wheelchair occupant can use it.

While some wheelchair travelers will improvise with portable toilet and basin facilities in order to be able to sail on an otherwise inaccessible ship, others are rightly indignant if a line promises accessibility and they don't get it. Unfortunately, many cruise line employees don't have access to the specific cabin measurements for all their ships. You're better off booking through a travel agency that specializes in trips for the disabled.

Going ashore by tender in some cases is difficult or impossible for wheelchair passengers. An exception is the broad-decked Little Norway from NCL's *Norway*, which can be loaded level with the gangway doors, allowing wheelchairs to be rolled on and off the tender. Other cruise lines such as American Hawaii can offload mobility-impaired passengers through the lower deck crew gangway, which is level with the dock, rather than the passenger gangway, which can be steep in many island ports.

Under the cruise lines and ship reviews beginning on page 77, we have tried to point out ships that have accessible cabins we have personally inspected.

AGENCIES SPECIALIZING IN TOURS AND CRUISES FOR THE DISABLED

Flying Wheels Travel
PO Box 382
143 West Bridge St.
Owatonna, MN 55060
☎ (800) 535-6790

Mada Edmonds
Cobb Travel Agency
905 Montgomery Highway
Birmingham, AL 35216
☎ (205) 822-5137

Joe Regan
Able to Travel
247 N. Main Street
Suite 308
Randolph, MA 02368
☎ (800) 557-2047

Joan Diamond & Jill Bellows
Nautilus Tours & Cruises Ltd.
17277 Ventura Blvd. Suite 207
Encino, CA 91316
☎ (818) 788-60004
Outside CA (800) 797 6004

Marilyn Ryback
Dahl's Good Neighbor Travel
7383 Pyramid Place
Los Angeles, CA 90046
☎ (213) 969-0660

Murray Vidocklor
SATH Handicapped Travel
347 Fifth Ave. Suite 610
New York, NY 10016
☎ (212) 447-2784

Judi Smaldino
Tri Venture Travel
1280 Court Street
Redding, CA 96001
☎ (916) 243-3101

Five Tips for Physically Challenged Travelers

1. Be honest with yourself about what you can and cannot do and pass that information on to the travel agent.

2. Be sure your doctor says your condition will allow you to travel.

3. Take it easy; don't try to do everything that's offered just to prove you can.

4. Do take along an aide or companion. Some agents have a list of retired nurses who'll accompany disabled travelers and share a cabin in exchange for the trip.

5. Seeing-eye dogs are accepted on some ships, but each case has to be individually arranged with the cruise line.

Nude Cruises

Nude cruising is the latest wrinkle, according to Roslyn Scheer, executive director of the American Association for Nude Recreation, who says 92 per cent of her organization's members are over 35, and half of them earn more than $50,000 a year.

Three nude cruises a year are offered by **Bare Necessities Tour & Travel** of Austin, Texas, who boast a database of 20,000 names. The company charters small to mid-sized vessels ranging from the sailing ships of Star Clipper to the *Cunard Dynasty.* **Travel Au Naturel** in Land O'Lakes, Florida,charters sailings with costume parties, dancing and a special celebrations. "Some nude shore excursions are also scheduled on certain sailings," says the agency's Christie Musick.

For more information, contact the **American Association for Nude Recreation**, *1703 N. Main Street, Suite E, Kissimmee, FL 34744-3396,* ☎ *(800) TRY-NUDE* or *(407) 933-2064.*

Cruises for Gays

RSVP Cruises, *2800 University Avenue Southeast, Minneapolis, MN 55414,* ☎ *(612) 379-4697.*

Our Family Abroad, *40 W. 57th Street, Suite 430, New York, NY 10019* ☎ *(800) 999-5500.*

Advance Damron Vacations, *Houston, TX* ☎ *(800) 695-0880.*

Cruises for Women Only

Olivia Cruises, *4400 Market Street, Oakland, CA 94608,* charters small cruise ships with sailings exclusively for women. In the past, Greek Islands and Mediterranean cruises have been a particular specialty. Call them at ☎ *(510) 655-0364.*

Cruises with College Classes

Semester At Sea sailings conducted by the Institute for Seaboard Education and the University of Pittsburgh gives a student academic credit for some 50 courses from Global Ecology to Caribbean Literature. Classes meet daily when the ship is at sea, and go on field trips when the ship is in port.

Some 500 students sail on each Semester at Sea program, which also operates a cruise ship in Alaska during the summer. The ship serves as the student dormitory, with sailing students sharing two- and three-berth cabins. All meals are provided on board.

An informational video is available from **Semester at Sea**, *University of Pittsburgh, 811 William Pitt Union, Pittsburgh, PA 15260,* ☎ *(800) 854-0195.*

Christian/Church-Oriented Cruises

Vacations-in-the-Son, *PO Box 91591, Longwood, FL 32791*, markets religion-oriented cruises for groups and charters with born-again Christians. Contact them at ☎ *(407) 862-6568.*

Alcohol-Free Cruises

Serenity Trips, a company that specializes in alcohol-free vacations, schedules family cruises. For details, call ☎ *(800) 615-4665.*

Friends of Bill W meetings are scheduled frequently on many cruise ships.

1997 WORLDWIDE CRUISING: WHO GOES WHERE

WORLD CRUISING

These ships move continuously throughout the world during the year. Those marked **World** do a long cruise in the winter/spring.

Costa Cruise Line	World	*Daphne*	*page 254*
		Mermoz	*page 262*
Crystal Cruises	World	*Crystal Symphony*	*page 270*
Cunard Line	World	*QE2*	*page 284*
	World	*Royal Viking Sun*	*page 298*
Delphin Seereisen	World	*Kazakhstan II*	*page 314*
Holland America Line	World	*Rotterdam*	*page 434*
P & O (Princess Tours)	World	*Canberra*	*page 514*
	World	*Oriana*	*page 518*
Renaissance Cruises		*Renaissance II –VIII*	*page 614*

ALASKA

BAHAMAS

Carnival Cruise Line	*Ecstasy*	page 165
	Fantasy	page 165
Canaveral Cruise Line	*Dolphin IV*	page 146
Dolphin Cruise Line	*OceanBreeze*	page 345
Majesty Cruise Line	*Royal Majesty*	page 456
Norwegian Cruise Line	*Leeward*	page 474
Premier Cruise Lines	*Star/Ship Atlantic*	page 532
	Star/Ship Oceanic	page 536
Regal Cruises	*Regal Empress*	page 604
Royal Caribbean Cruises, Ltd.	*Nordic Empress*	page 637
	Sovereign of the Seas	page 650

BERMUDA

Celebrity Cruises	*Meridian*	page 195
	Zenith	page 190
Cunard Line	*QE2*	page 284
Holland America Line	*Veendam*	page 422
Norwegian Cruise Line	*Dreamward*	page 468
Regal Cruises	*Regal Empress*	page 604
Royal Caribbean Cruises, Ltd.	*Song of America*	page 642

CANADA/NEW ENGLAND

American Canadian Caribbean Line	*Caribbean Prince*	*page 120*
	Mayan Prince	*page 120*
Clipper Cruise Line	*Nantucket Clipper*	*page 208*
Crystal Cruises	*Crystal Symphony*	*page 270*
Cunard Line	*QE2*	*page 284*
Dolphin Cruise Line	*IslandBreeze*	*page 342*
Holland America Line	*Veendam*	*page 422*
	Westerdam	*page 440*
Princess Cruises	*Royal Princess*	*page 561*
Regal Cruises	*Regal Empress*	*page 604*
Seabourn Cruise Line	*Seabourn Legend*	*page 670*
	Seabourn Pride	*page 670*
Silversea Cruises	*Silver Cloud*	*page 692*
Special Expeditions	*Polaris*	*page 712*
St. Lawrence Cruise Line	*Canadian Empress*	*page 723*

CARIBBEAN

American Canadian Caribbean Line	*Caribbean Prince*	*page 120*
	Mayan Prince	*page 120*
	Niagara Prince	*page 120*

CARIBBEAN

Carnival Cruise Line	*Celebration*	*page 159*
	Destiny	*page 155*
	Fascination	*page 165*
	Imagination	*page 165*
	Inspiration	*page 165*
	Sensation	*page 165*
	Tropicale	*page 173*
Celebrity Cruises	*Century*	*page 184*
	Galaxy	*page 184*
	Horizon	*page 190*
	Meridian	*page 195*
	Zenith	*page 190*
Clipper Cruise Line	*Nantucket Clipper*	*page 208*
	Yorktown Clipper	*page 208*
Club Med Cruises	*Club Med 1*	*page 216*
Commodore Cruise Line	*Enchanted Isle*	*page 224*
Costa Cruise Line	*CostaClassica*	*page 240*
	CostaPlaya	*page 246*
	CostaRomantica	*page 240*
	CostaVictoria	*page 252*
Crystal Cruises	*Crystal Symphony*	*page 270*
Cunard Line	*Cunard Countess*	*page 290*
	Cunard Dynasty	*page 294*
	QE2	*page 284*
	Sea Goddess II	*page 303*
	Vistafjord	*page 307*
Dolphin Cruise Line	*IslandBreeze*	*page 342*
	SeaBreeze	*page 349*
EuroCruises	*Black Prince*	*page 390*
Holland America Line	*Nieuw Amsterdam*	*page 428*
	Noordam	*page 428*
	Rotterdam	*page 434*
	Ryndam	*page 422*
	Statendam	*page 422*
	Veendam	*page 422*
	Westerdam	*page 440*
Majesty Cruise Line	*Royal Majesty*	*page 456*
Norwegian Cruise Line	*Dreamward*	*page 468*
	Leeward	*page 474*
	Norway	*page 478*
	Norwegian Crown	*page 484*
	Seaward	*page 488*
	Windward	*page 468*
P & O	*Victoria*	*page 522*

CARIBBEAN

Princess Cruises	Crown Princess	page 547
	Dawn Princess	page 578
	Star Princess	page 573
	Sun Princess	page 578
Radisson Seven Seas Cruises	Radisson Diamond	page 591
Regal Cruises	Regal Empress	page 604
Royal Caribbean Cruises, Ltd.	Grandeur of the Seas	page 626
	Majesty of the Seas	page 631
	Monarch of the Seas	page 631
	Nordic Empress	page 637
	Splendour of the Seas	page 626
	Song of Norway	page 646
	Sovereign of the Seas	page 650
Seabourn Cruise Line	Seabourn Legend	page 670
Sea Cloud Cruises	Sea Cloud	page 675
Seawind Cruise Line	Seawind Crown	page 684
Silversea Cruises	Silver Cloud	page 692
Special Expeditions	Polaris	page 712
Star Clippers	Star Clipper	page 730
	Star Flyer	page 730
Sun Line Cruises	Stella Solaris	page 760
Tall Ship Adventures	Sir Francis Drake	page 767
Windjammer Cruises	Amazing Grace	page 774
	Fantome	page 777
	Flying Cloud	page 777
	Mandalay	page 777
	Polynesia	page 777
	Yankee Clipper	page 777
Windstar Cruises	Wind Spirit	page 790
	Wind Star	page 790
World Explorer Cruises	Universe Explorer	page 797

WEST AFRICA AND CANARY ISLANDS

EAST AND SOUTH AFRICA

GREEK ISLANDS AND TURKEY

HAWAII/TAHITI

American Hawaii Cruises	*Independence*	*page 132*
Carnival Cruise Line	*Tropicale*	*page 173*
Crystal Cruise Line	*Crystal Harmony*	*page 270*
Holland America Line	*Statendam*	*page 422*
Princess Cruises	*Golden Princess*	*page 553*
	Sky Princess	*page 567*
Royal Caribbean Cruises, Ltd.	*Legend of the Seas*	*page 626*
Seabourn Cruise Line	*Seabourn Legend*	*page 670*
Windstar Cruises	*Wind Song*	*page 790*

MEDITERRANEAN

Classical Cruises	*Minerva*	*page 202*
Club Med Cruises	*Club Med 1*	*page 216*
Costa Cruise Line	*CostaAllegra*	*page 234*
	CostaClassica	*page 240*
	CostaRomantica	*page 240*
	CostaVictoria	*page 252*
Crystal Cruises	*Crystal Harmony*	*page 270*
Cunard Line	*Royal Viking Sun*	*page 298*
	Sea Goddess I	*page 303*
	Sea Goddess II	*page 303*
	Vistafjord	*page 307*

MEXICO WEST COAST

ORIENT/ASIA

PANAMA CANAL

SCANDINAVIA AND BALTIC

SOUTH AMERICA

Costa Cruises	*CostaMarina*	*page 234*
	EugenioCosta	*page 258*
Cunard Line	*Royal Viking Sun*	*page 298*
	Vistafjord	*page 307*
Crystal Cruises	*Crystal Harmony*	*page 270*
Ivaran Lines	*Americana*	*page 448*
Princess Cruises	*Pacific Princess*	*page 557*
Silversea Cruises	*Silver Cloud*	*page 692*
Sun Line Cruises	*Stella Solaris*	*page 760*

SOUTH PACIFIC

Club Med Cruises	*Club Med 2*	*page 216*
Esplanade Tours	*Bali Sea Dancer*	*page 372*
Orient Lines	*Marco Polo*	*page 506*
Princess Cruises	*Sky Princess*	*page 567*
Renaissance Cruises	*Renaissance V*	*page 614*
	Renaissance VI	*page 614*
Seabourn Cruise Line	*Seabourn Legend*	*page 670*
Silversea Cruises	*Silver Wind*	*page 692*

COASTAL AND RIVERS

American Canadian Caribbean Line
	Caribbean Prince	*page 120*
	Mayan Prince	*page 120*
	Niagara Prince	*page 120*

American West Steamboat Company — *Queen of the West* — *page 142*

Alaska Sightseeing/Cruise West
	Spirit of Alaska	*page 95*
	Spirit of Columbia	*page 95*
	Spirit of Discovery	*page 100*
	Spirit of Endeavor	*page 104*
	Spirit of Glacier Bay	*page 106*
	Spirit of '98	*page 110*

Clipper Cruise Line
	Nantucket Clipper	*page 208*
	Yorktown Clipper	*page 208*

Delta Queen Steamboat Company
	American Queen	*page 325*
	Delta Queen	*page 330*
	Mississippi Queen	*page 334*

Special Expeditions
	Sea Bird	*page 716*
	Sea Lion	*page 716*

St. Lawrence Cruise Lines — *Canadian Empress* — *page 723*

EXPEDITIONING

AF = Africa; ANT = Antarctica; ARC = Arctic; WW = Worldwide

Abercrombie & Kent	ANT, WW	*Explorer*	*page 84*
Esplanade Tours	AF, WW	*Caledonian Star*	*page 375*

EXPEDITIONING

Golden Bear Travel	ANT, WW	*Bremen*	*page 409*
Orient Lines	ANT	*Marco Polo*	*page 506*
Quark Expeditions	ANT, ARC	*Kapitan Dranitsyn*	*page 803*
	ANT, ARC	*Kapitan Khlebnikov*	*page 803*
	ANT, WW	*Alla Tarasova*	*page 803*
	WW	*Yamal*	*page 803*
	ANT, WW	*Professor Khromov*	*page 803*
	ANT, WW	*Professor Molchanov*	*page 803*
Radisson Seven Seas Cruises	ANT, ARC, AF, WW	*Hanseatic*	*page 587*
Society Expeditions	ANT, WW	*World Discoverer*	*page 703*
Special Expeditions	WW	*Polaris*	*page 712*

UP-FRONT AND PERSONAL

Your Guide to Our Guide

The main body of this book is a thorough compilation of cruise lines, ships and alternative cruises around the world, with 160 ships reviewed, plus details on dozens of other smaller and alternative vessels.

The cruise companies—most are cruise lines but a few are marketing companies who represent various foreign cruise lines—are described first, in alphabetical order, and following each company's description the ships are then described individually or, in the case of identical sister vessels, in a group, but rated individually.

You may note in the book and even within certain segments of it information repeated several times, because we feel many readers will dip into the book at random rather than read it in sequence.

Eight Terms You May Meet for the First Time in This Guide

1. Repositioning—When a vessel moves seasonally from one cruising area of the world to another, it makes a "positioning" or "repositioning" cruise; because the ship has to make the journey whether passengers are aboard or not, the cruises may be discounted, offer an eclectic and unusual itinerary or a lot of leisurely days at sea.

2. Refit—The redecoration or remodeling of a vessel, which can be in drydock (the ship above the waterlevel so hulls can be repainted) or wetdock (the ship in the water). "Soft furnishings" are all the upholstery, draperies, sheets, towels, tablecloths and so on. "Cosmetic" refits are sort of like face lifts—they don't make the ship's life longer, just help her look a little fresher.

3. The Jones Act—The term commonly applied to the 1886 Passenger Service Act, an obscure turn-of-the-century passenger cabotage act designed to protect American shipping by not permitting any foreign-flag vessel to transport people between two points in the United States without calling at one or two foreign ports in between. Since there is very little American passenger shipping left, movement has been underway to strike out the antiquated law, but cargo shipping interests zealously protect it because they feel if it were struck down it would threaten their cargo shipping as well.

4. U.S.-flag ship—For a ship to qualify as a U.S.-flag vessel, it must have been built and registered in the United States, be staffed by a primarily or totally American crew and never have been re-flagged to another country. The only exception to this rule was made in 1979 by Congress for American Hawaii's *Independence*, which lost its U.S. flag when it was sold to a Hong Kong shipping company. See American Hawaii Cruises, page 127.

5. Flags of convenience—A euphemism for ship registrations made in Panama, Liberia, the Bahamas, Cyprus and other nations with low ship taxes and non-hindering union requirements by ship owners who want to save money.

6. Cruise-only—The fare quoted is for the cruise itself and does not provide an air transfer from your home town to the port where you board the ship. You're responsible for getting yourself to the port on time, and getting yourself back home afterwards.

7. Air add-ons—Usually extra fees added on top of a cruise fare that may (or sometimes may not) already include some airfares. The usual routine is to book an air/sea package through the cruise line whenever it's available since the airfare will usually be lower than you could negotiate on your own. But some travelers want to use frequent flyer awards or fly a specific airline or upgrade to business or first class. While upscale lines may offer this option in their air add-ons, the normal cruise line is going to fly you in the cheapest seats on the most inconvenient schedule that can be blocked out. They don't like it; you don't like it. They're at the mercy of the air carriers, and that's why you don't get your air tickets until a few days before you leave on your cruise.

8. Meet-and-greets—These are land-based employees of the cruise line who do all the gathering up and shuttling of passengers between the airport and the ship. They are usually in a uniform of some sort and always carry a sign or clipboard with the name of your cruise line or ship on it. When you see them, check to make sure they have your name on their clipboard list or you may not get a seat on the bus that will take you to the ship.

Eight Things to Remember

1. Report Card—the ratings for ship cabins, food and entertainment based on the way your high school English teacher used to grade your book reports.

2. Average Price PPPD—the average per person per day price, based on double occupancy, for the cruise ship cabin under review.

3. The Bottom Line—Personal observations and ruminations about the vessel or cruise line under review.

4. GRT—Gross Registered Tonnage, not a ship's weight, but rather a measurement of a ship's enclosed cubic space which tallies all revenue-producing areas aboard for the purpose of harbor dues.

5. Passengers—Cabins Full—the maximum number of passengers aboard if all the beds, including upper berths, are filled.

6. Passengers—2/Cabin—The normal complement of passengers with two passengers to each cabin.

7. PSR—Passenger Space Ratio, a figure reached by dividing the number of passengers carried into the Gross Registered Tonnage, which gives a general idea of how much total enclosed space is available for each passenger; a sort of seagoing comfort index.

8. Seating—The number of meal seatings per evening; most ships have two seatings, a first, early or main seating, and a second or late seating. When there is a single seating, passengers often have some latitude in arrival time, unlike two seatings, which require on-time arrival.

The Ratings

When the *Fielding Worldwide Guide to Cruises* first began in 1981, the late Antoinette DeLand initiated the rating system of stars that has always been associated with this guide. As new authors for the guide, we have decided to simplify the system somewhat by eliminating all the pluses but adding an extra star.

The present authors have been aboard all the ships rated with black stars and anchors in the following pages, and the **black star ratings** reflect our personal opinion of the ship and the cruise experience it offers.

White stars represent ships that are in transition from one company to another, which we have been aboard in the vessel's earlier life, or new vessels that are sister ships to existing, already inspected vessels due to come on line in 1997.

Anchor ratings were created by the publishers to reflect a cruise experience that was enriching and rewarding aboard an adventure, expedition, river or coastal vessel where the pleasure of the journey far exceeds the physical quality of the cruise vessel. A few ocean-going ships that offer expedition and educational sailings will carry both star and anchor ratings.

Unrated ships are those the authors have not been aboard in the ship's present incarnation, most of them new ships not yet on line.

★★★★★★ The ultimate cruise experience

★★★★★ A very special cruise experience

★★★★ A high quality cruise experience

★★★ An average cruise experience

★★ If you're on a budget and not fussy

★ A sinking ship

ABERCROMBIE & KENT

1520 Kensington Road, Oak Brook, IL 60521
☎ *(708) 954-2944, (800) 323-7309*

History ....

Abercrombie & Kent started as a safari operator 34 years ago, founded by the father of present CEO Geoffrey Kent, who made up the mythical Abercrombie as his partner because he liked the way it sounded. One of the most respected of all luxury tour operators, A&K had booked a number of groups and charters on ships over the years, but got into the cruise business first-hand when it went into a marketing agreement with Seattle-based Society Expeditions in 1990, and ended up buying the company's 96-passenger expedition ship *Society Explorer* (the former *Lindblad Explorer*) in 1992 when Society Expeditions went into Chapter 11 bankruptcy reorganization. (The Seattle company is back in business again, operating its other expedition vessel *World Discoverer*. See Society Expeditions, page 699) The *Explorer*, as it was renamed, was refurbished in 1992 at a cost of $1 million.

—The first passenger ship to cruise to Antarctica (*Lindblad Explorer*, 1969).

—First passenger ship to successfully negotiate the Northwest Passage (*Lindblad Explorer*, 1984).

Concept ....

Expedition and adventure cruising as we know it today began with the late Lars-Eric Lindblad and his *Lindblad Explorer* in 1969, and has been going to the penguins ever since. Lindblad introduced a basic travel pattern that is still followed today—to bring along experts in geology, flora and fauna on every sailing, to use inflatable rubber landing craft called Zodiacs to leave the mother vessel to explore ashore or to get closer to icebergs or rocky cliffs where seabirds are nesting, and to rehash the day's events before dinner nightly in a recap, usually with the experts interpreting what the expeditioners had seen. Expeditioners would receive volumes of material and recommended reading lists before, during and after the sailing. Shore excursions would be included in the fare.

Signatures ....

Red expedition parkas issued to each Antarctic cruiser; Zodiac explorations ashore; follow-up trip logs prepared by lecture staff and issued to all passengers after they've returned home from the trip.

Gimmicks ....

The red hull of the *Explorer* stands out dramatically against the snow and ice in photographs. To this day, some of those early expeditioners think every expedition ship's hull has to be red.

Who's the Competition ....

There's plenty of competition these days for A&K, especially in the Arctic and Antarctic regions, although most of the organizers and operators came out of either Lindblad Travel or Society Expeditions in the late 1970s and early 1980s. Quark Expeditions and Zeghram Expeditions use Russian icebreakers to crunch through the ice to the North Pole and to make a full circumnavigation of Antarctica. Society Expeditions' *World Discoverer*, Radisson Seven Seas Cruises' *Hanseatic*, Golden Bear's *Bremen* (the former *Frontier Spirit*) and Orient Cruise Line's *Marco Polo* are the major competitors in the Antarctic, while Special Expeditions (founded by Lindblad's son Sven-Olof Lindblad) uses its *Polaris* for expeditions all around the world.

Who's Aboard ....

Older couples and singles who have the time and money to go adventuring; members of the Century Club; members of the Explorers Club; veterans of earlier expeditions. They're mostly North Americans and Europeans, particularly German and Swiss, although we often find Brazilians and Japanese on Arctic and Antarctic expeditions. It can be very clubby.

Who Should Go ....

Anyone interested in learning more about the world around us.

Who Should Not Go ....

Small children; people with impaired mobility (there are no elevators on the ship and exploring involves climbing down steep gangways into Zodiacs bobbing in icy water); and anyone who wants to know how many formal nights are scheduled.

The Lifestyle ....

Instead of oiling up to soak in the sun or sipping piña coladas on deck, expedition passengers stand at the ship's rail in the polar breeze watching for whales or icebergs, penguins or polar bears, tufted puffins or royal albatross. Shipboard life is casual; there is no need to dress up. Dining is at open seating, and everyone usually arrives right on time. If whales are spotted, everyone jumps up from the table and runs out on deck. If you've signed up to be called when the Northern Lights are out, you may be awakened at 3 a.m. to struggle out onto an open deck shivering.

Wardrobe . . . .

Because there is little closet space in the *Explorer's* cabins and no fashion police on board, take along practical and rugged outdoor clothing that can be layered so items can be donned or removed as the weather changes. In the Arctic and Antarctic, we find lightweight long silk underwear very practical, because it gives warmth without weight and dries quickly when you get wet wading ashore. In the evenings, expeditioners may or may not change into something clean, depending on their mood and how long the afternoon's excursion lasted. Some passengers bring jacket and tie for the captain's dinners, usually two per sailing. The important items to pack on most expedition cruises are headgear and footwear—rubber boots, some sort of raingear, hiking shoes or boots, rain hats, sun hats with strings that tie them down, and, if you must, safari hats.

Bill of Fare . . . . B

The food aboard is well prepared by European chefs. Breakfasts and lunches are usually built around buffet self-service items, while dinners are served course by course. Cocktails and wines are available.

Showtime . . . .

The nightly "recap" from the naturalists and expedition leaders tells you what you saw today and what you'll do tomorrow. On days at sea, lectures and films are scheduled frequently except for a two-hour window after lunch when most of the rugged expeditioners take their naps.

Discounts . . . .

Early booking discounts of $500 per person are available on Antarctic expedition sailings of the *Explorer*. Make consecutive bookings of two back-to-back sailings and get 20 percent off the lower priced cruise.

The Bottom Line

The intrepid little *Explorer* can tackle just about any part of the globe, and in her 28 years of wandering probably has. The cabins are small but comfortable, the food is good and your fellow passengers congenial, as a rule. Expeditioners are just cruisers who go to extremes.

Explorer   ★★, ⚓⚓⚓⚓⚓

As the days went by, the ice of the Antarctic began to seem like confectionery instead of glaciology—some of it cracked meringues, shiny and crunchy-looking; others the sculpted cold sheen of ice-blue marble where an iceberg had split. There was the window-display, fake-snow glitter of an ice floe in the sunshine with a dozen penguins perched on it out for a ride, and glossy marshmallow mountains, divinity peaks and sugar-dusted chocolate rocks.

The *Explorer* was built with polar cruising in mind, and has a double ice-hardened hull, shallow draft, extensive navigational equipment and bow thrusters to help her maneuver among the icebergs and floes of Arctic and Antarctic oceans. All cabins are outsides and have private baths with showers; there is a lounge, bar, library, lecture hall, dining room, gift shop, laundry service, beauty shop, English-speaking doctor and single seating meal service.

The Brochure Says

"After a day of adventure, return to the ship to enjoy all the amenities of a traditional cruising vessel: like-minded company, excellent Continental cuisine and comfortable, air-conditioned cabins."

Translation
You can see the world without hardly leaving the comforts of home.

INSIDER TIP

All shore excursions and on-board tips are included on the Antarctic and Amazon sailings.

Cabins & Costs

Fantasy Suites: C

Average Price PPPD: $562 in the Amazon, $855 in the Antarctic, both plus air add-ons.
There are two suites aboard the *Explorer*, not really on the fantasy level but more comfortable and spacious than the other quarters, each with a queen-sized bed, separate sitting area with sofa and chairs, a coffee table, mini-refrigerator and bath with shower.

Small Splurges: C

Average Price PPPD: $385 in the Amazon, $533 in the Antarctic, plus air add-ons.
Since there's no elevator, one of the two upper cabin decks is more convenient, say one of the ten standard cabins on the boat deck, with a window, two lower berths, a small desk/dresser with stool and five drawers, and a tiny bathroom with shower.

Suitable Standards: C

Average Price PPPD: $372 in the Amazon, $476 in the Antarctic, plus air add-ons.
Go for one of the Yacht Deck amidships cabins for the best ride in rough waters. These standard outside doubles have portholes instead of windows and the same furnishings (see "Small Splurges," above) in a smaller space.

Bottom Bunks: .... C-

Average Price PPPD: $281 in the Amazon, $372 in the Antarctic, plus air add-ons.
Portholes in the bottommost deck cabins get what we call the laundromat treatment—either you're watching the seas sloshing over them or they're covered against severe weather and you're in the equivalent of an inside cabin. They contain the same basic furniture as the other standards (see "Small Splurges," above) but are even narrower.

Where She Goes

The *Explorer* spends the winter months in the Antarctic, cruising along the peninsula and sometimes visiting nearby island groups like the Falklands, South Georgias or South Orkneys.

In the spring a series of Amazon River cruises is offered, some traveling between Iquitos and Manaus, and some between Iquitos and Belém, the entire 2000-mile length of the river.

For the remainder of the season, various companies charter the *Explorer*.

The Bottom Line

Nine of the bottom-category cabins designated as doubles are primarily sold as single cabins with a 50 percent single supplement added on. These cabins are located forward on Explorer and Yacht Decks. They're also the smallest cabins with the potential of offering the bumpiest ride in rough seas, plus the washing-machine porthole view of the oceans of the world. But the overall experience outweighs the small drawbacks of this vessel, as you can see from the two-star, five-anchor rating.

Five Essential Places

1. The lecture hall, where passengers gather for slide lectures and learned discussions (and sometimes a quick nap).

2. The sun deck with its small pool can be a shelter from the wind or a good place to read.

3. Explorer Lounge is where the expeditioners gather at the end of the day to compare notes, buy a drink and nibble on chips and pretzels.

4. The dining room is big enough to seat all the passengers in one seating, but can get noisy if everyone decides to talk at once.

5. The library, a great place to go to catch up on research between shore excursions; published material about the regions being cruised is all there.

Five Good Reasons to Book This Ship

1. To cruise the Antarctic Peninsula on the first passenger ship that ever sailed there.

2. To get the equivalent of a college course about geology, marine mammals, cacti, icebergs, parrots of the Amazon—whatever your interest.

3. To meet people you'll probably stay in touch with—perhaps even take other expedition cruises with—for years.

4. To go bird-watching in a Zodiac.

5. To take and bring back incredible photographs of icebergs, and a lot of mysterious shots of where the whale was.

Five Things You Won't Find On Board

1. A dance orchestra.

2. An elevator.

3. A Jacuzzi.

4. A casino.

5. A cabin designated wheelchair-accessible; this vessel is not appropriate for mobility-impaired travelers.

Explorer ★★, ⚓⚓⚓⚓

Registry	Liberia
Officers	European
Crew	International
Complement	61
GRT	2,398
Length (ft.)	239
Beam (ft.)	46
Draft (ft.)	14.7
Passengers-Cabins Full	114
Passengers-2/Cabin	105
Passenger Space Ratio	22.83
Stability Rating	NA
Seatings	1
Cuisine	Continental
Dress Code	Casual
Room Service	Yes
Tip	Included

Ship Amenities

Outdoor Pool	1
Indoor Pool	0
Jacuzzi	0
Fitness Center	Yes
Spa	No
Beauty Shop	Yes
Showroom	No
Bars/Lounges	1
Casino	No
Shops	1
Library	Yes
Child Program	No
Self Service Laundry	No
Elevators	0

Cabin Statistics

Suites	2
Outside Doubles	55
Inside Doubles	0
Wheelchair Cabins	0
Singles	9
Single Surcharge	150-200%
Verandas	0
110 Volt	No

Alaska Sightseeing CruiseWest

Fourth and Battery Bldg., Suite 700, Seattle, WA 98121
☎ *(206) 441-8687, (800) 426-7702*

History ....

The near-legendary World War II pilot Charles B. "Chuck" West came back from the China-Burma-India theater to start an Alaska bush pilot service in 1946, which he turned into world-famous Westours, Inc. After selling Westours to Holland America Line in 1973, he went on to found Alaska Sightseeing/Cruise West, at first offering day cruises on Prince William Sound and along the Inside Passage, and in 1990, adding overnight cruises in Alaska on the 58-passenger *Spirit of Glacier Bay.*

In May, 1991, West, by now also known as "Mr. Alaska," reintroduced U.S.-flag sailings between Seattle and Alaska for the first time since Alaska Steamship Company suspended its passenger operations in 1954. He used one 82-passenger ship the first year, adding a second 84-passenger vessel in 1992, then a 101-passenger ship in 1993.

Today, with West's son Richard as president and CEO, the family-owned company's vessels cruise in Alaska, British Columbia, Puget Sound, the Columbia and Snake Rivers and the San Francisco Bay/Sacramento Delta.

—AS/CW is the biggest little-ship cruise company in North America, with six overnight vessels and two day-cruise vessels, each carrying fewer than 101 passengers.

—All the line's vessels are under 100 tons, which allows the company full access to Glacier Bay without having to qualify for the limited number of permits issued annually for entrance.

—The company runs a longer sailing season in Alaska than its rivals, beginning in early April and continuing until October.

—Captain Leigh Reinecke and Captain Becky Crosby, two of the very few female captains at sea, command AS/CW vessels.

Concept ....

This Alaska-savvy company feels that putting passengers in small vessels is the best way to get a close look at and a feel for the true Alaska experience. Eco-tourism and the environment are primary concerns at AS/CW, and schedules are deliberately styled to be flexible so the captain can take a different course to show passengers a mother bear and her cubs feeding in a rich patch of grass, or spend an hour watching a chorus line of 15 orcas lined up across British Columbia's narrow Grenville Channel, so close to the ship that one frustrated passenger complained she couldn't get them all in one shot with her 50-millimeter lens.

Signatures....................................

A unique bow-landing capability on four of the line's vessels allows passengers to troop down a front gangway and right onto shore without using a tender or inflatable landing craft. This device was originally designed and built by Luther Blount of American Canadian Caribbean Line, whose company also promotes its own bow-landing vessels. Blount's Warren, Rhode Island, shipyard constructed the former *New Shoreham I* and *New Shoreham II*, which now sail as the *Spirit of Glacier Bay* and the *Spirit of Columbia*.

An open bridge policy gives passengers daytime access to the navigation bridge except in severe weather, letting wanna-be skippers chat with the captain, stare at the radar or study the charts. It's also a good place to watch for wildlife without getting wet when it's raining.

There is an emphasis on the foods, wines and boutique beers of the Pacific Northwest. Several regional wines are usually available by the glass as well as by the bottle.

CHAMPAGNE TOAST

Bartenders aboard these small vessels will let passengers who want a glass of wine at cocktail time in the bar, then another with dinner in the dining room, save money by buying a full bottle at the bottle price and keeping it in the bar refrigerator with the cabin number written on the label.

Gimmicks....................................

"Our Bear...Their Bear" ad campaign has a closeup photo of bears on a rocky shore taken by an amateur photographer from the deck of the *Spirit of Alaska*. Beside it is a long view photo of an Alaska shoreline with a circle pointing out a distant speck on the shore..."Their Bear."

DID YOU KNOW?

In addition to its overnight cruise ships, AS/CW also operates two highly successful day-cruise vessels which are not rated in this guide—the Glacier Seas, which makes daily eight-hour crossings of the Prince William Sound, and the Sheltered Seas, which takes passengers on five- or six-day cruises of the Inside Passage with overnights spent at land hotels.

Who's the Competition ....

AS/CW competes head-on with two similar vessels operated in Alaska by New York-based Special Expeditions, the *Sea Bird* and *Sea Lion*, which offer a somewhat more rugged version of Alaska and Pacific Northwest cruises with excursions in inflatable rubber landing craft and a permanent rather than transitory company of naturalists.

The AS/CW flagship *Spirit of '98*, a replica riverboat built in 1984, has a new competitor for its Columbia/Snake River itineraries in the *Queen of the West*, a replica paddlewheeler built by Seattle-based Bob Giersdorf, who operated now-defunct Exploration Cruise Lines with some of the vessels now in AS/CW's fleet, and who is a longtime rival of the West family in Alaska tourism services.

Who's Aboard. . . . .

American and Canadian couples and a few singles, most past retirement age, with a sprinkling of younger (read late 40s-early 50s) people and some parents with adult offspring. On each sailing there's usually a handful of foreigners—British, Germans, Australians and New Zealanders—who have come to experience Alaska for themselves after hearing about it from friends or relatives back home. For many aboard, it is their first cruise and they have deliberately chosen what they anticipate is an untraditional, non-fancy cruise experience.

These homey, unpretentious vessels are ideal for people who want to see Alaska close-up and personal.

Who Should Go. . . . .

These vessels are ideal for people who want to see Alaska up close and personal with a friendly and energetic staff of young Americans (most of whom are here because they love Alaska). While most of the passengers on the cruises we've taken are seniors, we feel younger couples interested in the environment and wildlife would also enjoy the bed-and-breakfast ambience of the vessels for a casual, low-key holiday. There are plenty of options for active rather than passive shore excursions, things like kayaking, river rafting, salmon fishing or bicycling down a mountain. As the company's brochure says, it's "for people who'd rather cruise in the wilderness than shop-till-you-drop."

Who Should Not Go ....

Families with young children, because there's nowhere on these small vessels for children to play or run about.

Night owls who like a lot of slick entertainment, casinos and discos.

People who want to dress up and show off their jewelry.

Anyone who decided to take a cruise after watching a Carnival commercial.

NO NOs

Smoking is not permitted anywhere indoors on this line's ships; passengers are requested to smoke only on the open decks.

The Lifestyle ....

Casual, very nature-oriented, friendly and unpretentious. Passengers dine at one seating, arriving soon after the meal call is broadcast and sitting where they please at tables for six. Most choose to wear their handwritten name tags that give first name and home state or country, to make casual conversation that much easier with fellow passengers.

All the ships have deck areas for brisk walking, as well as a couple of exercise machines tucked away in a corner somewhere, which is as close as they come to a fitness center.

Entertainment is provided by energetic young crew members who perform improvisational comedy and re-enact corny melodrama scenes so badly they break themselves up as passengers look on with paternal pride. Lectures are ad hoc, provided perhaps by a pair of wilderness rangers paddling in by kayak to show off their territory from an inside point of view (as in, "Right over there last week we found a mountain goat that had slipped and fallen a couple of thousand feet and drowned.") Daytime activity at sea consists of watching the scenery from indoors or out, chatting with each other, reading, playing cards and writing postcards. It's very relaxed and family-like, and passengers share many interests and common backgrounds.

Wardrobe ....

There is no dress code and no dressing up for dinner. You may show up in whatever you happen to be wearing, so long as it's decent. Casual clothing prevails, with sweaters and slacks or jeans with jogging shoes the Alaska uniform. An in-cabin booklet says it best: "Dress is always casual...(you can) save on dry-cleaning bills once you have returned home...(and) there is no time wasted changing clothes."

Bill of Fare ....B

Young chefs prepare American-style food that is quite tasty compared to the sometimes bland banquet cuisine aboard the big ships, even veering giddily close to the cutting edge for some passengers. One day when the breakfast special was described as lox and bagels, a woman at our table from California's Central Valley asked in sweet confusion, "And what exactly is that?"

Meals are served family-style; you sit where and with whom you please.

There is a set menu for each meal with one or two or, sometimes at dinner, three choices, perhaps fresh Alaska salmon, Cornish game hen or a vegetarian eggplant or lentil dish, but a limited range of alternatives can be ordered ahead of time by people who want something different. At the end of dinner each evening, the chef appears and describes what he's preparing for the next day. Passengers turn in their orders on a slip of paper, somewhat as one does in a railway dining car.

Hot hors d'oeuvres are served in the lounge before dinner, perhaps baked brie in a pastry crust with a garnish of grapes, a pâté, pizza or hot sausages with mustard.

The first course is often already on the table when passengers arrive, so that "yes" or "no" is more appropriate than "this" or "that." Desserts are usually familiar and tempting (a rich pecan tart and a Klondike pound cake were memorable).

Breakfast may be a choice of almond seven-grain pancakes or eggs, bacon and hash brown potatoes, enhanced by a self-service buffet at the room entrance with oatmeal, fresh fruit, juices and muffins. In addition, there's a self-service early riser breakfast of coffee, tea, juice and breakfast pastries.

At lunch, there's usually a substantial salad and/or sandwich, along with a hot soup, or you can request a hamburger or hot dog on special order.

Special dietary requirements—i.e., vegetarian, low salt, low-fat or Kosher—can be requested at time of booking.

There is no cabin food service (except in the Owners Suite on the *Spirit of '98*), but if you're feeling under the weather, one of the cheerful and caring Passenger Service Representatives (a euphemism for cabin and dining room stewardesses) would probably bring you something anyhow.

A modest selection of wines, most of them from California and the Pacific Northwest, are available by the glass or bottle at reasonable prices.

Discounts ....

No special fares or discounts are offered, but low-cost air add-ons from 75 gateway cities are available. Early booking is essential on these ships, which frequently sell out by spring for the entire season.

The Bottom Line

This is a particularly beguiling cruise experience for novices and veterans alike. Quintessentially American in style and cuisine, it should be a must for non-North Americans who want to get a sense of typical American hospitality, humor and food. The staff is young, dedicated and genuinely enthusiastic about what they're showing you, and there's never a discouraging word on board. This is due in equal measure to the passengers, who are the kind of people who travel cheerfully without a litigious attitude or complaint-driven monologue. While not pretending to claim they're perfect for everyone, AS/CW has a way of winning over even a dyed-in-the-wool curmudgeon, should one ever clomp aboard.

Interestingly, the company, like Carnival, has apparently chosen to compete with land-based vacations rather than other cruise products, and they structure their brochures and marketing efforts toward audiences who might book a Tauck Tour or Grand Circle Travel trip, spelling out the itinerary in coach tour terms. "Breakfast, lunch, dinner" is listed as included on each day's itinerary aboard ship, as if other cruise lines did not also provide them gratis. Photos of destination highlights far outnumber depictions of life on board in the land-oriented brochures.

On the down side, there is nowhere to get away from your fellow passengers except in the cabin or ashore. Most of the ships have a single lounge that doubles as bar, lecture room, card room, reading room and gift shop.

Spirit of Alaska   ⚓⚓⚓⚓
Spirit of Columbia   ⚓⚓⚓⚓

Our first cruise aboard the Spirit of Alaska was sailing through Washington's San Juan Islands, something like bopping along a scenic maritime road, watching the scenery and looking for wildlife, then pulling into sleepy little port towns. We found a whaling museum staffed by volunteers dedicated to the three pods of 89 or so orcas who inhabit the San Juans, a hotel where Teddy Roosevelt once slept (he'd still recognize it today) and evening concerts on an Aeolian pipe organ in a turn-of-the-century mansion turned resort hotel.

A forward seat in the lounge gives a good vantage point for seeing glaciers.

Seeing the gradual transformation on these two vessels from basic boats to attractive cruise options has been inspiring. The *Spirit of Columbia*, which we first sailed when it was ACCL's *New Shoreham II*, is dramatically changed after being stripped down to the bare bones and rebuilt in a somewhat more luxurious mode. The *Spirit of Alaska*, built in 1980 as the former *Pacific Northwest Explorer* from Exploration Cruise Lines, has also been considerably spiffed up recently.

These sister ships are clean and comfortable without a lot of big-cruise-ship extras like beauty parlor, casino or buffet restaurant. But then there's little need to have your hair groomed, since a few minutes in the fresh breeze (or fog and rain) can make it a mess again; gambling is not of interest to most of the passengers aboard; and having an alternative place in which to eat is superfluous when you have a menu of very tasty food at every meal and all-day self-service coffee and tea available. A bow-landing ramp on the front of the vessels allows passengers to disembark quickly and easily at remote island beaches.

The Brochure Says

"The sleek *Spirit of Alaska* is equipped for bow landings, with ample outside viewing areas and an open wheelhouse."

Translation

You can sometimes get off the ship by queueing up behind the rest of the passengers and trooping down a steep, narrow gangway onto land. There's a lot of open deck with railings and various items of nautical hardware underfoot where you can lounge about if you don't mind sharing space with the handful of smokers that are usually aboard, and you can drop by the bridge any time to share your navigational observations with the patient captain.

Cabins & Costs

Fantasy Suites: ....B

Average Price PPPD: $485 plus airfare.

The brand-new Owner's Suite added to the *Spirit of Columbia* forward on the Upper Deck, with its queen-sized bed, view windows, TV/VCR, mini-refrigerator, bathtub with shower and stocked bar, has generous storage space in both drawers and hanging closets.

Small Splurges: .... C-

Average Price PPPD: $456–$532 plus air add-ons.

While not strictly suites since the sitting area and the sleeping area are awfully close together, these accommodations will meet the requirements of most non-fussy passengers who don't like big cruise ships. What you get is a window or two, a sink that's in the cabin rather than in the bathroom and a shower.

Suitable Standards: .... D

Average Price PPPD: $395 plus air add-ons.

You get two lower beds, a nightstand, closet, in-cabin lavatory and bathroom with toilet and shower in an area that measures roughly nine feet by 11 feet.

Bottom Bunks: .... **D-**

Average Price PPPD: $228–$289 plus air add-ons.

Take the same facilities as above, push them into a somewhat smaller space, and eliminate the window in favor of a portlight, a hole high up on the cabin wall that you can't see through but that lets a little daylight in, and you have the bottom category C cabin. The good news is, there's only one of these on each ship.

The *Spirit of Alaska* offers two 10-day "adventure" (read "repositioning") cruises from Seattle to Juneau at the beginning and end of each season (late April and early September), with extra time in the Inside Passage to go exploring in rarely visited areas like Sea Otter Sound and Prince of Wales Island, as well as the more familiar ports and cruising areas that make up the regular season itineraries. Season-long, seven-night all-Alaska itineraries follow, exploring Alaska's Inside Passage in detail on two alternate itineraries. In the fall, the ship makes seven-night cruises roundtrip from Seattle along Canada's Inside Passage, cruising Powell River and Desolation Sound, Knight Inlet, Princess Louisa Inlet, Canda's Gulf Islands and Washington's San Juan Islands, and calling at Victoria, Chemainus, Vancouver, Friday Harbor and Orcas Island.

Spirit of Columbia spends the whole season from late March through mid-November sailing from Portland roundtrip on seven-night cruises along the Columbia and Snake Rivers.

The shallow-draft *Spirit of Alaska* was refurbished extensively in 1995, which got rid of most of her former ugly duckling features. The *Spirit of Columbia* was extensively rebuilt from the hull up in a style intended to suggest a national-park lodge, with a generous use of wood. Since there's no elevator on either vessel, mobility-impaired travelers should consider booking the line's *Spirit of '98* instead, which has an elevator (although no cabins designated for the disabled) and cruises some of the areas these ships do. While the per diem prices may seem high for these simple vessels, the product is so successful that the company does not need to discount or make any special two-for-one offers.

Fielding's Five

Five Good Spots to Stake Out

1. A seat on the sheltered amidships covered area on Bridge Deck on the Spirit of Alaska or on the warm Sun Deck on the Spirit of Columbia that gives a view to both port and starboard.

2. A dining room seat by the windows so you can see wildlife sightings on either side of the vessel; the best whale sightings almost always seems to happen at mealtimes.

3. A forward seat in the Glacier View/Riverview Lounge in order to view glaciers, rivers and other points of interest.

4. A vantage point on the Bow Viewing Area to chat with a visiting ranger or photograph a whale.

5. An Upper or Bridge Deck cabin with doors that open directly onto the Great Outdoors when a wildlife- spotting opportunity arises (or a nicotine addict has to have a cigarette).

Five Good Reasons to Book These Ships

1. The tireless and enthusiastic young American crew.
2. You never have to put on a tie.
3. You can sit anywhere you wish at mealtime.
4. You can walk or jog around the Upper Deck area as many times as you wish with no obstructions to slow you down.
5. You can go places in the Inside Passage or along the Columbia River that few if any other ships visit.

Five Things You Won't Find On Board

1. Breakfast in bed.
2. A blackjack table that takes real money.
3. A self-service laundry.
4. An intimate little hideaway lounge away from the other passengers.
5. Anywhere for children to stay or play.

Spirit of Alaska
Spirit of Columbia

Registry	U.S.
Officers	American
Crew	American
Complement	21
GRT	97
Length (ft.)	143
Beam (ft.)	28
Draft (ft.)	7.5
Passengers-Cabins Full	82
Passengers-2/Cabin	78
Passenger Space Ratio	NA
Stability Rating	Fair
Seatings	1
Cuisine	American
Dress Code	Casual
Room Service	No
Tip	$10 PPPD pooled among staff incl. bar

Ship Amenities

Outdoor Pool	0
Indoor Pool	0
Jacuzzi	0
Fitness Center	Yes
Spa	No
Beauty Shop	No
Showroom	No
Bars/Lounges	1
Casino	No
Shops	1
Library	Yes
Child Program	No
Self Service Laundry	No
Elevators	0

Cabin Statistics

Suites	3
Outside Doubles	24
Inside Doubles	12
Wheelchair Cabins	0
Singles	0
Single Surcharge	Yes
Verandas	0
110 Volt	Yes

Spirit of Discovery ⚓⚓⚓⚓

On Miner's Night the bartenders and dining room servers get down and dirty with raunchy red long johns, toy revolvers and popguns, and painted-on whiskers, which are especially funny on the females. While all the vessels in this line have a high degree of bonding among the passengers, Spirit of Discovery seems particularly sociable.

Miner's Night aboard **Spirit of Discovery** *leads to crew highjinks.*

Built in 1976 for now-defunct American Cruise Line and named the *Independence*, perhaps because of the bicentennial spirit we all had that year, this shallow draft coastal vessel went through a stint as the *Columbia* before being renovated and renamed by AS/CW in 1992. A favored spot on the ship whether at sea or in port is the trim, open Bow Viewing Area, the place to be to sip late afternoon cocktail in Ketchikan sunshine or watch for humpback whales in Glacier Bay. A colorful information bulletin board with pictures and details about the cruising area is changed daily. Cabins are compact but attractively furnished, and there is a gift shop with books, maps and logo sweatshirts and windbreakers.

Cabins & Costs

Fantasy Suites: .... NA
None

Small Splurges: C
Average Price PPPD: $529 plus air add-ons.
Each of the four 10 x 12-foot deluxe rooms on Sun Deck has a queen-sized bed, writing desk and chair, TV/VCR, minirefrigerator and bar, and big windows.

Suitable Standards: C
Average Price PPPD: $425 plus air add-ons.
The 10 category Three cabins on Lounge Deck open directly to the outside deck, with two lower beds, a full-length hanging closet, vanity with desk and chair and in-room lavatory. Baths have showers only.

Bottom Bunks: .... D
Average Price PPPD: $332 plus air add-ons.
The category six cabins with upper and lower berths, because they are forward on the Main Deck, are curved from the contours of the hull, eight-and-a-half feet at the widest point and narrowing toward the bathroom, which has a shower only. There is a view window, but no chair, and the lavatory is located in the cabin rather than in the bath.

Where She Goes

In spring, *Spirit of Discovery* cruises Canada's Inside Passage on seven-night roundtrips from Seattle, cruising Powell River and Desolation Sound, Knight Inlet, Princess Louisa Inlet, Canada's Gulf Islands and Washington's San Juan Islands, and calling in Victoria, Chemainus, Vancouver, Friday Harbor and Orcas Island.

In summer, the ship sails between Seattle and Juneau on seven-night itineraries, calling in Sitka, Petersburg and Ketchikan, and cruising Glacier Bay, LeConte Glacier, Misty Fjords and Desolation Sound. On shoulder seasons, the vessel sails Canada's Inside Passage roundtrip from Seattle on seven-night itineraries, calling in Campbell River, Chemainus, Victoria, Vancouver, Friday Harbor, La Conner and Port Townsend, and cruising Desolation Sound, Princess Louisa Inlet, Howe Sound and the San Juan Islands.

Tlingit teenagers from Ketchikan come aboard Spirit of Discovery *to talk about local culture and crafts.*

The Bottom Line

These cruises, while fascinating, are fairly pricey (*Spirit of Discovery* per diems are higher than some of the line's other ships), and optional shore excursions carry an additional cost. But the food and camaraderie on board are excellent, and it's pleasant to stand on the Bow Viewing Area with no nautical machinery to stumble over. If you want to make new friends and see some wildlife, this may be the ship for you.

Fielding's Five

Five Special Things About This Ship

1. The two single cabins, which may be booked at a flat rate rather than a singles' surcharge.

2. The food, especially the peanut butter pie and Dungeness crab.

3. On northbound Alaska cruises only, the riveting evening talk about Tlingit culture by Native American Joe Williams, along with songs and dances by teenagers from his extended family in Ketchikan.

4. The wall of floor-to-ceiling windows in the Glacier View Lounge.

5. The sign-up sheet for passengers who wish to be awakened for wildlife sightings or the Northern Lights.

Spirit of Discovery ⚓ ⚓ ⚓ ⚓

Registry	U.S.
Officers	American
Crew	American
Complement	21
GRT	94
Length (ft.)	166
Beam (ft.)	37
Draft (ft.)	7.5
Passengers-Cabins Full	84
Passengers-2/Cabin	82
Passenger Space Ratio	NA
Stability Rating	Fair
Seatings	1
Cuisine	American
Dress Code	casual
Room Service	No
Tip	$10 PPPD pooled among staff incl. bar

Ship Amenities

Outdoor Pool	0
Indoor Pool	0
Jacuzzi	0
Fitness Center	Yes
Spa	No
Beauty Shop	No
Showroom	No
Bars/Lounges	1
Casino	No
Shops	1
Library	Yes
Child Program	No
Self Service Laundry	No
Elevators	0

Cabin Statistics

Suites	0
Outside Doubles	43
Inside Doubles	0
Wheelchair Cabins	0
Singles	2
Single Surcharge	Yes
Verandas	0
110 Volt	Yes

Spirit of Endeavor   **Unrated**

This ship marks a slightly different profile and design type from AK/CW's previous vessels, with its long, low yachtlike profile. Formerly the *Newport Clipper*, the first vessel built for Clipper Cruise Line back in 1984, *Spirit of Endeavour* is scheduled to be introduced into the fleet in 1997 and will carry approximately 100 passengers in all-outside cabins. A dining room amidships on a lower deck, a spacious lounge with wide view windows opening to the deck outside, and a large area of open deck atop the ship make this ship similar to its sister vessels. Many of the cabins open directly onto the decks rather than an inside passage.

Spirit of Endeavor — Unrated

Registry	US
Officers	American
Crew	American
Complement	32
GRT	95
Length (ft.)	207
Beam (ft.)	37
Draft (ft.)	8
Passengers-Cabins Full	102
Passengers-2/Cabin	102
Passenger Space Ratio	NA
Stability Rating	NA
Seatings	1
Cuisine	American, contemporary
Dress Code	Casual
Room Service	No
Tip	$9 PPPD

Ship Amenities

Outdoor Pool	0
Indoor Pool	0
Jacuzzi	0
Fitness Center	No
Spa	No
Beauty Shop	No
Showroom	No
Bars/Lounges	1
Casino	No
Shops	1
Library	Yes
Child Program	No
Self-Service Laundry	No
Elevators	0

Cabin Statistics

Suites	0
Outside Doubles	51
Inside Doubles	0
Wheelchair Cabins	0
Singles	0
Single Surcharge	150%
Verandas	0
110 Volt	Yes

ALASKA SIGHTSEEING/ CRUISE WEST

Spirit of Glacier Bay   ⚓⚓⚓

The littlest and plainest vessel in the overnight fleet, the Spirit of Glacier Bay has a tougher style than the other "soft adventure" vessels and the capability of cruising into remote inlets and out-of-the-way places. We could imagine it dedicated to more rugged adventure and expedition sailing, and, since it offers the least expensive of AS/CW's cruises, it might attract younger people who want to experience Alaska in a more active fashion.

Small-ship fans who gravitate toward the *Spirit of Glacier Bay*, the smallest overnight vessel in this small-ship fleet, should know it's also the slowest, cruising at only 10 to 11 knots. But its size gives it unique access to wilderness inlets in Admiralty Bay, home of numerous black and brown (a.k.a. grizzly) bears. The top category cabins usually sell out first on this ship because they have windows. The lounge is forward, with banquette seating and view windows, and the dining room is aft on the same deck, with four cabins in between. Since it has only three passenger decks, space is at a premium.

INSIDER TIP

Claustrophobes should avoid all cabins on the Lower Deck on this ship because they have portlights (small portholes high up in the cabin that offer no view and only a minimum amount of light) instead of windows. Because they're over the engine room, they're also noisy.

Cabins & Costs

Fantasy Suites: . . . . NA
     None

Small Splurges: . . . . *C*
     Average Price PPPD: $417 plus air add-on.

One of the two Condominiums, category AA cabins, with views in two directions, two lower beds (that crowd it a bit in this 10 x 9 foot space), a lavatory actually in the bathroom instead of the sleeping area (but a shower that sprays over the entire bathroom).

Bottom Bunks: .... D

Average Price PPPD: $287 plus air add-on.

The largest number of cabins on this ship are 13 category B cabins with two lower berths and a portlight (see "Insider Tip," above) wedged into a seven x 10 foot space. These are so small you have to go out in the hall to change your mind, so we'll call them Unsuitable Standards.

> ## INSIDER TIP
>
> *One of the writers, a card-carrying claustrophobe, once had the misfortune of bunking in a cabin like this with a rival cruise line; if you're stuck with one, try turning on the bathroom light and pulling the shower curtain across the doorway so you can pretend it's a window.*

Where She Goes

The *Spirit of Glacier Bay* goes to—where else—Glacier Bay on three- and four-night cruises out of Juneau between May and mid-September, spending a full day in the bay and calling at Sitka. On the four-night itinerary you also get to cruise the inlets of Admiralty Bay to see the bears. In April, the ship sails on three- and four-night itineraries from Seattle into Vancouver Island's mural city of Chemainus and picturesque Victoria.

The vessel introduces a new Island Discoveries itinerary, seven nights roundtrip from Seattle through Puget Sound and the San Juan Islands. A salmon bake and Northwest Indian dance performance, a motorcoach tour of Mt. Rainier National Park, a day in Victoria, an inside look at the history of the Pig War, a walking tour of Port Angeles and a rare port of call on Whidbey Island are among the special stops.

Five Things You Won't Find On Board

1. An indoor ashtray.
2. An elevator.
3. A majority of cabins with windows.
4. An afternoon teatime.
5. Wash basins in the cabins; they're in the bathrooms.

The Bottom Line

As the smallest, plainest and oldest overnight ship in the fleet, the *Spirit of Glacier Bay* (or SGB, as the crew calls it) doesn't always get the proper respect. Built in 1971 as the *New Shoreham I*, it was one of Luther Blount's first no-frills vessels for American Canadian Caribbean Line. But there are two appealing upscale cabins, 309 and 310, plus two much-in-demand single cabins, 301 and 302. The doughty little vessel can go almost anywhere, including not only lots of places the big ships can't go, but even a few nooks and crannies the other AS/CW vessels can't visit. While remodeling goes on, the SGB is still not up to the modest glamour of her bigger sisters.

Fielding's Five

Five Good Reasons to Book This Ship

1. To cruise where nobody else can.

2. It's a little less expensive than the other overnight vessels in the fleet.

3. To sleep in one of "The Condominiums," a pair of freestanding cabins on the aft end of the upper deck, with one picture window facing aft and one facing the side.

4. The prime rib of Angus beef roasted on a bed of rock salt.

5. The new Island Discoveries itinerary.

Spirit of Glacier Bay ⚓⚓⚓

Registry	U.S.
Officers	American
Crew	American
Complement	21
GRT	97
Length (ft.)	125
Beam (ft.)	28
Draft (ft.)	6.5
Passengers-Cabins Full	57
Passengers-2/Cabin	54
Passenger Space Ratio	NA
Stability Rating	Fair
Seatings	1
Cuisine	American
Dress Code	Casual
Room Service	No
Tip	$10 PPPD pooled among staff incl. bar

Ship Amenities

Outdoor Pool	0
Indoor Pool	0
Jacuzzi	0
Fitness Center	Yes
Spa	No
Beauty Shop	No
Showroom	No
Bars/Lounges	1
Casino	No
Shops	1
Library	Yes
Child Program	No
Self Service Laundry	No
Elevators	0

Cabin Statistics

Suites	0
Outside Doubles	12
Inside Doubles	13
Wheelchair Cabins	0
Singles	2
Single Surcharge	Yes
Verandas	0
110 Volt	Yes

ALASKA SIGHTSEEING/ CRUISE WEST

Spirit of '98   ⚓⚓⚓⚓⚓

*We watched her sail into Ketchikan looking tiny and top-heavy, even a little
ungainly, compared to the Cunard Dynasty, which was approaching the dock
from the south, but as she got closer, she whizzed around the end of the pier
and into her little inside spot while the Dynasty seemed to be standing still.*

*Passengers on the bow of **Spirit of '98** get close in to shore.*

We first saw this ship, now the flagship of Alaska Sightseeing/Cruise West,
back in 1984 in St. Thomas, when it was the newly built *Pilgrim Belle* for
now-defunct American Cruise Line. As the *Colonial Explorer*, it sailed for
also-defunct Exploration Cruise Line, then was briefly the *Victorian Empress*
for Canadian-flag St. Lawrence Cruises.

A replica of a Victorian riverboat, the *Spirit of '98* is much more appealing
than you might expect, with fairly spacious cabins furnished in reproduction

Victorian antiques, good dresser and closet hanging space and large, if rudimentary, bathrooms with shower. Only the lavish owner's suite (see "Fantasy Suites," below) has a bathtub. Like the other vessels of the line, the *Spirit of '98* has only one major lounge where the passengers gather, although there is a smaller, quieter area called Soapy's Parlour aft off the dining room, where the bar is rarely if ever manned.

EAVESDROPPING

"I hate to go home," sighed an Arizona woman on the last morning of her cruise. "This has been the most wonderful trip of my life—beyond my wildest expectations."

INSIDER TIP

This is usually the most popular ship in the fleet, so if you want to sail aboard, book as early as possible or put yourself on a wait-list in case there's a cancellation.

*The **Small Splurge** cabin nomination for the **Spirit** of '98—the category one cabins on Main Deck forward.*

Fantasy Suites: .... A

Average Price PPPD: $733 plus air add-on.

The Owner's Suite is a lavish 552-square-foot apartment set all by itself on the topmost Sun Deck behind the navigation bridge, with big windows on three sides for optimum viewing. The living room has a sofabed, loveseat, two chairs, end tables and coffee table, as well as a full built-in entertainment center, wet bar stocked with complimentary drinks and a game and dining table with four chairs. A separate bedroom has a king-sized bed, and the green marble bath contains a tub/shower combination. This cabin is the only one on the ship that has full room service privileges, even at dinner, as well as complimentary beverages, including bar drinks, and cabin hors d'oeuvres service nightly.

Small Splurges: ....B

Average Price PPPD: $504 plus airfare add-on.

We particularly like the category one cabins all the way forward on Main Deck, because they're spacious with very little foot traffic passing by. You do hear the engines, but not with a deafening roar, just a quiet steady throb. Bigger than most of the other cabins, this pair narrows with the curvature of the ship's hull. There's a queen-sized bed, covered with a handsome dark-green-and-black-striped quilted spread and a clutch of lush pillows, including bolsters, in case you want to lie down and read in bed.

A three-drawer nightstand on either side, along with two drawers built in under the bed and a large wooden armoire, provides generous hanging and wardrobe space for anything you'd carry on a weeklong cruise. A desk, reading lamp, mini-refrigerator, TV/VCR and two chairs round out the furnishings, and the bath, large but basic, has a big shower, lavatory and toilet. A small basket of toiletries is also presented.

Suitable Standards: ....B

Average Price PPPD: $442, plus airfare.

Category two and category three cabins open onto outer decks, and have big windows, twin or queen-sized beds, chairs, closet and spacious bathroom. Furnishings are virtually identical to those described above.

Bottom Bunks: ....B

Average Price PPPD: $350 plus airfare add-on.

A pair of category five cabins on the Upper Deck have upper and lower berths, along with a built-in deck and chair, closets and bath with shower, not bad at all for minimum accommodations. They open directly onto the outdoor deck.

DID YOU KNOW?

Kevin Costner as Wyatt Earp was aboard to film the final scene of the Western of the same name; you can see his autograph, along with those of other cast and crew members, on the life ring displayed near the dining room entrance (look at the area where eight o'clock would be on a clock face).

Where She Goes

The *Spirit of '98* spends the summer—from late May through August—cruising on seven-night itineraries between Seattle and Juneau, with calls in Ketchikan, Sitka, Skagway and Haines, plus cruising through Desolation Sound and Tracy Arm. In September and October, the ship cruises the Columbia and Snake Rivers out of Portland on seven-night itineraries that include a jet-boat ride in Hells Canyon, Idaho, plus a winery tour in Washington.

Waitresses serenade passengers aboard the **Spirit of '98.**

CHAMPAGNE TOAST

When the time comes to disembark, all the officers and crew line up at the end of the gangway to say a personal goodbye, and only the most reserved passengers settle for a 'thank you' and handshake. Most of them exchange hugs and addresses, and take photos of each other.

The Bottom Line

This is a classy "soft adventure" with a roster of affluent and intelligent passengers, many of them taking a first cruise, who selected the vessel for its historic character and up-close-and-personal looks at Alaska. The American crew is young, energetic and enthusiastic, the food and service are quite good, and there's really nothing to complain about except the utilitarian, less-than-lavish bathroom facilities—and they're not THAT bad. *Spirit of '98* is a real winner for anyone who wants to travel through southeast Alaska in comfort and style.

Fielding's Five

Five Special Spots On Board

1. The forward viewing area on lounge deck, great for spotting orcas and bald eagles.

2. The giant checkerboard aft on Bridge Deck, good for a group game of checkers or chess.

3. Soapy's Parlour, a quiet hideaway for reading aft of the dining room where nothing ever happens in the daytime unless someone comes in to swap a video cassette.

4. The Klondike Dining Room, with big windows and tables for six, and open seating that allows you to sit where and with whom you please.

5. The Grand Salon with its small, appealing bar, Continental breakfast and cocktail hour hors d'oeuvres buffet, cozy and crowded with small tables, chairs and sofas for chatting, reading, card-playing or catching up on correspondence.

Five Good Reasons to Book These Ships

1. You can open the cabin windows.

2. The cruises begin and end in Seattle.

3. It's the only vessel in the line that has an elevator.

4. You can lounge in the sun or shade on the Sun Deck, feet propped against the rail, watching the gorgeous scenery along the Inside Passage.

5. Settle into the Owner's Suite in luxurious comfort (see "Fantasy Suites,").

Five Things You Won't Find On Board

1. Kevin Costner—at least not this year. (See earlier "Footnote.")

2. A library with hardback best-sellers.

3. A stuffy attitude.

4. A key to lock up your cabin.

5. A high crew-to-passenger ratio.

ALASKA SIGHTSEEING/
CRUISE WEST

Laconte fjord's blue iceberg

Alaska Sightseeing's *Spirit of '98*

Spirit of '98

Registry	U.S.
Officers	American
Crew	American
Complement	26
GRT	96
Length (ft.)	192
Beam (ft.)	40
Draft (ft.)	9.3
Passengers-Cabins Full	101
Passengers-2/Cabin	98
Passenger Space Ratio	NA
Stability Rating	Fair
Seatings	1
Cuisine	American
Dress Code	Casual
Room Service	No
Tip	$10 PPPD pooled among staff incl. bar

Ship Amenities

Outdoor Pool	0
Indoor Pool	0
Jacuzzi	0
Fitness Center	Yes
Spa	No
Beauty Shop	No
Showroom	No
Bars/Lounges	1
Casino	No
Shops	1
Library	Yes
Child Program	No
Self Service Laundry	No
Elevators	1

Cabin Statistics

Suites	1
Outside Doubles	48
Inside Doubles	0
Wheelchair Cabins	0
Singles	0
Single Surcharge	Yes
Verandas	0
110 Volt	Yes

ALASKA SIGHTSEEING/ CRUISE WEST

AMERICAN CANADIAN CARIBBEAN LINE, INC

"The Small Ship Cruise Line"

461 Water Street, Warren, RI 02885
☎ (401) 247-0955, (800) 556-7450

History . . . .

Captain Luther Blount of Blount Marine in Warren, Rhode Island, founded ACCL, "the small ship cruise line," more than 30 years ago. He grew up in a fishing family and when he was 17, influenced by reading Gifford Pinchot's book *To the South Seas*, set out for the Galapagos as part of the crew aboard a 30-foot yacht. "We never got there—the boat got shipwrecked—I don't know how my folks ever let me go." The energetic New England octogenarian (when we first interviewed him by phone in 1989, he said, "I'm 74 but I only look 58") built his own three vessels, plus several that sail at present for Alaska Sightseeing/Cruise West. His offbeat itineraries demand "a good sea boat that can't draw over six feet, and it has to go through the Erie Canal so the top has to fold down flat." His ships also have a stern swimming platform with steps to get in and out of the water, a mini-sailboat for passenger use in the Caribbean, a motorized skiff to take passengers ashore when the bow landing feature is not used (see below) and a glass-bottom boat to let passengers view underwater life.

—Inventor of the bow-landing ramp; the vessel noses into shore and opens a forward ramp, allowing passengers to walk from the ship directly onto land. Inventor of the retractable pilot house, which folds down to allow the vessel to sail under low bridges such as those on the Erie Canal.

Concept . . . .

To create ships that can offer a maximum of 90 passengers a chance to go where larger vessels can't, to provide a casual onboard ambience so passengers and crew get to know each other well, and to take people on "real adventures close to home," like the Erie Canal, Belize and Guatemala, Costa Rica, Nicaragua, Honduras, Trinidad and Tobago, the Orinoco, and a cruise between New Orleans and Chicago. The line says it's destination-oriented rather than ship-oriented.

Signatures . . . .

The unique bow-landing ramp and retractable pilot house, plus extremely shallow drafts, allow the ships to go under low bridges, into shallow waters and disembark passengers almost anywhere.

A BYOB (Bring Your Own Bottle) policy, because Blount doesn't believe in making money off a bar. The cruise line provides soft drinks and snacks, but passengers who want a cocktail or glass of wine have to bring their own.

Gimmicks...................................

After a passenger takes nine cruises with ACCL, his tenth cruise is free. This alone keeps 'em coming back year after year, comparing notes on how near they are to their freebie.

Who's the Competition ....

In the Caribbean, Blount's vessels compete (only slightly) with Clipper Cruises, and in some Central American programs, ACCL competes a bit with Special Expeditions' *Polaris*, which is a different type of vessel.

EAVESDROPPING

Captain Luther Blount: "I haven't gone whole hog in borrowing a lot of money and getting in the hole by trying to do too much, (and) I haven't tried to be the biggest guy on the lot." He makes it a point of pride to build a new ship only when he can do it without borrowing money. His new Mayan Prince debuted in 1992, the new Niagara Prince in 1994, and the new Grande Prince is due in the near future.

Who's Aboard ....

Couples and singles, most of them in the golden years beyond retirement, with an aversion to dressing up, gambling, hanging around bars and watching floor shows. Instead, they enjoy getting closeup looks at exotic parts of our own hemisphere. They love swimming and snorkeling (although none of them would make the *Sports Illustrated* swimsuit issue), exploring archeological ruins and visiting remote primitive villages, and all of them look forward to their 10th cruise with the company.

Who Should Go ....

Basically, the people who are aboard, plus middle-aged couples who'd like to go snorkeling in Belize, cruising the Erie Canal or bird-watching in Trinidad.

Who Should Not Go ....

Young couples and singles, families with small children (or teenagers, for that matter) or anybody who wants to live it up.

INSIDER TIP

The ships do not permit any passengers under 14 years of age.

The Lifestyle ....

Very casual, just as Captain Blount intends. No need to ever dress up, or even change clothes between the day's excursion and the evening's dinner unless you really want to. The closeness between passengers and crew that the boss advocates is nearly unavoidable, since these vessels are quite compact with a paucity of public space. Basically there's a dining room and a nearby lounge, and that's it except for open decks. Passengers sit where they wish at large informal tables in the dining room and food is served family-style, so everybody gets to know everybody pretty quickly, if only from passing the salt. Despite the absence of a bar, cocktail hour is diligently observed every night before dinner, with mixers and nibbles in abundance. The bottle-owners write their names on their bottles and stow them in the lounge between cocktail hours. Smoking is permitted only on the deck on the *Niagara Prince* and *Mayan Prince*, and only on deck and in designated cabin areas aboard the *Caribbean Prince*. Entertainment, when it occurs, may be a folkloric company on shore or a musician brought on board at a port of call. Or a passenger may play the piano or do birdcalls. Some shore excursions are free, some sold at a modest charge from $15-$30.

Wardrobe . . . .

Very casual, anything you'd wear to the Kmart, but polyester with elastic waistbands is very popular. These passengers are people who aim at practicality, traveling light and skipping wrinkles—they are not interested in being fashion plates. However, the men may don a tie or bolo (string tie) and the women put on a dress or pantsuit on a special evening. There is one very sophisticated couple we know who love these cruises and do like to dress up, so there are exceptions.

Bill of Fare C

It's American home cooking served family-style, and the quality relies heavily on what chef is in charge, but even if one of the less talented is in the galley, there's always plenty you will like. Once in a while a beach barbecue is scheduled, and coffee and snacks are available 24 hours a day. One special treat if you're in cabins near the galley is to smell the coffee brewing and breakfast cooking early in the morning.

> **EAVESDROPPING**
>
> *"The best thing about these ships," says a handsome La Jolla matron who sails them regularly, "is that you can go barefoot all the time."*

Discounts . . . .

Ten percent is discounted from the first trips of the season in both Erie Canal/Saguenay summer schedule and the Belize winter schedule aboard the Caribbean Prince. Back- to-back cruises on any of the ships get ten percent off on the price of the second cruise.

> **INSIDER TIP**
>
> *The big sellouts—available on a first-come first- served basis—are positioning and exploratory cruises, which are offered at a flat rate of $125 a day per person to a limited number of passengers (usually 12) who dine with the crew. Call ☎ (800) 556-7450 for dates and details.*

The Bottom Line

ACCL delivers just the sort of unpretentious, friendly and adventuresome cruise they promise, and the price is right. Loyal repeaters cite the casual lifestyle, the friendliness of the other passengers and the fact the vessels can go where nobody else can is the main reasons they continue to book. One regular calls the trips "senior citizen camping at sea."

Caribbean Prince   ⚓⚓⚓
Mayan Prince   ⚓⚓⚓⚓
Niagara Prince   ⚓⚓⚓⚓

In Guatemala, bouncing along a dirt road in the back of a banana truck on one of ACCL's offbeat excursions, we stopped by the roadside and bought a fresh heart-of-palm, a huge chunk four feet long and big around as an elephant foot, for about 50 cents, but when we presented it to the ship's chef—whose forte seemed to be blueberry muffins and chocolate chip cookies—he studiously ignored our plea to let us make it into a salad for dinner. Later we heard a suspicious splash that we suspect was our heart-of- palm being tossed from the galley window.

While the three ships are not identical, they are quite similar to each other with comparable furnishings (functional) and decor (no-nonsense). Our first cruise with them was also our only cruise in tiny inside cabins; we had one each. Shirley is claustrophobic and had to leave the bathroom light on all night with the shower curtain pinned across the open doorway to pretend it was a window with a street light outside, and Harry went into hibernation in the soothing darkness, sleeping some mornings until nearly noon.

The cabins we're talking about are the ones we call "the terrible 20s," the tiny bottom-category forward cabins on the lowest deck with numbers in the 20s.

The ship layouts are simple—a Sun Deck on top with the pilot house, top category cabins and deck space, a Main Deck with more cabins, the galley, dining room and lounge, and the lower deck (except on the *Niagara Prince*), with crew quarters and "the terrible 20s."

The Brochure Says

"We at ACCL have been offering the traveling public 'adventure' cruises for 29 years, but we've done so with certain self-imposed restrictions. We believe in challenging trips, but never at the expense of your well-being, your wallet or your general comfort and peace of mind."

Translation

This is Captain Blount speaking bluntly—as is his wont—to his passengers. On the back page, there is also a paragraph that begins, "American Canadian Caribbean Line believes in honesty, reliability and good business ethics." You get a very strong sense of honor, decency and character with this line.

DID YOU KNOW?

When Princess Cruises objected to the proposed name of Mayan Princess for Blount's new ship, he promptly announced, "The ship will undergo a sex change operation." It was christened Mayan Prince. He may be slyly getting back at them with the announced name for his new ship Grande Prince. Princess' 104,000-ton megaship is named Grand Princess.

Cabins & Costs

Fantasy Suites: .... **NA**

Are you kidding?

Small Splurges: .... *C-*

Average Price PPPD: $205 plus airfare.

We'd recommend springing for the biggest cabins you can afford on these ships. The Sun Deck amidships cabins are usually the costliest but not always the biggest so check the brochure diagrams carefully. Dimensions and furniture arrangements are given. Cabins on the *Niagara Prince* measuring 12 feet by eight feet are the largest in the fleet, along with the Sun Deck cabins aboard the *Caribbean Prince*, which come in at 11 feet by eight and a half. They have two lower beds (some of which can be made into a double berth if the request is made at the time of booking), picture windows, a closet, a couple of stools and a dresser, as well as a very compact bath with a European-style hand-held shower which (if you don't handle it right) will drench the entire bathroom.

Suitable Standards: .... *C*

Average Price PPPD: $185 plus airfare.

Main Deck outside cabins are perfectly acceptable, but we wouldn't recommend the inside ones unless you're interested in hibernating. You'll find the usual two lower beds, perhaps a desk/dresser and stool, a closet and the compact bathroom with European hand-held shower.

Bottom Bunks: .... F

Average Price PPPD: $122 plus airfare.

We told you about "the terrible 20s," but there's one cabin on the *Mayan Prince* and *Caribbean Prince* that's even cheaper, the A Cabin. It's beside the galley, which means an early morning wake-up from the minute the chef starts rattling those pots and pans. It's also somewhat smaller than even "the terrible 20s" and we can't in good conscience recommend it.

The *Mayan Prince* makes Panama cruises between Balboa and Colon, followed by spring Intracoastal Waterway itineraries. Summer sailings include some New York/Hyannis Islands programs and the Saguenay River, which segues into Fall Foliage sailings.

The *Niagara Prince* cruises the Caribbean and Orinoco River in the winter, then spends late spring sailing between New Orleans and Chicago on a Rivers of America itinerary. Summer Erie Canal cruises between Chicago and Warren, RI, meld into fall, and the year finishes with another Chicago-New Orleans sailing.

The *Caribbean Prince* winters in Belize with a dandy cruise for divers and snorkelers, then sails between Belize and Roatan, Honduras, for still more watersports fun before repositioning up the Intracoastal Waterway for a summer series of Saguenay sailings and the ever-popular fall foliage cruises.

DID YOU KNOW?

In fine print under the description of each cruise is the note: Every effort will be made to follow the published itinerary—wind, weather, tide and the good Lord providing. ACCL reserves the right to change, omit or add stops, change the route or consume extra days.

While we have a tremendous admiration for Captain Blount and his practical, no-ripoff approach to cruising, we have to caution readers that these ships are not for everybody. If you don't like mixing and mingling, you may not be happy aboard. You get to know everybody pretty well because there's nowhere to get away from them but in your cabin. You need to be footloose (or barefoot) and fancy free, able to take schedule changes or little annoyances in your stride. And look, at these prices, if you're a happy camper, you can earn your free cruise in no time.

Fielding's Five

Five Gathering Points

1. The Lounge, where passengers stash their booze, names neatly written on the bottles, and there's usually somebody who suspects somebody else has been sampling his stash. Pretzels, cheese puffs and potato chips are in good supply.

2. The Dining Room, where passengers may dine on a single seating (where the timing is usually the same as early seating on other ships) and the crew dines at the second seating.

3. The Sun Deck, the place to stand to see the sea, where a stretch of tarpaulin may serve as shade because it's "low bridge, everybody down" on some sailings.

4. The Pilot House, where passengers are permitted to visit a couple at a time (it's too small for any more people than that) and see "who's driving the boat."

5. The bow-landing ramp, the entrance and exit in many ports.

Five Good Reasons to Book These Ships

1. The above-mentioned honor, decency and character.

2. To buy nine cruises and get the tenth one free.

3. To see The Americas first.

4. The price is right.

5. On the *Niagara Prince* in most cabins, the windows open.

Five Things You Won't Find On Board

1. A swimming pool.

2. A bar.

3. A casino.

4. A ventriloquist.

5. Sequins.

Caribbean Prince   ⚓⚓⚓

Registry	US
Officers	American
Crew	American/Belizean
Complement	16
GRT	89.5
Length (ft.)	156
Beam (ft.)	38
Draft (ft.)	6'6"
Passengers-Cabins Full	84
Passengers-2/Cabin	78
Passenger Space Ratio	NA
Stability Rating	Fair to Good
Seatings	1
Cuisine	American
Dress Code	Casual
Room Service	No
Tip	$8 - $10 PPPD

Ship Amenities

Outdoor Pool	0
Indoor Pool	0
Jacuzzi	0
Fitness Center	No
Spa	No
Beauty Shop	No
Showroom	No
Bars/Lounges	1
Casino	No
Shops	0
Library	Yes
Child Program	No
Self-Service Laundry	No
Elevators	0

Cabin Statistics

Suites	0
Outside Doubles	32
Inside Doubles	6
Wheelchair Cabins	0
Singles	6
Single Surcharge	175%
Verandas	0
110 Volt	Yes

AMERICAN CANADIAN CARIBBEAN LINE, INC.

Mayan Prince ⚓⚓⚓⚓

Registry	**US**
Officers	**American**
Crew	**Amer & Panamanian**
Complement	**18**
GRT	**98.4**
Length (ft.)	**169**
Beam (ft.)	**38**
Draft (ft.)	**6'8"**
Passengers-Cabins Full	**92**
Passengers-2/Cabin	**90**
Passenger Space Ratio	**NA**
Stability Rating	**Fair to Good**
Seatings	**1**
Cuisine	**American**
Dress Code	**Casual**
Room Service	**No**
Tip	**$8 - $10 PPPD**

Ship Amenities

Outdoor Pool	**0**
Indoor Pool	**0**
Jacuzzi	**0**
Fitness Center	**No**
Spa	**No**
Beauty Shop	**No**
Showroom	**No**
Bars/Lounges	**1**
Casino	**No**
Shops	**0**
Library	**Yes**
Child Program	**No**
Self-Service Laundry	**No**
Elevators	**0**

Cabin Statistics

Suites	**0**
Outside Doubles	**44**
Inside Doubles	**1**
Wheelchair Cabins	**0**
Singles	**6**
Single Surcharge	**175%**
Verandas	**0**
110 Volt	**Yes**

AMERICAN CANADIAN
CARIBBEAN LINE, INC.

Niagara Prince ♨♨♨♨

Registry	US
Officers	American
Crew	American
Complement	17
GRT	99
Length (ft.)	177
Beam (ft.)	40
Draft (ft.)	6'9"
Passenger-Cabins Full	88
Passengers-2/Cabin	84
Passengers Space Ratio	NA
Stability Rating	Fair to Good
Seatings	1
Cuisine	American
Dress Code	Casual
Room Service	No
Tip	$8–$10 PPPD

Ship Amenities

Outdoor Pool	0
Indoor Pool	0
Jacuzzi	0
Fitness Center	No
Spa	No
Beauty Shop	No
Showroom	No
Bars/Lounges	1
Casino	No
Shops	0
Library	Yes
Child Program	No
Self-Service Laundry	No
Elevators	0

Cabin Statistics

Suites	0
Outside Doubles	40
Inside Doubles	2
Wheelchair Cabins	0
Singles	6
Single Surcharge	175%
Verandas	0
110 Volt	Yes

AMERICAN CANADIAN
CARIBBEAN LINE, INC.

Two North Riverside Plaza, Chicago, IL 60606
☎ *(312) 466-6000, (800) 765-7000*

History . . . .

The only ocean-going U.S.-flag ship, the *Independence* of American Hawaii Cruises, was designed by Henry Dreyfuss and built in 1951 at Bethlehem Steel in Quincy, Massachusetts. It started as a transatlantic liner for American Export Lines of New York, carrying such famous passengers as President Harry S Truman, King Saud of Saudi Arabia, Rita Hayworth, Walt Disney, Alfred Hitchcock and Ernest Hemingway.

But the arrival of transatlantic jets in the 1960s changed ocean travel, and the ship fell into hard times. The formerly dignified *Independence* was chartered by a New York travel company called Fugazi, painted in garish Pop Art colors that featured a sunburst with Bette Davis eyes, and sent sailing as a one-class "funship" for a new kind of cruising in which passengers paid for their meals restaurant-style. That lasted for about 20 minutes before the ship was laid up in Baltimore, Maryland, in 1969.

In 1974, C.Y. Tung, a Hong Kong shipping magnate, bought the *Independence* and sister ship *Constitution* for his Atlantic Far East Lines and renamed the pair *Oceanic Independence* and *Oceanic Constitution* under the Monrovian flag. This act decommissioned the ships, meaning they lost their U.S.-flag status when they were acquired by a foreign owner. (Tung had also been the owner of Cunard's great liner *Queen Elizabeth*, predecessor of the *QE2*, when she burned and sank in Hong Kong harbor in 1972.)

The *Independence* got in a couple of years of cruising before she was laid up in Hong Kong with the *Constitution*, which never cruised under her new name.

In 1979, a reorganization within the C.Y. Tung family created a New York-based company called American Global Lines Inc., which acquired the pair of ships and, after a special act of Congress signed by President Carter, allowed the vessels to be recommissioned with the U.S. flag to enable them to cruise in the Hawaiian Islands. The *Independence* started sailing again in 1980, and Princess Grace of Monaco returned to christen the *Constitution* in 1982 at the shipyard in Taiwan where it was refurbished and sent back into service. The *Constitution* was retired in 1996.

Delta Queen Steamboat Company bought American Hawaii Cruises in 1993 and a year later renamed the joint company American Classic Voyages, which is traded on NASDAQ.

Concept . . . .

Under American Classic Voyages, the *Independence* has been extensively renovated—they term it "reinvented"—to emphasize the culture and traditions of Hawaii in the decor, food, activities and shore excursions aboard.

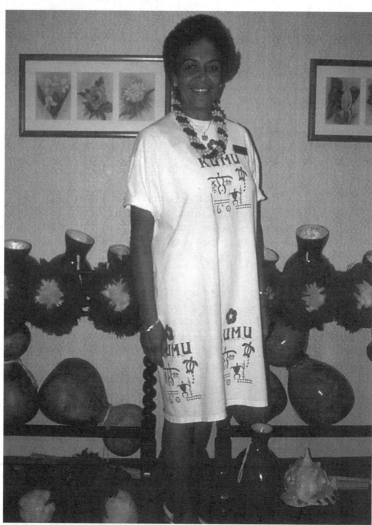

American Hawaii emphasizes the culture and traditions of the islands; a Kumu or Hawaiian teacher and storyteller such as Pua Lani Kauila, pictured here, is aboard every sailing.

Signatures . . . .

An Hawaiian teacher called a Kumu is aboard every sailing to talk about traditional culture, tell stories and demonstrate dances, and the famous Bishop Museum of Honolulu has helped set up a floating museum exhibit of Hawaiiana.

Gimmicks . . . .

Orchids, orchids everywhere, along with other fresh tropical foliage, decorate the ships. A Hawaiian "word of the day" is printed on the daily program, and passengers can learn Hawaiian crafts from weaving a ti leaf lei to playing the ukulele.

Who's the Competition. . . . .

Nobody, really, because the foreign flag vessels who cruise around the Hawaiian islands—among them Princess, Holland America and Royal Caribbean—have to begin or end their cruises in a non-U.S. port like Papeete, Tahiti, or Ensenada, Mexico because of an archaic cabotage law popularly called the Jones Act. There was once, very briefly, a competing U.S.-flag company called Aloha Pacific Cruises who brought the refurbished *Monterey* into Honolulu in 1988, but that company, hit with a flurry of lawsuits and other charges from American Hawaii, soon went into bankruptcy and the ship was laid up, then later sold to Star-Lauro, an Italian cruise company, now sailing as Mediterranean Shipping Cruises.

DID YOU KNOW?

One of the charges, ironically, was that the Monterey, which had never been decommissioned, should not be permitted to use the U.S. flag since some of her renovations were made in a foreign shipyard; this was strange coming from a company who had renovated its decommissioned vessels in Taiwan and needed an act of Congress to recommission them under the US flag.

Who's Aboard. . . . .

An interesting mix of families with young children, honeymooners, middle-aged couples, singles and retirees. When we were aboard recently, there were several affinity groups from businesses, churches or civic clubs in the southeast. Residents of Hawaii also get special cruise-only rates when sailings aren't filled.

Who Should Go. . . . .

More first-time visitors to Hawaii should experience the islands first by sea rather than spending a week on a package in Waikiki or Maui. Aboard ship, they can sample the best of four islands easily without flying between them or packing and unpacking. Also, families with children will find a cruise can usually save them money in the long run.

Who Should Not Go . . . .

Anyone looking for a live-it-up, Las Vegas-style cruise with lots of gambling and glitzy entertainment; American Hawaii does not have casinos and fog-and-laser production shows. They don't even permit smoking except on deck.

The Lifestyle . . . .

Casual best describes the daytime ambience. Naturally, with a port-intensive cruise, there are a large number of shore excursions available, from a helicopter flight over Kiluaea Volcano to tropical garden and macadamia nut farm tours. Passengers dine at assigned tables on one of two meal seatings. In port lunches and dinners are usually served open seating, which means passengers arrive during a set time period and are shown to a table.

> **DID YOU KNOW?**
>
> *The ride aboard is smooth, without vibration and motor noise, because it's operated by steam turbines.*

Dress aboard is casual during the daytime, as here during a deck hula lesson.

Wardrobe . . . .

The dress is casual on every night aboard except for the captain's welcome-aboard cocktail party and dinner, to which passengers are requested to wear semi-formal dress, usually interpreted as a jacket and tie for men, a dress or pantsuit for women. On deck and ashore in the daytime, shorts and T-shirts are acceptable most places except posh restaurants. There are always one or two nights that call for aloha wear (otherwise, why visit that muu muu factory?)

Bill of Fare . . . . .B+

We think the food has improved tremendously under the new ownership. The accent is now on Pacific Rim cuisine that incorporates more fresh foods made from island ingredients whenever possible. Breakfast offers all those familiar Honolulu hotel favorites, from fresh tropical fruits to macadamia nut pancakes, from Hawaiian Spam steak (yes, *that*

Spam; it's very popular in Hawaii) to Portuguese sausage. Lunch always features an authentic Hawaiian plate lunch, the sort served by little cafes in Hilo, like teriyaki beef with two scoops of rice and a macaroni-potato salad. But finicky eaters may also opt for Thai papaya-shrimp salad, a baked island fish or a paniolo (Hawaiian cowboy) burger with taro chips or curly fries. At the food court buffet lunch upstairs, you can hit the deli counter for an order-your-own sandwich if the regular hot, cold or grill items don't tempt you. Dinners offer two appetizers (perhaps Kona crab cakes or seared sashimi), two soups (wild mushroom or won ton), two salads, four main dishes (perhaps fresh Hawaiian fish, roast turkey, grilled New York steak or seared sea scallops) and a separate menu of desserts.

The Ohana Buffet is like a food court with various food stations from a deli counter for a choose-your-own sandwich to a hot area with carvery roasts.

CHAMPAGNE TOAST

One very good American Hawaii idea more ships should emulate is the Sack Lunch, a ready-packed paper bag to pick up and take along on your all-day shore visit.

Showtime C

Entertainment aboard is a blend of Hawaii and the mainland U.S., with both hula and line dancing classes, Big Band and Blue Hawaii theme sailings and the Newlywed/Not So Newlywed game following a Hawaiian standup comic. All-day movie screenings in the theater (from *An Affair to Remember* to *Sleepless In Seattle*), a passenger talent show, or dancing under the stars—there's always something to do.

Discounts . . . .

An early booking discount knocks down brochure prices; children 18 or younger sharing a cabin with two full-fare adults get special deals.

The Bottom Line

An authentic Hawaiian experience is what American Hawaii wants to offer its passengers, and they seem to be doing a very good job of it. They've integrated music, food, culture, history and traditions like "talk story," in which the Kumu, or teacher, relates island myths and legends. The ship is charming in its new guise, the food delicious, the all-American staff friendly and the scenery spectacular as you sail around the islands.

Independence ★★★

Before it became our 50th state, Hawaii was our myth, our sweet sugar-and-pineapple candyland, with romantic popular songs like "Blue Hawaii" and "Sweet Lelani" on the radio bringing crashing surf and sinuous hula rhythms into our living rooms. In those magical days, the lush landscape of Hawaii was our secret garden, and we sailed in fantasy on glistening white steamships to palatial pink hotels on golden beaches, to the ports of paradise.

If you haven't been aboard the *Independence* in the last couple of years, you've missed the big makeover—pots of fresh orchids and birds of paradise everywhere, showy lobby carpets with tropical floral border, bare wood floors and bamboo and wicker period furniture, balcony windows that open to the outside, bars with old movie posters and Cadiz shell lampshades, a free jukebox with all-Hawaiian melodies. There's even hallway carpeting with small swimming whales headed toward the bow of the ship, so if you follow the pattern, you're walking forward.

From a practical point of view, the renovation has improved the traffic flow tremendously with the new aft deck stairs, and added six lavish new solarium suites on Bridge Deck. One big change is the opening up of the formerly enclosed ocean liner areas to create more of an indoor-outdoor lanai atmosphere.

The Brochure Says

"Created by legendary American designer Henry Dreyfuss and built in 1951, this classic ship features a full array of 50 different configurations of fully-appointed suites, staterooms and cabins...Cabins, though similar in size and amenities, may vary within each category."

Translation

Back in the days of three-class ships, cabins came in all shapes and sizes, and that's what you'll find aboard. The bathrooms in particular on some of the cheaper cabins may remind you of the old Navy term "head." Some of the tiniest cabins on the lower decks make us remember the tearful bride complaining at the desk that there wasn't room in their cabin for both her luggage and her new husband. You should always book the highest category you can afford on this ship.

INSIDER TIP

Go easy buying aloha tropical wear; what looks hot on Oahu doesn't always work back home in Omaha.

Cabins & Costs

Hawaiian decor dresses up the cabin interiors.

Fantasy Suites: ....A

Average Price PPPD: $450 plus airfare for the Boat Deck suites, $379 plus airfare for the solarium suites.

A clutch of new AA suites on the *Independence*'s Bridge Deck and AAA suites on the Boat Deck provide from 300 to 575 square feet of space. Solarium suites have high ceilings with skylights and windows that open, best for passengers who like to see starlight and sunrises; they can't be darkened completely. The larger Boat Deck suites have separate living and sleeping rooms. All are prettily turned out with original Hawaiian art, Hawaiian quilts and fabrics, and most should offer you a double or queen-sized bed.

Small Splurges: .... A

Average Price PPPD: $335 plus airfare.
We particularly like some of the A category deluxe suites with separate sitting and sleeping rooms and big windows to the view. The new furnishings are in beautiful florals and pastels, and the carpeting repeats a traditional basketweave pattern.

Suitable Standards: .... B

Average Price PPPD: $292 plus airfare.
Opt for an outside double standard and you'll find a window or porthole, bathroom with shower and, in many, a sofa that converts to a single berth and a fold-away single berth, more comfortable than they sound.

Bottom Bunks: .... D-

Average Price PPPD: $159 plus airfare.
Cheapest are the inside category G budget cabins (the ones that made the bride tearful, see "Translation," above), with upper and lower berths. The last refurbishment added attractive furnishings but didn't increase the size.

INSIDER TIP

Suites and newly-added cabins are more apt to have real beds inside than the original cabins, many of which were furnished with a sofa that makes into a single berth and a second berth that folds out from the wall. But look, if Grace Kelly and Cary Grant could sleep on those, you should be able to.

Where She Goes

The *Independence* sets out from Honolulu's Aloha Tower every Saturday, has a day at sea, calls at Kauai, spends an overnight in Maui, Hilo and Kona on the Big Island.

The classic 1950s ocean liner offers a wonderful introduction to Hawaii.

The Bottom Line

Sailing the classic 1950s ocean liner from one island to the next provides the best possible introduction to Hawaii. But even old hula hands still get a thrill seeing the town of Lahaina from the sea or cruising past the rugged contours of Molokai. The way the *Independence* sparkles from its last renovation dramatically improves an already good product. Our only caveat is to try to stay out of the very cheapest inside cabins; spend a little bit more to get some space.

Fielding's Five

Five Happy Havens

Wood floors and koa wood doors open onto open-air lanais from the lounges; a cultural exhibit created by the Bishop Museum ornaments each lounge.

1. The signature Kama'aina Lounge, or living room, has koa wood doors that open onto open-air lanais on both sides; a cultural exhibit created by the Bishop Museum is the focus.

2. The redesigned deck areas greatly improve traffic flow.

3. The Commodore's Terrace is a handsome glass-walled room with two gold-and-royal-blue sofas with gold stars and gold fringe like a commodore's uniform; the carpet is dark blue with gold stars.

4. The Ohana Buffet is set up like a food court with various food stations—a deli counter for a choose-your-own sandwich, a station to pick up a sack lunch to go, a grill for hot dogs and hamburgers, a fruit juice area, a cold area with salads, a hot area with carvery roasts and side dishes and a dessert area.

5. The Hapa Haole Bar is reminiscent of old downtown Honolulu, filled with movie stills and posters from films shot in Hawaii, tacky Cadiz shell lampshades and a free jukebox with only Hawaiian songs.

The Hapa Haole Bar, reminiscent of old downtown Honolulu, sports movie stills, a jukebox and shell lamps.

Five Good Reasons to Book This Ship

1. To see Hawaii from the sea like the first Polynesian settlers did; these days there's virtually no inter-island boat service—everyone commutes by air.

2. To immerse yourself in a real Hawaiian experience with no Don Ho, Tahitian *tamare* or plastic grass skirt in sight.

3. To go resort-shopping if you want to come back and stay awhile; the ships stop in almost all the popular beach areas so you can pick out your beach and hotel for the next visit.

4. To visit four of Hawaii's islands without endlessly sitting around in airports waiting an hour for a 20-minute commuter hop, not to mention having to divulge your weight every time you check in for a flight.

5. To sightsee at your own pace by booking one of nearly 50 shore excursions, arranging for a rental car on every island to do your own touring or just walking around in the ports.

Five Things You Won't Find On Board

1. A casino.

2. Smoking areas anywhere inside the ship.

3. Bathtubs in standard cabins.

4. A Jacuzzi.

5. A library.

Independence   ★ ★ ★

Registry	US
Officers	American
Crew	American
Complement	315
GRT	30,090
Length (ft.)	682
Beam (ft.)	89
Draft (ft.)	26.5
Passengers-Cabins Full	1165
Passengers-2/Cabin	802
Passenger Space Ratio	37.51
Stability Rating	Good to Excellent
Seatings	2
Cuisine	Pacific Rim
Dress Code	Hawaiian casual
Room Service	No
Tip	$8.75 PPPD, 15% automatically added to bar check

Ship Amenities

Outdoor Pool	2
Indoor Pool	0
Jacuzzi	0
Fitness Center	Yes
Spa	No
Beauty Shop	Yes
Showroom	Yes
Bars/Lounges	3
Casino	No
Shops	Yes
Library	No
Child Program	Yes
Self-Service Laundry	Yes
Elevators	4

Cabin Statistics

Suites	32
Outside Doubles	171
Inside Doubles	188
Wheelchair Cabins	3
Singles	20
Single Surcharge	160-200%
Verandas	0
110 Volt	Yes

AMERICAN HAWAII CRUISES

AMERICAN WEST STEAMBOAT COMPANY

520 Pike Street, Suite 1400, Seattle, WA 98101
☎ *(206) 292-9606, (800) 434-1232*

Queen of the West *sails the Columbia River from Portland, Oregon.*

History . . . .

Brand-new American West Steamboat Company had some delays with
its first boat, the 165-passenger paddlewheel steamer *Queen of the West*.
Technical problems with its hydraulic system and paddlewheel were
adjusted before the end of the first season. The new U.S.-flag cruise line
is headed up by Seattle's Bob Giersdorf, whose eight-ship Exploration
Cruise Line folded in 1988 after a financial dispute with investor
Anheuser-Busch led to a declaration of bankruptcy and a dispersal of
the fleet to other cruise companies. Giersdorf was also president of Glacier Bay Tours and Cruises and Yachtship Cruise Line until early 1996,
when he sold the 49-passenger catamaran *Executive Explorer* and the

36-passenger *Wilderness Explorer* to Juneau-based Goldbelt, Inc., an Alaskan Native American corporation.

—The first overnight sternwheeler to operate on the Columbia river since 1917.

Concept . . . .

The boat follows an "American West" theme with historical material, nightly entertainment and complimentary escorted motorcoach shore excursions "to reflect the elements of the rich past of the historic Columbia, Snake and Willamette river regions."

Signatures . . . .

Showboat-style entertainment nightly. The big red three-story paddlewheel. A 45-foot bow ramp for shore access.

Gimmicks . . . .

All shore excursions are included in the price of the cruise.

Who's The Competition? . . . .

The only other riverboat-type vessel in the Pacific Northwest is Alaska Sightseeing/Cruise West's *Spirit of '98,* which has a turn-of-the-century ambiance but no paddlewheel, and the small expedition vessels from Special Expeditions and Alaska Sightseeing/Cruise West that cruise along the Columbia and Snake in the spring and fall. For a real head-to-head competition between paddlewheelers, the *Queen of the West* would have to be in the heartland of America along the mighty Mississippi and take on those three paddlewheel champions from Delta Queen Steamboat Company, the *Delta Queen* (a former Westerner herself), *Mississippi Queen* and *American Queen*—but those ladies don't seem to have a hankering to head west.

Who's Aboard . . . .

Most of the passengers are older couples 55 to 75, many from the east and midwestern U.S., but there's usually a sprinkling of young-to-middle-aged Americans as well as families with teenagers.

Who Should Go . . . .

Anyone who has an overwhelming desire to see America close-up and learn the history and culture of the Pacific Northwest from shipboard historian Alden Jencks.

Who Should Not Go . . . .

The vessel is not appropriate for babies and small children, because there are no child-care programs or playrooms on board.

The Lifestyle and Wardrobe. . . . .

Casual to informal wardrobe is the rule as well as layered clothing for spring and fall because of temperature changes, and walking shoes for deck and shore excursions. They prefer gentlemen don a jacket, with or without tie, for the captain's welcome aboard party. Meals are served in a single seating. Shore excursions specified in the itinerary are included in the fare. There are no telephones aboard for ship-to-shore calls; they should be made from the daily shore stops. Smoking is limited to outer deck areas only, and the vessel does not have medical service, laundry service, dry-cleaning or a beauty or barber shop. All these services are available ashore.

Bill of Fare . . . . B+

The food aboard is well-prepared by chef Michael Quick, who figures he rustles up 550 meals a day with all desserts and baking from scratch. Hot rolls are prepared fresh for lunch and dinner every day, and he takes on fresh local seafood frequently, with fresh salmon the first night out, followed on subsequent evenings by items such as fresh scallops, halibut and steamer clams. One of his lunch specialties is a luscious smoked pork sandwich from a tenderloin he lightly smokes on board. Heart-smart and vegetarian offerings are on every menu, and he uses all fresh produce and dairy products. Menu items include fresh clam chowder, Dungeness crab cakes, Washington state rack of lamb, Tillamook cheese, Oregon pears, Walla Walla sweet onions, fiddlehead ferns and Northwest fresh berries. Each breakfast features a special of the day—blintzes with Oregon berries, western omelette, Idaho potatoes with poached eggs and bacon, salmon frittata, French toast stuffed with cherries or smoked salmon with poached eggs on a bagel.

Showtime . . . . B+

Nightly entertainment is provided by entertainers who come aboard from shore, plus a resident three-piece band and a singer/pianist who belts out singalong ballads and blues in the Paddlewheel Lounge. The most popular evening combines close-up magic tricks by card sharp Matt "Maverick" Burton along with an Oregon trail music-and-narration by Dallas McKennon, one of the stars of TV's "Daniel Boone" series. Country/western musicians, "Golden Oldies" singers, a "Best of Broadway" musical evening and a 10-piece Big Band for dancing come aboard one evening each cruise.

Discounts . . . .

Special occasion group rates covering birthdays, 25th and 50th wedding anniversaries, family reunions and holiday getaways for groups of 10 or more qualify for group rates. With 15 paid staterooms in a group, a complimentary stateroom is provided. Early booking discounts are also offered.

Queen of the West   ⚓⚓⚓⚓

She's sailing the Columbia River, not the Mississippi, but a first glimpse of the Queen of the West with her tootling calliope, gold-flanged black smoke-stacks and bright red paddlewheel would remind most cruise buffs of the venerable Delta Queen Steamboat Company in New Orleans, something the western competition does not seem averse to.

Cabins & Costs

All 73 suites and staterooms are outsides, some with private verandas. There are nine price categories from a single top-category owner's suite down to the lowest priced pair of value staterooms (slightly smaller than the others with a single lower bed, pulldown upper berth and small sitting area). A choice of beds from twins, doubles, queens to twins that can convert to a queen is available; baths have showers only. All rooms have view windows, and all but two have inside corridor entries. The two Vista View Deck Suites on the topmost deck adjacent to the captain's quarters and wheelhouse open directly onto the deck, each with its own fenced "front porch." Prices range from $135 to $563 per person, double occupancy, based on a seven-day sailing.

Where She Goes

The *Queen of the West*'s itinerary is a major attraction, with cruises ranging from two to seven nights in length and a route that in its seven-night version goes roundtrip from Portland along the Willamette River to the Columbia, then through the Columbia Gorge National Scenic Area to the Hood River, where passengers get off for a rail excursion on the Mount Hood Scenic Railway. The Dalles Lock and Dam is transited, and visits are made to Maryhill Museum of Art and the American version of England's Stonehenge Monument. In the John Day Lock and Dam, the *Queen of the West* is raised 105 feet for the transit. Other highlights include a cruise along the Snake River, then a jet-boat ride through Hell's Canyon, a country-western day in Pendleton, Oregon, and wine-tasting in Washington and Oregon wineries.

The Bottom Line

Queen of the West (and a sister ship planned for a 1998 debut,) bring a classy riverboat operation to the northwest without slavishly copying the Delta Queen Steamboat product. Cabins are spacious and prettily furnished, public areas are large and hallways wide, and the crew young and friendly. So far, surprisingly, much of the clientele has come from distant rather than nearby cities.

Fielding's Five

Five Special Places

1. The top deck area with the Calliope Bar & Grill, covered with heavy plastic curtains in inclement weather, serves early bird continental breakfast, 24-hour coffee and fresh fruit, frozen yogurt, jumbo hot dogs and hot fresh popcorn.

2. The Paddlewheel Lounge overlooks the churning red wheel from a stunning, glass-walled aft area.

3. The Lewis & Clark Dining Room with hot fresh rolls served the minute you sit down for your lunch or dinner.

4. The Columbia Showroom with its big windows, long bar at one end and small dance floor.

5. The railed deck areas all around the ship, ideal for river-watching except for a few bitterly cold days in winter and early spring.

Five Reasons to Book This Ship

1. To meet Cincinnatus from the old "Daniel Boone" TV series.

2. To go jet-boating in Hell's Canyon.

3. To sample the foods and wines of the Pacific Northwest.

4. To play the steam calliope.

5. To buy a plaid wool shirt on sale at the Pendleton Woolen Mills.

Five Things You Won't Find Aboard

1. Assigned meal seatings.

2. A casino.

3. A gym.

4. A beauty shop.

5. An ash tray in any of the public rooms or cabins; smoking is permitted only on outside decks and verandas.

Queen of the West   ⚓⚓⚓

Registry	US
Officers	American
Crew	American
Complement	41
GRT	NA
Length (ft.)	230
Beam (ft.)	50
Draft (ft.)	NA
Passengers-Cabins Full	163
Passengers-2/Cabin	146
Passenger Space Ratio	NA
Stability Rating	Unrated
Seatings	1
Cuisine	American
Dress Code	Casual
Room Service	No
Tip	$7-$8 PPPD

Ship Amenities

Outdoor Pool	0
Indoor Pool	0
Jacuzzi	0
Fitness Center	No
Spa	No
Beauty Shop	No
Showroom	No
Bars/Lounges	3
Casino	No
Shops	1
Library	Yes
Child Program	No
Self-Service Laundry	No
Elevators	1

Cabin Statistics

Suites	6
Outside Doubles	67
Inside Doubles	0
Wheelchair Cabins	0
Singles	0
Single Surcharge	150%
Verandas	23
110 Volt	Yes

CANAVERAL CRUISE LINE, INC.

751 Third Avenue, New Smyrna Beach, FL 32169
☎ (904) 427-6892

Stunning Bahamian sunsets are a treat for cruise passengers.

History . . . .

The *Dolphin IV* was purchased from Dolphin Cruise Line by Kosmas Shipping Corporation in July, 1995, to be repositioned to Port Canaveral for two-day cruises to the Bahamas as part of a week-long Florida land/sea package. Kosmas named its new line Canaveral Cruise Line, Inc.

Dolphin IV

> *The most delicious things on the ship are the breadsticks, which disappear all too quickly from the breadbaskets. At the captain's table (where we joined an astonishingly large group of 19) the captain is given his own personal basket of them, from which no one had the audacity to swipe one. After making the breadsticks disappear, the captain entertained his guests with after-dinner magic tricks with coins and cigarettes.*

The ship, built in 1955 as the *Zion* for Zim Israel Line, was turned into the *Amelia de Mello* for Lisbon-Canary Islands service in 1966, laid up in 1971, sold to a Greek company in 1972 and renamed *Ithaca*, then sold again in 1979 to operate as the *Dolphin IV* under a joint agreement between Ulysses Cruise Line and Paquet. In 1984, Dolphin Cruise Line was formed to operate the vessel, which made three- and four-day cruises to the Bahamas out of Miami. At present, it makes short cruises from Port Canaveral to Grand Bahamas Island.

Cabins & Costs

Fantasy Suites: .... **NA**

N/A

Small Splurges: .... **C**

Average Price PPPD: $238 cruise-only.

There are some modest suites on the ship, five of them on the topmost passenger deck and four of them on the deck below the major public areas. Suites 500 and 501 are rather cramped, with double beds against the wall on one side and a sofa, coffee table and closet so close together you have to clamber over the coffee table to put clothes in the closet or sit on the sofa. Suites 513 and 515 are a little larger, but the view is partly obstructed from hanging lifeboats. In all the suites, the sofa makes into a bed, but we can't imagine how it opens up—there's no room.

Suitable Standards: .... D

Average Price PPPD: $198 cruise-only.
Most of the cabins are just big enough for two lower beds, a dresser and bathroom with shower, but some also have upper berths.

Bottom Bunks: .... D-

Average Price PPPD: $105 cruise-only.
The lowest-priced are inside cabins with upper and lower berths, five of them deep down into the ship and forward, where the ride is bumpier.

Where She Goes

The vessel sails from Port Canaveral to Grand Bahamas Island on two-night cruises, sold as part of a land package that also includes three days in Orlando theme parks and two days at the beach.

The Bottom Line

It's a high density ship with long lines for buffets, for teatime, or any other time food is set out. Still, it has a pleasing personality, and the large numbers of first-time cruisers aboard always seem to be having a wonderful time. We do hope the new owners will refurbish the deck areas, which really need work. The teak is badly worn and oil-spotted. And the self-service buffet, which is tucked into a niche just inside from the pool area, is laid out very inefficiently, forcing the lines to circle the room and come back out the same narrow door. At breakfast, they add a second outdoor buffet on deck which cuts down some on the traffic.

Fielding's Five

Five Favorite Places

1. The main lounge has a large metal dance floor and chrome-framed tub chairs that supplement long banquettes around the outside perimeters.
2. The library, with locked cases of books, a strip mirror wall and movable chairs, doubles as a film-screening room.
3. The casino, with one roulette wheel, three blackjack tables, a Caribbean stud table and 71 slots.
4. Two small plunge pools surrounded with tiny blue tiles ornament the aft end of the public rooms deck.
5. A disco buried deep in the bowels of the ship has a shiny, sunken dance floor and mirrored posts.

Five Things You Won't Find On Board

1. Elbow room at your dining table when the ship is full.
2. A peaceful game in the video games room; all 11 are about shooting, wrestling, fighting or car chases.
3. A performers' dressing room; they have to change in the card room off the main lounge. (At that, it's better than the old Royal Viking ships, when dancers used the public ladies' room to change costumes.)
4. Space to swim a lap in the swimming pools.
5. A cabin designated wheelchair-accessible.

Dolphin IV ★★

Registry	**Panama**
Officers	**Greek**
Crew	**International**
Complement	**285**
GRT	**13,007**
Length (ft.)	**501**
Beam (ft.)	**65**
Draft (ft.)	**26**
Passengers-Cabins Full	**670**
Passengers-2/Cabin	**588**
Passenger Space Ratio	**22.12**
Stability Rating	**Good**
Seatings	**2**
Cuisine	**Continental**
Dress Code	**Traditional**
Room Service	**No**
Tip	**$8.50 PPPD**

Ship Amenities

Outdoor Pool	**1**
Indoor Pool	**0**
Jacuzzi	**0**
Fitness Center	**No**
Spa	**No**
Beauty Shop	**Yes**
Showroom	**Yes**
Bars/Lounges	**2**
Casino	**Yes**
Shops	**1**
Library	**Yes**
Child Program	**Yes**
Self Service Laundry	**No**
Elevators	**1**

Cabin Statistics

Suites	**9**
Outside Doubles	**208**
Inside Doubles	**77**
Wheelchair Cabins	**0**
Singles	**0**
Single Surcharge	**150%**
Verandas	**0**
110 Volt	**Yes**

⟫Carnival.

3655 NW 87 Avenue, Miami, FL 33178
☎ *(305) 599-2600, (800) 327-9501*

Carnival designer Joe Farcus stands amid the flash and dazzle of his signature atrium lobby.

History ....

"The most popular cruise line in the world," as the slogan goes, was founded by Ted Arison, who had sold an air-freight business in New York in 1966 and headed back to his native Tel Aviv to retire. According to Arison's son Micky, now chairman and CEO of Carnival, his father never intended to go into cruising, but once he was back in Israel, he took over the management of a struggling charter cruise operation and turned it into a success.

When that vessel, a ship called *Nili*, was returned to the Mediterranean because of the owner's continuing financial difficulties, Arison had several cruises booked but no ship. As Micky tells it, "Ted heard the *Sunward* was laid up in Gibraltar, so he called (Norwegian shipping executive) Knut Kloster and said, "You've got a ship, I've got the passengers, we could put them together, and we'd have a cruise line.' So in effect, they started NCL (Norwegian Cruise Line) that way."

CARNIVAL CRUISE LINES

When that partnership dissolved in 1972 after some disagreement between the principals, Arison went out and bought the *Empress of Canada,* renamed it *Mardis Gras* and started Carnival Cruise Lines. The line's first sailing with 300 travel agents aboard ran aground. There was nowhere to go but up.

Today Carnival Cruise Lines operates a fleet of 10 ships with five more scheduled to arrive by 1998. Parent company Carnival Corporation also owns all or part of three other cruise lines, Holland America, Windstar and Seabourn. Founder Arison, an intensely private billionaire and philanthropist, has retired to Israel but still keeps an active eye on the company. *Mardi Gras* and *Carnivale* have also retired from the fleet; both were sold to Greek-owned Epirotiki Lines.

Carnival went public in 1987 and is traded on the New York Stock Exchange.

—The largest cruise line in the world, based on the number of passengers carried.

—Claims the largest staff of trained and qualified youth counselors in the industry (80 fulltime employees) to handle some 100,000 kid cruisers a year.

—First cruise line to build a dedicated performance stage in the show lounge (*Carnivale,* 1975).

—First cruise line to use TV commercials on a saturation schedule during the network news hour around the country (1984).

—Pays off a $1,065,428.22 "MegaCash" jackpot to two cruisers from Alaska (aboard the *Jubilee,* March 1994).

—Introduces the world's largest passenger ship, the 100,000-ton, $400 million *Carnival Destiny,* in November, 1996.

Concept . . . .

The fledgling company took off when Arison and a young vice president of sales and marketing named Bob Dickinson created a new concept. They cut prices and added casinos and discos to attract more passengers. By loosening the traditional structure of the cruise market with its formality and class distinctions, they created the "Fun Ships" concept for a vast new cruise audience, a segment of the population that had never cruised before. The company calls itself a "contemporary product" aimed at a mass market, and the cruises are meant to tap the fantasy element to stimulate passengers rather than soothe them, turning the ship into a theme park for adults. Carnival's architect, Joe Farcus, the Michael Graves of the cruise industry, says, "The ships give people a chance to see something they don't in their ordinary lives...Instead of sitting in a theater watching, they're in the movie."

EAVESDROPPING

"Carnival is Wal-Mart, value-oriented for Middle America, for the masses, and it always meets their expectations," cruise industry analyst Jim Parker told the Miami Herald in a 1993 interview.

Signatures . . . .

Carnival's distinctive winged funnel painted in bright red, white and blue is instantly recognizable in warm water ports all over the Caribbean and Mexico, as well as Alaska. Chosen originally as a design statement, the funnel, which vents the smoke off to each side, surprised everyone when it actually worked.

Almost as recognizable is the bright blue corkscrew slide into the amidships pool on every "Fun Ship."

Splashy, fog-and-laser shows with contemporary pop music and spectacular dancing are a regular feature aboard Carnival ships; the bigger the ship, the bigger the show.

> ### DID YOU KNOW?
>
> Carnival's ship designer Joe Farcus, famous for his splashy "entertainment architecture," got his start with the line when a Miami architectural firm he worked for was contracted to go to Greece in 1975 to turn the Empress of Britain into the Carnivale. When Farcus' boss got sick and no one else in the office was free to go, the young architect got the job, and the rest, as they say, is history.

Gimmicks . . . .

Smiling waiters in tropical colors circulate around the decks on embarkation day with trays of Technicolor drinks in souvenir glasses, which first-time cruisers sometimes accept without realizing they have to pay for them. And kids in the $1 million virtual reality entertainment complex aboard the *Holiday* can activate the high tech games by using their passenger I.D. cards; they don't need to go get money from Mom or Dad, once the initial use has been approved.

Who's the Competition. . . . .

In the Caribbean, Carnival competes with Royal Caribbean and Norwegian Cruise Line for under-40 couples and singles in the seven-day market and goes head-to-head with both in the mini-cruise market out of Miami and Los Angeles, as well as competing with Premier Cruises out of Port Canaveral. The line still perceives land-based resorts as its primary competition, and exerts a lot of effort to entice first-time cruisers. Dickinson himself says the former competitors are all "moving upscale" and leaving the field to Carnival and what he flippantly calls "the bottom feeders," low-budget cruise lines with old ships.

Who's Aboard. . . . .

Despite the line's early reputation for swinging singles' party ships, Carnival attracts a broad spectrum of passengers from newlyweds to families with small children to middle-aged couples to retirees. About 60 percent are first-time cruisers, down from 80 percent in the 1980s, and some 23 per cent have taken a Carnival cruise previously, up from nine percent in the 1980s.

Families comprise a large part of the line's mini-cruise business.

Who Should Go ....

Families with children and teenagers will find plenty of diversions for the kids aboard, but there's also a well-thought-out Camp Carnival program with youth counselors that divides them into four age groups—toddlers two–four (on all ships except the *Tropicale* and *Festivale*), intermediates five–eight, juniors nine–12 and teens 13–17. They'll find playrooms stocked with games and toys, a full program of daily activities at sea including special aerobics classes and karaoke parties, a kiddies' pool tucked away on its own deck area and the trademark slide at the adult pool (see "Signatures"). Babysitting is usually available as well.

Plus: Anyone who likes to spend a weekend in Atlantic City, Nassau or Las Vegas, anyone who wants to show off some new clothes and stay up late dancing, or anyone who adores glittering high-rise resorts.

Who Should Not Go ....

People whose favorite cruise line was Royal Viking; early-to-bed types; or anyone allergic to twinkle lights and neon.

The Lifestyle ....

About what you'd expect if you've seen the Kathy Lee Gifford commercials—you know, "If they could see me now..." (Gifford says that when she auditioned for the job she almost didn't get it; she was sixth down on the list of performers they wanted to see.)

While the ships are glitzy, they are also very glamorous if you like bright lights and shiny surfaces, and the humor and whimsy Joe Farcus brings to the designs comes closer to *gee-whiz!* than *omigod!* The casinos and the spas are among the biggest at sea, the disco stays open very late, there's often an X-rated midnight cabaret comedy show, singles get-togethers, honeymooner parties, around-the-clock movies on the in-cabin TV set, plenty of fitness classes, trapshooting, shuffleboard, knobby knees contests, ice carving demonstrations, bridge and galley tours and all the other usual shipboard folderol.

> **INSIDER TIP**
>
> *No passengers under 18 years of age are permitted to travel without a parent or adult guardian, and new I.D. cards issued to every passenger, including youths, flags a bar computer to report an underage wanna-be drinker.*

Wardrobe ....

While Carnival ships are a bit less dressy than more traditional lines, many of the passengers look forward to dressing up on the one to two formal nights a week, when formal dress or a dark suit is suggested. You will see more sequins and tuxedos those nights than sport coats without a tie. The pattern is usually two formal nights, two informal nights (the line suggests sport coat and tie for men) and three casual nights that call for resort wear. For daytime, almost anything goes (or almost nothing, if you opt to sunbathe in the secluded upper deck topless sunbathing area). To go ashore in the Caribbean, Mexico or Alaska, casual, comfortable clothing and good walking shoes are best. Don't forget to take a sun hat and sunblock.

Bill of Fare . . . . B+

From a predictable mainstream seven-day menu rotation on its ships featuring Beef Wellington and Surf 'n Turf several years ago, the line has made some changes in its menus after finding a 300 percent increase in the number of vegetarian entrees ordered and a 20 percent rise in chicken and fish. Fewer than half the passengers order red meat these days, says Carnival's food and beverage director; a popular fresh fish "catch of the day" is now offered on every dinner menu.

That's not to say Beef Wellington and Surf 'n Turf have disappeared—they haven't—but rather that menus have moved a little closer to the cutting edge without scaring diners with huitlacoche mushrooms or fermented soybean paste; "Fun Ship" fans will still encounter those ubiquitous theme nights (French, Italian, Caribbean and Oriental) and flaming desserts parade, and children can order from their own special menus of familiar favorites.

Three-quarters of all the passengers opt for buffet breakfast and lunches rather than going to the dining room to their assigned seating, so a much wider range of casual, self-service options has been added, from a 24-hour pizzeria on the new *Imagination* to across-the-fleet salad bars, hot daily breakfast and lunch specials, made-to-order pasta stations and spa cuisine. Table service has been upgraded in the buffet areas as well.

All the shipboard dining rooms are smoke-free on Carnival. You can breakfast in bed and order simple menu items like sandwiches and fruit and cheese 24 hours a day from room service. Big midnight buffets are followed by a second mini-buffet at 1:30 a.m. on these late-night ships.

NO NOs

The brochure warns that Carnival passengers are not permitted to bring alcoholic beverages of any kind aboard the ship or to consume any beverages purchased in a foreign port in the public rooms or on deck.

Showtime . . . . A+

Lavishly costumed, fully professional entertainment as good as (often better) than you'd see in Las Vegas is one of the line's hallmarks. The company produces its own musical shows in-house with high-tech lighting, sound and special effects. Different shows are featured on different ships (much as the Broadway shows on Norwegian Cruise Line ships vary from one vessel to another) so if you're a fan of big production shows, you'll want to cruise them all sooner or later.

Three different live bands and a piano bar are usually playing around the ship in the evening, along with a steel drum or calypso band on deck at midday in the Caribbean.

Except on the Alaska sailings, which carry a naturalist, the only lecturers you'll run across on the "Fun Ships" are the people who tell you where to shop.

Discounts ....

Deduct up to $1200 per cabin from the listed brochure rates if you book early. Savings amounts are reduced over time based on demand, so earliest bookings get the lowest rates. Some restrictions apply.

The Bottom Line

Carnival is not just for party-time singles any more. The new generation of sleek megaliners that began with the *Fantasy* in 1990 and continues through the *Ecstasy, Sensation, Fascination, Imagination, Inspiration,* and, in 1998, the *Elation* and *Paradise,* are real crowd-pleasers.

While the public areas pulse with their abstract sensory stimulation, fiber optics, neon, Tivoli lights, state-of-the-art stagecraft and virtual reality machines, there are a few quiet areas to get away from it all—in the massage rooms, the indoor whirlpool spas, the top deck jogging track or the outdoor deck wings aft behind the indoor Lido Deck bar. Cabins are adequate in size and comfortably free of glitz, with all-day movies and room service, although not so cushy you'll spend your whole cruise there rather than hitting the bars and casino.

On the other hand, if you want a quiet, relaxing cruise, better book another cruise line, because these are the "Fun Ships." While they're not to our own particular cruising taste—we find it hard to spend more than three or four days aboard before the color, lights and pinging slot machines get to us—most Carnival passengers think they've died and gone to heaven. For flat-out fun-and-games cruising, nobody does it better.

Carnival Destiny
Carnival Triumph

☆☆☆☆☆

Unrated

On a visit to Italy's Fincantieri shipyard, we were able to see under construction both the 101,000-ton *Carnival Destiny* and Princess Cruises' gigantic 104,000 ton *Grand Princess*, the first two cruise ships ever built in this size range.

The $400 million Carnival ship carries 2642 passengers based on two to a cabin, but with Carnival's increasing family business and the number of third and fourth berths available, the average number of passengers aboard is expected to be around 3000 a cruise.

Carnival Destiny has the first-ever three-deck showroom, a huge spa and fitness center 30 percent larger than the 12,000-square-foot facilities on the Fantasy-class ships and a Sun & Sea Lido restaurant with not only a 24-hour pizzeria operating, but also an Italian buffet, Chinese buffet, salad bar and mixed-menu buffet.

Four glass elevators serve the nine-deck atrium with a showy fiber optic cityscape the full nine decks simulating skyrockets exploding. "It's a show you can enjoy going up and down in the elevator," says designer Farcus modestly.

There are three large swimming pools, one of them with swim-up bar, one with a 15-foot-high platform and waterslide, and one with a sliding glass roof cover. Piano bar fans should particularly appreciate the Apollo Bar, where every table has its own microphone and spotlight for singing along, controlled, fortunately, by the piano bar host from a central console.

A series of stained glass windows created by Venetian artist Luciano Vistosi line the enclosed promenades, and the two dining rooms are roofed with skylights with clouds and stars overhead.

EAVESDROPPING

At the introductory press conference, one European reporter asked if the 124-foot-wide Carnival Destiny will be going through the Panama Canal, which is 110 feet wide. "We could do it only once," quipped line president Bob Dickinson.

Cabins & Costs

Fantasy Suites: .... A

Average Price PPPD: $363 including airfare.

Eight sensational suites with granite entry, granite desk/dresser, separate living room with leather sofa and chairs, and bedroom, dressing room, big Jacuzzi tub, huge windows, and private veranda with see-through balcony walls.

Small Splurges: .... B+

Average Price PPPD: $348 including airfare.

Forty suites have similar leather furnishings and granite counters, along with a similar bathroom and smaller dressing room, and private veranda.

A standard outside cabin without veranda aboard the **Carnival Destiny.**

Suitable Standards: .... B+

Average Price PPPD: $254 including airfare.

The majority of the standard outside doubles on the ship have private verandas, at a price only slightly higher than for those without. Twin beds convert to queen-sized, and there's a leather sofa, wall-mounted TV, chair, stool, coffee table, desk/dresser covered with glittery gold plastic laminate, a larger closet, big shower in pink tile bathroom, and plenty of storage space.

Bottom Bunks: .... B

Average Price PPPD: $200 including airfare.

An inside cabin with upper and lower berths, wall-mounted TV, desk/dresser, chair, and bath with shower.

Carnival Destiny sails on alternating eastern and western Caribbean itineraries, calling at San Juan, St. Croix and St. Thomas on the eastern sailings, at Playa del Carmen/Cozumel, Grand Cayman and Ocho Rios on the western sailings.

Carnival Destiny ★★★★★

Registry	**Panama**
Officers	**Italian**
Crew	**International**
Complement	**1050**
GRT	**101,000**
Length (ft.)	**892**
Beam (ft.)	**125**
Draft (ft.)	**27**
Passengers-Cabins Full	**3350**
Passengers-2/Cabin	**2600**
Passenger Space Ratio	**38.46**
Stability Rating	**NA**
Seatings	**2**
Cuisine	**International**
Dress Code	**Traditional**
Room Service	**Yes**
Tip	**$7.50 PPPD, 15% automatically added to bar checks**

Ship Amenities

Outdoor Pool	**4**
Indoor Pool	**0**
Jacuzzi	**7**
Fitness Center	**Yes**
Spa	**Yes**
Beauty Shop	**Yes**
Showroom	**Yes**
Bars/Lounges	**11**
Casino	**Yes**
Shops	**4**
Library	**Yes**
Child Program	**Yes**
Self-Service Laundry	**Yes**
Elevators	**18**

Cabin Statistics

Suites	**62**
Outside Doubles	**740**
Inside Doubles	**519**
Wheelchair Cabins	**0**
Singles	**0**
Single Surcharge	**150-200%**
Verandas	**418**
110 Volt	**Yes**

Celebration ★★★
Holiday ★★★
Jubilee ★★★

At the 1985 debut of the Holiday, first of this trio of then-new ships, we recall being vastly amused because the piano bar in Rick's Cafe American was literally a piano-shaped bar with black-and-white keys all the way round the bar area. But what seemed avant-garde in 1985—a whimsical late-night buffet inside a Danish bus permanently parked in a lounge, the grotto with an undulating blue "undersea" ceiling, the flashy Reflections discotheque—was only a modest forecast of the wonders to come from the imagination of Carnival's designer, Joe Farcus.

Covered promenade decks—here aboard the Jubilee—take passengers from bar to casino to disco.

These ships were the first to introduce a wide starboard "boulevard" with the casino and lounges on port side; the earlier *Tropicale* has a more traditional center casino flanked by enclosed promenades on either side. In fact, this trio forecasts many of the design features of the later Fantasy class, with veranda cabins forward on a top deck, then a Lido deck with amidships pool, two interior decks with lounges, dining rooms and showroom, then below them, all the other passenger cabins.

These are also the vessels that discreetly offered an "Adults Only, No Jogging, Top-Optional Sunbathing" deck, and pioneered the line's recycling separation of garbage.

EAVESDROPPING

An excited family group boarding the Holiday was cautioned by one of their party, "Now remember, everybody needs to take a Valium." We hope she meant dramamine.

The Funnel Bar & Grill aboard the Jubilee *carries through a fanciful and bright nautical cafe theme.*

The Brochure Says

"People that cruise with Carnival are all very different people, with unique tastes. It's the job of our cruise staff to make sure that there are hundreds of different activities and ways to have fun aboard our 'Fun Ship.' So there's truly something for everyone."

Translation

Take your pick—an average day at sea offers you 14 eating opportunities (including two late-night buffets), eight screenings of the day's feature film on the cabin TV, six exercise sessions, bingo, Knobby Knees Contest, trivia quiz, disco, passenger talent show, sing-along piano bar, Newlywed and Not-So-Newlywed game, calypso, pool games, trapshooting, ice carving demonstration, poker games, skin care demonstration and shopping opportunities, plus all the bars and lounges, the evening production show and late-night cabaret or comedy show and the casino.

Cabins & Costs

Fantasy Suites: .... B

Average Price PPPD: $348 including airfare.

Each ship has 10 Veranda Deck suites with sliding glass doors that lead to private balconies, separate sitting area with L-shaped sofas that can make into an additional bed, elegant wood cabinetry, large TV set, twin beds that convert to king-sized, a slightly larger than standard bathroom with tub and shower and a walk-in closet.

Small Splurges: C

Average Price PPPD: $265 including airfare.

The Empress Deck category Nine outside doubles are just one deck down from the dining rooms, show lounge and shops, and two decks down from the casino, disco and other lounges. If you run back and forth a lot and are too impatient to wait for the elevator, the convenience might be worth the slightly higher tariff. Otherwise, the size and furnishings are identical to all the other standard cabins. See "Suitable Standards," below.

Suitable Standards: C

Average Price PPPD: $251 including airfare.

You'll find twin beds that can convert into a king-sized bed, wall-mounted TV set, corner table, chair, two stools, desk/dresser, closet, bath with large shower.

Bottom Bunks: .... D

Average Price PPPD: $200 including airfare.

The cheapest cabins are in category One on the two lowest cabin decks, 19 of them altogether, with upper and lower berths, wall-mounted TV, chair, stool, desk/dresser with drawers, closet and bath with shower.

INSIDER TIP

Prices listed under Cabins and Costs (above) are based on seven-day fares. Three-day cruises will run slightly higher per day, four-day cruises slightly lower.

Where She Goes

The *Celebration* sails every Friday year-round from New Orleans to the Western Caribbean, calling in Tampa, Grand Cayman, and Playa del Carmen/Cozumel. You can also depart from Tampa on Sundays.

The *Holiday* makes three- and four-day cruises out of Los Angeles to Ensenada, Mexico; the three-day sailing leaves Fridays and the four-day sailing, which also visits Catalina Island, leaves Mondays.

The *Jubilee* makes seven-day sailings out of Los Angeles to the Mexican Riviera, leaving every Sunday and calling in Puerto Vallarta, Mazatlán and Cabo San Lucas.

The Bottom Line

While not as shiny as when they were brand-new, these vessels are holding up pretty well; the age shows primarily in deck and cafeteria areas where the natural teak is spotted from food spills. Housekeeping aboard is generally good.

The buffet meal service has been expanded beyond the original closet-sized pantries to add a big salad bar that holds Continental breakfast makings in the mornings. Despite the gimmicks, they have a more nautical feeling than the newer ships, especially in the Lido Deck bar and grill rooms with resin-covered wood tables decorated with period luggage tags and other cruise memorabilia, coils of rope, the suggestion of a tugboat and a big red, white and blue funnel in the middle of the room.

Fielding's Five

Five Fun Places

1. The Speakeasy Lounge on the *Jubilee* with its fire-engine red piano, wrought iron spiral stairs to the casino above, brick walls adorned with Prohibition-era auto posters, low-hanging pool hall lights and ceiling with faux skylights.

2. The *Jubilee's* Smuggler's Lounge with cargo-net ceilings, corrugated tin walls and burlap-covered bales and shiny oil drums lying around.

3. The *Jubilee's* Churchill's library with several suits of armor, a massive pseudo-stone fireplace with a baronial air and wood paneled walls.

4. The Trolley Bar on the *Celebration's* Bourbon Street enclosed promenade, with its vintage trolley and New Orleans-style sidewalk cafe.

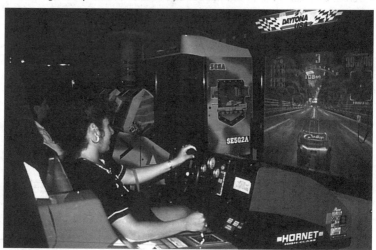

The new million-dollar entertainment center aboard the Holiday *includes games galore, including virtual reality.*

5. The *Holiday's* million-dollar entertainment complex (replacing the Blue Lagoon grotto) with virtual reality machines, a teen disco, ice cream/pizza parlor, motorcycle and car racing video machines, dozens of video games and R360, a strap-in aerial machine that spins around 360 degrees.

Five Good Reasons to Book These Ships

1. The fun and games (see "Translation").
2. The high-quality entertainment, especially on the *Holiday* with its high-tech shows like "Here's Hollywood" and "Broadway!"
3. To play MegaCash, the biggest slot jackpots at sea.
4. To enroll the kids in Camp Carnival.
5. To check out the virtual reality games on the *Holiday*.

Five Things You Won't Find On Board

1. Smoking in the dining rooms.
2. Elbow room in the little stainless steel closets where the buffet hot foods are served.
3. Single cabins.
4. A cinema.
5. A passenger with nothing to do.

Celebration
Holiday
Jubilee

★ ★ ★
★ ★ ★
★ ★ ★

Registry	**Liberia**
Officers	**Italian**
Crew	**International**
Complement	**670**
GRT	**47,262**
Length (ft.)	**733**
Beam (ft.)	**92**
Draft (ft.)	**24.7**
Passengers-Cabins Full	**1896**
Passengers-2/Cabin	**1486**
Passenger Space Ratio	**31.80**
Stability Rating	**Good**
Seatings	**2**
Cuisine	**International**
Dress Code	**Traditional**
Room Service	**Yes**
Tip	**$7.50 PPPD, 15% automatically added to bar checks**

Ship Amenities

Outdoor Pool	**3**
Indoor Pool	**0**
Jacuzzi	**2**
Fitness Center	**Yes**
Spa	**Yes**
Beauty Shop	**Yes**
Showroom	**Yes**
Bars/Lounges	**6**
Casino	**Yes**
Shops	**4**
Library	**Yes**
Child Program	**Yes**
Self-Service Laundry	**Yes**
Elevators	**8**

Cabin Statistics

Suites	**10**
Outside Doubles	**437**
Inside Doubles	**279**
Wheelchair Cabins	**15**
Singles	**0**
Single Surcharge	**150-200%**
Verandas	**10**
110 Volt	**Yes**

Ecstasy	★★★★★
Fantasy	★★★★★
Fascination	★★★★★
Imagination	★★★★★
Inspiration	★★★★★
Sensation	★★★★★

"All I can say is, Wow!" sings spokeswoman Kathy Lee Gifford in the Carnival commercials, and passengers walking for the first time into these ships with their soaring seven-deck atriums, glass elevators and moving sculptures are saying the same thing—except for an occasional, "Oh my God!" from those who pretend to more refined tastes.

On the Fantasy, the huge clear-glass skylight in the dome ceiling seven decks above drenches the atrium with natural light during the daytime, but as dusk approaches, the room is suffused with color from miles of neon tubing that circle every level of the space. The effect is strangely impressive, but disorienting, something like walking into a giant jukebox. If you don't like the color, hang around for a while and it will change.

This is no place like home.

Toto, I don't think we're in Kansas any more.

Are you listening, Elvis? Las Vegas is alive and floating.

The *Fantasy*-class ships are all virtually identical in superstructure and deck plan, but each is dramatically different inside. We find ourselves doing a lot of standing by the rail looking down, both inside from the upper atrium levels down into the lobby, watching the glass elevators glide up and down, and outside from the upper decks down into the amidships pool deck with its acres of bronzing bodies in all shapes and sizes, at kids (and adults) trying out the bright blue water slide, at the impromptu dancers in bathing suits who always begin to gyrate on deck when the band comes out on the raised stage.

The 12,000-square-foot Nautica spas with their large whirlpool spas and well-equipped gyms are among the best at sea.

On the topmost deck is a rubberized jogging track, then down one deck on Veranda Deck is the huge Nautica spa with one of every exercise machine known to man, 26 suites with private verandas and on the aft deck, a sun-bathing area and pool with two Jacuzzis.

One deck down on Lido is a large glass-walled self-service cafe with indoor and outdoor dining and the amidships pool area with its stage.

The Promenade Deck and Atlantic Deck contain most of the bars, lounges, showrooms and dining rooms, along with a galley on Atlantic Deck that makes the aft dining room a you-can't-get-there-from-here proposition. Directly behind that dining room is the teen club and children's playroom, and on the deck just above, the wading pool, all completely removed from the adult areas of the ship. Forward on the same deck is a second dining room, a small lounge and library, the atrium, shops and the main level of the showroom. One deck up on Promenade is the showroom balcony, the atrium, a vast casino on port side and an enclosed "avenue" on starboard side with sidewalk cafes and bars, another lounge and a disco, then still another lounge and a cabaret showroom aft.

The remainder of the cabins are on four decks below Atlantic; the base of the atrium with the ship lobby and information desk is one deck down on Empress. Three banks of elevators and three sets of stairs access the cabins.

These are "get up and get out and have fun" ships; the cabin TV runs the same daily feature over and over in any 24-hour period, and with only a minimal library of books, you mustn't expect to snuggle down and read.

CHAMPAGNE TOAST

On the Imagination, *the exquisite hand-set mosaics in Venetian glass sparkling with bits of gold-leaf-covered glass are framed in gilded wood to cover tabletops and inset in the granite floors. And don't overlook (as if you could) the gilded, bosomy Sphinxes staring down from the walls around the upper atrium levels.*

The Brochure Says

"The best vacation on land or sea! Children have plenty to do on a "Fun Ship" cruise. Relax on acres of sun splashed decks. Kick up your heels to one of our many live bands. Pamper yourself with our Nautica Spa program. Our attentive staff will wait on you 24 hours a day. Savor a fabulous array of food from around the world. We bet you'll have a great time in the largest casinos at sea. Enjoy lavish Las Vegas-style entertainment."

Translation

Every sentence is accompanied by a picture making the intent very clear—"Children" are eating pizza with a youth counselor serving them and no hovering parents in the background. "Relax" shows rows of sunbathing bodies holding flower-garnished drinks. "Kick up" depicts a pair of sedate middle-aged couples doing what kids today call close-dancing, meaning they're dancing while holding each other in their arms, like people over 50 do sometimes. "Pamper" shows shapely young bodies, mostly female, on gym machines with smiling male instructors. "Our attentive staff" is a waiter serving breakfast in bed to a happy couple. "Savor" shows a table of six-plus passengers (the table edge is cropped, but a six-top is the smallest table you can usually find on these vessels). "We'll bet" is a croupier at the roulette wheel with a lot of happy couples, all of whom seem to think they're winning. "Enjoy lavish Las Vegas-style entertainment" depicts a bevy of chorines in pink feathers and towering headdresses. Altogether, it's Cruising 101 Illustrated for first-timers.

INSIDER TIP

Sometimes passengers are so hypnotized by the dazzle that they just stand there staring indecisively at the elevator buttons, the buffet selections, the ice cream dispensing machine, the coffee dispensing machine, lost in space or reverie. You may have to nudge them to move them along.

DID YOU KNOW?

There are 226 slot machines, 23 blackjack tables, three craps tables, two roulette wheels and a giant wheel in the Crystal Palace Casino on the Ecstasy.

EAVESDROPPING

Designer Joe Farcus says passengers should feel romance, excitement and the anticipation of boarding a new ship, "and when they come on board, I don't want them to be disappointed; when they leave, I want them to feel they got more than they expected."

Cabins & Costs

Fantasy Suites: .... A

Average Price PPPD: $348 including airfare.

The *Fantasy*-class ships have some of the best veranda suite buys at sea, with 28 Upper Deck veranda suites and 26 Veranda Deck demi-suites. But opt for the top— one of the Upper Deck suites with separate sitting area is big enough for entertaining and furnished with an L-shaped sofa, two chairs, coffee table, cocktail table, built-in wood cabinetry that includes a mini-refrigerator, glassware and TV with VCR, and a teak-floored private veranda with lounger, two chairs and a small table. The bedroom area has twin beds that can convert to queen-sized bed and marble counter desk/dresser with five drawers. The bath is fairly large with a marbleized counter, inset porcelain sink, Jacuzzi tub and tile walls and floor. There's an entry with walk-in closet, one full-length and two half-length hanging spaces, shelves and a large safe.

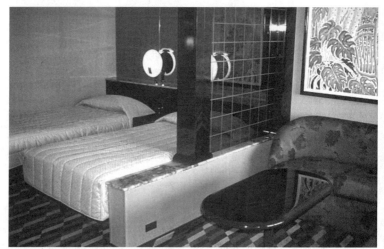

Fantasy-class suites like this veranda suite on the **Imagination** *are good buys.*

Small Splurges: .... A

Average Price PPPD: $320 including airfare.

The demi-suites on Veranda Deck have twin or queen-sized beds, big windows, private veranda with two chairs and a table, sitting area with sofa, table and chair and a bath with tile shower. Some have partially obstructed views due to hanging lifeboats.

Suitable Standards: .... B

Average Price PPPD: $251 including airfare.

Carnival's standard cabins are consistent throughout this class, 190 square feet with twin beds that convert to queen-sized, dark gray carpeting thinly striped in bright colors, an armchair and matching stool, a built-in corner table, wall-mounted TV set and desk/dresser with four drawers. The closets have one enclosed and one open full-length hanging space plus shelves. The tile bath has a big shower, a counter around the sink and a glass-doored medicine cabinet.

Bottom Bunks: ....D

Average Price PPPD: $200 including airfare.

The lowest category cabins are insides with upper and lower berths placed perpendicular to each other, considerably smaller than the standards (the brochure calls them "cozy"), similar closet space and a tile bath with shower. There are only nine of these on each ship, plus 28 more with upper and lower berths in higher price categories than are slightly roomier.

EAVESDROPPING

Carnival president Bob Dickinson: "We say we're 'Fun Ships'; we're not trying to be Royal this or Platinum that. People don't want to spend their vacations with the Queen Mum."

The *Ecstasy* sails from Miami every Friday on three-day cruises to Nassau and every Monday on four-day cruises to Key West and Playa del Carmen/Cozumel.

The *Fantasy* sails every Thursday and Sunday from Port Canaveral on three- and four-day cruises calling in Nassau; the four-day sailing also visits Freeport.

The *Fascination* cruises the Southern Caribbean on year-round itineraries leaving San Juan every Saturday and calling in St. Thomas, Guadeloupe, Grenada, La Guaira/Caracas and Aruba.

The *Imagination* sails every Saturday from Miami to the Western Caribbean, calling in Playa del Carmen/Cozumel, Grand Cayman and Ocho Rios.

The *Inspiration* sails every Sunday from San Juan into the Southern Caribbean, calling in St. Thomas, St. Maarten, Dominica, Barbados and Martinique.

These ships come to life at night when the dramatic colors and lighting are highlighted against the many glass surfaces. They are tactile (touch the surfaces of the chairs, tables, walls and floors on *Imagination*), aural (changing sounds of nature—the surf, rain, wind and chirping birds—wash by on *Sensation's* Sensation Boulevard) and intensely visual (fiber optics and neon panels "jump off" the walls as passengers walk by on the *Sensation*).

Elsewhere in this book, we call the *Fantasy* a lava lamp for the 1990s, but we mean it in a fond sense. This series of ships is constantly amazing and amusing, thanks to the ingenuousness and genius of Joe Farcus, whose own innocence and clarity of image keep them from being vulgar.

Are they gaudy? Sometimes. Do they tread dangerously close to maxing out? Perhaps. But they can match the much-praised pair of Crystal ships in marble, crystal and glove leather, dollar for dollar, ton for ton. Whether they strike you as glitzy or glamorous depends on your own individual taste, but they're never boring. Carnival delivers precisely what it promises, and if you've seen its advertising, you should already know whether it's the right cruise line for you.

Five Fabulous Spaces

1. The Old Curiosity Library aboard the *Imagination* boasts replicas of Bernini's altar columns from St. Peter's in Rome along with genuine and reproduction antiques to give the atmosphere of an antique shop.

2. Also on the *Imagination*, the classy Horizon Bar & Grill with its 24-hour pizzeria (also serving calzone, Caesar salad with or without grilled chicken and garlic bread), jukebox, elegant cast aluminum chairs, granite and aggregate floors, Matisse-like hand-painted fabric tabletops under resin, fresh flowers, cloth napkins and silverware already on the tables and lots of drinkable wines by the glass.

3. Diamonds Are Forever on the *Fascination* is a James Bond take on a disco, with fiber optic diamonds on the walls and ceilings, tabletops that glitter with handset "diamonds", and carpets woven with diamond shapes; the black granite floor and banquette bases emit smoke/fog at night when the disco is going full blast. It's hot, hot, hot!

4. The Universe show lounge aboard the *Fantasy*, which in the words of one passenger "looks like it's ready to blast off" with its carpet covered with comets and swirling ringed planets, its black upholstery flocked with tiny, intensely bright metallic microchips in red, blue, silver and gold, and its ability to turn from a gigantic stage with a 33-foot turntable in the center to a ballroom closed off by a wall of beveled gold mirrors with a sunken orchestra pit that rises to eye level.

5. The 12,000-square-foot Nautica spas on every ship with Steiner of London beauty services from facials to aromatherapy and massage, an abundance of state-of-the-art exercise machines facing a glass wall overlooking the sea, sauna and steam rooms, fully mirrored aerobics room and big twin Jacuzzis lit by the sun through an overhead skylight.

Five Off-the-Wall Places

1. Cleopatra's Bar on the *Fantasy*, patterned after an ancient Egyptian tomb, with stone floor, hieroglyphics on the walls, gilded sarcophagi and full-sized seated and standing Egyptian gods and goddesses. In the center of the room is a glossy black piano bar, and as random laser lights spotlight details around the room, you half expect to hear a chorus of "My Mummy Done Ptolemy."

2. Cats Lounge on the *Fantasy*, inspired by the set for the musical of the same name, with oversized tin cans and rubber tires, bottle cap and jar lid tabletops, and walls lined with soap and cereal boxes; you enter through a giant Pet milk can and the band plays atop a giant rubber tire laid on its side.

3. Touch of Class piano bar on the *Sensation*, entered through a doorway framed by hands with long red fingernails; the same supporting hands cup the barstool seats (making for some funny images from the back when the stools are filled) and support cocktail tables, while the walls are covered with ceramic tile handprints.

4. The movie star mannequins spotted all around the *Fascination*, from Vivien Leigh and Clark Gable standing by the faux fireplace in the Tara Library to Bette Davis sitting in a corner booth of the Stars Bar with her ubiquitous cigarette, amid delightful Al Hirschfeld drawings under glass on the tops of the small white cafe tables. Passengers stand in line to photograph each other hugging a movie star; it's a big hit.

5. The Rhapsody in Blue bar aboard the *Inspiration* with its rippling blue fabric ceiling and Manhattan-deco upholstery.

Five Good Reasons to Book These Ships

1. To have fun in an unintimidating, relaxed atmosphere without worrying about picking up the wrong fork or wearing the wrong clothes.

2. To try to win a million dollars.

3. To eat, drink, gamble, dance and watch movies all night long if you want to; it's your vacation.

4. To show the snapshots of the ships to your neighbors back home "so they can see you now..."

5. To get married on board (the line can arrange it) and spend your honeymoon at sea, all for less than a formal church wedding at home would probably cost; call Carnival's Bon Voyage Department at ☎ *800-WED-4-YOU* for details.

Five Things You Won't Find On Board

1. Lavish gift toiletries, even in the suites; all you get is a sliver of soap.

2. A table for two in the dining room.

3. A lot of books in the library.

4. A cruise director who spells Knobby Knees (as in the contest) with a "k"; every program we've seen calls it "Nobby Knees."

5. An atrium sculpture that doesn't move; some of them are inadvertently hilarious.

Ecstasy	★★★★★
Fantasy	★★★★★
Fascination	★★★★★
Imagination	★★★★★
Inspiration	★★★★★
Sensation	★★★★★

Registry	**Panama**
Officers	**Italian**
Crew	**International**
Complement	**920**
GRT	**70,367**
Length (ft.)	**855**
Beam (ft.)	**104**
Draft (ft.)	**25' 9"**
Passengers-Cabins Full	**2594**
Passengers-2/Cabin	**2040**
Passenger Space Ratio	**34.49**
Stability Rating	**Good**
Seatings	**2**
Cuisine	**International**
Dress Code	**Traditional**
Room Service	**Yes**
Tip	**$7.50 PPPD, 15% automatically added to bar checks**

Ship Amenities

Outdoor Pool	**3**
Indoor Pool	**0**
Jacuzzi	**6**
Fitness Center	**Yes**
Spa	**Yes**
Beauty Shop	**Yes**
Showroom	**Yes**
Bars/Lounges	**5**
Casino	**Yes**
Shops	**3**
Library	**Yes**
Child Program	**Yes**
Self-Service Laundry	**Yes**
Elevators	**14**

Cabin Statistics

Suites	**28**
Outside Doubles	**590**
Inside Doubles	**402**
Wheelchair Cabins	**20**
Singles	**0**
Single Surcharge	**150-200%**
Verandas	**54**
110 Volt	**Yes**

Tropicale

When Ted Arison announced in 1978 that he was ordering his line's first brand-new ship, the 36,674-ton Tropicale, 20,000 tons was considered large for a cruise ship. The wisdom of the day was that he'd never fill it. (Today the Tropicale is the smallest ship in the fleet.)

When it was delivered in 1982, he further confounded industry insiders by taking it out of the Caribbean and positioning in on the west coast for Mexican Riviera cruises out of Los Angeles. It wasn't very long until the vessel was operating at 100 percent-plus capacity.

The smallest ship in Carnival's fleet, the *Tropicale* might appeal particularly to people who like the "Fun Ship" cruise style but don't want to sail on megaships. With only 1022 passengers and a single dining room with two seatings, it's a little easier to get to know fellow passengers, at least by sight.

Some of the details on the *Tropicale* reflect design styles of older vessels, and again may have been influenced by the *Festivale*. The dining room, for instance, is on a lower deck with no windows, making it an awkward three-deck climb up to the show lounge, which is forward on Empress Deck.

At the same time, it modestly forecasts some of the bells and whistles that would distinguish the later new ships—the Exta-Z disco with its glass dance floor lit from below, the swimming pool with a slide leading down into it, the distinctive split T-shaped funnel that vents the smoke off to each side.

Cabins are modular, virtually the same size in all categories except for the slightly larger top deck veranda suites.

The Brochure Says

"You'll see more of Alaska's magical landscape when you cruise with Carnival. And because you're on a 'Fun Ship,' you can count on having Your Kind of Fun!"

Translation

We're a little bit nervous at Carnival about how many of our younger, with-it, sunbathe-and-piña-colada crowd will go for glaciers. And we're certainly not about to tell them about Alaska's ban on gambling within state waters which closes down the casinos a couple of nights every cruise. Maybe we can distract them with the Midnight Sun or something.

Cabins & Costs

Fantasy Suites: ....B

Average Price PPPD: $386 without airfare.

The veranda suites with private balconies are best, especially if there's a glacier or Northern Lights sighting on your side of the ship. The suites contain twin beds that convert to king-sized in a separate sleeping area, with a comfortable sitting area as well. There is a pulldown upper berth and a sofa that makes into a bed, in case you want to take two additional family members along. The private veranda has a couple of chairs, the bath has a tub, and a low room divider separates sleeping and sitting areas. It could work as a family suite, especially since the kids (or adult occupants) would pay only $599 apiece for the cruise.

Small Splurges: .... NA

There's nothing that really qualifies; all the rest of the cabins are standards, and prices change only according to the deck and whether the cabin is inside or outside (Carnival calls the latter Ocean View cabins).

Suitable Standards: ....*C*

Average Price PPPD: $285 plus airfare.

Upper Deck outsides in category Eight offer windows and twin beds that convert to king-sized beds. A corner table, wall-mounted TV set, chair and desk/dresser with drawers, closet and bath with shower are what you get. Eleven cabins have been modified for the physically challenged and provide 32-1/2 inch-wide doors.

Bottom Bunks: ....*C*

Average Price PPPD: $242 plus airfare.

A few bottom-price insides with upper and lower berths are on the *Tropicale* with furnishings similar to all the other ships in the fleet. The good news is they're larger than on most other vessels, the bad news is there are only nine of them.

Where She Goes

Between May and September, the ship offers Gulf of Alaska sailings between Vancouver and Seward (for Anchorage), calling in Skagway, Juneau, Ketchikan and Sitka (northbound) or Valdez (southbound), and cruising College Fjord, Columbia Glacier, Lynn Canal and Endicot Arm, Tracy Arm or Yakutat Bay.

September 24 the ship will test the waters in Hawaii, cruising from Vancouver to Honolulu on an 11-day itinerary that calls in Kahului, Hilo, Kona and Nawiliwili, then cruise from Honolulu with the same ports of call on an 11-day sailing to Ensenada (for Los Angeles).

November 14, the ship makes a 14-day Panama Canal transit between Los Angeles and San Juan, with calls in Puerto Vallarta, Zihuatanejo/Ixtapa, Acapulco, Caldera, Curacao and St. Thomas.

In winter it alternates 10-day Southern Caribbean cruises from San Juan with 11-day Panama Canal visits.

The Bottom Line

The ship is in very good condition except for some worn natural teak decking that appears to be gradually being replaced.

Since the *Tropicale* is the line's smallest ship and has cruised in Alaska before, it was a logical choice to check out the territory. The downside, of course, is the lack of a retractable glass roof over the pool and sunbathing area for sometimes inclement Alaska weather, but there are wind baffles that shelter the central area.

The enclosed promenades on each side of the casino make a comfortable and attractive place to sit between whale-watching and glacier-spotting. It's certainly cheerful enough with its school bus yellow and black chairs and floor squares, inset with a Mondrian-pattern carpet in primary colors on the floor and walls, along with plastic-topped tables in red, yellow, blue and purple.

One advantage Carnival's affiliation with Holland America Westours offers is a seasoned and well-tested program of CruiseTour options so passengers can take a luxurious glass-domed private railcar between Fairbanks and Anchorage with an overnight stopover in Denali National Park.

Fielding's Five

Five Fun Spots

1. Chopstix, a dazzling piano bar that was added to the ship in a remodeling, has table-tops bordered with piano keys, a carpet sprinkled with musical notes, arches that are neon-lit piano keys, and a black piano covered with piano keys and encircled with black barstools.

2. The Boiler Room Bar & Grill, with its deliberately exposed pipes painted in rainbow colors and industrial-looking tables of brushed chrome with a bottle of catsup sitting on each; this is where the buffet breakfasts and lunches are served.

3. The Tropicana Lounge with its sofas and long curved banquettes in a dark batik print shot through with gold threads and a Picasso-print carpet; the stage doubles as a raised dance floor.

4. The Paradise Club Casino, where the most comfortable barstools on the ship are—where else?—in front of the slot machines.

5. The Exta-Z Disco, with a glass floor lit from underneath with bright bands of neon plastic high-backed banquettes piped in shocking pink, chrome chairs and tables and Tivoli lights.

Five Good Reasons to Book This Ship

1. It offers two very good itineraries—northbound and southbound between Vancouver and Seward (for Anchorage) with an afternoon of cruising Prince William Sound and views of Columbia Glacier and College Fjord. (See Where She Goes, above, for full itineraries.)

2. If you book ahead of time, you can deduct as much as $1200 a cabin from the cruise price, perhaps enough to cover your airfare add-ons; contrary to the other sailings, Carnival's Alaska cruise prices do not include air.

3. To take one of the special Panama Canal or Hawaii sailings that bracket the Alaska season (see Where She Goes, above).

4. To join (Carnival hopes) a younger and livelier crowd on this traditionally senior destination; actually, we see more and more younger couples and families in Alaska every year.

5. Book the two winter itineraries back-to-back and visit 13 islands plus the Panama Canal in 21 days.

Five Things You Won't Find On Board

1. A 24-hour pizzeria; that's unique to the *Imagination*.

2. An outdoor Jacuzzi.

3. Ash trays in the dining room; Carnival has a no-smoking policy in all its dining rooms.

4. A view from the dining room.

5. A kosher meal.

Tropicale ★★★

Registry	Liberia
Officers	Italian
Crew	International
Complement	550
GRT	36,674
Length (ft.)	660
Beam (ft.)	85
Draft (ft.)	23' 1"
Passengers-Cabins Full	1400
Passengers-2/Cabin	1022
Passenger Space Ratio	35.88
Stability Rating	Fair to Good
Seatings	2
Cuisine	International
Dress Code	Traditional
Room Service	Yes
Tip	$7.50 PPPD, 15% automatically added to bar checks

Ship Amenities

Outdoor Pool	3
Indoor Pool	0
Jacuzzi	0
Fitness Center	Yes
Spa	No
Beauty Shop	Yes
Showroom	Yes
Bars/Lounges	5
Casino	Yes
Shops	4
Library	No
Child Program	Yes
Self-Service Laundry	Yes
Elevators	8

Cabin Statistics

Suites	12
Outside Doubles	312
Inside Doubles	187
Wheelchair Cabins	11
Singles	0
Single Surcharge	150-200%
Verandas	12
110 Volt	Yes

CARNIVAL CRUISE LINES

Celebrity Cruises, Inc.

5201 Blue Lagoon Drive, Miami, FL 33126
☎ (305) 262-8322, (800) 437-3111

A passenger volunteer assists executive chef Walter Lauer in a cooking demonstration aboard the Meridian.

History . . . .

The Greek-based Chandris Group, founded in 1915, began passenger service in 1922 with the 300-ton *Chimara*, and by 1939 had grown to a 12-ship family-owned cargo and passenger line. In the post-World War II years, the company acquired a number of famous cruise liners, most of which have been retired. Under the Fantasy label (see "Fantasy Cruises"), the company operates the *Amerikanis* but has retired the *Britanis.*

In April 1989, Chandris formed Celebrity Cruises with the intention of creating an upscale division with a premium cruise product. The *Meridian*, a massive makeover of the classic liner *Galileo Galeilei*, debuted in April 1990, followed the next month by the all-new *Horizon*. In April 1992, sister ship *Zenith* followed.

In October of that same year, Chandris formed a joint venture with Overseas Shipholding Group (OSG), a large publicly-held bulk-shipping company, and entered into the next expansion phase, ordering three 70,000-ton ships to be constructed by Joseph L. Meyer in Papen-burg, Germany. The first of these, the innovative *Century*, debuted at the end of 1995, followed in the fall of 1996 by sister ship *Galaxy*.

—Chandris introduced the fly/cruise concept in the Mediterranean in the early 1960s.

—Pioneered fly/cruise packages in the Caribbean in 1966.

—Celebrity pioneered affiliations with land-based experts from London's three-star Michelin restaurateur Michel Roux to Sony Corporation of America to create innovative onboard products and programs.

Concept . . . .

Celebrity from its beginning has aimed at presenting the highest possible quality for the best price, and offers luxury service and exceptional food with a very solid value for the money spent. These stylish ships illustrate the decade's new values—luxury without ostentation, family vacations that don't just cater to the kids and close-to-home getaways that provide pure pleasure.

Celebrity's celebrity came in part from its exceptionally good food, created and supervised by Guide Michelin three-star chef Michel Roux; here, a whimsical touch adorns a buffet dish at lunchtime.

Signatures . . . .

Perhaps the single best-known feature of this fleet is its superlative cuisine, created and supervised by London master chef Michel Roux, a longtime *Guide Michelin* three-star chef, who takes a hands-on approach, popping in for surprise visits to the ships, training shipboard chefs in his own kitchens and sending key supervisory personnel for regular culinary check-ups.

Gimmicks . . . .

The Mr. and Mrs. icebreaker game. At the beginning of each cruise, a man and a woman on board are chosen to represent Mr. and Mrs. (*Horizon, Zenith, Meridian, Century*). During the cruise, passengers are encouraged to ask individuals if they're the Mr. and Mrs. selected, and the first to find them gets a prize. In the meantime, everyone gets acquainted. Anyone for musical chairs?

Who's the Competition.............................

In its brief six years of service, Celebrity has managed to virtually create a class of its own by providing a product priced competitively with Princess and Holland America but with a level of food, and sometimes service, that approaches Crystal Cruises. Previously, the line limited its itineraries to Caribbean and Bermuda sailings, but has expanded to include Alaska and Panama Canal sailings, and very likely will enter the Mediterranean in 1998 with its mid-sized *Meridian*, oldest vessel in the fleet.

Who's Aboard.............................

Young to middle-aged couples, families with children, and, aboard the *Meridian* on certain early-season Bermuda sailings from southeastern ports, groups of senior citizens from Florida retirement communities who request early sitting dinners that start at 5:30 instead the normal 6 or 6:30 p.m. In winter season, Celebrity attracts some European and French Canadian passengers as well. Although the line is only six years old, it has many frequent cruisers with double-digit sailings.

Who Should Go.............................

Anyone looking for a good value for the money; discriminating foodies who will find very little if anything to complain about; families with children; couples of all ages. When the line was first introduced in 1990, Al Wallack, then Celebrity's senior vice president for marketing and passenger services, had several suggestions: "People who are joining country clubs but not necessarily the most expensive or exclusive country club on the block;" passengers of the former Home Lines and Sitmar ships who did not merge into Princess and who like "ships that look like ships, ships that have a European quality."

Who Should Not Go.............................

Anyone who calls for catsup with everything or after perusing the menu asks the waiter, "But where's the surf and turf?"

The Lifestyle.............................

Upscale without being pretentious, sleek and fashionable without being glitzy, the Celebrity ships offer a very comfortable seven-day cruise that is outstanding in the areas of food, service and surroundings. Evenings aboard are fairly dressy, with jacket and tie for men requested on both formal and informal nights; only casual nights suggest a sports shirt without jacket. Meals are served at assigned tables in two seatings.

Book a suite and you get all-day butler service; take the kids along during holiday and summer sailings and you'll find well-trained youth counselors on board. Ladies looking for a dancing partner will find social hosts on many sailings.

Evenings the ships present musical production shows and variety shows (except when they are docked in Bermuda, which does not permit professional entertainment other than live music on cruise ships in port), recent feature films, and duos or trios playing for dancing or listening in small lounges around the ships. Daytimes bring popular culinary demonstrations by the executive chef, arts and crafts lessons, trapshooting, napkin folding, golf putting, lectures on finance or current affairs, a trivia quiz, basketball, exercise classes and bingo.

Wardrobe . . . .

A seven-night cruise normally schedules two formal nights, in which the line suggests "both men and women may prefer more dressy attire, such as an evening gown for women and a tuxedo or dress suit for men." In our experience aboard the line's ships, a cocktail dress or dressy pants suit for women and a dark suit or blazer with tie will be acceptable. There is also a tuxedo rental service aboard the *Zenith*.

Two nights are designated informal, and men are asked to wear a jacket and tie, women a suit or dress, and three casual nights when a sport shirt and slacks are acceptable for men, dresses or pantsuits for women.

Daytime wear is casual, with good walking shoes a must. Bermuda-bound passengers in spring and fall should take a jacket or sweater, hat or scarf, for going ashore; there's often a cool breeze blowing.

A rolling cart of wines available by the glass serves the buffet restaurants.

Bill of Fare . . . . A+

Celebrity's executive chef, Vienna-born Walter Lauer, who goes from one ship to another constantly checking quality, describes it as "creating something new, where you can't cook everything in advance. Here there is the chance to do something new, more of the high standards in cuisine." One example: All the stock for soups is made from scratch on board rather than using prepared bases as many cruise kitchens do.

Lauer's mentor, Michel Roux, says, "The most important thing is to have a very good quality product and to rely on cooking skill more than the richness of the product." Fresh ingredients cooked to order figure prominently, and the menus are changed every six months.

Basically, the idea of serving simple but sophisticated dishes prepared from fresh ingredients as close as possible to serving time was revolutionary in the basic banquet/hotel catering kitchens of big cruise ships. But it succeeds splendidly. Usually if we find two or three dishes a meal that tempt us we're happy, but we could cheerfully order one of everything straight down the menu on these ships.

For lunch you might find a vegetable pizza or minestrone to start, then a main-dish salad of romaine with Mediterranean tabouli, hummus and pita bread garnished with garlic chicken; a piperade omelet with ham, tomatoes, peppers and onions; broiled ocean perch; roasted chicken with Provencale potatoes; spaghetti with fresh tomato sauce; grilled calf's liver with bacon and onions.

Dinner could begin with New England clam chowder or a pasta tossed with cilantro, oregano, ancho chile and fresh cream; a low-fat version of coquilles Saint-Jacques on vegetable tagliatelle; a pan-seared darne of salmon; roast lamb with garlic, thyme, fresh mint and olive oil with country roasted potatoes; broiled lobster tail or prime rib of beef. The dessert menu always includes one lean and light suggestion, along with fruit and cheese, pastries, ice creams and sorbets and a plate of showcase sweets presented to each table by the waiter, who describes them in mouth-watering detail. Full vegetarian menus are offered at every lunch and dinner.

A substantial 24-hour room service menu, gala midnight buffets, Caribbean barbecues on deck, continental breakfast in bed, late morning bouillon and afternoon tea are other meal options during a typical cruise.

Lunchtime buffets are reminiscent of Impressionist paintings, with displays of fresh fruits and vegetables, woven baked baskets holding bread and wonderfully crunchy homemade breadsticks, fresh and crisp salads, a huge display of fresh vegetables, a rolling cart of wines by the glass, cold and hot main dishes and plenty of desserts.

A variety of entertainment from production musicals to, as here, classical string quartets in the Horizon's Centrum.

Showtime. . . . . .A

The production musical shows have a lot of verve and are well-performed and well-costumed; they follow the usual musical revue formats with salutes to Broadway and/or Hollywood, but with fresh looks at vintage shows like *Hair* and *Jesus Christ Superstar*. Variety performers, musical soloists and duos and a Caribbean band round out the evening entertainment. Daytimes are chock-a-block with games, movies, lectures and exercise classes. The new *Century* and *Galaxy* introduce still more technological marvels from rooms with "video wallpaper" to a nightly light-and-sound spectacular.

Discounts . . . .

Special advance purchase fares save up to 45 percent for passengers who book well ahead of time; ask a travel agent for details.

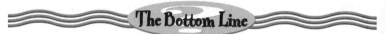

The Bottom Line

In today's world with value for the vacation dollar so important, it's comforting to sail with a cruise line that delivers high quality food and service on a stylish ship at moderate prices. We sense welcome and commitment from every employee, even the cleaning crew who polish the brass and chrome and the deck crew who pick up dirty dishes and wet towels more promptly than on many ships. All the ships in the line, even the not-built-from-scratch *Meridian*, have our highest recommendation for quality for the money.

Century
Galaxy

★★★★★

Unrated

During the inaugural sailing of this "ship of the future"—a joint venture between Celebrity and Sony Corporation of America—we found ourselves wandering around the decks trying to decipher this brave new world. There were

the very appealing intimate game booths for two or more in the Images Lounge, three high-back booths with very expensive built-in game screens on tabletops. While we never quite got the hang of them, a young couple in the booth next door was bent intently over the screen, playing with great concentration when we first saw them, then later, when we checked in again, they looked up at each other from the game and began kissing passionately. We wanted what they had, but apparently it was a different game.

Celebrity's chairman John Chandris calls his new pair of babies "the ships I've always wanted to build...ships for the next century" and tags them super-premium, saying they are for "discriminating consumers who demand the highest quality experience at the best possible value." There are a lot of exciting new features on board. Take the state-of-the-art spa with its hydropool underwater "air beds" to give the body a weightless sensation and jets of water that provide neck massages as well as another spa area with jets of water at different heights that are similar to a standup Jacuzzi. Along with the usual hydrotherapy and thalassotherapy is a seagoing first—a mud, steam and herbal treatment called rasul. All the AquaSpa programs can be booked in advance with a travel agent.

A lounge called Images utilizes "video wallpaper," hundreds of changeable, custom-designed backgrounds that can be punched up on a wall-sized video display system to change the room's ambiance from tropical palms to low-light jazz club to sports bar or wine cellar, whatever background fits the activity of the moment. Around one end is a series of interactive gaming booths big enough to seat several people at a time. For showtime, there's a Broadway-style theater with row seating, orchestra pit and four-deck fly loft for scenery. A glazed dome in the Grand Foyer changes in a slow transition from dawn to daylight to sunset to night, when astronomically correct "stars" appear in the dome "sky." Sony Corporation of America has created exclusive interactive guest services, touch-screen information kiosks, in-cabin entertainment systems, telephonic video service and special teleconferencing equipment for meetings.

"Welcome to the new *Century*, a vessel that recaptures the golden age of cruising blended with modern sophistication."

Translation
Perhaps too much emphasis was initially put into the joint venture between Celebrity and Sony. While we think passengers will certainly note the two dozen technological additions from Sony, they will be even more impressed by the elegant dining room, theater, casino, Michael's Club and the Crystal Room nightclub than electronic gadgetry.

Fantasy Suites: . . . . A
Average PPPD: $856 including airfare.
A pair of lavish penthouse suites measuring 1173 square feet offer a private veranda with its own outdoor hot tub, a living room, dining room, butler's pantry and 24-

hour butler service, master bedroom with walk-in closet, living room with wet bar and entertainment center and a guest powder room supplementing the marble bath with spa tub.

Small Splurge: .... A

Average Price PPPD: $585 including airfare.
The eight Royal Suites are spacious inside although the private verandas are fairly narrow. The living rooms have sofa and two chairs, dining table with four chairs and a separate bedroom. Museum "art boxes" in each suite displays themed pieces of art; the suite we saw featured African carvings.

Suitable Standards: .... B+

Average Price PPPD: $342 including airfare.
A typical cabin is furnished with a queen-sized bed under a large window with a striped Roman shade, a marble-topped desk/dresser, two armchairs, a cocktail table, TV set, minibar and big hinged mirror covering shelves and a safe in the wall behind it. The bathroom has a very large white tile shower (chairman John Chandris is very big on spacious shower stalls) with excellent shower head, marble counter and lots of storage.

Bottom Bunks: .... B

Average Price PPPD: $268 including airfare.
All the cabins contain safes, mini-bars, hair dryers, direct dial telephones and color TV sets, and the smallest is 171 square feet. The bottom units still contain two lower beds which can convert to a queen-sized bed, bath with spacious shower and all the amenities listed above.

Where She Goes

The *Century* sails alternating Eastern and Western Caribbean itineraries from Ft. Lauderdale every Saturday. The Eastern Caribbean sailing calls in San Juan, St. Thomas, St. Maarten and Nassau, while the Western Caribbean program visits Ocho Rios, Grand Cayman, Cozumel and Key West. The *Galaxy* also alternates Eastern and Western Caribbean itineraries with the same ports of call in winter and visits Alaska in summer.

The amidships pool on the Resort Deck of Century.

A lot of the public rooms strive mightily to look like Tomorrowland, especially the lounge called Images that combines elements of both video games and sports bars with a massive video wall and intimate high-backed booths with game screens inset into the tabletops. The overall design also skimps on the deck space, making the pool deck and sun walk above seem crowded when the ship is full. At the same time, only 61 cabins and suites have private balconies, so that means more people are out on deck. The suites aboard are lovely, well worth the splurge—and having your own private veranda means you can skip the deck sunbathing.

Images Lounge features sports bar type video walls plus one-on-one electronic game booths.

Fielding's Five

Five Good Reasons to Book This Ship

1. The exceptional AquaSpa from Steiners with an elaborate program of beauty and spa appointments that can be booked from home before the cruise via your travel agent.

2. To get a souvenir digital photograph that sets you against an unlikely backdrop of jet skis, yawning alligators, a painter's perch dangling from the bow or on the bridge with the captain.

3. To play video games almost anywhere and use interactive cabin TV service to order food, watch pay-per-view movies or wager on a few hands of video poker.

4. To dine in the elegant two-deck Grand Restaurant that evokes the dining room from the Normandie.

5. To watch a production show in a theater where there are no bad sightlines.

Five Favorite Spots

1. The dazzling casino, designed by California's Louis Periera, with its swirling gold ceiling and a carpet with a pattern of cherries and fanned cards.

2. Cigar aficionados will appreciate Michael's Club, a smoking room where a resident cigarmaker turns out Cuban- style stogies.

3. John McNeece's sensation theater complete with "floating" walkway entrances and an orchestra pit.

4. The sleek art deco nightclub called the Crystal Room, reminiscent of Radio City's Rainbow room, designed by New York hotel designer Birch Coffey on his first shipboard commission.

5. The popular little cafe bar called Tastings, where you can sip a cappuccino while you watch the lighted dome above the three-deck grand foyer change colors from dawn to midday to twilight.

Five Things You Won't Find Aboard

1. Obstructed sightlines in the showroom; the view is perfect from every seat.

2. Visitors.

3. Pets.

4. A golf cart at the simulated golf links.

5. A thoroughly worked-out low-fat, low-calorie menu program; the super light and lean menu is mysteriously heavy in fat and sodium on several suggested dishes like chicken fajitas and some pork entrees.

Century Galaxy

★★★★★ Unrated

Registry	Liberia
Officers	Greek
Crew	International
Complement	843
GRT	70,000
Length (ft.)	807
Beam (ft.)	105
Draft (ft.)	25
Passengers-Cabins Full	2056
Passengers-2/Cabin	1750
Passenger Space Ratio	40
Stability Rating	Excellent
Seatings	2
Cuisine	Contemporary
Dress Code	Traditional
Room Service	Yes
Tip	$9 PPPD, 15% automatically added to bar checks. Suites tip Butler $3 PPPD

Ship Amenities

Outdoor Pool	2
Indoor Pool	0
Jacuzzi	3
Fitness Center	Yes
Spa	Yes
Beauty Shop	Yes
Showroom	Yes
Bars/Lounges	4
Casino	Yes
Shops	0
Library	Yes
Child Program	Yes
Self-Service Laundry	No
Elevators	9

Cabin Statistics

Suites	52
Outside Doubles	517
Inside Doubles	306
Wheelchair Cabins	8
Singles	0
Single Surcharge	150-200%
Verandas	61
110 Volt	Yes

CELEBRITY CRUISES

Horizon
Zenith

Revisiting a ship you've known from its birth is sort of like being a godparent to a child and watching it grow up. The first time we saw the Zenith, at the Joseph L. Meyer shipyard in Papenburg, Germany, she was unprepossessing, a huge brooding structure of dark red steel with bare stairways, dangling wires and cords. Then, at her inaugural sailing in 1992, she was an elegant beauty decked out in expensive if understated finery, and when we saw her again not long ago she was prettier than ever, lovingly polished and primped within an inch of her life.

The **Horizon's** *Rendezvous Lounge is a popular before-dinner cocktail spot.*

The *Horizon* and *Zenith* are very similar sister ships, with a few modifications on the interior of the *Zenith*—an expanded health club, a much larger forward observation lounge and ten more passenger cabins (including two additional suites), giving her a higher gross registry tonnage than the *Horizon*. The children's playroom was moved to a higher deck on the *Zenith*, and the topmost deck's Mast Bar eliminated, along with Fantasia, the teen center ice cream and juice bar, which is replaced by a meeting room on the *Zenith*. The *Zenith* also has warmer colors and more woodwork in its decor.

Because most of the cabins aboard are modular design, insides and outsides are virtually identical in size (around 176 square feet) and furnishings, with the cabin's deck position determining the price.

INSIDER TIP

In the back of the balcony, tall barstools around a tall table look inviting to latecomers to the shows, but those seats don't swivel and are clumsy to get into and out of; move on down to a regular seat, but avoid the front row of balcony seats where the wooden balcony rail is right at eye level.

The Brochure Says

"Attention to detail...you notice it the minute you come on board."

Translation

The care and attention to detail goes beyond the design and decor into every part of the service. At a second seating luncheon our waiter was removing the cover plate when he noticed a tiny spot on the tablecloth underneath it and, horrified, immediately began apologizing profusely as he removed all the tableware, tore off the offending linen and snapped on a new cloth, then reset the entire table. When we tried to make a joke about it, he said, "No, this is very serious, and this is my mistake; I'm terribly sorry."

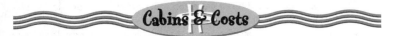

Cabins & Costs

Fantasy Suites: .... **A-**

Average Price PPPD: $570 including airfare in the Caribbean.
The two top suites, called Royal Suites on the *Zenith* and Presidential Suites on the *Horizon*, are 510 square feet with separate sitting room (the one we like has caramel leather sofas and chairs), glass dining table with four chairs, wood and marble counter, TV set and big windows; the bedroom has twin or king-sized beds, walk-in closet with generous storage space and built-in safe, and a second TV set. The marble bathroom is not large but does have a Jacuzzi bathtub. And there's butler service, hot cabin breakfasts if you wish, fresh fruit replenished daily and a welcome bottle of champagne.

Small Splurges: .... **A-**

Average Price PPPD: $456 including airfare in the Caribbean.
Deluxe suites, 18 on the *Horizon* and 20 on the *Zenith*, have two lower beds or a king-sized bed, sitting area with two chairs or loveseat and chair, glass table, large window and small TV, as well as a long marble-topped desk/dresser with chair. The bathroom is very like the one in the bigger suites (see "Fantasy Suites" above).

Perks: Butler service, terrycloth robes, hot breakfasts served in-cabin, fresh fruit, a welcome bottle of champagne.

An outside deluxe cabin aboard the Zenith.

Suitable Standards: . . . . B

Average Price PPPD: $335 including airfare in the Caribbean.
Most standard cabins measure 176 square feet and have two lower beds or a double, two chairs, table, window, large built-in desk/dresser, TV set and bath with shower. Four outside wheelchair-accessible cabins on each ship have generous bedroom and bathroom space for turning, a big shower with fold-down seat, extra-wide doors and ramp access over the low bathroom sill.

Bottom Bunks: . . . . B

Average Price PPPD: $268 including airfare in the Caribbean.
The cheapest insides are also 176 square feet with two lower beds or a double, two chairs, table, TV, wide dresser and bath with tile shower and white Corian self-sink and counter. A vertical strip of mirror on the wall where a window would be lightens and brightens the space. Some have third and fourth fold-down upper bunks.

Where She Goes

This summer the *Horizon* and new *Galaxy* travel far afield from Celebrity's usual Caribbean/Bermuda itinerary—to Alaska—with a series of seven-night sailings between Vancouver and Seward that covers both the Inside Passage and the Glacier Route. The sailings visit Ketchikan, Juneau, Skagway, Hubbard Glacier, Valdez and College Fjords on the northbound itinerary, and Hubbard Glacier, Sitka, Juneau, Tracy Arm, Skagway and Ketchikan on the southbound itinerary.

In winter the *Horizon* makes seven-night Caribbean sailings from San Juan calling at Barbados, Martinique, Antigua, St. Thomas and Catalina Island.

The *Zenith* operates seven-day Southern Caribbean cruises round trip from San Juan, calling at St. Thomas, Guadeloupe, Grenada, La Guaira and Aruba.

In summer, *Zenith* sails from New York on seven-day cruises to Bermuda, calling at Hamilton and St. George's.

The Bottom Line

When the line was first introduced, executives were careful not to over-hype the new product and bombard the public with extravagant promises. Instead, they let the product speak for itself, and it did—in volumes. Early passengers commented that they had not expected so much for the price, and Celebrity's reputation grew quickly among knowledgeable cruise passengers looking for a good buy.

After sailing aboard all the line's ships, we find very little to criticize, other than the captain's formal parties with their tepid, watery, premixed cocktails; and we often wish, in dining rooms aboard other ships, we had one of Celebrity's menus facing us instead.

Fielding's Five

Five Great Spaces

1. The shipshape navy-and-white nautical observation lounges high atop the ships and forward, America's Cup on the *Horizon* and Fleet Bar on the *Zenith*. Lots of wood and brass trim and snappy blue chairs with white piping around the edges.

2. The self-service cafe, with two indoor and one outdoor buffet line with an inviting array of dishes at breakfast and lunch, waiters on hand to carry passengers' trays to the tables, and a rolling wine cart of vintages available by the glass at lunchtime. The floors are wood and tile, the seats a pretty floral pattern.

3. Harry's Tavern, named for former company president Harry Haralambopoulos, is a small Greek taverna decorated with a mural depicting a Mexican fountain splashing under Greek trees occupied by South American parrots on a Tuscan hillside.

4. The elegant Rainbow Room on the *Zenith*, with its cabaret/nightclub ambience, wood-toned walls, gently curved bar, raised seating areas and blue leaf-patterned upholstery.

5. The show lounge offers optimum sightlines in most areas, with seven different seating levels on the two decks facing the large raised stage; multimedia projections and high-tech lighting design enhances the well-costumed shows.

Five Good Reasons to Book These Ships

1. Because the *Horizon* may very well be the best restaurant in Alaska this summer.

2. Because they represent perhaps the best value for the money in the whole world of cruising.

3. Because they take service seriously (see "Translation").

4. Because there's an excellent health center where you can work off the calories.

5. Because the whole family can experience a top quality cruise experience without mortgaging the farm.

Five Things You Won't Find On Board

1. Hot breakfasts served in standard cabins; you only get it in suites.

2. Private verandas.

3. Permission to bring your own alcoholic beverages aboard for cabin consumption; the brochure spells this out as a No No. You're expected to buy your drinks on board. (Other cruise lines permit passengers to use personal supplies while in the privacy of their cabins.)

4. A hungry passenger.

5. A cinema. Movies are shown daily on the cabin television.

Horizon ★★★★★
Zenith ★★★★★

Registry	**Bahamas**
Officers	**Greek**
Crew	**International**
Complement	**642**
GRT	**46,811**
Length (ft.)	**682**
Beam (ft.)	**95**
Draft (ft.)	**24**
Passengers-Cabins Full	**1752**
Passengers-2/Cabin	**1354**
Passenger Space Ratio	**34.57**
Stability Rating	**Good**
Seatings	**2**
Cuisine	**Contemporary**
Dress Code	**Traditional**
Room Service	**Yes**
Tip	**$9 PPPD, 15% automatically added bar checks. Suites tip Butler $3 PPPD**

Ship Amenities

Outdoor Pool	**2**
Indoor Pool	**0**
Jacuzzi	**3**
Fitness Center	**Yes**
Spa	**Yes**
Beauty Shop	**Yes**
Showroom	**Yes**
Bars/Lounges	**4**
Casino	**Yes**
Shops	**0**
Library	**Yes**
Child Program	**Yes**
Self-Service Laundry	**No**
Elevators	**7**

Cabin Statistics

Suites	**20**
Outside Doubles	**513**
Inside Doubles	**144**
Wheelchair Cabins	**4**
Singles	**0**
Single Surcharge	**150-200%**
Verandas	**0**
110 Volt	**Yes**

Meridian

★★★★

"I believe ships have a soul," says the Meridian's *Captain A. S. Varsamis.*
"You go on ships all these years and you can feel it." His ship started life in
1963 as the Galileo Galelei for Lloyd Triestino and sailed between Genoa and
Sydney. She was acquired by Chandris in 1984 and was sailing as the Galileo
when we first saw her a year later. There's not a lot of the old ship left on the
Meridian—she was dismantled and rebuilt from the hull up—except her soul,
but we agree with Captain Varsamis. You can feel it when you stand at the rail
on a wind-tossed night sailing from Bermuda.

Golfers en route to Bermuda practice on the **Meridian's** *putting green.*

This smooth-sailing former ocean liner has a 29-foot draft and a top cruising speed of 24.5 knots, so it's one of the fastest ships at sea. The deck crew
scrubs down the teak early every morning, when determined early-morning

walkers do their mile or two if they don't mind working their way through the water and suds.

The *Meridian* has a longer, sleeker line than the newer *Horizon* and *Zenith*, with the dining room on a middle deck amidships and the show rooms and lounges one deck above. The topmost decks house the skylight suites, swimming pool and whirlpool spas and a self-service cafe that doubles as a late-night disco.

DID YOU KNOW?

Sister ship of the Galileo Galilei *was the* Guglielmo Marconi, *also built in 1963 and now sailing as the* Costa Riviera.

The Brochure Says

"The decor: inviting and perfectly understated. Put simply, you feel right at home. Except at home, you don't have a steward bringing you whatever you need, whenever you need it."

Translation

Rather than setting out to astonish, Celebrity works quietly, training its staff to serve meals or make cabins in precisely the same way time after time after time. A most recent sailing five years after the first one found all the details we had admired from the beginning still in place, still being done exactly the same way, down to the presentation of various breakfast teas in a wooden chest.

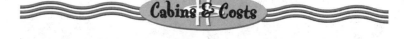
Cabins & Costs

Fantasy Suites: .... B+

Average Price PPPD: $414 in Bermuda plus air add-ons.

Eight romantic Skylight Suites on the top deck let you look up at the night sky. The sitting area is beside floor-to-ceiling windows with sofa, two chairs, coffee table and a long built-in wood dresser/desk with 16 drawers. Two lower beds or one double, a wide nightstand with three drawers and a big cabinet/console, plus a closet with four doors opening to full- and half-length hanging sections, shelves and a safe, can stow plenty of wardrobe for a week—even for Ivana Trump. The bath, just barely big enough, is marble with a spa tub. Occupants of suites have the use of terrycloth bathrobes during the cruise, fresh fruit daily, a complimentary bottle of champagne as well as the services of the butler, on our cruise happy Herbert from Honduras.

Small Splurges: .... B+

Average Price PPPD: $378 in Bermuda plus air add-ons.

A pair of category Two deluxe junior suites on Atlantic Deck are as large as the top-ranked Skylight Suites, and represent a best buy (on our cruise, one of them was occupied by two cabin-savvy travel agents). You'll find a sitting area, two lower beds, two chairs, a big closet, lots of storage shelves, mini-refrigerator and bathroom with tub.

The Royal Suite aboard the **Zenith.**

Suitable Standards: . . . . *C*

Average Price PPPD: $249 plus airfare in Bermuda.

Category seven outside cabins are on Caribbean Deck, one deck below the dining room, with a choice of twin beds or a double bed (have your travel agent specify which you want when booking), desk/dresser with five drawers, and bath with shower. Some of the vintage bathroom fixtures and mirrors—including a round chrome porthole-shaped mirror and a big mirror on a stand—date from the *Galileo*. All cabins have hair dryers, complimentary toiletries, bottles of mineral water, TV sets and most have safes. Cabins on Europa, Caribbean and Bermuda Decks have portholes rather than windows.

Bottom Bunks: . . . . *C+*

Average Price PPPD: $142 plus airfare in Bermuda.

The lowest-priced category 14 inside cabins offer double beds or upper and lower berths, with two dressers, plenty of storage. There are only six of them.

Where She Goes

The *Meridian* cruises in the Caribbean in winter on 10- and 11-night sailings from San Juan, alternating a 10-night itinerary calling at Aruba, La Guaira, Grenada, Barbados, St. Lucia, Martinique, St. Maarten and St. Thomas with an 11-night program visiting La Guaira, sailing into the Panama Canal, then calling at San Blas, Cartagena, Martinique, St. John and St. Thomas.

In summer, the *Meridian* sails to Bermuda on round-trip seven-night cruises from New York, spending three days docked at Kings Wharf on the island's eastern tip by the newly-restored Royal Dockyard complex of shops, restaurants, museums and movie theaters.

With slightly lower prices than Celebrity's newer ships and far-reaching Caribbean winter itineraries, the *Meridian* offers a good opportunity to passengers who want to see a lot of Caribbean islands on one cruise.

Because of the ship's deep draft (29 feet), the *Meridian* is relegated to Bermuda's only deepwater port at Kings Wharf, some distance from the capital of Hamilton, which is 30 minutes away by tender, 50 minutes away by taxi. Cabins aboard are fairly spacious and the food, as we have said before, is excellent. When the ship is full, however, the dining room gets a little crowded, with less space between tables than on the line's new ships.

A nice additional touch: In the suites, daily lunch and dinner menus, along with wine lists, are delivered in mid-morning.

Five Favorite Places

1. The Rendez-Vous Lounge always seems to be full of happy passengers comfortably ensconced in coral tub chairs at little marble tables to wait for dinner one deck below, to dance to a duo alternating rock 'n roll, Big Band favorites or 50s pop like "Blue Moon"—hey, a keyboard synthesizer helps—or watching a cooking demonstration or playing team trivia.

2. The Marina Cafe makes a pretty set-up out of buffet lunch, with an arrangement of wine bottles and grapes and a huge display of fresh vegetables at the entrance, then a chef in a crisp white toque carving a roast, plus salads, cold cuts and vegetables decorated with carved characters created from squash and onions, along with half a dozen hot dishes and a dessert table of sweets, including sugar-free pastries.

3. A two-level cinema that plays recent films on a reasonable schedule that lets someone who's missed everything since *Forrest Gump* play catch-up.

4. Two glass-enclosed promenade deck areas called Palm Court are divided into smoking areas on one side and nonsmoking on the opposite, with bamboo chairs and marble-topped tables, perfect for needlepoint, reading, playing Scrabble or having a quiet chat.

5. Interlude Bar, a great hideaway with pretty peach chairs and comfortable leather barstools, just the spot for a tête-à-tête.

Five Good Reasons to Book These Ships

1. The food, the food, the food, the food, the food!

2. The best martini at sea (from Franco in the Rendez-Vous Lounge).

3. A smooth and even ride in seas that can sometimes get rough.

4. A fresh and delightful production show called *Fifty Years of Broadway*.

5. A courteous and caring crew from the captain on down.

Five Things You Won't Find On Board

1. An empty dance floor.

2. A lot of passengers springing for the caviar, Russian vodka and champagne specials in the Zodiac Lounge—at least not on our sailing.

3. A glass of champagne on the tray of pre-mixed cocktails at the captain's welcome-aboard party.

4. A stale breadstick—they're always crisp and freshly baked.

5. An empty seat during the cooking demonstration (free samples are dispensed afterward), as with this "Filet Mignon Celebrity" demonstrated by executive chef Walter Lauer:

Four 8-ounce filet mignon steaks

3 oz olive oil

3 finely chopped shallots

2 TB peeled, seeded and cubed fresh tomato

8 black olives, chopped

2 TB green peppercorns

5 ounces heavy cream

2 ounces cognac (optional)

8 ounces brown veal stock

1 TB chopped fresh basil

Season the steaks with freshly ground black pepper and salt, then saute in a hot pan with olive oil until cooked to taste. Remove steaks from pan and keep warm. Add shallots to pan and saute until light brown. Add tomato cubes, black olives and green peppercorns and heat, then flame with cognac (optional). Add veal stock and cream, and cook down to reduce by half. Finish the sauce by adding the chopped basil, season to taste, and serve steaks with sauce to four.

CELEBRITY CRUISES

Meridian ★ ★ ★ ★

Registry	**Bahamas**
Officers	**Greek**
Crew	**International**
Complement	**580**
GRT	**30,440**
Length (ft.)	**700**
Beam (ft.)	**94**
Draft (ft.)	**29**
Passengers-Cabins Full	**1420**
Passengers-2/Cabin	**1106**
Passenger Space Ratio	**27.52**
Stability Rating	**Good to Excellent**
Seatings	**2**
Cuisine	**Contemporary**
Dress Code	**Traditional**
Room Service	**Yes**
Tip	**$9 PPPD, 15% automatically added to bar checks. Suites tip Butler $3PPPD**

Ship Amenities

Outdoor Pool	**2**
Indoor Pool	**0**
Jacuzzi	**3**
Fitness Center	**Yes**
Spa	**Yes**
Beauty Shop	**Yes**
Showroom	**Yes**
Bars/Lounges	**2**
Casino	**Yes**
Shops	**0**
Library	**Yes**
Child Program	**Yes**
Self-Service Laundry	**No**
Elevators	**4**

Cabin Statistics

Suites	**10**
Outside Doubles	**285**
Inside Doubles	**258**
Wheelchair Cabins	**0**
Singles	**0**
Single Surcharge	**150-200%**
Verandas	**0**
110 Volt	**Yes**

CLASSICAL CRUISES & TOURS

132 East 70th Street, New York, NY 10021
☎ *(212) 794-3200, (800) 252-7745*

One of the most enchanting ports in the western Mediterranean is Portoferraio, Elba, another Napoleon connection.

History . . . .

Classical Cruises is an offshoot of Travel Dynamics, a New York-based company that specializes in small-ship expeditions and educational cruises for university alumni associations and museum groups. While the ship also charters other vessels that are offered by various agencies, Classical Cruises always has a ship or two for which they are the major American charterer—such as Swan Hellenic's new *Minerva*.

Minerva   Unrated

Swan Hellenic's new *Minerva*, the former *Okean*, is just the size ship the company seems to prefer for its cultural and intellectual European programs. While the clientele is primarily British, a lot of Americans also enjoy these cruises because of their unusual itineraries and in-depth lecture programs.

Swan Hellenic's European tours have been offered since the 1920s; the company began Greek ship-based tours in 1952 when the war-torn country had little tourism infrastructure. Everyone from the former Archbishop of Canterbury to the Deputy Keeper at the British Museum takes a turn at talking about archeology, history, mythology, geology, military history, astronomy, marine biology, art, music, drama and medical history.

An open-seating policy in the dining room gives passengers a chance to get acquainted with a wider range of people, including the lecturers, than with the customary assigned seating. Passengers may arrive within a time frame and sit where they like. There is a no- tipping policy as well. Dress aboard is casual during the daytime, and gets a bit dressier (say, a floral frock or pantsuit) for evenings. There is one gala night where dressing up is expected. And while the Swan Hellenic cruises may sound like a serious matter, there's a lot of fun as well, with sunbathing around the pool and cocktails on deck or in the bar. There's a fitness center, beauty shop, library and self-service laundry, but no casino.

Twelve of the accommodations aboard are suites, with 130 outside double cabins and 52 inside double cabins. Single rates are offered on all cabins. Four of them are wheelchair-accessible, and the vessel has two elevators.

Anyone under 26 accompanying a full-fare adult gets a 50 percent discount on the regular adult fare. Group discounts are also available on request.

Swan Hellenic's usual cruising patterns include the Eastern and Western Mediterranean, the Aegean, Black Sea, Red Sea, North African coast and Iberian peninsula. All-inclusive rates cover air from London, tips and shore excursions.

Minerva — Unrated

Registry	**Bermuda**
Officers	**British**
Crew	**International**
Crew	**90**
GRT	**12,000**
Length (ft.)	**416**
Beam (ft.)	**65**
Draft (ft.)	**19.5**
Passengers-Cabins Full	**400**
Passengers-2/Cabin	**388**
Passenger Space Ratio	**30.92**
Stability Rating	**Good**
Seatings	**1**
Cuisine	**International**
Dress Code	**Casual**
Room Service	**No**
Tip	**No Tipping**

Ship Amenities

Outdoor Pool	**1**
Indoor Pool	**0**
Jacuzzi	**0**
Fitness Center	**Yes**
Spa	**No**
Beauty Shop	**Yes**
Showroom	**Yes**
Bars/Lounges	**1**
Casino	**No**
Shops	**1**
Library	**Yes**
Child Program	**No**
Self-Service Laundry	**Yes**
Elevators	**2**

Cabin Statistics

Suites	**12**
Outside Doubles	**130**
Inside Doubles	**52**
Wheelchair Cabins	**4**
Singles	**0**
Single Surcharge	**150%**
Verandas	**12**
110 Volt	**No**

CLASSICAL CRUISES & TOURS

CLASSICAL CRUISES & TOURS

❖ CLIPPER

7711 Bonhomme Avenue, St. Louis, MO 63105
☎ *(314) 727-2929, (800) 325-0010*

History . . . .

Founded in 1982 in his native St. Louis by travel entrepreneur Barney A. Ebsworth, who also founded Intrav tour company, Clipper Cruises owns and operates two small ships, the 138-passenger *Yorktown Clipper* and the 100-passenger *Nantucket Clipper*, both U.S. flag vessels built in Jeffersonville, Indiana. The company is privately held by parent company Windsor, Inc., a real estate and investment company.

The first ship on line was the 104-passenger *Newport Clipper*, which introduced the line's signature Colonial South cruises in 1984. That vessel was subsequently sold and now sails as *Spirit of Endeavor* for Alaska Sightseeing/Cruise West.

The two ships cruise the waterways of North and Central America from Alaska to Costa Rica, the Caribbean to New England, with an emphasis on local culture, art, history, golf and swimming and snorkeling off the side of the ship, depending on the cruising region.

Nantucket Clipper passengers spot a whale off the coast of Massachusetts.

Concept . . . .

Clipper uses small, shallow-draft vessels to explore America's waterways, tying up in small, out-of-the-way ports as well as urban areas in walking distance of the sightseeing. The line prides itself on being "a thoughtful alternative to conventional cruising," stressing substance over slickness, naturalist and lecture programs over musical productions and bingo and sneakers over sequins.

Clipper president Paul H. Duynhouwer likes to point out the misconceptions about adventure cruising—"Elitist, expensive, far away and long are common misconceptions," he says. Clipper, on the other hand, makes soft adventure trips that are as short as seven days and more affordable than many of the exotic journeys other lines offer.

Signatures . . . .

Clipper was one of the early providers of golf theme cruises with its southeastern U.S. itineraries offering passengers a chance to play courses like Kiawah Island, Palmetto Dunes, Wild Dunes, Dataw Island, Osprey Cove and St. Simons Island Club, all during a one-week cruise.

Open-seating meals served by friendly young Americans, many of them just past college-age, are prepared by chefs trained at the famous Culinary Institute of America in Hyde Park.

Gimmicks . . . .

Clipper Chippers—warm chocolate chip cookies served at teatime and other times.

Who's the Competition . . . .

While Clipper offers a fairly unique product because of the scope of its itineraries, it does compete somewhat with Special Expeditions in Alaska, Costa Rica, Panama and Mexico's Sea of Cortez, as well as rivaling American Canadian Caribbean Line in the Virgin Islands in winter. And the all-American style of its food and service, as well as an emphasis on lesser-visited ports and cruising areas, competes with Alaska Sightseeing/Cruise West in Alaska.

Who's Aboard . . . .

Couples and singles past 40, many from the south and midwest, dominate the passenger list. What the passengers have in common is an interest in history, culture and nature, and a desire to learn more about the world around them. They are destination-oriented rather than pleasure-driven, and would show little interest in a casino or production show, even if Clipper were to offer them. Most represent household incomes of over $70,000 with substantial discretionary income. They're the sort of people who would wear a name badge if issued one.

Who Should Go . . . .

We think more younger couples would enjoy the ship as much as their elders, the same people who would take a bicycling tour through a wine region or stay in bed-and-breakfast establishments. Also, Clipper would appeal to people who have taken package tours or bus tours because they feel safer being escorted around but are tired of all that regimentation, packing and unpacking.

Who Should Not Go

Families with young or restless children, because there are no places on these ships for them to get away; everyone congregates in one large indoor lounge more suitable to quiet adult activities. Because the ships have no elevators, they are not appropriate for travelers who require wheelchairs or walkers to get around.

The Lifestyle

Single seating meals with no assigned tables allow passengers to get acquainted more easily than on large ships, and many of the Clipper crowd find they have a great deal in common. Most days the vessels are in port for all or part of the day, with a range of organized excursions and suggestions for on-your-own activities. Naturalists and lecturers are scheduled frequently to talk about special features of the ports of call, and if there is any entertainment, it is apt to be someone from shore performing folk songs or playing jazz.

Wardrobe

Day dress is casual but in the east coast preppy or country club style, with topsiders, golf pants, plaid Bermuda shorts and such. Zippered windbreakers, soft hats rather than billed caps and sensible shoes are worn ashore. While there is no specific dress code, passengers usually dress up a bit for dinner, and men will sometimes wear jacket and tie.

Bill of Fare. B+

As mentioned above, chefs from the Culinary Institute of America are responsible for preparing the excellent contemporary American cuisine on board. We've found the food uniformly good and the menus consistent in their appeal and variety. Half-portions can be ordered for people with small appetites and "light" dishes are offered on every menu. Much of the food is prepared with fresh ingredients from scratch—including homemade crackers served with the day's soups.

A delectable—and very rich—Flourless Chocolate Cake is one of the specialties:

1 pound butter

1 cup brewed espresso or coffee

1 cup granulated sugar

1 pound semisweet chocolate chips, chopped

8 eggs

Bring butter, coffee and sugar to a boil. Remove from heat and stir in chocolate chips until melted. Mix in beaten eggs and pour into a buttered 10" springform pan. Bake at 350 degrees for 30 to 35 minutes. The cake should be wobbly but dry to the touch.

Cool and cover with Ganache:

4 cups heavy cream

2 pounds semisweet chocolate chips

Bring the cream to a boil and remove from the heat. Add chocolate chips and mix until melted. Pour over the cooled cake.

DID YOU KNOW?

A free 21-minute video is available for loan from Clipper for any potential passenger who'd like a closer look at the vessels and the life aboard them. Rather than using models as most cruise lines do, the video features actual Clipper passengers. Call ☎ (800) 325-0010 to borrow a copy.

The Bottom Line

These are rewarding and enjoyable cruises, with as many surprises and delights to be discovered in Charleston as in Costa Rica or in Annapolis as in Panama's San Blas Islands. The cruises are especially delightful when a passenger is following a subject of particular interest—whether golf, Civil War history, great art museums, Native American legends and lore, snorkeling or restored historic rail cars on a combination cruise/train journey into Mexico's Sea of Cortez and Copper Canyon.

Nantucket Clipper
Yorktown Clipper

A cruise along the coast of Maine brings back indelible memories of a lunchtime when a humpback whale mother swam by, her nursing calf clinging to her, lazily flapping her white fins in a backstroke wave just outside the dining room windows. On other days, we'd search out the lobster pound in every port, and feast on fresh steamed one-and-a-quarter pounders, promising each other it was in lieu of dinner—and then dinner was always so tempting we'd eat it anyhow.

The *Nantucket* and the *Yorktown Clippers* have four passenger decks reached by stairs; there are no elevators. Topmost is the Sun Deck, with lounge chairs and good observation points; it doubles as an outdoor dining venue from time to time, and, on the *Yorktown Clipper*, also has four passenger cabins. The Promenade Deck, as its name implies, is wrapped all around by a covered promenade, and cabins on this deck open directly to the outdoors, a boon except when it's raining. Lounge Deck has a forward observation lounge and an outdoor bow area in front of that, along with passenger cabins, some opening into an inside hallway, others at the aft end opening to the outdoors. Main Deck is where the dining room is located, along with additional passenger cabins. All cabins are outsides with windows or portholes.

The Brochure Says

"Lifestyle on board is casual and unregimented. The crowds, commercial atmosphere and hectic activities so often associated with conventional cruise ships are nowhere to be found on Clipper. Your fellow travelers are likely to remind you of the members of your own country club."

Translation
None needed; it's a very precise description of the lifestyle and passengers.

Cabins & Costs

Fantasy Suites: .... NA
Nothing on board really qualifies for this category.

Small Splurges: .... B
Average Price PPPD: $440 plus air add-ons.
The category Five outside double staterooms, three on *Nantucket Clipper* and eight on *Yorktown Clipper*, are the most expensive digs aboard, primarily because of being slightly larger with more desirable deck locations. Like all the other Clipper cabins, they contain twin beds, bath with shower, desk/dresser with chair plus windows rather than portholes.

Suitable Standards: C
Average Price PPPD: $340 to $400, plus air add-ons.
Same as the above (see "Small Splurges") except slightly smaller, the category Two, Three and Four cabins are very similar but vary slightly in price. The category Fours have twin beds in an L-configuration with a bit more floor space, while the others have the two beds parallel to each other with a small desk/dresser in between. All three categories have bath with shower only and windows instead of portholes.

Bottom Bunks: C
Average Price PPPD: $315 plus air add-ons.
The lowest-priced cabins on board are forward on the lowest passenger deck and have portholes instead of windows. Otherwise, each contains twin beds arranged parallel to each other with a small desk/dresser and chair in between. Baths have shower only.

In the winter the ships are in the Caribbean, then the *Nantucket Clipper* heads north along the Atlantic seaboard for golf, Colonial America and Civil War Battlefields sailings, then more coastal U.S. and Canada itineraries. Aboard the *Yorktown Clipper*, highlights of the season include spring and fall Copper Canyon and the Sea of Cortez sailings. Summer is spent in Alaska, and Costa Rica and Panama are highlighted with spring and fall repositioning sailings.

While the prices could be regarded as slightly higher than average—and there's no early booking discount advertised—the value is there. The vessels are comfortable, attractively decorated and always spotlessly clean, although when the ship is full, the lounge sometimes feels crowded. In a few areas they visit—notably off the coast of Maine—the shallow draft causes more ship motion than some passengers might like. The other downer is getting from the Promenade Deck cabins, which open onto a covered deck, down to the dining room when it's raining. But the food, service, itineraries and overall experience are so delightful that little annoyances about space or rain in the face seem minuscule. We like these ships very much.

Five Favorite Places

1. The tasteful Dining Room, just about everyone's favorite hangout three times a day, plus when it doubles as a cinema after dinner some evenings and the crew makes a batch of fresh popcorn.

2. The Observation Lounge, where passengers socialize, listen to lectures, play cards and games, write letters and do needlepoint, is prettily decorated in pastels and subdued pale tones. This is where the chocolate chip cookies are served at teatime.

3. The Promenade Deck, good for getting in a mile walk if you don't mind counting double-digit laps.

4. The bow observation area, a good place to watch for Alaska wildlife or denizens of the Darien jungle, also where you might sip a cup of hot coffee or glass of iced tea.

5. The Sun Deck, where you sit in lounge chairs and observe the scenery, is also the place where a New England clambake may be dished up.

Five Good Reasons to Book These Ships

1. To get tee times at the south's top golf courses.

2. To get special tours of famous American art museums conducted by your own shipboard art experts.

3. To enjoy some genuinely warm and friendly American service and delicious American food.

4. To cruise some unusual and interesting waterways, including the Great Lakes, the St. Lawrence Seaway, the Sea of Cortez, the Orinoco River and Intracoastal Waterway.

5. To meet other people around the same age who share the same interests.

Nantucket Clipper ⚓⚓⚓⚓

Registry	**US**
Officers	**American**
Crew	**American**
Complement	**32**
GRT	**95**
Length (ft.)	**207**
Beam (ft.)	**37**
Draft (ft.)	**8**
Passengers-Cabins Full	**102**
Passengers-2/Cabin	**102**
Passenger Space Ratio	**NA**
Stability Rating	**NA**
Seatings	**1**
Cuisine	**American, contemporary**
Dress Code	**Casual**
Room Service	**No**
Tip	**$9 PPPD**

Ship Amenities

Outdoor Pool	**0**
Indoor Pool	**0**
Jacuzzi	**0**
Fitness Center	**No**
Spa	**No**
Beauty Shop	**No**
Showroom	**No**
Bars/Lounges	**1**
Casino	**No**
Shops	**1**
Library	**Yes**
Child Program	**No**
Self-Service Laundry	**No**
Elevators	**0**

Cabin Statistics

Suites	**0**
Outside Doubles	**51**
Inside Doubles	**0**
Wheelchair Cabins	**0**
Singles	**0**
Single Surcharge	**150%**
Verandas	**0**
110 Volt	**Yes**

Yorktown Clipper   ⚓⚓⚓⚓

Registry	US
Officers	American
Crew	American
Complement	40
GRT	97
Length (ft.)	257
Beam (ft.)	43
Draft (ft.)	8.5
Passengers-Cabins Full	138
Passengers-2/Cabin	138
Passenger Space Ratio	NA
Stability Rating	NA
Seatings	1
Cuisine	American, contemporary
Dress Code	Casual
Room Service	No
Tip	$9 PPPD

Ship Amenities

Outdoor Pool	0
Indoor Pool	0
Jacuzzi	0
Fitness Center	No
Spa	No
Beauty Shop	No
Showroom	No
Bars/Lounges	1
Casino	No
Shops	1
Library	Yes
Child Program	No
Self Service Laundry	No
Elevators	0

Cabin Statistics

Suites	0
Outside Doubles	69
Inside Doubles	0
Wheelchair Cabins	0
Singles	0
Single Surcharge	150%
Verandas	0
110 Volt	Yes

Club Med® Cruises

40 West 57th Street, New York, NY 10019
☎ (212) 977-2100, (800) 453-7447

History . . . .

The vacation phenomenon that is Club Med started in the summer of 1950 in a small tent village on the island of Mallorca and has grown to more than 100 all-inclusive vacation villages around the world. In February 1990 the company introduced the first of two five-masted sailing ships, the *Club Med 1*, built by France's Société Nouvelle des Ateliers et Chantiers du Havre, the yard that also constructed the three Windstar sailing ships. Similar to the Windstar ships but larger, and also with computer-trimmed sails, the Club Med ships are sleek, handsome vessels carrying 376 passengers.

—At 14,745 tons, a length of 617 feet and a draft of 16.5 feet, they are the world's largest sailing ships.

The same emphasis on watersports as in the land clubs can be found aboard the Club Med ships with their marine platforms.

Concept

To offer a cruise vacation aboard a motor/sailing ship in "unparalleled comfort and elegance" with a relaxed atmosphere that "fosters freedom, intimacy and camaraderie."

Signatures

Some 64 to 77 GOs, *gentils organisateurs*, or "congenial organizers," as in the Club Med land resorts, operate as a sort of free-wheeling social staff aboard each ship.

Gimmicks

Usually once a cruise there's a shoreside lobster picnic lunch, along with a water-skiing exhibition by the GOs.

Who's the Competition

While the Club Med vessels are similar to those of Windstar, the lifestyle aboard differs because of the very strong presence of the GOs, who function as cheerleaders, entertainers and quasi-passengers. The end result is part-cruise, part-Club Med land village experience. Therefore, the real competition Club Med ships face is from Club Med land resorts.

Who's Aboard

Young to middle-aged singles and couples, families with children over 10 (kids under 10 are no nos), watersports enthusiasts, honeymooners, and destination-oriented young vacationers primarily from Europe and North America.

Who Should Go

Anyone young at heart who enjoys sun, sand, surf and sails, who has a sense of adventure, a dislike of formality but an appreciation for luxurious, if unpretentious, accommodations and surroundings.

Who Should Not Go

Children under 10.

Mrs. Pritchard, author James Thurber's quintessential cruiser: "If you travel much on cruise ships you are bound, sooner or later, to run into Mrs. Abigail Pritchard. She is not one woman, but many; I have encountered at least fifteen of her." Mrs. Pritchard, who appreciates Cunard, would be confused at the absence of a professional cruise staff, the lack of dress code and the babel of different languages with French predominating.

The Lifestyle

There is no assigned seating for meals. A variety of indoor and outdoor, self-serve and full-service restaurants are on board, plus the Hall Nautique, a watersports marina that can be lowered astern when the ship is at anchor. Daily ports of call are visited by passengers who shuttle ashore by tender to go to an island beach or shops or restaurants.

Wardrobe

Daytime dress is casual aboard ship and on shore, and topless sunbathing is popular aboard with both passengers and female GOs. Bathing suits and coverups are the most common daytime garb. While recent Club Med brochures show a formally dressed couple on deck, we can't recall seeing anyone wearing black tie on our cruise. "Stylish resort attire" is what is requested for evening, and a jacket without tie on men, a long skirt or silk slacks on women is about as dressy as it gets normally.

Bill of Fare . . . . B

An open-air snack bar, self-serve restaurant for breakfast and lunch plus a full-service restaurant for lunch and dinner offer meal choices for French-accented cuisine. A complimentary table wine is served at both lunch and dinner in generous quantity, with a wine list available offering premium wines for purchase. The cooking when we were aboard was more Continental rather than nouvelle. A room service menu offers additional choices at a surcharge—smoked fish, caviar and sandwiches.

Showtime . . . . D

As in the land Club Meds, the GOs perform a lot of the entertainment, lip-syncing to records and donning funny hats with the same enthusiasm Judy Garland and Mickey Rooney used to put into their shows in grandpa's barn in the old MGM movies. Sometimes a steel band from shore comes aboard.

Discounts . . . .

Land/cruise combination packages can save money when purchased as a package, but the cruise line does not routinely offer discounts.

The Bottom Line

Club Med has begun to diversify its land product during the last several years, emphasizing certain resorts for "romance and friendship" for couples and singles, and others as "togetherness" for families. Another recent creation is a separate brochure marketing Club Med's Finest, listing nine of the club's most luxurious resorts, plus the two Club Med ships, promoting them as upscale destinations. And this seems to be the precise placement for Club Med Cruises, which in the early days did not seem to be able to decide whether it wanted to be a cruise line or a floating Club Med vacation village. It is, in fact, both, but an upscale, luxurious version, one of Club Med's Finest.

Club Med 1
Club Med 2   ★★★

Her first captain, Alain Lambert, loves the Club Med 1. "She's like a fish, just like a fish when she's running. She's lovely. She puts her nose in the water, she likes the water." Her maximum list is two percent but he can control it from one degree to five degrees. "If I have sportive passengers, I can put it five degrees." The combination of sails and engine saves seven tons of bunker fuel a day. Twenty tons are consumed in the average day. The ship makes 14 knots under motor and sail with favorable winds, and he can raise or lower the sails in one-and-a-half minutes. "She's very stable."

Waterskiing demonstrations are performed by Club Med's GOs.

Instead of a professional cruise staff, pursers, hotel managers, entertainers and such, the cruise is run by a team of 64 to 77 energetic young men and women from various parts of the French-speaking world called GOs (for *gentils organisateurs*) who seem to be having more fun than anybody. Rather than hotel staffers in the traditional sense, they function as quasi-guests, taking part in the same activities with the guests. When they're not water-skiing or leading passengers in songs and dances, they're sunbathing by the pool or rehearsing lip-sync songs for shows. The chief purser/hotel manager is called the *chef de village*, or head of the village, and he may spend more time polishing his mono waterski technique than his hotel-keeping skills, while the ship's doctor may spend his days checking out scuba equipment to the passengers if no one is ill.

INSIDER TIP

Newlyweds on the Club Med ships get a bottle of sparkling wine, two bar coupons, two T-shirts and a VIP gift basket, plus a cocktail party with the chef de village. Honeymooners must be spending one week or longer aboard, must travel within three months of their wedding, must present their marriage certificate when checking in and should request the gift package when booking.

The Brochure Says

"The whisper of the wind along the sails above. On every side, a sea of ultramarine grandeur. Under your feet, eight elegant decks of Burmese teak...All the romance of the sea is yours when you fly on the wings of the wind in these sleek white ships."

Translation

The only problem is, you'll have to get up early in the morning to experience it since the ships tend to spend most of each day in port with the sails furled.

Cabins & Costs

Fantasy Suites: . . . . **NA**

There is nothing on board that fits this category.

Small Splurges: . . . .**A**

Average Price PPPD: $526 including airfare from New York in the Caribbean, $542 including airfare from Los Angeles in French Polynesia.
Suites (two measuring 321 square feet each on the *Club Med 1*, five measuring 258 square feet each on the *Club Med 2*) containing the same basic furnishings as standards (see "Suitable Standards," below) are also available.

Suitable Standards: . . . .**A**

Average Price PPPD: $325 including airfare from New York in the Caribbean, $400 including airfare from Los Angeles in French Polynesia.
All the *Club Med* cabins are outsides with portholes rather than windows and measuring 188 square feet, with white walls, mahogany trim, twin beds that can be made into a queen-sized bed and space module bathrooms that are trim and sleek

with excellent pulsating shower heads. Some 23 cabins have a third upper berth. Furnishings include a long dresser/desk with six drawers, a mirror wall, wide counter, built-in TV set fitted into a wooden base (most of the programming is in French) and a hotel-type folding suitcase rack. Niceties include attractive art, reading lights over the beds, hair dryers, terrycloth robes, fresh fruit in each cabin and Club Med label toiletries. A stocked mini-refrigerator and mini-bar carry price lists for the contents. Except for continental breakfasts, room service carries a charge.

Bottom Bunks: .... NA

There are no accommodations that fit this category.

INSIDER TIP

You have to join Club Med with a nonrefundable, one-time-only initiation fee when booking your cruise and pay an annual membership fee. Think of it as just another port tax.

EAVESDROPPING

"A real babble tower," is the way one of the Club Med executives described their 64 GOs that come from all over the world.

Club Med 1 spends winters in the Caribbean, sailing from Fort-de-France, Martinique, and summers in the Mediterranean, and Club Med 2 sails in French Polynesia and the South Pacific. Length of sailings varies from three to seven nights with land package combinations available. A few special Christmas holiday sailings may be seven to 15 nights.

While more emphasis has been placed on English-speaking personnel aboard the ships, these cruises still favor French-speaking passengers. Passengers have to hustle to get to the best deck chairs, watersports gear and barstools ahead of the GOs. While the ships are lovely in every way, the food perfectly acceptable and the wines drinkable, we find the bar prices extremely high and some of the GOs irritating. Club Med ships are primarily for the young at heart who want a casual, active holiday, or anyone who had the time of their lives at summer camp.

Club Med 1   ★ ★ ★

Registry	**Bahamas**
Officers	**French**
Crew	**International**
Complement	**178**
GRT	**14,745**
Length (ft.)	**617**
Beam (ft.)	**66**
Draft (ft.)	**16**
Passengers-Cabins Full	**399**
Passengers-2/Cabin	**376**
Passenger Space Ratio	**39.21**
Stability Rating	**Good to Excellent**
Seatings	**1**
Cuisine	**French**
Dress Code	**Casual elegance**
Room Service	**Yes**
Tip	**No tipping**

Ship Amenities

Outdoor Pool	**2**
Indoor Pool	**0**
Jacuzzi	**1**
Fitness Center	**Yes**
Spa	**Yes**
Beauty Shop	**Yes**
Showroom	**No**
Bars/Lounges	**5**
Casino	**Yes**
Shops	**1**
Library	**Yes**
Child Program	**No**
Self-Service Laundry	**No**
Elevators	**2**

Cabin Statistics

Suites	**2**
Outside Doubles	**186**
Inside Doubles	**0**
Wheelchair Cabins	**0**
Singles	**0**
Single Surcharge	**130%**
Verandas	**0**
110 Volt	**Yes**

Club Med 2 ★★★

Registry	**Bahamas**
Officers	**French**
Crew	**International**
GRT	**14,983**
Length (ft.)	**617**
Beam (ft.)	**66**
Draft (ft.)	**16**
Crew	**214**
Passengers-Cabins Full	**521**
Passengers-2/Cabin	**392**
Passenger Space Ratio	**38.22**
Stability Rating	**Good to Excellent**
Seatings	**1**
Cuisine	**French**
Dress Code	**Casual elegance**
Room Service	**Yes**
Tip	**No tipping**

Ship Amenities

Outdoor Pool	**2**
Indoor Pool	**0**
Jacuzzi	**1**
Fitness Center	**Yes**
Spa	**Yes**
Beauty Shop	**Yes**
Showroom	**No**
Bars/Lounges	**5**
Casino	**Yes**
Shops	**1**
Library	**Yes**
Child Program	**No**
Self-Service Laundry	**No**
Elevators	**2**

Cabin Statistics

Suites	**5**
Outside Doubles	**191**
Inside Doubles	**0**
Wheelchair Cabins	**0**
Singles	**0**
Single Surcharge	**130%**
Verandas	**0**
110 Volt	**Yes**

COMMODORE CRUISE LINE
Western Caribbean–Yucatan

4000 Hollywood Boulevard, South Tower, Suite 385, Hollywood, FL 33021
☎ *(305) 967-2100, (800) 237-5361*

History . . . .

In mid-1995, a financial group headed by Jeffrey I. Binder bought Commodore Cruise Line from its owners, Finnish-based EffJohn International, for $33.5 million, which included the line's two ships, *Enchanted Seas* and *Enchanted Isle.*

This transaction, plus Cunard's acquisition of the former *Crown Dynasty,* now the *Cunard Dynasty,* marked the end of EffJohn's long-time cruise operations in North America which at one time or another had included Bermuda Star Line (which was merged with Commodore in 1989) and Crown Cruise Line. Only the Effjohn-owned, NCL-operated *Leeward* remains

The two vessels are very likely the most-named passenger ships in the world. They started life as the *Brasil* and *Argentina* for New York-based Moore-McCormack Lines in 1958 in South American service. The *Brasil* became the *Volendam* and the *Argentina* the *Veendam* for Holland America in 1972, but after a year of service were laid up and subsequently the former *Argentina* was chartered out to Agence Maritime International, which, for some mysterious reason, renamed her *Brasil,* according to Arnold Kludas in *Great Passenger Ships of the World, Volume 5.* After that, things get even more confusing, but according to our reckoning, *Enchanted Seas* has had 11 names, *Enchanted Isle* 10. Two of them came out of waffling when Bermuda Star Line couldn't decide between *Bermuda Queen* and *Queen of Bermuda,* announcing first one and then the other, and later, on the same ship, Commodore was going to call her *Enchanted Odyssey* but decided it sounded too much like Royal Cruise Line's ships. (See "Did You Know," below.)

After a brief stint as a Russian hotel (*Hotel Commodore,* moored on the Neva River in St. Petersburg), the *Enchanted Isle* was returned to service in the Caribbean in 1995. The *Enchanted Seas* was leased to World Explorer Cruises in 1996 to become the *Universe Explorer.* (See World Explorer Cruises page 795).

DID YOU KNOW?			
1958	Brasil	**1958**	Argentina
1972	Volendam	**1972**	Veendam
1975	Monarch Sun	**1974**	Brasil
1977	Volendam	**1975**	Veendam
1984	Island Sun	**1976**	Monarch Star
1986	Liberté	**1978**	Veendam
1987	Canada Star	**1984**	Bermuda Star
1988	Bermuda Queen	**1990**	Enchanted Isle
1988	Queen of Bermuda	**1994**	Hotel Commodore
1990	Enchanted Odyssey	**1995**	Enchanted Isle
1990	Enchanted Seas		
1996	Universe Explorer		

Concept . . . .

The new Commodore aims "to provide top quality service to the markets we serve," according to the line's new chairman and CEO, Fred A. Mayer. The budget-priced cruises are slated to sail from New Orleans year-round.

Signatures . . . .

A distinctive line logo features the gold braid sleeve insignia of a commodore.

Gimmicks . . . .

In 1993-4, the line used a distinctive jazzy, neon-bright campaign called, "Tell Reality to Take a Hike," with some of the most innovative cruise brochure graphics in the industry. It was a shade more hip than the ships. In 1995 they went back to slimmer, more conservative brochures.

Who's the Competition . . . .

Since the ship sails from New Orleans year-round, the line will compete head-to-head with Carnival's Tampa/New Orleans sailings.

Who's Aboard . . . .

Lots of first-time cruisers drawn by the low prices and port-intensive itineraries. When we were aboard during the summer, there was an even mix of families with children, young and middle-aged couples and a good sprinkling of singles who seemed to have a grand time.

Who Should Go . . . .

People looking for a casual, moderately-priced getaway to the Western Caribbean.

Who Should Not Go . . . .

Veteran cruisers fussy about food and service.

The Lifestyle . . . .

Generally, things follow a traditional medium-sized cruise ship pattern, with self-service breakfasts and lunches available as well as dining room meals. A cruise staff leads fun and games, and helps with the evening's entertainment. This line is noted particularly for theme cruises.

Wardrobe . . . .

Plan to dress on the casual side of traditional. Two formal nights a week would find some men in tuxedos or dinner jackets but more in suits or sport jackets with tie. Women, as usual, can get by with just about anything except shorts.

Bill of Fare C

The passengers generally don't complain about the food (but some self-styled gourmets might). Portions are generous and service is usually friendly if not always proficient. The self-service buffet meals—breakfast, lunch and tea—were less appealing than the dining room meals. Generally dinners offer a couple of appetizers plus fruit juices, several soups, a couple of salads and four main-dish choices, including a Lite Cuisine selection. Desserts are showy, on the rich and elaborate side.

NO NOs

Shorts, tank tops and bare feet are not permitted in the dining room.

Showtime C

Evening musical and variety shows are supplemented with lots of cruise staff-led fun and games, from horse racing and bingo to audience participation lip sync shows, line dancing lessons, trapshooting and wine and cheese parties.

Discounts . . . .

Early booking discounts require a $200 per person deposit or a full payment 90 days prior to the confirmed sailing date. Groups traveling together also qualify for discounts.

The Bottom Line

The ships have fairly spacious cabins, many with third and fourth berths good for families with children. The relatively deep draft means they ride well, an asset in the sometimes-rough Gulf of Mexico. Although the ships are generally clean and attractively furnished, they're on the basic side, without such finishing touches as art in the cabins and hallways.

Enchanted Isle

Here and there on this ship, you can still glimpse a touch of the original vessel, or at least the Holland America version, with wood paneling, old wooden dressers with recessed vanity areas, etched glass folding panels to close off a bar area and bits of odd architectural details in the self-service cafes.

There are as many dissimilarities as similarities on this ship which has been through so many name and design changes through the years. The cinema deep down in the ship was turned into a disco. Cabin configurations, however, are virtually the same with high density passenger numbers vis-a-vis the open deck space and public room areas.

The Brochure Says

"Fine food is part of Commodore's unique New Orleans heritage."

Translation

Brennan's famous New Orleans restaurant is the inspiration for a special breakfast on each cruise.

Cabins & Costs

Fantasy Suites: . . . . NA

There are no cabins aboard that would qualify in this category.

Small Splurges: C

Average Price PPPD: $224 plus air add-ons.
The cabins are called deluxe suites and have a double bed, sitting area, desk/dresser with drawers, nightstands, good closet space and large tiled bathroom. The room is spacious and light. Some of the cabins in this category have old wooden dressers that look as if they date from Holland America days.

Suitable Standards: C

Average Price PPPD: $158 plus air add-on.

Since the ship was built in the days before modular cabins, don't expect any two standards to be exactly alike. Many have portholes and most are fairly spacious, with two lower beds (some can be put together into a queen-sized bed, others should be specified as twins or double bed when booking), desk/dresser with drawers, fair closet space and in designated cabins, there is a tub in the bathrooms.

Bottom Bunks: .... D

Average Price PPPD: $121 plus air add-ons.

Category 11 insides have upper and lower berths but are fairly spacious. They're not very luxurious, but then they're not very expensive either.

Where She Goes

The *Enchanted Isle* sails every Saturday from New Orleans, calling in Playa del Carmen and Cozumel, Grand Cayman and Montego Bay.

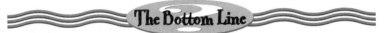

The Bottom Line

Prices are quite moderate, with some cabins coming at under $125 a day per person, double occupancy.

If you're a first-time cruiser, don't anticipate a ship that looks like, say, the ones in Carnival's TV ads or the ones you loved on "The Love Boat." This is an old ship and it shows its age in some spots on deck and in the cheaper cabins on the lower decks. There's a lot of sound seepage between cabins as well. But it has a deep draft and rides fairly smoothly in rough seas, and the air conditioning was overhauled a couple of years ago and should still be working O.K.

Fielding's Five

Five Social Spots

1. The observation lounge high atop the ship with a row of windows facing forward, a piano bar and late-night cabaret shows. Tub chairs, cocktail tables, a small bar with three stools and a large round center sofa furnish it.

2. The Monte Carlo casino is spacious but looks as if it's made up of several smaller rooms.

3. The Grand Lounge has some vintage wood paneling and a marble dance floor along with some murky upholstery on the banquettes and chairs and lots of columns which spoil the sightlines during shows.

4. Barnacle's Bar in the Bistro (try to say that three times real fast!) on the *Enchanted Isle* is a popular gathering spot for daytime drinks (and checking out the singles action).

5. Neptune's Disco on the *Enchanted Isle* replaced the cinema so now they project movies on the back wall of the disco.

Five Good Reasons to Book These Ships

1. The prices are very modest, as low as any you'll find anywhere these days—based on published brochure prices, before any discounting and dealing!

2.   To be able to sail from New Orleans.

3.   To find low-priced cabins big enough for a family of four to move around in (so long as you avoid the really small ones down on Dolphin Deck).

4.   To sample some theme cruises from Mardi Gras to Country and Western, Jazz, even Polka (left over from the days of the *Boheme!*)

5.   To see how well they used to build ships in Pascagoula, Mississippi.

Enchanted Isle ★★

Registry	Panama
Officers	European/American
Crew	International
Complement	350
GRT	23,395
Length (ft.)	617
Beam (ft.)	84
Draft (ft.)	28
Passengers-Cabins Full	840
Passengers-2/Cabin	729
Passenger Space Ratio	32.09
Stability Rating	Good
Seatings	2
Cuisine	International
Dress Code	Traditional
Room Service	Yes
Tip	$8.50 PPPD, 15% automatically added to bar check

Ship Amenities

Outdoor Pool	1
Indoor Pool	0
Jacuzzi	1
Fitness Center	Yes
Spa	No
Beauty Shop	Yes
Showroom	Yes
Bars/Lounges	6
Casino	Yes
Shops	2
Library	Yes
Child Program	Yes
Self-Service Laundry	No
Elevators	3

Cabin Statistics

Suites	4
Outside Doubles	286
Inside Doubles	77
Wheelchair Cabins	2
Singles	6
Single Surcharge	150-200%
Verandas	0
110 Volt	Yes

C O S T A *Italian Style* C R U I S E S

80 Southwest 8th Street, Miami, FL 33130
☎ *(305) 358-7325, (800) 462-6782*

Costa's distinctive bright yellow stack with a blue "C" is seen in many Mediterranean and Caribbean ports.

History . . . .

The parent company of Miami-based Costa Cruises is Costa Crociere of Genoa, which started back in 1860 with a family business that imported olive oil from Sardinia, refined it and exported it all over Europe. When patriarch Giacomo Costa died in 1916, his sons inherited the family business and bought a freighter to transport their oil themselves. By 1935 they had eight freighters.

They started passenger service after World War II with the the 12,000-ton *Anna "C"* cruising between Genoa and South America. A fleet of three others was added in just four years—the *Andrea "C"*, *Giovanna "C"* and *Franca "C"*.

229

The first brand-new ship came in 1957-58 when Costa constructed the 24,000-ton *Federico "C"*, now sailing as Dolphin's *SeaBreeze*. In 1959 they moved the *Franca "C"* to Florida and entered seven-day Caribbean cruising. It wasn't long before their entire fleet began spending winters in the Caribbean.

Today, with one of the youngest fleets in the Caribbean, Costa markets tropical cruises in winter and Mediterranean cruises in summer. The line's present fleet (including the *Mermoz*) numbers 10 with the *Costa Victoria*.

—Introduced three- and four-day cruises to the Bahamas from Miami (*Anna "C"*, 1964).

—Based a cruise ship in San Juan and began the first air/sea program between the U.S. mainland and Puerto Rico (*Franca "C"*, 1968).

—Launched "Cruising Italian Style" with toga night parties (*Costa Riviera*, 1985).

DID YOU KNOW?

Costa's Bianca "C", originally built as La Marseillaise for a French shipping company, burned and sank at the mouth of the harbor in St. George, Grenada, in 1961. You can still see the statue Costa erected in the harbor to commemorate the kindness and hospitality of the Grenadians, who took the 725 passengers and crew into their homes for two days until a rescue vessel could arrive. The statue depicts Christ of the Depths, and is a copy of the original statue in Portofino, Italy, dedicated to scuba divers. One crew member and two passengers died as a result of the fire, and another crew member was never accounted for.

Concept

"Italian Style by Design," Costa explains as "a product that combines the sophisticated elegance of a European vacation with the fun and spirit of the line's Italian heritage."

Signatures

The distinctive bright yellow stack with a blue "C" and a blue band across the top makes a Costa ship easily recognizable in any port in the world, especially on the new ships, with their clusters of three narrow vertical yellow stacks.

The use of "C" (meaning Costa) following the ship's name in earlier days and the present use of the ship's name following the Costa name in one word, as in *CostaClassica*, emphasize the fact that this is still a family-owned, family-run company.

The piazza, or town square, comparable to the lobby in a major hotel, is the heart of every Costa ship.

Gimmicks

Roman Bacchanal, better known as "toga night," has progressed from a fairly primitive form—passengers tying on sheets taken from their beds—to a very sophisticated routine—ready-made togas handed out by cruise staffers who also pass around gilded laurel wreaths and such.

From its very inception it's been wildly popular with North American passengers (they don't usually do it in Italy but offer a Venetian Carnival night instead). It used to be that on masquerade night, you often cringed in embarrassment if you had put on a costume and were one of the few—on toga night, you're embarrassed if you're wearing street clothes because you're very conspicuous. It's usually held the last night of the cruise, simplifying the what-to-wear question for people who pack before dinner. Also, at least one cruise director warns reluctant toga-wearers, "No sheet, no eat."

On Toga Night, almost every passenger dons one of the costumes, partly because it happens the last night aboard, when you've packed most of your clothes, but also because at least one cruise director threatens, "No sheet, no eat."

Who's the Competition . . . .

Costa used to face a lively competition from Sitmar and Home Lines, both Italian cruise lines that are now defunct, but doesn't really have to duke it out with Princess, despite Princess owning the former Sitmar ships; they appeal to different people.

Because of the stylish new hardware both lines have, we'd say Costa and Celebrity might compete in the Caribbean, since both are major names on the east coast. But in the Mediterranean, Costa dominates the upper price market, Epirotiki the lower price market.

Who's Aboard . . . .

Costa has always attracted a large segment of cruisers from the northeastern U.S., especially those with an Italian-American heritage. In both the Caribbean and Europe, French and Italian passengers are numerous, especially since Costa added the *Mermoz* from Paquet French Cruises to its roster. Young to middle-aged couples, young families, retirees and often three generations from the same family may all be seen cruising Italian style.

Who Should Go . . . .

More young couples, especially anyone wearing an Armani label, would love the newest Costa ships, because they have the same spare elegance with their chic Italian furniture and uncluttered cabins. Opera fans will enjoy the bigger-than-life dining rooms with their strolling musicians and La Scala-painted murals that change by the evening from a medieval street to an Italian garden. Anyone who wants to travel in Europe with more Europeans than fellow Americans. Anyone who never said "Basta!" ("Enough!") to pasta.

Who Should Not Go . . . .

Cunard first-class transatlantic passengers who might find the energy and noise level a little high; anyone who dislikes pasta and pizza; anyone unwilling to don a toga when everyone else on board does; anyone who doesn't want a multi-cultural experience on a European itinerary or can't stand to hear shipboard announcements broadcast in five languages.

The Lifestyle . . . .

Traditional cruise programs with an Italian accent characterize the Costa ships, with the usual dress code requests, two meal seatings, and a full onboard and shore excursion activities program. Lavish spas imitating Roman baths are on board the newer ships, and the pool decks encourage spending all day outside with cocoon cabana chairs, sidewalk-cafe tables and chairs, splashing fountains and lounge chairs with pale blue-and-white striped cushions. Overall, there's a lighthearted good humor on these ships, especially when a lot of unflappable Italians are aboard.

Because of the number of Europeans aboard in summer, Costa adds an American hostess program to perform as special liaison for the English speakers on board, usually a minority on European sailings.

Wardrobe . . . .

Costa says it would like its passengers to wear on gala evenings tuxedos or dark suits for gentlemen, evening gowns or cocktail dresses for ladies; there is at least one gala evening a cruise. On other evenings, men wear sports coats and slacks, ladies resort attire. In the daytime, casual resort wear is in order, including light cotton clothing and swimwear. Don't worry about toga nights if one is scheduled (they don't usually do it in Europe); the cruise staff delivers the costumes.

Bill of Fare . . . . .B+

Meals are served at two seatings, with early or main seating at noon for lunch and 6:15 p.m. for dinner, and late or second seating at 1:30 p.m. for lunch, 8:30 p.m. for dinner. All dining room breakfasts and occasional lunches are designated open seating, which on these ships mean any passenger may arrive within a set time and be seated at whatever table has space. It's not unusual on the larger *Classica* and *Romantica* to find a queue forming 15 or 20 minutes ahead of time; some Costa passengers always seem to be worrying needlessly about when their next meal is arriving.

Food and service are usually good to excellent, with a captain or maitre d'hotel always willing to toss a salad or pasta especially for you at tableside. While the chef may be an Austrian and the waiters Croatian or Honduran instead of Italian, the spirit is there. "They're all Italians at heart," says Costa's president.

Whoever's in the kitchen, we've found the pastas generally outstanding, along with vegetarian eggplant dishes, flambe shrimp, breadsticks, salads, cheeses, fresh fruits, grilled veal chops and pasta-and-bean soups. Less successful on most ships are the pizzas (with the notable exception of the *CostaRiviera*, which has a fine pizzeria on board), some of the meats and the desserts. We particularly miss the Italian-style gelati that has been replaced with American commercial ice creams on several ships.

A fresh fish "catch of the day" is sometimes on display on a decorated cart at the entrance to the dining room on the *CostaClassica* and *CostaRomantica*.

Showtime . . . . B-

Because passengers on board speak several different languages, Costa ships rely more on musical programs or variety performers like magicians, jugglers and acrobats rather than comedians or production shows that need an English-language narrative. The production shows we have seen aboard are produced by a British company and are handsomely costumed and well choreographed but seem dated beside some of the state-of-the-art shows coming out of Carnival, Princess and RCCL these days.

Films are shown on cabin TV sets throughout the day and evening on an alternating basis, and a late-night disco promises to keep going until the wee hours. Live music for listening or dancing is performed throughout the ships before and after dinner. In Europe, a small company of opera singers may be brought aboard to entertain for the evening.

Discounts . . . .

Passengers who book 90 days ahead of time get early booking discounts.

The Bottom Line

Costa has been through several ups and downs in the last few years, as in 1992 when U.S. advertising and marketing executives for Costa attempted to abandon the very successful "Cruising Italian Style" concept for a new EuroLuxe label heralding the debut of the *CostaClassica*, proclaiming "a standard of elegance, entertainment and personal service so unprecedented, there wasn't even a name for it until now—EuroLuxe." While the new ship was dramatic and dazzling with its bare marble floors and sleek, stark ambience, its debut was marred by passengers who complained they had been promised plusher surroundings and more pampering from the service staff than they were getting.

But a change of U.S. executives and a return to the Italian-style theme led to a quick recovery, and by the time sister ship *CostaRomantica* was introduced a year later, most passengers took the marble floors in stride.

While the overall fleet goes back to the 33-year-old *CostaRiviera* and the 30-year-old *EugenioCosta*, the ships positioned in North America for Caribbean cruises are all recently built or rebuilt.

Costa offers a good, middle-of-the-road traditional cruise with an Italian accent—you should have a lot of fun aboard if you like Italian-American food and have an easygoing sense of humor.

CostaAllegra ★★★★
CostaMarina ★★★★

When the CostaMarina was brand-new, we had two magazine story assignments to cover it, and through a series of mishaps had to chase the ship all around the Mediterranean, from Ibiza to Barcelona to Madrid to Tunis for three days, arriving in Tunisia just after Saddam Hussein had invaded Kuwait, only to be greeted by two machine-gun wielding teenagers who studied our U.S. passports muttering, "Bush, Bush," to each other, then turned us over to the Tunisian police to be interrogated. By the time we got aboard the CostaMarina, she was the most wonderful and welcoming ship we'd ever seen, and our fondness for her exists to this day.

The *CostaMarina* was the first of the pair to debut, in the summer of 1990, an extensive rebuilding from the hull up designed by Italian architect Guido Canali. The same architect designed the *CostaAllegra*, which was built in 1992 on an existing hull. The result is a pair of high-tech, mid-sized ships that are cost-efficient and trim but without a lot of extra flourish and furbelows. This is not to say they're not attractive—on the contrary, they are extremely handsome, even whimsical—but they're not traditional. They have a trim, clean, almost austere design that lets the bones, the very skeleton of the ship, show through here and there.

The stern is cropped off in a vertical wall of glass which looks strange from outside but makes a lot of sense when you're sitting inside in the dining room or lounge looking out through all that glass. We recommend them to anyone who doesn't want to sail aboard one of today's megaships, but particularly to those younger passengers, Europeans and Americans, who have no preconceived notions of what a ship should look like.

Venetian "canals" run along the pool deck of the CostaMarina between the whirlpool and the swimming pool.

The Brochure Says

"Sophisticated, stylish and architecturally stunning, the *m/v CostaAllegra* is a timeless masterpiece of color, light and water with an irrepressible Italian soul."

Translation

While the language is a bit effusive, we agree.

Cabins & Costs

Fantasy Suites: .... A

Average Price PPPD: $542 in Europe including airfare from New York.

On the *CostaAllegra* only, three forward-facing Rousseau Grand Suites offer a private veranda, separate living room with white sofa wrapped around two walls, wet bar, big portholes looking forward and mirrored walls. In the bedroom is a queen-sized bed and wood-toned walls, with a marble bathroom with toilet and bidet, Jacuzzi tub and separate stall shower, and a walk-in closet with dressing room area. The total space is 376 square feet. When you book a suite aboard at full tariff in the Caribbean, the second passenger pays the minimum cruise price.

Small Splurges: .... B+

Average Price PPPD: $609 in Europe including airfare from New York.
On the *CostaMarina*, eight deluxe outside staterooms with verandas just big enough for two lounge chairs also have a folding wood wall that can separate bedroom from living room. The bedroom has a queen-sized bed and the living room a pull-down berth and a sofa that can be made up as a bed, making room for two additional passengers. Bathrooms have a chic black-and-white tile floor and a Jacuzzi tub.

Suitable Standards: .... B+

Average Price PPPD: $428 in Europe including airfare from New York.
Most outside cabins aboard *CostaAllegra* in Category 7 on Gauguin deck have twin beds that can convert to queen-sized, two large portholes covered with solid shade and sheer curtains, walls covered in fabric wall hangings, a long desk/dresser with eight drawers plus a combination safe, color TV with remote control, three-drawer nightstands, bathroom with a futuristic round shower of clear curved plexiglass, gray marble counter with basin, big mirrors, good lighting and built-in hair dryer. The size is adequate but hardly generous at 156 square feet.

Bottom Bunks: .... C-

Average Price PPPD: $256 in Europe including airfare from New York.
Category Two inside cabins include some designated for disabled passengers (only on the *CostaAllegra*) with upper and lower berths; the others contain two lower beds that can be put together for a queen-sized bed, as well as furnishings similar to outside standards, including desk and chair. (See "Suitable Standards," above.) Inside cabins measure only 146 square feet.

INSIDER TIP

Playing the cabin radio is a good cover for your own in-cabin conversations, somewhat like a 50s spy movie.

Where She Goes

The *CostaAllegra* spends the winter in the Caribbean, sailing from San Juan with a new port of call every day, sometimes two ports—St. Thomas/ St. John, St. Maarten, Guadeloupe, St. Lucia, Tortola/Virgin Gorda, and Serena Cay, Costa's private island off Casa de Campo.

From May to September the *CostaAllegra* makes a variety of Baltic and Scandinavian cruises.

CostaMarina does seven-day cruises out of Copenhagen to the Baltic and Scandinavia, then moves to Genoa for a series of Mediterranean cruises.

The Bottom Line

These ships are particularly well designed for younger passengers, with considerable space devoted to spa, gym and disco. Particularly in Europe, we notice a number of young families, mostly Italian, with small children. There is a children's program and dedicated children's center on board the *CostaAllegra*; a meeting room on the *CostaMarina* is turned over to children when necessary.

Food and service in the dining rooms on both ships are quite good, with tableside service; here, aboard the **CostaMarina.**

Food and service in the dining rooms is quite good, with some tables for two available.

In the Caribbean, the great expanses of glass mean some parts of the ship—notably the disco and spa—get uncomfortably warm by late afternoon despite the air conditioning. A less structured daily program is offered in Europe, where passengers have a laissez-faire attitude. Sightlines are not very good in the showrooms, but the entertainment is not always riveting anyhow.

The real pleasure of these ships is the fresh design, the open and inviting decks and public rooms and the ease with which even first-time cruisers can find their way around.

COSTA CRUISES

CostaAllegra ★★★★

Registry	**Liberia**
Officers	**Italian**
Crew	**International**
Complement	**450**
GRT	**30,000**
Length (ft.)	**615**
Beam (ft.)	**84.5**
Draft (ft.)	**27**
Passengers-Cabins Full	**1066**
Passengers-2/Cabin	**810**
Passenger Space Ratio	**37.03**
Stability Rating	**Good**
Seatings	**2**
Cuisine	**Italian**
Dress Code	**Traditional**
Room Service	**Yes**
Tip	**$6 PPPD, 15% automatically added to bar checks**

Ship Amenities

Outdoor Pool	**1**
Indoor Pool	**0**
Jacuzzi	**2**
Fitness Center	**Yes**
Spa	**Yes**
Beauty Shop	**Yes**
Showroom	**Yes**
Bars/Lounges	**7**
Casino	**Yes**
Shops	**Yes**
Library	**Yes**
Child Program	**Yes**
Self-Service Laundry	**No**
Elevators	**4**

Cabin Statistics

Suites	**3**
Outside Doubles	**219**
Inside Doubles	**186**
Wheelchair Cabins	**8**
Singles	**0**
Single Surcharge	**150%**
Verandas	**3**
110 Volt	**Yes**

CostaMarina ★★★★

Registry	Liberia
Officers	Italian
Crew	International
Complement	395
GRT	25,000
Length (ft.)	571.5
Beam (ft.)	84.5
Draft (ft.)	27
Passengers-Cabins Full	1025
Passengers-2/Cabin	772
Passenger Space Ratio	32.38
Stability Rating	Good
Seatings	2
Cuisine	Italian
Dress Code	Traditional
Room Service	Yes
Tip	$6 PPPD, 15% automatically added to bar checks

Ship Amenities

Outdoor Pool	1
Indoor Pool	0
Jacuzzi	2
Fitness Center	Yes
Spa	Yes
Beauty Shop	Yes
Showroom	Yes
Bars/Lounges	70
Casino	Yes
Shops	Yes
Library	Yes
Child Program	Yes
Self-Service Laundry	No
Elevators	8

Cabin Statistics

Suites	8
Outside Doubles	180
Inside Doubles	173
Wheelchair Cabins	0
Singles	0
Single Surcharge	150%
Verandas	8
110 Volt	Yes

COSTA CRUISES

CostaClassica ★★★★★
CostaRomantica ★★★★★

The CostaClassica, *first of the two new ships, got off to a bad start because some former executives misled travel agents and potential passengers by tagging the new ship "EuroLuxe," creating the expectation of a plush Crystal-style ship rather than an austere but handsome contemporary Italian design. Expecting "luxury, elegance and sumptuousness," as the dictionary defines luxe, one disgruntled passenger looked at the bare marble floors and muttered, "The luxe stops here."*

The dining rooms change their looks when they change their background scenery, painted by a La Scala Opera House designer.

These sister ships are sleek and stylish with marble, tile, brass, polished wood, fountains and sculptures. So much hard surface lends a cool rather than warm ambience.

The ships have an angular bow, a boxy midsection and a rounded stern, with a vertical cluster of bright yellow funnels aft balanced by a forward glass-walled circular observation lounge set atop an all-glass deck housing the Caracalla Spa and amidships pool.

Two stairwells with bare stone floors and no risers provide the main vertical traffic flow through the ship, and on busy occasions like the lifeboat drill, sounds like changing classes at Woodrow Wilson Junior High.

Decks are handsome and well-designed. One pool is amidships, a second one aft, along with two Jacuzzis and several levels of teak decking for sunbathing.

"Created for those with a sense of adventure and an appreciation for style...(with) Italian hospitality, European charm and American comforts."

Translation
You can expect to find pasta and pizza; a cabin with TV, radio, hair dryer and safe; and a charming waiter who may just as likely come from Riga or Rijeka as Roma.

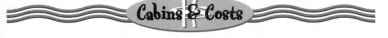

Fantasy Suites: . . . . A+
Average Price PPPD: $629 in Europe including airfare from New York.
Among our very favorite suites at sea are the 10 veranda suites on each ship, particularly those on the *Romantica* named for operas. Each is 580 square feet with private veranda, living room with burled brierwood furniture, a kidney-shaped desk, a small round table, two tub chairs and a long sofa; a separate bedroom with queen-sized bed, elegant wood dresser with round brass-framed mirror; floor-to-ceiling white window shades operated electronically, gauzy white undercurtains and a tied-back sheer green curtain at the windows; large whirlpool bathtub, stall shower and double lavatories in a wide counter. Butler service, mini-bar, terrycloth robes and reclining deck chairs on the veranda. Romantic? Yes!

Small Splurges: . . . . A
Average Price PPPD: $586 in Europe including airfare from New York.
Mini-suites, on the *Romantica* only, measure 340 square feet and contain a couch, two chairs, desk and chair, floor-to-ceiling windows, queen-sized bed, single trundle bed, bath with Jacuzzi tub, stall shower and double lavatories. Butler service, mini-bar and terrycloth robes.

Suitable Standards: . . . . B+
Average Price PPPD: $486 in Europe including airfare from New York.
More spacious than on many ships, the standard outside cabins measure 200 square feet and contain two lower beds, most of which convert to queen-sized; a few designated cabins have fixed queen-sized beds only. White marble counters and built-in hair dryers are in all bathrooms, hanging and storage space is generous and the

room has a dresser and a sitting area with two chairs and a table. Several inside cabins (cheaper than the price below) are designated wheelchair-accessible with extrawide doors, bathrooms with pulldown shower seats and generous turning space.

The lowest-priced inside cabins on the CostaRomantica can sleep up to four in style and comfort.

Bottom Bunks: .... *C*

Average Price PPPD: $343 in Europe including airfare from New York.

The cheapest cabins aboard are insides with a lower bed and upper berth, with two chairs, small table, dresser, TV set and bath with space-age shower. There are only six on each ship and they are sometimes assigned to staff. The next category up has two lower beds and is only marginally higher in price.

Where She Goes

Both ships cruise the Caribbean in winter, with the *CostaClassica* sailing from Pointeà-Pitre on seven-day cruises marketed exclusively to Europeans. From May through October there is a series of seven-day cruises from Venice calling at several Greek islands.

The *CostaRomantica* in winter makes alternate Eastern and Western Caribbean cruises out of San Juan, calling in Key West, Playa del Carmen/Cozumel, Montego Bay and Grand Cayman on the western itinerary, San Juan, St. Thomas, Serena Cay and Nassau on the eastern itinerary. The ship then sails across the Atlantic to spend the summer in Europe doing seven-day cruises from Genoa calling at Naples, Palermo, Tunis, Palma de Mallorca, Ibiza and Barcelona.

The Bottom Line

The "Italian by Design" theme emphasizes the architecture and decor of the ships and stresses Costa's Italian heritage, but most of the Italian waiters are gone, replaced over the years by other Europeans, many from the newly independent eastern countries and some of whom are still awkward with English.

Furnishings aboard are beautiful, with one-of-a kind high-style Italian chairs set about here and there like pieces of art.

In the dining room, despite the dangerous marble floors, meals are served on Limoges china and double-skirted Pratesi linen tablecloths while strolling musicians play. The food is most often very good.

Many standard cabins on the *Classica* have large wooden room dividers that steal floor space without adding any useful storage area; a better bet for couples are the cabins with fixed queen-sized beds and no room divider, the same size as the others but they seem much bigger.

Fielding's Five

Five Easy Places

1. With a pool, an Italian sidewalk cafe, beach cabanas with striped blue-and-white curtains, a striking blue marble "Trevi" fountain and a thrust overhead runway from the jogging deck above overlooking all the action, it's La Dolce Vita time.

2. The heart of each ship is the piazza—on the *Classica* the Piazza Navona, on the *Romantica* the Piazza Italia—where everyone seems to gather, with an all-day- and-evening bar and lounge and music for dancing before and after dinner.

3. The dining rooms aboard change their looks on special evenings when the staff unfurls background scenery to turn it into an Italian garden or medieval city, ancient Pompeiian villas or Renaissance town; the backgrounds are painted by a scenic designer for the La Scala Opera House in Milan.

4. The big open-air cafe aft on each ship is covered with a sweeping white canvas awning and furnished with apple green wicker chairs and marble-topped tables, just like the Via Veneto.

5. The glass-walled discos high atop the ship and forward, like see-through flying saucers, double as observation lounges in the daytime.

CostaClassica ★★★★★

Registry	**Liberia**
Officers	**Italian**
Crew	**International**
Complement	**650**
GRT	**54,000**
Length (ft.)	**723.5**
Beam (ft.)	**101**
Draft (ft.)	**25**
Passengers-Cabins Full	**1766**
Passengers-2/Cabin	**1300**
Passenger Space Ratio	**41.53**
Stability Rating	**Good**
Seatings	**2**
Cuisine	**Italian**
Dress Code	**Traditional**
Room Service	**Yes**
Tip	**$6 PPPD, 15% automatically added to bar checks**

Ship Amenities

Outdoor Pool	**1**
Indoor Pool	**0**
Jacuzzi	**2**
Fitness Center	**Yes**
Spa	**Yes**
Beauty Shop	**Yes**
Showroom	**Yes**
Bars/Lounges	**8**
Casino	**Yes**
Shops	**Yes**
Library	**Yes**
Child Program	**Yes**
Self-Service Laundry	**No**
Elevators	**8**

Cabin Statistics

Suites	**10**
Outside Doubles	**438**
Inside Doubles	**216**
Wheelchair Cabins	**6**
Singles	**0**
Single Surcharge	**150%**
Verandas	**10**
110 Volt	**Yes**

COSTA CRUISES

CostaRomantica ★★★★★

Registry	**Liberia**
Officers	**Italian**
Crew	**International**
Complement	**650**
GRT	**54,000**
Length (ft.)	**723.5**
Beam (ft.)	**101**
Draft (ft.)	**25**
Passengers-Cabins Full	**1782**
Passengers-2/Cabin	**1356**
Passenger Space Ratio	**39.82**
Stability Rating	**Good**
Seatings	**2**
Cuisine	**Italian**
Dress Code	**Traditional**
Room Service	**Yes**
Tip	**$6 PPPD, 15% automatically added to bar checks**

Ship Amenities

Outdoor Pool	**1**
Indoor Pool	**0**
Jacuzzi	**4**
Fitness Center	**Yes**
Spa	**Yes**
Beauty Shop	**Yes**
Showroom	**Yes**
Bars/Lounges	**8**
Casino	**Yes**
Shops	**Yes**
Library	**Yes**
Child Program	**Yes**
Self-Service Laundry	**No**
Elevators	**8**

Cabin Statistics

Suites	**16**
Outside Doubles	**462**
Inside Doubles	**216**
Wheelchair Cabins	**6**
Singles	**0**
Single Surcharge	**150%**
Verandas	**10**
110 Volt	**Yes**

COSTA CRUISES

CostaPlaya   **Unrated**

Formerly known as the *Pearl of Scandinavia*, *Ocean Pearl* and then just plain *Pearl*, this sturdy ship, which began in 1967 as a Scandinavian ferry called *Finnstar*, is best known for more than a decade of "soft adventure" cruising in the Far East. Acquired by Costa Crociere in 1993, the ship ceased its Orient service in September, 1995, and was turned into the *CostaPlaya* to be marketed in Europe and Latin America. The ship sails seven-day cruises from Puerto Plata calling at Santiago de Cuba, Montego Bay, Havana and Nipe Bay, Cuba. It is not marketed in the United States.

The former *Pearl* has been a favorite of country collectors since its earliest days in service, when it was one of the first cruise ships to sail into China. A major renovation in 1988 turned this former ugly duckling into a swan, albeit a glitzy one, with reflective ceilings and sleek cocktail lounges. A casino, cinema, disco, cabaret, indoor and outdoor swimming pools, skeet-shooting, shuffleboard, health club, library, card room, sauna and massage rooms are all on board.

Cabins & Costs

Suites and deluxe accommodations are spacious, but standard cabins are pretty compact. Each has two lower beds, dresser and bath with shower.

CostaPlaya — Unrated

Registry	Bahamas
Officers	Italian
Crew	International
Complement	232
GRT	12,475
Length (ft.)	517
Beam (ft.)	66
Draft (ft.)	20
Passengers-Cabins Full	740
Passengers-2/Cabin	489
Passenger Space Ratio	25.51
Stability Rating	NA
Seatings	2
Cuisine	Italian
Dress Code	Traditional
Room Service	Yes
Tip	$6 PPPD, 15% automatically added to bar checks

Ship Amenities

Outdoor Pool	1
Indoor Pool	1
Jacuzzi	0
Fitness Center	Yes
Spa	No
Beauty Shop	Yes
Showroom	Yes
Bars/Lounges	5
Casino	Yes
Shops	1
Library	Yes
Child Program	No
Self-Service Laundry	No
Elevators	2

Cabin Statistics

Suites	30
Outside Doubles	163
Inside Doubles	46
Wheelchair Cabins	0
Singles	11
Single Surcharge	150%
Verandas	0
110 Volt	Yes

CostaRiviera

> *We were aboard this ship in January, 1986, when then-Costa president Howard Fine introduced toga night by donning a handsome, custom-made red Roman centurion costume and a gold helmet with stiff red brush and marched through the dining room giving an imperial wave. "Cruising Italian Style" was the theme, and the then-new CostaRiviera, a massive makeover of the Marconi, was being introduced in the Caribbean. Howard's presidency lasted another year or two, "Cruising Italian Style" was axed in favor of "EuroLuxe" in 1992 and the CostaRiviera turned briefly into the kiddie cruise ship American Adventure in 1993-94. But everything that goes around comes around, and they're all back—"Cruising Italian Style," CostaRiviera, toga night—all except Howard.*

Until the *CostaMarina* entered the scene in 1990, the *CostaRiviera* was the closest thing to a "new" (read made-over) ship the company had, but when they joined then- Costa president Bruce Nierenberg (co-founder of Premier Cruises) in a project to create American Family Cruises, this was the ship AFC got. With both *CostaMarina* and *CostaClassica* in place, the *CostaRiviera* didn't look so shiny any more. But with the demise of AFC in late 1994, the *CostaRiviera* sailed back to Genoa, was quickly refitted into a more adult vessel and put out into the European cruise market. Fuzzy Wuzzy's Den and the Rock-O-Saurus Club turned into the dignified Vienna Ballroom, and Sea Haunt, formerly for ages eight to 12, became a computer center.

The Brochure Says

"The *CostaRiviera* is embarking on a limited number of sailings to some of the most unforgettable places on earth. Casablanca. Barcelona. Funchal. Lanzarote. Exotic destinations to faraway places on a ship that's as comfortable as your own backyard."

Translation

While we never had the luxury of a steamship in our backyard, we can agree that the *CostaRiviera* is comfortable and low-key, unpretentious and good for families. And this winter's Canary Islands and North Africa cruises out of Genoa look like fun.

Fantasy Suites: .... NA

There are no accommodations on board that fit this description.

Small Splurges: .... C-

Average Price PPPD: $497 in the Greek Isles including airfare from New York.

The top accommodations are in category Nine, an upper deck of cabins that was added on Amalfi Deck when the ship was extensively renovated in 1985, but take care making a choice—some of these are much larger than others, and many have views partly or totally obstructed by hanging lifeboats. All have twin beds or a queen-sized bed; specify which you want when booking. Some of the larger ones may have as many as three additional bunks for children from the American Family Cruises days. Baths have showers only, and closet space is usually adequate.

Suitable Standards: .... C-

Average Price PPPD: $469 in the Greek Isles including airfare from New York.

Capri Deck category Seven cabins also have two lower beds or a queen-sized bed, and most offer fold-down third and fourth berths as well.

Bottom Bunks: .... D

Average Price PPPD: $340 in the Greek Isles including airfare from New York.

The lowest-priced category of inside cabins provides upper and lower berths and baths with shower; they're pretty basic.

The *CostaRiviera* spends the winter cruising the Canary Islands from Genoa on 11-night itineraries (see "Five Good Reasons to Book This Ship,") and cruises in summer in the Eastern Mediterranean on seven-day cruises from Venice calling at Bari, Corfu, Heraklion, Piraeus, Hydra, Kithera and Tremiti Islands.

This ship had some hard use during its days as the *American Adventure*, with as many as 500 or more kids aboard at a time. The density is intense, with 972 lower bed spaces and 833 additional upper berths. But this plethora of cabins with two or even three additional berths can be a boon for the budget-minded. Among the specialty areas on board are a teen center, a two-level cinema, a small pizzeria, a fairly large beauty shop, a fitness center and a computer center. While the winter Canary Islands sailings are very moderately priced, the summer Mediterranean tariffs seem high for a ship of this vintage.

Five Focal Points

1. The Bella Napoli Pizzeria, which in our fond memory serves up the best made-to-order pizza at sea.

2. The Grand Prix Bar with its cushiony couches and chairs makes a grand place to meet friends for a drink before dinner; a long drinks-and-espresso bar along one side gives it the congeniality of an Italian town square.

3. In the Galleria Via Veneto you'll find the shopping, all the treasures from Milan, Florence and Venice as well as worldwide duty-free buys.

4. Portofino Restaurant provides a few tables for two along the sides of the room near the windows, but most are bigger round tables for six or eight; "Mangia, mangia!" ("Eat, eat!")

5. The La Scala Showroom is structured with a lot of sofa-like theater row seats, comfortable and with fair sightlines to the stage, as well as a covey of tables and chairs down front on the sides and center.

Five Good Reasons to Book This Ship

1. The aforementioned Canary Islands and North Africa winter/spring itineraries, calling at Malaga, Madeira, Tenerife, Lanzarote, Agadir, Casablanca and Barcelona.

2. The price is right on the winter sailings.

3. If you want to shoehorn a family of five in one cabin, *CostaRiviera* has the berths.

4. The Bella Napoli Pizzeria.

5. To follow the Road to Morocco.

CostaRiviera   ★★

Registry	Liberia
Officers	Italian
Crew	International
Complement	535
GRT	31,500
Length (ft.)	700.9
Beam (ft.)	94.1
Draft (ft.)	28.3
Passengers-Cabins Full	1805
Passengers-2/Cabin	972
Passenger Space Ratio	32.4
Stability Rating	Good
Seatings	2
Cuisine	Italian
Dress Code	Traditional
Room Service	Yes
Tip	$6 PPPD, 15% automatically added to bar checks

Ship Amenities

Outdoor Pool	1
Indoor Pool	0
Jacuzzi	3
Fitness Center	Yes
Spa	Yes
Beauty Shop	Yes
Showroom	Yes
Bars/Lounges	5
Casino	Yes
Shops	Yes
Library	Yes
Child Program	No
Self-Service Laundry	No
Elevators	6

Cabin Statistics

Suites	0
Outside Doubles	299
Inside Doubles	178
Wheelchair Cabins	0
Singles	0
Single Surcharge	150%
Verandas	0
110 Volt	Yes

COSTA CRUISES

CostaVictoria   **Unrated**

The *Victoria* is the first of two more new ships for Costa. The 75,000-ton, 1928-passenger vessel comes from the Vulkan Group's Shichau Seebeckwerft Shipyard in Bremerhaven, Germany, and it was briefly delayed because of the yard's financial problems.

The most striking area of the ship is the Observation Lounge, which spans four decks, with a waterfall and a floor-to-ceiling glass wall. The area will serve as the piazzetta, or town square, as well as a special events area and a theater for evening shows.

A second atrium in the Central Hall soars seven decks from the lobby up to a glass dome high atop the ship, with four glass elevators to sweep passengers to the upper decks.

A canvas-covered outdoor cafe similar to those on the *CostaClassica* and *CostaRomantica* is expanded to two decks on the aft end of the ship. Two swimming pools, a smaller splash pool and four Jacuzzis are on deck, as well as a tennis court and 1312-foot jogging track.

Fitness aficionados will find a super Caracalla Spa on board that includes an indoor swimming pool, Turkish bath, steam, sauna and fitness center.

Two dining rooms with two seatings each, a casino, centers for children and teens, a disco, library and show lounge are also on board.

Six suites and 14 mini-suites are among the 964 cabins aboard; 60 percent are outside. Per diem prices range from $400 to $686 per person double occupancy in the Greek Isles, including airfare from New York.

CostaVictoria cruises the Greek Islands on seven-day itineraries out of Venice to Athens, then repositions to the Caribbean, beginning seven-day cruises out of Miami.

CostaVictoria — Unrated

Registry	Liberia
Officers	Italian
Crew	International
Complement	0
GRT	75,000
Length (ft.)	824
Beam (ft.)	105.5
Draft (ft.)	NA
Passengers-Cabins Full	2250
Passengers-2/Cabin	1928
Passenger Space Ratio	38.9
Stability Rating	Good
Seatings	2
Cuisine	Italian
Dress Code	Traditional
Room Service	Yes
Tip	$6 PPPD, 15% automatically added to bar checks

Ship Amenities

Outdoor Pool	3
Indoor Pool	1
Jacuzzi	4
Fitness Center	Yes
Spa	Yes
Beauty Shop	Yes
Showroom	Yes
Bars/Lounges	0
Casino	Yes
Shops	Yes
Library	Yes
Child Program	Yes
Self-Service Laundry	No
Elevators	12

Cabin Statistics

Suites	20
Outside Doubles	561
Inside Doubles	383
Wheelchair Cabins	0
Singles	0
Single Surcharge	150%
Verandas	0
110 Volt	Yes

COSTA CRUISES

Daphne

The Daphne and her sister ship Danae (now sailing as the Danae Princess) used to call in Los Angeles in the 1980s, the Daphne on her way to Alaska, the Danae on her world cruise. Now the Daphne takes a mostly European crowd on very long cruises from Genoa to faraway places. We wonder if our friends Genevieve and Eve, veterans of the bargain end of the world cruise, are aboard; they figured out long ago they could share a modest inside cabin and live more cheaply at sea than at home in the winter. (Eva was from Orlando, Genevieve from Palma de Mallorca.)

The venerable and comfortable *Daphne* dates back to 1955 when she was built as the British cargo liner *Port Sydney* (the *Danae* was built a year later as the *Port Melbourne*), carrying 12 passengers first-class between London and Australia/New Zealand. In 1975 she was rebuilt as a cruise ship for Greek-owned Carras Cruises, leased to Costa, then sold to Costa in 1985.

Cabins are spacious and most are outsides with bathtub and shower. A deck gelateria and pizza counter by the pool and Jacuzzis is a popular place in the afternoon, as is the little Yacht Club bar at cocktail time. Riviera Deck is the center of shipboard life, with a bar and lounge at one end, the dining room, casino, library and shops at the opposite end.

The Brochure Says

"She is yacht-like and private, a ship of great taste and understated elegance, yet as warm and spontaneous as an Italian smile."

Translation

Weeellll…yacht-like, certainly. And understated, and warm and perhaps even spontaneous. Hey, the cabins are really spacious on this vintage ship!

Cabins & Costs

Fantasy Suites: .... B+

Average Price PPPD: $523 in Europe including airfare from New York.
The newest accommodations aboard are the group of six Amalfi Deck suites with
private verandas, surely the ideal vantage point from which to survey the world.
Bedroom with double bed, living room with sofa, chairs, table, mini-refrigerator
and TV set, bathroom with tub and shower.

Small Splurges: .... B

Average Price PPPD: $463 in Europe including airfare from New York.
The cabins on Portofino Deck are all outsides, spacious but varying slightly in size.
Some have queen-sized beds and some twin beds; several also have a sofa that can
make into an additional single or double bed. Each has a sitting area, mini-refrigerator, TV set and bathroom with tub and shower.

Suitable Standards: .... B

Average Price PPPD: $340 in Europe including airfare from New York.
On the three lowest passenger decks, the outside cabins are still fairly roomy, with
two lower beds (some have additional upper berths) and bathroom with tub and
shower.

Bottom Bunks: .... B

Average Price PPPD: $280 in Europe including airfare from New York.
There are only 22 inside cabins aboard, and all have two lower beds and bathroom
with tub and shower.

Where She Goes

The *Daphne* usually makes a long cruise from Genoa to the Far East in winter, then
she sails to Oman, Yemen, Egypt and Syria on her way back to Genoa in early April. Segments are available. In the summer she makes 12-day Eastern Mediterranean cruises from
Genoa.

The Bottom Line

Although marketed primarily to a European audience, the *Daphne* was a longtime favorite in North America and certainly offers long cruises that would appeal primarily to
adventuresome, self-reliant types who might have done some freighter travel.

Fielding's Five

Five Favorite Places

1. The Yacht Club Bar is just steps away from the pool, and conveniently close to the
   gelati and pizza.

2. The Trevi Restaurant, big enough to serve all its passengers in one seating, has
   tables for two, four, five, six and eight.

COSTA CRUISES

3. The Cinema doubles as a venue for lectures or meetings and, on long cruises, is a good place to screen movies you've missed.

4. The Rendezvous Bar and Riviera Lounge are lined with comfortable banquettes that were refurbished in some stylish new fabrics and colors.

5. The Monte Carlo Casino packs a fair amount of gaming in a small space; it even squeezes in a roulette wheel.

Five Good Reasons to Book This Ship

1. The spacious cabins.

2. The single-seating meals.

3. The fantastic winter itineraries.

4. The pasta.

5. To be the first on your block to visit Beirut, Parepare, Krakatau, Ningbo, Similan Sera and Tartus.

Five Things You Won't Find On Board

1. TV sets in cabins, except in suites.

2. Any cabins designated wheelchair-accessible.

3. An announcement delivered in only one language.

4. A lap pool.

5. Enough deck space for everybody.

COSTA CRUISES

Daphne ★★★

Registry	Liberia
Officers	Italian
Crew	International
Complement	235
GRT	16,330
Length (ft.)	532.7
Beam (ft.)	70.2
Draft (ft.)	28
Passengers-Cabins Full	540
Passengers-2/Cabin	422
Passenger Space Ratio	38.70
Stability Rating	Good
Seatings	1
Cuisine	Italian
Dress Code	Traditional
Room Service	Yes
Tip	$6 PPPD, 15% automatically added to bar checks

Ship Amenities

Outdoor Pool	1
Indoor Pool	0
Jacuzzi	2
Fitness Center	Yes
Spa	Yes
Beauty Shop	Yes
Showroom	Yes
Bars/Lounges	2
Casino	Yes
Shops	Yes
Library	Yes
Child Program	No
Self-Service Laundry	No
Elevators	2

Cabin Statistics

Suites	27
Outside Doubles	162
Inside Doubles	22
Wheelchair Cabins	0
Singles	0
Single Surcharge	150%
Verandas	0
110 Volt	Yes

COSTA CRUISES

EugenioCosta

Costa didn't always build a new ship every year or two the way they're doing now—there were no new-builds between the Federico "C" in 1958 and the Eugenio C, now EugenioCosta, in 1966, but they're certainly making up for lost time.

The *EugenioCosta* is a high-density ship, carrying a maximum of 1418 mostly-Italian passengers on cruises around the Mediterranean. It has all those features typical of 1960s ships—a cinema, bank, drugstore, barber shop, winter garden and chapel, plus, of course, Costa's signature Piazza Italia town square. With twin funnels aft, a sheltered pool amidships and a graduated series of sunwashed stern decks for the lounge-and-pool crowd, it's a comfortable vessel for cruising European-style.

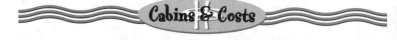

The Brochure Says

"All the world sails aboard Costa, which means your fellow-guests are just as likely to be from Paris, Texas, as Paris, France; Naples, Florida, as Naples, Italy. You may dine with folks from Milan or Milwaukee or have a nightcap with chaps from Frankfurt, Oxford or Prague."

Translation

Get ready for those interminable five-language announcements over the ship's public address system and those chaps from Frankfurt, Oxford and Prague who don't know what a "no smoking" sign means.

Cabins & Costs

Fantasy Suites: . . . . *C*

Average Price PPPD: $588 including airfare from New York.
Top digs are eight deluxe suites on Boat Deck forward, with double beds, an additional single sofa bed in the sitting area, bathroom with tub and bidet.

Small Splurges: C

Average Price PPPD: $468 including airfare from New York.
We'd opt for the next category down from the suites, which are outsides with double or twin beds plus a single sofa bed and bathroom with tub and bidet.

Suitable Standards: .... D

Average Price PPPD: $408 including airfare from New York.
Virtually all the standard outside cabins have either two lower beds and two upper berths or a single upper and lower berth; like we said, high density.

Bottom Bunks: .... D-

Average Price PPPD: $314 including airfare from New York.
The *EugenioCosta* has lots of these, including outsides with upper and lower berths, but for the sake of argument, we'll stick with the 11 bottom category insides on the lowest passenger decks, which are variously shaped, depending on the luck of the draw. The only consistency is that you'll have to toss a coin to see who gets the bottom bunk.

INSIDER TIP

While the cabins marketed in the U.S. all have private facilities, the Eugenio-Costa still contains a few budget accommodations without en suite bathrooms that are sold in other countries. Be sure to check it out when booking, especially if you book your cruise after you get to Europe.

The Bottom Line

There's nothing fancy about the *EugenioCosta*, not compared to the dazzling *Classica* and *Romantica* and the architecturally interesting *Allegra* and *Marina*, but she's a popular ship among the Europeans, who think of cruising as a less structured, more footloose family vacation with no particular mystique. Personally, we think the prices—pegged to the European market—are far too high for most Americans, especially on a vintage ship.

Fielding's Five

Five Favorite Places

1. The amidships pool, very 1960s with its freeform surround and random tile patterns, sheltered from errant winds and facing a series of little niches similar to those on the *CostaMarina*, just the right size for a table and four chairs.
2. The aft pool, surrounded by sunbathing bodies in all shapes and sizes.
3. The Piazza Italia, your own village square where you can sip an espresso, buy a gelati or piece of pizza and watch the world go by.
4. The big aft Boat Deck sports and tournament center.
5. The Cinema, with its box-like seats that line both sides of the balcony like an opera house.

Five Good Reasons to Book These Ships

1. To travel with all those cosmopolitan folks outlined previously.
2. To really cruise Italian-style.
3. To learn Italian (and French and German and Polish and so on).

COSTA CRUISES

4. To enjoy the convenience of cruising in Europe rather than taking a bus or train tour with constant packing and unpacking.

5. To dress up for the European-style masquerade party, a Venetian masked ball.

Five Things You Won't Find On Board

1. A pizzeria.
2. TV sets in cabins.
3. A library.
4. A smoke-free restaurant.
5. A table for two.

EugenioCosta ★★

Registry	**Liberia**
Officers	**Italian**
Crew	**International**
Complement	**568**
GRT	**30,000**
Length (ft.)	**713.4**
Beam (ft.)	**96.4**
Draft (ft.)	**28.3**
Passengers-Cabins Full	**1418**
Passengers-2/Cabin	**1002**
Passenger Space Ratio	**29.94**
Stability Rating	**Good**
Seatings	**2**
Cuisine	**Italian**
Dress Code	**Traditional**
Room Service	**Yes**
Tip	**$6 PPPD, 15% automatically added to bar checks**

Ship Amenities

Outdoor Pool	**2**
Indoor Pool	**0**
Jacuzzi	**1**
Fitness Center	**Yes**
Spa	**Yes**
Beauty Shop	**Yes**
Showroom	**Yes**
Bars/Lounges	**7**
Casino	**Yes**
Shops	**Yes**
Library	**Yes**
Child Program	**Yes**
Self-Service Laundry	**Yes**
Elevators	**5**

Cabin Statistics

Suites	**8**
Outside Doubles	**263**
Inside Doubles	**230**
Wheelchair Cabins	**0**
Singles	**0**
Single Surcharge	**150%**
Verandas	**0**
110 Volt	**Yes**

Mermoz

Our favorite memories of the Mermoz are all in French, from a transatlantic crossing combined with an intense Berlitz immersion course in intermediate conversational French. We went to class every day for several hours, then chatted in French with each other, and, as we gained courage, with our friendly Gallic shipmates, who were amused we were trying to speak their language well. By the time the ship reached Europe, we were using the right verb forms and idioms, but we had to get off in Spain to do a Bon Appétit story about trains. A week later, all the beautiful French was gone from our heads.

The *Mermoz* was for many years the flagship (and later the only ship) for Paquet French Cruises. Paquet also bought Pearl Cruises and now-defunct Ocean Cruise Lines in 1990, but Paquet/Pearl in turn was absorbed by Costa in 1994. This year marks the 41st annual classical Music Festival At Sea, one of the hottest and hardest-to-get tickets in cruising. The ship was named for Jean Mermoz, a charismatic French aviator during World War I, a male version of Amelia Earhart, who disappeared mysteriously in the Atlantic in December, 1936. You'll find a bust of him in the Bahamas Deck lobby, along with a ship's wheel, brass telescopes and other ship artifacts, and photos and posters of ships and ship models.

"A truly international cruise experience enhanced by those inimitable and irresistible touches of French style."

Translation

Cruising French-style.

Prices for the Music Festival at Sea include all shore excursions, cocktail parties, concerts, bar drinks and table wines. To get more information about the Music Festival at Sea, contact The Leonard Haertter Travel Company, 7922 Bonhomme Avenue, St. Louis, MO 63105, or call ☎ (314) 721-6200.

Cabins & Costs

Fantasy Suites: .... B

Average Price PPPD: $625 in Europe, $1,763 for the Music Festival at Sea.
There are four suites aboard, all located amidships on a middle deck in the old liner tradition. Each has a separate sitting room, some with two day beds, a long desk/dresser, built-in wood closet and art deco wall mirror. There are portholes instead of windows. The bedroom has a queen-sized bed, a chair and night tables, and there are two full bathrooms with tubs.

Small Splurges: .... C+

Average Price PPPD: $412 in Europe, $850 for the Music Festival at Sea.
Superior deluxe outside staterooms come with a choice of double or twin beds, and have a tub/shower combination in the bathroom. You'll also find a dresser with four big drawers and a chair or hassock.

Suitable Standards: .... C-

Average Price PPPD: $250 in Europe, $500 for the Music Festival at Sea.
Standard outside doubles are dispersed throughout the lower decks, but on Fjords Deck, the bottom passenger deck, remember that your porthole view of the sea will be akin to watching your washing at the laundromat. Twin beds and a bath with shower, a dresser and sometimes a small table are the furnishings.

Bottom Bunks: C

Average Price PPPD: $200 in Europe, $400 for the Music Festival at Sea.
Even with the very cheapest inside double, you'll still have two lower beds rather than upper and lower berths, a dresser, a shelf and a bath with shower only.

Where She Goes

The *Mermoz* cruises around the world in winter, not a formally announced world cruise but on a series of exotic sailings back-to-back. In summer the ship cruises in Europe. The Music Festival at Sea usually takes place in early September.

The Bottom Line

The *Mermoz* is a nice-sized ship for anyone who wants to avoid the megaliners, and while she shows her age, there's still enough left of the charming renovation performed by French architect Marc Held (who also designed the Windstar ships) 10 years ago to show her character. Don't expect elaborate bathrooms or huge cabins; both are on the standard-to-small size.

As Francophiles (and wanna-be Francophones) we're very fond of the *Mermoz*. One of the most delightful aspects of traveling aboard is to get to know the French, who are not nearly so formidable as we are led to expect. We have chatted in our rudimentary French or their basic English with retired manufacturers from Lyon, folk dancers from Provence and housewives from the Loire who are genuinely interested in meeting and talking with Americans, once the initial shyness of each wears off.

Five Easy Places

1. The Renaissance Grill, the smaller of two restaurants aboard, usually reserved for the upper category cabins, has big windows overlooking the sea, wicker chairs, rattan hanging lights and upholstered banquettes.

2. Grand Salon Mermoz is the showroom equivalent, arranged as the name suggests more like a salon for concerts, French folk dancing and mini-operas, with comfortable caramel leather tub chairs and some smaller folding chairs, a wood parquet dance floor and small bandstands.

3. The Winter Garden is a handsome enclosed promenade with wicker chairs and large potted palms that attracts readers, card players and conversationalists.

4. The Atlantic Salon, with an inlaid wood dance floor, a piano, ceiling fans and neo-Matisse sketches of nudes, plus, charmingly, a large porthole in the wall framed by a strip of ship's railing and framing a painted backdrop of sky and sea.

5. The Massalia Dining Room, with round tables, white stem chairs, a low ceiling ornament with plaster art deco swirls in pink, and slim silver vertical lights dropped from the ceiling over each table.

Five Good Reasons to Book This Ship

1. Because it carries only 500 passengers in a very civilized fashion.

2. Because (traditionally) wine is included with dinner.

3. Because it cruises to some exotic and interesting places.

4. Because the French you'll meet are more likely to be a biscuit manufacturer and his wife from Lyon or a florist from Avignon than a snob from Paris.

5. Because the annual Music Festival at Sea is one of the greatest theme cruises.

Mermoz ★★★

Registry	Bahamas
Officers	French
Crew	French/Indonesian
Complement	320
GRT	13,691
Length (ft.)	532
Beam (ft.)	65
Draft (ft.)	20
Passengers-Cabins Full	550
Passengers-2/Cabin	533
Passenger Space Ratio	25.68
Stability Rating	Good
Seatings	1
Cuisine	French
Dress Code	Traditional
Room Service	Yes
Tip	$8 PPPD, 15% automatically added to bar checks

Ship Amenities

Outdoor Pool	2
Indoor Pool	0
Jacuzzi	0
Fitness Center	Yes
Spa	Yes
Beauty Shop	Yes
Showroom	Yes
Bars/Lounges	4
Casino	Yes
Shops	1
Library	Yes
Child Program	No
Self-Service Laundry	No
Elevators	2

Cabin Statistics

Suites	4
Outside Doubles	198
Inside Doubles	58
Wheelchair Cabins	0
Singles	17
Single Surcharge	150%
Verandas	0
110 Volt	Yes

COSTA CRUISES

CRYSTAL CRUISES

2121 Avenue of the Stars, Los Angeles, CA 90067
☎ *(310) 785-9300, (800) 446-6620*

History . . . .

Los Angeles-based Crystal Cruises did the cruise line equivalent of coming from 0 to 60 in six seconds. Founded in 1988 by century-old NYK (Nippon Yusen Kaisha), one of the largest transportation companies in the world, the Japanese-financed company set up a long and elaborate program of introducing to the United States a new ship that was still two years away from completion.

The line's first ship, the 960-passenger *Crystal Harmony*, was built in the Mitsubishi shipyard in Nagasaki, Japan, and made its debut in Los Angeles in July, 1990, to great critical acclaim. A sister ship, the *Crystal Symphony*, built in Finland's Kvaerner-Masa Yard, made its debut in New York in May 1995.

—First line to offer two alternative dinner restaurants to all passengers at no surcharge (*Crystal Harmony*, 1990).

> ### DID YOU KNOW?
>
> *Interestingly, this very upscale line deliberately chose as godmothers for its ships actresses that are better-known for popular television series than for feature films or theater, Mary Tyler Moore for the* Crystal Harmony *and Angela Lansbury for the* Crystal Symphony.

Concept . . . .

From its inception, Crystal set out to define "luxury" by trying to provide the best of everything—food, entertainment, service and shipboard accommodation—and to offer "warm and personal service in an elegant setting." They say, "The line provides sophisticated travelers and experienced cruisers with an intimate and luxurious cruise experience."

Signatures . . . .

The turquoise seahorses on the Crystal stacks have become a recognized logo in most of the great ports of the world, and that particular shade is carried through on logo caps and T-shirts and other Crystal souvenir merchandise.

In the lobby of each ship is a "crystal" piano made of lucite, along with bronze-colored statuary, a waltzing couple on the *Harmony* and a pair of ballet dancers on the *Symphony,* and waterfalls with crystal cut-glass cylinders and Tivoli lights.

Gimmicks

Using costly Louis Roederer Cristal Champagne for special occasions like christenings.

Extension telephones in the bathrooms.

Who's the Competition

In its brief five years of cruising, Crystal has garnered an enviable reputation for service and overall quality, so that it virtually stands alone at the head of its class. It would have rivalled the former Royal Viking Line, and we do note some crossover from Cunard's *Royal Viking Sun.* It also attracts veterans of Princess and Holland America, as well as Seabourn and Sea Goddess.

Who's Aboard

Most of the passengers are successful couples between 40 and 70, with a sprinkling of older singles who enjoy the gentleman host program aboard. Very few of the passengers are Japanese, but those that do sail represent the upper strata of independent travelers rather than group tourism. Some 90 percent of the line's passengers are 45 and up with a median age of 60, and 80 percent are married. Of the line's total passengers, nearly half have traveled with Crystal before. A recent passenger list shows guests from the United States (primarily California), Canada, Saudi Arabia, Japan, Australia, Hong Kong, Mexico, Switzerland, Brazil, Germany and Belgium.

Who Should Go

Younger passengers and upscale first-time cruisers who will enjoy the excellent entertainment, the high quality of food and service and the only pair of Caesars Palace casinos at sea.

Who Should Not Go

Anyone who doesn't like to dress up and socialize.

The Lifestyle

These ships offer one of the finest versions of classic, traditional, luxury ship cruises available, with a fairly formal dress code and assigned dining at two seatings but with two alternative restaurants available most evenings as well by advance reservation. Lavish surroundings, pampering service, excellent housekeeping and superlative dining keep the same passengers coming back again and again. Daytime activities are frequent and fascinating, shore excursions very well handled and evening entertainment top-notch.

Wardrobe

Dressy, dressy, dressy. We're frequently carry-on people with only a little luggage, but we always check a large bag when we're flying to board a Crystal ship. Daytimes and shore excursions can be casual, but the passengers are almost attired in smart casual, or casual elegance (what the Crystal handbook calls "country club attire.") Evenings, women wear cocktail dresses or dressy pantsuits for informal (what some lines now are calling "semi-formal") nights, while men don jacket and tie; on formal nights, women wear evening gowns (we saw as many long gowns as short ones on the inaugural of the *Symphony*) and men don tuxedos or dark business suits.

Bill of Fare............................ A

Creative contemporary cuisine, much of it prepared to order, comes out of the Crystal galleys, which are under the direction of executive chef Toni Neumeister, former executive chef for Royal Viking Line. A dinner menu will carry suggestions for a full menu recommended by the chef, a lighter fare menu giving the calorie, fat and sodium counts, a vegetarian menu and cellar master wine suggestions by the glass or by the bottle. Traditionally, you can choose from three or four appetizers (perhaps tempura fried softshell crab with red pepper aioli), two or three soups (maybe a chilled tomato soup with goat cheese quenelles), three salads, a nightly pasta special (like fusilli with zucchini, garlic, olive oil and onions) and four main dishes (say, seared fresh ahi tuna steak, crisp baby hen, grilled tournedos of beef tenderloin Rossini or roasted Scandinavian venison loin) plus a vegetarian option such as a baby eggplant stuffed with ratatouille. The dessert roster runs to five desserts (maybe a tarte Tatin with vanilla ice cream or a souffle Grand Marnier) plus a cheese trolley and various frozen desserts. A little silver tray of freshly made petits fours always arrives with the coffee service.

But that's only the dining room. There are also two alternative restaurants with special evening menus, one Italian and one Asian (Chinese on the *Symphony* and Japanese on the *Harmony*) and a wonderful assortment of casual buffet lunch choices from an elegant spread of cold seafoods and meats and hot dishes in the Lido Cafe to our favorite gardenburger, pizza, grilled hot dogs or hamburgers on deck. There's also an ice cream bar.

Showtime.............................. A

The entertainment is dazzling, with highly professional productions that are constantly updated, along with prestigious lecturers, concerts, cabarets and game shows. Lecturers include names such as journalist and author Pierre Salinger, ship historian Bill Miller, novelist Judith Krantz and former Los Angeles mayor Tom Bradley. Production shows are gorgeously costumed (some of the hand-beaded wardrobe pieces cost as much as $10,000 each) and beautifully choreographed and performed.

Discounts..............................

Members of the Crystal Society (previous cruisers with the line) get a five percent discount with no advance booking deadline. If you book a future cruise while you're aboard one of the ships, you get a discount of $250 to $500 per person, and your travel agent gets her full commission as well. Pay in full six months ahead of sailing time and you get an additional five percent discount.

The Bottom Line

There are only two possible criticisms demanding luxury cruisers could make—the two seating dining and the shortage of really generous closet space on very long sailings like the full world cruise. To the first, we'd point out that you could book the alternative restaurants for 7:30 or order dinner in your cabin for those nights when you didn't want to dine at your assigned table. To the second, we'd suggest if you're taking a really long cruise and you like to dress up, book as high a cabin category as you can, say one of the penthouses or penthouse suites.

The Crystal ships are for those who want—and are willing to pay for—the very best in a traditional big-ship sailing experience.

Crystal Harmony   ★★★★★★
Crystal Symphony   ★★★★★★

The highly successful Crystal ships have had only a few gaffes in their career—and our favorite is the Viennese Mozart Tea, which used to be presented as one of the highlights of the cruise. On the inaugural of the Crystal Harmony in 1990, it was dazzling, with a string trio and all the waiters decked out in white wigs, gold lame frock coats and vests, long white stockings and slippers—visualize Tim Curry as Mozart in the film Amadeus and you get the picture. On our next outing aboard the Harmony in 1993, the procedure had gotten routine, and the Viennese Mozart tea on that sailing had only three of the waiters (the ones who looked as if they'd drawn the losing straws) garbed in white wigs and partial costumes, but wearing loafers and white tennis socks. The Manila Strings trio were only two, wearing their ordinary daytime garb of

white pants and shirts. (The third musician was missing, Harry pointed out, because Mozart didn't write for guitar.) On the inaugural of the Crystal Symphony, there were no white wigs, gold lame vests and knee breeches in sight, just the table of elegant cakes and pastries. The wigs had caused near-revolution in the ranks of waiters, as had the costumes, so the whole fancy-dress thing was written off.

This elegant pair of ships with their sleek, graceful lines offers a lot of sensational cabins with private verandas, a plethora of posh public rooms and an easy-to-get-around layout. The public areas are concentrated on the top two decks and two lower decks with most of the cabins in between. An amidships pool deck is sheltered enough with its sliding glass roof and glass side windows that it provides a cozy sun-trap even on a cool Alaska day. By limiting the major "avenues" to one rather than both sides of a deck, the traffic flows neatly without sacrificing space that could be devoted to a shop or bar. Craftsmanship is meticulous aboard both these ships. Comfortable cruising speed is 16 to 17 knots, but the *Crystal Symphony* on its inaugural was averaging 20 between New York and Bermuda.

An expansive amidships pool and raised whirlpool is surrounded by plenty of sunbathing area.

The Brochure Says

"From the moment you step aboard the gleaming white jewels known as *Crystal Harmony* and *Crystal Symphony*, you will feel you have arrived at a very special place and have been warmly embraced as part of the Crystal family."

Translation

They're serious about this, folks. There's something called The Crystal Attitude, a service philosophy that is a part of the intensive training each employee goes through, with motivational tapes and videos and classes for upper echelon employees in notable hotel schools like L'Ecole Hotelier in Switzerland and Cornell Hotel School. Crystal has the highest crew return factor of any cruise line, with more than 70 percent re-enlisting.

Fantasy Suites: . . . . A+

Average Price PPPD: $1306–$1843 with some airfare included.

The most lavish quarters aboard are the Crystal penthouse suites, each measuring 948–982 square feet, with large sitting room, dining area, private veranda, wet bar, big Jacuzzi tub with ocean view, separate master bedroom with king-sized bed, big walk-in closets and a guest bath. There's butler service, of course.

Fantasy suites like the Crystal Penthouse with veranda aboard the **Crystal Symphony** *are sought after by big spenders.*

Small Splurges: . . . . A+

Average Price PPPD: $790 to $1260 with some airfare included.

Eighteen penthouse suites with verandas that measure a total of 491 square feet and 44 penthouses with verandas that measure 367 square feet are spacious and prettily furnished. Butler service is offered in all the penthouses, along with complimentary bar, cocktail hour canapes, and in-room dining with dishes that can be ordered from the dining room or either alternative restaurant.

Suitable Standards: . . . . A+

Average Price PPPD: $541–$689 with some airfare included.

The deluxe stateroom with private veranda is the most numerous of the cabin categories on board, with 214 cabins (on the *Symphony*) each measuring 246 square feet, with a private veranda, king-sized bed, loveseat sofa, chair, built-in desk/dresser with plenty of storage space, a safe, mini-refrigerator, TV/VCR, plus a large closet with built-in shoe rack and tie rack, and a marble bathroom with tub/shower combination, double sinks and two hair dryers. Seven staterooms for the disabled are available on the *Symphony*, four on the *Harmony*.

Bottom Bunks: . . . . A

Average Price PPPD: $329 for the Harmony *insides with some airfare included.*

Inside cabins on the *Crystal Harmony* and outside cabins without verandas on the *Crystal Symphony* are the lowest-priced digs aboard. The latter number 202, and some have restricted views due to hanging lifeboats. The insides on the *Harmony* measure 183 square feet and have two lower beds, remote control TV/VCR, full bath with tub and shower, mini-refrigerator, safe, small sofa and chairs with desk/dresser and coffee table. You're not slumming here.

Where She Goes

The *Crystal Harmony* begins the year with a couple of transcanal sailings, then moves to the Amazon at the end of January, returns for more canal transits in March and April, then repositions to Alaska for the summer, her first visit there since her inaugural year of 1990. She'll sail between Vancouver and Anchorage on 10- and 11-day Gulf of Alaska itineraries. In the fall, the *Harmony* sets out for Asia, sailing from Anchorage to Xingang (for Beijing) on an unusual 13-night program that will also add three overland nights in Beijing. The ship then cruises between Hong Kong and Beijing/Xingang in September and early October, followed by sailings between Hong Kong and Bangkok (the port of Laem Chabang) in late October and November. The *Harmony* repositions from Singapore to Sydney in late November, followed by Down Under Sydney-Auckland itineraries and then a transpacific from Auckland to Los Angeles during the Christmas and New Year holidays.

The *Crystal Symphony* spends the first quarter of 1996 making the first-ever around-the-world cruise for the line, which positions the ship in Europe for a series of Mediterranean and Northern European summer cruises. A transatlantic crossing which visits the Canaries is set for late October, followed by transcanal and Caribbean sailings through the Christmas holidays.

The Bottom Line

While the ship's interior is handsome and dignified, the real sense of the luxury comes not from eye-grabbing architecture but rather fine attention to detail—items like the Wedgwood teacups in the Palm Court at teatime, Riedel hand-blown wine glasses in the Prego Restaurant, Villeroy & Boch china and Frette linens in the dining room, goose down pillows in each cabin, the designs on the Bistro plates and cups. Passengers are treated like adults rather than children at summer camp. Big-ship cruising doesn't get any better than this.

Fielding's Five

Five Spectacular Spots

1. The Palm Court, a sunny, airy winter garden with wicker chairs and ceiling fans, potted palms and a harpist playing for tea.

2. The Avenue Saloon, the "in" bar on board (you can always tell the "in" bar because that's where the officers and the entertainers hang out) with its wood floors and Oriental rugs, green leather bar rails and movable stools.

3. Caesars Palace At Sea, a truly classy shipboard casino operation that actually (in the Vegas style) gives free drinks to players.

4. The spectacular Crystal Spa and Salon on the top deck with lots of glass windows, aerobics area, gym with lots of machines, sauna, steam and massage.

5. The elegant Prego Restaurant aboard the *Symphony*, the Italian alternative dining option, with its red-and-white striped pillars and high-backed blue armchairs tied with red tassels and cord, the very essence of a classy Venetian restaurant.

Five Good Reasons to Book These Ships

1. To tell all your friends about your cruise.
2. To show off your wardrobe and jewelry.
3. To be pampered by a happy staff who have the best crew accommodations at sea plus their own gym and Jacuzzi.
4. Cabin telephones with voice mail, and bathroom extension phones.
5. To have a private veranda, which will change your whole picture of luxury cruising.

Five Things You Won't Find On Board

1. Portholes; all the outside cabins have windows.
2. Anyone inappropriately dressed on formal night.
3. A bad attitude or discouraging word.
4. A lot of children, even though there's a youth and teen area provided.
5. A really unhappy passenger.

Crystal Harmony ★★★★★

Registry	**Bahamas**
Officers	**Norwegian/Japanese**
Crew	**International**
Complement	**545**
GRT	**49,400**
Length (ft.)	**791**
Beam (ft.)	**104**
Draft (ft.)	**24.6**
Passengers-Cabins Full	**1010**
Passengers-2/Cabin	**960**
Passenger Space Ratio	**51.45**
Stability Rating	**Good to Excellent**
Seatings	**2**
Cuisine	**Contemporary**
Dress Code	**Traditional**
Room Service	**Yes**
Tip	**$10 PPPD, 15% automatically added to bar check**

Ship Amenities

Outdoor Pool	**2**
Indoor Pool	**1**
Jacuzzi	**2**
Fitness Center	**Yes**
Spa	**Yes**
Beauty Shop	**Yes**
Showroom	**Yes**
Bars/Lounges	**7**
Casino	**Yes**
Shops	**4**
Library	**Yes**
Child Program	**Yes**
Self Service Laundry	**Yes**
Elevators	**8**

Cabin Statistics

Suites	**62**
Outside Doubles	**399**
Inside Doubles	**19**
Wheelchair Cabins	**4**
Singles	**0**
Single Surcharge	**115 - 200%**
Verandas	**260**
110 Volt	**Yes**

Crystal Symphony ★★★★★★

Registry	**Bahamas**
Officers	**Norwegian/Japanese**
Crew	**International**
Complement	**530**
GRT	**50,000**
Length (ft.)	**781**
Beam (ft.)	**100**
Draft (ft.)	**24.9**
Passengers-Cabins Full	**1010**
Passengers-2/Cabin	**960**
Passenger Space Ratio	**52,08**
Stability Rating	**Good to Excellent**
Seatings	**2**
Cuisine	**Contemporary**
Dress Code	**Traditional**
Room Service	**Yes**
Tip	**$10 PPPD, 15% automatically added to bar check**

Ship Amenities

Outdoor Pool	**2**
Indoor Pool	**1**
Jacuzzi	**2**
Fitness Center	**Yes**
Spa	**Yes**
Beauty Shop	**Yes**
Showroom	**Yes**
Bars/Lounges	**7**
Casino	**Yes**
Shops	**4**
Library	**Yes**
Child Program	**Yes**
Self Service Laundry	**Yes**
Elevators	**8**

Cabin Statistics

Suites	**64**
Outside Doubles	**416**
Inside Doubles	**0**
Wheelchair Cabins	**7**
Singles	**0**
Single Surcharge	**115 - 200%**
Verandas	**278**
110 Volt	**Yes**

CUNARD

555 Fifth Avenue, New York, NY 10017-2453
☎ (212) 880-7500, (800) 221-4770

Cunard made headlines in 1994 when it acquired not only the posh **Royal Viking Sun** *with its swim-up bar on pool deck but all rights to the prestigious Royal Viking brand name and its subsidiary labels.*

History ....

"I want a plain but comfortable boat, not the least unnecessary expense for show," Samuel Cunard instructed the Scottish shipyard that built his 1154-ton wooden paddlewheel steamer *Britannia* in 1840. And when it set out on its maiden voyage from Liverpool to Halifax and Boston on July 4, with 63 passengers, 93 crew members and a cow to supply fresh milk on the voyage, the conservative businessman from Nova Scotia was more concerned about his cargo—he had a lucrative contract to carry Her Majesty's mails and dispatches across the Atlantic twice a month—than his passengers.

DID YOU KNOW?

One of the Britannia's early passengers was novelist Charles Dickens, who sailed the North Atlantic through severe gales in January, 1842, describing his feelings tersely as, "Not ill, but going to be." His cabin contained "a very thin flat quilt, covering a very thin mattress, spread like a surgical plaster on a most inaccessible shelf," and the dining room was "not unlike a gigantic hearse with windows in the sides."

That same year, Cunard quadrupled his fleet, eventually cutting down crossings from the usual six weeks of that era to two weeks.

DID YOU KNOW?

"Going to sea is a hardship," wrote one early Cunard executive in response to a query as to why the ships did not provide napkins in the dining room. "The Cunard Company does not undertake to make anything else out of it, and if people want to wipe their mouths at a ship's table, they could use their pocket handkerchiefs."

In its 157-year history, Cunard has operated more than 190 ships, including the famous *Queen Mary* and *Queen Elizabeth*, who saluted each other in the midatlantic as their paths crossed. They transported 4000 people a week between the U.S. and U.K.

In the late 19th and early 20th centuries, the Cunarders carried hundreds of thousands of immigrants from Europe to the U.S., and during World War II carried troops to and from Great Britain.

*Cunard's **Mauretania** is remembered today with a striking 16-foot model displayed aboard the **QE2** complete with lighted portholes.*

But the 1920s and 1930s were the heyday of ocean liners. Cunard's legendary *Mauretania* with its four red-and-black stacks and lavish wood-paneled, plaster-ceilinged public rooms, ruled the waves through the twenties. The *Queen Mary* was star from the thirties to the waning days of transatlantic crossings in the sixties, with guests such as the Duke and Duchess of Windsor, in perpetual, glittering exile with their 75 suitcases and 70 trunks; Noel Coward; Rex Harrison; Rita Hayworth; Richard Burton and Elizabeth Taylor.

DID YOU KNOW?

After 31 years of service, the Queen Mary *was retired in 1967, exactly a decade since the number of transatlantic travelers crossing by air first outnumbered those crossing by sea. The* Queen Mary *is today a landmark moored at the city of Long Beach, California, serving as a hotel and tourist attraction.*

Samuel Cunard would probably not be surprised at the size and diversity of his company's present fleet—seven sea-going ships ranging from the 1814-passenger *QE2* to the deluxe little 116-passenger *Sea Goddess* ships—but he would probably be astonished to find that people book passage by sea not by necessity but for the sheer pleasure of traveling slowly, emulating those shadowy companions of another day who enjoyed an infinite supply of the one travel luxury we lack—time.

DID YOU KNOW?

Cunard has been a wholly-owned company of London-based Trafalgar House, PLC, since 1971. The company was acquired in 1996 by Kvaerner.

—First company to take passengers on regularly scheduled transatlantic departures (*Britannia*, 1840).

—Introduced the first passenger ship to be lit by electricity (*Servia*, c. 1881).

—Introduced the first twin-screw ocean liner (*Campania*, 1893).

—Introduced the first steam turbine engines in a passenger liner (*Carmania*, 1905),

—Introduced the first gymnasium and health center aboard a ship (*Franconia*, 1911).

—Introduced the first indoor swimming pool on a ship (*Aquitania*, 1914).

—First cruise line to introduce an around-the-world cruise (*Laconia*, 1922).

—Held the record from 1940 to 1996 for the largest passenger ship ever built (*Queen Elizabeth*, 1940).

—The only cruise company to sail regularly-scheduled transatlantic service year-round (*Queen Elizabeth 2*).

DID YOU KNOW?

"Getting there is half the fun," was an ad slogan Cunard came up with in 1956 to promote its transatlantic crossings against the new competition from jet aircraft.

Concept . . . .

In the wide diversity of Cunard ships, the flagship *Queen Elizabeth 2* stands alone, providing an around-the-world cruise, regular transatlantic crossings and warm-water cruises.

The highly rated *Royal Viking Sun* and the prestigious *Vistafjord* offer very good quality food, service and accommodations at sea for the most demanding and sophisticated travelers.

Cunard's ultra-deluxe little *Sea Goddess* ships are among our very favorite vessels, because they give passengers the sense of sailing on their own private yachts.

In the mid-sized, moderately-priced range are two classic ships, the sparkling new *Cunard Dynasty,* making shorter cruises to popular destinations such as Alaska, the Caribbean and the Panama Canal, and the beloved, if somewhat vintage, *Cunard Countess,* which cheerfully cruises the Caribbean year-round with some interesting island ports of call.

Signatures . . . .

The distinctive red-and-black funnel that has characterized Cunard ships since the *Britannia* in 1840 has not been affixed to the *Royal Viking Sun* and the pair of *Sea Goddess* ships. The *Sun* retains the red RVL sea eagle, and the *Sea Goddess* ships carry a golden goddess.

The dark hull of the *QE2* is a modern-day version of the standard Cunard North Atlantic black as opposed to the white hulls more typical of cruise ships.

The Cunard lion, rampant, wearing a crown and holding a globe in his paws, first appeared in 1880 when the company went public; according to ship historian John Maxtone-Graham, rival sailors disparagingly called it "the monkey wi' the nut."

Serving caviar and champagne in the surf is an eye-catching Sea Goddess tradition; here, passengers and crew wading at Jost van Dyke in the British Virgin Islands.

Gimmicks . . . .

Serving caviar from the blue two-kilo tins is a trademark/gimmick aboard the *Sea Goddess* ships, where it adorns the serve-yourself appetizer table at cocktail time and is fetched ashore by waiters in black tie and swim trunks on beaches in the Caribbean.

Who's the Competition. . . . .

A unique vessel, the *Queen Elizabeth 2* has no real competition except herself, because of the intense love/hate relationship her passengers accord this most famous and most misunderstood vessel. They complain about signs of aging or inconveniences aboard the ship, then scream when things are changed. Every other year like clockwork, when the ship comes out of drydock in late autumn, something or other on board doesn't work. They complain to each other, rage to the media and threaten lawsuits—then book passage again the next time they're going to take a cruise.

Cunard's purchase of the *Royal Viking Sun* eliminated much of the direct competition facing *Vistafjord*; now the pair competes with the Crystal ships. *Sea Goddess*, almost always mentioned in the same breath with *Seabourn*, is really more like Radisson Seven Seas' *Song of Flower* or the Silversea ships since the admittedly-steep fares include all the beverage service on board, still an optional extra with Seabourn.

Who's Aboard. . . . .

Perhaps the broadest possible spectrum of passengers is aboard one of the short segments of the *QE2's* world cruise, everyone from the very rich penthouse passengers to the Miss Marples in the *Mauretania* dining room, who are signed up for the full cruise, and the transients taking a segment, a mix of middle-aged, middle-income couples and upscale singles and families. The Panama Canal transit and the transpacific segment between Los Angeles and Honolulu always sell out.

Older couples and singles, most of them North Americans with an upper-range income, are typically aboard *Royal Viking Sun* while the *Vistafjord* usually draws a more cosmopolitan and slightly younger crowd, a mix of North Americans, British and Germans.

Sea Goddess attracts almost exclusively couples who have money or want people to think they do and who may or may not be married.

Who Should Go. . . . .

Everyone who loves ships and cruising should make a transatlantic crossing at least once on the *QE2* to experience the tremendous difference between crossing and cruising. Families with children aged two to eight will also find *QE2* a good ship because of its nursery overseen by two professional British nannies and a special high tea (which correctly used means a light supper, not English-style afternoon tea) for kids at 5:30.

Anyone who loves luxury and can afford it should book one of the *Sea Goddess* ships, preferably in the Caribbean or Mediterranean, to be pampered with caviar and champagne around the clock as if it's your own private yacht. And aging baby boomers who've done well in business should reward themselves by sampling the *Royal Viking Sun* or *Vistafjord* to see if that's how they want to vacation when they retire.

Who Should Not Go ....

It's interesting that with most cruise lines, the crossover from one ship to another is easily made, even with a size disparity, as with Princess Cruises' mid-sized *Pacific Princess* versus the very large *Regal Princess*. But with the Cunarders, things are different. It's impossible to visualize a *Sea Goddess* passenger going over to the *Cunard Countess*, or even a *QE2* penthouse passenger who dines in the Queens Grill switching to the first seating in that ship's Mauretania restaurant. So when it comes to Cunard, "Who should not go on which ships?" is the real question, which will be addressed under the individual ships. (See "No Nos," under each ship.)

The Lifestyle ....

Because the lifestyle aboard Cunard vessels, unlike those of other cruise lines, varies depending not only on the ship but also the type of sailing—transatlantic, world cruise, warm-weather cruising—we'll describe it with each individual ship.

Wardrobe ....

Except for the *Cunard Countess* and *Cunard Dynasty*, which are termed "informal cruising," the Cunard ships call for a fairly dressy wardrobe. The exception, interestingly enough, is on a transatlantic crossing, when many businessmen, particularly Europeans, will wear a dark suit that doubles as business wear rather than a tuxedo. On the crossings, every night except first and last are formal.

Day wear aboard the ships is smart casual or "country club" garb. On informal nights, especially on the *Royal Viking Sun*, some of the men wear madras jackets with bright linen pants in what we think of as a preppy or southeastern resort look.

Even on the least dressy vessels in the line, the *Cunard Countess* and *Cunard Dynasty*, it is noted in the fine print that "women prefer evening or cocktail dresses, or other formal attire, and gentlemen wear black tie or dark suit. On informal evenings, regular cocktail dresses for women, and jacket and tie for men are the norm." We wonder how one can tell the difference between a "cocktail dress" and a "regular cocktail dress."

Bill of Fare ....A+ to B

Since the food on the *Queen Elizabeth 2* varies according to which restaurant room you're assigned, we'll discuss and rate that ship's food under its Cabins and Costs section.

The *Royal Viking Sun* and *Vistafjord* have good to excellent cuisine, with some dishes cooked to order and a pleasurable range of choices, including the option to order special meals. Wine lists are outstanding on both ships. *Sea Goddess* cuisine and service have always been superlative, even their deck buffet dishes. *Cunard Dynasty* and *Cunard Count-*

ess serve a varied menu of popular Continental and international dishes in the dining rooms, along with buffet breakfasts and lunches in the deck cafe.

Cuisine Report Card:

A+ *Sea Goddess, Royal Viking Sun*

A *Vistafjord*

B+ *Cunard Dynasty*

B *Cunard Countess*

Showtime . . . . B+

Cunard entertainment, while hewing to a general pattern, varies according to the size of the ship's show lounge facilities. The classic stars—*Royal Viking Sun* and *Vistafjord*—follow a traditional format of musical production shows and variety acts by magicians, ventriloquists, puppeteers and comedians, as well as audience participation game shows like Liars Club and Team Trivia. There's usually a dance team (yes, Velez and Yolanda live!) who perform on variety nights and teach dance classes during the daytime to groups or in optional private lessons. On the *Sea Goddess* ships, entertainment consists primarily of the passengers socializing with each other or dining alone in their suites, so except for a musical group that plays nightly for dancing, or a late-night cabaret artist, there is usually not much happening.

The *QE2* presents a full range of entertainment, especially on the world cruise, with gala balls, famous lecturers and entertainers, notable orchestras and big bands, authors signing their books and karaoke nights in the pub.

The entertainment aboard the mid-sized *Cunard Dynasty* and *Cunard Countess* also presents production shows and variety acts, but usually on a somewhat smaller scale. Entertainment

Discounts . . . .

Cunard gives a 20 percent early booking discount to passengers who book and place a deposit on a cabin 120 days before sailing.

The Bottom Line

With the current policy of acquiring rather than building ships, Cunard has set itself apart from the other major cruise lines who are introducing new builds almost annually. With seven ships, Cunard is outnumbered by Carnival, Costa Royal Caribbean, Holland America and Princess.

Queen Elizabeth 2   ★★★★★/★★★★

The storm seemed to spring full-blown from nowhere on the late May New York-to-Southampton crossing in 1987, buffeting the ship for 16 hours with hurricane-strength winds up to 50 miles an hour, registering Force 10 on the Beaufort scale and leaving in its wake smashed dishes and glassware, spilled vases and planters, granite lounge tables crumbled like cookies and overturned grand pianos looking like fallen elephants. A friend in a nearby cabin woke suddenly with icy water splashing across his chest and feared he had been thrown overboard, but it was only the pitcher of ice water his stewardess had thoughtfully placed on the table by his bed the night before.

The *QE2* is the only vessel reviewed in this guide that carries a dual rating—five stars for its Grill Room class, meaning passengers booked in cabins that are assigned to dine in the Queens, Britannia and Princess Grills in categories Q1 through P2, and four stars for the rest of the ship, which includes the Caronia and the Mauretania Dining Room cabins.

Built as a two-class turbine steamer in Brown's Clydebank yard in 1967 and 1968, the *QE2* set out on its maiden voyage to the Canary Islands December 23, 1968, prior to the official delivery of the vessel to the line. A fault developed in the turbines along the way and the ship was returned to the builder. Since the passenger accommodations were still unfinished, Cunard refused to accept delivery of the ship on the planned date of January 1, 1969, and the ship made its actual maiden voyage May 2, 1969, from Southampton to New York.

The classic ocean liner retooled its engines from steam turbine to diesel in 1987, and some of the crew say the plumbing has never worked right since. The most massive renovation since the engine retooling took place in late 1994, when 850 bathrooms were remodeled and most of the public rooms and deck spaces changed and/or relocated—"cosmetically the biggest renovation ever done to the *QE2*," according to Captain John Burton-Hall—and set up a howl from unhappy passengers who complained of unfurnished cabins, bad plumbing and "exploding toilets" which reverberated throughout the world media for a month.

Life aboard the *QE2* could be compared to living in a self-contained seagoing city with its own post office and city hall (the bureau), its own police force (on-board security, both uniformed and plainclothes), its own public library with a fulltime professional librarian, its own pub, five restaurants, a movie theater, a shopping mall, a travel agency (shore excursions and tour office), eight bars, a bookstore, a computer center, casino, photo shop, florist, daily newspapers, gymnasium, spa, beauty salon, barber shop, 40-car garage, kennel, hospital with operating room, a private club (Samuel Cunard Key Club), casino, laundromat, video rental shop, a sports center and bank. Even the staff demeanor is more serious and businesslike than on a cruise ship.

DID YOU KNOW?

Deja vu *all over again?* "Hindsight suggests that Cunard was overly optimistic in setting out with a shipload of full-fare passengers, and a not-quite-finished refit...where some passengers complained of unfinished staterooms, erratic air conditioning and leaking water pipes, making newspaper headlines and TV and radio newscasts around the world ..."

from the authors' Cruise Views
column, Los Angeles Times,
July 12, 1987

NO NOs

Who shouldn't go on the QE2? Anyone who dislikes large ships—you take a lot of long hikes getting around on this ship; young couples and honeymooners, because there are not a lot of young couples aboard.

The Brochure Says

"Everywhere she goes, in every corner of the globe, *Queen Elizabeth 2* creates excitement."

Translation

They got a lot of press in 1994-95, so everybody in the world knows the *QE* was refurbished again. Actually, the renovations are obligatory because of the ship's status as a troop carrier; every two years it has to be taken out of commission to carry out government-required surveys. As Captain Burton-Hall says, "We're like a 747, really, we have to be up and running all the time." The 1996 renovations dramatically reconfigure the ship.

Cabins & Costs

Fantasy Suites: .... A
    Average Price PPPD: $1713 on the transatlantic, including airfare.

Any of the 31 penthouse suites except #8184 (the only one without a private veranda) would do well, although some of them overlook lifeboats as well as the sea. Each has lounge chairs and table in the veranda, king-sized bed, sofa and two chairs, built-in desk/dresser, good storage space, mini-refrigerator, safe and bathroom with toilet, bidet, deep tub and double sinks. You'll dine in the elegant Queens Grill with its own private cocktail lounge on treats like fresh grilled Dover sole, fresh lobster and fresh foie gras by request, and from the breakfast menu, shirred eggs with caviar and cream, along with a rolling cart of more than a dozen different kinds of marmalade.

Small Splurges: .... A

Average Price PPPD: $1265 on the transatlantic, including airfare.
Ultra-deluxe outside cabins in category P1 are spacious and comfortable, nicely furnished in rich dark blue and beige fabrics, with sofa and chairs, a long desk/dresser in wood, a big walk-in closet, a bath with tub, mini-refrigerator and terrycloth robes, plus plenty of storage space. You dine in the Princess Grill, a red candybox of a room with small tables and an intimate atmosphere. Both the Princess and Brittania Grills have recently improved menus and food preparation.

Suitable Standards: .... C+

Average Price PPPD: $1011 on the transatlantic, including airfare.
Standard outside cabins in the C categories are not identical or even similar, and the size is the luck of the draw. But all are refurbished with attractive fabrics and colors and a renovated bathroom. Figure on twin beds and, in Category C4, a shower instead of those lovely long, deep tubs. You'll dine in the Caronia restaurant after cocktails, if you like, in the Crystal Bar, which serves the Princess Grill, Britannia Grill and Caronia. We found the food and service in the Caronia better than we recall from the old Columbia first-class restaurant although the room itself is less dramatic.

Bottom Bunks: C

Average Price PPPD: $532 on the transatlantic, including airfare.
A cabin with two lower beds and bath with shower located amidships on a lower deck is the least expensive cabin for two; remember that *QE2* also has a number of single cabins. You'll dine in the Mauretania restaurant. All the dining rooms on the ship carry the same basic menus, but the service, quality of preparation and availability of special order dishes may vary from one to another. The Mauretania features single meal seatings following the November, 1996 refit.

Where She Goes

The *QE2* sets out in early January every year on her around-the-world cruise, usually sailing from New York to Los Angeles, then on to the Pacific and Asia, Australia, India, Southern Africa, South America and the Caribbean.

The rest of the year the ship makes a series of transatlantic crossings between the U.S. and U.K., interspersed with warm-water cruises to Bermuda and the Caribbean.

The Bottom Line

While her newest scheduled renovation reduces the number of berths, the *QE2* will never be a perfect luxury cruise ship because she serves too diverse a group of passenger types and nationalities to offer one consistent across-the-board product. Aboard the world cruise, her entertainment is ambitious, particularly with renowned lecturers and soloists from the world of politics, media, music, theater and film, but the musical production shows still leave something to be desired, primarily because there's no venue devoted exclusively to them. Two decks of advanced spa areas, including a full thalassotherepy area, plus an indoor pool, make the ship a good destination for fitness- oriented travelers no matter what the climate in the area cruised. "We're looking for the over-40s professional people who know the meaning of quality service, style, people who want the best, whether it's in food or entertainment or sheer relaxation," says cruise director Brian Price. But despite the frequent intrusion of "cruise" activities, the ship retains the atmosphere of a transatlantic liner with places to go and things to do rather than the aimless fun-and-games ambience of a pure cruise ship.

Five Big Changes On the Ship

1. The Cunard history and artifacts exhibits along the Heritage Trail, with a four-panel mural of Cunard history in the Midships Lobby, a striking 16-foot model of the 1906 *Mauretania* with lights glowing from each porthole, and menus and silver serving pieces from the much-loved 1948 *Caronia*, nicknamed the Green Goddess for her unusual green livery.

2. The Golden Lion Pub, with its friendly publican drawing pints and half-pints of Carlsberg lager or Tetley bitter.

3. The greatly-enlarged Lido self-service buffet restaurant, which replaces an indoor/outdoor pool area that was rarely used; it has a sliding glass dome roof, pale wood floors and neon cove lighting and can seat 500 passengers at a time for breakfast, lunch, children's high tea and midnight buffet. A stairway leads down to the Pavilion, a new glassed-in casual buffet adjacent to the pool deck serving early Continental breakfast and lunchtime hot dogs, hamburgers, steak sandwiches and vegetarian specials.

4. The former Midships Bar has been replaced by the elegant little Chart Room, an intimate lounge where singer/pianists perform sophisticated music of Porter and Gershwin.

5. The already excellent library has been expanded into two rooms, one staffed with a professional librarian who checks out books and videotapes to passengers free of charge, the other a bookshop that sells volumes about ships and the sea plus an ever-changing collection of books written by lecturers sailing aboard.

Five Off-the-Wall Things to Do

1. Try and find the dog kennels.

2. Try and find the nursery.

3. If you're dining in the Queens Grill, make a special dinner order of bubble and squeak or baked beans on toast.

4. Go to karaoke night at the pub and see if you can sing "Moon River" without hitting a single note on key. (It isn't easy, but a dear little English lady in a Miss Marple frock did it one night when we were aboard.)

5. Enter the table tennis competition against the keen British and Australian players.

Five Good Reasons to Book This Ship

1. Because she's the *QE2* and there's no other ship in the world like her.

2. To shop at the only sea-going branch of Harrods, the famous London department store.

3. To earn Cruise Miles (like frequent flyer miles) for discounts or future free cruises.

4. To walk through the wonderful self-guided Heritage Trail chock-a-block with 150 years of Cunard artifacts and history; it's riveting for anyone who loves ships.

5. To take the shortest and cheapest possible segment of a world cruise (Ensenada to Honolulu every January); ask your travel agent since it's not promoted in the brochures.

Five Things You Won't Find On Board

1. A little entrance stage into the first-class dining room like there used to be, since the first class and tourist class eateries changed places.

2. The private lounge that used to distinguish the Princess Grill; now everyone has before-dinner drinks in the large Crystal Bar.

3. That indoor swimming pool under the sliding dome roof has gone; in its place, a 500-seat buffet restaurant that one disgruntled passenger said "looks like a big cafeteria." Funny, that's exactly what it's supposed to be. Anyhow, there's another indoor pool in the spa down on Deck 7.

4. Access to all the bars and lounges; one is a private key club for world cruise passengers only, another the Queens Grill bar, accessible only to passengers who dine in the Queens Grill.

5. A dinky little dance band—the *QE2* prides itself on its 15-piece dance orchestra.

NOTE:

In November, 1996, a scheduled drydocking reconfigures the QE2's statistics for 1997.

Queen Elizabeth 2 ★★★★/★★★★

Registry	England
Officers	British
Crew	International
Complement	1015
GRT	69,053
Length (ft.)	963
Beam (ft.)	105
Draft (ft.)	26.5
Passengers-Cabins Full	1550
Passengers-2/Cabin	1500
Passenger Space Ratio	46.1
Stability Rating	Good to Excellent
Seatings	1
Cuisine	Continental
Dress Code	Traditional
Room Service	Yes
Tip	$10- $15 PPPD, 15% automatically added to bar check

Ship Amenities

Outdoor Pool	2
Indoor Pool	2
Jacuzzi	4
Fitness Center	Yes
Spa	Yes
Beauty Shop	Yes
Showroom	Yes
Bars/Lounges	6/2
Casino	Yes
Shops	Yes
Library	Yes
Child Program	Yes
Self-Service Laundry	Yes
Elevators	13

Cabin Statistics

Suites	34
Outside Doubles	566
Inside Doubles	119
Wheelchair Cabins	4
Singles	62
Single Surcharge	175-200%
Verandas	34
110 Volt	Yes

Cunard Countess

The Cunard Countess used to offer a wonderful combination of Caribbean programs, a cruise and a resort stay, where you could book the Countess, get off in midweek at Barbados or St. Lucia and bop over to a Cunard-owned resort hotel, spend a week and then get back on the ship and finish your cruise. It was competitively priced with resort holidays and seemed a really good idea. But Cunard gradually got out of the hotel business, so the Sail 'n Stay Vacation went the way of the dodo.

After her multiple makeovers, the *Countess* looks much as a vintage Hollywood star would; you can't look too closely under the cosmetics. Even though she's not as glamorous as the *Dynasty*, a lot of people love the ship, and she offers year-round low-key, relaxed cruising in the Caribbean at an affordable price. Basically easy to get around, she carries most of her cabins on the three lower passenger decks and the public rooms and deck areas on the three upper passenger decks. A recent renovation redid the vessel's air conditioning system and overhauled the stabilizers for a cooler, smoother ride, redecorated many cabins, put a new sound system in the show lounge and redecorated several public rooms.

The Brochure Says

"Let *Cunard Countess* transport you to a world of lush emerald isles afloat in a shimmering turquoise sea. Experience the quintessential Caribbean vacation, where palm-fringed beaches, splendid tropical weather and golden sunsets are a way of life."

Translation

Our passengers, many of them from the U.K. and Europe, come for the islands, beaches and sunshine, and don't care that our ship is aging.

Cabins & Costs

Fantasy Suites: .... NA

Nothing on board qualifies for this category.

Small Splurges: .... B

Average Price PPPD: $286 plus airfare.
A big spender could book the category A1 deluxe outside double rooms, one of the pair located amidships on Five Deck. What you get is a cabin nearly twice the size of the next category down, plus sitting area, mini-refrigerator, two lower beds, TV and bathroom with tub and shower.

Suitable Standards: C

Average Price PPPD: $183 plus airfare.
Category C outside double cabins with windows have two lower beds and new bathrooms; some have a pull-down third berth as well. These are fairly basic although they were redecorated nicely on the last redo and had specially-commissioned watercolors added.

Bottom Bunks: .... D

Average Price PPPD: $139 plus airfare.
The lowest-priced cabins aboard are the H category minimums, some with two lower beds, some with upper and lower berths, and baths with shower only.

Where She Goes

The *Cunard Countess* sails from San Juan year round to the islands of the Southern Caribbean.

The Bottom Line

While not the prettiest ship to ever come along, the *Cunard Countess* is comfortable as an old shoe (but looks more like a new one, thanks to the recent renovations), non-fancy and non-intimidating. Her passengers come for the port destinations and the prices, which are very modest indeed in today's cruise world. Cabins are small, except for the very top pair, and walls are thin.

Fielding's Five

Five Newly Refurbished Places

1. The Meridian Restaurant, looking better than ever after the most recent refurbishment, offers a few tables for two along with its more usual tables for four, six and eight.
2. The Showtime Main Lounge sparkles with its new sound system and reupholstered chairs and banquettes.
3. The Starlight Piano Lounge forward on Sun Deck has been completely redecorated.
4. The Outdoor Center has had its worn teak replaced and repaired and new tables and chairs installed, along with new lounge chair cushions.

5. The Satellite Cafe, which doubles as disco and casual buffet restaurant, has been perked up with new furniture.

Five Good Reasons to Book This Ship

1. To get a second week in the Caribbean with all-new island ports for half-price, except during the Christmas holidays, in cabin categories A1-F.

2. To take a popular country music cruise with the Cowgirl Hall of Fame and Pat Cannon's Foot & Fiddle Dance Company.

3. To sail from San Juan, where you can add on a two-night pre- or post-cruise package at the Condado Plaza Hotel and Casino for only $199 per person, double occupancy.

4. To earn Cruise Miles which can add up to discounts or free cruises.

5. You'll be able to find your way around it easily.

Five Things You Won't Find On Board

1. Private verandas.

2. Cabins designated wheelchair-accessible.

3. Single cabins (although some are small enough to qualify).

4. A self-service laundry.

5. A predominance of American passengers; the British usually outnumber them.

CUNARD LINE

Cunard Countess ★★

Registry	Bahamas
Officers	British
Crew	International
Complement	350
GRT	17,593
Length (ft.)	536'7"
Beam (ft.)	74'10"
Draft (ft.)	18'8"
Passengers-Cabins Full	974
Passengers-2/Cabin	810
Passenger Space Ratio	21.71
Stability Rating	Fair to Good
Seatings	2
Cuisine	Continental
Dress Code	Traditional
Room Service	Yes
Tip	$8 PPPD, 15% automatically added to bar check

Ship Amenities

Outdoor Pool	1
Indoor Pool	0
Jacuzzi	2
Fitness Center	Yes
Spa	No
Beauty Shop	Yes
Showroom	Yes
Bars/Lounges	4
Casino	Yes
Shops	1
Library	Yes
Child Program	Yes
Self-Service Laundry	No
Elevators	2

Cabin Statistics

Suites	2
Outside Doubles	264
Inside Doubles	139
Wheelchair Cabins	0
Singles	0
Single Surcharge	150-200%
Verandas	0
110 Volt	Yes

CUNARD LINE

Cunard Dynasty ★★★★

We loved all three of the former Crown ships, and wish Cunard still had the Jewel as well as the Dynasty. It's an ideal size, elegantly decorated, with very good food and entertainment and the only problem is a lot of people never heard of it.

The pretty oval pool aboard the Cunard Dynasty *is surrounded by a Palm Beach-style deck with comfy loungers and umbrella-shaded tables.*

There used to be five mid-sized, moderately-priced ships in the fleet—the *Cunard Princess* (now sold to Mediterranean Shipping Company as the *Rhapsody*), the *Cunard Countess* and three leased ships built between 1990 and 1993 for Palm Beach-based Crown Cruise Line, owned by the Scandinavia- based Effjohn Group—*Crown Monarch*, *Crown Jewel* and *Crown Dynasty*. But the owners sold the *Crown Monarch* and the *Crown Jewel* to

Asian-based operators, leaving only the *Crown Dynasty*, renamed *Cunard Dynasty*.

The Brochure Says

"After dining amid magnificent sea views, take your seat for the Broadway-style revue. Dance in our lovely disco or choose your favorite game of chance in the casino. Watch a movie in the comfort of your cabin, or take a moonlight stroll on deck. Then, sample a delicacy or two from the Midnight Buffet."

Translation

It's all happening here, on a lovely ship that you share with fewer than 800 fellow passengers.

Cabins & Costs

Fantasy Suites: .... B+

Average Price PPPD: $493 including airfare.
Top digs are 10 suites with about 350 square feet of area each, with teak-decked private balconies, separate sitting areas, mini-refrigerator and extra-large closets. (Two other suites have extra-large sitting areas with bay windows instead of private balconies if you prefer.) The two lower beds can be converted to one double, and the bath has a shower only.

Small Splurges: .... B+

Average Price PPPD: $447 including airfare.
The seven extra-large category Two forward cabins on Deck Six give you a captain's-eye view of the sea through big angled glass windows, two beds that can be put together for a double, two chairs, cocktail table, dresser/desk and chair. These are about the same size as the Fantasy Suites above, but without the veranda.

Suitable Standards: .... B

Average Price PPPD: $358 including airfare.
Category C standard outside doubles are available on three different decks, average 140 square feet with two lower beds that can convert to a double, remote-control color TV, safe, mirrored built-in dresser/desk, satellite telephone and bath with shower.

Bottom Bunks: C

Average Price PPPD: $229 for the G, $183 for the H (as in, rare as hen's teeth), including airfare.
The two H category cabins would be so rare to be able to book—they're like the loss leader in a supermarket ad—that we might as well recommend the next category up, a 132-square-foot G inside double with two lower beds, TV, telephone and bath with shower.

Where She Goes

The *Cunard Dynasty* makes 11-day winter cruises from Ft. Lauderdale and Acapulco calling at Cozumel, Grand Cayman, Canal transit and Costa Rica. ten-day return cruises call at Costa Rica, transit the Canal, and visit Ocho Rios and Key West.

Summer finds the *Cunard Dynasty* in Alaska sailing between Vancouver and Seward, calling at Ketchikan, Tracy Arm, Juneau, Sitka and cruising Hubbard Glacier. The seven-day return substitutes Skagway and Wrangell for Sitka.

The Bottom Line

While big enough to give a sense of stability, the *Cunard Dynasty's* public rooms and lounges have an intimate ambience, so passengers can socialize easily. And its staterooms, while not overly spacious, are comfortable and handsomely furnished. There's something for everyone aboard this clean, pretty ship.

Fielding's Five

Five Super Spaces

1. The drop-dead gorgeous five-deck atrium with its spiral staircase and trompe l'oeil mural of Italian colonnades with blue skies and clouds beyond, and down at the very, very bottom on a parquet floor, a white piano.

2. The Palm Beach-style deck with comfy loungers covered in blue-and-white striped mattresses, matching umbrellas to shade the tables and pretty oval pool.

3. The Rhapsody Lounge showroom with wood-backed banquettes in dark pink and purple tapestry fabric and matching carpet.

4. The surprisingly lavish Olympic Spa that offers seaweed body wraps, massages, body-composition analysis, makeup and hair styling and full beauty salon services.

5. The Marco Polo Cafe, the casual buffet-service restaurant with wicker chairs and a sunny tropical atmosphere.

Cunard Dynasty ★ ★ ★ ★

Registry	Panama
Officers	British
Crew	International
Complement	320
GRT	20,000
Length (ft.)	537
Beam (ft.)	74
Draft (ft.)	18
Passengers-Cabins Full	856
Passengers-2/Cabin	800
Passenger Space Ratio	25
Stability Rating	Fair to Good
Seatings	2
Cuisine	Continental
Dress Code	Traditional
Room Service	Yes
Tip	$8 PPPD, 15% automatically added to bar check

Ship Amenities

Outdoor Pool	1
Indoor Pool	0
Jacuzzi	4
Fitness Center	Yes
Spa	Yes
Beauty Shop	Yes
Showroom	Yes
Bars/Lounges	6
Casino	Yes
Shops	Yes
Library	Yes
Child Program	Yes
Self-Service Laundry	No
Elevators	4

Cabin Statistics

Suites	12
Outside Doubles	268
Inside Doubles	120
Wheelchair Cabins	4
Singles	0
Single Surcharge	175-200%
Verandas	10
110 Volt	Yes

CUNARD LINE

Royal Viking Sun ★★★★★★

England's Princess Anne hosted a gala benefit on the ship's pre-inaugural in December, 1988, while it was moored in Greenwich in the middle of the River Thames. Dress instructions were precise: Men were to wear proper black tie attire and women were to wear modest gowns with long sleeves, and no one could photograph the Princess Royal except when she was presenting an award. Shirley noted that actress Joan Collins was appropriately modestly garbed. But la-di-da, you'd never believe what London's cafe society showed up wearing! One striking-looking woman had on a long skirt, all right, but it was totally see-through over the tiniest micro-mini we'd ever been exposed to, and another had on a long dress cut down to expose her cleavage—in the back. Still, the gala was a big success, with the princess dancing in the disco until well past midnight, and the London society types hanging in until nearly dawn. That's probably the latest that disco was ever open!

This extremely spacious ship with its graceful lines introduced the first swim-up bar at sea, as well as the first croquet court seen in many years. She's a quiet, smooth-riding ship. Rubber-mounted engines virtually eliminate vibration, and extra-heavy cabin insulation shuts out extraneous noise. Cabins are large and each includes rheostat light controls on the dressing table and bed lamps, a hairdryer, personal safe, terrycloth robes and TV with VCR. Dining is at an assigned table on a single seating, and the spa is operated by Golden Door Spa at Sea. The clubby wood-paneled Oak Room was to have had a wood-burning fireplace, but the Coast Guard prohibited it; now it glows from a cool red light buried in its ersatz logs. The sophisticated ship's tenders are air-conditioned with rest rooms in case there's an extra-long ride to shore.

CUNARD LINE

DID YOU KNOW?

The Royal Viking Sun garnered international publicity near the end of her 1996 World Cruise when she struck a reef in the Gulf of Aqaba on April 4. The vessel was towed into Sharm el-Sheikh, Egypt, where passengers were off-loaded and returned home or transferred to the QE2, while the ship was held by the Egyptian government who claimed damages of $23.5 million to the reef. On April 30, the ship was released after a promissary note was issued by Cunard and its insurers.

The Brochure Says

"Aboard *Royal Viking Sun*, you will enjoy the incomparable spaciousness and elegance of a ship that was made for classic, longer cruises. Decorated in bright Scandinavian style, her staterooms feature plush furnishings and warm wood tones throughout. Almost half her staterooms boast private verandas where you can watch the sun rise over a distant land."

Translation

This ship was made for cruising with really spacious cabins you could move into for a month or more.

Cabins & Costs

Fantasy Suites: ....A+

Average Price PPPD: $1157 in Europe including airfare.

Any of the penthouse suites would make a fantasy holiday; the Owner's Suite is the most expensive but also most often booked first. Fortunately there are 10 penthouses, each 488 square feet with its own private veranda, floor-to-ceiling windows, separate living room with sofa and chairs, TV/VCR, walk-in closet, big bathroom with tub, stall shower and extra vanity; bedroom with TV/VCR, desk/dresser, lots of built-in cabinetry, personal safe, stocked bar, mini-refrigerator and butler service. The Owner's Suite, if you're curious, is twice as large with two bathrooms and two glass bay windows and a double-sized veranda; the price is available "on request."

Small Splurges: ....A+

Average Price PPPD: $954 in Europe including airfare.

The A Deluxe staterooms make a splendid splurge, at 362 square feet big enough for modest entertaining. You'll have twin beds that can be converted to king-sized, sitting area with curved leather sofa, handsome dark wood and glass cabinetry, large marble bathroom with deep tub and shower, and separate water closet with its own marble washbasin and telephone.

Suitable Standards: ....A

Average Price PPPD: $606 in Europe including airfare.

Standard outside doubles are 191 square feet and have either bathtub or tile shower, along with large windows, twin beds, a loveseat, chair, table and corner cupboard for the TV set. Two outside cabins on Scandinavia Deck are designated singles, and there are four wheelchair-accessible cabins.

Bottom Bunks: ....B

Average Price PPPD: $468 in Europe including airfare.
There are 25 inside cabins measuring 138 square feet each, with two lower beds, large closet, desk/dresser with chair, TV/VCR, and bath with tub/shower combination or shower only.

Royal Viking Sun *can claim, if not the first croquet court at sea, certainly the first in many years.*

Where She Goes

The *Royal Viking Sun* sails around the world from Ft. Lauderdale between January and April, heading through the Panama Canal into the Pacific, via Los Angeles and San Francisco, then to Australia, the Philippines, Hong Kong, China, Japan, Vietnam, Thailand, the Seychelles, Kenya, Yemen, Jordan, Egypt, Lebanon, Israel, Cyprus and into the Mediterranean, before arriving back in Ft. Lauderdale. Summer and fall offers a variety of European and Mediterranean itineraries.

The Bottom Line

We disagree with some of the RVL regulars who complained about Cunard's takeover changing things, because we sailed with the same captain, hotel manager, staff and many crew members we remember from other cruises. The same seamless service in which things materialize just before you realize that's what you want, the genuine warmth and hospitality of the crew, the Scandinavian stewardesses who always remember to fill the ice bucket at 5 p.m.—all were still in place. The *Royal Viking Sun* provides one of the finest cruise experiences available at any price.

Five Great Spaces

1. The Midnight Sun Lounge, lively throughout the day and evening with its big glass windows facing aft; this is where you play team trivia, listen to cabaret entertainers and classical artists and have pre-lunch Bloody Marys.

2. The Norway Lounge, where you can take early morning stretch classes, watch evening production shows and dance with gentleman hosts.

3. The dining room has big glass windows all around and a spiral staircase leading down from the Compass Rose room above; this is where you enjoy beautifully served, well-prepared meals.

4. The Stella Polaris Room, high up and forward with a 180-degree view, serves an elegant afternoon tea and makes a quiet hideaway for pre-dinner cocktails.

5. The romantic 60-seat Venezia Restaurant, serving Italian dinners to passengers who reserve this alternative dining option in advance.

Five Good Reasons to Book This Ship

1. To enjoy some of the best food and service available anywhere on land or sea.

2. To take an around-the-world cruise that calls in such exotic ports as Savusavu, Fiji; Ambon, Indonesia; Keelung, Taiwan; Ho Chi Minh City, Vietnam; Aqaba, Jordan; Lanarca, Cyprus; and Beirut, Lebanon.

3. To spend a Scandinavian Christmas at sea with gingerbread houses, caroling children and fragrant fresh Christmas trees all over the ship.

4. To swim in one of the few lap pools at sea, conveniently located just outside a splendid spa and fitness center.

5. To take a cabin with private veranda and eat breakfast every morning by the sea.

Five Things You Won't Find On Board

1. A caddy in the golf simulator; you can, however, play Pebble Beach, and there is usually a golf pro aboard.

2. A concessionaire who'll take cash except in the Casino; you are requested to charge beauty, massage and photo services and gift shop items.

3. A children's play area, although there is a children's program when enough kids are aboard, as during the Christmas cruise.

4. A nightly midnight buffet; late-night snacks are usually served instead except on designated occasions.

5. A chance to get out of shape; the Golden Door Spa at Sea is on hand with as many as 10 exercise classes a day.

Royal Viking Sun   ★ ★ ★ ★ ★

Registry	Bahamas
Officers	Norwegian
Crew	International
Complement	460
GRT	38,000
Length (ft.)	673
Beam (ft.)	95
Draft (ft.)	23
Passengers-Cabins Full	843
Passengers-2/Cabin	766
Passenger Space Ratio	49.60
Stability Rating	Good to Excellent
Seatings	1
Cuisine	Continental
Dress Code	Traditional
Room Service	Yes
Tip	Included, 15% automatically added to bar check

Ship Amenities

Outdoor Pool	2
Indoor Pool	0
Jacuzzi	1
Fitness Center	Yes
Spa	Yes
Beauty Shop	Yes
Showroom	Yes
Bars/Lounges	3
Casino	Yes
Shops	1
Library	Yes
Child Program	Yes
Self-Service Laundry	Yes
Elevators	4

Cabin Statistics

Suites	19
Outside Doubles	338
Inside Doubles	25
Wheelchair Cabins	4
Singles	2
Single Surcharge	125-140%
Verandas	141
110 Volt	Yes

Sea Goddess I ★★★★★★
Sea Goddess II ★★★★★★

When we asked the founder of Sea Goddess back in 1984 how he came up with the basic concept, an expensive and luxurious alternative to the usual sea vacation, Helge Naarstad, a handsome young Norwegian businessman, said, "I sat down and made a list of all the things I myself would like to do on a cruise." What Helge and his beautiful wife Nini like is, quite simply, the best of everything.

The little extras that you can take for granted aboard Sea Goddess include a special afternoon tea and grandly themed afternoon fruit-and-cheese buffets.

Well, setting out to create your own ideal vacation and give your passengers the best of everything does not necessarily guarantee a profit margin, certainly not when you're the first on the block to come up with such an unusual idea. So a financially-troubled Sea Goddess was acquired by Cunard Line in 1986, which had the wisdom not to change a thing, including the legendary largesse with champagne and caviar. All the alcoholic and non-alcoholic beverages consumed on board (except special-order wines) are included in the basic fare, as are the tips for the exceptionally fine staff. As the forerunner of the super-deluxe small ships, the *Sea Goddesses* are good but far from ideal, something their designers, Pettar Yran and Bjorn Storbraaten, would readily admit. The duo has created the interiors for virtually all the ships in this class—Seabourn, Silversea, *Song of Flower*, *Queen Odyssey*—and acknowledge that each subsequent ship got design refinements they learned from doing the previous one. Cabins are comfortable but not particularly large, closet space is sparse and bathrooms are strictly mainstream rather than upscale-sybaritic as on the Seabourn class vessels. But all in all, these are among only a handful of our very favorite ships at sea.

"A certain world travels on Sea Goddess: people whose lives are diverse, experience wide, tastes high. Worldly company fills the ship with the warmth, elegance and intimacy of a private club."

Translation

This is a Rorschach test. Read it and you'll know if you're right for Sea Goddess and Sea Goddess is right for you.

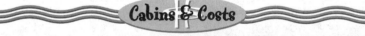

Two suite-rooms combine for a small splurge.

Fantasy Suites: . . . . NA

All the accommodations on board are suites.

Small Splurges: .... A

Average Price PPPD: $971 plus airfare, all tips and beverages included, in the Caribbean. You can either opt for a suite-room or a suite. The latter is two suite-rooms, and would represent a splurge. In 410 square feet you get two entry halls, two full baths, a his and a hers, a large sitting room with two sofas and table and lots of built-in cabinetry, a bedroom with queen-sized bed, and a study or smaller sitting room with two chairs and large windows.

Suitable Standards: .... A

Average Price PPPD: $642 plus airfare, all tips and beverages included, in the Caribbean. The suite-rooms are the standard outside doubles in these ships; there are 58 of them with about 205 square feet each. They contain an entry, bath with tub and shower, sitting area with sofa and chair, coffee/dining table, built-in cabinetry, mini-refrigerator, entertainment center, TV/VCR and stocked bar. The bedroom has a queen-sized bed, night tables, picture windows and vanity counter with stool and drawers. Closet space is adequate but not generous.

Bottom Bunks: .... NA

See "Suitable Standards," above.

Where She Goes

Sea Goddess I and II sail all over the world, alternating schedules that include the Caribbean, Alaska, the Med, Northern Europe, Greek Isles, Southeast Asia and the Orient.

The Bottom Line

The bathrooms and closets could be larger and the suites could have a private veranda, but there's little else we would change about these wonderful ships. They're not stuffy and not pretentious. Extra little surprises may include meals created by famous chefs (who just might be aboard to cook them for you), wine-tasting with famous vintners and unique shore excursions called Sea Goddess Exclusives. These ships fulfill the fantasies of sybaritic couples of all ages, but singles may find them frustrating.

CUNARD LINE

Sea Goddess I ★★★★★★
Sea Goddess II ★★★★★★

Registry	Norway
Officers	Norwegian
Crew	International
Complement	89
GRT	4,250
Length (ft.)	344
Beam (ft.)	47
Draft (ft.)	14
Passengers-Cabins Full	116
Passengers-2/Cabin	116
Passenger Space Ratio	36.63
Stability Rating	Good
Seatings	1
Cuisine	Contemporary
Dress Code	Traditional
Room Service	Yes
Tip	Included

Ship Amenities

Outdoor Pool	1
Indoor Pool	0
Jacuzzi	1
Fitness Center	Yes
Spa	No
Beauty Shop	Yes
Showroom	No
Bars/Lounges	3
Casino	Yes
Shops	0
Library	Yes
Child Program	No
Self-Service Laundry	No
Elevators	1

Cabin Statistics

Suites	58
Outside Doubles	0
Inside Doubles	0
Wheelchair Cabins	0
Singles	0
Single Surcharge	175-200%
Verandas	0
110 Volt	Yes

Vistafjord

★★★★★

The suite life: Every day at noon, Martina brings another big basket of fresh fruit swathed in cellophane and tied with a ribbon, "like an Easter basket, no?" she says, even if you haven't opened the one from yesterday yet. And every day at 5:30, she arrives with a silver tray of canapes—a bit of caviar or goose liver pâté, a shrimp with a feathery sprig of fresh dill, a curl of smoked salmon, strawberries dipped in chocolate, to go with the cocktails you can mix in your own wet bar. If you want to lunch on your private veranda, you can order from a room service menu or from the lunch menu from the dining room (always arranged on your bar in its own leather cover every morning). You can soak in a private hot tub on the veranda as you watch the sun go down, or relax in your private sauna, just off the living room in one of the two most lavish suites at sea, PH 1 and PH 2 on the Vistafjord.

Expect excellent food from executive chef Karl Winkler and his staff, who turn out luscious beauties like these.

The *Vistafjord* was introduced in 1973, eight years after her sister ship *Sagafjord*, and the pair sailed for Norwegian American Cruises before being acquired by Cunard in 1983. The ship is unique for its almost equal mix of North American, British and German passengers, plus a sprinkling of other Europeans, a few Australians and an occasional passenger or two from Asia. The passenger list is usually made up of 50 to 70 repeaters, and many of the Germans and British who sail regularly have become friends over the years. The *Sagafjord* was retired in 1996.

DID YOU KNOW?

On an average 14-day cruise, the Vistafjord serves 13,000 pounds of meat, 75 pounds of Russian caviar, 36,000 fresh eggs, 1800 quarts of ice cream and 13,690 bottles of beer.

The Brochure Says

"High atop the ship, *Vistafjord's* new glass-enclosed penthouse suites become a 'box seat' for the grandest views of sea and sky that cruising has to offer."

Translation

From these glass perches and big private balconies, you can even look down on the captain when he's on the bridge wing.

Cabins & Costs

The lavish new duplex penthouses include a private veranda with outdoor whirlpool plus an en suite private sauna and two marble bathrooms.

Fantasy Suites: .... A+

Average Price PPPD: $1401 in Europe including airfare.

Two brand-new penthouse duplex suites were added during the last refit, each of them 827 square feet with a glass window wall forward on the upper level that gives a captain's-eye view of the scenery ahead, and a huge private veranda with natural teak decking, a hot tub and plenty of room for a cocktail party. A private sauna, tiled shower and separate large marble and tile bath is also upstairs. Inside the big living room are two sofas and two easy chairs in dark green, an oval coffee table, wet bar with stocked liquor cabinet and mini-refrigerator, an entertainment center with color TV/VCR and CD player with a full stock of CDs and new hardback books, a deluxe Scrabble set, a Nordic Track treadmill. Outside, a forward private deck covered in royal blue astroturf looks down on the bridge wings. A spiral staircase leads down to the bedroom with its own private veranda and a large bath with Jacuzzi tub, double basins, toilet and bidet.

Small Splurges: . . . . B+

Average Price PPPD: $713 in Europe including airfare.
The Category B outside doubles with private veranda on Sun Deck have marble bathrooms with tubs, king-sized beds and mirrored dressing table, mini-refrigerator, TV/VCR, personal safe and terrycloth robes.

Suitable Standards: . . . . B

Average Price PPPD: $541 in Europe including airfare.
Category H outside double cabins have twin beds in a fairly small cabin, a chair, dresser/desk, marble bathroom (some with tub and shower, some with shower only). There are a number of single cabins available in various price ranges, including some with private veranda.

Bottom Bunks: . . . . B

Average Price PPPD: $521 in Europe including airfare.
With the refurbishment, even the lowest-priced inside category J cabins are prettily furnished with the new marble bathrooms (some have tub and shower, some shower only) and two lower beds, plus desk/dresser, chair, adequate closet space, TV/VCR, robes and safe.

DID YOU KNOW?

The Vistafjord *is "The Love Boat" of Europe; it starred in the German TV series "Traumschiff"–"Dreamboat"–as well as the 1983 Jon Voight/Millie Perkins feature film,* Table for Five. *Kevin Costner also played a small role in that film before he was famous.*

Where She Goes

The *Vistafjord* makes a lazy, easy circuit through the world's warm waters, starting in the Caribbean in January, moving through the Panama Canal to Los Angeles in early February, then across the Pacific to Tahiti and back, and south to the Amazon in March. She crosses the Atlantic in April for a summer of Mediterranean and Northern Europe cruises, covers Ireland to Iceland in August, the Black Sea and the Holy Land in the autumn, then sails via the Canary Islands back into the Caribbean in time for Christmas.

The Bottom Line

This is a classic, traditional vessel with nothing harsh, glitzy or noisy, no hard edges, and a staff and crew that have worked together for a long time. The recent renovation brings her into the forefront of traditional luxury ships, but a few areas still need improvement, primarily the food and service in the Lido Cafe, which is still not large enough for the numbers of people who use it. The overflow people take their breakfast trays into the ballroom and risk getting food all over the expensive new carpeting and upholstery. With just a little more effort and a larger staff, this ship could rival its new running mate *Royal Viking Sun*.

Five Favorite Places

1. Tivoli, a romantic 40-seat Italian restaurant on the balcony above the nightclub, serves as an alternative to the dining room by advance reservation; the food is delicious.

2. The North Cape Bar, intimate and evocative, in gray and taupe with a finely meshed black spiderweb pattern in the upholstery and putty leather barstools along the rosewood bar.

3. The library, with its comfortable dark green leather sofas, Oriental rug, mahogany and glass bookcases, gold drapes with knotted ropes and tassels, is very clubby but rich-looking, as is the adjoining writing room with black and gold fabric on the chairs and a pair of computers on writing tables in the corner.

4. The pale and elegant Garden Lounge, all in ivory and very light green, with tile-topped tables, bleached wood walls, sage and ivory-striped silk curtains with rope ties.

5. The dining room is leafy green with wood-framed chairs covered in green and gold striped silk, the carpet green with pale pink flowers, and lots of tables for two in the room.

Five Good Reasons to Book This Ship

1. The new penthouse suites high atop the ship are the most sybaritic at sea; nothing else can equal them.

2. It's a classy and classic ship with a Continental flair.

3. The traditional Bavarian Brunch, with aquavit and beer, sausages and sauerkraut, roast suckling pig and German potato salad, served once on every cruise; the crew always feasts on one as well.

4. To take an exotic winter cruise like the Los Angeles-to-Papeete itinerary that calls in Hawaii, American Samoa and the Cook Islands before arriving in Tahiti.

5. To dine on Chef Karl Winkler's salmon with horseradish crust in the dining room or sample the splendid Zuppa Valdostana in the Tivoli restaurant.

Salmon with Horseradish Crust
6 servings

6 six-ounce fresh salmon fillets, boneless and skinless

Salt and freshly ground white pepper

Horseradish Crust, prepared and chilled

Season salmon slices with salt and pepper and arrange them on a buttered baking dish. Top each with a piece of crust the same size as the fish. Bake in hot oven (450 degrees) for about 10 minutes or until crust is browned and fish cooked through. Chef Winkler serves it with a light white wine and chive sauce.

To make the Horseradish Crust, combine the following ingredients in a mixing bowl:

8 slices day-old bread, crusts removed, made into crumbs

6 ounces butter, softened

1/2 cup grated horseradish

1/2 cup smoked salmon cut into cubes

1/2 cup chopped fresh dill and parsley mixed

1/2 cup sour cream

Juice of one lemon

Put a large square of waxed paper or plastic wrap on a tray, spread the crust mixture on it and top with a second square. With a rolling pin, roll the mixture to a thickness of 1/4 inch, then refrigerate until set. Cut into six pieces the same size as the salmon fillets.

Five Things You Won't Find On Board

1. Enough space in the Lido cafe for the number of passengers who want to eat there.

2. A nonsmoking table in the Tivoli restaurant (although the sympathetic maître d'hotel will try to seat you by nonsmoking neighbors).

3. A nonsmoking table in the nightclub.

4. A lot of casino action; the small casino has a roulette table, two blackjack tables and 28 slot machines.

5. Single-language announcements; everything, including newspapers and daily programs, are in both English and German.

Vistafjord ★★★★★

Registry	**Bahamas**
Officers	**Norwegian**
Crew	**European**
Complement	**379**
GRT	**24,492**
Length (ft.)	**628**
Beam (ft.)	**82**
Draft (ft.)	**27**
Passengers-Cabins Full	**730**
Passengers-2/Cabin	**679**
Passenger Space Ratio	**36.07**
Stability Rating	**Good to Excellent**
Seatings	**1**
Cuisine	**Continental**
Dress Code	**Traditional**
Room Service	**Yes**
Tip	**$9 PPPD, 15% automatically added to bar check**

Ship Amenities

Outdoor Pool	**1**
Indoor Pool	**1**
Jacuzzi	**1**
Fitness Center	**Yes**
Spa	**Yes**
Beauty Shop	**Yes**
Showroom	**Yes**
Bars/Lounges	**3**
Casino	**Yes**
Shops	**Yes**
Library	**Yes**
Child Program	**No**
Self-Service Laundry	**Yes**
Elevators	**6**

Cabin Statistics

Suites	**16**
Outside Doubles	**254**
Inside Doubles	**33**
Wheelchair Cabins	**6**
Singles	**71**
Single Surcharge	**150%**
Verandas	**34**
110 Volt	**Yes**

DELPHIN SEEREISEN

Postfach 10 04 07 Offenbach/Main, Germany, 63004
☎ *(699) 840-3811*

The dolphin logo at the bottom of the ship's pool indicates its worldwide warm-weather itineraries.

History . . . .

This large German travel company has a longterm lease (through the year 2001) on the newly refurbished *Kazakhstan II*, owned by Black Sea Shipping, which is marketed almost exclusively to German-speaking passengers, but when we were aboard in the Caribbean, it carried Germans, Austrians, Swiss, Poles, French, Greek, and a sprinkling of both North and South Americans.

Kazakhstan II

The Russian ships we saw in the 1980s in various ports of the world always looked faintly threatening with that red flag and gold hammer-and-sickle on the stack. And inside they were utilitarian with a no-nonsense, no-tipping staff that could get grumpy at times. But after the breakup of the U.S.S.R., the Ukrainians, notably Black Sea Shipping, controlled the majority of the newer passenger ships, and with western-based joint venture travel firms, they upgraded the fleet to world-class standards, managing at the same time to keep the prices down in many cases.

The *Kazakhstan II* was originally built as the just plain *Kazakhstan* in Finland's Wartsila yard in 1975, around the same time the original three Royal Viking ships were being built, and it has very similar lines. But after a 1994 renovation in Bremerhaven, the ship has turned into a real dazzler—spotlessly clean and very elegant, but with a certain charming period quality (the cocktail of the day is a Sidecar, something few American bartenders under 60 have ever heard of).

The Brochure Says

"Mehr Komfort, mehr Spass, merh Erlaben: Den gestiegenen Anspruchen der Gaste entspricht die neu "Kaz" mit einem Erlebniskonzept, das das ganze Schiff umfasst."

Translation

"More comfort, more space, more experiences: the enriching fulfillment the guests talk about with the new "Kaz" with only one concept idea, that the whole experience on board is a total delight."

Cabins & Costs

Fantasy Suites: .... A

Average Price PPPD: $370 plus airfare.
The top suites are #1010 and 1011, very large suites with living room, dressing room and separate bedroom, pale green carpets, curved sofa and two chairs plus several pale wood chairs and a small TV set, then another small TV set and a lot of storage in the dressing room, then a bedroom with twin beds and a chest in between, plus a marble bath with several colors of marble arranged in a mosaic pattern, a bathtub and separate stall shower.

Small Splurges: .... B

Average Price PPPD: $325 plus airfare.
Junior suites like # 1014 are very spacious cabins with double bed, sofa, table, chair and two dressers, plus plenty of storage and a built-in hair dryer. The bathroom is tile with shower only.

Suitable Standards: .... A

Average Price PPPD: $281 plus airfare.
Category I cabins are outside doubles with lots of space, twin beds, a wooden armoire and wooden dresser and a tile bath with shower.

Bottom Bunks: C

Average Price PPPD: $118 plus airfare.
The lowest-priced inside category is S, with two lower beds, dresser and chair and tile bath with shower.

Where She Goes

The *Kazakhstan II* spends the first half of the year going around the globe from Italy to Germany, then cruises in Europe and the Mediterranean for the summer and fall before heading for the Caribbean for winter.

The Bottom Line

The main problem is the extremely steep stairs around the vessel, which require concentration for older passengers ascending or descending them. The shipboard announcements are made only in German, and the daily program printed only in German, but most members of the Russian and Ukrainian staff speak English as well as German. The upside is that the prices for very nice, newly redecorated inside cabins hover down near the $100-a-day mark on long cruises.

Fielding's Five

Five *Gemütlich* Spots

1. The Sky Club Disco, the ship's nightclub, on the topmost desk, reclaimed deck area to make this big handsome room with lavender carpet and lavender upholstery and

leather tub chairs and a long, glamorous, curved marble bar, glass dome, wood dance floor and DJ booth.

2. The Boat Deck, covered in natural teak with a sheltered overhang, ping pong tables, a mosaic tile swimming pool with a blue tile dolphin in the bottom, a children's wading pool, white plastic tables and chairs and a long curved pink marble bar.

3. The Delphin Lounge, a gorgeous room with golden yellow upholstery on chairs and banquettes, a navy and yellow carpet, a small splashing fountain in the room's center, tub chairs and banquette sofas and lovely art.

4. The Grand Salon music bar with its parquet wood floor, bar with black leather swivel stools, tub chairs and curved banquettes.

5. The Lido Bar serves a buffet for continental breakfast and lunch, with white wicker tub chairs made cushy with handsome upholstered cushions and booth banquettes along the window walls on both sides.

Five Good Reasons to Book This Ship

1. It's one of the most elegant vessels sailing today.

2. It literally sails around the world in a leisurely pattern without repeating a port to anywhere the sun is shining.

3. You can be a loner without offending anyone by simply saying you don't speak the language.

4. You can make the longest and most thorough world cruise anyone offers, from Genoa to Bremerhaven in 150 days.

5. You can learn German by ear, talking with Germans, which is much easier than trying to read it.

Kazakhstan II ★★★★

Registry	Ukraine
Officers	Ukrainian
Crew	Ukrainian
Complement	250
GRT	15,410
Length (ft.)	512
Beam (ft.)	72
Draft (ft.)	19
Passengers-Cabins Full	640
Passengers-2/Cabin	470
Passenger Space Ratio	32.78
Stability Rating	Good
Seatings	1
Cuisine	European
Dress Code	Traditional
Room Service	Yes
Tip	$10 PPPD

Ship Amenities

Outdoor Pool	2
Indoor Pool	0
Jacuzzi	0
Fitness Center	Yes
Spa	No
Beauty Shop	Yes
Showroom	Yes
Bars/Lounges	5
Casino	No
Shops	2
Library	Yes
Child Program	No
Self-Service Laundry	No
Elevators	2

Cabin Statistics

Suites	2
Outside Doubles	128
Inside Doubles	105
Wheelchair Cabins	0
Singles	0
Single Surcharge	NA
Verandas	0
110 Volt	No

DELTA QUEEN STEAMBOAT COMPANY

30 Robin Street Wharf, New Orleans, LA 70130
☎ *(504) 586-0631, (800) 543-7637*

A New Orleans jazz band parade around the dining rooms on special evenings, here aboard the **Delta Queen.**

History . . . .

In 1890, 28-year-old Gordon C. Greene bought his first riverboat, the 150-foot-long *H.K. Bedford*, and married Mary Becker, who began working alongside him in the pilot house. Later Captain Mary B. Greene, one of the few women to earn both a pilot's and a Master's license on the river, was often in command of Greene Line's new *Greenland*, which carried passengers to the 1904 St. Louis World's Fair as well handling the company's more profitable freight hauling. In the 1930s Greene Line added a steamboat for passenger cruises when diesel towboats took away their freight business.

After World War II, Gordon's son Tom paid $46,000 for the historic *Delta Queen*, built in 1926 to cruise California's Sacramento delta, and had it crated up and barged through the Panama Canal to the Mississippi; it began overnight passenger service in 1947.

In 1976, the company launched the new *Mississippi Queen*, and the *American Queen* made its debut in June, 1995.

The three-vessel fleet enjoys a high year-round occupancy rate, 93 to 96 percent a year. The 106-year-old company, which also owns American Hawaii Cruises, is traded on NASDAQ under the corporate name American Classic Voyages.

—*Delta Queen* is the only National Historic Monument that travels at eight miles an hour (riverboats measure in miles instead of knots).

—*Mississippi Queen* was designed by James Gardner, co-designer of Cunard's *Queen Elizabeth 2*.

—*American Queen* is the only vessel in history to be christened with a giant bottle of Tabasco pepper sauce. The 21.3 gallons of spicy sauce went into the Mississippi, "but we were told it wasn't a large enough amount to endanger the fish," says a spokeswoman.

Concept . . . .

The line intends to provide a warm, sincere, all-American experience with generous dollops of river scenery and history, a friendly and mostly-young American crew, a 19th century ambience and, according to former line president Jeffrey Krida, "good solid American food, hearty American fare with some regional dishes as the boats go through the country."

Signatures . . . .

A steam-powered calliope that can be heard for five miles up and down the river signals a Delta Queen steamboat's arrival and departure. The bright red paddlewheel tosses up drops of water that hang and glisten in the sunlight for a moment before falling back into the yellow-brown, mud-colored river. "Riverlorians," historians who give passengers infinite details about the route, scenery and river, are aboard every sailing.

Two long-standing traditions are the annual steamboat race between the *Delta Queen* and the *Belle of Louisville* at Kentucky Derby time and the Great Steamboat Race between the *Mississippi Queen* and the *Delta Queen* that recreates the famous contest between the *Natchez* and the *Robert E. Lee*. Book well ahead to be aboard one of these coveted sailings.

DID YOU KNOW?

When the Delta Queen looked as if it would be banned for its wooden superstructure by federal SOLAS (Safety of Life At Sea) legislation in 1973, congress granted it a nick-of-time reprieve at the end of what was to have been its last voyage.

Gimmicks . . . .

Mike Fink Day with its "floozie" competition and seafood buffet is a crowd-pleaser, along with Calliope Capers, when each passenger has an opportunity to play the steam calliope on deck. While the vessels have no casinos, real money is bet on Steamboat Races, bingo and Dollar Bill Drawings, where each passenger signs a bill and puts it in a winner-take-all pot.

> ## INSIDER TIP
>
> *Don't call them ships; these are boats.*

Who's the Competition . . . .

Delta Queen Steamboat enjoys a unique niche because of its midwestern river itineraries and very popular vessels, although some other small U.S. flag companies like Alaska Sightseeing/Cruise West with the *Spirit of '98* and the new *Queen of the West* from American West Steamboat Company also offer river cruises aboard steamboat replicas in the Pacific Northwest and Alaska. In Canada, little St. Lawrence Cruise Lines provides replica steamboat cruises on the St. Lawrence and Ottowa Rivers aboard the *Canadian Empress*.

Who's Aboard . . . .

Delta Queen is frank about concentrating on over-50 passengers, saying they don't need younger passengers or families with children to fill the boats, since the entertainment would have to be changed to appeal to a under-50 crowd. Some 70 percent of all its passengers are cruise veterans, many of them also Alaska cruisers. The average passenger age is 64, and there are a fair number of singles, mostly female. Some 26 percent of Delta Queen Steamboat's passengers come from California and the Pacific Northwest; three percent come from Europe, Australia and New Zealand.

Who Should Go . . . .

Anyone, especially foreigners, who want to get in touch with the real American heartland; people who like banjoes, sing-alongs and respectful young waiters and waitresses who always have a minute to chat; anyone who loves to tour stately homes and gardens; and travelers who want what the line calls "security, safety and predictability." (We were aboard the *Delta Queen* during the 1992 Los Angeles riots and had trouble imagining such a disturbance that could be threatening our residence as we cruised languidly along the Ohio River.)

Who Should Not Go . . . .

Small children or restless teenagers, although a bright, history-oriented preteen might have a wonderful time. Wheelchair-users should book only the *Mississippi* or *American Queens*, which have elevators, and avoid the *Delta Queen*, which does not.

INSIDER TIP

With so many repeat passengers sailing, you can count on new itineraries to sell out completely within a few days of being announced.

The Lifestyle . . . .

Steamboating is an amiable blend of down-home Americana, a history tour and a visit to Grandmother's house or a favorite Victorian bed-and-breakfast with plenty of books, games and puzzles. Self-service snacks can be found around the ship between the copious meals, and singing along to old songs, while not required, usually happens anyhow.

The river itself turns out to be as beguiling a sight as a campfire or clouds drifting overhead. Here and there white cranes, said to be reincarnated old riverboatmen, sit on the broken snags of a half-submerged tree trunks, watching the boats go by in the sunlight. But when a fog comes up, they fly from one snag to the next, resting on each until they are certain the pilot has seen them and knows to keep clear of the tree that could puncture the hull of his boat.

The boats tie up frequently at ports of call, historic small towns or cities where passengers can usually walk to points of interest if they don't want to spring for the optional shore excursions.

Dress is casual by day, only slightly more dressy in the evenings, although many men don jacket and tie for the captain's dinner. The two larger boats have two assigned meal sittings, while the *Delta Queen* has only one.

There are no casinos aboard any of the boats, although they may stop along the river near a moored casino boat so passengers can get off to gamble if they wish.

DID YOU KNOW?

A new company policy adopted several years ago praises crew accomplishments rather than punishing the failures. When hiring, the line looks for individuals with pleasing personalities. "We believe you can train people to do the technical aspects of the job more easily than training them to be nice people," Krida says.

Wardrobe . . . .

The dress code could be described as "clean and decent" with comfortable shoes and casual wear during the daytime and something only slightly fancier for the evenings. Trips ashore during the warmest months call for lightweight cotton or linen fabrics. Since there is a small swimming pool aboard the *Mississippi* and *American Queens*, a bathing suit might also be in order.

INSIDER TIP

Since the boats do not travel more than 12 miles away from shore at any time, there is no doctor or nurse required to be on board.

Bill of Fare. . . . . B+

Breakfasts with a southern accent include grits, ham and hot breads, along with fancier New Orleans brunch fare such as eggs Benedict and eggs Sardou. Lunches offer light fare like a New Orleans fried shrimp poor boy sandwich as well as more substantial dishes such as braised short ribs with vegetables. The normal dinner menu offers three appetizers, two soups, two or three salads and five main dishes, including a Heart Smart main dish and/or vegetarian offering, along with beef, chicken and fish. The vessels' hot breads and desserts are particularly delicious, and portions are medium to large. Special diets can be arranged at time of booking, and some simple dishes not listed on the menu may also be requested from the servers if you don't find what you want in the usual fare.

Between meals, you can help yourself to a great hot dog (with cooked or raw onions, sauerkraut, chili sauce and other condiments) from a rolling cart on deck near the outdoor bar aboard the *Mississippi* and *American Queens* or a basket of freshly popped corn in the indoor bar on all three boats, along with soft ice cream, fresh lemonade, and 24-hour iced tea and hot coffee.

INSIDER TIP

If you're boarding one of the boats in New Orleans and have your own or a rental car along, you can park free in a covered shed at the Robin Street Wharf, where passengers embark.

Showtime. . . . .

Quartets perform barbershop or Broadway melodies, soloists belt out cabaret numbers and banjo players, pianists, riverboat gamblers, harpists and clog dancers may appear at any time. A church gospel choir is sometimes brought aboard for a rousing evening of music, and Mark Twain has been known to show up on stage in his white linen suit with a few well-chosen remarks. Many on-board activities are passenger-generated, from making and flying kites to lessons in Victorian parlor crafts.

Discounts. . . . .

Early booking discounts from 10 to 15 percent are offered on certain sailings for passengers booking and making a deposit six months in advance. Some discounted air add-ons can also be booked in conjunction with a Delta Queen Steamboat sailing.

INSIDER TIP

On these early-to-bed vessels, pre-lunch Bloody Mary specials are apt to be put out at 10:30 a.m., cocktail hour starts at 4:30 p.m. and the Night Owls Club gathers for "late night entertainment" at 10 p.m.

The Bottom Line

To sit and watch the paddlewheel turning on a genuine historic river vessel is as good as it gets.

These very popular cruises draw a number of repeat passengers who enjoy the low-key excursions into the heart of America and are willing to pay somewhat higher tariffs than on a typical Caribbean cruise. The end product, however, is so unique that it cannot be compared to any other cruise.

With the new *American Queen* in place, this line is operating at the peak of its form. Over the last 10 years, we've watched "steamboating" evolve into a precise and polished vacation that just seems to get better and better for that spectrum of Americans—and we don't feel it should be limited to over-50s—who like Dixieland jazz and sing-alongs, kite flying and calliope music, and get misty-eyed when they hear "God Bless America."

American Queen   ⚓⚓⚓⚓⚓

On the good ship Serendipity you can go back to a magical summer afternoon in childhood, discovering hidden treasures in Grandmother's parlor, swinging in a creaky wooden porch swing, drinking tart-sweet lemonade and stealing an extra cookie when no one's looking. We barely managed to resist the temptation to take a book and lie stomach-down on the cool, polished hardwood floors to read. The atmosphere is so beguiling that we don't even mind the two meal seatings. Big family dinners in the south always had two seatings, adults first and children and some of the meal preparers later. Country roads can take you home on water as well as land.

The biggest steamship on the river doesn't feel like a behemoth when you're aboard, although the 89.3-foot width—21 feet more than the *Mississippi Queen*—gives the *American Queen* a vast sense of space. So counterbalancing the spaciousness and grandeur of the dining room with its tall gold-framed mirrors, crystal chandeliers and tables set comfortably apart are a number of smaller, more intimate spaces like the pretty little Captain's Bar off the dining room, the Gentlemen's Card Room and the Ladies' Parlor. Screened-in porches with wicker chairs are spotted at intervals around the boat.

A plus or minus, depending on the weather, is that many of the cabins open directly onto the outer decks rather than an interior hallway.

INSIDER TIP

Those A-category cabins 403 and 404 on Observation Deck with private screened porches look more appealing than they really are on a hot day, when the breeze is blocked by cabins on either side. It's cooler to sit out on the open deck.

The Brochure Says

"...entire towns will turn out to celebrate her arrival...the *American Queen* is the most elaborate paddlewheeler ever."

Translation

She looks like a gigantic floating wedding cake, except that instead of a bride and groom placed atop the cake, there are two black metal smokestacks with fancy "feathered" tops that sit 109 feet above the river and an all-glass wheelhouse with rococo birdcage trim situated between them. The folks will gather to watch, because in order to pass under some of the lower bridges, the captain has to flatten the smokestacks and lower the wheelhouse. One bridge is so low, the riverlorian says, that the captain, controlling the vessel from a wing bridge, has to get down on his knees to clear it.

Cabins & Costs

Fantasy Suites: .... A

Average Price PPPD: $589 plus airfare.

Any of the AAA suites can transport you back to the golden days of steamboating, but we especially like the Mississippi Queen suite, # 352, very ornate with a queen-sized bed with carved headboard, bath with tub and shower, a vanity mirror trimmed in Venetian glass beading, velvet and brocade draperies over the hanging closet that look just like the draperies Scarlett O'Hara turned into a new dress in *Gone With The Wind*, and a small private balcony overlooking the paddlewheel.

Small Splurges: .... A

Average Price PPPD: $425 plus air add-ons.

An A Outside Superior cabin has a lot of space inside; several even have private screen porches (which overlook the promenade so are not really secluded). You'll have one or two easy chairs, a dresser, queen or twin beds, French doors to the deck, big windows and mirrors, adequate storage space, and spacious bath with tub and shower.

Suitable Standards: .... B+

Average Price PPPD: $359 plus air add-on.

The standard outside doubles, including seven of the nine wheelchair-accessible cabins, have big bathrooms with black-and-white mosaic tile floors, twin beds in an L-configuration, sometimes a wicker chair, a desk and highboy with drawers and beautiful period wallpaper. There are also eight cabins designated singles.

Bottom Bunks: .... C+

Average Price PPPD: $249 plus airfare add-ons.

The lowest-priced inside cabins are cozy but livable accommodations on the Promenade Deck, with twin beds placed close together because the room is narrow. The wallpaper is elegant, and there's a handsome old-fashioned dresser, a chair and a bathroom with black-and-white mosaic tile floor and shower only.

Where She Goes

American Queen starts the year with a series of Dixieland Festival roundtrip sailings from New Orleans in January, followed by Big Band cruises in February and March, then heads north into the heartland for summer sailings from St. Paul, Cincinnati, St. Louis and Pittsburgh.

The Bottom Line

We think this is one of the best see-America cruises possible, especially recommended for foreign visitors who want a genuine American experience instead of a theme park ersatz America. While the line concentrates on marketing to the over-50 group, we could see a family with bright 10-12 year-olds really grooving on this cruise, despite the absence of video games and flashy entertainment. The ship is delightful for anyone who enjoys bed-and-breakfast establishments, but the food, entertainment and privacy are even better. It's worth every penny of the fairly pricey tariff!

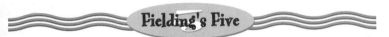

Fielding's Five

Five Evocative Places

1. The Front Porch, a glassed-in, air conditioned porch with wicker rocking chairs, carefully painted to look well worn on the seat and along the arms, with old-fashioned game tables, much-read copies of Tom Swift and Bobbsey Twins books, and help-yourself lemonade and cookies.

2. The Gentleman's Cardroom with green velvet sofas, a stuffed bear, a miniature billiards table, and a stereopticon with naughty French Postcards.

3. The Ladies' Parlor with its Victorian furniture and painted screens, a morning glory Victrola with round Edison wax cylinder recordings, a big table with a Ouija board on it and a screen porch with wicker chairs.

4. The Mark Twain Gallery, opulent, cool and dark, a perfect Victorian parlor with its Tiffany stained glass lampshades, bookcases and busts, and fringed lampshades. On either side, glass windows look down into the airy, sunlit dining room below, inspired by the grand restaurants aboard 19th century steamboats.

5. The Grand Saloon, with a balcony level of private boxes entered by doors labeled for such luminaries as Ralph Waldo Emerson and Harriet Beecher Stowe, a wooded stage with footlights and a main floor with banquettes, marble-topped tables and Victorian chairs.

Five Off-the-Wall Things to Do On Board

1. Drop a penny into the coin-operated stereopticon in the Gentleman's Card Room to flip through an innocently naughty set of turn-of-the-century French postcards.

2. Sit down in the Ladies' Parlor with a couple of friends and ask the Ouija board some questions.

3. Hang out in the engine room with the amiable engineers and watch the pair of 1932 steam engines salvaged from a submerged barge in Mississippi propel the bright red paddlewheel. (Get there from a marked doorway in the Engine Room Bar.)

4.   Earn a Vox Calliopus certificate by playing five consecutive notes on the steam calliope when the daily program lists Calliope Capers.

5.   Go fly a kite you've made yourself from the aft Calliope Bar aboard, but watch out for that kite-eating bridge near Oak Alley Plantation.

Five Good Reasons To Book This Boat

1.   It's more fun than visiting your favorite aunt.

2.   The yummy bread pudding with caramel sauce.

3.   To have a serious chat with Mark Twain.

4.   To enjoy the ambience of an antiques-filled bed-and-breakfast without having to tiptoe around.

5.   To sit in the Engine Room Bar watching the red paddlewhheels churning and sing "Proud Mary"…"big wheel keep on turning …"

American Queen ⚓⚓⚓⚓

Registry	U.S.
Officers	American
Crew	American
Complement	170
GRT	3,707
Length (ft.)	418
Beam (ft.)	90
Draft (ft.)	8.5
Passengers-Cabins Full	436
Passengers-2/Cabin	436
Passenger Space Ratio	NA
Stability Rating	Excellent
Seatings	2
Cuisine	American
Dress Code	Casual
Room Service	Yes
Tip	$10 PPPD, 15% automatically added to bar checks

Ship Amenities

Outdoor Pool	1
Indoor Pool	0
Jacuzzi	0
Fitness Center	Yes
Spa	No
Beauty Shop	Yes
Showroom	Yes
Bars/Lounges	2
Casino	No
Shops	1
Library	Yes
Child Program	No
Self-Service Laundry	Yes
Elevators	2

Cabin Statistics

Suites	24
Outside Doubles	144
Inside Doubles	54
Wheelchair Cabins	9
Singles	8
Single Surcharge	150-175%
Verandas	29
110 Volt	Yes

Delta Queen ⚓⚓⚓⚓⚓

You can arrange to cheer (and put money on) two famous races during a nine-day cruise if you can be aboard the Delta Queen for the annual steamboat race with the Belle of Louisville (one-and-a-half hours for 12 miles), then add on a visit to the Kentucky Derby three days later (two minutes for a mile-and-a-quarter). The year we did it was 1992, concurrent with the Los Angeles riots, and it was hard to imagine someone might be burning our house down while we were relaxing in the friendly, slow-moving heartland. PS: Our place was still standing when we got back home after the Derby, so our only losses were on the hosses.

This is a genuine National Historic Landmark listed on the National Register of Historic Places, the only national monument that steams along at eight miles an hour. It took an act of Congress to keep her in business (see "Footnote" under "History"). She's slow-moving, far from spacious (the dining room doubles as the show lounge and lecture hall) and hasn't the most luxurious accommodations on the river (those belong to her newer sister *American Queen*) but love and devotion from her dedicated fans have kept her afloat since 1948 and no one had better murmur about retiring her.

DID YOU KNOW?

They say the ghost of Mary "Ma" Greene still haunts the Delta Queen. If so, better avoid the bars, since Ma was a strict teetotaler and would never let liquor be served on board during her lifetime. The first time they installed a bar after her death, the steamboat was forcefully rammed by a barge which surprised officers noted was named the Mary Greene.

The Brochure Says

"Walk the decks where a princess or a president may have strolled before you. Immerse yourself in the inspiring beauty, nostalgic adventure and captivating history that so wonderfully exemplify the grand American tradition of Steamboatin'."

Translation

Famous previous passengers, many of them remembered with brass plaques fitted to the doors of the cabins they occupied, include Princess Margaret, Lady Bird Johnson, Jimmy Carter, Van Johnson, Helen Hayes and opera stars Roberta Peters and Jan Peerce.

Cabins & Costs

Fantasy Suites: .... B+

Average Price PPPD: $589 plus air add-ons.
The AAA Outside Superior Suites, a pair of posh cabins all the way forward on the Sun Deck with queen-sized beds, sitting area, big mirrors, bath with tub and shower and doors that open right onto the deck. There are two others, slightly smaller, down on Cabin Deck aft, that would do in a pinch.

Small Splurges: .... B

Average Price PPPD: $425 plus air add-ons.
Next best are the pair of AA Outside Luxury Suites located aft on Sun Deck with queen-sized bed, windows, a chair, a desk and bath with shower.

Suitable Standards: C

Average Price PPPD: $359 plus air add-ons.
All the cabins aboard are outsides, so in this category we'll look at some of the mid-range outside doubles, leaving the bottom-priced outsides for the category below. You should generally expect twins or double bed, mirror and bath with shower. Chairs are at a premium in these small cabins, but the decor is attractive and you won't suffer.

Bottom Bunks: C

Average Price PPPD: $155 plus air add-ons.
The very cheapest cabins aboard are the category F outside staterooms with extra-wide lower bed and upper berth. The cabins themselves are narrower than the others on board (which can be very narrow indeed; people were smaller or less demanding in the 1920s). Anyhow, the downside is, there's a partly obstructed river view; just open the door and wander down the deck to improve it. Tain't no big thang.

Where She Goes

The *Delta Queen* celebrates Christmas and New Years on a Memphis-Nashville-New Orleans run with guest stars Pete Fountain, Art Linkletter, Tammy Wynette, Steve Allen and the singing Modernaires aboard one or another sailing. February finds her sailing Dixie Fest jazz cruises out of New Orleans, followed by spring pilgrimages through the Old South. An April Kentucky Derby cruise between Memphis and Cincinnati is followed by Wilderness and Crossroads itineraries.

The Bottom Line

The food is delicious, the entertainment down-home but amusing, and all cabins are outsides, many of them opening directly onto the deck. Antiques decorate the few public rooms aboard, and porch swings and rocking chairs invite passengers to sit awhile on deck, watching the river go by, living in the rhythms of the 19th century. This is the only authentic period riverboat making overnight cruises in the United States.

Fielding's Five

Five Big-Easy Places

1. The Orleans Room on Main Deck fills triple duty as dining room, show lounge and lecture hall, but its wide windows, plank floor, pressed-tin ceiling and lace curtains set the mood of an earlier time.

2. The steam calliope, which, depending on your hearing, is a great boon or a great nuisance, trills out tunes as the boat goes up and down the river; passengers also get a turn at playing it.

3. The Forward Cabin Lounge is where passengers gather for afternoon tea or late-night (we hesitate to say "midnight" since it's usually much earlier) buffet amid handsome antique furniture.

4. The Grand Staircase, made of handcrafted of oak, teak, mahogany, Oregon cedar and other hardwoods, is accented with Tiffany stained glass and brass appointments.

5. The Texas Lounge, where spicy Cajun Bloody Marys are on special at 10:30 a.m., hot fresh popcorn is always available, and singalongs are frequent.

Delta Queen ♨♨♨♨♨

Registry	US
Officers	American
Crew	American
Complement	75
GRT	3,360
Length (ft.)	285
Beam (ft.)	58
Draft (ft.)	8.5
Passengers-Cabins Full	174
Passengers-2/Cabin	174
Passenger Space Ratio	NA
Stability Rating	Excellent
Seatings	2
Cuisine	American
Dress Code	Casual
Room Service	No
Tip	$10 PPPD, 15% automatically added to bar checks

Ship Amenities

Outdoor Pool	0
Indoor Pool	0
Jacuzzi	0
Fitness Center	No
Spa	No
Beauty Shop	No
Showroom	No
Bars/Lounges	1
Casino	No
Shops	1
Library	No
Child Program	No
Self-Service Laundry	No
Elevators	0

Cabin Statistics

Suites	6
Outside Doubles	87
Inside Doubles	0
Wheelchair Cabins	0
Singles	0
Single Surcharge	175%
Verandas	0
110 Volt	Yes

DELTA QUEEN STEAMBOAT COMPANY

Mississippi Queen   ⚓⚓⚓⚓⚓

The first time we went steamboatin' was aboard the Mississippi Queen, and we were thrilled to have our own tiny screened porch overlooking the river. We immersed ourselves in stories about Big Al the alligator, who when he smoked under the river created fog to bother the captains above, and the cranes, the souls of reincarnated boatmen, who appeared to show captains where the underwater snags (logs) were. It was a wonderful introduction to the romance of American travel.

A hoop-skirted hostess aboard the **Mississippi Queen** *greets passengers.*

On the other hand, until her recent reincarnation as a proper sister ship to the elegant *American Queen*, we were not particularly fond of the somewhat glitzy *Mississippi Queen.*

The Brochure Says

"...unlike early steamers, she features a pool on the Sun Deck, a beauty salon, a movie theater and elevators, as well as climate-controlled staterooms with steamboat-to-shore telephones."

Translation

This boat is for people who want to go steamboatin' on a cruise ship.

Cabins & Costs

Fantasy Suites: .... A

Average Price PPPD: $589 plus air add-ons.

There are four Superior Veranda Suites, the top digs on the *MQ*, with twin beds that convert to king-sized or a fixed queen-sized bed, depending on the cabin, along with sitting area with sofa bed, bathroom with tub and shower, and a private veranda. If you book 401 or 402, you're adjacent to the wheelhouse with a steamboat captain's view; if you book 274 or 275, your veranda overlooks the paddlewheel.

Small Splurges: .... B

Average Price PPPD: $425 plus air add-ons.

Again, we'd go for a suite with veranda, perhaps one of the Deluxe Veranda Suites on Texas Deck, with twin beds plus a day bed to sleep a third person, a big walk-in closet, bath with tub and shower and a small private veranda.

Suitable Standards: .... B

Average Price PPPD: $394 plus air add-ons.

The predominant cabin configuration on board is the category B Deluxe Veranda Stateroom. There are 68 of them, all with small private verandas, windows, a chair, a dresser, bath with shower and closet.

Bottom Bunks: .... D

Average Price PPPD: $155 plus air add-ons.

There are only eight of the very cheapest cabins, the category F Inside Staterooms, which have a lower bed, upper berth, bathroom with shower and a dresser. But all cabins have been handsomely redecorated in Victorian furniture, fabrics and wallpaper.

Where She Goes

In the winter, the *Mississippi Queen* sails from New Orleans on Big Band cruises, followed by Spring Pilgrimage sailings through the Old South, then Kentucky Derby cruises and in summer, Wilderness and Crossroads itineraries on the Arkansas, Tennessee and Cumberland Rivers.

The Bottom Line

What the *Mississippi Queen* offers that the *Delta Queen* doesn't is elevators, a swimming pool, Continental breakfasts served in the cabin, telephones and individual climate controls in the cabin, a movie theater, a self-service hot dog stand and ice cream bar, a sauna and fitness room, shuffleboard, hot hors d'oeuvres before dinner and a cage of pet birds in the lobby. With the glitz all gone and the decor brought up to speed with the new *American Queen*, the *Mississippi Queen* steams right along with her sister boats.

Fielding's Five

Five Favorite Places

1. The Paddlewheel Lounge has two-deck-high windows facing the churning red wheel; passengers sit, transfixed, watching the water like flames in a fireplace.

2. The Forward Cabin Lounge with its baroque bird cages and chirping finches doubles as lobby and shore excursions office.

3. The Calliope Bar, forward on the top deck, is the place to gather in the open air and listen to the ridiculously ornate gilded steam piano tootling out Stephen Foster songs from the balcony above or help yourself to a hot dog with all the trimmings from a rolling cart.

4. The Grand Saloon with its chandeliers and bay windows is the gathering spot after dinner for music from Dixieland to blues, Big Band sounds for dancing to tunes from Broadway.

5. The Sun Deck, with its swimming pool, shuffleboard and sunny lounging chairs is the place to be on a warm summer day.

Five Good Reasons to Book This Boat

1. It's a great introduction to the heartland of America.

2. The chocolate-peanut butter pie.

3. Steve Spracklen, a former student of pianist Eubie Blake, playing an evening of ragtime.

4. Waving at the people who line up along the river just to see her pass by, including whole classes of grade-school children.

5. To toodle when your turn comes on the steam calliope and be heard five miles up and down the river.

Five Things You Won't Find Aboard

1. Seasickness—the ride is quiet and smooth.

2. Speed measured in knots; on the river it's measured in miles per hour.

3. A children's program.

4. A casino.

5. A TV set in your cabin.

Mississippi Queen ⚓⚓⚓⚓⚓

Registry	US
Officers	American
Crew	American
Complement	165
GRT	3,364
Length (ft.)	382
Beam (ft.)	68
Draft (ft.)	8.5
Passengers-Cabins Full	458
Passengers-2/Cabin	414
Passenger Space Ratio	NA
Stability Rating	Excellent
Seatings	2
Cuisine	American
Dress Code	Casual
Room Service	Yes
Tip	$10 PPPD, 15% automatically added to bar checks

Ship Amenities

Outdoor Pool	1
Indoor Pool	0
Jacuzzi	1
Fitness Center	Yes
Spa	No
Beauty Shop	Yes
Showroom	Yes
Bars/Lounges	2
Casino	No
Shops	1
Library	Yes
Child Program	No
Self-Service Laundry	Yes
Elevators	2

Cabin Statistics

Suites	26
Outside Doubles	109
Inside Doubles	72
Wheelchair Cabins	1
Singles	0
Single Surcharge	175%
Verandas	94
110 Volt	Yes

DELTA QUEEN STEAMBOAT COMPANY

DELTA QUEEN STEAMBOAT COMPANY

DOLPHIN CRUISE LINE

901 South American Way, Miami, FL 33132
☎ *(305) 358-5122, (800) 992-4299*

History ....

Dolphin Cruise Line came about through a marketing agreement in 1979 between Peter Bulgarides, who formed Ulysses Cruise Line, and Paquet to operate the *Dolphin IV.* That agreement was terminated in 1984, and Dolphin Cruise Line was born to handle the ship.

A second ship, the former *Star/Ship Royale* from Premier Cruises, was acquired in 1989, and renamed the *SeaBreeze,* and when Admiral Cruises was disbanded by its parent company Royal Caribbean Cruise Line in 1992, Dolphin acquired the former *Azure Seas,* which it named *OceanBreeze.* The latter ship had been based in Los Angeles for more than a decade, making highly successful three- and four-day cruises to Baja California.

For three years, the company operated its trio of vessels, using the *Dolphin IV* for short cruises to the Bahamas and the other two for seven-day Caribbean sailings. In August 1995, Dolphin sold its *Dolphin IV* to Kosmas Shipping Group, Inc., a Florida-based company (see Canaveral Cruise Line, page 145). The *Oceanbreeze* was redeployed to Miami to take over the three- and four-day cruises to the Bahamas and Key West.

In 1996, Dolphin acquired the former *Festivale* from Carnival which became the *IslandBreeze.*

Majesty Cruise Line, which operates the *Royal Majesty,* is also affiliated with Dolphin Cruise Line. Both lines are headed up by Captain Paris Katsoufis. Peter Bulgarides resigned as chairman of the board in 1994.

Concept ....

Dolphin feels it established itself as a leader in the three- and four-day cruise market early on by providing quality and value, as well as offering "quality service and gourmet dining" on all of its ships. The vintage Dolphin vessels still carry details from their ocean liner days such as teak decks, wood paneling, etched glass and polished brass.

Signatures............................

The distinctive blue dolphin on the ships' white stacks makes an easily recognized and identified logo.

Theme cruises abound, such as Country Western sailings, '50s and '60s cruises, Motown, Oktoberfest, Big Band and Nostalgia.

On-board weddings were popularized by Dolphin and frequently take place on the ships.

Gimmicks............................

As the Official Cruise Line of Hanna-Barbera, Dolphin and Majesty ships are animated with cartoon characters such as Yogi Bear, Fred Flintstone and Scooby Doo.

Who's the Competition ....

Dolphin has long been a leader in the budget cruise arena and competes primarily in the price-driven market that also includes Commodore Cruise Line and Regal Cruises.

Who's Aboard ....

A great many first-time cruisers, family groups, singles, couples, many passengers in their 20s and 30s.

Who Should Go ....

Anybody who wants to sample a cruise to see what it's all about without having to make a big commitment in time and money should try one of the mini-cruises out of Miami.

Who Should Not Go ....

Fussy veteran cruisers will not like the very long lines that form anywhere food is being arranged, served or set out.

EAVESDROPPING

A man standing in line at tea time watching several family members heaping plates with cakes and sandwiches shakes his head in mock dismay and says, "I'm gonna hafta get some new springs for my car before I can drive the five of them back home."

The Lifestyle ....

The three- and four-day cruises are a little more hectic than the seven-day sailings, just because Dolphin tries to work in as many special activities as possible. The usual daily pattern always offers plenty of chances to eat, plus as many as eight shore excursions in port. Sports and exercise classes, movies, ping pong, dance classes, beauty salon demonstrations, napkin folding, fruit and vegetable carving, pool games, horseracing, tours of the navigation bridge, Name That Tune, captain's cocktail party, shore excursion sales, dance music, game shows led by the cruise director, a deck party under the stars, ice carvings, midnight buffet, disco and night owl movie—and that's just one day! Children's programs offer a variety of options from dolphin encounters to sand castle building and treasure hunts. The atmosphere on board is friendly, even ebullient, because people worried about whether they were going to have a good time realize they're having a great time.

Wardrobe. . . . .

Dolphin is very kind to its first-time cruisers on the three- and four-day sailings, requesting that they dress up for formal night to meet the captain and go to dinner, then letting them change back to casual garb for the rest of the evening. Not many cruise lines do that.

Generally, they expect men to wear at least a jacket and tie for formal nights; a lot of men bring tuxedos or dinner jackets. They do not permit shorts in the dining rooms after 6 p.m. On evenings designated semi-formal, they also expect men to wear a jacket. On Tropical and Casual dress code nights, almost anything goes.

Bill of Fare. . . . . B

Dolphin has always impressed us with the quality and quantity of its embarkation day buffets when many more-expensive cruise lines are doling out sandwiches. Breakfast buffets on the pool deck usually include bacon, eggs, potatoes, French toast, fruit and pastries. Dinners are fairly predictable hotel banquet-type meals, but the homemade breadsticks are delicious and there are always a lot of rich, elaborate desserts that seem to please the multitudes. Menus rotate on a fixed basis and are changed "every couple of years." Midnight buffets are especially big on the three- and four-day sailings, with a themed version scheduled every night, Italian Buffet, Fruit Buffet and Farewell Buffet, plus the Magnificent Buffet on four-night sailings. There's usually a diet dish on every lunch and dinner menu.

Showtime. C

The three- and four-day sailings depend a lot on audience participation games including "The Newlywed and Not-So-Newlywed Game," along with disco and casino action, male nightgown competitions and cash bingo. On longer sailings there are mini-musical revues, variety shows and karaoke contests. The ship's orchestras play quite well for dancing.

Discounts. . . . .

Dolphin's SaleAway Program promises, "The earlier you book, the more you'll save!"

The Bottom Line

These are good economy-priced ships for first-timers who want to take a mini-cruise or spend a week sampling popular Caribbean ports in a casual atmosphere. The staff is friendly and the food tasty, and the ships are kept very clean. The only vessel we felt badly needed some deck maintenance was the *Dolphin IV*, which the line has sold but will continue to operate for the new owners.

DOLPHIN CRUISE LINE

IslandBreeze

The former *Festivale* from Carnival was built in 1961 as the Transvaal Castle for Union Castle Lines. It carried mail and passengers between Southampton and Durban, South Africa, then was transferred to South African Marine Corporation and renamed Vaal. Carnival bought it in 1977 and Dolphin acquired it from Carnival in 1996. The *IslandBreeze* is long and sleek with ocean liner lines and vestiges of its previous decor, including a remarkable art deco-style steel stairway, but don't expect a classic cruise ship. This is basic but attractive. It has a lot of sunbathing deck, two swimming pools aft and a small wading pool forward. Most of the cabins are fairly spacious, although more than half of them are insides. The dining room, typical of vessels from this vintage, is amidships on a lower deck without windows. Lounges can get crowded when the ship is full, but you can usually find stretch-out room on deck.

The Brochure Says

"Outstanding award-winning cuisine is a Dolphin trademark, and our chefs' skill is especially evident at the midnight buffets."

Translation

You can pig out to the wee hours of the morn.

Cabins & Costs

Fantasy Suites: C
Average Price PPPD: $321 plus airfare.
Ten suites with private verandas have twin beds that can be converted to queen-sized, plus a sitting area with sofa that makes into a third bed. The bathroom has a tub.

Small Splurges: C
Average Price PPPD: $242 plus airfare.
Two forward-facing cabins on Veranda Deck are the biggest accommodations on board, larger even than the more expensive veranda suites. Both have queen-sized beds.

Suitable Standards: .... D
Average Price PPPD: $235 plus airfare.
The basic standards are similarly priced whether inside or out. You'll need to specify whether you want twin beds or a queen-sized or double, since they're not convertible. In many, the sink is in the main cabin rather than in the bathroom.

Bottom Bunks: .... D
Average Price PPPD: $142 plus airfare.
There are only a handful of cabins in the lowest-priced category, all insides with upper and lower berths and all on lower decks. Again, you can expect the sink in the main cabin rather than in the bathroom.

Where She Goes

The *IslandBreeze* sails from New York to New England and eastern Canada in summer on five-night weekday cruises, with a two-day cruise to nowhere every weekend. In winter, the ship sails on seven-night itineraries from Montego Bay, Jamaica, into the Panama Canal, calling at Cartagena, San Blas Islands and Puerto Limon, Costa Rica.

The Bottom Line

For the price, *IslandBreeze* offers a good getaway—an interesting itinerary on a vintage vessel that still looks like a ship.

Fielding's Five

Five Favorite Gathering Places

1. The Veranda Deck pool, where everyone pulls their sun loungers into a circle like wagon trains around a campfire.

2. The Gaslight Club Casino and Cafe, where a darkish period feeling prevails, is flanked by two enclosed promenades.

3. The Fanta-Z Disco with its mirrored ceiling and lighted dance floor that blinks in rhythm with the music.

4. The Copacabana Lounge, a vivid parrot carpet and bamboo bentwood chairs lend a tropical look, enhanced by a sunshine-bright ceiling.

5. The Tradewinds Lounge, all rattan tub chairs and ceiling fans; you half-expect to see Peter Lorre in a fez peering from behind a potted palm.

Five Good Reasons to Book This Ship

1. To travel aboard a vintage ship built for ocean crossings.

2. To walk up and down that magnificent steel staircase.

3. To meet the (man, woman) of your dreams at the singles' party (it does happen sometimes).

4. To book one of the modestly priced, fairly sizable cabins with third and fourth berths for the kids.

5. To sail with her into the Panama Canal and back out again.

Five Things You Won't Find On Board

1. A card room.

2. A gym with a view.

3. A cabin designated wheelchair-accessible.

4. A whirlpool spa.

5. A hot breakfast from room service.

IslandBreeze ★★

Registry	**Bahamas**
Officers	**Greek**
Crew	**International**
Complement	**580**
GRT	**38,175**
Length (ft.)	**760**
Beam (ft.)	**90**
Draft (ft.)	**27**
Passengers-Cabins Full	**1400**
Passengers-2/Cabin	**1146**
Passenger Space Ratio	**33.31**
Stability Rating	**Good**
Seatings	**2**
Cuisine	**Continental**
Dress Code	**Traditional/Casual**
Room Service	**Yes**
Tip	**$9 PPPD, 15% automatically added to bar checks**

Ship Amenities

Outdoor Pool	**3**
Indoor Pool	**0**
Jacuzzi	**0**
Fitness Center	**Yes**
Spa	**No**
Beauty Shop	**Yes**
Showroom	**Yes**
Bars/Lounges	**4**
Casino	**Yes**
Shops	**4**
Library	**Yes**
Child Program	**Yes**
Self-Service Laundry	**No**
Elevators	**8**

Cabin Statistics

Suites	**10**
Outside Doubles	**250**
Inside Doubles	**306**
Wheelchair Cabins	**0**
Singles	**0**
Single Surcharge	**150%**
Verandas	**10**
110 Volt	**Yes**

OceanBreeze

"We've never been on a cruise before," the young couple confided as they stood by the rail holding hands in the sunset. "Now we're going to save up for a longer one—14 days at least." He went on to say that he works as a mechanic for a municipal bus system; his wife bags groceries at a chain supermarket. Two chic and pretty African-American women who work for the post office were flirting with a Fijian bar steward, and a young punk rocker with purple hair spent most of his port time feeding the sea gulls perched on the ship's rail.

DID YOU KNOW?

One question we've been asked over the years is about timing–how we happened to get into the field of cruise writing 15 years ago before it was generally realized cruising would become a major industry. The answer is easy. The passage above was written on the Azure Seas back in 1981, showing that cruising is for everyone, not just the rich or retired.

A very young Queen Elizabeth II christened this ship as the *Southern Cross* in 1954, when it made the Australia/New Zealand run from Great Britain. It featured several design innovations, including the placement of the funnel and engines at the aft end and the elimination of cargo holds; both features have become commonplace on nearly every passenger ship constructed since. The ship was laid up in Southampton in 1971, then sold to a Greek company in 1973 to be refitted as a cruise vessel named *Calypso*. She sailed the Mediterranean for five years, primarily with British vacation package tourists aboard, then was sold in 1980 to Eastern Steamship Lines and renamed *Calypso I*. In 1981, she was sold to the company's West Coast associates, Western Steamship Lines, named the *Azure Seas* and began sailing on three- and four-day cruises out of Los Angeles to Ensenada, Mexico. Eastern and Western Steamship Lines merged to become Admiral Cruises in 1986, which was subsequently acquired by Royal Caribbean Cruises and disbanded in 1992.

Still handsomely maintained, the *OceanBreeze* shows more than a bit of her art deco background as well as a touch of glitter and glamour from recent makeovers. Cabins are larger than on many ships in this price and age range.

The Brochure Says

"Sit back. Relax. Sip a colorful, tropical cocktail and get to know some new friends. Or get to know each other even better. There isn't a better time or place to do all the things you haven't done in years. This is the cruise to do it all. Or nothing at all."

Translation

Try it, you'll like it.

Fantasy Suites: . . . . B+

Average Price PPPD: $248 plus airfare.

One of the 12 new penthouse suites they added on Boat Deck during a recent refit is called the owner's suite, and faces forward for a great view. With two big rooms—a living room with sofa and chairs, coffee table, minibar and TV, and a bedroom with queen-sized bed and plenty of storage, plus a bath with tub and shower—it's large enough to live in. The sofa makes into a double bed if you want to bring the kids along to share.

Small Splurges: . . . . B

Average Price PPPD: $198 plus airfare.

The spacious Category 2 double outside cabins on Barbizon Deck are bigger, cheaper and more private than the pricier category 1 cabins on Atlantis Deck, a promenade deck where you have people going past your window all the time. Most have two lower beds or double, and many have a third pulldown berth. The bath has shower only.

Suitable Standards: . . . . B

Average Price PPPD: $188 plus airfare.

The Category 3 outside double cabins on Caravelle and Dolphin Decks are adequate, although if you worry about motion sickness, we'd suggest avoiding the ones on Caravelle Deck, which are all forward from the dining room. A deck lower they're amidships for a smoother ride. Most of these have two lower beds but some of the choicest locations—# 239-244—have double beds instead and are near the elevators. Your bathroom will have a shower instead of a tub.

Bottom Bunks: C

Average Price PPPD: $108 plus airfare.

The cheapest cabins aboard are the Category 10 inside doubles on Emerald Deck, and there are only two of them. They have two lower beds or a double and a shower in the bathroom.

The *OceanBreeze* makes three- and four-day cruises from Miami to the Bahamas and Key West, sailing on Fridays and Mondays.

A graceful and dignified ship, the *OceanBreeze* offers a good, medium-priced vacation at sea for first-time cruisers or anyone who wants to get away for a few days. Larger and smoother riding than the *Dolphin IV*, she's ideal for the three- and four-day mini-cruises out of Miami.

Five Unforgettable Places

1. The elegantly refurbished two-deck casino with its art deco brass railings and light fixtures.

2. The Cafe Miramar, where buffet breakfasts and lunches are served and late-night cabaret shows sometimes happen.

3. The Mayfair Lounge with its wicker furniture, potted palms and ceiling fans evokes the past. Sunlit during the day, the bay windows offer pleasant sea views; softly lit at night with a pianist playing, it's an appealing spot for a quiet rendezvous.

4. On the other hand, the Rendezvous Show Lounge glitters and sparkles with the evening's main entertainment, which you watch from comfortable swivel tub chairs upholstered in a tight red-and-blue check that looks mauve from a distance. Don't sit behind a post or you'll miss some of the show.

5. The hard-to-find library has always been one of our favorites because it doesn't get much through traffic; books are locked in wood-and-glass bookcases and there are plenty of comfortable dark blue chairs and sofas.

Five Things You Won't Find On Board

1. TV sets in cabins that are not suites.

2. Windows in the dining room.

3. Windows in the disco—it's below the waterline.

4. Cabins designated wheelchair accessible.

5. A passenger that knows the difference between a boat and a ship.

OceanBreeze ★ ★ ★

Registry	Liberia
Officers	Greek
Crew	International
Complement	400
GRT	21,486
Length (ft.)	604
Beam (ft.)	78
Draft (ft.)	29
Passengers-Cabins Full	980
Passengers-2/Cabin	776
Passenger Space Ratio	28.00
Stability Rating	Good
Seatings	2
Cuisine	Continental
Dress Code	Traditional/Casual
Room Service	Yes
Tip	$9 PPPD, 15% automatically added to bar check

Ship Amenities

Outdoor Pool	1
Indoor Pool	0
Jacuzzi	1
Fitness Center	Yes
Spa	No
Beauty Shop	Yes
Showroom	Yes
Bars/Lounges	2
Casino	Yes
Shops	2
Library	No
Child Program	Yes
Self-Service Laundry	No
Elevators	1

Cabin Statistics

Suites	12
Outside Doubles	226
Inside Doubles	150
Wheelchair Cabins	0
Singles	0
Single Surcharge	150%
Verandas	0
110 Volt	Yes

SeaBreeze

The only mystery we kept bumping into was a sign in the main lobby, near the purser's desk, that said Pictures From An Exhibition. How classy, we said, perhaps an art show, an art auction is behind that locked door, or a lounge that presents classical music in the afternoons. The space was shown and neatly labeled in the deck plan bracketed by a pair of restrooms, with nothing more to illuminate it. Finally, the moment came when the doors were unlocked and open. It was the ship's photographer's display of the passengers arriving, shaking hands with the captain, coming down the gangway in port and posing in formal clothing on a dress-up night, perhaps the first time since the prom or the wedding pictures. Pictures From An Exhibition. Yes.

The *SeaBreeze* was built as Costa's *Federico C* in 1958 as a two-class ship, then became Premier's *Royale* in 1984. Dolphin acquired her in 1989. There are nine passenger decks, with cabins located on all but two, the topmost deck, where there is a buffet setup, and the bottom-most, where the disco is located. During its ownership of the vessel, Premier increased the density both by adding cabins in former deck areas and adding third and fourth berths, so that almost any cabin you book is likely to have additional overhead bunks. The idiosyncratic cabin layout means the configuration of the cabins varies; some have twin beds, some double beds, some bathrooms have tub and shower, some shower only.

CHAMPAGNE TOAST

To the hotel manager of the SeaBreeze, who not only keeps a superbly clean ship but who won't let passengers take their buffet breakfast and lunch trays from the cafe into the adjacent air-conditioned show lounge to eat. There's a sign on the door: No food permitted inside. That's the way it should be—If you want air conditioning, eat lunch in the dining room. If you want a buffet, eat it outdoors on the sunny or shaded deck. But don't spill your food and drink all over the lounges.

The Brochure Says

"As you'll find out, almost everything's included on Dolphin Cruise Line. So stop dreaming and wake up to Dolphin. One of the world's best cruise lines. And the best value in cruising."

Translation

The appeal is to first-time cruisers, reminding them that many more things are included in the basic fare on ships than they are accustomed to in resort hotels.

The dining room of the **SeaBreeze***, a very attractive, budget-priced ship.*

Cabins & Costs

Fantasy Suites: . . . . B+

Average Price PPPD: $206 plus airfare.

Seven suites on board are spacious, pretty rooms with king-sized bed, sitting area with sofa and chair, and a long built-in desk/dresser, along with two windows.

If you get B4, you'll have a view forward, a tile bath with tub and a frosted window in the bathroom, the last really rare on ships.

Small Splurges: . . . . B

Average Price PPPD: $171 plus airfare.

Category 2 outside superior cabins are fairly spacious, some of them (# D8, for example) with built-in cabinetry from the 1960s, lovely old coatracks fitted onto the cabin walls with pull-out hangers, brass temperature gauges made in Milan with all the instructions in Italian, left over from the *Federico C* days. We like the cabin despite its obstructed view and its two additional overhead berths.

Suitable Standards: C

Average Price PPPD: $156 plus airfare.

Category 4 cabins are outsides on the lower passenger decks with two lower beds or a double bed (specify which one you want when booking), bathrooms with shower and portholes instead of windows.

Bottom Bunks: .... D

Average Price PPPD: $99 plus airfare.
The very cheapest cabins on board are two very tiny Category 11 inside cabins with upper and lower berths forward on Isolde Deck, the lowest deck with passenger cabins. (The only one lower is the Juliet Deck where the disco is located.)

Where She Goes

The *SeaBreeze* sails from Miami every Sunday on alternate seven-night itineraries to the Eastern Caribbean and the Western Caribbean. In the Eastern Caribbean, she visits Nassau, San Juan, St. John and St. Thomas, and in the Western Caribbean, she stops at Playa del Carmen/Cozumel, Montego Bay and Grand Cayman.

The Bottom Line

When we were last aboard the *SeaBreeze*, we were tremendously impressed at how clean and fresh she looks, especially given her age and her background as a veteran of the children's crusades over at Premier, when she was the *Royale*. Frankly, this ship is kept more spic-and-span than a lot of fancy new vessels built in the 1980s. It's a good economy-priced vessel for first-timers who want to sample a lot of Caribbean islands in a non-intimidating atmosphere.

Fielding's Five

Five Special Places

1. The Water Music Whirlpool, a trio of Jacuzzi pools surrounded by rows of plastic loungers, is on the aft end of the Boheme Deck.

2. The Prelude Bar is an intimate little lounge with very comfortable swivel rattan barstools, a varnished teak floor and latticework walls, plus lots of healthy fresh green plants.

3. The Casino, with some rare five-cent slot machines among the 99 one-armed bandits, plus four blackjack tables, one Caribbean stud and one roulette.

4. Royal Fireworks Lounge, wide rather than deep, with curved sofas, wood tables, blue and mauve chairs and an oval dance floor in wood parquet.

5. The Carmen Lounge, a show lounge filled with swivel tub chairs in rose or sage, round wooden cocktail tables, bar with eight stools, and very poor sightlines.

Five Good Reasons to Book This Ship

1. The price is right.

2. The itineraries alternate from week to week—the Eastern Caribbean one week, the Western Caribbean the next—so you could add them together for a great 14-day full Caribbean tour, and take a substantial discount on the second week's price as well.

3. Let your kids meet Yogi Bear and Fred Flintstone.

4. To be one of the displays at Pictures From An Exhibition.

5. You could get married on board—and sail away on a wonderful honeymoon. Have your travel agent contact the Wedding Coordinator at Dolphin to find out about five different wedding packages from $275 to $750.

Five Things You Won't Find On Board

1. A chair apiece if you're not in a suite; in the cabins, you get one to share.

2. A look at the bottom halves of the chorus girls in the Carmen Lounge unless you're in the front row.

3. A table for two in the dining room; you'll be seated at a table for eight to 10. But look at the upside—you'll meet that many more people.

4. A movie projected on film; in the ship's cinema, videocassettes are what you get.

5. A horse in the Light Cavalry Arcade, which is occupied by 12 coin-operated video games.

SeaBreeze ★★★

Registry	**Panama**
Officers	**Greek**
Crew	**International**
Complement	**400**
GRT	**21,000**
Length (ft.)	**605**
Beam (ft.)	**79**
Draft (ft.)	**29**
Passengers-Cabins Full	**1100**
Passengers-2/Cabin	**840**
Passenger Space Ratio	**25.00**
Stability Rating	**Good**
Seatings	**2**
Cuisine	**Continental**
Dress Code	**Traditional/Casual**
Room Service	**Yes**
Tip	**$9 PPPD, 15% automatically added to bar check**

Ship Amenities

Outdoor Pool	**1**
Indoor Pool	**0**
Jacuzzi	**3**
Fitness Center	**Yes**
Spa	**No**
Beauty Shop	**Yes**
Showroom	**Yes**
Bars/Lounges	**3**
Casino	**Yes**
Shops	**2**
Library	**No**
Child Program	**Yes**
Self-Service Laundry	**No**
Elevators	**2**

Cabin Statistics

Suites	**7**
Outside Doubles	**253**
Inside Doubles	**160**
Wheelchair Cabins	**0**
Singles	**1**
Single Surcharge	**150%**
Verandas	**0**
110 Volt	**Yes**

€PIROTIKI
Make our world your world

One Rockefeller Plaza, Suite 315, New York, NY 10020-2090
☎ *(212) 397-6400, (800) 872-6400*

NOTE: Sun Line Cruises and Epirotiki Cruises have formed a merger called Royal Olympic Cruises (see page 663) which markets ships of the two lines in two different divisions. The Blue World of Sun Line consists of three classic-style vessels with hulls painted dark blue—*Stella Solaris, Stella Oceanis* and *Odysseus*—which we list under Sun Line. The White World of Epirotiki comprises a mainstream three-ship fleet with white hulls—*Triton, Orpheus* and *Olympic*—which we list under Epirotiki.

History . . . .

The company that is today Epirotiki started in shipping some 150 years ago, and was named for the founding Potamianos family's village of Epirus in northwestern Greece. While the line offered some specialized passenger service in pre-World War II, mostly archeological expeditions, Greek Islands cruises didn't come into prominence until after the war. In postwar Greece, war reparations vessels from Italy and later American war ships sold as scrap but rehabilitated in Greece as passenger vessels helped the Greek companies, including Epirotiki, rebuild their fleets to provide essential services along the coast and between the islands. In 1954 the *Semiramis* set out on the first scheduled tourist cruise in the Aegean for Epirotiki.

Over the years, in addition to operating a flourishing charter business, the company has owned, sold and lost countless ships, and even scrupulous record-keepers have trouble keeping track of Epirotiki's ships except those that bring particular notice to themselves. Ships such as the *Oceanos* when it sank off South Africa in August 1991; the almost-unsinkable *Pegasus,* which, after going down once as the *Sundancer* in British Columbia in 1984, was burned and scuttled in Venice harbor in 1991, then was turned into a ferry before it went down for the third and final time; and the *Pallas Athena* (the former *CarlaCosta/Flandre*), which burned at the dock in Piraeus during a fire while under reconstruction in 1994, caused, insiders say, by rehearsing performers who left sound and electrical equipment plugged in when they went home for the night.

The ships mentioned in the Royal Olympic Cruises agreement include the *Odysseus,* which will join the Sun Line Blue Ships, and the *Triton,*

Orpheus and *Olympic*, which will make up the Epirotiki White Ships. Three other longtime Epirotiki vessels—*Jason*, *Neptune* and *Argonaut*—will be made available for charter rather than scheduled sailings, along with Sun Line's lovely little *Stella Maris*.

Epirotiki also had previously entered into a marketing agreement with Carnival Cruise Corp. in 1994 that was terminated a year later by mutual agreement but resulted in Epirotiki's purchase, in effect, of two former Carnival ships, the *Carnivale*, which is now the *Olympic*, and the *Mardi Gras*, now the *Apollo*, leased to Royal Venture Cruises as the *Sea Venture*.

—Owns the oldest passenger ship still sailing for a major cruise company (*Argonaut*, built in 1929).

—Made the first-ever tourist cruise in the Aegean (*Semiramis*, 1954).

Concept

Epirotiki sails vintage Greek-flag ships with Greek crews on affordable-to-budget fares around the Greek Islands, Mediterranean and beyond. The owners describe their three basic principles as "the right ship, the right cruise, the right itinerary."

Signatures

The distinctive logo, a gold Byzantine cross on a field of blue, can be seen in ports around the Mediterranean as well as other parts of the world.

Gimmicks

Epirotiki traditionally has marketed cruise itineraries rather than ships, mixing and matching ships in homeports depending on what was operational or what might be going out under a lucrative charter contract.

Who's the Competition

With the potential end of Greek cabotage laws in sight, the exclusive advantage the Greek companies had of being able to sail roundtrip cruises from Piraeus is weakened as more and more cruise lines sail into the Aegean. While regarded as a budget line, Epirotiki's per diems on the vessels it will be operating under Royal Olympic Cruises vie with some of the U.S.-based mainstream lines that are cruising the Mediterranean, such as Royal Caribbean.

Who's Aboard

A lot of first-time cruisers and package travelers to Greece from all over Europe and North America have been the backbone of Epirotiki's passenger list, but it has fewer frequent repeat passengers than Sun Line. The line also attracts Latin Americans, Asians, Australians and South Africans.

Who Should Go

The same people that have gravitated to Sun Line in the past are the most likely to go with Royal Olympic's Blue Ships, and the Epirotiki veterans and price-conscious package travelers will probably continue to patronize the White Ships.

Who Should Not Go ....

With two different areas of style and service, the new company covers the waterfront of potential cruisers. Generally, Greek Islands, Turkey, Egypt and Israel sailings (which is what Royal Olympic seems to be concentrating on) are port-intensive and very tour and excursion oriented, perhaps not appropriate for families with small children.

The Lifestyle ....

Epirotiki's cruises follow a traditional Mediterranean cruise format, with numerous ports of call in the daytimes, shore excursions, two meal seatings, fairly casual dress code suggestions, five-language announcements and variety entertainment.

Wardrobe...................................

Casual clothing is suggested for daytime, and since it can be very hot in summer on shore excursions, lightweight clothes and sun hats are recommended, along with sturdy walking shoes for negotiating ruins.

Epirotiki suggests that men wear a jacket and tie and women a cocktail dress for the captain's welcome aboard and farewell parties. Since both the ship and the tour buses are air-conditioned, you may want to bring along a sweater to take off the chill.

Bill of Fare...............................*C*

The food aboard is Greek and continental, served in generous portions. Because of busy days in port, the deck buffets are particularly popular for breakfasts and lunches. Flaming desserts, baked Alaska and gala buffets are usually on the agenda, along with simpler treats such as hot dogs and hamburgers, Greek salads and taverna dishes.

Showtime..................................*C*

Because of the number of different languages spoken by the passengers, entertainment leans more to visual variety acts including magicians, musicians and dancers rather than aural performers such as comedians and ventriloquists. You can count on an evening (or two or three) of spirited Greek folk dancing along the lines of "Dance of the Wounded Sponge Diver." Classical concerts or recitals show up from time to time, and there's always dancing in the lounge or disco.

Discounts..................................

Cruise-only fares and all-inclusive air/land/cruise packages are offered. Singles sail without supplemental charges on the *Orpheus* except in deluxe cabins.

The Bottom Line

We have had some cavalier service on Epirotiki ships from time to time—brusque waiters or bartenders—but we've also had very friendly, caring treatment at other times. The new merger with Sun Line should bring an upgraded hotel management plus an expansion of marketing in North America.

Olympic

> *We've been with her through three names now, and that doesn't go back to the beginning. While she seems to do very well in the Aegean, our favorite incarnation was the brief time she spent as the FiestaMarina, a niche line aimed at the Latin American market, with some of the best food we ever had at sea, created by the chefs of Miami's trendy neo-Cuban Yuca and New York's Patria. Problem was, the Latin Americans didn't like fusion Latin food—the Brazilians said it was Mexican, the Colombians thought it was Peruvian and everybody wanted surf-and-turf and beef Wellington "like they serve on the other Carnival ships." FiestaMarina went out of business not because it wasn't good enough, but because it was too good and ahead of its time.*

The *Olympic* started life in 1956 as the *Empress of Britain*, built in Fairfield's Glasgow, Scotland, yard for London's Canadian Pacific line. In 1964, she was sold to the Greek Line to become the *Queen Anna Maria* and sailed for 10 years before being laid up in Piraeus in 1975. Later that year Ted Arison bought her for his Carnival Cruise Lines, sending a young Miami architect named Joe Farcus over to Greece to supervise a makeover. "I thought all cruise ships were white and sparkling and clean," Farcus remembers. "But you should have seen that rusty old tub lying there!" As the *Carnivale*, she sailed successfully for Carnival from 1976 until she was turned into the *FiestaMarina* in 1993. There are eight passenger decks, only four of them with cabins, on the *Olympic*, with a lot of sun-and-fun upper decks and a dining room and fitness club down on the lower decks.

"...one of the largest ships ever to sail the Eastern Mediterranean."

Translation

The Potamianos family, who never liked large ships, calling them "monsters of the sea," is adjusting to larger vessels.

Cabins & Costs

Fantasy Suites: C

Average Price PPPD: $330 plus airfare.
While not exactly a fantasy, there are five suites on the Olympic, four of them adequately roomy and the fifth one a bit smaller. A glass partition separates the sleeping
and the sitting area, and there's a dresser, hanging closets, sofa/bed, two double
beds, tub/shower combination, and some units have a separate water closet.

Small Splurges: C

Average Price PPPD: $298 plus airfare.
Category S outside double cabins have twin beds, double dressers, hanging closets
and a chair, plus a bath with tub and shower. A glass medicine cabinet in the bathroom provides additional toiletries storage.

Suitable Standards: C

Average Price PPPD: $235 plus airfare.
Some of the outside doubles on Venus Deck are large and comfortable with two
lower beds and bath with shower.

Bottom Bunks: .... D

Average Price PPPD: $180 plus airfare.
The 8-by-12 insides with upper and lower berths are the cheapest cabins on the vessel; in many, the wash basins are in the bedroom.

Where She Goes

The *Olympic* sails every Friday on three-day roundtrip cruises from Piraeus to
Mykonos, Patmos, Kusadasi and Rhodes on the Aegean Hellenic itinerary, and every
Monday on four-day roundtrip sailings from Piraeus to Mykonos, Kusadasi, Patmos,
Rhodes, Heraklion and Santorini on the Aegean Classical itinerary. The season runs from
April through November.

The Bottom Line

The *Olympic's* sleek ocean-liner figure makes her look less huge in the Eastern Mediterranean than if she were a boxy new vessel, so she doesn't necessary stand out as the
largest ship in the fleet and one of the biggest in the Aegean. But doing the three- and
four-day sailings does mean that's she needs more and better maintenance to keep from
getting beat-up.

Fielding's Five

Five Farcus Feats

1. The Nine Muses night club with its big curved bar and dance floor.

2. The Veranda, an enclosed promenade where you can sit and chat, write or read,
wraps around the Hera Deck.

3. The Monte Carlo Casino was one of the hearts of the ship when it sailed for Carnival.

4. The former Salsa Plaza from FiestaMarina where the Latins danced until 4 a.m. has turned into the more sedate Horizon Lounge, but the piano bar next door still has that snazzy black-and-white tile checkerboard floor.

5. A children's pool and children's playroom on the top deck are separated by a length of promenade deck.

Five Good Reasons to Book These Ships

1. Her several stylish makeovers in this decade.

2. Her three- and four-day sailings from Piraeus, the three-day cruise calling in four ports, the four-day cruise calling in six ports. She's a new face in the Med.

3. She has a more comprehensive casino and lounges that most of the other Epirotiki ships.

4. There's more dedicated space for kids than on many Med cruisers.

5. There's an indoor swimming pool, gym, sauna, massage and fitness club.

Five Things You Won't Find On Board

1. A lifeguard working the indoor pool.

2. Any of that fantastic *FiestaMarina* Latin fusion food.

3. Your way to the fitness club without a lot of searching. Clue: Take the elevator down from the reception desk to the beauty salon, then walk down stairs.

4. A way to watch the movie in the cinema without someone opening the door and whiting out the screen.

5. A view out of the dining room; the "windows" are photos of sunsets nicely framed and fitted around the walls.

Olympic ★★

Registry	**Greece**
Officers	**Greek**
Crew	**Greek**
Complement	**550**
GRT	**550**
Length (ft.)	**640**
Beam (ft.)	**87**
Draft (ft.)	**29**
Passengers-Cabins Full	**1364**
Passengers-2/Cabin	**959**
Passenger Space Ratio	**32.85**
Stability Rating	**Good**
Seatings	**2**
Cuisine	**Continental/Greek**
Dress Code	**Traditional**
Room Service	**Yes**
Tip	**$6 - $8 PPPD**

Ship Amenities

Outdoor Pool	**3**
Indoor Pool	**1**
Jacuzzi	**1**
Fitness Center	**Yes**
Spa	**Yes**
Beauty Shop	**Yes**
Showroom	**Yes**
Bars/Lounges	**5**
Casino	**Yes**
Shops	**1**
Library	**Yes**
Child Program	**Yes**
Self-Service Laundry	**No**
Elevators	**2**

Cabin Statistics

Suites	**5**
Outside Doubles	**216**
Inside Doubles	**252**
Wheelchair Cabins	**0**
Singles	**13**
Single Surcharge	**150%**
Verandas	**0**
110 Volt	**Yes**

EPIROTIKI CRUISES

Orpheus

We stood at the rail of a ship in Piraeus one Monday morning in June 1985, and noted the names of the vessels as they sailed in—Stella Solaris and Stella Oceanis from Sun Line. Galaxy and Constellation from K-Line. Cycladic's City of Rhodes and City of Mykonos. And Epirotiki's Jupiter, Atlas and Neptune, all but Neptune gone now. The Orpheus was one of that family group.

Chartered on a long-term basis with P & O's Swan Hellenic until the end of 1995, the *Orpheus* has been cherished and looked after for years by her devoted questers of knowledge and truth. Now, back in the fold with Epirotiki, she's part of Royal Olympic Cruises' White Ships, making Classic Aegean and Ionian Voyages every Saturday between May and October from Piraeus.

The Brochure Says

"To honor the centennial anniversary of the modern Olympic Games held in Greece, Royal Olympic Cruises is pleased to present the Classical Aegean and Ionian Voyage, a 7-day exploration of the varied and beautiful lands of Greece."

Translation

It also goes to Albania.

DID YOU KNOW?

Women were not permitted to watch the original Olympic Games because all the male athletes competed naked.

Cabins & Costs

Fantasy Suites: . . . . NA
N/A

Small Splurges: .... C+

Average Price PPPD: $300 plus airfare.

The eight deluxe outside cabins boast two lower beds and a bathroom with tub and shower and some handsome wood-crafted dressers and nightstands, plus a desk, hassock, table and chair.

Suitable Standards: C

Average Price PPPD: $286 plus airfare.

Outside cabins with the choice of two lower beds or a double bed are the standard offerings on the *Orpheus;* there's only one of the latter.

Bottom Bunks: ....D

Average Price PPPD: $192 plus airfare.

Inside cabins with upper and lower berths are the lowest-priced accommodations on board. The bath has shower only. There are also some inside single-bed cabins available.

Where She Goes

The *Orpheus* makes a seven-day Classical Aegean and Ionian Voyage with some different ports of call from the rest of the White Ships—cruising the Corinth Canal, visiting Delphi; Ithaca; Saranda, Albania; Corfu; Katakolon; Zante; Rethymnon; Santorini; Mykonos; and Nauplion, which is the gateway to Epidaurus and Mycenae. The ship sails every Saturday between May and October.

The Bottom Line

The cabins and public rooms are attractively furnished, and the ship was well taken care of during its long charter with Swan Hellenic. While the cabins are quite small, they're comfortable enough for the itinerary the ship is offering—you'll be ashore on a tour bus a lot of the time if you visit all the famous Greek sites you're offered.

Fielding's Five

Five Easy Places

1. The swimming pool is surrounded by padded benches and loungers and, while not huge, is adequate to cool down a few people at a time.

2. A small taverna aft on Venus Deck makes a casual spot to get together for a chat or a buffet breakfast, lunch or dinner.

3. The library gives a good read or a spot to admire the lovely Greek mythological murals on the walls.

4. The Apollo Pool Bar and overhead Solarium are laid-back spots to commune with nature.

5. The Lounge of the Muses is where after-dinner coffee is served and where you might be struck to turn out a poem or a sonata.

Five Good Reasons to Book This Ship

1. You could get an education by osmosis from the years of erudite lectures oozing from the walls.

2. There's a great sun deck and pool that could turn a scholar into a hedonist in no time flat.

3. You get to go to Albania—if only to note that you don't know why you ever wanted to go to Albania.

4. It's the only one of the White Ships that cruises the Corinth Canal.

5. You can visit the tomb of Agamemnon, the beaches at Rethymnon on Crete's northern coast and eat a fish soup called Psarosoupa Avgholemono in the wonderful waterfront seafood restaurants of Nauplion, where the Lion of Venice still stares down from the walls.

Five Things You Won't Find On Board

1. An elevator.

2. TV sets in the cabin.

3. A fitness center.

4. A children's playroom.

5. Cabins designated wheelchair-accessible.

Orpheus ★★

Registry	Greece
Officers	Greek
Crew	Greek
Crew	190
GRT	5,092
Length (ft.)	375
Beam (ft.)	50
Draft (ft.)	16
Passengers-Cabins Full	316
Passengers-2/Cabin	304
Passenger Space Ratio	16.75
Stability Rating	Fair
Seatings	2
Cuisine	Continental/Greek
Dress Code	Traditional
Room Service	Yes
Tip	$6 - $8 PPPD

Ship Amenities

Outdoor Pool	1
Indoor Pool	0
Jacuzzi	4
Fitness Center	No
Spa	No
Beauty Shop	Yes
Showroom	Yes
Bars/Lounges	3
Casino	Yes
Shops	1
Library	Yes
Child Program	Yes
Self-Service Laundry	No
Elevators	0

Cabin Statistics

Suites	0
Outside Doubles	116
Inside Doubles	35
Wheelchair Cabins	0
Singles	1
Single Surcharge	150%
Verandas	0
110 Volt	Yes

EPIROTIKI CRUISES

Triton

An English/Norwegian "Bahamarama boat" from Miami has hit the big-time in the Mediterranean because of its wide teak decks and large swimming pool and standard (if narrow) cabins that don't carom back and forth in all shapes and sizes but are fitted together neatly in an orderly fashion and have beds that can be changed in a whisk from twins to queen-sized. Triton himself was the son of Poseidon and Amphitrite, a demon of the sea with a fish tail. He serves as a helpmate on a good journey, which is sort of what Triton can do for you.

The former *Sunward II* from Norwegian Cruise Line, the *Cunard Adventurer* before that (1971–1976), has settled happily into the Aegean sunshine as Epirotiki's *Triton* since the ship debuted for the Greek line in 1992. With seven passenger decks, five of them containing some cabins, the vessel has a large swimming pool, some public rooms on the two topmost decks and two-seating dining. Lighter and brighter than many of the vintage vessels plying the Med, the *Triton* has easily adaptable cabins in which most allow twin beds to be put together instantly to make a queen-sized bed instead.

The Brochure Says

"The *Ms Triton* made her first voyage with Epirotiki in the spring of 1992. This 14,000-ton vessel has a special atmosphere and offers all the comforts of a modern liner."

Translation

Finally, she gets a little respect, and it's about time. Her Greek owners obviously dote on her. When she was NCL's *Sunward II*, she did the Bahamarama mini-cruise run and was the smallest ship in the fleet.

Cabins & Costs

Fantasy Suites: .... **NA**
N/A

Small Splurges: .... **C**
Average Price PPPD: $320 plus airfare.
The largest cabins on board are the outside doubles on Apollo Deck, about 13 by 17 feet, with twin or queen-sized beds, bathroom with tub, a small sitting area, dresser and nightstands.

Suitable Standards: .... **D**
Average Price PPPD: $289 plus airfare.
Standard outside doubles have two lower beds that in most cases can be combined into a queen- sized bed, plus a chair, desk/dresser with stool, nightstand with drawers and bathroom with shower. These rooms are quite narrow.

Bottom Bunks: .... **D**
Average Price PPPD: $220 plus airfare.
The lowest-priced cabins are the inside doubles with two lower beds that can be put together for a queen-sized bed; these are almost identical to the outsides (see Suitable Standards, above) except without a window or porthole.

Where She Goes

The *Triton* sails the Golden Fleece Route for the White Ships division of Royal Olympic, departing Piraeus on Friday mornings and calling in Santorini, Heraklion, Rhodes, Patmos, Kusadasi, Istanbul and Mykonos. The season begins in April and ends in November.

The Bottom Line

The *Triton* is a surprisingly sleek-looking ship with an interesting itinerary for a destination-oriented traveler, perhaps someone making a first visit to the Eastern Mediterranean. Cabins are fairly small but attractively furnished, and the pool and deck areas are expansive. We'd love to hear a comment from former owners NCL about her average per diem cruise-only prices in the Med, however, compared to what they were in the Caribbean (clue: much, much cheaper in the Caribbean).

Fielding's Five

Five Sensational Places

1. A great pool deck has an oval pool with tile surround and a curved teak deck filled with sun loungers.

2. The Nine Muses Nightclub has panoramic windows opening forward to the sea, the same view the navigation bridge has, only higher up.

3. A light and bright dining room makes a contrast to some of Epirotiki's below-decks windowless restaurants.

4. A full casino, operated by Casinos Austria, with discreetly patterned decor and small bar at one end.

5. The Nefeli Bar, a covered outdoor bar amidships on an upper deck with a big overhead awning for when you realize you're getting too much sun and want something cold to drink.

Five Good Reasons to Book This Ship

1. There's an around-the-ship jogging track, rarer than hen's teeth in the Aegean.

2. Her seven-day Golden Fleece itinerary that calls in seven ports in Greece and Turkey.

3. She's a bigger star in the Eastern Med than she was in Miami.

4. A friendly Greek staff who'd like to show you their Mediterranean.

5. To have an evening and all the next day in Istanbul to negotiate the purchase of a Turkish carpet.

Five Things You Won't Find On Board

1. A library.

2. Good sightlines in the Sirenes show lounge; but then it's pretty small, so you might not find a seat anyhow.

3. A self-service laundry.

4. Assigned seating at breakfast and lunch; only dinners have assigned tables and times.

5. A smoking section at meals; the White Ships have been designated entirely non-smoking in the dining rooms.

Triton ★★

Registry	Greece
Officers	Greek
Crew	Greek
Complement	285
GRT	14,110
Length (ft.)	449
Beam (ft.)	70.5
Draft (ft.)	19
Passengers-Cabins Full	912
Passengers-2/Cabin	706
Passenger Space Ratio	19.83
Stability Rating	Fair
Seatings	2
Cuisine	Continental/Greek
Dress Code	Traditional
Room Service	Yes
Tip	$6 - $8 PPPD

Ship Amenities

Outdoor Pool	1
Indoor Pool	0
Jacuzzi	0
Fitness Center	Yes
Spa	No
Beauty Shop	Yes
Showroom	Yes
Bars/Lounges	4
Casino	Yes
Shops	1
Library	Yes
Child Program	Yes
Self-Service Laundry	No
Elevators	2

Cabin Statistics

Suites	30
Outside Doubles	206
Inside Doubles	117
Wheelchair Cabins	0
Singles	0
Single Surcharge	150%
Verandas	0
110 Volt	Yes

EPIROTIKI CRUISES

ESPLANADE TOURS

581 Boylston Street, Boston, MA 02116
☎ (617) 266-7465, (800) 426-5492

The **Caledonian Star** *travels to the remotest and most untouched corners of the world; here enthusiastic dancers greet the ship's arrival in Takoradi, Ghana.*

Esplanade Tours of Boston is the North American marketing representative for Noble Caledonian Ltd. and Spice Island Cruises.

Spice Island Cruises, which sails among the islands of Indonesia, operates the *Bali Sea Dancer*, the former *Illiria*, on three- and four-day cruises out of Bali. Noble Caledonian Ltd. operates the *Caledonian Star* on worldwide expedition cruises.

Esplanade also markets the *MS Regency* on seven-night Nile sailings from Luxor.

ESPLANADE TOURS

Bali Sea Dancer ★★★, ⚓⚓⚓⚓

Bali has a way of softly and sweetly dictating its own terms. Tourism is the main industry here, and Bali is expert at it. It is street theater raised to an exquisitely detailed level, and everyone has to play. This is no place for a cynic, or even a pragmatist. It is a well-worn island, lush and green, most of it lovingly terraced and sculpted so often over the centuries that there is probably no inch of landscape that has not been rearranged a dozen times.

The *Bali Sea Dancer*, built as the *Illiria* in Italy in 1962, is quite pretty, long and low with yachtlike lines, a short wide funnel and a lot of wood and polished brass. The food aboard is tasty, with fresh fruit, big hearty breakfasts and—the culinary highlight—a big Dutch/Indonesian *rijsttafel*, the traditional Dutch planter's feast of rice topped with meats, seafood, vegetables, sauces, coconut and pickled and spiced side dishes. The Indonesian crew is fluent in English, eager to serve and always remembers your name and favorite libation.

The Brochure Says

"On shore there's even more to see and do. Dive the exquisite reefs with our onboard Dive Master. Or you can snorkel or just paddle about in the crystal clear waters. A number of enthralling cultural tours are offered at each destination. And each stop promises to be handicraft heaven for the shoppers amongst you."

Translation

Not only is it a lovely ship to cruise the waters of Indonesia aboard, but look at everything you can do in the ports of call.

Cabins & Costs

Fantasy Suites: .... NA
  N/A

Small Splurges: .... B
  Average Price PPPD: $310 plus airfare.
  A couple of deluxe cabins with floral bedspreads and matching easy chairs, wooden nightstand and bathroom with tub and shower are the most spacious and comfortable quarters aboard.

Suitable Standards: C
  Average Price PPPD: $220 plus airfare.
  All the cabins on the ship are on the small side; the outside mid-category doubles have two lower beds (some also with a third berth), a three-drawer wooden cabinet and a vanity stool, two hanging closets and a large tile bathroom almost as big as the bedroom, with shower, makeup mirror and storage for toilet articles.

Bottom Bunks: C
  Average Price PPPD: $150 plus airfare.
  The nine inside cabins are actually larger than many of the outside cabins, and contain the same furnishings as the Suitable Standards described above.

Where She Goes

The *Bali Sea Dancer* sails on Fridays for a three-day cruise to Komodo, home of the famous Komodo dragons, and Badas, Sumbawa, to see the buffalo races. A four-day cruise adds the unspoiled island of Lombok to the itinerary.

The Bottom Line

This is a comfortable, well-riding ship with more class and luxury than you would expect to find in short-cruise vessels going out of Bali. It is highly recommended for people who enjoy expedition cruises as well as people looking for a warm-weather, watersports-oriented holiday.

Fielding's Five

Five Easy Places

1. The library, one of the most charming at sea, displays reproductions of Greek art, and has a small ornamental fireplace, sofas, chairs, wooden game tables and writing tables, as well as a good collection of books about nature, geography and wildlife.

2. The pool deck has a buffet setup at one end, a sheltered area for chairs and tables; the pool is fairly large with a wide wooden rim that provides extra seating.

3. The Ikat Lounge has a small wood dance floor, six columns that support the ceiling wrapped in tree-trunk-like material, wood coffee tables, chairs and sofas and arrangements of fresh tropical flowers.

4. The reception area and purser's square are furnished with comfortable leather chairs and hassocks, wood walls with a rubbed satiny finish; glass-and-wood French doors open to the deck.

5. The Orchid Dining Room has very attentive service but can get crowded when the ship is full.

Five Good Reasons to Book This Ship

1. To see a Komodo dragon.

2. To dive the reefs.

3. To sample some of the delicious cuisine of Indonesia.

4. To sail from Bali on three- and four-day cruises, just right to add onto a land visit.

5. To watch the buffalo races in Badas.

Five Things You Won't Find On Board

1. A casino.

2. A large gym; the tiny one on board has a treadmill, two stationary bikes and an adjacent sauna.

3. A level cabin floor at either end of the ship.

4. A good view from the forward observation deck; the curve of the bow inhibits looking ahead.

5. A fire in the library's fireplace.

ESPLANADE TOURS

Bali Sea Dancer   ★★★, ⚓⚓⚓

Registry	Indonesia
Officers	Indonesian
Crew	Indonesian
Crew	90
GRT	4.000
Length (ft.)	329.5
Beam (ft.)	47.6
Draft (ft.)	16.3
Passengers-Cabins Full	150
Passengers-2/Cabin	146
Passenger Space Ratio	27.39
Stability Rating	Good
Seatings	1
Cuisine	International
Dress Code	Casual
Room Service	Yes
Tip	$4 PPPD

Ship Amenities

Outdoor Pool	1
Indoor Pool	0
Jacuzzi	0
Fitness Center	Yes
Spa	No
Beauty Shop	Yes
Showroom	No
Bars/Lounges	1
Casino	No
Shops	1
Library	Yes
Child Program	No
Self-Service Laundry	Yes
Elevators	0

Cabin Statistics

Suites	2
Outside Doubles	62
Inside Doubles	9
Wheelchair Cabins	0
Singles	0
Single Surcharge	150%
Verandas	0
110 Volt	No

ESPLANADE TOURS

Caledonian Star   ★★★, ⚓⚓⚓⚓⚓

She's not particularly handsome nor very lavish—there are no cabins with private verandas, for example, and our waiter—lovesick, homesick, the Hamlet of the dining room—never once got a single meal order correct at our table of four. But she's one of our very favorite ships in the world. Not just anybody can handle a mix of 76 very exacting British and American veteran travelers on a 24-day cruise along the coast of West Africa and leave them as happy at the end as at the beginning. We'd go again tomorrow.

Zodiacs carried aboard the **Caledonian Star** *ferry passengers ashore for expeditionary visits to unusual islands.*

The *Caledonian Star*, the former *North Star* from now-defunct Exploration Cruise Lines, is much better known in Great Britain than in the United States, and the company gets a tremendous amount of repeat business from there. Itineraries are exotic enough to titillate even the most-traveled members of the Century Club, and the lived-in, unpretentious vessel somehow manages to always make one feel at home. There are five passenger decks with cabins on three of them; all cabins are outsides. The topmost deck has sun deck and library/lecture hall, and the Veranda Deck is where the pool and main lounge are located. The dining room is one deck lower. Cabins are smallish and bathrooms are standard all over the ship with showers rather than tubs.

The Brochure Says

"Our 'Little Blue Ship,' as she is affectionately known by hundreds of our frequent travelers is large enough to go anywhere, yet small enough to allow exploration in the remotest and untouched corners of the world. Expedition cruising was little known to travelers in the U.K. until the arrival of the *Caledonian Star* in the late 1980s. Since that time she has developed a loyal following from those who prefer to travel aboard a ship which is dedicated to learning more about our world and taking part in detailed in-depth itineraries in the company of our expert expedition teams and knowledgeable guest speakers."

Translation

A very apt description of the ship and its lifestyle.

EAVESDROPPING

A travel agent who specializes in expedition cruises: "You're not going to take a Seabourn person and put him on an expedition cruise. You have to be very careful and be sure you know your client."

Cabins & Costs

Fantasy Suites: . . . . *C*

Average Price PPPD: $377 including airfare, land package program and all shore excursions.
There are two suites aboard, neither of them to die for, but spacious enough, with separate living room, bedroom and small bath with shower. The living room sofa can convert to a bed as well.

Small Splurges: . . . . **D**

Average Price PPPD: $331 including airfare, land package program and all shore excursions.
The three deluxe staterooms on the lowest passenger deck cannot really be recommended because of the water sloshing against the portholes in heavy seas, even though there's a sofa bed, built-in desk, and separate sitting room divided from the bedroom by a curtain.

Suitable Standards: . . . . *C+*

Average Price PPPD: $307 including airfare, land package and all shore excursions.
The standards are small but comfortable enough, with windows on upper decks and portholes on lower decks. There are two lower beds, one of which converts to a sofa for daytime, plus a desk/dresser with chair, a TV/VCR, a couple of large mirrors and a mini-refrigerator. There's limited drawer space but plenty of open shelf space in the hanging closets. The bathroom has a counter and sink, marine vacuum toilet

and shower, plus additional storage under the sink counter and in a mirrored medicine chest on the wall.

Bottom Bunks: ....D

Average Price PPPD: $253 including airfare, land package and all shore excursions.
The basic cabins are similar to the standards or a bit smaller (see "Suitable Standards") with two lower beds, but are located on the lowest passenger deck, with portholes instead of windows and that sloshing sea.

Expect the unexpected on the ship of exotic itineraries. In early 1997, she visits New Zealand, Australia, Indonesia and the Seychelles.

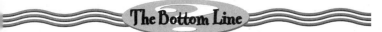

While not new and certainly not in the class of the glamorous *Hanseatic* and *Bremen*, the *Caledonian Star* is a handsome and comfortable expedition vessel. The food aboard is not haute cuisine, but it is well prepared and varied, with expansive breakfast and lunch buffets as well as à la carte hot dishes cooked to order. A baker prepares fresh breads, pastries and cakes daily. The Scandinavian officers keep the navigation bridge open to passengers except during severe weather or entering and leaving certain ports where local officials don't like to see passengers on the bridge. The lifestyle aboard is easygoing, and both passengers and crew are congenial. We would not recommend booking cabins on the lowest passenger deck because of the sea sloshing against the portholes like the water in an automatic washing machine.

Five Favorite Places

1. The library and lecture hall has a fascinating collection of esoteric books about nature, wooden armchairs, heavy fixed tables, and self-service coffee, tea and cookies around the clock.
2. The sun deck outside the library is also where barbecues and picnics are set up at long wooden tables, along with a grill and a buffet table.
3. The swimming pool, large enough for lap swimming, unusual on a ship this small, surrounded by white plastic chairs and tables.
4. The main lounge is a handsome, comfortable room with sofas and chairs and a long banquette along one side, and a small dance floor and patio, plus (when we were aboard) plenty of live green plants.
5. A small dining room with windows, and tables for four, six and eight.

Five Good Reasons to Book This Ship

1. The itineraries, the itineraries, the itineraries.
2. The open single meal seatings that let you sit where and with whom you please, giving a good chance to get to know the lecturers as well as the other passengers.
3. The Zodiac landing craft that can take you exploring to uninhabited islands.
4. Because all the shore excursions are included in the basic fare.
5. The excellent quality of the expedition leaders and lecturers.

Five Things You Won't Find On Board

1. An elevator; you do an awful lot of walking up and down companionways on this ship.

2. A closed navigation bridge; the bridge is always open to passengers, as are the bridge wings, so long as passengers don't get in the way.

3. Room service; you don't get waited on unless you're sick.

4. Casino; the passengers are not really interested in gambling.

5. Cabins designated wheelchair-accessible; the ship is inappropriate for anyone with limited mobility.

Caledonian Star ★★★, ♨♨♨♨

Registry	**Bahamas**
Officers	**Scandinavian**
Crew	**Filipino**
Complement	**63**
GRT	**3,095**
Length (ft.)	**292.5**
Beam (ft.)	**45.5**
Draft (ft.)	**21**
Passengers-Cabins Full	**134**
Passengers-2/Cabin	**120**
Passenger Space Ratio	**25.79**
Stability Rating	**Good**
Seatings	**1**
Cuisine	**Continental**
Dress Code	**Casual**
Room Service	**No**
Tip	**$7 PPPD**

Ship Amenities

Outdoor Pool	**1**
Indoor Pool	**0**
Jacuzzi	**0**
Fitness Center	**No**
Spa	**No**
Beauty Shop	**Yes**
Showroom	**Yes**
Bars/Lounges	**1**
Casino	**No**
Shops	**1**
Library	**Yes**
Child Program	**No**
Self-Service Laundry	**No**
Elevators	**0**

Cabin Statistics

Suites	**2**
Outside Doubles	**66**
Inside Doubles	**0**
Wheelchair Cabins	**0**
Singles	**2**
Single Surcharge	**150%**
Verandas	**0**
110 Volt	**Yes**

EURO⊙CRUISES

INCORPORATED

303 West 13th Street, New York, NY 10014
☎ (212) 691-2099, (800) 688-EURO

St. Xavier of the Spilled Blood in St. Petersburg is visited on **Kristina Regina**
cruises.

History . . . .

EuroCruises is the largest North American marketer of ships to Europe, representing ships and ferries owned and operated by various European companies.

Among the most unusual ships it represents are the icebreakers *Nordbris* and *Polarstar*, which cruise to polar bear country in Spitsbergen on four- and seven-night cruises. The *Nordbris* carries 38 passengers, the *Polarstar* 25.

Its river and canal cruisers are covered under Alternative Cruises (page 807) The 200-passenger *Kristina Regina* offers nine-day St. Petersburg and Baltic States cruises in summer.

Ausonia

She's laid out and ready for sun and fun, with a lighthearted Italian lilt, and she sails along the sparkling Turquoise Coast of Turkey and to the citrus-scented island of Cyprus, where the roadways are lined with cypress trees so dense they form a tunnel, and the "typical local lunch" we sampled consisted of 20 different hot and cold dishes.

Grimaldi Cruises' *Ausonia*, fourth in the line to carry this name, was built in Italy's Monfalcone yard in 1956-57 for Adriatica SAN as a three-class ship and put into Trieste-Beirut service before her long career as a popular Mediterranean cruise ship. Her most recent makeover was in 1991.

The vessel is literally all decked out for Mediterranean sunshine, with her expansive aft pool decks on two levels, both surrounded with plenty of teak deck as well as cooler, shaded areas with tables and chairs. The interior is clean and comfortable if not exactly cutting-edge decor. Eight passenger decks include five with cabins on them and elevators to most but not all passenger sleeping areas. A single public room deck has the dining room, show lounge, library, disco, shops, bars and card room packed in.

The Brochure Says

"A truly all-inclusive holiday, all meals, a la carte luncheons and dinners, afternoon tea with pastries, complimentary red wine (in carafe) at lunch and dinner, Captain's Welcome Cocktail, movie shows, dancing every evening to the orchestra, nightly entertainment, Piano Bar, Disco until early hours, deck games, swimming pool, card room, safe for your valuables, library, deck chairs, gymnasium, Jacuzzi."

Translation

Veteran cruisers take far too much for granted. It takes a page of copy like this, obviously aimed at first-time cruisers, to realize what a good deal we really get. And hey, did you notice the *vin ordinaire c'est inclus?*

Cabins & Costs

Fantasy Suites: .... B

Average Price PPPD: $280 plus airfare.

There are six junior suites on board named for Italian composers, of which we'd tout the Verdi and Donizetti, forward on Bahia Deck, over the others amidships two decks down on Delphi, because they have a better view. What you get is a two-room suite with living room—sofa, chairs, coffee table, built-in cabinetry and chests—a bedroom with two lower beds, nightstand and closets, and a bathroom with tub. Naturally, they include the Le Club perks described below (see Five Good Reasons to Book This Ship).

Small Splurges: C

Average Price PPPD: $250 plus airfare.

Category 9 cabins have two lower beds, a tub in the bathroom, a minibar, the Le Club extras, a banquette, TV, and desk/dresser with chair.

Suitable Standards: C

Average Price PPPD: $200 plus airfare.

An outside double with two lower beds, nightstand, bath with shower, and sometimes a fold-down third berth, plus a bathroom with shower.

Bottom Bunks: .... D

Average Price PPPD: $167 plus airfare.

The cheapest digs on this ship are the four-berth insides, spacious as a Scandinavian ferry (which means, not very). It does have a private bath with shower.

Where She Goes

The *Ausonia* perambulates around the Mediterranean between late March and late October, calling, depending on itinerary, in France, Spain, Italy, Greece, Egypt, Israel, Cyprus, Turkey, Tunisia, Morocco, Malta, Sardinia, Corsica and Syria.

The Bottom Line

When you get down to where the hoi polloi sleeps, the price gets reasonable and your fellow travelers are almost certainly young stay-up-late types. You'll be subjected to the usual five-language announcements, but they publish a daily program in English and think you'll enjoy meeting the continental crowd.

Fielding's Five

Five Special Spots

1. The big Jacuzzi pool, aft on Bahia Deck, is usually full of kids and young people—but this ship draws a lot of young people anyhow.

2. The Ball Room Majorca is the largest lounge on board; this is where the dancing girls come on and kick 'em high.

3. The disco goes on until the wee small hours with a lot of great (and not so great) bodies gyrating; the junior officers show up here.

4. The free-form pool and shallow-water surround on Athena Deck is a great place to lie in cool water while sunbathing.

5. The cozy Lounge Venezia is a good place to meet for a quiet drink.

Five Good Reasons to Book This Ship

1. Honeymooners and seniors get a discount off the published rate.

2. Because it's Italian; there are two meal seatings for that pasta, fashionably late, the early at 7 p.m., the late at 8:45.

3. Because it goes to some of the most exotic ports in the Med—Limassol, Casablanca, Antalya, Latakia, Alexandria, Tangier and Tartous.

4. Because you can book a Le Club cabin and get a bonus bottle of Italian champagne (a.k.a. Spumante) and fresh fruit daily.

5. Because in the European fashion (without those dreary cabotage laws) you can get on and off in any of several ports, completing a seven-day cruise from whichever city you prefer.

Five Things You Won't Find On Board

1. The certainty of a call at Capri; if the weather doesn't permit anchoring and tendering, the ship goes on to Naples instead.

2. Good sightlines in the show lounge—if you sit in the back during the dance routines, you'll see only the t and not the a.

3. A crew member who doesn't speak at least a little English—except maybe down in the engine room.

4. A casino; Italians don't want Italian-flag ships offering gambling in Italian waters.

5. A wheelchair-accessible cabin; companionways are steep and passageways narrow on this vintage vessel.

EUROCRUISES, INC.

Ausonia ★ ★ ★

Registry	Italy
Officers	Italian
Crew	Italian
Complement	220
GRT	13.000
Length (ft.)	523
Beam (ft.)	70
Draft (ft.)	17.5
Passengers-Cabins Full	550
Passengers-2/Cabin	497
Passenger Space Ratio	26.15
Stability Rating	Good
Seatings	2
Cuisine	Italian
Dress Code	Informal
Room Service	No
Tip	N/A

Ship Amenities

Outdoor Pool	1
Indoor Pool	0
Jacuzzi	1
Fitness Center	No
Spa	No
Beauty Shop	Yes
Showroom	Yes
Bars/Lounges	3
Casino	No
Shops	1
Library	Yes
Child Program	No
Self-Service Laundry	No
Elevators	1

Cabin Statistics

Suites	6
Outside Doubles	140
Inside Doubles	101
Wheelchair Cabins	0
Singles	3
Single Surcharge	140%
Verandas	0
110 Volt	No

Azur

We think of the Azur in the same fond terms we remember the longtime "Follies" show girl who triumphantly belts out "I'm Still Here" in the musical. We were aboard during her Paquet period in the early 1980s when the French cruise company was trying to build a U.S. market. They were so anxious they even offered a bacon and eggs breakfast and American coffee on board—and you know how the French hate that.

The *Azur*, which sails under the Azur-Bolero Cruises banner these days, was built as the deep-sea ferry *Eagle* in France in 1970-71 for P&O's ferry division, and in 1975 went over to Nouvelle Cie de Paquebots for ferry service out of Marseilles, when she was renamed *Azur*. She was rebuilt as a cruise ship in 1981, when cabins were added to her car-carrying decks, most of them obviously insides, which is why she has more inside than outside cabins. She sailed for Paquet until 1987, when she went over to Chandris Fantasy Cruises and was renamed *The Azur*, dropped out of sight for a while and then resurfaced later in the early 1990s when she was put out to charter under Classical Cruises, EuroCruises and other banners. With seven passenger decks, five of them carrying cabins, she's a fairly dense vessel but has all the traditional cruise ship niceties from the early 1980s, from cinema to playroom, two swimming pools and two major lounges. They suggest men wear a jacket and tie and women a cocktail dress to dinners. And like her passengers, the *Azur* looks spiffy these days.

The Brochure Says

"The 750-passenger vessel is made for leisurely cruising. It offers spacious cocktail bars, lavish midnight buffets, and a host of onboard program activities including aerobics, karaoke and casino gambling."

Translation

See how with-it we are—even offering karaoke.

Cabins & Costs

Fantasy Suites: .... **NA**
N/A

Small Splurges: .... **NA**
N/A

Suitable Standards: .... **C+**
Average Price PPPD: $195 plus airfare.
The cabins on board are fairly comparable, with all the outside standards similar in size and furnishings. Two lower beds, a desk/dresser with chair, perhaps a second chair and coffee table if you've booked one of the pricier categories. The top-priced cabins have tub/shower combinations, all others shower only.

Bottom Bunks: .... **C**
Average Price PPPD: $111 plus airfare.
The cheapest inside double cabins are fairly spacious with two lower berths (and some quads with two uppers as well) and have similar furnishings to the Suitable Standards, above.

Where She Goes

The *Azur* cruises the Greek Islands and Eastern Mediterranean roundtrip from Venice most of the summer, with a couple of longer repositioning spring and fall cruises to and from Genoa and winter sailings in the Canary Islands, Egypt and North Africa.

The Bottom Line

It's a good buy for cruisers watching their budgets. Even the lowest-priced inside cabins have two lower beds and enough room to change your mind. The itinerary is good, with some beach and shopping time worked in, not always common on seven-day Greek Islands sailings, and an added bonus is cruising through the Corinth Canal.

Fielding's Five

Five Special Places

1. The Lounge Deck swimming pool is a bit larger than the Sun Deck swimming pool, but the fact that there are two will brighten your Mediterranean cruise.

2. A really proper cinema with a balcony and rows of theater seats on a raked level makes the Rialto Cinema a favorite.

3. A casino, of course, on this Panamanian-flag vessel with Greek officers and no Machiavellian Italian rules to get in the way.

4. The Tahiti Lounge with its wicker chairs and tropical laziness is a combination disco, bar and buffet cafe.

5. The Azur show lounge with its reflective ceiling and swivel tub chairs is where you see the entertainment.

Five Good Reasons to Book This Ship

1. The airfare is included from New York with some good add-on package rates from other cities.

2. A seven-day roundtrip Greek Isles sailing from Venice with eight ports of call plus cruising the Corinth Canal and a technical call in Bari, where they don't let you get off the ship.

3. To visit the blue caves of Zakynthos.

4. To play squash at the only squash court at sea—now that the *Seawind Crown* removed hers.

5. The cabins are relatively spacious for a Mediterranean cruise ship in this price range.

Five Things You Won't Find On Board

1. A shop or bar that takes U.S. dollars; you spend Italian lira on this ship.

2. A private veranda.

3. A lunch without pasta.

4. A bad sport, not with squash, volleyball, ping pong, trap shooting, gymnasium and bodybuilding center available.

5. Late-night hunger; you get a midnight buffet followed an hour later, at 1 a.m., by pizza and a snack.

Azur ★★★

Registry	Panama
Officers	Greek
Crew	International
Complement	325
GRT	15,000
Length (ft.)	466
Beam (ft.)	72
Draft (ft.)	20
Passengers-Cabins Full	770
Passengers-2/Cabin	661
Passenger Space Ratio	22.69
Stability Rating	Good
Seatings	2
Cuisine	Italian
Dress Code	Informal
Room Service	Yes
Tip	N/A

Ship Amenities

Outdoor Pool	2
Indoor Pool	0
Jacuzzi	0
Fitness Center	No
Spa	No
Beauty Shop	Yes
Showroom	Yes
Bars/Lounges	5
Casino	Yes
Shops	1
Library	Yes
Child Program	Yes
Self-Service Laundry	No
Elevators	3

Cabin Statistics

Suites	0
Outside Doubles	146
Inside Doubles	180
Wheelchair Cabins	0
Singles	93
Single Surcharge	160 - 170%
Verandas	0
110 Volt	No

Black Prince

*We still remember being stunned by the watersports platform on the stern
of the Black Prince that was added in the 1987 refit. That was ahead of Seabourn's collapsible wire mesh swimming pool but after Sea Goddess's more
modest watersports platform.*

Fred. Olsen Cruise Lines' *Black Prince*, a favorite of the British cruise market, was built in Germany in 1966, and boasts not only one of the earliest
watersports marina platforms but also the biggest—60 feet long when it's all
in place. The Marina Park extends from the stern when the ship is at anchor
to allow passengers to swim in a collapsible wire mesh pool with teak decking
around it, or sail, waterski or windsurf off a watersports platform. It's used
most frequently in the Canary Islands or in quiet Mediterranean and Caribbean bays away from shipping traffic.

The *Black Prince* has seven passenger decks, with cabins concentrated on
four of them. The main public room deck is anchored with a lounge at either
end and restaurants amidships.

The Brochure Says

"These days there are all sorts of holidays to choose from. Beach holidays and city holidays, cultural holidays and holidays crammed full of activities. But there's one break that
combines them all and does it without you having to check in and out of countless hotels,
jump on and off planes, trains and automobiles. It's a cruise."

Translation

None necessary.

Cabins & Costs

Note: Unlike North America, European line's published rates are their actual prices.

Fantasy Suites: .... NA

N/A

Small Splurges: .... B

Average Price PPPD: $293 plus airfare.
There are four larger-than-average deluxe double outside on the topmost Marquee
Deck, attractively decorated, with two lower beds, a new in-house video system and
bath with tub and shower.

Suitable Standards: .... B

Average Price PPPD: $235 plus airfare.
Outside cabins with two lower beds may mean two real beds, one bed and one sofa,
or one bed and one pullman bed that folds into the wall. These cabins have bath
with shower only. There are also "family cabins" with a double bed, one lower and
one upper berth; a wide range of inside and outside singles; and the possibility of
creating a two-room suite out of certain adjoining cabins on Marina Deck.

Bottom Bunks: C

Average Price PPPD: $181 plus airfare.
The little inside three-berth cabins are the low man on the *Black Prince* totem pole,
with two lower beds and one upper berth. There is also fairly limited wardrobe
space in the lower category cabins.

Where She Goes

The *Black Prince* sails in the Canary Islands and Morocco in winter, then repositions
to the Caribbean for more winter sunshine, returns to the Canary Islands in springtime,
heads north to Norway in midsummer, then to the Western and Eastern Mediterranean
in late summer and fall. In the late autumn, the ship returns to the Canary Islands.

The Bottom Line

This is a sparkling clean, very sophisticated ship with a dedicated following in the United Kingdom. Cruises average 12 to 30 days in length, and discounts are offered for two
back-to-back sailings as well as early bookings. The main problem we find is that most of
the cabins don't offer a lot of wardrobe space, although the ship will store your "trunks
and suitcases" down the hall in special closets for you.

Fielding's Five

Five Favorite Principalities

1. The Aquitaine Lounge, a place to slip away and read in the daytime or sip before-
   dinner cocktails to piano music.

2. Neptune Lounge is where the evening entertainment happens with all those chorus
   girls, plus daytime fun and games when one of them just might be calling bingo.

3. The Video Lounge, where you can watch a movie on video (if you must).

4. The Marquee Restaurant is a top deck sidewalk cafe under canvas where you can
   breakfast or lunch alfresco.

5. The Sauna Deck, to steam out your aches, get a massage, exercise or have your hair done.

Five Good Reasons to Book This Ship

1. So you can become a member of the Fred. Olsen Cruise Lines Club and get perks on future sailings.

2. To take a games theme cruise, a whole sailing built around lots of Scrabble, Clue and Trivial Pursuit.

3. To visit the Canary Islands and Morocco for a little winter sunshine.

4. If you're over 62, you get a five percent senior discount; if you book certain soft sailings, you'll get 10 percent off.

5. To sail with the Norwegians to Norway.

Five Things You Won't Find On Board

1. Free 24-hour room service; there's a small fee for cabin service.

2. Ashtrays in the ship's indoor restaurant; smoking is not permitted there.

3. A visitor; Black Prince security systems do not permit them.

4. U.S. dollars; all accounts are run in pounds sterling.

5. Sloppy dressers; a jacket and tie are required for informal evenings, a dark suit or dinner jacket for formal evenings.

Black Prince ★★★

Registry	Norway
Officers	Norwegian
Crew	Filipino
Crew	200
GRT	11,209
Length (ft.)	460
Beam (ft.)	70
Draft (ft.)	19
Passengers-Cabins Full	433
Passengers-2/Cabin	395
Passenger Space Ratio	28.37
Stability Rating	Good
Seatings	2
Cuisine	International
Dress Code	Traditional
Room Service	Yes
Tip	$7 PPPD

Ship Amenities

Outdoor Pool	1
Indoor Pool	1
Jacuzzi	1
Fitness Center	Yes
Spa	No
Beauty Shop	Yes
Showroom	Yes
Bars/Lounges	3
Casino	Yes
Shops	2
Library	Yes
Child Program	No
Self-Service Laundry	No
Elevators	2

Cabin Statistics

Suites	0
Outside Doubles	149
Inside Doubles	33
Wheelchair Cabins	2
Singles	31
Single Surcharge	120%
Verandas	0
110 Volt	No

Black Watch

The first cruise we ever took, in what seems like eons ago, was aboard one of the Royal Viking ships in the days before the "stretch" (when the ship was cut in half and a new midsection of additional cabins and public space inserted). We cruised in Alaska, and thought it was the most magical vacation anyone could possibly have. Now, some 200 cruises later, we still do.

The *Black Watch* is the former *Star Odyssey/Royal Viking Star*, comfortably mid-sized, and carrying around 750 passengers. Cabins are built in the modular style, so all except the suites are about the same size with similar furnishings, and the prices differ only by the deck you choose.

Cabins & Costs

Fantasy Suites: .... A

Average Price PPPD: $427 plus air fare in the Mediterranean.

The three owner's suite apartments with private veranda have separate bedroom and sitting room, small veranda, large bath and walk-in closet. Twin or queen-sized beds, voluminous storage space, a graceful living room with sofa, several chairs and coffee table, adequate for entertaining, a bathroom with tub and shower, TV/VCR, hair dryer and mini-refrigerator provide all the comforts of home.

Small Splurges: .... B

Average Price PPPD: $292 plus air fare in the Mediterranean.

There are about three dozen of the S3 suites spread around the ship. These are comfortable cabins with picture windows, sitting areas with sofa, chair and coffee table, bathroom with tub and shower, TV, hair dryers and mini-refrigerator.

Suitable Standards: .... B

Average Price PPPD: $198 plus air fare in the Mediterranean.

Cabins aboard are built on a modular plan, so all are about the same size with the same furnishings; the major difference is which deck you're on and whether you're amidships, forward or aft. The F Category deluxe outside staterooms on Coral Deck are typical, with portholes rather than windows, bathroom with tub and shower (in a few cases, shower only—ask when booking if it's important), TV and hair dryer.

Bottom Bunks: .... B

Average Price PPPD: $173 plus air fare in the Mediterranean.

The lowest-priced category is I, a deluxe inside on the lowest passenger deck with two lower beds, bath with shower only, hair dryer and TV set, as well as a desk/dresser with chair, another chair and table, large closet.

Where She Goes

The *Black Watch* cruises around Africa in November, followed by year-round European sailings from Dover.

The Bottom Line

A lot of money was spent both on the cosmetic and the behind-the-scenes upgrading and updating of this vintage vessel. If anything, the makeovers have turned it into a more sophisticated vessel, particularly in the public rooms and bars, where there is more and longer cocktail service than there used to be. Older couples and singles in particular will find this ship offers an appealing, traditional cruise of the same high quality they used to enjoy on Royal Viking and Royal Cruise Line.

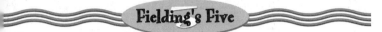

Fielding's Five

Five Favorite Spots

1. The Panorama forward observation lounge with its wide windows and swivel leather chairs where you can sit transfixed by the view all day long.

2. The Seven Seas Lounge and Terrace replaces what we used to call the morning bar, because everybody used to gather there about 11 or so with Bloody Marys and sing along to the pianist's popular melodies.

3. The bar adjacent to the show lounge with rose tapestry sofas and tub chairs, oval marble tables and a long bar with swivel leather stools where the regulars congregate before dinner.

4. The fitness area with enclosed gym and sauna on the top deck.

5. The deck area mini-galley.

Black Watch ☆☆☆☆

Registry	**Norway**
Officers	**Norwegian**
Crew	**Filipino**
Complement	**410**
GRT	**28,000**
Length (ft.)	**676**
Beam (ft.)	**83**
Draft (ft.)	**24**
Passengers-Cabins Full	**821**
Passengers-2/Cabin	**775**
Passenger Space Ratio	**36.12**
Stability Rating	**Good**
Seatings	**2**
Cuisine	**International**
Dress Code	**Traditional**
Room Service	**Yes**
Tip	**$7 PPPD**

Ship Amenities

Outdoor Pool	**1**
Indoor Pool	**0**
Jacuzzi	**3**
Fitness Center	**Yes**
Spa	**Yes**
Beauty Shop	**Yes**
Showroom	**Yes**
Bars/Lounges	**6**
Casino	**Yes**
Shops	**2**
Library	**Yes**
Child Program	**No**
Self-Service Laundry	**Yes**
Elevators	**5**

Cabin Statistics

Suites	**54**
Outside Doubles	**279**
Inside Doubles	**33**
Wheelchair Cabins	**4**
Singles	**48**
Single Surcharge	**120%**
Verandas	**9**
110 Volt	**Yes**

Bolero

As the Starward, *she was the first ship built especially for cruising in the Caribbean; the only ship sailing year-round ahead of her was the* Sunward I, *which had been repositioned from the Mediterranean.*

The last of the old Norwegian Cruise Line "white ships" to bite the dust, the former *Starward*, has become the *Bolero* for Azur-Bolero Cruises, and began service with the Christmas cruise at the end of 1995. *Starward* was also the first of the trio of newbuilds for Norwegian Cruise Line between 1968 and 1971.

Cabins & Costs

Fantasy Suites: C

Average Price PPPD: $198 plus airfare.
Not really fantastic, but adequate unto the need—the ship's five outside deluxe suites. A separate sitting area can be curtained off from the sleeping area, and has a sofa (that can be made into a bed), chairs, desk/dresser, coffee table, mini-refrigerator, and a big double closet with plenty of storage. The white tile bathrooms have tub, bidet and a long sink counter.

Small Splurges: C

Average Price PPPD: $181 plus airfare.
Two other similar suites amidships on a lower deck have a double bed and sitting area with a convertible sofa bed and lounge chair.

Suitable Standards: .... D

Average Price PPPD: $149 plus airfare.
The basic cabin has two lower beds, a window, a small nightstand with drawers, a tiny desk, a shelf in the window and a curtain rather than doors covering the hanging closet space, which allows only about 12 inches of free space before a built-in

cabinet underneath begins. The bathroom has a shower only, and an open two-shelf unit for toiletries.

Bottom Bunks: .... D

Average Price PPPD: $107 plus airfare.

A few really small cabins with upper and lower berths can be found forward on the lowest passenger deck, and some of them are outsides with portholes, but a tight squeeze to get into.

Bolero spends the winter season cruising the Canary Islands, Red Sea, Italy, Egypt, Greece and Israel, then repositions for summer and fall Eastern Mediterranean sailings.

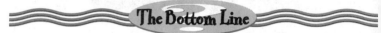

The *Bolero* has very small cabins with very thin walls, and was built on the premise that in the Caribbean everyone will spend the whole day ashore anyhow. Perhaps the same thing happens in the Med. The ship is probably best for young couples; on our sailing, one-third of the entire passenger list was on a honeymoon, making this a real love boat.

Five Special Spots

1. The cozy bar on the topmost deck overlooking the amidships swimming pool.

2. The amidships pool with tile surround, white plastic cafe chairs and loungers, sheltered with glass wings and partly covered overhead.

3. A second, aft swimming pool and sun lounging area and an adjacent buffet cafe.

4. A small, chic amidships lounge below the buffet cafe deck is near the casino and an intimate spot to meet for a drink.

5. The dining room has mostly tables for four, six, eight and 10, but a few for two are set so close together they might as well be a four.

Five Good Reasons to Book This Ship

1. Despite the small cabins with thin walls, the vessel itself is clean and well-decorated.

2. It sails to the Canary Islands, the Red Sea, Italy, Israel, Greece and Egypt.

3. Some very low introductory cruise deals this winter through EuroCruises, including the inaugural voyage, a five-night Christmas cruise Dec. 22–27, 1995, for $485-$895 plus airfare.

4. It's very handsomely decorated and small enough to find your way around easily.

5. To eavesdrop on your neighbors through the thin walls; we learned a lot about the private life of a certain football star and his wife in the cabin next door.

Five Things You Won't Find On Board

1. Good traction on an early morning jog; the decks can get slippery when wet.

2. Good sightlines in the show lounge.

3. Single cabins.

4. A self-service laundry.

5. An unwelcome breeze on the covered pool deck.

Bolero ★★★

Registry	**Bahamas**
Officers	**Italian/Greek**
Crew	**International**
Crew	**315**
GRT	**16,107**
Length (ft.)	**525**
Beam (ft.)	**75**
Draft (ft.)	**22**
Passengers-Cabins Full	**938**
Passengers-2/Cabin	**766**
Passenger Space Ratio	**21.02**
Stability Rating	**Good**
Seatings	**0**
Cuisine	**International**
Dress Code	**Traditional**
Room Service	**Yes**
Tip	**N/A**

Ship Amenities

Outdoor Pool	**2**
Indoor Pool	**0**
Jacuzzi	**0**
Fitness Center	**Yes**
Spa	**No**
Beauty Shop	**Yes**
Showroom	**Yes**
Bars/Lounges	**3**
Casino	**Yes**
Shops	**3**
Library	**Yes**
Child Program	**Yes**
Self-Service Laundry	**No**
Elevators	**4**

Cabin Statistics

Suites	**7**
Outside Doubles	**216**
Inside Doubles	**160**
Wheelchair Cabins	**0**
Singles	**0**
Single Surcharge	**160 - 170%**
Verandas	**0**
110 Volt	**Yes**

Funchal

It's difficult to think of the Funchal as a Scandinavian vessel because of its name and long Portuguese associations. But the Swedish officers and Portuguese staff do their best to remind you of both countries on this Panamanian-registry ship.

The *Funchal* from Fritidskryss has been around for a while but was extensively refurbished in 1991. Along with the former *Vasco de Gama* (see Seawind Cruise Line, page 681) this is the cruise ship so long associated with Portugal's George Potamianos who calls himself "a passionate lover of rea ships." Built in Denmark in 1961, the veteran ship has a lot of character, car feed all the passengers at a single seating in the two dining rooms and even includes an overnight and city tour in Gothenburg on Spitsbergen and North Cape itineraries. A $2 million refurbishment last year has upgraded cabins and public rooms.

The Brochure Says

"The *Funchal* is appointed in the simple, modern style preferred by Europeans."
Translation
Don't expect fancy.

Cabins & Costs

Fantasy Suites: . . . . NA
  N/A

Small Splurges: C
  Average Price PPPD: $341 plus airfare.
  An outside double cabin the company calls a suite (there are five of them) with two lower beds can be had.

EUROCRUISES, INC.

Suitable Standards: .... D

Average Price PPPD: $270 plus airfare.

There are a variety of double outside cabins on the *Funchal* with various bed arrangements—doubles, two lowers and a Combi, with extra pullman berths. The cabins are small, and a few have shared bathroom facilities, so double check the status before booking.

Bottom Bunks: .... D

Average Price PPPD: $131 plus airfare.

Oddly enough, the cheapest cabins aboard are not those singles with shared facilities, but rather the inside doubles with upper and lower berths and private bath on a bottom deck.

Where She Goes

Probably the two most popular itineraries in summer for the *Funchal* are the Spitsbergen run and the North Cape. The former is an 18-night roundtrip out of Gothenburg and the latter a 12-night cruise.

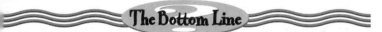

The Bottom Line

Basically an expedition vessel in itinerary, the *Funchal* still hews to traditional cruise patterns such as dressing up for dinner even in the high Arctic. Dr. Ian Fleming (no, not James Bond's creator) is a popular onboard lecturer on the subject of Arctic geology and Nordic cultures. Think expedition—perhaps Special Expeditions with its Swedish officers—to get a handle on these cruises.

Fielding's Five

Five Happening Places

1. The cozy Porto Piano Bar reminds us of the singalong piano bar on the Orient Express trains, both the VSOE and the Nostalgic Istanbul OE.

2. The comfortable bow deck with its tables and chairs and great views of the fjords and ice pack.

3. The *Funchal's* cabins are concentrated on five of the six passenger decks.

4. The Portuguese serving staff presents both a la carte and buffet offerings in the single-seating dining rooms.

5. The promenade decks are protected, ideal for passengers heading far above the Arctic Circle.

Five Good Reasons to Book This Ship

1. To go to Spitsbergen and look for polar bears.

2. To glory in the beauty of the Norwegian fjords.

3. To take advantage of very good transatlantic air rates offered by EuroCruises.

4. To sing along in that happy piano bar.

5. To get a free overnight in Gothenburg; as they used to say in vaudeville, second prize is two free nights in Gothenburg.

Funchal ★★

Registry	**Panama**
Officers	**Swedish**
Crew	**Portuguese**
Complement	**165**
GRT	**10,000**
Length (ft.)	**500**
Beam (ft.)	**63**
Draft (ft.)	**18**
Passengers-Cabins Full	**467**
Passengers-2/Cabin	**424**
Passenger Space Ratio	**23.98**
Stability Rating	**NA**
Seatings	**2**
Cuisine	**Continental**
Dress Code	**Informal**
Room Service	**No**
Tip	**N/A**

Ship Amenities

Outdoor Pool	**1**
Indoor Pool	**0**
Jacuzzi	**0**
Fitness Center	**No**
Spa	**No**
Beauty Shop	**Yes**
Showroom	**Yes**
Bars/Lounges	**2**
Casino	**Yes**
Shops	**1**
Library	**Yes**
Child Program	**No**
Self-Service Laundry	**No**
Elevators	**2**

Cabin Statistics

Suites	**5**
Outside Doubles	**129**
Inside Doubles	**58**
Wheelchair Cabins	**0**
Singles	**33**
Single Surcharge	**110%**
Verandas	**0**
110 Volt	**No**

FANTASY CRUISES

5200 Blue Lagoon Drive, Miami, FL 33126
☎ (305) 262-5411, (800) 423-2100

The angular whitewashed churches of Santorini.

History ....

Fantasy Cruises used to be the major marketing label of the Chandris Group, a distinguished family-owned Greek company that operated a number of vintage vessels on both long and short sailings from New York and Miami. But with the instant success of Celebrity Cruises, the Chandris upscale label introduced in 1990 with the *Meridian* and the *Horizon*, the Fantasy product was reduced gradually to only two ships, the *Britanis* and the *Amerikanis*. Today, the *Britanis* is laid up and the *Amerikanis* repositioned year-round in Europe.

Amerikanis

Notes from a first visit: "An ugly ship, chopped up and jerry-decorated with a little bit of everything. Gaudy dark carpet in the purser's lobby along with Chinese red and black lamps, rose floral walls, black leatherette chairs. An elaborate medieval fireplace in one room with a sofa shoved up in front of it." She obviously failed to win our hearts, but fortunately she's been refurbished a couple of times since.

Built in 1952 as the *Kenya Castle* for London's Union-Castle Line, the ship was purchased by the Chandris Group in 1967 and renamed the *Amerikanis*. There are eight passenger decks with passenger cabins on six of them. Because the vessel was originally built to transport families between Great Britain and Africa, cabins are fairly spacious with generous closet space. Two dining rooms split by the galley are inconvenient to get to, but both are served by elevators, as are the cabins on the lowest decks. The public rooms deck is anchored at the aft end by the Mayfair Ballroom, the show lounge, and forward by the slightly smaller Neptune Lounge. A recent refurbishment improved her cosmetically, getting rid of that neo-medieval decor that cluttered the public rooms. The Greek staff is affable.

"Aboard the *Amerikanis*, you'll be served by our caring, highly trained staff, which anticipates your every need."

Translation

Peel me a grape, Dimitri. While we've never counted noses, the company says there are 400 crew members on board to serve only 600 to 650 passengers. That's a very high service ratio.

Cabins & Costs

Fantasy Suites: .... **NA**
N/A

Small Splurges: .... **C**
Average Price PPPD: N/A.
There are 50 mini-suites on board that span three different decks, some of them on upper decks with large picture windows but less space than the ones on the Rome (dining room) Deck and Washington (purser's square) Deck. They have double or twin beds, a sitting area, TV and bathroom with tub. Several on Rome Deck are interconnecting for families traveling together.

Suitable Standards: .... **C**
Average Price PPPD: N/A.
Many of the outside double cabins have third and fourth berths as well, and a few have a double bed and a third lower bed. You'll need to specify whether you want double or twin beds.

Bottom Bunks: .... **D**
Average Price PPPD: N/A.
On the two lowest passenger decks, Ottawa and Lisbon, the cheapest cabins on board offer upper and lower berths and bath with shower only; there are 10 of them altogether.

Where She Goes

The *Amerikanis* begins her season in the Greek Islands, followed by a series of seven-night cruises calling at Mediterranean and North African ports for May and again in October. Summer sailings take her around Europe from Toulon to Zeebrugge at the end of May, then on a series of Norwegian fjords and Spitzbergen sailings in July, followed by North Cape and Baltic cruises in August and Eastern Mediterranean sailings in fall.

The Bottom Line

Five Favorite Spots

1. The Mayfair Ballroom has a large round dance floor and stage where four shows are usually presented during each seven-day cruise.

2. The Aquamarine pool bar with its Greek terrazzo mural makes a pleasant place to sit out by the pair of little free-form pools.

3. The circular Rendez-Vous Bar is perhaps the most striking room on the ship; it's adjacent to the casino action. Here's the area where you can still see bits of the vessel's original design details.

4. The wine cellar, a small, glass-enclosed niche by the entrance to the Silver Carte (forward) restaurant.

5. The covered promenade decks have wooden ceilings; unfortunately, they don't offer a full around-the-ship promenade.

FANTASY CRUISES

Five Good Reasons to Book This Ship

1. The very high service ratio (see Translation, above).
2. The European itineraries for the summer that cover the continent from Spitsbergen to Gibraltar.
3. The food, which is pretty good for a ship in this category.
4. Her large closets and bathrooms and fairly spacious cabins.
5. To mix and mingle with Europeans, who far outnumber the North Americans on board.

Five Things You Won't Find On Board

1. Cabins designated wheelchair accessible.
2. A Jacuzzi or spa, although there is a sauna.
3. Your dining room on the first try.
4. A self-service laundry.
5. Announcements in a single language; they'll often be in four or five.

Amerikanis ★★

Registry	**Panama**
Officers	**Greek**
Crew	**International**
Complement	**400**
GRT	**20,000**
Length (ft.)	**576**
Beam (ft.)	**74**
Draft (ft.)	**26**
Passengers-Cabins Full	**650**
Passengers-2/Cabin	**601**
Passenger Space Ratio	**33.27**
Stability Rating	**Good**
Seatings	**2**
Cuisine	**Continental**
Dress Code	**Smart Casual**
Room Service	**Yes**
Tip	**$7.50 PPPD**

Ship Amenities

Outdoor Pool	**2**
Indoor Pool	**0**
Jacuzzi	**0**
Fitness Center	**Yes**
Spa	**No**
Beauty Shop	**Yes**
Showroom	**Yes**
Bars/Lounges	**4**
Casino	**Yes**
Shops	**1**
Library	**Yes**
Child Program	**No**
Self-Service Laundry	**No**
Elevators	**2**

Cabin Statistics

Suites	**50**
Outside Doubles	**155**
Inside Doubles	**89**
Wheelchair Cabins	**0**
Singles	**13**
Single Surcharge	**150%**
Verandas	**0**
110 Volt	**Yes**

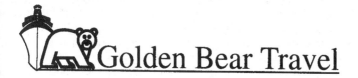

Golden Bear Travel

16 Digital Drive, Suite 100, Novato, CA 94948
☎ *(415) 382-8900, (800) 551-1000*

Expedition cruising offers closeups of nature.

GOLDEN BEAR TRAVEL

History . . . .

Golden Bear Travel, a tour wholesaler and retail travel agency, is exclusive North American sales agent for Hapag-Lloyd's *MS Bremen*.

Bremen ★★★★★, ⚓⚓⚓⚓

> *On remote Micronesian atolls such as Lamotrek in the state of Yap, supply barges are the only large seagoing vessels many of the villagers have ever seen, and as we were sailing in on the* Frontier Spirit *in 1990 early one Sunday morning, the chief's young son ran to his father and shook him awake, crying, "Papa, papa, an island is coming!"*

The *Bremen* began life as Salen-Lindblad's *Frontier Spirit*, and later SeaQuest's *Frontier Spirit*, the first new expedition ship to be built in 16 years when it debuted in 1990 under the command of the well-known expedition captain, Heinz Aye, master of Society Expeditions' *World Discoverer* for so many years. The ship was financed by a consortium of owners that included Salen-Lindblad, Hapag-Lloyd, Mitsubishi and Japan's shipping giant NYK, who also owns Crystal Cruises, and built by Mitsubishi in their Kobe shipyard. It carries a Super Ice-Class rating, the highest possible, and an impressive array of environmentally friendly features from refrigerated garbage compactors and glass-grinders to incinerators and bilge oil separators that skim off the waste oil to incinerate and return the water to the bilge. But the vessel's luxury details are equally impressive, with private verandas, a self-service laundry room, a separate heated drying room that can dry out wet sneakers overnight, mini-bars and mini-refrigerators in every cabin, along with remote-control color TV sets and built-in hair dryers.

EAVESDROPPING

"The old-timers said, 'We don't want so much luxury,'" one Salen-Lindblad executive told us after the first sailing. "They call me and say, 'Why do we need so many forks and knives? Why does dinner take so long?'"

The Brochure Says

"The popular *MS Bremen* offers passengers a special combination of exploration capability and luxurious accommodations not found on other ships."

Translation

A really luxurious, state-of-the-art expedition ship, the *Bremen* is rivaled only by the newer, perhaps even more luxurious expedition ship *Hanseatic* from Radisson Seven Seas Cruises.

DID YOU KNOW?

Captain Heinz Aye has circled the globe 33 times and made more than 60 voyages to the Antarctic, as well as claiming dozens of major seagoing expedition "firsts."

Cabins & Costs

Fantasy Suites: .... A
Average Price PPPD: $1000 including airfare in the Antarctic and gratuities.
There are two suites with verandas aboard, the only two accommodations on the topmost pool deck, one decorated in aqua, the other in rose. Each contains twin beds that can be made into a queen-sized bed, separate sitting area with curved sofa and two chairs, a desk and built-in cabinetry, a bath with tub/shower combination and wide counter with two wash basins.

Small Splurges: .... A
Average Price PPPD: $883 including airfare in the Antarctic and gratuities.
Almost as nice are the standard outside doubles with veranda, 16 cabins on Deck 6. (Cabins 615, 616, 617 and 618 are slightly smaller than the others.) Each has a small veranda with two chairs and a table, a sitting area with two chairs inside, plus a desk and built-in cabinetry and bath with shower. Wardrobe space is generous.

Suitable Standards: . . . . A

Average Price PPPD: $502 to $742 including airfare in the Antarctic and gratuities.
All the remaining cabins on board are outside doubles divided into cabin categories
that depend on deck location for the price.

Two are designated wheelchair-accessible with ample turning space and a ramp for
the bathroom doors. Each has twin or queen-sized beds, writing desk, two chairs,
bath with shower and generous wardrobe. All cabins and suites also contain color
TV, minibar/refrigerator and hair dryer.

Bottom Bunks: . . . . NA

There are no cabins in this category on this ship.

Where She Goes

The *Bremen* starts the year in the Antarctic. Several long cruises through the South Pacific follow in the early spring, then a Panama Canal transit and transatlantic crossing
from Venezuela to the Canary Islands and on to a summer in Europe and autumn in
North America.

The Bottom Line

Some discounts for early bookings are available from Golden Bear. The passenger
complement is international, but German-speaking travelers are the most numerous,
along with North Americans. Passengers who book through Golden Bear are part of a
group accompanied by Mariner Club hosts who look after many travel details.

The ship is extremely comfortable with state-of-the-art technical and environmental
niceties, even a helipad on the top deck. It carries inflatable Zodiac landing craft for exploring in remote areas.

Fielding's Five

Five Favorite Places

1. A main lounge with bar and comfortable conversational groupings of sofas and
   chairs serves as location for the nightly "recap" at cocktail time.

2. High atop the ship and forward is a glass-walled observation lounge that also serves
   as a lecture room, with a wide range of projection equipment, rows of blue banquettes on four levels along with fixed round tables and blue and chrome tub chairs
   that can be moved.

3. An expansive deck area with swimming pool, a rarity among expedition ships.

4. A small gym contains lifecycles, weights and other equipment and is adjacent to a
   large sauna.

5. A quiet library off the main lounge with beige leather chairs, long tables covered
   with recent magazines and newspapers in several languages and reference and paperback books.

Five Good Reasons to Book This Ship

1. To cruise with the charismatic Captain Heinz Aye, in command on "selected
   cruises," according to the brochure.

2. To see the Antarctic.

3. To stay in the same suite (# 704) that the Duke and Duchess of Bedford enjoyed on the inaugural cruise.

4. To visit the mythic islands of the South Pacific—Tuamotus, Gambier, Pitcairn, Henderson, Ducie and Easter.

5. To go on an expedition where you can actually keep your clothes clean and dry.

Bremen ★★★★★, ⚓⚓⚓⚓

Registry	**Bahamas**
Officers	**German**
Crew	**International**
Complement	**94**
GRT	**6,752**
Length (ft.)	**366**
Beam (ft.)	**56**
Draft (ft.)	**16**
Passengers-Cabins Full	**185**
Passengers-2/Cabin	**164**
Passenger Space Ratio	**41.17**
Stability Rating	**Good**
Seatings	**1**
Cuisine	**Continental**
Dress Code	**Casual**
Room Service	**No**
Tip	**Included in fare**

Ship Amenities

Outdoor Pool	**1**
Indoor Pool	**0**
Jacuzzi	**0**
Fitness Center	**Yes**
Spa	**No**
Beauty Shop	**Yes**
Showroom	**No**
Bars/Lounges	**3**
Casino	**No**
Shops	**1**
Library	**Yes**
Child Program	**No**
Self-Service Laundry	**Yes**
Elevators	**2**

Cabin Statistics

Suites	**2**
Outside Doubles	**80**
Inside Doubles	**6**
Wheelchair Cabins	**0**
Singles	**0**
Single Surcharge	**120-160%**
Verandas	**18**
110 Volt	**No**

HOLLAND AMERICA LINE

300 Elliott Avenue West, Seattle, WA 98119
☎ *(206) 283-2687, (800) 426-0327*

String trios play for teatime and after dinner, as here, aboard the **Statendam.**

History ....

One of the oldest and most distinguished of the cruise lines, Holland America was founded in 1873 as the Netherlands-America Steamship Company, a year after its young co-founders commissioned and introduced the first ship, the original *Rotterdam*, a 1700-ton iron vessel. The new ship left the city it was named for on Oct. 15, 1872, and spent 15 days sailing to New York on its maiden voyage. It carried eight passengers in first class and 380 in steerage. Only a few years later, because all its sailings were to the Americas, it became known as Holland America Line.

—A leading carrier of immigrants to the United States, Holland America transported nearly 700,000 between 1901 and 1914 alone; a steerage fare cost $20.

—After World War II, when middle-class Americans began touring Europe in large numbers, HAL concentrated on offering moderately priced tourist class service with two medium-sized ships that carried 836 tourist class passengers and only 39 first-class passengers.

—The line introduced educational and pleasure cruises to the Holy Land just after the turn of the century, and in 1971, suspended transatlantic sailings in favor of cruise vacations.

—The first line to introduce glass-enclosed promenade decks on its ocean liners.

—First line to introduce a full-service Lido restaurant on all its ships as a casual dining alternative.

—First cruise line to introduce karaoke, a sort of high-tech singalong (on the *Westerdam* in 1990).

—Through its subsidiary Westours, Holland America retains a strong tour profile in Alaska, and with another subsidiary company, Windstar, offers small-ship sailing vacations in Tahiti, the Caribbean and Mediterranean.

—In 1989, Carnival Cruise Lines acquired Holland America and its affiliated companies, but retains HAL's Seattle headquarters and separate management.

Concept . . . .

With its slogan "A Tradition of Excellence," Holland America has always had a reputation for high quality and giving full cruise value for the money, along with a strong program of security and sanitation. Since its acquisition by Carnival, the line has worked to upscale its product and sees itself now firmly entrenched in what is called the "premium" segment of the cruise industry, a notch up from mass-market lines such as Carnival but not in the highest-priced luxury segment.

HAL defines its premium status with such details as adding suites with private verandas to its four newest ships, *Statendam*, *Maasdam*, *Ryndam* and *Veendam*, along with more elaborate spas and advanced technology showrooms. The new vessels have also been designed to handle both short and long cruises equally well, with generous closet space and more-spacious staterooms.

There's also a strong undercurrent of "politically correct" behavior, consistent with its Pacific Northwest base, from specially packaged, environmentally safe cabin gift toiletries to taking a stand against the proposed Alaska aerial wolf-hunting program several years ago. The company also makes frequent, generous contributions to Alaskan universities and nonprofit organizations such as the Alaska Raptor Rehabilitation Center in Sitka.

Signatures . . . .

A "No Tipping Required" policy means that while tips are appreciated by crew members, they cannot be solicited. However, very few passengers disembark without crossing more than a few palms with silver.

The line's longstanding tradition of hiring Indonesian and Filipino crew members and training them in its own Jakarta hotel school results in consistently high-quality service.

The continuing use of museum-quality antiques and artifacts from the golden days of Dutch shipping adds dignity and richness to the ship interiors.

The classic ship names, taken from Dutch cities, are always repeated in new vessels, with the present *Statendam*, *Maasdam* and *Rotterdam* each the fifth to bear the name, the *Veendam* the fourth, the *Nieuw Amsterdam*, *Noordam* and *Ryndam* the third namesakes, and the *Westerdam* the second in the line with that name.

Gimmicks . . . .

The ubiquitous Holland America bag, a white canvas carry-all embellished with the company's logo and names of all the ships, can be glimpsed all over the world. Each passenger on each cruise is given one of these, so you can imagine how many frequent cruisers manage to amass. They're washable and last forever. "It's the single best investment we ever made," said one HAL insider.

Passport to Fitness, a folded card that has 48 separate areas to get stamped as the holder completes a qualifying activity, from the morning walkathon to aerobics class or a volleyball game. The prizes vary by the number of stamps, but are usually a Holland America logo item such as a T-shirt, cap or jacket. (We heard one eager-to-win passenger ask the librarian to stamp her passport for checking out a book about sports.)

Five Special Touches

1. Beautiful red plaid deck blankets.

2. Toiletries in each cabin wrapped in replicas of period Holland America posters and advertising art.

3. Museum-quality ship and seafaring artifacts in special display cases, along with antique bronze cannons and figureheads.

4. Fresh flowers flown in from Holland all over the ship.

5. Trays of mints, dried fruits and candied ginger outside the dining room after dinner.

Who's the Competition . . . .

Princess is the closest head-on competitor, vying to be top dog in the Alaska cruise market. The two lines can claim the two largest land tour operators, HAL's Westours and Princess's Princess Tours. For the past couple of years, Princess has had more ships in Alaska than Holland America, but Westours claims more tour departures. In the Caribbean, Celebrity Cruises is a major competitor with Holland America. HAL is also in the league to compete in the premium market with Princess for senior couples and singles.

The line's classic ocean liner *Rotterdam* on its long cruises competes head-on with Cunard's *QE2*, *Royal Viking Sun* and *Vistafjord*. The Rotterdam retires in 1997.

Who's Aboard . . . .

While the Alaska market is attracting more and more younger cruisers and families, Holland America's basic passengers can still be defined as middle-aged and older couples who appreciate solid quality in food, surroundings and service.

Perhaps the most interesting are those who sail on the *Rotterdam's* long cruises, many wealthy, set-in-their-ways dowagers who cruise together year after year, throwing lavish cocktail parties and luncheons and competing to see who brings the most gorgeous gowns (and the most agreeable rent-a-male escorts).

Who Should Go . . . .

More younger couples and families should be aboard Holland America's shorter sailings, especially to Alaska, where the line excels in the scope and variety of its land/cruise packages. Single women and families with children will find HAL is thinking of them—youth counselors coordinate activities for each age group, from an ice cream sundae party for the 5-to-8 set to teen disco parties and contests, and social hosts to dance with unattached women on all cruises 14 days or longer. Physically-challenged passengers will find suitable accommodations on board all the new ships, plus extra assistance from the attentive staff, who also lavish special care and attention on the elderly and small children.

Who Should Not Go . . . .

Young swinging singles looking to boogie all night or meet the mate of their dreams.

Nonconformists.

People who refuse to dress up.

The Lifestyle . . . .

A surprising amount of luxury and pampering go on aboard these ships, with string trios (two of them usually work each ship now) playing at teatime, white-gloved stewards to escort you to your cabin when you board, vases of fresh flowers everywhere, bowls of fresh fruit in the cabins, and most of all, what the Dutch call *gezellig*, a warm and cozy ambiance, defined with curtains in the cabins that can separate the sleeping area from the sitting area, friendly Dutch officers and caring Indonesian and Filipino crew members, who make it a point of pride to remember your name.

In Alaska, naturalists and longtime Alaska residents are always among the lecture staff. Kodak ambassadors are on board designated cruises to assist passengers with photo problems and show examples of good slide photography from the area. Movies are shown at three or four daily screening times, as well as on cabin TV, and shore excursions emphasize sightseeing and flightseeing, with floatplane and helicopter glacier flights, kayaking, raft trips and visits to cultural (Native American) areas and historical city tours.

Wardrobe...............................

Dress code follows a traditional pattern, with a week usually calling for two formal nights (and they do dress up on these ships, even in Alaska), two informal nights when men are expected to wear a jacket but a tie is usually optional, and three "elegantly casual" nights with no shorts, T-shirts, tank tops, halter tops or jeans permitted. During the daytime, comfortable, casual clothing—jogging outfits, shorts or slacks, T-shirts, bathing suits and cover-ups—are adequate deck wear.

Holland America consistently produces some of the most attractive buffets at sea; here, breakfast aboard the **Maasdam.**

Bill of Fare............................. A

"Genteel tradition" is important to Holland America, from a chime master who announces dinner to the Indonesian bellman in the bellboy outfit (similar to the doormen in white at the Peninsula Hotel in Hong Kong) who holds open the doors between the Lido buffet and the deck for every passenger.

Holland America consistently produces some of the tastiest and most appealing buffets at sea, from the lavish Dutch-style breakfasts to wonderfully varied luncheons. In addition to a full hot-and-cold buffet in the Lido restaurants, chefs on deck will grill hot dogs and hamburgers to order, serve up make-your-own tacos, stir-fry-to-order and pasta of the day, plus a very popular make-your-own-ice-cream-sundae counter with a bowl of homemade cookies.

Because of the scope and popularity of the buffet service, dining room breakfast and dinner are served open seating, which means you can arrive within a specified time and sit with whom you wish.

Dinner menus have grown increasingly sophisticated. A typical dinner might include six appetizers (among them warm hazelnut-crusted Brie with apple and onion compote and French bread, bay shrimp coupe with cocktail sauce, smoked king salmon with horseradish cream and herb crostini), two soups (one may be five-onion cream with frizzled onions), three salads (including field greens with smoked duck, Asia[n] pears and toasted pecans), six entrees, from a low-calorie, low-fat sau[teed] teed Alaskan snapper teriyaki or fresh halibut with asparagus and lemo[n] pepper mashed potatoes to a parmesan-crusted chicken breast or grilled New York steak with baked Idaho potato and onion rings. A cheese and fresh fruit course follows, then a choice of four desserts plu[s] pastry tray, ice creams and frozen yogurts, and sugar-free desserts. Chocoholics will adore the Chocolate Extravaganza late show, served once during each cruise as a midnight buffet.

Children's menus offer four standard entrees—hamburger and fries, hot dog, pizza or chicken drumsticks—plus a nightly chef's special, per-haps beef tacos, fish and chips or barbecued ribs. The more urbane kid may prefer to order from the regular menu, but he can't sample the fol-lowing winner for the line's executive chef in the seventh annual Inter-national Cruise Ship Recipe Competition:

Salmon Tart Scotch Mist
4 servings

1 pound thinly sliced salmon fillets

4 five-inch puff pastry discs, already baked (can use frozen ones)

1 ounce butter, melted

Sauce:

1 ounce butter

3 finely chopped shallots

1 ounce Scotch whisky

1/4 pint heavy cream

4 ounces unsalted butter cut into cubes

2 TB chopped fresh dill

Melt one ounce of butter in saucepan; add shallots and simmer until soft. Add whisky and reduce by half. Add heavy cream, bring to a boil. Whisk in the butter cubes a couple at a time. Add chopped fresh dill and salt and pepper to taste. Keep warm until serving time.

On each pastry disc, overlap slices of salmon, then brush with melted butter and place under a hot broiler for two to three minutes.

To serve, spoon a little of the sauce onto each plate, place the salmon tart near the center, and garnish with steamed baby vegetables, dill sprigs and rosemary sprigs.

CHAMPAGNE TOAST

Holland America serves Seattle's famous Starbucks coffee on board all its ships; on the big new liners–Statendam, Maasdam, Ryndam and Veendam– after-dinner espresso is complimentary in the Explorer's Lounge.

Showtime. . . . . .B+

A more sophisticated level of production shows was introduced recently, with each ship featuring its own specially tailored programs. On the line's long cruises and world cruises, headliner entertainers such as Rita Moreno, Roy Clark, Victor Borge and Vic Damone, plus noted lecturers and even a Las Vegas-style ice skating spectacular, may show up on the program.

Discounts. . . . .

Early booking savings can take off 10 to 20 percent for passengers who book and make a deposit on a specified timetable, which may mean anything from one to six months ahead of time. Passengers who book earliest get the lowest prices, and if a new money-saver is introduced after they book, their fare will be adjusted on request and verification. Past passengers also get added discounts and special mail offers on certain cruises.

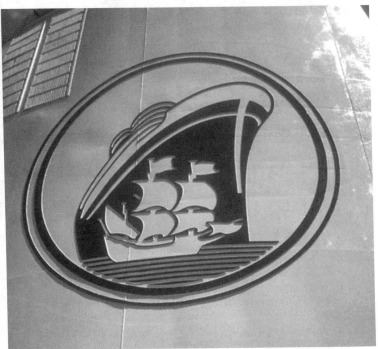

Holland America's distinctive logo is painted on the funnels of its ships.

The Bottom Line

This is an extremely high quality product with good fulfillment for the money, one that keeps getting better. As much as anybody in the business, Holland America delivers what it promises.

Officers are Dutch, with a no-nonsense attitude about safety and seamanship. The lifeboat drill is thorough and explicit, and cleanliness and sanitation are of an extremely high standard.

When we gave Shirley's parents their first cruise a few years ago for an anniversary gift, Holland America was the line we chose—and they're still saying it was the best vacation they ever had.

Maasdam   ★★★★★
Ryndam   ★★★★★
Statendam   ★★★★★
Veendam   ★★★★★

The Dutch, or more precisely the Netherlanders, have lent their name to some decidedly unglamorous expressions—in Dutch, Dutch treat, Dutch uncle, Dutch courage. Over the years, they have given us cozy and cliche images of dowager queens in sensible shoes, herrings, Hans Brinker, Gouda and Edam cheese, windmills and respectable burghers staring out at us from museum walls and cigar boxes.

But these ships are not apple-cheeked little Dutch girls in wooden shoes and stiff white bonnets. They're sophisticated and very elegant women of the world who know who they are and what they're doing.

The newest HAL ships are ideal for long cruises, with spacious cabins, each with its own sitting area, and generous closet and drawer space. A variety of lounges, public rooms and outdoor spaces offer enough entertaining alternatives to ensure that passengers won't get bored.

A 26-foot Italianate fountain ornaments the three-deck lobby of the *Statendam,* and a slightly smaller version of the same also decorates the *Ryndam* lobby, while the *Maasdam*'s centerpiece is a monumental $350,000 green glass sculpture created by Luciano Vistosi of Murano, Italy, that looks as though it's made from Superman's kryptonite. The *Veendam* also has a towering Vistosi glass sculpture in the lobby called "Jacob's Ladder."

From the gangway level, a graceful curved stairway and an escalator (convenient but unusual aboard ships) take passengers up one deck to the front

ffice and lobby, the bottom level of the three-deck atrium. Each ship shows
ff a $2 million art collection, along with dazzling two-deck theaters and
howy glass-walled dining rooms, sizable spas and expansive deck areas.

CHAMPAGNE TOAST

*For the charming artwork created for the Maasdam by whimsical Danish
artist Bjorn Windblad, especially in the beauty salon, where his mural of the
Judgement of Paris (when the handsome youth Paris had to choose the most
beautiful of the Greek goddesses) is accompanied by Windblad's handwritten
note wishing that all the salon's clients will leave feeling like Aphrodite, the
winner.*

The Brochure Says

"Floating resorts, our ships are our own private islands, destinations in themselves, offering everything you'd expect in a great resort on land. Fine dining. Dazzling entertainment. Activities galore. And it's all included in your cruise fare."

Translation

Holland America seems to be looking to appeal to a new group of passengers, younger, more resort-oriented people who may not have cruised before, by accenting entertainment, cuisine and variety. The previous emphasis on overall cruise value and nearly 125
years of service is still underscored as well.

Cabins & Costs

The lavish owner's suite aboard the **Maasdam**.

Fantasy Suites: ....A+

Average Price PPPD: $730 plus airfare in the Caribbean.
The penthouses on Navigation Deck, one on each ship, are huge—1123 square
feet—ideal for entertaining with a living room with wraparound sofa, four chairs,

big screen TV; a large private veranda, dining table that seats eight, butler pantry separate bedroom with queen-sized bed, built-in dressing table and walk-in dressing room lined with closets. The marble bathroom has double sinks, a whirlpool tub, a steam bath/shower combination and separate water closet with bidet; there's even a custom-tiled guest bath.

Small Splurges: .... A

Average Price PPPD: $366 plus airfare in the Caribbean.

A deluxe outside double with private veranda in categories A or B measure 284 square feet and have a sitting area with sofa that can be converted into a third bed, a TV with VCR, minibar and a refrigerator, as well as a whirlpool bath. Both categories are identical, but the As are one deck higher than the Bs.

Suitable Standards: .... B

Average Price PPPD: $261 plus airfare in the Caribbean.

Each large outside double contains twin beds that can convert to queen-sized, a sitting area with sofa and chair, a desk/dresser with stool, coffee table, hair dryer, safe, large closet, and bath with tub/shower combination. Six wheelchair-accessible cabins, outside doubles with shower only, are also available.

Bottom Bunks: .... B

Average Price PPPD: $226 plus airfare in the Caribbean.

Even the cheapest cabins on the luxurious vessels are pretty good. Inside doubles are 187 square feet with sitting area sofa and chair, twin beds that can convert to queen-sized, a desk/dresser with stool, coffee table, hair dryer, safe, and a four-door closet. Bathrooms have showers only, and a floral privacy curtain between beds and sitting area.

Where She Goes

The *Statendam's* itinerary includes 10-day roundtrip Southern Caribbean sailings from Ft. Lauderdale, calling in St. John, St. Thomas, Dominica, Grenada, La Guaira (for Caracas), and Curaçao. These are followed by a repositioning cruise via Hawaii to Alaska through the Panama Canal, then summer-long seven-day Inside Passage cruises from Vancouver that call in Ketchikan, Juneau and Sitka. An autumn Hawaii/Panama Canal transit is scheduled for September, followed by another series of 10-day Southern Caribbean cruises and seven-day holiday sailings in late December.

The *Maasdam* makes 10-day Panama Canal transits between Acapulco and Ft. Lauderdale or New Orleans (depending on the date), then offers a transatlantic crossing to Europe, followed by a summer of Mediterranean and Northern Europe itineraries.

The *Ryndam* makes a winter series of 10-day Southern Caribbean cruises through mid-April from Ft. Lauderdale, then repositions to Alaska through the Panama Canal before starting a summer season of seven-day Glacier Route sailings between Vancouver and Seward, calling in Ketchikan, Juneau, Sitka and Valdez. In September the ship is scheduled to return through the canal to the Southern Caribbean to resume its 10-day programs.

The *Veendam* makes a series of seven-day Caribbean itineraries roundtrip from Ft. Lauderdale that alternate between the Eastern and Western Caribbean in winter and cruises Alaska in summer.

The Bottom Line

A musical production show aboard the **Statendam** *illustrates HAL's younger, more energetic style that has emerged with the newest class of ships.*

Traditionalists as well as luxury loving passengers should like these vessels, which gleam with softly burnished wood and brass, with the added zing of dramatic showrooms that are themed from Dutch masterpieces by Vermeer, Rembrandt, Rubens and Van Gogh.

While the decorous gentility will attract well-heeled older passengers, there's enough spark and energy to appeal to upscale younger couples and singles as well. Almost anyone should feel at home aboard, especially if home were a palatial mansion with a smiling staff.

The message these newest Holland America ships seem to be sending is that the company is aiming in the direction of other luxurious large-ship companies, such as Crystal Cruises. Both hardware (the new ships) and software (the food, service and ambiance) just keep on improving on this very fine line.

Fielding's Five

Five Spectacular Places

1. The striking two-deck Rotterdam dining rooms on all the ships have a magnificent entry stairway ideal for making a grand entrance, window walls on three sides and a ceiling covered with a thousand frosted Venetian glass morning glories.

2. The Crow's Nest top deck observation lounges, especially on the *Maasdam* with its Alaska-themed decor of craggy granite "mountains" and silvery freeform fiber optic tubing that suggests waterways and fjords, with cross-cut wood slabs covering floors, bars and tabletops. On the *Ryndam*, designer Joe Farcus has taken the theme another step, with crackle-glass "glaciers" as flooring and a ceiling of glass cylinders cut at different angles like glacial ice surfaces.

3. The sumptuous and subdued Rembrandt show lounge on the *Maasdam* is like walking into a tasteful 17th century drawing room full of fluted mahogany columns, Delft tiles and upholstery fabrics in red and blue shot through with gold threads.

4. The full promenade decks on all the ships, covered in teak and lined with classic wooden deck loungers, invite you to stretch out in the shade with a good book.

5. The handsome covered Lido Deck pool area with its retractable sliding glass dome (ideal in Alaska's changeable climate), playful dolphin sculptures, spas and children's wading pools.

Five Good Reasons to Book These Ships

1. Sunbathers will like the blue terrycloth covers fitted to the loungers, much more comfortable for wet or oiled bodies than the usual plastic strips or removable cushions.

2. Buffets galore for nibbling and noshing, from an ice-cream-sundae bar to a make-your-own taco stand, free hot fresh popcorn at the movie matinees in the theater, the Chocolate Extravaganza late-night buffet, the hot hors d'oeuvres at cocktail time in the Crow's Nest, the Royal Dutch Tea, and a glass of fresh carrot juice from the juice bar in the Ocean Spa.

3. A good workout, from the Passport to Fitness program (see Gimmicks, above) to a jog around the *Statendam* or a fast game of deck tennis on the *Ryndam* or *Maasdam*, with some aerobics, massage, sauna and steam treatments in the expansive Ocean Spa with its Stairmasters, treadmills, bicycles and free weights.

4. You'll have plenty of closet and drawer space to store your wardrobe, no matter how much you've over-packed.

5. The romantic little piano bars on board each ship, especially the *Maasdam's* elegant candy box of a room with rich gold and crimson curtains swagged from the ceiling like a pasha's tent.

Maasdam
Ryndam
Statendam
Veendam

★★★★★
★★★★★
★★★★★
★★★★★

Registry	**The Netherlands**
Officers	**Dutch**
Crew	**Indonesian/Filipino**
Complement	**571**
GRT	**69,130**
Length (ft.)	**720**
Beam (ft.)	**101**
Draft (ft.)	**25**
Passengers-Cabins Full	**1613**
Passengers-2/Cabin	**1266**
Passenger Space Ratio	**54.60**
Stability Rating	**Good to Excellent**
Seatings	**2**
Cuisine	**International**
Dress Code	**Traditional**
Room Service	**Yes**
Tip	**No Tipping Required**

Ship Amenities

Outdoor Pool	**2**
Indoor Pool	**0**
Jacuzzi	**2**
Fitness Center	**Yes**
Spa	**Yes**
Beauty Shop	**Yes**
Showroom	**Yes**
Bars/Lounges	**8**
Casino	**Yes**
Shops	**5**
Library	**Yes**
Child Program	**Yes**
Self-Service Laundry	**Yes**
Elevators	**8**

Cabin Statistics

Suites	**29**
Outside Doubles	**485**
Inside Doubles	**148**
Wheelchair Cabins	**6**
Singles	**0**
Single Surcharge	**150%**
Verandas	**200**
110 Volt	**Yes**

HOLLAND AMERICA LINE

Nieuw Amsterdam   ★★★★
Noordam   ★★★★

In May 1984, two new ships, the Noordam and Sitmar's Fairsky (now Princess Cruises' Sky Princess) each made a debut cruise from Los Angeles to the Mexican Riviera a week apart along the same familiar route down to Puerto Vallarta and back. Cruise writers who were aboard both sailings had spirited arguments back and forth about which ship was prettier, the innovative Fairsky, the last big steamship to be built, or the solid, well-crafted and traditional Noordam. There was no decision, no winners or losers, although proponents of each went away certain their arguments had prevailed.

A tile surround on the aft swimming pool aboard the **Noordam** *keeps sunbathers cool.*

The *Nieuw Amsterdam* debuted in 1983, the first new ship for Holland America in nearly quarter of a century, and, like her identical sister *Noordam* a year later, was built in France's Chantiers d'Atlantique yard. Despite some noticeable vibration in certain areas, the ships are classy, traditional and comfortable, with museum-quality artifacts relating to sailing and the sea handsomely displayed.

All the cabins are relatively large with plentiful wardrobe space, from the minimum-priced insides to the deluxe staterooms with sitting areas. There are no large suites or private verandas. Outside cabins have windows on Main Deck and above; the portholes begin on A Deck and get more view-restrictive on B and C Decks. Inside cabins mark the imaginary "window" with fabric draperies that are always closed.

Once on board, passengers relax almost instantly in the spacious public rooms and tasteful, subdued decor. There's no glitz or jingle-jangle to bring in a jarring note, and the smiling, soft-spoken serving staff of Indonesians and Filipinos do nothing to break the mood. A few pockets of activity shelter night owls—the Horn Pipe Club on the *Nieuw Amsterdam*, the Pear Tree on the *Noordam*—but most passengers turn in fairly early.

The Brochure Says

"Attentive Filipino and Indonesian crew members offer gracious 'Five-Star' service, expecting no reward beyond your smile of thanks—because Holland America sails under a 'tipping not required' policy."

Translation

Note it does not say, Tipping not permitted. If you wanted to press the issue, you could claim tipping is not required on any cruise ship, but very obviously the passenger is expected to supplement the low base salaries on most major vessels with a tactfully "suggested" tip. Holland America does not permit its employees to "suggest" or even "hint" about a tip; instead, they simply provide excellent service the entire time you're aboard the ship, so that only a churl would even consider disembarking without dispensing some largesse.

INSIDER TIP

Happy Hour in the Crows Nest on the Noordam is from 4:45 to 5:45 and from 7 to 8 p.m., with the first drink at the regular price and subsequent ones at half price. Drinks are accompanied by a generous assortment of hot and cold hors d'oeuvres.

Cabins & Costs

Fantasy Suites: C
Average Price PPPD: $304 plus airfare in the Caribbean.
While there are no really big elegant suites aboard, the top category A cabins offer a great deal of comfort if not space. The wood furnishings are dark and polished, and all accommodations contain a king-sized bed, sitting area with sofa-bed, armchair, table, desk and double windows, as well as mini-refrigerator, closets with

good storage space and bathroom with tub/shower combination. The down side is
that every window in the A category cabins has a partially obstructed view from
hanging lifeboats. The part you'll see through your window is only the top half
which still lets you see some of the sea.

Small Splurges: ....B

Average Price PPPD: $293 plus airfare in the Caribbean.

We'd recommend opting for a B or C rather than an A category on these ships
because you'll get the same or even more space, along with tub and shower and sitting area, and may not, depending on deck location, have to look out over hanging
lifeboats. The best B cabins are 114 and 115 on Boat Deck, oversized quarters with
double bed, and our favorite C cabins are those forward on Boat and Upper Promenade Decks with a captain's-eye view of the sea ahead. On the Boat Deck, cabins
#100-103 are wheelchair-accessible quarters with bathroom grip rails, shower seat
and low hanging closet rack.

An inside cabin on the **Noordam** *is spacious and comfortable; notice the
curtains that suggest a window may be behind them.*

Suitable Standards: ....B

Average Price PPPD: $264 plus airfare in the Caribbean.

If you could nail down one of two E category Large Outsides (cabins E 711 or 716)
you'd find a very big cabin with twin beds, large TV, long desk counter, leather
headboards, and plenty of storage; these two cabins are almost double the size of
the others in this category. The others are also OK, just not so big.

Bottom Bunks: ....C+

Average Price PPPD: $207 plus airfare in the Caribbean.

All the lowest-priced inside cabins have two lower beds and are the same size with
the same furnishings as most of the other cabins aboard, including color TV, but on
a lower deck (C Deck) and forward.

ANNOYANCES

This is really nit-picking, but the friendly, polite servers stand and chat with well-meaning passengers in the dining room, asking questions about their families and home towns, slowing down the service to a crawl sometimes.

INSIDER TIP

One of the best views of the stage is from the five rows of black leather theater seats in the center back of the main level of the show lounge, where latecomers are often put.

On the balcony level of the show lounges, late arrivals have to sit on the outer edges away from the railing in tables and chairs arranged in conversational groupings, and they do just that—make conversation while the show is going on at a volume that competes with the performers.

Where She Goes

The *Nieuw Amsterdam* makes seven-day Western Caribbean sailings from New Orleans in winter, calling at Montego Bay, Grand Cayman, Playa del Carmen and Cozumel, and spends summer in Alaska on an Inside Passage seven-day roundtrip itinerary out of Vancouver, calling in Juneau, Sitka and Ketchikan.

The *Noordam* also makes seven-day Western Caribbean sailings in winter, sailing from Tampa and calling in Grand Cayman, Ocho Rios, Playa del Carmen and Cozumel, with a summer seven-day Glacier Route in Alaska between Vancouver and Seward, calling in Juneau, Sitka, Ketchikan and Valdez.

The Bottom Line

While more than 10 years old, both ships are kept remarkably clean in the traditional Holland America shine-and-polish style. Where the age and wear shows is on the few outer deck areas covered with astroturf, with spots, splotches and patches all too apparent. Inside, however, housekeeping is of the sort our mothers used to describe as, "You could eat off the floor."

We like the glass bowls of fresh fruit in the cabins and batik bedspreads with matching privacy curtains, one of the cozy touches the Dutch call *gezellig*, as well as the comfortable places to sit all around the ship with antiques, ship models and old maps to study.

Fielding's Five

Five Favorite Spots

1. The Crow's Nest, elegantly cozy forward observation lounges with hot hors d'oeuvres at cocktail time and piano music throughout the evening, as well as period ship models in plexiglass cases.

2. The Lido, where the art of the buffet comes to life; not only does everything look good enough to eat, but it really is. And you can make your own ice cream sundaes for dessert.

3. The Explorer Lounge on the *Nieuw Amsterdam*, with a wall lined with wooden ship figureheads holding lamps; this is where the Rosario Strings play after dinner while bar waiters offer espresso, cappuccino and liqueurs—on a tab, of course.

4. The Ocean Spa on both ships, with massage rooms, saunas, gym with bikes, rowing, treadmills and weights, and just outside, the pool and spas.

5. The broad natural teak deck all around both ships on Upper Promenade, with sheltered, covered reading spots and rows of traditional wooden deck loungers reminiscent of ocean-liner days.

Off-the-Wall

For the birds: The Partridge Bar on the *Nieuw Amsterdam* displays large paintings of peacocks on its back wall.

Five Good Reasons to Book These Ships

1. A tempting range of food opportunities, from light and healthful menus and sugar-free desserts to make-your-own-taco or ice-cream-sundae stations.

2. Hot, fresh popcorn served for movie matinees (but not evening screenings) in the theater.

3. The Dutch figures in traditional costume in the glass cases at the entrance to the Lido restaurant.

4. The broad expanse of Lido Deck in natural teak with fresh water swimming pool, wading pool and splash surround, only steps away from the hot dog/hamburger grill and the outdoor Lido Bar.

5. The classic Holland America tote bag, free to every passenger on every sailing.

Five Things You Won't Find On Board

1. A well-stocked library; if you want to read a current best-seller, bring it yourself.

2. A free self-service laundry; you pay $1 to wash your clothes, but soap and the dryer are free.

3. A bathroom mirror reflection in the designated handicap cabins if you're in a wheelchair; you can easily roll the chair under the sink rim, but can't see your reflection once you're there.

4. Slot machine gambling when the ships are in certain Alaskan waters in summer.

5. A good view of the stage from every seat in the two-deck show lounge, especially in the balcony; you'll have to search to find a good spot from which to see everything.

HOLLAND AMERICA LINE

Nieuw Amsterdam
Noordam

★★★★
★★★★

Registry	**The Netherlands**
Officers	**Dutch**
Crew	**Insonesian/Filipino**
Complement	**566**
GRT	**33,930**
Length (ft.)	**704**
Beam (ft.)	**89**
Draft (ft.)	**25**
Passengers-Cabins Full	**1378**
Passengers-2/Cabin	**1214**
Passenger Space Ratio	**27.94**
Stability Rating	**Good**
Seatings	**2**
Cuisine	**International**
Dress Code	**Traditional**
Room Service	**Yes**
Tip	**No tipping required**

Ship Amenities

Outdoor Pool	**2**
Indoor Pool	**0**
Jacuzzi	**1**
Fitness Center	**Yes**
Spa	**Yes**
Beauty Shop	**Yes**
Showroom	**Yes**
Bars/Lounges	**8**
Casino	**Yes**
Shops	**3**
Library	**Yes**
Child Program	**Yes**
Self-Service Laundry	**Yes**
Elevators	**7**

Cabin Statistics

Suites	**0**
Outside Doubles	**411**
Inside Doubles	**194**
Wheelchair Cabins	**4**
Singles	**0**
Single Surcharge	**150%**
Verandas	**0**
110 Volt	**Yes**

HOLLAND AMERICA LINE

Rotterdam

It's still possible on the Rotterdam, built in 1959, to see how it used to be divided into first and transatlantic classes (and could be again). A central stairway called "the secret staircase," inspired by stairs in the French chateau of Chambord, makes it possible for two people to go up or down on separate, adjacent stairs without seeing each other, except on the landings when sliding doors are open.

The Dutch say gezellig *for cozy, which describes these booths in the* Rotterdam's Lido Cafe.

One of the true grande dames of the sea, the elegant *Rotterdam* has been renovated numerous times without losing her original character. The gleam of polished wood interiors, plush and leather lounge furniture will remind you of the splendid ocean-liner days, and the number of intimate bars and ounges around the ship, each with its own dance floor, suggests one of the favorite onboard activities.

But even sun-and-pool fans will enjoy it. An extension of the upper promenade deck adds a permanent cover to the Lido pool deck below, and a horseshoe shaped wooden bar with 16 barstools supplements the white plastic loungers and deck chairs and umbrella-covered tables around the blue-and-white tile pool. A covered grill on the starboard side turns out hot dogs, hamburgers and sandwiches grilled to order. Tea and coffee are served throughout the day in the Lido restaurant.

The flagship of the fleet, the *Rotterdam* is the fifth ship with this name. Its replacement *Rotterdam VI* enters service the day this vessel is retired in September 1997.

EAVESDROPPING

A young Dutch officer just transferred to the Rotterdam: *"I told them, I'll do anything, work long months with a short vacation, just put me on the Rotterdam instead of one of those new hotels with a little hull wrapped around it so it'll float—the* Rotterdam *is a real ship!"*

The Brochure Says

"Holland America's Grand Voyage service begins the moment you step aboard. A string quartet plays. An officer smiles. A white-gloved steward escorts you to your stateroom, where everything has been laid out for your imminent arrival; personalized stationery, fresh flowers, even a plush terry robe to slip into."

Translation

Posh is an understatement on a long voyage aboard the *Rotterdam*, where every day seems to bring another special gift from the line. We'd suggest you carry an extra bag to bring them home in, except that HAL gives you a canvas carry-all as well.

Cabins & Costs

Fantasy Suites: . . . . A-

Average Price PPPD: $483 plus airfare for the final holiday sailing.
While not as plushly evocative as some of the public rooms, the A category staterooms aboard have king-sized beds, sitting area with sofa, two chairs and oval black granite table, a long dresser with 10 drawers, safe and shelves, mini-refrigerator, built-in dressing table and stool, separate dressing room and bath with tub and double sinks.

Small Splurges: . . . . B+

Average Price PPPD: $425 plus airfare for the final holiday sailing.
Deluxe outside double cabins in category B provide plenty of room and some of the custom cabinetry from the 1950s, including vanity tables with tall mirrors, built-in drawers and clips to secure bottles of perfume or other toiletries. A separate sitting area has a sofa and chairs with coffee table, and a dresser with nine drawers stores lots of clothing. Bathrooms usually have tubs and heated towel racks. We particu-

larly like the forward-facing cabins on Boat Deck, B 33 and B 34, with three windows each.

Batik fabrics and built-in wood cabinetry decorate this standard outside cabin with portholes aboard the Rotterdam.

Suitable Standards: ....B

Average Price PPPD: $379 plus airfare for the final holiday sailing.
Because the original ship was built before modular cabins came into play, standard cabins vary somewhat in size and shape. All the standard doubles have two lower beds or double bed, private bath (some with tubs and heated towel racks), TV, batik bedspreads and curtains, a chair or two, built-in cabinetry with lower drawers and upper shelves, plus sometimes a pullout writing desk or vanity table.

Bottom Bunks: C

Average Price PPPD: $271 plus airfare for the final holiday sailing.
The cheapest economy inside doubles are category O, with upper and lower berths and bath with shower only. The ones we've looked at are very small, but still have a chair, dressing table with mirror, dresser with six drawers, some of them with locks, and a tile bath with shower only.

> **INSIDER TIP**
>
> *Note that the Rotterdam also has number of small single inside and outside cabins with one lower bed and bath with shower.*

Where She Goes

The *Rotterdam* is one of HAL's long-voyage vessels, setting out January 18 on her last Grand World Voyage, her 29th world cruise.

In the summer the ship will make seven-day sailings along Alaska's Glacier Route between Vancouver and Seward, calling in Ketchikan, Juneau, Sitka and Valdez, followed by a nostalgic cruise from Vancouver to Ft. Lauderdale, her last sailing before retirement.

The Bottom Line

This is one of our very favorite ships, and it makes us sad to note a few signs of age, such as the worn teak decking aft on Promenade Deck. Cozy, clean and comfortable cabins and gracious, understated public rooms; an around-the-ship promenade, part of it glassed in, lined with old-fashioned wooden steamer chairs; a plethora of fresh flower arrangements everywhere; a big, bright gym and sun room; the stylish, art deco nightclub and lounges—all add up to a classy and classic shipboard experience that cannot be duplicated. We all bid her farewell in September, 1997.

Fielding's Five

Five Classic Places

1. The Ritz-Carlton Lounge, a two-deck nightclub that impeccably recalls the glorious days of ocean liners, with a shimmering 90-foot wall mural from 1959 with Aegean scenes and a grand curved staircase for a movie-star entrance. The furniture is upholstered in jewel-toned velvets in sapphire, emerald and topaz, and the dance floor is incised brass.

2. The two high-domed dining rooms, the La Fontaine decorated with ceramic scenes from the famous fables, and the Odyssey with ceramic scenes from Homer's epic poem.

3. The dual "secret staircase" left over from the days when the ship was divided into two classes, structured so people can go up or down at the same time without seeing each other.

4. The Ambassador Lounge, like a New York bar of the 1950s with its bull's-eye glass, long velvet banquettes, inlaid wood parquet dance floor and tiny red plush barstools for fashion-model derrières.

5. The easy-to-love Ocean Bar, one of the great small bars at sea, with its comma-shaped bar lined with stools and its handful of tête-à-tête cocktail tables.

Five Off-the-Wall Hideaways and Secret Spots

1. The Tropic Bar, a tiny pseudo-tropical late-night drinking-and-singalong spot tucked away behind the Ritz-Carlton night club. It's usually open only on long cruises.

2. An indoor swimming pool down on D Deck with marble benches, saunas and massage rooms nearby, tile fish on the pool bottom and sculptured fish on the walls.

3. The Sky Room, on Bridge Deck above the Sun Room, a little piano bar with over-stuffed plush chairs (you can find the stairs leading up there near the Wireless Office).

4. A tiny terrace with tables and chairs outside the Sky Room, where nobody will ever think to look for you.

5. The shuffleboard courts outside the gym and sun room on Sun Deck, where spectators gather on wooden benches during the numerous hotly-contested tournaments.

Five Good Reasons to Book These Ships

1. To experience what the grand days of ocean-liner travel were all about.

2. To make a complete round-the-world cruise for her final season.

3. To admire the one-of-a-kind wood paneling and marquetry, the exquisite restored 90-foot wall mural of the Aegean that adorns the two-deck walls of the Ritz-Carlton nightclub, to seek out (behind the slot machines) the unique tapestry murals created for the 1959 ship in the former card room, now the casino, and the original wood chairs in a 1950s moderne design in the Queen's Lounge.

4. To read or write in the Reading Room with its dictionary stand, writing tables, wing chairs with batik upholstery and dark blue velvet hassocks piped with gold.

5. To get a last sad look at a ship of this type, since the corporate owners in their infinite wisdom decided not to make the sizable investment it would take to bring her up to the new SOLAS (Safety of Life At Sea) standards after her 1997 World Cruise.

Five Things You Won't Find On Board

1. A disco, although there are two piano bars.

2. A wheelchair-accessible cabin, although ramps are available to help get over the doorsills.

3. A children's playroom (don't bring the kids along on this ship).

4. An unobstructed sea view from the cabin windows on Sun Deck; they're partially blocked by hanging lifeboats.

5. A real fire in the fireplace in the casino.

HOLLAND AMERICA LINE

Rotterdam	★★★★★
Registry	**The Netherlands**
Officers	**Dutch**
Crew	**Indonesian/Filipino**
Complement	**603**
GRT	**38,000**
Length (ft.)	**748**
Beam (ft.)	**94**
Draft (ft.)	**30**
Passengers-Cabins Full	**1347**
Passengers-2/Cabin	**1065**
Passenger Space Ratio	**35.68**
Stability Rating	**Excellent**
Seatings	**3**
Cuisine	**International**
Dress Code	**Traditional**
Room Service	**Yes**
Tip	**No tipping required**

Ship Amenities

Outdoor Pool	**1**
Indoor Pool	**1**
Jacuzzi	**1**
Fitness Center	**Yes**
Spa	**Yes**
Beauty Shop	**Yes**
Showroom	**Yes**
Bars/Lounges	**7**
Casino	**Yes**
Shops	**4**
Library	**Yes**
Child Program	**Yes**
Self-Service Laundry	**Yes**
Elevators	**8**

Cabin Statistics

Suites	**29**
Outside Doubles	**307**
Inside Doubles	**268**
Wheelchair Cabins	**0**
Singles	**15**
Single Surcharge	**150%**
Verandas	**0**
110 Volt	**Yes**

HOLLAND AMERICA LINE

Westerdam

Built in Papenburg, Germany, by Meyer Werft as the Homeric for now-defunct Home Lines, the Westerdam is Holland America's largest ship, thanks to a "stretching" from the same shipyard in 1989. How do you stretch a ship? Very, very carefully. Cut through the superstructure with acetylene torches, then check to make sure all the units have been completely severed by running a piano wire along the cut from top to bottom. Drop in a prefabricated midsection, then put it all back together again.

The distinctive Sun Deck pool area with its sliding glass roof and enclosed glass-walled veranda offers optimum comfort both in Alaska's cool climate and the Caribbean when it gets hot and muggy. The same walls and roof that let in the sun and keep out the rain also hold in the air conditioning.

Nine passenger decks, two separate self-service buffet restaurants, two outside swimming pools, a two-deck showroom and a number of lounges keep the 1494 passengers well dispersed around the ship, while a wood-and-plexiglass dome with special lighting brightens the lower-deck dining room.

Perhaps a little less formal than the line's other ships, the *Westerdam* offers some competitive prices on seven-day cruises. The Big Apple teen disco and video center make this a good ship for families.

DID YOU KNOW?

The original Westerdam, *which made crossings between Rotterdam and New York from 1946 to 1965, had its keel laid in 1939, but when the Germans invaded Holland in 1940, work was suspended. The partly constructed vessel survived three sinkings at her berth during World War II before she made her maiden voyage. She was bombed by the Allies in 1940 and raised by the Germans, then bombed by the Dutch underground resistance forces in 1944 and again raised by the Germans, and sunk for the third time in 1945, again by the Dutch underground. After the war, the Dutch raised the vessel and completed construction. The first* Westerdam *was sent to be broken up in Alicante, Spain, in 1965.*

The Brochure Says

"It is a balmy Saturday afternoon as the *Westerdam* charts an easterly course through the Caribbean...First there will be two full days at sea. Great!"

Translation

Veteran cruisers treasure days at sea, lazy times when the ship is the destination and there's no getting up early to catch a shore excursion or rushing up and down the gangway in the tropical heat. Days at sea develop their own rhythms.

Cabins & Costs

Fantasy Suites: .... B+

Average Price PPPD: $464 plus airfare in the Caribbean.
The five top suites on board are located on Lower Promenade Deck amidships, the traditional place for the most expensive cabins on classic vessels because the ride is smoother. Larger than two standard cabins, each of the suites has a separate bedroom with two lower beds that can convert to king-size, a living room with sofa bed that can sleep an additional two persons, as well as several comfortable upholstered chairs, a bathroom with tub and shower and some handsome cabinetry.

Small Splurges: .... B

Average Price PPPD: $283 plus airfare in the Caribbean.
Deluxe double cabins in C category are long rooms with with separate sitting area which has sofa and matching chair, plus a sleeping area that can be set off with curtains that close. The entry hallway is lined on one side with two closets, on the other with tile bathroom with tub/shower combination. A desk/dresser with stool and a coffee table round out the furnishings.

Suitable Standards: C

Average Price PPPD: $257 plus airfare in the Caribbean.
Standard outside cabins with two lower beds are somewhat smaller than the deluxe, without the sofa and sitting area, and bathrooms have shower only. There is a desk/dresser with good storage drawers and a mirror over and stool underneath.

Bottom Bunks: C

Average Price PPPD: $221 plus airfare in the Caribbean.

The cheapest standard inside cabins, which are N category, have two lower bed that can convert to queen-sized bed, a nightstand, desk/dresser, TV set and bath with shower only, but are surprisingly spacious for bottom-of-the-line. However there are only nine of these, so don't expect to nab one right off the bat. You may have to move up a grade or two on a popular cruise, but HAL has always been good about upgrading passengers when space permits.

The *Westerdam* cruises the Eastern Caribbean in winter from Ft. Lauderdale on seven-day itineraries, calling in St. Maarten, St. John, St. Thomas and Nassau. In fall she makes a series of Canada/New England cruises before returning to the Caribbean.

While the *Westerdam* is the only vessel in the fleet not built from the hull up by Holland America, she still has been rebuilt to fit almost seamlessly into the fleet. (A hint: If you're looking for her "stretch" marks, begin in the smaller dining room addition amidships on Restaurant Deck, the Bookchest library on Promenade Deck, the self-service laundries on Upper Promenade and Navigation Decks or the Veranda Deck and restaurant on Sun Deck.)

A very good value for the money, *Westerdam* provides bigger-than-average cabins and a sense of comfort throughout.

Five Favorite Places

1. The beautiful Veranda restaurant with live music during luncheon and tea is one of the prettiest self-service cafes at sea; there's a second Lido Cafe two decks below.

2. The amidships Veranda pool area adjacent, with a sliding glass dome so you can sit comfortably in a lounge chair, loll in the Jacuzzi or swim in the heated pool even on a chilly day.

3. The 127-seat Admiral's Terrace balcony overlooking the main stage has some good sightlines for the evening's entertainment, but late arrivals have to stand to see the show. The 680-seat Admiral's Lounge below provides big, cushy theater-type seats and couches and is probably a better bet.

4. The volleyball and paddle tennis courts on Sports Deck, covered at the sides and top with nets, get a good workout on short cruises.

5. The 17th-century bronze cannon, cast in Rotterdam in 1634, once defended a Dutch admiral's warship, then lay at the bottom of the sea for 300 years until a Dutch fisherman dragged it up in his nets.

Five Good Reasons to Book This Ship

1. It sails to some of the most popular ports in the Eastern Caribbean—Philipsburg, St. Maarten; Nassau, Bahamas; and St. Thomas and St. John in the U.S. Virgin Islands.

2. To try and find the seams from the "stretch," which added 130 feet in length, 13,872 more gross registry tons and capability for 494 more passengers.

. Because four laps on the all-around-the-ship Upper Promenade Deck make one mile.

. Because for the price range the cabins are unusually spacious.

. The little hideaway Saloon with a Victorian accent and singalong piano bar.

Five Things You Won't Find On Board

1. Private verandas.

2. An indoor swimming pool.

3. A single cabin.

4. Skimpy cabins for wheelchair users; designated mobility impaired cabins E002, D068, J021 and D087 are all on upper decks with plenty of extra turning space.

5. A long walk to an elevator; with four different locations along each deck, it's an easy stroll to a lift.

Westerdam ★★★★

Registry	The Netherlands
Officers	Dutch
Crew	Indonesian/Filipino
Complement	639
GRT	53,872
Length (ft.)	798
Beam (ft.)	104
Draft (ft.)	25
Passengers-Cabins Full	1833
Passengers-2/Cabin	1494
Passenger Space Ratio	36.04
Stability Rating	Good to Excellent
Seatings	2
Cuisine	International
Dress Code	Traditional
Room Service	Yes
Tip	No tipping required

Ship Amenities

Outdoor Pool	2
Indoor Pool	0
Jacuzzi	2
Fitness Center	Yes
Spa	Yes
Beauty Shop	Yes
Showroom	Yes
Bars/Lounges	8
Casino	Yes
Shops	3
Library	Yes
Child Program	Yes
Self-Service Laundry	Yes
Elevators	7

Cabin Statistics

Suites	5
Outside Doubles	495
Inside Doubles	252
Wheelchair Cabins	4
Singles	0
Single Surcharge	150%
Verandas	0
110 Volt	Yes

HOLLAND AMERICA LINE

IVA'RAN
Lines
Since 1925

111 Pavonia Avenue, Jersey City, NJ 07310-1755
☎ *(201) 798-5656, (800) 451-1639*

*Aboard Ivaran's **Americana** is a surprisingly spacious pool and deck area.*

History . . . .

The distinguished freighter-cruise company Ivaran Lines began in 1925, but its freight-carrying vessels started way back in 1902. The company's funnels bear a white "C" on a field of red for its founder, Norwegian-born Ivar Anton Christensen, who signed himself Ivar An. Christensen. Over the years, the company has had a number of notable executives, include Anders Wilhelmssen, co-founder and co-owner of Royal Caribbean Cruises Ltd., who was made general manager of Ivaran in 1950.

The *Americana*, hands-down the most luxurious of the cargo-carrying passenger ships, was built in Korea by Hyundai Heavy Industries and made its maiden voyage in 1988. It remains the world's only container/cruise vessel. Ivaran had the option to build two more, but the Korean authorities refused to grant export license when the options were declared, and the building of any similar vessels was put on hold indefinitely.

The vessel sails from ports in the southeastern United States to port along the Atlantic coast of South America, selling both full voyages o some 53 days and segments of five or more days. One reason the *Americana* is an exceptional vessel is because it carries 88 passengers, wherea the usual freighter takes a maximum of 12 passengers. That's because o a ruling that any seagoing ship with more than 12 passengers has tc have a doctor aboard. The line also has a more traditional new 12- passenger cargo ship *San Antonio*, with six single and three double cabins, a small dining room, lounge, bar and conference room.

—Operates the world's only container/cruise vessel (*Americana*, 1988).

Concept . . . .

The *Americana* is a hybrid, a small luxury cruise ship riding atop a workaday cargo vessel.

Signatures . . . .

The white C on the red stack.

Gimmicks . . . .

A Norwegian dinner is served once during each cruise, making the officers in particular happy, since otherwise they have to eat the same continental menu the passengers do.

Who's the Competition . . . .

Nobody at all, because there's no other comparable vessel in passenger service today. Purists sniff that the *Americana* is too luxurious for a freighter, which suits us just fine.

Who's Aboard . . . .

On our sailing, while there were some younger people—a California psychiatrist and his wife in their early 40s, two young Norwegian men, the captain's 16-year-old daughter—most passengers are singles and couples past retirement age, one a sprightly retired priest from New York near 90. There's no maximum age limit like most freighters have since the *Americana* carries a doctor.

Who Should Go . . . .

The *Americana* represents a good travel buy for the right kind of passenger—including veterans of freighter travel, for example, who are beyond the age limit set by some freighters with no doctors. Other candidates are single passengers tired of paying surcharges for occupying a cabin alone—Americana has a number of single cabins that cost little more than the per-person, double-occupancy rate—and anyone who hankers to write The Great American Novel. The late Alex Haley wrote most of his books aboard freighters.

Who Should Not Go . . . .

Mobility-impaired travelers will find there are no wheelchair-accessible cabins, although there is an elevator for the passenger decks. But the long steep gangway from the dock is difficult to negotiate.

No families with children, because there's nowhere for children to play.

Anyone who needs a cruise staff to keep him or her entertained.

The Lifestyle . . . .

Since there may be as many as nine days at sea between port calls, the ambiance on board takes on a long-cruise flavor, with groups of two or three chatting quietly together in the lounge, others reading on the spacious sunny deck or in the quiet, well-stocked library, still other swimming in the deck pool, working out in the gym or screening a feature film on the ship's video system or their own in-cabin VCR. In port, optional shore excursions are sometimes available. The cruise experience of posh cabins and dining room service is expanded with an easygoing freighter ambiance and the unpredictability of arrival and departure times.

Wardrobe. . . . .

Casual clothing is acceptable on the vessel and in the ports in the daytime, but the passengers like to dress up a little on special evenings like the captain's welcome aboard party. On many evenings men are requested to wear jacket and tie in the public areas after 6 p.m. Don't forget a bathing suit; there's a pool and Jacuzzi on board. And bring good walking and deck shoes. Forty cubic feet of baggage is permitted aboard for each passenger.

Bill of Fare. C

Meals are served in one seating, with large buffet breakfasts and lunches, and sit-down dinner service with a choice of two soups, three main dishes (one is always a reliable grilled steak with baked potato) and several desserts. Homemade pastries and baked goods are particularly nice, but since the galley is five decks below the passenger dining room, most of the hot dishes have been waiting in the finishing kitchen on a steam table.

Showtime . . . . N/A

Unlike regular cruise ships, the *Americana* has little in the way of organized shipboard activities, only an occasional after-dinner program of Trivial Pursuit, dancing to recorded music, blackjack, or entertainment brought on from shore, such as a lively samba group. Although there are six slot machines on board, we never saw anyone playing them.

Discounts. . . . .

Passengers sailing a full southbound or northbound voyage may discount 5 percent on cruise only fares, and Fly/Sail passengers may discount 5 percent on that package.

The Bottom Line

Because it is primarily a cargo vessel, the *Americana* does not have stabilizers, so the ride, while not uncomfortable, is less smooth than on many new cruise vessels, with a little more vibration discernible in some parts of the ship. You'll have to climb up and down a very steep gangway in port, although once you reach the passenger decks, there is an elevator. Regulations vary in ports; don't expect to be permitted to casually stroll around during loading and unloading operations.

Americana

Most people have only a day in a port of call such as Santos, South America's busiest port, a two-hour drive away from the continent's largest city, São Paulo. But those of us aboard the Americana, a passenger-carrying cargo ship, have two whole days to explore the area while our vessel is loading and unloading some of 1120 containers of automobile parts or animal hides. Another two days is spent in Buenos Aires, perhaps taking on canned corned beef and taking off coffee beans. Since all containers look alike, we're never sure which one holds what.

The same designers that did the Sea Goddess and Seabourn ships created the interiors for the *Americana*. The passenger areas cover six decks, with three decks of cabins connected by a graceful center staircase with curved chrome railings. Both public rooms and cabins are elegantly decorated and extremely comfortable; you won't be roughing it on this vessel!

The Brochure Says

"Here's your dream. You want to go to sea on a cargo vessel. You want to visit all those exciting, colorful ports that big cruise ships don't stop at. The problem is that you're used to living and traveling with a certain standard of luxury, and you're not sure you want to give up that standard, especially for a period of several weeks. With *M/V Americana* there's no problem at all."

Translation

You can run away from home but take all the comforts of home along with you.

IVARAN LINES

Cabins & Costs

Fantasy Suites: .... A

Average Price PPPD: $341 including airfare.
The two top suites aboard are called the Americana Suite and the Presidential Suite, but also sometimes referred to as the owner's suites, presumably because they overlook the containers, surely a view only an owner could love. The suites—really apartments—have an entry foyer, a large living room with sofa, two chairs, coffee table, lots of windows, separate bedroom and one and a half baths, as well as two TV/VCRs and two minibars.

Small Splurges: .... A

Average Price PPPD: $309 including airfare.
The deluxe suites with big private balconies are like the standard cabins (see Suitable Standards, below) but have the outside area with two lounging chairs facing aft on a painted green deck.

Suitable Standards: .... A

Average Price PPPD: $280 including airfare.
Standard double cabins measure 258 square feet, with king-sized or twin beds, sofa and chair in a sitting area, two built-in desks with chairs, five closets and plenty of enclosed shelf space, a refrigerator and mini-bar, TV and VCR, combination safe, hair dryer, fresh fruit, fresh flowers and a welcome-aboard bottle of champagne. Each large bathroom has a tub/shower combination and bidet, as well as plenty of storage shelves in the mirrored medicine cabinets and a lavish gift kit of toiletries.

Bottom Bunks: .... B

Average Price PPPD: $237 for an inside, $289 for an outside, including airfare.
Singles get a break on the *Americana* because the company has installed 8 outside and 12 inside singles and priced them at a flat rate with no surcharge. Singles measure 133.5 square feet and contain a bed that makes into a sofa for daytime, a coffee table, chair, built-in desk/dresser, TV/VCR, bath with shower and adequate closet space.

Where She Goes

The *Americana* goes from New Orleans to South America on 53-day roundtrip sailings, usually calling at Houston, Puerto Cabello and La Guaira, Venezuela; Rio de Janeiro and Santos, Brazil, and Buenos Aires, Argentina on the southbound route; and Rio Grande do Sul, Itajai, Santos, Rio de Janeiro, Salvador de Bahia and Fortaleza, Brazil; Bridgetown, Barbados; San Juan, Puerto Rico; Rio Haina, Dominican Republic; and Veracruz and Altamira, Mexico on the northbound itinerary. Passengers may book the full cruise or only the northbound or southbound portions, along with a package that includes airfare and hotel stays in New Orleans or Buenos Aires.

The Bottom Line

The *Americana* is best for self-reliant people with good sea legs who don't require constant entertainment and diversion, especially singles who want to avoid punishing surcharges and couples who want big, lavish cabins at moderate prices. Because cargo scheduling takes priority, potential passengers must be flexible about departure and arrival dates and ports of call. The housekeeping and service aboard are outstanding, and tipping is not required. Friendly South American staffers fluent in English call passengers by name and know each one's drink preferences within a day or two. The Norwegian officers are always around at mealtime and in the evenings to socialize, and the navigation bridge is open at all times to passengers. If you fit the profile of a freighter passenger, this vessel has our highest recommendation.

Five Sociable Spots

1. The Neptune Lounge has a white piano, a bar with six or eight stools, a long row of windows, fixed round tables and nicely upholstered sofas and chairs.

2. The teak sports and pool deck has a bar (that is rarely open), a pool, Jacuzzi and shower, shuffleboard court, lots of lounge and regular deck chairs and round tables bolted down.

3. Glass-doored bookcases, leather sofas and chairs and leather-topped tables make the library a good place for reading or playing cards.

4. The dining room has double glass doors and two rows of tables set for five or six places each; meals are served at a single open seating with a long center buffet used for food service at breakfast and lunch, for appetizer and cheese displays in the evening.

5. The large gymnasium has mirrored walls and an array of exercise equipment.

Five Good Reasons to Book This Ship

1. It has niceties freighters don't always offer—a gift shop, beauty shop, masseuse, sauna and self-service laundromat with ironing boards.

2. To get an in-depth look at the east coast of South America.

3. To write or read The Great American Novel.

4. To be treated like an individual rather than a number.

5. To get away from it all.

Five Things You Won't Find On Board

1. A singles surcharge.

2. A children's program; this ship is inappropriate for small children.

3. A cabin designated wheelchair-accessible; the ship is not appropriate for mobility-impaired passengers.

4. Tips. There's no tipping required.

5. Age limits.

Americana ★★★

Registry	**Norway**
Officers	**Norwegian**
Crew	**South American**
Complement	**53**
GRT	**19,500**
Length (ft.)	**578**
Beam (ft.)	**85**
Draft (ft.)	**32**
Passengers-Cabins Full	**102**
Passengers-2/Cabin	**84**
Passenger Space Ratio	**NA**
Stability Rating	**Good**
Seatings	**2**
Cuisine	**Continental**
Dress Code	**Casual**
Room Service	**No**
Tip	**No Tipping**

Ship Amenities

Outdoor Pool	**1**
Indoor Pool	**0**
Jacuzzi	**1**
Fitness Center	**Yes**
Spa	**No**
Beauty Shop	**Yes**
Showroom	**No**
Bars/Lounges	**1**
Casino	**No**
Shops	**1**
Library	**Yes**
Child Program	**No**
Self-Service Laundry	**Yes**
Elevators	**2**

Cabin Statistics

Suites	**10**
Outside Doubles	**22**
Inside Doubles	**0**
Wheelchair Cabins	**0**
Singles	**20**
Single Surcharge	**None**
Verandas	**4**
110 Volt	**Yes**

CRUISE LINE

901 South America Way, Miami, FL 33102
☎ *(305) 530-8900, (800) 645-8111*

History

Majesty Cruise Line, an upscale spin-off of Miami-based Dolphin Cruise Line, inaugurated its $220 million, 1056-passenger *Royal Majesty* in July 1992 when it was christened in New York by actress/singer Liza Minelli. The new line came up with some fresh ideas, including a totally nonsmoking dining room and a number of nonsmoking cabins and was built in less time than normal because the hull had already been completed for a ship that was never finished at Kvaerner-Masa Yard in Finland.

—The first Miami-based ship in the mini-cruise market to split itineraries between the Bahamas and Mexico, so a passenger could book two back-to-back cruises with different itineraries (1993).

Concept

After years of sailing the popular *Dolphin IV* from Miami on three- and four-day budget cruises, Dolphin Cruise Cruise Line decided to start up a sister company to operate a new, upscale ship offering to an increasingly younger market cruises that were elegant but still affordable, with an emphasis on hospitality and service.

Signatures

The distinctive crown logo is visible on the ship's superstructure.

The most attention-getting detail about Royal Majesty is the nonsmoking rule—no smoking in the dining room, show lounge or in 132 designated cabins, 25 percent of the total.

"It's a unique selling point," commented one of the travel agents on the inaugural sailing. "A few clients out there among the smokers won't like it, but for every one of them you lose, you'll pick up three others that are thrilled to be in a dining room without any smoking."

Gimmicks

The Hanna-Barbera costumed characters aboard are equally popular with kids and adults, and when they appear, which they do frequently, video and still cameras pop up all over the ship as loved ones run to be photographed with Fred and Barney.

Who's the Competition

One prominent travel agent said he did not see that the *Royal Majesty* was competing with Carnival's *Fantasy* in the three-day market but that it would compete with RCCL's *Nordic Empress*. In the seven-day Bermuda market, it does compete head-to-head with Celebrity's *Meridian* and *Horizon*.

Who's Aboard

Younger couples and singles, a lot of families with small children on holidays and, in summer, around 200 non-U.S. citizens from Canada, Latin America and the United Kingdom are on each cruise. Also in summer, on the Bermuda sailings, a number of yuppie couples and as many as 300 children. In winter, many of the cruisers are older Florida residents, but once spring and summer arrive, the ship fills with yuppies, singles, couples and families with kids.

Who Should Go

It's a good ship for seniors because it's not too large, has a warm atmosphere and a caring cruise staff. Children love the Hanna-Barbera characters, of course, and families have enough options to be together when they wish or apart and still have a good time. But it's also a happy hunting ground for single guys looking for great-looking, single, thirty-something women.

Who Should Not Go

Dowager veterans of the world cruise, and anyone who would be a party-pooper with a lot of families with children, yuppies and singles having a really great time.

The Life-style

It's a young, active ship with exercise classes such as tai chi, aerobics and stretch-and-tone scheduled before 9 a.m., plus quiz, Scrabble and ping pong competitions, dance and golf lessons, ice-carving demonstrations and art auctions. A Medieval Royal Fest with knights and jesters, face painting and fun and games is held on board during most cruises. A Club Nautica watersports program provides optional shore excursions with deep-sea fishing, snorkeling, scuba and sailing. Besides the daily program for adults, children are issued their own colorful activities booklets with Fred Flintstone on the cover. Particularly during spring and fall, *Royal Majesty* will have conference and incentive groups on board wearing badges and going to meetings in the ship's conference rooms.

Wardrobe

Because there are usually a number of first-time cruisers aboard, some of them group and incentive travelers, dress codes are not as strictly adhered to as on some ships. But the line does observe two formal nights when men are asked to wear "proper attire," and two semi-formal nights that usually call for jacket and tie. Casual-dress evenings call for resort-wear rather than shorts, T-shirts or jeans.

> ## NO NOs
> *Shorts are not allowed in the dining room after 6 p.m. and bathing suits are never permitted in public rooms without a coverup.*

Bill of Fare . . . . B+

In the dining room, dinner menus usually offer a choice of four or five main dishes, say, Cornish game hen, steak, veal, grilled fish and a vegetarian pasta dish. A choice of three or four appetizers, two soups, two salads and a range of desserts presented at the table fills out the menu.

The buffet breakfasts are copious, with ready-made omelets, scrambled eggs, bacon, sausage, ham, potatoes, herring, smoked salmon, bagels, fruits, cereals and all kinds of freshly made pastries.

A "Light at Sea" menu lists calories, cholesterol and sodium count (but not fat grams). We tried the low-calorie pita pockets with chicken, cucumber, tomatoes and onions that were delicious. Other lunchtime options that day were a California frittata, sauteed ling cod, mignons of turkey supreme Cacciatore, braised round of beef, plus an onion, tomato and white bean salad garnished with black olives.

One of our favorite food venues on board is the Piazza San Marco out on deck, serving pizza, hot dogs, ribs, hamburgers, French fries and ice cream, along with optional wine, beer and soda on ice. Steps away are tables with umbrellas and red-checkered cloths, like an Italian sidewalk cafe with a big stretched canvas canopy overhead in a sort of Sydney Opera House sail shape. (OK, like an Australian sidewalk cafe then.)

Dining room service is friendly and generally efficient, except for the open-seating breakfasts. One morning every order delivered to our table of six was confused. There's also 24-hour room service with cold plates, desserts, coffee tea or milk.

Showtime . . . . B+

Royal Majesty presents live theatrical productions such as "Star-Spangled Girl" and "Murder at the Howard Johnson's" during each cruise by a resident acting company. A Medieval Feast highlights one evening during each cruise, and a "Big Chill" '50s and '60s party, karaoke sing-alongs, fun and games with the cruise staff and some musical production and variety shows round out the programs.

Discounts . . . .

The AdvanSaver promises that the earlier you book, the more you'll save.

The Bottom Line

The line is already prepared for the millennium because their ship is fully sprinkler-equipped, all windows are double-glazed and equipped with thermal and sound insulation. Environmental systems include fully automatic sewage treatment plant and fully automatic garbage handling plant that shreds, then burns waste in a smoke-free incinerator. Glass and metal are stored aboard for recycling ashore.

As with many lines today, there's a big push for onboard revenue, with countless bingo games, heavy shop promotions, skeet shooting, art auctions and a lot of bar and wine merchandising.

Royal Majesty

In the dining room of the Royal Majesty, when we are ushered to our table, three pretty young women already seated there are stunned; we suspect they expected the other two seats to be occupied by handsome young men. We think of them later as Thelma and Louise and Louise, very nice women from a southern state, three pals, one of them married and two single, on their very first cruise, and they expect more romance and adventure than is reasonable. Fortunately, we have a flirtatious waiter who fills some of the gap.

A white piano is the centerpiece of the **Royal Majesty's** *marble lobby.*

It's an elegant ship with some of the most distinctive fabrics and carpeting we've seen anywhere, along with a generous use of wood that lends a warm ambiance.

Cabins are located on six of the nine passenger decks, with a top deck sunning area, below which is the Majesty Deck pool and spa area. Deck 5, the Countess Deck, is where most of the public rooms are located, starting from the forward observation deck and lounge and moving back through a series of small rooms that double as meeting areas when a conference is on board and bars, card rooms and such when there's no group. Amidships is the Crossroads lobby area, directly below the casino, and the dining room is aft. The show room is conveniently located one deck above the dining room, making it an easy progression from dinner to entertainment.

The Brochure Says

"From the beginning a ship designed for conferences."

Translation
We met a lady in the elevator who was wearing a name tag on her bathing suit.

EAVESDROPPING

A recently coiffed champagne blonde shrieked at one of the crew who tried to help her don her life jacket, "Stop that, you're ruining my hair!"

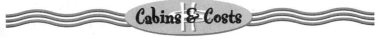

Cabins & Costs

Fantasy Suites: .... A
Average Price PPPD: $439 plus airfare.
Two royal suites are the top digs aboard, two large separate rooms with floor-to-ceiling bay view windows, a living room with paisley sofa, coffee table, two chairs, glass dining table with four chairs and long built-in granite counter, and a bedroom with queen-sized bed, covered in a paisley print bedspread, nightstands, desk/dresser with chair, TV/VCR, minibar, safe, hair dryer, ironing board, bathrobes and 24-hour butler service. There's also a marble bath with long tub and a big walk-in closet/dressing room with good hanging storage.

Small Splurges: .... A
Average Price PPPD: $359 plus airfare.
The 14 deluxe suites have twins or queen-sized beds, a granite-topped built-in desk and dresser with blue tweed chair, a granite-topped nightstand with four drawers, a big window in the bedroom side and a sliding fabric panel in strips of beige fabric that can be pulled across the room to separate the bedroom from the sitting area. The latter has a large sofa and two chairs, plus a wood-and-glass coffee table. A built-in wood console has TV/VCR and underneath is a wooden cabinet with glassware and minibar. In the marble bathroom is a tub, sink with marble counter and big mirror with good makeup lights, a built-in hair dryer, shower over the tub and complimentary toiletries. There is a glass bay window in the sitting area, and the artwork in the cabin consists of three pleasant watercolors. You also get 24-hour butler service in these suites.

Suitable Standards: ....B

Average Price PPPD: $243 plus airfare.

The outside standard cabins are very attractive because of the elegant fabrics used throughout the ship. These are crisp brick red, apple green and black plaids with a smaller patterned carpet in the same colors. You can request queen-sized, double or twin beds, and also get a picture window, color TV, safe, hair dryer, ironing board (ingeniously built into a dresser drawer) and signature kimonos for use during the cruise. The bath is adequately sized with shower only, and there's also a pair of nightstands with drawers, a desk/dresser with chair and a closet with two full-length hanging spaces and one half-length hanging space with four drawers under, quite adequate for a week's cruise. Four cabins are designated wheelchair-accessible.

Bottom Bunks: ....B

Average Price PPPD: $146 plus airfare.

Even the lowest-priced inside doubles have two lower beds, and a handsome mirror wall where the window would be successfully presents the illusion of light and space, brightening the room inside. There's a nightstand with drawers, a desk/dresser with chair, bath with shower only, adequate closet and wall-hung TV set. Some of these cabins have upper berths as well.

INSIDER TIP

Watch out for cabins with partially obstructed views from hanging lifeboats, especially on Empress and Queen's Deck, where most of the more expensive cabins are located. They are indicated in the brochure and a price adjustment is made for the dozen cabins with fully obstructed views on Queen's Deck. Only 19 of the 46 cabins on Empress Deck offer totally unobstructed views—numbers 901, 902, 904, 905, 907, 910, 912, 914, 915, 917, 919, 930, 935, 940, 942, 944, 945, 947 and 949.

Where She Goes

Royal Majesty makes three-day cruises to the Bahamas and Key West every Friday from Miami, and four-night cruises to Mexico and Key West every Monday during the winter season. In spring the ship repositions to Boston for seven-night roundtrip sailings to Bermuda during the summer.

The Bottom Line

This is a classy ship and the prices are right. The deck sunbathing areas are a bit small and can be crowded when the ship is jam-packed full, as it was on an Easter weekend last spring when we were aboard, along with some 200 children.

The *Royal Majesty* is one of the rare new ships that offers a full promenade around the ship for inveterate walkers and joggers. Rubberized red matting covers the entire deck, with a special track laid out in green in the center; five laps around is a mile.

It's a good vessel for fitness-conscious people, with plenty of exercise options on board and ashore, including walking tours with cruise staff members. The only thing that surprises us is, for a ship with such an active nonsmoking policy, there are an awful lot of smokers aboard and it's hard to get completely away from the smell of it in the corridors,

ven when you book a smokefree cabin, eat in a smokefree dining room and watch the
how in a smokefree lounge.

Five Special Places

1. The dining room, one of the first nonsmoking cruise dining rooms at sea in 1992, now one of many, has lights bright enough to see but not flat cafeteria lighting, and there is enough sound baffle on the ceiling to reduce the room noise a bit.

2. Body Wave, the really hot gym on board with every imaginable kind of equipment, plus an adjacent exercise room with wood floor, windows, mirrors, barre and sauna.

3. Royal Fireworks, where a resident theater company performs two one-act comedies each cruise, with two-seat sofas and swivel chairs in autumn leaf tones, a wood parquet dance floor and bandstand, and elegant blond-burled wood-covered walls.

4. Royal Observatory, with striped red-and-black tub chairs, antique ship models and drawings, a curved wood bar with brass rail and curved glass walls facing forward.

5. The Polo Club, one of the most sophisticated bars at sea, low key, with excellent music, whether a late-morning jazz session with some of the musicians from the ship's orchestra or a cocktail-hour classical guitarist playing music you can hear and converse over at the same time.

Royal Majesty *passengers pose with Hanna Barbera characters George Jetson and Yogi Bear.*

Five Good Reasons to Book This Ship

1. To take an Elvis birthday theme cruise.

2. To cruise with Fred Flintstone, Barney Rubble, Yogi Bear and George Jetson—all Hanna-Barbera characters licensed to Majesty.

3. To combine a three-day cruise to the Bahamas and a four-day cruise to Cozumel and Key West for a fascinating week-long sailing.

4. To take a Pro-Am Golf Classic Cruise.

5. Safety and security are taken very seriously on board; in addition to our boarding passes, we are required to show photo IDs to reboard the ship, and the lifeboat drill is one of the most thorough at sea, which starts indoors with indoctrination and

putting on lifejackets, then moves outside in orderly rows so that passengers end up lined up on boat deck with men in the back, women in front of them, and women with children in the very front.

Five Things You Won't Find On Board

1. The chance for someone in your family to eat up a fortune in the tempting but expensive minibar; it cannot be opened until authorized by the cabin occupants and unlocked by the cabin steward.

2. A delay getting back your laundry and dry cleaning; same-day service is provided.

3. A child under 2 or not potty-trained accepted into the Little Prince playroom, which has a kiddies' pool, child-scaled furniture and toys, a slide that ends in a pool of bright plastic balls, a rope-climbing area and some white wall panels waiting to be decorated with crayons.

4. A moment of silence in the serene-looking Crossroads lobby with its white piano, white marble floor and potted palms, because just above in the open atrium is the Winners Circle Casino with slot machines constantly ringing and pinging.

5. A self-service laundry.

Royal Majesty ★★★★

Registry	Panama
Officers	Greek
Crew	International
Complement	500
GRT	32,400
Length (ft.)	568
Beam (ft.)	91
Draft (ft.)	20.5
Passengers-Cabins Full	1225
Passengers-2/Cabin	1056
Passenger Space Ratio	30.68
Stability Rating	Good
Seatings	2
Cuisine	Continental
Dress Code	Traditional
Room Service	Yes
Tip	$9 PPPD, 15% automatically added to bar check

Ship Amenities

Outdoor Pool	2
Indoor Pool	0
Jacuzzi	2
Fitness Center	Yes
Spa	Yes
Beauty Shop	Yes
Showroom	Yes
Bars/Lounges	3
Casino	Yes
Shops	3
Library	Yes
Child Program	Yes
Self-Service Laundry	No
Elevators	4

Cabin Statistics

Suites	16
Outside Doubles	327
Inside Doubles	185
Wheelchair Cabins	4
Singles	16
Single Surcharge	150%
Verandas	0
110 Volt	Yes

NORWEGIAN CRUISE LINE

95 Merrick Way, Coral Gables, FL 33134
☎ (305) 445-0866, (800) 327-7030

The sports bar on the **Windward** *underscores NCL's emphasis on active and theme cruises.*

History ....

Norwegian Caribbean Lines was founded in 1966 by Knut Kloster and Ted Arison (see Carnival Cruises, History, above) to create casual, one-class cruising in the Caribbean in contrast to the more formal, class-oriented tradition of world cruises and transatlantic crossings. That partnership soon broke up, however, leaving Kloster to begin a rapid expansion of the line while Arison went off to found Carnival Cruise Lines.

NCL's first ship was the *Sunward*, but the fleet soon grew to include the *Starward* (1968), *Skyward* (1969), *Southward* (1971) and, also in 1971, a replacement for the original *Sunward* called *Sunward II* (the former *Cunard Adventurer*).

But the real coup came in 1979 when the Kloster family bought French Line's *France*, which had been laid up in Le Havre for five years, made a major rebuilding to convert the former ocean liner into a cruise ship and renamed her *Norway.* From her debut in 1980, she was the flagship of the line, and the other four vessels came to be called "the white ships" for their white hulls that contrasted sharply with the dark blue hull of the *Norway.* (All the original "white ships" have been retired from the fleet, the last in September, 1995.)

In 1984, Kloster Cruise Limited, the parent company of Norwegian Cruise Line, bought Royal Viking Line, promising to make minimal changes to the highly respected company. Two years later, Kloster changed the Norwegian registry of the RVL ships to Bahamian, then a year after that closed down the long-time San Francisco headquarters and moved the entire operation to Florida.

In 1987, the former Norwegian Caribbean Lines changed its name to Norwegian Cruise Line with an eye to long-range marketing of Alaska, Bermuda and European cruises, and in 1989 acquired San Francisco based Royal Cruise Line. This time, however, Kloster left the company in San Francisco with most of its executive roster intact.

The dismantling and sale of RVL happened in the summer of 1994, with the flagship *Royal Viking Sun* and the Royal Viking name, logo, past passenger list and general goodwill sold to Cunard, who promptly (but only briefly) named their new division Cunard Royal Viking Line (see Cunard, above). The *Royal Viking Queen* was soon transferred over to Royal Cruise Line and renamed the *Queen Odyssey.* Two earlier RVL ships, *Royal Viking Star* and *Royal Viking Sea*, also went to Royal to become *Star Odyssey* and *Royal Odyssey.*

In 1996, Royal Cruise Line was dismantled, the *Crown Odyssey* becoming NCL's *Norwegian Crown*, the *Queen Odyssey* becoming *Seabourn Legend* and the *Star Odyssey* becoming the *Black Watch* for Fred Olsen Lines.

In the late 1980s, Knut Kloster began taking a less active role in the company in order to pursue his dream of building the world's biggest passenger ship, the 250,000-ton, 5600-passenger *Phoenix World City.* Despite its detractors who say the project's dead, the giant ship may still be a viable possibility, pending funding.

—The first three- and four-day cruises to the Bahamas incorporating a private island beach day.

—First line to restage hit Broadway musicals aboard cruise ships; the *Norway's* first production was "My Fair Lady."

—The official cruise line of the National Basketball Association, the Basketball Hall of Fame and the National Football League Players Association; NCL presents a number of sports theme cruises throughout the year (see Theme Cruises, page 1125).

—First cruise line to broadcast live NFL and NBA games live aboard its ships.

Signatures . . . .

Theme cruises—especially the annual *Norway* jazz festival, now in its 14th year, and the sports theme cruises which are aboard all the ships.

The "Dive-In" program—the first and perhaps most successful of the watersports packages found on cruise ships combines onboard instruction and equipment rentals with shore excursions to snorkel and dive spots. A Sports Afloat T-shirt is given to participants in designated activities who accrue seven tickets by the end of the cruise.

Gimmicks

The line's award-winning advertising campaign built around a sexy young couple who look like they might star in lingerie or perfume ads and the slogan, "It's different out here." The campaign itself is great, but it could be argued they're barking up the wrong mast, because we've never seen that couple on an NCL ship.

Who's the Competition

The main competitors in all its cruising areas (now that Carnival has entered Alaska) are the ships owned by Kloster's old nemesis Arison and the rapidly-growing Royal Caribbean Cruise Line. The *Norway*, unique in the otherwise modern fleet because of her history as the famous ocean liner *France*, should be competing with other classic ships like the *Rotterdam* and the *Queen Elizabeth 2*, but with a year-round, seven-day Caribbean itinerary and the same food and entertainment as the rest of the NCL fleet, she doesn't.

Who's Aboard

A lot of sports-oriented young couples from the heartland; yuppies and baby boomers; jazz fans for two weeks every autumn on the *Norway*; people who want to see a Broadway show without actually having to set foot in Times Square.

Who Should Go

Young couples and singles looking for a first-time cruise; music fans who'll enjoy not only the two-week annual jazz festival but the annual blues festival and two country music festivals; TV quiz show fans to take the annual "Wheel of Fortune" cruise; comedy aficionados for the summer comedy cruise; rock 'n rollers for the 50's and 60's cruise; Big Band devotees for the November sentimental journey; and fitness buffs for the annual fitness and beauty cruise each fall aboard the *Norway*.

Young families who will appreciate NCL's "Kids Crew" program for kids 3 to 17, with special kids-only activities onboard and ashore. They're divided into four different age groups: Junior Sailors, 3–5; First Mates, 6–8; Navigators, 9–12; and teens, 13–17.

Who Should Not Go

Longtime cruise veterans looking to check out a new line, senior singles, and urban sophisticates who've "been there, done that."

The Lifestyle

"Elegant, yes; stuffy, never," was the way they described themselves a couple of years ago, and it's fairly apt. NCL's ships offer traditional cruising, with themed sailings (see Who Should Go, above), international themed dinners several times a sailing, live calypso music on deck, and something going on around the ship every minute. Not long after boarding, passengers are offered free spa demonstrations, free casino lessons, a rundown on the children's program for the week, a free sport and fitness orientation, dive-in snorkeling presentation and as many a three singles parties—one each at 8 p.m. for college-aged spring brea celebrants and over-30 singles (a Big Band dancing session is usuall scheduled at the same time for the over-50s set), plus a third at 11:3 for any singles that couldn't find a friend at the first two parties.

In other words, you'll stay busy aboard—and that's before the dozen o so shore excursions offered in each port of call!

Wardrobe . . . .

NCL calls for less stringent dress codes than its Caribbean competitor good news for guys who hate to wear ties. A seven-day cruise usuall calls for two formal outfits, two informal outfits and a "costume" for theme country/western or Caribbean night if you wish. Short cruise schedule one formal night and two informal nights. Formal garb described by NCL as "cocktail dresses or gowns for the ladies and th men wear a jacket and tie or tuxedo." On informal nights, "just abou anything but shorts is fine." For daytimes, take along some exercis clothing, bathing suits, shorts, T-shirts and sandals, plus light cotto clothes and walking shoes for going ashore. NCL also reminds passen gers not worry about clothes—if they forget something, they can bu anything they need in the shipboard shops.

Bill of Fare . . . . £

The food is big-ship cruise fare with some new cutting-edge options.

The dinner menu usually provides five appetizers, three soups, two sal ads, a pasta and four main dishes, one of which is fish, along with a fu vegetarian menu offered nightly. There are four desserts plus ice crear and fruit, and low fat, low calorie dishes are indicated on the menu with an asterisk. Dinners are served in two assigned seatings at assigne tables, with first seating 6:30 p.m. and second seating 8:30 p.m.

A welcome-aboard buffet is typical of lunchtime self-service offerings— a make-your-own taco table and a vegetarian buffet with hot and col selections, plus carved roast beef, turkey goulash with rice and pre cooked hamburgers, along with a dessert table and separate beverag service area.

An alternative restaurant called Le Bistro, on board the *Norway*, *Sea ward*, *Dreamward* and *Windward*, requires an advance reservation an a tip to the waiter but makes no surcharge for the food. The menu described as "South-Beach style" by the Miami-based line (meanin Miami Beach's trendy art deco district), offers for starters a Norwegia seafood medley, escargots, French onion soup or clam chowder, thre salads including Caesar and a warm spinach, then a vegetable mai course, two pastas and three main dishes—chicken Provençale, peppe steak Madagascar and veal medallions with a wine/herb sauce an polenta. Dessert choices include a warm apple tart, a chocolate desser and a selection of fruit and cheese.

Showtime . . . . A

NCL was the first cruise line to create a buzz about its onboard entertainment, presenting shipboard versions of popular Broadway shows from "My Fair Lady" to the relatively current "The Will Rogers Follies" and the popular revival "Grease." In addition to the Broadway shows, each ship presents a song-and-dance Sea Legs revue as well as variety performers on other evenings.

Also aboard: Q and A sessions with sports stars, several different lounges offering live music for dancing, art auctions, games, dance lessons, and pop psychology lectures about astrology or fashion colors.

Discounts . . . .

Early booking discounts knock off as much as 15 percent of the cruise price.

Children under two sail free; a maximum of two adults and two children per cabin is the limit for this offer.

The Bottom Line

These are good, moderately-priced traditional cruises that will particularly appeal to first-time cruisers, honeymooners, couples, families and singles up to the outer perimeters of Baby Boomdom. Filled with nonstop activities, music, very professional entertainment and sports-themed programs for watching or doing, NCL is never boring for middle-of-the-road mainstreamers, although very sophisticated travelers may (despite the "It's different out here" commercials) stifle a yawn now and again.

Dreamward
Windward

It was the water curtain on the Dreamward that really grabbed attention. On the inaugural sailing, we sat in the front row scribbling notes about traffic "flow" and "splashy" production numbers while watching a dazzling revue staged behind a unique curtain of water. A Gene Kelly-lookalike splashed about in "Singin' in the Rain," marine creatures frolicked "Under the Sea" and not a drop of water fell on the front row. The water spurts from below like fountains or drizzles from above like rain, and the big finale incorporated fireworks, fog and film clips of Esther Williams swimming with cartoon characters Tom and Jerry.

How do you make a big ship look like a little ship? The answer is clearly illustrated aboard NCL's new *Dreamward* and *Windward*, ships that carry 1246 passengers but offer so many intimate spaces they actually seem cozy. There are no soaring atriums or double-decker dining rooms; instead, three separate dining rooms that seat from 190 to 282 passengers appear to have more smaller tables seating two to four than big ones seating six to eight. Instead of a vast self-service buffet area, the ships have incorporated quick pickup breakfasts and lunches into a small snack bar adjacent to the Sports Bar & Grill, with a continental breakfast and lunchtime hot dogs and hamburgers. Salads, desserts and beverages are laid out buffet-style. Many areas, including some of the dining rooms and deck sunbathing spots, have been terraced to give an illusion of smaller space but with more privacy.

INSIDER TIP

If you're not assigned to one of the dramatic terrace restaurants, you can still eat breakfast or lunch in one of them any time you wish, since those meals are served open seating at your choice of restaurant. And the view is even better in the daylight.

The Brochure Says

"No matter where you choose to go, you are certain to have a lot of fun getting there: full-court basketball, a jogging track and fitness center, golf driving nets, outdoor hot tubs, a two-story casino, a Sports Bar & Grill with ESPN, NFL and NBA games beamed in live, dozens of top-notch entertainers—they're all here, just waiting for you."

Translation

We're ready for the young and the restless, and double-dare anyone to get bored aboard.

Cabins & Costs

Suite # 20 aboard the Windward.

Fantasy Suites: .... A

Average Price PPPD: $600 including airfare in the Caribbean.
Top digs are six 350-square-foot grand deluxe suites with concierge service, all facing forward on three different decks for a captain's-eye view of the world. The living room is sumptuously furnished with a brocade sofa and three chairs, a long desk and dresser with eight drawers and glass coffee table. In the bedroom, you can choose either twin or queen-sized beds. The bathroom has tub and shower, and additional perks include a mini-refrigerator and a private safe.

Small Splurges: .... B

Average Price PPPD: $453 including airfare in the Caribbean.
Penthouses with private balconies are 175 square feet inside plus a veranda that is large enough for two chairs and a table. A separate sitting area with love seat and chairs, floor-to-ceiling windows, twin or queen-sized bed, private safe, TV set, mini-refrigerator and concierge service are included.

Suitable Standards: .... B

Average Price PPPD: $343 including airfare in the Caribbean.

Standard outside staterooms are virtually identical in size (160 square feet) and furnishings—sitting area and twin or queen-sized bed, TV set, built-in cabinetry—with the price varying according to deck location. "I'd advise clients to book one of the lower-category outsides," one travel agent told us, "because the differences in deck and amenities isn't that much." Accordingly, we'd recommend the D category outsides; get any lower on the totem pole and you're facing partial or full obstruction from hanging lifeboats. Six wheelchair-accessible cabins have shower seat and hand rails plus spacious turn-around room and no sills to impede the wheels.

Bottom Bunks: C

Average Price PPPD: $290 including airfare in the Caribbean.
The lowest-priced cabins aboard are category J inside double cabins with two lower beds in 150 square feet of space. Needless to say, you shouldn't expect a sitting area with sofa.

INSIDER TIP

If you want to book a category A outside cabin and value your privacy, opt for those on Atlantic Deck instead of Promenade Deck. While Promenade Deck is considered posh by old-time cruisers, it also means the joggers and strollers are walking around the deck outside your windows day and night, while on Atlantic deck only the gulls and flying fish can look in while the ship's at sea.

In winter, *Dreamward* offers a seven-day Western Caribbean program sailing Sundays from Ft. Lauderdale and calling in Grand Cayman, Playa del Carmen/Cozumel, Cancun and Great Stirrup Cay, NCL's own private island, for a beach day.

The *Dreamward* spends summers in Bermuda with seven-day sailings every Saturday from New York, spending one full day and night in St. George's, then repositioning to Hamilton for two-and-a-half days there.

In winter, the *Windward* sails the Exotic Caribbean on seven-day cruises from San Juan every Saturday, calling at Barbados, St. Lucia, St. Barts, Tortola, Virgin Gorda, St. John and St. Thomas.

The *Windward* summers in Alaska with seven-day sailings every Monday from Vancouver that alternate Misty Fjords and Glacier Bay as all-day cruising destinations. The ship also calls in Skagway, Haines, Juneau and Ketchikan.

Fall and spring repositioning cruises take the *Dreamward* between Ft. Lauderdale and New York on 13- or 15- day sailings, and the *Windward* on two transcanals and two Pacific Coast cruises.

The Bottom Line

This is a very special pair of ships, stylish enough for frequent travelers but accessible to first-time cruisers as well. They offer everything an active young passenger might wish without appearing intimidatingly huge. While the cheaper cabins are not as spacious as you might wish, they're a lot bigger than many NCL cabins used to be. And the fact that hese vessels return to the human scale in contrast to the awesome new megaships is a great plus.

The aft pool deck aboard the **Dreamward** *has terraced sunbathing.*

Five Fabulous Places

1. The sunbathing deck, not acres of astroturf lined with sunbathers sprawled everywhere, but lounge chairs arranged in a series of teak terraces separated by low wooden planters filled with clipped boxwoods, rather like an ampitheater.

2. Sports and Sky Decks include two golf driving areas, Ping-Pong tables in an enclosed alcove, a volleyball-basketball court and shuffleboard on rubberized mats, plus a full fitness center with sauna and massage.

3. The big forward Observation Lounge doubles as a late-night disco with marble dance floor and a pair of electronic route maps that show the ship's itineraries.

4. Le Bistro, originally a fourth dining room, has turned into a 76-seat specialty restaurant with no surcharge, only a request for advance reservations and a tip for the waiter afterwards. It's a good place for a quiet dinner for two, perhaps celebrating a romantic occasion, or a place to get together with other new friends.

5. The 150-seat Sun Terrace dining room, three levels set high atop the ship and aft, facing a wall of windows to the sea, and one deck below, The Terraces, 282 seats on several levels that also overlook the sea through an expanse of glass with a huge undersea mural on the back wall.

The Sun Terrace dining rooms aboard the **Dreamward** *and* **Windward** *offer sweeping views to the sea.*

Five Good Reasons to Book These Ships

1. To meet jocks, both professional and amateur.

2. To sail aboard a ship christened by ex-first lady Barbara Bush (the *Windward* 1993).

3. To luxuriate aboard a ship that was designed especially for new, younger cruise passengers who want everything a shoreside resort can offer, including an oceanfront room.

4. The Sports Bar & Grill, which brings in live sports telecasts from around the world daily on big-screen TV sets, with small snack bars not far away in a quiet corner if you want a hot dog with your beer or soda.

5. To venture aboard a young-minded ship beyond the Caribbean into Alaska or Bermuda.

Five Things You Won't Find On Board

1. A single cabin.

2. A self-service laundry.

3. Anyone wearing shorts in the dining room after 6 p.m.

4. A giant atrium with revolving sculpture.

5. A lavish lunchtime deck buffet.

Dreamward / Windward ★★★★★ ★★★★★

Registry	**Bahamas**
Officers	**Norwegian**
Crew	**International**
Complement	**696**
GRT	**41,000**
Length (ft.)	**624**
Beam (ft.)	**94**
Draft (ft.)	**22**
Passengers-Cabins Full	**1502**
Passengers-2/Cabin	**1246**
Passenger Space Ratio	**32.90**
Stability Rating	**Good**
Seatings	**2**
Cuisine	**Themed**
Dress Code	**Traditional**
Room Service	**Yes**
Tip	**$9 PPPD, 15% automatically added to bar checks**

Ship Amenities

Outdoor Pool	**2**
Indoor Pool	**0**
Jacuzzi	**2**
Fitness Center	**Yes**
Spa	**Yes**
Beauty Shop	**Yes**
Showroom	**Yes**
Bars/Lounges	**5**
Casino	**Yes**
Shops	**3**
Library	**Yes**
Child Program	**Yes**
Self Service Laundry	**No**
Elevators	**7**

Cabin Statistics

Suites	**101**
Outside Doubles	**428**
Inside Doubles	**92**
Wheelchair Cabins	**6**
Singles	**0**
Single Surcharge	**150-200%**
Verandas	**48**
110 Volt	**Yes**

Leeward   ★★★★

*We are struck by how many young male passengers stay aboard the ship
watching ESPN in the sports bar rather than going ashore on the idyllic private
island with its sandy beaches, barbecue buffet and watersports. Perhaps NCL
has stumbled across the answer to the dilemma: Wife wants to take a cruise;
husband, accustomed to spending his weekends watching sports on TV, is
promised the same thing at sea. Ergo: everybody's happy.*

This joint-venture ship owned by Finland's Effjohn International and operated by NCL is far more attractive in total than the sum of its component
parts. The size, 25,000 tons carrying 950 passengers, seems ideally human-
scale in these days of megaliners, and the decor, evocatively art deco-style
smudges most of the outline of the former Baltic ferry Sally Albatross.

The Brochure Says

"Your heart is saying, 'Go ahead, take a long vacation.' Unfortunately, your schedule
is saying, 'Uh-uh, just a few days.' Oh boy, have we got a cruise for you.'"

Translation

As a mid-sized ship in the three- and four-day market, Leeward offers a more intimate,
refreshing change from the big ships of Carnival and RCCL.

Cabins & Costs

Fantasy Suites: . . . . A

Average Price PPPD: $553 including airfare.
A pair of owner's suites, one dubbed the Presidential Suite because ex-President
George Bush once stayed there, provides large private balconies with outdoor hot
tub, living room spacious enough for a modest party, separate bedroom with two
lower beds, picture windows, mini-refrigerator, walk-in closets and bath with tub
and shower.

The owner's suite aboard the Leeward goes for $553 a day per person, double occupancy.

Small Splurges .... A

Average Price PPPD: $470 including airfare.

Eight deluxe penthouses with small private verandas and living rooms with sofa and large picture window, mini-refrigerator, queen-sized bed in separate bedroom area, wall-mounted TV, and generous storage space.

Suitable Standards .... B

Average Price PPPD: $306 including airfare in category E.

We deem categories D and E as "suitable," but not categories F and G, outsides with partially or fully obstructed views because of hanging lifeboats. You'll find two lower beds, some sitting areas, and, in many, very handsome black-and- white tile bathrooms with shower. All passengers get a basket of toiletries in the bathroom and a silver dish of fresh fruit in the cabin. Nonsmoking cabins are available on request.

Bottom Bunks .... B

Average Price PPPD: $226 including airfare.

This quartet of small outsides on Promenade Deck are the lowest-priced accommodations on board. While most of the inside cabins priced slightly higher have two lower beds, these upper and lower berth cabins have a window and a good location just steps away from the open deck.

Where She Goes

The *Leeward* makes year-round three-day cruises every Friday, with alternate itineraries from Miami to Nassau and Great Stirrup Cay, the line's private island, or from Miami to Key West and Great Stirrup Cay. On Mondays, two alternating itineraries are also offered on the four-day sailing, one roundtrip from Miami to Key West, Cancun and Cozumel, the other roundtrip from Miami to Playa del Carmen, Cozumel and Key West.

All in all, this is a handsome and winning ship. We only wish we couldn't glimpse so much untreated steel superstructure under the cosmetic surface.

The busy Sports Bar and Grill shows sports events from ESPN.

Five Fabulous Places

1. The Sports Bar and Grill aboard means nobody has to miss any important play of a televised sports event.

2. Gatsby's Piano Bar with angled glass walls, raised curved banquettes and tapestry-covered seating offers a nightclub ambiance.

3. Le Bistro, an alternative restaurant for couples who want to dine alone or with new friends they met aboard.

4. The Stardust Lounge with its entrance that is reminiscent of an art deco movie house.

5. The Four Seasons Dining Room, with a shipboard art deco entrance that reinforces the sense of being at sea.

Five Good Reasons to Book This Ship

1. If you're an art aficionado, you'll find plenty to admire aboard.

2. To dine in one of the two dining rooms that seem no larger than your favorite upscale restaurant.

3. To hang around the Sports Bar amid museum cases of vintage sports equipment.

4. To enjoy a rousing production of "Pirates of Penzance."

5. To visit the super port of Key West.

Leeward ★★★★

Registry	Bahamas
Officers	Norwegian
Crew	International
Complement	400
GRT	25,000
Length (ft.)	524
Beam (ft.)	82
Draft (ft.)	18
Passengers-Cabins Full	1409
Passengers-2/Cabin	974
Passenger Space Ratio	25.93
Stability Rating	Fair
Seatings	2
Cuisine	Themed
Dress Code	Traditional
Room Service	Yes
Tip	$9 PPPD, 15% automatically added to bar checks

Ship Amenities

Outdoor Pool	1
Indoor Pool	0
Jacuzzi	1
Fitness Center	Yes
Spa	Yes
Beauty Shop	Yes
Showroom	Yes
Bars/Lounges	5
Casino	Yes
Shops	1
Library	Yes
Child Program	Yes
Self Service Laundry	No
Elevators	4

Cabin Statistics

Suites	16
Outside Doubles	309
Inside Doubles	162
Wheelchair Cabins	6
Singles	0
Single Surcharge	150-200%
Verandas	10
110 Volt	Yes

Norway

Ship buffs and historians know the Norway was built in 1962 as the France, the last of the great French Line fleet that also included the Ile de France and the Normandie. While the last major makeover added two additional decks that thickened her sleek line, she's still one of the most beautiful vessels at sea. She makes us think of the 1954 film The French Line with Jane Russell and a lot of U.S. Olympic athletes working out down by the indoor pool area, which has been remodeled lots of times since then but still looks glamorous. While most people visualize Jane Russell leaning against a shock of hay eyeing a baby-faced Billy the Kid in "The Outlaw", our favorite shipboard film is "Gentlemen Prefer Blondes," filmed aboard the Ile de France in 1953 with her co-star Marilyn Monroe.

The sybaritic Roman Spa aboard the Norway.

On our most recent *Norway* visit the ship looked very clean and spiffy from a recent makeover—she could rival any Hollywood star in number of facelifts, and she's only 34. Over the years, new luxury cabins and penthouses have been added, each with big windows or private balconies overlooking the sea. But because of the ship's vintage, the original cabins come in all shapes and sizes rather than the neat, identical modules you find on new ships. It's worth spending some extra time studying the deck plan and cabin specifics to be sure you're getting the sort of cabin you want.

The heart of the ship is the International Deck with its enclosed promenade most of the way around on both sides, like fashionable boulevards lined with sidewalk cafes and elegant boutiques. Two separate dining rooms, remnants of the two-class ocean liner days, are divided by the galley in a you-can't-get-here-from-there arrangement, and cabins are dispersed throughout the 10 passenger decks in random configuration.

Even from a distance (she usually lies at anchor in her ports of call) you can recognize her twin stacks and dark blue hull.

The Brochure Says

"Ever since her launch as the *S.S. France*, she has been hailed for her plush splendor and architectural marvels. Now, after the finishing touches of a three-year, $60 million refurbishment...she has emerged with her classic features intact: the hand-laid tile mosaics, Art Deco murals, marble statuary, teak rails, two-story Broadway theater, and the magnificent Club Internationale ballroom."

Translation

The real joy of cruising on the *Norway* for a ship buff is to recreate some of the glory and nostalgia from an ocean liner, even a liner-come-lately like the *France*. In many of the cabins, touches remain from the original; some bathrooms still have the 1960s plumbing fixtures like old-fashioned bathtubs, heated towel racks and tile mosaics. And look for the five antique slot machines on exhibit in the new marble-floored casino, probably not from the original ship but antiques nevertheless.

INSIDER TIP

Enjoy the free ice cream from Sven's Ice Cream Parlor on the International Deck; passengers used to have to pay for it because, as one staffer said back then, "Otherwise it would be full all day with people eating ice cream." There was no crowd when we sampled some at 3 p.m. on a hot afternoon last spring—we were the only customers.

Cabins & Costs

Fantasy Suites: . . . . A

Average Price PPPD: $778 including airfare.

While we admire the original two-bedroom, two-bath grand suites on Viking Deck (Jerry Lewis always occupied one of them when he was the headline entertainer on a cruise), today's luxury-loving passengers would probably prefer one of the two new owner's suites forward on the top deck. Each has its own wrap-around terrace; a living room with leather sofa and chairs, desk, tape/CD deck, large TV, fully stocked bar, marble table, built-in cabinetry, and plenty of room for entertaining; a bedroom with queen-sized bed, big walk-in closet, marble bath with Roman tub, marble floor, separate stall shower and powder room; and concierge service.

Small Splurges: .... A

Average Price PPPD: $392 including airfare.

The junior suites on Pool Deck are marvelously light, bright rooms with three big picture windows, two lower, queen-sized or king-sized beds, sitting area with sofa and chair, dressing table with make-up lights and good mirror, mini-refrigerator, tub and shower, and concierge service.

This standard outside double cabin aboard the **Norway** *is actually a bit more spacious than some in that category.*

Suitable Standards: .... C-

Average Price PPPD: From $300 to $321, including airfare.

Cabins vary widely, with the four standard outsides and one superior inside categories more or less falling into the standard cabin range. Each has a bed arrangement that sleeps two people in some fashion in lower beds, a bath with tub or shower, a chair, dresser, TV set and table. If you don't mind an inside, O 88 has a lot of room, twin beds, two dressers, two chairs and table.

Bottom Bunks: .... F

Average Price PPPD: $228 in category N, $256 in category K, including airfare.

The category N inside doubles with upper and lower berths are the bottom-of-the-line on the *Norway*, and the one we looked at recently—V 248—we could not recommend, even to the most forgiving first-timer. A tiny space with a stool, TV set, single bed and overhead bunk, with fresh carpeting and upholstery but an original bathroom with shower only and the smell of bad drains. We'd suggest spending another $190 each for the week and take a category K inside like A 023 with a double bed and upper pulldown (making it workable even for roommates who want separate beds), chair, dresser, TV set and bath with shower only.

INSIDER TIP

Make sure your travel agent books a specific bed arrangement—twins, double, queen- or king-sized—because in many cabins on the Norway beds cannot be put together.

Where She Goes

The *Norway* follows the same seven-day itinerary year-round, sailing from Miami on Saturdays and anchoring off St. Maarten, St. John, St. Thomas and Great Stirrup Cay, the line's private island in the Bahamas, for a beach day.

The Bottom Line

It's important for a potential passenger, especially an ocean liner aficionado, to make a clear mental distinction between the *Norway*, a seven-day mass-market cruise ship featuring dinner menus with fixed themes that rotate every seven days, and the *France*, an ocean liner that offered superb first-class food and service that rivaled the three-star Michelin restaurants of France on crossings in the 1960s. While the *Norway* offers extremely good seven-day Caribbean cruises for vacationers, honeymooners and first-time cruisers, you must not expect to sail in the legendary style of the French Line.

Fielding's Five

Five Lovely Locales

1. The Club Internationale looks like the kind of nightclub Nick and Nora Charles would have frequented, except perhaps for the tuxedoed mannequin seated at the player piano and those gesso gods of the sea in the side niches. Elegant green and gold silk tapestry covers the banquettes and chairs, and original light fixtures from the 1960s still adorn the walls and ceilings.

2. The Champs Elysees on starboard side and Fifth Avenue on port side are almost as grand as the originals, enclosed promenades that let you saunter past shop windows glittering with jewelry, crystal, perfumes and sequinned gowns, even a fur shop, and a sidewalk cafe where you can sit down in white wrought iron chairs for a drink.

3. The sybaritic spa compound built around the ship's indoor pool, operated by Steiner of London, a 6000-square-foot Roman spa with hydrotherapy baths, steam rooms, saunas and aquacise pool with spa treatments sold individually or part of a package, plus a 4000-square-foot health and fitness center, basketball court and jogging track.

4. The charming children's playroom called Trolland on the Norway, still has its original fairytale wall mural from the *France*; three youth counselors are always aboard, but the number swells to seven during holiday sailings and summer.

5. The Saga Theatre is a proper theatre with its comfortable row seats and balcony, just the place to watch Will Rogers ropin' and chattin' in "The Will Rogers Follies," to catch the Gerry Mulligan Quartet during the jazz festival or the Shirelles singing "Dedicated to the One I Love" during a '50s and '60s theme cruise with great rock 'n roll era names.

Five Good Reasons to Book This Ship

1. To look for details from the original *S.S.France*. Where to start: The first-class dining room was the one now called the Windward, amidships on Atlantic Deck with its magnificent staircase for grand entrances; its original name was the Chambord Restaurant.

2. Because there's no extra charge for all that jazz—you can hear the world's greatest jazz musicians gathered together for concerts and impromptu jam sessions all over the ship at any hour of the day or night during the two-week annual autumn jazz festival.

3. To win a free T-shirt with seven vouchers proving you took part in seven Motion on the Ocean fitness and sports activities.

4. If you cruise before the fall of 1996, you can claim you've sailed on the world's biggest cruise ship; once the 100,000-ton *Carnival Destiny* arrives, *Norway's* record 76,049 gross registry tons falls into second place.

5. To enroll in a full spa program and get The Body Beautiful at the Roman Spa; each October there's a fitness and beauty cruise with top Olympic athletes and experts in fitness, health and beauty.

Five Things You Won't Find On Board

1. A gangway down to the dock in ports of call; passengers go ashore by tender, since the ship docks only in Miami.

2. A bad sport.

3. That nice couple you met on deck the other day; the ship is so big you'll want to get names and cabin numbers from anyone you'd like to see again.

4. A cabin designated single, although there are a lot of teeny-tiny ones that should be.

5. A self-service laundry (but can you imagine all the rich and famous who crossed the Atlantic on the *France* running down and washing their undies themselves?)

Norway ★ ★ ★ ★

Registry	**Bahamas**
Officers	**Norwegian**
Crew	**International**
Complement	**900**
GRT	**76,049**
Length (ft.)	**1035**
Beam (ft.)	**110**
Draft (ft.)	**35.5**
Passengers-Cabins Full	**2548**
Passengers-2/Cabin	**2122**
Passenger Space Ratio	**35.83**
Stability Rating	**Excellent**
Seatings	**2**
Cuisine	**Themed**
Dress Code	**Traditional**
Room Service	**Yes**
Tip	**$9 PPPD, 15% automatically added to bar checks**

Ship Amenities

Outdoor Pool	**2**
Indoor Pool	**1**
Jacuzzi	**3**
Fitness Center	**Yes**
Spa	**Yes**
Beauty Shop	**Yes**
Showroom	**Yes**
Bars/Lounges	**4**
Casino	**Yes**
Shops	**9**
Library	**Yes**
Child Program	**Yes**
Self Service Laundry	**No**
Elevators	**11**

Cabin Statistics

Suites	**165**
Outside Doubles	**473**
Inside Doubles	**423**
Wheelchair Cabins	**9**
Singles	**0**
Single Surcharge	**150-200%**
Verandas	**58**
110 Volt	**Yes**

Norwegian Crown

Notes from the inaugural sailing, 1988: The overwhelming first impression is a feeling of total luxury, a relaxed sense of being in the best of all possible worlds where only pleasant things can happen to you. It's a world of marble, polished granite, glove leather, meltingly soft suede, gleaming brass.

Christened in 1988 as the *Crown Odyssey*, the ship turned into the *Norwegian Crown* almost overnight in 1996.

The glittering lounges and intimate bars, comfortable cabins and attractive dining room create an upscale ambiance that should please most NCL passengers very well. Especially appealing is a state-of-the-art cinema on board.

The Brochure Says

"We suggest you book early. Because when a new ship like this comes around, word travels fast."

Translation
Not fast enough to save it in its previous incarnation, apparently.

Cabins & Costs

Fantasy Suites: . . . . A

Average Price PPPD: $571 with airfare in the Caribbean; $625 plus air in Europe.
The Owner's Suite apartments with private verandas are named for their decor; Sandringham and Balmoral, for instance, follow a Scottish theme with lace curtains, plaid carpeting and darkish upholstered furniture, while Portofino has a lot of white and Bel Air an art deco look with lots of black. Each is about 615 square feet with separate living room, bedroom and dressing room, two sofas and a dining table with four chairs, TV/VCR, whirlpool tubs in the bathroom, a queen-sized bed and plenty of storage.

The bay window suites on the **Norwegian Crown** *make a special small splurge.*

Small Splurges: .... A

Average Price PPPD: $378 w/air in the Caribbean; $542 plus air in Europe.

The S1 suites with bay windows let in a lot of light and give a bit of a view in three directions (and sometimes into the edge of the bay window cabin next door when the shades are open). Push buttons raise and lower the shades automatically from the bedside, and a pair of peach suede tub chairs flank a glass cocktail table in the bay, while a six-foot marble-topped desk/dresser provides four big storage drawers on each side. Twin or queen-sized beds, marble nightstands and mirror with lucite wall fixtures dominate the sleeping area. There are two closets, each with full-length and half-length hanging areas, built in drawers and shoe storage, a white tile bathroom with marble-faced tub/shower combination and marble sink counter.

Suitable Standards: .... B

Average Price PPPD: $314 w/air in the Caribbean; $292 plus air in Europe.

All the deluxe outside doubles (there are apparently no standard cabins on the ship; all are deluxe inside or outside doubles) are around 165 square feet with two lower beds, nightstand with drawers, desk/dresser with chair, a second chair and table, generous closets and bath with shower (some have bathtubs as well). Four are designated suitable for wheelchairs and have shower only.

Bottom Bunks: .... C+

Average Price PPPD: $267 w/air in the Caribbean; $233 plus air in Europe.

A K Category inside with two lower beds has a desk/dresser, two chairs and bathroom with shower plus generous closet space.

The *Norwegian Crown* sails to the Western Caribbean from Ft. Lauderdale in winter and makes 12-day cruises around Europe in summer.

The Bottom Line

It's interesting to observe this ship as odd man out in the NCL fleet.

The former *Crown Odyssey* was a custom-designed vessel built just for Royal Cruise Line loyals by the two people who knew them best, Richard Revnes and Pericles Panagopoulos. And it's still a dandy ship for older NCL passengers, who are health- and image-conscious but also want to have fun with a little dancing, sharing cocktail chatter and taking an occasional whirl in the casino.

Norwegian Crown ★★★★

Registry	**Bahamas**
Officers	**Norwegian**
Crew	**International**
Complement	**470**
GRT	**34,250**
Length (ft.)	**614**
Beam (ft.)	**92.5**
Draft (ft.)	**23**
Passengers-Cabins Full	**1240**
Passengers-2/Cabin	**1052**
Passenger Space Ratio	**32.55**
Stability Rating	**Excellent**
Seatings	**2**
Cuisine	**Themed**
Dress Code	**Traditional**
Room Service	**Yes**
Tip	**$9 PPPD, 15% automatically added to bar checks**

Ship Amenities

Outdoor Pool	**1**
Indoor Pool	**1**
Jacuzzi	**4**
Fitness Center	**Yes**
Spa	**Yes**
Beauty Shop	**Yes**
Showroom	**Yes**
Bars/Lounges	**6**
Casino	**Yes**
Shops	**3**
Library	**Yes**
Child Program	**No**
Self-Service Laundry	**No**
Elevators	**4**

Cabin Statistics

Suites	**90**
Outside Doubles	**322**
Inside Doubles	**114**
Wheelchair Cabins	**4**
Singles	**0**
Single Surcharge	**150-200%**
Verandas	**16**
110 Volt	**Yes**

NORWEGIAN CRUISE LINE

Seaward

★★★

Of all the ships in NCL's fleet, including the now-departed white ships, the Seaward has been the hardest for us to warm up to, perhaps because of its cool, almost darkish interiors and upper decks, acres of painted metal and indoor/outdoor carpeting instead of teak. But a recent drydocking that added more pastels, mirrors and art work lightens it up, at least on the inside. Now, if they could do something about that painted metal Promenade Deck surface...

This is a ship for the young and active, with a fitness center, golf driving range, a basketball court and a full, around-the-ship jogging track on promenade deck labeled with arrows so everyone runs or walks in the right direction (counter-clockwise). The Big Apple Cafe serves a lot of breakfasts and lunches for passengers too busy to go down to the dining room. Down on Atlantic Deck is a small children's playroom called Porthole. Traffic flow through the dining room areas moves smoothly along a port side walkway called Park Avenue that links the Four Seasons Dining Room with the Seven Seas Dining Room.

The Brochure Says

"She boasts a lounge featuring the Broadway hit musical 'Grease,' an extravagantly designed casino, and marvelous places to dance. As well as some of the finest four-star cuisine to be found anywhere..."

Translation

"Grease" was indeed playing on board during our most recent visit. The showroom is dark, cool and elegant, with generally good sightlines and row seats in back with pull-down drink tables fitted between the seats. The casino is also classy, but we're not sure what four-star cuisine is (the French food Bible Guide Michelin only goes up to three). However, there's a wide range of choices and what it lacks in subtlety it makes up for in copious portions.

INSIDER TIP

There's a tuxedo rental shop aboard if you've forgotten to bring one or don't own formal wear and want to dress up to match your wife's finery.

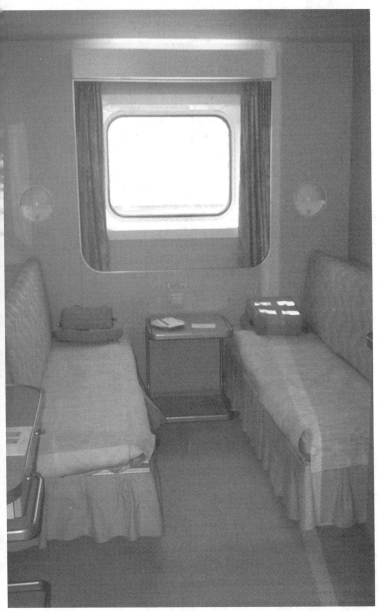

Cabin 4228 is a standard outside double with portholes on the Seaward; lifejackets are laid out on the beds on embarkation day, when the boat drill takes place.

NORWEGIAN CRUISE LINE

Cabins & Costs

Fantasy Suites: .... A

Average Price PPPD: $414 each for two occupants, including airfare.

Four newly added Owner's Suites sleep up to five passengers in 280 to 360 square feet, with sitting area with sofa double bed, dining area, separate bedroom, two TV sets, mini-refrigerator and bathroom with tub and shower.

Small Splurges: .... B

Average Price PPPD: $378 including airfare.

Three forward deluxe suites on Norway deck share a captain's eye view of the scenery ahead, along with a sleeping area with two lower beds, sitting area with a sofa that can convert to a bed for an additional occupant, a mini-refrigerator, lounge chair and bath with tub and shower.

Suitable Standards: C

Average Price PPPD: For category E outside doubles, $321 including airfare.

Twin sofa beds with a small table in between, a built-in cabinet tower with desk, four drawers, complimentary bottle of Evian, TV, ice bucket, slender full-length mirror and full hanging cabinet inside, as versatile a storage area as we've seen outside the Hold Everything catalogue. There are also two additional full-length hanging areas on the opposite wall, as well as a bathroom with tile floor, shower, and pastel bath fixtures. Cabin described is in category E.

Bottom Bunks: .... D

Average Price PPPD: $253 including airfare.

Six category N cabins with a fairly large lower bed and a pulldown berth that folds up during the day because otherwise there's not enough room to walk between the beds. These cabins might work for two very slender, very close friends. There's also a built-in desk/dresser, a chair, TV set, a small table and a lime green cabinet tower (see Suitable Standards, above). And all cabins are issued a bowl of fresh fruit and a bottle of mineral water.

Where She Goes

The *Seaward* offers alternating seven-day Barbados Series and Aruba Series sailings roundtrip from San Juan every Sunday. The Barbados Series calls at Barbados, Martinique, St. Maarten, Antigua, St. John and St. Thomas, while the Aruba Series calls at Aruba, Curaçao, Tortola/Virgin Gorda, St. John and St. Thomas.

The Bottom Line

While this ship was one of the last to come out of the respected Wartsila shipyard in Finland before its subsequent conversion to Kvaerner-Masa Yard, the construction is not nearly so sturdy. In areas of the deck, you may step on a patch of thin, buckled steel plating under the indoor/outdoor carpet. The ship went through a major refurbishing in May, 1995, to freshen carpeting and upholstery, as well as adding additional suites. (Lavish suites are big sellers on this line that caters to so many honeymooners.) After being

ntenced to the short-cruise market, which adds so much wear and tear to a ship, she
eeded a cosmetic make-over.

Fielding's Five

Five Dramatic Spaces

1. The Crystal Court two-deck entry lobby with a fountain dripping water down glass pipes, slick white marble squares, wide dark green curved leather benches, plants, a rock garden—a dark, cool contrast to the bright, hot tropics outside.

2. Gatsby's is billed as a wine bar/nightclub, but when we were aboard recently in Miami, it was the setting for a small private wedding and luncheon, and showed it could be turned into the most romantic little restaurant at sea. It's pretty dreamy with its tall ladderback black chairs and round tables, granite floors and white piano.

3. Oscar's Piano Bar, with its very comfortable barstools, could entice a passenger to linger awhile around the curved piano bar, perhaps even join in on a chorus or two.

4. Hallways and landings, an often-ignored part of a ship's decor, here are filled with art, including pretty original water colors, wall hangings and majestic marble and granite, endowing the space with richness.

5. The Pool Deck with its shaded outdoor dining areas lashed with panels of fabric on the sides and ceiling, wood-trimmed tables and woven plastic armchairs.

Five Good Reasons to Book This Ship

1. The Chocoholic Buffet, served once a cruise at midnight, the chocoholic's witching hour, with every fantasy dessert you ever dreamed of.

2. To learn snorkeling with the well-organized, comprehensive Dive-In program.

3. Lickety-Splits ice cream stand, with free cones or dishes of ice cream in four flavors, plus sherbet, frozen yogurt and any toppings you'd like to add; open all afternoon.

4. Le Bistro for alternative dining at no extra charge except a tip for the waiter; an advance reservation is required, however. It's the place to be alone together for a special occasion or a quiet evening, or to get together with new-found friends.

5. To check out the seagoing mall called Everything Under the Sun, with lots of shops and gold chains by the inch.

Seaward ★★★

Registry	**Bahamas**
Officers	**Norwegian**
Crew	**International**
Complement	**630**
GRT	**42,000**
Length (ft.)	**700**
Beam (ft.)	**96**
Draft (ft.)	**21**
Passengers-Cabins Full	**1796**
Passengers-2/Cabin	**1494**
Passenger Space Ratio	**28.11**
Stability Rating	**Fair**
Seatings	**2**
Cuisine	**Themed**
Dress Code	**Traditional**
Room Service	**Yes**
Tip	**$9 PPPD, 15% automatically added to bar checks**

Ship Amenities

Outdoor Pool	**2**
Indoor Pool	**0**
Jacuzzi	**2**
Fitness Center	**Yes**
Spa	**Yes**
Beauty Shop	**Yes**
Showroom	**Yes**
Bars/Lounges	**5**
Casino	**Yes**
Shops	**1**
Library	**Yes**
Child Program	**Yes**
Self Service Laundry	**No**
Elevators	**6**

Cabin Statistics

Suites	**7**
Outside Doubles	**494**
Inside Doubles	**246**
Wheelchair Cabins	**4**
Singles	**0**
Single Surcharge	**150-200%**
Verandas	**0**
110 Volt	**Yes**

OCEANIC CRUISES

5757 West Century Blvd., Suite 390, Los Angeles, CA 90045
☎ *(310) 215-0191, (800) 545-5778*

History . . . .

When the *Oceanic Grace* was introduced in 1989, it was the first time a year-round luxury vessel had been based in the Japanese Islands. Parent company Showa Line, Ltd., one of Japan's largest shipping companies, built the ship in the Tsu Yard of Nippon Kokan but had it designed in Holland with an eye toward attracting European and American passengers.

Concept . . . .

The company's early sales promotions were built around selling a western-type cruise product to the Japanese market and promising a Japanese cruise experience in the west, but that dual approach has been toned down in recent years, and the ship attempts to provide a comfortable and luxurious way to tour around Japan with high-quality western and eastern food and service.

Signatures . . . .

The profile head of a sea princess, long hair flowing and flower tucked behind her ear, is the line's distinctive logo.

Who's the Competition. . . . .

Nobody really, because the other Japanese ships sailing year-round in these waters are mass-market rather than upscale vessels.

Who's Aboard. . . . .

North Americans make up around 20 percent of the passengers on an average cruise; the rest are primarily upscale Japanese couples including honeymooners and young marrieds on anniversary sailings to renew vows. A high percentage of the passengers are repeaters.

Who Should Go. . . . .

Anyone who wants to travel in Japan in low-key but familiar surroundings but at the same time get a truer local experience than passengers on big western cruise ships.

Who Should Not Go . . . .

Children under 12 years old are not permitted on board.

The Lifestyle . . . .

During a seven-day sailing, there are usually two formal nights, two eve nings calling for informal garb and three casual nights. A trio plays fo dancing in the evenings, but, as on Sea Goddess, there are few planne activities.

Shore excursions and sightseeing jaunts are provided in ports of call.

Watersports are emphasized, particularly diving, since the *Oceani Grace* carries air-conditioned dive boats with 22 tanks aboard and ha professional divers on the staff. Windsurfing boards, catamarans canoes, Boston whalers, waterskis, fishing gear, wet suits and aqualung are all on board and use of them is free.

Wardrobe . . . .

The *Oceanic Grace* is a fairly dressy ship with men wearing dark suits o tuxedos for the two captain's dinners during each weeklong cruise Women usually wear formal kimonos, long gowns or dressy cocktai outfits. During the daytime, comfortable casual clothes like joggin suits and running shoes are the norm.

Bill of Fare . . . . .B+

The menu includes traditional Japanese dishes as well as continenta dishes prepared by chefs trained in Tokyo's top western-style restau rants, headed up by an executive chef from the Palace Hotel. Ar evening menu might feature medallions of beef, lobster newburg and grilled salmon on the western side, and crabmeat, shinjou soup, Mat susaka beef and fried lobster in green sauce on the eastern side. There is a single seating in unassigned seats, meaning you may sit where and with whom you please.

Showtime. C

A musical trio plays for dancing in the main lounge and there's also some other organized evening entertainment as well, sometimes folk-loric groups from shore, but no casino. Casino nights with make-believe money do take place on occasion.

Discounts . . . .

The line rarely offers discounts.

The Bottom Line

The company is doing well enough to stay in business year-round but not so well that it's ordering a second ship. It's very difficult to establish a solid cruise market in Japan because few people want to take a full week, let alone two weeks, off for vacation. Three- and four-day cruises are much more common here than seven.

Oceanic Grace ★★★★

The ship itself looks like a cross between Sea Goddess and Seabourn, with a yachtlike sleekness and a gleaming white finish. And the owners admit that the 116-passenger Sea Goddess ships were the image they had in mind when the project began, except that they wanted to have a bigger ship that would carry only 120 passengers. So they went for a gross registry tonnage of 5050 tons compared to Sea Goddess's 4260 and Seabourn's 10,000. (Seabourn carries 212 passengers.)

Cabins are spacious and modular, all almost precisely the same size, and are laid out forward and amidships on four decks, with public areas aft on the same four decks. Above is a Sun Deck with jogging track. A very well-equipped watersports platform lets passengers try windsurfing, sailing, diving, snorkeling, fishing and waterskiing, with all equipment provided free of charge.

The Brochure Says

"The *Oceanic Grace* opens new worlds. You can embark on a voyage of discovery along Japan's western coastline (Sea of Japan), the Inland Sea, or along Japan's subtropical Pacific coastline. You can explore castles, shrines, samurai mansions, cathedrals, temples, fish markets, tropical gardens, and white sand beaches at your own pace."

Translation

You'll see a lot more of the real Japan than any other way of traveling can show you.

Cabins & Costs

Fantasy Suites: . . . . NA

All cabins aboard are suites but they are all virtually identical, so there is nothing that fits this category.

Small Splurges: .... *A*

While all the cabins are the same general size and rated at the same value in the brochures, eight of them, the cabins on Deck 6 numbered 601-608, have private balconies, worth making a play for.

Suitable Standards: .... *A*

Average Price PPPD: $500 including tips and plus airfare; price varies widely dependin
on season, destinations and length of cruise.
On this all-suites ship, the 60 cabins measure 185 square feet each and contain
choice of twin or queen-sized beds, loveseat, chair and table, built-in desk/dresse
with wide counter and TV set with VCR, generous use of mirrors and wood panel
ing, fairly good closet space, a mini-bar, mini-refrigerator, vanity, terrycloth robes
toiletries and safe. The marble-trimmed bathroom has a Japanese-style tub, shor
and deep; if you're tall, you'll sit with your knees tucked under your chin.

Bottom Bunks: .... *NA*

See Suitable Standards, above.

The *Oceanic Grace* cruises around the islands of Japan's Inland Sea with occasiona
forays into whale watching in the semi-tropical Ogasawara Islands. Many special theme
sailings are built around Japanese holidays.

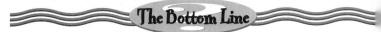

Although the per diems are fairly steep, anyone who wants to tour Japan might find
the ship's prices reasonable compared with the same quality beds and restaurants ashore
each paid for individually instead of in an inclusive price. Tips are included but bar and
wine are extras—and fairly pricey extras.

The *Oceanic Grace* is a good choice for someone who wants a Japanese experience in
western surroundings with a chance to meet and exchange views with upscale Japanese
couples.

Five Special Spots

1. The main lounge with its reflective ceiling, lively musicians and dancing couples is a
   festive after-dinner spot.

2. The pretty deck is equally appealing night and day with its small freshwater pool and
   Lido Bar.

3. The sizable gym, with a trainer, sauna, beauty salon, Jacuzzi and jogging course,
   will help keep you in shape.

4. The watersports marina has a wide variety of gear from Boston whalers for fishing
   and waterskiing to Zodiacs for snorkeling and scuba.

5. The Main Bar is another sleek public area off the Main Lounge with ultrasuede-cov-
   ered swivel bar stools and cozy banquettes and chairs for a more private conversation.

Five Good Reasons to Book This Ship

The opportunity to travel to smaller towns and villages in Japan that overland tours never include.

A chance to have an easy introduction to Japanese life-styles, food and culture with an omnipresent western safety net in case you want a break from it.

To have an entire dinner of top-quality sashimi and sushi without having to pick up the bill at the end.

To cruise around Japan hitting the major local festivals at exactly the right time.

To enjoy still another Sea Goddess-like experience.

Five Things You Won't Find On Board

A casino.

An inside cabin.

A single cabin.

A children's program; children under 12 are not permitted aboard.

As many Japanese-style mattresses and pillows as when the line debuted.

Oceanic Grace ★★★★

Registry	Japa…
Officers	Japanes…
Crew	Japanes…
Complement	7…
GRT	5,05…
Length (ft.)	33…
Beam (ft.)	5…
Draft (ft.)	1…
Passengers-Cabins Full	12…
Passengers-2/Cabin	12…
Passenger Space Ratio	42.0…
Stability Rating	Goo…
Seatings	
Cuisine	Japanese and Continenta…
Dress Code	Traditiona…
Room Service	Ye…
Tip	Included in far…

Ship Amenities

Outdoor Pool	…
Indoor Pool	…
Jacuzzi	…
Fitness Center	Ye…
Spa	N…
Beauty Shop	Ye…
Showroom	N…
Bars/Lounges	3
Casino	N…
Shops	…
Library	Ye…
Child Program	N…
Self-Service Laundry	N…
Elevators	…

Cabin Statistics

Suites	60
Outside Doubles	0
Inside Doubles	0
Wheelchair Cabins	1
Singles	0
Single Surcharge	150%
Verandas	8
110 Volt	Yes

OCEANIC CRUISES

OdessAmerica.

Cruise Line of the Czars

170 Old Country Road, Suite 608, Mineola, NY 11501
☎ *(516) 747-8880, (800) 221-3254*

History . . . .

OdessAmerica is North American sales agent for Galapagos Cruise Line and its *Ambasador I*, as well as the *Terra Australis*, an expedition vessel in Patagonia. The company is also a North American representative for CTC, which operates several vessels from the Black Sea Shipping Company of Odessa.

Ambasador I   ★★, ⚓⚓⚓⚓

She's been around in expedition cruises for a long time, and used to sail for Salen Lindblad when it was in business. We used to see her in Piraeus and Dubrovnik and always wondered about the single "s" in her name. We still do.

Built in the former Yugoslavia in 1958, the *Ambasador* has had a long career as an expedition ship. Now registered in Ecuador in order to cruise the Galapagos Islands—only Ecuadorean-flag ships have been permitted to cruise there for the past few years—the ship carries only 86, the maximum permitted because of environmental impact in the islands, instead of the 160 she was built to carry. Spruced up again with some fresh fabrics and new soft furnishings and looking fairly chipper—anyhow, more luxurious than most of the Galapagos vessels—the *Ambasador* affords a comfortable way to go see the Sally Lightfoots and giant tortoises. The ship anchors on most stops and you go ashore by 20-passenger *pangas* (Boston whalers). Dress aboard is casual, but you need cotton shorts and pants, T-shirts, a sweater or windbreaker, walking shoes or sneakers, a swimsuit and a wide-brimmed sun hat, preferably with a string to tie it down.

 The Brochure Says

"With *MV Ambasador I*, an extraordinarily well-equipped, environmentally friendly ship, you can experience all of this without endangering any life forms that make the Galapagos Islands one of the most extraordinary natural environments in the world."

Translation

It's a guilt-free way of enjoying the wilderness without discomfort.

Cabins & Costs

Fantasy Suites: .... NA
N/A

Small Splurges: .... NA
N/A

Suitable Standards: C
Average Price PPPD: $337 plus airfare.
A deluxe twin-bed cabin on Floreana Deck has floral bedspreads, reading lamps over the bed, a private bath with shower only, a telephone, radio and dresser.

Bottom Bunks: .... D
Average Price PPPD: $182 plus airfare.
Some of the inside double cabins are quite small but have private facilities with a shower, upper and lower berths and small dresser.

Where She Goes

The *Ambasador I* cruises in the Galapagos Islands year-round.

The Bottom Line

The cabins are small, the lifestyle casual and the amenities simple, but the reward here is exploring the unique islands of the Galapagos with excellent guides who take you out in groups of 20 or fewer. Be prepared for the heat with cool clothing and sunscreen; the ship provides bottled water to carry ashore with you.

Fielding's Five

Five Special Spots

1. The Grand Salon is a large bar and lounge with swivel tub chairs and chrome tables where the social life and the lectures are slated because there's nowhere else to go but the deck and the dining room.

2. The swimming pool on Sun Deck is a popular favorite in the sizzling equatorial climate of the Galapagos. After an arduous overland trek to the tortoises, a dip in the pool is irresistible.

3. The Lido Bar, equally popular for the same reasons and the ice-cold beer or soda that's waiting after a hot morning of learning the love life of the lava lizard.

4. There is a small library with materials about the islands, bird guides and such, plus a boutique selling souvenirs and sun screen.

5. The restaurant serves all passengers in a single seating, and the cuisine is continental with some Ecuadorean specialties such as the fresh local shrimp and the wonderful potato cakes called llapingachos covered with cheese and peanut sauce.

Llapingachos
6 servings

2 pounds potatoes, peeled, boiled and mashed

2 TB butter

1 large onion, finely chopped

1 1/2 cups grated mild cheese, such as Monterey Jack

Oil for frying

Peanut sauce

Lettuce, tomato and avocado slices (optional)

Melt the butter in a small pan and gently sauté the onion until very soft but not browned. Mix with the mashed potatoes and shape into 12 balls. Poke a hole into each and stuff it with some of the cheese, then pat the potato mixture into a round cake about an inch thick. Chill 15 or 20 minutes or until firm. Then sauté in a little hot oil until browned on both sides. Serve with a garnish of lettuce, tomato and avocado, if desired, and top with peanut sauce for a first course.

Peanut Sauce

2 TB peanut or olive oil

1 onion, finely chopped

1 tomato, seeded and finely chopped

1 clove garlic, minced

2 TB crunchy peanut butter

Salt and pepper to taste

Heat the oil and saute the onion, tomato and garlic until tender. Stir in the peanut butter, season to taste and cook until thin enough to pour, adding water if necessary.

Five Good Reasons to Book This Ship

1. To watch the courting displays of the majestic frigate birds.

2. To see the mating dance of the blue-footed booby.

3. To learn the soap opera ups and downs of the love life of a lava lizard.

4. To wonder how even another marine inguana could love that face.

5. To watch Sally Lightfoot strip (see crabs shed their carapaces).

Five Things You Won't Find On Board

1. A gym or fitness center.

2. Room service.

3. Children under 7 years old.

4. A cabin designated wheelchair-accessible; this ship and the cruise are not suitable for the mobility-impaired because of the amount of tendering that has to be done.

5. An elevator.

Ambassador I   ★★, ⚓⚓⚓

Registry	Ecuador
Officers	Ecuadorean
Crew	Ecuadorean
Complement	68
GRT	2,573
Length (ft.)	296
Beam (ft.)	43
Draft (ft.)	14.7
Passengers-Cabins Full	160
Passengers-2/Cabin	86
Passenger Space Ratio	29.91
Stability Rating	Fair
Seatings	1
Cuisine	Continental/Ecudorean
Dress Code	Casual
Room Service	No
Tip	$10 PPPD

Ship Amenities

Outdoor Pool	1
Indoor Pool	0
Jacuzzi	0
Fitness Center	Yes
Spa	No
Beauty Shop	Yes
Showroom	Yes
Bars/Lounges	2
Casino	No
Shops	1
Library	Yes
Child Program	No
Self-Service Laundry	No
Elevators	0

Cabin Statistics

Suites	4
Outside Doubles	40
Inside Doubles	13
Wheelchair Cabins	0
Singles	10
Single Surcharge	120%
Verandas	0
110 Volt	No

ODESSA AMERICA CRUISE
COMPANY (ODESSAMERICA)

ORIENT LINES ℠

1510 S.E. 17th Street, Fort Lauderdale, FL 33316
☎ (305) 527-6660, (800) 333-7300

The dining room aboard **Marco Polo** *serves the kind of sustenance a weary explorer needs after a day of discoveries.*

History . . . .

British entrepreneur Gerry Herrod has been in the travel and cruise business since he founded Travellers International in the 1970s, which grew to be the largest European tour operator for Americans. He is also former chairman of now-defunct Ocean Cruise Lines and Pearl Cruises; the latter pioneered year-round cruises in the Far East and was among the first ships to visit China. His newest company, Orient Lines, was founded in 1992 and introduced its 800-passenger *Marco Polo* in December 1993.

Herrod is very much a hands-on CEO. During the inaugural of the *Marco Polo*, he was fussing over his ship like a mother hen, prowling the vessel, talking to passengers, fine-tuning details such as lighting and sound levels.

ORIENT LINES

Concept . . . .

Herrod calls his product "destinational cruising," and says it is designe
for "inquisitive people who want to see something more than Freepo
and Nassau but don't necessarily want to go catching butterflies,
which we interpret to mean a destination-oriented program of so
adventures. His passengers, he says, like to dress up, eat good food an
dance in the evenings after dinner, even when they're in a remote c
exotic corner of the world, which he feels differentiates Orient Lin
from some of the more solemn expeditioners. Still, there is a reading li
of 77 recommended books about the line's destinations published i
the back of the 1995-96 brochure.

Signatures . . . .

The distinctive logo of a stylized wave and a globe symbolizes "th
world of Marco Polo."

To bring on board local folkloric performers in as many ports of call a
possible.

Gimmicks . . . .

Bright red parkas they get to keep are issued to every passenger on th
Antarctic cruises. "We need to be able to see them against all that sno
and ice," one executive admitted.

Who's the Competition . . . .

Interestingly, the main competition for Orient Lines would have bee
Pearl Cruises, had that company remained in business, but these days i
would probably be Radisson Seven Seas' *Hanseatic* and Hapag-Lloyd'
Bremen, both upscale expedition ships with destination-oriented pas
sengers; the *Caledonian Star*, particularly popular in the United King
dom for its exotic itineraries; the destination-driven Renaissance ships
and the mid-sized, globe-trotting pair of veteran Princess ships, th
Pacific Princess and *Island Princess*, with their Pacific and Asia itinerar
ies.

Who's Aboard . . . .

The *Marco Polo* on its longer, more exotic itineraries attracts mostl
well-heeled North Americans and British 55 and up (when we wer
aboard in South Africa, they looked more like 65 and up). They're a
mix of people who've taken land tours along with some cruise veterans
About 80–85 percent are North Americans, most of the rest British o
Australian. The Australians, interestingly enough, flock to the seven-da
New Zealand cruises because many of them have never been to New
Zealand. In the Antarctic, the ship draws younger-than-average passen
gers because prices are lower than on the small expedition ships.

Who Should Go . . . .

More younger couples, even honeymooners, will enjoy the affordabl
new seven-day, island-intensive Mediterranean sailings.

ORIENT LINES

Who Should Not Go . . . .

Although you'll find a few children sailing with their grandparents during the summer and Christmas holidays, it's not really a ship for families with kids.

The Lifestyle . . . .

"The destinations influence the life on board," says Deborah Natansohn, senior vice president, sales and marketing, "with a guest lecture program and local entertainment in each port. In the menus, we try to use local specialties and serve regional wines when we're in South Africa, Australia and New Zealand, as we will this summer in the Mediterranean."

We found the onboard pattern follows a traditional cruise style, with formal nights, lectures and activities, and an intensive shore excursions program that even includes some overnight overland journeys. Orient Lines places an emphasis on shoreside excursions and looks for specialty tours not always offered by other cruise lines.

Wardrobe. . . . .

Orient Lines says to pack as for any resort destination, suggesting lightweight, easy-to-care-for daytime casual sportswear and good walking shoes for shore visits. Formal attire requests a tuxedo, dinner jacket or dark suit and tie for men, a "party dress or gown of fashionable length" for women. On informal evenings, men are expected to wear a jacket and women a cocktail dress or pantsuit. Casual nights call for dressy sportswear or khakis. Raffles, the alternative restaurant, does not require jackets. Dress is a little more casual on the Antarctic sailings.

Bill of Fare. . . . . A

The food is excellent aboard the *Marco Polo*, just the type of sustenance a weary explorer needs after a day of discovering South Africa or New Zealand. When we were aboard, one dinner started with a salad of lamb medallions on lettuce with vinaigrette and red peppers, followed by a delectable white truffle risotto with sweetbreads and shrimp. The main course was grilled red snapper with puréed white beans and grilled baby zucchini, and dessert featured an old-fashioned apple and raisin pie with vanilla bean sauce and vanilla ice cream.

Executive chef Terence Greenhouse prepares California and continental cuisine, and there is an alternative restaurant called Raffles, open several nights a week, that serves specialty menus based on the region of the world the ship is cruising in. This summer in the Greek Islands, for instance, Raffles menus will feature Italian, Spanish and Mediterranean seafood specialties. Passengers make reservations the same day of the dinners and are requested to leave a gratuity for the servers, although there is no surcharge for the meal. The same cafe also offers self-service breakfast and lunch dishes. Breakfast may offer scrambled eggs, bacon, sausages, fried potatoes, yogurt, juices, cereals, fruits and pastries. Meals in the dining room are served at assigned tables in two seatings.

Showtime. . . . . .B

The dominant entertainment is local and regional troupes brought on board in the various ports—a Zulu dance troupe, Maoris in New Zealand, Australian aborigines, Balinese legong dancers, a Kenyan dance company, and wonderful performers in Cape Town reminiscent of New Orleans parade bands.

To supplement the local talent is a complement of singers and dancers who double as cruise staff and perform musical revues and variety shows. A singer/pianist alternates with a Romanian string trio in the Cafe Concerto.

Discounts . . . .

Early booking discounts take from 5 to 20 percent off the fare for passengers making reservations and a deposit 120 days or more ahead of sailing date. The precise amount depends on the cruise.

The Bottom Line

Herrod is going back to his own travel roots as a land tour operator, building a variety of broader land/sea packages for Orient Line passengers—adding on African safaris, Taj Mahal visits, excursions to Kathmandu or Australia's Ayers Rock and Alice Springs. In the summer of 1996, the vessel made its first Mediterranean sailings, offering seven-day port-intensive cruises in the Greek Islands. Because the company uses many of the key employees from Pearl Cruises, veterans of that line will be welcomed on board by familiar faces.

Marco Polo

It was hard to tell who was enjoying the evening more, the Marco Polo's passengers or the exuberant Zulu dance troupe from the Valley of the Thousand Hills in KwaZulu, which had been brought aboard to entertain us in Dur-

ORIENT LINES

ban. *Because we had earlier toured Johannesburg on a land excursion with a Zulu guide from the Soweto township named Nicholas, we had more than a passing interest in the traditional dances.*

This 800-passenger, mid-sized ship started life as the *Alexandr Pushkin*, one of five vessels of the same class—the others being the *Ivan Franko, Taras Shevchenko, Shota Rustaveli* and *Mikhail Lermantov*—built in Wismar, East Germany, between 1963 and 1972. An extensive renovation in 1993 turned the 1965 motorship into the glamorous, art deco-accented *Marco Polo*.

Cabins are dispersed among seven of the eight passenger decks, most of which also have public areas on them. The Belvedere Deck is where the main public rooms are located, and it's an easy stroll from the forward show and lecture lounge through the convivial Polo Lounge, past the purser and excursion offices and shops, through the casino, past the library and card room into the self-service restaurant called Raffles and then on to the pool deck aft. The restaurant is located on a lower deck amidships, a health and beauty center on Upper Deck, outdoor Jacuzzis on Sky Deck and the Charleston Club and an aft sun lounging area on Promenade Deck. A small casino provides roulette, blackjack and slot machines for passengers, most of whom take less interest in gambling than going to enrichment lectures and port talks. A splendid collection of Oriental art and antiques decorates the public areas. Outstanding is a stone Buddha on a glass-and-marble base at the entrance of the dining room, and pair of gold Buddhas above the cruise staff desk.

The *Marco Polo* has an ice-hardened hull, a helipad on the uppermost deck for helicopter take-offs and landings and high-speed launches as passenger tenders; it carries 10 inflatable Zodiac landing craft.

The Brochure Says

"Like the great explorer for which it is named, the cruise ship *Marco Polo* journeys to the most exotic corners of the earth in a spirit of friendship and discovery. Never before have inquisitive travelers had the opportunity to visit so many wondrous lands in such style."

Translation

This boat's for you if you love to visit offbeat destinations and go exploring all day long but want to get out of those sweat-wet clothes and into a dry martini at the end of the day.

Cabins & Costs

Fantasy Suites: . . . . B+

Average Price PPPD: $600 in South Africa including airfare.

Two deluxe suites, the Mandarin and the Dynasty, are the top digs aboard; both face forward with a captain's eye view of the world. You get a separate living room and bedroom, with a sofa, loveseat, two chairs, two chests, marble counters, a stocked bar that is replenished regularly, a queen-sized bed in the bedroom, generous storage space, robes, a safe and a marble bathroom with tub and shower.

Small Splurges: ....B

Average Price PPPD: $409 in South Africa including airfare.

Category A cabins have queen-sized beds, and large seating areas with sofa, chair, stool, coffee table, mini-bar and double dresser. Cabins in category C and above get robes and safes; suites and A cabins have queen-sized beds and marble bathrooms with tubs as well as showers. We'd suggest going for one of the two Category A cabins amidships on Main Deck; the ones on Sky Deck have partially obstructed views due to hanging lifeboats.

Suitable Standards: .... B+

Average Price PPPD: $352 in South Africa including airfare.

Category C cabins on main deck are fairly spacious, with a large window, twin beds, a wood-toned double dresser with eight drawers and a second smaller dresser with four and a pull-out desk top, handsome furnishings, wall-mounted TV set with remote control, three closets and a bathroom with shower only. All cabins have international direct-dial telephones. Some cabins can accommodate third and fourth passengers in pulldown berths.

Bottom Bunks: .... B+

Average Price PPPD: $234 in South Africa including airfare.

The category I inside we saw is large with twin beds, double dresser and chair, while the category H was narrower, also with twin beds and dresser plus a pulldown third berth. Deadlights may be closed in rough seas on the lowest passenger deck.

INSIDER TIP

The fares given above are for the southern Africa itineraries and reflect the average exotic sailing; fares will be lower for the summer Mediterranean cruises and higher for the winter Antarctic sailings.

Where She Goes

The *Marco Polo* spends alternate winters in the Antarctic and Southeast Asia, shoulder seasons in the Indian Ocean and summers in the Mediterranean and Greek Islands. A new Aegean Odyssey for 1997 features a 12-day land and sea package from $1445 to $3850 plus low air add-ons.

The Bottom Line

Pearl Cruises lives—and with a more luxurious ship! But the *Marco Polo* is not a copy of the *Pearl;* it is a subtler and more upscale rendering of a highly successful, destination-oriented cruise line that specializes not only in cruises in the Far East but all over the globe, including Antarctica. Could all we port-and-country collectors ask for anything more?

Fielding's Five

Five Spots to Explore

1. The Charleston Club, a charming spot in the evenings for cocktails and dancing, its tub chairs covered in a confetti-pattern fabric and glass cocktail tables, a curved bar with granite top, swag draperies and pleated paper shades.

2. Raffles, the self-service cafe and evening specialty restaurant with a wood-toned tile floor, glossy blue walls and ceiling, wood chairs with blue/green upholstery, and two buffet feedlines.

3. The Palm Court, with lots of potted palms, wicker and rattan with floral fabrics and marble-topped tables, is where you read or write postcards in the morning and take afternoon tea.

4. The chic black-and-white Casino Bar is faintly art deco with its black-and-white photographs of Fred Astaire and Ingrid Bergman and its intimate atmosphere.

5. The Polo Lounge is the central meeting place with leaf-patterned upholstery and carpet, glass cocktail tables, granite bar with green leather barstools and green swag curtains.

Five Good Reasons to Book This Ship

1. To sail into Cape Town, one of the world's most beautiful harbors, sitting on deck in a traditional Queen Mary-style wooden deck chair.

2. To hit all the highlights of the Greek Islands in one seven-day cruise at a price as low as $1395 per person, double occupancy, cruise-only.

3. To get a free red polar parka you can keep as a perk for booking the lowest-priced Antarctic cruise on the market.

4. To dine on a special menu once each cruise created by London's famous Cafe Royal.

5. To participate in intensive Workshops at Sea on longer sailings, classes that teach you how to photograph icebergs and penguins in the Antarctic or how to capture Mount Kilamanjaro in watercolors while you're cruising off the coast of Kenya.

Five Things You Won't Find On Board

1. Great sightlines in the Ambassador Lounge, because the performance area is almost the same level as the audience and there are lots of posts in between.

2. A hot breakfast from room service; they serve only continental breakfasts in the cabins.

3. Specially designated cabins and some areas of the ship that are accessible for wheelchairs, although there are elevators on board.

4. Anyone who can identify the subject of that statue resembling the late Rudolph Nureyev in an exaggerated balletic pose that stands between the ship's twin exercise rooms in the Health and Beauty Center.

5. A self-service laundry.

Marco Polo ★★★★

Registry	**Bahamas**
Officers	**Scandinavian**
Crew	**Filipino**
Complement	**350**
GRT	**20,502**
Length (ft.)	**578**
Beam (ft.)	**77**
Draft (ft.)	**27**
Passengers-Cabins Full	**922**
Passengers-2/Cabin	**848**
Passenger Space Ratio	**24.17**
Stability Rating	**Good**
Seatings	**2**
Cuisine	**Contemporary**
Dress Code	**Traditional**
Room Service	**Yes**
Tip	**$8 PPPD**

Ship Amenities

Outdoor Pool	**1**
Indoor Pool	**0**
Jacuzzi	**3**
Fitness Center	**Yes**
Spa	**Yes**
Beauty Shop	**Yes**
Showroom	**Yes**
Bars/Lounges	**5**
Casino	**Yes**
Shops	**1**
Library	**Yes**
Child Program	**No**
Self-Service Laundry	**No**
Elevators	**4**

Cabin Statistics

Suites	**6**
Outside Doubles	**286**
Inside Doubles	**131**
Wheelchair Cabins	**2**
Singles	**2**
Single Surcharge	**125%**
Verandas	**0**
110 Volt	**Yes**

ORIENT LINES

P & O CRUISES

c/o Princess Cruises; 10100 Santa Monica Boulevard, Los Angeles, CA 90067-4189
☎ *(310) 553-1770, (800) LOVE-BOAT*

Princess Cruises is a North American agent for P & O Cruises' new *Oriana*, the *Canberra* and the *Victoria* (the former *Sea Princess*).

History . . . .

Peninsular and Oriental Navigation Company is the oldest and largest of the British shipping companies, founded in 1837, shortly before Samuel Cunard founded his company. Cunard looked west to America, P&O looked east, first to Spain and Portugal, later to India. The founders of P & O, Arthur Anderson, a one-time Shetland Islands "beach boy" (itinerant worker) and Brodie McGhie Willcox, were serious young men only a few years away from poverty when they invested in their first ship, a small American schooner run aground near Dover which they salvaged. Soon they acquired additional vessels, including the steamer *William Fawcett*, usually credited as being their first passenger ship.

P & O's India-bound passengers in the 1840s had the option of traveling across the Suez overland three decades before the famous canal was built. First-class on P&O was the only socially acceptable way to travel to the raj.

In the 1880s, the *British Medical Journal* recommended sea voyages for health, and by 1898, a P & O poster was advertising a 60-day pleasure cruise to the West Indies.

Not only were generous quantities of food always included on the P & O sailings, but until 1874, unlimited quantities of wine, beer, spirits and mineral water were also included. On Sundays, sailing days and holidays, champagne was also thrown in. In the days before refrigeration, whole barnyards of live animals were taken along to be slaughtered and cooked as needed.

In 1914, P & O merged with British India Company. In 1932, the company had 41 cargo and passenger ships, only three pre-World War I, but in 1939 its ships, including 21 passenger vessels, were requisitioned by the government to serve as armed merchant cruisers and transports. In 1946, there were 13 left; eight had been sunk. Between

511

1946 and 1950, the government returned the requisitioned hardware to P & O, and in 1960, the first of two new ships debuted, the *Oriana* followed a year later by the *Canberra*.

—The word "posh," according to popular lore, is said to have originated from the cabin reservation stamped P.O., S.H. for "Port Out Starboard Home" for passengers traveling between England and India who demanded the coolest staterooms in each direction. Some authorities say that claim is without foundation; others say the word actually came into slang usage from the snobbishness of P&O passengers themselves.

—P & O claims it invented leisure cruising in 1844 when British author William Makepeace Thackery sailed around the Mediterranean on a free ticket to publicize the service and wrote a travel book about his cruise— *From Cornhill to Grand Cairo*—under the pseudonym Michael Angelo Titmarsh. He was not a happy camper—he hated Athens and was often seasick—and because his trip was during the religious holidays of Ramadan, he complained bitterly about missing all the grandly advertised wonders of the East, from the whirling dervishes to the harem at the seraglio in Istanbul.

—One of the three largest cruise lines in the world.

Concept . . . .

To take English-speaking passengers all over the English-speaking world and beyond, on world cruises, warm-weather getaway cruises and seasonal travels between a home on one continent and one on another

Signatures . . . .

Cruising "British style," which appeals to many Anglophiles in North America in addition to the large number of travelers from the United Kingdom.

Gimmicks . . . .

The children's tea, an early supper served just to kids at 5:30, before the early seating dinner begins.

Who's the Competition . . . .

Naturally the Cunard ships compete head-on with the P & O ships, the difference being that P & O does not participate in active U.S. marketing except through companies like Princess Tours, while Cunard maintains very active U.S.-based offices.

Who's Aboard . . . .

Primarily British passengers, but some Americans, Australians, New Zealanders and others; families with children on holiday cruises; singles of all ages.

Who Should Go . . . .

The people that do, plus American and Canadian Anglophiles.

Who Should Not Go . . . .

Anyone who can't mix and mingle with people from another country; any passionately chauvinistic American who thinks everyone else is disadvantaged (much as the British used to feel about the rest of the world).

The Lifestyle . . . .

Since P & O virtually invented the pleasure cruise, many of the familiar traditions of the genre are practiced aboard these ships, from dress codes to shipboard games.

Wardrobe. . . . .

We remember being aboard the *Victoria* when it was the *Sea Princess*, and a wealthy Texan showed up on a formal night in a resplendent custom-made outfit, a cowboy tuxedo in white with red patent leather lapels and matching red and white cowboy boots. The irate British at the next table summoned the maitre d'hotel and demanded that the Texan be sent back to his cabin "to change into proper attire." They may run around in frocks and undersized bathing suits and even terry-cloth bathrobes all day long, but when black tie is required in the evening, they're sticklers for correctness.

Bill of Fare. . . . . B

The meal pattern is British rather than American, with kippers, kidneys and finnan haddie on breakfast menus, kedgeree and curries and such for lunch, along with a roast, called a joint. Afternoon tea is much more important than midnight buffet, and high tea (correctly used, the term means a light early supper rather than fancy little sandwiches and scones with cream and jam) a tradition for the children on board. The British like to see the entire array of silverware to be used for the meal arranged in front of them at the beginning, perhaps to scrutinize the setting to anticipate marrow on toast as a savory or the ever-so-fussy little mother-of-pearl server for caviar. And of course the sweet (dessert) comes before the savory (cheese, marrow or smoked oysters on toast or chicken livers grilled with bacon) that finishes the meal.

Showtime . . . . B+

Since P & O also invented the amusements that go with cruises—a letter written from before the turn of the century lists "quoits, bull, potato race, egg-and-spoon race, tugs-of-war, skipping contests, thread-needle races"—you can expect a daily quiz, team trivia games, a ship's mileage pool, duplicate bridge, even cricket games. Evenings offer music for dancing, some fairly routine production shows (except on the new *Oriana* with its professional theatrical stage) and the usual variety artists from Butlin's.

Discounts. . . . .

On some cruises early booking discounts on the *Oriana*, *Canberra* and *Victoria* should be available.

The Bottom Line

"Cruising British style" means less glitz and glamour in the decor but a more traditional shipboard experience. If you wonder what that's about, pick up almost any book by W. Somerset Maugham, (he's still famous, and quite obviously was a writer!) who traveled extensively by ship.

Canberra

This classic ocean liner harkens back to the days when people on a ship were going somewhere—maybe for the season, maybe for the rest of their lives— not just cruising lazily from port to port comparing shopping bargains. When she was new in the 1960s, she used to sail into San Francisco from Australia and dominated the docks with her gleaming white superstructure and prim little twin funnels aft. Last time we saw her, she was tied up at a remote pier waiting for parts and mechanics to be flown in, stranded for more than a week during her world cruise, and desperately helicoptering passengers all over the place to keep them amused. We all get old, but it's sad to see it happen to ocean liners.

The more technically advanced *Canberra* was built one year after the former *Oriana*, and made her maiden voyage in 1962 from Southampton to Sydney and Auckland. In the Falklands War, she was called the "Great White Whale" when she served as a main troop ship. The *Canberra* is one of the few cruise ships still sailing today that does not offer private, en suite bathroom facilities with every cabin. There are three swimming pools, a children's pool, gym, cinema, theater, nightclub, disco, casino and nine bars, plus a children's night nursery, teen club, library, hair salon, shops and a launderette on every deck to take care of that washing that piles up. The ship has a cruising speed of 26 knots.

The Brochure Says

"The *Canberra* is a one-class ship and therefore all public rooms and facilities are there for all passengers to enjoy."

Translation
A delicate little reminder that some things have changed since the days of the raj.

antasy Suites: .... B+

Average Price PPPD: $621
There are four AA suites amidships on C deck, each of which in size seem equivalent
to four cabins nearby. These have a large sitting room, bedroom and full bath.

Small Splurges: C

Average Price PPPD: $347
An H category twin-bed cabin with bathroom that has a tub and beds that turn into
day sofas, along with a desk/dresser with drawer storage.

Suitable Standards: .... D

Average Price PPPD: $224
An upper and lower berth in the Court category R grade that sleeps only two. If one
of you can tolerate an upper berth, the storage is good, and there's a window and
bath with shower.

Bottom Bunks: .... F

Average Price PPPD: $118
The absolutely cheapest digs on the ship are the Z category (you kind of get the
feeling from the nomenclature, don't you?) inside four-berth cabins without private
facilities. Since that sounds to us like Folsom Prison without a reprieve, we won't
dwell on the details.

The *Canberra* makes her annual world cruise during the first quarter of the year, then
cruises around Europe and the Caribbean.

A number of the *Canberra's* cabins still do not have private bathroom facilities but require a passenger to use the loo down the hall. Passengers are assigned by the cabin category to one of two restaurants where meals are served in two seatings. While she's no
longer the state-of-the-art darling she used to be in world cruising, she's still an appealing
if vintage entry.

Fielding's Five

Five Favorite Places

1. The Pacific Restaurant, the former first-class dining room, is for passengers in cabins
   1 through 103, and the Atlantic Restaurant for passengers in cabins 201 to 333.
   Families with children are generally assigned to the early seating.

2. The Crows' Nest piano bar offers a great view through its floor-to-ceiling windows.

3. Alice Springs Pool & Bar, sure to make some homesick Aussie happy with its tile
   pool surround and plenty of Fosters. It's the former second-class pool, but who's
   counting?

4. The children's playroom, large and well laid-out with a professional staff.

5. The amidships Bonito Pool area is a good place to gather on a cool or windy day because it's sheltered from the breeze.

Five Good Reasons to Book This Ship

1. They take very good care of children on board.

2. The cabins without en suite facilities are among the lowest-priced cruise buys anywhere.

3. You can wash out your smalls in the self-service launderettes that are located on almost all passenger decks.

4. The court cabins if you have one or two good friends and don't mind delicately roughing it; they are blocks of inside cabins with small corner windows that face a large window at the end of the corridor, letting a trickle of daylight. All have a private tub or shower and a toilet.

5. To take a world cruise for under $100 a day if you book a lower-priced inside cabin (with private facilities) early enough to get a second-person-free deal.

Five Things You Won't Find On Board

1. Silence if you're in Deck A cabins 71, 73, 74, 76, 78 and 80, because you're under the nightclub.

2. Private bathroom facilities in nine different cabin categories; the loo is down the hall.

3. A branch of Harrods; only Cunard's *QE2* has that.

4. A predominance of Americans.

5. Tables for two in the Atlantic Restaurant.

Canberra ★★

Registry	**Britain**
Officers	**British**
Crew	**British**
Complement	**805**
GRT	**44,807**
Length (ft.)	**818**
Beam (ft.)	**102**
Draft (ft.)	**32**
Passengers-Cabins Full	**1615**
Passengers-2/Cabin	**1388**
Passenger Space Ratio	**32**
Stability Rating	**Good**
Seatings	**2**
Cuisine	**British**
Dress Code	**Traditional**
Room Service	**Yes**
Tip	**$8 PPPD**

Ship Amenities

Outdoor Pool	**3**
Indoor Pool	**0**
Jacuzzi	**0**
Fitness Center	**Yes**
Spa	**No**
Beauty Shop	**Yes**
Showroom	**Yes**
Bars/Lounges	**9**
Casino	**Yes**
Shops	**3**
Library	**Yes**
Child Program	**Yes**
Self-Service Laundry	**Yes**
Elevators	**5**

Cabin Statistics

Suites	**4**
Outside Doubles	**270**
Inside Doubles	**351**
Wheelchair Cabins	**0**
Singles	**138**
Single Surcharge	**NA**
Verandas	**0**
110 Volt	**No**

Oriana

We remember the previous Oriana from the 1960s, but this new one is ever so much lovelier. The drollest touch of British whimsy aboard the Oriana turns up in the least expected place, the navigation bridge, where a grandly antlered reindeer head hangs on the wall. It is "Sven the ever-watchful," the captain says, a gift from the mayor of Olden, Norway, which none of the designers would permit in any of the ship's public rooms, so it ended up there. "We've found lots of uses for it," says one officer, "like hanging tinsel from the rack and putting a red nose on it for Christmas."

The *Oriana* is that increasingly rara avis, a ship that still looks like a ship. Built for the British market and christened in April, 1995, by Queen Elizabeth, the newest P&O vessel has a magnificent expanse of teak stern decks, three full-sized swimming pools and the most complete and spacious children's center at sea. It's exhilarating to stand at the stern on an upper deck and gaze down at the vast expanse of natural teak decking on five deck levels, the first four curving gently at both sides in a crescent-shaped ending that allows still more attractive nooks and hideaways for readers, dozers and sunbathers. The full professional theatre has an orchestra pit and flawless sightlines; every seat in the house is good.

Cabins & Costs

Fantasy Suites: . . . . **A**

Average Price PPPD: $859 in the Canary Islands including some airfare.
Suites with private balconies provide twin beds that can be converted to queen-sized, sofa, cocktail table, five-drawer desk, coffeemaker and generous closet space.

Small Splurges: . . . . **A**

Average Price PPPD: $559 in the Canary Islands including some airfare.
Category B deluxe doubles with private verandas have two lower beds that can convert to queen-sized, bookshelves, built-in safe, binoculars, robe and slippers, cur-

tains to close off sleeping area from sitting area, and a sofa that can double as a bed for a child.

Suitable Standards: .... A

Average Price PPPD: $446 in the Canary Islands including some airfare.
All cabins are furnished with twin or double beds, nightstands with drawers, desk/dressers with drawers and large mirrors, mini-refrigerators, combination safes, TV sets with remote control, plentiful closet space, and most bathrooms have tubs as well as showers.

Bottom Bunks: .... B

Average Price PPPD: $372 in the Canary Islands including some airfare.
The smallest inside doubles are 150 square feet with two lower beds, corner love seat, mirrored cabinets and hair dryers. There are eight designated wheelchair-accessible cabins that measure 257 square feet each.

Where She Goes

The *Oriana* begins her year with an around-the-world cruise, followed by Northern European and Mediterranean itineraries in summer, the Aegean in autumn, and the Canary Islands, Holy Land and Caribbean in winter.

The Bottom Line

While Princess Cruises will be the North American representatives for its parent company, there's no way the *Oriana* could ever be mistaken for a love boat. Strikingly handsome and dignified, this ship is perfect for traditionalists because it looks more like an ocean liner than a floating resort. Young families with small children will really appreciate the extremely good child care facilities and experienced staff. It offers a very British cruise experience that would also be appreciated by American Anglophiles, fans of British country house hotels, experienced cruisers who yearn for proper dress codes and decorum, the return of fancy dress parades and passenger talent shows and enjoy the absence of frenetic onboard revenue pushes from multiple bingo games to art auctions. All in all, the ship has a lot to offer travelers of all ages.

Fielding's Five

Five Fantastic Places Aboard

1. Theatre Royal, a full-fledged theatre with rows of red velvet seats and no smoking or drinking inside.

2. Harlequin's, a nightclub with traditional dancing on a large dance floor until midnight, when the disco sound takes over.

3. Lord's Tavern, a cricket-oriented pub that's packed with people at the pre-luncheon hour and decorated with a mural of Lord's Cricket Ground on one wall.

4. Thackeray Room, an elegant library and reading room lined with wood and furnished with handsome tapestry wing chairs and green leather chairs with brass nail studs and floor lamps.

5. The quiet, sedate European-style gaming room, with noisy slots relegated to a soundproofed room next to the pub.

P & O CRUISES

Five Good Reasons To Book This Ship

1. To see the kids fed at a special children's tea at 5:15, after which they can go to the night nursery for free supervised care until 2 a.m.

2. To feast on traditional British breakfasts, complete with kippers, black pudding, fried bread and tinned baked beans.

3. To enjoy some sybaritic beauty treatments in an elegant art nouveau spa.

4. To bask in the limitless acres of teak deck, so nicely laid out that everyone aboard can find his own special spot for sun or shade.

5. To engage in the most dedicated quoits competitions we've ever seen at sea.

P & O CRUISES

Oriana ★★★★★

Registry	**Britain**
Officers	**British**
Crew	**British**
Complement	**760**
GRT	**69,153**
Length (ft.)	**850**
Beam (ft.)	**105**
Draft (ft.)	**26**
Passengers-Cabins Full	**1804**
Passengers-2/Cabin	**1760**
Passenger Space Ratio	**38**
Stability Rating	**Good**
Seatings	**2**
Cuisine	**British**
Dress Code	**Traditional**
Room Service	**Yes**
Tip	**$8 PPPD**

Ship Amenities

Outdoor Pool	**3**
Indoor Pool	**0**
Jacuzzi	**5**
Fitness Center	**Yes**
Spa	**Yes**
Beauty Shop	**Yes**
Showroom	**Yes**
Bars/Lounges	**9**
Casino	**Yes**
Shops	**2**
Library	**Yes**
Child Program	**Yes**
Self-Service Laundry	**Yes**
Elevators	**10**

Cabin Statistics

Suites	**8**
Outside Doubles	**477**
Inside Doubles	**340**
Wheelchair Cabins	**8**
Singles	**110**
Single Surcharge	**NA**
Verandas	**114**
110 Volt	**Yes**

Victoria

In the grand tradition of Hollywood films, where a classy, intelligent but plain Jane, usually played by Rosalind Russell, takes off her glasses, lets down her hair and suddenly becomes glamorous, Princess Cruises briefly turned P & O's stalwart Sea Princess (now the Victoria), a sedate British dowager, into a Princess ship in 1987. This move infuriated the British, and after a relative brief whirl in her glamour garments, the Sea Princess returned to the fold. So great and long-standing was their wrath that eight years later the ship was renamed Victoria to erase any confusion in the U.K. that it might be one of those gaudy American Princess ships.

This elegant and classic ship started life as the *Kungsholm* for Swedish American Lines, and was one of the last great ships built by John Brown on the River Clyde. Today the vessel combines a stateliness and solid seaworthiness with the big deck dazzle of a fun-in-the-sun ship. It has a lot of action for active outdoorsy types, two outdoor pools and one indoor one, plus a whirlpool spa, sauna and gym, and a special sports afterdeck with shuffleboard and quoits, table tennis and golf. There are enough bars and lounges on board to visit a different one every day of the week, and several big comfortable reading rooms overlooking the sea. Staterooms are unusually large and beautifully fitted, with enough closet and storage space for a three-month cruise.

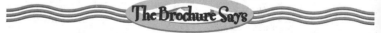

The Brochure Says

"Her sleek lines reflect the elegance of her interior. As soon as you step on-board, you'll notice a little extra refinement, a touch more style. Wood paneling gleams in the subdued lighting. You'll see fine paintings and delightful floral arrangements everywhere you look. The *Victoria's* small size lets her slip into out-of-the-way ports, and gives you a chance to meet your fellow passengers."

Translation

None needed—well said!

Cabins & Costs

antasy Suites: .... A

Average Price PPPD: $598

Six big suites added during the major refurbishment in 1986 are named for classic P & O ships and have sitting areas, double beds, mini-refrigerators and bathrooms with Jacuzzi tubs.

mall Splurges: .... A

Average Price PPPD: $344

Spacious BA category cabins have sitting area, built-in desk/dresser with stool and mirror, twin or double beds, bathroom with tub.

uitable Standards: .... B

Average Price PPPD: $259

Many of the standard cabins have two lower berths, one of which folds away during the day to lend more space, while the other can be made up as a sofa. There are some tubs, some showers only in these middle categories. Some 16 inside and outside single cabins are a boon for the solo traveler, so often overlooked in today's new ships or hit with a hefty surcharge for occupying a double cabin alone.

ottom Bunks: .... A

Average Price PPPD: $212

Bottom category inside cabins on the lowest passenger decks are fairly spacious, fitted out with the lovely wood interiors like the other cabins are, and usually have a desk/dressing table and a chair as well as two lower beds, one of which folds away during the day.

Where She Goes

The *Victoria* does a series of Caribbean itineraries out of San Juan throughout the spring including one that offers a cruise into Gatun Lake in the Panama Canal. A 13-day transatlantic sailing on April 12 moves the ship to Europe for a summer/fall group of European Cruises.

The Bottom Line

A graceful and elegant classic ship since her days as the *Kungsholm*, the *Victoria* is an antidote to megaliners and glitz. If you're a traditional cruiser who loves polished wood interiors and glass-enclosed promenades, and you subscribe to British understatement, *Victoria* is your ship come in.

Fielding's Five

Five Favorite Places

1. Warm wood paneling and finely detailed carpentry show the extraordinary custom work that went into the ship, especially in the International Lounge.

2. The Coral Dining Room is an attractive medium-sized room with two meal seating and two entrances, one forward and one aft, for anyone who gets mixed up on the way to dinner.

3. The circular bar in the Carib Lounge is a popular gathering spot because the casino is nearby.

4. The International Bar is an intimate place for a drink or two with a very close friend

5. The Starlight Lounge was our favorite venue for hotly contested Trivial Pursuit games; it helped that if only one table out of the six or eight teams got the right answer, the bar sent over free drinks.

Five Good Reasons to Book This Ship

1. It's a longtime classic and you can tell that by being aboard.

2. It goes to some fascinating places you may not have been before, including Fethiye, Turkey; Mytilene, Greece; Tasacu, Turkey; the Dalmatian Islands (there are no 101 of them); Sinop, Turkey; Cephalonia, Greece; Nesebur, Bulgaria; and Tartous, Syria.

3. Two outdoor pools and one indoor one, plus whirlpool spa, sauna and gym, mean you can work out every day, and a special sports afterdeck provides an out-of-the-traffic area for shuffleboard and quoits, playing table tennis or driving golf balls.

4. Because if you book the right sailing far enough in advance through Golden Bear you may be able to take the second person in the cabin along free.

5. Because there's a launderette and ironing room on virtually every deck.

Five Things You Won't Find On Board

1. TV sets in the lower-category cabins.

2. A shortage of closet space.

3. A hot breakfast served in your cabin; only continental breakfasts are offered by room service.

4. A private veranda.

5. A skimpy bathtub; all the cabins with tubs have those great deep British tubs.

Victoria ★★★★

Registry	**Britain**
Officers	**British**
Crew	**British**
Complement	**400**
GRT	**27,670**
Length (ft.)	**660**
Beam (ft.)	**87**
Draft (ft.)	**26**
Passengers-Cabins Full	**847**
Passengers-2/Cabin	**722**
Passenger Space Ratio	**38**
Stability Rating	**Good**
Seatings	**2**
Cuisine	**British**
Dress Code	**Traditional**
Room Service	**Yes**
Tip	**$8 PPPD**

Ship Amenities

Outdoor Pool	**2**
Indoor Pool	**1**
Jacuzzi	**2**
Fitness Center	**Yes**
Spa	**No**
Beauty Shop	**Yes**
Showroom	**Yes**
Bars/Lounges	**4**
Casino	**Yes**
Shops	**2**
Library	**Yes**
Child Program	**Yes**
Self-Service Laundry	**Yes**
Elevators	**10**

Cabin Statistics

Suites	**6**
Outside Doubles	**262**
Inside Doubles	**87**
Wheelchair Cabins	**10**
Singles	**12**
Single Surcharge	**NA**
Verandas	**0**
110 Volt	**No**

PREMIER CRUISE LINES

400 Challenger Road, Cape Canaveral, FL 32920
(407) 783-5061, (800) 327-7113

History . . . .

Premier Cruise Lines, founded in 1984, got some notice as a cruise line dedicated to families and as the first multi-day cruise ship sailing from Port Canaveral, but it catapulted to attention in November 1985, when it became "the Official Cruise Line of Walt Disney World," selling combination week-long land/sea vacations that allowed passengers to take a three- or four-day cruise and spend the remaining four or three days at Disney World with hotel room, rental car and admissions included in the package.

It was a great idea, first conceived around 1980 or 1981 by Bruce Nierenberg (who also later founded now-defunct American Family Cruises) and Bjornar Hermansen, when both were with Norwegian Caribbean Line (now Norwegian Cruise Line). So it was to NCL they first took the idea of basing a cruise ship in Port Canaveral to take advantage of the nearness of Disney World and tap into some of that rapidly growing leisure travel market. NCL wasn't interested, so in 1983, Nierenberg and Hermansen started up Premier with the backing of the Greyhound Corp. (later to become part of The Dial Corp) of Phoenix, Arizona.

The first ship Premier operated was the *Star/Ship Royale*, the former *Federico C* from Costa, which carried 1050 passengers when all the berths were filled, which they usually were. They bought and renovated the ship for $14 million, painted the hull bright red with orange and yellow trim, and sent it on its maiden voyage in March 1984.

In November 1985, on the heels of the Disney deal, Premier bought the *Oceanic* from Home Lines and made a major conversion that increased the ship's maximum passenger capacity from 1096 to 1800.

Premier acquired the six-year-old *Atlantic*, which became the *Star/Ship Atlantic*, after Home Lines went out of business in 1988. From a maximum of 1167 passengers, the *Atlantic* was remodeled to carry 1600. Later that same year Premier bought the 686-berth *Sun Princess* from Princess Cruises and turned it into the 950-berth *Star/Ship Majestic*, and then sold the *Royale* in January 1989 to Dolphin to become the *SeaBreeze*.

Heading into the 1990s, Premier decided to start calling itself The B: Red Boat, which was picked up instantly by TV-watching children. : also made marketing sense, because it meant instead of calling an requesting a ship by name, the passenger would take whichever Big Re Boat was handy despite the dissimilarities in the fleet.

Carnival Cruise Lines entered into negotiation to buy Premier in Apr 1991, then in May rescinded the offer. In June, co-founder Nierenber resigned and sold his stock to Dial Corp. Co-founder Hermanse stayed on, trimming and streamlining company operations until his re ignation in June 1992.

In March 1994, the 10-year agreement with Disney came to an enc but the line still offers Disney World vacation packages in combinatio with its cruises. Disney decided to start its own cruise line, called Disne Cruise Lines, with the first of two new ships scheduled to debut in Jar uary 1998. Premier went out and got itself some other 'toons fro: Warner Brothers' Looney Tunes—Bugs Bunny, Daffy Duck, Tweet Bird, Sylvester, the Tasmanian Devil—that Premier employees animat on board the ships.

The line operated three vessels until early 1995, when the *Majestic* wa leased to CTC, a European cruise operator. At present, the *Atlantic* an *Oceanic* compose the fleet of The Big Red Boat.

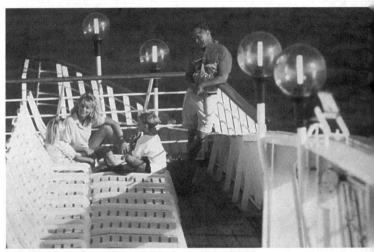

Family cruises aboard the Big Red Boat mean parents spend quality time wit: kids, but don't have to constantly entertain them because of the plethora o, activities and programs.

Concept . . . .

While other cruise lines, particularly Sitmar, had introduced very good children's programs, nothing anywhere near the scale of Premier's fam ily program had been seen before. Children divided into age group. have their own daily programs as full of activities as the adults', ever their own shore excursions, so parents could take the kids on a cruise without having to constantly entertain them, making it a real vacation for everybody.

ignatures . . . .

Bright red hulls on both Big Red Boats.

Cartoon characters on board—currently Looney Tunes favorites such as Bugs Bunny, Elmer Fudd, Porky Pig and Tweety Bird.

Extensive children's programs that run from 9 a.m. to 10 p.m. with a staff of professionally trained counselors who divide the kids into five different age groups. At the end of the scheduled program, babysitting is available at a nominal charge. Child care for children ages 2 to 12 is offered on an around-the-clock basis.

The Tasmanian Devil tucks kids in at bedtime—for a fee.

immicks . . . .

Tuck-in bedtime service for kids by one of the costumed characters ($10) or a character breakfast in a special dining room ($30 for a family of four).

Chocolate Ship cookies for kids at bedtime.

Who's the Competition

In the short range, it's Carnival, who put its glittering new *Fantasy* int
Port Canaveral on three- and four-day cruises with a Disney Wor'
package similar to the one offered by Premier. In the long haul, it's t'
Mouse, of course. Both lines profess to be excited about the Disn'
cruise ships coming into Port Canaveral in 1998 because they expe
them to draw into the area many more potential passengers for ever
body.

Who's Aboard

Kids, lots and lots of kids, some 500 or so children on an average summer or holiday cruise. At the same time, the line promotes the romant
aspects of cruising to honeymooners and frequently offers singles an
senior citizen specials as well.

Who Should Go

Parents, single parents and grandparents with children. Couples an
singles who enjoy being around other people's children.

Who Should Not Go

Anyone who doesn't adore children.

The Lifestyle

A lot of attention is paid to the adults on board, because the line inten-
to provide a vacation for the whole family, not just the children. Mon
and Dad can enjoy a full day working out in the gym, taking a snorke
ing tour, signing up for golf lessons, having a massage or beauty trea
ment at Steiners Beauty and Fitness Salon/Massage, betting on th
horse races, attending the captain's champagne reception, gaming i
the casino, playing family snowball bingo, hitting a late-night cabar
party before going to the gala midnight buffet at 12:30 and havin
some French onion soup and made-to-order omelets between 1 and
a.m.

CHAMPAGNE TOAST

*The new Voyage of Discovery series that brings the whole family together for
special entertainment has been introduced, including a mock version of the
TV quiz game "Family Feud" in pirate costume, called "Pirates Feud," a moonlight harbor cruise in Nassau, a family karaoke session and a "History of the
Caribbean" tour in Port Lucaya. Some of the programs carry a surcharge.*

Wardrobe

The garb for these cruises is casual most of the time, although everyon
in the family should bring something a little dressy for the captain'
party. After dinner, unlike many lines, Premier doesn't mind passenge
changing back to casual clothing for the rest of the evening on form;
night.

Bill of Fare..............................C

The dinner menu offers three appetizers, three soups, two salads and seven entrees, plus a special children's menu with familiar favorites such as cheeseburgers, chicken nuggets, hot dogs and fish fingers, along with a "health boat" selection that includes cheese pizza, beef kabob, beef and bean burrito and Spaghetti O's. Buffet breakfast and lunch is served in the cafe as well as full-service breakfast, lunch and dinner in the dining room. The Big Dipper ice cream parlor with "make-your-own-sundaes" is open throughout the afternoon. An "America the Beautiful" menu with the Looney Tunes characters strolling around the dining room is usually scheduled the last night of the cruise, with other themed dinners—French, Italian and Caribbean—also on the schedule, depending on the length of the cruise. Meals are served in the dining rooms at assigned tables during two seatings.

Showtime............................B

In addition to daylong activities and shore excursions, evening production shows such as "Legends in Concert" with clones of Elvis, Madonna and the Blues Brothers performing, a Carlos & Charlie's Mexico-themed party, and lots of audience participation, from costumed '50s twist parties and Country Western Jamborees to karaoke contests.

Discounts............................

A family reunion plan gives 10 percent off the tariff for the first two guests in each of three cabins with a minimum of 10 people and six full-fare guests. Single parents traveling with one to three children under 17 can take a category 3 through 8 cabin, pay 125 percent of the per person, double occupancy rate, and the kids pay the cheaper third, fourth and fifth guest rate for sharing the same cabin. And seniors (anyone 60 or over) and a guest traveling with them can take 10 percent off the cruise fare during the season (summer and holiday weekends) and 15 percent apiece off during the rest of the year.

The Bottom Line

Premier has always attracted a great many first-time cruisers because it has been selling a vacation package rather than a cruise, with the emphasis on the fun and activities on land and sea rather than on a ship.

But now the line seems to be dividing its emphasis: First, it's promoting its three- and four-day cruises as a primary destination in a separate brochure, using the variety of shore excursions it has set up at Port Lucaya and a day and evening in Nassau as the main attraction. Secondly, it's issued a second brochure that promotes the seven-day family cruise vacation incorporating visits to the Orlando theme parks, including Disney World, with various packages priced depending on which hotel is used. And thirdly, it's testing seven-day Caribbean cruises out of Port Canaveral for repeat passengers who have asked for longer cruises. If this is successful, the line may begin stressing the cruise aspect even more.

Star/Ship Atlantic

> *Our first surprise aboard Star/Ship Atlantic was that the ice cream parlor was filled with more adults than children, many of them seniors on special discounts, spooning up the make-your-own sundaes with obvious delight. Next door in the pub not much was happening.*

Built in 1982, the *Atlantic* is a durable vessel with high passenger density thanks to those 452 upper berths in the cabins. A sliding plexiglass roof over the amidships terrace and pool makes the area comfortable year-round. Passenger activity is concentrated on the Pool Deck and Lounge Deck with most of the cabins and the dining room below. A group of cabins is also located forward on Lounge Deck, and the major children's play area, Pluto's Playhouse, is aft on the deck below Lounge Deck with its own kiddies' pool outside.

The Brochure Says

"While you're having fun, we provide five separate programs for kids and teens that keep them occupied every day until 10 p.m. After that, group baby-sitting is available for a nominal fee as part of our 24-hour child-care service. We'll watch the kids overnight so you can relax and dance the night away!"

Translation

You can bring the kids on a cruise and hardly ever have to see them at all—but that's not what we observe on board. On the contrary, many parents seem to want to spend more time with their kids—or the kids with their parents—on the ship and ashore, so that the children's play room is often not as busy as we'd expected. The new Voyages of Discover program (see Champagne Toast, above) acknowledges this and introduces more activities for the whole family to do together.

Cabins & Costs

NOTE:

Average per person per day prices below are for three- and four-day cruises; seven-day packages including theme park stays will be less-expensive on a per-day basis. The prices are for two full-fare cabin occupants; third, fourth and fifth cabin occupants pay $449-$569 apiece including airfare from some cities for the three- or four-day cruise, depending on the season.

Fantasy Suites: C

Average Price PPPD: $399 including roundtrip airfare.
The largest accommodations on board the Atlantic are the category 9 apartment suites, which have a sitting room with sofa-bed and TV set and a bedroom with queen-sized bed, enough space for a family of four. While not huge, these are twice the size of the suites in the next category down, and have bathrooms with tub.

Small Splurges: C

Average Price PPPD: $329 on category 8 suites, $299 on category 6 cabins, including airfare.
All category 6 outside staterooms are almost the same size as category 8 suites, but can sleep only one child. Both categories are considerably smaller than the apartment suites. Category 8 suites have queen-sized bed or two lower beds plus third and fourth upper berths. Both have sitting area, TV sets and bathroom with tub.

Suitable Standards: C

Average Price PPPD: $293 including airfare.
Category 5 outside cabins are about the same size as the 6s and 8s but on a lower deck. A few have one upper berth for a third child, but most have two lower beds or a queen-sized bed plus two or even three additional berths, sitting area, TV and bathroom with tub. Four outside cabins are designated wheelchair accessible.

Bottom Bunks: .... D

Average Price PPPD: $213 including airfare.
The cheapest cabins are category 1 insides or outsides, 12 very tiny cabins forward on the lowest passenger decks, which means more ship motion. They have upper and lower beds and bathroom with shower only.

Where She Goes

The *Star/Ship Atlantic* sails every Thursday evening from Port Canaveral to Nassau, arriving at noon on Friday and staying past midnight so you can enjoy the local nightlife if you wish. Saturday morning you wake up anchored off Port Lucaya, a special island for beach parties, the dolphin experience, a barbecue and lots of fun and games. You sail Saturday night and arrive back in Port Canaveral early Sunday morning.

On Sunday afternoon, the ship sails at 4:30, spends Monday at sea so the whole family can explore the ship and enjoy its activities, then arrives in Nassau Tuesday morning and stays until well past midnight. On Wednesday it anchors off Port Lucaya for the same activities described above, then sails back to Port Canaveral Wednesday at 6 p.m., arriving early Thursday morning.

It's an interesting thing to see the changes Premier made in this ship to make it suitable for families with one, two or even three children when it had been a ship serving adult vacationers sailing from New York to Bermuda and from Ft. Lauderdale into the Caribbean. The density was tremendously increased by the addition of third and fourth berths in most of the cabins, along with sofa bed or rollaway bed options for additional passengers where floor space would permit. There was also the necessity to create small individual areas for the various age groups of children to meet for activities, so bars were turned into teen centers, shops converted to video arcades and deck areas enclosed for children's play rooms. But the menus from Home Lines' *Atlantic* bear little resemblance to the menus from the *Star/Ship Atlantic*. There's nary a mention on the latter of essence of capon broth with quail eggs or roast pheasant with Bordeaux garnish. But let's face it, the kids— and probably their parents—wouldn't order it anyhow.

Five Family Favorites

1. The Sunrise Terrace, formerly an observation lounge, has been turned into a cafe with ice cream tables and chairs and two buffet service lines leading into it from the terrace.

2. The Galaxy Dining Room with its dome overhead serves meals at assigned tables in two seatings, with dinnertime visits from Looney Tunes characters.

3. Club Universe is a handsome room where shows are presented, along with port talks, family snowball bingo and the captain's cocktail party; don't sit behind one of the big posts, however, or you'll miss some of the show.

4. Lucky Star Casino is Mom and Dad's equivalent to Pluto's Playhouse; it has a roulette table, craps table, six blackjack tables and lots of slots.

5. The Calypso Pool is aft on the pool deck, surrounded by a natural teak deck, a lot of lounge chairs, a couple of whirlpools and a small bandstand.

Star/Ship Atlantic ★★★

Registry	Liberia
Officers	Greek
Crew	International
Complement	535
GRT	35,143
Length (ft.)	671
Beam (ft.)	90
Draft (ft.)	25
Passengers-Cabins Full	1550
Passengers-2/Cabin	1098
Passenger Space Ratio	32
Stability Rating	Good
Seatings	2
Cuisine	Themed
Dress Code	Traditional
Room Service	Yes
Tip	$9 PPPD

Ship Amenities

Outdoor Pool	2
Indoor Pool	1
Jacuzzi	1
Fitness Center	Yes
Spa	No
Beauty Shop	Yes
Showroom	Yes
Bars/Lounges	5
Casino	Yes
Shops	2
Library	Yes
Child Program	Yes
Self-Service Laundry	Yes
Elevators	4

Cabin Statistics

Suites	6
Outside Doubles	371
Inside Doubles	178
Wheelchair Cabins	4
Singles	14
Single Surcharge	125%
Verandas	0
110 Volt	Yes

Star/Ship Oceanic

At the champagne reception, the captain in his neatly pressed white uniform bows and shakes hands formally with a little girl in a ruffled dress and hair ribbons, and Bugs Bunny pads down the corridor to greet an arriving family and pose for snapshots. Inside, at the party, an orchestra plays, and among the many couples are dressed-up little girls dancing with their dads and scrubbed, self-conscious little boys stiffly leading their moms around the floor.

A classic cruise vessel built by Italy's Fincantieri shipyard for now-defunc Home Lines in 1965, the *Oceanic* still has some charming details from th period, including the two free-form Riviera pools and the bright tile floor The ship is clean and kept in very good shape but seems much darker in th public areas than the Atlantic. The layout is a bit different, too, with verand suites on the topmost deck, a magrodrome sliding glass roof over the amic ship pool areas, more cabins aft on the pool deck, a full deck below that large cabins and suites, then a deck of public rooms. Below that are mor cabins and the dining room. When Premier christened the ship in 1986, th godmother was Miss Minnie Mouse.

"Whether you're honeymooners, single parents, or grandparents...whether you'r getting together for a family reunion or just want a vacation filled with fantasy, excite ment and wonder, no other cruise offers you more than The Big Red Boat's 7-nigh Cruise and Orlando Theme Park Vacations."

Translation

There are two brochures from Premier, one with the theme park vacations detailed anc priced and the other with the cruise itself detailed and priced. If you don't know which program interests you more, ask your travel agent or the cruise line to send you both.

NOTE:

Average per person per day prices below are for three- and four-day cruises; seven-day packages including theme park stays will be less expensive on a per-day basis. The prices are for two full-fare cabin occupants; third, fourth and fifth cabin occupants pay $449–$569 apiece including airfare from some cities for the three-or four-day cruise, depending on the season.

Fantasy Suites: .... B+

Average Price PPPD: $399 including airfare.
Eight spacious suites with private verandas high atop the Sun Deck give a great view of the sea as well as having plenty of room for a family of four. There's a king-sized bed plus two other berths, sitting area and bathroom with tub.

Small Splurges: ....B

Average Price PPPD: $329 including airfare.

Category 8 suites on the *Oceanic* are larger than those on the *Atlantic*, and have a separate sitting area with sofa and chairs, twin or queen-sized bed with room divider and bathroom with tub. Some have room for a third passenger, some a third and fourth. Specify whether you want a double or twin beds. You may prefer the suites on Pool Deck, although slightly smaller, because many of those on Premier Deck have partially obstructed views from hanging lifeboats.

ꭰuitable Standards: . . . . B

Average Price PPPD: $272 including airfare.
Most of the category 5 outside cabins have berths for third, sometimes fourth and fifth passengers, along with a choice of double or twin beds. Bathrooms have tubs and the rooms are fairly spacious and prettily furnished in pastels. Some connecting cabins are available for family groups.

ꭰottom Bunks: C

Average Price PPPD: $213 including airfare.
The cheapest cabins aboard are 15 category 1 inside cabins with upper and lower berths, quite small and designated for only two passengers.

Where She Goes

The *Star/Ship Oceanic* sails Friday afternoons from Port Canaveral, arriving in Nassau late Saturday morning and staying at the dockside until past midnight. On Sunday, the ship anchors off Port Lucaya at 9 a.m. and gives you a full day ashore at the beach with lots of things to do. The ship sails at 6 p.m. and arrives back in Port Canaveral early Monday morning.

On Monday afternoons, it sails again with the midweek passengers, spending Tuesday at sea so everyone can enjoy the ship, arriving early Wednesday morning in Nassau with a whole day for shopping and sightseeing, and doesn't sail until after midnight in case you want to check out the local casinos and nightclubs. Thursday the ship spends all day at anchorage off Port Lucaya with lots of activities for both kids and grownups ashore and on the ship. It sails at 6 p.m. and arrives back in Port Canaveral Friday morning.

The Bottom Line

We like a lot about the *Oceanic*—its nice big cabins (well, some of them are!), the lovely pool deck, the cool, darkish public rooms on Lounge Deck that are a good respite from the bright Bahamian sunshine. Kids will like the big play area and supervised wading pool. Some of the former bright yellows, oranges and reds have been subdued into lavenders and burgundies on a recent refit. Now, if that maintenance man could just stay ahead of all those sticky little fingerprints everywhere and the popcorn ground into the carpeting!

Fielding's Five

Five Fun Places

1. The Riviera pools on pool deck, a pair of free-form shapes almost touching with blue tile surrounds and shady niches along the sides with tables and chairs.

2. Pluto's Playhouse, a big children's play area with a wading pool outside, bright carpeting, lots of toys and games and children's videos, an arts and crafts center, and jungle gyms.

3. Heroes and Legends, a pub and karaoke club, is a cozy little spot with Victorian decor, frosted glass and big, belly-up bar.

4. Seasport Health Center has a gym with weight room, exercycles and other machines plus a massage room.

5. Starlight Cabaret has a 1960s nightclub look with mushroom-type lights fixed into tabletops, dance floor and bandstand.

Five Off-the-Wall Things to Do

1. Hit the adults-only karaoke contest in the Heroes and Legends Pub.

2. Have a tequila shooter at the Carlos & Charlie's Party in the Starlight Cabaret.

3. Swim with the dolphins at Port Lucaya; you can have your travel agent book your appointment when you book your cruise.

4. Get in a poker game in the Heroes and Legends Pub.

5. Take golf lessons from the golf pro on board at poolside.

Five Good Reasons to Book This Ship

1. To see what a 1960s ocean liner looked like.

2. To get photographed with Bugs Bunny or have the Tasmanian Devil tuck you in bed at night.

3. To take a cruise and stay on-site at Disney World for a family of four for around $525 a day including all meals on the ship, admissions and hotel room at Disney, rental car and roundtrip airfare to Florida.

4. To get away on a quiet midweek vacation (when there are fewer children on board) at a 15 percent discount if one of the two of you is over 60.

5. To enroll the kids in a professionally run children's program tailored specifically for each one's age group.

Star/Ship Oceanic ★★★

Registry	**Bahamas**
Officers	**Greek**
Crew	**International**
Complement	**565**
GRT	**38,772**
Length (ft.)	**782**
Beam (ft.)	**96**
Draft (ft.)	**28**
Passengers-Cabins Full	**1800**
Passengers-2/Cabin	**1180**
Passenger Space Ratio	**32.85**
Stability Rating	**Fair**
Seatings	**2**
Cuisine	**American**
Dress Code	**Traditional**
Room Service	**No**
Tip	**$9 PPPD**

Ship Amenities

Outdoor Pool	**1**
Indoor Pool	**2**
Jacuzzi	**3**
Fitness Center	**Yes**
Spa	**No**
Beauty Shop	**Yes**
Showroom	**Yes**
Bars/Lounges	**6**
Casino	**Yes**
Shops	**2**
Library	**Yes**
Child Program	**Yes**
Self-Service Laundry	**No**
Elevators	**5**

Cabin Statistics

Suites	**65**
Outside Doubles	**190**
Inside Doubles	**335**
Wheelchair Cabins	**1**
Singles	**0**
Single Surcharge	**125%**
Verandas	**8**
110 Volt	**Yes**

PRINCESS CRUISES

10100 Santa Monica Boulevard, Los Angeles, CA 90067
☎ (310) 553-1770, (800) LOVE-BOA(T)

A new tradition aboard the newest Princess ships is to stage the captain's cocktail party in the three-story atrium lobby.

History . . . .

While the popular TV series "The Love Boat" catapulted Princess Cruises to worldwide fame, the company had been a household name on the west coast, at least among cruise aficionados, from the 1960s.

In the winter of 1965-66, Seattle entrepreneur Stan McDonald chartered the 6000-ton *Princess Patricia* from Canadian Pacific Railway and offered cruises along the Mexican Riviera from Los Angeles. From the ship's name came the company name, Princess Cruises. The first season went so well aboard the "Princess Pat," as everyone began to call her, that McDonald soon chartered a newly-built Italian ship called the *Italia* and renamed her the *Princess Italia*. In 1968, the *Princess Carla* (the former French Line *Flandre*), then Costa's *Carla C*, was chartered, and in 1971 the *Island Princess* (the only one of these still in the fleet).

Then London-based Peninsular and Orient Steam Navigation Company, better known as P&O (see P & O under Cruise Lines, above), the largest and oldest shipping company in the world, eyed the action and decided to come into the cruise scene with its new *Spirit of London* which it positioned on the west coast in the winter of 1972–73 to compete with Princess. There was little competition; McDonald continued to dominate Mexican Riviera cruising, despite one travel writer's comments that aboard the Princess Pat "the standard dessert was canned peaches" and the decor "was on a par with a good, clean $7-a-night room in a venerable but respected Toronto hotel."

So in 1974, P & O acquired Princess Cruises, including its key marketing staff, and set about upgrading the fleet hardware. The *Carla* and *Italia* went back to Costa Cruises in 1974, and the *Island Princess* was purchased outright. P & O's new *Spirit of London* was added to the fleet as the *Sun Princess*, and the *Sea Venture*, sister ship to the *Island Princess*, was acquired to become the *Pacific Princess*.

Things were already going well, but destined to improve even further when TV producer Doug Cramer showed up in 1975 with a new series he wanted to film aboard a cruise ship. *Et voila!* "The Love Boat" was born.

In 1988, continuing its "if you can't beat 'em, buy 'em" strategy, P & O/Princess acquired Los Angeles-based rival Sitmar Cruises, which added three existing ships and one nearly-completed new ship, *Star Princess*, to the fleet, to bring it up to nine vessels.

Today there are still nine Love Boats cruising the seven seas, five of them from the 1988 fleet, with a 10th, the 104,000-ton giant *Grand Princess*, due to arrive in the spring of 1997 to sail the Caribbean year round. (A prudent move, since the ship is too big to go through the Panama Canal.)

—Parent company P & O claims it invented leisure cruising in 1844 when British author William Makepeace Thackery sailed around the Mediterranean on a free ticket to publicize the service and wrote a travel book about his cruise—*From Cornhill to Grand Cairo*—under the pseudonym Michael Angelo Titmarsh.

—One of the three largest cruise lines in the world.

—Offers the largest number of world-wide destinations of any major line.

—First to introduce all outside cabins with a high proportion of private balconies (*Royal Princess*, 1984).

—First major cruise line to introduce multimedia musical shows produced in-house.

—First to install a "black box" recorder on each of its ships for additional safety data in case of an incident at sea.

—Introduced easy-to-use phone cards to make local or long distance calls from anywhere in the world with a push-button phone; the card (good for $20 worth of phone time) was originally developed as a convenience for the Princess crew (sold across the fleet, July 1995).

—TV's "The Love Boat" is seen in 93 countries and heard in more than 29 different languages. The title comes from a book written by a former cruise director named Jeraldine Saunders about her life onboard.

> ### DID YOU KNOW?
>
> *While the* Pacific Princess *is the vessel most associated with "Love Boat" over the years, the pilot episode was actually filmed aboard the* Sun Princess, *the former* Spirit of London, *now retired from the fleet.*

Concept . . . .

"It's more than a cruise, it's the Love Boat," a beaming Gavin MacLeod said on the Princess commercials.

What does that make you think of? The TV series, of course, with its glamorous, friendly crew, never too busy to intercede in someone's love affair. Luxurious staterooms and elegantly garbed passengers. Nubile nymphs in bikinis. Exotic ports, perpetual sunshine and cloudless blue skies. In other words, the perfect vacation—a cruise.

With its varied fleet of vessels, ranging from the homey, mid-sized 610-passenger *Island Princess* and *Pacific Princess* to the new 1950-passenger *Sun Princess* and the upcoming 2600-passenger *Grand Princess*, the line feels it offers "something for everyone" from "endless activity" to "total relaxation."

> ### DID YOU KNOW?
>
> *Princess says it has trademarked both the name Princess and the Love Boat slogan (see "Concept") and has in the past even brought legal action against two smaller cruise lines for infringement of copyright—American Canadian Caribbean Line for attempting to name one of its 90-passenger vessels* Mayan Princess *(ACCL changed it to* Mayan Prince *rather than go to court) and now-defunct Ocean Cruise Line for advertising its* Ocean Princess *Antarctica sailings with the slogan "Cruise Antarctica with a Princess."*

Signatures . . . .

The line's distinctive stack logo, the "sea witch" with the flowing hair, provides instant identification when a Princess ship is in port. Just as distinctive, but less well known, is the Princess tradition of furnishing each of its new ships with an exquisite museum-quality million dollar-plus art collections from contemporary artists such as Andy Warhol, David Hockney, Robert Motherwell, Frank Stella, Laddie John Dill, Billy Al Bengston, Richard Diebenkorn and Helen Frankenthaler.

On-board pizzerias with special ovens serve up pizzas and calzone cooked to order aboard the line's *Crown Princess, Sky Princess, Regal Princess, Star Princess* and *Sun Princess*.

Gimmicks . . . .

Declaring St. Valentine's Day as Love Boat National Holiday aboard all the line's vessels, with renewal of vows ceremonies in which some 4000 couples participate. The holiday also features a poetry contest and read-

ing, romantic feature films, a Hearts card game tournament and honey
mooner and singles parties.

Who's the Competition

In Alaska, Princess has been competing head-on with Holland Americ
for some years, and usually outnumbers HAL in ships positioned ther
for the summer. In the Caribbean, HAL is also a main competitor, bu
Love Boats face some Costa competition for fans of pizza, pasta an
Italian waiters.

Who's Aboard

Romantic couples of all ages who saw "The Love Boat" on TV; long
time loyals, both couples and singles, over 45; a group of younger cou
ples who've met on board and continue to take vacation cruise
together (see "Footnote" to follow); some families with children, wh
gravitate toward those ships that have dedicated playrooms and full
time youth counselors (*Sky Princess, Golden Princess* and *Star Princess*)
people with glints of gold from head (hair coloring) to toe (gold lam
sandals or ankle bracelets), neck (gold chains) to fingertips (gold pink
rings, a gold lamé tote).

Who Should Go

Anyone who wants a very traditional cruise experience with a chance to
dance and dress up; admirers of avant-garde Pompidou Center architec
Renzo Piano, who designed parts of the *Crown* and *Regal Princess;* fam
ilies whose teenagers like the pizzeria and the zany fountain drink
aboard the *Star, Crown* and *Regal;* young women who want to mee
some Italians; anyone who loves pasta, pastries and cappuccino; fans o
the Cirque du Soleil who'll adore the new avant-garde show *Mystiqu*
on the *Crown, Regal, Sun* and *Star.* More younger passengers should b
boarding, because Princess is becoming expert at giving them what the
want, at least on the big new ships—a less-structured captain's cocktai
party; music for listening and dancing all over the ship; lots of sundeck
and water areas with swim-up bars, waterfalls, swimming pools and
Jacuzzis. Families with children now that Princess is welcoming them
with open arms.

Who Should Not Go

Anyone with children under 18 months of age (babies are not permitted on board); anybody who refuses to wear a tie on any occasion; anyone who would answer "Huh?" to the query, "Fourth for bridge?"

The Lifestyle

Set in the framework of traditional cruises, a day aboard a Princess ship
includes a plethora of activities and entertainment, from an exercise
class in the gym or a facial in the beauty salon to language lessons, pool
games, bridge classes, aquacise in the ship's pool, indoor and outdoor
game tournaments, bingo, golf chipping, feature films in the ship's theater or in the cabin, port lectures, shopping lectures, cooking demonstrations, galley and bridge tours, fashion shows and karaoke singing.
Even kids have their own karaoke contests, along with coketail parties,
coloring contests and ice cream parties.

Many evenings are relatively formal aboard, with passengers wearing their finest clothes and jewelry and Italian or British officers hosting dinner tables, but other nights, such as the traditional London Pub Night, casual wear is prescribed and beer and pub dishes are on the agenda, along with rowdy music hall songs and dances.

Wardrobe............................

Princess passengers usually have two formal nights, two or three semi-formal and two or three casual nights during a week. For formal nights, men are requested to wear tuxedos, dinner jackets or dark suits and women cocktail dresses or evening outfits. Semi-formal evenings call for men to wear jacket and tie, women to wear dresses or dressy pantsuits.

On casual evenings, men may wear open-necked sport shirts, slacks and sports outfits; women, slacks, dresses or skirts. Daytime clothing can be quite casual, but coverups over bathing suits are expected for passengers walking through the ship.

Bill of Fare........................... B+

Cuisine is Continental with an emphasis on Italian dishes. A pasta or risotto specialty is featured every day at lunch and at dinner, along with a low-fat, low-calorie selection and a vegetarian dish.

Late-night buffets aboard the Princess ships are themed, with fish and chips following London Pub Night, a pasta party, a pizza party, a champagne fountain and Crepes Suzette on French Night, and a gala buffet among the other offerings.

Meals are served in two assigned seatings, with dinners somewhere between 6-6:30 p.m. for first seating, 8–8:30 p.m. for second seating. Breakfast and lunch are also served at assigned seatings when the ships are at sea, but may be open seating when the ship is in port. Your travel agent should request your seating preference when booking. All Princess dining rooms are smoke-free.

Pizzerias that cook pizzas and calzones to order are aboard some of the line's ships (see "Signatures").

The captain's gala dinner may offer Sevruga Malossol caviar, shrimp cocktail, liver pâté Strasbourg and fresh fruit cup with Triple Sec, following by a choice of three soups, a salad, ravioli with porcini mushroom sauce, rock lobster tail, salmon en croute, pheasant breast flambé or tournedos, along with four desserts plus cheese and fruit. Wine prices aboard are generally reasonable.

Meals in the dining room and pizzeria are usually somewhat better than the buffets, but the latter are improving. The new *Sun Princess* is leading the way to better cuisine on board.

Showtime.............................. A

Princess pioneered elaborate multimedia shows with film clips projected onto screens beside the stage and pre-recorded "click track" sweetening to swell the musical accompaniment. As other lines began using many of the same techniques, the company started updating its entertainment to include Nolan Miller costumes (he did the wardrobe for TV's

"Dynasty"), sometimes with as many as 60 costume changes a show (nearly as many as Joan Collins made each week).

The audience gets to participate in the popular "Love Boat Legends," playing on all the line's ships, with 24 passengers selected from volunteers who audition the first day, rehearse all week and join the cruise staff and entertainers in performing the last night of the sailing.

Perhaps the most sensational production is *Mystique*, an innovative and elaborately costumed production with a company of 23 performers including nine European and Asian acrobats, set under the sea in Atlantis, with inflatable scenery that literally "grows" in front of your eyes; it's remarkable. *Mystique* appears only on board the *Crown Princess*, *Regal Princess*, *Star Princess*, and *Sun Princess*.

Big Band music, a splashy new Caribbean revue, a show-biz production called *Let's Go to the Movies*, a full lecture program, trivia quizzes, "Baby Boomer" theme nights, London Pub Night and A Night at the Races fill out the fun.

On the new *Sun Princess*, big-name entertainers are scheduled for some sailings.

Discounts . . . .

Love Boat Savers are discounts that take off from $500 to $1150 per person from the cruise-only price, but the offer is restricted to residents of the U.S. and Canada. The lowest fares are for the earliest bookings; discounts may decrease as the sailing date approaches. Discounts vary according to the price and season.

Frequent cruisers who belong to the Captain's Circle are mailed notices on special savings for designated sailings, including deals like two-for-one buys, 50 percent off for the second passenger in a cabin or free upgrades.

The Bottom Line

Princess prides itself on little extra details that make a cruise more luxurious, such as stocking each passenger cabin with robes to be used during the sailing, a bowl of fresh fruit replenished daily, CNN on cabin TV sets, designer toiletries, pillow chocolates and 24-hour room service.

Housekeeping aboard all the ships is excellent and service generally good, particularly in the dining room where Italian waiters and captains really seem to enjoy taking special orders and preparing tableside dishes such as Caesar salad and crêpes suzette.

All in all, these are good cruises for almost everyone except fussy foodies and families with infants.

Princess' familiar flowing-haired logo atop the funnel of the **Crown Princess.**

Crown Princess ★★★★★
Regal Princess ★★★★★

"Euclid alone / Has looked on beauty bare." Edna St. Vincent Millay

The most beautiful ship interior we ever saw was the Crown Princess dome when it was under construction at the Fincantieri shipyard in Italy in early 1990. Architect Renzo Piano walked us through the pristine space that from the outside forms the "dolphin brow" of the ship. Inside it resembles what Piano called "the inside of a whale," with polished, rounded bone-colored ribs arching from ceiling to floor framing wide curved glass windows. As Piano talked about metaphor and magic, we stroked the silky, eggshell finish of the glossy plaster ribs.

> *When we came back to Europe a few months later to sail on the maiden voyage, the dome was filled with slot machines and potted palms, red leather chairs and cocktail tables. It was never so beautiful again.*

This elegant pair of ships, while similar in size to sister ship *Star Prince* are far from identical to her. They were built in Italy's Fincantieri yard, whi *Star Princess* came out of France's Chantiers d'Atlantique.

The *Crown Princess* and *Regal Princess* are unmistakable, even at a dis tance, because of their sloped, dolphin-like brow and strong vertical funne Controversial Italian architect Renzo Piano dislikes too much emphasis o the dolphin-like shape he designed—"A ship is a ship, it's not a dolphin."

The vertical funnel, a bold departure from the broad raked funnels o most of the Love Boats, he terms "a frank, clear, strong statement...and works beautifully, by the way, to take the smoke away."

If an award were given for spacious cabins, these ships would win hanc down. Cocktail lounges on board are lovely, as is a wine-and-caviar bar, a pa tisserie/sidewalk cafe in the lobby, a wonderful shopping arcade and a wel planned show lounge with fairly good sightlines except from the back of th main lounge.

CHAMPAGNE TOAST

On our most recent visit to these ships, the wood bars at eye level that had once sabotaged the observation facility of The Dome had been removed and lower wooden benches put in their places. Now the area really works as an observation lounge; finally, passengers are using it during the daytime as well as after dark.

The Brochure Says

"Her teak is from Burma, her marble from Carrera, and her fittings were forged by Italian craftsmen in shipyards over 200 years old...a masterpiece of the sea created by one of the world's most gifted architects."

Translation

Just what it says. These ships are the the the last word in design and decor, luxurious, graceful, stylish and very comfortable, and they whisper about their $200 million-plus price rather than shout it the way Carnival's megaliners do.

EAVESDROPPING

One purportedly cruise-savvy matron to her friend just after boarding, "Don't they have to go three miles out before they can open the bars? I'm sure they do." (PS: They don't.)

Cabins & Costs

Fantasy Suites: . . . . A+
Average Price PPPD: $409 plus airfare on Caribbean sailings.

Top accommodations are the 14 suites, each with a double-size private veranda large enough for two lounging chairs with a small table between as well as a bigger table with two chairs, ideal for private breakfasts in the sun and sea breeze. A wide wooden doorway divides the living room with its sofa, chairs, tables and mini-refrigerator from the bedroom with its king-sized bed (which has a single mattress top rather than the two divided mattresses one usually gets when two beds are pushed together). Each room has its own TV set. A large dressing room lined with closets and enough storage space for an around-the-world cruise leads to the spacious marble bathroom with separate bathtub and stall shower. The toilet and second lavatory are adjoining, with another door that opens for the living room so it can double as a powder room when you're entertaining.

A prettily furnished deluxe cabin on the **Regal Princess.**

Small Splurges: ....A

Average Price PPPD: $369 plus airfare in the Caribbean.
The category A mini-suites with private veranda are a bit smaller on both balcony and interior, but still very comfortable with bed (twins or queen-sized), sitting area with sofa and chairs, TV, mini-refrigerator, bath with tub and shower and spacious closet space.

Suitable Standards: ....A

Average Price PPPD: $235 in the Caribbean plus airfare.
Category GG outside double cabins forward on Plaza Deck provide queen-sized beds and a convenient location, but there are only four of them. All the standards contain amenities usually found only in suites—mini-refrigerators, remote-control TV sets, guest safes and walk-in closets. Baths have showers only. Other standards offer two lower beds that can be made into a queen-sized bed.

Bottom Bunks: ....A

Average Price PPPD: $200 in the Caribbean plus airfare for category M, $230 for category G.
Even the lowest category inside double cabin, the M category forward on Plaza Deck (only steps away from the lobby), measures 190 square feet and contains the same amenities and furnishings as the mid-range standards (see "Suitable Stan-

dards," above). The cheapest outside cabins are category G on Fiesta Deck with upper and lower berths and portholes instead of windows.

In winter, the *Crown Princess* cruises the Southern Caribbean roundtrip from Ft. Lauderdale on 10-day itineraries calling at Nassau, St. Thomas, Guadeloupe, Barbados, Dominica, St. Maarten and the private beach at Princess Cays. For the summer Alaska season, she repositions through the Panama Canal, then sails every Saturday on a seven-day Gulf of Alaska sailing between Vancouver and Seward. For fall, she returns to the Caribbean with another Panama Canal sailing.

The *Regal Princess* sails the Panama Canal and the Caribbean in winter. For the summer Alaska season, she repositions through the Panama Canal, then sails every Saturday on a seven-day Gulf of Alaska sailing between Vancouver and Seward. For fall, she returns to the Caribbean with another Panama Canal sailing.

This is an exquisite pair of ships, and generally everything runs smoothly. Newly embarking passengers are serenaded by a Filipino string trio and greeted by white-gloved stewards to escort them to their cabins. Everything you need to know is spelled out in the daily "Princess Patter" programs or advance cruise materials mailed ahead of time, making these very good vessels for first-time cruisers. With the improvements in The Dome (see "Champagne Toast"), Piano's vision seems clearer, although a lot of the magnificent view windows between the "whale ribs" are still blocked by slot machines. As for people who worry that there's nothing to do on a cruise, we'd like to take them on a stroll around these ships at almost any hour of the day or night, and they'd never fret again.

Five Super Places

1. The chic 1930s-style cocktail lounges on promenade deck, the Adagio on the *Regal*, the Intermezzo on the *Crown*, where you half-expect to see Cary (but not Hugh!) Grant at the next table.

2. The Italian garden ambience in the Palm Court Dining Room on the Regal Princess, with its ivy-patterned carpet, pastoral garden murals and pastel rose and teal decor.

3. The Patisserie in the three-deck atriums, the true gathering spot on the ships (architect Piano had hoped The Dome would fill that function but it doesn't); you can get cappuccino and espresso all day long, accompanied by freshly baked pastries, and observe the comings and goings of fellow passengers.

4. The Bengal Bar aboard the *Regal Princess* takes you back to the raj with wicker chairs, ceiling fans and a life-sized Bengal tiger, plus some tiger balm—a menu of rare single malt whiskies or a classic Bombay Sapphire gin martini, all under $4.

5. The Presto Pizzeria on the *Crown Princess* with its Italian food-and-wine print red tablecloths, red-and-white glazed tile walls and natural teak floors, warm and inviting, serving five types of pizzas including vegetarian, plus calzones, garlic focaccia and Caesar salad, open 11 a.m. to 5 p.m., then again from 9 p.m. to 1 a.m.

Dancing in The Dome on the Regal Princess.

Three Off-the-Wall Things to Do

1. Order one of the zany drinks from the boldly illustrated menu in Characters Bar, perhaps the Strip & Go Naked or Ta Kill Ya Sunrise.

2. Converse with the talking elevators, which announce each deck and caution you when you exit to watch your step.

3. Check out the photo of ex-president George Bush on board wearing a *Regal Princess* cap and chatting with Captain Cesare Ditel; you'll find it with other trophies in the corridor between the library and the Stage Door lounge.

Five Good Reasons to Book These Ships

1. To see the spectacular shows, especially *Mystique*, go to the pizzeria afterwards, talk about the performance show with other audience members, then watch the stars come in for an after-show snack.

2. To get scuba certification in the New Waves program; the course costs $370 and passengers must sign up ahead of cruise departure or at the very beginning of the cruise.

3. To attend a captain's cocktail party where you don't have to stand in line for ages to shake hands and be photographed with the captain; on these ships everyone circulates throughout the three-deck atrium, drinks in hand, and anyone who wishes to be photographed can pose on the curved staircase for the ship's photographer.

4. To spend a day at a private beach in Mayreau or Princess Cays.

5. To get more spacious cabins for the money than almost anywhere else afloat.

Five Things You Won't Find on Board

1. A gym or spa with sea views.

2. Jogging permitted before 8 a.m.

3. Locked bookcases; Princess trusts these passengers not to steal books or games.

4. The best seats for the show in the front row; third row from the back, one level up from the main seating area, is better.

5. Captain Stubing (although his alter ego, Princess spokesman Gavin MacLeod, does show up sometimes).

PRINCESS CRUISES

Crown Princess / Regal Princess ★★★★★ / ★★★★★

Registry	Liberia
Officers	Italian
Crew	International
Crew	696
GRT	70,000
Length (ft.)	811
Beam (ft.)	105
Draft (ft.)	26
Passengers-Cabins Full	1792
Passengers-2/Cabin	1590
Passenger Space Ratio	44.02
Stability Rating	Good to Excellent
Seatings	2
Cuisine	Continental
Dress Code	Traditional
Room Service	Yes
Tip	$7.75 PPPD, 15% automatically added to bar checks

Ship Amenities

Outdoor Pool	2
Indoor Pool	0
Jacuzzi	4
Fitness Center	Yes
Spa	Yes
Beauty Shop	Yes
Showroom	Yes
Bars/Lounges	6
Casino	Yes
Shops	4
Library	Yes
Child Program	Yes
Self-Service Laundry	Yes
Elevators	9

Cabin Statistics

Suites	14
Outside Doubles	604
Inside Doubles	177
Wheelchair Cabins	10
Singles	0
Single Surcharge	150-200%
Verandas	184
110 Volt	Yes

PRINCESS CRUISES

Golden Princess

NOTE: The *Golden Princess* is scheduled to retire from the fleet December 1996.

We'll always think of this ship as the Royal Viking Sky, an elegant seagoing lady, and remember sailing her to the Norwegian fjords and North Cape, watching the Norwegian crew grow warm, fulsome and joyous as they got closer and closer to home. Another summer we saw her in Stockholm in her startlingly garish livery as the Birka Queen, looking over-rouged and altogether inappropriate. ("The Finns were cooking sausages in the sauna!" sniffed one beauty salon attendant who had stayed aboard). The ship came back to Miami in 1991-92 for a humiliating season as NCL's Sunward, making three- and four-day cruises to the Bahamas, then reverted to her new Finnish owners, Birka Line. They leased her in 1993 to Princess to make Alaska sailings as the Golden Princess, which called for a major renovation, and when we visited her in Ketchikan, she looked like her old self again. Thank you, Princess, for treating her like a lady.

Through her various name changes, the *Golden Princess* has lost her original single-seating dining room. The area now offers two seatings, standard for Princess, with an extra lounge area called the Rendezvous filling what used to be the outer dining room. It's used for daytime activities and before-dinner seating with cocktail service and live music. Part of the former dining room has been turned into a children's playroom, and another space opposite it into a six-game video arcade. Pretty area rugs, another Princess touch, have been worked into each hallway by the elevators, and the casino is much bigger than in the old RVL days, despite an Alaska restriction that closes it down in state waters.

"Sun-loving, activity-minded guests will also appreciate her two sparkling pools, spa, sauna, paddle tennis court, driving range and fitness center."

Translation

The passengers on board are a lot younger and more active than the Royal Viking passengers used to be.

Fantasy Suites: .... A

Average Price PPPD: $827 plus air add-on for an Australia/New Zealand itinerary.
Category AA suites with veranda provide a large living room with leather sofa and two or three chairs, table, desk, TV set, mini-refrigerator, bath with Jacuzzi tub and shower, separate bedroom with twin or double bed, divided bathroom with tub and lavatory in one area, toilet and a second lavatory accessible from both bedroom and living room to double as guest powder room. Storage space is plentiful.

Small Splurges: .... C+

Average Price PPPD: $518 plus air add-on for an Australia/New Zealand itinerary.
Category C deluxe outside doubles on Promenade Deck have a fabric sofa, two chairs, coffee table and mini-refrigerator in the sitting area, two lower beds, desk/dresser and chair in the sleeping area. The bathroom has a tub with shower.

Suitable Standards: .... C+

Average Price PPPD: $428 plus air add-on on an Australia/ New Zealand itinerary.
Category FF outside double cabins on Atlantic Deck are typical of the modular inside and outside doubles on board, with two lower beds, one made up as a sofa during the day, a desk/dresser with stool and two chairs, TV and a bath with tub (in most cabins; a few have shower only).

Bottom Bunks: .... C+

Average Price PPPD: $341 plus air add-ons on an Australia/New Zealand itinerary.
Remember the magic word "modular." The very cheapest K category inside is the same size with the same furnishings as the FF above, except you'll have a shower instead of a bathtub.

DID YOU KNOW?

A popular Drink of the Day is a Bailey's Banana Colada, an accidental discovery that happened when a passenger ordered a piña colada made with Bailey's Irish Cream, and the bartender dropped a banana in the blender by mistake but served the drink anyhow.

The *Golden Princess* sails Alaska, Hawaii and Mexico until the end of 1996, when she retires from the fleet.

The Bottom Line

Only slightly larger than the *Island Princess* and *Pacific Princess*, the *Golden Princess* so appeals to the same audience, who prefer their ships smaller and less showy. Instead f big lavish production shows that this stage can't handle, you'll have more variety shows d passenger-participation events. On the other hand, lines are short to nonexistent, it's sy to find a sunny or shaded lounger on deck, and there's a well-qualified youth coun-lor in the playroom. Don't get too excited about the *Golden Princess*, however, since er days in the fleet are numbered; she'll be history by the time a couple of the new Love oats now under construction are delivered.

Golden Princess ★★★

Registry	Bahama
Officers	Italian/British
Crew	Internationa
Complement	41(
GRT	28,00(
Length (ft.)	67-
Beam (ft.)	8:
Draft (ft.)	2-
Passengers-Cabins Full	101)
Passengers-2/Cabin	83(
Passenger Space Ratio	33.7:
Stability Rating	Good to Excellen
Seatings	:
Cuisine	Continenta
Dress Code	Traditiona
Room Service	Ye:
Tip	$7.75 PPPD, 15% automatically added to bar checks

Ship Amenities

Outdoor Pool	:
Indoor Pool	(
Jacuzzi	1
Fitness Center	Yes
Spa	Yes
Beauty Shop	Yes
Showroom	Yes
Bars/Lounges	3
Casino	Yes
Shops	4
Library	Yes
Child Program	Yes
Self-Service Laundry	Yes
Elevators	5

Cabin Statistics

Suites	9
Outside Doubles	342
Inside Doubles	64
Wheelchair Cabins	0
Singles	0
Single Surcharge	150-200%
Verandas	9
110 Volt	Yes

Island Princess
Pacific Princess

We once sailed aboard that most legendary of Love Boats, the Pacific Princess, into the equally legendary city of Casablanca. Play it again, Captain Stubing. It makes you wonder what becomes a legend most. Casablanca looked nothing like the film of the same name, but then the movie was shot on the studio backlot and nothing in it looked like Casablanca anyhow. And there we were on the Love Boat in a cabin that bore no resemblance whatsoever to the palatial accommodations where Lana Turner, Ethel Merman, Stewart Granger, Anne Baxter and all the other gone-but-not-forgotten guest stars lived during their cinematic cruise. Those cabins are on the back lot too, along with Rick's cafe and Paris and the whole thing.

The aft pool deck on **Pacific Princess** *gets a lot of sunbathing action.*

Princess takes very good care of its hardware, and these two dowagers of the fleet have undergone plenty of facelifts over the years. The most recent ones, 1992 for the *Pacific Princess* and 1993 for the *Island Princess*, not only introduced new colors and fabrics throughout the cabins and public rooms but also brought operational and technical systems up to date.

In the showrooms, new tiered floors were added to improve sightlines; gyms were moved from the port side of Riviera Deck to the starboard side where some of the slot machines used to be, and furnished with all-new equipment; casino space was improved and a video arcade added. Cabins were totally refurbished and furnished with TVs, new telephones and hair dryers.

"Following the design standard set by our newest ships, these timeless vessels are resplendent with woolen carpets and custom fabrics in tones of aquamarine, rust, burgundy and blue."

Translation
The interior decoration on the *Crown Princess* and *Regal Princess* turned out so well they decided to go back and add some of its details to the older ships. Good idea!

DID YOU KNOW?
According to Princess president Peter Ratcliffe (try to say that seven times without tripping), the line's most popular dessert is Grand Marnier Soufflé, so the menus during most cruises will offer as many as five different dessert soufflés.

Fantasy Suites: .... P
Average Price PPPD: $727 plus air add-on in Pacific and South America.
Two of the four top suites are forward on Promenade Deck with a captain's-eye view; the other two are aft on the same deck. Each contains a separate sitting area with sofa and chairs, coffee table, dining table and chairs, mini-refrigerator and TV set, plus a bathroom with tub and shower and a bedroom with twin beds.

Small Splurges: C
Average Price PPPD: $637 plus air add-on in Pacific and South America.
The mini-suites in B category are a bit smaller but cheaper, and there are nine of them, two facing forward, and seven more aft. All have sitting area with sofa and coffee table, sleeping area with two lower beds, mini-refrigerator, color TV, hair dryer and bathroom with tub and shower.

Suitable Standards: .... D
Average Price PPPD: $399 plus air add-on in Pacific and South America.
The standard outside double cabins on these ships are small—there's no getting around that (or much getting around in that)—many of them only 126 square feet. They have a sofa that converts to a bed and a second recessed lower bed that slides

under the sofa/bed. There's also a built-in counter, desk/dresser with stool, TV set, bath with shower and adequate but far-from-generous closet space.

Bottom Bunks: . . . . **D**

Average Price PPPD: $351 plus air add-on in Pacific and South America.
The K category inside doubles on Fiesta Deck are really not any smaller than the outside doubles (see "Suitable Standards") and with the same furnishings basically. They just don't have a window or porthole.

Island Princess starts the year with some exotic itineraries in Southeast Asia and moves on to South Africa.

For summer, the *Island Princess* sails the Mediterranean, Baltic and Aegean.

Pacific Princess sails in the Caribbean and South America, then crosses to spend the summer in the Mediterranean.

While the cabins on these two ships are quite small compared to the rest of the fleet, the intimate quality of life onboard makes up for it for passengers who don't want to travel aboard a megaship. The recent $40 million refurbishment for the pair totally redecorated them in the style of the newer, more elegant vessels. An appealing range of exotic cruises from 10 to 23 days will attract Love Boat veterans, especially older couples and singles, who have time and money to go shopping and country-collecting.

Island Princess ★★★
Pacific Princess ★★★

Registry	Britis
Officers	Britisl
Crew	Internationa
Complement	35
GRT	20,00
Length (ft.)	55
Beam (ft.)	8
Draft (ft.)	2
Passengers-Cabins Full	72
Passengers-2/Cabin	61
Passenger Space Ratio	31.2
Stability Rating	Good to Excellen
Seatings	
Cuisine	Continenta
Dress Code	Traditiona
Room Service	Ye
Tip	$7.75 PPPD, 15% automaticall added to bar check

Ship Amenities

Outdoor Pool	
Indoor Pool	
Jacuzzi	
Fitness Center	Ye
Spa	N
Beauty Shop	Ye
Showroom	Ye
Bars/Lounges	
Casino	Yes
Shops	4
Library	Ye
Child Program	Ye
Self-Service Laundry	Ye
Elevators	5

Cabin Statistics

Suites	4
Outside Doubles	234
Inside Doubles	67
Wheelchair Cabins	0
Singles	0
Single Surcharge	150-200%
Verandas	0
110 Volt	Yes

Royal Princess ★★★★★

In a simpler, more romantic time back in 1984, the glowing, recently wed Princess Diana christened the Royal Princess, and while the bloom may be off the royalty these days, the Royal Princess is as lovely as ever, proving that class acts last. The inaugural sailing was a media event, with an episode of "The Love Boat" being filmed aboard, as well as a segment of "Lifestyles of the Rich and Famous," starring Connie Stevens (her first cue card read, "Hi, I'm Connie Stevens"), and a number of regional and local TV teams, including a then-little-known host of "AM Chicago" named Oprah Winfrey.

DID YOU KNOW?

Passengers vied with each other on the inaugural cruise through the Panama Canal to work all day for nothing as extras on "The Love Boat," and more passengers were usually inside watching the filming than outdoors watching the canal transit they'd booked the cruise to see.

The *Royal Princess* began as a study design for "the most advanced cruise ship ever built" from the research and design team headed up by Kai Levander at Wartsila in Helsinki, Finland. In a radical design departure for a ship this size, all 600 cabins are outside on upper decks, while the public rooms are located below them, and 150 staterooms have private verandas overlooking the sea.

This was the first ship to introduce private balconies in quantity, adding them to cabins as well as suites and mini-suites. This was also one of the first ships to offer twin beds that could easily be put together into one queen-sized bed. One of the two outdoor swimming pools allows energetic passengers to swim laps instead of just plunge in and get wet. The other is a cluster of pools and whirlpools that is reminiscent of the Crystal pool aboard the *Pacific Princess.*

Circles and curves are a recurring motif—the overlapping large and small circles of the Lido Deck spa pools, the rippling circles of the International

Lounge spreading outward from the dance floor, the arc of the double sta
way leading down into the dining room and the graceful curved stairways
five aft decks.

DID YOU KNOW?

Captain Ian Tomkins, who often served aboard the Royal Princess *before his retirement, compared her handling to "dancing with a beautiful lady in a crinoline dress when a Viennese waltz is playing."*

The Brochure Says

"Her series of terraced observation areas both fore and aft, her acres of teak decks ar her lavish, floor-to-ceiling windows make her the perfect ship for experiencing the Pan ma Canal."

Translation

With the expansive deck areas, big windows and numerous private verandas, the *Roy Princess* is indeed ideal for the Panama Canal or any other close-in cruising where t view is important.

Cabins & Costs

The gala suites aboard the **Royal Princess** *have large private verandas.*

Fantasy Suites: . . . . A

Average Price PPPD: $962 in the Panama Canal, including airfare.

The 806-square-foot Royal and Princess, the pair of penthouse suites aboard th *Royal Princess*, were once the largest suites at sea, and while they may have bee eclipsed in size by more recent vessels, they're still among the most posh. The cate gory AA suites contain whirlpool tubs in a huge tiled and mirrored bathroom, si ting room with picture window, separate bedroom with queen-sized bed, a dinin table and chairs, TV/VCR, mini-refrigerator, Oriental rugs and original art, plus a big private veranda.

Small Splurges: .... A

Average Price PPPD: $649 in the Panama Canal, including airfare.

A category B mini-suite with private balcony has twin beds that convert to queen-sized, sitting area with sofa and chairs, balcony with two chairs and a table plus a stretch-out lounger, picture window, bath with tub and shower, dressing area, plenty of closet space, TV and mini-refrigerator.

Suitable Standards: .... B

Average Price PPPD: $384 to $406, depending on cabin location, on a Panama Canal cruise, including airfare.

An outside double has twin beds that convert to queen-sized, built-in desk/dresser with stool, an easy chair and table, bathroom with tub and shower, color TV and mini-refrigerator. If you want to see the sea from your picture window, stick to categories EE, E, F or G. One of the twin beds folds into the wall during the day to give more floor space inside the cabin.

Bottom Bunks: C

Average Price PPPD: $334 to $349, depending on cabin category, on a Panama Canal Cruise, including airfare

While there are no inside cabins on the *Royal Princess*, some of the outsides have very limited views because of lifeboats hanging outside—notably, categories JJ, J and K, which have windows totally obscured by boats. Still, you'll get enough daylight in to tell day from night and probably enough sky view to get a read on the weather without going out on deck. Otherwise, furnishings and size are identical to the cabins previously discussed (see "Suitable Standards").

INSIDER TIP

Princess restricts the number of wheelchair passengers to six per cruise on this ship. While the staterooms can accommodate a standard wheelchair (22"-23" in width) the bathroom floor rises seven inches above the cabin floor. Public rooms and decks are accessible and some public restrooms are designed to accommodate wheelchairs.

Where She Goes

Royal Princess makes Panama Canal transits in winter and spring between Acapulco and San Juan; the 10- and 11-day itineraries include calls at Puerto Caldera, Cartagena, St. Maarten and St. Thomas eastbound, and at St. Thomas, Martinique, Grenada, La Guaira (for Caracas) and Curaçao westbound.

For summer, she will return to Europe, where she offers cruises from 12 to 19 days long. A new Scandinavia/Russia itinerary spends two full days in St. Petersburg and calls in Stockholm, Helsinki, Amsterdam and Denmark. The Atlantic/Mediterranean itinerary includes Santorini, Rome, Florence/Pisa, Barcelona, Monte Carlo, Gibraltar, Vigo and Lisbon.

In fall, *Royal Princess* sails to New England and Canada, then comes back in early winter for more Panama Canal sailings.

The Bottom Line

An elegant ship, the *Royal Princess* presents a seamless blend of classic liner and contemporary cruiser with the best features of each. British officers host dining tables on every cruise, with the kind of first-class courtesy and attention an around-the-world passenger would expect. The natural teak decks provide generous strolling, lounging and games space, and the top deck Horizon Lounge opens up splendid views in three directions. For those passengers with private verandas, one of the most pleasurable parts of a day is to sit in the fresh breezes looking at the ocean, wearing pajamas and robe if you like.

It's hard to find fault with the *Royal Princess*, but we'll do it anyhow. The Lido buffets, as on several of the other ships, are disappointing, but the cafe itself is delightful with its bright tile-topped tables and contemporary patio chairs. Thankfully the aft end of Lido deck has been partially enclosed to get rid of the wind tunnel effect.

Now that we've got that out of the way, let us confess—this was our favorite Princess ship, at least until we saw the new *Sun Princess*.

Fielding's Five

Five Elegant Areas

1. The Plaza and Princess Court is a two-deck atrium from the early days of atria, centered with a sculpture called *Spindrift*, a polished arc with soaring birds, waterworn rocks and splashing fountain, and surrounded by cushy chairs and the strains of piano music.

2. The Horizon Lounge with its angled glass window walls overlooks everything to see at sea, but at night turns into a disco, with dancing, a DJ station and projectors and screens around the U-shaped room.

3. The Lido Bar, only steps away from the cluster of pools and Jacuzzis, will always remind us of the late Stewart Granger, who used to order an entire pitcher of Bloody Marys made to his own recipe, then walk around the deck refilling glasses for sunbathing passengers.

4. One of the first top-deck beauty and fitness centers, The Spa is built on Sun Deck between the lap pool and a second, smaller pool with sunbathing platform, and offers massage, sauna, beauty salon and gym.

5. The two acres of teak decks, especially the long sweeping curves of the stern stairways, five beautiful decks of them, that draw the eye inevitably up to the curved stack on top.

Five Good Reasons to Book This Ship

1. She's a classic beauty, perhaps the last of her kind in these days of floating hotels.

2. To have a front-row seat on your own private balcony going through the Panama Canal.

3. To make an entrance—down the curved staircase in the Plaza Foyer, down the stairs into the dining room from the Terrace Room or along the stern deck stairs, which was the setting for Lana Turner's "wedding" to Stewart Granger on "The Love Boat."

4. To have a watery wonderland choice from among three outdoor swimming pools and lots of Jacuzzis.

- To be able to do your morning walk around a full promenade deck, rarer than ever these days.

Five Things You Won't Find on Board

. An inside cabin.

2. Everybody up early and out on deck; veranda cabin passengers linger inside until late morning, usually breakfasting on their private balcony.

3. Cabins with shower only.

4. A pizzeria.

5. Prince Charles.

Royal Princess ★★★★★

Registry	British
Officers	British
Crew	International
Complement	520
GRT	45,000
Length (ft.)	757
Beam (ft.)	106
Draft (ft.)	26
Passengers-Cabins Full	1323
Passengers-2/Cabin	1200
Passenger Space Ratio	37.5
Stability Rating	Good to Excellent
Seatings	2
Cuisine	Continental
Dress Code	Traditional
Room Service	Yes
Tip	$7.75 PPPD, 15% automatically added to bar checks

Ship Amenities

Outdoor Pool	3
Indoor Pool	0
Jacuzzi	2
Fitness Center	Yes
Spa	Yes
Beauty Shop	Yes
Showroom	Yes
Bars/Lounges	5
Casino	Yes
Shops	4
Library	Yes
Child Program	Yes
Self-Service Laundry	Yes
Elevators	6

Cabin Statistics

Suites	14
Outside Doubles	580
Inside Doubles	0
Wheelchair Cabins	0
Singles	0
Single Surcharge	150-200%
Verandas	150
110 Volt	Yes

Sky Princess

The TSS Sky Princess, *constructed in 1984 in France's CNM shipyard near Toulon as Sitmar's* Fairsky, *was the last big steam turbine passenger ship to be built, probably the last that will ever be. TSS means turbine steamship, and while steamships are more expensive to operate than motor ships, they also offer a smoother, quieter ride. "She has an underwater body that is a masterpiece," said one of the officers who oversaw her construction. Smooth-riding but unfinished, she had to slip out of the shipyard in the dead of night, according to some crew members aboard at the time, because shipyard workers, fearful of losing their jobs when the project was done, were sabotaging their own work, building things during the daytime and breaking them again at night. The interior finishing was completed on the long crossing from France to Los Angeles.*

The welcome-aboard buffet on the Sky Princess *in Alaska was far more lavish than the other Love Boats.*

Sky Princess was one of the early ships to be decorated by a team of designers, some of them noted for hotel rather than naval architecture. As a result materials such as silk wall coverings, burled blond wood paneling, marble Venetian glass and glove leather upholstery (instead of the Naugahyde prevalent then on many cruise ships) and subtle, harmonious shades of beige gray, pale sage greens and soft rose were introduced into a sea of cheerful Scandinavian woolens in coral, marine blue and bright green. A recent refurbishment has kept the original design features virtually intact.

DID YOU KNOW?

When Sitmar operated the ships that became Sky Princess, Dawn Princess *and* Fair Princess *(only the* Sky Princess *remains in the fleet today) the late Boris Vlasov, who owned the line, insisted that white Swedish rubber rather than carpet lined all the stairwells, so passengers could see how clean everything was kept.*

"Passengers looking for comfort and understated elegance need look no further tha the *Sky Princess.* Ultra-spacious, her casual, easy-going atmosphere pleases everyone fro couples to teens."

Translation

Cabins aboard are larger than on the *Island, Golden* or *Pacific Princess,* the decor sub tle, and the friendly Italian waiters like to joke with passengers. Children and teens find lot to like aboard, including three pools, a fully supervised youth and teen center and th pizzeria, of course.

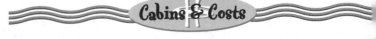

Fantasy Suites: . . . . A

Average Price PPPD: $774 plus air add-on in the South Pacific.
Book one of the 10 AA category suites and you'll enjoy a private veranda as well a a separate living room with leather loveseat, four leather chairs, glass-and-chrom dining table, long marble-topped desk, stocked mini-bar and mini-refrigerator an TV. In the bedroom is a queen-sized bed (except Malaga and Amalfi suites, whic have twin beds), robe and slippers, marble nightstand with four drawers, a dressin room with marble-topped table, three-way mirror, leather chair, big safe, built-i dressers with six drawers each, and two separate hanging closets with safes in each The marble bathroom has a deep Jacuzzi tub.

Small Splurges: . . . . B

Average Price PPPD: $608 plus air add-on in the South Pacific.
Category B mini-suites on the Lido don't have private verandas but they do hav picture windows, a bedroom with twin beds and wooden nightstand with two draw ers, and a sitting room with long leather sofa, three leather armchairs, desk/dresse with marble inset, color TV, handsome marble lamp with linen shade, cabinet fo bar glasses, mini-refrigerator, plenty of good mirrors, two full-length hanging clos ets with safe and bath with shower and long marble counter.

Cabin 148 is a Category C outside double.

Suitable Standards: .... C+

Average Price PPPD: $387–$424 plus air add-on in the South Pacific; price varies depending on deck location and whether cabin is inside or outside.
All the standard inside and outside cabins are similar, with twin beds, nightstand, desk/dresser, two chairs, small table, generous closet space and bathroom with shower. Nearly half also have optional pull-down berths for third and fourth occupants. Six cabins are designated wheelchair accessible, including C 207 and C 208, outsides which are slightly larger than standards, with no lip on the doors, a shower with seat and pull bars, a roll-under sink, lower handles on the closets and a low-hanging rod accessible from a wheelchair; very wide inside with three windows.

Bottom Bunks: .... C+

Average Price PPPD: $358 plus air add-on in the South Pacific.
The category M inside doubles are the least expensive accommodations on board, but are still fairly spacious and similar to the "Suitable Standards". Two lower beds, TV, very large closets, bath with shower, desk/dresser with chair and a second chair with small table.

INSIDER TIP

Library books must be checked in and out on the Sky Princess, and anyone planning to abscond with an unfinished novel faces a $50 fine added to his cabin account.

DID YOU KNOW?

Don't try this at home! The Love Boat cocktail is a blend of tequila, creme de cacao, Galliano, grenadine and cream.

Sky Princess cruises the Caribbean and into the Panama Canal without transiting it in winter, offering 10-day itineraries round trip from Ft. Lauderdale, calling in Playa de Carmen/Cozumel, Limon, Cartagena and the private beach at Princess Cays.

Some longer 15-day Ft. Lauderdale-Los Angeles sailings are also available, calling in Montego Bay, Cartagena, Puerto Caldera, Acapulco and Cabo San Lucas.

In summers, she sails the Gulf of Alaska on seven-day itineraries with Monday departures between Vancouver and Seward.

In fall, she moves into the Far East, with Orient, Asia, Hawaii and South Pacific itineraries.

This ship, one of the most elegant at the time of its inaugural sailing in 1984, has held up very well. The top deck indoor spa, including a whirlpool with raised stairs, was one of the first top deck, glass-walled spas; before that, indoor pools and a modest exercise area were usually found on a bottom deck amidships.

While the deck areas show their age in spots—worn astroturf, oil-stained teak—the interiors are as clean and pristine as when the ship was new.

Sky Princess is particularly good for families with children because the cabins with upper berths are spacious enough you won't feel cramped and because the child-care and teen programs on board are so well-arranged. The Youth Center is particularly pleasant with linoleum floor, lie-down sofas and sturdy play tables. The Teen Center has lots of curved banquettes and game tables with industrial lamps overhead and a video game room with six games. The two dining rooms are light and bright with big windows, so if you're lunching during Alaska whale-spotting or Gatun Lake sightseeing, you won't miss much. The buffets on this ship are much more elaborate than most of the others.

Five Special Spots

1. Veranda Lounge, the venue for dancing before and after dinner, is a lovely room with its swirl marbleized carpet in gray and teal, with teal leather and fabric chairs, teal glass-topped tables with leather trim, sheer Austrian shades at the windows and pale wood walls.

2. The Pizzeria with its black bentwood chairs with red seats, big tile kitchen decorated with faux salamis, cheeses and hams, big round booths big enough for six or eight, and atop every table jars of crushed red pepper and oregano. For people who want a full lunch, a blackboard promotes a soup of the day and a pizza of the day.

3. The Horizon Lounge, an observation lounge with a forward-facing wall of windows, lots of cushy leather chairs in teal and caramel, and squashy cushions in the window ledges for additional seating with a view.

4. A beautiful library with two separate reading rooms, each with deep black leather chairs and wood-paneled walls, along with curved modern desks in wood and black leather for writing diaries or postcards.

6. The intimate little Melody Bar with its long granite bar lined with black leather swivel barstools, burled wood and mirrors on the walls, a perfect little hideaway for two.

Five Good Reasons to Book This Ship

1. The Pizzeria for its made-to-order pizza.

2. The big, lavish showroom with its thrust stage where you might see comedian Dick Gold, harmonica virtuoso Harry Bee, the juggling Zuniga Brothers and the Love Boat singers and dancers.

3. To buy some Lladro porcelain in the new Alaska-themed pieces, Eskimos ice-fishing and such; Lladro must sell like crazy on cruise ships if the Spanish are creating whole new groups. What's next? The characters from "The Love Boat"?

4. To compete in the passenger talent show.

5. To experience the smooth ride of the last passenger steamship ever built.

Five Things You Won't Find on Board

1. Alcoholic drinks available for 18-to-21 year-olds.

2. Silent elevators—the ones on the *Sky Princess* talk to you.

3. No full promenade deck all around the ship; the green astroturf-covered walking deck (no jogging) says 11 times around its perimeter is one mile and the textured dark red jogging track above the Sun Deck says 15 laps is a mile.

4. Marble bathroom counters on inside cabins.

5. Gambling within a three-mile limit of the Alaska coastline.

Sky Princess   ★★★★

Registry	**British**
Officers	**British**
Crew	**International**
Complement	**535**
GRT	**46,000**
Length (ft.)	**789**
Beam (ft.)	**98**
Draft (ft.)	**25**
Passengers-Cabins Full	**1806**
Passengers-2/Cabin	**1200**
Passenger Space Ratio	**38.33**
Stability Rating	**Good to Excellent**
Seatings	**2**
Cuisine	**Continental**
Dress Code	**Traditional**
Room Service	**Yes**
Tip	**$7.75 PPPD, 15% automatically added to bar checks**

Ship Amenities

Outdoor Pool	**3**
Indoor Pool	**0**
Jacuzzi	**1**
Fitness Center	**Yes**
Spa	**Yes**
Beauty Shop	**Yes**
Showroom	**Yes**
Bars/Lounges	**5**
Casino	**Yes**
Shops	**4**
Library	**Yes**
Child Program	**Yes**
Self-Service Laundry	**Yes**
Elevators	**6**

Cabin Statistics

Suites	**10**
Outside Doubles	**375**
Inside Doubles	**215**
Wheelchair Cabins	**6**
Singles	**0**
Single Surcharge	**150-200%**
Verandas	**10**
110 Volt	**Yes**

PRINCESS CRUISES

Star Princess

It was a unique experience to tour France's Chantiers de L'Atlantique shipyard in late 1988, to see a ship nearing completion that began life as Sitmar's FairMajesty and by a stroke of a pen was turned into Princess' Star Princess overnight. That's why the Star Princess is not just like its sister ships Crown and Regal. When P&O bought Sitmar in July 1988, it acquired one ship under construction and two others on the drawing board, so because of the long planning and building time—two to three years—all three ships still carry many Sitmar characteristics, including Italian instead of British officers.

Particularly memorable for us was sailing aboard the Star Princess inaugural cruise with her godmother, the late Audrey Hepburn, as a fellow passenger.

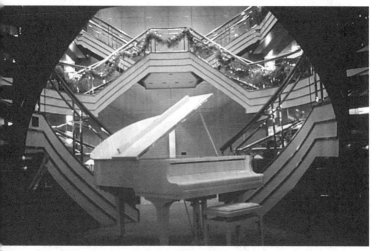

The atrium lobby and piano are framed by a dramatic staircase.

The *Star Princess* has one of the best pool-and-sun decks at sea. It runs most of the length of the vessel and stars two large swimming pools spanned by a raised sun deck. The area is filled out by an aft buffet cafe and a forwar bar and pizzeria. Overall, she heralded a "new Princess," bigger, brighte livelier than her predecessors, with a wider appeal and more accessibility t younger passengers than any of the previous ships from either Princess (Sitmar. A little more than a year after *Star Princess* first entered service, it median passenger age was seven years lower than the line's fleetwide average

A three-deck atrium with a stainless steel kinetic sculpture dominates th amidships area. This is the vessel that first introduced the very popular La Pa tisserie cafe and pastry shop in the lobby area.

The spa, beauty salon, gym and massage areas, on the other hand, were re egated to below-decks without windows rather than given a prominent an sunny spot atop the ship as on the *Sky Princess*.

The Brochure Says

"...*Star Princess* also offers some of the largest standard staterooms in the industry Connoisseurs of fine cruising will be dazzled by this modern-day floating resort."

Translation

An apt description. It's hard to think of anything you'd get at a big Caribbean resor hotel that you can't find on the *Star Princess*, except for sand between your toes.

Cabins & Costs

Fantasy Suites: . . . . A

Average Price PPPD: $464 in the Caribbean including airfare.
The 14 AA category suites are top-of-the-line, measuring 530 square feet and named for popular Mediterranean ports. Inside the sliding glass doors is an open, L shaped room divided into sitting and sleeping areas with sofa, two chairs, coffee table, queen-sized bed, nightstands and built-in desk. There's plenty of closet and storage space, two TV sets, a dressing room with mahogany built-in dressing table and large mirror, a spacious marble bathroom divided so the tub, separate shower stall and wash basin can be closed off to let the toilet and second wash basin double as powder room. A mini-bar is stocked with complimentary beverages, and a mini-refrigerator keeps everything cold.

Small Splurges: . . . . B

Average Price PPPD: $407 in the Caribbean including airfare.
The 36 category A mini-suites are 370 square feet each, with private veranda, sitting area with built-in desk and counter as well as sofa and chairs, and a large bath with tub/shower combination.

Suitable Standards: . . . . A

Average Price PPPD: $221–$285 in the Caribbean, including airfare.
All cabins aboard have twin beds that can be rearranged into one queen-sized bed, walk-in closet and separate dressing area, refrigerator and mini-bar, guest safe, ter-rycloth robes, hair dryers and color TV. Both outsides (with picture windows) and insides are the same size—180 square feet. Ten are designated wheelchair-accessible, and these measure 240 square feet with extra-wide doors and no thresholds.

Bottom Bunks: . . . . A

Average Price PPPD: $157 in the Caribbean, including airfare.
The cheapest cabins are M category with two lower beds, only seven of them, located forward on Plaza Deck. Furnishings are the same as "Suitable Standards."

Where She Goes

Star Princess sails the Eastern Caribbean on a seven-day roundtrip itinerary out of Ft. Lauderdale, calling in Nassau, St. Thomas, St. Maarten and the private beach at Princess Cays in winter and spring.

In summer the ship cruises the Gulf of Alaska, sailing on Mondays for a seven-day itinerary between Vancouver and Seward.

Before and after the summer, the ship repositions through the Panama Canal and returns to the Caribbean for seven-day sailings.

The pool deck on the **Star Princess** *has a very popular waterfall.*

The Bottom Line

When a ship is this perfect for warm-weather cruising, we're puzzled as to why Princess sends it up to Alaska in the summer. But wherever it goes, it's a natural magnet for families and younger cruisers.

Fielding's Five

Five Great Places

1. The Lido Deck pools have a raised sunbathing deck between the Oasis pool, with its waterfall and in-pool bar, and the Paradise pool, which is flanked by four whirlpool spas.

2. Characters, a colorful Lido Deck bar serving up outrageous drinks, both alcoholic and non-alcoholic, including a margarita big enough for four in a goldfish bowl-sized glass with four straws.

3. Windows to the World, a circular glass-walled observation lounge above the bridge where The Dome is located on the Crown and Regal, doubles as an observation

lounge and after-dark entertainment center with music. The French shipyard work ers called it Le Camembert because its round shape reminded them of a cheesebox

4.   The Club House Youth Center and Off Limits Teen Center get a lot of space, mak ing this a good ship for kids and teens.

5.   The Sports Deck, with its basketball, volleyball and paddle tennis court, jogging track, state-of-the-art gymnasium and aerobics room.

Five Good Reasons to Book This Ship

1.   You can spend all day on the pool deck for optimum fun in the sun.

2.   It's a great place for kids, who keep busy with supervised activities from 9 a.m. to midnight, plus a kids- only wading pool.

3.   Teens have their own social life on board, with special hours in the adult disco, the chance to film an episode of "Love Boat," Italian lessons, arts and crafts, video games, karaoke talent shows and PG-13 movies nightly.

4.   A museum-quality art collection of contemporary works valued at $1 million plus.

5.   You'll be traveling with younger passengers that get involved with a more active shore excursion and onboard sports program.

Five Things You Won't Find Aboard

1.   A small intimate bar for a quiet getaway for two.

2.   Fuddy-duddies.

3.   An ocean view from the gym or the disco; they're on a lower deck hidden away for privacy and noise control.

4.   Smoking in the dining room or show lounge.

5.   The very expensive swan logo commissioned for this ship by Sitmar shortly before Princess bought the company.

Star Princess ★★★★

Registry	Liberia
Officers	Italian
Crew	International
Complement	600
GRT	63,500
Length (ft.)	805
Beam (ft.)	105
Draft (ft.)	27
Passengers-Cabins Full	1838
Passengers-2/Cabin	1490
Passenger Space Ratio	42.61
Stability Rating	Good to Excellent
Seatings	2
Cuisine	Continental
Dress Code	Traditional
Room Service	Yes
Tip	$7.75 PPPD, 15% automatically added to bar checks

Ship Amenities

Outdoor Pool	3
Indoor Pool	0
Jacuzzi	4
Fitness Center	Yes
Spa	Yes
Beauty Shop	Yes
Showroom	Yes
Bars/Lounges	3
Casino	Yes
Shops	4
Library	Yes
Child Program	Yes
Self-Service Laundry	Yes
Elevators	9

Cabin Statistics

Suites	14
Outside Doubles	570
Inside Doubles	165
Wheelchair Cabins	10
Singles	0
Single Surcharge	150-200%
Verandas	50
110 Volt	Yes

PRINCESS CRUISES

Sun Princess
Dawn Princess

★★★★★

☆☆☆☆☆

> *It was love at first sight when we walked aboard the Sun Princess, still under construction in Italy's Fincantieri shipyard. An orchestra was playing, the magnificent marble atrium glowed with polished brass and an Italian barman was handing out cups of freshly made cappuccino. Later, we would see the many unfinished sections of the vessel, but for that one magic moment, it was as if the ship were completed and ready to sail."*

The first of the new Grand Class ships for Princess, the *Sun Princess* at her debut was the largest cruise ship in the world. Two sister ships are upcoming, *Dawn Princess* in the spring of 1997 and *Sea Princess* for early 1999, plus, of course, the world's largest cruise ship on the record, the 104,000-ton *Grand Princess*, due in 1998. The most remarkable thing about the *Sun Princess* is that when you're aboard, she really doesn't seem as large as she is, 77,000 tons and carrying 1950 passengers. Nobody ever seems to be standing in line; even the captain's welcome aboard cocktail party is held in the soaring four-deck central atrium, allowing passengers to enter immediately at any level from any direction. Sunbathing space on deck is generous, and 410 of the cabins have their own private verandas. A full-time gardener tends to the $1 million-plus worth of plants on board.

The Brochure Says

"We're also taking a great Princess tradition and making the ultimate luxury, a stateroom with a private balcony, affordable for everyone. With up to 80 per cent of outside accommodations—over fifteen hundred staterooms—featuring private balconies, (this ship) truly opens up a new world in cruising: Cruising in Grand Style!"

Translation

Princess pioneered the concept of private verandas for more than just penthouse suites ᴴen the *Royal Princess* was introduced in 1984. Now, aboard the *Sun Princess*, almost ᵉryone gets a private veranda.

ᴀntasy Suites: ....**A+**

Average PPPD: $464 in the Caribbean, including airfare.
Six spacious aft suites, each measuring between 536 and 754 square feet, with private balcony, separate bedroom, large living room, dining table with four chairs, wet bar, granite counter, big divided bath with stall shower and Jacuzzi tub, dressing room, desk/makeup area in bedroom, two TV sets, mini-refrigerator.

ᴹmall Splurges: ....**A**

Average PPPD: $407 in the Caribbean, including airfare.
Thirty-two mini-suites are almost as lavish, with private veranda, sitting area with sofa and chair, queen-sized bed, walk-in closet, two TV sets, bath with tub and shower and mini-refrigerator.

ᴹuitable Standards: ....**A**

Average PPPD: $299 in the Caribbean, including airfare.
The least expensive cabins with private balconies also have twin or queen-sized bed, big closet, desk/dresser with chair, TV and mini-refrigerator.

ᴰottom Bunks: ....**A**

Average PPPD: $267 in the Caribbean, including airfare.
The smallest inside doubles are a comfortable 175 square feet with two lower beds that can convert to queen-sized, desk/dresser, chair, bath with large tile shower and generous storage space.

Where She Goes

The *Sun Princess* cruises the Western Caribbean in winter on seven-day round-trips ᶠrom Ft. Lauderdale, calling in Montego Bay, Grand Cayman, Playa del Carmen/Cozumel and Princess Cays. In summer, the ship goes to Alaska for Inside Passage sailings ᵂeekly from Vancouver, calling in Juneau, Skagway and Sitka. She is the largest ship ever ᵗo sail in Alaska.

The Bottom Line

While the ship and its technology are cutting edge, traditional touches are everywhere—the Wheelhouse Bar with its ship models from the P&O archives, a "museum" of opera costumes in glass cases outside the theater, Queen Mary deck chairs on the natural teak promenade deck, and handsome real wood laminates in cabins and public rooms. The deck space is broken up into different levels with free-form "islands" of green Astroturf resembling landscaping. The casino is huge, but is not permitted to dominate the ship. While passengers are aware of where it is, they are not forced to constantly walk through it. The ship works extremely well and rides very smoothly.

Five Favorite Spots

1. Verdi's, an elegant pizzeria that resembles a terraced winter garden with its verdigr wrought iron trim.

2. The Horizon Court, a gala buffet area serving food 24 hours a day, plus a night alternative dinner menu with table service and music for dancing from 7:30 p.m. t 4 a.m.

3. The magnificent Princess Theatre, as professional as anything on Broadway or in th West End, with flawless sightlines from every seat.

4. The Vista Lounge, a second show lounge arranged in a cabaret style, again with per fect sightlines from every seat because of a cantilevered ceiling designed withou support posts underneath.

5. The elegant Compass Rose piano bar with its wood paneled walls and rich uphol stered banquettes and chairs.

Five Good Reasons to Book This Ship

1. To be able to dine in the Horizon Court when you don't feel like dressing up fo the dining room.

2. To see brilliant entertainment in a professional theater with red plush row seats from the Schubert Theater in Los Angeles.

3. To participate in the New Waves watersports program with a scuba certificatio course and snorkeling instruction.

4. To enjoy really delicious pizza baked to order in Verdi's.

5. To try out the "listening chairs" in the library, the sophisticated golf simulator ($1! for 9 holes at Mauna Kea) or browse among the $2.5 million worth of art, all com missioned especially for the ship.

Sun Princess ★★★★★

Registry	**Italian**
Officers	**Italian**
Crew	**International**
Complement	**900**
GRT	**77,000**
Length (ft.)	**856**
Beam (ft.)	**106**
Draft (ft.)	**26**
Passengers-Cabins Full	**2270**
Passengers-2/Cabin	**1950**
Passenger Space Ratio	**39.48**
Stability Rating	**NA**
Seatings	**2**
Cuisine	**Continental**
Dress Code	**Traditional**
Room Service	**Yes**
Tip	**$7.75 PPPD, 15% automatically added to bar checks**

Ship Amenities

Outdoor Pool	**4**
Indoor Pool	**1**
Jacuzzi	**5**
Fitness Center	**Yes**
Spa	**Yes**
Beauty Shop	**Yes**
Showroom	**Yes**
Bars/Lounges	**7**
Casino	**Yes**
Shops	**7**
Library	**Yes**
Child Program	**Yes**
Self-Service Laundry	**Yes**
Elevators	**11**

Cabin Statistics

Suites	**6**
Outside Doubles	**597**
Inside Doubles	**408**
Wheelchair Cabins	**18**
Singles	**0**
Single Surcharge	**150-200%**
Verandas	**411**
110 Volt	**Yes**

PRINCESS CRUISES

PRINCESS CRUISES

RADISSON SEVEN SEAS
C R U I S E S

600 Corporate Drive, Suite 410, Fort Lauderdale, FL 33334
☎ *(305) 776-6123, (800) 333-3333*

History . . . .

This hybrid cruise line with three very different ships—what they have in common is superlative quality—came about through a series of marketing agreements. Radisson, of course, is a long-time hotel brand name which entered the cruise industry with the first major twin-hulled cruise vessel, the 354-passenger *Radisson Diamond*, owned by Finland's Diamond Cruise Inc., which debuted in 1992. Seven Seas was a San Francisco-based company marketing the elegant little 172-passenger *Song of Flower*, a Sea Goddess-like ship owned by Japan's "K" Line freight and container company under its "K" Line America subsidiary in New Jersey, and the 188-passenger *Hanseatic*, arguably the most luxurious expedition vessel in the world, is owned by Germany's Hanseatic Cruises. Radisson Seven Seas Cruises was launched January 1, 1995, with 500 employees in the Ft. Lauderdale-based offices of the former Radisson Diamond Cruise.

—First cruise ship to be christened in the stern; it has no discernible bow. (*Radisson Diamond*, 1992, Greenwich, England).

Concept . . . .

Radisson Seven Seas says it aims to bring together three ultra-deluxe ships, exotic destinations worldwide and innovative shipboard programming to create three distinct styles of luxury cruising offering excellent service, intimate ambience and strong value for the dollar throughout the fleet.

Signatures . . . .

The *Radisson Diamond's* twin hull is an unmistakable sight in every port in the world, warranting at least a double-take if not a "What the hell is that?" Less known but almost equally unique is the ship's policy of using female rather than male servers in the dining room.

Song of Flower is among a handful of luxurious cruise vessels that distinguishes itself by not proffering tabs to be signed; virtually everything on board from bar beverages to tips is included. You pay extra only for laundry, beauty shop services, casino gambling and shop purchases. The distinctive blue lyre on the ship's twin funnels is now the logo for the entire line.

The *Hanseatic* is notable for its state-of-the-art environment-saving features, including an advanced non-polluting waste disposal system and
pollution-filtered incinerator which enable it to call in remote and environmentally sensitive areas.

Gimmicks . . . .

The *Radisson Diamond's* "An Evening at Don Vito's" is the liveliest
and most delicious of all the cruise line alternative restaurants, with
waiters in red aprons singing "O Sole Mio" between serving up bites of
everything that comes out of the special Italian kitchen that evening.

A "welcome back" libation greets *Song of Flower* passengers at the gangway when they return from grueling shore excursions—cold lemonade
or chilled champagne if it's a hot day in Southeast Asia, hot chocolate,
hot buttered rum or mulled wine if it's a cold day in the Black Sea.

A "passenger bridge" on the *Hanseatic* is furnished with ocean charts
and radar. In addition, passengers are free to visit the ship's real bridge
whenever they wish.

Who's the Competition . . . .

The *Hanseatic* faces competition only from the *Bremen*, also a state-of-
the-art expedition vessel which cruises with a similar mix of Europeans
and North Americans. *Song of Flower* was competing mainly with the
Sea Goddess ships until the debut of Silversea; now *Silver Cloud* and *Silver Wind*, although somewhat larger, are rivals. Seaborn also provides
a bit of competition but lacks the all-inclusive policy that makes the
other ships appealing to luxury-loving penny-pinchers. As for *Radisson
Diamond*, that's a different situation entirely; it would seem to compete
more with shoreside resorts and tours than other ships, except perhaps
its own associate *Song of Flower*. Word of mouth has been the primary
factor in attracting more and more passengers to these three vessels.

Who's Aboard . . . .

On all three ships, upscale middle-aged couples are the major passengers, along with older singles and younger, baby boomer pairs. *Radisson
Diamond* has a number of incentive groups aboard on some sailings—
the ship was originally created for that market but has found a huge
acceptance from individual travelers as well. *Hanseatic's* luxurious version of soft adventures attracts a more cosmopolitan crowd than the
earnest expedition types who like to rough it.

Who Should Go . . . .

People who don't like the idea of having to tip—tips are already
included in the fares on all three vessels but passengers may offer additional money for special service at their own discretion.

People who worry about ship motion triggering seasickness should try
the smooth-riding, twin-hulled *Radisson Diamond* with its four computer-operated, non-retractable stabilizers that correct pitch and roll
after only one degree.

Who Should Not Go

There are some ship purists who would never set foot on the *Radisson Diamond* because of its boxy shape and twin hulls, and we can understand that reluctance, but it offers one of the finest food and hotel operations at sea, and when you're aboard, you're not really looking at its shape, are you?

The ships reserve the right to limit the number of children on board, but all except very mature teens and well-behaved 10-to-12-year-olds should not be aboard in any case.

The Lifestyle

What the three ships have in common is a small number of passengers in a relaxed but luxurious atmosphere with impeccable service and very good food. Entertainment, while it is provided, is a minor concern, as are casinos and gift shops, while enrichment lecturers, beauty services, fitness centers and alternative dining options are major on-board pluses.

Tips are included in the basic fares on all three ships, which makes the interrelationship between crew and passenger less forced, and all three provide a single open seating at mealtimes, letting passengers sit where and with whom they please.

Wardrobe

All three ships are relatively dressy, except that the *Hanseatic* says it wants the penguins to wear the tuxedos, and male passengers are perfectly O.K. in a dark suit. That's fine, but they also hint that they want him to be in a jacket, not necessarily with a tie, every night. The other vessels are a little more laid-back, with formal night meaning black tie or its equivalent, but casual nights dotted throughout the cruise where no jacket and tie at all are necessary.

Bill of Fare . . . . A+ to B+

The *Song of Flower* and *Radisson Diamond* outshine the *Hanseatic* a bit in the kitchen, but perhaps that's because they're dealing with a more homogenous passenger list and don't mind pushing the envelope when they've found something really interesting they want people to taste. On the *Radisson Diamond*, passengers are served beautiful meals in the most gorgeous dining room at sea, but when they wish, they can book the alternative dining experience, "An Evening at Don Vito's," a rollicking, finger-licking evening of home-cooked Italian food where you end up sampling a little bit of everything. The *Song of Flower* chefs and waiters are the ones we'd hire to run our own mansion if we were rich and famous.

Cuisine Report Card:

Radisson Diamond A+

Song of Flower A+

Hanseatic B+

Showtime . . . . B

Even on the *Hanseatic*, there's life after dinner, what with a quartet playing for dancing and an occasional folkloric troupe showing up to perform esoteric routines they learned from a Peace Corps voluntee But showtime is not bigtime on these smallish ships, and it shouldn be. We enjoy the singer/dancer foursome that performs on the *Radi son Diamond's* scenery-less stage, as well as the amiable variety artis who double as shore excursion escorts on the *Song of Flower*, but thes ships are not Broadway nor were meant to be. They're luxurious hid aways where you might just as soon spend an evening dining wit friends or having dinner brought into your cabin and watching a vide film.

Discounts ....

Early booking bonuses of $500 per person off the listed fares are i effect for the *Hanseatic* if you book by designated deadlines, and yo get $500 off if you combine two back-to-back cruises. *Song of Flowe* offers from $250 to $2050 per person for early bookings made 12 days before sailing, and includes free round-trip airfare and many sho excursions in its base rate. Combine two or more cruises back-to-bac to total 15 nights and subtract another $1500. On *Radisson Diamon* selected sailings deduct 50 percent of the fare of the second passeng in the cabin, plus adding airfare and free overnights on pre- and pos cruise stays.

The Bottom Line

We can think of no other cruise line that has three such dissimilar but ver comparable ships. They're all small, intimate and upscale, with flawless Eu ropean service and excellent food, fascinating itineraries and lavish accom modations. More remarkably, they give you a lot of value for the admittedl top-market prices. Strange bedfellows? Perhaps, but what they have in com mon is more important than how they are different from each other.

At the end of 1997, a fourth, all-new ship, totally unlike the other three joins the fleet for year-round cruises in the South Pacific. The 320-passenge vessel has 80 cabins with private balconies.

Hanseatic ★★★★★, ⚓⚓⚓⚓⚓

"Penguins, whales, seals—we can guarantee you'll see them," the captain says cheerfully. On this autumn stopover in San Diego, he's between a successful transit of the Northwest Passage and the beginning of the Antarctic season, and feeling particularly chipper because he believes the Hanseatic, the largest ship ever to make the transit, has established a new time record for it—14 days. We find ourselves remembering not only a much longer transit on a less sophisticated ship a decade before but also the constant wondering about whether we'd make it through at all.

Until the last year or so, the ship was marketed primarily in Germany and still attracts a mixed bag of Europeans and North American passengers who laud the no-tipping policy, polished European serving staff and open bridge rules which allow passengers access to the navigational bridge at all times. Elegant and luxurious, with spacious cabins and beautifully decorated public rooms, the *Hanseatic* seems almost too lavish for an expedition ship, but who says you have to rough it just because you're going into the wilderness?

The Brochure Says

"After a day of observing penguin rookeries, (a passenger) could ease into the glass-enclosed whirlpool or enjoy a relaxing massage and sauna; perhaps snuggle up with a favorite book from the library, order room service and enjoy the view from the picture window of his spacious stateroom. For guests on Bridge Deck, there's the added luxury of private butler service."

Translation
Wake me when the Northern Lights come on, Jeeves.

RADISSON SEVEN SEAS CRUISES

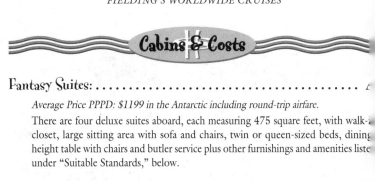

Cabins & Costs

Fantasy Suites: .... *£*

> *Average Price PPPD: $1199 in the Antarctic including round-trip airfare.*
>
> There are four deluxe suites aboard, each measuring 475 square feet, with walk-in closet, large sitting area with sofa and chairs, twin or queen-sized beds, dining height table with chairs and butler service plus other furnishings and amenities listed under "Suitable Standards," below.

Small Splurges: .... N∤

> It's not necessary to splurge on this ship; the standards are more than adequate.

Suitable Standards: .... *£*

> *Average Price PPPD: $649 to $980 in the Antarctic, depending on cabin category including airfare.*
>
> Each accommodation, even the least expensive, has twins or queen-sized bed, marble bathroom with tub and shower, a separate sitting area with chaise or sofa, TV set with VCR, writing desk, hair dryer, mini-refrigerator stocked with non-alcoholic beverages and generous closet and drawer space. The standards measure 23 square feet.

Bottom Bunks: .... N∤

N/A

DID YOU KNOW?

Although the full capacity of the ship is 188, the line claims it never cruises with more than 170 passengers.

Where She Goes

The *Hanseatic* goes to the ends of the earth—literally. The ice-hardened vessel cruises from the Arctic to the Antarctic, and is as equally at home in Spitsbergen or Patagonia, the Galapagos or the South Georgias. She begins her year in the Antarctic, then sails north.

The Bottom Line

The *Hanseatic* is an elegant and luxurious ship with rich wood-toned paneling in all cabins and public rooms and spacious staterooms, all outsides with windows or portholes. It's also an extraordinarily tough expedition ship with a 1A1 Super ice class rating, just one notch below the icebreaker classification. A friendly young European staff and a very high crew-to-passenger ratio of one crew member to every 1.4 passengers mean the service is exemplary, and the food, while not cutting-edge contemporary, is quite tasty. A thumbs-up recommendation!

Five Record-Breaking Rooms

- In the Explorer Lounge with its pretty upholstered, wood-framed tub chairs and leaf-patterned carpet, a quartet plays for dancing before and after dinner, and a pianist accompanies afternoon tea.

- Darwin Hall is a large and comfortable lecture room that doubles as a cinema; this is where the experts tell you about the local wildlife—and we don't mean pub-crawling.

- Casual breakfast and lunch buffet service takes place in the Columbus Lounge with its rattan chairs and big windows.

- The Marco Polo Restaurant manages a miracle—it seats all the passengers at once with every chair near enough to one of the big windows to watch the scenery go by.

- Passengers have their own "bridge" to monitor the ship's route and progress on ocean charts and a radar monitor in the glass-walled observation lounge with its 180-degree view.

Five Good Reasons to Book This Ship

- Because they leave the tuxedos to the penguins—male guests need only wear a dark suit for formal nights—but it's still the dressiest expedition vessel afloat, with jackets requested for men every night.

- Because they supply the parkas and rubber boots you need to go ashore in polar regions; you don't have to go and buy bulky gear you'll probably never use again and figure out how to pack it to get it to the ship.

- Because they carry 14 Zodiacs to take you ashore or cruising around an iceberg.

- Because you can travel with the ease of knowing you and your vessel are doing nothing to damage the environment.

- Because shore excursions are included.

Hanseatic ★★★★★, ⚓⚓⚓⚓

Registry	**Bahama**
Officers	**Europea**
Crew	**Internationa**
Complement	**12**
GRT	**9,00**
Length (ft.)	**40**
Beam (ft.)	**5**
Draft (ft.)	**15.**
Passengers-Cabins Full	**18**
Passengers-2/Cabin	**17**
Passenger Space Ratio	**52.9**
Stability Rating	**Good to Excellen**
Seatings	
Cuisine	**Continenta**
Dress Code	**Informa**
Room Service	**Ye**
Tip	**Included in far**

Ship Amenities

Outdoor Pool	**?**
Indoor Pool	**?**
Jacuzzi	**?**
Fitness Center	**Ye**
Spa	**N**
Beauty Shop	**Ye**
Showroom	**N**
Bars/Lounges	**2**
Casino	**N**
Shops	**?**
Library	**Ye**
Child Program	**No**
Self Service Laundry	**No**
Elevators	**1**

Cabin Statistics

Suites	**4**
Outside Doubles	**86**
Inside Doubles	**0**
Wheelchair Cabins	**2**
Singles	**0**
Single Surcharge	**150%**
Verandas	**0**
110 Volt	**No**

Radisson Diamond   ★★★★★

The first time we ever saw the Radisson Diamond *the brand new ship was moored in Tilbury, the Port of London, and right next to her was the long, sleek* Royal Princess. *The effect was like seeing the short wide robot R2D2 from* Star Wars *hanging around with Cary Grant.*

The swimming pool on **Radisson Diamond.**

The *Radisson Diamond* has a unique SWATH design—Small Waterplane Area Twin Hull—with an extra-wide superstructure atop two pontoons. There are four special-design stabilizers, two forward and two aft, inside the well, permanent rather than retractable, and computer-controlled to negate rolling, pitching and heaving. The vessel roll is only one-fifth that of a conventional monohull ship with one-tenth of the noise and vibration levels, the captain says.

Inside, the extra-wide beam gives a great sense of spaciousness. A cent
atrium with stairs and two glass elevators makes it simple to get around tⁱ
ship; all the passenger cabins and public rooms are clustered around it.
rubberized, nonskid jogging track, spa, beauty salon, fitness center, golf pⁱ
ting area and driving cage are on the upper deck areas, and a self-containⁱ
watersports marina allows passengers to go water-skiing, windsurfing, sailiⁱ
or riding wave runners when sea and weather conditions permit.

"The *Diamond* is truly one-of-a-kind, the only twin-hull passenger vessel in the worl
Her innovative design offers you a smooth and stable cruise. This unique configuratiⁱ
allows us to provide our guests with more spacious surroundings than any ship at sea."

Translation

They're so proud of their ship they've got to exaggerate a little. It is innovative aⁱ
spacious, but not completely unique. There are several twin-hull passenger vessels thⁱ
have been around longer than the *Radisson Diamond*, although none of the others aⁱ
quite as large. The 49-passenger *Executive Explorer*, for instance, has been carrying paⁱ
sengers for more than a decade and was still in business when we saw her in Alaska a feⁱ
months ago. And while the *Diamond's* passenger space ratio of 57.33 is impressive, it
still smaller than the *Europa's* 61.68.

Fantasy Suites: . . . . A

Average Price PPPD: $952 including airfare from the east coast.
A hand-painted mural in the style of Henri Rousseau decorates each of a pair ⁱ
master suites measuring 522 square feet, with a large sitting area with puffy paⁱ
blue leather sofa, two chairs, a full-sized desk, mini-refrigerator, fully stocked liquⁱ
cabinet and TV/VCR. A king-sized bed has a beige and blue coverlet with greⁱ
hounds stitched on it; a sliding etched glass panel can close off the bedroom froⁱ
the entry hallway and closet area. On the private veranda outside are two chairs anⁱ
a table. The bathroom has a double basin in a marble counter, separate water closeⁱ
stall shower and Jacuzzi tub.

Small Splurges: . . . . Aⁱ

Average Price PPPD: $660 including airfare from the east coast.
Most of the cabins on board have private balconies, and in 243 square feet you'ⁱ
find queen-sized or twin beds, a sitting area with sofa, chairs and built-in desk,
marble bathroom with tub and shower—short, deep Finnish-style tubs—and TVⁱ
VCR, minibar and refrigerator and built-in dresser and storage area.

Suitable Standards: . . . . Aⁱ

Average Price PPPD: $532 including airfare from the east coast.
The third cabin type aboard is the same size as the veranda cabin (243 square feet
but with a larger sitting area instead of the veranda. You'll have a white leather sofⁱ
and two chairs, built-in desk and dresser, wide window wall and marble bathrooⁱ
with tub/shower combination. Two cabins are designated wheelchair-accessible.

ɔttom Bunks: .... NA
N/A

Where She Goes

The *Radisson Diamond* transits the Panama Canal between Puerto Rico and Costa
ɔa in winter, making nine-day cruises that visit St. Thomas, Curaçao, Cartagena and the
n Blas Islands, along with a two-night overland excursion to San Jose and the Poas Vol-
ɲo. These cruises are followed by a series of Caribbean sailings out of San Jose that
ɹge from four to 14 nights. The vessel's crossing sets out in April, followed by seven-
ɟht Mediterranean sailings between Rome and Barcelona, and a series of seven-night
ltic Republics cruises between Stockholm and Copenhagen. The ship then makes its
·stbound transatlantic crossing back to the Caribbean in autumn.

n art deco style bar with chrome barstools aboard the **Radisson Diamond.**

The Bottom Line

We chose to sail on a transatlantic cruise to see how the ship rides in the sometimes-
ugh Atlantic. At first the sea was smooth, but as we got closer to Portugal it turned
ɩoppy. While there was no traditional roll or pitch, the ship would start into a rolling
ɔtion, only to have the stabilizers correct it after one degree. We think the motion in
ɩugh seas for a passenger walking or standing is similar to standing aboard a moving
ɹin.

Despite the ship's unconventional looks, it offers a supremely appealing cruise experi-
ʌce. Our eleven days on the crossing were gloriously relaxing without any ports of call.
'hy eleven days, you may ask? The ship's maximum comfortable cruising speed is only
ɔout 12 or 13 knots; she'd never win the Blue Riband.

Fielding's Five

Five Splendid Spots

1. The Grill, a cluster of several teak-floored rooms with glass walls to the deck both sides, where buffet breakfasts and lunches supplemented with cooked-to-ord à la carte dishes are served at wooden tables; it turns into Don Vito's most evenin with red tablecloths, singing waiters and a constantly changing Italian menu.

2. In the coolly elegant Club, mushroom-colored leather chairs trimmed in ebon mirrors and potted palms, lend a movie-set 1930s look; you expect to see Willia Powell and Myrna Loy make an entrance.

3. The most romantic dining room at sea is wide and airy and almost two decks hig with plenty of tables for two against an aft window wall, gilt frame armchairs wi striped silk upholstery, art deco pillars and a 1930s frieze of figures, all in tones copper, silver and bronze. On the evenings when candlelight dinners are serv against a background of the fading sunset, it is indescribably lovely.

4. The Windows is a multi-level lounge with ice blue leather furniture, black gran bars and silver and gray barstools, a wide wood dance floor and raised stage wi bandstand in front of a window wall; a lavish tea is set out here every afternoon.

5. The Constellation Center, a meeting room and lecture hall with rows of red leath chairs in blond wood frames; this is where art auctions, slide lectures and fil screenings (with a big silver punch bowl of hot popcorn) take place.

Five Good Reasons to Book This Ship

1. If you're worried about ship motion that might cause seasickness, the twin hulls pr vent pitching and rolling.

2. If you're a claustrophobe worried about ships being confining, check out the ext width and spaciousness.

3. If you enjoy female servers in the restaurant.

4. To squeeze through the Panama Canal with only inches to spare on either side.

5. If you love real Italian home cooking, "An Evening at Don Vito's" trattoria pass around trays of antipasto, followed by platters of lobster risotto, penne with porci and tomato sauce and tortellini in butter and fresh sage—and those are just th starters. Then comes veal scaloppine with fresh vegetables and a rolling cart of Ita ian desserts like tirama su and cannoli, all of it served with generous complimenta portions of chilled Soave and Ruffino Chianti.

Five Things You Won't Find on Board

1. A bathtub you can stretch out in; the Finnish tubs are so short that tall bathers en up with their knees under their chins.

2. A place on deck where you can stand and watch the lines cast off; the configuratio of the ship doesn't allow a view straight down to the water.

3. A traditional lifeboat drill; instead, passengers are shown where the jackets ar stored on deck.

4. A self-service laundry.

5. A children's program.

Radisson Diamond ★★★★★

Registry	Finland
Officers	Finnish
Crew	International
Crew	192
GRT	20,295
Length (ft.)	420
Beam (ft.)	103
Draft (ft.)	23-26
Passengers-Cabins Full	354
Passengers-2/Cabin	354
Passenger Space Ratio	57.33
Stability Rating	Excellent
Seatings	1
Cuisine	Contemporary
Dress Code	Traditional
Room Service	Yes
Tip	Included in fare

Ship Amenities

Outdoor Pool	1
Indoor Pool	0
Jacuzzi	1
Fitness Center	Yes
Spa	Yes
Beauty Shop	Yes
Showroom	No
Bars/Lounges	3
Casino	Yes
Shops	1
Library	Yes
Child Program	No
Self Service Laundry	No
Elevators	2

Cabin Statistics

Suites	2
Outside Doubles	175
Inside Doubles	0
Wheelchair Cabins	2
Singles	0
Single Surcharge	115-125%
Verandas	123
110 Volt	Yes

Song of Flower   

A frequent question about Song of Flower is where the name came from. At the beginning, one of the vessel's co-owners was Meiyo Corporation, represented in the person of Miss Tomoko Venada of Kobe, very much a hands-on person whom her devoted crew called Madame. "Serving all western food was Madame's policy," one of her former executive chefs told us, "along with European chefs and serving staff, and she wanted a western rather than Japanese ambience on board...but I usually sneaked in sushi, soba (buckwheat noodles) and California rolls at the midnight buffet." Another of Madame's ideas—not currently in use—was to create glittering formal nights and masquerade parties that involved everyone. So the ship carried formal gowns, dinner jackets and tuxedos that could be rented, altered by an onboard seamstress, and worn on captain's nights. Then for masquerade night, other racks of costumes, wigs, sequins and feather boas were set out for passengers to rummage through and borrow, free, for the evening. It made for a lot of hilarity.

Song of Flower was commissioned in 1986 as the *Explorer Starship* for now-defunct Exploration Cruise Lines when she was rebuilt in a German shipyard from the hull of a ro-ro (roll-on roll-off) cargo vessel called *Begonia*. In 1989, she underwent another major refurbishment in Norway to become *Song of Flower*, a Japanese/Norwegian joint venture, and, after a February 1990 christening in Singapore, was marketed primarily in Asia for the first year.

But in 1991 the marketing emphasis switched to North America, and the ship began attracting a passenger balance of about half Asian, mostly Japanese, and half North Americans for its summer season in Alaska. In 1993, the ship was repositioned for European sailings in summer, and from that point on the vessel has sailed with predominantly western passengers. The winter cruises in Asian waters were lengthened to appeal to western preferences and varied ports of call were introduced with more of an emphasis on Oriental culture and history than holiday resorts. Although Japanese-owned, the ship carries Scandinavian officers, European hotel staff, British and

American cruise staff and entertainers, international crew and a Norwegian flag.

The Brochure Says

"On *Song of Flower* our shipboard staff takes pride in providing you with outstanding service. Enjoy many of life's finer pleasures on your voyage, each one with our compliments...order room service at any hour, cocktails in any lounge, specialty drinks poolside and fine wines to accompany lunch and dinner...all without signing a bill. We try our best to anticipate your needs rather than merely fulfill them."

Translation

You're going to get some of the best service and most relaxing vacation hours you ever spent anywhere, and there's nobody nickel-and-diming you at every turn.

The pool deck on **Song of Flower** *has recently been retiled in a handsome dark blue with teak facing.*

DID YOU KNOW?

*When it is necessary to go ashore by tender, you shuttle aboard the—are you ready?—***Tiny Flower***.*

Cabins & Costs

Fantasy Suites: . . . . A

Average Price PPPD: $889 including some airfare, tips, beverages, transfers and some shore excursions.

The top accommodations on board are two-room, two-bath suites with a living room, separate bedroom with sitting area, color TV and VCR, mini-refrigerator, dressing room, walk-in closet and two baths, one with half-tub and one with shower only. Spacious enough for entertaining, the suites have only one drawback in our eyes—no private veranda.

Small Splurges: .... A

Average Price PPPD: $835 including some airfare, tips, beverages, transfers and som.
shore excursions.
We like the top deck ocean view suites in category B for their private verandas, spaciousness (321 square feet) and full-sized bathtubs. You'll find a queen-sized bed sofa, three chairs, a desk with four drawers, a small foyer, large closets, stocked mini-refrigerator and bar, color TV and VCR, robe and slippers and bath with tub/shower combination.

Suitable Standards: .... A

Average Price PPPD: $632 including some airfare, tips, beverages, transfers and som
shore excursions.
All the cabins in C, D and E categories are similar, around 200 square feet with twins or queen-sized bed (specify which you want when booking), sitting area, desk/dresser with chair, nightstands, bathroom with half-tub and/or shower, TV/VCR, hair dryer and so on.

Bottom Bunks: .... A

Average Price PPPD: $482 including some airfare, tips, beverages, transfers and som
shore excursions.
The least expensive cabins aboard are the category F outsides available with twin beds or queen-sized bed (specify which when booking) and bathroom with shower only. You're not exactly slumming in this 183-square-foot cabin with full-length sofa, chair, coffee table, desk/dresser with chair, stocked bar, mini-refrigerator, TV/VCR and double closets.

Deck meals are served under blue umbrellas on **Song** of **Flower.**

Where She Goes

Song of Flower has some of the most fascinating itineraries in the cruise industry, since she spends her winters in Asia and her summers in Europe. She starts the year on Hong Kong-Singapore sailings that visit five ports in Vietnam, then moves on to Burma/Myanmar, Indonesia, more Burma, Borneo, the South China Sea and more Vietnam to round out the winter season. The ship moves to Europe, then spends the summer in the Mediterranean, Baltic and the Norwegian fjords, moves back into the Mediterranean for autumn, then back into Asia in late October.

The Bottom Line

We've taken three cruises on this ship as the *Song of Flower*, and one earlier as the *Starship Explorer*. The minute we walk aboard, we always experience that warm-and-fuzzy feeling of being home, and say to each other, "She looks better than ever." She's sparkling clean, impeccably run, and just plain fun. It's easy to see why she has so many loyal repeat passengers and has gone from being, "Song of *what*?!" to "Oh, yes, I've heard about *Song of Flower*, they say it's wonderful."

Fielding's Five

Five Places You'll Love

1. The dining room, where tables are always set with fresh flowers, the full gamut of silver and the biggest starched white linen napkins at sea; wonderful things arrive on your plate and waiters never hover but are always there to pull out your chair, unfold your napkin and anticipate every need.

2. The pool deck cafe is a welcoming blue-and-white haven of deck tables and chairs and big umbrellas, a grill that cooks breakfast bacon and eggs, lunchtime hamburgers and hot dogs to order, in addition to a cold buffet and made-to-order pasta.

3. The nightclub and disco is a well-mannered room in purples and pinks that gets moderate use all day long because of its big windows and luscious afternoon tea.

4. The main lounge is where the captain has his cocktail parties, the entertainers perform, the lecturers show slides and the five-piece orchestra plays for dancing. It's done in pastel tapestry upholstery with a bar at the rear, screen and projection equipment and a marble tile dance floor that doubles as a stage.

5. The library, tucked away behind the main lounge with a spiral staircase connecting it to the deck below, has apricot leather sofas and chairs, wood-and-glass bookcases always unlocked, and plenty of books and videos.

Five Good Reasons to Book This Ship

1. It's the ideal cruise ship for the 1990s after the excesses of the 1980s—elegant but unpretentious, friendly and accessible, and it provides the kind of pampering people dream about at prices lower than many of its competitors.

2. A concierge-style shore excursion staff that goes beyond selling tours into helping to arrange independent shore tours for you on an individual basis.

3. The ease of traveling where everything is included, even airfare, transfers and shore excursions, so you know up front how much your cruise is going to cost.

4. The ratio of staff to passengers, one crew member to every 1.2 passengers when the ship is full, perhaps the highest in the industry.

5. To see Komodo dragons, Krakatau, the Torajans of Sulawesi and the "wild man of Borneo," all slated on winter itineraries for *Song of Flower*.

Five Things You Won't Find on Board

1. A self-service laundry.

2. A sense of regimentation.

3. Cabins designated wheelchair-accessible; there are elevators aboard.

4. A lot of glitz and glitter.

5. Theme cruises.

RADISSON SEVEN SEAS CRUISES

Song of Flower   ★★★★★★

Registry	Norway
Officers	Norwegian
Crew	International
Complement	144
GRT	8,282
Length (ft.)	409
Beam (ft.)	52.5
Draft (ft.)	15
Passengers-Cabins Full	200
Passengers-2/Cabin	172
Passenger Space Ratio	48.15
Stability Rating	Fair to good
Seatings	1
Cuisine	Contemporary
Dress Code	Traditional
Room Service	Yes
Tip	Included in fare

Ship Amenities

Outdoor Pool	1
Indoor Pool	0
Jacuzzi	1
Fitness Center	Yes
Spa	No
Beauty Shop	Yes
Showroom	Yes
Bars/Lounges	4/3
Casino	Yes
Shops	1
Library	Yes
Child Program	No
Self Service Laundry	No
Elevators	2

Cabin Statistics

Suites	20
Outside Doubles	80
Inside Doubles	0
Wheelchair Cabins	0
Singles	0
Single Surcharge	125-150%
Verandas	10
110 Volt	No

Regal Cruises™

4199 34th Street, Suite B 103, St. Petersburg, FL 33711
☎ *(813) 867-1300, (800) 270-SAIL*

History

Regal Cruises was founded by executives from Liberty Travel and GoGo Tours in 1993 when the companies acquired the venerable *Caribe I*, "the happy ship" from Commodore Cruises, and turned it into the *Regal Empress* almost overnight. "The world's smallest cruise line" is based in St. Petersburg and is a privately-held company.

Concept

While a few longer cruises may be offered, Regal depends primarily on short-term "cruises to nowhere" for first-time cruisers and budget-minded vacationers.

Signatures

Two-day party cruises jamming onboard a capacity quota of the-more-the-merrier types.

Gimmicks

An adults-only spa to keep the kids out; candy bar bingo for the kids; 60s music and theme cruises with waitresses in poodle-cloth skirts.

Who's the Competition

There's nobody who can match the *Regal Empress's* low, low published brochure rates out of New York or St. Petersburg, Florida.

Who's Aboard

A lot of young first-time cruisers, singles and couples and families, party-hearty types who arrive ready for a good time.

Who Should Go

Just who's aboard, plus a New Yorker or West Coast Floridian who'd like a really low-priced getaway on a lovely old ocean liner with a friendly, if sometimes unpolished, staff.

Who Should Not Go

Traditional cruise veterans who have specific ideas about wardrobe and behavior; fussy eaters; people who demand top-notch service.

The Lifestyle . . . .

Cramming everything from cruises that's fun or interesting into the format. The line itself calls it "Regal Revelry on the High Seas" on the daily programs. There's a lot going on all day and a plethora of shore excursions, plus mealtimes happening every hour or so.

The dress aboard is well-groomed casual.

Wardrobe . . . .

The line specifies no tank tops or shorts in the dining room, but as often happens with first-time cruisers, they may forget to read the program and so enter in happy ignorance in inappropriate costume and are rarely corrected by the friendly crew, who don't want to hurt any potential tipper's feelings. What Regal Cruises would like to see are people who dress up a little bit for formal nights, even if it's only a jacket without a tie for men. The brochure models, always a tip-off to what the line imagines is right, are studiously casual but well-groomed, shown in polo shirts or sport coats without ties as a rule.

Bill of Fare C

Feeding times are frequent on the *Regal Empress*, with early-bird coffee at 6 a.m., dining room breakfast 7 to 9 and poolside buffet breakfast 7 to 10. Lunch open seating buffets on shore days run from 11 to 1:30 in the dining room; on days at sea lunch is served later. Teatime with sandwiches and cookies is served at 4. First seating dinner is at 6, second seating at 8:15, and there is usually a midnight buffet.

The food is delivered in generous portions, but during our time aboard did not seem particularly well prepared, especially from the buffets, where meats were dry and tough from being too long on the steam table. We may have hit an off-period, however, because friends (actually, a friend—we don't know that many other people who have ever sailed aboard this ship) says it was acceptable to good during his cruise. A newly added Pietro's Pizza Palace serves pizza, hotdogs and Cuban sandwiches.

Showtime C

The entertainment format follows the usual mass-market cruise pattern: lots of bingo and game shows with the cruise staff, dancing to the ship's orchestra, late-night disco with a DJ and a few variety artists of varying capabilities. The biggest hit aboard is the lip sync show in which passengers recruited ahead of time double in ship-provided costumes and wigs as, say, Sonny and Cher to mime "I Got You Babe" and suchlike amusements. A new "Hooray for Hollywood" revue salutes movie musicals.

NO NOs

In the show lounge on the Regal Empress, video and flash cameras are not permitted during the performance, the first two rows do not get drink service during the show and there is no smoking permitted in the entire lounge during the show.

Discounts . . . .

They don't really need to offer discounts with their low brochure prices.

The Bottom Line

You get more than you pay for on this line, partly because of the lovely old ship itself, graceful and beautiful in many areas like the library and Mermaid Bar, plus the warm and friendly crew, from the captain and hotel manager down to the ebullient youth counselor Casey and the friendly Filipino crew. It's not a fancy cruise, and isn't meant to be. You're supposed to be ready for a good time or a party-time, and Emily Post ain't nowhere in sight. Let 'er rip!

Regal Empress

Captain Uwe Bunsen, master of the Regal Empress, has been at sea for 40 years and was for many years captain of the Boheme from Commodore Cruises, which now belongs to the Scientology group, and was 28 times in the Antarctic when he worked for Society Expeditions. But the former Caribe I is his favorite ship, and now he's back with her as the Regal Empress. "She's still one of the traditional ships, with beautiful design...only the plastic is missing."

The *Regal Empress*, the former *Caribe I*, was built as the *Olympia* for the Greek Line in 1953 as a two-class ocean liner, making her maiden voyage from Glasgow and Liverpool to New York. In 1974 she was laid up in Piraeus, a victim of the overall cruise malaise brought on by the success of the transatlantic jet planes. In 1981, a German company purchased her and renamed her *Caribe*, but left her laid up in Piraeus, changing the flag from Greek to German. In 1983, with a major refit, she sailed from Piraeus to become the *Caribe I* for Commodore Cruise Lines. Very few changes have been made since she became the *Regal Empress*, so it's a wonderful experience for a ship buff to wander around and spot the beautiful spaces. A recent $3 million refurbishment makes her look spiffy.

The Brochure Says

"We take pride in our decor, a study in quiet elegance with warm woods, tasteful fabrics and the occasional Art Deco touch. The *Regal Empress* boasts some of the largest staterooms afloat."

Translation

This is a lovely old ship and even the two-day party cruisers to nowhere fall silent when they peek into the elegant library. And for the money, you can get some very nice cabins. (See "Cabins and Costs".)

*A classic wood-paneled suite aboard **Regal Empress**; you could almost imagine Fletcher Christian sleeping here.*

Fantasy Suites: .... B

Average Price PPPD: $133 cruise only in the Caribbean.

While not huge nor unrelievedly lavish, there are two suites forward on Upper Deck that call back the grand old days of ocean cruising, even perhaps the captain's quarters on the *Mayflower*, but who's counting? The Admiral Suites forward on upper deck (accept no substitutes; there are other less admirable Admiral Suites on this ship), in particular the Commodore Suite # F, has a lovely wood interior, two rooms with the bedroom separate, windows facing forward, built-in dresser, glass coffee table, hair dryer, fresh flowers, mini-refrigerator, and the sofas in the sitting room convert to beds if you want to put friends or family inside at a reduced rate.

Small Splurges: C

Average Price PPPD: $109 cruise only in the Caribbean.

The category Two deluxe mini-suites with mini-refrigerator, double bed plus two lower berths, sitting area with sofas, two windows and hair dryer are quite acceptable for the price.

Suitable Standards: .... C-

Average Price PPPD: $101 cruise only in the Caribbean.

A category Four cabin on Upper Deck may have portholes instead of windows, twin beds and an optional upper berth, but you'll also find floral bedspreads, a chair, adequate closets and a bathroom with shower only.

Bottom Bunks: .... C-

Average Price PPPD: $78 cruise only in the Caribbean.

In one of the lowest cabin categories, 10, in cabin B 24, you can find an inside with two lower beds, two dressers and two closets that will be perfectly adequate for a budget getaway for two.

Where She Goes

In the winter, *Regal Empress* sails from Port Manatee in St. Petersburg, Florida, on Mexico and Caribbean cruises to Key West, Cozumel and Playa del Carmen on four- five- and six-day cruises, some including calls in Grand Caymen and Jamaica. In summer the ship does a number of two-day party cruises out of New York, interspersed with Bermuda, Bahamas and New England/Canada sailings.

The Bottom Line

If the ship looks a little weary around the edges, think a little tenderness. She's had a long, hard life with party-time passengers who don't always appreciate her finer points. But for some impecunious people who would love to get even a tiny taste of what cruising is all about, this is a wonderful entry-level product—so long as you're not a cruise veteran who's just looking for a cheap thrill.

Fielding's Five

Five Good Reasons to Book This Ship

1. The price, perhaps the lowest in all cruising today.

2. To poke around and discover some of the lovely little architectural and decorative surprises aboard.

3. If your budget is strapped and you need to get away for a couple of days of r&r.

4. If you'd like to take a cruise to Bermuda on a budget.

5. If you'd like to take a cruise to Cozumel that doesn't cost too much.

Five Beautiful Spaces

1. The Mermaid Lounge, a lovely room with beautiful brass mermaids clinging to the corners of the bar, a brass rail at the feet, of course, and frosted glass "aquarium" windows with mermaids etched on them and light falling down from a clear glass skylight above.

2. Commodore Club, a piano bar adjoining the Mermaid Lounge, small and intimate with two sunken seating areas, an ideal hideaway where you can talk and still hear the music from the lounge next door.

3. The Library, perhaps the most gorgeous library at sea, paneled in dark wood with bull's eye windows that open, oil paintings, books in glass cases and a rich red patterned carpet on the floor. On the short cruises to nowhere, we suspect nobody ever lingers in this lovely room.

4. The enclosed promenade deck that makes a nice area for reading or chatting or doing needlework. Tables and chairs and potted trees line both sides of the glass-enclosed deck, which also has ping pong tables, shuffleboard and varnished decking in good shape.

5. The Grand Lounge, the showroom with a big round dance floor in marble, a small bar in one corner, curved floral banquettes all around the room and fair to good sightlines. Drink holders are fitted on the backs of the sofas in front.

Five Things You Won't Find On Board

1. A little kid who can't make his parents happy; if he'll forgo the evening in their company he can get a free after-dinner kids' program in the youth center so his parents can dine alone.

2. Hunger in the afternoon; not only is teatime a "happening thing," but you can scarf down hot dogs, cookies and ice cream from that oh-so-genteel spread.

3. Cabins designated wheelchair-accessible.

4. A passenger without proof of citizenship on most sailings; people don't realize a driver's license doesn't count. You need a passport, a voter registration card or a copy of your birth certificate.

5. Baby-sitting available in cabins; while the child care program is generous, they will not do in-cabin child care because of insurance liability problems.

Regal Empress ★★

Registry	Bahamas
Officers	German/European
Crew	International
Complement	358
GRT	23,000
Length (ft.)	612
Beam (ft.)	80
Draft (ft.)	28
Passengers-Cabins Full	1180
Passengers-2/Cabin	904
Passenger Space Ratio	22.5
Stability Rating	Good
Seatings	2
Cuisine	American
Dress Code	Traditional
Room Service	Yes
Tip	$7.50 PPPD, 15% automatically added to bar check

Ship Amenities

Outdoor Pool	1
Indoor Pool	0
Jacuzzi	2
Fitness Center	Yes
Spa	No
Beauty Shop	Yes
Showroom	Yes
Bars/Lounges	6
Casino	Yes
Shops	2
Library	Yes
Child Program	Yes
Self Service Laundry	Yes
Elevators	3

Cabin Statistics

Suites	7
Outside Doubles	224
Inside Doubles	128
Wheelchair Cabins	0
Singles	0
Single Surcharge	150%
Verandas	0
110 Volt	Yes

RENAISSANCE
CRUISES

1800 Eller Drive, Ft. Lauderdale, FL 33335
☎ *(305) 463-0982, (800) 525-5350*

History ·

Originally launched in 1989 by the Norwegian-based shipping company Fearnley and Eger, Renaissance began with an innovative idea—to build eight virtually identical 100-passenger luxury ships in a two-year period (actually, it took two-and-a-half years).

Before all the ships were completed, however, Fearnley and Eger foundered, filing for bankruptcy in May, 1991, and Renaissance was acquired by a partnership of Italy's Cameli Group and a holding company controlled by Edward B. Rudner, a travel entrepreneur who headed up Certified Tours and had a long association with Alamo Rent-A-Car.

Today, Renaissance sails in the Mediterranean, Northern Europe, the Seychelles and African islands and Indonesia, plus the *Aegean I* in the Mediterranean..

—First company to market a fleet of eight interchangeable ships.

—First cruise line to concentrate its marketing almost exclusively by direct mail to previous cruisers.

—First cruise line to charter a super-luxury airline to ferry passengers nonstop between Los Angeles and Antigua (aboard MGM Grand Air for *Renaissance III*, 1992).

Concept ·

Renaissance concentrates on destination-oriented seven- and 14-day cruises built around pre- and post-cruise land packages, on-board lecture programs to enrich the passenger's travel experience and in-depth shore excursions. The company describes the ships as having a "private club atmosphere," promoting open seating at mealtimes and the all-outside-suites configuration of the vessels. A shallow draft allows the Renaissance ships to go into ports larger ships must avoid.

Signatures......................................

The repetition of the company name in the ship's names, each followed by its own Roman numeral, creates a strong identity factor for the line. With emphasis on the brand name rather than an individual ship, Renaissance is free to substitute one vessel for another or shuffle the fleet around when necessary. "Besides," the line's former president Mark Conroy (now president of Radisson Seven Seas) once quipped, "it's impossible to remember eight different names. I can't even remember the Seven Dwarfs."

Gimmicks......................................

Renaissance often sells the destination more than the ship by distributing single-product flyers advertising only one cruise in detail rather than a full cruise brochure, and putting more pictorial emphasis on the scenery and activities at the destination rather than the ship and its lifestyle.

The direct mail brochures touting two-for-the-price-of-one sailings or freebies from roundtrip airfare to African safaris to low-cost upgrades to business class are designed primarily to attract the line's predominantly yuppie/baby boomer audience which can afford to buy whatever cruise it wants but which likes to feel it's getting something for nothing.

Who's the Competition ....

Nobody really fits into the niche where Renaissance has positioned itself, although there are certain similarities with Sea Goddess in ship size, open meal seatings and the all-suites concept, and with Windstar in a "casual elegance" dress code and day-long visits to beach-oriented islands. While a cursory glance at itineraries might bring some expedition lines to mind, Renaissance is strictly a mainstream "soft adventure" product with no bird-watching or desert hikes.

Who's Aboard ....

Well-traveled first-time cruisers who are booking for the itinerary rather than the ship; repeat Renaissance veterans who found out they loved the ships as much as the destinations; and bargain hunters who could never resist a two-fer. They're mostly couples, mostly between their late 20s and mid-50s, with an easy camaraderie with fellow passengers.

Who Should Go ....

Anyone who wants to travel to faraway places and be guaranteed a comfortable suite, good to excellent food and a non-regimented on-board life.

Who Should Not Go ....

Families with young children—there's nowhere for the kids to play or get out of the way of the adults; senior singles who'll complain "there's nothing to do"; anyone expecting a big-time gambling and nightlife cruise—the casino is limited to one blackjack table and four slot machines and the entertainment is a musical trio playing for dancing.

The Lifestyle ....

People who like Sea Goddess, Radisson Seven Seas, Seabourn, Silversea and Windstar sailings will immediately be at home with the dine-when-you-wish and sit-where-you-like freedom; the tendency to treat passengers as adults rather than children who have to be constantly entertained and herded about (except during the overland portions, where some organization is essential); and the lack of a regimented dress code.

Wardrobe

The dress code calls for "comfortable elegance," meaning no jacket and tie is ever required although plenty of passengers do dress up in the evening. Resortwear is the operative word—things like silk shirts, linen pants, gauzy cotton skirts and the like.

Day wear is casual clothing from jogging suits to shorts and T-shirts, whatever is appropriate to the climate and destination.

NO NOs

The line specifically requests that jeans, shorts, T-shirts and tennis shoes not be worn in the dining room at dinner.

Bill of Fare ....A-

The cuisine is contemporary restaurant-style cooking, much of it prepared to order. While simple breakfast and lunch buffets are served on deck for people who don't want to change from their bathing suits, most passengers take all their meals in the dining room. At lunchtime, there is usually an expansive buffet of salads, shellfish, cold meats, sandwiches, breads, cheese and desserts, and guests are also offered a full à la carte menu for hot orders. All-day room service sandwiches are available in the cabins as well as Continental breakfast.

Low-calorie dishes are available every meal, and all dinners provide five main dish choices plus two always-available options, broiled steak with baked potato and broiled chicken.

During our three cruises with Renaissance, the food has always been good to excellent, but we have encountered some veterans in port during the past year that felt the quality of food they'd enjoyed on one ship had not been duplicated on a different ship. This may go back to the chef in the kitchen at the time, although a good head of operations should strive to keep things up to par throughout the fleet.

Discounts

Past passengers get enticing two-for-one cruise buys or free airfare and overland package offers constantly in the mail, good if they book by a certain deadline. Groups qualify for discounts, and some frequent-flyer organizations also provide Renaissance discounts.

The Bottom Line

On our most recent sailing, we found the basic Renaissance cruise experience that we had enjoyed twice previously still very much intact, with the same care to food and service that we found on earlier sailings. But despite the ships' handsome, spick-and-span interiors, the exteriors and deck are always look as if they need more spit-and-polish maintenance than they get

Given the moderate prices for the quality of accommodations, more people should sample Renaissance if they enjoy small-ship, unstructured cruising. Unfortunately, the line is still not as well known as it should be among the travel agent community or the general public.

Aegean I   Unrated

The former Aegean Dolphin has become the Aegean I for Renaissance Cruises with sailings in, naturally, the Aegean Sea. But even Renaissance veterans need to be extra-cautious with this one. Accustomed as they are to all-outside cabins on the Renaissance series of ships, they may cheerfully book a "Classic Cabin," "Superior Cabin," or "Deluxe Cabin" without realizing all three categories are in fact inside cabins.

The ship, built in 1974, has been refurbished several times in simple bright colors, and has a trim line and a low, wide funnel. Typical of its size and vintage, it has a dining room amidships on a lower deck, and a cinema beauty salon and gym in the very bowels of the vessel. Still, it's fine for travelers who want to get a lot of Greece in a few days. To introduce the vessel for the summer and fall of 1996, Renaissance offered a nine-day package for as little as $1695 per person, double occupancy, including roundtrip air transfers and a two- night hotel package. The cruise itself lasts five days and visits Santorini, Heraklion, Rhodes and Kusadasi.

Cabins & Costs

With eight cabin categories on a 288-cabin ship, there is a wide range of choices and prices. The best lodgings are cabins 501 and 502, which the previous line designated suites, facing forward on the Sun Deck. Oddly enough, there are 14 other cabins in the same price category that are about half the size of 501 and 502. Termed "Renaissance Cabins," they average around $456 a day per person, double occupancy. Coming down a peg or two, the "Premium Cabin" is the lowest-priced outside accommodation at around $314 a day per person, double occupancy. The bottom of the heap is the "Classic Cabin" at $242 a day per person, double occupancy.

Aegean I   Unrated

Registry	**Greece**
Officers	**Greek**
Crew	**Greek**
Complement	**175**
GRT	**11,563**
Length (ft.)	**461**
Beam (ft.)	**67**
Draft (ft.)	**20**
Passengers-Cabins Full	**701**
Passengers-2/Cabin	**576**
Passenger Space Ratio	**20.07**
Stability Rating	**NA**
Seatings	**2**
Cuisine	**Continental**
Dress Code	**Traditional**
Room Service	**Yes**
Tip	**$5 - $8 PPPD**

Ship Amenities

Outdoor Pool	**1**
Indoor Pool	**0**
Jacuzzi	**1**
Fitness Center	**Yes**
Spa	**No**
Beauty Shop	**Yes**
Showroom	**Yes**
Bars/Lounges	**4**
Casino	**Yes**
Shops	**1**
Library	**Yes**
Child Program	**No**
Self Service Laundry	**No**
Elevators	**2**

Cabin Statistics

Suites	**16**
Outside Doubles	**186**
Inside Doubles	**86**
Wheelchair Cabins	**0**
Singles	**0**
Single Surcharge	**150%**
Verandas	**4**
110 Volt	**No**

Renaissance I–IV

Renaissance V–VIII   ★★★★

It was aboard the inaugural cruise of the Renaissance I *that we learned Krakatau is not east of Java, as the old movie title had it, but west of Java and east of Sumatra in the Sunda Straits. We had gone ashore on the hot black volcanic sand to photograph a beach picnic for a* Bon Appétit *article about small luxury cruise ships, and when we uncorked the sweating, chilled bottle of California Chardonnay to pour it into the glasses, half a dozen ragged Sumatran fisherman surrounded us, holding out their own cups for a sample. We wonder how many cruise lines other than Renaissance have put their passengers ashore on the black sand beach at Krakatau.*

The ship layouts are very simple, basically five decks, each with some cabins amidships and forward, and public areas concentrated aft. The lowest passenger deck houses the restaurant, the next deck up the lobby and main lounge, the next up the piano bar and casino, the next up the swimming pool, whirlpool spa and outdoor pool bar, and the topmost the sun deck, which is forward of the four top category cabins.

Renaissance I, II, III and *IV* are identical sisters, while *Renaissance V–VIII*, all identical to each other, are slightly larger than the first pair.

All accommodations on board are suites, but some are more suite-like than others. (See "Cabins and Costs", for more detail.) Tucked away here and there are a small beauty salon, a gift shop, card room, library, sauna and a couple of exercise machines in a makeshift gym area.

The Brochure Says

"Relax in...our intimate Piano Bar in The Club, or try your luck in the Casino. Peruse The Library full of best-sellers and current videos."

Translation

And all without taking more than ten steps in any direction.

A standard cabin provides twin beds or queen-sized bed.

Fantasy Suites: .... B+

Average Price PPPD: $400 on tour packages with air.

The top-priced suites on these vessels are literally on the top and called Renaissance Suites. They have private verandas, sitting area with sofa, two chairs, cocktail table, mini-refrigerator and desk/dresser with TV/VCR in 250 square feet of space. The bed can be arranged as twins or queen-sized, and there's generous closet space, bathroom and, in some, separate dressing area.

Small Splurges: .... A

Average Price PPPD: $280 on tour packages with air.

Unless you're set on having a private veranda and don't mind portholes instead of windows, we think the best buys aboard these vessels are the Superior Suites on the I, II, III and IV, two large rooms with big walk-in closet and large bath with marble counter. They're 287 square feet, the biggest suites on any of the vessels, and conveniently steps away from the restaurant. On the V-VIII, they measure 210 square feet, have big windows and walk-in closets.

Suitable Standards: .... B+

Average Price PPPD: $215 on tour packages with air.

The standard suite is an outside suite with an average of 210 square feet, with separate sitting area with sofa and chairs, bath and plenty of storage space.

Bottom Bunks: .... NA

There are no accommodations in this category on the Renaissance ships; the cheapest cabins are the suites described under "Suitable Standards," above.

The small casino aboard has one blackjack table.

Where She Goes

In the first year, the line proudly named just about every sea and continent in the world short of Antarctica, but as realism settled in, based on balance sheets and bookings, the itineraries were narrowed to a few choice spots in the world—the Seychelles and Indonesia in the winter, the Mediterranean and the Baltic in summer. Ask not which ship goes where—they're all more or less alike and it doesn't really matter. Just call and request to be put on their brochure mailing list. (See "Cruise Line Contacts," page xlv.)

INSIDER TIP

You can save money over the brochure price by taking advantage of one of the many discount possibilities. (See "Discounts".)

Renaissance cabins are large enough for entertaining.

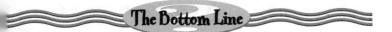

The Bottom Line

While not quite in the league of Sea Goddess, Seabourn, Silversea and Radisson Seven Seas, Renaissance offers excellent itineraries and a pleasurable on-board experience. Three caveats: The shallow draft of these vessels means sometimes bumpy rides in rough seas. Exercise equipment and self-service buffets sometimes get short shrift on these compact little ships. Last time we were aboard, the buffet filled the space originally designated for the gym and the exercise equipment (both pieces) had been relegated to a covered outdoor area on a lower deck.

But worst of all, the "suggested tipping guidelines" are outrageous.

Fielding's Five

Five Favorite Spots

1. The pretty Restaurant (terminology can be basic on ships this small) has plenty of tables for two, but passengers often want to gravitate to larger tables as they get to know each other, so there are also 4s and 6s, some sofa/banquettes and very comfortable chairs.

2. The sleek beige piano bar called The Club, where afternoon tea is usually served, card games are played and the casino operates to a piano background when the pianist is not needed to fill out the trio in the lounge downstairs.

3. The Lounge is where passengers gather for lectures, pre-dinner cocktails and dancing, and after-dinner dancing.

4. The Lobby, a cool, comfortable spot where the information desk is located, as well as (on the I–IV), a seating area convenient for waiting for friends or sinking into to cool off after a hot visit ashore.

5. The Library, where books and videotapes can be taken out whenever you wish; all cabins have TV sets with VCR capability.

Five Good Reasons to Book These Ships

1. To go to some of the world's most exotic ports in complete comfort and ease.

2. To be guaranteed an outside suite, no matter how much or how little you pay.

3. To travel in a full, luxurious, well-planned land-and-sea program that is not a bags-in-the-hall-at-six a.m., everybody-on-the-bus-at-seven package.

4. To have the luxury of dining when and with whom you please instead of being regimented into a set time and table.

5. To get on that repeat passenger mailing list that sends you two-for-one offers.

Five Things You Won't Find on Board

1. A children's program or playroom; don't bring small children aboard because you'll be punishing yourselves, them and your fellow passengers.

2. Space for two people at a time in the swimming pool; these birdbath-size waterholes are strictly plunge pools to dip into and get wet.

3. Inside cabins.

4. Wheelchair-accessible cabins, although the vessel does have an elevator.

5. Roulette; the casino consists of one blackjack table and a couple of slot machines.

Renaissance I–IV   ★★★★

Registry	Liberia
Officers	Italian
Crew	International
Complement	67
GRT	4,500
Length (ft.)	290
Beam (ft.)	50
Draft (ft.)	12
Passengers-Cabins Full	100
Passengers-2/Cabin	100
Passenger Space Ratio	45
Stability Rating	NA
Seatings	1
Cuisine	Contemporary
Dress Code	Traditional
Room Service	Yes
Tip	$17 - $23 PPPD, 15% automatically added to bar check

Ship Amenities

Outdoor Pool	1
Indoor Pool	0
Jacuzzi	1
Fitness Center	No
Spa	No
Beauty Shop	Yes
Showroom	No
Bars/Lounges	2
Casino	Yes
Shops	1
Library	Yes
Child Program	No
Self Service Laundry	No
Elevators	1

Cabin Statistics

Suites	50
Outside Doubles	0
Inside Doubles	0
Wheelchair Cabins	0
Singles	0
Single Surcharge	150%
Verandas	4
110 Volt	Yes

RENAISSANCE CRUISES

Renaissance V–VIII ★ ★ ★ ★

Registry	Liberia
Officers	Italian
Crew	International
Complement	72
GRT	4,500
Length (ft.)	297
Beam (ft.)	50
Draft (ft.)	12
Passengers-Cabins Full	114
Passengers-2/Cabin	114
Passenger Space Ratio	39.47
Stability Rating	NA
Seatings	1
Cuisine	Contemporary
Dress Code	Traditional
Room Service	Yes
Tip	$17 - $23 PPPD, 15% automatically added to bar check

Ship Amenities

Outdoor Pool	1
Indoor Pool	0
Jacuzzi	1
Fitness Center	No
Spa	No
Beauty Shop	Yes
Showroom	No
Bars/Lounges	2
Casino	Yes
Shops	1
Library	Yes
Child Program	No
Self Service Laundry	No
Elevators	1

Cabin Statistics

Suites	57
Outside Doubles	0
Inside Doubles	0
Wheelchair Cabins	0
Singles	0
Single Surcharge	150%
Verandas	12
110 Volt	Yes

⚓ROYAL CARIBBEAN

1050 Caribbean Way, Miami, FL 33132
☎ (305) 539-6000, (800) 327-6700

The signature Viking Crown Lounge and RCCL logo.

History . . . .

In 1969, three Norwegian shipping companies, I.M. Skaugen, Gotaas Larsen and Anders Wilhelmsen, founded RCCL for the purpose of offering year-round seven and 14-day cruises out of Miami. Now owned by Wilhelmsen and the Hyatt Hotels' Pritzger family of Chicago, Royal Caribbean Cruises Ltd. is a publicly traded company on the New York Stock Exchange.

The spring 1996 delivery of the *Splendour of the Seas* brought the line's total to 10 vessels. Just past its 25th anniversary, RCCL is definitely one a handful of major players in the cruise industry.

—First cruise line to commission three new ships expressly for the Caribbean cruise market, *Song of Norway* (1970), *Nordic Prince* (1971) and *Sun Viking* (1972).

—First cruise line to "stretch" a ship, cutting it in half and dropping in a new midsection, then putting it back together (*Song of Norway*, 1978).

—First cruise line to commission a specially designed ship for three- and four-day cruises (*Nordic Empress*, 1990).

—First seagoing, 18-hole miniature golf course (on *Legend of the Seas* 1995).

—First cruise line to open shoreside hospitality centers in popular ports where passengers can leave packages, make phone calls, bone up on local shopping or sightseeing, get a cold drink and use toilet facilities (1995).

Concept

Consistency is the key word here. RCCL aims to provide a cruise experience to mainstream, middle-of-the-road passengers that is consistent in style, quality and pricing, with a majority of the ships following a consistent year-round schedule. Rod McLeod, head of sales and marketing, calls it "the doughnut factor" from a travel agent who once commented that what he liked best about RCCL was that all the doughnuts on all the line's ships taste exactly the same.

Signatures

RCCL ships are easily recognized at a distance because of the Viking Crown Lounge, a cantilevered round glass-walled bar and observation lounge high atop the ships projecting from or encircling the ship's funnel; company president Edward Stephan dreamed it up after seeing the Seattle Space Needle.

DID YOU KNOW?

When RCCL sold its Nordic Prince to British-based Airtours last spring, the new owners didn't get to keep the Viking Crown Lounge; the cantilevered signature bar was removed before delivery.

Lounges, bars and restaurants on board are named for Broadway musicals and operettas, sometimes with unintentionally funny results, as with the *Sun Viking's* Annie Get Your Gun Lounge. (That's also a musical that few of today's RCCL passengers would remember.)

DID YOU KNOW?

We fantasize over musical titles they haven't yet used on the RCCL ships, like a dining room named for Grease or Hair, or a gym called Black and Blue.

Gimmicks

ShipShape Dollars, given out each time a passenger participates in an exercise or sports activity; with six you get egg roll. Actually, you get egg-yolk yellow T-shirts proclaiming the wearer ShipShape. Passengers compete wildly for them and proudly wear them for years afterward aboard cruise ships of competing lines.

Who's the Competition

RCCL competes directly with Carnival and Norwegian Cruise Line for Caribbean passengers, but it also vies price-wise with more upscale lines like Celebrity and Princess. The line's new megaliners have brought in a more glitzy sheen, with flashy gaming rooms created by a Nevada casino designer instead of a ship designer. The company has also gone head-to-head with Carnival in the mini-cruise market in south Florida, pitting its ladylike *Nordic Empress* against the neon-throbbing *Fantasy* and glow-in-the-dark *Ecstasy,* and in Los Angeles, where its glitzy *Viking Serenade* is getting some lively competition from Carnival's even glitzier *Holiday.* For 1997, *Sovereign of the Seas* takes the three- and four-day Bahamas run, and *Nordic Empress* moves to San Juan.

Who's Aboard

All-American couples from the heartland between 40 and 60, with new clothes, new cameras and nice manners; families with fairly well-behaved children; two or three 30-something couples traveling together; born-to-shop types who find the line's newer ships with their mall-like galleries familiar and comforting; clean-cut young couples on their honeymoons; single 20-somethings on holiday sharing an inexpensive inside cabin, more often females than males.

Statistically, the median age is a relatively low 42, with a household income from $40,000 to $75,000. One-fourth are repeat passengers, half are first-time cruisers. More Europeans, Australians and Latin Americans are also gravitating to the line.

Who Should Go

These are ideal ships for first-time cruisers because the staff and the signage instruct and inform without appearing to lecture, putting everyone at ease right away. Also for honeymooners, fitness freaks (except on the *Sun Viking* and *Song of Norway,* which don't have gyms), sunbathers, big families on a reunion and stressed-out couples who want some time together in a resort atmosphere. Baby Boomers and their juniors 25 to 45 years old will always be warmly welcomed: RCCL wants YOU!

Who Should Not Go

Dowager veterans of the world cruise.

Small ship enthusiasts.

Anyone who dislikes regimentation.

The Lifestyle

RCCL's ships follow a traditional cruise pattern, with specified dress codes for evening, and two meal seatings in the dining room at assigned tables for a minimum of four and a maximum of eight or ten; very few if any tables for two are available. A day-long program of games, activities and entertainment on board is supplemented by shore excursions that emphasize sightseeing, golf and watersports. In the Caribbean, private beach areas at CocaCay in the Bahamas and Labadee in Haiti are beach destinations for swimming and lunch barbecues.

Wardrobe

RCCL makes it easy for passengers by spelling out dress-code guidelines in the brochure. A normal seven-day Caribbean cruise has four casual nights where sport shirts and slacks are suggested for men, two formal nights where women wear cocktail dress or evening gowns and

men wear suits and ties or tuxedos, and one or more theme night
where passengers may don '50s or country/western garb if they wish
During the daytime, comfortable casual clothing—jogging outfit
shorts or slacks, T-shirts, bathing suits and coverups—is appropriate o
deck but sometimes not in the dining room.

NO NOs

No bathing suits, even with coverups, are allowed in the dining room at any time. Shorts, jeans and tank tops are not permitted after 6 p.m.

INSIDER TIP

Tuxedos are for rent on board most RCCL ships; ask your agent to check when booking if you think you may want to rent one.

Bill of Pare . . . . B+

Non-threatening, special-occasion food is produced by an affiliate
catering company on a rotating set menu that is similar but not identic
on the different ships. There's a wide variety and good range of choice
and the preparation is capable if not inspired. Dinner includes seve
appetizers (four of them juices), three soups, two salads, five mai
dishes and six desserts (three of them ice creams). On a typical day mai
dishes may include crabmeat cannelloni, sole Madagascar, pork loin a
jus, roast duckling and sirloin steak. In addition, a nightly vegetaria
menu, a kids' menu and a ShipShape low-fat, low-calorie menu ar
offered.

Our very favorite from the latter seems tailored to The Ladies Wh
Lunch—it starts with a shrimp cocktail without sauce, then consomme
hearts of lettuce salad with carrot curls and fat-free dressing, followe
by poached fish and vegetables, then rich, sugary Key Lime Pie with
whopping 12 grams of fat per slice.

Except on cruises of 10 days or longer, when cabin occupants can orde
from set lunch or dinner menus, 24-hour room service is limited t
breakfast and cold snacks such as sandwiches, salads and fruit-and
cheese plates. Breakfast and lunch buffets are served in a self-service caf
eteria with hot and cold dishes available, and early morning coffee
afternoon tea and midnight buffets fill out the legendary eight-meals-a
day format.

Captain Sealy's menu for kids includes fish sticks, peanut butter an
jelly sandwiches, tuna fish, pizza, hamburgers and macaroni and cheese
plus chocolate "ship" cookies. On a recent sailing aboard the *Splendour of the Seas*, we felt the food preparation and presentation had greatly
improved.

CHAMPAGNE TOAST

Just like their competitors, RCCL bar waiters on embarkation day on Caribbean cruises are hustling around with trays of brightly colored fancy drinks in souvenir glasses, but unlike some of their competitors, they prominently display signs showing the drink price at $4.95 so an unwary first-timer doesn't assume that they're free.

Showtime . . . . A/C

The major production shows produced by the line, complete with Broadway-style playbills and computerized light cues, are sensational on the bigger ships with their state-of-the-art technical facilities. Unfortunately, on the smaller vessels, the shows still come out of the under-inspired and overworked south Florida production companies and suffer from make-do stagecraft and poor sightlines. Passengers entertain each other at karaoke nights, masquerade parades and passenger talent shows, and pack appropriate garb for country/western night and '50s and '60s rock 'n roll night.

Discounts . . . .

Booking six months in advance earns discounts of 10 to 20 percent off the brochure rate.

The Bottom Line

Very nice but over-priced, especially when the line's consistency of pricing puts its older vessels in the same general range as its newer ones. Cabins are small throughout the fleet except in the newest Project Vision ships, but are very quiet in all the newer ships, thanks to modern soundproofing techniques that provide a 42-decibel reduction in the walls and 40 at the door from hallway noise. RCCL delivers a consistency across the fleet just as they intend to, even though the ships represent four different design groups and sizes.

Grandeur of the Seas ☆☆☆☆☆
Legend of the Seas ★★★★★
Splendour of the Seas ★★★★★

They call it "The Ship of Light" and claim it has more glass than any other ship afloat, more than two acres of windows, from the atrium hotel lobby with its soaring glass elevators to a Roman spa with clear crystal canopy that can be opened to the air or covered against temperature extremes. The two-deck dining room walls are glass, the Viking Crown Lounge wrapped around the ship's funnel is almost all glass, and a glass-walled cafe that doubles as observation area is high atop the ship and forward. People who cruise on glass ships should take along their sunglasses.

The most talked-about feature on these ships are their nine-hole miniature go courses, the first at sea.

Legend of the Seas and sister ships *Splendour of the Seas* and *Grandeur of th Seas* are the first of a projected six vessels in RCCL's Project Vision serie ships that are slightly smaller but considerably faster than the line's giant *So ereign, Monarch* and *Majesty.* They cruise at 24 knots as compared to th usual 20 or less, allowing passengers a longer time in port or shorter transi between ports.

Despite their size, these ships give the impression of intimacy, particularl in the soaring seven-deck Centrum with its glass skylight ceiling, where eac deck level has its own small sitting areas, library or cardroom.

The Brochure Says

"Your accommodations aboard the *Legend of the Seas* are exceptionally roomy an comfortable, with large staterooms, more expansive public areas and more cabins with ve randas."

Translation

Cabins are a bit bigger than the previous RCCL norm, although the one we occupied called a Larger Outside, begged the question, Larger than what? The ship's extra width—

ith a 105-foot beam, it's barely slim enough to squeeze through the Panama Canal—
gives a greater sense of space throughout the ship. The passenger-space ratio of 38.32 is
much higher than on the line's megaships.

KEELHAUL

*The gaudy casinos with Tiffany stained glass lamps over the tables, tacky
carpeting and far too many pinging slot machines and neon lights resemble
early downtown Reno.*

Cabins & Costs

Fantasy Suites: ....A+

Average Price PPPD: $586 including airfare in the Caribbean.
The 1148-square-foot Royal Suite with its gleaming white baby grand piano is
drop-dead gorgeous, from its private veranda to its sumptuous marble bathroom
with separate WC and bidet, three wash basins, stall shower and oval Jacuzzi tub.
For entertaining, there's a wet bar, mini-refrigerator, full entertainment center with
TV, VCR, CD and the rest of the alphabet. Two sofas, two chairs, a glass dining
table for four, separate bedroom with king-sized bed, easy chair and super storage
space.

Small Splurges: ....A

*Average Price PPPD: $471 each for two, $289 each for four, or $211 each for seven,
including airfare in the Caribbean.*
The two family suites, each with two bedrooms, two baths (one with tub and one
with shower), private veranda, sitting area with sofa-bed and chair, and a pull-down
berth, big enough to sleep seven and certainly comfortable enough for four.

*A spacious Category D deluxe outside cabin on Legend of the Seas has sitting
area and private veranda.*

Suitable Standards: ....C+

Average Price PPPD: $336, with airfare included in the Caribbean.
Category F Larger Outsides provide twin beds that can convert to queen-sized, a
sitting area with loveseat, small glass table with a brass wastebasket fitted under-

neath, nice built-in cabinetry, desk/dresser with three big drawers on one side, three little ones on the other, two nightstands with two drawers each and floral curtains with sheer drapery underneath. A small TV set, closet with one full-length and two half-length hanging areas, safe, full-length mirror and cabinet with shelves above make the basic unit more spacious and comfortable than on most RCCL ships. Bathrooms have showers only.

Wheelchair Accessible:

Seventeen cabins from Standard Insides to C category suites are designated accessible for the physically-challenged; all are near elevators. Doors are an extra-wide 32 inches across; there are no doorway sills; the bathrooms have shower stalls with stools and grab bars, and both bathrooms and passenger corridors are wide enough for a wheelchair to turn around.

Bottom Bunks: C

Average Price PPPD: $243 apiece for two, $175 apiece for four, with airfare in the Caribbean.

Even the standard quad insides with two lower and two upper berths have a sitting area with TV and a little space to move around. Storage is adequate, if not overly generous, and you can always take turns sitting on that cute little sofa.

CHAMPAGNE TOAST

For outstanding attention to disabled passengers: the large number of wheelchair-accessible cabins (17); Braille elevator signs; special cabin kits for hearing-impaired passengers with strobe-light door knocker and telephone ringer, mattress-vibrator alarm clock, telephone amplifier and enhancing FM receivers for sound in the show lounge.

Where She Goes

The *Legend of the Seas* transits the Panama Canal on 10- and 11-night sailings between San Juan and Acapulco in winter, then sails to Hawaii in spring and fall, and spends summers in Alaska cruising the Inside Passage.

Splendour of the Seas sails in Europe in the summer. For the winter, the ship returns to the Caribbean with a San Juan home base, Saturday departures and a new Southern Caribbean itinerary that includes Aruba and Curaçao, St. Maarten and St. Thomas.

The Bottom Line

Legend of the Seas and *Splendour of the Seas* look like moneymakers for the company. They feel like smaller ships than they are, because of the number of intimate areas tucked away here and there.

Cabins are somewhat more spacious than on previous RCCL ships—even another 24 square feet is a bonus. A total of 17 staterooms are designated for the disabled. Practical touches like removable coat hangers, some with skirt clips, along with good mirrors and makeup lighting will be appreciated, too.

Since several different designers created the public areas, there is a pleasurable variety of decorating styles. Deck areas are handsomer than on the line's megaships. There are

anvas-shaded seating areas and pools with arcs of water spraying, although the golf
ourse takes up a lot of sunbathing area.

We can already hear the cash registers ringing as this formerly conservative company
tarts crowding Carnival on the outer edges of Glitz World.

Fielding's Five

Five Fabulous Places

. A spectacular solarium with a "crystal canopy" sliding roof, pool with water jets and
spas, Roman marble floors and walls, fountains, even a convivial marble bar; also
there—a full spa, gym and beauty salon, steam baths and saunas.

?. The first 18-hole golf course at sea, in miniature of course, complete with water
hazards, sand traps, halogen lights for night play, wind baffles and a clear dome roof
in bad weather; reserved tee times, club rentals, $5 a game or $25 for unlimited play
throughout the seven-day cruise.

. The Centrum, the seven-deck, glass-ceilinged heart of the ship with two glass elevators, marble terraces and champagne bar.

. The two-level dining room, where diners are surrounded by glass walls and a dramatic curving stairway lets well-dressed couples make a dramatic entrance.

. The theater, the best showroom at sea from an audience point of view because all
the seats are good—and comfortable. High-tech professional shows, an orchestra
pit and retractable 50-screen video for multimedia productions.

Five Off-the-Wall Fun Facts

1. Sitting in the Viking Crown Lounge on these ships puts you at eye level with the
Statue of Liberty.

2. If these two ships sailed through your neighborhood at normal cruising speed,
they'd be ticketed for exceeding 30 mph.

3. The steel used in *Legend of the Seas* could build two Eiffel towers.

4. The ships are twice as wide as Rodeo Drive in Beverly Hills, and twice as long and
three times as high as the Hollywood sign.

5. Passengers on a seven-day cruise on *Splendour of the Seas* devour 4200 chickens,
2150 bagels, 3065 pounds of watermelons, 600 cases of beer and 383 cases of soda.

Five Good Reasons to Book These Ships

1. If you've always wanted to play miniature golf at sea.

2. If you like translating basic Latin phrases like those adorning the marble walls of the
Solarium—Bene Lava, Omnia Vincet Amor, Genius Loci and Carpe Diem.

3. To enjoy the excellent collection of original art on board, 1939 pieces altogether.

4. To hit the steam room and sauna, Jacuzzi and stand-up Solarium Bar.

5. To stargaze from a special deck with state-of-the-art starwheels that rotate on a
"star-time" clock mechanism to show where constellations are in synchrony with
real time and place. The cruise staff has been trained to explain it.

Five Things You Won't Find on Board

1. A self-service passenger laundry.

2. A golf cart on the 18-hole course.

3. A bad seat (or a smoking seat) anywhere in the show lounge.

4. A lot of space around your dinner table.

5. Public rest rooms in the Viking Crown Lounge.

Grandeur of the Seas ☆☆☆☆☆
Legend of the Seas ★★★★★
Splendour of the Seas ★★★★★

Registry	Liberia
Officers	Norwegian
Crew	International
Complement	720
GRT	69,130
Length (ft.)	867
Beam (ft.)	105
Draft (ft.)	24
Passengers-Cabins Full	2076
Passengers-2/Cabin	1804
Passenger Space Ratio	38.32
Stability Rating	Good to Excellent
Seatings	2
Cuisine	Themed
Dress Code	Traditional
Room Service	Yes
Tip	$7.50 PPPD, 15% automatically added to bar checks

Ship Amenities

Outdoor Pool	1
Indoor Pool	1
Jacuzzi	4
Fitness Center	Yes
Spa	Yes
Beauty Shop	Yes
Showroom	Yes
Bars/Lounges	7
Casino	Yes
Shops	4
Library	Yes
Child Program	Yes
Self Service Laundry	No
Elevators	11

Cabin Statistics

Suites	8
Outside Doubles	575
Inside Doubles	327
Wheelchair Cabins	17
Singles	0
Single Surcharge	150%
Verandas	231
110 Volt	Yes

Majesty of the Seas   ★★★★
Monarch of the Seas   ★★★★

One of the most fascinating phenomena of late twentieth-century life is the mall, that vast enclosed emporium of shops, bars, theaters and restaurants that has become a meeting place for teenagers and a weekend and evening destination for the young and upwardly mobile. In a sheltering, climate-controlled environment, surrounded by glittering options for spending money, people get dreamy-eyed and slow-moving. Majesty of the Seas and her sister megaliner Monarch of the Seas remind us a lot of hangin' out at the mall.

Starting with the first ship in this series, the slightly smaller *Sovereign of the Seas*, RCCL concentrated on positioning the cabins forward and the public rooms aft so that passengers can make their way vertically from, say the cocktail bars to the dining room to the show lounge to the casino, and horizontally from their cabins to the public areas.

But we would still recommend that a passenger traveling from a modest B deck inside forward cabin to the sports deck area atop the ship aft take along a compass and a brown bag lunch.

The plus side of big is that the soaring sense of space makes these huge ships especially appealing to first-time cruisers accustomed to hotels and resorts. And you shouldn't get lost too often—a three-dimensional plexiglass ship directory is set in each elevator/stairwell landing to help passengers find their way around.

They're good for kids because of the way the age groups are divided into five-to-eight-year-olds, "tweens" eight to 12, and teens from 13 to 17. Teens can hang out at their own soft drink bar with its adjacent video games center and even run the special effects and light show in the teen disco.

A whole new subculture of passengers has developed around these me gaships. They call themselves Trekkies (after the "Star Trek" TV series) i honor of their own journeys into space.

INSIDER TIP

People in bathing suits should avoid settling into those handsome woven plastic mesh bar seats at the pool bar if they don't want waffle patterns on the back of their thighs when they stand up again.

EAVESDROPPING

"Isn't this something!," gushes a 40ish blonde woman in awe as she enters the Majesty lobby at embarkation. "I'll certainly enjoy this week. You just can't believe it's a ship!"

The Brochure Says

"Big-city dazzle with its elegant dining rooms...as tall as the Statue of Liberty...unlimited freedom to curl up with a good book, eat all the ice cream you want (and) tell the kids to ship out..."

Translation

It's a big ship but you're going to kick back and have a great time. Head up to the Viking Crown Lounge and fantasize being on eye level with Miss Liberty (only in your imagination, since these ships don't sail into New York). Dazzling, come-hither bright lights and a sense of action draw young and first-time cruisers who know how to have fun. As for good books, see "Insider Tip" below.

For unlimited ice cream, the line's *Nordic Empress* with its own free ice cream bar might be a better bet. But you can certainly tell the kids to ship out, with three child care programs that split age groups between 5 and 8, "tweens" 8 to 12, and teens. The last have their own club and disco called Flashes, created by a line that realizes teens are only a decade or so away from buying cruises for themselves. Attention must be paid.

OFF-THE-WALL

The On Your Toes nightclub/disco on the Majesty of the Seas with its neon signage, optical illusion glass-and-neon entryway and state-of-the-art DJ station strains to send a "with it" message which is sabotaged by the saccharine central sculpture of a pair of ballet dancers.

INSIDER TIP

The elegant library aboard has 2000 books, an impressive number until you realize the ship carries 2354 passengers, presumably leaving 354 people with nothing to read during the cruise. Check out your book ASAP.

CHAMPAGNE TOAST

To the splendid new ShipShape Center, open daily from 8 a.m. to 8 p.m., with a padded floor and enough space so aerobics and exercise classes don't have to be scheduled on deck or in one of the lounges, as on many vessels.

Cabins & Costs

The Royal Suite on **Majesty of the Seas** *is a true fantasy suite.*

Fantasy Suites: .... A

Average Price PPPD: $571 including airfare.

The Royal Suite, #1010 on both ships, provides ideal digs for anyone who wants to entertain in nearly 1000 square feet indoors and out. A separate living room with private veranda, dining table with six chairs, L-shaped sofa and two chairs, wet bar stocked with liquor, soft drinks and snacks and an entertainment center with CDs and VCRs headlines the suite. In the bedroom is a king-sized bed, lovely wood dresser, a marble bathroom with double basins, Jacuzzi tub, stall shower and walk-in dressing area with large safe.

Small Splurges: .... B+

Average Price PPPD: $457 per person for first two passengers, $107 per person for third and fourth sharing the suite. Includes airfare.

The Family Suite, #1549 on both ships, has two bedrooms and two baths, adequate sleeping, lounging and wardrobe space for a close family of five, with private veranda, sitting area, master bedroom and bath, and second bedroom with two lower beds, a pulldown berth and small bathroom with shower.

Suitable Standards: C

Average Price PPPD: $321 including airfare.

F is the predominant category of standard outside double cabins, each with its twin beds in L-shaped configuration, the ends at the L overlapping by 18 inches. In the 127 square feet, you'll find one chair (flip a coin for it), a small TV set, a tripod glass-topped table with a brass wastebasket as its base (we tried to chill champagne in it but were sternly corrected by a Bahamian stewardess), a built-in cabinet with four drawers, a closet with one full length and two half-height hanging areas plus drawers and a safe and a small tidy tile bath with shower.

Wheelchair Accessible:

Two inside category N cabins and two outside category D cabins are designated as physically-challenged accessible. They're larger than others in their price category, with good turning room for the wheelchair, and twin beds with pastel covers, along with sofa and chair. The baths have no sills, and provide grab rails by the toilet and in the shower, along with a pull-down plastic seat. Some low hanging closet racks are accessible, but the safe, located on an upper shelf, would be out of reach for someone in a wheelchair.

Bottom Bunks: C

Average Price PPPD: $229 including airfare.

With the modular cabin design common to new ships, the cheapest digs often offer two lower beds and a bathroom identical to those in higher-priced categories. The bottom-dollar beds are in category Q, insides that measure only 114 square feet and are situated well forward on the lowest passenger cabin deck, but hey, they're livable unless you hit a heavy storm, which could toss you out of bed.

DID YOU KNOW?

At the French shipyard a week before delivery of the Monarch of the Seas, a group of American media touring the vessel were bemused to note that in the Ain't Misbehavin' Lounge, the life-sized sculpture of the noted black pianist with his derby hat was labeled Fats Domino instead of Fats Waller.

Where She Goes

Majesty of the Seas sails year-round, seven-day Western Caribbean round-trips from Miami (Sundays) calling at Playa del Carmen and Cozumel, Grand Cayman, Ocho Rios and, depending on the cruise, Labadee, Haiti, or CocoCay, Bahamas, for a beach day.

Monarch of the Seas sails year-round seven-day Southern Caribbean round-trips from San Juan (Sundays) calling at Martinique, Barbados, Antigua, St. Maarten and St. Thomas.

The Bottom Line

The acres of astroturf and anodized bronze loungers, glittering shops and glass elevators, leather sofas, potted palms and lobby pianist make the *Majesty* and *Monarch of the Seas* look more like Marriott of the Seas to a purist.

While the cabins and interiors are as spotless as ever, the deck housekeeping is sometimes lax. A well-decked-out lady deserves better than this.

Solid mainstream ships, the *Majesty* and the *Monarch* set out to impress from the moment a passenger boards, just as Carnival does, but they aim for a slightly more sophisticated audience. Only dedicated traditional ship buffs will find much to grouse about here.

Fielding's Five

Five Great Space Stations

1. The Centrum, a four-deck lobby with two glass elevators, a two-level marble floor and a pianist, looking for all the world like a Hyatt Regency hotel lobby.

2. Boutiques of Centrum, 10 storefronts in the shopping gallery circled like pioneer wagons around a campfire, each with its own character and line of duty-free products. In the center of it all, a plaza with luggage-brown leather chairs where non-shoppers can sit and wait—just like at the mall.

3. The tri-level show lounge (A Chorus Line on *Majesty*, Sound of Music on *Monarch*) with its curved cantilevered box seats, eye-catching murals and neon entrance signage adds glitz to this fairly conservative line, although kilowatt-wise, it can't compete with the Casino Royale.

4. The spacious Schooner Bar, everybody's favorite piano bar, with a decor that includes plank floors, brass ship lamps, ship models in plexiglass cases and spars and rigging. While the house music is closer to "My Way" than "Blow the Man Down," it's still pretty nautical.

5. The two-deck Windjammer Cafe is open to the sea, with an enclosed cafe forward and a covered, outdoor cafe amidships, sheltered with window walls and a glass dome overhead; unique "waterfall" columns sandwich a cascade that ripples through plexiglass cases and towers of glass blocks.

Majesty of the Seas ★★★★
Monarch of the Seas ★★★★

Registry	**Norway**
Officers	**Norwegian**
Crew	**International**
Complement	**822**
GRT	**73,941**
Length (ft.)	**880**
Beam (ft.)	**106**
Draft (ft.)	**25**
Passengers-Cabins Full	**2744**
Passengers-2/Cabin	**2354**
Passenger Space Ratio	**31.4**
Stability Rating	**Fair to Good**
Seatings	**2**
Cuisine	**Themed**
Dress Code	**Traditional**
Room Service	**Yes**
Tip	**$7.50 PPPD, 15% automatically added to bar check**

Ship Amenities

Outdoor Pool	**0**
Indoor Pool	**0**
Jacuzzi	**0**
Fitness Center	**Yes**
Spa	**Yes**
Beauty Shop	**Yes**
Showroom	**Yes**
Bars/Lounges	**0**
Casino	**Yes**
Shops	**10**
Library	**Yes**
Child Program	**Yes**
Self Service Laundry	**No**
Elevators	**0**

Cabin Statistics

Suites	**13**
Outside Doubles	**732**
Inside Doubles	**445**
Wheelchair Cabins	**4**
Singles	**0**
Single Surcharge	**150%**
Verandas	**62**
110 Volt	**Yes**

Nordic Empress

*Our favorite memory of the Nordic Empress was sitting on our cabin's pri-
vate veranda late one Saturday night in the summer of 1990 when the then-
new ship ship was docked in Nassau, and watching the equally new Fantasy
from Carnival, docked across the way, change colors as its computer-pro-
grammed neon tubing strung throughout the vessel shifted from red to blue
to fuchsia to lime to pink. The Fantasy, a sort of lava lamp for the 1990s, serves
to delineate the differences between the two, the first brand-new ships that had
ever been scheduled for profit-generating three- and four-day cruises.*

*Until then, only the oldest vintage vessels from a line were shoved over into
that high-density, high-attrition market once perceived as a one-time-only
whoopee cruise for guzzling undergraduates and singles on the make.*

*Now, suddenly, right before our eyes, the whole scene had changed, and we
were witnessing the cruise equivalent of a stare-down confrontation between
genteel Melanie Wilkes and flamboyant Scarlett O'Hara.*

The *Nordic Empress* actually started on the drawing board as a rather pre-
tentiously named vessel called *Future Seas*, designed expressly for three-and
four-day cruises for a now-defunct company called Admiral Cruises, an affiliate of RCCL.

Company executives define the differences on the mini-cruise vessels:

—"We try to cram a seven-day cruise into three days."

—More hectic.

—In port daily.

—More steak and lobster, fewer unfamiliar dishes on the menu.

—"Passengers want to eat and drink as much as they would in seven days."
(Passengers also spend roughly the same amount of disposable income for
on-board extras as they would in seven days.)

—Deck plan must be easy for the passenger to learn and find his way
around in a limited time.

Pool deck areas are shaded with canvas umbrellas on the **Nordic Empress.**

The Brochure Says

"A cascading waterfall. Lush tropical plants. The kind of sunlight you never get back home. Wait. This isn't an exotic port. This is your ship. The Centrum Lobby, actually."

Translation

The heart of the ship is a hotel-like lobby that connects to all the passenger decks and so helps passengers learn their way around. (It's no fun when you're on a three-day cruise and can't find your cabin for hours.) The Centrum, as it's called, is drop-dead dramatic, a great place for photographing each other. (It's also a good backdrop for a wedding, if you have romance in mind. See page 55, "Getting Married Aboard".)

CHAMPAGNE TOAST

For their subtle how-to's for first-timers: at the first night's dinner, the waiter, busboy and headwaiter introduce themselves to each table, each explaining what his particular duties are so the uninitiated cruiser doesn't have to worry about which server to summon for a glass of water or a cup of coffee. Cabin stewards greet each arriving guest and point out cabin features, and the welcome-aboard presentation on embarkation day introduces personnel from the ship's shops, sports and fitness program, beauty shop, casino and photography concessions to explain the services and prices, and that there's no charge for being photographed unless you want to buy the finished picture.

Cabins & Costs

Fantasy Suites: . . . . A

Average Price PPPD: $623 including airfare.
The one-bedroom Royal Suite is big enough for entertaining with a wet bar, large dining or conference table, curved sofa and chairs, teak-floored veranda, walk-in

closet, Jacuzzi tub, and separate marble-and-glass shower. While the price is about $100 a day more than the owner's suites, the Royal Suite incorporates space from an owner's suite and two standard cabins.

Small Splurges: .... B+

Average Price PPPD: $406 including airfare.

One of the 56 category C deluxe outside cabins with private balcony, two lower beds which can be arranged as one, a sofa, chair and coffee table, built-in dresser/ desk, good reading lamp, built-in vanity table and terrycloth robes.

Suitable Standards: .... B

Average Price PPPD: $316 including airfare.

Cabins were designed with women in mind, according the ship designers, who say females comprise 60 percent of all cruise passengers. There's generous counter space in the bathroom, subdued pastel fabrics, floral watercolors and a beauty table with its own makeup lights. H and I category cabins have twin beds that convert to queen-sized, color TV, built-in dresser with stool, one chair, good storage space and small bathroom with shower only.

Bottom Bunks: C

Average Price PPPD: $233 including airfare.

Q category cabins forward on B deck are the bottom-dollar digs; expect all the standard cabin amenities in a slightly smaller space.

Where She Goes

Fridays three-day roundtrips from Miami to Nassau and CocoCay.

Mondays four-day roundtrips from Miami to Freeport, Nassau and CocoCay.

Beginning Dec. 20, three- and four-day roundtrips from San Juan to St. Thomas and St. Maarten, plus St. Croix as well on the fours.

The Bottom Line

The *Nordic Empress*, like Carnival's glittering new short-cruise megaships, is attracting a whole new set of first-time cruise passengers of all ages and ethnic backgrounds, a welcome sight in an industry that spent too many years competing for the same narrow stratum of cruise regulars.

This ship offers a gentler, quieter version of the party cruise without soft-pedaling the fun. On both three- and four-day itineraries, passengers have a full day at the beach on a private island for swimming, snorkeling, sailing and windsurfing with a calypso band and beach barbecue lunch, while competitor Carnival provides a day at sea to enjoy (read: spend money in) the ship's games, bars, shops and casinos.

The *Nordic Empress* is highly recommended for first-time cruisers of all ages, including families and three-generation groups. It's a good introduction to mainstream cruising.

ROYAL CARIBBEAN CRUISES, LTD.

Five Sensational Spots

1. The Centrum, a nine-deck open atrium with a glass skylight on top, then a waterfall that cascades, sometimes framed in glass or caught up in pools, sometimes splashing free, faced with pink begonias and white marble and a crystal-drop sculpture of a ship's prow, all of it best viewed from the two glass elevators.

2. The two decks of the glass-walled Carmen Dining Room, the first of the nearly one dozen double-deckers now at sea, with a great view of the port as the ship sails away. It's bright and airy for breakfast and lunch, and spectacularly lit at dinnertime when musicians on a raised marble platform serenade diners.

3. The tri-level Casino Royale with 10 blackjack tables, two roulette tables, two craps tables, 40 sit-down poker machines and 220 slot machines is catnip for sporting cats.

4. Kids Connection Playroom has a slide that lets small children fall into a sea of brightly colored plastic balls; there's also a cave-like hidden TV room with carpeted seating levels, great for watching scary videos like *Jurassic Park*.

5. The Strike Up the Band Showroom in coral tones with white marble and gleaming brass cantilevered curved balcony boxes is lovely to look at, and a wooden thrust stage with splendid turntable and technical equipment offers state-of-the-art stagecraft. The only flaw is the over-exuberance of curved rails in the balcony that limit access and force late arrivals to vault over the railings into their seats.

Five Things You Won't Find on Board

1. The usual blank wall in inside cabins. Where the window would be on an outside cabin, the line has decorated with artwork and vertical fabric and plexiglass strips framing wall sconces.

2. A panoramic ocean view from outside cabins amidships on Mariner Deck (cabin 7100–7652, plus cabins 7032 and 7352) because lifeboats are hanging outside the windows. For the same price, ask your travel agent to book category F cabins well forward or aft to avoid the obstructions.

3. A library or card room.

4. A self-service laundry.

5. Consistently good sightlines in the show lounge; arrive early so you don't have to sit in the balcony.

Nordic Empress   ★★★★

Registry	Liberia
Officers	Norwegian
Crew	International
Complement	671
GRT	48,563
Length (ft.)	692
Beam (ft.)	100
Draft (ft.)	25
Passengers-Cabins Full	2020
Passengers-2/Cabin	1600
Passenger Space Ratio	30,35
Stability Rating	Good
Seatings	2
Cuisine	Themed
Dress Code	Traditional
Room Service	Yes
Tip	$7.50 PPPD, 15% automatically added to bar checks

Ship Amenities

Outdoor Pool	2
Indoor Pool	0
Jacuzzi	4
Fitness Center	Yes
Spa	Yes
Beauty Shop	Yes
Showroom	Yes
Bars/Lounges	6
Casino	Yes
Shops	3
Library	Yes
Child Program	Yes
Self Service Laundry	No
Elevators	7

Cabin Statistics

Suites	6
Outside Doubles	471
Inside Doubles	329
Wheelchair Cabins	4
Singles	0
Single Surcharge	150%
Verandas	69
110 Volt	Yes

ROYAL CARIBBEAN CRUISES, LTD.

Song of America

It was a windy but memorable December day in 1982 in Miami when opera star Beverly Sills christened Song of America. It took the durable diva five swings before she broke the bottle of champagne across the bow. Moments before, she had cautioned the crowd of well-wishers not to spill anything on "my carpets—I like to run a tight ship." At the time, Wartsila-built Song of America was the biggest cruise ship ever constructed in Scandinavia, and perhaps the only modern Caribbean ship to boast an ex-president (Jimmy Carter) and his family as passengers on the maiden voyage. The Carters still return periodically, but also travel aboard the Sovereign of the Seas, where Mrs. Carter is godmother.

A deluxe cabin on **Song of America** *with its own sitting area and desk/dresser.*

Unlike this ship's many fervent fans, we dismissed her as Nordic high-tech razzle-dazzle when she was new because of her popsicle interior colors, but n a more recent renovation, some of the original orange cabin furnishings have been muted to beige tones and the former grape-and-raspberry upholtery in the Can Can Lounge and Guys & Dolls Lounge has quieted down as well. It's been some time since the Schooner Bar was introduced and the outdated cinema removed (now that the cabins have color TV sets for video movies) in favor of a conference and meeting area and expanded casino. The soundproofing has been beefed up since the early days as well.

Traditionalists like the long sleek lines compared to today's shoebox shapes, and sunbathers find plenty of room to stretch out on the expansive Compass and Sun Decks. For nightlife, the ship has three spacious lounges for shows, music and dancing, plus the smaller Schooner piano bar.

The Brochure Says

"We'll do everything, so you have the option of doing nothing. We'll clean up your room (twice a day), cook for you (six times a day), entertain you and take you to far-away places with strange-sounding names."

Translation

A cruise is an easy vacation, because you buy everything in a neat package, even your round-trip airfare and transfers. You have a cabin steward who cleans your cabin twice a day, replacing towels and refilling the ice bucket, and you can eat every couple of hours if you concentrate. Best of all, your cruise ship takes you to exotic spots like the U.S. Virgin Islands where the inhabitants speak English and welcome U.S. dollars.

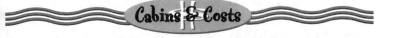

Cabins & Costs

Fantasy Suites: .... B

Average Price PPPD: $464 including airfare.
The Owner's Suite, #7000, on Promenade Deck, is double the size of the deluxe outside suites, with sitting area with sofa, chairs and coffee table; mini-refrigerator, color TV, twin beds and an optional third berth, wide desk/dresser, three picture windows and bathroom with tub. On the down side, you're overlooking a public deck area from your picture windows.

Small Splurges: .... C+

Average Price PPPD: $407 including airfare.
A deluxe suite in B category, not as lavish space-wise as the Owner's Suite, but comfortable enough, with sofa, chairs, desk/dresser, color TV, separate sleeping area with twin beds and big window, and bath with tub.

Suitable Standards: .... C-

Average Price PPPD: $307 including airfare.
The modular cabin design means all standards are virtually identical, with the category and price difference reflected in the deck location. The H category A deck outside doubles have two lower beds (one sofa/daybed and one fold-up twin) except for cabins 3207–3210, 3147–3150 and 3013–3018, all of which have twin beds that can be put together into a queen-sized bed. Most of these also have a pulldown third berth. All have bathrooms with shower only.

ROYAL CARIBBEAN
CRUISES, LTD.

Bottom Bunks: .... (

Average Price PPPD: $235 including airfare.

The B Deck inside doubles in the forward part of the ship, Q category, are the low
est-priced accommodations. Each has two lower beds that can be put together t
make a queen-sized bed, a bath with shower, wall-mounted color TV set and
desk/dresser with stool.

INSIDER TIP

*Only about half the cabins on board have twin beds that can be converted to
queen-sized beds, so specify your preference when booking.*

Song of America cruises the Southern Caribbean from San Juan in winter, sailing on
Saturdays and calling in St. Croix, St. Kitts, Guadeloupe, St. Maarten, St. John and St.
Thomas. In summer, she sails to Bermuda from New York every Sunday, and spends one
day in St. George's, then two-and-a-half days in Hamilton.

This long, sleek beauty is one of only three classic non-mega-sized ships remaining in
the rapidly-growing RCCL fleet, and it has retained its popularity over the years, with
some loyals claiming as many as two dozen sailings aboard since its debut.

Because the cabins are on the small side (around 120 square feet for standard doubles),
the passenger space ratio is a modest 26.8, but deck areas and lounges are spacious and
comfortable, and warm-weather cruisers shouldn't have to spend too much time in their
rooms.

Anyone sensitive to cigarette smoke may find, as we do, that although the Viking
Crown Lounge with its expansive (and unopenable) glass windows offers dramatic sea
and sunset views, it also retains the smell of smoke despite the line's zealous attempts to
clean and freshen the air.

Five Special Spots

1. The cozy Schooner Bar, just the right size on this ship compared to the bigger version aboard the megaliners.

2. The Sun Walk that overlooks the amidships pool deck, which allows you to get in
   your daily mile or two while checking out the scenic sunbathers below.

3. The 360-degree view from the Viking Crown Lounge, the first one for the line that
   was wrapped completely around the stack instead of just part of it.

4. The Oriental Terrace and Ambassador Room, two narrower dining ells that branch
   off the big Madame Butterfly dining room on both port and starboard sides.

5. The Mast Bar on Compass Deck with its 14 barstools that overlook the onboard
   action.

Song of America ★★★

Registry	**Norway**
Officers	**Norwegian**
Crew	**International**
Complement	**525**
GRT	**37,584**
Length (ft.)	**705**
Beam (ft.)	**93**
Draft (ft.)	**22**
Passengers-Cabins Full	**1552**
Passengers-2/Cabin	**1402**
Passenger Space Ratio	**26.8**
Stability Rating	**Fair**
Seatings	**2**
Cuisine	**Themed**
Dress Code	**Traditional**
Room Service	**Yes**
Tip	**$7.50 PPPD, 15% automatically added to bar checks**

Ship Amenities

Outdoor Pool	**2**
Indoor Pool	**0**
Jacuzzi	**0**
Fitness Center	**Yes**
Spa	**No**
Beauty Shop	**Yes**
Showroom	**Yes**
Bars/Lounges	**7**
Casino	**Yes**
Shops	**2**
Library	**Yes**
Child Program	**No**
Self Service Laundry	**No**
Elevators	**7**

Cabin Statistics

Suites	**1**
Outside Doubles	**406**
Inside Doubles	**295**
Wheelchair Cabins	**0**
Singles	**0**
Single Surcharge	**150%**
Verandas	**0**
110 Volt	**Yes**

ROYAL CARIBBEAN CRUISES, LTD.

Song of Norway

> *RCCL was certainly music-minded when it launched its first ship with rooms named after musicals—South Pacific Lounge, The King and I Dining Room, My Fair Lady Lounge—but the first time we went aboard this ship in the early 1980's, we were struck more by the Kool-Aid colors everywhere, raspberry, tangerine, lemon-lime and strawberry. All these, fortunately, have gone the way of RCCL's old cash-only policy. (The company was one of the last to institute a credit card policy for onboard purchases, a sure way to raise revenue but nervous-making for the conservative Norwegians.*
>
> *(We asked them once why they charged a refundable $15 for checking a book out of the library. "Because someone might steal it," was the answer.)*
>
> *Now with the SuperCharge card, passengers can take a cashless cruise, using the card for drinks, gift shop purchases, beauty shop services—yes, even that refundable book checkout deposit.*

When the *Song of Norway* debuted back in 1970, she had a capacity for 740 passengers, probably considered quite enough in those days, but the demand was soon such that the line decided to lengthen the vessel in 1978 in the first-ever "stretching" operation (see "History") and now carries 1004 passengers. Second-smallest in the fleet (only *Sun Viking* is smaller), she manages to retain some intimacy but is big enough to give passengers a sense of choice when they're out and about, with three big lounges and a good expanse of deck space, plus a full round-the-ship promenade.

We wish we could say passengers get a sense of personal space as well, but most of the cabins are quite small—around 120 square feet—with the exception of three modest suites.

INSIDER TIP

You have to walk up an outdoor stairway to get into the Viking Crown Lounge, something that can really destroy your hairdo on a wet or windy evening.

The Brochure Says

"Like the beautiful and cultured countries she visits, our *Song of Norway* is known for her understated elegance...No wonder she visits such irresistible places—otherwise, you might never go ashore."

Translation

She's not very glitzy or glamorous, but you'll find her comfortable enough as a floating hotel to take you to some places you want to go without packing and unpacking all the time.

Cabins & Costs

Fantasy Suites: . . . . *C*

Average Price PPPD: $460 including airfare.

The Owner's Suite, while a little short on fantasy, is the biggest accommodation on board (266 square feet) with sitting area, mini-refrigerator and bar, larger-than-usual wardrobe area, bathroom with tub and shower and two lower beds that cannot be pulled together for a queen-sized bed.

Small Splurges: . . . . *C*

Average Price PPPD: $400 including airfare.

The category C deluxe staterooms are up around the Owner's Suite but a bit smaller. Still, they're adequate, with two lower beds and bathroom with tub. Strollers along the Promenade Deck outside the window add an additional diversion.

Suitable Standards: . . . . *C-*

Average Price PPPD: $280 including airfare.

Lots of "outside staterooms" and "larger inside staterooms" (read "smallish cabins") are in the mid-range categories on A and B decks. Expect a double or two lower beds, sometimes configured in an L-shape in the larger ones, or parallel in the smaller ones.

Bottom Bunks: . . . . *D-*

Average Price PPPD: $220 including airfare.

Q category bottom-of-the-line inside cabins have a single double bed suitable for petite romantics who don't want any sunlight coming in to wake them up. Bathrooms have showers only. There are only four of these.

INSIDER TIP

Young singles shouldn't plan on crowding four into a cheap inside cabin, no matter how appealing the prices are, without taking into consideration how little dressing, showering and storage space is available. If you travel really light, however, you might be able to manage it.

Song of Norway makes 10- and 11-night Southern Caribbean sailings between Miami
and San Juan in winter at the conclusion of her summer Alaska season.

A sentimental favorite with both RCCL's executives and its repeat passengers, *Song of
Norway* nevertheless shows her age in dated furniture and interior design and lack of specialized facilities now common on RCCL ships—for instance, there is a gym but it's tiny.

Standard accommodations still feature what we call the "interlocking knees" double
cabin, from a long-ago RCCL brochure photograph that showed an attractive pair of
models ensconced in that small, chairless cabin, gamely smiling, one sitting on each bed
facing each other with, yes, their knees interlocked.

And this high-density vessel has a low passenger-space ratio, meaning when the ship is
full, which it frequently is, conditions can get crowded.

Overall, this ship is best for competitive types, who can vie in the fitness/sports program to win free T-shirts and visors; couples, who can rekindle romance in the very cozy
cabins; and kids, who fit into the upper Pullman-style berths easier than adults.

A future is still possible for ships of this size and vintage in European cruising, where
many of the vessels are older and smaller, but RCCL has opted to replace her in Europe
with the bigger, glossier *Splendour of the Seas*, so her days may be numbered.

Five Special Spots

1. The pool on Sun Deck, a convivial gathering spot just steps away from the Pool Bar
   and the Pool Cafe; a dedicated sun worshipper could spend most of the day here
   without missing a thing.

2. The Sun Walk, a balcony which looks down on the pool but offers a peaceful getaway from the pool activity.

3. The My Fair Lady Show Lounge, redecorated in subtler, deeper shades instead of
   its formerly flashy orange, raspberry and green.

4. The King and I Dining Room, trim and shipshape and with windows big enough to
   see out from, as well as nightly themed dinner menus to take you around the world.

5. The very first Viking Crown Lounge ever built, still cozy and warm with a wonderful glass-walled view. (See Insider Tip above)

Song of Norway ★★

Registry	Norway
Officers	Norwegian
Crew	International
Complement	423
GRT	22,945
Length (ft.)	637
Beam (ft.)	80
Draft (ft.)	22
Passengers-Cabins Full	1138
Passengers-2/Cabin	1004
Passenger Space Ratio	22.85
Stability Rating	Fair
Seatings	2
Cuisine	Themed
Dress Code	Traditional
Room Service	Yes
Tip	$7.50 PPPD, 15% automatically added to bar checks

Ship Amenities

Outdoor Pool	1
Indoor Pool	0
Jacuzzi	0
Fitness Center	Yes
Spa	No
Beauty Shop	No
Showroom	Yes
Bars/Lounges	5
Casino	Yes
Shops	3
Library	Yes
Child Program	No
Self Service Laundry	No
Elevators	4

Cabin Statistics

Suites	3
Outside Doubles	325
Inside Doubles	177
Wheelchair Cabins	0
Singles	0
Single Surcharge	150%
Verandas	0
110 Volt	Yes

Sovereign of the Seas ★★★★

In the awesome five-story open lobby, brass-trimmed glass elevators glide up and down, their gleaming reflections glancing off marble walls. Elegantly-clad guests lean against a brass railing to look far below at a white baby grand piano where a man in a red coat is playing light classics beside three fountain pools. Almost every major city has one of these grand hotels with majestic staircases and soaring, ethereal space. The only difference is, this one is scheduled to sail off into the Caribbean sunset at 5:30.

The pool deck on Sovereign of the Seas *after embarkation.*

Sovereign of the Seas was the largest ship ever built for cruising when it came into service in 1988. Like its newer sister ships *Monarch of the Seas* and *Majesty of the Seas,* it has a "bigger than life" theatricality and showy design that lends excitement. From the moment its mostly youngish, often first-timer passengers first board, they have the sense of arriving at a major resort. It's ideal for couples, singles and young families shopping for a Caribbean vacation that just happens to be aboard a cruise ship.

How far does the average passenger have to walk between the show lounge and the midnight buffet on a ship that is almost three football fields long? Theoretically, only a short stroll and a stairway or elevator separate the chorus girls from the cheesecake, because the ship's design concentrates the public rooms aft and the staterooms forward.

In fact, your evening could go something like this: You start at the bottom in your assigned dining room (Gigi is on A Deck and Kismet on Main Deck), then walk up one deck to the casino, to the lower level of the show lounge or the shops, then up another deck if you want to sit in the show lounge balcony or have a quiet drink in Finian's Rainbow Lounge or the champagne bar. Walk up one more deck to catch the late show in the Music Man Lounge, then up another deck to check out the disco. Finally, if you want a nightcap in the Viking Crown Lounge, catch the elevator outside the disco and ride three more decks to the top of the ship. Whew!

DID YOU KNOW?

When this ship was new, we speculated about how many hands a captain can shake at a captain's cocktail party. RCCL set two parties for each of the two dinner seatings, so that the captain had to press the flesh of only 1141 passengers in two shifts, while his second in command was in another lounge handling the other half.

The Brochure Says

"Big. You may wonder if that's what you want in a cruise ship. Won't you get lost just trying to find your stateroom? Not with Royal Caribbean—there's always a staff member who'll point you the right way—or take you there."

Translation

None necessary.

DID YOU KNOW?

When this ship was brand-new, we saw her docked in San Juan as we sailed in on another vessel. The passengers lining the rail wondered aloud what it was, until one man proclaimed, "I know, that's the new Severance of the Seas!"

Cabins & Costs

Fantasy Suites: .... A

Average Price PPPD: $666 including airfare.
The Royal Suite, #1010, some 1000 square feet of luxury, with private veranda, whirlpool tub, living room with wet bar, refrigerator and entertainment center—plus plenty of room for entertaining, and a big walk-in closet with generous storage space and personal safe.

Small Splurges: .... B

Average Price PPPD: $466 including airfare.

One of the eight Bridge Deck suites, with large windows, sitting area with sofa an
chairs, two lower beds plus a sofa-bed for a third person, mini-refrigerator and bat
with tub.

Suitable Standards: .... (

Average Price PPPD: $366 including airfare.
In categories F and G, you'll find twin beds in an L-configuration, small tripo
brass-and-glass table, one chair, desk/dresser, bath with shower and skimpy storag
space in an area approximately 120 square feet.

Bottom Bunks: .... (

Average Price PPPD: $233 including airfare.
The Q category inside cabins forward on B Deck are the cheapest on board, wit
two lower beds in parallel configuration, bath with shower, one chair and dresser.

Where She Goes

The seven-day Eastern Caribbean itinerary aboard *Sovereign of the Seas* ends in De
cember when the ship begins three- and four-day cruises year-round from Miami to th
Bahamas.

The Bottom Line

We're still not crazy about the vertical stacking that puts the cabins forward and th
public areas aft. While it saves long strolls down hallways (unless your cabin is well for
ward) it still means a lot of stair climbing for impatient passengers who don't want to wai
for the elevators.

Families with teenagers would be wiser to book one of the four newer ships—*Mon
arch, Majesty, Legend* or *Splendour*—because all of them have better youth facilities than
Sovereign.

Other than that, however, you'll probably find *Sovereign of the Seas* is like your favor
ite resort hotel gone to sea, with everything aboard but the golf course; you'll have to
book RCCL's *Legend of the Seas* or *Splendour of the Seas* for that.

Fielding's Five

Five Favorite Space Stations

1. The Centrum, a five-deck atrium with glass elevators, pools and fountains, glittering
    curved staircases, all dazzle and splash.

2. Touch of Class Champagne Bar, ideal for a romantic early evening glass of the bub-
    bly and a nibble of Camembert amid cushy leather sofas in an intimate step-down
    sitting room.

3. Boutiques of Centrum, the ship's shopping mall and a veritable town square with its
    own sidewalk cafe.

4. Anything Goes, the disco/nightclub aft on Commodore Deck, with its laser optics
    and holograms, pulsating neon and throbbing music.

5. The Music Man Lounge, with 76 trombones etched on the windows and three
    musicians sculpted in metal by the door, presents late cabaret shows and country/
    western music on theme nights.

Sovereign of the Seas ★★★★

Registry	**Norway**
Officers	**Norwegian**
Crew	**International**
Complement	**808**
GRT	**73,192**
Length (ft.)	**880**
Beam (ft.)	**106**
Draft (ft.)	**25**
Passengers-Cabins Full	**2524**
Passengers-2/Cabin	**2276**
Passenger Space Ratio	**32.15**
Stability Rating	**Good**
Seatings	**2**
Cuisine	**Themed**
Dress Code	**Traditional**
Room Service	**Yes**
Tip	**$7.50 PPPD, 15% automatically added to bar checks**

Ship Amenities

Outdoor Pool	**2**
Indoor Pool	**0**
Jacuzzi	**2**
Fitness Center	**Yes**
Spa	**Yes**
Beauty Shop	**Yes**
Showroom	**Yes**
Bars/Lounges	**9**
Casino	**Yes**
Shops	**6**
Library	**Yes**
Child Program	**Yes**
Self Service Laundry	**No**
Elevators	**13**

Cabin Statistics

Suites	**12**
Outside Doubles	**722**
Inside Doubles	**416**
Wheelchair Cabins	**0**
Singles	**0**
Single Surcharge	**150%**
Verandas	**0**
110 Volt	**Yes**

Sun Viking

While the name itself connotes rows of golden Scandinavian gods and goddesses lazily rotating as they turn themselves tan, we think instead of Finnish shipyard workers laboring away in the chill damp of a Helsinki winter morning as they create a fantasy Caribbean cruise ship for the 1970s. A swimming pool—yes!—and no shade to come between the sun and the sunbathers, say the shivering architects.

Everything on the top three decks is centered around a deep oblong pool big enough for modest laps; the decks are swathed in enough robin's egg blue AstroTurf to carpet a small stadium. The top three decks stare at that pool and the pair of saunas tucked away just behind it, the Sun Walk looking down from above, and rows of wooden benches like an ampitheater where an audience might applaud a particularly shapely body in a swimsuit. A mural on the sports deck says it all—a 1970's Op Art rendition of a pretty blonde riding a seahorse. You almost expect to see a yellow submarine.

Tidy as the line's ShipShape promotions, the *Sun Viking* offers beige-on-beige rows of cabins and passageways lined with porthole-shaped photographs that look like a Kodak shop window display, some of them faded. As the line's smallest ship, the *Sun Viking* has served as bellwether from the beginning, pioneering new destinations like Alaska, Europe and now Asia, once the line made the gigantic hurdle to venture beyond the Caribbean.

The Brochure Says

"...intimate...might have been crossbred with a cozy yacht...generous ratio of staff to passengers..."

Translation

The *Sun Viking* is small enough that it's easy to find your way around and meet fellow passengers, and cabins are about the size you'd find on a very cozy yacht but adequate unto the need, given that dedicated pool deck. The staff is pleasant and friendly, and the ratio of 2.1 passengers to one crew member is better than most ships in this price range.

Cabins & Costs

Small Splurges: C

Average Price PPPD: $393 including airfare.

"Small" is the operative word for almost all RCCL cabins, but the category C cabins on Promenade Deck are slightly roomier than most and worth the extra money for the additional storage space, mirrors on the sliding closet doors, a bathtub with shower and the fact that the two of you can sit down on the twin beds without bumping knees. You also get one chair and one hassock.

Suitable Standards: C

Average Price PPPD: $314 including airfare.

Inside and outside cabins in the H category are termed Larger Staterooms, meaning larger than a breadbox. Many are interconnecting, making this a possibility for families, and if you pick an amidships location, the ride is smoother.

Bottom Bunks: .... D

Average Price PPPD: $257 including airfare, dropping to $204 a day per person when four people share.

Four slim-hipped people could squeeze into one of the budget-priced N category cabins like 746, a quad, with two lower and two upper beds, providing they traveled light and took turns getting up and dressing, then going out of the cabin so the next one could get up and dress. The good news: With four very close friends sharing the space, the rate drops considerably.

INSIDER TIP

Try to get table assignments at one of the tables for four along the window wall in the L-extension of the pretty HMS Pinafore Dining Room for optimum viewing pleasure.

KEELHAUL

We note both a bellstand on board and a printed suggestion sheet saying "Bellboys are tipped when service is rendered." On most lines, cabin stewards lend a hand with baggage without the other hand extended for tips.

Where She Goes

Sun Viking makes a series of 14- and 15-night sailings—round-trip from Singapore to Indonesia, Malaysia and Thailand; Singapore to Hong Kong with calls in Thailand, Vietnam and China; Beijing to Tokyo with calls in Korea, China and Japan; Hong Kong to Beijing with calls at six Chinese ports; 13-night cruises between Beijing and Hong Kong that call at five China ports; Bangkok to Singapore calling in Malaysia and Indonesia; and between Bangkok and Hong Kong, calling in Malaysia, Singapore, Vietnam and China.

As the smallest and second-oldest vessel in the fleet, the *Sun Viking* is a sentimental favorite with long-time loyal passengers. This also makes it the obvious choice to pioneer new destination areas, since RCCL frequent cruisers always want to check out new places especially when they get frequent-passenger introductory discounts.

Warmer and cozier than the megaliners, *Sun Viking* is not likely to be around much longer for RCCL because of increasingly stricter international safety regulations and the upcoming series of new vessels under order for the rest of the decade. Book soon while she's still here. Although neither elegant nor deluxe, she's a trim and comfortable ship and you'll probably love her if you're not a world-class fussbudget.

Best of all, these Asia cruises are great buys, priced, even with roundtrip airfare, not much higher than Caribbean prices aboard the line's other ships.

Five Good Reasons to Book This Ship

1. To take a mainstream American-style cruise in Asia.

2. To enjoy the RCCL lifestyle on a more intimate vessel.

3. To get a great perch for sightseeing high atop the ship on the Compass Deck's built-in wood benches.

4. To stake out one of the comfortable barstools in the pretty Merry Widow Lounge with its Tiffany-like stained glass dome and expanse of shining mahogany bar.

5. To be able to say to new shipboard friends, "I'll meet you in the Annie Get Your Gun."

Sun Viking ★★

Registry	**Norway**
Officers	**Norwegian**
Crew	**International**
Complement	**341**
GRT	**18,445**
Length (ft.)	**563**
Beam (ft.)	**80**
Draft (ft.)	**22**
Passengers-Cabins Full	**818**
Passengers-2/Cabin	**714**
Passenger Space Ratio	**25.84**
Stability Rating	**Fair**
Seatings	**2**
Cuisine	**Themed**
Dress Code	**Traditional**
Room Service	**Yes**
Tip	**$7.50 PPPD, 15% automatically added to bar checks**

Ship Amenities

Outdoor Pool	**1**
Indoor Pool	**0**
Jacuzzi	**0**
Fitness Center	**No**
Spa	**No**
Beauty Shop	**Yes**
Showroom	**Yes**
Bars/Lounges	**6**
Casino	**Yes**
Shops	**2**
Library	**Yes**
Child Program	**No**
Self Service Laundry	**No**
Elevators	**4**

Cabin Statistics

Suites	**1**
Outside Doubles	**240**
Inside Doubles	**117**
Wheelchair Cabins	**0**
Singles	**0**
Single Surcharge	**150%**
Verandas	**0**
110 Volt	**Yes**

Viking Serenade

You've come a long way, baby, from your start as a Scandinavian ferry back in 1981, then a stint as the car-carrying Stardancer *in Alaska for Sundance Cruises, the short-lived company operated by Stan MacDonald, founder of Princess Cruises and grandaddy of TV's "The Love Boat." But you kept on truckin' until your fairy godmother RCCL picked you up and dusted you off with a $75 million full-body makeover to turn you into the dazzler you are today. Lucky, lucky LA to have you all to herself alone. Twice a week for 52 weeks all year round, Ensenada here we come!*

Few makeovers have been as startling as the 1991 changeover from the 996-passenger plain-Jane *Stardancer* to the glittering 1514-passenger *Viking Serenade* with 260 new cabins, 144 of them neatly slipped in where the vessel's under-utilized car ferry used to be. And these newest cabins are also the lowest-priced outside doubles (see "Suitable Standards").

You'll find spacious lobby areas, a large shopping center, a big lavish casino and two handsome restaurants featuring theme dinners, everything a first time cruiser or a weekender would expect. A little neon here, some brass and marble there, and voila, a glamorous weekend getaway at Palm Springs prices.

DID YOU KNOW?

You may remember Viking Serenade *as the ship that was struck by an outbreak of Shigella flexneri in late August 1994, sickening 650 passengers. Prompt action by the line and U.S. Public Health Service inspectors prevented any further outbreaks; two subsequent cruises were cancelled while all areas of food preparation and all food handlers were tested. Everything aboard the ship was completely sanitized before she sailed again; even telephones and hand-held hair dryers were taken apart and sanitized.*

DID YOU KNOW?

At the time of the random incident, the ship's public health sanitation score was 92, and a subsequent inspection in January 1995 resulted in an 88. Scores of 86 and above are termed satisfactory by the Centers for Disease Control, who make regular unannounced inspections of all ships sailing from U.S. ports. Go figure.

The Brochure Says

"She's beautiful. She's romantic. And she's always fun…If we don't see you on deck for coffee and fresh pastries at 6 a.m., *hasta la vista*."

Translation

You're going to have fun aboard, probably stay up very late, but you'll enjoy some really classy decor aboard this ship.

DID YOU KNOW?

Although Whoopi Goldberg is godmother of the Viking Serenade, *the original vessel, named* Scandinavia, *was christened by actress Liv Ullmann in 1981.*

Cabins & Costs

Fantasy Suites: .... **B+**

Average Price PPPD: $593 with airfare, $543 cruise only.
The Royal Suite, # 9566, fills an area that previously held four standard cabins, with a large living room with wet bar and dining area, a TV set with VCR and CD player, a separate bedroom with king-sized bed, a big marble bathroom with oversized Jacuzzi tub, and a walk-in closet.

Small Splurges: .... **A**

Average Price PPPD: $453 with airfare, $403 cruise only.
We'd opt for one of the five aft suites on Star Deck, which have their own private balconies. These category B quarters, built where the officers' quarters were previously, are a bit bigger than the standard cabins. A great bonus: private sunbathing or reading area away from the sometimes-crowded public decks. They have two lower beds, sitting area with sofa and chairs and plenty of storage space for a short cruise.

Suitable Standards: .... **B**

Average Price PPPD: $326 with airfare, $276 cruise only.
If you don't mind a porthole instead of a window, you can save money by booking the cheapest outside double cabins, category I on B deck. They're the same size as the other standard cabins on board (around 150 square feet) with modular German-built bathrooms, two lower beds and plenty of storage space.

Bottom Bunks: .... **C**

Average Price PPPD: $226 with airfare, $176 cruise only.
And that's literally the case with the cheapest digs aboard, the category Q insides with upper and lower bunks. The good part is, you're on Main Deck rather than

down in the dungeons somewhere, and the cabin is attractively furnished and ever so slightly larger than some of the more expensive outside doubles across the hall.

INSIDER TIP

Check sailing dates in the brochure to find "value" or "economy" season sailings because prices are somewhat lower than peak season (summer) rates given above.

Where She Goes

The *Viking Serenade* sails from Los Angeles to Ensenada and back every Monday and Friday, calling at Catalina Island on the four-day midweek cruises. (She used to call in San Diego as well, until the attorney general of California announced a ruling against cruise ship gambling.)

With a 6 p.m. Friday departure and an 8 a.m. Monday morning arrival it makes a good weekend getaway for southern Californians—so long as they remember to get aboard before 5:30 p.m. and realize they can't disembark until 9:30 or 10 a.m.

The Bottom Line

The *Viking Serenade* is handsome, the price is right, and if you've already done Ensenada, you can stay on board and enjoy the pool, spa and sundeck.

Fielding's Five

Five Hot Hot Hot Spots

1. The Sunshine Bar, the best singles' bar at sea, 50-feet long and dotted with comfortable barstools stretching almost the width of the vessel on the Sun Deck.

2. The Aida Dining Room with its Egyptian art, honey-colored burled wood and marble trim, smaller than the Magic Flute Dining Room one deck above.

3. The Viking Crown Lounge, a combination observation lounge and jazzy disco after dark, was prefabricated in a San Diego shipyard, lifted in one piece (all 144 tons of it) and carefully settled into its allotted space by the funnel during the massive renovation in 1991.

4. The Bali Hai Lounge, with its copper trim, etched glass panels and shiny surfaces, makes a dazzling cabaret and nightclub.

5. The children's playroom with its jumble of brightly colored plastic balls to dive into.

Five Good Reasons to Book This Ship

1. To take a weekend break without going to Las Vegas or Palm Springs.

2. To check out the best bodies as they parade between the swimming pool and the fitness center on Sun Deck.

3. It's the only way to get to Catalina Island, 22 miles across the sea (yes, we know the song says 26, but it's wrong) in peak season and still be assured you have a place to sleep. (Catalina is a port of call on four-day cruises only.)

- The kids will love it—teenagers because there's a teen club with its own dance floor, DJ booth, video games and cola bar, younger kids for the playroom with pint-sized furniture in Crayola colors.

- Because actress Whoopi Goldberg is the ship's godmother (she christened the vessel in LA in June, 1991), and it carries on in her special blend of worldly-wise humor and from-the-heart sentiment.

Five Things You Won't Find on Board

1. A car-carrying deck; that was removed in 1991.

2. A bunch of early-to-bed types.

3. Papageno in the Magic Flute Dining Room.

4. The wooden bust of Stan MacDonald that used to grace the Schooner Bar when it was called Stanley's Pub. (RCCL sent it back to MacDonald after the renovation.)

5. A lot of empty deck space; every inch seems to be covered with tables, chairs or sun loungers.

Viking Serenade ★★★★

Registry	Bahamas
Officers	Norwegian
Crew	International
Complement	320
GRT	40,132
Length (ft.)	623
Beam (ft.)	89
Draft (ft.)	24
Passengers-Cabins Full	1863
Passengers-2/Cabin	1512
Passenger Space Ratio	26.54
Stability Rating	Fair
Seatings	2
Cuisine	Themed
Dress Code	Traditional
Room Service	Yes
Tip	$7.50 PPPD. 15% automatically added to bar checks

Ship Amenities

Outdoor Pool	1
Indoor Pool	0
Jacuzzi	0
Fitness Center	Yes
Spa	No
Beauty Shop	Yes
Showroom	Yes
Bars/Lounges	5
Casino	Yes
Shops	3
Library	Yes
Child Program	Yes
Self Service Laundry	No
Elevators	5

Cabin Statistics

Suites	8
Outside Doubles	478
Inside Doubles	278
Wheelchair Cabins	4
Singles	0
Single Surcharge	150%
Verandas	5
110 Volt	Yes

Royal Olympic Cruises

One Rockefeller Plaza, Suite 315, New York, NY 10020-2090
(212) 397-6400, (800) 872-6400

History . . . .

Two Greek-owned cruise lines, Sun Line and Epirotiki Cruises, announced a merger to form a new cruise line called Royal Olympic Cruises.

The new cruise line operates as two separate divisions. The upscale division is called the Blue Ships and includes three ships, the 620-passenger *Stella Solaris*, the 300-passenger *Stella Oceanis*, and the 400-passenger *Odysseus*. The popular-priced line, called the White Ships, will include the 670-passenger *Triton*, the 300-passenger *Orpheus* and the 900-passenger *Olympic*. The ships sail in the Greek Islands, Turkey, Egypt and Israel.

The remaining vessels in the combined fleet, which includes the *Stella Maris, Jason, Neptune* and *Argonaut,* would be made available primarily for charter service in various geographical areas. Under the agreement, each company would continue to own its own vessels.

For convenience, this guide will place the ships' ratings and reviews under the banner of their parent company. For this reason, see Sun Line, page 749, for reviews and ratings for the *Stella Solaris, Stella Oceanis* and *Odysseus,* and Epirotiki Cruises, page 355, for ratings and reviews on the *Triton, Orpheus* and *Olympic.*

SEABOURN
CRUISE LINE

55 Francisco Street , San Francisco, CA 94133
(415) 391-8518, (800) 929-4747

History . . . .

The buzz started in 1987 with a full-color ad in the travel trades depicting the dapper and distinguished Warren Titus, recently retired head of Royal Viking Line, clad in a tuxedo and standing on a pier at night to announce the impending arrival of a new super-luxury cruise line to be called Signet Cruises. But while the new company's first ship was still under construction, it was learned a small Texas-based company had registered the name Signet Cruises, presumably in case they might start a cruise line in the future. So the fledgling new line, owned by young Norwegian industrialist Atle Brynestad, changed its name to Seabourn and—the cliché is inevitable—the rest is history.

On a rainy mid-December morning in 1988 in San Francisco, ambassador and former child star Shirley Temple Black smashed the customary bottle of champagne against the bow of the 200-passenger *Seabourn Pride* with aplomb (to the rhythm of what some of us imagined was "On the Good Ship Lollipop") and later requested a tour of the engine room.

The *Pride* was followed in 1989 by almost-identical sister ship *Seabourn Spirit*, both achieved great acclaim, especially in the luxury travel press. In 1991, Carnival Cruise Lines, having long touted an upscale "Tiffany product" they intended to introduce, purchased 25 percent of Seabourn, and acquired an additional 25 percent in 1996, as well as the former *Royal Viking Queen/Queen Odyssey*, now *Seabourn Legend*.

—First cruise line to implement a timeshare-at-sea program called WorldFare, in which passengers purchase 45, 60, 90 or 120 days of Seabourn cruising and use them over a period of 36 months on any cruises (1993).

SEABOURN CRUISE LINE

Concept . . . .

To offer discriminating passengers all the amenities they expect aboar
a full-sized cruise vessel of 10,000 tons carrying 200 in an onboar
ambiance that is "casual, but elegant." Service is "warm and friendl
but impeccable. And there is absolutely no tipping."

Signatures . . . .

The blue-and-white shield logo that adorns the double funnels of bot
ships.

The Signature Series of shore excursions, custom-designed especiall
for Seabourn passengers. The Celebrity Chefs series that brings wel
known chefs from restaurants around the world to prepare signatur
dishes or special menus to complement the ship's already superb cui
sine.

EAVESDROPPING

*Then-mayor of San Francisco Art Agnos, touring the newly christened ship
with its godmother Shirley Temple Black and other local officials, quipped,
"If the Pilgrims had come over on the Seabourn Pride rather than the Mayflower, they never would have gotten off the ship."*

Gimmicks . . . .

Seabourn WorldFare advance purchase plan in which a passenger ca
buy a certain number of days aboard and use them within three years o
any cruises offered by the line.

Who's the Competition . . . .

The usual suspects, of course. Silversea Cruises will give Seabourn
good run for the money-passengers if it maintains its present high qual
ity product (which, unlike Seabourn, includes all beverages in a less
pricey base fare) and keeps prices down. And of course, the one an
only Sea Goddess, which had a four-year head start on Seabourn.

EAVESDROPPING

*Carnival CEO Micky Arison to Seabourn founder Atle Brynstad, "No one has
ever tried to copy Carnival (the most profitable of Carnival Corporation's
three cruise lines) but everyone tries to copy Seabourn (at that time, the least
profitable)."*

Who's Aboard . . . .

Veteran cruisers from Royal Viking and Sea Goddess, first-time cruiser
who only want the best and can afford it, a few families traveling ir
three-generational groups with interconnecting suites, ranging in ag
from thirtysomething two-income professional couples to retired
CEOs. About half the passengers on any cruise are under 50. On our
several cruises with Seabourn, we've met English country squires, Sar
Francisco restaurateurs, Hong Kong journalists, a young California-
based New Zealand executive, a romance novelist, a noted jazz musician, and numerous doctors, dentists, lawyers, financiers and psychoan-

alysts. They're more often old money rather than nouveau riche. Passengers are always falling into small-world conversations, finding they have close mutual friends or children attending the same schools. It's a small world in that tax bracket.

Who Should Go.........................

Anyone who books a suite at the Pierre, lunches at The Club in Pebble Beach, has a house in Vail or a condo in Deer Valley. Clubby and very posh, these ships are for couples who are rich and successful. If you want to see a cross-section of typical passengers, ask the line to send you a copy of their pretty publication for repeat passengers called Seabourn Club Herald. There, on several back pages, are color photographs of recent passengers—Stirling Moss, the legendary British motorcar racer; actress Rhonda Fleming; Teddy Roosevelt's granddaughter Sarah Gannett—along with a number of the rich and unfamous.

Who Should Not Go ....

Children or even restless teenagers would not find places to go and things to do on these ships. Anyone unwilling to dress for dinner would be out of place. And anyone who doesn't know what "out of place" means should certainly not go.

The Lifestyle ....

The ships are large enough to give passengers a sense of privacy when they wish but with a variety of indoor and outdoor spaces to be social or be secluded. Obviously the luxuriously comfortable cabins with seating areas, TV/VCR and full meal service entice passengers to spend more time inside. Days are casual, with many passengers lounging on deck in bathing suits reading a book, but evenings get much more formal. There are not many organized activities on board since passengers prefer to plan their own time, but they will attend outstanding lecturers.

Wardrobe.............................

While daytimes may be spent in casual, but never sloppy, garb, people dress up in the evenings, not because a dress code tells them they must, but because they like to, and because they are at ease in tuxedos and dressy gowns, silk or linen suits and top-label sportswear.

Bill of Fare........................... A+

Sophisticated contemporary cuisine prepared a la minute (when it's ordered) and served in small portions to encourage passengers to try the suggested menu rather than simply one or two dishes. We remember one chef's suggestion menu from Stefan Hamrin that we followed all the way through—an avocado fan with jumbo shrimp and scallion sauce, followed by creamy onion garlic soup with croutons, then a field salad of arugula and radishes, roast rack of spring lamb Dijonnaise, and hot macadamia nut soufflé with Tia Maria sauce. The food was light enough and the portions small enough that we were satiated but not stuffed at the end of the meal.

The Veranda Cafe on the Seabourn Spirit is a delightful place to have breakfast on a sunny morning.

Mornings you can breakfast on deck under the shade of a canvas canopy or inside the jade green-and-white marble Veranda where the fresh fruits are arranged on the buffet like gemstones and the thinly sliced smoked salmon and gravlax are draped like silk with caper beading.

The recipe for a delectable raspberry dessert was given to us by Seabourn chef Stefan Hamrin when we were writing a *Bon Appétit* article about luxury cruise ships in the Mediterranean several years ago.

Raspberry Parfait
10 servings

5 egg whites

1/4 cup sugar

1 1/8 cups sugar

4 ounces (1/2 cup) water

3 pints fresh raspberries

1/2 cup sugar

1 tsp lemon juice

4 cups whipping cream, whipped stiffly

Beat egg whites and 1/4 cup sugar together until stiff peaks form. Cook 1 1/8 cups of sugar with 4 ounces water to soft ball stage (when a bit of the mixture dropped into a cup of cold water forms a soft ball).

Carefully add this sugar syrup in a thin stream to the beaten egg whites, beating all the time to incorporate it, until the mixture is evenly cool.

Purée the raspberries and strain through a fine sieve to remove the seeds. Combine raspberry purée with 1/2 cup sugar and lemon juice and fold into the egg white mixture.

Finally, gently fold in the whipped cream and place in a mold or freezer form; place in freezer for several hours until firm. Serve with additional raspberry purée and whipped cream if desired.

Showtime . . . . A

When the ships began operation, the evening's entertainment was done by the Styleliners, a quartet of singers who perform music by Sondheim, Porter, Berlin, Gershwin and other notables in a choreographed concert style. The ships still offer musical caberet shows on the modest stage using the variety of principal artists performing during the cruise, as well as bringing in regional entertainers from the ports of call. Lecturers from celebrity chefs to contract bridge teachers, jazz artists, pianist-humorist Victor Borge and other celebrities. TV personality Dick Cavett, actress Brenda Vaccaro, Paris-based food writer Patricia Wells and astronaut Wally Schirra were among the recent guests.

Discounts . . . .

Seabourn never allows the "D" word to creep into a discussion, but a rose by any other name can still save some money on a cruise. Repeat passengers in The Seabourn Club get "savings on the cruise tariff" of 10 percent from having made a previous cruise, plus 5 percent off the fare for friends they bring along who occupy a separate suite. Cumulative days of cruising with the company also brings "substantial fare reductions," and anyone who completes 140 days aboard the ships gets the next cruise of up to 14 days free. An "early payment program" means if you book and pay for your cruise 12 months ahead of time you save 10 percent, six months ahead of time and you save 5 percent. A "single traveler savings option" on certain cruises reduces the normal 200 percent surcharge to only 110, 125 or 150 percent.

The standard suite-like cabins aboard **Seabourn Pride** *and* **Seabourn Spirit** *are large enough to have friends in for cocktails.*

The Bottom Line

When the *Seabourn Pride* had been running for a year and the *Seabourn Spirit* just introduced, we asked Warren Titus about the difference between operating Seabourn and operating Royal Viking. "It's much easier for us to cater to a single strata of people...They basically come form the same background and tastes...and it's so much easier to satisfy people on this ship than on a Royal Viking ship with a variety of cabins and prices."

Seabourn ships are the ultimate in patrician elegance without ever being stuffy. Your dinner table partner might turn out to have a title preceding his name, but he's unlikely to ever mention it. Everything works on these ships from the food to the service to the ambiance. You get, quite simply, a superbly satisifying cruise experience.

Seabourn Legend ★★★★★★
Seabourn Pride ★★★★★★
Seabourn Spirit ★★★★★★

Day after day, time after time, we find ourselves agreeing that there is nowhere else on earth we would rather be than right here, right now, aboard the Seabourn Pride *listening to Page Cavanaugh at the piano playing "Rainy Day" at cocktail time in the understated elegance of The Club.*

Notes from the inaugural sailing
December 1988

Nothing makes the folks at Seabourn madder than to hear their 10,000-ton cruise ships called "small," "little," or "yacht-sized." They have, as Warren Titus pointed out on the first sailing of the *Seabourn Pride*, "all the amenities and facilities of a full-sized cruise ship but only for a few people." Everything here is scaled to the human passenger rather than cruise industry statistics, and they spent a lot of time determining what the experienced cruise passenger who books the upper end of the market would like. Suiterooms are a spacious 277 square feet with very lavish bathrooms and sitting

.reas large enough to host six people comfortably at cocktail time. There are .ll sorts of beautiful public rooms and deck spaces, along with, at one time, a mysterious flying saucer-like device called the Star Observatory, where passengers could climb in and lie back on cushy leather seats to star-gaze through a telescope; that's not easy on a moving ship, which is why we've never saw anyone try it.

The Brochure Says

"To some, Seabourn may be expensive; but Seabourn is not overpriced. Some cruise ines say they provide a 'Seabourn-like' experience at half price. We know it can't be done and so do you. New and so-called luxury cruise lines are cropping up and claiming five stars even before their ships are launched. At the same time, old and established cruise ines, as we knew them, are either disappearing or being modified and downgraded in price wars that offer the 'deal.' The authentic Seabourn Experience is a good value for the money, because we believe we provide an experience that exceeds your expectations."

Translation

This is an example of what we meant when we said above that Seabourn is "the ultimate in patrician elegance without ever being stuffy." They're not above taking off their white gloves to duke it out with the competition.

Cabins & Costs

Fantasy Suites: ....A+
Average Price PPPD: $1831 in the Mediterranean including airfare.
Owner's Suite Type E (there are two per ship) are 575 square feet with veranda, large living room with curved sofas, chairs and coffee table plus a dining table with four chairs, a marble bath with tub and twin sinks plus a second half-bath for guests, and a separate bedroom with all the amenities listed below (see Suitable Standards).

Small Splurges: ....A+
Average Price PPPD: $1676 in the Mediterranean including airfare.
Each of the 16 Regal C suites is 400 square feet with a small private veranda, queen-sized bed in a separate bedroom, curved sofas and chairs in the living room and lots of built-ins, plus all the amenities listed below (see Suitable Standards).

Suitable Standards: ....A+
Average Price PPPD: $1055 in the Mediterranean including airfare.
The standard suite-rooms are 277 square feet each with a five-foot picture window placed low enough on the wall that you can lie in bed (either twins or queen-sized) and watch the sea. A tapestry-print sofa, three chairs and two round stools provide plenty of guest seating, along with a mini-refrigerator, full array of crystal and a fully stocked liquor cabinet. The coffee table can be raised to dining table height if you want to dine in, and there's a walk-in closet with lots of storage, a built-in dresser/desk with drawers and mirror, and a marble bathroom with tub, twin sinks set in a marble counter and a mirrored storage area for toiletries.

Bottom Bunks: .... NA
There's no such thing on Seabourn ships.

EAVESDROPPING

Famous Last Words Department: A quartet of San Francisco travel agents, invited for the christening-day tour of the Seabourn Pride, walked from the gangway into the reception hall and turned up their noses at the last-minute touch-ups of artificial greenery to replace plants damaged in the stormy crossing, accepted a glass of champagne from a white-gloved waiter and flounced into the Magellan Lounge, where they sat at the back table just long enough to empty their glasses. "Hmph," one sniffed, "I don't like this room; it's too dark." "Well, this ship'll never touch the Sea Goddesses," her friend commented. "I've seen enough—ready to go?" And away they went, back down the gangway without looking at anything else.

DID YOU KNOW?

We have had innumerable conversations with heads of certain ultra-deluxe cruise lines about why they don't include as largesse the relatively inexpensive duty-free bar drinks (even if it's house brands only) and dinner wines like Song of Flower, Silversea and Sea Goddess ships do, and the answer we invariably get is, "The passengers who don't drink don't want to subsidize those that do."

The *Seabourn Spirit* begins 1997 in southeast Asia with cruises from Singapore to Malaysia, Myanmar and Thailand, then moves to Bali, back to Hong Kong and China in the spring, and sails into the Mediterranean for the summer, then to Africa and the Seychelles.

The *Seabourn Pride* starts 1997 in South America, then offers Caribbean cruises before setting on its transatlantic sailing March 31 to Lisbon. The ship spends the summer in Europe, with an early and late summer series of Mediterranean sailings interspersed with some Scandinavian June and July cruises, then sails to New York for autumn Canada/New England cruises.

The *Seabourn Legend* cruises the Caribbean then repositions via the West Coast to Hawaii, Asia and the South Pacific.

Yes, it's expensive, but not even the worst nit-picker could find anything to complain about with the food, service and accommodations. And there are really exotic and interesting itineraries, calling at some rarely visited ports, along with appealing mix-and-match cruises that can be combined for a sizable savings. Go for the standard suite-rooms unless you want to splurge to get a veranda. When you head for the deck, there's a steward in white shirt and tie to turn your deck chair toward the sun hourly or spritz you with mineral water. In the evening, you can slip away for cocktails in the club while the pianist plays your favorite sentimental song, or don something dazzling for dinner dancing between courses in the restaurant. Or enjoy breakfast in bed while gazing at the sea through a five-foot picture window with its own automatic window washing system.

Fielding's Five

Five Unforgettable Places

1. A watersports marina that can be thrust out from the ship when it's at anchor, letting passengers swim in a giant submersible steel mesh tank with its own teak deck around it, or go windsurfing, sailing or waterskiing.

2. Forward on the top deck is the Horizon Lounge with wrap-around glass windows, cushy blue leather chairs and couches, a polished granite bar, a radar screen for passengers to play with and a computer-animated wall map of famous historic voyages as well as itinerary information.

3. The Sky Bar, a wooden bar with a circle of barstools around it plus wooden tables and lower stools fixed on the teak decking, is a popular gathering spot.

4. The Club, cool white and beige with wood, marble and woven textures, is equally handsome in the daytime with sunlight streaming in its glass dome or in the evening with the shades lowered and a pianist playing Duke Ellington compositions.

5. The Restaurant, with quiet, comfortable tables placed well apart, tapestry-patterned chairs and silky curtains; a pianist plays during dinner and there's a small dance floor for those evenings when dinner dancing is scheduled.

Five Good Reasons to Book These Ships

1. Because service is so good you don't have to lift a finger; you can let things come to you, rather than having to go fetch them.

2. Because you can buy an air/land program that includes economy-class airfare or optional upgrades, premium hotel accommodations, hospitality desks at the hotels and transfers to and from the ship.

3. Because tipping is not only not requested, but not permitted.

4. The little extras that mean a lot—bathrobes, hair dryers, combination safes, walk-in closets with four different kinds of hangers, personalized stationery, a sewing kit with the needles already threaded, a 24-hour room service menu that includes everything from sandwiches to grilled steaks, complete sets of bathroom towels in two colors, peach and pewter gray, and exquisite almond-scented toiletries.

5. Instead of aspic-encased show buffets and parades of baked Alaska, you can find sevruga caviar whenever you want to order it, fresh broiled sea bass, sautéed pheasant breast with Calvados sauce, chocolate truffle cake.

Five Things You Won't Find On Board

1. A lap swimming pool; the smallish pool is adequate but wedged between the Veranda Cafe and a stairwell. The Jacuzzi is more popular than the pool.

2. A view of undersea life in the underwater viewing room on the bottom deck when the ship is moving; all you see are bubbles.

3. A delay on getting your laundry and dry cleaning back; same-day service is available.

4. A surprise when you get to the dining room; copies of the menus are delivered daily to the cabins so you can plan ahead.

5. Bar drinks and dinner wine included in the fares; you'll pay extra for those.

Seabourn Legend ★★★★★
Seabourn Pride ★★★★★
Seabourn Spirit ★★★★★

Registry	**Norway**
Officers	**Norwegian**
Crew	**European**
Complement	**140**
GRT	**10,000**
Length (ft.)	**439**
Beam (ft.)	**63**
Draft (ft.)	**16.4**
Passengers-Cabins Full	**208**
Passengers-2/Cabin	**200**
Passenger Space Ratio	**50**
Stability Rating	**Good**
Seatings	**1**
Cuisine	**Contemporary**
Dress Code	**Traditional**
Room Service	**Yes**
Tip	**No tipping allowed**

Ship Amenities

Outdoor Pool	**1**
Indoor Pool	**0**
Jacuzzi	**3**
Fitness Center	**Yes**
Spa	**Yes**
Beauty Shop	**Yes**
Showroom	**Yes**
Bars/Lounges	**3**
Casino	**Yes**
Shops	**1**
Library	**Yes**
Child Program	**No**
Self-Service Laundry	**Yes**
Elevators	**3**

Cabin Statistics

Suites	**104**
Outside Doubles	**0**
Inside Doubles	**0**
Wheelchair Cabins	**4**
Singles	**0**
Single Surcharge	**110-150%**
Verandas	**6**
110 Volt	**Yes**

SEA CLOUD CRUISES

c/o Elegant Cruises & Tours, Inc.
31 Central Drive, Port Washington, NY 11050
☎ *(516) 767-9302, (800) 683-6767*

Sea Cloud   ★★★★, ⚓⚓⚓⚓⚓

While any vessel with white sails puffed by the wind is romantic, the sailing yacht Sea Cloud *is the most romantic of all the tall ships, not only because of her grace and beauty, but also because of her history. The yacht was built for a glamorous heiress by a fabled financier who loved her, became a nursery garden of delights for a child who would grow up to become a famous actress, and was briefly a home during the holidays for many of the world's rich and famous, as well as the rich and infamous. The legendary ship went on to become the toy of a Latin American dictator, a playpen for movie starlets, then an impounded derelict rotting away in Panama before being rescued by a group of German yachtsmen who restored her to her original glory.*

The *Sea Cloud* was built for $1 million in 1931 in the Krupp yard in Kiel, Germany, and was the largest privately-owned yacht in the world when she

was delivered to cereal heiress Marjorie Merriweather Post and her then-hus
band financier E. F. Hutton. The four-masted barque was first named *Hussar V*, since she was fifth in the series of yachts Hutton had built under that
name. (See Windjammer Barefoot Cruises, the *Mandalay*, page 777 for the
Hussar IV.) Their daughter, actress Dina Merrill, remembers in her child
hood spending six months of every year sailing around the world with guest
such as the Duke and Duchess of Windsor.

DID YOU KNOW?

*Marjorie rented a large warehouse in New Jersey where she chalked out the
deck plan on the floor and endlessly arranged and rearranged the antique
furniture until it suited her, then transferred it to the ship. All the bric-a-
brac and ornaments were glued to the mantels and tabletops where she
meant for them to stay.*

The Brochure Says

"The *Sea Cloud's* graceful style still inspires awe and admiration today, whether in port
or under sail. And the exhilaration of being on board, under full sail in warm tropical waters, is without comparison."

Translation

You're an instant celebrity in any port when you disembark this unique and glamorous
vessel, and you'll find yourself fending off street vendors in the Caribbean who think you
must be very, very rich.

DID YOU KNOW?

*Rafael Trujillo had come into possession of the Sea Cloud by trading a 44-pas-
senger Viscount propjet to Marjorie for it. He then put a cannon on the side
of the yacht, named it Angelina, termed it a man-of-war and rented it back
from the Dominican Republic's Navy for $1 a year. His favorite illegitimate
son Ramfis took it to college with him when he was enrolled in law school in
Southern California. When Trujillo was assassinated in 1961, family members
and loyal aides fled the country aboard the yacht with some $5 million in
cash and the dictator's body in an elaborate mahogany coffin in the smoking
room. After they were intercepted by a Dominican Republic gunboat, the
dictator's body was permitted to go on for burial in Paris' Pere Lachaise cem-
etery while the yacht—and presumably the $5 million—was returned to the
country to become the Patriot.*

Cabins & Costs

Fantasy Suites: .... A+

Average Price PPPD: $1184 plus airfare.
Owner's Suite #1, decorated in Louis XVI style with a marble fireplace (non-working), marble bathroom with gold faucets, French canopy bed with damask covers,
chairs and ottomans in satin brocade, flower-etched mirrors and gilded moldings, is
sumptuous and spacious.

The elegant owner's suite aboard the sailing yacht Sea Cloud *has marble fireplaces (non-working) and gold faucets.*

Small Splurges: .... A+

Average Price PPPD: $1070 plus airfare.

Suite #7 is warm and sophisticated with its softly burnished pale pine paneled walls and lower wainscoting accented with darker wood strips. The bath, a bit smaller than those in the two owner's suites, is marble with gold faucets on the tub. Best of all, there's a deep, walk-in closet with handcrafted storage cubicles.

Suitable Standards: C

Average Price PPPD: $656 plus airfare.

Now, here's the rub. There are only eight original staterooms on the ship; the remaining 24 were built in a refit when the ship was turned into a cruise vessel. They are divided into Categories A and B. The As are "large outside staterooms" which means they're slightly bigger than the tiny B cabins, and contain two lower beds with storage drawers built in underneath, a window, a built-in dresser with four drawers, and a small bathroom with shower. There is no desk, table or chair, nor anywhere to sit except on the beds, but you do get a hair dryer, terrycloth robes, a bowl of fruit, fresh flowers and a bottle of German champagne. In these cabins, you take turns getting up, showering and dressing, then one of you goes outside so the other can get up, shower and dress.

Bottom Bunks: .... C-

Average Price PPPD: $570 plus airfare.

B Category staterooms are furnished similarly to A, above, but are smaller.

Where She Goes

The *Sea Cloud* usually includes Caribbean cruises in winter and Mediterranean sailings in summer. Sailing from Antigua, the *Sea Cloud* cruises among the Windward Islands.

The Bottom Line

The food, prepared by German and Austrian chefs, is delicious although menus are limited in scope. Set dinner menus are posted in the mornings; if passengers spot something they don't like, they report promptly to the bartenders, who double as major-domos, and a substitute dish or entire menu will be arranged. Breakfasts are self-serve affairs set up in the dining room; lunches are elaborate buffets of hot and cold dishes with complimentary wines and beer usually eaten on the Lido deck, and dinners are formally served on linen-covered tables by candlelight, again with complimentary wines. Despite the cozy little shipshape cabins, we would go again tomorrow; it's that special.

Fielding's Five

Five Glorious Places

1. The Main Deck, natural teak with brass trim, glossy wood-paneled walls and polished benches, above which you can watch young sailors, male and female, climb the rigging to set the sails in the time-honored fashion.

2. The Lounge with its elegant wood bookcases, piano and oil paintings of classic tall ships doubles as part of the dining room during candlelight dinners.

3. The dining room with its original carved wood ceilings and panels and elegant wood-and-upholstery chairs is where the captain invites each passenger to dine at his table one evening during the cruise.

4. The Lido, a big deck shaded with a tarp, is where you sit out in the breeze and enjoy the casual buffet lunches. Complimentary wines are served at lunch and dinner.

5. The Blue Lagoon, a big cushioned area aft on the middle deck where lolling sunbathers recline on a raised platform upholstered with puffy blue mattresses.

Five Off-the-Wall Places

1. Owners Suite # 1 is Marjorie's own suite, grandly done up in marble and gold.

2. Owner's Suite # 2 was E. F. Hutton's equally grand but more masculine quarters, pine-paneled with a Carrera marble fireplace.

3. Suite # 4, all its furnishings original, was where the Duke of Windsor slept when he and the Duchess cruised with Mrs. Post to Cuba. (We don't know where the Duchess slept.)

4. Suite # 7 was Dina's bedroom and nursery, with a lavish marble bathroom and walk-in closet.

5. We're not sure which cabin was occupied by Zsa Zsa Gabor in the 1950s when her friend Ramfis Trujillo had the yacht anchored off the coast of Santa Monica, but people ashore still remember waking up one morning to see a banner hanging across the Sea Cloud's side painted in foot-high bright red letters, "Zsa Zsa Slept Here."

Five Good Reasons to Book This Ship

1. Because it's there.

2. To pretend to be one of the rich and famous, if only by getting up and going out on deck early in the morning to make believe it's 1935 and this is your own private yacht.

3. To explore the Caribbean or Mediterranean on a sailing expedition with all shore excursions included.

4. To have an unimaginably wonderful experience that you'll never forget.
5. To sleep in the bed where the Duke of Windsor once slept.

Five Things You Won't Find On Board

1. A wheelchair-accessible cabin; with no elevators and extremely steep stairs, this vessel should not be booked by anyone with limited mobility.
2. A children's program; children should not be aboard this ship because there's nowhere for them to play or be looked after.
3. A casino.
4. A beauty shop.
5. A swimming pool, although sometimes when the ship is at anchor, the gangway is lowered for passengers to swim in the Caribbean or Mediterranean.

Sea Cloud ★★★★, ⚓⚓⚓⚓

Registry	**Malta**
Officers	**International**
Crew	**International**
Complement	**65**
GRT	**2323**
Length (ft.)	**360**
Beam (ft.)	**49**
Draft (ft.)	**16.5**
Passengers-Cabins Full	**70**
Passengers-2/Cabin	**64**
Passenger Space Ratio	**NA**
Stability Rating	**Good**
Seatings	**1**
Cuisine	**Continental**
Dress Code	**Casual**
Room Service	**No**
Tip	**$7 PPPD, 15% automatically added to bar check**

Ship Amenities

Outdoor Pool	**0**
Indoor Pool	**0**
Jacuzzi	**0**
Fitness Center	**No**
Spa	**No**
Beauty Shop	**No**
Showroom	**No**
Bars/Lounges	**2**
Casino	**No**
Shops	**1**
Library	**Yes**
Child Program	**No**
Self-Service Laundry	**No**
Elevators	**0**

Cabin Statistics

Suites	**2**
Outside Doubles	**30**
Inside Doubles	**0**
Wheelchair Cabins	**0**
Singles	**0**
Single Surcharge	**150%**
Verandas	**0**
110 Volt	**No**

SEAWIND
CRUISE LINE

4770 Biscayne Boulevard, Miami, FL 33137
☎ *(800) 223-1877*

History

Seawind Cruise Line was founded in 1991 by a mix of Portuguese, Swedish and Greek interests to market the classic Portuguese ocean liner *Vasco de Gama* in the Caribbean on sailings out of Aruba. Until mid-1995, the ship retained the name *Vasco de Gama* while it sailed as and was marketed under the trade name *Seawind Crown*. Now it is officially *Seawind Crown*, and the double names painted on the bow are gone.

The ship was christened in Aruba on Aug. 11, 1991, by Maria Kyriakidis, wife of charterer Takis Kyriakidis, whose charter agreement was abruptly terminated Sep. 20, 1991. The then-owners, doing business as Trans World Cruises, picked up the charter themselves, and the ship resumed sailing Oct. 6, 1991, under the direction of Bo Paulson, George Potamianos and Jan Hygrell. Paulson and Hygrell represented the Swedish shipping giant Nordisk, which sold the vessel in July 1995, to a group of New York investors named Capital Holiday.

Concept

Sailing from Aruba with two alternating southern Caribbean itineraries at modest prices in a very gracious and spacious classic liner.

Signatures

The dual names on the ship's bow certainly made it stand out in a crowd, but, alas, that whimsical touch is gone now. There's an elegant wood-paneled chapel that can be used for weddings or renewal of vows. And there's always the Great American Cookout/Picnic on deck with down-home American music from barbershop quartets and such.

Gimmicks

Honeymoon and anniversary celebrations for people married within seven days of their cruise or couples celebrating an anniversary during the cruise.

Who's the Competition.

Dolphin Cruise Line withdrew the *OceanBreeze* from Aruba last May, leaving little real competition year-round for Seawind except in the general Caribbean marketplace itself.

Who's Aboard

A mix of 70 percent veteran and 30 percent first-time cruisers drawn b
the price and itinerary, many of them young to middle-aged couple:
The median age aboard is 45–50.

The ship also attracts a sizable contingent of Europeans, Latin Ameri
cans and Asians.

Who Should Go

Veteran cruisers will love the classic ship and the excellent itineraries
while first-timers will find all the traditional cruise touches they expec
presented in an un-glitzy fashion. An extra bonus for island collectors
If you take the two cruises back-to-back, you'll visit eight islands.

Who Should Not Go

Passengers who need a wheelchair-accessible cabin; there are non
aboard. Families with small children, since there's no children's pro
gram or counselor. Anyone who thinks it's not a Caribbean cruise if i
doesn't call in St. Thomas.

Teak and tile ornament the pool deck of this classic Portuguese liner.

The Lifestyle

Basically, a traditional cruise pattern is followed, with exercise classes,
musical and variety show entertainment, skeet-shooting, scuba and
snorkel lessons. There are two formal nights during the week.

EAVESDROPPING

*Travel agent on board: "My cabin I can get to in three minutes. On a three-
day cruise on those big ships, you spend the whole three days trying to find
your way around. Everything is right here—you don't have to walk five
blocks just to get to the lounge."*

Wardrobe

Casual island resort wear is proper daytime and shoreside apparel.

There are two formal nights aboard during each week, the captain's welcome-aboard and farewell parties, which call for men to wear a tuxedo, dinner jacket or suit, or at least a jacket and tie.

Bill of Fare.................................. B

The food is generally good, but the caterers lean toward large show buffets, flaming desserts and displays to impress first-time cruisers. There are some innovative Caribbean and Latin American dishes, as well as a couple of Greek specialties, that show up from time to time to supplement the run of oxtail consomme, duckling à l'orange and cherries jubilee. There are two meal seatings at assigned tables. First dinner seating is usually 6:30, the second at 8:30.

Showtime............................... .C+

There's a lot of entertainment with different musical productions nightly from Vanoff Productions of Miami, featuring feather-clad chorus girls who, when they exit, leave the stage looking like it's molting season. Caribbean bands play poolside in the daytime, and a combo plays dance music in the Panorama Lounge. Movies run daily in the cinema and on the cabin TV sets.

Discounts.................................

Seawind does some aggressive marketing, with advance purchase rates for anyone booking with a deposit 60 days ahead of sailing and a discounted second week for anyone booked 14 days back-to-back. A special Aruba land package called Free-Aruba adds on a free seven-night resort stay in Aruba at La Cabana All-Suite Beach Resort and Casino for passengers who have booked in cabin categories A through D. If you buy a cheaper cabin, in categories E through G, you'll still get three nights free at La Cabana. The airfare is included in that package too. You can also, if you prefer, opt for a free Caribbean wilderness adventure in Dominica or St. Lucia. If you cruise five nights on board in a cabin category A through G, you get four nights in Dominica's The Castaways (a beach and dive resort) or Fort Young Hotel (an urban hotel built in an old fort). If you cruise five nights on board in cabin categories A through D, you get seven nights free in The Harmony (a 30-room hotel at Rodney Bay) or Orange Grove Hotel (a hilltop hotel with its own private beach below) in St. Lucia.

The Bottom Line

This is a very good buy for anyone interested in cruising on a mid-sized classic ship to Caribbean islands a little off the beaten track.

Seawind Crown

It was an object lesson in how not to initiate a new cruise line—compared with, say, Crystal, which spent more than two years paving the way. The erstwhile charterer picked up the ship in a dock in Aruba at the end of a chartered Brazilian cruise (and some of the Brazilians refused to get off, so they sailed on the inaugural with us). He also flew out from Miami carrying two tons of excess baggage that consisted mostly of printed materials for the vessel. The costumes for the entertainers were impounded by Aruban officials (probably because of all the feathers), and the final blow came when the line's new president, while describing to the press all the 11th-hour travail, picked up a packet of sugar to sweeten his coffee and saw that it was marked Premier Cruise Line, a rival line that shares the same catering company.

The *Seawind Crown*, previously the *Vasco de Gama*, was built as the *Infante dom Enrique* in 1961 for the Portugal-to-Mozambique service and was laid up in Lisbon in 1976 after the African colony won its independence from Portugal and there was no further need to transport bureaucrats and their families back and forth.

In 1988, a major refurbishment supervised by George Potamianos was done in Greece to turn the ship into the *Vasco de Gama*, the name of the street in Lisbon where George lives. It would be interesting to ship buffs to make a walk-through figuring out which areas were what when it was a two-class ship. We got some clues from George. The smaller Madeira Restaurant adjoining the big dining room was the first-class dining room, the casino the first-class bar. There were even separate children's playrooms, presumably so the kids of the first-class passengers didn't have to associate with the kids of the second-class passengers. Turns out they didn't pray together either, since there was a second-class chapel where the mural behind the pool is located now. The existing chapel is, of course, the old first-class chapel. There was even, George said, a Tourist Class B, the next thing to steerage, and a lot of the cabins didn't have private baths in the old days. He also built what we

>elieve is one of the few seagoing squash courts, but it was supplanted not
>ng ago, alas, by an ordinary mirrored gym and fitness center.

The Brochure Says

"A half-century ago, when cruising was still the exclusive domain of the very rich, there
/as a certain style of life aboard cruise ships, a simple, classic style of service that is rarely
>und in the world today. Here, in the balmy waters of Seawind's Caribbean, time has
tood still, and thoughtful, gracious service still awaits you."

Translation

Although the international crew may represent as many as 34 different nationalities,
here is a warmth and friendliness from them that most cruisers will enjoy.

Cabins & Costs

Fantasy Suites: .... B

Average Price PPPD: $406 including airfare and free Aruba land stay.
The two owner's suites are spacious apartments with a large living room and separate bedroom, lots of windows facing forward, a couch that can convert to additional sleeping, coffee table, two chairs, color TV set, mini-refrigerator, built-in
desk and entry hall. In the bedroom are two single beds, a long built-in table with
console and nightstands, two large closets, and a huge bathroom with two wash
basins, tub and shower and storage shelves.

Small Splurges: .... B

Average Price PPPD: $364 including airfare and free Aruba land stay.
Also on the topmost deck are eight suites not quite as large as the owner's but very
handsomely furnished, part of the 12 suites that were created out of 24 original cabins in the 1988 refurbishment.

Suitable Standards: C

Average Price PPPD: $249 including airfare and free Aruba land stay.
In category H, fairly good-sized cabins with chest, dresser, three closets, optional
overhead bunks, and bath with shower.

Bottom Bunks: .... B

Average Price PPPD: $178 including airfare and free Aruba land stay.
The very lowest-priced category are the 32 inside cabins with upper and lower
berths, a small three-drawer chest, dresser, TV, mini-refrigerator, terrycloth robes,
hair dryers, bathroom with shower, a large mirror, altogether quite adequate unto
the need.

DID YOU KNOW?

*On the inaugural sailing of the Seawind Crown, everyone was so frantic and
flustered that the theme from "Gone With The Wind" played over and over on
the cabin radios, every day of the cruise until Friday, when someone, perhaps a bored Brazilian, put on samba tapes, which then played nonstop for
the remaining two days.*

Where She Goes

The *Seawind Crown* sails two alternate itineraries in the Caribbean out of Aruba, on week calling in Curaçao, Grenada, Barbados and St. Lucia, and the next week visiting Trinidad, Tobago, Barbados and Martinique, giving a real collector eight islands in 14 days, including Aruba.

The Bottom Line

We like the ship and the line for the money they charge, and the Free-Aruba package makes it a very good buy, throwing in on one package price roundtrip airfare, a seven night cruise and overnight stays in Aruba, the number of nights and type of hotel depending on the accommodations you booked aboard the ship. There are also new packages for Dominica and for St. Lucia, which let you cruise five nights on the ship, then stay in an island resort for four to seven nights and fly home from that island. That's a creative solution to the problem of airlift into Aruba to get the passengers all in and out.

Fielding's Five

Five Super Places

1. The chapel, a quiet, elegant little room on an upper deck, with an original inlaid wood mural outside, where passengers can participate in a renewal-of-wedding vows ceremony.
2. The Panorama Lounge, used for cabaret acts and dancing in the evenings.
3. The spiffy lower-deck gym, replacing a unique squash court but probably more popular among the North American passengers.
4. The Taverna doubles as a casual breakfast and lunch buffet area but is a bit small to handle the passenger numbers. However it makes a warm and cozy hideaway between meals.
5. The pool deck has a raised platform for the musicians, a horseshoe-shaped bar, white plastic loungers, chairs and tables, plus a large, lap-sized swimming pool; there's a second, smaller one on the deck above.

Five Good Reasons to Book This Ship

1. To go back to the days of elegant transatlantic liners.
2. The price is right.
3. The itineraries let you discover a lot of the Southern Caribbean on a seven-day cruise.
4. You can get a free Aruba, St. Lucia or Dominica vacation before or after your cruise; see Discounts, above, for details.
5. Cabins are spacious and the ship never feels crowded.

Five Things You Won't Find On Board

1. That wonderful squash court that used to be there.
2. Two names painted on the bow—with the new ownership, it's now officially the *Seawind Crown*.
3. A self-service laundry.
4. Theme cruises.
5. Ushers in the cinema.

Seawind Crown   ★ ★ ★ ★

Registry	**Panama**
Officers	**International**
Crew	**International**
Complement	**324**
GRT	**24,000**
Length (ft.)	**642**
Beam (ft.)	**81**
Draft (ft.)	**27**
Passengers-Cabins Full	**824**
Passengers-2/Cabin	**728**
Passenger Space Ratio	**32.96**
Stability Rating	**Good to Excellent**
Seatings	**2**
Cuisine	**International**
Dress Code	**Traditional**
Room Service	**Yes**
Tip	**$7.50 PPPD, 15% automatically added to bar check**

Ship Amenities

Outdoor Pool	**2**
Indoor Pool	**0**
Jacuzzi	**0**
Fitness Center	**Yes**
Spa	**No**
Beauty Shop	**Yes**
Showroom	**Yes**
Bars/Lounges	**5**
Casino	**Yes**
Shops	**2**
Library	**Yes**
Child Program	**No**
Self-Service Laundry	**No**
Elevators	**9**

Cabin Statistics

Suites	**20**
Outside Doubles	**210**
Inside Doubles	**121**
Wheelchair Cabins	**2**
Singles	**4**
Single Surcharge	**150%**
Verandas	**2**
110 Volt	**No**

SILVERSEA CRUISES

110 East Broward Boulevard, Ft. Lauderdale, FL 33301
☎ (305) 522-4477, (800) 722-9055

History

Founded in 1992 by the Francesco Lefebvre family of Rome and the
Vlasov Group of Monte Carlo, the former owners of now-defunct Sitmar Cruises, Silversea built its line around two 296-passenger super-
luxury vessels instead of returning to big- ship cruising in the Sitmar
style.

The *Silver Cloud*, which debuted April 2, 1994, and the *Silver Wind*,
which debuted Jan. 29, 1995, were designed by Norwegian architects
Pettar Yran and Bjorn Storbraaten, who also designed the interiors of
the Seabourn and Sea Goddess ships as well as the renovated *Song of
Flower* for Radisson Seven Seas Cruises.

—The Silversea name ties in with the Vlasov Group's 80-year-old British-based shipping company called the Silver Line.

—V.SHIPS, Inc., of Monte Carlo, also part of the Vlasov Group, provides many cruise lines around the world with officers and crews and
other operational services.

Concept

The intent to provide full all-inclusive packaging in one price, including
onboard beverage service, all gratuities on board, port taxes, baggage
handling and selected shore excursions. Air/sea packages also factor in
air travel, transfers, porterage and a choice of overnight or day deluxe
five-star hotel room prior to embarkation. All-inclusive fares are available on cruise-only or air/sea packages. Free shuttles between the port
and town are also offered in many ports of call.

Signatures

The Silversea Experience—a special shore excursion that is included for
all passengers that explores some special aspect of local culture or hospitality, perhaps dinner in a Victorian castle, a private wine tasting in
Bordeaux or a Turkish wedding party with camels and belly dancers and
a lavish picnic in a pine forest.

Gimmicks

Special affiliations with prestigious companies lets Silversea produce
themed sailings such as a series of Le Cordon Bleu voyages featuring

chefs from the famous Paris cooking school preparing meals and demonstrating culinary techniques, along with wine tastings conducted by the head of Domaines Lafite Rothschild.

Who's the Competition

It's pretty obvious that Silversea's competition is other players in the small-ship ultra-luxury market. But with larger ships, a higher proportion of private verandas, increasingly finer food and service, and all-inclusive fares at very competitive prices, this newcomer can give Seabourn, Sea Goddess, and Radisson Seven Seas a run for the money.

Who's Aboard

Everybody from Charlton Heston (guest-starring in a recent film festival aboard the *Silver Cloud*) to your friendly neighborhood travel agent (if your zip code is 90210). On one recent sailing aboard the *Silver Wind,* the guest list ranged from two college-age passengers from New Jersey traveling with their parents to an Italian principessa and a number of doctors and professors; passenger home addresses included the United States, Britain, Hong Kong, Italy, Germany, The Netherlands, Mexico, Bermuda, Switzerland and Austria. Passengers are predominantly middle-aged couples, many of whom have sailed aboard some of the other super-luxury lines.

Who Should Go

Anyone who likes a lot of options, with, say, a choice of lunch in the dining room, on the canvas-shaded terrace of the Terrace Cafe, on the private veranda of your cabin or ashore in a waterfront cafe; people who stay in Relais & Chateaux hotels; people who want individual service and attention.

Who Should Not Go

Anyone whose idea of a really great meal is a Big Mac with fries; anyone whose all-time favorite vacation was a week at Disney World or a weekend in Las Vegas; anyone with small children, because there's no program or playroom for kids on these ships.

The Lifestyle

Life on board the Silversea ships will feel familiar to any veteran of the other super-deluxe vessels—luxurious, sociable, stress-free without schedules and regimentation. Two well-traveled British couples on a recent sailing around Italy never got off the ship.

Shipboard activities are low-key, ranging from nine fitness classes a day to a printed quiz, duplicate bridge, trivia, a galley tour or water volleyball. A sports marina that can be opened off the stern of the ship when it is at anchor allows passengers a chance for windsurfing, snorkeling, and sailing from the ship. A larger-than-average swimming pool on board is long enough for modest laps.

Arriving guests find chilled champagne, fresh flowers and a bowl of fruit in their suites, as well as a fully stocked bar and mini-refrigerator. With a high ratio of staff to passengers (one crew member for every 1.5 passengers) and an extremely high passenger-space-ratio of 56.75, you can anticipate a leisurely, pampering cruise experience. But many veteran travelers say the detail they appreciate most about an all-inclusive cruise is the freedom from signing bar chits or figuring out tips.

Wardrobe

The Silversea ships are fairly dressy with passengers fashionably attired daytimes as well as evenings when we've been aboard (except for a couple of elderly Brits who wandered around most of the day in the terrycloth robes from their cabins). Formal wear is requested for two evenings a week, with most men wearing either a tuxedo or dinner jacket and women in their most glamorous outfits. It's telling that the daily programs do not find it necessary to tell passengers exactly what formal dress requires. Informal dress, usually requested two or three nights out of seven, calls for men to wear a jacket and tie, while casual garb on the remaining evenings is still fairly dressy on these ships. Anyone who doesn't feel like dressing for dinner can always order dinner from the dining room menu to be served course-by-course in the cabin.

Bill of Fare . . . A

The cuisine is contemporary, restaurant-style cooking with a nice mix of simple and sophisticated dishes and an emphasis on fresh foods. Very early or late risers will find coffee, tea, pitchers of freshly-squeezed orange and grapefruit juice, and fresh-baked croissants and other pastries in the Panorama Lounge on an upper deck between 6 and 11 a.m., followed by bouillon and crackers at 11. Full breakfast and lunch buffets and a la carte menu of hot dishes is set out daily in the Terrace Cafe, and The Restaurant serves all meals on an open seating arrangement that lets guests arrive when they wish and sit where they please. In addition, a special themed dinner may be served in the Terrace Cafe or on deck once or twice a cruise.

Showtime . . . A

The entertainment aboard usually includes a couple of variety acts, a team of magicians and a puppeteer, for instance, plus some singers and dancers, usually a quartet of Americans called the Styleliners who present music from the Gershwin/Cole Porter era as well as more contemporary show tunes and pop music, or the Matrix Dancers, a British group that perform scaled-down versions of traditional cruise production shows.

A pianist or harpist is on hand to play during teatime and dinner, a quartet plays for dancing, the casino is open when the ship is at sea and films are screened on cabin TV sets or available anytime day or night in the library for your cabin VCR.

Discounts

Besides a full air/sea, all-inclusive package price, Silversea also offers an early booking incentive of 10 percent off for passengers who book and pay a deposit four months ahead of sailing date; a combination cruise program that saves up to $3,000 off the published air/sea fare for passengers booking two or more consecutive sailings; and an advanced

payment bonus for 15 per cent when payment is received in full s
months prior to sailing.

The Bottom Line

These all-inclusive, very luxurious ships should appeal to almost everyor
who's extra-demanding about food, accommodations and service. With
sizable contingent of former Royal Viking Line personnel in the hotel ope
ations on Silversea, you can expect the same quality that RVL always provi(
ed. The vessels themselves are well-designed, with spacious decks and publ
rooms, very comfortable suites, many of them with verandas, and alert ar
personable cabin stewardesses. A concierge is always on duty to help wit
any shipboard or shoreside requests. For what it costs, Silversea sailings re|
resent a very good upscale cruise buy. (One passenger recently figured th,
he saved $1813 on items included in the 11-day air/sea package that h
would have had to pay for on similar lines without inclusive packages.)

Silver Cloud   ★★★★★★
Silver Wind   ★★★★★★

*While we thought the Silversea concept was excellent, we didn't consider it
really earthshaking, at least not until the day we drove back to Monte Carlo,
having spent the day touring the Silver Cloud, under construction at the shipyard in Genoa, to learn that at the same time we were aboard the ship, the
Northridge earthquake, the most costly natural disaster in the history of the
U.S., was taking out parts of the Los Angeles area. While we found nothing
damaged when we got home, we still think of that 6.8 temblor every time we
board a Silversea ship.*

The pretty pink dining room of the **Silver Cloud** *serves very good cuisine cooked a la minute.*

On check-in, passengers find a bottle of champagne in the suite, chilling in a silver ice bucket, a bud vase of fresh flowers, maybe orchids, a mini-refrigerator stocked with Evian and soft drinks, a liquor cabinet with several large bottles of different spirits, an epergne of fresh fruit, foil-wrapped chocolates on turndown, a mini-refrigerator (to keep the champagne cold if you don't want to drink it right away), and a full set of glassware in a cocktail cabinet. Everything is replenished frequently. The only extra expenses you'll have are laundry and dry cleaning, the casino, shopping and extra-premium wines and champagnes if you want to pay a surcharge. Otherwise, the wines they pour with meals are quite acceptable; there are usually two or three choices.

The layout of the sister ships makes it easy to find your way around—Vista Suites, The Restaurant, photo shop and self-service laundry on the lowest passenger deck, then The Bar, casino, boutique and entry lobby on the next deck up, along with Veranda Suites. Take one more deck up the stairs or one of the elevators to the main lobby, show lounge, card room, concierge and information desks. The Terrace Cafe, fitness center and beauty salon are one more deck up, then the pool deck and Panorama Lounge. High atop the ship is a walking/jogging track and the glass-walled observation lounge.

The Brochure Says

"Silversea cruises are truly all inclusive as everything you could possibly desire on board is included in your fare: All suite accommodations, complimentary alcoholic and non-alcoholic beverages, select wines with lunch and dinner, all gratuities, all port taxes, 24 hour room service, in suite a la carte dining, all entertainment, on board lectures and a special shoreside event."

Translation

Who could ask for anything more?

CHAMPAGNE TOAST

A glass of the bubbly to Silverseas for including port taxes in their all-inclusive fare. This annoying and oft-times overpriced head tax is almost always an extra on other ships.

INSIDER TIP

There are two suites for the physically challenged on the Silver Wind (640 and 643) but none on the Silver Cloud.

Cabins & Costs

Fantasy Suites: .... A+

Average Price PPPD: $1050 for air/sea package on Grand Suite with one bedroom, i the Americas.

The term could aptly apply to virtually all the accommodations on board these ships, certainly any of those with a private veranda, but if you really wanted to book the top digs, one of the 1314-square-foot Grand Suites should do fine. A two-bedroom suite with three small private verandas, a huge living room and a second smaller sitting room, dining area with ocean view, entertainment center with CD, TV, and VCR, mini-refrigerator, two walk-in closets and two marble bathrooms with full-sized tubs.

Small Splurges: .... A+

Average Price PPPD: $850 on air/sea package in the Americas.

The Silver Suite (three to each ship) is usually the first to be booked on board these ships. At 541 square feet, it's almost twice the size of the standard suites, and has a large veranda, big living room and dining ell, a separate bedroom, walk-in closet and marble bath with tub. Also inside: Twin beds that convert to queen-sized, an entertainment center, two TV sets, VCR, refrigerator, cocktail cabinet, writing desk, wall safe, dressing table and lots of storage space.

Suitable Standards: .... A

Average Price PPPD: $600 on air/sea program in the Americas.

We regard the Silversea Veranda Suite as standard, and the Vista Suite (without veranda, see below) as slumming because we love being able to sit out in the fresh sea breezes anytime day or night. The Veranda Suite has 295 square feet, including a small private veranda, with the sitting area adjacent to the veranda and furnished with sofa, three chairs, table, built-in desk/dresser, entertainment center, mini-refrigerator, cocktail cabinet, wall safe, walk-in closet, dressing table with hair dryer, twin or queen-sized bed and marble bathroom with tub.

Bottom Bunks: .... A

Average Price PPPD: $500 on air/sea program in the Americas.

Despite our flip comment above, booking a Vista Suite is not exactly slumming, even if it is the lowest-price cabin category on the ships. With 240 square feet of space and all the furnishings detailed above except the private verandas (see Suitable Standards, above) it would be quite acceptable.

Where She Goes

The *Silver Wind* starts the year in Singapore with roundtrip 13- and 14-day cruises to ¹donesia, followed by two 10-day series of Hong Kong-Tianjin sailings calling in China, ¹en a pair of 13- and 14-day cruises to Vietnam and a spring repositioning voyage to In-¹a. A 16-day sailing from Bombay to Haifa sets the ship up for its European summer ¹ith 12-day sailings between London and Copenhagen, visiting major ports of Scandina-¹a and Russia. In September the *Silver Wind* crosses from Cork to New York on an eight-¹ay transatlantic, then cruises New England and Canada between New York and Mont-¹al in the fall, followed by winter in the Caribbean.

The *Silver Cloud* starts the year in the Caribbean and South America with seven-, 10-, ¹- and 14-day cruises, then makes a transatlantic crossing to start the summer European ¹eason. The ship covers the eastern Mediterranean through mid-October, when she repo-¹tions from Haifa to Mombasa for a fall series of Seychelles and East African itineraries. ¹ December, *Silver Cloud* sails from Mombasa to Singapore for a winter season in Asia.

Looking down at the pool deck from the jogging track on the **Silver Cloud.**

The Bottom Line

After a tentative start, Silversea has really come a long way. The infusion of new staff from the Royal Viking ships and *Song of Flower* has sharpened the hotel staff, and the kitchen is turning out a more-polished version of contemporary cuisine than at the beginning.

At the same time, it's a comfortable, non-intimidating cruise experience where everything is done just right without someone hovering at your elbow all the time.

While not as showy as Seabourn (you won't find silver cloches lifted in unison in the dining room here) or as sybaritic as Sea Goddess (we haven't run across serve-yourself tins of caviar among the canapes), Silversea ranks right up there on our happy vacation roster.

Five Fabulous Places

1. The natural teak pool deck with its 30 x 12 foot swimming pool, long enough fc modest laps, two Jacuzzis, sunny and shaded lounging areas, long wooden bar wit wood barstools in one corner, loungers covered with blue/white striped cushior and tables with umbrellas.

2. The hideaway Observation Lounge high atop the topmost deck sits out on its ow like a glass bubble furnished with wicker chairs, glass tables, cactus gardens an monitors showing wind speed and other operational ship's data.

3. The elegant double stairway with brass rails that is the heart of the ship; if you loo up from each landing you can see the shape of a ship's keel overhead.

4. The Bar and the adjoining Parisian Lounge, Art Nouveau-style with art glass inset and Erte painted figures on each side of the stage, elaborate period lamps wit wrought iron and copper trim, and glass doors etched with champagne glasses an bubbles.

5. The Terrace Cafe, more like your favorite restaurant than a ship's casual buffet cafe with wood walls and green and yellow tapestry print chairs, lots of green plants.

Five Good Reasons to Book These Ships

1. Because everything is included in one neat package (see "The Brochure Says" above).

2. Because a special Silversea Experience is included with every cruise; our favorite wa. on the *Silver Cloud* when we were taken to a pine forest near Antalya for spectacula Turkish wedding feast—Turkish wines, two dozen cold appetizers, six or eight dif ferent kind of kebabs grilled over charcoal, a table of desserts and fresh fruits, and costumed wedding couple who rode through the trees on decorated camels greet ing guests while folk dancers and belly dancers performed on a small open-air stage.

3. For an extremely smooth ride despite the vessels' shallow drafts; in the Aegean we didn't notice any motion until we looked out and saw a 40 mph wind blowing the lounge chairs all over the deck.

4. For a toning and trimming spa routine with Steiner of London, including thalasso- therapy, massage and beauty treatment rooms, saunas and steam rooms, ionother- apy, and nine exercise classes a day plus personal trainers.

5. For the super-gourmet, Cordon Bleu food and wine cruises are offered several times a year.

Five Things You Won't Find On Board

1. A snob; despite the elegance, all the passengers are very friendly and socialize easily.

2. A baby; the line doesn't permit infants under one and severely limits small children.

3. Enough days at sea; no matter how well-planned the itineraries, passengers never feel they have enough free time to luxuriate aboard these lovely ships.

4. A crowded shore excursion bus; the line's routine is to book enough tour buses to allow everyone to spread out and be comfortable with a maximum of 60 percent of the seats occupied and a carry-on kit of mineral water, soft drinks, etc.

5. A closet hanger with skirt clips; nitpicking, we admit, but on board both *Silver Cloud* and *Silver Wind* (a year apart) we've requested these from housekeeping and have been told "they're on order."

Silver Cloud
Silver Wind

★★★★★★
★★★★★★

Registry	**Bahamas**
Officers	**Italian**
Crew	**International**
Complement	**196**
GRT	**16,800**
Length (ft.)	**514.14**
Beam (ft.)	**70.62**
Draft (ft.)	**18**
Passengers-Cabins Full	**315**
Passengers-2/Cabin	**296**
Passenger Space Ratio	**56.75**
Stability Rating	**Good to Excellent**
Seatings	**1**
Cuisine	**Contemporary**
Dress Code	**Traditional**
Room Service	**Yes**
Tip	**Inclusive**

Ship Amenities

Outdoor Pool	**1**
Indoor Pool	**0**
Jacuzzi	**2**
Fitness Center	**Yes**
Spa	**Yes**
Beauty Shop	**Yes**
Showroom	**Yes**
Bars/Lounges	**3**
Casino	**Yes**
Shops	**1**
Library	**Yes**
Child Program	**No**
Self-Service Laundry	**Yes**
Elevators	**4**

Cabin Statistics

Suites	**148**
Outside Doubles	**0**
Inside Doubles	**0**
Wheelchair Cabins	**2**
Singles	**0**
Single Surcharge	**150%**
Verandas	**110**
110 Volt	**Yes**

Society Expeditions

2001 Western Avenue, Suite 710, Seattle, WA 98121
☎ *(206) 728-9400, (800) 548-8669*

Passengers aboard an expedition cruise in the Bering Strait on the World Discoverer *go birdwatching in a Zodiac.*

Society Expeditions, Inc.

History . . . .

Seattle adventurer and entrepreneur T. C Swartz founded Society Expeditions in 1974 under the name Society for the Preservation of Archeological Monuments, dedicated to saving the giant moai statues on Easter Island, and got into the cruise business when he chartered the 138-passenger *World Discoverer* in 1979 for a five-year series of museum and university charters and independent expeditions to exotic areas of the world.

In 1984, when that charter was up, the owner of the vessel, Heiko Klein, head of a German travel company called Discovery Reederei, leased the ship to a short-lived cruise company called Heritage Cruises, which had also chartered the sailing yacht *Sea Cloud*. Heritage hired the famous decorator Carleton Varney to turn the doughty expedition vessel into a chic luxury ship that would offer exotic expeditions with music and entertainment (i.e., life after dinner).

When Heritage went out of business at the end of 1984, Klein again chartered the *World Discoverer* to Swartz. Society also acquired the *Lindblad Explorer* in 1985 when Lindblad Travel went out of business. Klein ultimately ended up buying out Swartz in 1988 to become the owner of Society Expeditions. The company ordered a new expedition ship called the *Society Adventurer*, to be built in Finland and delivered in 1991. Then Klein entered into a marketing agreement with Abercrombie & Kent to promote the two existing expedition ships and the new one coming up.

When the *Society Adventurer* was almost completed, Society Expeditions refused to accept delivery of the $68 million vehicle and started a contractual dispute with the shipyard. In January 1992, Society filed a Chapter 11 reorganization plan bankruptcy. The *Explorer* was acquired by business associate Abercrombie & Kent and the *World Discoverer* leased to Clipper Cruises, which operated the vessel through the end of April 1995. Society Expeditions came back into business in 1994.

—First line to offer a seven-continent world cruise (1982).

—First company to attempt commercial marketing of a tourist space ship cruise into outer space (1984).

DID YOU KNOW?

The erstwhile Society Adventurer *languished in the shipyard another two years before making its 1993 debut as the* Hanseatic, *now part of Radisson Seven Seas Cruises.*

Concept . . . .

To offer expedition cruises to a loyal coterie of repeat passengers, along with "the opportunity to visit small, out-of-the-way ports that are inaccessible to larger ships and the delight of traveling with like-minded individuals with whom you share common interests."

Signatures . . . .

The soaring bird logo over the blue-and-white D with the globe inside; the Zodiacs, inflatable landing craft, carried aboard and used almost daily; the inclusion in basic rates of all shore excursions, lectures and special programs; the largesse of throwing in small unadvertised "surprises" during the cruises; the strict environmentally responsible onboard program of waste management.

Gimmicks . . . .

The Ship's Log from every cruise, compiled by the captain and naturalists aboard and mailed to passengers long after they have returned home, reminding them afresh of what a good time they had. On Antarctic cruises the line sends each passenger a bright red parka, so he or she won't get lost in the ice and snow.

Who's the Competition . . . .

There was a time when Society Expeditions and Lindblad Travel virtually dominated the upscale expedition market in the US, but while Society was away the newcomers began to play, many of them former associates and/or employees of the two leaders. Now we have Quark Expeditions, which took up the Lindblad/Salen Lindblad banner; Zegrahm Expeditions, founded by a group of ex-Society Expeditions executives and expedition leaders; and the two new luxury expedition ships, the *Bremen* and the *Hanseatic*, originally everyone's hope for the future growth of expeditioning but both operated by companies that are more upscale-mainstream than expedition-oriented.

> ### DID YOU KNOW?
>
> *The late Lars-Eric Lindblad of Lindblad Travel also had chartered the* World Discoverer *briefly but let it go because regulars on his 80-passenger* Lindblad Explorer *thought the 138-passenger ship was "too big."*

Who's Aboard.......................

Mostly well-traveled, well-read, upper-income couples and singles over 45—weeelllll, over 65 in most cases, but who's counting? On the *World Discoverer's* historic first Northwest Passage west-to-east crossing, one of the youngest of our fellow passengers was celebrating his 50th birthday. They are alert, curious, quizzical, argumentative, politically conservative but environmentally active, warm, friendly and loving.

Who Should Go.......................

Perhaps the cost and the length of the cruises have been deterrents to younger passengers in the expedition field, but the last under-35 passenger we can recall was a stowaway on the *World Discoverer's* 32-day transit of the Northwest Passage in 1985.

> ### DID YOU KNOW?
>
> *The young stowaway, who got aboard by wearing a Society Expeditions membership pin he had cajoled from a disembarking passenger in Nome and said he was "desperate" to be among the first to transit the Northwest Passage from west to east, was mentally noted by all the other passengers who averaged 50 years his senior but not remarked on, until crew members found him sleeping in a lifeboat (the usual hideaway for a stowaway) the first night out.*
>
> *Captain Heinz Aye, a stickler for rules, put him off at the first port of call, Little Diomede Island, Alaska, in the Bering Strait three miles from Siberia. The local tribal chief promised the young man could stay for the two weeks until the next plane arrived but "would have to work for his keep." We never saw him again and have often wondered what happened after that day we sailed away and left him on Little Diomede.*

Who Should Not Go.......................

Stowaways, obviously (although Captain Aye is now master of the *Bremen*, see Golden Bear Travel). Infants and small children, because there are no facilities for them aboard. Wheelchair passengers because there are no easily accessible cabins. Anyone looking for life after dinner.

The Lifestyle . . . .

Almost everyone becomes obsessed with observation and record-keeping, scribbling in journals, making photographs and sketches, even videotaping with murmured commentary into the side of the camera. We hunt the ship's library for books about the area, flock to 25-year-old documentary films and attend rambling discourses on anything having faintly to do with the subject at hand. Dress is casual in the extreme, the food is good to excellent, and life aboard becomes more comfortable and insular day by day.

Wardrobe . . . .

Comfortable, sensible clothes that do not need a lot of care, practical shoes for walking and hiking, rain gear and rubber boots, spare walking shoes to replace the pair you got wet on the last Zodiac landing.

Bill of Fare . . . . .B+

In the Arctic and Antarctic, passengers always feel a pang of guilt when they hear about the deprivations of the early explorers, then step on the scales to find they've gained another pound or two from the excellent cuisine on board. Fresh fruits and vegetables are air-lifted, by charter plane, if necessary, into some of the most remote airports of the world to keep *World Discoverer* passengers happy and well-fed.

Showtime. . . . . N/A

Unless watching ancient Film Board of Canada documentaries like "Group Hunting on the Spring Ice, Part III" with a soundtrack entirely in the Netsilik Eskimo dialect is your cup of tea, you'll go to bed after dinner with a good book.

Discounts . . . .

Previous cruisers with Society Expeditions frequently get direct-mail brochures with early booking discounts on upcoming journeys. Call and ask to get on their mailing list, even if you're not a previous passenger; it just may work.

Explorers meet seals in the Antarctic.

The Bottom Line

Out of the 200+ cruises we've made during the past 15 years or so, we've spent more days at sea aboard the *World Discoverer* than any other ship—something like 109 days in the Arctic, the Antarctic, Burma, India, Singapore, Indonesia, Fiji, Alaska and Siberia—more than three months altogether, under the auspices of at least three different cruise lines. Obviously we like the ship and its programs very much, but at the same time, we feel the improvements that have been made in expedition cruising with the introduction of the *Bremen* and the *Hanseatic*—private verandas, elegant dining rooms and lounges, state-of-the-art lecture halls—should not be disparaged in the reverse snobbery of the old-time expeditioners. The new ships are more environmentally correct, and they have the opportunity of attracting a larger, younger international market who might appreciate a cabin TV set that receives satellite news or a trio playing for dancing after dinner. We haven't heard the Germans or Japanese on these new ships complaining about "too much luxury."

World Discoverer ★★★, ⚓⚓⚓⚓⚓

Along the horizon, as far as the eye could see, shimmering cliffs of ice towered, as if Dover had frozen over. It was a surrealist fantasy. The Beaufort Sea was calm and the sky was blue. Our little blue-and-white ship World Discoverer *seemed trapped between the icy cliffs on one side and the glittering sand-colored skyscrapers of an Arctic Metropolis twinkling with lights and belching flames on the other. Fire and ice in a vast, flat sea. We were five days north of Nome, looking at something no map had prepared us for, one of the Arctic's more devious tricks, a mirage called "looming." The flames and towers to our starboard side were part of the oil equipment at Prudhoe Bay. The stark icy cliffs to our port side were illusions, the flat ice cap of the Beaufort Sea reflect-*

ing against itself in the morning sunlight. How many explorers desperately searching for the Northwest Passage during the last 400 years had seen a similar wall of ice ahead and turned back?

Icebergs off the coast of Greenland during a Northwest Passage transit.

Her dark blue hull, which still reduces pre-1984 passengers into fits of muttering, "But it was always red!" came courtesy of Heritage Cruises' decorator Carleton Varney ("The blue looks more nautical, don't you think?"). There are three decks with passenger cabins, all of them fairly small with basic furnishings and baths with showers only, plus a lavish owner's suite on the Boat Deck and two smaller suites on A Deck. A restaurant and two lounges, one forward and one aft, plus a film/lecture hall on the topmost deck, make up the basic layout. There is a small swimming pool aft on deck and access to the forecastle forward on Boat Deck to see whales, Northern Lights and icebergs.

The Brochure Says

"The *World Discoverer* is a small cruise ship accommodating only 138 passengers in a relaxed and casually elegant atmosphere. On board, a genuine camaraderie prevails among travelers. Her attentive staff presents every comfort. Each cabin has an outside view, lower beds, private bathroom and individual comfort control."

Translation

Everything is on hand to please the people "who want their adventure and their dry martini too!," as the late Antoinette DeLand, first author of the Fielding cruise guides, observed.

Cabins & Costs

Fantasy Suites: .... B+

Average Price PPPD: Owner's suite $666, other suites $569 in the Antarctic plus airfare. Although there are three suites on board, the owner's suite on Boat Deck is the largest, a big cabin with large sitting area, king-sized bed, a wall of storage closets and a spacious bath. If that's spoken for, the two two-room suites on A Deck will do very well, each with two lower beds, dresser and nightstands in the bedroom, sofas and cabinets in the living room, and a bathroom with tub and shower.

Small Splurges: C

Average Price PPPD: $510 in the Antarctic plus airfare.

The deluxe double cabins are a bit bigger than the others and conveniently located on Odyssey Deck. They contain two lower beds, window and bathroom with shower. Closet space is barely adequate.

Suitable Standards: .... C-

Average Price PPPD: $431 in the Antarctic plus airfare.

The category 4 cabins on Voyager Deck are where we've spent many of those 109 days; we can still see them in our sleep. There are two lower beds, one of which folds into the wall during the daytime, and one of which makes up as a day sofa. We draw straws to see which one has to sleep in the pulldown bed. Two of them have a third pulldown bunk, which takes up even more of the limited space. Then you have a desk/dresser with mirror, chair and three drawers, one of which locks, a space where clothes are hung back to front rather than the more standard side by side, a couple of storage shelves with wire baskets and a tiny bath with shower.

Bottom Bunks: .... D

Average Price PPPD: $333 in the Antarctic plus airfare.

Although the eight forward cabins in Category 1 on Discoverer Deck have two lower beds, they also have those washing-machine portholes with the sea splashing against the glass—when you're lucky enough not have them covered because of rough seas. Baths have shower only, of course, and the rest of the furnishings approximate those in Suitable Standards, above.

Where She Goes

The *World Discoverer* spends each winter in the Antarctic, as she has for the past 17 years, then sails north along the coast of South America.

The Bottom Line

The peripatetic *World Discoverer* offers single-seating meals (you can sit where and with whom you please but tables for two are grabbed up quickly) with fairly sophisticated cuisine, along with top-notch lecturers and wildlife experts to help passengers identify seabirds, spot and identify whales, or look for lichens. Late-night activities run more to aurora borealis gazing than disco dancing. There are no casinos or dance bands aboard—there used to be a pianist who doubled as a Zodiac driver, or was it a Zodiac driver that doubled as a pianist?—so entertainment is usually limited to lectures, films and passenger accounts of discoveries from the latest shore explorations, which on a slow day in the high Arctic sometimes deteriorated into a show-and-tell of desiccated animal droppings. It's expensive but rewarding; you should know after reading this whether it's right for you.

Five Favorite Spots

1. The Crow's Nest, a tiny forward observation area higher than anything else on the ship, situated about where the crow's nest would have been on a sailing ship, with standing room only for half a dozen people at the most, a rail to get a firm grip on and a view into the crashing, churning sea that is more exciting than any roller coaster ride in any amusement park in the country, especially when you're rounding Cape Horn.

2. The Discoverer Lounge, scene of the nightly "recaps" and once home to the long-gone brass palm trees, a nightclub touch decorator Varney borrowed from Los Angeles' Cocoanut Grove and added to the structural support posts around the room. He wrapped them in brass strips, then hung a cluster of brass "palm fronds" from the low ceiling like foliage on a tree. Unwary dancers ran the risk of getting maimed when they waltzed under them, and the captain pruned them regularly until one day they were entirely gone.

3. The Marco Polo Restaurant, once pretty in pink with chairs that used to be too big and heavy to pull up under the tables, has been trimmed down but still looks lovely, and offers open seating.

4. The lecture hall is the most popular after-lunch nap spot on the ship, especially if the documentary of the day is a couple of decades old.

5. The Lido Lounge, a big comfortable aft lounge with banquettes, tables and chairs, used all day long from buffet breakfast and lunch through needlepoint, reading, postcard writing and chatting.

Five Good Reasons to Book These Ship

1. To go to the Antarctic and see the penguins.

2. To visit the captain and navigator on the open bridge.

3. To have the optimum opportunity for spotting marine mammals—this ship detours for whales.

4. To get a free red coat—the Arctic/Antarctic parka that is one of the perks of booking a polar cruise.

5. To check out Christmas Island or Kirabati Atoll.

Five Things You Won't Find On Board

1. A room key; passengers leave their cabins unlocked during the day, bolting them from the inside when they go to bed.

2. Room service (unless you're sick).

3. Cabins designated wheelchair accessible; but there is an elevator aboard, albeit a small one.

4. An inside cabin.

5. Frivolous reading in the library.

World Discoverer   ★★★, ⚓⚓⚓⚓

Registry	Liberia
Officers	German
Crew	International
Complement	75
GRT	3153
Length (ft.)	285
Beam (ft.)	50
Draft (ft.)	15
Passengers-Cabins Full	138
Passengers-2/Cabin	129
Passenger Space Ratio	24.44
Stability Rating	Good
Seatings	1
Cuisine	Continental
Dress Code	Casual
Room Service	No
Tip	$8 PPPD

Ship Amenities

Outdoor Pool	1
Indoor Pool	0
Jacuzzi	0
Fitness Center	Yes
Spa	No
Beauty Shop	Yes
Showroom	No
Bars/Lounges	2
Casino	No
Shops	1
Library	Yes
Child Program	No
Self-Service Laundry	No
Elevators	1

Cabin Statistics

Suites	3
Outside Doubles	59
Inside Doubles	0
Wheelchair Cabins	0
Singles	0
Single Surcharge	140%
Verandas	0
110 Volt	No

SOCIETY EXPEDITIONS, INC.

SPECIAL EXPEDITIONS

123 South Avenue East, Third Floor, Westfield, NJ 07090
☎ *(908) 654-0048, (800) 348-2358*

History . . . .

Launched in 1979 as a travel company offshoot of Lindblad Travel by Sven-Olof Lindblad, son of the late expedition pioneer Lars-Eric Lindblad, Special Expeditions has also carved out its own very special niche in expedition cruising. Sven bought the division in 1984 and acquired the line's first ship, the 80-passenger *Polaris*, the former *Lindblad Polaris*, in 1987, followed by the *Sea Lion* in 1989 and the *Sea Bird* in 1990. With Captain Hasse Nilsson, longtime captain for the Lindblad vessels, Sven co-owns the *Swedish Islander*, a 128-foot ship that carries 45 passengers around the Stockholm Archipelago for a program called "Impressions of a Swedish Summer," putting them up overnight in small country inns. Special Expeditions is also the best-known North American charterer of the famous sailing yacht *Sea Cloud*, built for cereal heiress Marjorie Merriweather Post.

Concept . . . .

The logo for Special Expeditions, a giant eye in dark blue, "stands for a different way of looking at the world, with more of an in-depth perspective," says Lindblad. Many of the places his expeditions visit are fresh and fascinating, not always as gee-whiz name-dropper stops but visited rather for their own unique environments, and the company's excellent expedition leaders and naturalists devote considerable time and attention to interpreting them for passengers.

Signatures . . . .

The blue eye logo on the stack of the line's flagship *Polaris* and the sides of the smaller *Sea Lion* and *Sea Bird*.

Zodiacs, inflatable rubber landing craft used to explore ashore or venture in close to icebergs and cliffs of nesting seabirds.

Allowing a serendipitous flexibility in the schedule when something special occurs.

Including all shore excursions and sightseeing, as well as some transfe and shore meals, in the basic fares.

A generosity of spirit in refusing to exploit on-board revenue—visits t the ship's doctor are free and the staff frequently offers free drinks beer and wine with meals.

Gimmicks............................

Publishing individual brochures for each sailing or series of similar sai ings rather than an entire catalogue of cruises by the year.

Who's the Competition ....

The *Polaris's* classic competitors in the expedition field are the *Explore* from Abercrombie & Kent, once its Lindblad Travel stablemate, an Society Expeditions' *World Discoverer.* In Alaska and the Pacific North west, the *Sea Lion* and *Sea Bird* come head-to-head with Alaska Sight seeing/Cruise West's very similar small vessels, which offer fewe expeditioning extras than Lindblad. The *Sea Cloud,* in our opinion, ha no competition; it stands alone.

Who's Aboard ....

Mostly seniors and retirees who have the time and money for expedi tioning and the thirst to learn more about the world around them.

Who Should Go ....

Birdwatchers of the world—these are some of the most fantastic voy ages for birding we've ever been aboard; whale watchers and wildlife spotters; photographers; more young people who enjoy hiking and eco tourism.

Who Should Not Go ....

Families with very young children—there's no program for children and no place for them to play.

People with wheelchairs or walkers—these ships have no elevators but do have numerous steep stairs and gangways to negotiate.

The Lifestyle ....

The overall ambiance is one of fun and discovery, due in part to the energetic young naturalists and expedition leaders. Dress is casual, and single-seating meals are served at unassigned tables. Aboard the *Polaris,* you'll be able to have your hair done, see a doctor or take a sauna, but don't expect a swimming pool, cabin TV set, casino, slot machines or after-dinner entertainment. You may, however, go ashore on an unin habited island for a barbecue dinner or set out in a glass-bottomed boat on a balmy moonlit night to sip champagne while drifting over lumi nous seas sparkling with rainbow-colored fish, or go swimming or snor keling from empty beaches in clear turquoise waters. You'll also go back to school if you wish—and everyone does—attending lectures, reading supplementary materials and watching films and slides when not actu ally ashore or in a Zodiac exploring.

Wardrobe...

Very casual, sturdy expeditioning clothes—jeans, twills, shorts and T-shirts, swimsuits, sweaters, depending on the climate, plus sturdy shoes for deck wear and hiking ashore and rain gear in some climates. Most passengers take along one sort of dress-up outfit, not black tie and sequins but more on the order of bolo tie and knit dress.

Bill of Fare........................... B

Food is not an obsession with Sven-Olof's passengers—most require only that it be healthful, substantial and digestible with no strange seasonings or ingredients a lifelong New Englander can't recognize. The chefs do a nice job in spite of the guests. Meals are served at a single open seating, allowing passengers to sit where and with whom they please. They do, however, as we have observed over the years, tend to stake out the same table and tablemates for most of the cruise.

Showtime............................... N/A

Unless you count the nightly 7 p.m. "recap"—the recapitulation of what happened today and the forecast of what may or may not happen tomorrow—as entertainment, these ships have none.

SPECIAL EXPEDITIONS

Polaris passengers explore the islands off Baja California by Zodiac.

The Bottom Line

Special Expeditions has moved ahead carefully and cautiously, concentrating on its strong suits rather than trying to spread itself too thin and offer too many different options to its dedicated repeaters, many of whom sailed with Sven's father before him. It is a solid, predictable cruise product of very high quality and dignity, worth every penny of the sometimes substantial price.

Polaris   ★★★, ⚓⚓⚓⚓⚓

Expeditioners would rather actively participate than passively observe, would be more intent at a slide lecture on seabird migration than a big-money game of jackpot bingo and are unruffled when schedules and itineraries are juggled without notice because of weather conditions or other unexpected problems. There's little ostentation—dressing for dinner may mean changing into clean clothes, and the only one-upmanship practiced at cocktail time is about rare birds spotted or offbeat destinations visited previously.

Homey, low-key and comfortable, the 82-passenger *Polaris* provides single-seating meals at unassigned tables for four or six, allowing everyone a chance to get acquainted, and wide windows in the dining room mean no one has to miss a whale sighting during lunch. On one *Polaris* cruise, our well-traveled fellow passengers, many near or past retirement age, included an archeologist from New Mexico, a New York architect, a Hollywood screenwriter-director, a rice farmer from California's central valley, attorneys, university professors and stockbrokers.

The Bahamian-registry ship is sturdy rather than glamorous, but the cabins are well-furnished and comfortable and the Filipino service staff and Swedish officers friendly and efficient. The captain usually allows visitors on the bridge on an informal basis.

DID YOU KNOW?

The Polaris was the only cruise ship that passed through the Panama Canal during the U.S. military action against Panama's president Manuel Noriega in 1989. The ship was already in the canal when the firing started, and was stalled at the locks nearest Panama City for an hour or so, with some gunfire and a lot of helicopters flying overhead. The passengers were brought inside and below decks since there was shooting going on. "It was terrible for our bird list," one of the naturalists observed later.

The Brochure Says

"Where can you snorkel on the largest barrier reef in the New World, search for tou-ns and howler monkeys in the rain forest, discover vibrant native cultures, and walk 1ong the temples of ancient Mayan cities? You can do all this between Panama and Be-:e—a region of coral reefs, wildlife reserves, archeological treasures and welcoming peo-e."

Translation

This is the strong suit aboard the *Polaris*, the chance to explore and discover all the onders listed above. If you take all the shore excursions—they're included in the fare—u'll discover at least three-quarters of what they promise, if not a hundred percent. Un-:e many cruise line brochures, those of Special Expeditions never promise what they n't have a good chance of delivering.

Cabins & Costs

'antasy Suites: . . . . B

Average Price PPPD: $775 plus airfare.
The owner's suite has two full-sized beds and a lot of space (but it's no bigger than the slightly cheaper #321 down the hall). Sitting areas are handsomely furnished in navy blue with sofa and matching chair piped in red, and there is a desk/dresser with its own chair and a coffee table. Two windows.

'mall Splurges: . . . . B

Average Price PPPD: $683 plus airfare.
The aforementioned #321 (see above) has much the same decor and furniture as the owner's suite and is also convenient to the public area and decks. Two windows.

'uitable Standards: . . . . B

Average Price PPPD: $470 plus airfare.
The largest category of standard cabins is Category 2 with 22 examples, all but one with windows instead of portholes. (Cabin #101 one deck lower has a porthole). All cabins are outsides. Twin beds, windows, a desk/dresser with chair, lamp and tele-phone, and bathroom with shower are typical of this category.

'ottom Bunks: C

Average Price PPPD: $415 plus airfare.
Four outside doubles with portholes instead of windows are the lowest-priced cab-ins aboard, and contain the same general decor and furniture arrangement as the suitable standards, above. Your portholes will sometimes look like washing machines when seas are churning.

Where She Goes

The *Polaris* starts the year in Central America where she transits the Panama Canal be-tween Panama and Costa Rica with "A Journey on the Wild Side" itineraries, then crosses the Atlantic in April to Lisbon to begin her cultural and historical explorations of Europe, including the islands of Britain and Ireland and the Norwegian Fjords. Then she sets out for the Scandinavian and Canadian Arctic before turning south toward the Caribbean.

Basically it's a no-frills cruise with some largish, some smallish cabins, lectures and sli[de] shows on every subject from seabird migration to the life cycle of lichens; inflatable rub[ber] landing craft to take passengers ashore on deserted islands or navigate through na[r]row river channels; and no-nonsense dinners, briskly served and sometimes eaten withou[t] a change of clothes from the last expedition of the afternoon. But the ship is a favorite [of] well-traveled people for its warmth and friendliness. It's expensive, but we've never bee[n] disappointed with a cruise aboard the *Polaris*.

Five Good Reasons to Book This Ship

1. To get an incomparable introduction to an exotic corner of the world that [is] unique.

2. To travel with like-minded fellow passengers who care intensely about nature an[d] the environment.

3. To listen to some of the brightest and best naturalist/lecturers on the expeditio[n] circuit.

4. To be able to scoot around the seas of the world in Zodiacs or the ship's own glass[-] bottomed boat.

5. To be able to go on the "open bridge" and look at the radar and navigation chart[s] and chat with the officers.

olaris ★★★, ⌄⌄⌄⌄⌄

Registry	**Bahamas**
Officers	**Swedish**
Crew	**Filipino**
Complement	**44**
GRT	**2214**
Length (ft.)	**238**
Beam (ft.)	**43**
Draft (ft.)	**14**
Passengers-Cabins Full	**82**
Passengers-2/Cabin	**82**
Passenger Space Ratio	**27**
Stability Rating	**Good**
Seatings	**1**
Cuisine	**Continental**
Dress Code	**Casual**
Room Service	**No**
Tip	**$7 PPPD, 15% automatically added to bar check**

Ship Amenities

Outdoor Pool	**0**
Indoor Pool	**0**
Jacuzzi	**0**
Fitness Center	**No**
Spa	**No**
Beauty Shop	**Yes**
Showroom	**No**
Bars/Lounges	**1**
Casino	**No**
Shops	**3**
Library	**Yes**
Child Program	**No**
Self-Service Laundry	**Yes**
Elevators	**1**

Cabin Statistics

Suites	**1**
Outside Doubles	**40**
Inside Doubles	**0**
Wheelchair Cabins	**0**
Singles	**0**
Single Surcharge	**150%**
Verandas	**0**
110 Volt	**No**

Sea Bird ★★, ⚓⚓⚓

Sea Lion ★★, ⚓⚓⚓

Both ships cruise the Sea of Cortez in winter, where sea lions sunning them-selves on rocky ledges slide off into the creamy foam to swim over to our rub-ber craft for a closer look. They show great curiosity, playfully swimming and rolling about and deliberately splashing us, then swimming away again. One large dominant male, who felt our presence threatened his harem, followed us doggedly, bellowing loudly and showing his teeth in the most aggressive dis-play he could summon. Overhead, the tropic birds darted around gossiping shrilly with each other, and the blue-footed boobies honked hoarsely across the guano-covered rocks. This is the noisiest island in the unspoiled group that are North America's equivalent of the Galapagos.

This pair of sturdy little American-built expedition vessels have been re-configured since their days with now-defunct Exploration Cruise Line when they sailed as the *Majestic Explorer* and *Great Rivers Explorer*. Now they carry only 70 passengers instead of the 92 they used to handle. Meals are single-seating. Cabins are all outsides, but instead of windows or por-holes, the four lowest-priced accommodations on the lower deck have portlights located high up in the walls, which let in a little light but don allow a view. The ships carry Zodiacs, inflatable rubber landing craft, in order to take passengers exploring ashore or in the sea. A shallow eight-foot draft permits these small vessels to get into small ports and visit uninhabited islands.

The Brochure Says

"Your voyage is led by historians and naturalists rather than conventional tour guides specialists who share their enthusiasm for the area with informal talks, slide presentations nd anecdotes over drinks at the end of the day. You join them for frequent trips ashore, nd on forays in Zodiac landing craft to explore remote areas."

Translation

This is not a cruise, this is a learning expedition that will enrich a part of your life, or t least teach you how to recognize a frigate bird in flight.

Cabins & Costs

'antasy Suites: . . . . NA

There are no cabins on board in this category.

Small Splurges: . . . . B

Average Price PPPD: $325 plus airfare.
The Category 4 aft cabins on Upper Deck, #216 and #219, are large and comfortable and only steps away from the deck when you want to run out and see the (choose one: bear, whale, porpoises, sea lions, pelicans). They have twin beds or double beds, depending on which cabin you select, a dinette seating arrangement with benches and table and large window. The bathrooms throughout the ship are quite compact with shower only.

Suitable Standards: . . . . C-

Average Price PPPD: $290 plus airfare.
Upper Deck category 2 cabins are a bit smaller than the category 4 (see Small Splurges, above) but contain twin beds and a big window.

Bottom Bunks: . . . . D

Average Price PPPD: $237 plus airfare.
The four cheapest category cabins are on the lowest passenger deck with portlights instead of windows, meaning you have a little daylight but don't get to look outside. One double bed and a single that converts to a couch in the daytime round out the furnishings, and there is a small bathroom with shower.

Where She Goes

Both *Sea Lion* and *Sea Bird* cruise in Mexico in the winter, offering Copper Canyon Railway packages in conjunction with Sea of Cortez cruises, as well as whale-spotting expeditions around Baja California. In summer they sail the coastal waterways of western Canada and Alaska, and spend spring and fall cruising from Portland along the Columbia River and Hells Canyon, Idaho, "In the Wake of Lewis and Clark."

The Bottom Line

Shore excursions, visits to the ship's doctor, non-alcoholic beverages and use of snorkeling equipment are all included in the basic fare. Most of the cabins open directly onto an outer deck, which could be a nuisance in cold rainy weather like you get sometimes in Alaska. To avoid this, book one of the cheaper Category 1 or Category 2 cabins on a lower deck. While dress is casual, do bring along a change of sneakers, since you often get wet feet on Zodiac landings.

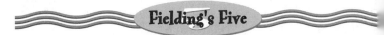

Fielding's Five

Five Familiar Places

1. The dining rooms, big enough for everyone in one open seating with passenger free to sit where they please, have round and rectangular tables for five to eight.

2. In the observation lounges, the furniture is arranged in conversational grouping with swivel chairs and fixed small tables; lectures, "recaps" and social gathering take place here.

3. The Sun Deck makes a good place for lounging and reading between wildlife spot ting and bird-watching.

4. The upper deck forward is where to gather to watch the dolphins that swim with th ship in the warm waters of the Sea of Cortez.

5. Despite their modest sizes, *Sea Bird* and *Sea Lion* have full around-the-ship prom enade decks for inveterate walkers who don't mind a double-digit number of laps t make a mile.

Five Good Reasons to Book These Ships

1. To learn how to identify frigate birds, tropic birds and blue-footed boobies in flight.

2. To explore the rivers, deltas, fjords and seas of the American west.

3. To ride Mexico's dramatic Copper Canyon Railway and go whale-spotting in th Sea of Cortez, all on the same unforgettable eight-day trip.

4. To take a comfortable, affordable expedition close to home in little more than week.

5. To venture into places such as Princess Louisa Inlet looking for black bears an Point Adolphus, where the humpback whales feed.

Five Things You Won't Find On Board

1. A children's program.

2. Cabins designated wheelchair-accessible.

3. Room service.

4. Spa and beauty shop.

5. Elevators.

Sea Bird ★★, ⇓⇓⇓⇓
Sea Lion ★★, ⇓⇓⇓⇓

Registry	**Bahamas**
Officers	**Swedish**
Crew	**Filipino**
Complement	**22**
GRT	**99.7**
Length (ft.)	**152**
Beam (ft.)	**31**
Draft (ft.)	**8**
Passengers-Cabins Full	**76**
Passengers-2/Cabin	**72**
Passenger Space Ratio	**NA**
Stability Rating	**Good**
Seatings	**1**
Cuisine	**American**
Dress Code	**Casual**
Room Service	**No**
Tip	**$7 PPPD, 15% automatically added to bar check**

Ship Amenities

Outdoor Pool	**0**
Indoor Pool	**0**
Jacuzzi	**0**
Fitness Center	**No**
Spa	**No**
Beauty Shop	**No**
Showroom	**No**
Bars/Lounges	**1**
Casino	**No**
Shops	**1**
Library	**Yes**
Child Program	**No**
Self-Service Laundry	**No**
Elevators	**0**

Cabin Statistics

Suites	**0**
Outside Doubles	**36**
Inside Doubles	**0**
Wheelchair Cabins	**0**
Singles	**0**
Single Surcharge	**150%**
Verandas	**0**
110 Volt	**Yes**

SPECIAL EXPEDITIONS

ST. LAWRENCE CRUISE LINES, INC.

253 Ontario Street, Kingston, Ontario, Canada, K7L 2Z4
☎ *(613) 549-8091, (800) 267-7868*

History . . . .

The 66-passenger *Canadian Empress*, the only Canadian-flag cruise vessel, has been sailing through the Thousand Islands since 1981, when Bob Clark, a Kingston real estate developer, got the idea one afternoon when he and a neighbor were watching excursion boats carrying as many as 13,000 sightseers a day. But nobody went out overnight.

Clark set to studying river boats, since a cruise ship patterned after a traditional river boat sounded like a good idea. He went to Connecticut's Mystic Seaport Museum where he "crawled all over and measured," then sailed aboard the *Mississippi Queen* and the *New Shoreham II* (now Alaska sightseeing/Cruise West's *Spirit of Columbia*).

He named his company Rideau St. Lawrence Cruise Ships, with the intention of cruising the mild-weather Rideau Canal between Kingston and Ottawa at the beginning and end of the St. Lawrence season. But when he set out that first year with his new vessel "the canal wasn't as we were told she was," and his four-day-old *Canadian Empress* struck an obstruction that was not on the charts and tore a 34-foot gash in the hull.

The sadder but wiser Clark later changed the name of his cruise line to St. Lawrence Cruise Lines, Inc., and cut out the Rideau Canal.

Concept . . . .

"Calm-water cruising on Canada's beautiful waterways" aboard a replica of a 1908 steamship that might have toured the St. Lawrence.

Signatures . . . .

A brass steam whistle, pressed-tin ceilings and Tiffany-style lamps and polished brass in the Grand Saloon.

Gimmicks . . . .

An after-dark campfire ashore with a hot dog and marshmallow roast is usually scheduled once during every cruise.

Who's the Competition

The closest competition is American Canadian Caribbean Line, a U.S. flag line that cruises in the United States, Canada and the Caribbean with small, shallow-draft vessels. ACCL makes fall foliage cruises along the St. Lawrence Seaway, the Saguenay River and Erie Canal. The former vessel *New Shoreham II* was one of the prototypes Bob Clark sailed aboard before building the *Canadian Empress*.

Who's Aboard

People who love talking with each other, an Ontario man celebrating his 86th birthday, a couple making their 18th cruise aboard the vessel. The average age is 60 to 70, but there are some in their 50s, some in their upper 80s. They're the type of folks that would never complain, who adore the pretty young girls and boys who cheerfully wait on them and gently flirt.

Ten of the 62 passengers on our sailing were from Ontario, 10 from California, and the rest from other states and provinces.

Who Should Go

Anybody who wants a low-key look at life along the St. Lawrence in down-home Canadian style.

Who Should Not Go

Anybody looking for glamour, glitz and gambling; families with small children.

The Lifestyle

The passengers are an agreeable group who enjoy sitting on the top deck watching the progress through the seven locks of the St. Lawrence Seaway, going ashore to a historic re-creation of an Upper Canada Village, engaging in a cutthroat game of Trivial Pursuit or singing along with a lively piano player after a home-cooked dinner served by pretty waitresses in Victorian garb.

EAVESDROPPING

"The only people who wouldn't like this," said one passenger, "are the people who wouldn't be happy if you gave them a million dollars."

Wardrobe

There's nothing dressy about the *Canadian Empress*. Most of the time the women wear polyester pants or dresses and the men plaid Bermuda shorts.

Bill of Fare ....B+

Most meals are served on open seating, often two seatings when the ship is full, with breakfast between 7:30 and 9, lunch at 12 and 1:30 p.m., dinner at 6 and 7:30 p.m.

The traditional first-night dinner is prime rib (with some rum punch served beforehand), plus a French-Canadian dinner of pea soup and *tourtière* (meat pie) another night, roast pork loin, steak, breast of duckling and a fish fillet. These are the main courses served on different days; there is usually one set menu. Breakfast might be scrambled eggs and ham with toast, grapefruit, juice and cereal, and lunch could be hamburgers with potato and macaroni salads, raw vegetables with a dip and fruit and cheese for dessert. It's all pretty much the same menu every cruise, according to the couple who've taken 18 of them, but since there are two different cooks, they say it tastes different each time.

Showtime . . . . N/A

Unless you count singing along from the songbook to a tune-thumping pianist or watching the antics of a troupe of performers from Upper Canada Village, the real entertainment aboard is the sightseeing along the river.

Discounts . . . .

The highly successful *Canadian Empress* offers no discounts, but you do get five percent off the second cruise and a $25 credit for onboard purchases if you book two of them back-to-back.

The Canadian Empress sails from late May to the end of October, with the busiest season the fall foliage months of September and October. The ride is smooth, the crew is wholesome and friendly and your fellow passengers polite and unpretentious.

Canadian Empress ⚓⚓⚓⚓

In the Thousand Islands, your window can drift by the autumn leaves. Most of the 1870 islands in this part of the St. Lawrence River have stands of hard-wood trees, so when they put on a fall foliage show you can count on high-voltage displays in scarlet, gold, russet and orange, set off by the jade green of jack and pitch pines.

Informal and completely unpretentious, the *Canadian Empress* has n swimming pool, gambling, masquerade parties or dress-up dining. It do have a taped narration about points of interest along the river, homemac brownies and chocolate chip cookies for snacks, and a shallow five-foot dra that allows it to tie up every night at small marinas along the river. Square the aft and high-riding in the water, she's an unlikely looking vessel whe you're ashore looking at her, but when you're on board she moves smooth and gracefully.

The Brochure Says

"Sail on a replica steamship. The *Canadian Empress* is a grand ship with a warm an friendly personality. The interior is designed in charming early heritage style. Whether i is elegant furnishing, or the brass handrails complemented by ornate metal ceilings, you ship recaptures the grace of a turn-of-the-century lifestyle."

Translation

You can get away from the pressures of the 20th century by languidly moving along the river in a 19th-century atmosphere.

Cabins & Costs

Fantasy Suites: .... NA

N/A

Small Splurges: C

Average Price PPPD: $245
Two of the larger cabins aboard are the premier staterooms forward on St. Lawrence Deck with double beds, folding director chairs, and small bath with shower.

Suitable Standards: C

Average Price PPPD: $230
Most of the cabins are very small, with two lower beds, one folding up into the wall during the daytime to allow space for a director's chair. While closet and drawer space is limited, the relaxed dress code and casual ambiance don't call for any fancy apparel. Basic bathrooms contain shower and toilet, with a washbasin and mirrored medicine chest in the cabin. All cabins are outside, with windows or portholes that can be opened.

Bottom Bunks: .... NA

N/A

Where She Goes

The *Canadian Empress* cruises between Kingston and Montreal on four-night excursions, between Kingston and Quebec City on six-night cruises, and between Kingston and Ottawa on five-night sailings.

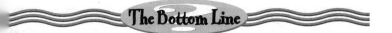

The Bottom Line

The total experience of sailing along the St. Lawrence aboard this casual and friendly vessel is seamless, with no jarring adjustment between life on board and life on shore. The guides who take you around the sights on shore are proficient, and the experience of going back into the 1860s in Upper Canada Village is alone worth the price of the cruise. While the cabins are small—we think they may be the smallest quarters we've ever occupied on a ship—they're clean and comfortable and prettily furnished, and you can open the window for fresh air at night when the ship ties up along the shore. The only disturbance is the generator noise when we're tied up at night and the motor noise and vibration when we're running during the day.

Fielding's Five

Five Down-Home Places

1. The topmost Sun Deck offers shuffleboard and a giant checkerboard behind the wheelhouse, plus yellow-and-white director's chairs for watching the scenery.

2. The Grand Saloon, a combination bar, lounge and dining room, is where indoor games are played, meals are served, the captain holds his welcome-aboard cocktail party and people sit around and talk.

3. The corner store is tucked away on the lowest passenger deck with a small stock of sundries and logo T-shirts and such.

4. A forward observation deck below the wheelhouse makes a good vantage point to watch the river ahead of you.

5. An aft observation deck below the Sun Deck makes a good vantage point to watch the river behind you.

Five Good Reasons to Book This Ship

1. To choose one of three different itineraries, each covering a pretty part of Canada.

2. To visit Upper Canada Village, included on all three itineraries, a living museum animated with costumed interpreters who show you what life used to be like along the river.

3. To watch the busy shipping along the St. Lawrence Seaway.

4. To see the rich green spring foliage or the glowing autumn leaves, or pick out one of the For Sale islands you might want to buy.

5. Because the price is right—from around $800 for a four-night cruise.

Five Things You Won't Find On Board

1. A children's program, because children under 12 are not permitted.

2. An ashtray indoors; smoking is permitted only on the outer decks.

3. A Jacuzzi.

4. A cabin designated wheelchair-accessible.

5. A nurse or doctor.

ST. LAWRENCE CRUISE LINES, INC.

ST. LAWRENCE CRUISE
LINES, INC.

Canadian Empress ⚓⚓⚓

Registry	Canad
Officers	Canadia
Crew	Canadia
Complement	1
GRT	46
Length (ft.)	108
Beam (ft.)	30
Draft (ft.)	9
Passengers-Cabins Full	66
Passengers-2/Cabin	64
Passenger Space Ratio	NA
Stability Rating	Good
Seatings	2
Cuisine	Canadian
Dress Code	Casual
Room Service	No
Tip	$7 - $9 PPPD

Ship Amenities

Outdoor Pool	0
Indoor Pool	0
Jacuzzi	1
Fitness Center	No
Spa	No
Beauty Shop	No
Showroom	No
Bars/Lounges	1
Casino	No
Shops	1
Library	No
Child Program	No
Self-Service Laundry	No
Elevators	0

Cabin Statistics

Suites	0
Outside Doubles	32
Inside Doubles	0
Wheelchair Cabins	0
Singles	0
Single Surcharge	175%
Verandas	0
110 Volt	Yes

STAR CLIPPERS, LTD.

4101 Salzedo Avenue, Coral Gables, FL 33146
☎ *(305) 442-0550, (800) 442-0551*

History

Swedish-born yachtsman and shipping executive Mikael Krafft introduced the first of his two classic square-rigged, four-masted clipper ships in June 1991, in the reverse order from what he had planned. Since the name of his company is Star Clipper, he naturally intended to debut the *Star Clipper* first, but found himself embroiled in litigation with St. Louis-based Clipper Cruise Line over the proprietary use of the name "Clipper." The Missouri-based Clipper, which operates motor vessels, not sailing ships, claimed the use of the word entailed copyright infringement. So the *Star Flyer* debuted first (same ship, different name) while the case was pursued, then settled by the time the *Star Clipper* arrived in the Caribbean at the end of 1991.

—The tallest ships in the world (226 feet in mast height).

Concept

To experience the essence of sailing in its purest form, says the line, on a ship where computerized systems have not replaced human hands in the ancient ritual of raising sails.

Signatures

The 30 sails with 36,000 feet of canvas snapping taut in the wind is as distinctive an image as a cruise line could wish.

Daily sail-training classes conducted on both ships teach sailing a square rigger to every interested passenger and award diplomas of Nautical Achievement on the final night of the cruise.

Gimmicks

The taciturn parrot named Captain Loreto was brought on board *Star Flyer* and trained to talk by owner Mikael Krafft, but the trauma of actually sailing resulted in long spells of silence in the early days. Later, either he perked up or another parrot replaced him, because he became loquacious and a popular feature of the ship.

Who's the Competition

Traditional sailing vessels such as the *Star Clipper* ships differ from the windcruiser vessels such as the Windstar and Club Med ships but would attract some of the same thirtysomething couples because of the romance of it all. Classic tall ships such as the Windjammers lack the luxurious cabins and public rooms the Star Clippers provide. "Wow," one Windjammer veteran said about the *Star Clipper*, "this is so luxurious compared to Windjammer," which she described as "sort of like camping out with cold showers and stuff."

Who's Aboard

Sophisticated travelers who are successful and live well but may not have taken a cruise before; sailing enthusiasts from both Europe and America; mostly couples. It may be a person who made a safari in Africa last year who wants to cross the Atlantic on a square-rigged sailing ship this year.

The average passenger is 47, a professional, married. Half are first-time cruisers.

"A lot of our passengers," one executive says, "are people who have done a bare boat charter in the Caribbean and the wives have found out it wasn't as much fun as they thought; the husband was out fishing while the wife was in scrubbing the head."

Who Should Go

A New Jersey travel agent we sailed with aboard the *Star Clipper* said she would gear the ship toward people to whom relaxation is paramount, to couples in their mid-30s and older, to outgoing singles and to honeymooners when the ships call at romantic ports. Or to someone who doesn't cruise but takes a condo in Maui or goes skiing in Aspen for a week.

Who Should Not Go

The ships are not appropriate for people in wheelchairs or who have difficulty walking, since there are no elevators and plenty of stairs and extra-high sills. Bookings for children under 8 years old are also discouraged.

The Lifestyle

There's a wonderful sense of casual camaraderie aboard, appealing to anyone looking to unwind from a stressful job. The ports are colorful and interesting with few "must see" destinations so the obligation of shore excursions is removed. Most passengers set out on their own to stroll through the ports, perhaps lunching or dining ashore. Passengers are allowed to lend a hand with the sails if they wish, and, when seas permit, the ship anchors for swimming, sailing and windsurfing from the gangway platform. Informal classes in navigation and sail-handling are also offered. A team of sports directors supervises aerobics classes, snorkeling lessons and diving trips for passengers with certification.

Wardrobe...

Dress is casual aboard, although some passengers don fashionable resortwear for dinner. Jackets are never required, but shorts and T-shirts are not considered acceptable at dinner. The term "casual elegance" crops up in the brochure a couple of times. The right footwear is particularly important, with rubber-soled deck shoes of some sort essential for getting around the ropes and gear on deck.

Bill of Fare.......................... B

Out of necessity, food is less elaborate aboard sailing vessels because the galleys are smaller and don't allow banquet-type catering preparation. Breakfasts and lunches are often served buffet-style with a choice of several hot and several cold dishes, and dinner is served course by course but with a limited selection—two appetizers, one soup, one salad, a pasta, a choice of two main dishes and two desserts plus ice cream. A table of hot and cold hors d'oeuvres is set out on deck daily at 5:30.

Showtime............................... C

To supplement a resident singer/pianist, local entertainment is brought on in some ports. In the Mediterranean, a pair of opera singers from Elba entertained during dinner one evening. Another night, a Corsican quartet headed up by a Dean Martin lookalike in a pin-striped suit played European pop music and American '50s rock for dancing on the deck under the stars. TV sets in the cabins play movies during the day and evening on two channels when the hotel manager remembers to load the videos. A 24-hour news crawl is updated regularly.

Discounts..............................

From time to time, special pricing promotions on designated sailings may also include one category upgrades for early booking and special air/sea package fares. Have your travel agent inquire.

The Bottom Line

One important detail to remember is that sailing ships do not stick to itineraries as steadfastly as bigger cruise liners, since winds and sea conditions may necessitate last- minute port changes. But flexibility is part of the fun.

Star Clipper

Star Flyer

Sailing represents romance to a woman, adventure to a man, we were told while standing at the rail of the Star Flyer off the Isle of Wight in 1991. The new ship had just sailed from Belgium and along with a BBC-TV crew and some British press, we sailed out from Southampton to meet her. At the last minute, we were given permission to come aboard, and climbed up the Jacob's Ladder against the steep, sheer side of the ship for what seemed a mile before being pulled over the rail onto her deck.

While passengers are not usually permitted to climb the Jacob's Ladder up the side, they can venture out on the bowsprit, which has a safety net underneath, to lie back and see the ship's sails from that vantage point, to stand on the outdoor bridge and watch the helmsman at work, or go out in an inflatable Zodiac landing craft to photograph the ship under full sail. The Star Clippers are very hands-on vessels for passengers, who lend a hand with the sails if they wish. The forward deck is where the serious work goes on; amidships and aft deck are swimming pools and lounging chairs for serious sunning.

The Brochure Says

"Perhaps nothing stirs the spirit so much as the romantic era of the great clipper ships. Today, a new name proudly carries on the tradition of the tall ships with two new sailing vessels—the first passenger sailing vessels to be classified by Lloyds since the early 1900s."

Translation

It's rare and wonderful to be able to sail aboard a square-rigger and recall the brief days of the clipper ships, the two decades between the California Gold Rush of 1849 and the opening of the Suez Canal in 1869. These classic vessels, built by Scheepswerven Langer-

rugge in Ghent, Belgium, were rated A-100 by Lloyds, and passed U.S. Coast Guard in-
•ection on the first try, a rarity in the port of Miami.

Cabins & Costs

Fantasy Suites: .... NA

Average Price PPPD: N/A
There is a "secret" owner's suite on board—at the extreme aft end of Clipper
Deck—that is sometimes put on the market or used as a special charity auction item
or for the CEO on incentives and charters. With a queen-sized bed, sofas, mini-
refrigerator, TV in a built-in cabinet, four bedroom portholes, a large closet, a marble bathroom with a gold faucet Jacuzzi tub and porthole, it's pretty lavish. There's
even an escape hatch to the pool deck above.

Small Splurges: .... B+

Average Price PPPD: $370 plus airfare.
Category 1 cabins aft on Sun Deck near the pool have twin beds that can be put
together into a queen-sized, a mini-refrigerator stocked with complimentary beverages, and a large bathroom with Jacuzzi tub. Four portholes are built up high so no
one looks in while walking past. Cellular satellite direct-dial phones are in every
cabin, along with TV/VCR and hair dryers.

Suitable Standards: .... B

Average Price PPPD: $320 plus airfare.
We booked a category 2 double with a king-sized bed (two lower beds pushed
together with a thin fill mattress across the top) and built-in storage underneath. A
built-in corner chair has a drawer underneath, and there's fairly good hanging space,
one full-length about two feet wide and one half-length, a safe and three open
shelves below, plus a third cupboard that is all open shelves top to bottom. The
bathroom has a medicine chest, some counter space around the sink (with a faucet
water control that you push on but goes off by itself just when you're ready to rinse
your toothbrush), and a shower that also saves water by turning off just when
you've soaped up.

Bottom Bunks: C

Average Price PPPD: $213 plus airfare.
Standard inside cabins with upper and lower berths have plenty of shelving, wall
lamps and privacy curtains across doorway; these are the only cabin category aboard
that doesn't have TV sets.

Where She Goes

Star Clipper is based in Barbados year-round, setting out every Saturday for seven-day
sailings on two alternate itineraries, one to Tobago, Grenada, Cariacou, St. Vincent and
St. Lucia, the other to Union Island/Tobago Cays, Bequia, Dominica, Martinique and
St. Lucia.

Star Flyer cruises the Mediterranean, Greek Isles and Turkey in summer. In Septem-
ber, 1996 the ship makes a 35-day repositioning cruise from Rhodes to the Thai island of
Phuket, sailing through the Suez Canal, the Gulf of Aden, the Arabian Sea, the Indian
Ocean, the Bay of Bengal and the Andaman Sea. The ship then introduces new Southeast

Asia winter itineraries beginning Nov. 2, featuring islands and scuba dive sites visited usually only by private sailing yachts—Surin Island, Similan and Rok Nok Island,Thailand Langkawi, Malaysia—then to Malacca and into Singapore. On alternate weeks the ship will call in Pangkor and cruise the Butang group of islands in Malaysia; then in Thailand Phi Phi Island, the Pang Archipelago Channel, Dam Hok Island, Krabi and Khai Nok Island, arriving at the end of the cruise in Patong Beach Bay on the southern tip of Phuket at a private mobile pier.

A passenger lends a hand with the sails aboard the **Star Clipper.**

The Bottom Line

The Star Clippers spend more time under sail than the modern windcruisers, particularly in the Caribbean out of Barbados where the winds are favorable; the *Star Clipper* is under sail at sunset every day but one, and spends a full 36 hours nonstop under sail on alternate weeks in the Tobago Cays, a real treat for a sailor. While the service in the dining room may not be as polished as on the Sea Goddess, these ships are beautiful and unique, and will provide a lifetime of wonderful memories of being under sail.

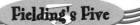

Fielding's Five

Five Fine Places

. The Tropical Bar, outdoors with a white tarp covering the area, two fixed high wood tables with six built-in wood and chrome barstools at each, plus a big outdoor bar with 16 wooden stools around it.

. The Library, cozy and comfortable, with a non-burning fireplace, a belle époque fixture from a 19th century home in Ghent, print armchairs, fixed wooden tables, cream leather sofas, oil paintings of sailing ships, CD player, and lots of hardback books and games.

. The Piano Bar has a royal blue carpet and 12 blue leather and brass stools at the indoor marble-topped bar (which connects with the outdoor bar so one bartender can work them both). Tables, paisley-covered chairs and built-in leather banquettes make this a comfortable place to chat, and you can look through portholes into the underwater pool.

. The dining room has royal blue carpet with a rope pattern, rose flame print chairs with wood and wicker backs but no arms, tables for six and eight and side booths set up for four but big enough for six. It's open seating, so you can sit where and with whom you wish.

. The bowsprit, the perfect place to slip away to see the ship's sails in full glory; there's a net underneath for safety.

Five Good Reasons to Book These Ships

. The romance of it all.

. To learn how to sail a square-rigger.

. To kick back and relax in a luxurious but unstuffy setting.

. To have a once-in-a-lifetime experience at the cost of an ordinary cruise.

. To take a 35-day repositioning cruise from Rhodes to the Thai island of Phuket, sailing through the Suez Canal, the Gulf of Aden, the Arabian Sea, the Indian Ocean, the Bay of Bengal and the Andaman Sea aboard the Star Flyer (see Where She Goes, above).

Five Things You Won't Find On Board

. A casino.

. A beauty shop.

. Laundry service (they can send it out for one-day service in certain ports).

. Smoking permitted in the cabins.

. An elevator.

Star Clipper / Star Flyer

★★★
★★★

Registry	Luxembour
Officers	Europea
Crew	Internationa
Complement	7
GRT	302
Length (ft.)	36
Beam (ft.)	5
Draft (ft.)	18.
Passengers-Cabins Full	18
Passengers-2/Cabin	170
Passenger Space Ratio	17.79
Stability Rating	Good
Seatings	1
Cuisine	Continenta
Dress Code	Casual elegance
Room Service	Yes
Tip	$8 PPPD, 12.5% automatically added to bar check

Ship Amenities

Outdoor Pool	2
Indoor Pool	0
Jacuzzi	1
Fitness Center	No
Spa	No
Beauty Shop	No
Showroom	No
Bars/Lounges	2
Casino	No
Shops	1
Library	Yes
Child Program	No
Self-Service Laundry	Yes
Elevators	0

Cabin Statistics

Suites	1
Outside Doubles	78
Inside Doubles	6
Wheelchair Cabins	0
Singles	0
Single Surcharge	150%
Verandas	0
110 Volt	Yes

STAR CRUISE

391B Orchard Road #13-01, Ngee Ann City, Tower B, Singapore, 0923

☎ *(65) 733-6988*

History . . . .

Star Cruise, which began in 1993 and already has five ships, is headed up by a hotel, casinos and resort executive named Eddy Lee, who has been associated with Sheratons in Asia and the Pacific, the Genting Highlands Resort in Malaysia, the Burswood Resort in Australia and CDL Hotels International in Hong Kong. Lee and his investors acquired and converted two passenger ferries from Sweden, the former *Athena* and *Kalypso*, into the *Star Aquarius* and the *Star Pisces*, and began cruising in December 1993. Subsequently, the new company acquired three existing cruise vessels, the *Cunard Crown Jewel*, sister ship to the *Cunard Dynasty*, and the *Aurora I* and *Aurora II*, two small luxury vessels formerly owned by a German bank and leased to New York-based Classical Cruises.

Officers for the new cruise line are English-speaking Scandinavians. Four of the ships are based in Singapore and one in Hong Kong, and the fleet, one of the world's youngest, has an average age of four years.

Concept . . . .

This vibrant Malaysian-owned, Singapore-based cruise line, after studying the Carnival and Royal Caribbean operations in the Caribbean, created a three-label cruise line tailored to very specific markets. "*Star*" ships make short, high-density, mass-market, Asian-oriented sailings from Singapore and Hong Kong; "*MegaStar*" ships offer deluxe charters particularly targeting the upscale Asian market; and "*SuperStar*" ships are marketed internationally with particular emphasis on Australia, New Zealand and the United Kingdom. Another stated intention of the cruise line is to create a year-round rather than seasonal cruise industry in Singapore to utilize the new Singapore Cruise Centre.

Signatures . . . .

The Star Cruise logo is a broad funnel with a dark blue base and red-and-white striped top ornamented with an eight-point gold star.

Who's Aboard ....

Hong Kong and Singapore residents make up the greater portion of travelers on the "Star" label vessels, while the other ships draw from other urban areas in Asia as well as Europe.

Who Should Go ....

Besides first-time cruisers from the region, anyone visiting in Singapore, Malaysia or Hong Kong who wants a short, luxurious break from business. Families with children will find teen video arcades and child care available. Meetings and incentive groups will find a variety of meeting rooms and business services offered. The five-day *SuperStar Gemini* cruises from Singapore to Malaysia, Indonesia and Thailand give a good cross-section view of the area for a cruiser with limited time. British travelers usually buy a two-week package that includes land programs as well, while Australians buy a one-week package that is basically transportation, transfers and the cruise.

Who Should Not Go ....

Traditional cruisers will find the ambiance aboard the Star label ships more similar to a Scandinavian ferry than a cruise ship, while the deluxe MegaStar vessels are marketed almost entirely to charters, particularly Korean honeymooners and incentive groups.

The Lifestyle ....

Star Cruise has created a uniquely Asian-style leisure product patterned loosely on traditional western cruises. The differences include a much wider range of food options for far longer hours; private karaoke and mah jongg booths; a membership club that provides special lounges at the port as well as on board some of the ships; and 24-hour child care. There are more surcharge options, particularly for meals, than on traditional cruise ships.

Wardrobe ....

Given the tropical climate and the general lifestyle of the area residents, any idea of dress code is out the window. On the Star ships, passengers come aboard in whatever they wear at home and continue to follow what the line terms "smart casual" dress style throughout the cruise. The Australians and British on the *SuperStar Gemini* are usually in sport shirts for the men, cotton frocks for the ladies. But some of the honeymooners and incentive groups on the *MegaStar* ships do dress up.

Bill of Fare ....A to B+

The Star label ships provide passengers with vouchers for three meals a day, which may be taken at any hour in the buffet restaurant, or which serve as a base price for dining in the optional restaurants—Chinese, Japanese, Italian, seafood—with a surcharge added, depending on which dishes are ordered. On the *Star Aquarius* we noted a live fish tank, surely the only one at sea, in the surcharge seafood restaurant. The *SuperStar Gemini* sets out a copious eastern and western buffet that stretches for miles—from cream of tomato soup to sushi, roast beef to fried rice—plus offering at no extra charge a choice of western or Chinese meals in the dining room. The little MegaStar ships offer "the ulti-mate gastronomical adventure" for passengers willing to spring for caviar, Peking duck, fresh lobster and rack of lamb.

Cuisine Report Card: Asian dishes A, western dishes B+

Showtime . . . . C+

The *Star Aquarius* and *Star Pisces* include a karaoke nightclub, adult disco, children's disco, cinema, a mah-jongg and card room, a 400-seat cabaret and show room, and an activity center where you can rent library books, videotapes, karaoke discs, cards and games. In Asia, the mah-jongg and card room, along with the karaoke facility, is customar-ily rented to users on a reservation basis rather than being a free, public area. The Admiral Club, a private membership club, offers extra perks such as a private lounge aboard and in the cruise center.

On the *SuperStar Gemini*, a large show lounge, a cabaret lounge, karaoke lounge, disco and a number of indoor and outdoor bars are sited where their equivalents were on the former *Crown Jewel*. The Admiral Club is located where the casino used to be, and the casino is in the Star Club.

On the former Auroras, the very small vessels, there's a main lounge, a karaoke room, an auditorium (for groups and meetings when the ships are chartered) and another Admiral Club houses the casino.

Discounts . . . .

There are no discounts.

The Bottom Line

While there have been ocean-going cruise lines based in Asia for some time—primarily in Japan—this is the first major, English-speaking, main-stream cruise company aiming primarily at the Asian market with its first ves-sels, but also eyeing the international cruise market with the last three ships. The construction design and quality of all the ships is excellent; they have been altered only enough to add items westerners would consider optional but easterners think essential, niceties such as private mah-jongg and karaoke rooms and larger casinos.

MegaStar Aries ★★★★
MegaStar Taurus ★★★★

> *When we boarded the pretty little* Aurora II *in Topolobampo, Mexico, it was love at first sight, not only for us but for a frequent-cruiser couple traveling with us. She had lovely sleek yachtlike lines, a dark blue hull, big windows, elegant cabins with big tile bathrooms, broad expanses of teak deck.*

This pair of elegant little ships were actually ordered in the late 1980s by a now-defunct German company called Windsor Cruises (reflecting the German fascination with the British royal family), and the two ships were going to be Sea Goddess clones named the *Lady Diana* and the *Lady Sarah*. Given the way that whole affair turned out, it's probably just as well they weren't delivered under those names. A German bank ended up as the reluctant owner of the pair and chartered them out to Classical Cruises, a division of New York's Travel Dynamics, which books university and museum groups on educational cruises aboard a variety of small ships. We first met them on a Sea of Cortez nature cruise in the spring of 1994 and were enchanted. For the record, the *Aurora I* is now the *MegaStar Taurus*, the *Aurora II* the *MegaStar Aries*.

The Brochure Says

"It's not true we're exclusive. We're very, very exclusive. Few hear of it. Even fewer experience the luxurious high life on a Star Cruise MegaStar vessel. Because each cruise is limited to a select number of guests who barely outnumber the impeccably discreet staff."

Translation

Wow, a textbook case in subliminal selling, aiming at everyone from someone who wants to be au courant ("Few hear of it") to a business executive out for a fling with his secretary ("impeccably discreet staff"). But actually, more and more of the Asian market are hearing of it, because most sailings are sold-out charters..

Cabins & Costs

antasy Suites: .... **A**

Average Price PPPD: Available by request only.

The Commodore Suite is a large two-room suite with a king-sized bed, a marble bathroom with tub off the bedroom, a living room with chairs and sofa and a second bathroom with shower instead of tub off the living room.

mall Splurges: .... **A**

Average Price PPPD: $265, cruise only.

The 34 Admiral Suites (we would call them deluxe cabins) have twin beds that can be cranked up or down by remote control, TV/VCR, desk, mini-refrigerator, large corner table, reading lamps, two chairs, two chests, two large closets, and a tile bathroom with tub/shower, marble counter and good storage.

uitable Standards: .... **A**

Average Price PPPD: $250, cruise only.

"Deluxe cabins"—there are only two of them, would be the cheapest cabins aboard—and they are very similar to the Small Splurges, above, except the bathrooms have shower only.

Bottom Bunks: .... **NA**

N/A

Where She Goes

The *MegaStar Taurus* is based in Singapore, and makes one-night luxury cruises to nowhere on weekends, leaving Singapore at 8:30 p.m. on Saturdays and returning at 4 p.m. on Sundays. Weekdays, the vessels sails from Singapore on Sundays, Tuesdays and Thursdays to Port Kelang, Malaysia, returning on Mondays, Wednesdays and Fridays.

The *MegaStar Aries* sails from Singapore on Mondays, Wednesdays and Fridays to Port Kelang and returns on Tuesdays, Thursdays and Saturdays. A free city tour is included.

Both vessels are frequently under charter and not available for individual bookings.

The Bottom Line

Obviously aimed at a short cruise getaway market, these pretty little ships should be able to charge whatever the traffic will bear, so the prices seem relatively modest for the quality of accommodations being offered. There's no tipping aboard, and there are some theme cruises built around holiday celebrations such as Christmas (a major big deal in Singapore) and Chinese festivals such as New Year and Autumn Moon. Most often, however, the vessels go out under charter. They are particularly popular with groups of Korean honeymooners.

Fielding's Five

Five Special Spots

1. The expanded aft deck Admiral's Club contains blackjack, roulette, slots and baccarat.
2. Oscar's Unisex Salon beauty shop is actually operated by Steiners.
3. The Aquarius Lounge, a warm living room with wood-paneled walls and comfortable sofas and chairs in bright silk tapestry.
4. The Pisces Dining Room, also wood-paneled, serves all the guests at one seating.
5. The Aurora Auditorium is comfortable enough to nap in, with padded blue theater seats in rows, and a full video and slide presentation facility.

Five Good Reasons to Book These Ships

1. They're small, elegant and exclusive.
2. Cabins are extremely comfortable and the bathrooms are some of the largest at sea.
3. To become a member of the Admiral's Club for those special perks.
4. To sail into smaller ports than the big ships can.
5. To have all the Beluga caviar and Peking duck you ever wanted—so long as you order it in advance.

Five Things You Won't Find On Board

1. Tables for two.
2. Elevators; you'll have to walk.
3. A children's program; this is not really a family cruise.
4. Tipping; there's no tipping necessary.
5. A private veranda; if they'd been as routine in 1991 as they are now, you can bet these ships would have had them.

MegaStar Aries ★★★★
MegaStar Taurus ★★★★

Registry	Panama
Officers	International
Crew	International
Complement	80
GRT	3264
Length (ft.)	267
Beam (ft.)	45.5
Draft (ft.)	11
Passengers-Cabins Full	72
Passengers-2/Cabin	72
Passenger Space Ratio	45.33
Stability Rating	Good
Seatings	1
Cuisine	Continental and Asian
Dress Code	Smart Casual
Room Service	Yes
Tip	No Tipping

Ship Amenities

Outdoor Pool	0
Indoor Pool	0
Jacuzzi	1
Fitness Center	Yes
Spa	No
Beauty Shop	Yes
Showroom	Yes
Bars/Lounges	2
Casino	Yes
Shops	1
Library	Yes
Child Program	No
Self-Service Laundry	No
Elevators	0

Cabin Statistics

Suites	1
Outside Doubles	35
Inside Doubles	0
Wheelchair Cabins	0
Singles	0
Single Surcharge	176%
Verandas	0
110 Volt	No

Star Aquarius ★★★
Star Pisces ★★★

This good-looking pair of ferry-like vessels are a major introduction to cruising for the Asian market, offering short, snappy getaways tabbed "resort vacations" for one of the world's biggest yuppie markets. Since many of Singapore's ethnic Chinese have friends and relatives on the island of Penang in Malaysia and like to vacation there, it was a logical destination choice when the first ship, *Star Aquarius*, was introduced in December 1993. The savvy marketing arm of Star Cruises made a big selling pitch to young singles, couples and families to get rid of "the popular misconception of cruise holidays as being only suitable for the middle-aged or retirees."

Frankly, we've never seen a middle-aged, white-collar worker in Singapore in the dozen or so times we've been there. Everyone we meet is 35 or under. We've never been able to figure out what they do with citizens over 40, but we suspect they're put out to pasture in those endless blocks of high-rise apartment complexes in the suburbs.

"An all-inclusive package in a fabulous cruise resort."

"Bring your staff for a seminar or convention they'll never forget."

"Every night is party night on *Star Aquarius.*"

"Fettucini yesterday, sashimi last night. How about shark's fin soup for now?"

"A nonstop party for the whole family."

The public rooms run the gamut from optional specialty restaurants and fast-food counters to private karaoke and mah-jongg parlors. Activities for kids and teens, conference meeting room facilities, a computer center, duty-free shopping, cabaret and showroom and separate discos for kids and adults,

ven a Singapore-style satay stand selling skewers of meat or chicken with
eanut sauce—what's not to like?

Cabins & Costs

Cabins on the two ships are shipshape Scandinavian ferry-style accommodations in the
ower categories. There's a standard family quad with four beds two desk/dressers with
hair, TV, phone and small bathroom with shower; a standard twin with twin or double
ed, two chairs and a small table, desk/dresser and bathroom with shower. Per diem
rices range from $221 to $442 per person.

Where She Goes

The *Star Pisces* sails from Hong Kong on a weekend cruise to nowhere, and two week-
ay cruises, a two-night and a three-night, to the Chinese beach resort of Hainan. The
tar Aquarius makes a two-night cruise to nowhere from Singapore every Friday night,
lus a two-night sailing to Penang and a three-night sailing to Port Kelang, gateway to
Kuala Lumpur, Malaysia, and the island of Langkawi.

The Bottom Line

Embarkation is like a replay of the early 1980s in Los Angeles or Miami, when the
three-night cruises loaded with first-timers starry-eyed with excitement set out for the Bahamas or Ensenada. Star Cruise is making cruising a high demand holiday for mass market travelers in Singapore and Hong Kong. This could be the start of something big.

STAR CRUISE

Star Aquarius ★★
Star Pisces ★★

Registry	Panama
Officers	International
Crew	International
Complement	750
GRT	40,000
Length (ft.)	574
Beam (ft.)	94
Draft (ft.)	11
Passengers-Cabins Full	1900
Passengers-2/Cabin	1378
Passenger Space Ratio	29.02
Stability Rating	Good
Seatings	2
Cuisine	International
Dress Code	Smart Casual
Room Service	No
Tip	No Tipping

Ship Amenities

Outdoor Pool	1
Indoor Pool	2
Jacuzzi	2
Fitness Center	Yes
Spa	Yes
Beauty Shop	Yes
Showroom	Yes
Bars/Lounges	4/2
Casino	Yes
Shops	4
Library	Yes
Child Program	Yes
Self-Service Laundry	No
Elevators	5

Cabin Statistics

Suites	6
Outside Doubles	299
Inside Doubles	360
Wheelchair Cabins	0
Singles	48
Single Surcharge	176%
Verandas	0
110 Volt	No

SuperStar Gemini ★★★★

The Star Cruise team, some recruited from existing cruise lines, some hired and trained in Singapore, really pitch in and work hard to meet and greet their passengers. From Charley Penguin (the mascot) to pretty female staffers at the gangway dressed in exotic regional costume, everyone seems to be right where they're supposed to be doing what they're expected to do with a bright, wide smile—and there's no tipping.

The former *Crown Jewel*, which made a splashy debut during the Barcelona Olympics in 1992, is a jewel box of a ship, big enough to give a sense of stability and comfort, but intimate in its public rooms and lounges so guests can meet each other and socialize easily. Cabins are dispersed among five of its seven passenger decks, with a topmost deck housing a fitness center, video arcade, teen and youth center, beauty salon, pool, pool bar and mah-jongg and card room where the former teen area was located. The other major public rooms deck is Deck 5, anchored by a show lounge forward and a casino aft.

The Brochure Says

"In Singapore, home port of the *SuperStar Gemini*, you can breakfast with hundreds of colorful exotic birds on the celebrated terrace of the Jurong Bird Park, with the world's largest walk-in aviary. You can share morning tea with Ah Meng, the friendly orangutan at the famed Singapore Zoological Gardens. And in the evening when you sail through the glittering city of lights that is the world's busiest port, you may even find yourself seated with the Captain. He may not be as exotic. But we guarantee he has better manners."

Translation

(Also from the brochure) "Breakfast with the birds. Tea with the Orangutans. Dinner with the Captain." He's a Scandinavian, and he speaks English.

INSIDER TIP

Even if you never plan to take a cruise from Singapore, write to this line and request a copy of the SuperStar Gemini brochure; it's one of the wittiest cruise brochures we've seen in a long time.

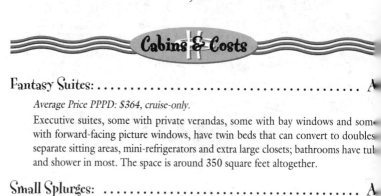

Fantasy Suites: .... A

Average Price PPPD: $364, cruise-only.

Executive suites, some with private verandas, some with bay windows and some with forward-facing picture windows, have twin beds that can convert to doubles, separate sitting areas, mini-refrigerators and extra large closets; bathrooms have tub and shower in most. The space is around 350 square feet altogether.

Small Splurges: .... A

Average Price PPPD: $210, cruise-only.

Junior suites have sitting areas with sofa and coffee table, twin beds that can convert to queen-sized, and desk/dresser with chair.

Suitable Standards: .... B

Average Price PPPD: $168, cruise-only.

While they're called Admiral Suites, they're really standards measuring around 146 square feet, with twin or queen-sized bed, chair, coffee table, desk/dresser with chair.

Bottom Bunks: .... B

Average Price PPPD: $140, cruise only.

The cheapest quarters are the inside cabins, measuring around 132 square feet each, with two lower beds that can be combined, remote-control color TV, combination safe, mirrored built-in dresser/desk, telephone and bath with shower.

The *SuperStar Gemini* sails Sunday nights from Singapore, calling Mondays in Port Kelang, Malaysia; Tuesdays in Medan, Sumatra; Wednesdays in Phuket, Thailand; and spends a day at sea on Thursdays before sailing back into Singapore on Friday afternoon. On weekends, she makes a two-night cruise to nowhere.

If you were a resident of this tiny but prosperous little country, say, a young, single Singaporean making a good living working in a bank or office, perhaps still living at home with your parents, and you loved western-style amusements, wouldn't you take a short cruise on one of these ships?

Fielding's Five

Five Special Spots

- The Star Club casino offers dai sai (Chinese roulette), blackjack, roulette and mini-baccarat.

- The Galaxy of the Stars main lounge has four graduated levels, swivel club chairs and cocktail tables, and handsome draperies. Sightlines are spotty.

- The pool deck area with natural teak and green astroturf underfoot, padded sun loungers and a pool flanked with Jacuzzis in a three-step teak platform.

- The Universe Fitness Center is surprisingly elaborate for a ship this size, with exercise equipment and beauty services, plus the Star Track for jogging.

- The children's playroom with a slide into colored balls, a special nap area and 24-hour babysitting.

Five Good Reasons to Book This Ship

- To have tea with the orangutan at the Singapore Zoo.

- To visit the James Bond Islands of Phi Phi from the film *Man With the Golden Gun*, and "be shaken, not stirred."

- To meet the Batak people of Sumatra, who were said to be cannibals. "Now," says the brochure, "they'd like to have you for lunch."

- To relax on the Palm Beach-style pool deck in a trim blue-and-white cushioned lounger.

- To take a three-country cruise in only five days, visiting Malaysia, Indonesia and Thailand from Singapore.

Five Things You Won't Find On Board

1. Durian fruit; it is forbidden on board due to its strong aroma.

2. A limited version of mealtimes; since many Singaporeans snack frequently from the street carts in their spotless city, they expect to be able to eat anytime. *SuperStar Gemini* tries to have something around to munch on all the time.

3. Anyone chewing gum; it's forbidden in the country of Singapore.

4. A self-service laundry.

5. A gratuity envelope. There is no tipping.

STAR CRUISE

SuperStar Gemini   ★ ★ ★

Registry	Panam
Officers	Internation.
Crew	Internationa
GRT	19,08
Length (ft.)	53
Beam (ft.)	7
Draft (ft.)	17.
Crew	47
Passengers-Cabins Full	80
Passengers-2/Cabin	80
Passenger Space Ratio	23.8
Stability Rating	Fair to goo
Seatings	
Cuisine	Continental and Asia
Dress Code	Smart Casua
Room Service	Ye
Tip	No Tippin

Ship Amenities

Outdoor Pool	
Indoor Pool	
Jacuzzi	
Fitness Center	Ye
Spa	Ye
Beauty Shop	Ye
Showroom	Ye
Bars/Lounges	3
Casino	Ye
Shops	
Library	Ye
Child Program	Ye
Self-Service Laundry	No
Elevators	5

Cabin Statistics

Suites	17
Outside Doubles	260
Inside Doubles	123
Wheelchair Cabins	4
Singles	0
Single Surcharge	150 - 200%
Verandas	17
110 Volt	No

SUN LINE CRUISES

One Rockefeller Plaza, Suite 315, New York, NY 10020-2090
(212) 397-6400, (800) 872-6400

NOTE: Sun Line Cruises and Epirotiki Cruises have formed a merger called Royal Olympic Cruises (see page 663) which markets ships of the two lines in two different divisions. The Blue World of Sun Line consists of three classic-style vessels with hulls painted dark blue—*Stella Solaris, Stella Oceanis* and *Odysseus*—which we list under Sun Line. The White World of Epirotiki comprises a mainstream three-ship fleet with white hulls—*Triton, Orpheus* and *Olympic*—which we list under Epirotiki.

History . . . .

Sun Line was founded by the late Ch. (Charalambos) A. Keusseoglou in 1957, after he had been a co-founder and former executive vice president of now-defunct Home Lines. Keusseoglou had been in the shipping industry since he left the Greek Army in 1947, going first to Sweden to work with Swedish American Line, then becoming one of the founders of Home Lines later that same year, along with Swedish American Line and Greek interests. He worked with Home Lines until after the acquisition of his first vessel for Sun, a Canadian frigate he turned into the yacht-like *Stella Maris I* in 1959. This ship was followed by the *Stella Solaris I*, then in 1963 the present *Stella Maris* replaced the original and four years later the *Stella Oceanis* was added to the fleet to replace the *Stella Solaris I*. In 1973, the flagship *Stella Solaris* was put into service, bringing the fleet to its present three ships.

The Marriott Corp. acquired an interest in Sun Line in 1971, but the family purchased back those shares in 1987.

Isabella Keusseoglou from the beginning has taken the responsibility for decorating the line's ships and hiring the cruise staff and entertainers, and with her sons and daughter in key executive positions, has overseen the operation of the cruise line since her husband's death in 1984.

In August 1995, Mrs. Keusseoglou, with George Potamianos of Epirotiki Cruises, made a joint announcement of the merger of the two companies into a new cruise line to be called Royal Olympic Cruises. Two of the three present Sun Line ships will compose two-thirds of the upscale Blue Ships division of the new company, while the third, the little *Stella Maris*, will be made available for charter under the auspices of

the new line. The New York marketing offices will remain in the Su
Line quarters in Rockefeller Plaza, while operations will be headqua
tered in Epirotiki's Piraeus offices.

Concept . . . .

To create itineraries to take passengers to "the unusual and the une:
pected," with destinations in Greece and Turkey, the Caribbean an
South America, and the services of a warm, loyal Greek crew, many
whom have been with the line for years.

Signatures . . . .

"Luxury Cruises in the Exotic Zone," with winter sailings up the Am:
zon and into the Yucatan, timed to coincide with special events fror
Carnival in Trinidad to the Maya Equinox at Chichen Itza.

Gimmicks . . . .

The hot homemade potato chips served in the Bar Grill room on th
Stella Solaris keep passengers like us coming back.

Who's the Competition . . . .

Under the new merger with Epirotiki, this pair of Greek lines perforn
very solidly in the Aegean, at least until the Greek version of the Jone
Act is eroded, as industry watchers expect it to be, because of demand
from European Community members who would like to see their ship
be able to make roundtrip cruises out of Piraeus. Orient Lines' *Marc
Polo*, the surprise entry in the Mediterranean, at about the same size an
a slightly lower price range than the *Stella Solaris*, could be competition
But if Celebrity's *Meridian* is repositioned to the Mediterranean, i
would be the toughest competition for the upscale Blue Ships becaus
of the extremely high quality of its hardware, food and service.

Who's Aboard . . . .

The *Stella Solaris* appeals mainly to older, more experienced cruise pas
sengers, many of them frequent travelers with the line. Sometimes 4:
percent of the passengers aboard are repeaters. Young couples and sin
gles, particularly in the Greek Islands, like all three ships.

Who Should Go . . . .

The new line's division between Blue and White Ships should broade:
the market base for both Sun and Epirotiki and reach more of the lan
tour travelers to the Aegean, including more young singles, couples anc
families.

Who Should Not Go . . . .

Any curmudgeon who won't join in the Greek dancing on Greek
Night.

The Lifestyle . . . .

The Greek Islands and Turkey itinerary on Sun Line ships is the perfec
answer for people who worry that "there's nothing to do" on a cruise
With its port-intensive itinerary, onboard lecturers and land guides, it':
the most information-packed trip imaginable, so long as your stamina
and curiosity hold up.

"I'd never book honeymooners on this cruise," one American travel agent sighed after a morning tour in Delos and an afternoon in Mykonos.

Passengers are a cosmopolitan lot, particularly in Greece, but language groups are sorted out and multilingual guides travel with each group. Social hosts accompany many of the cruises aboard the *Stella Solaris* in winter, when there are more days at sea and an older clientele aboard.

Wardrobe...................................

Both the Aegean and the South American cruises are casual by day, somewhat dressy by evening. The line suggests that on formal nights men wear dark suits or tuxedos and women gowns, cocktail dresses or dressy pantsuits. On informal nights, men are expected to wear suits or jacket and tie, while women are requested to don dresses, skirts or pantsuits. Casual evenings call for slacks and sportshirts for men, similar attire for women. There are usually two formal nights, one informal night and four casual nights during a seven-night cruise. Laundry and pressing services are available on board but there is no dry cleaning.

Bill of Fare........................... B

While the food is variable, depending on the chef aboard, the Greek dishes are always uniformly delicious, and we've found the deck buffets tasty as well.

The chief steward, if alerted the day before, can arrange a light cuisine or special order meal. Dinners usually provide three main dish choices, fish, fowl and meat, plus light or vegetarian fare, and a passenger can always order broiled chicken or grilled steak on the spot if nothing on the menu seems appealing. All breads and desserts are made on board, and hot homemade potato chips and thick, creamy homemade yogurt are two of our favorite treats.

An appealing deck buffet offers Greek salad, cold meats, hamburgers, moussaka, batter-dipped fried zucchini, fruit and cheese, in case you want to get an early start on an afternoon ashore.

Showtime............................. B

Mrs. Keusseoglou usually selects both the cruise staff and the entertainers who work on board and tends to keep certain passenger favorites over the long haul, including the charming and talented Caesar, a cocktail pianist. During our several cruises aboard, we've seen every sort of entertainment from the infamous Mr. Blackwell doing wildly popular fashion makeovers for volunteers from the audience to a dance team so exquisitely untalented they could bring back Velez and Yolanda. Magicians, ventriloquists and other variety artists are usually aboard, along with some really gifted performers such as jazz artists Steve and Bonnie Cole.

Discounts.................................

Early booking discounts from 10 to 50 percent, depending on itinerary and departure date, are offered by Sun Line. Royal Olympic Cruises had not established a discount policy as we went to press.

The Bottom Line

The Sun Line ships are well-suited to the Royal Olympic venture, and the marketing clout of the combination should be good for both companies. But there's a wide disparity in shipboard style between the two lines, and we wonder how that will be reconciled. We would like to think the Blue Ships will reflect the careful, warm and fastidious service so typical of Sun for all these years.

Odysseus

A ship anchored off Santorini is actually in the deep blue waters of the caldera itself and the island, thought by some to be the remnants of the lost continent of Atlantis, is the core of the volcano. We clambered up and down all over the town trying to get a photograph of the ship against the backlit sea, finally settling instead for stark white buildings with patches of vivid red, blue and yellow flowers. Late in the afternoon, as the wind grew fiercer and colder, we walked to the edge of the stone terrace that surrounded the cathedral to look at the other side of the island, and found ourselves backstage in the real Santorini, where a gaggle of tourist buses were parked and heavy traffic was bumper-to-bumper along the roadway that connects the small towns of the island. Our fantasies of a rugged remote island with no vehicles but donkeys and funiculars were dashed forever.

The former *Aquamarine* (only the last of many of her names), built in 1962, was virtually rebuilt when acquired by Epirotiki in 1988. When she made her debut in the spring of 1989, owner George Potamianos praised her extra-large cabins, 90 percent of them outside, and called her deck area "for a ship of her size more ample than any ship afloat." Cabins are located on five of the seven passenger decks, awkwardly divided on the lowest of them, where neither forward nor aft sections has elevator service. The topmost deck is given over to exercise, beauty salon treatments, massage and

una, with a large solarium aft and an observation deck forward. The prima-
public room deck is Jupiter, with a main lounge forward, a cocktail
unge, casino, library, card room and nightclub amidships, and a pool and
ck area aft.

The Brochure Says

"Nearly every day brings a new island or city to explore."

Translation

These are port intensive cruises with a number of optional shore excursions.

Cabins & Costs

antasy Suites: .... B

Average Price PPPD: $337 plus airfare.

The top pair of suites on board are the two forward on Apollo Deck with corner
sofas, a chair, coffee table, double bed, dresser, lots of closet space, a bathroom with
tub and shower and four windows in a 17-by-20-foot space.

mall Splurges: C

Average Price PPPD: $320 plus airfare.

Next best are a row of a dozen cabins measuring roughly 17-by-12, with three
lower beds, nightstands with drawers, four hanging closet areas and a bathroom
with shower only.

uitable Standards: C

Average Price PPPD: $260 plus airfare.

They're getting smaller, folks. While configurations vary, outside double cabins
range from 10-by-12 to 12-by-15, but all of them are attractively furnished with
two lower beds or a double bed, bath with shower and some closet hanging space.

ottom Bunks: .... D

Average Price PPPD: $182 plus airfare.

The very tiniest are a handful of outside cabins with upper and lower berths scat-
tered around on several decks; these have bath with shower.

Where She Goes

The *Odysseus* sails every Friday from Piraeus on a roundtrip three-day Aegean Discov-
ry cruise to Mykonos, Kusadasi, Patmos and Rhodes, and every Monday on a roundtrip
our-day Aegean Venture cruise to Mykonos, Heraklion, Santorini, Rhodes, Kusadasi and
'atmos. The season runs between March and November.

The Bottom Line

Much depends on the latest renovations. The vessel is in fairly good shape from its last
efurbishing. Cabins are attractively furnished although some of those on the lower decks
un on the small side. Eleven of them are marketed as singles, and the line says there are
ome wheelchair-accessible cabins available, although we've never seen them. That may

be part of the most recent refit. Certainly, under Sun Line operation the *Odysseus* com
up a notch or two.

Five Special Spots

1. The Solarium, a sheltered sun trap for serious basking on Kronos Deck aft.

2. The Trojan Horse is a cozy night club with bar just off the pool deck near tl
   library.

3. The Sirenes, a large main lounge with wood parquet dance floor and tub chairs, h
   a charming semi-circular bar with swivel stools at one end.

4. A buffet restaurant called Ulysses Marine Club located aft of the dining room al
   doubles as a video and film room.

5. The top deck fitness and beauty area boasts a sauna, massage room, gymnasiu
   beauty salon and fitness club.

Five Good Reasons to Book This Ship

1. To see how it matches up with Sun's *Stella Solaris* in the Blue Ships fleet.

2. To set out on port-intensive three- or four-day cruises to the Greek Islands and Tu
   key, hitting four ports in three days or six ports in four days.

3. To snuggle into that Solarium on a breezy fall day in the Aegean.

4. To luxuriate around the pool on that lovely teak deck.

5. To splurge on a suite with lots of windows.

Five Things You Won't Find On Board

1. A private veranda.

2. A self-service laundry.

3. A single-meal seating.

4. Elevator service to all the passenger cabin decks; it stops short of Poseidon.

5. A paucity of deck lounging chair space; there's plenty.

Odysseus ★ ★ ★

Registry	Greece
Officers	Greek
Crew	Greek
GRT	10,000
Length (ft.)	483
Beam (ft.)	61
Draft (ft.)	24
Crew	190
Passengers-Cabins Full	486
Passengers-2/Cabin	452
Passenger Space Ratio	22.12
Stability Rating	Good
Seatings	2
Cuisine	Continental/Greek
Dress Code	Traditional
Room Service	Yes
Tip	$6 - $8 PPPD

Ship Amenities

Outdoor Pool	1
Indoor Pool	0
Jacuzzi	4
Fitness Center	Yes
Spa	Yes
Beauty Shop	Yes
Showroom	Yes
Bars/Lounges	4
Casino	Yes
Shops	1
Library	Yes
Child Program	Yes
Self-Service Laundry	No
Elevators	1

Cabin Statistics

Suites	14
Outside Doubles	168
Inside Doubles	38
Wheelchair Cabins	0
Singles	11
Single Surcharge	150%
Verandas	0
110 Volt	Yes

SUN LINE CRUISES

Stella Oceanis   ★★★

Our favorite thing, more than browsing through the vegetable market or sitting at one of the seafood cafes of Mikrolimano, is to stand at the rail of a passenger vessel sailing in or out of the port of Piraeus looking at all the ships and deciphering the Greek letters—ships you'd forgotten existed, ships that used to be somebody, ships that only an owner could love. One thing Piraeus has plenty of is ships.

With cabins on four of the six passenger decks, the *Stella Oceanis* has onl one real public deck, Oceanis Deck, with the dining room forward and th main lounge aft. One deck up on Lido is the popular Plaka Taverna with i wood paneling and nautical accents. The Sun Deck and pool are larg enough for most of the passengers to get in some sunning and swimming be tween island tours.

The Brochure Says

"On our cruises to Egypt and Israel, you'll have the chance to marvel at the Pyramids of Egypt and visit Jerusalem, alive with history and sacred to three great religions. The mysterious Sphinx has enthralled visitors throughout the ages, inspiring countless myths and legends concerning its origin, construction and meaning."

Translation

This is a destination-oriented cruise, and you'll have plenty of time ashore with your guides to ponder the mystery of it all.

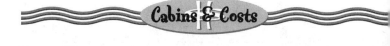
Cabins & Costs

Fantasy Suites: C

Average Price PPPD: $360 plus airfare.

There are 10 accommodations designated as suites on board, two of them amidships on Stella Deck, the remainder aft on Lido Deck. Each has two lower beds, two chairs, a coffee table and a bathroom with tub and shower.

Small Splurges: . . . . *C*

Average Price PPPD: $300 plus airfare.
Two categories of deluxe cabins line the Pelagos Deck, varying a bit in size. Each has two sofa/beds with dresser, smaller table and stool, chair and two portholes, plus a tile bathroom with tub.

Suitable Standards: . . . . *C*

Average Price PPPD: $289 plus airfare.
Most standard outside doubles have two lower beds, small tile bath with corner shower, built-in desk and dresser, and two small individual closets with good hanging space. In some of them, one bed folds up during the daytime to make more floor space. Some have third and fourth upper berths as well.

Bottom Bunks: . . . . D

Average Price PPPD: $192 plus airfare.
The cheapest quarters aboard, suitable for students on a generous budget, perhaps, are quite small, with upper and lower berths and tiny baths with shower only. The two lowest passenger decks provide small, chopped-up accommodations.

Where She Goes

The *Stella Oceanis* makes seven-day roundtrip Lands of Antiquity sailings from Piraeus on Fridays, visiting Santorini, Heraklion, Port Said (for Cairo), Ashdod (for Jerusalem), Patmos and Kusadasi, beginning in April, with the last scheduled departure in November.

The Bottom Line

The least glamorous of Sun Line's three vessels, *Stella Oceanis* nevertheless has sleeker external lines than her smaller sister *Stella Maris* and draws the youngest crowds on Greek Islands land/sea packages in summer. The ship is kept spotlessly clean, and the decking always seems to be in good shape. Still, the cheaper cabins are quite small and halls in the lower passenger decks narrow. The seven-day itinerary that visits Cairo and Jerusalem as well as Turkey and the Greek Islands is a good introduction to the area for first-time visitors.

Fielding's Five

Five Favorite Places

1. The Minos Salon is decorated with murals of Greek mythology and plush furniture in autumnal shades, plus a bar with four barstools and a dance floor.

2. In the Aphrodite Restaurant, tables seat four, five or six; windows are large and let in light but the ceiling is awfully low.

3. The swimming pool is fairly large for a ship this size, and surrounded with teak decking and dark brown and blue lounge chairs. The deck buffet is served here, and just inside is a cozy bar.

4. The popular Plaka Taverna is a cozy bar that doubles as disco, decorated in nautic theme with a ship's wheel, rope knots and figurehead.

5. The Club, a tiny cardroom tucked away aft beyond the Minos Salon, makes a goo hideaway when the world is too much with you.

Five Good Reasons to Book This Ship

1. To visit Cairo, Jerusalem and Ephesus plus three Greek islands, all in a week.

2. The warmth and friendliness of the Greek crew.

3. The expanse of pool and sun deck for R&R between must-see monuments.

4. To learn Greek—as well as a smattering of the other four or five languages publ announcements are made in.

5. To have a Greek salad for lunch every day.

Five Things You Won't Find On Board

1. A children's program.

2. 110-volt electrical current.

3. Cabins designated wheelchair-accessible.

4. A full-fledged casino, although there are slot machines.

5. A gym or fitness center.

tella Oceanis ★ ★ ★

Registry	**Greece**
Officers	**Greek**
Crew	**Greek**
Complement	**140**
GRT	**5500**
Length (ft.)	**350**
Beam (ft.)	**53**
Draft (ft.)	**16**
Passengers-Cabins Full	**369**
Passengers-2/Cabin	**300**
Passenger Space Ratio	**18**
Stability Rating	**Good**
Seatings	**2**
Cuisine	**Continental/Greek**
Dress Code	**Traditional**
Room Service	**Yes**
Tip	**$9 PPPD**

hip Amenities

Outdoor Pool	**1**
Indoor Pool	**0**
Jacuzzi	**0**
Fitness Center	**Yes**
Spa	**No**
Beauty Shop	**No**
Showroom	**No**
Bars/Lounges	**3**
Casino	**No**
Shops	**1**
Library	**Yes**
Child Program	**No**
Self-Service Laundry	**No**
Elevators	**1**

Cabin Statistics

Suites	**10**
Outside Doubles	**103**
Inside Doubles	**46**
Wheelchair Cabins	**0**
Singles	**0**
Single Surcharge	**125-200%**
Verandas	**0**
110 Volt	**No**

Stella Solaris

It's hard to imagine anything more romantic than a balmy evening at midnight standing at the rail of the Stella Solaris with moonlight rippling on the Aegean Sea. Even the captain had fallen in love with one of his American passengers during one of these Greek Islands cruises and later got married aboard his own ship. Yes, these week-long sailings are exhausting, exciting, exotic, fulfilling and hectic—and they're also very, very romantic.

The largest of the three Sun Line ships is *Stella Solaris*, built in 1959 as the *Stella V*, then the *Camboge*, with eight passenger decks and a great expanse of teak decks aft. The topmost Lido deck is where you'll find the swimming pools, sunbathing loungers and Lido Bar. Down one deck from here are the suites, with a full around-the-ship promenade deck outside and a small reading and card room aft that doubles as a meetings venue. The main public lounges are on Solaris Deck, with the dining room and galley forward, a couple of bars, the lobby and purser's desk amidships, and the main lounge and a piano bar aft. Below are cabins, plus a cinema, gym, beauty shop, disco and hospital

The ship's new 2600-square foot Daphne Spa has a full menu of beauty and health treatments that can be booked ahead of sailing individually or in package.

The Brochure Says

"Our Greek officers and crew are experts when it comes to welcoming you on board in the true tradition of Greek hospitality."

Translation

The new merger of Sun and Epirotiki becomes the largest Greek cruise company Royal Olympic Cruises, who have taken the blue and white of the Greek flag as their colors and it will set you sailing with that wonderful crew.

INSIDER TIP

Better take those free Greek dancing lessons when they're offered, because on Greek night, you can count on being whirled out on the floor by an enthusiastic crew member.

DID YOU KNOW?

Celebrity passengers aboard Stella Solaris *have included Cary Grant, Rock Hudson, Jimmy and Rosalyn Carter, Eva Marie Saint and Ernest Borgnine, in whose honor the staff screened* The Poseidon Adventure.

Cabins & Costs

Fantasy Suites: .... B+

Average Price PPPD: $397 plus airfare.

The 34 deluxe suites on Boat Deck have various configurations, but all usually contain a large sitting area with sofa and chairs and coffee table, plus built-in wood cabinetry, and a bedroom with twin or queen-sized bed, huge walk-in closet and spacious bath with tub and shower.

Small Splurges: .... B

Average Price PPPD: $360 plus airfare.

Smaller deluxe suites amidships on Ruby Deck have the advantage of the smoothest ride aboard as well. Two lower beds, four small closets, sitting area and bath with tub and shower, and, on this deck, portholes instead of windows.

Suitable Standards: .... B

Average Price PPPD: $295 plus airfare.

Superior outside doubles on Emerald Deck also have portholes, plus two lower beds, built-in desk and dresser, stool, bathroom with tub and shower, and, in some, the possibility of booking adjoining cabins.

Bottom Bunks: .... D

Average Price PPPD: $192 plus airfare.

The least expensive digs are the Category 11 inside cabins on Sapphire Deck, which do not have elevator access; you have to walk down from the elevator on the deck above. These cabins are small with upper and lower berths and bath with shower only.

EAVESDROPPING

Captain Michael Benas, for many years master of the Stella Solaris, *when asked about passengers fraternizing with crew, chuckled, "When we miss a passenger, we call the crew cabins."*

Stella Solaris spends the winter in the Caribbean and South America, sailing from F Lauderdale through the Caribbean and into the Amazon, than makes a 23-day Primave repositioning cruise to Piraeus for Aegean service under the Royal Olympic Cruises ba ner. Throughout the summer, she makes seven-day roundtrip cruises from Piraeus, ca ing in Istanbul, Mykonos, Kusadasi, Patmos, Rhodes, Heraklion and Santorini.

With a deep 28-foot draft and steam turbine engines, the *Stella Solaris* offers a ve. smooth ride. Safety procedures get high marks as well, with a thorough boat drill that ir cludes lowering the launches in front of the passengers at each boat station. One of th main assets of this ship is also one of its problems—the Greek dining room stewards wh have been here forever sometimes get more involved in the logistics of "Head 'em uj move 'em out" on open seatings than is appropriate with a ship of this class. Bear in minc too, that the *Stella Solaris* is one of those ships that changes personality by season. Th longer winter voyages attract older, more affluent passengers than the seven-day summe sailings. Some of the winter passengers come back every year, stay on board 40 or 45 day and may not get off the ship in ports they've seen before. "They don't care where the shij goes," said one longtime staffer, "they want to travel with their favorite steward."

Five Familiar Places

1. The Grill Room Bar with its classic dark leather sofas and chairs, its horseshoe shaped bar and clubby New York ambience, is one of our favorite spots at sea.

2. The Solaris Lounge is divided from the Piano Bar by an open sculpture wall and fur nished with gold plush chairs and patterned plush banquettes, plus raised seating levels around the sides of the room facing the dance floor and stage.

3. Teatime takes place in the Piano Bar with a pianist playing pop and show tunes as waiters serve tea and cookies. A long, low bar with wide view windows behind it offers a great view of the sea.

4. The pool deck has two overlapping oval pools surrounded by a sunning platform, umbrella-covered tables and sun loungers.

5. The dining room with its wide windows lets you watch the scenery while you're cruising, or you can puzzle over the murals of legends and heroes decorating the walls.

Five Good Reasons to Book This Ship

1. Because the same Greek waiters, stewards and bartenders seem to have been here forever.

2. Because the ship never feels crowded, even when it's full.

3. For unique special event cruises such as the Maya Equinox Cruise, when passengers visit the El Castillo Pyramid in Chichen Itza for the vernal equinox, when the set- ting sun makes a pattern of seven triangles, one appearing at a time, along the north face of the temple, depicting the mystic descent of the "feathered serpent" that illus- trates the arrival of the Maya god Kukulkan on earth.

To take a seven-day crash course in Greek history and culture.

To socialize with some of Sun's celebrity passengers.

Five Things You Won't Find On Board

TV sets in most of the cabins except suites.

A bumpy ride in rough seas; the deep draft of the ship adds a lot of stability.

A chance to sit where you want to at open seating breakfasts and lunches, when the waiters rush you into whatever empty space is up.

Plenty of soundproofing between cabins; many allow eavesdropping through the walls.

A wheelchair-accessible cabin.

SUN LINE CRUISES

Stella Solaris ★★★

Registry	Greec
Officers	Gree
Crew	Gree
Complement	31
GRT	18,00
Length (ft.)	54
Beam (ft.)	7:
Draft (ft.)	28.!
Passengers-Cabins Full	70
Passengers-2/Cabin	62
Passenger Space Ratio	2!
Stability Rating	Goo
Seatings	2
Cuisine	Continental/Greel
Dress Code	Traditiona
Room Service	Yes
Tip	$9 PPPD

Ship Amenities

Outdoor Pool	2
Indoor Pool	0
Jacuzzi	0
Fitness Center	Yes
Spa	Yes
Beauty Shop	Yes
Showroom	Yes
Bars/Lounges	4
Casino	Yes
Shops	2
Library	Yes
Child Program	No
Self-Service Laundry	No
Elevators	3

Cabin Statistics

Suites	66
Outside Doubles	166
Inside Doubles	58
Wheelchair Cabins	0
Singles	0
Single Surcharge	125-200%
Verandas	0
110 Volt	No

TALL SHIP
ADVENTURES

1389 South Havana Street, Aurora, CO 80012
☎ *(303) 755-7983, (800) 662-0090*

History . . . .

The three-masted schooner *Sir Francis Drake* was constructed in Germany in 1917 as the *Landkirchen* and carried copper from Chile around Cape Horn to Europe. Then, with an engine added in the 1920s, it spent 40 years carrying cargo in the Baltic and North Seas. In 1988 Eckart Straub and Captain Bryan Petley purchased the vessel and renamed it after the dashing English buccaneer. Captain Petley, a New Zealander, has been sailing since he was 13, and brings a cheerful, offbeat attitude of fun that rubs off on all the passengers.

—One of fewer than 100 tall ships remaining that was built to transport cargo solely under sail.

Concept . . . .

"We advertise ourselves as a middle-of-the-road soft adventure," says Captain Petley, "not as luxurious as the Star Clippers or *Sea Cloud* but a bit less basic than the Maine Windjammers or the Windjammer Barefoot Cruises." What he means is that the cabins are carpeted, air-conditioned and have private bathrooms, but you can still show up to dinner barefoot and in shorts.

Signatures . . . .

The B.L.T. party, every Tuesday night, when passengers are required to wear (1) Buccaneer dress, (2) Lingerie or (3) Toga.

Gimmicks . . . .

Pirate's Punch is free.

Who's the Competition. . . . .

Probably the Windjammer ships come the closest in style and authenticity, but the cabins don't all have private facilities on those vessels.

Who's Aboard. . . . .

Young to middle-aged couples and singles, with a median age in the mid-40s, but they can be as young as 20 or as old as 80, plus an occa-

sional family with children over 8. Captain Petley discourages childr
any younger than 8.

Who Should Go ....

People who want to relax. One veteran of many Tall Ship Adventu
says, "The first day you're a little uptight, the second day you begin
unwind and by the seventh day, you don't have a clue what's happeni
in the world and you don't care."

Who Should Not Go ....

Fussbudgets and nitpickers; clothes horses; shoppers (there are very fe
shopping stops on the itinerary); people who hate sun, sand and sea.

The Lifestyle ....

The usual drill in the U.S. and British Virgin Islands is to sail in tl
mornings, anchor at midday and have lunch on the beach, spending tl
afternoon snorkeling, swimming, windsurfing, sailing or waterskiin,
Dinner is served on board, and afterwards the captain and whoev
wishes to join him usually go ashore "to where the bands are" and part
For a 10-minute video preview of the ship, send a refundable $1
deposit to Tall Ship Adventures (address above).

Wardrobe ....

Anything goes. Bare feet and shorts are acceptable dinner attire excer
perhaps on the Sunday night captain's dinner. "That's when I dress i
my uniform," Captain Petley says.

Bill of Fare ....(

In the tiny galley below decks, the chef prepares a mix of popular star
dards including hamburger and barbecued ribs with elegant lobste
sandwiches on homemade bread or Caribbean-accented specialties suc
as chicken-and-shrimp stir-fry and West Indian baked chicken. Lunch i
often served on the beach, and deck barbecues are popular. This is che
Patrick Browne's recipe:

Chicken and Shrimp Stir-Fry
4 to 6 servings

1 cup diced raw chicken breasts, skin and bones removed

1 cup chopped raw shrimp, shells and veins removed

Salad oil

1 cup each thinly sliced and chopped fresh cabbage, carrots, broccoli
cauliflower and onions, or other vegetables if preferred

Seasoned salt

Soy sauce

Hot steamed rice

Heat 1-2 TB oil in wok or large deep skillet until smoking, then drop in
chicken and shrimp and cook, stirring constantly, two minutes. Remove
from oil with slotted spoon and keep warm. Put vegetables in oil and
stir quickly to mix, then cover and steam just until vegetables are
crunchy-tender, about 15 minutes. Ten minutes into the cooking,
return the chicken and shrimp to the pan, add seasoned salt and soy

sauce to taste and cook an additional five minutes or so. Serve over hot rice.

howtime . . . . **N/A**

Going ashore after dinner to small island nightclubs with the unflappable Captain Petley.

)iscounts. . . . .

Early booking bonuses up to 20 percent are available on certain cruises; call the company for details. A group of 10 to 19 passengers gets a 5 percent group discount, while a group of 20 or more gets a 10 percent discount.

The Bottom Line

This is Captain Petley's ship, run in his own inimitable fashion. He former-y sailed as a captain with Windjammer and describes one primary difference etween his ship and theirs: "They sail at night every night and stop during he day. We sail during part of the day and anchor at night."

Sir Francis Drake ⚓⚓⚓⚓

The first time we saw the Sir Francis Drake *was in the Boston Harbor during the Tall Ships celebration in 1992, and even there amid so many vessels its three masts stood out above the crowd.*

You won't get lost aboard the ship if you can just remember which companionways go where. There are only 14 cabins, a dining room, a lounge and the open deck, but a recent refitting has spruced it up, and if you had 33 like-minded friends could probably arrange your own charter. The last going price we heard was $4000 a day, which would work out to about $118 apiece a day if you had the full 34 people.

The Brochure Says

"• It's swimming and watersports and relaxing on the beach.
- It's sunfish sailing and windsurfing and fabulous sunsets.
- It's picnics on the beach and snorkeling and diving.
- It's delightful parties and dancing the nights away.
- It's exploring tropical islands and exciting ports of call.
- It's making new friends that will last a lifetime."

Translation

There's the answer to the question, What's there to do?

EAVESDROPPING

"The people we get don't ever want to go back on a floating hotel or a wimp cruise again," says Captain Bryan Petley.

Cabins & Costs

Fantasy Suites: C

Average Price PPPD: $199 plus airfare.
There is one luxury suite on board, contoured into the aft corners of the vessel, not huge but it certainly seems spacious beside the others. Anyhow, the bed is big enough for two, it's carpeted, air-conditioned and has a wall-mounted chest for a modicum of storage.

Small Splurges: C

Average Price PPPD: $170 plus airfare.
Small is the operative word here. You can book the next category down, a double bed with upper twin (there are six of these), carpeting, air conditioning and private toilet and shower.

Suitable Standards: C

Average Price PPPD: $170 plus airfare.
Side-by-side twin beds mean only one of you gets up and gets dressed at a time; there are four of these, with very compact bathrooms.

Bottom Bunks: .... D

Average Price PPPD: $142 plus airfare.
And you thought the small splurges were small! Three of these with upper and lower bunks are pretty basic; one is aft, opposite the suite, and the other two forward, but you can't get from the aft one to the forward ones without going up, across the next deck and back down.

Where She Goes

While the captain changes itineraries frequently, he stays in the Caribbean, usually around the British Virgin Islands. Most recently the ship sails from Tortola on the first, third and fifth Saturday of each month to most of the little islands in the BVI, and on the

:ond and fourth Saturdays to the rest of them. In summer, the ship sails between Sim-on Bay, St. Maarten, and English Harbour, Antigua, visiting St. Barts, Tintamarre, Sta-t, St. Kitts and Nevis southbound, and Antigua's snorkeling beaches, Barbuda's coral :efs and the remote volcanic island of Saba on the northbound route. Combine both neraries and you can knock off 10 percent from your 14-day cruise.

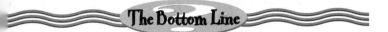

The Bottom Line

The *Sir Francis Drake* is a handsome old ship, especially after its recent refurbishment, ut housekeeping is not always pristine and the casual lifestyle may verge on the raffish :casionally. Still, the prices are very low, the beach activities super and the food isn't bad ther. If you're not fussy and want a relaxed and relaxing barefoot cruise, you should try

Fielding's Five

Five Shipshape Spaces

. The lounge, which doubles as bar, video room, gift shop, TV room, library, gathering spot and lecture hall. (Only kidding—they don't do lectures aboard.)

. The deck, clean, natural teak bleached to a weathered gray, is ringed with chairs, lounges and small tables.

. The dining room, elegantly wood-paneled and prettily redecorated in beige with wood armchairs.

. The bowsprit has a safety net underneath that can support a foolhardy passenger or two.

. The deck bar, sometimes the setting for an onboard wedding.

Five Good Reasons to Book This Ship

1. To join Captain Petley at the Tuesday night B.L.T. (buccaneer, lingerie or toga) party; he himself may appear in filmy lingerie with his captain's bars pinned to one spaghetti strap.

2. It's a good blend of land and sea vacations for a watersports-and-party crowd.

3. Because all you need to pack are shorts, T-shirts and tennis shoes.

4. Because you can cruise through the unspoiled British Virgin Islands.

5. Because you can take a seven-day cruise for as little as $796 if you get in on an early booking discount.

Five Things You Won't Find On Board

1. Room service.

2. A concierge.

3. Anybody with a stuffy attitude.

4. Anyone wearing pantyhose and high heels—except maybe on B.L.T. Night.

5. An elevator.

Sir Francis Drake ⚓⚓⚓

Registry	Hondura
Officers	Internation:
Crew	Internation:
Complement	1
GRT	45
Length (ft.)	16
Beam (ft.)	2
Draft (ft.)	
Passengers-Cabins Full	3
Passengers-2/Cabin	2
Passenger Space Ratio	N/
Stability Rating	Fai
Seatings	
Cuisine	Caribbear
Dress Code	Casua
Room Service	Nc
Tip	$10 PPPD

Ship Amenities

Outdoor Pool	0
Indoor Pool	0
Jacuzzi	0
Fitness Center	No
Spa	No
Beauty Shop	No
Showroom	No
Bars/Lounges	2
Casino	No
Shops	1
Library	Yes
Child Program	No
Self-Service Laundry	No
Elevators	0

Cabin Statistics

Suites	1
Outside Doubles	13
Inside Doubles	0
Wheelchair Cabins	0
Singles	0
Single Surcharge	NA
Verandas	0
110 Volt	No

WINDJAMMER BAREFOOT CRUISES, LTD.

1759 Bay Road, Miami Beach, FL 33139
☎ *(305) 672-6453, (800) 327-2602*

History . . . .

In 1947, Captain Mike Burke, just out of the U.S. Navy after serving four years in submarines, says he headed first for Miami, then after a few drinks, on to the Bahamas with $600 back pay in his pocket. He woke up the next morning on the deck of a 19-foot sloop with no money and a splitting headache. He had bought a boat. He named it the *Hangover*.

Soon Burke found himself taking paying friends and guests on cruises to the Bahamas, and after a year or so of that, combined his entrepreneurial skills with his love of tall ships and founded Windjammer Barefoot Cruises. His first boat was a 150-foot schooner named *Janeen* that had been run aground. Burke fixed her up and renamed her *Polynesia I*. By 1958, his fleet numbered four, *Polynesia I, Polynesia II, Brigantine Yankee* and his prize, the *Yankee Clipper*, originally built for German industrialist Alfred Krupp and confiscated as a prize of war by the U.S. in 1945.

Burke says his secret is to buy the ships in bad shape and then fix them up. In that way he acquired his present fleet of six tall ships (the newest, the former *France II*, has a new name pending) and one motor vessel, *Amazing Grace*, his supply ship. His six children have joined him in his company.

—The largest single fleet of tall ships in the world (six). Burke says the Norwegian government comes in second with three tall ships.

DID YOU KNOW?

The Polynesia I was confiscated by Fidel Castro in 1971 when a storm blew her off course into Cuban waters and government officials seized her. Burke had to bail his crew out of jail in Cuba; fortunately, there were no passengers aboard. But Castro kept the vessel as his own private yacht.

Concept . . . .

To provide "memorable, affordable vacations for would-be "ol' salts o all ages" where informality rules. Passengers set their own pace, doin as much or as little as they like, from helping hoist a sail to lolling in th sun doing nothing.

Signatures . . . .

The logo tall ship and the word "barefoot" in the company nam describe the product clearly to would-be passengers. Four or five desig nated singles cruises are among each year's big sellers, in which a entire sailing is devoted only to singles, sometimes within a certain ag bracket, and always promising an equal mix of men and women. Th line claims five marriages so far from couples that have met on single sailings. Their longtime sailaway anthem is "Amazing Grace."

Gimmicks . . . .

"Drinker's Doubloons" are tokens you buy from the bartender o board to pay for drinks without having to carry cash around.

"Story hour" is the daily morning briefing (8:45 a.m.) from the captain telling you what is likely to happen during that day.

Who's the Competition . . . .

The only really comparable product is Tall Ship Adventures' *Sir Franci. Drake* (see above) but with only one ship, it doesn't really put a dent ir Windjammer's business. None of the more upscale sailing ship cruise lines—Star Clipper, Windstar or Club Med Cruises—come close to the bargain prices and informality on board the Windjammers.

Who's Aboard . . . .

The company says, "Singles, nearlyweds, newlyweds, retirees and fami- lies alike," which pretty much covers the waterfront.

Who Should Go . . . .

People who love sailing and the sea and want to meet like-minded folks.

Who Should Not Go . . . .

Tradition-mined cruisers; Sea Goddess veterans; anyone susceptible to mal-de-mer; infants and toddlers.

NO NOs

Open bottles of personal liquor in the cabins are not permitted; smoking is forbidden anywhere except on the open decks; and flip-flops are not advised for deck and island wear.

The Lifestyle . . . .

"Barefoot" is the operative word here; you'll never need dress-up clothes or even shoes, if you don't feel like wearing them. Free Bloody Marys before breakfast, Rum Swizzles at sunset, free wine with dinner (which is served in two seatings), and always time for a party. Passengers may help the crew with the sails or take a turn at the helm, and swim- ming, diving and snorkeling are favorite pastimes. Cabins range from dorm-like rooms to doubles to suites, most but not all with private bathroom facilities.

Wardrobe. . . . .

As little as possible, because the cruises are very casual with no dressing up even considered, let alone required, and because there's very little storage space in the cabins. Take plenty of bathing suits, shorts and T-shirts, perhaps a long-sleeved shirt and long pants or skirt to cover up from the sun.

Bill of Fare. . . . . C+

The food is hearty, simple and family-style. Breakfasts feature freshly baked breads and pastries, preceded, if you wish, by a complimentary Bloody Mary. Lunch may be a picnic on the beach or a buffet on deck. At cocktail time, hors d'oeuvres are served with rum or soft drinks, and dinner includes wine, beer or soft drinks of your choice. A late-night snack provides "midnight munchies." Many of the dishes have a Caribbean accent, including these ribs:

Guava Glazed BBQ Spare Ribs
6 servings

3 racks baby back ribs

6 cloves of garlic, minced

1 TB dried thyme

4 bay leaves, crumbled

2 TB dried parsley

1 TB ground allspice

2 TB liquid smoke

2 ounces soy sauce

4 ounces white wine

Parboil ribs for 10 minutes to rend fat. Combine the remaining ingredients into a marinade. Pat ribs dry with paper towels, then place in baking pan and brush liberally on both sides with the marinade. Cover and bake at 325-350 degrees for one hour and 30 minutes, basting with marinade from pan every half-hour. Remove from oven, cool pan drippings and prepare Guava Glaze. Finish on a grill (or return to the oven at 450 degrees); brush frequently with Guava Glaze.

Guava Glaze

1 cup pan drippings with fat removed

4 TB guava jelly

1 Scotch bonnet or jalapeno pepper minced
or, 1/2 TB West Indian hot sauce

Defat the drippings by pouring them from the baking pan into a saucepan and putting ice cubes in until the fat congeals on the ice. Then remove ice and fat, return pan to heat and reduce the drippings by half. Add jelly and minced pepper or hot sauce and continue reducing until sauce reaches a thick consistency.

Showtime. . . . . N/A

Drinking Rum Swizzles and nibbling hot hors d'oeuvres on deck is the evening's pre-dinner entertainment. What you do later is up to you.

Discounts . . . .

Windjammer Club members ($25 initiation fee) get to take along friend on a fall cruise for half-price on the "bosom buddy" program good through early December.

The Bottom Line

Windjammer delivers exactly what it promises its passengers, which explains its high repeat factor, with one loyal who's passed his 160th sailing Like Carnival, you know pretty much what you're getting so you can figur ahead of time whether it's what you want. The prices are right and the supply of food and grog plentiful; what's not to like?

Amazing Grace Unrated

The supply ship *Amazing Grace*, built in 1955 in Scotland as the *Pharos* and acquired by Windjammer in 1988, is a former British Navy motor vessel that sails on 13-day voyages between Freeport, Bahamas and Trinidad. She rendezvous with Windjammer's tall ships and delivers their monthly supplies, just as she once delivered supplies to lighthouse keepers along the rugged North Sea coast in Scotland on weekdays and entertained royalty at tea on weekends.

A period dignity has earned her the nickname "Orient Express of the Caribbean," and both a smoking room and a piano room with fireplace have been preserved in their original style. A spacious deck gives passengers room to move around or relax with a book.

Cabins are somewhat larger than on the tall ships, a few with twin or double beds. Some have private toilet facilities and some offer a wash basin in the room and toilet down the hall. The **Fantasy Suite** equivalent is Burke's Berth, which has a sitting room, sleeper sofa, TV/VCR and CD stereo with tape player and honor bar, a separate bedroom with double bed and a marble and teak bath with its own Jacuzzi.

Suitable Standards with private toilet and shower facilities include cabins 1BB, 1BI and the Officer's Deck cabins. All have upper and lower berths.

Bottom Bunks would include 1TP, 2TP and 2BP; the first two have twin beds and wash basin, porthole and desk or vanity, the latter upper and lower berths with porthole and wash basin.

Prices for the 13-day cruise range from $950 to $2800 per person, double occupancy, the latter, of course, for Burke's Berth. Add $100 a person for sailings between the first of November and the end of May. Calls are made at any of nearly three dozen islands between Freeport, to the north not far off Florida, and Trinidad.

Amazing Grace — Unrated

Registry	Honduras
Officers	British/West Indian
Crew	West Indian
Complement	40
GRT	1526
Length (ft.)	254
Beam (ft.)	38
Draft (ft.)	17
Passengers-Cabins Full	94
Passengers-2/Cabin	94
Passenger Space Ratio	NA
Stability Rating	Fair
Seatings	2
Cuisine	Continental
Dress Code	Casual
Room Service	No
Tip	$7.50 PPPD

Ship Amenities

Outdoor Pool	0
Indoor Pool	0
Jacuzzi	1
Fitness Center	No
Spa	No
Beauty Shop	No
Showroom	No
Bars/Lounges	1
Casino	No
Shops	1
Library	Yes
Child Program	No
Self-Service Laundry	Yes
Elevators	0

Cabin Statistics

Suites	10
Outside Doubles	36
Inside Doubles	1
Wheelchair Cabins	0
Singles	0
Single Surcharge	140-200%
Verandas	0
110 Volt	Yes

WINDJAMMER BAREFOOT CRUISES, LTD.

Fantome   ⚓⚓⚓⚓

Flying Cloud   ⚓⚓⚓⚓

Mandalay   ⚓⚓⚓⚓

Polynesia   ⚓⚓⚓⚓

Yankee Clipper   ⚓⚓⚓⚓

"Romantic" is the word most commonly used to describe sailing ships, perhaps because these age-old craft take us back to what we imagine as a more stress-free time. Shirley says white canvas sails puffed by the breeze are the perfect accessory to romance, far better than a ruffled parasol or a bearskin rug, because they seem to make most men act like Mel Gibson.

This fleet of tall ships—the four-masted stay-sail schooner *Fantome*, built in 1927 for the Duke of Westminster; the *Flying Cloud*, a former French naval cadet training ship decorated by General Charles de Gaulle for sinking two Japanese submarines when she was carrying nitrates from Tahiti; the *Mandalay*, the former luxury yacht of financier E. F. Hutton, originally the *Hussar IV* and predecessor to the famous *Sea Cloud*; the *Polynesia*, a former Grand Banks fishing schooner acquired by Windjammer in 1975, previously the *Argus*, subject of a National Geographic feature and an Allen Villers book; the two- masted sailing ship *Yankee Clipper*, probably the only armor-plated yacht in the world, built in 1927 for German industrialist Alfred Krupp as the *Cressida*; and the former *France II*, a meteorological research and exploration vessel owned by the French government, being converted into a four-masted ship.

DID YOU KNOW?

The Fantome *was purchased by Aristotle Onassis from the Guinness Brewing family to present as a wedding gift to Princess Grace and Prince Rainier. When he wasn't invited to the wedding, he didn't send the gift. Captain Mike picked her up in 1969 as the flagship of his fleet.*

DID YOU KNOW?

The Yankee Clipper, *originally a yacht named* Cressida *built for German munitions king Alfred Krupp, hosted Adolf Hitler during World War II, was acquired by the Vanderbilt family after the war and raced regularly off Newport Beach, California, as the* Pioneer, *once clocked at 22 knots under sail. She's still considered one of the fastest tall ships sailing.*

The Brochure Says

"Informality rules! T-shirts and shorts are all you'll need to pack, so trash the tuxes and ballgowns. Stow your gear in your air-conditioned cabin. From dorms to Honeymoon Suites, all feature modern amenities. Who said anything about roughing it?"

Translation

This is the ultimate in casual cruising, and Windjammer's multiple repeaters like it like that. Some of the cabins are pretty basic, however, and while everything is more or less air-conditioned, the modern amenities aboard may or may not include a private toilet facility.

Cabins & Costs

Fantasy Suites: . . . . .B

Average Price PPPD: $187 plus airfare.
The best digs (apart from Burke's Berth on the *MV Amazing Grace*, above) would be the Honeymoon Suite aboard *Flying Cloud*, which is below Main Deck with its own private entrance, windows, a queen-sized bed, mini-refrigerator, private toilet and shower, TV/VCR, CD and wet bar.

Small Splurges: . . . . *C*

Average Price PPPD: $170 plus airfare.
The Admiral's Suite on the *Fantome* with a queen-sized bed, private bathroom with toilet and shower and a mini-refrigerator, relatively lavish comfort for Windjammer.

Suitable Standards: . . . . *C-*

Average Price PPPD: $154 plus airfare.
Par for the course double cabins on the Windjammers are compact but livable, as in the *Yankee Clipper's* Main Deck cabins with upper and lower berths, mini-refrigerator, picture window, private toilet and shower.

Bottom Bunks: . . . . D

Average Price PPPD: $107 plus airfare.

There's a wide range to choose from on the fairly basic Windjammers. Typical would be the Bachelor/ette dorm rooms on the *Polynesia* or *Flying Cloud,* which sleep six in bunks with a private shower and toilet for the dorm. It's sold to all-male, all-female or a family of five or six.

Where She Goes

There's never a hard and fast schedule on the Windjammers; that's part of their charm. The captain chooses where to go based on a certain group of islands, and every time there's a fifth Monday in the month, it's a Captain's Choice cruise hitting all his top favorites.

The *Fantome,* based in Antigua, checks out the British, French and Dutch West Indies, visiting from among them St. Barts, St. Kitts, Nevis, Montserrat, Guadeloupe, Iles des Saintes and Dominica.

The *Flying Cloud* covers the British Virgin Islands from its home in Tortola, choosing among Jost van Dyke, Beef Island, Virgin Gorda, Peter Island and Norman Island.

The *Mandalay,* home-ported in Grenada and Antigua, visits the Windwards and the Grenadines, selecting from Nevis, Montserrat, Iles des Saintes, Dominica, Martinique, St. Lucia, St. Vincent, Bequia, Canouan, Mayreau, Palm and Carriacou.

From Sint Maarten, the *Polynesia* sails out to see Anguilla, St. Barts, Saba, Statia, St. Kitts, Nevis and Montserrat.

The *Yankee Clipper* is based in Grenada and sails to several of the following islands: St. Vincent, Bequia, Canouan, Mayreau, Union, Palm and Carriacou.

The Bottom Line

Prices are very modest on the Windjammers, so much so that if it's a special occasion like a honeymoon, you should spring for the best you can afford. If you're footloose and fancy free, book anything and spend your spare time on the deck. Don't worry about sailing experience; you don't need it. Just go with the flow. If you're concerned about getting seasick, take a dramamine or other approved medication in the prescribed amount of time before boarding rather than waiting until you feel queasy. But bear in mind that seasickness is much rarer than people think—neither of us has ever experienced it in more than 200 cruises in some of the roughest seas in the world. (See Seasickness, page 1064 for more about the malady and the treatment.)

Fielding's Five

Five Fun Places

1. The *Mandalay* interior, extensively renovated in the style of its period (the 1920s) has always been considered one of the most luxurious private yachts in the world. Reminiscent of the *Sea Cloud* in her original rosewood-paneled cabins and marble bathrooms, and of the modern-day ultra-luxury vessels with a pair of suites with private verandas.

2. The *Fantome's* dining room is a trim and shipshape wood-paneled area with comfortable booths and resin-coated tables.

3. The deck on any Windjammer, where you sun, hang out, chat or read, meet you fellow passengers or learn about sails and charts from the captain during a sailin lesson.

4. The beach, a frequent part of any Windjammer cruise, where you may have a barbe cue or buffet lunch, a swim or rum and nibbles at sunset.

5. The deck bar, where you check in with your $10 paper doubloon and have the ba tender nick it with a hole punch every time you buy a drink.

Five Good Reasons to Book These Ships

1. To take advantage of the modest prices that include a lot of things other line charge extra for such as sunset cocktails and wine with dinner.

2. To take a singles cruise and meet the mate of your dreams.

3. To learn how to handle the sails on a tall ship.

4. To see (and be seen in) the Caribbean aboard a classic ship, which automaticall makes you a celebrity.

5. To kick back and relax and take off your shoes.

Five Things You Won't Find On Board

1. Elevators.

2. Jacuzzis.

3. Fitness centers.

4. Swimming pools; they claim theirs is the Caribbean sea.

5. Casinos.

Fantome   ⚓⚓⚓⚓

Registry	**Honduras**
Officers	**British/West Indian**
Crew	**West Indian**
Complement	**45**
GRT	**676**
Length (ft.)	**282**
Beam (ft.)	**40**
Draft (ft.)	**17**
Passengers-Cabins Full	**128**
Passengers-2/Cabin	**128**
Passenger Space Ratio	**NA**
Stability Rating	**Fair**
Seatings	**2**
Cuisine	**Continental**
Dress Code	**Casual**
Room Service	**No**
Tip	**$7.50 PPPD**

Ship Amenities

Outdoor Pool	**0**
Indoor Pool	**0**
Jacuzzi	**0**
Fitness Center	**No**
Spa	**No**
Beauty Shop	**No**
Showroom	**No**
Bars/Lounges	**2**
Casino	**No**
Shops	**1**
Library	**Yes**
Child Program	**No**
Self-Service Laundry	**No**
Elevators	**0**

Cabin Statistics

Suites	**24**
Outside Doubles	**20**
Inside Doubles	**22**
Wheelchair Cabins	**0**
Singles	**0**
Single Surcharge	**175-200%**
Verandas	**0**
110 Volt	**Yes**

Flying Cloud ⚓⚓⚓⚓

Registry	**Honduras**
Officers	**British/Australian**
Crew	**West Indian**
Complement	**28**
GRT	**400**
Length (ft.)	**208**
Beam (ft.)	**32**
Draft (ft.)	**16**
Passengers-Cabins Full	**74**
Passengers-2/Cabin	**66**
Passenger Space Ratio	**NA**
Stability Rating	**Fair**
Seatings	**2**
Cuisine	**Continental**
Dress Code	**Casual**
Room Service	**No**
Tip	**$7.50 PPPD**

Ship Amenities

Outdoor Pool	**0**
Indoor Pool	**0**
Jacuzzi	**0**
Fitness Center	**No**
Spa	**No**
Beauty Shop	**No**
Showroom	**No**
Bars/Lounges	**1**
Casino	**No**
Shops	**1**
Library	**Yes**
Child Program	**No**
Self-Service Laundry	**No**
Elevators	**0**

Cabin Statistics

Suites	**7**
Outside Doubles	**12**
Inside Doubles	**15**
Wheelchair Cabins	**0**
Singles	**0**
Single Surcharge	**175-200%**
Verandas	**0**
110 Volt	**Yes**

Mandalay ⚓⚓⚓

Registry	**Honduras**
Officers	**Irish/US**
Crew	**West Indian**
Complement	**28**
GRT	**420**
Length (ft.)	**236**
Beam (ft.)	**33**
Draft (ft.)	**15**
Passengers-Cabins Full	**72**
Passengers-2/Cabin	**72**
Passenger Space Ratio	**NA**
Stability Rating	**Fair**
Seatings	**2**
Cuisine	**Continental**
Dress Code	**Casual**
Room Service	**No**
Tip	**$7.50 PPPD**

Ship Amenities

Outdoor Pool	**0**
Indoor Pool	**0**
Jacuzzi	**0**
Fitness Center	**No**
Spa	**No**
Beauty Shop	**No**
Showroom	**No**
Bars/Lounges	**1**
Casino	**No**
Shops	**1**
Library	**Yes**
Child Program	**No**
Self-Service Laundry	**No**
Elevators	**0**

Cabin Statistics

Suites	**9**
Outside Doubles	**12**
Inside Doubles	**0**
Wheelchair Cabins	**0**
Singles	**0**
Single Surcharge	**175-200 %**
Verandas	**0**
110 Volt	**Yes**

Polynesia   ⚓⚓⚓

Registry	Hondura
Officers	South African/U
Crew	West India
Complement	4
GRT	43
Length (ft.)	24
Beam (ft.)	3
Draft (ft.)	1
Passengers-Cabins Full	12
Passengers-2/Cabin	11
Passenger Space Ratio	N.
Stability Rating	Fai
Seatings	
Cuisine	Continenta
Dress Code	Casua
Room Service	N
Tip	$7.50 PPP

Ship Amenities

Outdoor Pool	
Indoor Pool	
Jacuzzi	
Fitness Center	N
Spa	N
Beauty Shop	N
Showroom	N
Bars/Lounges	
Casino	N
Shops	
Library	Yes
Child Program	No
Self-Service Laundry	No
Elevators	0

Cabin Statistics

Suites	14
Outside Doubles	3
Inside Doubles	40
Wheelchair Cabins	0
Singles	0
Single Surcharge	175-200%
Verandas	0
110 Volt	Yes

Yankee Clipper ⚓⚓⚓

Registry	**Honduras**
Officers	**British/Australian**
Crew	**West Indian**
Complement	**29**
GRT	**327**
Length (ft.)	**197**
Beam (ft.)	**30**
Draft (ft.)	**17**
Passengers-Cabins Full	**64**
Passengers-2/Cabin	**64**
Passenger Space Ratio	**NA**
Stability Rating	**Fair**
Seatings	**2**
Cuisine	**Continental**
Dress Code	**Casual**
Room Service	**No**
Tip	**$7.50 PPPD**

Ship Amenities

Outdoor Pool	**0**
Indoor Pool	**0**
Jacuzzi	**0**
Fitness Center	**No**
Spa	**No**
Beauty Shop	**No**
Showroom	**No**
Bars/Lounges	**1**
Casino	**No**
Shops	**1**
Library	**Yes**
Child Program	**No**
Self-Service Laundry	**No**
Elevators	**0**

Cabin Statistics

Suites	**12**
Outside Doubles	**5**
Inside Doubles	**15**
Wheelchair Cabins	**0**
Singles	**0**
Single Surcharge	**175-200%**
Verandas	**0**
110 Volt	**Yes**

WINDJAMMER BAREFOOT CRUISES, LTD.

WINDSTAR® CRUISES
A HOLLAND AMERICA LINE COMPANY

300 Elliott Avenue West, Seattle, WA 98119
☎ *(206) 281-3229, (800) 258-7245*

History ·

In Helsinki, Finland, in the early 1980s, ship designer Kai Levandar and his Finnish workshop group came up with a number of revolutionary cruise vessel concepts, including several that looked like major high-rise urban hotel towers floating on a ship-like hull, somewhat similar to the long-in-progress Phoenix World City project. But following a suggestion from an imaginative entrepreneur named Karl G. Andren, owner of Circle Line sightseeing boats, they created a design in 1983 called Windcruiser, a motor-sailing vessel with computer-trimmed sails.

In 1984, Andren contacted a French-born, Miami-based cruise line veteran named Jean-Claude Potier to make a feasibility study and find a yard to build it. Potier, who subsequently became the line's president, announced the project, Windstar Sail Cruises, in December 1984, and hired a French shipyard (Societe Nouvelle des Ateliers et Chantiers du Havre) to build it and French architect-designer Marc Held to create an interior design. The French government assisted in the financing.

Jean-Claude Potier saw romance in the design. "A sailing ship, unregimented, not organized, fun, an experience in feeling, not glittery, beautiful." He coined the term "casual elegance" to describe the onboard dress code for the vessels.

The 148-passenger *Wind Star* was the first of the trio, debuting in 1986 to immediate acclaim. The *Wind Song*, to be based year-round in Tahiti, followed in 1987, and the *Wind Spirit* in 1988. Andren sold the company to Holland America Line in August 1988, and Carnival Cruise Lines subsequently acquired Holland America in January 1989, and with it Windstar. Potier departed not long afterward, and the company subsequently changed its name to Windstar Cruises, eliminating the word "Sail." The ships do a substantial number of charter and incentive sailings.

In 1990, a new division of Club Mediterranee called Club Med Cruises introduced the first of two similar but larger motor/sail vessels, *Club Med 1*. (See Club Med Cruises, page 213)

—First cruise passenger vessels with computer-operated sails.

DID YOU KNOW?

How does it work? Sails on these sophisticated 440-foot, four-masted ships are set and trimmed by computers that monitor wind velocity and direction and control heeling to less than six degrees. This, in combination with the usual cruise-ship stabilizers and bow thrusters, gives the comfort of a cruise vessel with the romance and grace of a sailing ship. If you want to see it work, the captain welcomes passengers to the navigation bridge anytime.

Concept . . . .

A relaxed, non-regimented, non-dressy version of a cruise with an emphasis on watersports, tropical and Mediterranean ports and an upscale onboard lifestyle.

Signatures . . . .

The four-masted sailing vessels maintain an open bridge with passengers permitted to come inside and watch the computers trim the sails.

Gimmicks . . . .

In some seasons on certain itineraries, two of the ships may meet to sail side-by-side, so each vessel's passengers can photograph or videotape the other.

Who's the Competition . . . .

Windstar has found itself a fairly solid niche with a lot of repeat passengers in the younger, non-traditional cruise area. Club Med Cruise competes in all three of Windstar's cruising areas, Tahiti, the Med and the Caribbean, but attracts a slightly different crowd and more Europeans. Star Clippers, although more traditional sailing vessels, also compete somewhat with Windstar, but Windjammer Barefoot Cruises is not a strong competitor.

Who's Aboard . . . .

Mostly urban thirtysomething-and-up couples in high-pressure jobs out to relax. A few sailing enthusiasts (but purists turn their noses up at computer-trimmed sails), a lot of destination-oriented passengers (particularly on the Tahiti itinerary). One executive described the average Windstar passenger as 45, affluent, well-traveled, pays a lot of attention to travel plans and is interested in the sports activities available. He may or may not have taken a cruise before.

Who Should Go . . . .

Anyone who wants to have an upscale but casual resort sort of holiday. The ships are beautiful and the cabins and bathrooms efficient and well-designed. All are identical, so there's no problem deciding what cabin category you'll book.

Who Should Not Go . . . .

Sometimes there are families with children on board, but this doesn't work as well with kids under 12 because there's nowhere for them to call their own and they end up belly-flopping in the swimming pool and being general nuisances. The line discourages toddlers and young children specifically. Also, because there's no elevator, anyone with mobility impairment should not book because getting from cabin to breakfast cafe can mean climbing as much as four flights of stairs.

The Lifestyle . . . .

There is no regimentation. No mileage pool or deck games, no ship's photographer treading on the punch line of your best joke to ask everyone to sit closer together, no table assignments or specified meal seatings, no waiter choruses of "Happy Birthday" in the dining room, no tipping required, and no dress code beyond the genially vague "casual elegance."

These are ships for those who eschew a standard cruise, for couples who want to be alone together on a remote island beach instead of a bus tour of St. Thomas, for erstwhile or would-be skippers who like to stand on the bridge with the captain instead of lying in the sun, and for anyone who would rather snorkel and go windsurfing than play bingo or line up to photograph the midnight buffet.

Wardrobe . . . .

"Casual elegance," the ambiguous dress code term suggested by Jean-Claude Potier, has been variously interpreted over the years, but generally means elegant resort wear with jacket and tie optional. You see a lot of open-necked silk shirts and linen pants on both men and women. Daytime wear is very casual, usually a lot of shorts and swimsuits, and going ashore garb, except in the fashionable Mediterranean resorts, is equally basic.

Bill of Fare . . . . A

With Los Angeles' super-chef Joachim Splichal, owner of Patina, creating his signature cuisine on board all three ships, you can count on delicious fare. Splichal is not the type to wander away after stamping his name on a menu; the name of the cuisine concept is "180 Degrees from Ordinary." Consider marinated salmon with horseradish, potatoes and creme frâiche; chilled gazpacho with cilantro creme; roast young chicken with creamy polenta, artichoke, truffle oil and crispy Parmesan chips; chocolate croissant pudding with Wild Turkey bourbon sauce.

The seating at meals is open, meaning you arrive when you wish and sit where and with whom you please. Besides the dining room, there is a casual buffet cafe atop the ship where breakfast and lunch is served; it doubles as a cabaret or disco late at night.

Showtime . . . . N/A

Entertainment is too organized a concept for the Windstar ships, but there is usually a trio playing for dancing and a small casino, as well as a large library of videotapes, some of them X-rated.

Discounts . . . .

The Advanced Sailings Advantage Program allows discounts for early bookings on a first-come first-save basis; a limited number of cabins is available. From time to time, two-for-one sailings are also announced. The best idea is to get on the Windstar mailing list, either by requesting

it from the 800 number above or by being a repeat passenger. The
you'll get all the information as soon as the deals come up.

The Bottom Line

Since the emphasis is on low-key camaraderie and offbeat, noncommerci
ports of call in Tahiti and the Caribbean, people looking for nightlife, dis
and casino action and born-to-shop types should opt only for the Medite
ranean itineraries. While the sails initially attract the passengers, it is the ple
surable experience—friendly, relaxed and low-key—along with the very ni
staff and crew, that keeps everybody on board happy. Windstar is a real wii
ner.

Wind Song   ★★★★★

Wind Spirit   ★★★★★

Wind Star   ★★★★★

*They are most uncommon cruise ships, their long, trim hulls cutting
through the indigo sea like a knife through silk, their sails catching the breeze
and rising like romantic whispers from four tall white masts. The ports of these
dream ships are fantasies themselves, fragments of the world's surreal estate—
the wave-worn black sand beaches of Tahiti where Paul Gauguin spilled out
his life painting women as lush as overripe mangoes...the fortress fastness of
Elba, where Napoleon would sit for hours on a cold marble bench in a prim
little garden staring across the sea toward France...the elemental water-
smoothed stones of The Baths rising from the sapphire-and-turquoise Caribbean Sea at Virgin Gorda.*

WINDSTAR CRUISES

Sleek and sexy, these high-tech 148-passenger ships are fitted out like ▪chts, with dark wood and brass, rich colors and glove leather. The futuris-▪ gray modular bathrooms, a marvel of design by France's Marc Held, ▪ake you want to say, "Beam me up, Scotty!" when you step into the show-▪. Casual elegance is the keynote for the lifestyle on board. A coverup over ▪ur bathing suit will allow you to lunch in the handsome glass-walled Ve-▪nda Cafe, and after a busy day ashore or a bare-feet-and-bikini day in the ▪n, you can slip into sandals and something loose, soft and silky for evening.

DID YOU KNOW?

On the 1986 maiden voyage of the Wind Star, *in Mustique, William F. Buckley came over from his yacht and requested permission to board, and David Bowie wangled an invitation to lunch. In St. Lucia, Princess Margaret admired the ship, and Colin Tennant, Lord Glenconnor, was so enchanted he invited the ship and its passengers to spend the afternoon at his private beach (later to become the posh resort Jalousie) with his pet elephant Bupa, along with steel drummers, fire eaters, limbo dancers and acrobats.*

The Brochure Says

"It's not like any other travel experience you've ever known. The sails are your first ▪ue that it's different."

Translation

If you've booked this vessel for a vacation and didn't know about the sails—let's face ▪, they no longer mention them in the company name—you may not notice they're there ▪ntil a shadow suddenly falls across your body when you're sunbathing, and you look up ▪ith faint annoyance.

Cabins & Costs

▪antasy Suites: . . . . **NA**

All the cabins aboard are fantastic but not in the sense Fantasy suites implies.

▪mall Splurges: . . . .**A**

Average Price PPPD: $581 plus airfare.
There is an Owner's Suite, cabin # 107, that is somewhat larger than the standard cabins and sold at a 30 percent higher price than the standard cabins.

▪uitable Standards: . . . .**A**

Average Price PPPD: $449 plus airfare.
All the cabins on board, with the single exception of the Owner's Suite (see above) are identical, clean-lined and efficient rooms that have twins or queen-sized bed, color TV with VCR, mini-refrigerator and bar, makeup table, safe, desk, book-shelves and drawers. Bathrooms have space-age showers, hair dryers, plenty of counter space and thick terrycloth robes. Some have a pull-down third berth and some an adjoining private door to make a two-room suite.

Bottom Bunks: . . . . **NA**

This category does not apply; all cabins have two lower beds.

Twilight on the **Wind Song** *in Tahiti.*

Where She Goes

The *Wind Song* stays year-round in Tahiti, sailing from Papeete every Saturday and visiting Huahine, Raiatea, Bora Bora and Moorea, as well as cruising around Taha'a.

The *Wind Star* alternates north and southbound Caribbean cruises out of Barbados in winter, visiting Nevis, St. Martin, St. Barts, Montserrat and Martinique on the north-

und itinerary, and Bequia, Carriacou, Grenada, Tobago, Tobago Cays and St. Lucia on
e southbound. In summer, *Wind Star* cruises the Mediterranean out of various ports on
-, 11-, 12- 13-, and 14-day sailings.

The *Wind Spirit* cruises the Virgin Islands in winter from St. Thomas, visiting St.
roix, Saba, Montserrat, St. Barts, Virgin Gorda and St. John, and in summer sails the
reek Islands and Turkey.

The Bottom Line

These unique vessels, which capture the imagination of all who see them, the admira-
on of all who sail on them, have changed the face of small-ship cruising, offering an al-
ring alternative to sophisticated travelers looking for a fresh and more personal vacation
xperience. They have our highest recommendation.

Fielding's Five

Five Fun Places

.   The lounge is filled with natural light flooding in from a large skylight in daytime,
    and furnished with a lot of comfortable chairs and sofas in convivial groupings.

.   The glass-walled Veranda is a casual breakfast and lunch cafe that sometimes dou-
    bles as a disco when somebody can figure out where to turn on the fog machine and
    turn out the lights.

3. The Restaurant is a charming room with wood paneling and windows that let in the
    view. While there are plenty of tables for two, the ambiance onboard is such that
    passengers tend to clump together in larger groups.

4. The outdoor Piano Bar is conveniently close enough to the outdoor bar that joining
    in on a familiar song is irresistible.

5. The instruction wheel is on the top deck, a fixed ship's wheel that offers some sailing
    lessons to passengers, and makes a dandy place to be photographed.

Five Good Reasons to Book These Ships

1. Romance, romance, romance.

2. To eat the delectable cuisine of Joachim Splichal without having to pay the Patina
    price.

3. To go to the remote islands of French Polynesia and see it almost like Gauguin did.

4. To use the watersports deck in the balmy Caribbean, the sunny Mediterranean or
    exotic Tahiti to swim off the ship.

5. To enjoy an unusually smooth ride, even in notoriously temperamental waters.

Five Things You Won't Find On Board

1. A cruise director leading the fun and games.

2. A children's program.

3. An inside cabin; all accommodations have a view.

4. Anyone nudging you for a tip; tipping is at the passenger's discretion.

5. An elevator.

WINDSTAR CRUISES

Wind Song ★★★★
Wind Spirit ★★★★
Wind Star ★★★★

Registry	Baham:
Officers	Europea
Crew	Internation:
Complement	8
GRT	535
Length (ft.)	44
Beam (ft.)	6
Draft (ft.)	1
Passengers-Cabins Full	15
Passengers-2/Cabin	14:
Passenger Space Ratio	36.1
Stability Rating	Goo
Seatings	
Cuisine	Contemporar
Dress Code	Casual elegance
Room Service	Ye:
Tip	Not require

Ship Amenities

Outdoor Pool	1
Indoor Pool	0
Jacuzzi	1
Fitness Center	No
Spa	No
Beauty Shop	Yes
Showroom	No
Bars/Lounges	3
Casino	Yes
Shops	2
Library	Yes
Child Program	No
Self-Service Laundry	No
Elevators	0

Cabin Statistics

Suites	1
Outside Doubles	74
Inside Doubles	0
Wheelchair Cabins	0
Singles	0
Single Surcharge	150%
Verandas	1
110 Volt	Yes

WORLD EXPLORER CRUISES

555 Montgomery Street, San Francisco, CA 94111-2544
☎ *(415) 393-1565, (800) 854-3835*

History . . . .

San Francisco-based World Explorer Cruises was a division of the wide-spread C.Y. Tung family shipping interests, marketing the *Universe* for summer Alaska sailings when the vessel was not in use as a floating university.

The Seawise University concept had been a passion in this family since the late Mr. Tung acquired the *Queen Elizabeth 1* for the purpose of creating a university that would sail around the world. Unfortunately, that poor ship never got out of Hong Kong harbor, where she burned and sank during the refitting in 1972.

Concept . . . .

Education, eco-tourism and a close-up, first-hand look at Alaska are the main aims of the summer sailings. The slogan, "a 14-day adventure for the heart, mind & soul" seems to be the company's concept.

Signatures . . . .

Classical music instead of production shows, a full audience listening to lecturers instead of playing blackjack, hands-on crafts lessons.

Gimmicks . . . .

Fitness class hearts—12 laps around the deck net you one heart, and 20 hearts gets you a T-shirt that says Sound Mind, Sound Body, Universe.

Who's the Competition. . . . .

Nobody really offers a cruise like this one—14 days hitting more ports in Alaska than any other ship, and promoting the educational and cultural level of the cruise.

Who's Aboard. . . . .

The entire membership of Elderhostel, families with children, staffers from the University of Pittsburgh (who accredit the Semester at Sea program), grandparents bringing their grandchildren on a cruise, one family with several children including an infant. Many, many repeaters.

According to one longtime staffer, "Our passengers are those that ha[ve] never taken a traditional cruise and didn't want the glitz."

Who Should Go

People interested in getting a close-up look at Alaska and a lot of le[c]tures; people who don't want to dress up.

Who Should Not Go

Anyone fussy about food and service; anyone who usually books a su[ite] on a cruise ship; anyone who likes to dress up.

The Lifestyle

While the educational and eco-tourism aspects of the voyage ar[e] emphasized almost constantly, they still get passengers stirred up wit[h] typical cruise ship frivolities including bingo, singalongs, horse racin[g], mileage pools, a masquerade parade, passenger talent shows, bridg[e] competitions and dancing gentlemen hosts. This is not exactly Men[sa] on vacation.

INSIDER TIP

Unlike expedition ships, the Universe Explorer *does not include shore excursions in its fare; passengers pay from $12 for a botanical walk in Wrangell to $275 for a flightseeing excursion to Mt. McKinley.*

Bill of Fare

Breakfast usually offers a blackboard special of the day, with one fres[h] fruit, one egg dish, and side dishes that include oatmeal, blueberry pan cakes and such.

A typical lunch starts with three appetizer choices—perhaps fresh asparagus, fruit or a cheese plate, a smoked chicken risotto soup, a salad bar, and a choice of pan-fried fillet sole of lemon butter and almonds; Seafood Louie salad; beef Stroganoff over noodles; or the "light" selection of the day. There is also a continental self-service breakfast served on the enclosed promenade deck.

Dinners also feature several appetizers, one soup, the salad bar and a choice of several main dishes, perhaps salmon, barbecued chicken and steak, along with a vegetarian main dish.

Showtime

The staff musicians are Peggy Wied and the Voyagers, who bill themselves as "seniors playing for seniors." Classical concerts are interspersed with folk singers and a belting country, blues and pop singer who also leads singalongs.

The Bottom Line

This is the favorite Alaska cruise for a great many people, but we were amused to find the passengers being so self-congratulatory—"Aren't we clever not to be on some tacky cruise ship that doesn't really show you Alaska?"—every time a more handsome ship passed us along the Inside Passage.

e restrained ourselves from pointing out that they're taking the same op-
>nal, land-operated shore excursions in Alaska that, say, Princess and Hol-
1d America passengers do.

Universe Explorer   Unrated

The weary, sagging old *Universe*—still sentimentally recalled by both Semester-at-Sea students and Alaska cruisers—has been sent to the breakers in
India and replaced with Commodore's *Enchanted Seas*, which carries a new
name, *Universe Explorer II*, the twelfth name-change this ship has had in its
39-year-history. During the years, a second swimming pool was added on
deck and the casino and boat deck stern extended so the latter could house a
disco. For World Explorer sailings, the casino has been turned into the library, complete with all the former Universe's 12,000 volumes, and a computer room has been added.

The Brochure Says

"On a World Explorer cruise, you'll have the chance to participate rather than just
spectate. Because we give you more time on shore to really discover the land. Chances
are, you'll find yourself doing things you never imagined. Like flightseeing over majestic
fields of ice. Fishing for King Salmon. Or learning the history and spirited folklore of the
Tlingit Indians. We pride ourselves on being the uncommon route to Alaska. And we invite you to take part in this unique adventure...at unusually low fares."

Translation
To the unusually low fares, add another $350 or so, what those three shore excursions
described above will cost.

Cabins & Costs

Note: For general cabin types and descriptions, see Commodore Cruises' *Enchant Isle*, page 224, sister ship to the *Universe Explorer*. Commodore's prices, however, w not be in effect on the latter ship. Per diems will be around $103 to $221 per person do ble occupancy, in Latin America

Where She Goes

With its new vessel, 19-year-old World Explorer Cruises has announced some bas itinerary changes. On December 28, 1996, and January 12, 1997, the ship will sail fro Nassau to some rarely-visited ports in Latin America, including Calica, Mexico; Puert Cortes, Honduras, an overnight in Limon, Costa Rica; and a call in rarely-visited Cristo bal, Panama. The itinerary also includes more familiar ports like Cartagena and Och Rios. Shore excursions in Latin America will include fishing, climbing Mayan ruins an scaling waterfalls by torchlight in Ocho Rios. Prices range from $1445 to $3095 per pe son, double occupancy. In summer, the ship will continue to offer its unique 14-day Alas ka explorations, visiting eight ports of call. The increased speed ability of the new ship wi allow longer stays in the ports of call.

Universe Explorer ★★

Registry	**Panama**
Officers	**European/American**
Crew	**International**
Complement	**330**
GRT	**23,500**
Length (ft.)	**617**
Beam (ft.)	**84**
Draft (ft.)	**28**
Passengers-Cabins Full	**840**
Passengers-2/Cabin	**726**
Passenger Space Ratio	**32.36**
Stability Rating	**Good**
Seatings	**2**
Cuisine	**International**
Dress Code	**Casual**
Room Service	**No**
Tip	**$8.50 PPPD, 15% automatically added to bar check**

Ship Amenities

Outdoor Pool	**1**
Indoor Pool	**0**
Jacuzzi	**1**
Fitness Center	**Yes**
Spa	**No**
Beauty Shop	**Yes**
Showroom	**Yes**
Bars/Lounges	**6**
Casino	**No**
Shops	**2**
Library	**Yes**
Child Program	**No**
Self-Service Laundry	**No**
Elevators	**3**

Cabin Statistics

Suites	**4**
Outside Doubles	**286**
Inside Doubles	**74**
Wheelchair Cabins	**2**
Singles	**2**
Single Surcharge	**130%**
Verandas	**0**
110 Volt	**Yes**

OTHER CRUISE COMPANIES

The following are cruise marketing companies that represent various lines or charter various vessels seasonally over a period of years.

Airtours

Wavell House, Holcombe Road, Helmsmore, Lancashire BB4 4NB, Great Britain
☎ *(01706) 260000*

In early 1996, Carnival Cruise Lines invested $310 million to purchase 29.54 percent of British-based Airtours, the second largest tour operator in the United Kingdom. The company also owns Scandinavian Leisure Group AB, formerly a travel property os SAS airlines, and Sunquest Vacations of Canada.

The two companies complement each other in air/land/sea packages throughout Europe and North America.

Airtours operates two ships familiar to many North American cruisers—the former *Nordic Prince* from Royal Caribbean Cruise Ltd. is now the *Carousel*, and the former *Southward* from Norwegian Cruise Line has become the *Seawing*. Neither ship has been dramatically changed since going into Airtours service, except for the removal of the Viking Crown Lounge from the former Nordic Prince, a stipulation made when the contract was drawn up.

English breakfasts, "elevenses" mid-morning snacks, luncheon in the dining room or on deck, afternoon tea, a four-course dinner and a midnight supper are on the menu daily.

In summer the ships cruise the Mediterranean, in winter the Caribbean, Canary Islands and North Africa.

Bergen Line, Inc.

405 Park Avenue, New York, NY 10022
☎ *(212) 319-1300, (800) 323-7436, (reservations), (800) 666-2374 (brochures)*

The Bergen Line represents a group of shipping companies in Norway that offer a variety of coastal and canal cruises, ferry services and summer Spitsbergen expeditions.

Norwegian Coastal Voyages are year-round sailings aboard 11 working coastal steamers that carry passengers and goods to nearly three dozen communities between Bergen and Kirkenes. Three new vessels are in service—the 480-passenger *Polarlys*, the 490-passenger *Nordkapp*, and the 490-passenger *Nordnorge*. As each new ship is brought into service, one of the old ones is retired. The *Ragnvald Jarl*, present *Nordnorge* and *King Olav* will be phased out of service.

Gota Canal cruises cross the middle of Sweden from Gothenburg to Stockholm, negotiating 65 locks on the way, with three colorful period steamers, the *Juno*, built in 1874, the *Wilhelm Tham*, built in 1912, and the *Diana*, built in 1931. The *Diana* makes six-day cruises, the other two four-day cruises.

A series of Arctic Adventures aboard a traditional coastal vessel with an ice-hardened hull is offered by Bergen Line from Tromso to Spitsbergen and back to the North Cape on an eight-day itinerary.

Jadrolinjia Cruises

c/o Malta National Tourist Office
Empire State Building, 350 Fifth Avenue, Suite 4412, New York, NY 10118
☎ *(212) 695-8229*

This Croatian cruise line, marketed by two German companies, is also being touted by the New York office of the Malta tourism people for the 300-passenger *Dalmacija*, one of the former Yugoslavian vessels that got sidetracked during the long war. Built in 1965, the ship has five passenger decks, a single-seating restaurant, two bars, a lounge, an indoor swimming pool and a German/Croatian crew.

It has a fairly good-sized sun deck and basic cabins with tiny bathrooms, but modest per diem prices, from $76 for an inside quad to around $190 for an outside cabin with two lower beds and a sitting area.

13 Hazelton Avenue, Toronto, Ontario, Canada M5R 2E1
☎ *(416) 964-9069, (800) 263-9147*

Marine Expeditions is a Canadian company that offers polar expeditions aboard six oceanographic research vessels, the *Livonia/Marine Challenger*, registered in Estonia, and the *Akademik Ioffe/Marine Adventurer*, registered in Russia. Programs include a series of Antarctic expeditions aboard the *Marine Adventurer*.

Mediterranean Shipping Cruises

420 Fifth Avenue, New York, NY 10018 (212) 764-4800
☎ *(800) 666-9333*

Formerly known as StarLauro, this Italian line operates three ships, their flagship, the 600-passenger *Monterey*, a classic American-built vessel; the 800-passenger *Rhapsody*, the former Cunard *Princess*; and the 664-passenger *Symphony*, the former *EnricoCosta*. The ships sail primarily in the Mediterranean.

QUARK
EXPEDITIONS

980 Post Road, Darien, CT 06820
☎ *(203) 656-0499, (800) 356-5699*

Quark Expeditions was founded in 1990 by veteran expeditioners of countless Arctic and Antarctic programs who were able, thanks to the thaw in U.S./Russian relations, to charter former Soviet atomic fleet icebreakers to cruise not through balmy oceans but pack ice as thick as 16 feet. Many of the nuclear-powered vessels were built in Finland's Wartsila shipyard in the early 1980s, during the period when we were there observing construction

of more traditional cruise ships like the *Royal Princess* and Carnival'
Fantasy.

Quark's Russian icebreakers sail both polar regions.

The fleet employed by Quark include the *Kapitan Dranitsyn*, *Kapitan*
Khlebnikov, *Alla Tarasova*, *Yamal*, *Professor Khromov* and *Professor Molcha·*
nov. The because-it's-there adventurers will need big bankrolls though—
most of the North Pole sailings run into five figures sans decimal point, starting around $16,900. The "first-ever Antarctic Circumnavigation," two
months aboard the *Kapitan Khlebnikov* for November 1996, costs in the
neighborhood of $35,000 a passenger.

The only nuclear icebreaker we've seen first-hand is the *Yamal*, which was
briefly disabled and awaiting repairs off the Siberian coast in September
1993, when we met up with them while we were on another, more traditional expedition vessel. It was filled with wanna-be North Pole adventurers
champing at the bit to get moving, passing their days with Zodiac explorations of the area.

Royal Seas Cruise Line

507 North Florida Avenue Tampa, FL 33602
☎ *(813) 421-4222, (800) 290-6222*

This new cruise company began a year-round series of two-day cruises to
nowhere and five-day cruises from Tampa to the Mexican Caribbean in the
spring of 1996. The *Royal Seas*, the former *Ukraina*, carries 460 passengers.
Two-day cruises cost around $129 to $295 per person, double occupancy,
while the five-day itineraries range from $289 to $845.

Royal Venture Cruise Line

2727 Ulmerton Road Clearwater, FL 34699
☎ (813) 571-1400, (800) 396-3900

Takis Kiriakidis, formerly associated with the startups of Regency Cruises
nd later Seawind Cruises, announced his new company for a mid- to late-
996 beginning. The ship *Sun Venture* is scheduled for two- and five-day
ruises from Tampa, a two-night Gulf Spree Getaway and a five-night Mex-
can Fiesta to Merida, Playa del Carmen/Cancun and Cozumel. *Sun Venture*
s the former *Apollo* from Epirotiki, which in turn is the former *Mardi Gras*
rom Carnival. Prices start at $119 for the two-day sailing per person, double
occupancy, and $329 for the five-day sailing per person, double occupancy.
Kiriakidis had originally announced he would operate the former *Ikraina*
see Royal Seas, above) but later said he wanted a larger ship. *Sun Venture*
carries 942 passengers.

Zeus Tours and Cruises

566 Seventh Avenue, New York, NY 10018
☎ (212) 221-0006, (800) 447-5667

Zeus, a New York-based, 47-year-old company that specializes in Eastern
Mediterranean tours and cruises, is operating an extensive range of mainstream Aegean cruises as well as sailings aboard its sailing ships and private
yachts (See Alternative Cruises, below.)

Largest is the longtime Mediterranean veteran *La Palma*, an old friend we
often see in ports, built in 1951-52 as the *Ferdinand de Lesseps* for a French
line that sailed her between Marseilles and Mauritius. In 1968 she was sold
to a Greek company and renamed *Delphi*, then sold to Spanish breakers
(companies that destroy ships for their scrap metal value) in 1974, but that
deal fell through, so she's still here. After a brief three-year stint as *La Perla*
with a Cypriot flag, she's now *La Palma*, which should have offered an easy
transition job on the bow and stern name change.

She's a comfortable if well-worn old 800-passenger ship, with seven passenger decks and cabins on five of them. A disco is dungeon-deep down in
the ship, as usual on vessels from the 1950s (we're not sure what they were
before they were discos, because discos didn't come in until the late 1960s).
On the next-lowest passenger deck, there is the usual you-can't-get-there-
from-here cabin layout, with some cheap inside and outside cabins forward,
others aft, and never the twain shall meet. The darkish, low-ceilinged restaurant is also on a lower deck, as usual in that vintage, with cabins on the deck
above, more cabins and the main lounge on the deck above that. Promenade
Deck is the main public area, anchored with a pool deck aft and a nice expanse of observation deck forward, and two enclosed promenades spanning
the full amidships area, bracketing a casino and two smaller lounges. On the
topmost Boat Deck is a small but jovial Bavarian Beer Garden, a lot of hang-

ing lifeboats and some fair-sized patches of deck for sunning. There are als
six deluxe cabins and an owner's suite. The ship was cosmetically freshene
and lightened up in 1991.

Per diem price on the cabins ranges from around $138 for an inside wit
two lower beds to around $350 for a deluxe cabin in pretty, tropical whit
with double bed, bathroom with tub/shower combination and an extr
sofa-bed or pulldown berth. Kids 2 through 12 travel free if they share the
parents' cabin, so you can count on a lot of little ones aboard in summer.

The *La Palma* also has a beauty shop, large owner's suite (for which price
are not quoted), a private nudist sunbathing deck, and nice-sized swimmin
pool.

Zeus also markets the sleek 50-passenger *Lady Caterina*, a brand-new, 25
cabin, 70-foot mega-yacht, one of those long white jobbies with the dar
windows that remind us of Darth Vader in *Star Wars*. She makes seven-da
Mediterranean and Aegean cruises.

Another new ship for the company is the two-masted sailing ship *Galile*
Sun, carrying 36 in outside air-conditioned cabins with private bath.

ALTERNATIVE CRUISES

In Burgundy, barging and ballooning often go hand-in-hand.

The captain of the *QE2* is not likely to give you a turn at the wheel, and you won't be wading ashore at some tiny Caribbean island from the *Sovereign of the Seas*. Big cruise ships are like seagoing deluxe hotels, lavishly appointed, self-contained cities.

But just as travelers seek out little country inns and bed-and-breakfast establishments in off-the-beaten-track locations, cruise passengers seek alternative cruises, smaller vessels that sail to out-of-the-way corners of the globe.

You'll probably never see these ships in TV commercials. They don't have glittering casinos and Las Vegas-style shows, glamorous passengers dolled up in sequins and satins, miles of midnight buffet and cruise directors organizing fun and games.

Not all of them sail the ocean blue, and few of them boast sleek, streamlined curves and acres of teak decks. Some of them, in fact, are downright funny-looking—squat, sturdy barge-hotels that meander along the canals of Europe at five or six miles an hour, beetle-browed Russian icebreakers capable of moving through pack ice, old-fashioned paddlewheel steamers churning down the Mississippi, ferries and freighters, mail boats and coasta steamers from Alaska's panhandle to the fjords of Norway.

Barging Along the Burgundy Canal

Lazing along the canal at six or eight miles an hour is a wonderful way to see the French countryside.

A perfect antidote for an exhausting if-it's-Tuesday itinerary is a leisurely. luxurious cruise aboard a hotel barge along France's scenic and historic Burgundy Canal. Instead of eight countries in seven days, you'll get a close-up acquaintance with a handful of French towns, a couple of vineyards where you sample vintages with the winemaker himself, several chateaux where you may have tea with the titled owners, and perhaps a lunch or dinner in a *Michelin Guide* three-star restaurant, along with breakfast croissants and brioche bicycled back, still warm, from a village bakery.

Lolling lazily on the deck sipping a glass of champagne, you see Burgundy at eye level, waving at farmers in dazzling canary-yellow fields of rapeseed or fishermen in blue work smocks dozing along the banks of the canal as you glide past, almost close enough to touch the scarlet poppies and wild iris, purple lupine and feathery white Queen Anne's lace that bloom there. Life on a barge is as lighthearted as a floating house party with a dozen congenial friends.

The historic 600 miles of canals in Burgundy, like the rest of France's 3000 miles of manmade waterways, were begun in 1604 by Henry IV as a commercial artery. Today, trucks and trains have taken over the shipping, and Burgundy's canals are used for recreational sailing.

There are usually bicycles on board, one for each guest, so when you feel curious or energetic, you can disembark at one of the locks and ride along the towpaths, or explore nearby villages and countryside.

Days are easy and effortless, perfect for people who want to let city-jangled nerves slow down to a gentle, contented purr. While almost everyone promises get-away-from-it-all vacations, barge companies really deliver them, because once you're afloat, you won't hear the headlines or be paged for a long-distance call—there are no telephones, radios or TV sets on board. If fact, we spent most of a day driving in a van on barge towpaths along the Burgundy Canal with a barge company president who couldn't find his boat for hours. On the other hand, if you want to reach out and touch someone, it's easy to hop off and make a phone call from one of the towns along the way, or pick up a copy of the International Herald Tribune if you must.

Average per diem: $335–$400 PPPD, cruise only.

The best local wines and cheeses are served aboard French luxury barges.

The following are some of the companies that provide barge cruises in Burgundy and other scenic parts of Europe. If you think there seem to be an inordinate number of barges plying the canals, be aware that many of the barge owners may use several different companies to sell their sailings. Most of the following are American travel wholesalers or barge marketing firms.

Abercrombie & Kent

1520 Kensington Road, Oak Brook, IL 60521, ☎ *(800) 323-7308.*
Twelve barges in France, Holland, Belgium, Germany and Austria; features antiques, golf theme barge cruises in Britain.

Cruise Company of Greenwich

31 Brookside Drive, Greenwich, CT 06830, ☎ *(800) 825-0826.*
Provides barge tours of Ireland aboard the little *Shannon Princess*.

European Waterways

c/o Le Boat, Inc., PO Box E, Maywood, NJ 07607, ☎ *(800) 922-0291.*
Sixteen barges in France, England, Holland and Belgium, including the new *Belle Époque*, the first hotel barge with a spa pool, fitness room and sauna, and the barge *L'Impressionniste* for 12 passengers.

Fenwick & Lang

100 W. Harrison, South Tower, Suite 350, Seattle, WA 98119, ☎ *(800) 243-6244.*

Fourteen barges in France, England and Holland; optional hot air ballooning is also available with your barge cruise.

French Country Waterways

PO Box 2195, Duxbury, MA 02331, ☎ *(800) 222-1236.*
Four barges in France, special early and late season discounts.

Kemwel's Premier Selection

106 Calvert Street, Harrison, NY 10528, ☎ *(800) 234-4000.*
Twenty-five barges for charter and scheduled sailings in France, England and Holland.

Lanikai Charter Cruises

98-985 Kaonohi Street, Aiea, Hawaii 96701, ☎ *(808) 487-6630.*
A six-passenger crewed barge available for seven-day charters in France between April and October.

The Barge Lady

225 North Michigan Avenue, Suite 324, Chicago, IL 60601, ☎ *(800) 252-9400.*
The new *Saint Louis,* specialized French food and wine cruises (and an on-board cellular telephone—*quel dommage!*)

River and Coastal Cruises

Aboard Regal China Cruises on the Yangtze, the top category suites are quite luxurious; the lesser ones much less so.

It is so quiet as we move along the river, we can hear the birds singing in the nearby trees when our cabin's French doors are open. There's no deck or balcony outside, just waist-high metal bars, but the open doors provide fresh air and a closer rapport with the scenery.

From our mooring in the Czech Republic village of Decin, we can see a fairy-tale castle atop the hill. An oompah brass band in bright costume greeted us on our return from a day in Prague with some loud and lively tunes. Along the river we have seen ducks, swans, geese, a few storks, even a blue heron, and once we glimpsed deer standing stock-still in a misty green meadow.

This vessel, the *Prussian Princess*, is the most luxurious European river vessel we've sailed aboard, with its antique-style furnishings, oil paintings, Tiffany stained glass and big vases of fresh flowers. Passengers sit at sociably small tables set with crisp white linen. Service is swift and sophisticated and the cuisine is continental, with elaborate evening menus that often include a sorbet between the fish course and the meat course. Desserts from the Viennese chefs, not surprisingly, are delectable.

Some of the other river boats we've cruised aboard through the years have not been as lavish, but all have offered a unique close-up look at a lovely part of Europe, delicious meals, regional wines and a silk-smooth ride.

Average per diem: $350 PPPD, cruise only.

The following are some of the companies offering river and coastal cruises round the world:

Abercrombie & Kent

> *1520 Kensington Road, Oak Brook, IL 60521,* ☎ *(800) 323-7308.*
> Three river cruisers in France, Holland, Germany and Austria, including the *Anacoluthe*, which emphasizes art-oriented cruises in France; the Nile aboard three *Sun Boats*, and the new *Road to Mandalay* river cruises in Myanmar (Burma) between Mandalay and Rangoon with a call at Pagan.

AHI International

> *701 Lee Street, Des Plaines, IL 60016,* ☎ *(800) 680-4244.*
> River cruises in Europe on the Rhine, Main, Danube and Moselle, along Russia's Volga and China's Yangtze.

ATS Tours

> *2381 Rosecrans Avenue, Suite 325, El Segundo, CA 90245,* ☎ *(800) 423-2880.*
> Handles catamaran cruises aboard the new *Reef Escape*, *Coral Princess* and *Kangaroo Explorer* along Australia's Barrier Reef.

Berrier Enterprises, Ltd.

> *1 Sutter Street, Suite 308, San Francisco, CA 94104,* ☎ *(415) 398-1443.*
> Various waterways journeys in Portugal, Russia and other European areas.

Blue Lagoon Cruises

> *c/o Fiji Visitors' Bureau, 5777 West Century Blvd., Suite 220, Los Angeles, CA 90045,* ☎ *(800) YEA-FIJI.*
> Six small vessels that sail on short, casual cruises to Fiji's Yasawa Islands from Lautoka near Nadi Airport.

Cruise Company of Greenwich

> *31 Brookside Drive, Greenwich, CT 06830,* ☎ *(800) 825-0826.*
> Provides cruises to the national parks of Costa Rica and Belize aboard the 62-passenger *Temptress*.

Esplanade Tours

> *581 Boylston Street, Boston, MA 02116,* ☎ *(800) 426-5492.*
> For 20-passenger sailings aboard the *Myat Thanda* along the Irrawaddy in Myanmar.

EuropAmerica River Cruises

> *1800 Diagonal Road, Alexandria, VA 22314,* ☎ *(703) 549-1741 or (800) 348-8287.*
> Five luxurious river vessels that sail the Danube, the Rhine, the Elbe and the Rhone, including the *Prussian Princess*, described above, the *Mozart*, *Danube Princess*, *Dresden* and *Princesse de Provence*.

EuroCruises

303 West 13th Street, New York, NY 10014.
For Europe Cruise Lines' new *Rhine Princess* and *Blue Danube* on the Rhine, Moselle and Danube, Gota Canal sailings, the *Lady Ivy May* on Portugal's River Douro and the *Anton Tchekhov* on the Yenisey River in Siberia.

Glacier Bay Tours and Cruises

520 Pike Street, Suite 1400, Seattle, WA 98101, ☎ (800) 451-5952.
Alaska Inside Passage cruises aboard the 49-passenger catamaran *Executive Explorer*, as well as Glacier Bay study tours aboard the 36-passenger *Wilderness Explorer*.

Hebridean Island Cruises

c/o British Tourist Authority, 551 Fifth Avenue, New York, NY 10176-0799, ☎ (800) GO 2 BRITAIN.
Scottish coastal cruises aboard the 48-passenger *Hebridean Princess*.

KD River Cruises of Europe

2500 Westchester Avenue, Purchase, NY 10577, ☎ (800) 346-6525 from the eastern U.S., or Suite 619, 323 Geary Street, San Francisco, CA 94102, ☎ (800) 858-8587 from the western U.S.
Now 169 years old, the oldest and largest river cruise line in Europe, with 13 vessels sailing the Rhine, Danube, Elbe, Moselle, Main, Seine, Rhone and Volga. KD's river vessels are *Deutschland, Britannia, Austria, Europa, Italia, France, Wilhelm Tell, Clara Schumann, Theodor Fontane, Heinrich Heine, Normandie, Arlene* and *Kirov.*

Nabila Cruises/Naggar Tours

605 Market Street, Suite 1310, San Francisco, CA 94105, ☎ (800) 443-NILE.
For (what else?) cruises along the Nile, as well as yacht cruises along the Turquoise Coast of Turkey.

Regal China Cruises

57 West 38 Street, New York, NY 10018, ☎ (800) 808-3388.
Three new luxury river vessels, *Princess Sheena, Princess Jeannie* and *Princess Elaine*, that cruise the Yangtze, plus a Shanghai harbor overnight cruise on *Spirit of Shanghai*.

Roylen Endeavour Cruises

c/o Queensland Tourist and Travel Corporation, 516 Fifth Avenue, New York, NY 10036, (212) 221-4505, or 2828 Donald Douglas Loop North, Santa Monica, CA 90405, (310) 452-1225.
Offers two-, three- and five-night cruises in the Whitsunday Islands, off eastern Australia, on vessels carrying up to 50 persons each.

Special Expeditions

720 Fifth Avenue, Department 232, New York, NY 10019, ☎ (800) 762-0003.
Cruises the Danube and the Nile, the latter aboard the 15-cabin *Hapi*.

Sunny Land Tours

166 Main Street, Hackensack, NJ 07601, ☎ (800) 783-7839.
Offers tours of Siberia and the Ukraine aboard the *Russ*, the *Leonid Krasin* and the *Kirov*.

Uniworld

16000 Ventura Blvd., Encino, CA 91436, ☎ (800) 733-7820.
Offers cruises on the Amur River in the Russian Far East, Russia's Volga, Svir and Moscow Canal, China's Yangtze, and the Rhine, Moselle, Main and Danube in Western Europe.

ictoria Cruises Inc.
57-08 39th Avenue, Woodside, NY 11377, ☎ *(800) 348-8084.*
Has a fleet of new luxury river vessels cruising the Yangtze.

In addition, under Cruise Lines, above, see Alaska Sightseeing/Cruise
Vest, American Canadian Caribbean Line, American West Steamboat Com-
any, Bergen Line, Delta Queen Steamboat Company, EuroCruises and St.
awrence Cruise Lines.

Adventure and Eco-tourism Sailings

Penguins check out the visitors in the Antarctic.

The little pier is lined with people, a hundred or more, curious for the sight
of us. They have been waiting since 8 a.m., and it is now 3 p.m. We have ar-
ived on a expedition ship commanded by Captain Heinz Aye, and we are
he first group of white tourists ever to appear on Jamdena Island in the Tan-
mbars. As we come down the gangway, a dozen hands reach to touch our
oare arms...

In one house, preparation is under way for a wedding feast, with a pig tethered ready to kill and roast and hundreds of coconuts piled up in heaps. An
old woman, her mouth stained with betel nut, approaches, holding out a
small and intricately woven basket. We are not sure whether she is showing it
to us or trying to sell it, so we smile politely and nod. Later, after we're back
on the ship, one of the other passengers flaunts it. "Look what I got for only
$5!"

The next day we are ferried by Zodiac to a seemingly deserted island opposite the town of Tual. By the time the first Zodiac-load has waded into the
soft, sandy beach, two small boats have arrived from town to have a look at
us, and other islanders materialize from the bushes with white paste smeared
on their faces against the relentless sun. They stare gravely and silently as
these peculiar pale visitors don snorkeling gear and splash into the water.
The film star and her sister have stretched out on towels in the sand, and are
soon surrounded by young men staring with open curiosity. The sand is

clean and golden and dappled with tiny, elegant shells. Evelyn has unfurled
silk Chinese umbrella for shade as she strolls along collecting shells. Seth h
put up the windsurfer, to the great delight of the little boys watching, an
they touch the vivid, silky sail with tentative strokes.

Expedition ships go to extremes, to the icebergs of Antarctica, the steam
jungles of the Amazon, through the Northwest Passage or to some of the r
mote islands of Indonesia (as in the Tanimbars, above).

Average per diem: Around $400 PPPD for cruise only aboard the majo
expedition ships, much less from the small family operations.

The following are some companies who offer expedition and eco-touris
cruises:

Canadian River Expeditions Ltd.

3524 W 16th Avenue, Suite 1A, Vancouver, BC, Canada V6R 3C1, ☎ *(604) 738-444*
A family operation making river expeditions into the Queen Charlotte Islands, th
Yukon and coastal British Columbia.

Captain Al Parce

X-Ta-Sea, PO Box 240250, Douglas, AK 99824, ☎ *(907) 364-2275.*
Takes four people at a time out in his 49-foot vessel into Tracy Arm, Frederic
Sound and Admiralty Island on various itineraries from one to six nights.

Cruceros Australis

The Chilean Desk, 10250 SW 56th Street, Suite A-201, Miami, FL 33165, ☎ *(80*
541-8938.
The *Terra Australis,* previously one of the U.S.-built coastal cruisers of now-defunc
American Cruise Lines, sails in Tierra del Fuego from Punta Arenas. Although ther
are hints that she also ventures into the Antarctic, she should not, since there's n
ice-hardened hull on this vessel.

Eco-Expeditions

1414 Dexter Avenue N., #327, Seattle, WA 98109, ☎ *(800) 628-8747.*
Operates out of the same office as Zegrahm Expeditions (below), with a series o
Galapagos sailings and a cruise around Britain on the *Caledonian Star.*

The Explorers Club

46 East 70th Street, New York, NY 10021, ☎ *(800) 856-8951.*
Makes adventure expeditions, including occasional Antarctic sailings on the Russian
icebreaker *Kapitan Khlebnikov.*

Glacier Bay Adventures

PO Box 68, Gustavus, AK 99826, ☎ *(907) 697-2442.*
Makes eco-tour explorations of Alaska's Glacier Bay Country aboard the *Stellar,* a
research vessel built for the Alaska Department of Fish and Game.

InnerAsia Expeditions

2627 Lombard Street, San Francisco, CA 94123, ☎ *(800) 777-8183.*
Once again offering Alaska coastline cruises on its little 12-passenger *Discovery* after
several years of inactivity while the vessel was under charter during the Exxon oil
spill cleanup.

Lifelong Learning, Inc.

101 Columbia, #150, Aliso Viejo, CA 92656, ☎ *(800) 854-4080.*
Programs in the Antarctic, Costa Rica, the Amazon, North Africa, Asia Minor, the
Yucatan, Japan, Europe, Canada and the U.S.

Metropolitan Touring/Adventure Associates

13150 Coit Road, Suite 110, Dallas, TX 75240, ☎ *(800) 527-2500.*

Markets the *Santa Cruz*, *Isabella II* and hotel/yacht *Delfin* in the Galapagos.

WT Marine Group

17 England Crescent, Yellowknife, N.W.T., Canada, X1A 3N5, ☎ *(403) 873-2489.*
A family-run company that cruises Canada's Arctic along the Great Slave Lake and MacKenzie River aboard the 20-passenger *Norweta*.

Special Expeditions

720 Fifth Avenue, Department 235, New York, NY 10019, ☎ *(800) 762-0003.*
Cruises the Galapagos Islands aboard the *Isabela II* and the Amazon aboard the *Flotel Orellana*.

CS Expeditions

2025 First Avenue, Suite 830, Seattle, WA 98121, ☎ *(800) 727-7477.*
Veteran expeditioner T.C. Swartz, former head of Society Expeditions, provides adventure cruises to Iceland, Greenland, the Canadian Arctic and the North Pole.

Zegrahm Expeditions

1414 Dexter Avenue N., #327, Seattle, WA 98109, ☎ *(800) 628-8747.*
Longtime expedition leader Werner Zehnder and his team of experts explore the Arctic and Antarctic, and offer dive excursions to Galapagos, cruises of the Seychelles aboard the *Caledonian Star* and catamaran explorations of Australia's Kimberley Coast.

In addition, see under Cruise Lines, above, Abercrombie & Kent, Bergen Line, Caledonian Travel, Golden Bear Travel, Odessa America Cruise Company, Quark Expeditions, Radisson Seven Seas Cruises, Society Expeditions and Special Expeditions.

Sailing Ships

We drive through endless back roads of Maine trying to link up with the motorless sailing ship *Victory Chimes* we are to board for a *Bon Appétit* story. Finally the variable winds wind down and she slips easily into the harbor at Stonington on Deer Isle. Maine Windjammers don't follow a precise itinerary but sail with the wind.

The three-masted "ram" schooner, so called for her prominent thrust-bow profile, was built in Bethel, Delaware, in 1900 and christened *Edwin & Maud*. As no-nonsense as her name, she hauled lumber up and down the Chesapeake Bay.

Like the ship, our 30 or so fellow passengers are doughty, no-nonsense types with their birding binoculars, stout deck shoes and windbreakers with Elderhostel patches sewn on them.

We stow our small carry-on bag of casual clothing atop one of the two bunk beds in the compact cabin, noting an adjacent wash basin while realizing that both toilet and shower are elsewhere on the vessel. Since there's no need to change for dinner, we return up on deck in our rumpled traveling clothes. Nobody cares or even notices, because Monday night is the highly anticipated lobster night, and most of our fellow passengers, veterans of more than one cruise aboard, stand around chatting and sipping their BYOB cocktails with one ear cocked for the dinner bell.

As soon as it sounds, everyone hurries down to the dinner tables, where platters heaped with the huge, steaming crustaceans are plopped without

ceremony into the center of each table, enough lobsters for everyone to ha
two apiece. Accompanying them, corn on the cob, potato salad, and late
for dessert on deck, a crumbly double-crusted fresh strawberry and rhuba
pie topped with a huge dollop of hand-whipped cream.

Everything aboard is cleaned, polished and shined with a palpable pride l
the crew of nine, so that the *Victory Chimes* gleams like burnished gold in th
setting sun. As the ship's colors are lowered in the lingering dusk, the pa
sengers spontaneously applaud.

"She's the only one left of the three-masted schooners," Captain Kip Fil
says softly, "she's the only one to survive."

Average per diem: Around $125 PPPD.

The following are some of the companies that offer sailing ship cruises:

Absolute Asia

155 West 68th Street, Suite 525, New York, NY 10023, ☎ (800) 736-8187.
Indonesian culture and wildlife cruises aboard SongLines Cruises' new luxury sai
boat *Maruta Wind*.

Captains Ken & Ellen Barnes

70 Elm Street, Camden, ME 04843, ☎ (800) 999-7352.
Operate the schooner *Stephen Taber* along the coast of Maine in summers, as we
as the 1948 motoryacht *Pauline*.

Cruise Company of Greenwich

31 Brookside Drive, Greenwich, CT 06830, ☎ (800) 825-0826.
Offers sailing cruises aboard the new 50-passenger sail cruiser *Lili Marleen*, startin
in the Azores in April, the Med in May, the Baltic in midsummer and the Atlanti
coast of Europe and the Canary Islands in autumn.

Maine Windjammer Association

PO Box 137, Rockport, ME 04856, ☎ (800) MAINE-80.
Operates a fleet of ten individually owned, historic, two- and three-masted vessel
including the 132-foot *Victory Chimes* (see above), that sail along the coast o
Maine in summer.

Metropolitan Touring/Adventure Associates

13150 Coit Road, Suite 110, Dallas, TX 75240, ☎ (800) 527-2500.
Offers sailings in the Galapagos aboard two historic sailing vessels, the 12-passenge
brigantine *Diamant* and the 8-passenger ketch *Rachel III*.

Worldwide Travel & Cruise Associates, Inc.

400 SE 12th Street, Suite E, Ft. Lauderdale, FL 33316, ☎ (800) 881-8484.
Book several notable sailing yachts, including the *Savarona*, *Sea Cloud* and *L
Ponant*.

Yankee Schooner Cruises

PO Box 696FL, Camden, ME 04843, ☎ (800) 255-4449.
Sails the historic, two-masted 137-foot schooner *Roseway* off the coast of Maine i
summer and in the Virgin Islands in winter.

Zeus Tours & Yacht Cruises, Inc.

566 Seventh Avenue, New York, NY 10018, ☎ (800) 447-5667.
Markets the 24-passenger sailing cruiser *Pan Orama* in the Caribbean as well a
small ships in Greece and Turkey, including the yachts *Zeus I, II and III*. In the Sey
chelles, under the Galileo Cruises label, the line also books the 18-cabin sailing
cruiser *Galileo Sun*.

In addition, see under Cruise Lines, above, Club Med Cruises, Special Expeditions, Star Clippers, Tall Ship Adventures, Windjammer Barefoot Cruises and Windstar Cruises.

Freighters

It's a rare person who hasn't daydreamed about getting away from everyday routine by hopping a freighter to some distant port to stand gazing across the rail, pretending to be Somerset Maugham or Jack London—or even Alex Haley, the late author of *Roots*, who wrote many of his books while on long freighter cruises.

A few years ago it looked like freighter travel was fading into the sunset as more and more familiar companies such as San Francisco-based Delta Lines began closing down their cargo carriers to passengers. ("Cargo doesn't eat and doesn't complain," said one.)

Now, in the wake of the fast-growing cruise industry, freighters are seeing a resurgence of passenger travel as well.

The biggest misconception about freighter travel, according to Freighter World Travel executives, is that people expect the accommodations to look like something out of an old Humphrey Bogart movie, whereas actually, some lines are adding new ships and upgrading public areas for passengers.

But before you dash out and book passage on a slow boat to China, there are some things you need to know, both about yourself and about freighter travel. Here's a quick quiz.

Freighter Fitness: A Quiz

. Are you fussy about food and service?
   Very, add 5. Sort of, add 4. Occasionally, add 3. Rarely, add 2. Never, add 1.

. How flexible are you?
   Very, add 1. Sort of, add 2. Occasionally, add 3. Rarely, add 4. Never, add 5.

. Are you self-reliant and can easily amuse yourself?
   Very, add 1. Sort of, add 2. Occasionally, add 3. Rarely, add 4. Never, add 5.

. Do you get along easily in close quarters with strangers?
   Always, add 1. Sort of, add 2. Occasionally, add 3. Rarely, add 4. Never, add 5.

. Are you worried about getting bored aboard a ship?
   Very, add 5. Sort of, add 4. Occasionally, add 3. Rarely, add 2. Never, add 1.

Here are some helpful hints to guide you through the quiz.

. On 12-passenger freighter cruises, your meals will be the same served to the officers, which means on a foreign-flag vessel, say, Greek or German, you should be prepared to enjoy the cuisine of that country, because that's what the galley usually cooks for the crew. You'll also usually be sharing the officers' cabin steward, so don't expect breakfast in bed or lots of pampering.

. If the itinerary lists a port you've always wanted to visit, but the ship cancels that call at the last minute; if you're expecting to spend three days in Rio but end up getting only eight hours; if you plan to be home on the 58th day but actually don't get back until the 67th day—can you handle it?

. On a freighter, you won't have a cruise director to cajole you into fun and games, nor a shore excursions manager selling guided bus tours to Yokohama, nor an orchestra playing for after-dinner dancing. You may have to take your own readin materials and games (although most freighters have small libraries and a few car and games on hand), or even, in the case of Lykes Lines, your own dinner wine ar liquor.

4. Remember that you'll be sharing a dinner table with the same 10 or so other pa sengers for a lot of days, and what seems only vaguely irritating at the beginning ca be infuriating after a week or two. We remember a woman on the *Americana* nam Janet who constantly made pronouncements at the dinner table, like "This is not real freighter; I know, because I've taken 35 freighter cruises," or "I'm the po relation on board, because I'm the only one in an inside cabin."

5. Amiable loners and couples whose world is complete within themselves make goo freighter passengers, as do creative people with portable projects they need to wo on free of interference or telephone calls. It's a laid-back atmosphere where yo make your own entertainment.

SCORES:

If you scored higher than 20, book a cruise ship, not a freighter.

If you scored 15, the only cargo-carrier you'll be happy aboard is Ivaran's *Ame cana* (page 448).

If you scored under 10, you should be able to manage a freighter cruise.

Five Things You Need to Know Before You Go

1. There's no doctor aboard; if a vessel carries fewer than 12 passengers, he's n required.

2. There may be an age limit. Because of the medical rule above, many cargo comp: nies have stringent upper age or medical condition rules. You can expect to aske for a medical certificate.

3. No special dietary requests can be handled.

4. Most freighter companies refuse to carry children or pregnant women.

5. The per diem cost of a freighter trip is slightly lower than most cruise ships, bu don't book just because it's cheaper. You'll pay a flat rate, and if it lasts longer, yo won't have to pay any more, but if it ends early, you don't get a refund.

The following companies can help you book passage on a freighter:

Compagnie Polynesienne de Transports Maritime

595 Market Street, #2880, San Francisco, CA 94105, (415) 541-0677.
The 64-passenger *Aranui* carries mail, cargo, deck passengers and tourists aroun the islands of French Polynesia.

Freighter World Cruises, Inc.

180 South Lake Avenue #335, Pasadena, CA 91101, (818) 449-3106.
Represents virtually every freighter company that takes passengers, notably CAST Columbus Line, Bank Line ATW, Mineral Shipping, Reederei Bernhard Schulte NSB, Ivaran, Egon Oldendorff and the new *Cielo di Los Angeles* that cruises fro the west coast of Canada and the U.S. to the Mediterranean.

TravLtips Cruise and Freighter Travel Association

Box 188, Flushing, NY 11358, (800) 872-8584.
This group handles bookings for the cargo liner and Royal Mail Ship *RMS St. He ena*, which cruises to the remote South Atlantic island of St. Helena, where Napo leon spent his last years in exile. They also book Blue Star Line's *Columbia Star* an *California Star* from the west coast to Australia, New Zealand and Fiji.

In addition, see under Cruise Lines, above, Ivaran Cruise Line.

WHERE ARE THEY NOW?

A Work in Progress

We all wonder whatever became of our favorite ships when they seem to have dropped off the planet or at least out of the travel agencies. Too many times cruise lines either never mention them again or say they "retired" them. That doesn't necessarily mean the ships are sent out to pasture, mothballed or sent to the breakers; it may mean they've been sold or leased to another cruise company. So we set out in chase of recently-familiar ships, the vintage vessels which are changing hands rapidly these days because of the coming 1997 SOLAS (Safety of Life at Sea) and IMO (International Maritime Organization) safety requirements that will be difficult and expensive to implement. Here's where they were and what they were doing in mid-1996. To Be Continued...

Achille Lauro

This ship was little-known in the United States until the dramatic events on board in October, 1985, when terrorists took control of the vessel as it was sailing between Suez and Alexandria, while most of the passengers were on an overland excursion, and killed an American passenger. The bad-luck ship was built as the *Willem Rhys* in Holland, with its keel laid in 1939 but the vessel not launched until 1946 and delivered in 1947, for service between Rotterdam and Indonesia. She sailed around the world with two-class service for Rotterdamsche Lloyd until she was sold to Flotta Lauro, renamed the *Achille Lauro*, and rebuilt in Palermo in 1965. The work was delayed by an explosion and fire. She made her first voyage under the new name in 1966, then suffered another fire in 1972 during a refit in Genoa. In 1975, she collided with the livestock carrier *Yousset* in the Dardenelles, which sank with the loss of one life (plus some of the livestock, presumably). In 1982 she was impounded in Tenerife because of unpaid repairs, and then laid up the following year. In 1984 she returned to Mediterranean service. Despite being engulfed in world-wide publicity after the terrorist attack, the ill-fated ship continued cruising for Lauro; by then the line was renamed *StarLauro*. We passed her in the Bosphorus Straits in the summer of 1990, rusty, weary, and listing heavily to port. A disastrous fire aboard when she was off the Horn of Africa in 1994 totally destroyed the ship. She sank as rescuing tugs came in sight of her.

American Adventurer

The kids' cruise line ship spent only a year in extra-heavy duty with high-density family cruises before returning to Genoa to revert to its previous identity as *Costa Riviera*. (See Costa, page 248)

Aurora I, Aurora II

Sold to Singapore-based Star Cruises (see above, page 738) to become the *MegaStar Taurus* and the *MegaStar Aries*.

Boheme

Once a popular budget cruise ship sailing the Caribbean. Since 1985, it's the *Freewinds*, owned by the Church of Scientology. According to insiders, members get a free cruise if they make a donation of $5000 to the church.

Britanis

At this writing, the beloved old American-built *Britanis* is no longer under US government charter as offices and housing in Guantanamo Bay, Cuba. Instead, the ship is laid up.

Carnivale/Fiestamarina

Carnival's short-lived *FiestaMarina* version of its longtime "fun ship" *Carnivale*, directed at the Latin American market fizzled, despite the high quality product, and with running mate *Mardi Gras*, was sold to Epirotiki during another short-lived marketing agreement that ended with the Greek company, in effect, buying the two ships from Carnival.

Constitution

The *Constitution* has been retired by American Hawaii, who said it would be too expensive to renovate the ship and bring it up to new SOLAS standards.

Cunard Crown Jewel

Sold to Singapore-based Star Cruises (see above, page 745) to become the *SuperStar Gemini*.

Cunard Princess

Now sails as the *Rhapsody* for Mediterranean Shipping Cruises.

Danae

After being burned and scuttled in Venice harbor, the ship was resurrected as the *Baltica* for Sunshine Cruises (aka Greek-based Festival Shipping) and subsequently renamed *Danae Princess* by new operators Italia Cruise Lines.

Dawn Princess

The former *Fairwind* for now-defunct Sitmar, the *Dawn Princess* reverted to Vlasov's V.Ships in Monaco, its former owners, and was leased to a German travel company, which renamed her *Albatros*, with one 's.' With a name like that, what can you expect?

Dolphn IV

Sold to a central Florida shipping company named Kosmas, a.k.a. Canaveral Cruise Line Inc (page 146) in July, 1995, the vessel makes two-night cruises out of Port Canaveral.

Emerald Seas

Last seen sailing in the Mediterranean as the *Sapphire Seas*.

Enricocosta

Now sailing as the *Symphony* for Mediterranean Shipping Cruises.

Fair Princess

After a potential sale to now-defunct Regency Cruises fell through, Princess towed the *Fair Princess*, the former *Fairsea*, to Mazatlan where the ship is laid up awaiting purchase.

Majestic

Leased by Premier Cruises to London-based CTC Cruises for a four-year period.

Mardi Gras

After being leased out for a year as *Pride of Galveston*, the ship was renamed *Apollo* by owner Epirotiki. It was leased to Takis Kiriakidis' Royal Venture Cruise Line in mid-1996 and scheduled for two- and five-night cruises from Tampa as the *Sun Venture*.

Mermoz

The ships remaining from the trio of cruise lines owned at the end of 1994 by the French-based Accor Group went to Costa. The *Mermoz*, at press time still marketed to European cruisers and music lovers (for its annual classical music festival at sea), is described under Costa, above, page 262.

Monterey

It's been nearly five years now that the US-built *Monterey* has been sailing as flagship of the former StarLauro Cruises, now Mediterranean Shipping Cruises. It was picked up at bank auction for a song by a Panamanian company called Cia Naviera Panocean SA in Honolulu after parent company Aloha Pacific filed for bankruptcy in 1989.

Nordic Prince

Sold by Royal Caribbean Cruises Ltd. in early 1995 to Airtours, a British travel company, who renamed it *Carousel*. (See Airtours, "Airtours" on page 801)

Ocean Islander

This trim, mid-sized vessel that sailed for Ocean Cruise Lines in Europe, the Caribbean and South America, is now the *Royal Star* for Star Line Cruises in Mombasa.

Ocean Princess

Ran aground and was badly damaged in South America in 1993; we had gone aboard her only a couple of days before in Rio. Two decks were partly flooded and she was declared a total loss. Ellice Navigation in Piraeus bought her and towed her to Greece, where she was reconstructed as the *Sea Prince*. A subsequent sale to Louis Cruise Line of Cyprus has netted still another new name— *Princesa Oceanica*.

Odessa

The recently refurbished vessel from Black Sea Shipping was impounded in Italy a year ago, joining a number of other Black Sea vessels being detained by creditors in various ports of the world.

Pearl, Pearl of Scandinavia, Ocean Pearl

Poor pitiful *Pearl* had a lot of names during her illustrious career. Now she's the *CostaPlaya*, marketing cruises to Cuba from the Dominican Republic, sold only to Europeans and Latin Americans by parent company Costa Crociere in Genoa to circumvent US trading-with-the-enemy restrictions. See Costa, page 246.

Sagafjord

Cunard decided to retire this prestigious and beloved ship after an engine room fire off the Philippines interrupted her 1996 world cruise. She had previously been scheduled to leave the fleet at the end of her 1996 Alaska season.

Sea Princess

The *Sea Princess* was renamed *Victoria* in mid-1995, in order to free the name for a new Princess ship due in 1998. See P & O Cruises, page 522.

Southward

The longtime Norwegian Cruise Line vessel was sold to Airtours to become the *Sea wing* for the British-based travel company. See Airtours, "Airtours" on page 801.

Starward

The last of the Norwegian Cruise Line "white ships" to leave the fleet, the *Starward* has been turned into the *Bolero* for Greek-based Festival Shipping's Azur-Bolero Cruises. See EuroCruises, page 397.

The Victoria

Now at Louis Cruise Line in Cyprus as the *Princesa Victoria*.

Ukraina

In the spring of 1996, this former Black Sea Shipping vessel began sailing as the *Royal Seas* for Royal Seas Cruise Line on two- and five-day cruises out of Tampa. See Royal Seas Cruise Line, "Royal Seas Cruise Line" on page 804.

Universe

The doughty old *Universe*, which served for years as the Semester-at-Sea ship and made summer Alaska sailings for World Explorer Cruises, was sent to the breakers. She has been replaced by the *Universe Explorer*, the former *Enchanted Seas*. See World Explorer Cruises, page 797.

Vasco De Gama

The schizophrenic, dual-named vessel—its other monicker and present legal name is *Seawind Crown*—was finally offically renamed and able to sail under only one name, thanks to its purchase in July, 1995, by a group of New York investors called Capital Holiday.

World Renaissance

Sold in August, 1995, by Epirotiki (it was the line's flagship) to an Indonesian travel company.

CRUISING TO THE WORLD'S TOP PORTS PLUS THEIR RATINGS

The following are the 220 most popular cruise ports in the world and are rated based on the **port's appeal to the day visitor from a cruise ship**. We take into consideration the following factors:

Access to town from the port.

Courtesy or attitude of locals.

Interesting shore excursions.

Access to local beaches or beachfront hotels.

Shopping.

Cultural opportunities.

Photo opportunities.

Each port is rated from one to five stars. Our port star ratings are based on the needs of a day visitor rather than a vacationer who may spend several days in this area, and ratings are affected by visitor security and local politics as well as safety on the streets and accessibility of attractions.

★★★★★   A great port of call for a day, with plenty to do on tour or on your own.

★★★★   An appealing port that offers well-planned shore excursions and has some attractive shopping and independent sightseeing options.

★★★   A port that offers a variety of traditional shore excursions and some on-your-own things to do ashore.

★★   Perhaps not as polished and scenic as you would like, but you can find something interesting to do.

★   You may want to stay on the ship.

In addition to the rating, the major attractions of each port will be depict
in Fielding Rating Icons (see front of book). Also given at the head of ea
port listing is the local language and currency, whether English is genera
spoken and U.S. dollars accepted, and the best way to get to town from t
pier. Shore excursion price estimates are reflected in $ signs.

$	Under $20
$$	$20–$50
$$$	Over $50

THE CARIBBEAN CRUISE

Everybody has the image of what they'd like to do on a Caribbean cruise.

The Caribbean is **the most popular cruise area in the world**, drawing more than half of all cruise passengers. The appeal of its always warm and sunny weather is obvious, especially when most North Americans are shivering on a cold winter day. But the Caribbean, once considered seasonal sailing, is **big-time all year round in cruising** as more and more families take summer vacations afloat and more first-timers hop on mini-cruises to the Bahamas.

For some, a Caribbean cruise is the most comfortable route to a multi-island **shopping spree to stock up on duty-free items** from liquor to perfume, jewelry to cameras. For others, it's **a handy sampler of beaches and resort hotels** to check out for future vacations, or coral reefs and clear turquoise or cerulean water for diving or snorkeling, or a multicultural dip into a dazzling variety of languages, currencies, architecture and tropical foods.

Most cruise ships offer several basic shore excursions for sale for each port of call—a **general island tour that will include scenery, history and a shopping stop**; a boat excursion that may be anything from a rum punch party raft to a yacht cruise that stops at an uninhabited island to a submarine ride; and a beach, snorkeling or resort visit. On some islands, golf, tennis or helicopt sightseeing is also available.

Since per-person prices for excursions range from $15 to $85 or more, large family or group of three or four friends may choose to negotiate **an i dependent island tour with a local cab driver** or hire a cab to go to and from th beach. Be sure to agree on the price before getting into the vehicle; on man islands the fares are fixed and posted.

On the other hand, passengers making their first trip outside the mainlan U.S. or who are uneasy or uncomfortable about striking out on their ow will probably prefer the shore excursions sold on board the ship in order t travel with a group from the ship and have the services of an English-speak ing guide.

Select your excursion choices carefully, because on many ships the tickets ar not refundable if you change your mind about going.

Five Tips for Caribbean Touring

1 **Don't overtax yourself** in the hot, humid weather. An excursion that sounds supe while you're sitting in the air-conditioned lounge may not be as nice when you're standing in the broiling sun, say, at St. Lucia's Soufrière looking at bubbling volca nic mud pots and sniffing sulphur.

2 **Never take a full-day tour if a half-day tour will do**. You see almost exactly the same things on both; the full day just throws in a longer shopping stop and a hotel buffet lunch that's not nearly as good as what you get on the ship.

3 Unless you're a tireless trouper with unlimited funds, don't sign up for everything, or they'll all start running together in your memory. **Every island offers an island tour, whether there's anything interesting to see or not**.

4 If **you hire a cab** to take you to a remote beach for a swim, make a deal to have him wait (otherwise you might not get a cab back before the ship sails) and **don't pay him until you get back** to the pier.

5 Don't succumb to the urge to have your hair done in **cornrow braids** on the first day of your Bahamas cruise if you plan to spend the second day in the sun and water; you could get some painful, serious sunburn on your scalp.

Big, Mid-sized or Little Ship?

Big splashy megaliners carrying as many as 2600 passengers ply the waters of the Caribbean all year, with sophisticated spa facilities, glittering casinos, nightclubs with Las Vegas-style entertainment, shopping mini-malls and experts to teach you everything from bridge to line-dancing to aerobics or *tai chi*. There's never a dull moment, you'll get to know at least two or three other couples in your age range pretty well by sharing mealtimes at the same table, and you can have a drink in a different bar almost every day of the cruise.

Mid-sized ships carrying 500 to 1000 passengers have a lot of the same features but scaled down in size and glitz a bit. Many of these are older ships that still have real cinemas instead of films running on your cabin TV set, and full, all-the-way-around-the-ship promenade decks for brisk morning walks.

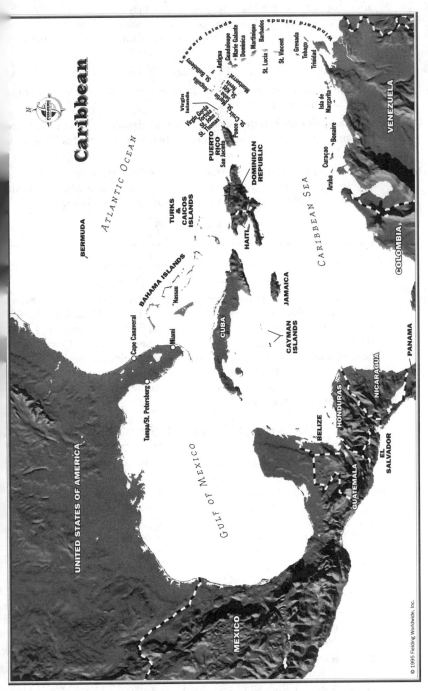

These vessels are more likely to offer midmorning bouillon and a white glo
afternoon tea than the big babes above. You may spend more time readir
or sunning on deck, and you may get to know more people than just those
your dinner table since you see them frequently on deck and at lectures ar
activities.

The **small ships** that cruise the Caribbean can be divided into several type

- **Ultra-deluxe**, with posh cabins, dressy evenings and a minimum of org;
nized entertainment and activities.

- **Expedition ships**, with basic cabins, not much dressing up but lots of lec
tures on the environment, flora and fauna and inflatable landing craft t
take you to island beaches.

- **Casual ships**, from sailing craft to bow-landing exploration boats, wher
everybody gets to know everybody else, almost anything goes in th
way of clothes, and you get to go swimming and snorkeling.

How Long?

Bahamas cruises generally last three or four days and may be combined
with a land tour such as an Orlando Theme Parks stay.

The most typical Caribbean cruise is a seven-day round trip sailing from ;
Florida or Puerto Rican port and offering an Eastern Caribbean, Wester
Caribbean or Southern Caribbean itinerary. Those that sail from San Juan o:
other island ports like St. Thomas, Aruba, Antigua, can sail more of th
"deep Caribbean" than ships that have to spend a first and last day just getting there from south Florida. Many ships have two alternate itineraries so ;
passenger can sign up for 14 days, two back-to-back seven-day cruises, without repeating ports of call.

Ten Best of the Best in the Caribbean

1   **Most elegant beach barbecue**: Aboard Cunard's *Sea Goddess* where waiters in
white mess jackets and swim trunks serve champagne and caviar to passengers wading in the surf at Jost van Dyke in the British Virgin Islands, followed by a lunch of
grilled fresh Caribbean lobster, steaks, even plebeian hot dogs and hamburgers.

2   **Adventuring with the rich and famous**: Sailing on the unique four-masted sailing
yacht *Sea Cloud* with Special Expeditions' splendid shore excursions in search of
rare flora and fauna, or swimming off the lowered gangway at a quiet anchorage.
Once owned by cereal heiress Marjorie Merriweather Post, the yacht maintains its
1930s ambience, complete with marble fireplaces (nonworking) and gold faucets on
the tubs in the grandest suites.

3   **Best fantasy beach**: The Baths at Virgin Gorda, where small-ship passengers may
arrive by Zodiac or bow-landing tender—or overland by van—then swim among
the boulders and into the hidden grottos or snorkel offshore.

4   **Most casual cruise**: Forget about tuxedos. If you don't even want to wear shoes on
your vacation, check out Windjammer Barefoot Cruises and their classic sailing
ships. You can sleep out on deck, if you wish, and there's a free Bloody Mary for
breakfast every morning.

Best port performers: The stylish and handsome Ballet Folklorique of Martinique, who come aboard to perform on many ships that call in Fort-de-France.

Most elegant beach barbecue is the caviar-and-champagne beach picnic aboard Cunard's **Sea Goddess I or II** *at Jost van Dyke.*

6   **Busiest port**: If you like crowds, you'll love Charlotte-Amalie, St. Thomas, where four to seven cruise ships a day may call and you can hardly move inside the popular shops.

7   **Rarest ports of call**: If you want to name-drop, see if you can find a ship that calls at any of the following islands—Anguilla, Saba, Barbuda, Montserrat, Nevis, Marie-Galante and Canouan. A few do.

8   **Best private island beach day**: Royal Caribbean's Coco Cay in the Berry Islands of the Bahamas, with a day of exploration and watersports—snorkeling with underwater cameras, diving, rides on watercycles, rocket rafts and pedal boats, underwater caves and nature trails to explore, native straw markets for shopping, steel drum bands and a lavish barbecue buffet for lunch.

9   **Best whole family experience**: A day at Port Lucaya with The Big Red Boat, swimming with dolphins, joining a junkanoo, hanging out with Bugs Bunny, scuba diving, straw markets and parasailing.

10 **Best island spotting**: Two swivel telescopes are bolted to the handsome teak decks aboard the *Club Med 1* for spotting distant islands or identifying ships that pass in the night (or day).

Rating the Ports of the Bahamas and Bermuda

Freeport/Lucaya, Bahamas ★★

Language:	**English**	*English Spoken?:*	**Yes**
Currency:	**B$=US$**	*US$ ok?:*	**Yes**
To town:	**Walk, taxi, tender, depending on dock or anchorage**		

Only 60 miles from Florida, Freeport is the **closest foreign port to the Unite States**, and as such, has long been a major **shopping port-of-call for day cruise** off the Florida coast. It's full of **tacky shopping bazaars**, which is a pity, sinc Grand Bahama Island also has 660 miles of beaches with watersports, sno keling, golf and tennis plus birdwatching at Rand Memorial Nature Centr and Garden of the Groves. Shore excursion options here range from swim ming with dolphins ($$$) to dancing to a junkanoo band ($). Lucaya has highly developed stretch of beach for cruise ship daytrippers with water sports, dolphins and rum party cruises.

Nassau, Bahamas ★★★

Language:	**English**	*English Spoken?:*	**Yes**
Currency:	**B$=US$**	*US$ ok?:*	**Yes**
To town:	**Walk**		

The Duke and Duchess of Windsor were posted to what they regarded as a colonial backwater during the turbulent days of World War II. These days, Nassau is a bigtime cruise port, especially for three- and four-day cruises sailing from the U.S. For many Americans, it is their very first foreign city, and despite the daytrippers, they still manage to scrape up some charm with **horsedrawn carriage city tours** and **the freewheeling straw market**. Your ship is steps away from downtown, so **duty-free shopping is a snap**. If you want to explore the **nightlife**, sign up for a tour to Paradise Island, or do it on your own by taxi. **Good buys** include British woolens and china, Colombian emeralds, hand-embroidered Irish linens, Gucci bags and Rolex watches. **Shore excursions** usually include the Seaworld Explorer semi-submarine ($$), a snorkeling expedition ($$), diving ($$, certification required), catamaran cruise ($),

ty and island tour ($), Coral World tour ($), beach tour ($) and a look at
he marching flamingos at Adastra Gardens ($).

Hamilton, Bermuda ★★★★

Language:	**English**	*English Spoken?:*	**Yes**
Currency:	**B$=US$**	*US$ ok?:*	**Yes**
To town:	**Walk, tender**		

This Atlantic island offers temperate rather than tropical weather, a pretty-
n-pink **honeymoon hideaway** popular in spring, summer and fall, but very few
ruise ships call during the island's mild winter. **Don't plan to rent a car**; there
are none available on the island, but taxis are plentiful. Many tourists **rent bicycles or mopeds** to get around to the many different beaches. The speed
imit on the island is 20 miles an hour, and traffic drives on the left, as in England. **Bus service** is excellent, aboard clean and uncrowded vehicles. Expect
high prices, clean and pretty small resorts and **pink sand beaches**. Good buys
include English bone china, Irish crystal and Louis Vuitton luggage, as well
as locally produced fragrances, straw bags, watercolors, liqueurs and oceanographic charts. **Shore excursions** include beach tours ($$), island tours ($$),
glass-bottom boat rides ($$), golf packages ($$$) and nightclub shows at
local resorts ($$$). The first game of tennis in the western hemisphere was
played here in 1873.

Kings Wharf/Dockyard, Bermuda ★★★★

Language:	**English**	*English Spoken?:*	**Yes**
Currency:	**B$=US$**	*US$ ok?:*	**Yes**
To town:	**Bus, ferry or taxi ($$$)**		

British troops set out from **the Royal Naval Dockyards** in 1812 to sack and
burn Washington, including the White House, but today ships with deep
drafts tie up here in Bermuda's only deepwater port. It's a **long way from
Hamilton** with sketchy public transit, but Bermuda has made an effort in re-
creating a **charming shopping and restaurant area** with maritime museum,
pub, restaurants and movie theater. In the nearby town of Somerset, the film
A Touch of Mink with Doris Day and Rock Hudson was filmed. **Good buys** include the local crafts, fashions and food products displayed and sold in Island
Pottery, the Bermuda Arts Centre, Dockyard Linens and Island Fever at the

Royal Naval Dockyard. **Shore excursions** include most of the options abov
(see "Hamilton").

*The beautifully restored Kings Wharf/Dockyard at the eastern tip of the islan
is the deepwater port for Bermuda.*

St. George's, Bermuda ★★★★

Language:	**English**	*English Spoken?:*	**Yes**
Currency:	**B$=US$**	*US$ ok?:*	**Yes**
To town:	**Walk**		

Bermuda's original capital is colorful and filled with history and pageantry, self-guided walks that pause at art galleries and tiny boutiques, and Feather-bed Alley Printery where a 350-year-old printing press is still in use. The replica of the 1609 Bermuda-built *Deliverance* is open for tours, but the most popular spot in town is a 17th century pillory on the square that lets visitors check out the stocks and ducking stools once used for punishment. A costumed town crier is often on hand as well. Good buys do not abound; if serious shopping is on the agenda, a taxi or bus over to Hamilton is a good idea if your ship doesn't reposition there later in your cruise. Shore excursions include a cruise on the glass-bottomed *Calypso* ($$), a tour to the island's west end ($$) or a tour around St. George's ($$). Golf ($$$) is sometimes also available.

DID YOU KNOW?

Albert Einstein once said the only thing in the world he did not understand was the Bermuda ferry timetable.

Rating the Ports of the Caribbean

St. John's, Antigua ★★★

Language:	**English**	*English Spoken?:*	**Yes**
Currency:	**EC$**	*US$ ok?:*	**Yes**
To town:	**Walk, taxi**		

Your ship will call in either St. John's or out at English Harbour near Nelson's Dockyard National Park, an excursion bus tour or taxi ride away from the capital of St. John's. Feisty, cricket-loving Antigua claims **365 beaches**, one for every day of the year, but yachting is an even bigger draw for the world's yachtsmen, who come from everywhere for **Sailing Week in April**. Traffic moves on the left, and roads are rough, potholed and poorly marked. Since taxis are fairly expensive, **shore excursions** may be cheaper than a cab tour here. Choose from the Nelson's Dockyard and island tour ($$), a half-day bus ride with time allowed for shopping and exploring at English Harbour ($$), and a swimming and beach tour ($$). Windsurfing, waterskiing, sailing, snorkeling and diving to see the wreck of the *Andes* are sometimes also available. **Good buys** include attractive silk-screened cotton garments at Coco's and the West Indian Sea Island Cotton Shop in St. John's. Ask whether prices quoted are in U.S. or EC dollars, since they use the same symbol and it takes nearly three of the latter to make one of the former.

Oranjestad, Aruba ★★★

Language:	**Dutch, Papiamento**	*English Spoken?:*	**Yes**
Currency:	**Guilder**	*US$ ok?:*	**Yes**
To town:	**Walk, taxi**		

Dutch-style buildings painted in pastel and tropical colors lend Aruba a distinct charm, but outside town it's flat and desertlike with dry, hot winds, dotted with cactus and weird, windblown divi divi trees. **White sugar-sand beaches** lined with palm trees stretch for seven miles along the west coast, a short taxi ride from the port. Good buys include Delft pottery, Swiss watches, pens, jewelry and hand embroidered linens. The **Hyatt Regency Aruba** with its lush gardens and waterfalls makes a good place to lunch. **Shore excursion** options include a not terribly interesting island tour ($$), the excellent Atlantis submarine ride ($$$), the Seaworld Explorer semi-submarine ($$) and a routine glass bottom boat ride ($). Divers should head directly for the submerged wreck of a WWII German freighter ($$$). Windsurfing ($$) and the new sport of sandsurfing ($) are other possibilities. Bustling Aruba now independent from its erstwhile Dutch Leeward cousins Curaçao and Bonaire; the three were once called the ABCs.

Bridgetown, Barbados ★★★★★

Language:	**English**	*English Spoken?:*	**Yes**
Currency:	**B$**	*US$ ok?:*	**Yes**
To town:	**Taxi, long walk**		

The colorful new Bridgetown port area makes shopping fun and easy, and has turned Barbados into one of the best day calls in the Caribbean.

The **new port area** in Bridgetown makes this one of the most appealing home ports or day calls in the entire Caribbean. **Great shops**—Caribbean Sounds, Duty-Free Liquor, Colombian Emeralds, Local Colour, plus **free samples** of a lot of local liqueurs (it's ok, you're walking back to the ship), a restaurant and a tourist information office. If you want to **lunch ashore**, you have two very different options—a posh hotel like the elegantly renovated **Sandy Lane Hotel**($$$) and the funky **Brown Sugar Restaurant** ($), near the **Barbados Hilton** on the outskirts of Bridgetown, with a moderately-priced sampling of the best of Barbados food from **fried flying fish** to homemade soursop or coconut ice cream. Stroll afterward on the sugar-fine beach by the Hilton amid the sheltering shade of palm trees. **Shore excursions** here inlude a city and island tour ($$), an underground walk through Harrison's Cave ($$), a Jolly Roger rum party cruise along the coast ($$) or an Atlantis submarine ride ($$$).

Kralendijk, Bonaire ★★★★

Language:	**Dutch, Papiamento**	*English Spoken?:*	**Yes**
Currency:	**Guilder**	*US$ ok?:*	**Yes**
To town:	**Walk**		

The sandy desert island of Bonaire, noted primarily for its snorkeling, also has miles of empty beaches and an easygoing ambiance.

Bonaire sits atop a coral reef, making it one of the **best snorkeling and diving destinations** in the Caribbean. Not many cruise ships call here, which is a mixed blessing. Its very isolation and serenity makes it one of the most appealing places in the Caribbean. **Eco-tourism** outweighs commercial development by policy. Bonaire's visitors are primarily **divers, snorkelers, hikers and birdwatchers**, there's little in the way of duty-free shopping, evening entertainment or organized shore excursions. Roads are narrow and often rough, but there's not much traffic; an adventurous visitor could **rent a four-wheel drive vehicle** and drive all around the island in a day, looking at bright **pink flamingos** feeding in salt ponds, prowling the 13,500-acre Washington-Slagbaai National Park in search of **Amazon parrots** and bright green and yellow native parakeets, or go underwater to look at Redlip Blennies, Parrotfish and Trumpet Fish. Divers head for the submerged 1000-ton freighter *Hilma Hooker* in Angel City, to the double reef at Alice in Wonderland and to

Thousand Steps. A number of dive operators are based in Bonaire includin the famous pioneering company that operates **Captain Don's Habitat**, wher you can book a Bonaire Night dinner and folk dance on Tuesdays.

Cartagena, Colombia   ★ ★

Language:	**Spanish**	*English Spoken?:*	**Yes**
Currency:	**Peso**	*US$ ok?:*	**Yes**
To town:	**Taxi, bus; don't walk**		

Cartagena can be dangerous, which is why we urge you not to walk around a lot, even in daytime; and, yes, we've often broken this rule without prob- lems. The only details that keep the city from being a one-star port are it **beautiful historic buildings and budget souvenir shopping.** This is one place to **take a group shore excursion and stick close to the guide. Don't change money on the street**, don't chat with strangers, don't wear or carry any valuable ashore. And yes, this is **where the emeralds come from**. You're usually safe buying them from the major dealers; cruise ship shore excursions always make a shopping stop at a modern, upscale mall with air-conditioned jewelry shops that take credit cards. **Souvenir hunters** will be happy with the other obligatory shopping stop, Los Bovedas, **old dungeons** built in the city walls that have been turned into cute, sometimes kitschy, shops. Good buys are coffee beans, embroidered textiles and handicrafts; bargaining is expected. The **historical city tour** ($) visits the old town, the fortress, the dungeon shops and a modern suburban mall; it's often the only shore excursion of- fered here.

Havana, Cuba   ★ ★ ★ ★

Language:	**Spanish**	*English Spoken?:*	**A little**
Currency:	**Peso**	*US$ ok?:*	**Yes**
To town:	**Shuttle bus**		

The Dominican Republic-based *CostaPlaya* is homeported there for short cruises to Cuba, marketed in Europe and Latin America, but not the United States unless travel restrictions are lifted. Anyhow, they're the first cruise line to Cuba on regularly scheduled service in many years. More than **half a mil- lion tourists visited Cuba in 1995** despite the travel restrictions laid down by the U.S. government. Many of them, of course, were not from the United States; the ones who were flew in from Mexico or Canada. As journalists, we ere able to visit on a German cruise ship call in 1988 (*Wilkommen in Cuba* aid the big banners spread across the dock area), and we found a sleepy, very lean Caribbean port filled with lovingly tended American cars from the exggerated tail fins days, so cannibalized for parts over the years that it was npossible to recognize the original model. The tourist infrastructure is rowing rapidly because of the influx of international hotel and resort mony. And there's always **Hemingway's favorite restaurant**, the Floridita, where he daiquiris are still made as he requested them, and **Bodeguita del Medio**, where he drank *mojitos* (rum, sugar and fresh mint leaves).

Willemstad, Curaçao

Language:	**Dutch**	*English Spoken?:*	**Yes**
Currency:	**Guilder**	*US$ ok?:*	**Yes**
To town:	**Taxi or long walk**		

Sailing into Curaçao brings everyone out on deck to snap photographs of the pastel old Dutch buildings.

One of the pleasantest arrivals in Caribbean cruising is sailing into Willemstad past rows of **pastel old Dutch gabled houses**, most of them turned into duty-free shops. It's so **charming and easy to get around** that there's little point in taking the pedestrian city and island tour ($$) around the outlying desert terrain unless you're avidly curious about Curaçao or want to taste **the island's eponymous orange-flavored liqueur** at the distillery where it's produced. **On your own walking tour**, the don't-miss details are the Queen Emma Pontoon Bridge and the floating market nearby, lined with brightly painted schooners that sail over from Venezuela or Colombia to sell fresh fruits, vegetables and fish. Across the street is a local **open-air crafts market**, and step away the pedestrian shopping mall chockablock with **duty-free shops**. Penh & Sons, in a building dating from 1708, sells perfumes, clothing and co metics. Divers will love Curaçao's 12-1/2 miles of coral reefs, and snorkele will find **the largest protected underwater park in the Caribbean**, with 1 marked and 10 unmarked trails.

La Romanna, Dominican Republic ★★★

Language:	**Spanish**	English Spoken?:	**Some**
Currency:	**Peso**	US$ ok?:	**Yes**
To town	**Tender, shuttle bus**		

The famous resort of Casa de Campo is a regular port of call for Costa's Caribbean cruises, which use one of the resort's beaches as a private out island.

Little La Romanna on the island's eastern edge, adjacent to the **world-famous resort Casa de Campo**, is a popular port of call for Costa Cruises. Golf on a Pete Dye course, tennis in the **"Wimbledon of the Caribbean,"** horseback riding and polo at The Equestrian Center, fishing, clay pigeon shooting, swimming and a shopping and sightseeing excursion to the Old World fantasy village of Altos de Chavon are all shore excursion options here, but if **a passenger does not buy a shore excursion, he doesn't get to go to the resort** itself, only to the cruise line's private beach resort. **Elegant shopping**, hardly budget but very artistic one-of-a-kind items, especially some stately amber and silver necklaces, can be found in the Altos de Chavon village. Amber is one of the Dominican Republic's best buys.

Puerto Plata, Dominican Republic   ★

Language:	**Spanish**	*English Spoken?:*	**Some**
Currency:	**Peso**	*US$ ok?:*	**Yes**
To town	**Walk or taxi**		

The Dominican Republic occupies half of the island of Hispaniola; the other half is Haiti. Despite its lush landscapes, rivers, white sand beaches, coral cliffs and old Spanish towns, the country still remains largely undiscovered by Americans outside a few resort hotels.

In Puerto Plata, there's not much to do except **shop for amber** or **head for the beach**, unless you're one of the passengers on Costa's new *CostaPlaya* **headed to Cuba** on the first regularly scheduled cruise calls to that island in a long time. **Shore excursions** here are usually limited to guided mini-bus tours that are not terribly interesting, and even the price of amber has escalated in recent years. If you want **to eat ashore**, you can find grilled chicken and plantain chips in the cheap restaurants, good local seafood in the expensive restaurants.

Santo Domingo, Dominican Republic   ★★

Language:	**Spanish**	*English Spoken?:*	**Some**
Currency:	**Peso**	*US$ ok?:*	**Yes**
To town:	**Taxi**		

Santo Domingo, the capital, has a lot of history, including the claim that Columbus, whose son was governor here, is or was at one time buried in the 1514 cathedral, oldest in the New World. As the **oldest city in the New World**, Santo Domingo can also claim the oldest house, street, hospital and university. The major **shore excursion** here, of course, is a tour of the Old Town and the appropriately old monuments ($). **Beaches are about half an hour away**; lively, anything-goes Boca Chica is the most popular. The food is quite good in the Dominican Republic, with shrimp, chicken and beef readily available. Local *empañadas* (pastry turnovers) filled with ground beef are sold from street carts and served in restaurants.

Portsmouth, Dominica ★ ★ ★

Language:	**English**	*English Spoken?:*	**Yes**
Currency:	**EC$**	*US$ ok?:*	**Yes**
To town:	**Shuttle bus, taxi**		

Dominica is going the way of eco-tourism rather than high-rise development, so more and more cruise ships are discovering this lush and unspoiled island.

Eco-tourism is the name of the game in lush and unspoiled Dominica, beginning to see a number of cruise ship calls thanks in part to a **new port facility** constructed at the north end of the island near **Cabrits National Park** and the town of Portsmouth. Previously, the few cruise ships that called usually arrived in the capital city of Roseau, and some still do call there. Rain forests, national parks, **rare birdlife and equally rare surviving Carib Indians** are among the highlights of "the nature island." **Shore excursions** usually include a walking tour of the renovated Cabrits fortress ($ or free) or a drive to the rain forests and the Carib Reservation, where the last remaining Carib Indians still live ($$). An adventurous visitor can **rent a beat-up Jeep** in town ($$) and cover a surprising amount of territory in a day. The drive along the coast between Portsmouth and Roseau is scenic, as is the Layou River Valley, inland from Roseau, but the roads are sometimes rough and potholed. **Get a local driving license** at the police department before setting out.

Key West, Florida   ★ ★ ★ ★ ★

Language:	**English**	English Spoken?:	**Yes**
Currency:	**US$**	US$ ok?:	**Yes**
To town:	**Walk**		

Key West is a dandy day tripper destination; you can walk anywhere you really want to go, or you can hop aboard the open-air Conch Train for a tour.

We love Key West as a port of call for daytrippers; if it were in another country, it would probably attract more cruise ships than St. Thomas. **Easily accessible and passenger-friendly**, this colorful town has not been a regular cruise port of call until fairly recently. While it's easy enough just to walk around town and see most of the historic sights, few can resist buying a ticket for the **open-air Toonerville Trolley-type Conch Train** and its cousin the Old Town Trolley Tours, which meander around the island while driver-guides, many of them seniors, spiel a combination of corny jokes and local anecdotes. It's not really necessary to take a shore excursion here, but a few are offered anyhow. You can **rent a bicycle** and pedal around, or simply walk around town and catch the sights—the **Ernest Hemingway house** with multiple descendents of his original six-toed cats still in residence, **Mel Fisher's gold treasures** salvaged from the sunken 17th century Spanish galleon *Atocha*, the Little White House where Harry and Bess Truman vacationed, the Tennessee Williams house and the Robert Frost cottage. Stop by **Sloppy Joe's** for a drink, but remember that the original Sloppy Joe's where Hemingway used to hang out is a few doors down the street. Snack on a Cuban sandwich or some conch fritters from a sidewalk stall. **Best buys** are locally made cotton sportswear and aloe vera skin products.

George Town, Grand Cayman   ★★★

Language:	**English**	*English Spoken?:*	**Yes**
Currency:	**CI$**	*US$ ok?:*	**Yes**
To town:	**Tender from ship**		

The **Switzerland of the Caribbean** has even more banks than duty-free shops, and the Cayman Islands dollar is often worth more than the U.S. dollar, so check prices carefully if you're tempted to shop here in the **posh, duty-free shops**. Locals live well; there are a lot of U.S. expatriates who moved down to stay with their money. Traffic moves on the left in this British Crown Colony. **Shore excursions** include the wildly popular **Stingray City Tour**, a snorkel-with-stingray opportunity that also includes snorkel equipment and instruction ($$), Scuba two-tank dive ($$–$$$, **bring certification**), Seaworld Explorer Semi-Submarine Tour ($$), Atlantis Submarine ($$$), a cruise aboard the Calypso Mermaid ($$), snorkeling ($$) and an island tour ($$) that includes Seven Mile Beach, the turtle farm, a black coral factory and a brief stop in **Hell**. (Locals find it amusing.) On your own, cab it to the Hyatt Regency Grand Cayman, a splendid resort hotel **on the sand at Seven Mile Beach**, or walk around in town hitting the shops. Then, perhaps, sit on the terrace at **Jamin**, a few steps away from the dock, sip a cold soda or beer and **crunch on conch fritters** while admiring your ship at anchor.

The harbor at St. George's, Grenada, is one of the loveliest in the Caribbean; the area where the bright boats are tied up is called the Carenage.

St. George's, Grenada ★ ★ ★

Language:	**English**	*English Spoken?:*	**Yes**
Currency:	** EC$**	*US$ ok?:*	**Yes**
To town:	**Walk**		

There's no way, José, no matter how tough you may think you are, to get
out of Grenada without forking over a dollar or two for the must-buy souvenir from this spice island, a tiny **handwoven basket filled with local nutmegs**,
cloves, mace and other spices. Because they're dried and not fresh, you can
bring them back into the United States, and they make cheap, compact and
unusual gifts for friends at home. Have your camera ready for the sail into this
picture-book harbor, one of the prettiest in the Caribbean, and stroll around
the Carenage in the harbor to shoot the vividly painted fishing boats, each
with its own special name painted on the bow, while fending off spice sellers
along the way. (It doesn't do any good to hold up the baskets you already
bought; the Grenadans think you can never have enough souvenir spice bas-
kets.) **Shore excursions** include the island tour ($$), often with a driver who
gives his memories of the 1983 U.S. invasion of Grenada, a stop at Grand
Etang National Park, and a half-day beach tour to two-mile-long Grand
Anse Beach, easy enough to do on your own with a taxi, either a regular cab
from town or a water taxi from the Carenage, across to the beach. For divers,
the **biggest shipwreck in the Caribbean** is here, an Italian cruise ship called the
Bianca C from Costa that caught fire and sank in 1961; a 350-pound grou-
per was living in the smokestack, the last we heard. Take a break at The Nut-
meg to sample **the island's famous rum punches** with fresh grated local
nutmeg on top. Two will make you careen along the Carenage back to your
ship.

The Grenadines ★ ★ ★ ★

Language:	**English**	*English Spoken?:*	**Yes**
Currency:	**EC$**	*US$ ok?:*	**Yes**
To town:	**Tender from ship**		

A treasure chest of **100 or so craggy green islands** set like emeralds in the
sapphire blue sea, a yachtsman's treasure with some of the best sailing in the
world. Sail cruisers, small expeditioners and champagne-and-caviar ships all
stop here, especially at the **jet-set island of Mustique** and the whaling outpost
of Bequia, where the few surviving whalers like to share their memories with

interested visitors. Best buys, if you can afford them, are the **elegantly han**‑
crafted boat models to order. (Queen Elizabeth has one.) The silk screen fa‑
rics from The Crab Hole are also attractive. Carriacou, an offbeat call f‑
smaller vessels, also has traditional boat builders at work. **Mayreau**, whic
provides a beach island day for many of Princess Cruises' Caribbean passe‑
gers, is privately owned and very tiny. **Palm Island**, even smaller and also pr
vately owned, is filled by a resort called the Palm Island Beach Club. Sm‑
vessels occasionally call there. None of these islands offers organized sho
excursions. Your best bet is to stroll around or hire a local taxi (often a
open-bed pickup with built-in benches) for a bumpy but fascinating loc
around.

Pointe-à-Pitre, Guadeloupe ★ ★ ★

Language:	**French**	*English Spoken?:*	**Some**
Currency:	**Franc**	*US$ ok?:*	**Yes**
To town:	**Walk**		

The dock in Guadeloupe is adjacent to the heart of Pointe-à-Pitre, and one o
the Caribbean's top restaurants, La Canne à Sucre, is only steps away.

One of the best restaurants in the Caribbean is only a few steps away from th
dock in Pointe-à-Pitre, if you can afford it and are there in the evenings whe
it's open—the sophisticated **La Canne à Sucre** ($$$). But real Caribbean food
freaks swear by the ebullient female Creole chefs who run simple restaurant
with local cooking, often in their own homes. You have to call ahead in orde
to get directions and be sure the place is open; ask locals what's currentl
good. The cooks proudly parade through the streets during **the annual**

ooks' Festival every August, wearing their traditional Madras headdresses and eating on pots and pans with kitchen utensils. Butterfly-shaped Guadeloupe is really two islands, Grande-Terre, more heavily populated, with a gentle landscape, and sparsely settled Basse-Terre with rugged, mountainous terrain. **Shore excursions** include an island tour ($$), with a visit to a rustic rum factory, a short hike to a waterfall in the national park and a brief shopping stop in town.

Iles Des Saintes ★ ★ ★

Language:	**French**	*English Spoken?:*	**Little**
Currency:	**Franc**	*US$ ok?:*	**No**
To town:	**Tender**		

The seldom-visited Iles des Saintes are clean, colorful and totally French.

For cruise ship day trippers from small sail cruise ships like Star Clippers, Windstar and Club Med, going off on your own and strolling around is the real pleasure—walking down a narrow road with more chickens than cars, photographing brightly painted fishing boats and whimsical cottages with flower gardens in the front yard, swimming or snorkeling in clear waters, **lunching on conch or sea urchins** or a French-style court bouillon of fresh fish. These eight tiny, idyllic islands off Guadeloupe inhabited by fishermen descended from Breton sailors who arrived more than a century ago are **like going back to yesterday's French West Indies**. Some French is handy if you want to have dialogue or commerce with the islanders.

Montego Bay, Jamaica ★★

Language:	**English**	*English Spoken?:*	**Yes**
Currency:	**J$**	*US$ ok?:*	**Yes**
To town:	**Taxi, shuttle**		

Skip the town itself unless you're really into local crafts and local food (th **jerk chicken at the Pork Pit** near Doctor's Cave Beach is to die for!) becaus you'll have some heavy hustling by vendors (including ganja—locally-grow marijuana—if you're under 50) and what many perceive as a lot of attitud Some of the island's most elegant resorts are in the vicinity, including **Roun Hill, Half Moon Bay** and **Tryall**. **Shore excursions** include rafting ($$) which w can't recommend since some tourists were robbed and shot while on a grou excursion on the Rio Grande a couple of years ago; a visit to **Rose Hall Grea House** ($$), said to be haunted by a "white witch" who murdered three hus bands; a half-day at a private beach club ($$); golf at Half Moon Bay ($$$ snorkeling ($$), scuba ($$$, **certification required**) or trimaran sailing t Doctor's Cave Beach ($$), within walking distance of the Pork Pit.

Climbing Dunn's River Falls near Ocho Rios is the must-do shore excursion in Jamaica; give your guide your camera to carry and he'll snap a picture of you.

Ocho Rios, Jamaica   ★ ★ ★

Language:	**English**	English Spoken?:	**Yes**
Currency:	**J$**	US$ ok?:	**Yes**
To town:	**Walk**		

Ocho Rios gets **more cruise ship calls** than Mo Bay these days. The **top ore excursion** is a splashy 600-foot climb up Dunn's River Falls ($$). **Wear bathing suit under your street clothes** and take a camera; your guide will arry it up the climb for you and snap your picture as a bonus. Slightly longer ours may include a combination of Carinosa Gardens, Fern Gully and unn's River Falls ($$), Prospect Plantation ($$) to see bananas, coffee, ineapple, sugar cane and other tropical plants growing; or coastal yacht ruises ($$-$$$). As we said in the copy above about Mo Bay, **we cannot rec- mmend river rafting** ($$) since two Pennsylvania men were robbed and shot n one of those in a group tour a couple of years ago. Craft vendors are ometimes aggressive in the streets around the port, some pushing you to uy ganja. **Ask about prices**, since **the Jamaican dollar sign is written like the .S. dollar sign**, and vendors hope you'll pay in the more valuable U.S. dollars ithout double-checking. The smoothly-functioning port facility is within alking distance to malls and craft markets, and if your mouth is set for some picy jerk chicken and ice-cold Red Stripe beer**, the Jerk Center is a short stroll om the ship; just ask the cruise staff how to find it.

Fort-de-France, Martinique   ★ ★

Language:	**French**	English Spoken?:	**Some**
Currency:	**Franc**	US$ ok?:	**Yes**
To town:	**Long walk, taxi**		

Despite the sultry heat and the rather longish (about a mile) and dull (ex- ept for the stunning Schoelcher Library) walk into town, we usually grit our eeth and hoof it because the local cabbies, heavy on attitude, are now charg- ng **$8 to drive you into town**, nearly double what it was a couple of years ago. On a recent visit, the cab drivers would not let the pre-arranged tourist buses ome into the port to take the passengers on the island tours unless the cabs ould get half of the pre-sold shore excursion business. The fact that the tour guides are fluent in English and history of the island and many cab drivers hardly speak English at all didn't seem to bother them. If you're comfortable driving a small rental car on a French-speaking Caribbean island and can ar-

range the rental ahead of time, we'd recommend going out on your own
you can't take the usual half-day island tour. The single most dramatic eve
in the history of the island, **the eruption of Mt. Pelée** in 1902 that kill
30,000 people from gas fumes, with the only survivor a prisoner in an und
ground cell, is dramatically illustrated in the local museum in St. Pierre. Y
can **buy French perfumes**, cosmetics and Lalique crystal at air-condition
duty-free havens like Roger Albert's gigantic shop.

Cozumel, Mexico ★ ★ ★

Language:	**Spanish**	English Spoken?:	**Yes**
Currency:	**Peso**	US$ ok?:	**Yes**
To town:	**Walk, taxi or tender**		

*At Cozumel's new port facility two miles from the old town, vendors promot
tropical drinks.*

On a busy winter or spring day, the port of Cozumel may be **chockabloc**
with cruise ships, some of them tendering from anchorage into the tow
dock in the heart of little San Miguel, others alongside at the new dock faci
ity a couple of miles away with its own port shopping complex. On a Wester
Caribbean itinerary, Cozumel is the star, and the drill is that your ship usu
ally calls first briefly at the port of Playa del Carmen on the mainland jus
long enough for **the shore excursions to Maya ruins** to disembark, then sails o
to the island of Cozumel. The local shops have really gotten tarted up th
last few prosperous years, but traces of the funky old Mexican village tha
used to be here are still in evidence. The handsome **Inter-Continental Hotel** is
short cab ride from the new pier and makes a nice place to lunch at the out

oor bar by the pool. If you're in the middle of town, try the casual, inex-
ensive **Palmeros** on the main square by the crosswalk to the town pier.
norkeling and shopping head the list of things to do in Cozumel. **Good buys**
iclude fine black coral jewelry made locally, hand-embroidered garments,
arved alabaster knick-knacks, straw hats and bags, woven hammocks,
rightly painted pottery and the ubiquitous t-shirt in all its guises. **Shore ex-**
ursions may offer a ho-hum island tour ($$), interesting but hardly riveting;
norkeling on famous Palancar Reef ($$), which includes instruction and
quipment; a one-tank dive at the Santa Rosa Wall ($$$, **certificate required**);
r a beginner dive at Paraiso Reef ($$), including instruction and equip-
nent.

Playa del Carmen, Mexico ★ ★ ★

Language:	**Spanish**	*English Spoken?:*	**Yes**
Currency:	**Peso**	*US$ ok?:*	**Yes**
To town:	**Walk**		

*Tulum, shown here, is the easier, half-day tour; it usually takes all day on the
bus or an expensive roundtrip flight to visit Chichen Itza.*

Playa del Carmen is used primarily as a disembarkation port for passengers
taking in **the wonders of the Maya ruins** at Tulum or Chichen Itza, but it's also
possible to visit the resort beach strip at Cancun ($$) on an excursion from
Playa del Carmen, although few ships offer the option. More common is **an
all-day excursion to Tulum's Maya ruins** by the sea and **the "sacred lagoon" of
Xel-Ha**, with a box lunch provided by the ship ($$). Even more spectacular
(and pricey) is the flight tour to Chichen Itza's ruins ($$$) to see the pyra-

mid of Kukulcan, the ball court, Temple of the Warriors and Well of Sacrifices. The bus tour to Chichen Itza from Playa del Carmen is **more than three hours each way**, and using a video camera at any of the ruins carries a surcharge of around $10. **Take a bottle of mineral water** from the ship to sip as you're walking around the ruins. If you have a whole day in Playa del Carmen, as ships occasionally offer, you'll find a good beach right by the pier backed by a pretty pink resort hotel, and not far away, south of Tulum, **Sian Ka'an Biosphere Reserve**, one of the UNESCO World Heritage Sites, with tropical forests and marine habitats protecting endangered mammal, bird and reptile species. Guides are on the premises to take you around ($$$).

San Juan, Puerto Rico ★★★★

Language:	**Spanish**	*English Spoken?:*	**Yes**
Currency:	**US$**	*US$ ok?:*	**Yes**
To town:	**Walk to old town, taxi elsewhere**		

Most cruise ships dock at the edge of San Juan's colorful Old Town at one of the city's spiffy new piers (or the old one) but if there's an overflow, your ship may sometimes be a mile or two away in an industrial port area. The Old Town is the main point of interest, and something you can easily do on your own unless you want a guide to fill you in on all the history. Pick up the latest copy of *Que Pasa* magazine (free but you'll have to ask for it) from the tourist information office near the dock. **Ship buffs should make a detour** (by taxi) over to the **Radisson Normandie Hotel**, a great eccentric art deco hotel designed to look like one of the French Line ships. The famous **Caribe Hilton** is a half-block away if you want to walk over there for a look. **Shore excursions** include a half-day Bacardi Rum Factory tour in combination with a visit to El Morro Castle and Old San Juan ($$), a city tour of new and old San Juan ($), a drive through the El Yunque rain forest ($$), golf at Cerromar Beach ($$$), deep-sea fishing ($$$), horseback riding with beach visit and barbecue lunch included ($$$), snorkeling ($$) or diving ($$$ for a one-tank with certification required, $$ for a first-timer's dive with equipment and instruction). Nightclub or casino evening tours ($$) are also offered when ship stays in port until midnight or later, but the last one of these we took was **dreadful, a lot of milling about and waiting for the cultural show in a stuffy, sleazy, smoke-filled casino** and nowhere smoke-free you could even sit down and get a quiet drink. We ditched the tour and took a cab back to the ship where it was much nicer.

Six stars, two ships and a singular commitment to you.

The promise of all-inclusive value and exceptional luxury distinguishes Silversea from all other cruise lines. Leaf through this cruise guide – you won't find another cruise line that offers more. All-suite accommodations (most with verandas), exacting service, acclaimed cuisine, worldwide itineraries and a shipboard atmosphere that puts guests first. Come, experience what ultra-luxury cruising is all about aboard the yacht-like *Silver Cloud* and *Silver Wind*. After all, *Fielding* doesn't award Six Stars to just anybody for two years in a row.

*Y*our all-inclusive fare includes:

A spacious outside suite, most with
   private verandas
Roundtrip air and pre-cruise hotel stay
Gratuities, wines and spirits
Port charges, transfers and porterage
Shoreside event on special sailings

SILVERSEA

Ships' Registries: Italy and Bahamas

MEDITERRANEAN   BALTIC   CANADA & NEW ENGLAND   CARIBBEAN   SOUTH AMERICA
AFRICA & INDIA   FAR EAST   SOUTH PACIFIC

Dolphin's *Ocean Breeze*, Bahamas

Scenic barge view in France

Norwegian Cruise Line's *Windward* in San Juan

Gustavia, St. Barts ★ ★ ★ ★ ★

Language:	**French**	*English Spoken?:*	**Yes**
Currency:	**Franc**	*US$ ok?:*	**Yes**
To town:	**Tender from ship**		

Quiet beaches and sheltered inlets like this make St. Barts a favorite hideaway of the rich and famous.

This lovely little island is the kind of French tropical island we used to dream about—gorgeous sandy beaches, **discreet topless sunbathing**, secluded resorts and restaurants, **chic shopping for Paris labels** and a glamorous, if laid-back, clientele. Now we just hop aboard one of the small, elegant cruise ships that visits there, rent a mini- Moke or Jeep ($$) and take off for the day for a beach or two and whatever hotel is trendy favorite of the year. One was **Le Toiny**, where we sat on the terrace watching the cobalt blue swimming pool shimmer and seem to slip seamlessly over the edge into the twinkling sea beyond. We ate grilled fresh fish, nibbled a plain green salad and drank an icy bottle of Muscadet, and tried to be suave enough not to raise an eyebrow at the $100 check. (No, no soup, no dessert, no coffee, just the fish and wine.) Off-the-wall fun in St. Barts (the real name is St. Barthélemy but nobody calls it that) includes parking on the hill above the airport and watching the planes barely clear the top of your head, then nose steeply downward to **land downhill on an STOL runway**! You could, of course, also spend your time wandering through the cool and costly shops of Gustavia checking out Cartier, Cardin, Animale St. Tropez, Hermés, Libertine, Hervé Leger and so on. Absolutely fabulous, darling!

St. Croix, U.S. Virgin Islands ★★★

Language:	**English**	*English Spoken?:*	**Yes**
Currency:	**US$**	*US$ ok?:*	**Yes**
To town:	**Walk to Frederiksted; shuttle to Christansted**		

St. Croix is the largest of the U.S. Virgin Islands, with an underwater national park for snorkeling and a lot of duty-free shops with less crowds than St. Thomas.

Only a few very small ships such as those from Renaissance and Sea Goddess can dock in the capital city of Christiansted. Large cruise ships usually come alongside or anchor off the second city of Frederiksted, across the island, whose port **was rebuilt recently** after severe damage from hurricane Hugo. **St. Croix is different** from sister islands St. Thomas and St. John, lower key, more affordable, with a wide range of beaches and watersports. It's Teddy Kennedy's Caribbean hideaway; you may run into him at **Duggan's on the Reef** chowing down on chowder or a flying fish sandwich. Only a few miles offshore is **Buck Island Reef National Monument**, the only underwater national park in the United States, with its marked underwater snorkeling trails. Shopping is best in Christiansted; shuttle service across the island is usually available for a nominal fee. **Shore excursions** here usually include an island tour and visit to Whim Great House ($$), a rum-tasting tour to the Cruzan Rum Distillery ($$), golf at a Robert Trent Jones course ($$$), horseback riding in the rain forest and at the beach ($$$), sailboat ride ($$), snorkeling at Buck Island ($$) or scuba at Long Reef ($$$, certificate required).

St. John, U.S. Virgin Islands ★★★★★

Language:	**English**	*English Spoken?:*	**Yes**
Currency:	**US$**	*US$ ok?:*	**Yes**
To town:	**Tender from ship**		

You'll disembark your big cruise ship in the early morning and board the tender for a balmy shuttle into the village of Cruz Bay, then be herded by groups into the local "taxis," the backs of pickup trucks with canvas-shaded benches built across them. Never fear, it's cool and nice once you head out into the woods, far nicer than an air-conditioned bus with windows that don't open. The **drivers are congenial**, stopping whenever anybody wants a photo, chatting about life on the island and just generally being cool and laidback. **Shore excursions** to Trunk Bay ($$) board these St. John taxis for a ride through pristine forest to an immaculate white sand beach fringed with coconut palms. If Trunk Bay looks crowded, ask the driver if he can drop you off at Hawksnest Bay (one cove closer to Cruz Bay) instead, and tell him to pick you up when he fetches the rest of the group from Trunk Bay. Slip him a tip, of course. If you lose your tour group, you can take one of the frequent ferries from Cruz Bay back to Red Hook on St. Thomas, then grab a cab back to the dock. Just remember your ship's sailing time and allow at least three hours to get back to St. Thomas. **Campers should check out Cinnamon Bay Campground** for future visits, two bays beyond Trunk Bay, if the driver will take you farther; some of these national park sites have cottages or rental tents and can be reserved in advance. The famous ecologically-oriented **Maho Bay Campground** is a bit farther away and a lot of drivers won't go in there because the road is so bad. It sure keeps out the riffraff.

Basseterre, St. Kitts ★★★★

Language:	**English**	*English Spoken?:*	**Yes**
Currency:	**EC$**	*US$ ok?:*	**Yes**
To town:	**Taxi shuttle from dock**		

There's no way you can take a shore excursion in St. Kitts and miss the island pride and joy, the fortress at Brimstone Hill.

We think one of the **most charming shore excursions** in the whole Caribbean for first-time visitors is the half-day island tour ($$), which usually includes a visit to the restored 17th century British fortress at Brimstone Hill, called the Gibraltar of the Caribbean because it was never conquered. You'll glimpse at least a couple of the 125,000 **wild vervet monkeys** that run amok all over the island (a pair of them are displayed in a roadside cage on the way into town) and have a chance to buy a few garments at **Caribelle Batik**, where silkscreen fashions are produced in the manor house of a 17th century plantation. There's even a quick tour around the raffish capital with its Caribbean versions of Big Ben, Piccadilly Circus and Pall Mall. While going around on your own isn't difficult, there's little need to do so when the **island tour is so well done**. The favorite local beaches, none of them up to the sandy classics on some of the other islands, include Banana Bay, Cockleshell, Conaree Beach, Frigate Bay and Friar's Bay, the last open to both the Atlantic and the Caribbean with some wild surf. While Nevis is very near here, it's almost impossible to get over there and back on a day tour from your ship because of local transportation times.

Castries, St. Lucia ★★★★

Language:	**English**	*English Spoken?:*	**Yes**
Currency:	**EC$**	*US$ ok?:*	**Yes**
To town:	**Taxi**		

The Pitons, twin peaks on the island of St. Lucia, and the still-active volcano of Soufriere are at the less-visited end of the island.

Lovely, lush St. Lucia has two ports, and most ships, because of size, must call at the less-interesting capital of Castries rather than anchor off the town of Soufrière at the foot of the needle-like Pitons and the still-seething volcano on the other end of the island. A few small vessels are able to anchor off Soufrière and take passengers in by tender for shore excursions to the bubbling mud pots and steaming sulphur pools of the volcano, but major ships call only at Castries' handsome new port facility of Pointe Seraphine, with an assortment of **duty-free shops just steps away from the gangway**. Old Caribbean hands will like funky downtown Castries, where **the lively vegetable market** still has posters stapled around its perimeters forbidding urinating in public. **Shore excursions** offered here include a sailboat trip to Marigot Bay ($$) where *Dr. Doolittle* was filmed; a daylong boatride with lunch along the coast to see Soufrière and the Pitons from the sea ($$); a city and environs tour which includes a shopping stop at Bagshaw's silk screen studios ($$); and, on occasion, a daylong bus tour to Soufrière ($$), which we'd hesitate to recommend unless you're *really* into fumaroles.

Philipsburg, St. Maarten   ★ ★ ★

Language:	**Dutch, Papiamento**	*English Spoken?:*	**Yes**
Currency:	**Guilder**	*US$ ok?:*	**Yes**
To town:	**Tender from ship**		

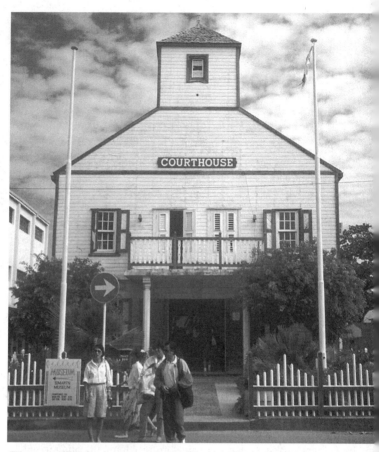

When you disembark your tender at the town pier in Dutch St. Maarten, the historic courthouse will probably be the first building you'll notice.

You'll land at the pier in the heart of town when you disembark the ship's tender, and getting around couldn't be simpler—there are **two main streets**, Front Street, the one nearer the water, and Back Street, the one farther away from the water. See how easy it is? But it's more complicated than it seems. The **schizophrenic 37-square-mile island is divided not quite equally between the Netherlands and France**; the French have more land but the Dutch have the international airport. But it's painless passing between the two sectors, just hail a taxi van, spend three bucks or so to ride up to Marigot and hail another one back to Philipsburg. The Dutch town has most of **the shopping and the casinos**, and the duty-free shopping here is pretty good; we'd stack it up against St. Thomas any day, except Americans get an extra break on the goods they buy in St. Thomas. The streets are usually thronged with shoppers and the occasional pickpocket. **Shore excursions** offered in Philipsburg include an island tour ($-$$), a sightseeing boat cruise up to Marigot, the French capital ($$), golf at Mullet Bay ($$$), **a cruise on an America's Cup yacht**—everyone loves this one—($$$), a sail and snorkel half-day aboard a

tamaran ($$), snorkeling ($$) and a one-tank scuba dive to a reef at a
epth of 50 to 60 feet ($$$, bring certification).

Marigot, St. Martin ★★★★

Language:	**French**	*English Spoken?:*	**Yes**
Currency:	**Franc**	*US$ ok?:*	**Yes**
To town:	**Tender from ship or shuttle from Philipsburg**		

Smaller ships sometimes call in Marigot on the French side of St. Martin, where a crafts and vegetable market often takes place in the town square.

This is the Gallic half of the island above, and a few valiant ships, notably the sail cruisers from Windstar and Club Med, still anchor in the bay here. The **waterfront area has been gentrified** in the last several years, and has turned what used to be a photogenic island vegetable market into a crafts and flea market with more junk than art. Still, the port area is lined with appealing (and expensive) sidewalk cafes that might make you think of the Côte d'Azur if you've never actually been there. **Culinary capital** of the island is the town of **Grand Case**, a short and inexpensive ride away on a local bus. **Stroll around town reading menus** to pick out a spot to lunch. Some **outdoor food sellers line the road** by Grand Case Beach if you prefer a snack. The island's **best-known clothing-optional beach** is Orient Beach, several miles east of Grand Case. You could also **take the ferry over to Anguilla**, where almost no cruise ships call, to have a look around, but you'd have to rush to squeeze it in. Walking is easier than driving in the one-way streets of downtown Marigot.

St. Thomas, U.S. Virgin Islands ★★★

Language:	**English**	*English Spoken?:*	**Yes**
Currency:	**US$**	*US$ ok?:*	**Yes**
To town:	**Shuttle, tender**		

The streets of Charlotte-Amalie, St. Thomas, are lined with shops and touts hustling you to come into each one of them.

The **most popular cruise port in the Caribbean** has four different areas where your ship may be positioned—the main port at West India dock (a.k.a. Havensight), two miles east of downtown Charlotte Amalie; the Crown Point (a.k.a. Sub Base) about two miles west of downtown Charlotte Amalie, the downtown pier (only small ships like ACCL's *Mayan Prince* tie up here), and anchoring offshore, as the elegant *Norway* has to do every week on its call. From West India Dock the **shuttles will charge you around $3 a person** for the ride into town. If a little light shopping is the only thing on your agenda and you don't like crowds, we'd recommend you stroll from the pier into the very nice and usually **uncrowded shops of Havensight Mall**, where we promise you'll find a branch of virtually every major downtown shop with the same prices but without the touts crowding the sidewalks. **Liquor is a bargain** if you don't mind lugging it home, but **never check it with your baggage**. **Shore excursions** include a beach day at Magen's Bay or island tours in open-air jitneys ($-$$); Kon Tiki rum punch party boats, Coral World's underwater observatory or a beach expedition to St. John ($$); the Atlantis Submarine, helicopter tours or golf at Mahogany Run ($$$). The harbor with its turquoise water, rows of red-roofed white buildings climbing green hills, and fluorescent foliage—bougainvillea, hibiscus, yellow trumpets—is gorgeous.

on't be tempted to rent a car to ride around; you drive on the left and roads re narrow, winding and often unmarked. While Hurricane Marilyn wreaked avoc a while back, the island is back up to speed now.

Kingstown, St. Vincent ★ ★

Language:	**English**	*English Spoken?:*	**Yes**
Currency:	**EC$**	*US$ ok?:*	**Yes**
To town:	**Walk**		

Lush, rural St. Vincent is primarily a banana port and administrative center for the Grenadines; you'll have a chance at an island tour to see the breadfruit.

A beautiful and unspoiled island with winding country roads and farming communities, St. Vincent really doesn't open itself up to the daytripper with limited time. In the port, you'll see **bananas being loaded onto Europe-bound freighters**, an activity that seems to go on night and day. A posh resort that is part of and at the same time not part of St. Vincent—it's on its own island with a severely restricted transportation policy—is **Young Island**; they only allow a few visitors on the private island at a time and you have to literally telephone from the boat landing to see if they'll let you come over or not. Frankly, when we finally were permitted to come over—hours after we first applied—we found it a bit **overrated if you're into creature comfort. Shore excursions** usually offered include an island tour ($$) that visits the botanical gardens dating from 1765, oldest in the Caribbean; you'll see a living **breadfruit tree brought back from Tahiti by Captain Bligh**. Diving and snorkeling tours ($$-$$$) to the Falls of Baleine, a 60-foot cascading waterfall spilling into a 15-foot-deep fresh water pool, are also sometimes available. **Stamp col-**

lectors treasure St. Vincent's beautiful postage stamps; you can find them
St. Vincent Philatelic Services Ltd. in Kingstown.

Scarborough, Tobago ★★★

Language:	**English**	*English Spoken?:*	**Yes**
Currency:	**TT$**	*US$ ok?:*	**Yes**
To town:	**Walk or shuttle, depending on dock or anchorage**		

A golf course in Tobago—but you'll see more cricket than golf played here.

The new port facility in Scarborough accesses one of the prettiest beaches
in the Caribbean, Pigeon Point. It used to be that small ships anchored off
the point and took passengers ashore by Zodiac or tender, but that doesn't
seem to happen much any more. On our most recent arrival, we were greeted by **a fine steel drum band** that seemed to consist mostly of local students,
both male and female. **Shore excursions** accent the island's emphasis on **eco-
tourism**, with glass-bottom boat rides and snorkeling at Buccoo Reef ($-$$),
an island tour ($$) visiting the capital of Scarborough, the 18th century En-
glish fortress of Fort George, the town of Portsmouth with its mysterious
riddle on an 18th century tombstone inscription, and a modest history mu-
seum. **Offshore reefs attract divers and snorkelers**; local operators offer dive
excursions to Buccoo Reef ($$$, **bring your certification**). Golfers will find an
18-hole course adjacent to Mount Irvine Bay Hotel.

Road Town, Tortola ★★★★

Language:	**English**	*English Spoken?:*	**Yes**
Currency:	**US$**	*US$ ok?:*	**Yes**
To town:	**Taxi, shuttle vans**		

We adore the British Virgin Islands, secluded and laid-back compared to the U.S. Virgin Islands, but with a distinctive character all their own. **Don't expect fancy or fussy**, glitzy or glamorous. What you get are pretty tropical islands with friendly people who are not in a bit of a hurry—heaven forfend—so you'd better not be either. Yachtsmen enjoy sailing around the 40 or so islands and cays, of which Tortola is the largest, as well as being the administrative center of the group. The **U.S. dollar is the official currency** here in these British islands. **Shore excursion options** are modest, with sailing, snorkeling and scuba ($$-$$$) heading the list, along with a tour to the Baths at Virgin Gorda ($$) or a glass-bottom boat ride over the **1867 wreck of the Royal Mail Ship *Rhone* near Salt Island** ($$). If you want to just walk around Road Town, Pusser's Company Store is the place to sample **killer rum drinks**, rated by number for strength, and to buy tropical safari wear. If you can drive on the left and negotiate narrow, winding, potholed roads, a self-drive rental car tour of the island ($$) could take you to the beach at Cane Garden Bay, Sage Mountain National park, Soper's Hole, and **Apple Bay's Sugar Mill** and its beachfront restaurant **Islands** for lunch.

The streets of Port-of-Spain, Trinidad, are lined with handsome Victorians.

Port-of-Spain, Trinidad   ★★

Language:	**English**	*English Spoken?:*	**Yes**
Currency:	**TT$**	*US$ ok?:*	**Yes**
To town:	**Walk**		

First there was **a single scarlet ibis**, feeding on a mud flat alongside som⟨e⟩ egrets and blue herons, then another and then after the guide anchored ou⟨r⟩ boat 500 feet away so as not to scare them, they began coming home i⟨n⟩ flocks, like groups of flashily dressed commuters off the 6:19. Trinidad h⟨as⟩ some of the **best birdwatching** in the hemisphere, with 400 varieties, many ⟨of⟩ them rare or unique, plus 600 species of butterflies. Until not long ag⟨o⟩ Trinidad was prosperous enough from oil and international business, bu⟨t⟩ with a soft economy has begun to look at tourism, **primarily eco-tourism**. Th⟨e⟩ few cruise ships that call here arrive at a handsome new cruise port in down⟨⟩ town Trinidad; walking is the best way to get around here since traffic sti⟨ll⟩ clogs the streets throughout the day. **Shore excursions** offered include an is⟨-⟩ land tour with a visit to Maracas Beach ($$); an early morning or late after⟨⟩ noon visit to Caroni Bird Sanctuary to see huge flocks of those scarlet ibi⟨s⟩ described above ($$); or an occasional expedition to Asa Wright Natur⟨e⟩ Centre ($$), a rain forest bird sanctuary with more than 160 species, som⟨e⟩ very rare. If you hire a taxi to take you out to Asa Wright and back, mak⟨e⟩ sure he knows where it is before you set out (our driver didn't) and agree o⟨n⟩ the price in advance. On your own in town, have **lunch at Veni Mange** (Come and Eat), a moderately priced spot in a tiny cottage on a side street where **two sisters cook up great local food**. If you can get here for the **pre-Lenten Carnival**, Trinidad's biggest tourist event of the year, you'll see a costume parade t⟨o⟩ rival Rio's.

La Guaira, Venezuela   ★

Language:	**Spanish**	*English Spoken?:*	**Yes**
Currency:	**Bolivar**	*US$ ok?:*	**Yes**
To town:	**Taxi**		

The port of La Guaira (for Caracas) has one shore excursion — a drive uphill to the capital of Caracas, of which this is part of the capitol complex.

La Guaira is the port for Caracas, which lies an hour or so away via a boring bus ride, and is the primary shore excursion offered here. Like the old joke, first prize is **a half-day tour of Caracas**, second prize is a full-day tour. You can see just about as much on the half-day tour ($$) and may get to miss an interminable two-hour shopping stop and a banquet lunch at a local hotel. Unless you're dying to see the birthplace of Simon Bolivar, the cathedral, the cardinal's palace and government buildings, a glass factory and a restored plantation house turned into a museum of colonial art, **we'd suggest staying on the ship**. That way you don't have to be part of the total bedlam that seems to fill the port whenever a large ship arrives.

Spanish Town, Virgin Gorda ★★★★

Language:	**English**	English Spoken?:	**Yes**
Currency:	**US$**	US$ ok?:	**Yes**
To town:	**Shuttle vans**		

Virgin Gorda is home of The Baths, as well as some off-the-beaten-path resorts.

The world-famous **Baths of Virgin Gorda** with their gigantic water-smoothed boulders and turquoise pools and grottos are the primary excursion here ($$). A boat brings you to Gun Creek, where you board an open-air safari bus or tourist van for an island drive which takes you through Spanish Town and ends at the Baths. You'll be let out at the top of the hill with a short walk down a narrow, uneven path into the area. Here you can explore, swim or snorkel amid the boulders for an hour or so before going back up the hill to get into your bus. A **sailing excursion** ($$$) aboard a 75-foot catamaran that sails around Peter, Pelican and Cooper Islands is also sometimes offered. After the cruise, the boat anchors off a sheltered beach for swimming, sunning or snorkeling. Laurance Rockefeller's famous **Little Dix Bay** has been a top luxury resort here since it opened back in 1964, but other famous resorts such as **Bitter End Yacht Club** and **Biras Creek** can only be reached by sea. Divers can explore Anegada Reef, the wreck of the *RMS Rhone* (where the film *The Deep* was shot) and the wreck of the *Chikuzen*. British entrepreneur Richard Branson owns **Necker Island**, a posh and private island with a 10-room hotel available for **$10,000 a night** for a maximum of 16 guests.

THE ALASKA CRUISE

Alaska's native people call them **children of the snow**, those craggy icebergs born from the snowfalls of an ancient time. From the ship's rail, passengers watching gasp and shriek as a sharp, rifle-shot sound from the glacier announces a "calving," or birth, of another iceberg ripped from the mother glacier and tumbling into the icy seas.

From a smaller ice floe, **a harbor seal** observes us, his head lifted in curiosity. We can hear peeps from **colonies of black-winged kittiwake**, and watch **cormorants diving for fish**. **A bald eagle** sits calmly on another iceberg surveying his domain. Sometimes whales indulge in a flirtatious game with the ship, coming in closer and closer, rolling and glistening in the sea, as if posing for the countless snapping cameras.

But **cruising among the glaciers**, while perhaps the most spectacular and eagerly anticipated activity, is only part of an Alaskan cruise. Contrary to what you may think before your first visit, it's a journey you can make over and over with a different experience every time.

INSIDER TIP

Jokes you'll hear more than once:

A sourdough is "sour on Alaska but without enough dough to get out."

A cheechako (tenderfoot) can become a real Alaskan after wrestling with a grizzly, urinating in the Yukon and surviving an amorous bear encounter.

Five Essential Items to Take On an Alaska Cruise

1. A **camera** with telephoto or zoom lens for wildlife shots.

2. A lightweight **down vest** or jacket for cool mornings on deck.

3. **Binoculars**.

4. Sturdy **walking shoes** or hiking boots.

5. **Lightweight silk long underwear** for glacier-watching days.

Dramatic totem poles are seen throughout southeastern Alaska; this particular one is in Haines.

DID YOU KNOW

Conversations about Alaskan wildlife can sometimes jolt an environmentalist from the lower 48; we were listening to an avid outdoorsman in Fairbanks talking about the indigenous wild animals. "And Dall sheep," he said, eyes glowing, "makes about the best eating there is."

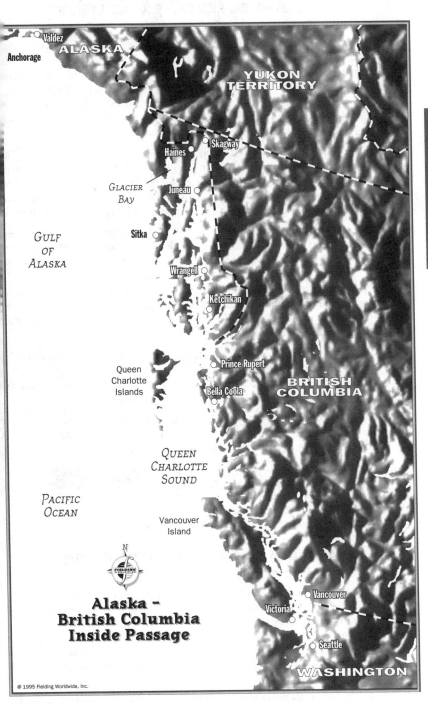

Valdez

Anchorage

ALASKA

YUKON TERRITORY

Skagway

Haines

GLACIER BAY

Juneau

GULF OF ALASKA

Sitka

Wrangell

Ketchikan

Queen Charlotte Islands

Prince Rupert

Bella Coola

BRITISH COLUMBIA

QUEEN CHARLOTTE SOUND

PACIFIC OCEAN

Vancouver Island

N

FIELDING WORLDWIDE

Alaska –
British Columbia
Inside Passage

Vancouver

Victoria

Seattle

WASHINGTON

@ 1995 Fielding Worldwide, Inc.

Classic and Alternative Alaska Cruises

There are two basic Alaska itineraries. **The classic Inside Passage,** the orignal and still highly popular, usually sets out from Vancouver for a seven-d; round-trip cruise up the Inside Passage, with most, but not all, vessels spen ing a day cruising around famous Glacier Bay. The **Gulf of Alaska cruise,** newer itinerary, has gotten tremendously popular in the last few years, bot for its cruise past the mighty Columbia Glacier and for repeat Alaska cruise: who have already done the classic Inside Passage.

Most of the Alaska ships are large cruise vessels that offer a traditional ship board experience and all the luxury and comfort passengers associate wit cruises. You can enjoy standing or sitting on deck (or on your own privat veranda on some ships) all day watching glaciers and wildlife, then dress u and dance the night away or watch an evening of professional entertainment

Don't make the assumption, as many do, that if you're on a large ship you miss out on a real Alaska experience. **Alaska residents and park rangers are aboard all the ships, large and small,** to give first-hand commentary, answe; your questions and share with you their feelings about their home state. The shore excursions, too, are run by the same few tour operators in every town so whether you're on a big elegant Princess or Holland America liner or the smaller World Explorer sailings, you're all seeing virtually the same shoreside sights with the same guides.

The small ships in Alaska can cruise into areas some of the larger vessels have to miss and may be able to get you a little closer to the glaciers. But some of the large ships have their own excursion boats that can take you still closer than the small cruise vessels, so it's all a tossup.

On the small ships, the dress code is normally casual and the atmosphere relaxed, with very little in the way of formal entertainment. The emphasis is on an educational experience and a personal discovery.

DID YOU KNOW?

"People from the lower 48 are used to seeing Alaska and Hawaii reduced to the same size in identical little boxes at the side of the maps," Alaskans like to remind us. "They don't know how big Alaska really is."

Ten Best of the Best in Alaska/British Columbia

1. **Alaska Highway Cruises,** a one-two combination punch for someone doing that once-in-a-lifetime Alaska trip, lets you buy a combination land/cruise trip with your own easy-to-drive rental RV. We tried this and loved it; you fly to Seattle (or Anchorage), pick up the vehicle and drive the Alaska Highway (or whatever other combination of drives and cruises you want) in one direction, turn in the rig and cruise the other way to your starting point to fly home. Call them at ☎ *(800) 323-5757* for a free brochure.

2. The **luxury glass-domed rail cars** of Princess Tours and Westours that are hooked on the Alaska Railroad engines to chug between Fairbanks and Anchorage through

some of the most dramatic scenery in Alaska; you can add one of these unforgettable journeys onto your Alaska cruise easily.

- The **White Pass & Yukon railway's** day tour out of Skagway (ok, so we love trains) past Dead Horse Gulch up to White Pass Summit, giving a dizzying look down at the trails the miners of '98 had to traverse.

- The **Klondike Gold Rush National Park Service Visitors Center** (free) for films, exhibits and brochures, plus free guided walking tours, of the historic gold rush town of Skagway.

- **Dawson City**, an optional overland excursion offered on many Alaska cruises that will give a wonderful and authentic look at the past.

- **Denali National Park**, another once-in-a-lifetime opportunity for game-spotting on the park-led tours into the wilderness aboard school buses (moderate but require a waiting list for boarding) or safari buses (more expensive but will take an advance reservation) from ARA Tundra Wildlife Tours, $45, ☎ *(907) 683-2215* in summer, ☎ *(907) 276-7234* in winter.

7. **Glacier Bay**, the icing on the cake for many first-time Alaska visitors who cruise the Inside Passage. This protected national park has 15 active glaciers, numerous seabirds and humpback whales, and the National Park Service until recently limited the number of large ships that could visit during the season because they feared too much traffic might disturb the whales. A weakening of this policy has been implemented with more vessel permits issued for the 1997 season.

8. **The Columbia Glacier**, at 400 square miles as big as the sprawling city of Los Angeles, a highlight of the Gulf of Alaska itineraries.

9. Crystal Cruises and Cunard Sea Goddess are two of the most **deluxe cruise lines**. If you like your glacier-gaping gala, check out itineraries for *Sea Goddess I* and the *Crystal Symphony*.

10. The scenery along **Turnagain Arm south of Anchorage** on the road to Seward, named when Captain James Cook told his first mate to turn around again when it turned out not to be the Northwest Passage he was seeking; the interesting footnote here is, the first mate was William Bligh, later to command the ill-fated *Bounty*.

Rating the Ports of Alaska and British Columbia

Chilkat dancers at Fort Seward in Haines present a program of tribal dances.

Anchorage, Alaska ★★★★

Language:	**English**	*English Spoken?:*	**Yes**
Currency:	**US$**	*US$ ok?:*	**Yes**
To town:	**Walk; shuttle from Seward**		

Only a few ships actually sail into the city of Anchorage. Most Gulf of Alaska cruises disembark passengers in the **port of Seward** (or occasionally Whittier) for an overland transfer to Anchorage. For all its northern exposure, Anchorage is a surprisingly urbane city. In fact, Alaskans call it "Los Anchorage" and quip that it's only 40 miles from Alaska. **Shore excursions** include a bus tour down Turnagain Arm to Portage Glacier, one of the state's most accessible ice-choked lakes ($$) or a city tour ($$) that includes the landscape of Earthquake Park, tilted and broken in the disastrous 1964 quake. But the top option is a two- or three-day cruise extension to Fairbanks ($$$) aboard a **luxury dome railway car** (both Westours and Princess Tours operate them daily) and an **overnight stopover at Denali National Park** and a bus ride into the wilderness to glimpse moose, mountain goats, Dall sheep, perhaps even brown bears. (Private vehicles are not allowed on the road into the park in

ımmer.) Getting a glimpse of majestic Mt. McKinley itself is a bit rarer;
.ark rangers estimate one clear day out of three as a rule. On your own in
.nchorage, check out the art museum and the Imaginarium science museum
ith its polar bear den and Northern Lights exhibit.

Homer, Alaska ★★★

Language:	**English**	English Spoken?:	**Yes**
Currency:	**US$**	US$ ok?:	**Yes**
To town:	**Shuttle bus, taxi**		

Familiar to many Americans as the town where humorist Tom Bodett settled to broadcast his radio show and Motel 6 commercials, Homer is also **an
artists' community**. Cruise ships dock at a new port facility off Homer Spit, a
five-mile sandbar in Kachemak Bay, and transfer passengers into town by
tour bus. The city tour ($$) is the basic **shore excursion** here, generally **a bus
ride from one art gallery or homemade jam shop to another**. Sometimes buses go
to the top of Baycrest Hill for the vista of Kachemak Bay or stop at Pratt Mu-
seum to see Aleut, Russian and Indian artifacts. Helicopter tours ($$$) take
a limited number of passengers aloft, four at a time, to see the "river of ice"
snowfields and perhaps, conditions permitting, land on Droshin Glacier.
The most colorful spot in town, and far too crowded on cruise ship days with
crew members and passengers, is the famous **Salty Dawg Saloon**, a log cabin
on the spit with a lighthouse tower above it. Scarcely big enough for dozen
drinkers at a time, the landmark is notable for surviving both the town's big
fire of 1907 and the earthquake of 1964. **Best buys** include jars of Alaska
Wild Berry Products' jams and jellies, watercolors or oil paintings, canned or
smoked Alaskan salmon and lighter-than-air scarves, stoles or caps made
from **qiviut, the soft, feathery underwool of the musk ox**, expensive but worth it
for its light weight and warmth.

Juneau, Alaska ★★★

Language:	**English**	English Spoken?:	**Yes**
Currency:	**US$**	US$ ok?:	**Yes**
To town:	**Walk**		

Juneau remains **Alaska's capital city**, even though it has no roads leading
into it. The setting is striking with the featureless cement high-rise government buildings clumped klutzily against a solid backdrop of green-covered

mountains. Ships dock at the edge of town, where it's an easy stroll to **the f: mous Red Dog Saloon** with its sawdust-strewn floor. You could spend a bund on the **shore excursions** here, with six of the options topping the $100 mar: They include a Mendenhall Glacier and city tour by motorcoach ($$) or v. ($$$), an all-you-can eat salmon bake ($$), a Mendenhall Glacier float tr ($$$), a very popular flight to remote Taku Lodge ($$$), a float-plane fligl "back to the ice age" ($$$), a glacier helicopter flight with a walk on the gl: cier ($$$), gold-panning ($$), sportfishing ($$$), the musical Lady Lo Revue ($), Taku Glacier and Scenic Wilderness cruise ($$$), kayaking ($$$ and the old duffer's ultimate tour, nine holes of **golf with a Mendenhall Glacie view** from every hole ($$$). The bottom line is, Mendenhall is called **th "drive-in glacier"** because it's an easy 10-minute cab ride from town if yo don't want to bother with a tour. On your own in town, walk over to th fine Alaska Historical Museum, take a carriage ride or tour the historic Wick ersham House. Get free maps at the Davis Log Cabin on Third Street.

Ketchikan, Alaska   ★★★★

Language:	**English**	*English Spoken?:*	**Yes**
Currency:	**US$**	*US$ ok?:*	**Yes**
To town:	**Walk or tender**		

Ketchikan brags about its cloudy weather, but the sun is always shining when we're there; this is the famous Dolly's bordello on Creek Street.

Ships either dock right in town in Ketchikan's pretty harbor, filled with fishing boats and framed by snow-capped mountains, or anchor and tender into the dock. While the town has a reputation for being rainy and overcast,

e've found it bright and sunny on almost all our visits. **Totem poles** are the
g attractions here—it claims to be the totem pole capital of the world—
d shore excursions offered include a town and totem tour ($$), a visit to a
aditional Tsimshian village ($$), a very popular flight to Misty Fjords ($$$),
historical waterfront cruise ($$), mountain lake canoeing ($$$), kayaking
$$$), sportfishing ($$$), jetboat excursion to Salmon Falls with lunch
$$$) and a **mountain bike tour** ($$$). The small ships of Alaska Sightseeing/
ruise West also offer a **delightful walking tour** of Ketchikan ($) with Native
merican Joe Williams, who'll tell you a lot about Tlingit culture. You could
lso take a cab on your own to **Totem Bight State Historical Park**, 11 miles
orth of town, to go inside a hand-carved ceremonial house. Walking
round on your own in town you can visit the Totem Heritage Center and
Nature Path, then cut across to the Deer Mountain Hatchery and Salmon
alls fish ladder at Ketchikan Creek, where you'll learn **more than you ever
vanted to know about spawning salmon**. Visitors always go to Dolly's House
$) on Creek Street, which operated as a brothel until the 1950s, and a sign
oints out it's "the only place in the world where **both the fish and the fisher-
nen went upstream to spawn**." Tourist shopping is centered around Creek
Street and Saxman Village, the latter a good place to find Native American
:rafts and the world's largest collection of standing totem poles. On our last
visit here, we took the outdoor elevator up the hill from town to the hand-
some **Westmark Cape Fox Lodge** and had a delicious lunch, as well as a great
overview of the harbor. The new **Southeast Alaska Visitor Center**, just across
from the pier, has some excellent exhibits of Northwest Indian life (free, op-
tional film screening $1).

Seward, Alaska ★ ★

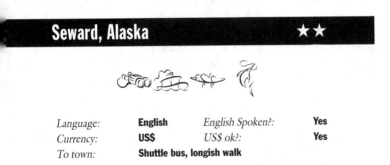

Language:	**English**	English Spoken?:	**Yes**
Currency:	**US$**	US$ ok?:	**Yes**
To town:	**Shuttle bus, longish walk**		

Seward is the most frequently used port for Anchorage on seven day itiner-
aries to and from Vancouver, so if you're signed up for a Gulf of Alaska itin-
erary, you're sure to see Seward. It's a fairly nondescript town surrounded by
spectacular scenery that includes **Kenai Fjords National Park** with its fjords, sea
lion colonies and bird rookeries at Resurrection Bay. Shore excursions here
include **flightseeing trips over the Kenai Peninsula** ($$$), a float trip and salm-
on bake on the Kenai River ($$$), a sled-dog demonstration and visit to Exit
Glacier ($–$$), and a bus tour to Chugach National Forest and Moose Pass
($$). If you want to walk around on your own, drop by the public library to
catch a showing of *Seward Is Burning*, **shots of the 1964 Good Friday earth-
quake** that destroyed 90 per cent of the town. The Resurrection Bay Histor-
ical Museum also includes earthquake artifacts. The misnamed Millionaires'

Row designates bungalows and cottages built just after the turn of the century by railway officials and bankers. The hill behind the town, Mt. Marathon, is the scene of a famous Fourth of July footrace. August brings the even more renowned Silver Salmon Derby; the winner gets **$10,000 for the biggest salmon caught**.

Sitka, Alaska ★★★

Language:	**English**	*English Spoken?:*	**Yes**
Currency:	**US$**	*US$ ok?:*	**Yes**
To town:	**Tender from ship**		

Sitka's big story is that it was once **the capital of Russian America**, and the town still retains more than a little of its exotic accent, notably the pretty onion-domed **St. Michael Russian Orthodox Cathedral**, rebuilt in 1966 after a fire, and the **New Archangel Russian Dancers**, a group of local women who perform folk dances. Shore excursions include a town tour and dance performance ($$), a motor launch cruise to Silver Bay with a chance of spotting eagles and old gold mines ($$), a visit to the eagle center and historic tour ($$), a sea otter and wildlife quest ($$), kayaking ($$), sportfishing ($$$) and a catamaran wildlife-spotting cruise ($$$). But if none of these excursion ideas thrill you, Sitka is a very easy town to stroll around on your own, looking inside the cathedral at the **original icons**, an 18th century jeweled chalice, a 19th century silverbound Bible and tablecloths hand-embroidered by the wife of the last Russian governor of Alaska. There's an old Russian cemetery, the restored Bishop's House, a replica of the blockhouse and, most beguiling of all, **Sitka National Historic Park**, where you can wander through an evergreen forest on cushiony brown pine needles past some splendid standing totem poles. In the visitor center, craftsmen demonstrate the making of Haida button-ornament red capes and Tlingit totems. The Sheldon Jackson Museum is between the park and town.

Skagway, Alaska ★★★★

Language:	**English**	*English Spoken?:*	**Yes**
Currency:	**US$**	*US$ ok?:*	**Yes**
To town:	**Walk**		

*he White Pass & Yukon Railway is a turn-of-the-century narrow-gauge
*ain that takes you up to the White Pass the same way the miners went to the
Klondike in '98.*

Our favorite shore excursion here is the **White Pass & Yukon Railway** ($$$), a
journey by vintage narrow-gauge train up the Dead Horse Pass, but big
spenders also have a shot at historical Skagway by motorcoach ($$)—**this is
really a waste of money unless you have trouble walking, because the park rang-
ers give free historic walking tours of town**—a bus tour to White Pass summit
and a gold rush trail camp ($$), a streetcar tour of Skagway ($$), a van tour
to White Pass Summit ($$), a helicopter lift to the Chilkoot Trail and a gla-
cier walk ($$$), an overflight of Glacier Bay ($$$), a bus and walking flora
and fauna tour ($$$), a glacier flightseeing and bald eagle float trip ($$$),
sportfishing ($$$), a mountain bike tour ($$$), a glacier hike and train tour
in Tongass Forest ($$$) and a deluxe helicopter tour ($$$). We have to con-
fess we liked Skagway better in the old days before the main street was paved
and helicopter tours roared off every few minutes from the field between
town and the cruise ship dock, but it's still a terrific port of call. Gold rush
historians fall in love with this colorful town where 100,000 would-be min-
ers paused on their way to the Klondike to be fleeced by con man Soapy
Smith and his gang. Today most of the town is included in the **Klondike Gold
Rush National Historic Park**, and park rangers show **free films and slide shows
and conduct free historic walking tours** for interested visitors. Impeccably re-
stored buildings make Skagway look today very much the way it did at the
turn of the century.

Valdez, Alaska ★

Language:	**English**	*English Spoken?:*	**Yes**
Currency:	**US$**	*US$ ok?:*	**Yes**
To town:	**Shuttle or taxi**		

Valdez is synonymous with oil for many people, first its connection as **te**-**minus of the 800-mile Trans-Alaska pipeline** and then, from 1989, as the cent of cleanup activities for the **11-million gallon *Exxon Valdez* oil spill**. Unless yo would find the pipeline tour riveting—and some people do—**you might wa** **to stay on board**. Today's Valdez, despite its beautiful setting against th Chugach mountains, is singularly lacking in charm. The town itself was r built in a different location after the devastating earthquake of 1964 d stroyed virtually every building. The major shore excursion here is a bus tr to the pipeline terminus ($$), which usually includes a look at the termin complex, oil storage tank farm, ballast treatment facility and perhaps th sight of a tanker taking on oil. Participants may not leave the bus except one viewpoint and smoking is not permitted. Other options here are a tou to Thompson Pass and the Worthington Glacier ($$), rafting in Keyston Canyon ($$) and a helicopter tour of Prince William Sound ($$$). On you own in town, you might want to wander into the Valdez Museum to se pipeline models, earthquake and mining exhibits, or take a look from th **Salmon Spawning Viewpoint** on Crooked Creek, where you can observe th fish spawning in July and August.

If you're on one of the few cruises that calls at Wrangell, the local citizenry will get themselves up in period costume and come down to meet your ship.

Wrangell, Alaska

Language:	**English**	*English Spoken?:*	**Yes**
Currency:	**US$**	*US$ ok?:*	**Yes**
To town:	**Walk**		

Costumed greeters sometimes meet the few cruise ships that call regularly at Wrangell. The area's Stikine River is one of the **fastest-moving rivers in North America**, so a day-visitor highlight here is the shore excursion on the Stikine River Jet Boat ($$$). Other options here are a botanical walking tour ($) and a city tour ($$). **Take your umbrella**, because Wrangell is often cool and misty. On your own, you can strike out for the visitor's center (beside the tall totem pole) where you can also pick up maps and brochures. Some petroglyphs—carved ancient stones—on a rocky beach, the **eagles who live in the trees nearby** and a building full of local memorabilia and junk called Our Collections are the highlights of the city tour. The town's biggest employer is a Japanese lumber mill.

Vancouver, British Columbia ★★★★★

Language:	**English**	*English Spoken?:*	**Yes**
Currency:	**US$**	*US$ ok?:*	**Yes**
To town:	**Walk from Canada Place, taxi or shuttle from Ballentyne Pier**		

The bustling home port for most Alaska cruises, Vancouver uses both the handsome, **sail-shaped Canada Place pier** downtown, built for the 1986 Expo, and the edge-of-town Ballentyne Pier, a bus or taxi ride away from downtown. Surrounded by mountains and water and set like a jewel amid the coastal mountains on a peninsula thrust into the Georgia Strait, Vancouver is **one of the most beautiful cities in the world**. The colorful bars and shops of Gastown are a short walk away from Canada Place, as are the elegant shops and European cafe ambience of Robson Street. Stanley Park is great for jogging or walking, and Vanier Park has the Maritime Museum with the Royal Canadian Mounted Police patrol ship *St. Roch*, and Vancouver Museum's planetarium, Indian galleries and historic exhibits, including a Hudson Bay Company trading post. Shore excursions offered here (if you're taking a pre- or post-cruise package) include a city tour ($$) that usually takes a look at Stanley Park, Granville Island Public Market, the Lions' Gate Bridge, colorful Gastown with its unique steam clock, Chinatown and downtowr handsome art deco buildings.

Vancouver's Canada Place cruise terminal and the city skyline.

Victoria, British Columbia ★★★★★

Language:	**English**	*English Spoken?:*	**Yes**
Currency:	**US$**	*US$ ok?:*	**Yes**
To town:	**Taxi shuttle**		

The stately Empress Hotel in Victoria is famous for an afternoon tea that is so in demand these days it goes on from 11 a.m. to 5 p.m.

The two must-do things here are the **famous afternoon teas and a stroll through beautiful Butchart Gardens**. And surprise! Your cruise ship will have a shore excursion offering both—but not on the same tour. You get a city tour and Butchart Gardens visit ($$) or a city tour and tea at a seaside hotel (not the famous Empress Hotel, $$), but not tea and Butchart Gardens. You could also visit Butchart Gardens on your own by cab (it's 13 miles from town, and be warned that tour groups often get entry priority over individual tourists) or pick up a local bus tour at the Empress Hotel just to the gardens that may be cheaper than the one sold on board the ship. If you want to do tea at the Empress on your own, reserve well ahead of time; in summer it's served at regular intervals between 11 a.m. and 5 p.m. **If you don't like gardens and don't want tea**, a third shore excursion option is a city tour and Craigdarroch Castle ($$), a 39-room mansion built by a local coal baron. But **you're gonna get that city tour** no matter what excursion you book! And hey, it's a lovely city, almost **more English than England** these days, with its cream teas, red double-decker buses, shops selling tweeds and English bone china, and Olde English Inn replica of Anne Hathaway's cottage in Stratford-upon-Avon. On your own, head first for the splendid **Royal British Columbia Museum** ($) with its reconstructions of a turn-of-the-century street and a section of George Vancouver's ship *Discovery*. The handsome Parliament Buildings and Empress Hotel are also in the same vicinity.

THE ALASKA CRUISE

CRUISES TO MEXICAN RIVIERA, PANAMA CANAL AND CENTRAL AND SOUTH AMERICA

Recife's pride and joy is the Misericordia Church in nearby Olinda, done to the ines in gilded baroque and dating from 1540.

Down Mexico Way

For some people, cruising down Mexico way means spotting whales, porpoises and sea lions off the rocky tip of Baja; for others, it may be strolling
the sometimes less-than-sanitary beaches of once-chic Acapulco; for still others, hoisting a beer at Hussong's in Ensenada or the Shrimp Bucket in Mazatlan.

The term **Mexican Riviera** was born, we think, in the late 1960s or early
1970s, when Princess Cruises' presiding genius Stan McDonald coined it, a

bit of image-making that dovetailed with the movie star and jet set mystiq
mushrooming around Acapulco and Puerto Vallarta in those days of *Night
the Iguana*, Liz-and-Dick, and all that stuff.

What can you expect from a Mexican Riviera cruise? **A lot of sunshine**, sor
low-cost souvenir shopping, a nodding acquaintance with the people and cu
ture of Mexico and an easy introduction to traveling in a foreign coun
without venturing far afield from the homelike security of your ship.

Except for Ensenada, which can be cool in the winter, you'll want to ta
lightweight cotton or linen clothing, bathing suits and sunblock, comfo
able flat shoes for walking around in port and a sweater or sweat shirt f
breezy days at sea or the superchill the air conditioning seems to take c
when sailing down Mexico way.

Five South-of-the-Border Travel Tips

1. When you're negotiating a city tour with a cab driver and ask if he speaks Englisl
   if he replies, "*Si, un poco*," don't go.

2. Remember as you lift that margarita to your lips that **ice is frozen water**.

3. Don't take the word of the silver sellers who'll greet you almost everywhere alon
   the Mexican Riviera with silver jewelry at very low and always negotiable price
   Unless it is stamped with the numerals 0.935 or the word "sterling," it's **only
   blend of silver and lead that can turn your neck green**.

4. Remind yourself that souvenir handicrafts like that four-foot-wide sombrero wit
   the mirrors and silver braid **looks better on a mariachi musician** than on you
   your next Cinco de Mayo party.

5. For **last-minute questions** and quick answers, ☎ *(800) 44-MEXICO*.

Transiting the Panama Canal

The audience arrives early for the spectacle, gathering in the morning ligh
cameras at the ready to photograph the star who, at 83, is still as graceful an
professional as ever. Eager for a front-row seat, they line the rails of the shij
some taking possession of folding deck and lounge chairs, others movin
constantly from one gallery to another to gain the best vantage point.

Just as explorers scale mountains because they're there, passengers on
Panama Canal transit admit they're fulfilling a lifelong dream when they **sai
from one great ocean to another in seven to 10 hours**, squeezing into locl
chambers hardly wider than the ship itself and navigating by stair-step lock
from sea level to 85 feet above and then back down to sea level again.

And, as audience members look up to envy those in private boxes, so d
cruise ship passengers envy those fortunate ones who have a private verand
on their own transit of the canal.

Five Trivia Items About the Panama Canal

1. The first recorded thought about a canal here may have been from Christopher
   Columbus, who made notes in 1502 about natives on the east coast of South America telling him there was a "narrow place" that led to another great sea.

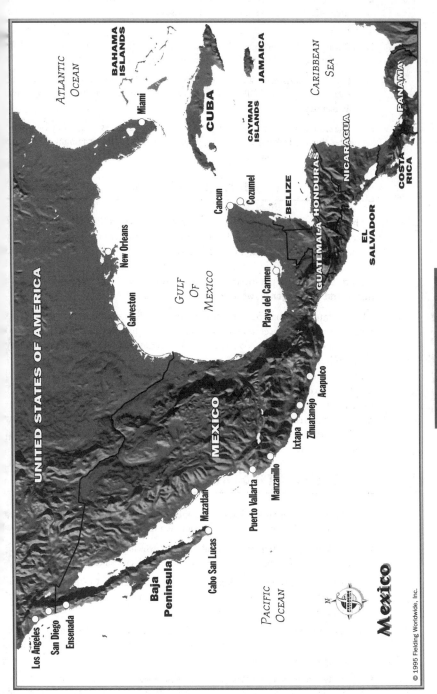

© 1995 Fielding Worldwide, Inc.

2. The French, led by Vicomte Ferdinand de Lesseps, who later built the Suez Canal, attempted an expensive and ultimately disastrous Panama Canal construction in the 1880s.

3. During the construction of the awesome Gaillard Cut, the "big ditch," more than 6000 workers died in the 10 years it took, most of them from yellow fever.

4. Poet John Keats made a boo-boo when he identified Hernando Cortez as staring "with eagle eyes" at the Pacific from a peak in Darién; actually, it was Vasco Nuñez de Balboa.

5. The cheapest transit fee paid for going through the canal was coughed up by adventurer Richard Halliburton in 1928, when he spent nine days swimming through it and paid only 36 cents.

Cruising Down to Rio

The giddy, gorgeous and gaudy **pre-Lenten Carnival in Rio is the spectacle of a lifetime**, like the Pasadena Rose Parade on amphetamines, costumed by Frederick's of Hollywood and orchestrated by the chain saw marching band from the Doo Dah Parade. Some 70,000 lavishly costumed and nearly naked singers and dancers parade through Rio de Janeiro's Sambadrome during a **three-night extravaganza** every year the weekend before Ash Wednesday.

But because Rio has been on the caution list for many travelers due to its high rate of crime directed toward tourists, a cruise ship is the safest way to travel there. That way, you don't have to take any valuables or jewelry ashore; they can stay locked up on board. When you're on a ship during Carnival, you don't have to worry about room reservations or some local hotel employee not showing up to make your bed or cook breakfast—*cariocas* in the throes of Carnival often don't go to work at all. During the collective annual madness, they drop everything for four days of partying, getting little or no sleep, dozing on the beaches in their dental floss bikinis so they can samba all night.

The Five Worst Shore Excursions in Latin America

1. The **all-day tour to São Paulo** from the port of Santos, the highlight of which, besides the city's unbelievable traffic jams, is a visit to a snake farm (page 891)

2. The **half-day city tour of Guayaquil**, Ecuador, which drives you past the same half-dozen mildewed and moldering public buildings several times (page 894)

3. The **Dole Banana Packing Plant** and train in Puerto Limon, Costa Rica, little more than a factory tour even if you do get an explanation of the sex life of a banana (page 893)

4. **La Bufadora** (the Blowhole) in Ensenada, Mexico; besides the long, bumpy bus ride and the dispiriting rows of truly tacky souvenirs, the blowhole itself sometimes spits up less than a dyspeptic baby (page 898)

5. The **two-hour shopping stop in downtown Caracas** when the guides disappear mysteriously is the high point of the all-day city tour of Caracas, Venezuela, from the port city of La Guaira.

South America

© 1995 Fielding Worldwide, Inc.

Rating the Ports of Latin America

Buenos Aires, Argentina ★★★★★

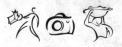

Language:	**Spanish**	*English Spoken?:*	**Yes**
Currency:	**Peso**	*US$ ok?:*	**No, use credit cards or change money**
To town:	**Taxi**		

Almost more European than South American, this lively, lovely city has a temperate climate and a sophisticated populace. We love its tango clubs, steak restaurants, the **Sunday morning flea market of San Telmo** and the great shopping on pedestrian-only Florida Street. A city tour ($$) covers the highlights, from the brightly painted buildings of the old Italian district called La Boca to the fashionable purlieus of Recoleta, including **the cemetery where Evita Peron is buried**. The Teatro Colón opera house from the turn of the century, the artists' quarter of San Telmo, the presidential palace of Casa Rosada where Juan and Evita used to wave from the balcony and the historic Plaza de Mayo are all usually included. Some ships offer an all-day or overnight flight excursion to the majestic but usually muddy brown cascades of **Iguassu Falls** ($$$), recommendable only if you've already seen Buenos Aires. Other options include a day visit to a **working ranch with a gaucho rodeo and barbecue** lunch ($$–$$$) or a nightlife **tango tour** ($$). On your own, you can hop into a taxi ($) to visit special areas, but bear in mind that most cabs are only big enough for two passengers.

Belize City, Belize ★

Language:	**English**	*English Spoken?:*	**Yes**
Currency:	**BZ$**	*US$ ok?:*	**Yes**
To town:	**Taxi (don't walk)**		

New and hot on the Western Caribbean cruise circuit is the small, proud, poor democratic nation of Belize, once known as British Honduras. With an equatorial climate, a heavy reputation for drug smuggling and a lot of petty street crime, Belize City is not anywhere you'd want to spend a lot of time. But the **diving areas to the north, the Maya ruins to the west and lush jungles to**

the south have attracted small and/or adventuresome vessels including ACCL, among others, in the winter season. We wandered all around Belize City in the daytime without any problems several years ago, and it's probably still okay so long as you take normal precautions. The allure of diving into the **longest barrier reef in the western hemisphere**, snorkeling in the clear blue waters of Laughing Bird Cay or South Water Cay off Placentia and Ambergris Cay and Goff's Cay off San Pedro, or visiting Maya ruins at Altun Ha, 35 miles north of Belize City, make it an appealing destination despite its problems.

DID YOU KNOW?

Author Evelyn Waugh once commented that if the earth had any ends, British Honduras would certainly be one of them.

Amazon River, Brazil ★ ★ ★

Language:	**Portuguese**	*English Spoken?:*	**Some**
Currency:	**Cruzeiro**	*US$ ok?:*	**Yes**
To town:	**Varies by village**		

Any nautical-minded romantic can tell you about the **Fitzcarraldo**, *built to steam along the Amazon and flown in and reconstructed on the river banks.*

The **reality of the Amazon** is not quite the traveler's fantasy of sailing through narrow jungle rivers looking at parrots and jaguars and wild orchids across the ship's rails. The truth of the matter is that you're on a mid-sized to large ship on one of the world's widest rivers, sometimes so wide you can hardly see across. The best way to see the Amazon close-up is on **small expe-**

dition ships with a fleet of Zodiac landing craft that can set out up narrow tributaries in search of more exotic surroundings. On the other hand, passengers who want to go someplace new on a favorite ship with all their creature comforts, from Broadway musical revues to blackjack dealers and snowball bingo close at hand, will still be able to wander through **exotic markets and backwater villages** without having an up-close-and-personal encounter with Mother Nature. Most Amazon itineraries **sail between Belem and Manaus**, but a few smaller vessels can make it all the way to Iquitos, Peru; beyond here, the river is not navigable for passenger ships. In Boca da Valeria barter for local crafts; swim at a sandy beach in Alter do Chão; photograph the variety of floating craft in the trading port of Santarem; take a city tour ($$) around bustling Belem at the mouth of the river.

Fortaleza, Brazil   ★ ★

Language:	**Portuguese**	*English Spoken?:*	**Yes**
Currency:	**Cruzeiro**	*US$ ok?:*	**Yes**
To town:	**Shuttle bus, taxi**		

The Centro de Turismo, a **renovated jail with crafts shops**, a folk art museum and tourist information stand, is the heart of the tourist area for this otherwise undistinguished commercial city in northeastern Brazil. Look for **hand-embroidered table linens**, handmade lace, leather goods, hammocks, and wood carvings, including images of saints. Asking prices are low and bargaining is expected. Most ships make a half-day call here, just long enough for the half-day city tour ($$), which includes a shopping stop at the center, as well as a visit to whatever museum may be open that day, probably the Museo Histórico e Antropológico do Ceará. The **strangest exhibit** here is outside the building, the wreckage of a small plane in which an area right-wing politician named Castello Branco died in 1967. You may also be shown the Coco ecological park that protects mangrove swamps on the city's outlying areas or the art nouveau Teatro José de Alencar from 1910. As in all Brazilian cities, **watch out for pickpockets** and **don't wear or carry anything valuable**; leave your jewelry on the ship. You should also avoid swimming at most of the city beaches because **the water is polluted**. The best beach is Praia do Futuro near the yacht club, where beachfront *barracas* (thatch-roofed stalls) serve fried fish and shrimp.

Recife, Brazil   ★ ★ ★

Language:	**Portuguese**	*English Spoken?:*	**Some**
Currency:	**Cruzeiro**	*US$ ok?:*	**Yes**
To town:	**Taxi**		

In Olinda, tourists have ample opportunities to purchase lace tablecloths; in fact, it's nearly impossible to avoid it unless you're very strong-willed.

Recife is a clean and attractive city with nice beach areas, a nearby historic hilltop town filled with artists and craftsmen and more modestly dressed beachgoers than Rio. Cruise ships are often greeted at the dock by *frevo* dancers with twirling umbrellas, and all in all, it's more appealing than many better-known Brazilian ports. A city tour usually includes the Pernambuco Culture Center, a **former prison turned into a crafts market** in 1975, with each cell converted into a different shop selling clay figurines, wood sculptures, leather goods, tie-dyed clothing, table linens and woven straw items, all charming and idiosyncratic. The tour also stops at Republic Square to see the pink-and-white Teatro Santa Isabel from 1850 and the Palace of the Governors from 1841, as well as the prettily **painted iron bridges** across the Capibaribe River. The most famous local sight is Olinda's **Misericordia Church in gilded baroque style**, dating from 1540. Coming and going, you'll be **besieged by sellers of lace tablecloths** and wood carvings. At Boa Viagem, the beaches are lined with vendors selling refreshing fresh coconuts. While we felt secure and comfortable in Recife, the guides cautioned us about taking photos out of an open window while the bus was stopped because **"street urchins" might try to steal the cameras**.

Rio de Janeiro, Brazil ★★★★

Language:	**Portuguese**	English Spoken?:	**Yes**
Currency:	**Cruzeiro**	US$ ok?:	**Yes**
To town:	**Taxi**		

Rio's Carnival brings out gala costumes and high spirits.

We know, we know, Rio is a **dangerous and politically incorrect city**, but for all its bad press, it is still one of the most magnificent ports in the world to sail into, and its annual **Carnival is one of the world's great spectacles**. While we've never experienced or seen street crime first-hand in Rio, we know it exists and would never disembark wearing or carrying anything valuable or walk alone anywhere in the city, day or night. Carnival parades take place for two nights, Sunday and Monday, in the week preceding Ash Wednesday. While things get underway around 8 p.m., the last (and best) samba schools usually come on after midnight, sometimes as late as dawn. The *cariocas* (citizens of Rio) arrive late, planning to stay and party all night, whereas cruise ship shuttle buses usually ferry their passengers back to the port before midnight, missing the real highlights. When you **come in a group from the cruise ship**, you are taken in private buses and escorted with a lot of security through the mobs and into the stadium, where you are supposed to sit together as a group. Actually, the *cariocas* don't pay any attention to things like reserved seats, so **you may find your seat already occupied**, in which case you take one nearby and fight off the next interloper who claims that's *his* seat. The usual shore excursions cover the gamut—a city tour ($$) with a cablecar up Sugar Loaf and/or cog train up Corcovado, a look at Ipanema and Copacabana beaches, a glance at the modern Metropolitan Cathedral and a drive through the tropical jungle of Tijuca while the guide tells riveting stories about black magic and white magic. Rio-bound ships always have **jewelry salesmen aboard** as paying passengers; they'll socialize, host cocktail parties, be generally charming and then **hit on you when you get to Rio.**

Salvador de Bahia, Brazil   ★★★★

Language:	**Portuguese**	*English Spoken?:*	**Some**
Currency:	**Cruzeiro**	*US$ ok?:*	**Yes**
To town:	**Taxi**		

We've always loved Bahia, despite the fact that the historic Pelourinho District with its splendid Baroque buildings is looking **a little tatty these days**. Our last arrival coincided with Ash Wednesday and an appalling morning-after scene of smelly, dirty streets and a few dazed revelers in costume still reeling around. To be fair, local street cleaners were out by ten a.m. with brooms, trucks, hoses and disinfectant cleaning up the mess, but not before an unfortunate impression had been made on about 900 *Crystal Harmony* passengers, most of them visiting for the first time. The city tour ($$) includes some walking through the old town and shopping (and bargaining) for handicrafts at the Mercado Modelo. A fascinating museum of candomblé saints, a local blend of traditional Catholic saints and African gods and goddesses, can be found in Pelourinho Square. The author Jorge Amado *(Doña Flor and Her Two Husbands)* lived in this area. Look for **Baianas clad in white dresses with white turbans** selling local dishes made with manioc meal and dende oil in the parks and along the beaches; sugar cane machines still cranked by hand to squeeze out the sweet juice into a glass or pitcher; street vendors who try to tie a fetish ribbon from the **shrine of Bonfim** around your wrist. You're supposed to make three wishes, then wear the ribbon until it rots and falls off your wrist to have them come true. And, of course, **you're expected to pay for the ribbon.**

Santos, Brazil   ★

Language:	**Portuguese**	*English Spoken?:*	**Some**
Currency:	**Cruzeiro**	*US$ ok?:*	**Yes**
To town:	**Shuttle bus or taxi**		

Santos, the largest port in Latin America, accesses the huge city of São Paulo. For some reason, cruise ships who call here think their passengers might enjoy **an all-day excursion to São Paulo** ($$$). Wrong! It's **the worst all-day excursion in Latin America** because once you reach the outskirts of São Paulo 45 miles from the port, you spend most of the day on a bus stalled in traffic The cathedral square is the best part of the day because you are allowed to get out of the bus for a moment and take in the local color—herbalists gathered on the steps vending medicinal oils and plants, and swarthy women in shiny dresses squatting on the sidewalk reading fortunes. Several sidewalk entertainers, all of them oddly enough performing the same trick with knives, draw small knots of people around the square. The apparent highlight of the trip is saved for last, a visit to the museum at Butantan Institute snake farm, where one could see spiders, scorpions and tarantulas and **watch snakes feeding on white mice** that scrabbled desperately against the glass cage walls trying to get away. On our next visit, we found Santos itself is not so bad—you can walk around in the central part of town without being run over. Or, if you want, you can stay on board the ship in the port and watch them load bananas.

Puerto Caldera, Costa Rica ★★

Language:	**Spanish**	English Spoken?:	**Yes**
Currency:	**Colon**	US$ ok?:	**Yes**
To town:	**Excursion bus**		

The town church in Sarchi, Costa Rica, is less famous than the boldly painted oxcarts that are sold in miniatures and full sizes, the latter as tea carts.

There's really not much in Puerto Caldera on Costa Rica's west coast except a large deepwater port used by cruise ships which dock here so passengers can **visit the capital city of San José**, about 60 miles away, much closer than Puerto Limón on Costa Rica's Caribbean coast, the other port alternative. A full-day tour to the cool mountain city ($$$) may include historic buildings like the **National Theater**, filled with gilt and red plush like the inside of a candy box; La Sábana Park; the Metropolitan Cathedral; the National Library; an art museum; plus a Costa Rican buffet lunch with strolling musicians and, time permitting, a shopping stop in the **crafts village of Moravia**, where wooden necklaces, toys, wood puzzle boxes in animal shapes, hand-painted ceramics and other items are for sale. The crafts town of Sarchi with its unique **oxcart factory** ($$) is where the elaborately decorated oxcarts crafted a century ago have become in demand as lawn art, garden furniture or even barbecue or tea carts to use indoors or out. Inlaid boxes, trays, wooden salad bowls, unique jewelry made from rare hardwoods and sculptures are also produced here. Some ships also add excursions to the **Poas Volcano National Park** north of San José ($$), either as a day trip or a pre- or post-cruise extra, as well as a full day **sailing and snorkeling trip** and beach adventure ($$$) on the island of Tortuga.

Puerto Limón, Costa Rica ★

Language:	**Spanish**	*English Spoken?:*	**Yes**
Currency:	**Colon**	*US$ ok?:*	**Yes**
To town:	**Walk in daylight only**		

Ships that call here usually offer an **all-day excursion to San José** ($$$), the cool capital city in the mountains. While San José itself is well worth a visit, the **three hours in transit** by bus in each direction could deter all but the most determined sightseer. The trip usually includes visits to the National Museum, the National Theatre, a big buffet lunch, a shopping stop, and a drive through the **Braulio Carrillo National Park** and rain forest to and from the port. Our driver glimpsed a sloth in the trees by the side of the road and pulled over to point him out. Other options include the "Goin' Bananas" narrow gauge train ride and bus tour through banana plantations ($$$). While the country of Costa Rica itself is a delightful cruise ship destination, **Puerto Limón** is muggy and humid, funky and tropical, filled with pickpockets by day, muggers by night. Don't venture into town alone at any time, but especially not after dark. **Costa Rican souvenirs** include brightly painted miniature carts, handmade wooden animal puzzles and bargain-priced bags of **freshly-roasted Costa Rican coffee beans**.

Galápagos Islands, Ecuador ★★★★★

Language:	**Spanish**	*English Spoken?:*	**Yes**
Currency:	**Sucre**	*US$ ok?*	**Yes**
To town:	**Tender from ship**		

Several years ago, the country of Ecuador made a rule that no foreign-flag cruise ships could call in the Galápagos, giving themselves more control over their **zealously protected Galápagos Islands**. Most, if not all, Galápagos cruises, therefore, are marketed by tour and expedition companies who charter part or all the space on one of the Ecuadorean-flag vessels. With all the unique wildlife and the chance for a visitor to observe it so closely, it's no wonder the islands and wildlife of the Galápagos are at the top of the list of dream destinations for many environmentally concerned travelers. **Experienced naturalists** take passengers ashore in groups of 20 or fewer after a full orientation session that lays down the rules—no smoking anywhere on the islands; no collecting of rocks, feathers, plants or anything at all; **no touching** of the wildlife; no surrounding of the wildlife; **no wandering off the trails**. You'll want **sturdy, lightweight cotton clothes**, mostly garments and footwear that can take getting wet but still perform well on an overland hike uphill and down in search of the gigantic land tortoises that gave the islands their name. Even a Caribbean wardrobe is too dressy and too hot for this equatorial heat. The memories of a Galápagos visit will last for a lifetime—swimming among the sea lions, watching courting frigate birds puff out huge red throat sacs to display, marveling over the prehistoric-horror-flick faces of marine iguanas, and far from least, seeing Darwin's finches, the birds that led to his masterpiece, *The Origin of Species.*

Guayaquil, Ecuador ★

Language:	**Spanish**	*English Spoken?:*	**Some**
Currency:	**Sucre**	*US$ ok?:*	**Yes**
To town:	**Taxi**		

The only reason we would ever go back to this hot, muggy banana port is to buy some more **Panama hats** (we lost the last ones) which are, of course, really made in Ecuador. While they're not as cheap in what locals call "the Indian market" as they used to be, they're still a pretty good buy. The city is also used as a jumping-off point to the Galápagos or the cool mountain capital city of Quito, which sparkles in the thin air at 9350 feet above sea level.

But **Guayaquil swelters**, whether during the rainy season, January through April, or the dry season the rest of the year. There is **a totally forgettable city tour** ($$) that drives past most parks, buildings and monuments, including a 1970s Sports Complex the Ecuadorian taxpayers call "the white elephant of Guayaquil." Most are nondescript, pseudo-modern structures from the 1960s and 1970s. A few graceful old buildings remain, including the gray and white Victorian City Hall, the tower-like Public Clock and the artists' quarter called Barrio Las Peñas. Watch out for pickpockets in the latter, however. About the only memorable thing about Guayaquil (except the Panama hats) are the land iguanas who lurk in the trees of the Parque Bolivar and are coaxed down by local children, who feed them mangos, potato chips and candy. A small Museo Municipal displays, among its treasures, five shrunken heads, and the Museo de Arqueologia del Banco Central shows gold and ceremonial masks. If you want to eat out, you'll find good fresh stone crab and grilled fish in local restaurants.

Port Stanley, Falkland Islands ★★★

Language:	**English**	*English Spoken?:*	**Yes**
Currency:	**Fl Pound**	*US$ ok?:*	**Yes**
To town:	**Walk or shuttle bus**		

Dolphins lead expeditioners into West Point Island in the Falklands.

With so much **cruise traffic going to the Antarctic** these days, Port Stanley has become a busy little port of call. This British self-governing colony has had its title disputed since 1760, first by Spain and then Argentina. In 1982, a 75-day war between the Argentines and British is said to have killed 225

British troops and 1200 Argentines; the entire population of the Falklands is little more than 5000. Sheep raising is the main livelihood here, and **Falklanders call mutton "365" because it's eaten every day of the year**. On your own, walk around the small, simple town, where one of the local "kelpers" (because the people that don't raise sheep harvest kelp commercially; some do both) will be happy if you stand him to a drink at the **Globe Hotel**, the local men's pub, or the **Upland Goose**, where women are also permitted to drink. Expedition ships have their own excursions here, which are usually always included in the fare. You may go to see the **tiny Magellenic penguins on Carcass Island** or the extremely rare Peal's dolphins near West Point Island. Carcass Island is beautiful in the southern hemisphere summer, with bright yellow gorse and rich green grass, wind-twisted evergreens and faded wooden buildings. Magellenic penguins wander through, along with kelp geese and black-browed albatross, and one tree is thick with nesting black-crowned night herons, the only birds we ever have photographed close-up and in focus because they just sit there like lumps. But **tromping through marshy, waist-high tussock grass and penguin guano** while trying to avoid stepping on one of those little bastards or its eggs isn't easy; you might want to hang around the Upland Goose instead.

Devil's Island, French Guiana ★★

Language:	**French**	English Spoken?:	**Yes**
Currency:	**Franc**	US$ ok?:	**Yes**
To town:	**Tender from ship**		

Remember the 1973 film *Papillon,* starring Steve McQueen and Dustin Hoffman? That was about Devil's Island, a **notorious 19th century French penal colony** where prisoners were kept in leg irons, sent naked into the jungles to work every day and when executed, had their heads severed and put on display, their bodies thrown to the sharks. Its most famous prisoner was French Army officer Alfred Dreyfus, about whom Émile Zola wrote his famous newspaper article "J'accuse." Well, Devil's Island, along with two nearby islands called Île Royale and St. Joseph, gruesome and esoteric as they are, are visited by a number of cruise ships sailing to the Amazon or east coast of South America. Passengers are taken ashore by tender and usually walk around the hot, humid island on their own, ending up atop a hill at a small hotel where cold drinks are a welcome option. **T-shirts and postcards** are the most common souvenir purchases in the hotel's gift shop, although some books about the prison are also on sale. Ironically, the now-deserted island is a vacation destination for residents of mainland French Guiana. Tangles of vines, mango trees, flowering hibiscus and coconut palms grow freely, and the peace and quiet can almost—but not quite—silence the ghosts.

Acapulco, Mexico   ★ ★ ★

Language:	**Spanish**	*English Spoken?:*	**Yes**
Currency:	**Peso**	*US$ ok?:*	**Yes**
To town:	**Taxi, longish walk**		

Sailing into Acapulco Bay at dawn before the air is smudged with pollution or sailing out after dark with a curve of lights twinkling against the shoreline is the stuff of dreams. But the last time we were there, the fabled bay, beaches and sidewalks were disappointingly dirty. We'd advise swimming only in the ship's pool, not at the beach. Ships sail into the famous horseshoe-shaped bay of one of the world's prettiest ports, and most stay a day and an evening to allow passengers time to enjoy the city's busy nightlife as well its daytime attractions. **Shore excursions** offered here usually include a half-day city tour ($$) by air-conditioned motorcoach that makes a stop to watch the cliff-divers of La Quebrada and a shopping call at the **Acapulco Princess Hotel**. Another option is an all-day tour to the silver city of Taxco ($$$). Passengers who want to explore on their own can take a taxi downtown from the pier for about $5 or out to the Acapulco Princess (away from the most polluted beach areas) for about $15 each way. The hotel welcomes day visitors. (But the posh **Las Brisas Hotel** will not admit daytrippers.) In Acapulco, there are morning beaches, afternoon beaches, beaches for sunset-watching, each lined with **thatch-roofed palapas** selling cold beer, fresh coconuts and seafood. On your own, you can go shopping along the Costera or bargaining with the crafts vendors in the market near the main square. A good place to pick up **inexpensive souvenirs** easily is in the air-conditioned Sanborn's department store crafts section.

Cabo San Lucas, Mexico   ★ ★ ★

Language:	**Spanish**	*English Spoken?:*	**Yes**
Currency:	**Peso**	*US$ ok?:*	**Yes**
To town:	**Walk, taxi**		

Los Arcos in Cabo San Lucas, where the Sea of Cortez meets the Pacific.

Cabo San Lucas and nearby San José del Cabo make up the booming resort area called **Los Cabos**, which has some **3500 hotel rooms and seven new golf courses**. In Cabo, most ships make **a half-day morning call**, anchoring in the bay and tendering passengers ashore. Under certain tidal conditions, the captain may opt to cruise by rather than anchor. The most popular shore excursion here is the **glass bottom boat ride** ($$) to Los Arcos, the dramatic rock arches where the Pacific meets the Sea of Cortez, which offers a view of the undersea world as well as of pelicans and sea lions en route. The excursion can be booked aboard ship, but it's also possible to pick up a boat in port at a lower price (but without the insurance the ship's tour operator carries). Other options include a **submarine ride** for fish watching ($$) and a drive along the coast to see posh desert hotels and have a margarita or two ($$). On your own, a taxi ride into town costs about $3 a person, but it's only a ten-minute walk. There are **open-air crafts markets** right at the pier where your tender comes in, as well as several attractive new market areas in town. Food is very inexpensive in some of the pretty little cafes, and the sanitation level has always been high in this part of Mexico. While the area is famous for its **golf courses and deep-sea fishing**, daytrippers on a half-day cruise call don't have enough time to participate in these activities. You'll need to come back and stay longer next time.

Ensenada, Mexico ★ ★

Language:	**Spanish**	*English Spoken?:*	**Yes**
Currency:	**Peso**	*US$ ok?:*	**Yes**
To town:	**Shuttle van, long walk**		

Hand-painted clay animals for sale in Ensenada.

If you take a mini-cruise out of Los Angeles to Baja California, Ensenada will be your primary port of call. Most people are content to wander the streets of the town and perhaps peek into the **sometimes-jumping Hussong's Cantina**, but organized shore excursions are also available here—a bumpy bus ride to La Bufadora (The Blowhole), which we don't recommend ($$); a **wine-tasting expedition to the Califia Valley**, which is ok ($$); a scenic coast tour ($$); horseback riding or golf ($$$). A van ride into town costs $3. Only vans are waiting at the pier to shuttle people into town, but taxis can bring you back to the port for the same $3 (or sometimes $2 if you negotiate and they're not busy). If you want to walk in, you'll be perfectly safe; the way is not long nor difficult, but it's also not very scenic. The fishing and shrimping town has really worked hard during the dozen or so years it's been a primary port of call to clean up its image and create attractions for its cruise visitors. One caveat: The weather is cooler than mainland Mexico temperatures in winter and early spring; bring a sweater. Shoppers will find everything from well-made **locally woven baskets and hand-painted pottery** to tacky Tijuana-type giant spangled sombreros and serapes. Take a moment to look in the convention center, a restored casino from the 1930s once managed by boxer Jack Dempsey.

Ixtapa, Mexico   ★ ★ ★

Language:	**Spanish**	*English Spoken?:*	**Yes**
Currency:	**Peso**	*US$ ok?:*	**Yes**
To town:	**Shuttle taxi or tour bus**		

Ixtapa is strictly a secondary port of call for passengers whose **ship stops Zihuatanejo**, but many travelers want to see for themselves this tourist des nation that aims to be the west coast equivalent of Cancun. A van excurs over to the resort development is offered from most ships (\$\$) and usua includes **a shopping mall stop** and a beach hotel pause with a cold beer margarita (the ice is safe). Passengers may also take a taxi over from Zihu tanejo for around \$7 one way if they want to create their own agenda. A g **tour** (\$\$\$) is also usually sold on board The problem with the shore exc sion from Zihuatanejo is that it may afford only the most rudimentary glan at a resort hotel you may be considering for a future vacation. If you kno you want to come back for a longer stay, consider negotiating with one the very amiable cabbies for a **taxi tour to Ixtapa** (\$\$) and have the driver st and wait wherever you want to take a closer look. The resort hotels are lin up along a broad two-mile white sand beach; across the street are boutiqu and crafts shops, restaurants and discos. Golf on an 18-hole Robert Tre Jones course, tennis, deep-sea fishing, parasailing, horseback riding alor the beach, scuba and snorkeling are all readily available for the resort visit who stays longer than a cruise daytripper.

Manzanillo, Mexico ★ ★

Language:	**Spanish**	*English Spoken?:*	**Yes**
Currency:	**Peso**	*US\$ ok?:*	**Yes**
To town:	**Taxi**		

The opulent resort of **Las Hadas, a Moorish fantasy** of white arches and ten cabanas built by a Bolivian tin millionaire and the location for the Dudle Moore/Bo Derek film *10*, is the main claim to fame for Manzanillo today although for the Spanish in the 16th century, it was the jumping-off poin for the expedition that led to Spain's conquest of the Philippines and to th discovery of Baja California. Very **few cruise ships call** here at present, al though several years ago it was on the regular circuit. Half-day city tour from the ship (\$\$) usually include a visit to Las Hadas, which welcomes day visitors, or one of the area's other not-quite-so-luxe resorts, plus the ubiqui tous shopping stop. But otherwise, there's little to see and do here short o going **deep-sea fishing** (\$\$\$), swimming, snorkeling or surfing. Between Manzanillo and Puerto Vallarta lies a stretch of still largely undeveloped beach area called the Gold Coast, including **Careyes**, which is beginning to get touristic attention for its **eight-mile white sand beach. Club Med's Playa Blanca** is also on this part of the coast.

Mazatlán, Mexico ★★★

Language:	**Spanish**	*English Spoken?:*	**Yes**
Currency:	**Peso**	*US$ ok?:*	**Yes**
To town:	**Taxi, shuttle bus**		

Bustling Mazatlán is the biggest city on Mexico's west coast and a **major shrimping port**. Cruise ship passengers here can opt for **game-fishing excursions for sailfish and marlin** ($$$) as well as half-day or full-day **excursions to colonial towns and handicraft villages** in the Sierra Madre like Concordia and Copola ($$-$$$) with a tasty local lunch at a restaurant in the countryside; a city tour ($$) that covers the main square, historic district, beach areas, Malecón (beach wall) divers and a shopping stop; or a beach day with lunch ($$). For passengers who prefer to strike out on their own, the fairly sedate **Shrimp Bucket** and the rowdier **Señor Frog's** are popular spots for lunch. The *Zona Dorade* (Golden Zone) is the main tourist area, with good crafts shopping as well as some of the best hotels and beaches. In the center of the city, the vast covered produce market is fascinating, and there are more shoe and boot dealers per block than anywhere else in the world. The culture and history here are fascinating as well, from the recently restored Angela Peralta Theatre, the town's **candy box of an opera house**, to a pretty Mexican Gothic-style cathedral. Shoppers will find lots of treasures in Mazatlán's craft areas, malls and boutiques, from gauzy, inexpensive clothing so practical in the area's hot climate to handicrafts painted every color of the rainbow.

One of Mazatlan's cliff divers takes off for a rapt audience.

Puerto Vallarta, Mexico   ★ ★ ★

Language:	**Spanish**	*English Spoken?:*	**Yes**
Currency:	**Peso**	*US$ ok?:*	**Yes**
To town:	**Shuttle van, long walk**		

An enterprising hat vendor has lined up his merchandise in Puerto Vallarta a a scenic spot where the tour buses stop.

Although you're perfectly safe walking into town, it is a long way and usually hot. If you decide to do it, be aware that you cannot walk along the beach from the pier all the way into town because of a stream that crosses a one point. A lot of cruise passengers are drawn by the **cobblestone streets and chic boutiques** of Puerto Vallarta and the new hotel and marina development across the bay, Marina Vallarta. Half-day city tours ($$) usually include photo stops at Mismaloya Beach to see the crumbling remains of the **film set for "Night of the Iguana"** and the area called Gringo Gulch, where Elizabeth Taylor and Richard Burton had their famous adjoining villas. The last tour we took there also included two very long shopping stops, which absorbed most of the time allotted for the tour. Game fishing ($$$), horseback riding on the beach ($$) or a sail along Banderas Bay to a swimming beach ($$). with drinks and snacks and the inevitable shopping stop are also possible. The new **Hard Rock Cafe** on the seafront Malecón has eclipsed Carlos O'Brien's in tourist popularity. City regulations now require that all water and ice in restaurants be purified, so you can enjoy that margarita with impunity. Attractive shopping options include artist Sergio Bustamente's two galleries on the Malecón, **Mar de Plata silver shops** and a row of cowboy-boot shops down near the old city market.

INSIDER TIP

When you're walking on the beach or in the tourist areas and are not interested in buying anything from a street or beach vendor, keep moving, say "no" politely when approached, but don't make eye contact or stop to look at the merchandise or the vendor will think you're interested.

Zihuatanejo, Mexico ★★★★

Language:	**Spanish**	*English Spoken?:*	**Yes**
Currency:	**Peso**	*US$ ok?:*	**Yes**
To town:	**Tender to town pier**		

Playa La Ropa, probably the best beach in Zihuatanejo, where cruise ship day visitors are welcomed at chic little Villa del Sol.

For an Ixtapa/Zihuatanejo call, ships anchor in the pretty bay off the fishing town of Zihuatanejo and tender passengers to a pier near midtown. On our most recent visit we noticed the vendors that used to throng the pier selling souvenirs are gone, perhaps into the sidewalk crafts stalls that dot the streets. The loveliest beach here is Playa La Ropa, where the luxurious little **Villa del Sol** (a member of the prestigious French Relais & Chateaux group) offers a **beach day with lunch for cruise-ship visitors**. It's a very civilized alternative to taking the bus tour to Ixtapa, we think. The minimum charge is $30 a person, from which food and beverage charges are subtracted. A fresh grilled seafood lunch, a thatch-roofed outdoor bar, changing rooms and showers and the use of beach loungers are all included in the fee. A taxi ride from the pier costs around $5 each way. Zihuatanejo is a **kick-back-and-enjoy** sort of town, unpretentious and moderately priced compared to its big-sort neighbor Ixtapa.

Panama Canal

Language:	**Spanish**	English Spoken?:	**Yes**
Currency:	**Balboa**	US$ ok?:	**Yes**
To town:	**You don't go**		

The longest-running show on earth—a full transit of the Panama Canal.

In recent years few if any cruise ships call at either end of the canal but simply proceed to move through it, which takes about eight hours. It's th **greatest engineering show on earth**, and most passengers stay on deck for th entire transit so as not to miss a moment. The ship squeezes into lock chambers hardly wider than its beam and navigates by stairstep locks from sea leve up to 85 feet and back to sea level. The canal cuts **50 miles across a narrow isthmus** between the Atlantic and Pacific oceans, passing through Gatur Locks, the man-made Gatun Lake, steep Gaillard Cut excavated through eight miles of rock and shale, Pedro Miguel Locks and Miraflores Locks. The drama of the transit is explained step by step by an onboard lecturer, as electric towing locomotives called mules pull ships into each lock chamber. A the chamber fills with water that pours in at three million gallons a minute the ship rises to the level of the next chamber, the gates open, the mules move forward, and the whole process is repeated all over again. The most **mystifying moment** occurs through a quirk of geography in the S-shaped isthmus. Passengers sailing from the Atlantic to the Pacific are sailing southeast, while ships bound from the Pacific to the Atlantic travel northwest.

San Blas Islands, Panama   ★★★★

Language:	**Cuna**	*English Spoken?:*	**Some**
Currency:	**Balboa**	*US$ ok?:*	**Yes**
To town:	**Tender, local boats**		

*These women of the San Blas Islands are very photogenic—and they know it.
You pay per shutter click.*

The most **colorful and photogenic** people in the Caribbean, the Cuna Indians of Panama, inhabit some 365 islands, most of them tiny flat cays with a few coconut palms and thatch-roofed dwellings. An autonomous, matriarchal society, the Cuna are pretty much left alone by the rest of Panama. The women wear elaborately appliqued blouses called *molas* with **gold necklaces, anklets, beaded bracelets, earrings, even nose rings**. With their vivid colors and short shiny black hair cropped into a cap on their heads, they are instant **prize-winning photographs**. And they know it. You don't snap a picture for free, but most subjects will pose for you at a fixed price per shutter click (50 cents last time we were there). They can count faster than you can shoot, so you won't get any free snaps. Subjects with props, such as the ubiquitous **child with the parakeet on her head**, get double. A tender from the ship is the only way you get ashore, and what you find is a combination of shopping and photo opportunities, a lecture about Cuna traditions and lifestyles, which distinctly set them apart from the rest of Panama, and sometimes a cultural performance. But the photos and the shopping are the real attractions for most daytrippers. The Cuna hang *molas* for sale, along with *mola* T-shirts, purses and pillowcases, on clotheslines throughout the village. Best buys are the most finely stitched *molas*, those with political or commerc‹ themes, or **those depicting your own cruise ship**.

Montevideo, Uruguay   ★ ★ ★ ★

Language:	**Spanish**	*English Spoken?:*	**Some**
Currency:	**Peso**	*US$ ok?:*	**No**
To town:	**Walk, taxi**		

An excursion to an estancia (ranch) outside Montevideo lets you watch roundup, then feast on the local barbecue.

The port is only a few blocks away from the heart of the city, and there a‹ some attractive sidewalk cafes in the area. The central part of the city alwa› reminds us of a Middle European city in the 1930s—**clean, faintly shabby ar filled with grandiose statuary**. The country's greatest hero, José Gervasio A‹ tigas, is depicted in the Independence Square as a heroic 30-ton equestri‹ statue standing atop his own mausoleum. Equally heroic statues of José Ma‹ tí, Suarez and Argentina's General San Martín are also around town. Mo‹ appealing are *The Struggle*, *Covered Wagon* and *The Stagecoach* by José Be‹ loni, depicting the country's founding and settling in images similar to tl‹ American west. All are in local parks beside reflecting pools. **You'll see ther all** and more on the city tour ($$), which the first-time visitor should prob ably make, although recently we enjoyed an all-day *estancia* (ranch) vis‹ with barbecue lunch ($$$). You could also take an excursion to the beach r‹ sort of Punta del Este ($$), and sometimes a **gaucho riding demonstration an barbecue** is offered at a nearby colonial ranch ($$$). Shopping for local‹ made **leather products** is quite good; handknit sweaters and furs are also so‹ at modest prices. Semi-precious stones, copper and silver are good buys her‹

you strike out on your own, bear in mind that most local taxi drivers **speak** **le or no English**.

Punte del Este, Uruguay

Language:	**Spanish**	*English Spoken?:*	**Some**
Currency:	**Peso**	*US$ ok?:*	**No**
To town:	**Walk from dock, tender from ship**		

The streets of Punta del Este, one of the most **fashionable seaside resorts** in outh America, are thronged with Argentinians during the southern hemi- here's high season from Christmas through March. The peninsula is lined th **white or golden sand beaches** where watersports from skiing to windsurf- g and surfing are available. Beaches on the eastern side of the peninsula are chnically ocean beaches, while those on the west are river beaches. For imming and watersports, however, there's very little difference between em. A few small ships call here, and the resort is also a full-day shore excur- on from Montevideo ($$$). Local options include a two-hour boat trip to la de los Lobos reserve ($$) to watch some 300,000 **southern fur seals** frol- in water or sun themselves on rocks; passengers are not permitted to go hore. Also available are the usual resort diversions—golf, tennis, deep-sea shing, yachting and horseback riding ($–$$$). **Two casinos** are open during ie season, and the town is jam-packed with good restaurants and chic bou- ques. Among the shopping temptations are shops selling **elegant leather** lothing like Zinca's Leather in the Galleria Shopping Center and a shop car- ying the name and labels of Calvin Klein.

NEW ENGLAND, CANADA AND EAST COAST CRUISES

A lot of ships cruise one of our favorite parts of the world—**we call it Lobster Land**, that wonderfully sinuous coast that winds its way from Boston up to the northern tip of Nova Scotia, where we can feast on those delectable crustaceans at an "early-bird lobster dinner." If you can eat before 5:30 or so, you can buy a whole fresh steamed lobster with all the trimmings for $10 or so. That way, if you're on second seating on the ship, you can think of it as a little appetizer before dinner.

Autumn is the favorite season for the Canada and New England cruises, sometimes called "the Northeast Passage", although many are scheduled in summer as well. Major embarkation or disembarkation points are usually New York, Montreal, Boston or Halifax, but the cheerful little *Canadian Empress* (page 723) sails the St. Lawrence River from Kingston, Ontario, and American Canadian Caribbean Line's exploration vessels cruise the Erie Canal and Saguenay River from Warren, Rhode Island.

The region has a broad appeal, especially during fall foliage time, but people generally like the scenery, history, local seafood as well as the autumn splendor. Add to that the ease of travel, the **value for the dollar** and the strong sense of security compared to cruises in many more distant port areas.

Even **first-time cruisers are comfortable** with the English language and dollar currency of Eastern Canada while getting a taste of a foreign experience in French-accented Quebec.

And the quieter, more culturally oriented sailings suit a lot of younger as well as older travelers.

Many Americans are charmed and delighted with the longer east coast cruises some lines—notably Clipper, Seabourn, Silversea and ACCL—offer into Colonial America and the inland waterways. You can study the battlefields of the Civil War, the antebellum south, the ecology and history of the Chesapeake Bay and the St. Lawrence Seaway and Thousand Islands and learn a lot of things you never knew about your own country.

Three American/Canadian Cruise Newcomers

1. Holland America's new *Veendam* joins the Westerdam to offer cruises of the N England Coast en route to Nova Scotia, Prince Edward Island, Quebec City a Montreal.

2. Budget-minded cruisers might want to book Dolphin's new *IslandBreeze*, former *Festivale*, or Regal Cruises' vintage *Regal Empress* on low-priced five-(sailings roundtrip from New York to Canada and New England.

3. The new *Seabourn Legend*, formerly the *Royal Viking Queen* and *Queen Odyss* has finally joined her sister ships *Seabourn Pride* and *Seabourn Spirit*, and sails Canada and New England in the fall

In Halifax, Nova Scotia, they still fire the noon gun every day and do a tatt with fife and drum corps up at the Citadel.

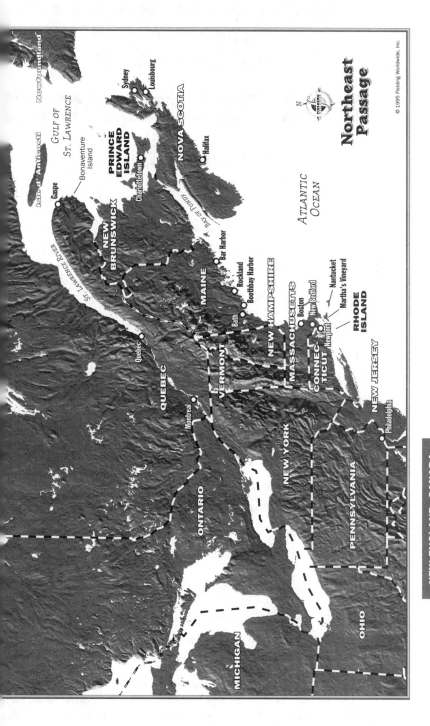

© 1995 Fielding Worldwide, Inc.

Northeast Passage

Rating the Ports of Canada and Eastern U.S.

Halifax, Nova Scotia ★★★

Language:	**English**	*English Spoken?:*	**Yes**
Currency:	**C$**	*US$ ok?:*	**No**
To town:	**Taxi or medium walk**		

Halifax claims the **second largest natural harbor in the world**, and has a lo history of shipbuilding and sailing, as Halifax's **Maritime Museum of the Atla tic** attests, with its displays of figureheads, scale models of vessels and **the tanic exhibit** (the Titanic went down off Halifax). A half-day shore excursi here ($) covers the Citadel National Historic Site; Nova Scotia Museu with flora and fauna displays including an unusual mushroom exhibit; Paul's Anglican Church from 1749, the first Protestant church in Cana Dalhousie University and The Historic Properties, a group of restored 19 century buildings including Privateer's Warehouse and the Old Red Store full-day scenic tour ($$$) to the picturesque **fishing village of Peggy's Cov with a lobster lunch** included, is another good idea. On your own, you cou walk around town or take a harbor tour. Some **diving around 50 wrecks alo the coast** is offered by Aqua Dive Shop and Northern Shore Diving Cent Early July's Nova Scotia Tattoo is the biggest local extravaganza. Listen the famous noon gun when you're strolling around town.

Sydney, Nova Scotia ★★★★

Language:	**English**	*English Spoken?:*	**Yes**
Currency:	**C$**	*US$ ok?:*	**No**
To town:	**Excursion bus to Louisbourg**		

Excursions set out from here to **Alexander Graham Bell's home**, laborator grave and a splendid museum to him in Baddeck, a little seaside village, an you'll probably be offered a chance for an all-day tour covering some of th Cabot Trail and **Cape Breton Highlands National Park**—but steel yourself an refuse both of those in favor of **Fortress Louisbourg, an extraordinary recre ation** by Canada Parks of a history that is detailed, honest and sometim

re gritty than respectful. The year is 1744, and each inhabitant of the re-
~red French fortress represents a particular individual who was there that
~r. You meet housemaids and officers' wives, sloppily-dressed soldiers and
ir jailers, alehouse keepers and fishermen. You can **drop by a tavern for a**
~ter tankard of ale, a hunk of cheese and a wedge of brown bread, or sit in the
~taurant and eat a hot meal typical of the period with the utensils of the
~e. One officer's bedroom has a canopy bed (it looks short, but so were
~ French soldiers in the 18th century), a card table covered with green felt
~ze, a nail-studded leather trunk, a bear rug on the floor by the bed, and a
~nch porcelain wash basin and pine armoire. Some July and August eve-
~gs, candlelight tours, which are particularly evocative, are scheduled. Syd-
~y's own history is tied up with coal mining, and there are some attractions,
~tably the **Miner's Museum and the colonial miner's village**, that interpret that
~e that is now past. Bird Islands a mile offshore provide nesting areas for
~usands of seabirds and land species from **the Atlantic puffin to the bald ea-**
~.

*~e entrance to Fortress Louisbourg takes you back into 1744 at this brilliant
~creation by Parks Canada.*

Charlottetown, Prince Edward Island ★ ★ ★

Language:	**English**	*English Spoken?:*	**Yes**
Currency:	**C$**	*US$ ok?:*	**No**
To town:	**Walk, taxi**		

Everything seems to be in miniature on charming little Prince Edward Is-
~nd, famous as the home of fiction's beloved **Anne-of-Green-Gables**, and pop-
~larly called PEI. Shopping for handicrafts and antiques, taking historical

walking tours that visit refurbished 19th century sandstone houses, incl
ing Fanningbank (1834), the Lieutenant Governor's residence on a
above the sea, and several **scenic island drives, are some of the half- or full-
shore excursion options**. Blue Heron Drive makes a circle tour past the w
sandy north shore beaches through fishing villages such as North Rus
Harbor, covering the Anne of Green Gables country. Lady Slipper Drive
lows the western end of the island in a figure-eight loop, passes Malpe
Bay, famous for its tiny, flavorful oysters, and the Acadian museum
homes around Summerside. The Kings Byway drive covers the eastern
of the island, where Irish moss seaweed is harvested. The **House of Green
bles** is in Cavendish town, and Prince Edward Island National Park has so
fine beaches. There's also a shipbuilding museum near Port Hill
Woodleigh, a collection of scale model replicas of famous British landma
But what we usually go searching for is a lobster, either at one of the isla
all-you-can-eat fresh lobster suppers in a community or church hall or, if
ship sails before dinnertime, in a commercial lobster restaurant on an e
bird special.

Montreal, Quebec ★ ★ ★ ★ ★

Language:	**French**	*English Spoken?:*	**Yes**
Currency:	**C$**	*US$ ok?:*	**No**
To town:	**Walk**		

   Cruise ships, depending on their size, dock alongside or very near Mont
al's old town, making it a snap to go exploring on your own at any ti
Many summer and fall season cruises begin or end in Montreal, connect
the city with New York, Boston or other northeastern ports. Shore exc
sions here include an all-day drive into the lovely **Laurentian Mountains**
spectacular in autumn when the first frost turns leaves to glowing jewel c
ors, taking you to areas famous as ski resorts in winter, Ste-Agathe, Val-D
id, St-Saveur, Ste-Adéle and St-Jovite near Mont Tremblant. A fast freev
speeds visitors up the mountain. A **city highlights half-day tour** ($$) is usu
offered, and may include views from atop Mont Royal Park or the cable
ride to the top of Olympic Park. Old Montreal and its Place Royale and Pl
de l'Armes is always on the agenda, along with the Sulpician Semina
boasting the **oldest public clock (1700) in the Western Hemisphere**. On yc
own, explore Montreal by the horse-drawn carriages called *caleches* in Vie
Montreal (the old town) or check out the the restaurants, shops and sights
walking distance. The **Montreal Jazz Festival** in late June and early July tu
the whole city into a concert hall.

Quebec, Quebec ★★★★★

Language:	**English**	*English Spoken?:*	**Yes**
Currency:	**C$**	*US$ ok?:*	**No**
To town:	**Walk up the stairs**		

We call it Quebec City, but don't be surprised when Canadians refer to it as Quebec. Even more European than Montreal, Quebec welcomes many cruise-ship visitors right at **the foot of its old town and the famous Chateau Frontenac Hotel, built in 1892**. A half-day tour here ($$) covers the Plains of Abraham, where British General Wolfe defeated the French commander, the Marquis de Montcalm, in a 20-minute battle; Petit Champlain, the oldest (and perhaps narrowest) street in North America, where the historic Louis Jolliet House (1683) is located; Dufferin Terrace, the scenic boardwalk with its fine views of the St. Lawrence River; the Citadel, constructed in 1820 for the Duke Wellington; the view from Boulevard Saint Cyrille Est; and the Place des Armes, once a military parade ground. A full-day excursion ($$$) includes all the above, plus a drive up to the shrine of **Ste-Anne-de-Beaupré** (also a famous ski area) and a stop at Montmorency Falls. The Beaupré area has been famous since 1658, when Pilgrims arrived to use the water to which they attributed "miraculous cures." On your own, walk around the old town, **window-shop the restaurants** where posted menus provide the means to peruse the choices and prices; visit the Musée de Quebec in Battlefields Park and the Musée de la Civilisation on Dalhousie.

Savannah, Georgia ★★★★★

Language:	**English**	*English Spoken?:*	**Yes**
Currency:	**US$**	*US$ ok?:*	**Yes**
To town:	**Walk, tender**		

Old Savannah is a **romance novel of a city**, its town squares bursting with vivid pink azaleas and camellias in early spring, and its trees draped with lacy Spanish moss like mantillas. This is especially true in the city's historic downtown area, a place where you expect to see gallant swashbucklers, sad-eyed heroes and swooning ladies in hoopskirts. **Hand me my smellin' salts, Aunt Pittypat**. If you're aboard a small ship, you've sailed up the Savannah River and into the old Factors Walk area, where cobbled streets are paved in ballast stones and the old Cotton Exchange flourished in the days when this port shipped its cotton to Europe. Explore on your own to find **the very bench** where **Forrest Gump sat** to tell his life's story in the film of the same name (one of the guides driving the local horse-drawn carriages will be glad to point out) or take the hottest new tour based on the best-selling book about Savannah, *Midnight in the Garden of Good and Evil.* Slip into the **Planter's Tavern** (in the lower level of The Olde Pink House on Abercorn), which looks like something out of a Gothic novel, or check out the City Market, which was replaced by a parking garage in the 1950s, but that was torn down a few years ago and the market rebuilt with a clutch of trendy cafes and restaurants.

Bar Harbor, Maine ★★★

Language:	**English**	English Spoken?:	**Yes**
Currency:	**US$**	US$ ok?:	**Yes**
To town:	**Walk or tender**		

Bar Harbor, Maine, a great place to get an early bird lobster dinner.

From Bar Harbor you can take shore excursions to nearby **Acadia National Park**. All of them take you to the top of Cadillac Mountain for the view, and some include a pause for **afternoon tea** in the old-fashioned, flower-filled gardens of Jordan Pond Lodge. John D. Rockefeller, who didn't like automobiles, commissioned 50 miles of gravel carriage roads in the park that are still used today by joggers, hikers and bicyclists. We found several good **early-bird lobster restaurants** in Bar Harbor, but think the **Cook House Pound** is best, where they sell it by the pound to take out, along with wonderful lobster rolls, fried clams and crab rolls; you don't have to take them any farther than the picnic tables outside. Many of the grandiose "cottages" that once filled fashionable Bar Harbor were destroyed in a five-day fire in 1947, and the

:nter of town is not so grand these days, filled as it is with ye olde kitschy-
ɔo and jammed with day-trippers who didn't look in the mirror after they
ɔnned those plaid Bermuda shorts and tank tops.

Nantucket, Massachusetts ★ ★ ★ ★ ★

Language:	**English**	*English Spoken?:*	**Yes**
Currency:	**US$**	*US$ ok?:*	**Yes**
To town:	**Tender**		

The island of Nantucket, even when thronged with summer day visitors, provides some serene getaways; here, the village of Siaconset, called "Sconset."

The thing we like most about Nantucket is very islandness, that **quirky cantankerousness** that dictates its idiosyncracies. Here the world is divided into two camps, "on island," which is Nantucket, and "off island," which is everywhere else in the world. If the shore excursions list offers a **walking tour with Roger Young** ($), sign up, because he's full of great Nantucket tales. You can **rent a bicycle** ($) and pedal around the mostly flat island past cranberry bogs to Sankaty Light and Sconset (really Siasconset but the locals don't say it that way), or you can while away a morning in the splendid Whaling Museum or splurge on an elegant **Nantucket Lightship basket purse** ($350 up) that is supposed to last a lifetime. (We splurged instead on **chocolate almond buttercreams in a hand-painted tin** in Sweet Inspirations at India Street.) The town's streets fill up on summer days with day visitors who arrive by ferry from Hyannis, as well as people from the occasional visiting cruise ship. The winter population of 7500 swells to over 50,000 in high season, but it's easy enough to hike, walk, bike or drive away from them, since the Nantucket

Conservation Foundation owns a lot of empty space being preserved arour the island.

Newport, Rhode Island   ★★★★

Language:	**English**	*English Spoken?:*	**Yes**
Currency:	**US$**	*US$ ok?:*	**Yes**
To town:	**Tender, then short walk or shuttle**		

Aficionados all know the famed **Newport Jazz Festival** which happens ever summer, and that some of America's most famous sailboat races take place the waters between Block Island and Narragansett Bay, but this pretty litt city is also sometimes included on cruise itineraries. This is where Jack an Jackie Kennedy got married, where **Claus von Bulow's trial** took place, an where various Vanderbilts, Astors and Belmonts built 70-room "cottages" dizzying excess, some of which are restored, converted to museums an open to the public. Shore excursions will usually offer a tour of one or two the **millionaire's cottages** lined up on Bellevue Avenue, plus some lovely 18t century buildings along the waterfront area with boatyards, ship chandler wharves and shops. The Newport Art Museum has some fine Winslow Hon ers.

Charleston, South Carolina, is a popular port of call on the east coast New York-to-Caribbean repositioning cruises.

Charleston, South Carolina ★★★★★

Language:	**English**	*English Spoken?:*	**Yes**
Currency:	**US$**	*US$ ok?:*	**Yes**
To town:	**Walk**		

Not only Americans but foreign tourists as well are beginning to pick up on the fascinating history and shore excursions offered on U.S. coastal cruises (really repositioning sailings between seasons, usually from New York to the Caribbean in spring and fall). And Charleston, **greatly spiffed up since its terrifying bout with Hurricane Hugo in 1989**, is a real star on the circuit. It's easy enough to get around on your own with a city map or walking-tour leaflet, but you can also take one of the good historic walking tours ($) offered around the **elegant homes of the Battery**, and of course a *de rigeur* visit to Fort Sumter, where the Civil War began when Confederate troops at Fort Johnson fired on federal troops at Fort Sumter in 1861. Golf packages to Kiawah Island's Pete Dye-designed Ocean Course ($$$) are part of a special Clipper theme cruise that visits Charleston, and other ships offer passengers in Charleston a chance to take a horse-drawn carriage through the streets or tour to nearby Boone Hall Plantation ($$). On your own, don't miss the old market area where Gullah-speaking women from the islands off the coast are busy weaving sweetgrass baskets for sale. The brick halls were built in 1841, and while most of the vendors today sell souvenirs and crafts instead of fruits and vegetables, you can buy tins of delectable "benne" (the Gullah or African word for sesame seed) cookies and wafers, **cinnamon-roasted pecans** and 13-bean soup mix. If time permits, hie yourself to **Louis's Charleston Grill** for some of the **world's finest southern cooking**, contemporary, sophisticated and downright delicious. Catfish Row, famous from Gershwin's folk opera *Porgy and Bess*, is also in the old downtown area of Charleston.

Williamsburg, Virginia ★★★★★

Language:	**English**	*English Spoken?:*	**Yes**
Currency:	**US$**	*US$ ok?:*	**Yes**
To town:	**Shuttle from dock**		

Williamsburg inhabitants dressed in 18th century costumes stroll the streets of old Williamsbury.

To visit the historic city of Williamsburg, your ship, if it's small, will probably dock in Yorktown, 15 miles away, Newport News, 23 miles away, if it's mid-sized to large. **Colonial Williamsburg** was recreated slowly, beginning in 1926 with some funding from John D. Rockefeller, Jr. Today the historic area fills 173 acres with 88 original and 50 more reconstructed buildings from the period, many of them occupied by costumed animators, which means **you are immersed in another time**. As a respite from the pressures of modern-day life, Colonial Williamsburg is wonderful, and as street theater enthralling. That elegantly dressed couple, their fur-trimmed capes swirling as they step down from their carriage, may be the governor and his wife; that man in knee breeches hurrying down the street may be a shoemaker on his way to his shop. While the tourists generally eat in one of the famous costumed taverns, **the best food in Williamsburg** is just outside the historic district at **The Trellis**, where French-Canadian chef Marcel Desaulniers creates the finest food in the region from fresh lump crabmeat, game and local produce. If you're a chocoholic, save room for his famous **Death by Chocolate** dessert. He's open for lunch and dinner, but it's a good idea to reserve ahead. ☎ *(804) 229-8610.*

CRUISING IN
NORTHERN EUROPE

The Houses of Parliament on the Thames in London.

The most comfortable way to see Europe close-up is from a cruise ship, with no packing and unpacking, no bags-in-the-hall-at-five-a.m. And reading through a cruise brochure reminds you of just how many places you can go—around the British Isles, the Norwegian Fjords, the North Cape, to Scandinavian Capitals, the Canary Islands, the Baltic.

A **North Cape or Norwegian fjords cruise** takes you traveling along the intricate indentations of the Norwegian coast from Oslo around past Bergen and north to Honnigsvaag, with Midnight Sun that fades into twilight around midnight and brightens up again at 3 a.m., past rainbow-streaked waterfalls splashing into deep, silent dark blue waters to the north of the 72nd parallel where patient, smiling Lapps sit in a cold drizzle selling vivid, jesterlike caps and racks of reindeer antlers from the door flaps of their roadside tents.

One of the newest itineraries takes you from a **great wine region of France** to many of **Europe's northern capitals**. Until recently, most travelers had to decide between a leisurely river or canal cruise for an intimate look at a small area, or take a wider-ranging ocean cruise that did not always come in for

close-ups. But several years ago the *Seabourn Pride* offered a cruise that s
out from Bordeaux and sailed along the Gironde and the Seine in Franc
Germany's Elbe, Holland's series of canals from the Atlantic into Amste
dam and England's Thames, as well as negotiating the locks of St. Malo.

Finally, there is the **Baltic cruise**, sailing along the Neva into St. Petersbur,
calling perhaps at newly independent Riga or Tallinn, the former East Ge
man port of Travemunde or in wonderful, wonderful Copenhagen.

Who knows, maybe the Grand Tour was meant to be by sea after all.

Five Virile Viking Excursions

Massive sculptures by Gustaf Vigeland ornament Oslo's Frogner Park.

1. **Oslo's Frogner Park** (get there on the #2 Frogner tram) where 192 massive sculptures of **650 human beings in bronze, granite and wrought iron** by Gustav Vigeland seem to writhe, leap joyously, fall in love, procreate, play with babies and children, argue, fall sick and, in the case of one monumental tower, climb over each other on the way to the top.

2. The **Dalsnibba mountain road** near Geiranger, called the **"eighth wonder of the world"** at the Paris Exhibition of 1900, where it shared billing with the Eiffel Tower, climbs above timberline to a bare, rocky 5000-foot summit where you see patches of snow and a few scruffy-looking reindeer.

3. **The North Cape**, cold, bleak and wet, the roadside lined with miserable reindeer and enterprising Lapp ladies selling reindeer antlers for $5; **you walk to the edge of the cliff and look over a fence** to the sea far below.

4. **Flydalsjub** (on the same excursion as Dalsnibba) offers a sensational view of a fjord, the same one you've seen in all those Norwegian cruise brochures; the tourist office even arranges for **two hikers in bright colors** to stand on a rocky ledge below you for foreground.

5. **Tromso, "gateway to the Arctic"** and one of the largest urban areas in the world— **its city limits cover 960 square miles** inhabited by 40,000 people and a lot of reindeer.

British Isles

Shetland Islands

Orkney Islands

Lewis

Harris

Hebrides Islands

SCOTLAND

NORTH SEA

ATLANTIC OCEAN

Edinburgh

NORTHERN IRELAND

Belfast

York

Hull

Dublin

Holyhead

Liverpool

Conway

GALWAY BAY

IRELAND

ENGLAND

Waterford

Stratford–upon–Avon

WALES

Oxford

London

Windsor

Dover

BANTRY BAY

ST. GEORGE'S CHANNEL

Calais

Southampton

Plymouth

ENGLISH CHANNEL

Le Havre

Channel Islands

© 1995 Fielding Worldwide, Inc.

Rating the Ports Of Northern Europe

Copenhagen, Denmark

Language:	**Danish**	*English Spoken?:*	**Yes**
Currency:	**Krone**	*US$ ok?:*	**No**
To town:	**Taxi or long walk**		

The famous peacock curtain at the commedia dell' arte theater in Copenhagen's Tivoli Garden.

Wonderful, wonderful Copenhagen gets our vote as the **happiest port in northern Europe**. The delightful 150-year-old **Tivoli Gardens amusement park**, said to have inspired Walt Disney to create Disneyland, is fun for all ages with its lush flowers, *commedia dell' arte* pantomime theatre with peacock curtain, marching bands and rides and games galore. Half-day city tours ($$) usually offer a visit to the Little Mermaid, the Gefion Fountain, Christiansborg and Amalienborg Palaces, the old harbor at Nyhavn and Kongens Nytorv and its Royal Theatre. A full-day excursion ($$$) takes you to **Elsinore, where Shakespeare's** *Hamlet* **agonized about whether to be** or not to be, and also includes a stop at the Viking Ship Museum in Roskilde and a scenic drive through North Zealand. An evening tour to Tivoli Gardens is also offered, but that's something simple enough to do on your own by taxi; the park is open until midnight with some 29 restaurants serving everything from inexpensive polser (hot dogs with fried onions) to expensive French dinners at

© 1995 Fielding Worldwide, Inc.

NORTH CAPE

Honningsvag

Hammeerfest

BARENTS SEA

GREENLAND SEA

Scandinavia

Tromso

RUSSIA

Narvik

NORWEGIAN SEA

FINLAND

SWEDEN

Trondheim

GULF OF BOTHNIA

Geiranger

Turku

Helsinki

St. Petersburg

NORWAY

Tallinn

Bergen

Oslo

Stockholm

Stavanger

ESTONIA

Visby

Riga

LATVIA

NORTH SEA

DENMARK

LITHUANIA

Copenhagen

BALTIC SEA

RUSSIA

Warnemunde

Gdynia

BELARUS

Bremerhaven

Hamburg

POLAND

GERMANY

the elegant **Belle Terrasse**. On your own, you can wander along the **Stroge** **shopping street** or tour the Carlsberg Brewery.

Channel Islands, English Channel ★★★★

Language:	**English**	*English Spoken?:*	**Yes**
Currency:	**CI Pound**	*US$ ok?:*	**No**
To town:	**Tender or walk**		

Our favorite of the Channel Islands is Guernsey, which looks like a clutch of **pop-up illustrations from a children's book** about flowers and fishing boats and whitewashed cottages. It's like being in *The Wizard of Oz* when the film goes from black-and-white into Technicolor. The only problem is, not many cruise ships call in the islands, but there is an occasional visit scheduled, usually to Guernsey or Jersey, the latter flatter and a bit less scenic, not quite as sweet as Guernsey. Tourists come to Guernsey to eat the island's famous tomatoes and strawberries, fresh lobster and sole. If you take a shore excursion you'll be guided to the **Guernsey Tomato Centre** where you get a complete history of that fruit. Then there's the Hanging Strawberry Farm, and, on a more serious note, the German Occupation Museum (the islands were occupied from 1940–1945 by Hitler's troops). Victor Hugo was exiled here, where he engaged in furious bouts of interior decorating between finishing *Les Misérables* and signalling from his window at his mistress, who lived in a house on the next hill.

DID YOU KNOW?

The only part of the Duchy of Normandy still loyal to the British Crown, the Channel Islands have no allegiance to Her Majesty's government and rely on it only for foreign policy and defense. They are part of the British Isles but not part of the United Kingdom, and will tell you that since they were on the winning side in 1066, Great Britain should belong to them.

London, England　　　　　★★★★★

Language:	**English**	*English Spoken?:*	**Yes**
Currency:	**Pound**	*US$ ok?:*	**No**
To town:	**Shuttle bus or taxi, depending on port**		

London's Tower Bridge celebrated its 100th birthday several years ago.

Most cruise ships bound for London actually **tie up at Tilbury** or Harwich, anchor in the middle of Thames in Greenwich or, as the *QE2* and other large ships do, come alongside in Southampton, the traditional transatlantic port for the city. But a few lucky smaller vessels like the Seabourn ships and the new Silversea vessels actually **sail up the Thames to the Tower Bridge, and disembark passengers in the city itself**. The only awkward moment here comes when you realize your early arrival that caused the bridge to be raised is also stalling the morning commute. It doesn't matter where you arrive for London so long as you get to this fantastic city. Because the airlift in and out of London is so good, many cruise lines use it as a seasonal home port and so offer a range of pre- and post-cruise options in London, **theater packages with tickets to the latest hits** ($$$), hotel and sightseeing packages ($$$), even three-night English Countryside packages ($$$) that take you to the Cotswolds, Oxford and Stratford-upon-Avon. Other day excursions include an all-day visit to Windsor Castle and surrounding countryside with lunch ($$$). A London city tour ($$) usually includes Big Ben and Parliament, Westminster Abbey, the Tower of London, St. Paul's Cathedral and the Strand, so if it's your first visit, by all means sign up for one. Then you can come back later and explore an area in more depth. On your own, **you can get around the city more easily than you might expect**, using a judicious combination of underground (subway), taxi and double-decker city bus. A little advance planning makes it even simpler.

Tallinn, Estonia ★★

Language:	**Estonian**	English Spoken?:	**Some**
Currency:	**Kroon**	US$ ok?:	**No**
To town:	**Taxi or walk**		

The colorful main square in Tallinn, Estonia, one of the best-preserved medieval cities in Europe.

Tallinn, the capital of Estonia and **one of the best-preserved medieval cities in Europe**, was once a port in the Hanseatic League, and over the years has been overrun by Danes, Germans and Russians eager to leave their mark. On a half-day city tour ($$) you will usually visit the **magnificent grand square** called Raekoha Plats, dating from the 11th century. The town hall still has a **set of chains permanently affixed to the walls** where any misbehaving citizen—a merchant who cheated a customer, a musician who played out of tune, a pair of ladies who gossiped too much—was strung up for a certain number of hours. The city is surrounded by a stone wall with six gates, each having its own nickname, from **"Stout Margaret"** to **"Tall Herman,"** which gives a little insight into the Estonian character. In the middle ages, the Upper Town of Toompea looked down on the Lower Town in more ways than one; **barons and counts lived in the Upper Town, and runaway serfs who hid in the lower town would be given their freedom if they could live there undetected for one year and one day**. A folkloric performance by the Folk Dance Group Soprus may be offered at the end of your tour, along with some typical Estonian refreshments like **unsweetened cakes with sour cherries and apple slices** and strong black coffee.

Helsinki, Finland ★★★

Language:	**Finnish**	*English Spoken?:*	**Yes**
Currency:	**Markka**	*US$ ok?:*	**No**
To town:	**Walk**		

Near the port in Helsinki is a fish and vegetable market in Kauppatori Square.

Cruise ships usually dock in downtown Helsinki only a short walk from the **colorful fish and vegetable market** at Kauppatori Market Square. Here in spring you can buy tiny new potatoes the size of your thumbnail, fresh and smoked fish, intensely sweet baby strawberries, feathery fresh dill, baby carrots and cabbages, handknit socks, caps and gloves, Lapp dolls and mittens, even fresh coffee and pastries. A half-day city tour ($$) will cover the Senate Square, the **Temppeliakuio Rock Church** (literally blasted from solid rock), the Lutheran Cathedral, **Sibelius Monument**, Finlandia Concert Hall, the market square and the planned suburb of Tapiola. A longer tour ($$$) goes to the outskirts of town to Hvittrask, the commune-like studio and residence of **designers Eliel Saarinan, Armas Lindgren and Herman Gesellius**, who, according to the guides, all swapped wives periodically. Shopping is good but fairly pricey. **Finnish crafts are spare and elegant**, but not cheap. It's easy to **stroll from your ship along the Pohjoisesplandadi** past Aarikka (toys, wood and silver articles), Marimekko (fabrics and clothing), Pentik (leather garments), Arabia (glass, ceramics, crystal and china), Wahlmans (Russian fur hats), Karvinen Anniki (handwoven blankets, wall hangings, placemats) and Academic Book Store, designed by Alvar Aalto.

Bordeaux, France   ★ ★ ★

Language:	**French**	*English Spoken?:*	**Some**
Currency:	**Franc**	*US$ ok?:*	**No**
To town:	**Walk**		

The elegant city of Bordeaux on the Gironde is undergoing a resurgence of cruise ship visits.

Most of the mid-sized to small ships that visit Bordeaux **sail along the river past the vineyards**, then dock in the heart of the city with **a magnificent view across to the Bourse** and the elegant 18th century city hall. As a port, the city has become quite popular in the last five or six years. Naturally, a **full-day wine country tour** ($$$) heads most shore excursion offerings here, with a visit to a couple of the vineyards of St.-Julien, Graves or Médoc and a luncheon en route, perhaps in St.-Emelion. A half-day city tour ($$) usually visits the historic buildings around the Bourse, the city's **magnificent Girondin monument with its galloping horse fountains**, the gentrifying Dockland sector, the Grand-Théâtre with 12 goddess columns supporting the exterior balcony, and the **Cité Mondiale du Vin** (for wine purchasing and other shopping). Bordeaux is also a pleasant city to **wander around on your own**, with bustling sidewalk cafes and fish restaurants around Parliament Square and pretty outdoor restaurants tucked away in leafy courtyards. **La Tupina** on rue Porte-de-la-Monnaie along the river is lively and fun, with wood-roasted meats and shellfish. When walking around the historic areas of Bordeaux, make a point to stop and look up, especially around the Bourse, where some **200 individually carved faces called** *mascarons* ornament doorways and walls, no two of them alike.

Le Havre, France ★

Language:	**French**	*English Spoken?:*	**Some**
Currency:	**Franc**	*US$ ok?:*	**No**
To town:	**Shuttle bus to Paris**		

The classic transatlantic crossing port of Le Havre is not a cruise day-triper's destination in any sense of the word. It's an ugly city that happens to be ⁊ the sea, and the only reason cruise vessels call here is **to ferry passengers to Paris** on a very long day-trip or a pre- or post-cruise overland journey ⁊$$$). From here, it's **three hours to Paris and three hours back**, leaving very :tle time to shop or sightsee on a one-day tour. From Rouen, also used as a ⁊rt of call for Paris, the commute is some 40 miles shorter each way. You ᴧn also set out from here to **the Normandy beaches** ($$$), a much shorter ᴧd more bearable day trip for most passengers. Other optional side trips inᴧde a visit to the charming little fishing village of Honfleur ($$), where ⁊me of the **early French Impressionists** came to join Eugene Boudin. **La ⁊rme St-Simeon**, a rustic country inn in those days, traded rooms and meals ⁊r paintings; a few can still be seen on the premises. Today it's a very elegant ⁊ember of the prestigious French Relais & Chateaux group. The fashion⁊ble **seaside resort of Deauville** is also often included on the Honfleur day ᴧur from Le Havre. But whatever you do, don't expect to spend a day ⁊trolling around the charming old port of Le Havre. None of its charm reᴧains after devastating bombardment during World War II, and the modern ᴧity, while functional, is also **graffiti-splattered and ugly**.

Rouen with its medieval streets and half-timbered houses is often used as the port for Paris.

Rouen, France ★★★★

Language:	**French**	English Spoken?:	**Some**
Currency:	**Franc**	US$ ok?:	**No**
To town:	**Shuttle bus or taxi**		

While Rouen is **a delightful port of call in its own right**, some cruise lines u[se] it as **a port for Paris** with a full-day trip with lunch ($$$). This excursion usually **covers the highlights fairly quickly**—the Arc de Triomphe, Champs El[y]sees, Place de la Concorde, Eiffel Tower, Les Invalides, Le Marais distri[ct,] the Opera Square and a brief pause for shopping—but it's a long ride. A d[ay] shuttle bus ($) for passengers who want to visit Paris on their own for sho[p]ping or museum-going is also occasionally offered. A much better day tr[ip] from Rouen is a **visit to Monet's home and gardens at Giverny** ($$), less than [an] hour in each direction. In Rouen, the city tour ($$), much of it on foot, vi[s]its the old city and its famous cathedral, the facade featured in so many [of] Monet's paintings; the rue de Gros-Horloge with **cobblestoned streets an[d] sidewalk cafes**, passing under the famous medieval mechanical clock; t[he] church of Saint-Maclou; the Renaissance Law Courts; the modern churc[h] dedicated to **Joan of Arc**; and the Old Marketplace **where she was burned at th[e] stake as a heretic** in 1431. Not least of the pleasures of Rouen as a port is th[e] beautiful voyage along the Seine coming into the city from the Atlantic. Th[e] ship passes by medieval castle ruins and under **the dramatic new bridge at Tan[]carville** and follows the wide lazy curves of the river into the port.

Bremerhaven, Germany ★★

Language:	**German**	English Spoken?:	**Yes**
Currency:	**Mark**	US$ ok?:	**No**
To town:	**Walk, taxi**		

Bremerhaven was created as an alternate port for Bremen in the early 19th century as the river Weser began to silt up, and thrives today as a North Se[a] fishing, passenger and cargo port. The early weekday morning fish auction attracts an audience, but perhaps the most interesting sightseeing in Bremer-haven is **the National Maritime Museum**, which has both an indoor museum with ship models and artifacts, and an open-air museum with seven historic old ships. More often, the port serves as **access to the historic and beautiful old city of Bremen 37 miles away**. Excursions ($$) usually include time to walk around the beautiful old Market Square with its Gothic Rathaus (City Hall)

d 11th-century cathedral. The most-photographed feature in the square is
30-foot statue of the medieval knight Roland, but the most appealing stat-
ry are **the Street Musicians of Bremen** by the Rathaus, a donkey, a dog, a cat
id a rooster from the fairytale by the Brothers Grimm. Bremen, a market
ort since 965, is an ideal town for walking. Don't miss the old quarter
illed **the Schnoor with its narrow 500-year-old streets** lined with gable-roofed,
ilf-timbered houses. The early wealth that created the city came from the
anseatic League**, an association of medieval towns that concentrated on
ade, became rich and powerful and paid no taxes or allegiance to other
owers.

Hamburg, Germany ★★★★

Language:	**German**	English Spoken?:	**Yes**
Currency:	**Mark**	US$ ok?:	**No**
To town:	**Walk**		

The city of Hamburg seen from the Elbe River.

Smaller cruise ships can come alongside in the heart of **old Hamburg's colorful port area** after a scenic cruise down the Elbe River from the North Sea.
Gracious brick houses along canals and some fine museums head the list of
independent sightseeing here. While there are several shore excursions offered, there's no problem in making your way around on your own. If you
arrive on a Sunday morning, you should head down the waterfront toward
the lively fish market, where a combination of **rock and jazz music happenings,
fish-selling and beer drinking** takes place; leave your valuables behind. Shore
excursions in Germany's second-largest city include a half-day tour ($$) with

a glass-topped motor launch ride through the **canals of Hamburg**, a look the Parliament and Stock Exchange, and the **St. Pauli red light district**, n nearly so raunchy as it used to be. A longer drive goes out of the city abo 30 miles to the medieval towns of Moelln, Ratzeburg and Lübeck ($$ Moelln is the place where the jester Til Eulenspeigel died, Ratzeburg where Henry the Lion founded the cathedral in in the mid-12th centur and Lübeck, medieval capital of the Hanseatic cities, still has its gates, towe and medieval houses. Lübeck is also **the home of marzipan**, the almond past sweet made into fruit, vegetable and animal shapes; buy some to take hon at I. G. Niederegger Konditorei by St. Mary's Church.

Warnemunde, Germany ★★

Language:	**German**	*English Spoken?:*	**Yes (in Berlin)**
Currency:	**Mark**	*US$ ok?:*	**No**
To town:	**Excursion bus to Berlin**		

Warnemunde, once part of the former East Germany, is now **the favorit cruise port of call for Berlin** because of its relative proximity. Some lines use train to transfer passengers to Berlin on a full-day excursion ($$$). (Ham burg, which is also sometimes used, is three hours' drive each way.) The Ber lin tour here usually includes **the former Checkpoint Charlie, now a museum**; visit to 17th century Charlottenburg Palace; the rewarding **Egyptian Museum** across from the palace, with its famous sculpture of Queen Nefertiti; an **evocative Unter den Linden street**, long shut off from the west. Other visit may be made to the **magnificent Pergamom Museum** where the classic Perga- mom Alter and the Roman Gate of Miletus, huge pieces from the 2nd-cen tury B.C., and other antiquities are on display; **the Brandenburg Gate**; the ruins of Kaiser Wilhelm Memorial Church; the Reichstag and Congress Hall Shoppers given some time to wander around on their own should make beeline to the **fabulous food department (6th floor) of the KaDeWe Department Store** on the Kufürstendamm for a Harrods-like display of edibles and drink- ables. Also interesting: the Berlin Zoo and the Tiergarten Public Park. An al- ternative tour from Warnemunde visits nearby medieval Rostock ($$), also a former East German city. En route, passengers also see other medieval towns and ride on the narrow-gauge Molli railroad. If you elect to stay in Warne- munde, walk around the Alter Strom, the **picturesque old harbor area lined with fishermen's cottages**.

Reykjavik, Iceland ★★★

Language:	**Icelandic**	*English Spoken?:*	**Yes**
Currency:	**Krona**	*US$ ok?:*	**No**
To town:	**Taxi, walk**		

The story goes that the Vikings blundered naming two territories—icy Greenland should have been named Iceland, and **lush, volcanic Iceland is more correctly Greenland**. In any case, when visiting Iceland, expect a great deal of scenic beauty with **abundant geothermal features from geysers and hot springs to craters and volcanoes** on this still-volatile island. A full-day excursion ($$$) visits hot springs, gardens and the Golden Waterfall; a half-day city tour ($$) covers the Folk Museum and Parliament House. The small capital city of Reykjavik ("Smoky Bay") has 150,000 of the country's quarter-million population. Most interesting walking areas in the central district are a pedestrian-only **shopping street called Austurstraeti** and an Old Town district near the harbor. The oldest structure here, rebuilt in 1764, is now a **rustic restaurant called Fogetinn**, serving local seafood dishes, lamb and game. Nearby is the Tjorn town pond, **where Arctic terns spend their summers**. A sampling of the **Icelandic Saga manuscripts** is on display in the Arnagardur (free), and the National Museum of Art and the National Culture Museum are also free. Don't be shocked by the prices. Everything in Iceland is expensive because almost everything has to be imported. One small consolation—**there's no tipping**. Shoppers will find plenty of occasions to purchase handknit wool sweaters (around $100 for top quality, cheaper for seconds).

Dublin, Ireland ★★★

Language:	**English**	*English Spoken?:*	**Yes**
Currency:	**Irish pound**	*US$ ok?:*	**No**
To town:	**Taxi**		

The traditional cruise ship arrival **port for Dublin is Dun Loaghaire** (pronounced "dun leary"), only eight miles or so from the city. The **James Joyce Museum** is located in a Martello Tower near the port, where the opening action in Joyce's novel *Ulysses* took place. The National Maritime Museum is also nearby. Most cruise ships that call here offer both half- and full-day shore excursions ($$–$$$). The half-day covers Trinity College and Library, with the **illuminated manuscript Book of Kells**; the classic Georgian mansions; the Bank of Ireland building; St. Patrick's Cathedral, founded in the 12th

century; **the Abbey Theatre**, founded by W. B. Yeats, Lady Augusta Grego
and John Millington Synge; and Grafton Street for shopping. The full-d
tour covers all the above and drives out to Glendalough in the Wicklc
Mountains, a little more than 30 minutes from the center of town, whe
you can visit a modest sixth century sanctuary that became a great mon;
tery. A drive along the coast to Malahide Castle, one of the country's olde
is another shore excursion option. Wandering around Dublin on your ov
can lead you into **colorful pubs like the Horseshoe Bar in the Shelbourne Hote**
the Bailey on Duke Street, or Ryans on Parkgate Street. You can also **tour th**
Guinness Brewery and Hopstore on Crane Street or the Irish Whisky Corner c
Bow Street.

Riga, Latvia ★★

Language:	**Latvian**	*English Spoken?:*	**Some**
Currency:	**Lat**	*US$ ok?:*	**No**
To town:	**Taxi, walk**		

Port calls at Riga are scheduled occasionally, but not as often as they were
year or two ago. The city was founded by an archbishop from Bremen i
1201 as a fortress town and springboard for conquering the Baltic province:
Remnants of the **unique Hanseatic League architecture** can still be seen in th
medieval part of town. Shore excursions include a city tour ($$) that visit
the medieval old town with its spired churches and merchants' houses, **13th**
century St. George's Church (oldest building in Riga), and the 15th centur
Livonia Knights' Castle, today an art and history museum. If you choose te
walk around on your own, you'll find **locals are generally helpful and courte**
ous, with a few exceptions; it's still a good idea to leave your valuables aboar
ship. Don't be surprised to see **a fair amount of public drunkenness**. The olc
town is mostly pedestrian-only streets, so walking is easy. Many building
date back to the 17th century. Several cultural and art museums are in the
13th century Riga Castle, built by German knights. In the same area you car
find the picturesque Three Brothers House, a 15th century dwelling that is
the oldest house in town, and the Swedish Gate and Powder Tower at the
city walls.

Amsterdam, Netherlands ★ ★ ★

Language:	**Dutch**	*English Spoken?:*	**Yes**
Currency:	**Guilder**	*US$ ok?:*	**No**
To town:	**Walk or taxi**		

Amsterdam's distinctive old buildings line the city's canals.

Sailing into Amsterdam is fascinating, because you enter the city through **a series of canals and locks**, then dock very near the heart of town and the Central Railway Station. Because the country is small, a day visitor can cover more territory than in many places. Shore excursion options here include a half-day city tour by canal boat and motorcoach ($$) that visits **the Rijksmuseum, home of Rembrandt's *Night Watch*,** Dam Square and the Royal Palace, along with a shopping stop; a full-day tour ($$$) heads out to the polders (reclaimed lands) and a stop at the **costume villages of Volendam, Marken or Edam**; an excursion to The Hague and Delft ($$-$$$) to see the famous blue porcelain made; or a drive to **the windmills of Zaanse Schans**, a restored village, and the cheese town of Edam. If you strike out on your own, other options include a tour of the **poignant Anne Frank House** (too small to handle group tours); the **diamond cutting district**, where several historic firms welcome visitors; a tour of the Heineken Brewery with samples, even an after-dark walk around the red light district (don't go alone and don't take your camera) where the **ladies of the evening display themselves behind plate glass windows**. If it's springtime, you may be offered an all-day excursion to the **spectacular Keukenhof Gardens** ($$$) near Lisse where you can not only tip-toe through the tulips but order bulbs to be shipped home.

Bergen, Norway ★ ★ ★

Language:	**Norwegian**	*English Spoken?:*	**Yes**
Currency:	**Krone**	*US$ ok?:*	**No**
To town:	**Walk or taxi**		

The walk from the cruise ship pier into town is interesting because it pass through the fish market area and along the painted facades of the love Hanseatic wooden houses in the Bryggen district built by the Hanseat League merchants and among the most beautiful wooden buildings in tl world. Since Bergen is the **gateway to Norway's fjords**, any cruise with "fjord in its title is likely to call here. The city itself is quite handsome in summe when the trees are green and leafy. The half-day tour ($$) usually include several of the following: Troldhaugen, the **home of composer Edvard Grie** the 12th-century **Fantoft Stave Church**, made of wood with dragons decorating the roof; the Bryggen waterfront area; medieval Haakon's Hall; Bergen shus Fortress; Rosenkrantz Tower; and sometimes the **Old Bergen Open Ai Museum** or the funicular ride up Mt. Floyen for the view. **If your tour doesn' cover the open air museum, make an effort to go over on your own**; the number 1 and 8 buses go there from downtown. The buildings are occupied by cos tumed inhabitants, and there are several appealing cafes and restaurant where you can have lunch or tea. There's also a fine Bryggens Museum rec reating medieval life; it's next to the **SAS Royal Hotel**. Don't worry abou brushing up on your Norwegian; almost all the locals will speak fluent En glish. **Bergen shopping options** include fine quality silver and wood objects furs, hand-knit socks and caps and smoked salmon in shrink wrap from th outdoor fish market.

North Cape, Norway ★

Language:	**Norwegian**	*English Spoken?:*	**Yes**
Currency:	**Krone**	*US$ ok?:*	**No**
To town:	**Excursion bus**		

Yes, we know this northern destination is so famous it gives its name to an entire cruise, but it's **one of those places people visit just to say they've been there**. The first comment most have about this bleak headland is, "Is that all there is?" We're not saying a North Cape Cruise is disappointing; the itinerary includes a number of **breathtakingly beautiful fjords, cascading waterfalls** and sometimes the rarely visited Lofoten Islands. But the cape itself is down-ght dreary—and, as if to add insult to injury, the so-called North Cape is **t even the northernmost point on the European continent**. It's on an island off e continent, and, even if that counted, an adjacent cape to the west is ac- ally further north. Occasionally a line has the right idea—a cruise past the orth Cape without stopping. But with most lines, the usual cruise visit in- ides a docking at the **tiny Arctic village of Honnigsvaag**, where the sightsee- g consists of a small fishing museum. The North Cape itself is 21 miles rther by bus, and is usually muffled in fog. The only thing worse than the cursion bus ride ($$$) past those encampments of cheery Lapps selling **ash ays made from reindeer hooves** is arriving at the combination post office-gift op-general store and being offered **a certificate priced at $10 that proves** u've been there.

Norwegian Fjords, Norway ★★★★★

Language:	**Norwegian**	*English Spoken?:*	**Yes**
Currency:	**Krone**	*US$ ok?:*	**No**
To town:	**Tender ashore in most ports**		

Even large ships are diminished by the awesome grandeur of Norway's fjords.

The Norwegian Fjords, one of the **most splendid scenic areas on earth**, wel- comes cruise passengers into its hidden depths. You sail into quiet, deep, lue waters guarded by evergreen-covered mountains and reflecting glaciers n the slopes above, the stillness broken only by the sound of a white water- all crashing down. How deep are these fjords? Sognefjord, one of the most najestic, has been measured at 4290 feet deep. Most cruises visit several jords, among them **Geirangerfjord**, where passengers can take an excursion

($$) up Mt. Dalsnibba, past herds of grazing reindeer, to the Eagle's N for a fantastic view of their ship lying far below; Flaam, for a side trip Sognefjord ($$–$$$) on **a tiny train that goes through a dozen tunnels** acrc the top of Norway; and Gudvangen, home of a spectacular waterfall call Stalheimfoss. Flightseeing excursions over the fjords ($$$) are also availab at Geiranger. But just as enchanting as the scenery are Norwegian villag like Voss, where the **13th-century town church has twisted and painted wood posts** inside and gates that close on each pew. From here, between 1836 ar 1914, some 10,000 people emigrated to America, including **a to-be-famor football coach named Knute Rockne**. All around the village, sheep graze c lush green pastures so thick and loamy you expect to bounce and spri when you step on it.

Oslo, Norway ★★★★

Language:	**Norwegian**	*English Spoken?:*	**Yes**
Currency:	**Krone**	*US$ ok?:*	**No**
To town:	**Walk, taxi**		

A day ashore in Oslo is **not really enough time** to see all of this beautiful cit because there's so much here to choose from. The relatively small city 500,000, set amid evergreen forests and craggy rocks, is located **at the end a 60-mile-long fjord**. A half-day shore excursion ($$) usually includes th Royal Palace, the Hollmenkollen ski jump, a visit to **Frogner Park with it unique life-sized sculptures of families by Gustav Vigeland** and a tour of th rather dour city hall. A few lines offer a shore excursion that concentrates o the city's fine maritime museums—the **Viking Ship Museum** with three wel preserved Viking vessels; the **Kon-Tiki Museum** containing Thor Heyerdahl famous rafts; the **Maritime Museum** with its cruise ship models; and the **Fra Museum**, with the polar vessel used by Fridtjof Nansen and Roald Amund en. If your ship doesn't offer this excursion, it's easy enough to get to th museums on your own; they're all near each other on the Bygdoy Peninsul where you can also visit the **wonderful Norwegian Folk Museum, with 150 his toric houses** from all over the country. On your own, you may wish to see th fine Edvard Munch collection in the **Munch Museum**. Shoppers should chec out the Husfliden, the Norwegian Association of Home Arts and Crafts, fc handmade Norwegian products.

Spitsbergen, Norway ★★

Language:	**Norwegian**	*English Spoken?:*	**Yes**
Currency:	**Krone**	*US$ ok?:*	**No**
To town:	**Tender**		

The Land of the Midnight Sun is nowhere more evident than in Svalbard Lands, notably its main group Spitsbergen, inhabited primarily by Norwegian and Russian coal miners. These **Arctic islands**, which lie far above the northern tip of Scandinavia roughly halfway between Greenland and Russia's Nova Zemla, are primarily glacier-covered. But **because of the Gulf Stream, ships are able to navigate as far as 83 degrees north, within seven degrees of the North Pole**, or sometimes farther or not as far, depending on the outer edge of the permanent ice floe. One ship you can count on visiting this remote group of islands in the Scandinavian Arctic virtually every summer besides the ever present coastal vessels from Bergen Line is Special Expeditions' sturdy little expedition vessel *Polaris. Polaris* passengers usually concentrate on **geology, flora and fauna** rather than more traditional sightseeing, which is scarce up here. All shore excursions aboard that ship are included in the fare. The best sightseeing options include visiting **nesting areas of the arctic tern** where passengers are sometimes attacked by the brave little birds in scenes (like Alfred Hitchcock's film *The Birds*), watching some of the other rich bird life—auks, guillemots, ivory gulls, puffins, kittiwakes or purple sandpipers. You may also have a chance to **hike to Waggonwaybreen glacier**. If you spot an occasional walrus or polar bear, you'll agree this a once-in-a-lifetime destination.

St. Petersburg, Russia ★★★

Language:	**Russian**	*English Spoken?:*	**Yes**
Currency:	**Rubles**	*US$ ok?:*	**Yes**
To town:	**Taxi or shuttle bus**		

Only small vessels like Cunard's Sea Goddess ships and Seven Seas' *Song of Flower* can come alongside on the River Neva in the heart of St. Petersburg; other larger ships are usually relegated to the commercial port area a short commute away. Some ships which call here stay overnight to allow passengers more time to explore this fascinating city. The most popular city shore excursions ($$) visit the **Hermitage, the world-famous museum in the Winter Palace** (its incredible collection of pictures is poorly lit and displayed); **St.**

Isaac's Cathedral; Peter & Paul Fortress; and drives along the Nevsky Pr pect shopping street. The major evening shore excursion is a cultural eve usually **tickets to a ballet, circus or folkloric evening**. Because ships visit duri **the summer's White Nights**, the sun will still be shining when you come out the performance near midnight. Excursions outside the city include a visit the summer palaces at Petrodvorets or the Pushkin Palace and Pavlovsk. T notation above that U.S. dollars are acceptable in Russia is really an und statement; they are **in great demand** by the street vendors who are everywh in St. Petersburg selling nesting dolls, T-shirts, lacquer boxes, rabbit fur h and even **copies of Tsarist-era peasant clothing like band-necked, full-slee shirts and embroidered blouses**.

The Catherine Palace in St. Petersburg.

Leith, Scotland ★★★

Language:	**English**	*English Spoken?:*	**Yes**
Currency:	**Scottish pound**	*US$ ok?:*	**No**
To town:	**Five-minute cab ride to Edinburgh**		

Leith, **the port of Edinburgh**, offers the day visitor a wide range of sidewalk fes, wine bars and seafood restaurants that have sprung up during the past ecade, but there's little of architectural or historic significance. Since the ajestic city of Edinburgh is only five minutes away, you should head direct- there. The standard half-day tour ($$) will take you to the ramparts of Ed- burgh Castle; **Holyrood House, where Bonnie Prince Charlie held court in the id-18th century and Mary Queen of Scots' secretary David Rizzo was murdered n the stairs**; the Royal Mile road between the two; St. Giles Cathedral and rinces Street. Some ships offer an evening folkloric excursion to a Scottish staurant for dinner ($$$), okay **if you like haggis, bagpipes and recitations om Robert Burns**; others provide daylong excursions into the countryside $$$). If you set out on your own, you can cover all the top attractions from ie tour plus perhaps a visit to the **Scotch Whisky Heritage Centre**, an audiovi- ual about the country's most famous drink; going antiques shopping in the ld Town's Victoria Street; checking out the National Gallery of Scotland nd its excellently displayed **paintings by Rubens, El Greco, Raphael, Titian, enoir and Pissaro**. The incredible **Edinburgh Military Tattoo, a twilight fife-and- rum parade par excellence**, is held during the July/August Edinburgh Festi- al; reserve in advance.

Stockholm's Grand Hotel.

Stockholm, Sweden ★★★★

Language:	**Swedish**	*English Spoken?:*	**Yes**
Currency:	**Krona**	*US$ ok?:*	**No**
To town:	**Taxi, walk**		

Stockholm is a **clean and beautiful city surrounded by lakes, canals and wate ways**. A half-day highlights shore excursion ($$) usually includes the O Town, with a brief opportunity to walk around the colorful streets; Storto get Square with its old stock exchange building and Storkyrkan Church; t Old House of Parliament; the Royal Palace, where **the changing of the gua takes place at noon**; the City Hall, site of the Nobel Prize presentations; and brief visit to **the Wasa, an excavated and restored 17th century warship**. A ha day trip ($$) to the **lovely Drottningholm Palace with its well-preserved 18 century theatre** and gardens, only five miles from town, provides a delightf day. A few ships, notably *Sea Goddess*, sometimes offer this as a separate po of call and anchor just outside the palace. If you've done the obligatory hig lights before, you can concentrate this visit on perhaps strolling through t **Skansen Open-Air Museum with its fine collection of 150 period Swedish house churches and farm buildings**, most housing a craftsman at work. You'll als find restaurants, a zoo, aquarium and forestry pavilion. You can take a fer for the short ride across from the city center. **The Old Town, called Gamla Sta** is a delightful place to stroll around on your own. Shoppers like the pret boutiques nestled here, as well as the showier shops and department stor like Nordiska Kompaniet in the main shopping district around Sergelsto Square.

THE MEDITERRANEAN CRUISE

he sidewalk cafes of Venice are alluring —and expensive. If you decide to sit, der a small, simple libation and nurse it carefully.

To Homer it was **the "wine-dark sea"** over which the fresh west wind came ging with a favorable breeze for Odysseus' ship. Perhaps that 2700-year-d phrase is **once again an apt description for the Mediterranean**, particularly the eastern part, where cautious travelers nervously eye **the trouble spots of e month**, from the former Yugoslavia to Egypt to Israel.

Surely the **most rewarding culturally and culinarily** of all shipboard destina-ons, a Mediterranean itinerary read aloud is a **litany of daydreams** that roll f the tongue like a magical incantation—Barcelona, Cannes, St. Tropez, lonte Carlo, Portofino, Capri, Sorrento and Venice.

A Mediterranean cruise virtually guarantees sunshine glinting off indigo lue water, daily ports of call with **sidewalk cafes in colorful village squares**, ophisticated shopping and dining ashore and an opulent array of museums, ionuments, theaters and concert halls.

945

The season used to run from April to October, but there's more and m[...] sloshing over into the shoulder seasons on Aegean sailings that may begi[...] early as March and go into November. Cruises range in length from thre[...] 14-plus days. You can buy an **air/sea package** that flies you from home to [...] Mediterranean port and back again, with the cruise and perhaps some l[...] programs included, or you can simply buy **the cruise only** and fit it into y[...] own vacation program.

Eastern Mediterranean cruises visit the Aegean, the Black Sea and sail i[...] the Red Sea, while Western Mediterranean cruises sail along the coasts [...] Spain, France and Italy, to the offshore islands of each and the coast [...] North Africa.

Five French Riviera Footnotes

1. The first tourist on the French Riviera was very likely one Tobias Smollett, a peri[...] tetic Scottish novelist who stopped off in Nice in 1763 and two years later publish[...] a two-volume treatise titled *Travels Through France and Italy, With Particu[...] Description of the City, Surroundings and Climate of Nice*.

2. **Queen Victoria used to vacation there** in winter (the fashionable season in the 1[...] century) traveling under the pseudonym Countess Balmoral; of course, everyo[...] knew who she was. It was her custom to distribute money to street beggars duri[...] her afternoon carriage ride, and one enterprising mendicant on her regular ro[...] painted on his card, "**By Appointment to Her Majesty the Queen**."

3. If Archduke Ferdinand had taken **the Train Bleu to the French Riviera** instead [...] going to Sarajevo, World War I might have been avoided.

4. The most considerate hostess on the French Riviera was **the Russian Princess S[...] varov**, who in the days of the Belle Époque purchased a villa rather than end the s[...] cessful party she'd rented it for. Later, after fleeing the Russian revolution, s[...] returned to find it a money-making property that took care of her the rest of h[...] days.

5. **The fashion for becoming sun-tanned** was introduced by designer Coco Chan[...] who spent the summer in the sun at Juan-les-Pins in the 1920s and came back [...] September to shock all Paris with her dark skin.

Rating the Ports of the Western Mediterranean

Corsica, France ★★★

Language:	**French**	English Spoken?:	**Some**
Currency:	**Franc**	US$ ok?:	**No**
To town:	**Walk**		

The tough, rugged island of Corsica with its rocky beaches and fragrant wild maquis was the birthplace of Napoleon.

The rugged island of Corsica is **fragrant with wild herbs and maquis** (the scrub that gave its name to the French resistance during World War II) that grows on its hillsides. Parts of it might still look familiar today to native son Napoleon. Tough but resilient, and famous for its blood feuds, Corsica has been **a reluctant part of France since 1769**. Cruise ships that call usually stop at one of three ports, **Bonifacio** (when sea conditions permit), a walled city atop steep cliffs; the **capital of Ajaccio**, birthplace of Napoleon; or **Calvi, a handsome citadel town** on the north coast. In each port you're usually offered a town and countryside half-day tour ($$). Bonfacio's excursion includes a walking tour around the historic citadel; in Ajaccio you'll be shown **countless museums, monuments and memorials to Napoleon** (who never came back to the island after becoming emperor); and in Calvi the bus tour usually visits several villages outside town as well as the fortress itself. If your ship docks in

Calvi, you can easily explore the fortress and upper town, set atop an 80-fo
granite cliff, on your own wearing good walking shoes. There is som
unique, if esoteric, shopping available here for the local **pâté called *mer***
made from blackbirds, and for candied local chestnuts called *marrons glacé.*

Nice, France ★★★★

Language:	**French**	English Spoken?:	**Some**
Currency:	**Franc**	US$ ok?:	**No**
To town:	**Taxi**		

Small ships can dock in the old port of Nice, but larger vessels usually an
chor in nearby Villefranche and bring passengers to Nice on a half-day tou
($$). For most visitors, the heart of Nice is the **Promenade des Anglais**, the
wide seafront avenue named for the sturdy English visitors, including Quee
Victoria, who promenaded here during the 1880s' winters. On one side i
the grand old Negresco Hotel, on the other, the rocky shingle beach. The
city is an intriguing mix of French and Italian (it was called Nizza for man
years) with some excellent museums—the **Musée Chagall, the Musée Matisse**
the International Museum of Naive Art and the offbeat Beaux-Arts Museum
with art nouveau works by Mossa. The **Marché aux Fleurs**, a bright melange
of floral colors and fragrances, and its adjoining vegetable and fruit market, i
on Cours Saleya in the old town, surrounded by **restaurants and cafes on the**
huge square. If you decide to lunch here, sample one of the local soups, *soupe*
de poisson (fish soup) or *soupe au pistou* (vegetable soup with a *soupçon* of pes-
to). If you wander into the side streets of the Old Town, especially in the
mornings, you'll find tiny cafes selling *socca*, the city's unique chick-pea pan-
cakes.

DID YOU KNOW?

When Nice was under the control of Sardinia in the early 19th century, the
Niçois called all foreigners English. The novelist Alexandre Dumas ques-
tioned an innkeeper about new arrivals and was told, "They are the English,
but I don't know whether they are French or German."

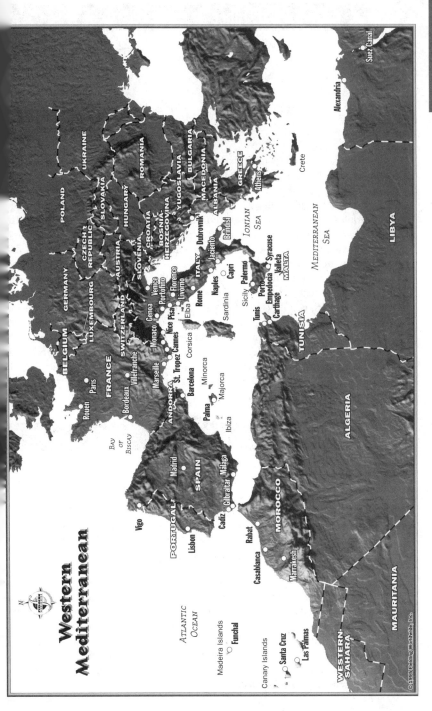

Western Mediterranean

ATLANTIC OCEAN

Madeira Islands
Funchal

Canary Islands
Santa Cruz
Las Palmas

WESTERN SAHARA

MAURITANIA

Casablanca
Rabat
Marrakesh
MOROCCO

ALGERIA

Vigo
PORTUGAL
Lisbon
Cadiz
Gibraltar
Málaga
SPAIN
Madrid

Bay of Biscay

Rouen
Paris
Bordeaux
FRANCE
ANDORRA
Barcelona
Palma
Ibiza
Minorca
Majorca

BELGIUM
LUXEMBOURG
GERMANY
SWITZERLAND
Villefranche
Marseille
St. Tropez Cannes
Nice Monaco
Genoa
Portofino
Corsica
Sardinia

POLAND
CZECH REPUBLIC
AUSTRIA
SLOVAKIA
SLOVENIA
HUNGARY
CROATIA
Venice
Florence
Pisa
Livorno
Elba
ITALY
Rome
Naples
Capri

UKRAINE
ROMANIA
BULGARIA
YUGOSLAVIA
BOSNIA HERZEGOVINA
MACEDONIA
ALBANIA
GREECE
Athens
Crete

Dubrovnik
Brindisi
Taciento
IONIAN SEA
Sicily Palermo
Syracuse
Empedocia
Carthage
Tunis
TUNISIA
Valleta
MALTA
Porto

MEDITERRANEAN SEA

LIBYA

Suez Canal
Alexandria

© 1995 Rattling Worldwide, Inc.

St-Tropez, France ★★★★

Language:	**French**	English Spoken?:	**Some**
Currency:	**Franc**	US$ ok?:	**No**
To town:	**Tender from ship**		

The colorful town of St-Tropez, which looks as if it's been here foreve was actually **recreated in the late 1940s** after being totally destroyed in Worl War II by retreating German soldiers. Even mobbed with tourists, the Côt d'Azur's **in-again, out-again resort** still has a drop-dead style. Nothing bea people-watching from the waterfront cafes as jaded *jeunes-filles* prowl th port area in somewhat outlandish garb. The **best beaches** are Tahiti Plag about a mile out of town, and du Pinet and Camarat on the Caps de St.-Tro pez about seven miles out of town. The town beach, in easy walking distanc from where the tender drops you, is a handkerchief-sized pocket of sand nea the Tour Vielle (Old Tower) past the harbor breakwater or mole. At most c the beaches, you'll be asked to pay for a beach towel and the space you oc cupy on the sand. Shoppers can find some **chic and sometimes surprisingly af fordable sportswear** in the waterfront boutiques here and in the 400 shop tucked away on the winding streets and alleyways of town. Art-lovers shoul check out the pleasant little Musée Annonciade in the harbor with its sun filled canvases by **Dufy**, **Bonnard** and **Matisse**. Shore excursions are rarely of fered here, except an occasional wine-tasting tour into the local vineyards.

Villefranche, France ★★★★

Language:	**French**	English Spoken?:	**Some**
Currency:	**Franc**	US$ ok?:	**No**
To town:	**Tender from anchorage**		

In one of the prettiest settings on the Côte d'Azur, the town of Ville-franche is often used as the central port of call to **access Monte Carlo, Cannes and Nice** for larger cruise ships. While shore excursion programs will proba-bly offer you a half-day tour to each of the three, you can strike out on your own easily enough by strolling over to the railway station and taking the train to whichever city you prefer; it runs frequently in both directions until nearly midnight. A bus tour to Cannes ($$) will also probably include **An-tibes**, **Port Vauban** and **Vallauris**, where **Picasso's studio** is usually on the agen-da. Still active as a pottery-making center today, the town has some outstanding studios and galleries. Shore excursion options also include a ance to visit the fortified little town of St.-Paul-de-Vence, where locals may be playing an intense game of *boules* in the town square, and a stop at the famed **Maeght Foundation museum** nets you artworks by Miro, Leger, Matisse, Chagall, Braque, Giacometti and dozens more. For travelers who have been to the Côte d'Azur several times, spending the morning sitting in one of the harborfront sidewalk cafes in Villefranche may be more satisfying than another shore excursion. **Mère Germaine** on Quai Courbet is particularly pleasant. Peek into the tiny Chapelle St.-Pierre at the harbor, decorated with frescoes by **Jean Cocteau**.

Gibraltar ★★

Language:	**English**	*English Spoken?:*	**Yes**
Currency:	**British Pound**	*US$ ok?:*	**No**
To town:	**Taxi or longish walk**		

Gibraltar's half-day shore excursion ($$) is as stolid and unchangeable as **the Rock of Gibraltar** itself—the same drive to the village of Catalan Bay to see the rain catchment area; a drive through the tunnel in the rock to see Europa Point and its lighthouse; and St. Michael's Cave, where you'll be taken inside to see the enormous cavern, scene of many **rock concerts** over the years. The guide will probably point out the house where **Lord Nelson's body** was preserved in a barrel of rum after the battle of Trafalgar. Finally there is the obligatory stop to see the famous **Barbary apes** of Gibraltar. Watch out; **they'll try to steal anything you have**, from sunglasses to billed caps to purses and cameras. Located at the southern tip of Spain at the entrance to the Mediterranean, the famous rock stands guard over this British colony, now self-governing but dependent on Britain for its defense. The struggle with Spain that closed the border for many years seems to be resolved, and visitors can once again arrive overland as well as by sea. The Gibraltar Museum in town is moderately interesting if you strike out on your own, and you'll find pubs serving **fish and chips, steak and kidney pie** and the like. Star Bar in Parliament Lane is said to be the oldest.

Capri, Italy ★★★

Language:	**Italian**	*English Spoken?:*	**Yes**
Currency:	**Lira**	*US$ ok?:*	**No**
To town:	**Tender from ship**		

Except for a few small ships like those from Windstar, which anchor o
shore when weather permits, the isle of Capri is **more often a shore excursi**
from Sorrento or Naples than a port of call on its own. Long legendary for
breathtakingly **beautiful Blue Grotto cave**, the lovely island is jam-packed wi
tourists in summer despite its **high prices and paucity of swimming beaches**.
shore excursion ($$) usually includes the obligatory boat ride into the Bl
Grotto (with more people jammed into the boats than should be), the Ga
dens of Augustus, one or more of the villas built by the Emperor Tiberius
the Villa Jovis offers fantastic views—and perhaps a ride up Monte Solaro f
an equally awesome view. The rocky islets of Faraglioni are particularly dr
matic from the Punta Tragara belvedere. If you start from Sorrento, you'll t
taken by hydrofoil for the **45 minute ride to the island**, then by funicular to th
town of Capri, a beguiling place to sit at a sidewalk cafe in the sun, drinkin
in the atmosphere. If you go on your own, from there you can take a loc
bus up a spectacular winding cliffside road to Anacapri. The boat ride to th
Blue Grotto costs around $15 from the Marina Grande, where ferries fror
the mainland arrive.

Civitavecchia, Italy   ★ ★ ★

Language:	**Italian**	*English Spoken?:*	**Yes**
Currency:	**Lira**	*US$ ok?:*	**No**
To town:	**Excursion bus to Rome**		

Civitavecchia (for Rome) appears written that way in the itineraries of virtu
ally every Western Mediterranean cruise. What it means is that you sail inte
the port town of Civitavecchia in order to be driven to Rome and back dur
ing the daylight hours. The town has been the port of Rome since the days
of Emperor Trajan in the first century A.D. but was extensively rebuilt after
WWII and has little of interest for the visitor. The **tiring full-day tour to Rome**
($$) is obligatory for visitors who have not been there before, although the
drive will take an hour and a half each way, more if traffic is snarled, as it
often is, and it's not the ideal way to see Rome in anything more than a cursory fashion. Among the stops on this site-filled tour—**a crash course in
Roman history** that is simplified if you do some reading in advance—are the
Coliseum, the Sistine Chapel, the Vatican and St. Peter's, Trevi Fountain,
sometimes the Spanish Steps and a shopping stop, and, wedged somewhere
in the midday, a stop for lunch. If you're lucky (as we have sometimes been),
you may have an excellent guide who adroitly pulls together the three separate cities—**Ancient Rome, Imperial Rome and Modern Rome**—into one under-
standable narrative. If you're not, take along a green *Guide Michelin* or other
guidebook to keep from getting terribly confused. For repeat visitors, some
cruise lines offer an **optional shuttle into Rome** ($$) that drops you off in the

orning, then picks you up at a set time in the afternoon to return to the
ip.

Elba, Italy   ★ ★ ★ ★

Language:	**Italian**	*English Spoken?:*	**Some**
Currency:	**Lira**	*US$ ok?:*	**No**
To town:	**Walk**		

*One of the most enchanting ports in the western Mediterranean is Portoferraio,
Elba, another Napoleon connection.*

The island of Elba is a **popular port of call for Windstar and Star Clipper vessels**, which can sail into the picturesque port past the fortress and the marina
filled with brightly-painted fishing boats. The modest and moldering little
villa where **Napoleon spent much of his exile** is at the top of the hill and easy
enough to visit on your own. He had a wonderful view to France (on a clear
day) from a marble bench in the garden. If you've a real Napoleon buff,
you'll want to take a shore excursion ($$) that includes a visit to his country
residence/prison, the Villa San Martino, a few miles outside town. On one

visit, **we rented a car with friends from the ship** (there are several car rent
places steps away from the docks) and drove around the island. While t
beaches in the port town of Portoferraio are mostly rocky and handkerchie
size, a drive can lead you to delightful beach resorts and outdoor seafoo
cafes. Shoppers will enjoy a stroll around the waterfront, browsing in **o**
handedly elegant little shops selling handmade leather bags, high-style r
sortwear and local semiprecious stones made into chunky jewelry. Wa
uphill through the town gates and you're in another world, an Italian villag
with a tree-shaded square, beautiful old churches and terraced stree
reached by stairways at each level.

Genoa, Italy ★★

Language:	**Italian**	*English Spoken?:*	**Some**
Currency:	**Lira**	*US$ ok?:*	**No**
To town:	**Taxi; don't walk in the port area**		

Genoa appears most often as a port of embarkation for **ships from Costa**
Cruises, whose parent company is located here. A major port since long be
fore the birth of its most **famous son, Christopher Columbus**, the city's harbo
today is still chockablock with ferries and freighters. The city itself, a bi
shabby around the edges, houses a conglomerate of gently moldering ol
buildings and ultramodern edifices; locals love to point out the pair of hug
white "washing machine buildings" with their round porthole windows. A
half-day city tour ($$), lasts longer than that if you get stuck in traffic, and
usually visits the rebuilt **house where Columbus was born**, the Cathedral of San
Lorenzo with its magnificent black-and-white Gothic facade, and the medi-
eval quarter, second-largest in Europe. On the north edge of town is the **fan-**
tastic Staglieno Cemetery, a glorious burst of sumptuous plaster tombs
dotting the hillside like wedding cakes. If you strike out on your own, have
the taxi take you to via Garibaldi, lined with elegant palaces and art galleries,
and **lunch on pasta al pesto**, perhaps at **Zefferino** on via 20 Septembre, where
everyone from Sinatra to the pope has eaten the famous dish sauced with ba-
sil, garlic, pine nuts and olive oil.

Livorno, Italy ★★★

Language:	**Italian**	*English Spoken?:*	**Some**
Currency:	**Lira**	*US$ ok?:*	**No**
To town:	**Excursion bus to Florence**		

Like Civitavecchia-for-Rome, this is Livorno-for-Florence, the port where our ship docks so you can be **shuttled to Florence** on an all-day tour ($$$) that usually drops by Pisa for a quick look at the leaning tower on the way over or back. Look fast, you'll usually have only half an hour. In Florence, the longest stop is normally at the **Piazza del Duomo** for a fast tour of the magnificent cathedral, its bell tower and baptistry, the latter with the famous **gilded bronze doors by Ghiberti and Pisano**. If you've visited Florence in spring or summer and stood in those long queues at the Accademia Gallery waiting for a look at Michaelangelo's David, **you'll be glad you're on a tour** this time as your group is herded past the independent tourists for priority entrance. **Excursions don't usually visit the famous Uffizi Gallery** (some of it closed after the 1993 car bomb explosion) or the Pitti Palace; if you want to see them, you're best on your own. Cruise lines often offer an **optional shuttle bus** ($$) to Florence for visitors who want to spend more time shopping or walking around on their own. Shoppers look for the city's **fine quality leather goods** (not cheap), jewelry, Pucci clothing and exquisite patterned papers. The famous Ponte Vecchio bridge over the Arno is lined with shops, some of them quite elegant.

Naples, Italy ★

Language:	**Italian**	English Spoken?:	**Some**
Currency:	**Lira**	US$ ok?:	**No**
To town:	**Taxi, walk**		

Naples gets more and more congested with foot and motor traffic, and **petty crime such as purse snatchings** is rampant, especially by thieves riding on motorbikes who can reach out and easily grab purses, cameras, even sunglasses. Don't carry or wear valuables ashore here. The **traffic, too, is dangerous to pedestrians**; no one stops for traffic lights or obeys traffic signs. The most popular shore excursions here are to Pompeii or Capri ($$–$$$). You should plan to stick with the ship's excursion bus if you want to get out of town; **car and bike rentals are not available** here because of the extremely high rate of theft. On a visit last summer, we had to hire a car and driver to get from the Naples airport to board a ship in Sorrento. The Pompeii tour ($$) spends half a day visiting the city covered in lava and ash by **eruptions of Mt. Vesuvius** in 79 A.D. Remains of the villas, shops and chariot-rutted streets still fascinate visitors. A half-day tour of the city of Naples ($$) usually includes a visit to the National Archeological Museum, housing a world-class collection of Greco-Roman artifacts including the **famous Farnese Bull**. The Duomo with its San Gennaro Chapel is a pilgrimage site in May, September and December when the faithful gather to pray that two vials said to contain the blood of St. Januarius (Gennaro) will liquefy and save the city from impending disaster.

Palermo, Italy　★

Language:	**Italian**	*English Spoken?:*	**Some**
Currency:	**Lira**	*US$ ok?:*	**No**
To town:	**Taxi; don't walk in the port area**		

This once-beautiful capital city of Sicily is still reeling from the Mafia tria and assassinations of the past several years, and where we once walked free all over the city, **we would think twice now about even getting off a ship tha called here**. Not that many do—usually just Italian lines call now. A typica half-day city tour ($$) includes a drive out to the lovely 12th century hillto cathedral of **Santa Maria la Nuova**, a striking blend of Norman, Arab, Byzan tine and classical architecture with handsome mosaics; the **Capuchin cata combs** with some 8000 skeletons lined up against the wall; and the exuberan (and decaying) palaces of the old town. Street vendors sell the handsome **Si cilian puppets**, usually paladins and Saracens dressed in metal armor witl swords; performances are noisy with all the clanging but delight local chil dren. The **International Puppet Museum** is on Piazza Marina. The **Vucciria frui and vegetable markets** are on the route to the port. Among Italy's most col orful, the market sells sausages, cheeses, tomatoes and garlic, a veritabl pizza in the raw.

Portofino never changes; by law, no one can change any of the colors of the building facades or the types of shutters, doors and windows.

Portofino, Italy ★★★★★

Language:	**Italian**	*English Spoken?:*	**Yes**
Currency:	**Lira**	*US$ ok?:*	**No**
To town:	**Tender from anchorage**		

One of the favorite ports of the rich and famous —as well as the not so rich and famous—is the elegant little village of Portofino. It looks like a mirage when you first glimpse it from the sea, its ocher, rose and gold buildings tucked into rocky cliffs. It starred in a lushly romantic film called *Enchanted April* not long ago, and yes, it really does look like that. A ship's tender will deposit you at the cobblestoned square at the waterfront, steps away from appealing (and expensive) sidewalk cafes, understated but posh little shops and boutiques and very fashionable restaurants. If **you're feeling flush**, turn right and walk uphill to the **Hotel Splendido**, sit on the terrace where so many movie stars have and order the house special, a—guess what?—Splendido, a mix of **champagne and framboise with a few fresh raspberries** dropped in for ballast. Hey, it's a bargain at $12, right? And you've got that great view down to your ship at anchor. If you're feeling poor (not poorly, however, because this is a steep climb) hike up the hill on the left side of the harbor from the stairs behind the Church of San Giorgio to the Castle of San Giorgio, where you'll discover why Portofino never changes—there is a scale model of the village inside that's used by the city fathers to dictate the precise tint each building facade must be painted, as well as the angle of each shutter and the slant of each roofline. Splurge on **a fresh sea bass baked in a coat of rock salt at Ristorante Puny** on the main square, or buy a foccacio-to-go from the **Canale family bakery** behind Puny. If you feel restless, walk or catch the inexpensive local bus over to the larger, less costly community of Santa Margharita about three miles away.

Portovenere, Italy ★★★★

Language:	**Italian**	*English Spoken?:*	**Some**
Currency:	**Lira**	*US$ ok?:*	**No**
To town:	**Tender**		

A newly discovered port is one of the Cinque Terre (five towns) of the Liguria coast, Portovenere.

Portovenere is one of the charming Cinque Terre villages of the Italian Riviera. Only a few small ships like the sailing vessels from Star Clippers call here, but it's a rewarding port for curious travelers who love **exploring and poking around on their own. Roman galleys used to stop here** on their way to Gaul in 161 A.D. The dramatic, gray-striped stone Church of St. Peter from 1277 is prominent at one end of the harbor and a 13th century Genovese castle is atop the hill; you walk up a long, broad, stone stairway, stopping off at intervals to peer through holes in the rocky cliffs at **people splashing about in the Grotto Aparia below**. It's called Byron's Grotto, because the English poet and exhibitionist Lord Byron jumped off here to swim to Lirici. Seafood restaurants like **Ristorante Elettra** (where we had some good mussels, calamari and pasta for lunch) line the waterfront, and **prices are fairly moderate** for this coast. We also found a wonderful deli called **G. Capellini** which sells salami, olives, foccacio and wine.

Sardinia, Italy ★★★★

Language:	**Italian**	English Spoken?:	**Some**
Currency:	**Lira**	US$ ok?:	**No**
To town:	**Depends on port**		

This **bone-dry desert island** plopped in a cerulean sea is renowned as a European jet-set paradise with its gorgeous **luxury hotels built by the Aga Khan** and its harbor full of gleaming yachts. But don't hope to hop a cab for lunch at the chi chi **Cala di Volpe** unless you're a friend of Gianni's (of the Fiat gnellis). Smaller cruise ships usually come into Porto Cervo (where the Aga han's modest summer residence can still be spotted across the bay) or ,olfo Aranci, the hot condo development. Some ships, however, dock in the ss interesting cities of Olbia or Cagliari. If you don't take a shore excursion, ɔu'll need a rental car (hard to find) or a car and driver, which the ship's con- ierge can arrange ahead of time. To buy? **Semi-precious stones**, leather ɔods, filigree gold or silver jewelry, rustic crafts. Lunch on grilled local sea- ɔod and cold white Sardinian wines at the **Hotel Sporting in Porto Rotondo**.

DID YOU KNOW?

On our first visit to Sardinia more than a decade ago, we innocently asked our driver guide to take us to "the villages," meaning those primitive moun- tain towns we'd heard about where women still wore native costume and farmers rode in burro-drawn carts. We couldn't understand why she kept driving us to time-share and condo hotels until we realized the term "vil- lages" means vacation condos in much of today's Europe.

Sorrento, Italy ★ ★ ★

Language:	**Italian**	*English Spoken?:*	**Some**
Currency:	**Lira**	*US$ ok?:*	**No**
To town:	**Tender from ship**		

On our most recent cruise from here, we learned small ships are no longer permitted to come alongside at the town pier as they used do; that's now re- served for ferries. **Cruise vessels anchor out in the picturesque harbor** with a wonderful view of the city walls rising steeply from the sea and palm trees and hotels lining the sea wall. A stairway with 200 steps and various private elevators glide up and down from the pier and the waterfront cafes. From here a number of shore excursions take off in different directions. A **Sorrento, Positano and Amalfi drive** ($$) takes in a portion of the world-famous Amalfi Drive lined with pine and lemon groves, pausing perhaps at Amalfi and Pos- itano for shopping and cafe stops. Anyone frightened by winding roads and a lack of guard rails may prefer another tour. For **Capri, passengers board a hy- drofoil** ($$) to the idyllic island for a boat tour of the Blue Grotto and a shop- ping stop in the hillside town. Passengers wanting to see **Pompeii**, buried by the sudden eruption of Mt. Vesuvius in 79 A.D., are taken on a half-day tour ($$–$$$) by bus to the town, stopping at sites like the House of the Danc- ing Faun and the House of the Vetti Brothers. **Herculaneum**, the latter also buried by Vesuvius but excavated much later than Pompeii, is smaller but better preserved. Passengers on the shore excursion ($$–$$$) visit the House of Neptune, House of the Drunken Satyr and **House of the Carbonized Furniture**, which should give you a good idea of the scenery.

Taormina, Italy ★★★

Language:	**Italian**	*English Spoken?:*	**Yes**
Currency:	**Lira**	*US$ ok?:*	**No**
To town:	**Shuttle or excursion bus**		

Your ship will actually dock at Catania, near the foot of Mt. Etna, or at Messina, and shuttle passengers uphill to the outskirts of this charming hilltop town. From here, most make their way easily on foot into the **pedestrian only streets**, which are lined with sidewalk cafes, elegant boutiques and pastry and candy shops specializing in the **ultra-rich sweets of Sicily**. The first tourists here were the Greeks and Romans 2000 years ago, but traffic fell off after repeated eruptions of Mt. Etna and didn't catch fire again until the English and German romantics rediscovered it early this century. A **magnificent third century Greek ampitheater** is perched precariously on the hillside with a great view of Mt. Etna and the Mediterranean; it's still used for Italy's summer film festival where the Davids (Oscar equivalents) are awarded. If you're on a shore excursion ($-$$), you'll have the bus shuttle from the port and a guided walk-through of the theater included in your ticket price. At the end of the main street, Corso Umberto I, you'll find a tiny funicular which will whisk you down to the beach of Mazzaro.

The highlight of a Mediterranean cruise for many is a call at Venice, where a stroll around St. Mark's Square is de rigeur.

Venice, Italy ★★★★★

Language:	**Italian**	*English Spoken?:*	**Yes**
Currency:	**Lira**	*US$ ok?:*	**No**
To town:	**Vaporetto (water bus) or water taxi**		

From the city's docks, it's 15 minutes by water taxi, a bit longer by vaporetto, to the **Piazza San Marco**, the sublimely beautiful square Napoleon called Europe's finest drawing room. But we sometimes feel as Truman Capote did when he said, "Venice is like eating an entire box of chocolate liqueurs in one go." If it's your first visit, you should take a half-day guided tour ($$) around the Piazza into the Basilica San Marco, the Doge's Palace, the Treasury and Basilica Museum, but stick close to your guide. In summer there are **so many tourists and so many languages being shouted simultaneously** that it's hard to understand everything. On your own, set out on foot and wander; you won't stay lost very long, since piazzas and alleyways are usually posted with yellow signs and arrows pointing you to familiar tourist landmarks. Do **stop by Harry's Bar** ($$$) for a drink or a meal; the most famous drink is a peach juice and champagne concoction called a Bellini, but they also make the world's best martinis. When you need to travel where you can't go on foot, remember that **Venice's water-borne bus system works well and cheaply**; water taxis and gondolas are unbelievably expensive and should be used sparingly.

Valletta, Malta ★★★

Language:	**Maltese**	*English Spoken?:*	**Yes**
Currency:	**Maltese Lira**	*US$ ok?:*	**No**
To town:	**Walk**		

As your ship sails into the bay, the city of Valletta with its **medieval castles and fortress walls** looks like a movie set; you half expect to see Kevin Costner swinging in on a rope. In 1530, Malta was given to the **Knights of the Order of St. John of Jerusalem**, and after soundly defeating Turkish foes in a three-month siege, the Knights, then called Knights of Malta, were hailed as the heroes of Europe. Many of Valletta's historic buildings date from that period. Don't worry if you haven't mastered Maltese; **many of the local residents speak English** because the strategically located island was also a British colony for 160 years. A half-day shore excursion here ($$) usually drives over to **Medina, the old capital** of Malta, where a chance to shop in **Ta Qali Crafts Village** lets you see craftsmen at work making lace, jewelry and decorative glass. Then you return to Valletta for a stop at **St. John's Cathedral**. A shopping stop at the Malta Crafts Centre opposite the cathedral will net you some of the country's lacework, gold and silver filigree jewelry, leather products, Oriental rugs or decorative glass. A short audio-visual production called **"The Malta Experience"** ($) can be seen in the Mediterranean Conference Center on Merchants Street.

Monte Carlo, Monaco

Language:	**French, Monegasque**	*English Spoken?:*	**Yes**
Currency:	**Franc**		
US$ ok?:	**No**	*To town:*	**Walk**

The fabled Casino of Monte Carlo at night.

On our most recent visit it was January and the sun was shining, the blue skies clear, the air comfortably warm (too warm for the parade of fur coats that are apparently obligatory in winter), the streets were cleaner than Disneyland and the throngs of summer had disappeared. An **elegant little jewel of a town**, Monte Carlo offers **perfection, at a price**, admittedly, but an hour of cafe-sitting and people-watching at the fashionable Cafe de Paris costs no more than the price of a cup of coffee or glass of wine. A half-day tour ($$) includes a visit to the casino, a look at the posh Hotel de Paris and L'Ermitage, a visit to the palace for the changing of the guard, sometimes a visit to the Oceanographic Museum or a look into the **hushed cathedral where Princess Grace is buried**. But you can easily do all this on your own if you don't mind climbing up and down a few hills. (In some places, there are public el-ators.) Visit the delightful Musée National with its animated dolls and **18th century automatons**. The city's parks offer gorgeous views of the harbor and ..., the shops are tempting but expensive, and the casino square looks **like omething out of a movie set (which it often is)**.

One caution: the casino is not like those you may be accustomed to in Las ...gas; except for the slots area, you **pay admission and must meet a dress code gamble**. If you want American-style gambling, go to the casino at Loews ...otel.

Casablanca, Morocco   ★★★

Language:	**Arabic**	English Spoken?:	**Yes**
Currency:	**Dirham**	US$ ok?:	**No**
To town:	**Walk, taxi**		

While the modern city of Casablanca is fairly interesting (**don't expect it to ook like it did in the Humphrey Bogart movie**), the best reason to come here is ...o take the all-day tour through the desert 150 miles to the 11th century im...erial city of Marrakech ($$$) or Rabat, the capital ($$$). Marrakech is fa...mous for its rosy-pink palaces, lush gardens and the **huge Djemma El Fna marketplace where snake charmers, jugglers, acrobats, fire-eaters and fortune-ellers congregate** to separate you from your pocket change. Make one move ...oward the market stalls and a hundred freelance "guides" will leap to your ...ide and importune you in English to hire their services. (It looks very much ...he way it did in the Hitchcock movie; remember Jimmy Stewart and Doris Day in *The Man Who Knew Too Much?*) The lavish **La Mamounia Hotel**, where Winston Churchill used to stay, would be an ideal place to slip away for a ...uiet lunch if you can afford the prices. Should you prefer to **stay in Casablan-ca**, you will probably be offered a half-day city tour ($$) that usually visits ...he old medina (Arab quarter), points out the French colonial- and Moroc-can-style architecture in the *ville nouvelle*, perhaps visits the Hassan II Mosque and shows you a couple of local beaches en route. On your own, you can enjoy a relatively hassle-free walk through the medina, although prices are higher than in other Moroccan cities.

Lisbon, Portugal   ★★★★

Language:	**Portuguese**	English Spoken?:	**Yes**
Currency:	**Escudo**	US$ ok?:	**No**
To town:	**Taxi**		

Lisbon's monument to Henry the Navigator is also one of the most striking sculptures in the world.

Sailing into Lisbon under the dramatic April 25th Bridge over the River Tagus makes for a memorable moment (and some **memorable photographs**). A half-day city tour ($$) may include the famous **monument to Prince Henry the Navigator**, perhaps a stop at the handsome antique coach museum nearby, a look at Lisbon's colorful old Alfama Quarter and a stop at Praça do Rossio in the middle of town with time for shopping. Other shore excursions here head out of town, offering a drive to the **seaside resort of Estoril**, a stop at Sintra's National Palace, and the beautifully restored Royal Palace at Queluz ($$–$$$) or a port wine tasting ($$). On your own, you might want to take a taxi over to the **incredible Gulbenkian Foundation Museum** to see the fine collections of French Impressionists, Oriental carpets and sculpture. Shopping can still be a **bargain** here; look for **leather goods**, hand-embroidered textiles, pottery (especially the handsome blue-and-white tiles) and filigree

velry. Note that prices are written with a $ sign between the number of es-
dos on the left and centavos (cents) on the right, the way we use the dec-
al point to separate the figures. A woman out walking on her own may
ar **a strange sort of hissing sound** when she passes several men; it's the Por-
guese equivalent of a wolf whistle.

Barcelona, Spain ★★★

Language:	**Spanish**	*English Spoken?:*	**Some**
Currency:	**Peseta**	*US$ ok?:*	**No**
To town:	**Walk or taxi**		

You may, like us, really enjoy wandering around on your own in Barcelona,
ut **be careful around the Ramblas** and the Gothic Quarter near the docks, be-
ause there's more petty crime than there used to be including a scam with
arnations by pickpockets. If you go for a stroll, leave your valuables on
oard. City tours here ($$) usually include a drive to the top of Montjuic for
he view, a look at **Gaudi's surrealistic Church of the Sagrada Familia**, a glimpse
f the Columbus statue and replica of the Santa Maria in the port, a look at
he back streets of the old town's 14th century Barri Gotic (Gothic Quarter),
nd sometimes a visit to **the Picasso Museum** or the Spanish Village with its
rafts shops and architectural recreations. If you're interested in art, you
might take a taxi up to **the extraordinary Museum of Catalonian Art** with its
rescoes from small Pyrenees churches, plus canvases by great painters like
Velazquez, Zurbaran and El Greco. If you didn't take an excursion that in-
luded the Picasso Museum, go by there as well, and take a look inside the
St. Joseph's Market on the Ramblas. The Maritime Museum will also interest
hip fans. A glass of sherry and some tapas in a bar along the Ramblas can
ound out the day nicely.

Cádiz, Spain ★★★

Language:	**Spanish**	*English Spoken?:*	**Some**
Currency:	**Peseta**	*US$ ok?:*	**No**
To town:	**Taxi, or excursion bus to Seville**		

Sailing into Cádiz with its **brooding medieval ramparts** is more dramatic than
the city itself turns out to be, so most visitors, at least on a first visit, opt for
the shore excursion to Seville instead of staying in the port city. From the
port of Cádiz, an all-day tour ($$$) visits the **historic Moorish city of Seville,**

including the 15th century cathedral, the **largest Gothic cathedral in the wor** with its Giralda Tower and Orange Tree Court; the Moorish **Alcazar fortre and gardens**; the Golden Tower, so-called because it was where the go laden galleons arrived from the New World; and the Barrio de Santa Cr the 17th century quarter favored by aristocrats. After lunch, the tour conti ues to the Plaza de España, where **the bullring featured in the opera *Carmen*** located, and to the Maria Luisa Park and its sunken gardens. If you dor want to take the 60-mile bus ride to Seville, it's usually possible to book two-hour walking tour around Cádiz ($) that visits the 18th century cath dral, the Fine Arts Museum with its **excellent collection of Zurbaran**, the Co gress Court of Spain and the Plaza de Mina. On your own in Cádiz, you m want to drop by the Historical Museum to see a curious 18th century ivo and mahogany model of the town. On the other hand, you may not.

Ibiza, Spain

Language:	**Spanish**	*English Spoken?:*	**Yes**
Currency:	**Peseta**	*US$ ok?:*	**No**
To town:	**Walk**		

The **port area is lined with seafood and sidewalk cafes where you can go gaz pacho-tasting**, and the nearby Marina Quarter is chockablock with trend and hippy shops and boutiques. If you can get out of town and away from the tourist areas, this little Balearic Island still seems unhurried and tradition al. A half- or full-day excursion ($$) will show you **whitewashed houses alon village streets** with bright shutters, groves of pine and almond trees, sand beaches and rocky cliffs. And a shopping stop en route may net you some **very fine quality Mallorca pearls** (they're made here on Ibiza as well on Mal lorca) at excellent prices. On your own, head uphill for **great views from the old city walls**. The cathedral with its massive 13th century belfry and the ar cheological museum are on the way up or down. In the latter, you'll fin Punic art from the seventh century B.C., Egyptian jewelry, Roman coins anc Greek amphorae. Lots of **clothing-optional beaches** and lively nightlife are also available; check locally for the latest word.

INSIDER TIP

While Ibiza makes a delightful stop for a one-day excursion, it should be avoided for a longer stay during July and August because it's packed with tourists from the UK, Germany and Scandinavia busy getting sunburned.

Málaga, Spain ★★★

Language:	**Spanish**	English Spoken?:	**Yes**
Currency:	**Peseta**	US$ ok?:	**No**
To town:	**Walk**		

Located at the eastern edge of Spain's **famous (and very tourist-driven) Costa del Sol**, Málaga is best visited in the spring or fall unless you don't mind **mobs of package tourists**. Traffic is congested, the coast is lined with high-rise hotels and time-share condos and the beaches are full of **northern Europeans grilling themselves lobster red**. Still, the **Arab-Spanish mix of Málaga** can be intriguing for a daytripper who can go back on board ship in the evening and avoid the crowds. The fortresses of Gibralfaro and Alcazaba offer grand views and Moorish gardens, and the Museo de Bellas Artes includes paintings by **native son Pablo Picasso**, who was born at 15 Plaza de la Merced, now a museum funded by the Picasso Foundation. While a few of the artist's sketches and pottery pieces are on hand, most interesting are the **family and personal pictures** that decorate the walls. An optional half-day shore excursion ($$) includes a driving tour of the Costa del Sol, a sampling of Málaga wines, a visit to the resort town of Torremolinos (**nicknamed "Terrible Torre" for its mobs**), and the mountain village of Mijas. A full-day excursion to **Granada's Alhambra** ($$$) is also offered on some sailings.

Palma de Mallorca, Spain ★★★

Language:	**Spanish**	English Spoken?:	**Yes**
Currency:	**Peseta**	US$ ok?:	**No**
To town:	**Walk**		

Largest of Spain's Balearic Islands, Mallorca is better-known for its beaches and resorts than its sightseeing and shopping, but even with only a day in port, you can squeeze in a bit of each. Just keep in mind that it gets very **crowded with tourists** during the summer months. The half-day city tours here ($$) usually visit the **Gothic cathedral, begun in the 13th century but finished in the 17th**; the 14th-century Bellver Castle on the edge of town, later used as a prison; and sometimes the Spanish Pueblo, a recreated Spanish village and crafts center, and the white sand beaches along the bay. If you prefer to set out **on foot from the port, you can easily cover most of the sites** except Bellver Castle, which really isn't that special. To explore the island outside town on your own, however, you're better off with a taxi or car and driver;

roads are narrow and curvy. A countryside half-day tour ($$) drives out
Valledemosa's monastery of La Cartuja, where **Chopin and George Sand spe**
the winter of 1838. Other notable native sons include painter Joan Miró a
Father Junipero Serra, who founded California's chain of missions. Shopp
will find **Mallorca pearls in a wide range of prices and lengths**, as well as ine
pensive olive wood beads and bracelets, leather goods and locally-made p
tery and raffia.

Tunis, Tunisia ★

Language:	**Arabic**	*English Spoken?:*	**Some**
Currency:	**Dinar**	*US$ ok?:*	**No**
To town:	**Taxi**		

Every traveler has **one never-go-again spot** in the world, and ours is Tunis.
had something to do with our timing—we arrived in August of 1990, rig
after Saddam Hussein had invaded Kuwait and the Arab world was hostile t
the U.S. passport, and particularly journalists carrying a U.S. passport. (Fc
the story, see *CostaMarina*, page 234) There is a half-day city tour ($$) o
fered; we had planned to take it but changed our minds and refused to leav
the port area. The city "is **not a wildly exciting city**" except perhaps for pokin
around **the ruins of Carthage**, and the medina is only "mildly interesting" (tc
quote our peers who write the Lonely Planet books). We refused the oppor
tunity to explore it.

Rating the Ports of the Eastern Mediterranean

Varna, Bulgaria ★ ★

Language:	**Bulgarian**	*English Spoken?:*	**Little**
Currency:	**Lev**	*US$ ok?:*	**No**
To town:	**Excursion bus**		

Bulgarian folk dancers are often on the program if your ship calls at Varna.

We were aboard a small ship on our most recent visit to Varna, and passengers were offered a choice of a full-day ($$$) or a half-day excursion ($$). Almost everyone chose the half-day, but **since the Bulgarians had already planned a full-day program, they just accelerated events** to cram everything into slightly more than half a day because they are so anxious to build up their tourism. We were taken first to visit in a private home, where we were served **homemade wine and Easter cakes** by the host and hostess and watched a weaving demonstration by the grandmother. Then we were driven to a seaside resort, crumbling a bit now that the big spenders from the Party are gone and the normal citizen can't afford it. In a picturesque peasant-style restaurant we were served **sweet local champagne, toasted hazelnuts and palatshinken** (pancakes) while we watched a very energetic folkloric show that lasted about an hour. After that we visited the museum of art and history to see **antique icons and a magnificent collection of Thracian gold** from 4000 B.C. discovered in a 200-grave necropolis in 1972. There was no shopping, because the state-owned shops are closed and no one could remember where

the crafts and crystal dealers have moved. While there's no particular dan⌐
here in striking out on your own, there's **not a lot to see**.

Limassol, Cyprus ★★★

Language:	**Greek**	*English Spoken?:*	**Yes**
Currency:	**C Pound**	*US$ ok?:*	**No**
To town:	**Taxi**		

The Cyprus countryside is fragrant from the scent of orange and lem⌐
blossoms and bright with flowers. We took an all-day island tour ($$
which included a stop at a **typical Greek Cypriot restaurant in Paphos where w⌐
were served a meal with 20 to 25 hot and cold dishes**, one after another in da⌐
zling array, including white beans in a rich tomato sauce, eggplant and pe⌐
pers in olive oil, pita bread with grilled *halloumi* cheese, tiny whole frie⌐
sardines, lamb kebabs and wine-marinated meat cooked in a tightly seale⌐
dish called *ofto kleftico*, finishing off with mushrooms and garlic, then a bi⌐
tray of fresh local oranges and bananas. **Paphos is the main tourist area**, one ⌐
the UNESCO world heritage sites and home of the tombs of the kings (the⌐
weren't really kings but public officials) carved out of underground rock b⌐
the sea, and the **magnificent mosaics of Paphos**, seen by walking along wood⌐
en boardwalks raised above the floors of a nobleman's house from the thir⌐
century B.C. Souvenirs to buy to take home include the very sweet Cypru⌐
delight candy, similar to Turkish delight. Then of course, there's the eve⌐
popular stop at the birthplace of Aphrodite, Petra Tou Pomiou; a tour of th⌐
handsome modern resort **Coral Beach Hotel**; and a stroll along the Papho⌐
waterfront with its famous resident pelicans. Cyprus is a partitioned island⌐
nation with the south Greek and the north Turkish, each using a differen⌐
currency and language.

Alexandria, Egypt ★★★

Language:	**Egyptian**	*English Spoken?:*	**Yes**
Currency:	**Egyptian Le**	*US$ ok?:*	**No**
To town:	**Taxi**		

Some ships call at Alexandria, one of the major port accesses for Cairo, be-
cause it offers a more interesting route for an all-day tour ($$$) than the bor-
ing desert drive from Port Said. One of the great cities of the ancient world,
Alexandria looks a little shabby today, with only a few hints of its grand past. In

Eastern Mediterranean

© 1995 Fielding Worldwide, Inc.

Cairo, the major destinations are **the pyramids and the magnificent, albeit du**
and badly-lit, Cairo Museum. The latter is well worth several hours if you h
an excellent guide. If your excursion group is large, struggle to stay near
guide because that's the only way you'll understand what you're seeing.
Pyramids, on the other hand, have been **experienced second-hand so ma**
times that, like the Grand Canyon, you tend to say, Yeah, that's how
thought they'd look. **Learn the word "baksheesh,"** which is often hissed
you by someone who feels he deserves a tip, like the man who helps you
the camel, should you be so misguided as to get up there in the first pla
Egypt is intermittently a troubled port of call with concerted acts of terr
ism committed against tourists by religious fundamentalists. For that reas
check with the U.S. State Department for the latest travel advisory about t
region before booking your journey, especially if you're planning to tra
on a vessel that is not a ship frequently used by North Americans, as, say, t
late *Achille Lauro*, no matter how good a bargain you got.

Suez Canal, Egypt   ★ ★

Language:	**Egyptian**	English Spoken?:	**Yes**
Currency:	**LE (pound)**	US$ ok?:	**No**
To town:	**Cruise through**		

Neither **Port Said**, the town at the north end of the canal, nor Suez at t
south end, holds any particular interest for the average traveler except as
gateway to Cairo, two hours or so away. Occasionally, passengers may emba
or disembark here, but it's best to **stay with the group for transfers** and n
wander off on your own, since it's very difficult to reenter the port without
distribution of *baksheesh* (tips) to the gate guards.

The transit of the Suez, unfortunately, is not as interesting as the Panan
Canal, except for the area **still littered with broken military hardware** from th
1967 Israeli War. The canal was closed at the beginning of that military a
tion and not reopened until 1975. The **normal Suez transit takes about 1**
hours, but it's possible for a cruise ship to be required to anchor to allow
convoy of cargo ships to pass through, lengthening the transit to 18 hours
even longer. It can be **stultifyingly hot** on deck when you're anchored in th
canal without a breeze stirring. From the Red Sea port of Safaga, south
Suez, passengers are sometimes taken on shore excursions through th
desert to **the Nile city of Luxor** ($$$).

Corfu, Greece ★★★

Language:	**Greek**	English Spoken?:	**Yes**
Currency:	**Drachma**	US$ ok?:	**No**
To town:	**Walk, taxi**		

Corfu, the westernmost of the Greek Islands, is where you'll find tiny Mouse Island; England's Prince Philip spent much of his early life in Corfu.

An all-day tour ($$$) is the best way to cover this large island if you haven't een here before. On one recent visit, we took a tour that included an excellnt **seafood lunch by a beach in Paleokastitsa** between visits to monasteries, ncient baths, temples, palaces and gardens. The **westernmost of the Greek Isands**, Corfu has a multicultural history with a dash of Venetian, British and urkish influences over the centuries. Big, lush and gray-green from its **milons of olive trees**, the island looks nothing like its cousins to the east. At live harvest time, islanders spread black mesh nets around each tree to catch he fragile fruit. On your own in Corfu town, you can hire a **horse-drawn carage**, explore the old town or just stroll through the Liston, a graceful arade lined with sidewalk cafes and charming little shops selling olive wood ecklaces and bowls, strings of amber and gold jewelry. The morning market s bright with rows of silver sardines, glass jars of topaz island honey, bunches f dark green parsley and heaps of golden oranges. Glifada is perhaps the **est and most popular beach**; it lies about a half-hour's drive from Corfu own. A beach club provides changing rooms, sun lounging chairs and umrellas for a small fee.

Crete, Greece

Language:	**Greek**	English Spoken?:	**Yes**
Currency:	**Drachma**	US$ ok?:	**No**
To town:	**Walk, taxi**		

Most cruise ships arrive in the capital of Heraklion, which is divided into modern and an ancient city. **Home island to Zorba the Greek**, Crete has the same bigger-than-life swagger and appetite for joy as Nikos Kazantzakis' fictional hero. Few tours include the grave of Kazantzakis, which is in Heraklion off the Plastira by the old city walls, or the museum devoted to him which is nine miles southeast of town. If you want to visit on your own, call ahead to make sure the museum is open. The half-day shore excursions here ($$) take in the two obligatory sights of Crete, the 4000-year-old **Minoan palace of Knossos**, five miles from town, and the **magnificent archeological museum in Heraklion** with its frescoes and artifacts from Knossos. If you have some time to wander around on your own, the **morning fruit and vegetable market** is colorful, with Greek Orthodox priests in black cassocks and black hats browsing among the vegetables with their shopping bags in hand, a blind lottery salesman hawking tickets, a fishmonger repelling flies from his merchandise with a flourishing spray of insect repellent. The unique fuzzy green herb dittany of Crete is sold here as a folk remedy for colds.

Delos, Greece

Language:	**Greek**	English Spoken?:	**Some**
Currency:	**Drachma**	US$ ok?:	**No**
To town:	**Tender from anchorage**		

The **uninhabited island of Delos** has been a major pilgrimage point since the days when it was a sanctuary dedicated to Apollo. It's usually a half-day port of call on a Greek Islands cruise, coupled with a stop at nearby Mykonos for the other half-day. Morning is the best time to visit, the earlier the better, because as the day goes on, more and more day-trippers arrive and are herded around by guides speaking every known language at the tops of their lungs. The **famous crouching stone lions of Delos have been worn down by generations of visitors climbing on their backs**; today they are protected by small ropes that make them off-limits only to law-abiding adults. Only five remain of the original nine carved of marble from the neighboring island of Naxos in the 6th century B.C. Step away from the crowds to contemplate the lions or

ok at the beautiful mosaic floors remaining from Greek villas like the **House
the Masks and House of the Dolphins** that date from the second century BC.
en you can still imagine the ghosts of the past whispering in the winds
t rustle through the dried grass and ruffle the crimson petals of the pop-
s that bloom everywhere.

Mykonos, Greece ★★★★

Language:	**Greek**	*English Spoken?:*	**Yes**
Currency:	**Drachma**	*US$ ok?:*	**No**
To town:	**Tender from anchorage**		

*n the island of Mykonos, the pelican is the official town mascot, but that
esn't mean he has good manners. He's a surly bird who'll snap at anyone.*

Mykonos is that rare port in the Greek islands where there is **no obligatory
ightseeing**, no ancient temples or palaces, no birthplace of gods or site of
lood-gushing familial slayings, just a colorful town of **seafood restaurants,
indmills and magnificent sunsets**. The town mascot is a **curmudgeonly pelican**
ho'll stab nastily at you with his beak if you get too close. Despite regula-
ons that prohibit painting a house anything but white (even the streets are
hitewashed), the town is **a riot of color**, bright blue trim painted on daz-
ling whitewashed houses piled up against the hills like a spilled box of sugar
ubes, a shock of red geraniums and fuchsia bougainvillea, punctuated by
ternly garbed men and women in black who sit outside their homes in the
te afternoons, eyes closed against the glare and the prowling mobs of Euro-
outh. There is **no organized shore excursion** on what is usually an afternoon
nd evening call, a bit of a respite from your cruise ship's cram course in

Greek Culture 101. Most people are content to wander around the stree pausing for a cold drink at a sidewalk cafe or a browse in one of the chic a expensive boutiques. By sunset, many are checking out spit-roasted lamb grilled fresh fish at one of the outdoor cafes near the harbor.

Piraeus/Athens, Greece ★★★

Language:	**Greek**	*English Spoken?:*	**Yes**
Currency:	**Drachma**	*US$ ok?:*	**No**
To town:	**From port to Athens, by train, taxi or shuttle bus**		

The tiny island of Hydra is on just a few cruise itineraries, most often feature on a one- or two-day cruise out of Piraeus.

Piraeus, the port of Athens, is **chockful of cruise ships** year-round. In th winter months, many are laid up; in the summer, all in working condition s out for cruises into the Greek Islands from one to 14 days. It takes about ha an hour to get to Athens, depending on the often-horrendous traffic. **Th electric train**, its station within walking distance of the port, is the quicke and most economical way to get there if you're setting out on your own Half-day shore excursions here ($$) usually include the obligatory visit t the **Parthanon in the Acropolis** (a difficult-to-impossible climb for people wh have problems walking), a pause at Constitution Square to watch the *evzon* guards in the stiff tutus marching back and forth at the Tomb of the Un known Soldier, **one or more archeological museums** (most are excellent), an at least **one shopping stop at a souvenir shop operated by a friend or relative o the guide**. Still, this is the best way to see this great, historic city. For som visitors, the unsightly problems of modern Athens spoil the enjoyment of th ient city, with heavy pollution taking its toll on ancient buildings and ffic jams so dense that 50 percent of the vehicles in the area are banned m entering the city every other day. Friends who picked us up for lunch ologized for the beat-up VW van they were driving; it was their second car h license plate numbers permitted for that alternate day.

Rhodes, Greece ★★★★

Language:	**Greek**	*English Spoken?:*	**Yes**
Currency:	**Drachma**	*US$ ok?:*	**No**
To town:	**Walk from dock, tender from anchorage**		

his lovely lady is perhaps the most-photographed citizen of Rhodes; she lives in indos on the route uphill to the Acropolis and sells handmade lace.

Most ships, especially larger ones, dock or anchor at the city of Rhodes, hich lies at the north end of the island, but a few smaller vessels may anchor f Lindos toward the south. The **Acropolis of Lindos** is the island's most important site, reached on foot or donkey back (we prefer the former) from the wn square. The narrow route passes **lacemakers sitting in front of their hitewashed cottages**. Shore excursions from the city of Rhodes include a alf-day to Lindos, a half-day to Mt. Philermos and city tour, a half-day Kairos and Mt. Phileremos tour and a Rhodes Jewish and Turkish Quarter ur ($$). If you take the Lindos tour, you usually have **a stop at a ceramics ctory** (required by the local government, we were told) on the way back to hodes. Other excursions offer a city tour of Rhodes, but enterprising passengers could manage this on their own. The entrance to the ancient port as, they say, once straddled by the 100-foot bronze **Colossus of Rhodes**,

which later toppled in an earthquake. The bronze deer that flank the p
today are still charming, if not awe-inspiring. The medieval walls and cas
grandiloquently reconstructed during a Mussolini moment in 1940, and
Turkish market and baths are usually included on the city tour ($$). C
bled Knights' Street reminds travelers of the medieval history of Rhodes,
of bastions of the Knights of St. John.

Santorini, Greece ★ ★ ★

Language:	**Greek**	*English Spoken?:*	**Yes**
Currency:	**Drachma**	*US$ ok?:*	**No**
To town:	**Tender, then cable car or donkey up the hill**		

A pair of passengers look at their cruise ship anchored far, far below in
caldera of this volcanic island.

Some claim Santorini is the remains of the **lost island of Atlantis**, not unlik
ly when you consider how many earthquakes and volcanic eruptions it h
undergone. The **capital city of Thera** is perched on a steep peak rising out
the sea, bristling with whitewashed houses and churches along its spine. T
ship's anchorage is the caldera, the central crater filled with sea water. T
tender takes passengers ashore and deposits them at the harbor to sort o
their transportation uphill. There's a cartoon posted in the souvenir shops
Santorini showing a melancholy donkey looking out at a cruise ship in t
harbor while a balloon from his imagination shows an obese tourist sittii
on his sagging back. This is why we never ride the donkeys uphill, but ta
the newer cable car at roughly the same price. There are usually **no organize
shore excursions** offered here, but it's simple to wander around the tow

oking into churches and shops and cafes for the half-day most ships allot
r this call. There is no natural water on the island, only that gathered in cis-
rns or brought in by barge. Sunset is particularly splendid here, so if your
ip is staying late, find a cafe on the hillside and sit outside to enjoy it.

Ashdod, Israel ★

Language:	**Hebrew**	*English Spoken?:*	**Yes**
Currency:	**Shekel**	*US$ ok?:*	**No**
To town:	**Taxi**		

Except as **port access for Jerusalem and Bethlehem**, there's not much reason
o go to Ashdod. As ports go, Haifa has a lot more character and interest,
nd can also access those historic cities. Ashdod is a new, planned city with a
deepwater port, a lot of modern buildings and industrial sites, the navy's
nautical school and some rather pedestrian hotels and restaurants. It's a pity,
because **historically it was a fortress that predated the Crusades**, one of the five
great Philistine cities. The new city was founded in 1957, which should give
you a **quick read on the local architecture**. If you land here and have a full day,
you can go out on your own and hop the local Egged bus to Tel Aviv (except
on the Sabbath, of course) about 20 miles north, or **take all-day tours to Be-
thlehem or Jerusalem** ($$$), each roughly 50 miles away. Some all-day circle
tours ($$$) include both cities. If you have to choose one over the other,
Jerusalem is the more interesting of the two with its Western (Wailing) Wall,
Dome of the Rock, Mount of Olives, Gethsemene, Via Dolorosa and
Church of the Holy Sepulchre. **Guides here can be officious**; we were hurried
by all the holiest sites because the lines were too long to suit our leader.

Haifa, Israel ★★

Language:	**Hebrew**	*English Spoken?:*	**Yes**
Currency:	**Shekel**	*US$ ok?:*	**No**
To town:	**Taxi**		

Haifa, a pretty port town in its own right, is the **jumping-off point for all-day
excursions ($$$) to Jerusalem, Bethlehem, Nazareth and/or the Sea of Galilee**.
Each tour operator has his own schedule and priorities, so it pays to check in
detail exactly where you'll be going. Nazareth, 15 miles east of Haifa, and
the Sea of Galilee another 15 miles farther, are usually paired on a half- or
full-day excursion. Likewise, **Jerusalem and Bethlehem are usually covered on**

one full-day excursion since they lie only seven miles apart but are two hou
from Haifa. Helicopter tours to Massada are also offered by some ships. I
Bethlehem, the **Church of the Nativity on Manger Square** is the primary dest
nation, with the Milk Grotto, the Tomb of Rachel and the souvenir baza
also included. **Jerusalem's Western (or Wailing) Wall, Dome of the Rock, Churc
of the Holy Sepulchre**, Mount of Olives, the Via Dolorosa and the Garden c
Gethsemene are among the spots visited. Nazareth's sightseeing include
Mary's Well, the Basilica of the Annunciation, and several churches built o
Biblical sites. En route to the Sea of Galilee, most excursions visit Can
Tiberias, Capernaum and the Mount of the Beatitudes. Strolling aroun
Haifa, you may want to **sample the street food**, especially falafels, balls of frie
ground garbanzos in pita bread.

Constanta, Romania ★

Language:	**Romanian**	*English Spoken?:*	**No**
Currency:	**Leu**	*US$ ok?:*	**No**
To town:	**Taxi or excursion bus; don't walk**		

Brightly-dressed Gypsies crossing the street in Constanta, Romania.

Every time we visit Constanta, it seems to get worse. On our most recent stop,
our guide welcomed us to "the Democratic Romanian country" and then,
after cautioning us to not change money on the street and saying there
wasn't time to stop at a bank, proceeded to **rip off passengers eager to buy
souvenirs with an inequitable currency exchange**. When we were there, the official rate was 600, the street black market rate 900, and our guide's rate 500
to the $. The harbor is full of rusting hulls, the town pocked with potholed

reets and worn-out rolling stock on the railroads, and the money changers, ightly costumed Gypsies and con artists rife on the streets. **Take an escorted hore excursion by bus here; don't strike out on your own.** The Archeological Museum usually tops the sightseeing list on the half-day excursion ($$), fol-wed by the excellent Folk Art Museum and perhaps a shopping visit to the **mis Department Store**, a five-floor mart with creaky escalators and light so 'm one can hardly see the merchandise. We opted for a second shore excur-on in the afternoon ($$), **a wine tasting** in the state-owned Murfatlar vine-ards area on the Danube Canal, interesting less to wine aficionados (all even vintages were undistinguished) than to students of Romanian culture or the folk music performed.

Alanya, Turkey ★★★

Language:	**Turkish**	*English Spoken?:*	**Yes**
Currency:	**Lira**	*US$ ok?:*	**No**
To town:	**Walk**		

This colorful little port on Turkey's Turquoise Coast is **bright with painted ishing boats and horsedrawn carts** and the traditional wooden boats called gulets. In perfect view from the dock, **capturable in a single photograph**, are he main attractions of Alanya: the fortress, built across the crest and he ides of the mountain behind the town, and the Kizil Kule, the Red Tower, built in the 13th century to protect the town's shipyard. A two-mile trail eads steeply uphill to the fortress, which dates from the Selcuk period. **The waterfront is lined with lively restaurants, cafes and bars**. The town was **once given as a present to Cleopatra** from Marc Antony, and the most popular beach today is called Cleopatra's Beach. "You can swim every day of the year if the sun is shining," says the guide. The **Damlatas Cave, filled with stalag-mites, stalactites and asthma patients**, is the first stop on a city tour; the pa-tients, mostly elderly Turkish women, have a prescribed treatment of spending four hours a day for 21 consecutive days lying in a lounge chair in-haling the damp air in the cave, which is supposed to be beneficial. They are chased out if a tour bus arrives. Next stop is **the Roman theater at Aspendos**, the best preserved Greco-Roman theater in Asia Minor, built in the time of Marcus Aurelius, then the ruins of the ancient city of Perge, and that fills the half-day tour ($$).

Antalya, Turkey ★★★

Language:	**Turkish**	English Spoken?:	**Yes**
Currency:	**Lira**	US$ ok?:	**No**
To town:	**Taxi**		

Antalya is a modern city, complete with Sheraton, **archeological museur and duty-free supermarket**, but there's also an old town, marina and the oblig atory Turkish fortress. The Turquoise Coast is semi-tropical, with sweet litt local bananas growing, greenhouses of tulips and carnations (the Turks actu ally export flowers to Holland) and Gypsy encampments with tethered can els by the roadside. It's a good place to see people dressed in tradition Anatolian costume. When we were here aboard Silverseas' *Silver Cloud,* special shore excursion called the Silversea Experience and free to all the pas sengers was a Turkish wedding picnic held in a shady pine forest and par called Kursunlu Selalesi. The Antalya Sheraton catered it; there were 20 o more cold *mezes* (appetizers) from dolmas to orzo; charcoal-grilled sword fish kebabs threaded with bay leaves; chicken, shrimp and lobster, lamb an sausages; hot mixed vegetables; breads; a table of ornate desserts. **Belly danc ers entertained**, and the bride and groom appeared in **Anatolian costume ridin camels**. It was an unforgettable experience.

Bodrum, Turkey ★★★★

Language:	**Turkish**	English Spoken?:	**Yes**
Currency:	**Lira**	US$ ok?:	**No**
To town:	**Tender**		

When Bodrum was the ancient city of Halicarnassus, it housed **one of the seven wonders of the ancient world**, the tomb of Mausolus, called the Mausoleum, with 36 Ionic columns and a statue of the king riding in the chariot. But the Knights Templar tore it down and used the stones to erect the Castle of St. Peter, destroying one of the great masterpieces of world building to put up one more medieval castle/fortress in an area thick with them. Still, it's a pretty sight from the sea as you sail in. The waterfront area is **filled with shops selling jewelry and leather coats**, and the harbor crowded with wooden boats called gulets which can be rented for a week-long cruise along the Turquoise Coast for around $400 a day for six or eight people. We took a half-day shore excursion to the rural villages of Yalikavak, where the weekly market was in full swing, and Gumusluk, where a woman in Anatolian dress sit-

ıg by an outdoor fireplace prepared *lokma*, a sort of **fritter dipped in honey**,
ːr us. The village has several shops selling Turkish crafts, including one with
meerschaum pipe carver.

Dikili, Turkey   ★ ★ ★ ★

Language:	**Turkish**	*English Spoken?:*	**Some**
Currency:	**Lira**	*US\$ ok?:*	**Yes**
To town:	**Walk, tender**		

The charming little seaport of Dikili is replacing Izmir with most cruise
ınes as the port for the **ancient hilltop city of Pergamum**. It's much closer,
ːliminating that nearly two-hour bus ride from Izmir, and making the visit
ossible on a half- or three-quarter day tour (\$\$). Pergamum, built atop a
300-foot hill, once had **a great library that rivaled the one in Alexandria**.
ːVhen the jealous Egyptians put an embargo on papyrus, a local shepherd
ːame up with parchment, called Pergaminac Charte at the time. The ruins of
ːhe Acropolis dominate the scene today. Pergamum was also where **a primi-
ːive form of psychiatry** was first practiced in the Asclepion hospital before the
ːirst century A.D. To be permitted to enter, a patient had to be able to walk
ːhe one mile from the town to the hospital, where a big banner over the gate
ınnounced, **"Death is not acceptable in the hospital.**" Patients were fed herbs
ːike parsley, set to running laps around the area and, if difficult, were im-
ːnersed in tubs of ice water, something akin to shock treatments. If a patient
ːlisobeyed and died anyhow, he was hastily disposed of in the middle of the
ːnight. Passengers who don't go to Pergamum will enjoy a morning stroll
ıround the **lively market in Dikili which spills out into the streets in all direc-
ːions**.

Istanbul, Turkey   ★ ★ ★ ★ ★

Language:	**Turkish**	*English Spoken?:*	**Yes**
Currency:	**Lira**	*US\$ ok?:*	**No**
To town:	**Walk**		

Fish sellers in the harbor at Istanbul.

This magnificent city is **one of the world's greatest ports**, as infinitely fascinating on the 10th visit as the first. The history-minded are faced with a cornucopia of treasures, far too many to visit in one arduous day, while **shoppers are dazzled by the 4000-boutique bazaar** and its assortment of exotic finds. **Be on deck when sailing in and out** of Istanbul, no matter what time of day or night. Early morning is the best, when the mists gradually fade and the rising sun gilds the mosques and minarets. A lot of shore excursions are available, but the first-time visitor should opt for a half-day tour ($$) that visits Topkapi Palace, the Blue Mosque, Hagia Sofia and the Grand Bazaar. On a return cruise to Istanbul, consider a boat cruise along the Bosporus or a bus excursion that takes you to lunch at one of the splendid seafood restaurants along the Bosporus. You can **safely walk around Istanbul on your own** in the daytime if you don't mind crowds and people that sometimes stare at foreigners with open curiosity. An easy stroll from the dock can include the **Egyptian vegetable market**, near the New Mosque, and the vendors that sell fish from brightly-painted boats by the Galata Bridge.

Kusadasi, Turkey ★★★★

Language:	**Turkish**	English Spoken?:	**Yes**
Currency:	**Lira**	US$ ok?:	**Yes**
To town:	**Walk**		

The marble columns at Ephesus, reached by shore excursions from Kusadasi

Kusadasi is the port for the **great ancient city of Ephesus**, built all in marble in the Roman style the Greeks considered gaudy. Don't miss the shore excursion here ($$); the city has been so extensively restored that even the most unimaginative **visitor can stroll into the ancient past**. Along the mile-long marble street, you can stop to see the chariot wheel ruts still incised in the stone, a crudely scratched **street corner advertisement for a brothel**, a six-story building that was an early condominium with running water. Photographers love the **big public toilet** with its rows of stone seats like a giant outhouse. Citizens would gather here in groups to gossip, and on cold mornings, a wealthy man would send a servant ahead to warm up his seat. The **great library, third largest in the ancient world**, is restored, along with the ampitheatre, which still presents plays and concerts. While there are hawkers of books, clothing and souvenirs around Ephesus, the **best shopping** is in the streets of Kusadasi, where vendors sell imitation Izod shirts for $2 or $3, sweaters, fishermen hats, green almonds and almost anything else you can imagine. Shops vend copperware, gold and silver jewelry, alabaster vases, Turkish carpets, leather and suede clothing. **Bargaining is obligatory** on the street and in the shops.

Odessa, Ukraine   ★ ★

Language:	**Ukrainian**	*English Spoken?:*	**Some**
Currency:	**Kupon**	*US$ ok?:*	**Yes**
To town:	**Taxi or shuttle bus**		

The famous Potemkin Steps in Odessa lead down to the harbor.

Odessa, the "Pearl of the Black Sea," is dominated by the **magnificent Potemkin Staircase**, immortalized in Sergei Eisenstein's 1925 silent film *Potemkin*, leading up from the docks of this major port and health spa on the Black Sea; it is definitely the highlight of the city. On our most recent visit our small **ship required nearly three hours to clear into the country,** forcing the half-day morning city tour ($$) to be postponed until the afternoon. Since the Ukraine severed itself from the USSR, it seems to have held on to all the previous bureaucratic red tape and added even more. Newly in evidence around the city are **leather-jacketed hoods wanting to change money and hard-eyed young prostitutes in micro-minis**. Gangs of teen-aged boys who should be in school are instead on the streets vending post cards and nesting matriosh-ka dolls in broken English. "They are taking practical training in free market enterprise," our guide comments dryly. The **gilt-and-red-velvet Academia Opera and Ballet Theatre** is magnificent; Tchaikovsky himself conducted the premiere of *The Queen of Spades* here. Pushkin, Gogol and Gorky all spent part of their creative lives in this energetic city. Sometimes a folkloric performance on board ship may also be scheduled.

Yalta, Ukraine ★ ★ ★

Language:	**Ukrainian**	English Spoken?:	**Some**
Currency:	**Kupon**	US$ ok?:	**Yes**
To town:	**Walk**		

Yalta's famous Livadia Palace where the 1945 conference was held between U.S. President FDR, England's Winston Churchill and Russia's Joseph Stalin.

A **popular seaside and health resort in its Russian days**, Yalta is still a beguiling town to walk around. Setting out on your own should present no problem here; you can stroll the beach, walk along the waterfront amusement park and through the vegetable market, one of the first free enterprise zones we encountered in the former USSR. The half-day shore excursion ($$) takes passengers by bus to the **White Palace in Livadia**, where Stalin, Churchill and Roosevelt met in the famous 1945 conference that carved up Europe. The tour also usually, but not always, stops to **visit the Chekhov House museum and garden**, where the famous writer spent his last years. His masterpieces *The Cherry Orchard* and *The Three Sisters* were written here. Rachmaninov, a frequent guest, played the piano that is on display. During its days as part of the USSR, Yalta, because of its mild climate, was a highly regarded health and spa resort with **huge hospitals built as R&R getaways for the country's rank-and-file**. These, plus the deluxe seaside resorts that flourished as getaways for Party heads, are having a tough time making it in these new economic days without state-subsidized vacations.

CRUISING IN AFRICA, THE SOUTH ATLANTIC AND INDIAN OCEANS

The Indian Market in Durban.

One of the hot destinations for cruisers during the past several years has been South Africa, back in the real world again after the abolition of apartheid and the lifting of international sanctions. Sailing into the **beautiful port of Cape Town** rivals Rio, Monte Carlo and San Francisco for sheer scenic wonder.

North African ports are usually part of an Eastern Mediterranean or Red Sea itinerary, and will be found in "Rating the Ports of the Mediterranean," page 945. **East Africa, famous for its safaris and game parks**, may be included as a pre- or post-cruise add-on with a Seychelles sailing (see below). The east coast of this continent has usually eclipsed West Africa in the tourist eye, but travelers who enjoy people, crafts and diverse cultures will find **West Africa an unforgettable jolt to the senses**.

In the Indian Ocean, the **Seychelles have become a major cruise base**, wi
many itineraries also including calls at Madagascar, Kenya and Tanzania, a
sometimes Mauritius. We also include India and Sri Lanka in the Indi
Ocean section, since many ships **cruise between Bombay and Mombasa** on r
positioning cruises.

The islands off West Africa in the southern Atlantic—the Canaries and M
deira—double as **winter cruising grounds** for a few European-based vesse
and as welcome landfalls on a transatlantic crossing. The Azores, also out
the Atlantic but farther northwest, are primarily **landfalls for transatlant
cruisers**.

Five Special Sights—Not for the Cynical

1. An all-day excursion to Kandy ($$$) in Sri Lanka's central highlands includes a vis
    to a temple where **Buddha's tooth** is displayed on a golden flower.

2. According to **General Gordon**, who took a holiday **from Khartoum** to visit the Sey
    chelles in 1881, the **Garden of Eden** lies in the Valle de Mai on Praslin. He believe
    the unique *coco de mer* palm tree with its **giant voluptuous coconut, suggestive c
    female genitals**, was the Tree of Knowledge of good and evil used to test Adam an
    Eve.

3. On the island of San Miguel in the Azores, there are **two lakes in the volcanic cra
    ter**, one blue and one green. It seems there was a goatherder with green eyes whc
    fell in love with a girl with blue eyes. She was promised in marriage to another, the)
    met for a **final farewell**, and cried so much his tears filled the green lake, her tear;
    filled the blue lake, and a flood came which drowned them both.

4. Loro Parque in **the Canary Islands has the largest collection of parrots in the
    world** (wait, that's not the joke), including one we somehow missed seeing and
    hearing (surely the only one we missed) **that whistles the Triumphal March from
    Aida**.

5. In West Africa's Togo, where cruise ships like *Caledonian Star* used to call, we had
    an exclusive audience with one Adidan Zonontin, a **Guerisseur Traditionnel, Expli-
    cateur des Forces Voodoo Africaines (at least that's what his printed calling card
    said)**, who showed us the African fetish version of a St. Christopher medal; there are
    two sticks, a small twig put into a gouged hole in the larger stick. You pull out the
    small twig, talk into the hole about where you're going and how you're traveling,
    then insert the small twig into the large one and put it in your left pocket. Check it
    periodically, and if it has come apart and does not willingly go back together, **don't
    take the journey** you told it about.

> ## DID YOU KNOW?
>
> *When Togo's President Etienne Eyadema, who took over in a coup in 1963, set
> out for what turned out to be his famous 1974 plane crash, he found his sticks
> apart and forced the two pieces back together and went anyhow, which is
> why the plane crashed. (Although it occurred to us later that he could have
> claimed because he had the fetish with him is why he survived the crash
> when the other four passengers didn't.) Afterwards, Eyadema put up posters
> all over Lome depicting himself in his military uniform with angel wings
> sprouting from his shoulders.*

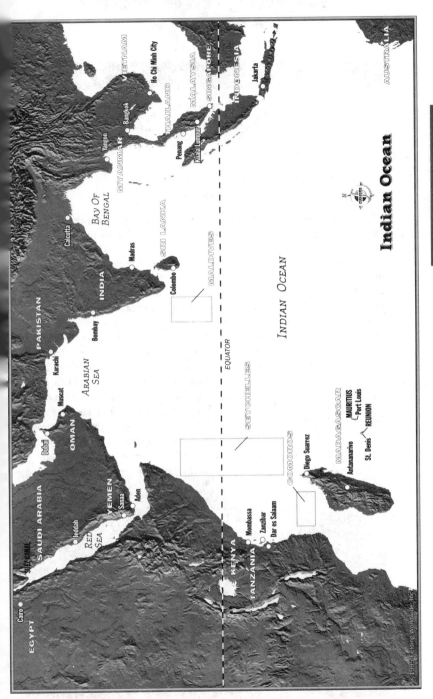

Indian Ocean

Rating the Ports of Africa

Mombasa, Kenya ★★★

Language:	**English**	*English Spoken?:*	**Yes**
Currency:	**Shilling**	*US$ ok?:*	**Yes**
To town:	**Taxi or walk**		

While Kenyans are **proud of the long stretches of white beachfront south of Mombasa**, most North American tourists prefer a visit to the **famous game parks**. From Mombasa, the best way to see the game parks is with a two- or three-day overland excursion; **a day trip does not offer the best animal viewing times**, which are early morning and late afternoon. An all-day game park drive to Tsavo East National Park ($$$ and exhausting) is offered, but since the route takes **three hours each way from the pier to the park** and lunch is served, you'll have little time left for game-spotting, even if there are some animals out and about in the midday. If your time is limited, a half-day tour ($$) around historic Mombasa may be more rewarding. The drive goes through the **famous gateway made of crossed elephant tusks**, followed by a walk in the Old Town with its **heavy Arab influence**, mosques, colorful bazaar and carved houses with overhanging balconies. Fort Jesus is the **16th century Portuguese fortress** near the harbor entrance; you'll find vendors selling crafts—**kanga fabrics, Makonde wood carvings**, drums and stone chess sets—at fair prices. English and KiSwahili are the official languages of Kenya; most people who work in and around the tourist industry will speak English.

The Senegalese are the merchant princes of street vending.

Dakar, Senegal ★

Language:	**French**	*English Spoken?:*	**Some**
Currency:	**CFA franc**	*US$ ok?:*	**Yes**
To town:	**Taxi**		

Dakar is a bustling, sometimes frenetic, port filled with the **Senegalese merchant princes of street vending**, who exude so much charm you're torn because what sounds like a good deal might be a ripoff. The price is right and the guy is being so very nice you get suspicious, **wondering if an associate is picking your pocket**. He may well be. The most annoying of the local scams is the giving of "presents" for which a return gift or payment is expected; **don't accept anything handed to you on the street**. Local touts can be most persistent; it takes a very firm "no" repeated often to get rid of them. The primary shore excursion (a half-day, $-$$) is a boat ride (via ferry) over to the **island of Goree**, an old fortified slaving station with a historical museum, slave houses and colonial mansions, as well as a beguiling collection of beachfront cafes and restaurants. A half-day city tour ($$) may include a visit to the Ifan Museum with its excellent **collection of West African masks**, furniture and royal artifacts; the Sandaga and Kermel street fruit markets; the city view from the top of the Hotel de l'Indpendence; the medina (old Arab quarter); and the **handicrafts village of Soumbedioune**.

One of the world's most beautiful ports, Cape Town, South Africa, with Table Mountain looming in the background on a clear day.

Cape Town, South Africa ★★★★★

Language:	**English**	English Spoken?:	**Yes**
Currency:	**Rand**	US$ ok?:	**No**
To town:	**Walk, taxi**		

To sail into the exquisite port of Cape Town on a sunny day with **Table Mountain standing out clear against a bright blue sky** is an unforgettable experience. A standard half-day excursion around the city and its environs ($$) includes a look at **St. George's Cathedral, Bishop Desmond Tutu's church**; the City Hall; the 1666 Castle of Good Hope, built by the Dutch East India Company; Signal Hill for its views; the recently developed Victoria and Alfred Waterfront area with its trendy shops and cafes; and the Clifton beaches along the Atlantic Coast. Another optional half-day ($$) takes you to the **Table Mountain cablecar** for a 10-minute ride up, then glorious views in all directions. This tour is offered only on clear, non-windy days. The **Stellenbosch Wine Country** ($$) makes a splendid half-day tour, visiting a charming country town famous for its university, its Cape Dutch architecture and jacaranda trees; you visit four restored period homes, then tour a winery and do a tasting of very pleasant South African wines. It takes a full day excursion ($$$) to drive down to the **Cape of Good Hope with its magnificent stands of protea**, which bloom in November and early December. Not long ago, with another couple from the ship, we rented a car and did that drive on our own, stopping for lunch in Stellenbosch.

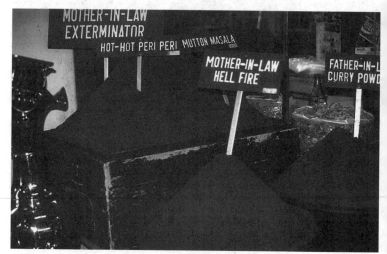

Durban's spice market has some intriguing products for sale, including Mother-in-Law Exterminator at the upper left.

Durban, South Africa ★★★

Language:	**English**	*English Spoken?:*	**Yes**
Currency:	**Rand**	*US$ ok?:*	**No**
To town:	**Walk or Taxi**		

It was hard to tell who was enjoying the evening more, the passengers aboard the *Marco Polo* or the exuberant **dance troupe from the Valley of the Thousand Hills in KwaZulu,** who were brought on board to entertain. The port city of Durban is the largest city in Natal, the coastal area first sighted by Vasco da Gama in 1497. While 19th century history here is long on the battles between the Boers, the British and **the fierce local Zulus**, the 20th century has had its share of conflicts as well, primarily political, between the Zulus and the Xhosa during the formative years of the changeover in South Africa. There are also a million East Indians in Natal adding to the melting pot. A half-day city tour ($$) drives along the **palm-lined Victoria Embankment** for a look at a 19th-century Portuguese clock presented on the 400th anniversary of Vasco da Gama's sighting of Natal province; the statue of Dick King, a teenager who rode 1000 kilometers in 10 days in 1842 to bring help to the British garrison; the Durban Club; the Yacht Club; **the colorful Indian Market**; the Botanical Gardens and orchid house; the stately homes of Morningside; and the Durban Country Club. A full-day tour ($$$) may visit the Valley of the Thousand Hills in KwaZulu country, stopping at the Zulu village where the dancers on the ship came from, or Shakaland ($$$), a different Zulu area in the Ekweleni Valley, where a lecture on history, culture and tradition is supplemented by native dancing and a **traditional Zulu meal is served in the main hut**. On your own, walk around the pretty Victorian beachfront at Marine Parade, where the resort hotels are located, if you can bear the muggy heat.

Zanzibar, Tanzania ★★

Language:	**English**	*English Spoken?:*	**Yes**
Currency:	**Shilling**	*US$ ok?:*	**Yes**
To town:	**Walk or taxi**		

Zanzibar, while a part of Tanzania, also considers itself an autonomous entity and requires **its own separate immigration and customs** procedures. There are a lot of entrepreneurial "guides" in Zanzibar who want to sell you something, take you on a tour or tout a hotel or restaurant to you; they're best ig-

nored. This **colorful old Arab trading center** was renowned for shipping clo
(and notorious for shipping slaves) all over the world in the 19th centu
Some of the Arab influence can still be seen in the **colorful, crowded baza**
and old Stone Town. English and KiSwahili are the official languages of T
zania. In Zanzibar, **foreign currency is preferred**, sometimes required, as p
ment rather than local currency. A half-day island shore excursion ($$) vi
the **spice shops of the island's bazaar, the site of the old slave market** (now
church), the ruins of Maruhubi Palace, the House of Wonders sultan's p
ace, and the home of David Livingstone, who lived here while getting rea
for his final journey into the heart of Africa. Another half-day excursion ($
goes to Changuu or Prison Island, where slaves were shipped for punis
ment. The shackles imbedded in the prison walls lend mute testimony abo
this terrible time. You may even have a chance to ride a giant tortoise and
go to the white sand beaches.

INSIDER TIP

*The currents off the east coast beaches are very strong and dangerous for
swimming; settle for a beach stroll instead.*

Rating the Ports of the Indian Ocean

Bombay, India ★★★★

CRUISING IN AFRICA, THE SOUTH ATLANTIC AND INDIAN OCEANS

Language:	**English**	*English Spoken?:*	**Yes**
Currency:	**Rupee**	*US$ ok?:*	**No**
To town:	**Taxi**		

To the left, the Taj Hotel, to the right, the famous Gate of India, both in the fascinating city of Bombay.

India is a **rich, complex, exhilarating and frustrating** country to visit, and most Americans may prefer to **tackle it first by ship and escorted shore excursion**, avoiding the congested and confusing airports and railway stations. Bombay, our own favorite city, is the most frequently visited port, although **Goa, Madras and sometimes Cochin, Mangalore and Calcutta** are also on itineraries. A half-day city tour ($$) covers a lot of the most interesting sights—from the *dhobi ghats* (public laundries where hundreds of men are beating wet garments against cement slabs) and Jain Temple, to the closely-guarded towers of silence, where **the Parsi dead are left to the elements and vultures**; the Gandhi house and museum; the Prince of Wales Museum; the Hanging Gardens. You have to go out on your own for some of the more lurid sights Bombay offers, like the **child prostitutes in cages** in the red light district or the busy open-air crematoriums that serve the poor. We like watching the **dabba wallahs** (lunch-bucket deliverers) thronging into Churchgate railway station at midmorning from all the suburbs bringing office workers hot lunches that were cooked at home by their wives. Each man balances an unbelieva▮ stock of lunch-buckets somehow coded for the mostly illiterate workers that the right meal always gets to the right desk. The very Victorian Cra▮ ford Market, **designed by Rudyard Kipling's father**, is best visited with one the market guides who'll pick you up near the entrance and for a modest ▮ protect you from being maimed by the frantic pandemonium inside. Ano▮ er day, you could take the **launch to Elephant Island and its sixth century te▮ ples carved out of rock caves**. You'll have an English-speaking guide if y▮ book the luxury launch ($); they leave from the Gate of India. Shopp▮ tempted by the bright fabrics and crafts, grabbing armloads of bangles a▮ gilded sari fabrics, semiprecious stones and Kashmir shawls, crewel embr▮ dery and carpets, **mustn't forget to bargain**. Counter with half the seller's fir price and work out the deal from there. Note: We designate **English as t▮ language of India because it is still used in the courts and most people speak** fluently; there are 15 other languages also legally recognized.

Nosy Be, Madagascar   ★ ★

Language:	**Malagasy**	*English Spoken?:*	**Little**
Currency:	**Madagascar franc**	*US$ ok?:*	**No**
To town:	**Tender to shore**		

   Madagascar is not only a **very poor country, but fractious to boot**, with spo▮ radic riots popping up now and again. What makes it appealing for tourists ▮ its unique ecosystem and the native courtesy of the Malagasy people, plus, ▮ course, a chance to see the lemurs. The name Nosy Be means Great or Bi▮ Island. The crystal beaches of Tanikely are enticing, but if you swim here **watch out for sea urchins and sometimes sharks**. Some experts say the snorkel ing and diving here are not as good as touted. Excursions available include ▮ half-day visit to the Lemur Park of Nosy Komba ($$) where black-brow▮ and ruffled lemurs can be seen swinging from branch to branch in the trees Lemurs look something like a cross between a monkey and a raccoon with ▮ fox-like face, indescribably appealing. **Ylang-ylang perfume** gathered from the fragrant yellow-flowering trees can be purchased in tiny bottles; it's the pri mary local product. Diego Suarez is also occasionally used as a port, prima rily **to access the rare lemurs** of Montagne d'Ambre Park.Otherwise it's a hot, dry, dusty and often unfriendly little town. French is widely spoken in Mada gascar, but English is much less common. There is a demanding currency form required from tourists as well.

Port Louis, Mauritius   ★ ★

Language:	**French,**	*English Spoken?:*	**Yes**
Currency:	**Rupee**	*US$ ok?:*	**Some places**
To town:	**Walk or taxi**		

Set in the Indian Ocean east of Madagascar, the island of Mauritius was colonized by both France and Britain, and became an independent nation in 1988. Most of the population is East Indian, descendents of workers brought to the sugar fields along with Chinese, Creoles and Franco-Mauritians. A half-day city tour ($$) offers glimpses of **tropical beaches** and rugged peaks en route to the **Royal Botanical Gardens** to see tree ferns, orchids and giant amazonica lilies, as well as what the locals call the **marmalade box tree, the chewing-gum tree, the fish poison tree and the sausage tree**. Also included is a stop at the beach at Grand Baie, a visit to the town market to see some of the local spices, fruits and vegetables, and a shopping stop at a row of fashionable boutiques selling everything from seashell necklaces to duty-free diamonds. An alternative half-day excursion is a visit to the Casela Bird Park ($$) on the west coast, home to 2000 birds representing 140 species. More than **100 aviaries enclose peacocks, pheasants, parrots, owls and rare pink pigeons**, plus some animals such as leopards, tigers, monkeys, deer and giant tortoises, one of them 150 years old. If you have several days free, you can sail to remote Reunion Island aboard the *Mauritius Pride* from Port Louis.

Mahe, The Seychelles   ★ ★ ★

Language:	**English**	*English Spoken?:*	**Yes**
Currency:	**Rupee**	*US$ ok?:*	**No**
To town:	**Tender to shore**		

Picture **a James Bond spy fantasy set on a tropical island** of golden beaches and swaying palms surrounded by a cerulean sea, and you get a sense of what the Seychelles is like—breathtakingly beautiful and faintly, almost whimsically, dangerous with its background of coups and political skullduggery. One of the pretty little **100-passenger Renaissance ships** sails from Mahe between November and February, visiting seven different islands; the cruise can be booked as a **package with an African game parks** overland excursion. A half-day Mahe island tour ($$) usually includes a view of Victoria from the mountains above; Mission Lodge, the ruins of a former school for children of freed slaves; the Marine Park; and Botanical Gardens to see the **giant Al-**

dabran tortoises and fruit bats. On Praslin Island, a visit to the Vallee de M nets a look at the unique **coco-de-mer palms**, which live 800 years and pr duce a suggestive looking fruit weighing up to 60 pounds. **Native black pa rots** are also usually seen, and there's time for a swim before returning to t ship. On your own, head for the beach, take a glass-bottom boat trip at St Anne Marine National Park or go diving at the Coral Gardens; **don't take a valuables to the beach**. Shoppers will find **batik, pottery, paintings**, ship mode and coconut crafts. English and French are both official languages.

Colombo, Sri Lanka ★

Language:	**English**	*English Spoken?:*	**Yes**
Currency:	**Rupee**	*US$ ok?:*	**No**
To town:	**Walk or taxi**		

Despite a decade of political unrest, Sri Lanka still greets a few cruise ship **Formerly known as Ceylon**, this predominantly Buddhist island country in th Indian Ocean has three designated languages—English, Sinhala and Tami Sri Lanka lies 30 miles off the southern tip of India very near the equator; th climate is **tropical and humid** year-round. Over the centuries, the island wa ruled by Arabs, Portuguese, Dutch and British, the latter until 1948. Ship usually dock opposite the former fort, now a business and banking cente Beyond the walls of the fort is the bazaar, a tangle of shops and kiosks, half them, it appears, **selling semiprecious gemstones**. Half-day shore excursion here ($$) usually visit Victoria Park, the President's Palace and Clocktowe the Colombo Museum and the ancient shrine at Kelaniya where Budda said to have bathed in the river. An all-day excursion to Kandy ($$$) in th central **highlands tea plantation area** includes a visit to the temple where Bud dha's tooth is displayed on a golden flower.

Rating the Ports of the South Atlantic

Ponta Delgado, The Azores ★ ★ ★

Language:	**Portuguese**	*English Spoken?:*	**Yes**
Currency:	**Escudo**	*US$ ok?:*	**No**
To town:	**Walk**		

CRUISING IN AFRICA, THE SOUTH ATLANTIC AND INDIAN OCEANS

Ponta Delgado in the Azores has intricately patterned black-and-white sidewalks created, it is said, for illiterate people to be able to find an address.

These remote Portuguese islands, which lie **2000 miles off New York and almost 1000 off Lisbon**, are visited occasionally on transatlantic cruises. Of the nine islands, San Miguel and its capital of Ponta Delgado seems to attract the most traffic. San Miguel is filled with neat villages with whitewashed cottages and **tumbles of nasturtiums blooming all around, blue and pink hydrangeas that locals call hortensia**, pineapples grown in greenhouses, whaling stations, black sand beaches and flocks of dairy cattle. Passengers can easily **walk around the clean, pretty town** and sightsee on their own. The harbor is filled with big white **wooden dories with red and blue trim** that sail out of the harbor every morning for fishing. **Sidewalks are swirled black and white stone**, each street a different pattern, a custom that originated, it's said, when most of the islanders were illiterate but needed to find their address. Locals who went away from the islands to make their fortunes returned and put up flags that salute the country where they made it; a lot of stars and stripes can be seen flapping in the wind. There are a number of historic churches in these

very religious islands, including Esperanca, where the Santo Christo stat (Christ of the Miracles) is kept, and São Sebastian, started in 1527, on own grand square with its adjacent monastery. Organized shore excursio ($$) take day-trippers around the island, including a visit to the Seven Citi towns built inside sheltered volcanic craters.

DID YOU KNOW?

In 1811, the HMS Sabrina saw smoke and a heavy wave from a subterranean earthquake that pushed up an island from the sea they named Sabrina, after the vessel. The British, American and Portuguese consuls quickly rowed out to the spot, each putting a flag on the island to claim it. They bickered about ownership for two months, when the island, still bearing the flags, sank back into the sea as suddenly as it had appeared.

Tenerife, Canary Islands ★ ★ ★

Language:	**Spanish**	*English Spoken?:*	**Yes**
Currency:	**Peseta**	*US$ ok?:*	**No**
To town:	**Bus or taxi**		

On Corpus Christi day in late spring, Canary Islanders make elaborate "sand paintings" of flowers, colored sand and crushed rock.

The Canary Islands, only 70 miles off the African coast, offer a sunny, generally warm climate all winter long, and a mild, sometimes breezy, summer. **Several ships usually cruise the Canary Islands in winter** with calls not only at Tenerife but also **Lanzarote, La Palma and Las Palmas**, the latter ports with similar names but on two different islands. Shore excursions may include a visit to the 200-year-old Botanical Gardens in Puerto de la Cruz; Lago Marnez, a **resort play area of saltwater pools and lagoons created around the astal volcanic rock** (the island has no sandy beaches); and, on occasion, ro Parque, **the largest collection of parrots in the world, including one that istles the "Triumphal March" from Aida.** If you find yourself in the Canary ands on **Corpus Christi day in late spring** or early summer, as we were once, u can see the famous **"sand pictures" made with colored sand, flowers, ushed rocks**, dried beans and peas, most of them constructed around a re- ious theme. The oldest city on Tenerife, La Laguna, celebrated its **500th thday in 1996**.

Madeira, Portugal ★★★★

Language:	**Portuguese**	*English Spoken?:*	**Yes**
Currency:	**Escudo**	*US$ ok?:*	**No**
To town:	**Taxi, walk**		

Generations of British tourists have left their mark, so virtually everyone on ower-filled Madeira, the **most delightful island cruise port in the Atlantic**, eaks English. The most time-honored half-day excursion ($$) in Funchal, e capital, is to **take a toboggan ride in a woven basket sled down a steep, slick bblestone hill, pulled by two local youths wearing straw boaters.** (This is what e Victorians did for fun; you have to see it to believe it!) Afterwards, you o for a **tasting at the Madeira Wine Institute.** Another half-day shore excur- on ($$) visits banana plantations and terraced vineyards in the countryside, ausing at the picturesque fishing village of Camara de Lobos and scenic abo Gairao, the world's second-highest sea cliff. On your own, head for the overed **fish, vegetable and flower market** to see the island's bounty, including e ferociously ugly espada fish; drop by **Reid's Hotel**, one of the great classic rn-of-the-century resorts, for a **traditional English tea**; walk through the bo- nical gardens; or **shop for blue-and-white Portuguese tiles**, hand-embroi- ered linens and wickerwork. Note that with the Portuguese escudo, prices re written with the dollar sign inserted between the escudo figure and the entavo figure, as 5$25.

CRUISING TO ASIA

You will appreciate the **comfort and convenience of a cruise ship** when traveling through the exotic Far East, especially in developing nations like Vietnam, Myanmar and China. While Danang is still a far cry from St. Thomas, the **ports of Vietnam** are welcoming more and more American cruise passengers. Ho Chi Minh City, the former Saigon, is on most itineraries. Here tiny new Hondas vie with pedal bikes, everyone wears sunglasses instead of conical straw coolie hats, and **pretty young women in long silky white tunics** and wide-legged pants called *ao dai* (required apparel for high school seniors) stream by on motor scooters, delicately holding up one corner of the tunic to keep it from getting tangled in the spokes.

A morning in the **breathtaking Shwedagon Pagoda in Yangon** (Rangoon) is alone worth the price of the voyage. This glittering complex contains a hundred different temples whose towers grow thicker and taller every time the faithful contribute more tissue-thin sheets of hand-hammered gold leaf in offerings for prayers or thanks. The main stupa (tower) is covered with a **ton of beaten gold** studded with 5500 diamonds, 2317 rubies and sapphires and, at the very top like the maraschino cherry on a sundae, a single 76-carat diamond.

Hong Kong and **Singapore** continue to be the most popular home ports for Asian cruises. North American passengers enjoy the shopping and sightseeing in both cities. Singapore's new port facility with its airline-type baggage claims carousel offers efficient embarkations and debarkations.

Ports not very long ago perceived as distant and exotic, once-in-a-lifetime destinations, are suddenly on **nearly every cruise line agenda**. Even Royal Caribbean, which rarely ventured outside the Caribbean, Bermuda and Baja California a few years ago, has headed for Asia with its smallest ship, *Sun Viking* (well, they've got to put all those ships somewhere!) Princess is practically a household word in the Pacific and Far East.

But sadly, the ship that did the most to popularize cruises to China, Japan and South Korea, the *Pearl*, was pulled out of the Orient and shipped to the Caribbean to pioneer short cruises to Cuba from the Dominican Republic.

Five Off-the-Wall Tourist Attractions in Asia

1. The **Temple of the Azure Cloud** in Penang looks like something out of *India Jones and the Temple of Doom*, **a temple filled with dozens of deadly poisono pit vipers** who drape themselves around the altar and lie across cartons of eg brought to them by admirers but, logy from the incense of burning joss sticks, too indolent to strike visitors.

2. **The freshest sashimi in town** is served at a restaurant built around a fish tank n Nagasaki at Ikesu Kawatoro in Fukuoka. Your choice of live fish is netted up a sliced without severing the spine, so the remains of the **fish, still wriggling**, or ment the platter of sashimi as it's served.

3. About an hour north of Nagasaki is Huis ten Bosch and nearby Holland Village, former a huge Dutch canals theme park, the latter a tourist-oriented **Dutch villa complete with tulips, windmills and Japanese hostesses in wooden shoes a white Dutch caps**. A wildly popular local cake called Castella originated with Dut settlers who carried on trade here in the 19th century and is still the obligatory so venir.

4. **Ho Chi Minh's Mausoleum** in Hanoi permits no bags or cameras inside, no shor tank tops or hats to be worn and no hands in pockets as one files through to see t **body encased in a glass dome**, the famous wispy white beard and thinning whi hair neatly combed, the hands resting against the severe black suit slightly curle like a pianist getting ready to play. For two months each year the body is returne to Russia "for maintenance."

5. Given its politically incorrect position in today's Vietnam, **The Museum of Ame can War Crimes in Ho Chi Minh City** may be closed by the time you get there; whe we saw it, there were lots of tanks and helicopters outside, some unsettling tortu pictures of Vietnamese victims with captions in English as well as Vietnamese and **war souvenirs shop** with old dog tags (or copies of them) in a glass case.

© 1995 Fielding Worldwide, Inc.

Rating the Ports of Asia

The Three Gorges area of China's Yangtze River is gradually being filled in
a gigantic new dam.

Beijing, China ★★★

Language:	**Mandarin**	*English Spoken?:*	**Some**
Currency:	**Yuan**	*US$ ok?:*	**No**
To town:	**Long ride via excursion bus or train to Beijing**		

eijing has modernized tremendously in the past decade; we hardly recog-
ed it on our last visit. There's **even a Bloomingdale's-like department store**
h every western luxury one could imagine stocked and for sale. Several
es have served over the years as ports of entry for Beijing, but the major
is Tianjin. **The train journey overland is two hours, the bus three.** Beijing
re excursions are usually two to three days in length, with passengers as-
ed to designated hotels for the overnights, and day trips provided for the
jing area. Meals, sightseeing and lodging are arranged by the ship and in-
ded in the overall price. The Beijing city tour includes a visit to **vast**
nanmen Square, where only a few rural Chinese tourists still wear blue
o suits; the **incredible Forbidden City** with its palaces, temples and muse-
s; the Beihai Park; and the Temple of Heaven and its Echo Wall. All-day
rs take you out to **the Great Wall** (wear comfortable walking shoes) and
Ming Tombs. At some point, you'll be served **a meal featuring Peking**
k, probably the best dish available in Beijing, and see a **performance by**
nese acrobats, sometimes simultaneously. Best buys: Silk long underwear,
ps, brushes, inks, silk scarves, T-shirts, Buddhas, paper lanterns and kites
among the souvenirs to take home.

Canton, China ★★

Language:	**Mandarin, local dialects**	English Spoken?:	**Some**
Currency:	**Yuan**	US$ ok?:	**Some**
To town:	**Excursion bus**		

Canton, also known as **Guangzhou**, has, sadly, some of the most polluted air
the world. Because foreigners have been coming here since 1957, they are
gely ignored or treated brusquely by the locals. **Traffic is horrendous**, with
any of the former bicycle riders switching to motorcycles and cars. Busi-
ss and money, enterprise and industry are the primary characterics of the
antonese, with a more frenetic and less orderly lifestyle than Beijing. An all-
y tour ($$$) here may offer a visit to the **Sun Yatsen Memorial Hall**, the **Mau-**
leum of the 72 Martyrs, the **Chen Clan museum** with its ornate carved sculp-
res, a visit to a children's school for a charming musical performance and a
ulti-course Chinese luncheon at a local hotel like the **White Swan**. If you
ant to make a visit to the local zoo to see the pandas, **allow plenty of time for**
e traffic.

CRUISING TO ASIA

Shanghai, China   ★★★

Language:	**Mandarin**	*English Spoken?:*	**Yes**
Currency:	**Yuan**	*US$ ok?:*	**No**
To town:	**Walk or taxi**		

Shanghai was **one of the most westernized cities in China during the 193** The Bund with its European buildings shows how much foreign influe was felt, most embarrassingly in the famous, perhaps apocryphal, sign in park along the Bund that refused entrance to dogs and Chinese. Shore cursions usually visit the Reclining Buddha, a **Children's Palace where photogenic kids are delighted to pose for pictures**, a woolen carpet fac (prices are much lower than at home), lunch and a cultural show. Other sibilities on the city tour include a home visit, jade and ivory carving pl and a shopping opportunity. An alternative all-day tour takes a train to city of Wuxi to tour a silk factory, visit the famous **gardens of Suzhou cruise on the Grand Canal,** watching barges at work on the canal and farr at work with some very primitive equipment in the fields that line the ba Passengers who are disabled or have trouble walking along briskly may to sit out some tours. You can also set out on your own for some fascina peeks into the back streets and alleyways of this teeming city.

Hong Kong, has a constantly changing skyline.

You stay there, we'll bring Asia to you.

Explore South East Asia on board a's finest cruise ship, the luxurious perStar Gemini. Each week, the erStar Gemini takes you to four tly different countries and cultures in incredible voyage.

Singapore. Kuala Lumpur. Medan. uket. Temples. Mosques. Markets. ches. Golf. Water sports.

As you finish a day's exploring, with

the betel-nut chewing mountain tribes of Sumatra, or in the awesome caverns of Malaysia's Batu Caves, or from sunning yourself on one of the world's most beautiful beaches on the Thai island of Phuket, there is nothing like retreating to the unparalleled dining, entertainment and leisure facilities that await you on the SuperStar Gemini.

And there is nothing like waking to discover we have brought a whole new destination right to you.

STAR CRUISE
A Touch of the Orient!

gapore : 391B Orchard Road, #13-01 Ngee Ann City Tower B, Singapore 238874. Tel: (65) 733 6388 Fax: (65) 733 3622
aysia : Tingkat 22, Wisma Genting, Jalan Sultan Ismail, 50250 Kuala Lumpur Tel: (603) 200 6363 Fax: (603) 201 6191
g Kong : 1501 Ocean Centre, 5 Canton Road, Tsimshatsui, Hong Kong. Tel: (852) 2317 7711 Fax: (852) 2314 1677

Sunset on Windstar Cruises' *Wind Spirit*

Cruising the Panama Canal

World Explorer passengers discover a waterfall

The Bund, Shanghai

Glittering Hong Kong view from the Peak

Abercrombie & Kent's *Anacoluthe* in France

Hong Kong ★★★★★

Language:	**English**	*English Spoken?:*	**Yes**
Currency:	**HK$**	*US$ ok?:*	**No**
To town:	**Walk, taxi**		

Most Hong Kong eyes are on the calendar for 1997, when, at midnight on
July 1, the British Crown Colony of Hong Kong is slated to become the
Hong Kong Special Administrative Region of the People's Republic of China, what some locals are calling **"the world's greatest Chinese takeaway."**
Hong Kong is probably the most exciting, certainly the most ephemeral city
on earth. Turn away for a moment to admire the outline of a stiff-sailed junk
in the harbor, and when you look back, **the skyline is altered with two or three
new skyscrapers**, each bristling higher than the last, and rendering all previous photographs obsolete. Shopping is famous here, but we find ourselves
less tempted on each subsequent trip; many times, we **can buy things as
cheaply or cheaper by judiciously shopping at home**. Passengers who feel the
way we do about shopping will perhaps be interested in the shore excursions
ships offer here—or will want to strike out on their own. Excursions that go
out of town to **mainland China and Macau** ($$$) are offered on pre- and post-
cruise packages from Hong Kong. Closer to home are city tours that visit
Victoria Peak, the Wanchai (Suzie Wong) district, the resort of Repulse Bay,
Deepwater Bay, the houseboat village of Aberdeen with sampans, floating
seafood restaurants and junks, and the central district's banks, high rise ho-
tels and shops. The more energetic will like a walking tour of the city ($$),
with an emphasis on **colorful side streets, markets and curio shops with a local
guide**.

Kyoto, Japan ★★★

Language:	**Japanese**	*English Spoken?:*	**Yes**
Currency:	**Yen**	*US$ ok?:*	**No**
To town:	**Excursion bus or bullet train from port**		

Kyoto, the **capital city of Japan for 11 centuries**, is most easily reached from
the ports of Kobe (by bullet train) or Osaka on all-day tours ($$$). The
Kinkakuji (Gold Pavilion), the Heian (Honeymoon) Shrine and the Sanju-
sangendo Temple (also sometimes called the Hall of the 1001 Buddhas) are
the major sights to visit. A **familiar Japanese lunch (usually tempura or sukiya-
ki)** will be served at a local restaurant on the all-day tour ($$$) and you'll also

visit the beautiful **wisteria and cherry gardens. Damascene-inlaid jewelry, Sat ma pottery and woodblock prints and scrolls** will appeal to shoppers. In Osa a half-day tour ($$–$$$) usually visits the 16th-century Osaka Castle and 6th-century Shitennoji Temple. Tours to Tokyo are sometimes offered a pre- or post-cruise option.

Nagasaki, Japan   ★★★

Language:	**Japanese**	*English Spoken?:*	**Yes**
Currency:	**Yen**	*US$ ok?:*	**No**
To town:	**Walk, taxi**		

Although most old Asia hands may disagree, Nagasaki is **our favorite Jap nese port** for its accessible size, friendly attitude and generally scenic su roundings. If you're **a *Madame Butterfly* fan**, strike out uphill at once for th lovely 1863 Glover House, the **setting for Puccini's opera amid a cluster 19th century European-style houses on a hillside bright with cherry blossom** Here poor Madame Butterfly watched in vain for her English lieutenant ship to sail back into the harbor. (You may remember the same plot line be ter from *Miss Saigon*.) Far more haunting is the **A-Bomb Museum or Interna tional Cultural Hall**, a four-floor museum of the horrors of the atomic bom that was dropped here in 1945 by U.S. forces. **The Peace Park is a landscape garden brightened with folded paper origami birds** traditionally left by th groups of Japanese school children that are brought on field trips to th park. One pleasant excursion from the city is to the **Arita pottery-making cen ter. A huge new Dutch village theme park** named Huis ten Bosch is also in tha area.

Yokohama (for Tokyo), Japan   ★★★★

Language:	**Japanese**	*English Spoken?:*	**Yes**
Currency:	**Yen**	*US$ ok?:*	**No**
To town:	**Excursion or shuttle bus to Tokyo**		

An hour away from the port of Yokohama is the vibrant city of Tokyo, with its **fashionable neon-lit Ginza shopping and restaurant district**, a park filled with **drooping cherry trees that frame the Imperial Palace** and high-tech Akihabara electronics street. Several shore excursions are available from Yokohama. The most popular is a full-day tour to Tokyo ($$$) which visits the Imperial Palace Plaza, Meiji Shrine with its heavily wooded grounds, and the Senso-ji

mple (formerly called Asakusa Kannon Temple) with its vibrant Nakamise
:ade of colorful market stalls. **Lunch at one of the local hotels is also includ-**
An all-day bus tour ($$$) to Japan's 234,290-acre Fuji-Hakone-Izu Na-
nal Park gives you a boat excursion on the lake, an **aerial ropeway ascent to**
Komagatake, and, if the weather permits, a **great view of snow-capped Mt.**
i. Lunch at a hotel is also included. Passengers who don't wish to take the
ve to Tokyo and back are offered a half-day journey ($$) to the nearby
aside resort of Kamakura, a shogun capital in the 13th century, where a visit
made to a gigantic bronze Buddha more than 42 feet high. Buses return
:m to the ship in time for lunch.

Penang, Malaysia ★★★★

Language:	**Bahasa**	*English Spoken?:*	**Yes**
Currency:	**Ringgit**	*US$ ok?:*	**No**
To town:	**Walk or taxi**		

*One of the temples of Penang, the popular beach resort and predominantly
ethnic Chinese island in northern Malaysia.*

Malaysia is a country we are very fond of, particularly the resort island of
Penang, where posh hotels line the beach and a **Sikh fortune-teller pads softly
from one suntanned Scandinavian blonde to the next reading palms**. In the Chinese market district of Chowrasta, a dignified gentleman squats anxiously
beside a **heap of prickly and noxious durian fruit**, so highly esteemed in southeast Asia, examining each one as intently as a jeweler grading diamonds. At
the Temple of the Azure Cloud, the few faithful (and the many tourists) crowd
in among the deadly poisonous pit vipers that are draped around the alter

and lying all about the temple, logy enough from the incense of burning j
sticks that they don't strike. Some foolhardy souls even pose with the sna
draped around their necks. A half-day tour ($$) usually visits a batik facto
the Kek Lok Si Temple, largest Buddhist temple in Malaysia; the 19th-ce
tury **Fort Cornwallis and its big cannon, where childless women place flowers a
offer special prayers for fertility**; and the beach at Batu Ferringhi where
big hotels are located. Sometimes a demonstration of rubber-harvesting a
curing is included as well. At Batu Ferringhi, the **Eden Seafood Restaura**
grills giant tiger prawns and serves cracked crab in a fiery tomato-and-ch
sauce. If you were in Singapore on business, **you could cruise up to Penang
one of the two-night Star Cruise ships**, big and glittering like new Scandinavi
ferries, which is what they were.

Port Kelang, Malaysia ★ ★ ★

Language:	**Bahasa**	*English Spoken?:*	**Yes**
Currency:	**Ringgit**	*US$ ok?:*	**No**
To town:	**Excursion or shuttle bus to Kuala Lumpur**		

Port Kelang (or, in some spellings, Port Klang) is the port for Kuala Lum
pur, the capital of Malaysia, 19 miles to the northeast. **KL, as most call it, is
fascinating combination of modern skyscrapers, Islamic mosques and minaret
and elaborate British Victorian gentlemen's clubs**. Mostly Malay and Chinese
KL thrives on business deals, rubber and tin, palm oil and banking. English
spoken almost everywhere. A half-day shore excursion here ($$) usuall
drives by the **Victorian railway station** (but doesn't stop), the Nation
Mosque (a massive and featureless modern building, where, unfortunately,
does stop), Chinatown (sometimes stops), the Selangor Pewter Factory (a
ways stops), a batik factory (usually stops) and the excellent Muzium Nega
ra, a mix of Malay architecture and crafts with some odd and fascinatin
artifacts, traditional wedding costumes and the like (usually stops). On you
own, you might want to explore colorful Chinatown on foot. Crafts shop
ping is especially good in Malaysia. Look for **cotton or silk batik and the high
quality pewter made from local tin**.

Yangon, Myanmar (Burma) ★ ★ ★

Language:	**Myanmar**	*English Spoken?:*	**Some**
Currency:	**Kyat**	*US$ ok?:*	**No**
To town:	**Walk, taxi**		

e sweepers at the Shwedagon Pagoda in Yangon (Rangoon) are fulfilling igious duties.

Somewhere east of Suez on the road to Mandalay, Kipling's sloe-eyed, slim-pped Burma girl may still be sitting, smoking her cheroot and staring spec-ively, not to the sea but to a new tide of tourist dollars routed into ngon/Rangoon. Burma sealed itself up in the early 1960s, opened the oors a crack to tourism in 1986, then slammed them shut again in 1988 to rn itself into Myanmar. While the income is apparently steady from its il-it production of **opium poppy—it's the world's largest producer**—Myanmar back on the cruise itineraries. Besides the ship calls at Yangon, the new ri-rboat *Road to Mandalay*, operated by Venice-Simplon-Orient Express and astern & Oriental Express cruises between Pagan and Mandalay. When we ere last there, the **old Stanley Hotel**, recently renovated into a luxury prop-ty again, was a dump, with nonworking plumbing and furniture that ooked like rejects from a Bulgarian flea market. The not-to-be-missed sight ere is the monumental, **golden Shwedagon Pagoda, gleaming in the sun.** Ev-ryone, pilgrim and tourist alike, is required to take off shoes and socks and alk barefoot into the temple complex; the white marble pavement is com-ortable in the evenings and early mornings, if a bit crunchy underfoot with its of raw rice from offerings, but it can be hot on tender feet in midday. Rows of sweepers, young people fulfilling religious duties, glide past fre-quently, swishing buckets of water in front of them, then sweeping with long hythmic strokes to keep it clean. Not far from the ferocious painted lion hat guards the entrance is **the modest tomb of U Thant.**

DID YOU KNOW?

One of our Burmese guides confided solemnly, "I hope to be reincarnated next as an American, so I too can travel about and see the world."

Singapore is poised to be the hub of business and banking for Southeast Asia.

Singapore ★★★★★

Language:	**English**	*English Spoken?:*	**Yes**
Currency:	**S$**	*US$ ok?:*	**No**
To town:	**Taxi**		

Singapore boasts **one of the finest cruise port facilities in Asia**, as well as having a great deal to offer a day visitor. Don't expect something quaint and charming, however; it's **a modern city filled with high-rise buildings** and so clogged with traffic that complicated rules govern what days and which cars can drive into the city center. It's cleaner than Disneyland, the streets are safe to walk day and night, nobody jaywalks and you can safely eat from street foodstalls. There are rigid restrictions on behavior; both **drugs and chewing gum are prohibited**, for instance, and fines are severe. Shore excursions here usually include a half-day city tour ($$) that visits sanitized versions of Little India and Chinatown, the Museum at Empress Place, drives past Raffles Hotel, Parliament House, the Padang, then to the Botanical Gardens to see the orchids. A half-day visit to **Jurong Bird Park** ($$) combines walking through aviaries with a Birds of Prey show and the World of Darkness display of nocturnal birds. Another half-day tour visits Chinatown and the market, the gaudy and vivid **Sri Mariamman Temple** and a crafts center. English is one of the island nation's four official languages; the others are Malay (Bahasa), Chinese and Tamil.

Pusan, South Korea ★★

Language:	**Korean**	*English Spoken?:*	**Yes**
Currency:	**Won**	*US$ ok?:*	**No**
To town:	**Taxi or shuttle bus**		

usan, South Korea's major port and second largest city, is interesting primarily for its beaches and its **enormous Chagalchi fish market**, best in early morning, where vendors sell fresh fish, live eels and dozens of varieties of shellfish just unloaded from boats. A half-day sightseeing tour ($$) may visit the fish market, as well as the Pusan Tower, the central business district, the beaches at Haeundae (which get jammed with people in summer), bucolic Keshin Park above the city, and the ever-popular shopping stop. Bargaining in order. Another half-day excursion ($$) drives up to the beautiful **Pomo-Buddhist Temple**, set in a quiet wooded park. Before or after the temple, you visit Kumgang Park and the mountaintop Kumjongsansong Fortress with its incredible views (on a rare clear day). A full-day excursion to Tongdosa Temple ($$$), founded in 646, is exceptionally rewarding; it is perhaps the most impressive and evocative Buddhist/Zen temple in Asia. Some 200 monks are in residence and can be heard chanting as you walk around the buildings. Hangul is the written alphabet for the spoken language of the Koreans, which has some interesting **similarities with North American Indian languages**.

Bangkok, Thailand ★★★

Language:	**Thai**	*English Spoken?:*	**Yes**
Currency:	**Baht**	*US$ ok?:*	**Yes**
To town:	**Taxi or shuttle bus**		

Laem Chabang, a newly developed wharf area, is the **closest cruise-ship port to Bangkok**, about 2-1/2 hours away along a good highway. Because of the distance, a lot of **lines use Bangkok as a home port** or spend two days on the call so passengers don't have to be driven that distance twice in one day. A highlights tour ($$$ and exhausting) from the port includes the **Royal Palace Grounds**, Wat Trimit and its **solid gold Buddha**, lunch at a local hotel, Wat Phra Keo and its Emerald Buddha, the Pantheon of Kings and the Golden Chedi. Another more leisurely tour beginning in Bangkok is a **boat trip along the Chao Phraya River**, poking into the *klongs* (canals) and visiting the floating market. Wat Aran, the Temple of the Dawn, is also on the itinerary. On your

own, **ride in one of the noisy open-air tuk-tuks** (passenger-carrying three-wh
taxis that sound like buzzsaws) to Jim Thompson's house and/or the ex
lent **Thai silk and cotton shop** nearby that he founded.

Phuket, Thailand ★ ★ ★

Language:	**Thai**	*English Spoken?:*	**Yes**
Currency:	**Baht**	*US$ ok?:*	**Yes**
To town:	**Van or excursion bus**		

*The white sugar sand beaches of Thailand's Phuket are a major draw fe
western tourists.*

Phuket Island is another popular cruise stop in Thailand. It's very hot a
year and populated by Chinese, Portuguese and local Chow Li people, mar
originally brought in to work in the tin mines and rubber plantations. An al
day tour includes colorful Wat Chalong monastery, Rawai Beach, **shoppin
for local cultured pearls in Phuket town** and a hotel lunch. Along the way, yo
see wooden houses on stilts, water buffalo in the fields, wood-and-wire en
closures where fighting cocks are sparring and brightly striped open-air buse
called "chicken buses." At Chalong stalls **sell everything from durian to plasti
machine guns** and fried cakes made of batter funneled through a tin can wit
holes punched in the bottom. The Chinese buy tissue-thin sheets of ham
mered gold to affix to the Buddhas and the paintings in the temple pavilion
along with offerings of lotus flowers or orchids, after which they stick a littl
flag in a mound of dirt and then set off firecrackers to make sure the gods are
listening. Afternoons are spent at **Kata Beach, a long, hot stretch of sand**. An
all-day James Bond Island Tour ($$$, includes lunch) goes up to Phang-Nga
where one of the Bond movies was filmed.

Haiphong (for Hanoi), Vietnam ★★

Language:	**Vietnamese**	*English Spoken?:*	**Yes**
Currency:	**Dong**	*US$ ok?:*	**No**
To town:	**Excursion or shuttle bus to Hanoi**		

Three fishing boats sail through Vietnam's Ha Long Bay.

From Haiphong, the port of **Hanoi**, it is an arduous **62-mile journey along bad roads** but riveting roadside scenery from the capital. It takes three hours or longer to cover the distance. Farmers in rice paddies wearing conical straw hats, **bicyclists pedaling along with a brace of live ducks tied to the handlebars** or a fat market-bound pig lashed onto the back, women trotting along the roadside with bamboo yokes balancing baskets filled with bok choy, mandarin oranges, live chickens—the scene is colorful and fascinating. An all-day shore excursion ($$$ and exhausting) takes you to **Ho Chi Minh's Mausoleum**, the One Pillar Pagoda from 1049, the Museum of Fine Arts and Temple of Literature and an Army Museum (that fascinated the Vietnam veterans on our tour). The **site of the notorious "Hanoi Hilton" prison** is pointed out. Visits are also made to the Lake of the Restored Sword and the **street market in the old town**, and passengers are served lunch and a well-performed program of Vietnamese folk music and dance. Shopping for inexpensive but **well-made Vietnamese crafts may net you great buys** in lacquerware, mother-of-pearl inlay, sandalwood statuettes, ceramic elephants, embroidered tablecloths, wall hangings, watercolors and offbeat T-shirts.

Ho Chi Minh City, Vietnam   ★ ★ ★

Language:	**Vietnamese**	*English Spoken?:*	**Yes**
Currency:	**Dong**	*US$ ok?:*	**Yes**
To town:	**Walk, taxi or pedicab**		

Cruise ships sail **four miles up the Saigon River to dock in Ho Chi Minh Cit** few steps away from the Ho Chi Minh Museum. In this bustling, hustli city, shiny new Honda motorcycles vie with pedal bikes, everyone wears su glasses, and only a few vendors in from the country sport conical straw ha The half-day shore excursions here ($$) usually visit the **Reunification Pala (the former presidential palace), preserved much as it was when the Commun tanks burst through the wrought iron gates in 1975.** The War Museum (al called the Museum of American War Crimes) is a bit grimmer, embarrassi some of the guides, who apologize later to the passengers, explaining t government requires it on all tours. An historic museum with exhibits fro all 54 racial groups that make up the country also features **a unique water pu pet show** that is splashy and diverting. The former American Embassy (wi rememberences of the frantic helicopter evacuation from the rooftop) pointed out en route. A shopping or cold drink stop in the heart of dow town Saigon lets you stroll to the **Rex or Continental Hotel** or into the Muni ipal Theatre for a look around.

THE HAWAII CRUISE

n the 1920s and 1930s, the only way to get to Hawaii was by ship, usually ¬e of the gleaming white Matson Lines vessels that sailed into Honolulu on ¬at everyone called Boat Day. The Royal Hawaiian Band would be on the ¬er playing "Aloha Oe," canoe paddlers would race out to meet the arriving ¬ip, hula dancers would be swaying and people would be waving flags and ¬reamers, strewing confetti and carrying armloads of flower leis.

¬Later, of course, going to Hawaii became almost too easy, with mass-pro-¬ıced vacations complete with ersatz grass skirts, hoi-polloi luaus and low-¬ɔst jet flights to air-conditioned bedrooms and balconies towering over the ¬ınds of Waikiki. It's enough to take the romance out of paradise. What's a ¬aveler to do? One possibility is to book a cruise around the islands, sort of a ¬awaii sampler aboard a ship that spends a day or more at each of the major re-**¬ɔrt islands**, allowing enough time ashore to window-shop among the lavish ¬ew resorts for a future holiday booking. Cruise passengers have the best of ¬oth worlds in Hawaii—the option of taking an easy look at shore from a ¬omfortable deck chair with a good book and a cold drink close at hand, or ¬ıining in an excursion with transfers to bus, small boat or helicopter.

The ships almost **always cruise within sight of land,** with frequent ports of all, and it's usually possible to arrange for a rental car on any of the islands ¬hrough the shore excursions office on board. Active sports ranging from **¬cuba diving, snorkeling and kayaking to bicycling or tennis** can also be booked ¬rom the ship.

Five Places to Find Old Hawaii

1. **Lahaina,** where once as many as 400 whaling ships anchored annually in Lahaina Roads and on a typical night **1500 brawling, drunken sailors** who had spent months sailing around Cape Horn in search of sperm whales went careening through the town looking with equal fervor for women and whiskey. Today, the whalers have been supplanted by tourists from Japan and the mainland seeking the perfect t-shirt. Check out **the Pioneer Inn** for authenticity.

2. **Kona coast,** where Kamehameha the Great trooped up and down in the early 19th century visiting the **royal fishponds** and deciphering the **ancient petroglyphs**; you can still see some of the ponds and the petroglyphs today on the grounds of the very posh hotels that line the coast.

3. **Kauai** has always been considered the home of Hawaii's two-foot-high *menehu* or leprechauns, who dug the fish ponds and canals and built gardens and intri structures in the old days. More recently, a tall *menehune* called Chris Hemm was responsible for building some of the most extravagantly overstated hotels in world; one of them, once the Westin Kauai and badly damaged by hurricane I in 1992, can be glimpsed as you sail in and out of the harbor at Nawiliwili.

4. Also in Kauai, on the north side, look down on the **Hanalei Valley** from the road of Princeville to see the **taro farms**, then proceed into town to look at the Wa Huiia Church and Mission House, **hit the Tahiti Nui** for a drink, and you get an i of what old Hawaii was really like.

5. Still in Kauai, on the west side, the dusty **old sugar town of Hanapepe** is gradu gentrifying but still carries a lot of character.

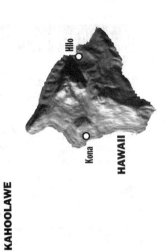

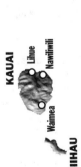

Hilo

MAUI

Kahului

Kona

HAWAII

KAHOOLAWE

MOLOKAI

LANAI

OAHU

Honolulu

KAUAI

Lihue

Nawiliwili

Waimea

NIIHAU

PACIFIC
OCEAN

N

Hawaiian Islands

© 1995 Fielding Worldwide, Inc.

Rating the Ports of Paradise

Big Island, Hawaii ★★★★★

Language:	**English**	*English Spoken?:*	**Yes**
Currency:	**US$**	*US$ ok?:*	**Yes**
To town:	**Walk or tender into Kona, taxi into Hilo**		

Mauna Lani's velvet golf courses are a main attraction to the Big Island.

The Big Island of Hawaii has two main ports. **Hilo, where the major shore excursion is to Volcanoes National Park** and you can almost count on a morning rain shower when sailing in, is where the orchids and anthuriums come from. The all-day bus tour to the park ($$) includes a stop at the lava tubes and a visit to the macadamia-nut factory that gives out free samples and sells lots more. Sometimes there is a **dramatic helicopter overflight of Kiluaea volcano** ($$$) but tightened restrictions on the local pilots have cut back on some of these tours. Shorter tours ($$) cover Akaka Falls or tropical botanical gardens. Over on the Kona Coast, you can opt for a day of golf ($$$), snorkeling and swimming tours ($–$$), the Atlantis submarine ($$$), a visit into *paniolo* (cowboy) country at Parker Ranch and a jeep tour into **lush, secluded Waipio Valley** ($$$). A general overview for first-time visitors is offered on a Kona Discovery Tour ($$). On your own, **you can rent a car in the Kamehameha Hotel** near the pier when the tender docks and drive up to Waimea and the Parker Ranch (don't miss **the colorful Kamuela Museum with its eclec-**

collections), or toodle along the Kohala coast, where the rich and famous ...cation in lavish resort hotels.

Kauai, Hawaii ★★★★★

Language:	**English**	*English Spoken?:*	**Yes**
Currency:	**US$**	*US$ ok?:*	**Yes**
To town:	**Taxi or shuttle bus**		

The lush headlands of the Ne Pali coast are accessible to kayakers and hikers, as well as day visitors aboard excursion boats.

Your ship will arrive at the port of Nawiliwili near Lihue. This lush and dazzling island may look familiar—**even if you've never been here before, you've seen Kauai's verdant landscapes** in *Raiders of the Lost Ark*, its golden sand beaches in *South Pacific*, its hideaway resorts in *Blue Hawaii*. The reason it's so green? At the center of the island is **the rainiest spot on earth**, Waialeale, with 451 inches of rainfall a year. Shore excursions include a full-day excursion to Waimea Canyon and the Fern Grotto ($$$), a half-day excursion to either of them ($$), a four-hour **Hanalei sea and snorkeling tour** ($$$), a boat excursion around the Ne Pali cliffs ($$$) and a kayak trip along the Huleia River ($$), as well as various snorkeling, sailing or swimming options ($–$$). On your own, renting a car lets you cover much of the island if you move briskly. Head toward Hanapepe to see the beach area of Poipu, the **recreated "old Hawaii" sugar town of Koloa** with its colorful shops and delectable Lappert's ice cream, a scenic drive to Waimea Canyon and, at the road's

end, a view down to the sea from atop Ne Pali. Head toward Princeville a
you can visit the fern grotto ($), see Kiluaea Lighthouse and the **clas**
Princeville Resort.

Maui, Hawaii   ★★★★★

Language:	**English**	*English Spoken?:*	**Yes**
Currency:	**US$**	*US$ ok?:*	**Yes**
To town:	**Taxi into Kahului, tender into Lahaina**		

*The old whaling port of Lahaina on Maui is still one of the most interesting
calls in the islands.*

Most ships, including American Hawaii's *Independence* (page 127), dock
at Kahului's pier, but a few anchor off the historic whaling town of Lahaina
with a gorgeous view of the island of Lanai on the opposite side. One of the
most popular shore excursions on Maui is **the drive up to Haleakala** National
Park through the cool upcountry ($$), a bicycle trip down Haleakala ($$$)
with breakfast and lunch included, a picnic and snorkel trip to Molokini
($$$), and an all-day van trip along the famous Hana Highway, ($$$), ex-
pensive and exhausting). Other options include a luau ($$-$$$), a tropical
plantation visit and tour of Iao Valley ($$) and an Atlantis submarine tour
($$$) that goes down 150 feet to see coral, fish and turtles. Between Christ-
mas and Easter, some **400 humpback whales winter off Lahaina**; small boat ex-
cursions ($$) can take you fairly close. On your own in Lahaina, you can
stroll the often-crowded streets lined with shops and vendors touting tours

THE HAWAII CRUISE

remarkably low prices (it's usually part of a time-share come-on, so take ~re). More fun is to hop aboard the narrow-gauge sugar train ($) for a short ~rrated tour through the cane fields or take a self-guided historic walking ~ur. From Kahului, you can drive up to **Ho'okipa beach to watch great wind-rfing**, but resist the urge to drive to Hana. You don't have time to get there ~d back on a cruise ship day visit.

Oahu, Hawaii ★★★★★

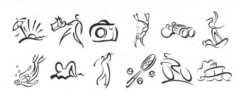

Language:	**English**	*English Spoken?:*	**Yes**
Currency:	**US$**	*US$ ok?:*	**Yes**
To town:	**Walk, taxi to Waikiki**		

In Honolulu, your cruise ship will be docked at Aloha Tower, within easy ~valking distance of downtown but a bus or taxi ride away from Waikiki. ~hore excursion options may include a Honolulu City Tour ($$), a Bishop ~Iuseum tour ($$), a **visit to the Arizona Memorial** and Punchbowl Crater and ~emetery ($$), the Polynesian Cultural Center with its living museum, a ~uffet meal and Polynesian show ($$$), a half-day visit to Pearl Harbor, Ar-zona Memorial and Honolulu highlights ($$), a Honolulu and environs ~ightseeing tour ($$) that includes downtown, Pali Lookout and lastly a stop ~n Waikiki, where you may leave the tour and return to the ship on your own. ~A full-day circle island tour with lunch ($$$) is also usually available, as are ~evening luaus and/or entertainment shows ($$-$$$). Among the more ac-tive options are beach, snorkel and scuba tours ($$). On your own, you can ~take a bus or taxi out to the superb Bishop Museum; hit the beach at Waikiki and catch some rays; take a **historic walking tour around Waikiki** or the old downtown area (☎ *(808) 524-0722* for info). But to really soak up the aloha spirit, drop by the **Halekulani Hotel's open-air cocktail terrace called House Without a Key and watch the hula-and-Hawaiian-music sunset show** for the price of a drink or two.

CRUISING THE SOUTH PACIFIC AND INDONESIA

For anyone who can hum "Bali Hai" or conjure up the memory of Dorothy Lamour in a sarong or Brooke Shields in a blue lagoon, the allure of the South Pacific needs no explanation. A South Pacific cruise is for sun worshippers and beach strollers, for people who dream over back issues of *National Geographic*, for sailors and island-collectors, for neo-Gauguins and erstwhile Fletcher Christians. Lush green islands are set in **a sea of aquamarine and cobalt blue**, sunsets are fiery displays of crimson and gold, tropical flowers are fragrant and **intense as fluorescent perfume**.

The ghosts of Sadie Thompson and Captain Bligh, Robert Louis Stevenson and Somerset Maugham still inhabit these islands. Brightly painted open-air buses garlanded with red ginger blossoms bounce along rural roadways, and markets are lively with heaps of papayas and breadfruit, clusters of orchids and strings of parrot fish, wraparound cotton pareus and clunky shell necklaces.

One caution: Anyone who ventures ashore should be able to withstand the **sometimes-extreme heat and humidity**, enervating enough to leave a sightseer limp and damp as a dishrag.

For any South Pacific or Indonesian cruise, you'll want to take along lightweight and loose-fitting cotton and linen garments, a couple of bathing suits and some coverups, a sun hat or umbrella for shade when walking on shore and a strong sunblock for protection against sunburn. Don't forget comfortable sandals or running shoes for shore excursions, and **sneakers or plastic wading shoes for venturing into the coral-bottomed waters**. Even what seems a minor scratch from coral can blossom into a serious infection if you're not careful.

Many cruise passengers buy inexpensive woven fans for practical use during shore stops, then recycle them as souvenirs or small gifts afterward.

Only a cruise ship gives you the luxury and freedom to wander from island to island in this vast sea, carrying bed and board with you in air-conditioned comfort, letting you adjust to the languorous rhythms of local life and come home to your stateroom when the heat gets you down. **A South Pacific cruise** is adventuring the easy way in a rare and exotic part of the world that won't ▶ able to keep its pristine charm much longer.

Glossary: Tokkin Pidgin

In parts of the South Pacific, a simplified version of English has grown up in tradin ports in countries with multiple languages and dialects like Papua New Guinea and Va uatu, reaching a semi-official status as the nation's language. Terms are sometimes colo ful; these are a few of our favorites.

1. Papua New Guinea: a bicycle is **wilwil** (pronounced wheel-wheel).

2. Also PNG: freight is **kago**, sometimes arriving as **hairkago**, sometimes as **sikago**.

3. PNG: telling a lie is **tokples blong satan**.

4. Vanuatu: a brassiere is **basket blong titi**.

5. Vanuatu public library sign: **Tabu Blong Smok**.

South Pacific

@ 1995 Fielding Worldwide, Inc.

Rating the Ports of the Pacific

Easter Island, Chile ★★★

Language:	**Spanish**	*English Spoken?:*	**Yes**
Currency:	**Peso**	*US$ ok?:*	**Yes**
To town:	**Tender to shore**		

The **mysterious monoliths** of Easter Island attract a surprising number of expedition vessels to this **very remote island 1250 miles from the nearest land**. While the island was annexed by Chile in 1888, the population is primarily Polynesian. The main town is Hanga Roa on the west end of the island, but the main attraction is the *moai*, the **giant stone heads** from six feet to over 60 feet high found around the island. No one knows who carved them or exactly how they were moved to their stone platforms from the quarries at the top of the mountain. It has been said that the figures "walked" under the power of the priests to the sites. The figures were cut from basalt from the Rano Raraku volcano; the 60-foot *moai* is still there, carved but not separated from the rock. Unfinished *moai* and fallen *moai* are all around the area; evidence shows some 600 were carved. Shopping here is limited to small stone *moai*, **replicas of wooden rongo-rongo tablets** with hieroglyphics that may have been genealogical tables, obsidian earrings and cloth rubbings of petroglyphs.

Rarotonga, Cook Islands ★★★

Language:	**English**	*English Spoken?:*	**Yes**
Currency:	**NZ$**	*US$ ok?:*	**No**
To town:	**Tender to town**		

No captain who observes the wreck of the *Yankee*, almost gone now after decaying off Rarotonga since its unhappy grounding in 1976, tries to come in beyond the island's unforgiving reef. The tourist traffic here is mostly from New Zealand (the island is a protectorate of NZ), and neighboring Australia. If the waters are too rough to tender passengers ashore, the **warm, winsome, English-speaking Cook Islanders** will be happy to come out through the surf to your ship and introduce themselves and their culture and crafts to ou. A 19-mile road goes around the island from the capital of Avarua, and Ɪe **dancing is some of the best in the entire South Pacific**. Local crafts include ꞮIique, finely woven, pandanus fans with a bit of polished abalone shell for ꞮIe handle, pandanus hats and hand-carved ironwood kitchen utensils. BarꞮining is not customary here; you pay the initial asking price. Tipping also ꞮIes against local custom, since any gift traditionally must be repaid in kind. ꞮIhere is a tiny fruit and vegetable market in town, where unsold items are ꞮIft overnight on the market tables rather than being lugged back home, beꞮause nobody is likely to steal a coconut in Rarotonga.

Suva, Fiji   ★ ★ ★

Language:	**English**	English Spoken?:	**Yes**
Currency:	**F$**	US$ ok?:	**Yes**
To town:	**Walk**		

Suva, exotic and colorful with its mixed population of Fijians, Indians, Chinese and Europeans, has an outstanding museum, the Fiji Museum in Suva's Thurston Gardens, with the finest collection of Fijian artifacts in the world. Don't miss it. You'll see "cannibal forks," war clubs and rare golden cowrieshell chief's necklaces. This was where we came up with the title for our *Bon Appétit* Fiji story that for some reason the editors chose not to use, "**Eating Your Way Through the Cannibal Isles**." Lucky cruise ship passengers may be treated to one of the South Pacific's special concerts if the **Fiji Police Band** comes down to play for the arrival or departure. Marching along the dock in precise formation **in their navy tunics and saw-toothed white sulu skirts**, they may play a medley of "Blue Suede Shoes," "Love Me Tender" and "South of the Border (Down Mexico Way)" but they always finish up with the moving **Fijian song of farewell**, "**Isa Lei.**" Shore excursions offered here often include an excellent tour ($$) out to Pacific Harbour and the Fijian Cultural Center to see the **Dance Theatre of Fiji** or the **fire walkers of Beqa perform**. A shorter half-day tour of Orchid Island ($$) gives a glimpse of village life and traditions including a sip of kava in a *bure* (thatched hut). A coral reef cruise in a glass-bottom boat ($$), a Fiji "fun night" buffet ($$$) and a tour of Thurston Gardens and Suva's stately homes ($$) may also be offered. If you choose to set out on your own to wander around, **be wary of the street vendors hawking wood carvings**; most are cheaply made and finished off with shoe polish that comes off on your hands. You can buy inexpensive local crafts and souvenirs from the **crafts market** near the dock or walk through the **lively fruit-and-vegetable market**, also near the dock.

Bora Bora, French Polynesia ★★★★★

Language:	**French**	English Spoken?:	**Yes**
Currency:	**CFP Franc**	US$ ok?:	**Yes**
To town:	**Tender from ship**		

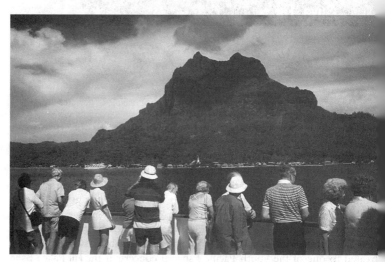

The arrival in Bora Bora draws all the passengers on deck.

Sailing into **Bora Bora delivers a scenic punch right to the solar plexus**—impossibly steep jagged peaks that seem to be upholstered in thick green velvet; sapphire and turquoise and lapis lazuli waters lap at the palm-lined shore, strung with a thin circlet of coral reef. **Bring on the dancing girls**! Take an early morning excursion by rented bicycle ($) or moped ($$) before it gets too hot and humid, perhaps pedaling all around the island (there's a rough hilly stretch where you'll have to walk your bike on the far side) or at least along the southwestern coast (turn right from the pier) past the white New England-style mansion left over from the movie set of *Hurricane*. Shore excursions are usually not offered here, since there is little in the way of organized tourism. Most passengers wander in and out of the **handful of shops at the dock,** then head back to the ship. A few may work their way over to Bloody Mary's for some fresh (and pricey) grilled fish or barbecued lobster. **You can't get lost**, since the 19-mile road around the island is the only one and forms a full circle. There are raffish little local cafes and bars where you can stop for a snack or a cold drink. You can buy a **lovely pareu in tie-dyed or floral pattern from a beautiful vendor** at a beachside boutique. She'll cheerfully show you how to drape and tie it; it isn't her fault you forget how before the end of the day.

Huahine, French Polynesia   ★ ★ ★

Language:	**French**	*English Spoken?:*	**Some**
Currency:	**CFP Franc**	*US$ ok?:*	**Yes**
To town:	**Walk**		

Small ships like Windstar's *Wind Song* visit this offbeat, **archeologically-rich** pair of twin islands year-round. The only organized sightseeing here is an open-air tram excursion to the archeological treasures at Maeva ($$). Huahine has been determined to be the oldest known settlement in the Society Islands, dating back perhaps to 1450 AD. At Maeva, there are 16 restored *narae* (temples), ancient stone fish traps and ancient village foundations. While the beaches of Huahine are nothing to write home about, there is some **surfing and diving** available. During one visit, virtually everyone on the island was lolling around watching the girls' volleyball game at the local Church of Latter-Day Saints. A few older men were engaged in a game of *petanque* (bowls) in classic French style. One hefty Polynesian, weighing in at perhaps 350 pounds, wore a crown of leaves and flowers as he sat atop his tractor to watch the games. What we enjoy most about Huahine are places like the village of Fare where a **Chinese grocery called Wing Wong** is filled with bright pareus, canned cassoulet in three sizes, Coleman lanterns and New Zealand canned corned beef. Three small children had just been given candy, and were leaping up and down in joy. When they saw us, they seemed to stop in midair, gaping in surprise; the store got very quiet as if everyone was holding his breath. We left quietly.

Moorea, French Polynesia   ★ ★ ★ ★ ★

Language:	**French**	*English Spoken?:*	**Yes**
Currency:	**CFP franc**	*US$ ok?:*	**Yes**
To town:	**Tender to shore**		

After that initial disappointment at the first sight of Tahiti, the teeming streets of Papeete, the visitor usually manages to find his "dream Tahiti" on Moorea. **Cook's Bay is a favored anchorage** on the beautiful island, which is as craggy and velvet-green as Bora Bora but much bigger. Excursions here include a half-day Highlights Tour ($$) that calls for some walking and includes a drive through the Opunohu Valley and a visit to a distillery that makes **French-style clear eau-de-vies from tropical fruits**, some 22 varieties produced in the classic Alsatian method; the ginger is particularly interesting.

An island drive ($$) is similar but stops at a *marae* (temple), the Belvedere vista for photographs and a beach resort with thatched-roof rooms for a chance to swim. Some excursions also visit a Tiki Village with dance show, crafts village and fishing demonstrations ($$). A Land Rover island tour by four-wheel drive ($$$) is also sometimes offered. On one visit we spent the morning cruising aboard a 70-foot sailing yacht through the bays and beyond the reef, followed by some snorkeling and a beach barbecue of grilled fresh tuna, then a ride on small vans through the forested interior of the island ($$$). More active excursion possibilities include snorkeling, scuba (**bring your certification**), **lessons in underwater photography**, parasailing, water-skiing, jet-skiing and deep-sea fishing. If you want to strike out on your own, you can book **beach horseback rides** from Rupe Rupe Ranch, Tahura Ranch or Centaure Ranch ($$). To buy: **Locally produced tie-dye pareus**.

Tahiti, French Polynesia ★★★

Language:	**French**	*English Spoken?:*	**Yes**
Currency:	**CFP franc**	*US$ ok?:*	**No**
To town:	**Walk or taxi**		

Papeete buzzes with motor scooters and automobiles and can be **heart stoppingly expensive** for even simple pleasures, so you know already that shore excursions, even the blandest half-day bus tours, are going to cost plenty. Cruise ships may dock right in the heart of Papeete, a short stroll from anywhere in town, or at the newer commercial docks a short shuttle away. Shore excursions here usually include a full-day circle island tour with lunch ($$$), a **half-day tour ($$$) to Point Venus for the view**, the city of Papeete and its governor's mansion, legislature, shopping centers and waterfront, then a stop at the Museum of Tahiti and Her Islands at Fisherman's Point to see archeological and nature exhibits, and a visit to the *marae* (temple) of Arahurahu. The **Gauguin museum and botanical gardens** ($$$) is popular, but don't be disappointed in the museum, which has only reproductions of the artist's works; there are some poignant photographs and artifacts from his time in Tahiti. A Tahitian *hima'a* serves you a very expensive Tahitian dinner cooked in hot rocks underground, along with wine and some dancing ($$$). On your own, stroll over to the **flower market in early morning** to see the lush flora of the island and the shivering vendors in heavy wool sweaters in the 80-degree cool. Some of the tastiest and least expensive meals around—crepes, pizza, steaks and *pommes frites*—are served by the *roulettes* (food wagons) that gather at the waterfront every evening.

Agana, Guam

Language:	**English**	English Spoken?:	**Yes**
Currency:	**US$**	US$ ok?:	**Yes**
To town:	**Taxi**		

Most of this **hot, humid island** is still under the control of the **U.S. military**. Shore excursions ($$) generally include a pause at several World War II **Japanese gun sites**, including the War in the Pacific National Historic Park Visitor Center, which also has a 15-minute slide show about the war. Once a Spanish colony and since the Spanish-American War a territory of the United States, Guam serves today as **a sort of surrogate America for budget-package tourists from Japan** who don't want to spring for the airfare to Hawaii or California, and so come here to spend dollars, eat hamburgers and stay in a Hilton. The Spanish influence becomes apparent with a stop at the Plaza de España downtown, a visit to the Guam Museum and the cathedral, first built in 1699, rebuilt in 1955. The ancient Latte Stone Park, **monoliths from prehistoric structures** perhaps, Government House and Two Lovers Point, where two Chamorro lovers tied their hair together and jumped from the cliff into the sea, are also popular stops. Each stop has a few vending booths with Chanel t-shirts and other merchandise aimed primarily at the Japanese market. Since the Marianas Trench is not far away, Guam is considered a **good diving and snorkeling destination**, although some areas are restricted by the military. The Blue Hole is a favorite spot for scuba divers.

Bali, Indonesia ★ ★ ★ ★ ★

Language:	**Indonesian**	English Spoken?:	**Some**
Currency:	**Rupiah**	US$ ok?:	**Yes**
To town:	**Tender from anchorage**		

On this lovingly tended and contoured lush green island, comically fierce stone guardians keep watch over the 20,000 or so stone-and-brick temples around the island. You can shop for exquisite arts and crafts created by a people who have no word for "artist" in the language, because all Balinese are artists. Shore excursions often visit the various art colonies where you'll be able to deal directly with the artist himself in many cases. The standard shore excursion here is the full-day tour ($$$) with lunch (usually a **tasty Balinese buffet** at a breezy hilltop restaurant), a stop to see the **Barong Dance** or the Monkey Dance, a visit to the wood **carvers and artists at work at Ubud and**

Mas, a trek to the Mother Temple of Besakih or Tampaksiring, as well **Klungkung's open-air Hall of Justice**, where the condemned had plenty of tin to study graphic descriptions of their punishments painted on the wall You'll be **surrounded at every stop by relentless hawkers** who tirelessly thru wood carvings, batik tablecloths, shell necklaces and tropical fruits in yo face, even pushing them in open bus windows when you're trying to get little air; you can haggle the modest prices down even further if you wish, a though **the full asking price is cheap enough**. When a cruise begins or ends i Bali, many lines offer an included or optional pre- or post-cruise; take advan tage of it if you want to check out the beaches.

Java, Indonesia ★★

Language:	**Indonesian**	*English Spoken?:*	**Yes**
Currency:	**Rupiah**	*US$ ok?:*	**Yes**
To town:	**Taxi or excursion bus**		

The **densely-populated island** of Java offers a mixed bag of attractions, de pending on where the ship docks. **Teeming, tumultuous Jakarta** with its heav traffic and **unsightly pockets of squalor** is the most-visited port. Shore excur sions here usually include a look at a couple of **grandiose and tasteless monu ments to Sukarno**, a visit to the somewhat **dark and musty Indonesian Nationa Museum** and perhaps a look at the Buginese Makassar schooners, traditiona wooden sailboats being loaded with modern cargo from TV sets to refriger ators for outlying islands. Check out the **handicraft shopping**—leather pup pets, silver filigree, batiks—at the **Sarinah department store**, frequently included on excursions. On your own, you might enjoy a visit to **Taman Mini Indonesia** a few miles out of town, where **traditional architecture** from the whole sprawling country is one display in one area, along with cultural per formances and crafts. The majestic temple of **Borobudur, one of the world's greatest Buddhist monuments**, is perhaps the most rewarding overland excur sion in Java ($$$); it's a busy and tiring full-day trip from Semarang, an over night two-day haul from Yogyakarta. You'll stop for a typical Indonesian meal on the full-day journey, as well as having a chance to watch batik made and perhaps purchase some. **Bargaining is customary with street vendors**, less frequent in shops.

Spice Islands, Indonesia ★★★

Language:	**Indonesian**	*English Spoken?:*	**Some**
Currency:	**Rupiah**	*US$ ok?:*	**Yes**
To town:	**Walk or tender, depending on port**		

An archipelago of some 17,000 islands stretches between **Sumatra and Borneo**, most of them part of Indonesia. The so-called Spice Islands, **a popular cruise itinerary with expedition vessels**, usually covers **Flores, Komodo, Lombok, sometimes Timor, Sumbawa and Lesser Sunda**, all part of the Nusa Tenggara group. Shore excursions are usually included in the fare aboard expedition vessels. You can expect a trip into the forest on Komodo to see the **legendary Komodo dragon**, a prehistoric monitor lizard that grows to ten feet long; a village visit with **crafts and dance exhibitions** from the rare Hindu Sasak people of Lombok; a look at the **volcanoes and rugged forests** of Flores, plus a village welcome with toddy and **betel-nut ceremonies** and a chance to watch ikat weaving. Trips into the isolated mountain villages of Sumbawa, the bustling Portuguese/Dutch port city of Kupang in Timor, and a greeting from costumed horseback riders astride the **"dancing sandalwood" horses** of Lesser Sunda are also sometimes on the agenda. Swimming, diving and snorkeling are daily options in most of the islands.

Noumea, New Caledonia ★★★

Language:	**French**	*English Spoken?:*	**Some**
Currency:	**CFP franc**	*US$ ok?:*	**No**
To town:	**Walk, taxi**		

Like Tahiti, New Caledonia is a **part of France**, with duty-free shops selling French perfumes, crystal and clothing. These islands got rich from nickel mines, and you can't miss the smelting plants nor the **rusty red overlay dusting the sandstone colonial buildings, fallout from the smelter**. The residents are a mix of **Melanesian, Polynesian, Chinese, Vietnamese and European French** who wear anything from traditional lace-trimmed Mother Hubbards in gaudy floral prints to American-style jeans and t-shirts. In town, there's a small aquarium whose star exhibit is a room filled with **living corals which glow under black light** in the darkness. But to fall in love with New Caledonia, you

have to **go to the beach**—to Anse Vata and Baie des Citrons, lined with feat
ery palms and *niaouli* eucalyptus and topless European sunbathers; t
Melanesians prefer umbrellas for shade and modest coverups. A **thousar
miles of coral reef** protect the island, and there's a dazzling casino on Ar
Vata beach. You can strike out for a walk around the town and find sor
charming little French cafes and restaurants with creditable local cookin
Other New Caledonian ports of call include the Loyalty Islands, Isle of Pin
and Hienghene.

Port Moresby, Papua New Guinea ★

Language:	**Pidgin**	*English Spoken?:*	**Yes**
Currency:	**Kina**	*US$ ok?:*	**Yes**
To town:	**Taxi**		

Port Moresby, unfortunately, is **one of the most dangerous ports in the worl
for petty theft and crime**. Passengers who arrive here on cruise ships are cau
tioned by locals not to go out alone even in the daytime; in the evening
parties wanting to go out to dinner are urged to group themselves in sixes c
eights and take taxis portal to portal. While Papua New Guinea's peop
speak an astonishing 740 different languages, **pidgin**, a charming corruptio
of basic English words overlaid with touches of German and other languag
es, is **the lingua franca**. English is understood and spoken in virtually all tou
ist areas. Shore excursions here may include a half- or full-day city an
countryside tour ($$–$$$) that covers the Parliament House, opened i
1984 by Prince Charles; the National Museum and Art Gallery with a **fin
collection of masks**; a drive up Paga Hill for the view; the **Motuan stilt villag
of Hanauabada; crafts and souvenir shops; and, on the full-day, a drive out t
Vairata National Park where you can often see **rare birds of paradise** betwee
June and November. Take an escorted shore excursion here; **don't attempt t
go around on your own, even in the daytime, around Paga Hill**. Visitors are no
welcome at Hanauabada except with local guides. Women should dress con
servatively and valuables should be left on board ship.

Manila, Philippines ★ ★

Language:	**Filipino**	*English Spoken?:*	**Yes**
Currency:	**Peso**	*US$ ok?:*	**Yes**
To town:	**Taxi, walk**		

Manila is a **crowded, colorful, sprawling city** with **extremely rich and extremely poor ghettos**, lively nightlife and flower-filled parks. You'll do best to **stay with shore excursions here**. They usually include a visit to Intramuros, the old **walled city from the 16th century** where the Spanish and Muslims lived. Sometimes a museum stop is made at the popular Museo ng Malacanang, the former **palace of Ferdinand and Imelda Marcos, where Filipino historical artifacts** are on display. The half-day tour ($$) also usually visits **Fort Santiago** and **San Augustin Church**. Another half-day tour ($$) is a scenic drive through the countryside to Tagaytay Ridge and its Taal Volcano, one of the deepest and most active volcanic craters in the world. En route, the tour passes local villages and coconut plantations, and **"jeepney" factories, where the brightly decorated local taxis are customized**. A full-day tour to Pagsanjan ($$$) requires a lot of exertion; passengers travel by **native dugout canoe** up the Lana River to see the waterfalls, **ride a bamboo raft through the falls, then shoot the rapids on the way back down**. But the most memorable, perhaps, is a half-day visit to **Corrigedor Island** ($), with its moving sound-and-light show about the Japanese attack and occupation during WWII.

Pago Pago, (American) Samoa ★★★

Language:	**English**	*English Spoken?:*	**Yes**
Currency:	**US$**	*US$ ok?:*	**Yes**
To town:	**Walk**		

An enthusiastic group of Samoan dancers, most of them high school kids who got to skip school for the occasion, greets the arrival of a cruise ship in Pago Pago.

There are **two Samoas**—American Samoa, a U.S. territory with its cap
Pago Pago, its language English and its currency the U.S. dollar, and in
pendent Western Samoa, a constitutional monarchy with its capital Apia,
language Samoan and its currency the tala (see below.) Pago Pago, like
erstwhile resident of fact and fiction, Miss Sadie Thompson, is **brash, lo
and untidy; money, booze and traffic flow freely**, and pragmatic romantics v
love it. Shore excursions in American Samoa—perhaps aboard a hand-pai
ed, open-air jitney decorated with fresh torch ginger and birds of paradise
may show you the self-styled supermarket, now selling Spam and canned e
chiladas, that is the location of the **rooming house where Somerset Maugh**
scribbled out the opening pages of *Rain*, the story of reformed prostitute Sa
Thompson. A class of Samoana High School students who cut class to co
and perform traditional Samoan songs and dances at the dock may include
many fair-skinned haoles as Polynesians. On your own in American Sam
you could do as we once did, hop aboard a local bus and ride to the end
the line to the Star-Kist tuna canning factory, then pay a second fare and r
back again. It's a very inexpensive way to get to know the island and its pe
ple. **Fellow passengers barraged us with questions about America and prou**
pointed out their homes, cars and coconut palms at each stop, teaching us mo
about American Samoa than any guided tour could have done.

Apia, (Western) Samoa   ★ ★ ★

Language:	**Samoan**	English Spoken?:	**Yes**
Currency:	**Tala**	US$ ok?:	**Yes**
To town:	**Walk**		

The most famous residents of Western Samoa were Tusitala, Teller of Tal
(a.k.a. English writer **Robert Louis Stevenson**), who lived in a home that
now at Samoa College and Valima Grounds and occupied by the head
state, and **Aggie Grey**, the charming hotelier said to be the model for Bloo
Mary in James Michener's *Tales of the South Pacific*. When we met her at he
hotel during the latter part of her life, she was a slender, small woman wh
looked astonishingly like a miniature version of the late writer Lillian Hel
man and was not averse to getting up on the stage to dance. The Apia Tow
ship and Environment tour ($-$$) takes you to Fagalii Bay, to the college t
see the home of Robert Louis Stevenson and for a shopping stop at a *tap*
factory. Ava and Umu, local cooking techniques, will also be demonstrate
for anyone interested in underground food preparation. On your own i
Western Samoa, if you're in good shape and get an early start in the coole
part of the morning, you can **climb to the grave of Robert Louis Stevenson, wh**
is buried atop Mt. Vaea. If you're not in good shape, **stop by Aggie Grey's fa**
mous hotel for lunch and more Samoan dancing. That's sometimes also offere
as a shore excursion ($$).

Nuku'Alofa, Tonga ★ ★

Language:	**Tongan**	*English Spoken?:*	**Yes**
Currency:	**Pa'anga**	*US$ ok?:*	**Yes**
To town:	**Walk**		

Tonga is an anomaly, the **last remaining Polynesian kingdom in the South Pacific**, ruled by a benign 400-pound king who is adored by his subjects. Tonga was **called "the friendly islands" by Captain Cook** on his visit in 1777 for its amiable residents. The captain didn't realize that the then-cannibalistic islanders were considering doing away with him, and scowling and being rude would obviously chase the quarry away before mealtime. Luckily, they couldn't agree on when to kill him, and so he survived. As with most of the other peoples of the South Pacific, the **Tongans were converted to Christianity by diligent 19th century missionaries, who brought them Victorian modesty, harmonious hymn-singing and rigorous rules for Sundays**. Twentieth century interpretations include **no fishing, no aircraft landings or takeoffs, no digging of taro root, no hanging out washing**. The rules have been altered slightly to allow taxis and hotels to operate, and cruise passengers to embark or disembark. Passengers calling here will probably be taken to watch *tapa* (mulberry bark cloth) being pounded and painted, to see the Royal Palace, Royal Chapel and Royal Tombs, to the Talamahu Market and the Fa'onelua Tropical Gardens, which displays a model Tongan village. Crafts shopping includes wall hangings, purses and placemats made of *tapa*, wood carvings and giant woven baskets.

Vila, Vanuatua ★ ★ ★

Language:	**Pidgin**	*English Spoken?:*	**Yes**
Currency:	**Vatu**	*US$ ok?:*	**Yes**
To town:	**Taxi, Walk**		

We confess a partiality to Vanuatu, if only because most of our friends haven't the foggiest idea where it is. Vanuatu used to be called the New Hebrides, and was ruled jointly by France and Britain in what was called a condominium government (which the locals called a pandemonium government), until its independence in 1980. Sailing into Port Vila past **Melanesian villages beginning to wake and stir as the bright morning sun spills into their dwellings** is magical. Dogs yawn and stretch, and proudly tusked **pigs, considered walking bankbooks and stock portfolios by the rural Vanuatans, stalk about,**

secure in their Dow Jones averages. The Main Wharf is a longish walk from center of town. At an open market shy vendors sit under a giant banyan t with their wares spread out on a mat in front of them—bananas, candlenu cherimoyas and live crabs, the last tethered in pairs so they can't get very away. Shore excursions here may include town and island tours, glass-b tom boat tours over the reef, sailing, game fishing, scuba and snorkeling, are not usually very organized, so may not be offered when you arrive. I more fun to just walk around and talk to the Vanuatans anyhow. Shopp will find a vivid collection of hand-screened t-shirts, **eerie carved masks wi paint and feathers,** and small stone figures like the *moais* of Easter Island bargain-basement prices for collectors patient enough to lug them hon We're still looking for a ship that calls at the island of Tanna, where **the Jo Frum cargo cults flourish,** and Pentecost Island, where the now-popular spo of **bungee-jumping was invented** by islanders who dive from a tower with lia vines tied around their ankles.

NEW ZEALAND/
AUSTRALIA SAILINGS

marching band crosses the street in Sydney.

After the enervating heat and humidity of the smaller South Pacific islands, **ew Zealand and Australia** feel more like Southern California, **warm but dry nd tolerable**. New Zealand is divided into two islands, called (rather logical-) North Island and South Island, while Australia is one huge island/conti-ent and some offshore islands including the tiny and often-forgotten asmania off its southeastern tip. Orient Lines and Princess Cruises offer ome particularly interesting itineraries in these areas.

New Zealand's main North Island ports are Auckland and Wellington, the atter **a dead ringer for San Francisco about 20 years ago**, and the two primary outh Island ports of call are the veddy veddy British Christchurch and sce-ic Milford Sound. New Zealand likes to think of itself as a miniature sam-ler of the world's great scenery, for **nowhere is more quiet beauty packed into ne small country**. Even the cities are modest enough not to overwhelm.

Australia, on the other hand, sets out deliberately to overwhelm. **Sailing nto Sydney's great harbor and smack up to the façade of the famous Opera**

House, frozen sails in mid-billow, constitutes **one of the great moments** cruising. Americans are immediately at home in this gregarious country.

Five Fair Dinkum Things to Do in Australia

1. **Collect aboriginal art**, which one Sydney critic says has saved the world from "boomerangs." See specialized galleries in The Rocks in Sydney or visit the Natic Gallery in Canberra with its splendid contemporary collection of dreamtime wc from the Kimberley region.

2. Forget the tinnies of Foster's lager, and **savor upscale tipples like boutique be and elegant Australian wines**, especially Tasmanian whites, Victorian vintages ; Western Australia's wines.

3. Take a pre- or post-cruise holiday where bedtimes are *bonzer* ("terrific") in upscale private resort like **Kewarra Beach** near Cairns, or a country hideaway **Lilianfels in the Blue Mountains**.

4. Despite the fact that the Aussies never let go the mini and continued to smear vivid shades of bright zinc sunblock, there is **some chic shopping** in every ci Check Sydney's Double Bay, Melbourne's South Yarra and Perth's Peppermi Grove.

5. Learn **Australian football rules**.

Rating the Ports of New Zealand and Australia

Brisbane, Australia ★★★

Language:	**Strine, similar to English**	*English Spoken?:*	**Yes**
Currency:	**A$**	*US$ ok?:*	**No**
To town:	**Taxi**		

Brisbane is a big, lively city, friendly as an overgrown pup, with no pretensions to class and style but a very stylish ambience anyhow. In the land of Oz, the Ozzies (we call them Aussies) will welcome you when you hop over. Shore excursions include a half-day city and Lone Pine Sanctuary tour ($$), the latter an introduction to Australian wildlife, where you can **cuddle a koala, feed a kangaroo and meet a hairy-nosed wombat**. (Don't mix up the order, however; we got bitten trying to feed the wombat!) A half-day countryside tour ($$) goes to Lamington National Park's rain forest with some gentle walking, followed by afternoon tea. The Gold Coast and Currumbin Bird Sanctuary ($$–$$$) visits the beaches and Surfer's Paradise, then takes a train ride around the sanctuary to **see emus, lorikeets, koalas and kangaroos**. On your own, visit the fine Queensland Cultural Centre with an art gallery, hands-on museum, state library and performing arts center, stroll along the winding Brisbane River through the heart of town, **visit the XXXX (Four X) Brewery** if you can find several friends to make up a group, or take a free guided walk (daily at 11 and 1 except Mondays) through the splendid Mt. Coot-tha Botanic Gardens. You could also head over to the immensely popular **Breakfast Creek Spanish Garden Steak House and Pub** for lunch. Service is casual (you stand in line to order; they deliver it to your table).

Cairns, Australia ★★★

Language:	**English**	*English Spoken?:*	**Yes**
Currency:	**A$**	*US$ ok?:*	**No**
To town:	**Taxi or walk**		

As the **jumping-off point for the Great Barrier Reef**, Cairns is the hear▪ Queensland's Far North, with a tropical climate that can be very hot tween November and April. The city came into being in 1876 as a port the Hodgkinson River gold field but soon profited from the Atherton Ta▪ land "tin rush" as well. From here, you can take a full-day excursion ($$$ the reef's Michaelmas Cay, **a national park that is home to thousands of birds**, for snorkeling and picnic lunch, accompanied by a marine biolog Game fishing ($$$) is another local option, along with **white-water raft▪ canoeing, horseback riding and bungee jumping** ($$$). For non-sportive typ a full-day excursion to Kuranda ($$$) for a beautiful train ride through rain forest aboard the **Kuranda narrow gauge railway** usually also includes aboriginal dance performance and lunch. Local tour operators offer visit Nerada tea plantation and Atherton Tableland waterfalls ($$) or half-day tours or two-hour cruises ($–$$) along Trinity Inlet. On your own, you walk around the **charmingly restored Gold Rush town**, along the Pier, the Tr ity Wharf and the Esplanade. Cairns Museum has aboriginal artifacts. If y want to go over to the reef on your own, ask locally about dive and cru operators ($$–$$$).

Melbourne, Australia   ★ ★ ★ ★

Language:	**English**	*English Spoken?:*	**Yes**
Currency:	**A$**	*US$ ok?:*	**No**
To town:	**Taxi**		

Melbourne, which reminds us of San Francisco to Sydney's Los Angel▪ considers itself the cultural, finance and banking center for Australia, a▪ prides itself on the Melbourne Cup races. Every visitor is urged to check o **the city's trams**, the beloved local equivalent of San Francisco's cable ca▪ The other irresistible (they think) local attraction is the **daily sunset fairy pe▪ guin parade** at Phillip Island, where the tiny creatures come out of the sea a▪ waddle to their nests on the beach, ignoring the mobs of people gathered ▪ gush over them. Shore excursions offered here include the ubiquitous ci▪ tour ($$) that covers gracious homes and gardens, the cathedral, Old Me bourne Gaol (jail) and some chic shopping at Toorak Village. A full day e▪ cursion ($$$) heads into the outback to Sovereign Hill and Ballarat, wher **the gold mining days of the 19th century** have been recreated. Highlights with in the city include the War Memorial, Arts Centre and City Square. Anoth▪ full day option is to the Dandenong Ranges and Healesville Sanctuary ($$$ the former some **surprisingly cool, lush forests** within an hour of Melbourn▪ the latter a refuge for the **platypus, koalas, kangaroos, birds of prey and othe▪ unique fauna indigenous** to Australia. A barbecue lunch (**and what's more indig enous than a barbie?**) is also included.

Perth, Australia ★★★

Language:	**English**	*English Spoken?:*	**Yes**
Currency:	**A$**	*US$ ok?:*	**No**
To town:	**Taxi or shuttle bus**		

Western Australia's capital city of Perth is located on the Swan River, which, because of its salt water, is one of the few rivers in the area that doesn't have **a flock of resident black swans**. Fremantle, 11 miles southwest, is the city's port and was **the host city when Australia won the America's Cup** in yacht racing in 1987. Botany enthusiasts flock here in Australia's spring (August-October) for the **unique and exotic wildflowers** like kangaroo paws. Shore excursions include half-day city tours of Perth and Fremantle ($$), a full-day beach and horseback riding tour with lunch ($$$), or all-day excursions ($$$) to the Pinnacles Desert and/or Yanchep National Park. On your own, you may enjoy wandering around the very pretty town of **Fremantle with its pubs, galleries, cafes and crafts markets**. The game fishing, surfing, diving and swimming are also considered by many as better than on the country's east coast. Perth's King's Park has an excellent botanical garden with some 3,000 different regional plant species. The Western Australia Museum has a good collection of aboriginal artifacts, plus an astonishing collection of meteorites up to 11 tons from the Outback. The Perth Zoo has **the world's only collection of numbats** (banded anteater), a wildlife park and a nocturnal house where visitors can observe the creatures of the night at work.

Sydney, Australia ★★★★★

Language:	**English**	*English Spoken?:*	**Yes**
Currency:	**A$**	*US$ ok?:*	**No**
To town:	**Walk**		

One of the most gorgeous harbors in the world greets the passengers of a cruise ship sailing into this spectacular city. The scene is a knockout—the angular Coathanger Bridge in the background, the Opera House with its white "sails" roof in the foreground. Great beaches for sunning and surfing abound, and for **the most photogenic city skyline** and Opera House view, take a boat ride across the water to the beguiling Taronga Zoo. Shore excursions here include city sightseeing and Opera House tour ($$), a half-day that visits the historic Rocks area, restored 19th-century homes, the southern beaches, cosmopolitan Kings Cross, Watson's Bay, **the famous surfing beach**

at **Bondi** and picturesque Paddington. Another half-day tour ($$) crosses
Coathanger Bridge for a dramatic view of the Opera House, then go
through the garden suburbs to Manly and its beaches, ending up at Penna
Hills Koala Sanctuary for a close-up look at Australia's sometimes peculi
looking wildlife. Also offered—an all-day motor coach tour to Katoom
and the Blue Mountains, with a stop at a koala park ($$$) and a helicop
overview ($$$). On your own, check out the **new Argyl Stores, restored wa
house shops** and the seafood cafes, galleries and boutiques along The Roc
a notorious district built by convicts in the 19th century. **Buy Australian opa
aboriginal art and—if you must—boomerangs**.

Auckland, New Zealand ★★★★

Language:	**English**	*English Spoken?:*	**Yes**
Currency:	**NZ$**	*US$ ok?:*	**No**
To town:	**Taxi or walk**		

Auckland's **yacht-filled Waitemata Harbour** is surrounded by volcanic hil
and this appealing and visitor-friendly city **offers more to do than the averag
day visitor has time for**. The city highlights tour ($$) visits Underwater Wor
Aquarium, stops at Mt. Eden for the view, the Domain park, the War M
morial Museum with its excellent collection of Maori war canoes, and Pa
nell's quaint shopping area and rose gardens. A three-quarter da
countryside tour ($$$) goes to St. Helier's Bay, then to Braeburn Farm for
demonstration of sheep dog herding and shearing, followed by a barbecu
lunch with New Zealand wines. A half-day version of the same tour with te
instead of lunch ($$) is also available. For passengers wanting to explore far
ther afield, the **Waitomo Glowworm Grotto**, much more interesting than i
sounds—think of Capri done up in organic Tivoli lights—makes a full-da
excursion ($$$), and an airplane or motor coach tour ($$$) to Rotorua'
smelly, bubbling thermal pools and Maori village and crafts center is als
sometimes offered. Rotorua is both the Maori homeland and a geotherma
center filled with bubbling mud pools and spouting geysers. Fishermen frea
out at the **giant brown and rainbow trout that look like they've been on a diet o
steroids**. On your own, you may wish to visit Parnell's artsy-craftsy boutique
and Victoria Park Market's flea market with great finds for collectors. The
there's always the **optimum New Zealand sport, bungy (bungee) jumping ($$$)**.

Bay of Islands, New Zealand ★★★

Language:	**English**	*English Spoken?:*	**Yes**
Currency:	**NZ$**	*US$ ok?:*	**No**
To town:	**Tender**		

When an already low-key New Zealander tells you where he goes to wind down, you can count on its being **a pretty relaxed place**. Bay of Islands is an area the kiwis like to call semi-tropical (actually it seems temperate to a couple of Californians), dotted with some 150 islands and discovered and popularized as a **deep-sea fishing capital** by American western novelist Zane Grey in the 1920s. It used to be a whaling port with a rowdy reputation—we dropped by Russell, "the hellhole of the Pacific," one Sunday afternoon but the bars were closed—that has softened in recent years. The number one excursion here is the **quaintly-named Fuller's Cream Trip ($$)**, a bay cruise aboard a vintage vessel that picks up dairy products from farms around the bay. Today tourists vastly outnumber milk containers but the trip is still folksy and fun; most people bring their own picnic lunch to munch on deck. The boat gets close to the Black Rocks to let you look nesting gulls in the eye, and when a dolphin or blue penguin is spotted, the captain maneuvers his craft so everybody gets a good picture. Sea kayaking and diving is also available. A bus tour around the area ($$) usually includes stops at the **Bay of Islands Maritime and Historic Park**, historic Waitangi where the Maoris signed a treaty of Queen Victoria's government in 1840, the Waitangi National Preserve where there's a magnificent war canoe and Maori meeting house on display, and the Opua Forest of rare kauri trees.

Christchurch, New Zealand ★★★

Language:	**English**	*English Spoken?:*	**Yes**
Currency:	**NZ$**	*US$ ok?:*	**No**
To town:	**Taxi**		

Christchurch is **more English than England**, with its schoolboys in Eton jackets; punts and swans on the River Avon, which meanders along grassy banks in the heart of town; spired Anglican cathedrals and English parks; and lawn bowling on trimly clipped greensward. A half-day city bus tour ($$) takes in the cathedral, Canterbury Museum, the Arts Centre, Botanic Gardens and Mona Vale Elizabethan homestead, with some free time for shopping. A half-day countryside tour ($$) covers the hills, coastline and harbor, plus a

short harbor cruise and a stop for tea. A wildlife excursion ($$) visits Ora
Park Wildlife Trust, where you can see **nocturnal kiwi in a special exhibit an**
drive-through lion reserve, and Peacock Springs animal reserve. A full-day vi
to Akaroa on the Banks Peninsula ($$$) includes a boat cruise on the *Ca*
terbury Cat. On your own, you can hop aboard a red London double-decl
bus called the English Connection (it runs between December and Febi
ary) for a short city tour ($) that lets you get on and off at several central I
cations. The Canterbury Arts Centre has some good **locally produced cra**
for sale, including pottery, jewelry, handmade toys, Maori carvings and a
tiques. Canoes can be rented along the Avon River or punts hailed at t
corner of Worcester Street and Oxford Terrace.

GETTING READY TO GO

If you have a special occasion to celebrate, let the line know ahead of time and they'll bake you a cake, as Cunard did for this couple.

Timetable

Two Months or More Ahead of Time:

—Get a passport (see Appendix, page 1073) or get your old one renewed if it's within six months of expiring.

—Apply for any visas you may need for ports of call. Some countries let you travel on a group visa so long as you stay with group excursions when ashore. If you want to strike out on your own, check to see if you need an individual visa. Then get it either through a visa service (usually quite costly and time-consuming) or, if you're in a city where there is a consulate or embassy from the country you're planning to visit, go down in person and apply. It takes only a few days, as a rule.

When Your Tickets Arrive:

—Sit down and examine carefully everything in the package, because the may be forms you need to fill out and mail or fax back to the line. At the ve least, there are forms that you should fill out at home before leaving rath than at the check-in counter at embarkation, when you may be holding up long line. And there will be valuable information dealing with life aboard th ship, wardrobe and how to communicate with you on the ship for those home.

—Give a copy of the satellite communications telephone number for th ship to whomever should contact you in an emergency, and threaten vic lence if they call when there is no emergency. (There's nothing scarier tha to be relaxing aboard a ship miles from land and have the radio officer rin your cabin with a call from home.)

—If you're traveling independently to the ship, take with you the nam and telephone number of the port agent for the city of embarkation, becaus sometimes a ship isn't where it's supposed to be when you arrive.

The Day or Night Before:

—Pack your bags, being sure to affix to each one the baggage tags th cruise line has sent, with your name and cabin number clearly written o each.

The Day of Your Flight
or Transfer to the Ship:

—Get to the airport (or the ship) comfortably early in case there's a traffi delay. Pay careful attention to boarding time and sailing time instructions. I you're too early, you'll sit around on a folding chair in a large terminal wait ing until you can board.

Carry casual clothes to wear on deck in the daytime, like this couple aboard the **Star Clipper;** *bathing suit coverups are always useful.*

Eleven Tips To Lighten Your Luggage

Lightweight Bags: We carry soft-sided but durable bags in small to medium sizes, tucking in an empty folding bag to bring dirty laundry or souvenirs back home. Try never to carry more than you can handle yourself, since you may arrive in some primitive place where there are no baggage carts, as in the Miami airport. While a ship doesn't care how much baggage you bring on board, the airline that gets you there can be sticky about overweight luggage. Also, cabin closet and drawer space may be limited on smaller ships or in lower category accommodations.

List: Work out a wardrobe list in advance to avoid those just-in-case clothes that get thrown in at the last minute and never worn. Remember that separates multiply, you can wear an outfit more than once, and sticking to basic color combinations means fewer shoes and accessories to coordinate.

Laundry: Virtually every cruise ship has a laundry, either self-service or send-out. Daytime clothes are casual and if they're washable as well, you don't need to take many. Dry-cleaning is available on most of the newer ships, and you'll often find irons and ironing boards in self-service laundries or from the housekeeping department for last-minute touch-ups.

Layering: Bulky garments add weight and take up space; instead, layer lightweight garments for air-conditioned areas and cool mornings on deck. You'll have more wardrobe variety as well. Wear your bulkiest clothing and shoes to the ship to save having to pack them.

Lightweight fabrics: Carry more light natural fibers such as cottons and linens to tropical climates; avoid synthetics, which tend to cling and don't breathe. Silks are nice for dressy evenings but wrinkle in the humidity on shore.

Location purchasing: Since you're going to be tempted by clothing in ports of call—T-shirts, caftans, pareus—you might as well plan for it. Take fewer casual items and shop with a clear conscience.

7. Little sizes: No, we don't mean clothing but toiletries; save those samples that come in the mail or buy the smallest possible tubes and containers before leaving. All but a few ships have complimentary toiletries in the cabins; we've tried to point out those that don't. (See Five Things You Won't Find Aboard under the cruise ship you're sailing aboard.)

8. Less is more: We've long ago limited gifts and souvenirs for friends back home to small, unbreakable, easily packed items such as scarves, flat placemats, leather goods including wallets or belts, rather than outsized, fragile items that have to be hand-carried.

9. Libraries: Don't carry a collection of hardbound best-sellers to read aboard; every ship has a library of some sort, from the *QE2's* magnificent collection to a small group of dog-eared paperbacks on an ACCL expedition vessel. Tuck a paperback or two into your luggage and then trade with someone else when you've finished.

10. Logic: Carry essentials including passport, tickets, traveler's checks, cash, extra glasses, cameras and prescription medications in hand baggage you always keep with you; never put them in a suitcase that may be checked.

11. Leave it out when in doubt: We've never yet come back from a cruise without at least one garment we carried and never wore. Other passengers usually don't notice if you're wearing the same thing several times; it's the pleasure of your company, not your wardrobe, that counts.

For many people, dressing up for formal night is a special part of the cruise.

Wardrobe Tips: Sequins Don't Wrinkle

Chances are, everything you need to pack for your cruise is already in your closet—(we know this doesn't make a good argument for someone using the cruise as an excuse to buy some smashing new clothes)—because people on ships wear the same clothes as people on land, regardless of what some department store fashion buyers seem to think.

In the daytime, casual shorts and T-shirts or jogging suits pass muster all over the ship, and in the evening, dress-up clothes of the sort you'd wear to a dinner party or nice restaurant will do just fine.

On the most classic and elegant ships, the dreaded words "formal night" do mean a tuxedo, dinner jacket or dark suit for a man, and a cocktail outfit or evening dress for women, but a blazer or sports jacket and tie for men, a

:ss or pantsuit for women, will be acceptable on most big Caribbean mass
irket lines such as Carnival, RCCL or NCL.

. few lines such as Star Clipper and Windstar ask only for "casual elegance"
the evenings and never require a jacket or tie. And Windjammer Barefoot
uises in their clever little "Windjammer Survival Booklet" (☎ 800-327-
01 to get a copy) says "With us dressing for dinner means putting on a
:an T-shirt."

Five Essentials to Pack in Your Hand Baggage

Prescription medications in their original containers.

Sunblock and a hat.

An extra pair of prescription eyeglasses or contact lenses.

A sweater to combat overzealous air conditioning on board.

Proof of citizenship—passport, copy of birth certificate or voter registration card; a driver's license is not acceptable.

Nice to Take Along

Camera and film (if you're a novice, practice at home with a roll or two before you leave).

Lightweight binoculars.

Small, packable guidebooks for the area.

INSIDER TIP

It's a good idea not to pack anything firm whether valuable or not in your checked baggage. In several major airports that handle a lot of cruise traffic (including New York's JFK) cameras and jewelry have a way of disappearing between the time the bag comes off the plane and when it gets into the baggage area.

Air/Sea Packages

If you've bought an air/sea package, the travel agent or cruise line has for-
arded your air tickets to you a distressingly short time before departure.
Nevertheless, take a moment and double-check the departure times and other
etails to be sure they coincide with the date and departure time of the
ruise. If you're traveling with a spouse, you may or may not be seated to-
:ether on the plane, since the block of tickets is run through a computer that
ouldn't care less about your marital bliss. If this happens to you, see if an-
•ther member of your group will change seats with one of you if you're all
lumped together.

Your route between home and the port may also be circuitous because of
:he airline hub system. If there's a long way to get there, you can count on
hat being your route. Should you have plenty of frequent flyer miles, you
:ould book the cruise at the cheaper cruise-only price and use your mileage
:o get to and from the port. The only downside there is if your cruise is can-
:elled at the last minute, the cruise line would probably not refund you the
•alue of your lost mileage.

Arriving at the Airport of Your Port City

With an air/sea package, you will find somewhere in the arrival airpor uniformed meet-and-greet holding a sign with the name of your ship cruise line on it. She may be at the gate or in the baggage area. She will you to claim your luggage and then mill about with the rest of your gro until everyone has his or her bags, or until the couple whose bag was lost to the baggage window and fill out the lost luggage forms.

Then you'll all be led as a group to your vehicles, and the meet-and-gre will supervise loading you and your baggage into the same or different ve cles. It's not a bad idea for a couple traveling together for one to get into t bus and get a seat for the two of you and the other watch the baggage unti is actually put into a vehicle.

Arriving at the Pier

The main difference between the port of Miami and the port of Los Ang les is that you'll be surrounded by porters to help you with your luggage the former, and you'll be surrounded by passengers trying to find a porter the latter. The porter will ferry your baggage from the taxi to the baggag loading area for the ship, or, if you've arrived by transfer on an air/sea pac age, the meet-and-greets will see to its transfer. Again, it's a good idea keep an eye on your bags as they're transferred.

You'll be ushered into a large hall where a lot of people are milling about standing in line. There will be from one to 10 counters with letters of the phabet above them. Queue up under the letter for your surname; if you are couple with different surnames, as we are, select the shorter of the two line You will turn in your cruise tickets, passports, and (please, please, pleas your already-filled-out forms, give them a credit card to imprint for o board charges, and they in turn will give you a boarding card, perhaps cabin key and part of your ticket. You will then be directed to the securi point where you'll put everything through the machines again, just as yo did at the airport. (If you're carrying 1000 ASA film for your cameras, th second X-ray dose could damage the film.)

> ### INSIDER TIP
> *You'll be expected to turn in your passport to the purser's staff when check-*
> *ing in aboard a ship and should not expect to see it again until the morning*
> *you disembark, except in certain Baltic and Black Sea ports where you pick*
> *it up from the purser and immediately turn it in to the port security officers*
> *at the bottom of the gangway. They return it to you when you come back to*
> *the ship and you turn it back into the purser's office.*

Security

Cruise passengers have gotten accustomed to the same security drills as air line passengers, running baggage through the X-ray devices and showing

rding pass to reboard the vessel. The newest precautionary safety mea-
introduced on some lines recently is the requirement of a photo ID to
k up the usual boarding card for passengers boarding and reboarding the
. This is particularly enforced in the Bahamas, where illegal immigrants
e been caught boarding ships with legitimate passengers by using another
eler's boarding card.

hipboard security officers like this Holland America stalwart stand at the
angway when ships are in port to enforce the "No Visitors" rule.

Visitors who have not made previous arrangements are not permitte[ ] board most ships in port. If you want to invite a friend on board for lunc[ ] a drink, be sure to ask well ahead of time at the purser's desk if it can be ranged.

Boarding

You will follow a long line of people carrying their hand baggage along interminable gangway, perhaps up some stairs or an escalator, perhaps al[ ] a covered walkway, to the point where a strip of tape has been stuck ac[ ] the floor and a man with a camera will order you to stop by a life ring [ ] smile. Try to look as cheerful as you can, because this photograph will be on display the next day for everyone on the ship to see.

When you cross over the threshold from the gangway into the ship, [ ] will be simultaneously greeted with a smile, handed some sheets of pa[ ] that you don't have anywhere to put, told to watch your step and watch y[ ] head, and have a white-gloved steward try to wrestle your hand baggage your shoulder while asking you your cabin number. He'll lead you to y[ ] cabin, where you may or may not be greeted by your cabin steward or st[ ] ardess, who introduces himself or herself politely and explains how to t[ ] on the TV and flush the toilet.

Check to see that your dining table assignment card is waiting in your cabin; [ ] not, go immediately to the maitre d'hotel and arrange it. The Rotterda[ ] *dining room here shows the variety of table sizes available.*

The First Five Things to Do After Boarding

1. Check the shipboard program to see when the lifeboat drill is held and what tim[ ] the welcome-aboard buffet lunch service shuts down.

2. Be sure your dining table assignment is set. If not, hie yourself to the maitre d[ ] table and get one.

Go to the spa or beauty salon in person to book all upcoming appointments for hair, nails, massage and facials.

Hurry to the library to check out that new best-seller or videotape you want to see; if the library is not staffed and things are locked up, make a mental note of what you want and check the shipboard program for the first opening time.

Unpack.

On Board

–Establish credit for your shipboard account.

On check-in or after boarding, you'll be asked to leave a credit card imprint establish your shipboard charge account. Most ships make it impossible to nd cash until check-out time. (On a few small vessels without a complete-computerized billing system, you may find that sales revert to cash at mid-ght the night before disembarkation to facilitate billing.) The purser's ice slips a bill under your cabin door the last night of the cruise, usually ıg after bedtime, and you don't need to stop by the desk at all unless you ve a question about it.

very ship sailing today has some sort of gym and fitness center, as well as door and outdoor pools where water exercises are held; this is aboard the lap ool on Princess Cruises' Royal Princess.

Spas

Almost every ship today sails with some sort of gym or fitness center; a jog-ing or walking track, either a specially surfaced ring around an upper deck r the passenger promenade deck; a daily exercise program that includes aer-bics and other energetic activities; and a menu that includes designated ow-fat, low-salt, low-calorie dishes. In addition, most have a full range of eauty, hair, nail and spa services, including manicures, pedicures, massage, ream baths, hydrotherepy, facials, herbal wraps and even mud/steam baths. he bigger the ship, the more the facilities.

Like most casinos, shops and photographic services, spas and beauty sh
at sea are operated by concessionaires. Steiner of London, which dates b
to 1903 when the company got its first royal warrent for hairdressing,
the lion's share of ship contracts, some 104 vessels at last count.

Passengers are urged to book massage and beauty services as quickly as p
sible after boarding, since the best times go quickly. Busiest days are w
the captain's formal welcome aboard and farewell parties are held.

Five Ways to Get Invited to the Captain's Table

1. Occupy the most expensive cabins aboard.
2. Be a many-time repeat passenger.
3. Be rich and/or famous, a travel agent or a member of the media.
4. Be an extremely attractive blonde, preferably Norwegian.
5. Have your travel agent make the request, describing you as a rich, famous, beauti
    Scandinavian, blonde travel writer.

The Lifeboat Drill

A mandatory lifeboat drill for all the ship's passengers and crew will
called within 24 hours after sailing from the port of embarkation. You will
told to go to your cabin and get your life jacket, then report to your lifeb
station as designated on a sign affixed to your cabin wall or door. Sometin
you report to a public lounge on the ship, sometimes directly to your b
station on deck. Crew members will be posted in each stairwell and hallw
to direct you to your station. It is requested that you not use the elevat
since in a real emergency, they might be disabled. The signal to gather
the lifeboat drill is seven short and one long blast on the ship's whistle. Y
stay at your station until released by the crew member in charge. Do
worry about struggling into your life jacket in the cabin; a crew member w
help you at the boat station if you need assistance. Smoking and drinki
during lifeboat drill is prohibited.

Steer clear of the ship's casino, like this one aboard RCCL's Majesty of th
Seas, *as well as the bingo games, if you're on a tight budget.*

Five Money-Saving Tips On Board

Take along your own soft drinks, wine or liquor (or buy them along the way in port) for pre-dinner libations in your cabin (but don't take your own drinks into the ship's public areas—that's a no-no). A few lines state that bringing your own liquor to your cabin is not allowable, but we've yet to see it enforced.

Ask the shore excursion staff about ways of doing your own sightseeing program ashore instead of buying a costly shore excursion; a group of four can sometimes negotiate a Caribbean island tour with a local cab driver for less than the cost of four excursions, and a couple can walk around a town in Alaska on their own and catch the highlights, using the shore excursion booklet as a guide.

If you have kids along, persuade them to participate in the youth programs and activities rather than hang out in the video arcades, where quarters have a way of melting away quickly.

Steer clear of the casino and bingo games on board if you're on a tight budget, or set aside the amount of money you can afford to lose and don't dip any deeper.

If your shopping resistance is low, concentrate on sightseeing instead; otherwise you'll end up with bulky shopping bags full of things that are not as irresistible as you thought when you get them home.

INSIDER TIP

To get better service than the other passengers doesn't cost a thing; just read a crew member's name tag, look him in the eye, call him by name, smile and say thank you and show an interest in him as an individual. And remember the name next time without having to look at the name tag.

KEELHAUL

Many cruise lines now offer "port lecturers" who hand out maps to what they call "recommended" shops where the merchandise is "guaranteed." All this means is that the shops listed on the maps have paid to be listed and give commissions to both the "lecturer" and the cruise line. Most promise a 30-day opportunity to return or exchange defective merchandise, but any legitimate shopkeeper should promise the same. Too many passengers read these maps without realizing they are commercial ventures, and become fearful of going into a "non-guaranteed" shop and getting ripped off.

Shore Excursions

A few cruise lines, primarily expedition vessels, include shore excursions in the base price, but aboard most ships, you'll be offered a variety of optional group port tours that may range from an inexpensive walking tour of Key West to a costly helicopter flight over a glacier or volcano.

Early in the sailing, the shore excursions director will hold one or more sessions to describe the tours as well as shopping pointers and ways to tour on your own. You're usually given a printed form with the excursions and prices on them, which you fill out and turn in to the shore excursions office. The excursions are then charged against your shipboard account, and the tickets or vouchers delivered to your cabin. Take care of your tickets and remember to have them along with you, "ripped and ready" as one shore excursions manager used to say, when you go ashore to take the tour. No ticket, tour.

If you're on a budget, you'll want to weigh carefully which excursion take and which to skip. Consider taking your own walking tour in a sr port rather than getting on a bus or in a van with the others. The shore cursions manager can usually give you some advice.

Remember too that certain excursions have limited participation, s there's something you can't live without, get to the shore excursions of as soon as possible after that tour is open for booking. Some cruise lines let your travel agent book a tour for you ahead of time so you're guarant a spot.

The usual shore excursions offered in each port will be described under name of the port, starting on page 823.

Scoping Out Seasickness

The recent removal of the Transderm Scop seasickness "patch" from market was a better-late-than-never move for this often-dangerous drug p ceived as innocuous by its users because it resembled the harmless and fan iar Band-Aid. Over the years we've encountered numerous serious med incidents because of the patch, whose main medical ingredient was scopo mine. The former prescription-only medication carried a lengthy caution sheet in fine print inside each package which we are confident few if any of users ever read. Adverse reactions ran from dryness in the mouth (two-thi of its users) to disorientation and loss of memory, particularly in older use

There are much safer and equally effective treatments for seasickness, well as some unusual remedies, included in the following roster:

1. Sea Band or Travel Garde bracelet-like knit bands worn around the wrist at acupre sure points to relieve symptons of nausea.

2. Ginger root capsules, available in health food stores or Asian pharmacies, tak before meals.

3. Nonprescription antihistamine remedies such as Dramamine, Antivert or Boni can be taken one or two hours before sailing but may cause drowsiness.

4. Some shipboard doctors recommend a Dramamine injection, which works mo quickly than an ingested tablet for a sudden or severe onset of seasickness.

Sidestepping Seasickness

But we have a more revolutionary cure for seasickness—a malady we mu confess we've never suffered, but we do have sympathy for its victims. He are three things to do if you're worried about a little mal de mer.

1. Select the right ship.

2. Sail the smoothest waters.

3. Sleep in the steadiest beds.

Pick a ship with little rolling and no pitching motion, such as the uniqu twin hulled *Radisson Diamond,* which moves smoothly (if rather slowl through the water with little discernible side to side motion and no back t front motion. Fixed inboard stabilizers counteract both roll and pitch, an pitch and heave are reduced because the water is funneled between the tw pontoons of the catamaran-like ship.

he sail-cruise vessels such as the Windstar and Club Med ships have com-
ter-trimmed and operated sails that keep the ships at an even keel when
ey proceed under sail, with heeling kept well under 6 percent.

hips with a deeper draft (the measurement of the ship's waterline to the
west point of its keel) usually perform better in rough seas than ships with
allow drafts. For instance, Norwegian Cruise Line's *Norway*, built as the
ansatlantic liner *France*, has a 35-foot draft that forces her to anchor rather
an come alongside in her Caribbean ports but sure does make getting
ere smoother.

Destinations and itineraries can make a big difference for passengers con-
rned about ship motion. Plan to sail in sheltered waters such as Alaska's In-
le Passage or along one of the great rivers of the world, where land is in
ght and waters are calm. Conversely, in areas where two seas meet—Cabo
n Lucas, Mexico, where the Sea of Cortez meets the Pacific, for instance,
South Africa's Cape of Good Hope or South America's Cape Horn—are
otorious waters. Areas with powerful currents that have a speed greater
an 0.8 knots an hour—the Falklands, South Indian Ocean, Bay of Bengal,
ay of Biscay, Solomon Sea, Java Sea, Bering Strait, Spitsbergen and the An-
ulhas Current along the southern tip of Africa—can really stir up the water.

Other rough sea reliables include the North Atlantic, the South China Sea,
e Aegean in summer, the Shetlands and west coast of Scotland. In our ex-
eriences over the years, areas that stand out dramatically are an April cross-
g on the North Atlantic, Cape Horn and the Drake Passage on a January
ntarctic sailing, a November sailing along the coast of West Africa off
Jamibia, and the seas around Nome, Alaska, anytime.

The smoothest ride on most ships is on a lower deck in an amidships cabin.
he higher-priced sun and boat deck cabins give more bounce and roll. But
ook a cabin too close to the bow or stem, and you may feel every swell.
aking an outside cabin near the waterline bothers some cruisers, because
he seas slosh across the little round window like a washing machine in the
undromat.

Take your camera manual and spare batteries with you on your cruise,
especially if you're going into severe weather areas such as the Antarctic to
photograph icebergs from the deck of the **World Discoverer.**

Ten Tips for First-Time Photographers

1. Take your camera manual with you on the cruise so if you have problems, a mo experienced photographer on board can help you figure it out.

2. Always take a set of spare batteries and have them along with you when you ashore.

3. When photographing people on deck or ashore against bright backgrounds, u your flash to fill in extra light on their faces.

4. Don't rest your elbows or camera against the ship's rail to steady it; the ship's vibr tions will make your photo blur.

5. If you want to shoot pictures through the window of a tour bus, put your camera close as possible to the glass without touching it; be aware tinted windows can c down on your light and alter the colors of the subject. And using the flash will gi you a beautiful picture of a white light in the bus window.

6. On deck, in small boats and Zodiacs, carry a plastic bag to slip over your camera keep the salt spray from splashing it.

7. If you're traveling with a borrowed camera, get it far enough in advance so you ca shoot a practice roll and develop it before leaving home.

8. When photographing lounge shows or lecturers indoors on a cruise ship, be awa how far the light from your flash will carry; it may be necessary to move forward in a better position to get your shot, but do it quietly and don't block anyone else view. Some ships do not allow flash pictures during a show and almost all ban th use of video cameras.

9. If you hold your camera firmly in both hands, push your elbows against your ri cage, begin mentally counting backwards from 10 to 1 and midway squeeze th camera button strange as it may sound, you can get a steadier shot in a low light si uation.

10. Think in terms of telling a story with your cruise photographs—photograph the li ring with the ship's name on it, your cabin, your waiters and stewards, even yourse in the mirror dressed for the captain's dinner.

The purser's or hotel manager's desk, usually in the main lobby, as here aboard **Renaissance III,** *is the place to take your complaints in most cases.*

Where to Complain

Cruises score higher on passenger satisfaction surveys than any other form leisure travel. But if things go wrong, the worst thing you can do is seethe ently and complain to your travel agent after you get back home, or mutter out it to fellow passengers. That only aggravates the annoyance.

Instead, when you have a specific problem during your cruise, take it immediately to the person responsible for that area of service, speak calmly and plain the situation in a reasonable tone of voice.

—Cabin or cabin service complaints should go to the housekeeper; if it oesn't work out, go to the hotel manager.

—Dining room complaints should be taken up with the maitre d'hotel or ne dining room captain responsible for your table area; if you don't get satfaction, go to the hotel manager or chief purser.

—Ship charges or procedures should be discussed with the purser's desk or nformation desk.

—Always point out any problems or complaints on the questionnaire ou're given at the end of the cruise. Everyone up to and including the chairnan of the board and the ship owner read these whenever there is a serious omplaint. And don't be coerced by an anxious waiter or steward to give an xcellent rating when not warranted just because he says he may lose his job s a result.

KEELHAUL

We give a punishing Keelhaul Award to those litigious passengers who threaten to sue cruise lines because there happened to be a hurricane or storm at sea that spoiled their vacation. When was the last time they sued Holiday Inn or Marriott under similar circumstances?

The Romance of Sail!

S AIL into the past in modern-day comfort. Described by the press as one of the most elegant of the remaining tall ships, SIR FRANCIS DRAKE is restored to meet the high standards of today's discriminating traveller.

Built in 1917, you'll share this historic 165' schooner with 30 fun-loving sailmates while cruising the crystal-clear waters of the British Virgin Islands and other exotic Caribbean ports of call. This is cruising as it was meant to be done! The winter itinerary departs every Saturday from Roadtown, Tortola, BVI, on delightful 7-night cruises, between November and June each year. Summer itineraries vary from year to year so that returning passengers can experience new island getaways. Accommodations are comfortable double- and single-berth, air-conditioned cabins, each with private bath and shower. Great for singles, couples, and groups.

Anchor in secluded coves and bays with brilliant beaches and a rainbow of tropical fish in balmy turquoise waters. Visit lush, unspoiled islands with quaint local cultures.

Full-ship charter rates and group rates available.

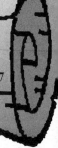

Tall Ship Adventures, Inc.

1389 S. Havana St. • Aurora, CO 80012
(303) 755-7983 • 800-662-0090 • Fax (303) 755-9007

THE END OF THE CRUISE

Despite the highly polished service, the cadre of dining room stewards aboard the Seabourn Spirit does not accept gratuities.

Tipping

It used to be that any article on shipboard tipping—"shipboard gratuities," as the cruise line brochures like to call it—dealt simply with whom, how much and when. At some point in his disembarkation lecture, the cruise director would say, "So many passengers have asked us about whom and how much to tip..." and launch into an easy-to-compute per-person-per-day figure for the waiters and the cabin stewards.

Then you would go back to your cabin and figure out how much to tip each, get some change and slip that amount into the little envelopes that had a way of appearing in your cabin just when needed. You might put a little extra cash in for someone who was extra solicitous, knock off a little from someone else who had done less than you expected.

That was the way it used to be.

In the late 1970s, Holland America Line, which trains its own employee special hotel schools in Indonesia and the Philippines, implemented a " tipping required" policy. "We don't say tipping is not permitted," a spokesman explained, "simply that it is not required. A passenger is free tip any of our serving personnel if he wishes, but those personnel are not p mitted to solicit tips in any fashion."

Then in 1984, Sea Goddess Cruises came along with an even more expl rule—"If you are concerned about tipping, the Sea Goddess concept is qu simple: gratuities are discouraged."

Seabourn went them one further in 1990; the company "strictly prohib all staff for any solicitation or acceptance of gratuities."

Even more astonishing is that we were getting excellent service on all th lines, erasing that notion that the word "tip" was an acronym "to inst promptness."

Well, if that isn't case, what is a gratuity? Is it a voluntary reward extra-special service, or is it, as in most European hotels and restaurants percentage charged for service and as routine a part of the bill as taxes? Anc that's so, why couldn't it be added into the base cruise fare?

An automatic up-front payment would eliminate the problem crew mei bers face called "stiffing"—a passenger leaving no tip whatsoever on a cru where tipping is expected.

Aboard some ships, tips are automatically calculated and added to the pa senger's shipboard account. And on most ships, bar service charges of percent are automatically added to the drink tab. Cunard established a poli a couple of years ago of letting passengers who were uncomfortable with tl matter of tipping pay the usual amount up-front.

On Crystal's ships, you can even charge your tips on your shipboard a count and receive in exchange small printed cards to sign and present to you waiters and cabin steward, who later turn them in for cash. This relieves yc of adding and multiplying chores and the necessity of going down to tl purser to get change.

Some of the confusion about tipping comes from ships with open-seatir policies. Since you may have a different waiter each time, how do you kno whom to tip?

The Greek stewards' union requests each passenger set aside a prescribe amount that is pooled and divided among the crew under a prescribed foi mula. The usual argument that a crew member will work harder if he's hop ing for a tip doesn't apply here, since everyone's going to get the same (Insiders say peer pressure shapes up any lazy stewards on a Greek ship.)

Some of the smaller American ships and expedition vessels also use the poc system for tips.

Anytime we mention tipping in our newspaper columns, the mail is fast an furious, very little if any of it defending the practice of tipping. The most au dible complaints come not from first-timers but veteran cruisers.

Here are some of the questions raised—Should the person who eats break fast and lunch from the self-service buffet and goes ashore for dinner when the ship is in port be expected to leave the same amount as the passenge

⊃ shows up in the dining room for all three meals every day? And should
couple in the small inside cabin on the lower decks give the same stew-
's tip as the couple in the big boat deck suite?

hese are questions for which there are no easy answers. In the meantime,
find out the recommended tip amounts for each ship, check that ship's
ing in the guide.

The Last Day: Don't You Love Me Any More?

veryone at your table has hugged goodbyes the night before, after each
s discreetly handed out the tips in their proper little envelopes and ex-
ssed a heartfelt thanks to the dining room stewards. The evening is always
g and loud after a short cruise, with everyone getting in their last few
urs of drinking and gambling and dancing, and quiet and downbeat after
ong cruise, when the difficult transition to going home has to be made.

3ags go into the hall at midnight or sometime before 6 a.m. They'll be
thered up and ferried to a central area on the ship and transferred ashore
:er the ship has been secured the next morning.

No passengers are permitted to disembark until all the luggage has been
loaded and put ashore.

> **INSIDER TIP**
>
> *Obvious as this may seem, you must be scrupulously careful setting aside the
> clothing you need to travel in the next day, all the items including shoes and
> underwear, before putting your bags outside your door for collection. You
> won't see them again until you're back on shore. Pajamas are not proper
> debarkation attire.*

Breakfast service is more limited on disembarkation day, with the added ag-
ravation in American ports that the tea is terrible because there's so much
hlorine in the water in case the kitchen has a surprise public health inspec-
on, and there are no poached eggs because for some mysterious reason, the
itchen cannot poach eggs if the public health inspectors are aboard.

If your waiters are friendly but a little withdrawn, it's because, on many
hips, they're the same busy beavers that spent the night lugging luggage
own the halls and so have had maybe two hours of sleep maximum. Your
ablemates, your best friends for life during the past week or so, may seem in-
ordinately concerned with airport and getting home details, but you all ex-
hange addresses and phone numbers.

You say goodbye a dozen times to everyone while you're milling about
vaiting for the ship to be cleared by customs and immigration and for your
group's turn to depart.

Getting Off

You have been given color-coded baggage tags depending on aircraft departure times or ongoing arrangements, and your baggage will be waiting in
the customs hall in the color-coded group. Do not panic; it is probably there

somewhere. Gather it up, getting a porter if you need one or lugging it by yourself if you don't.

You will have been given a U.S. customs form to fill out, which you turn in at the gate as you leave. Most cruise ships arriving in U.S. ports h customs and immigration officials on board who have precleared your p. port and customs forms before you disembark the ship.

INSIDER TIP

It's a good idea to take a close look at your bag before setting it out in the hall. When you get on the dock, you'll see a dozen just like it. The idea is to pick up the one belonging to you. We have seen passengers wandering around with no idea of what their bags actually look like.

Going Home

If you're on the air/sea package, your return to the airport and home v be very similar to your arrival, with the meet-and-greets on hand with th signs and advice. If you're in the port of Miami or Ft. Lauderdale and flyi with a major airline, after you claim your baggage and clear customs at t port, you can trundle it right over to the airline's baggage truck at the p and check it in there, trusting it will arrive in your home airport when y do. It usually does.

APPENDIX: THE NUTS AND BOLTS

w to get a passport:

Apply in person at one of the 3500 clerks of court or post offices which accept applications, or at one of the 13 passport agencies in the United States.

Present two passport photographs (go to a photographer who specializes in these), a photo ID with your signature such as an active driver's license, and proof of citizenship or nationality—a certified copy of a birth certificate, a Certificate of Naturalization or an expired U.S. passport.

Pay $65 if you're over 18, $40 if you're under 18, and turn in or mail in the completed printed form you were given to fill out. If you're renewing your passport, pay $55.

w to select a travel agent:

Take as much time and care with your choice as when choosing a mate, looking for intelligence, warmth, patience, friendliness and diligence. A knowledge of basic geography is helpful too.

Look for professional associations; the agent should be a member of ASTA (American Society of Travel Agents), ARTA (Association of Retail Travel Agents), CLIA (Cruise Lines International Association) and/or NACOA (National Association of Cruise Only Agents). The latter specialize in cruises, but it does not mean they are more qualified on the subject than "full service" agents, only that they are specialists.

Whenever you book a cruise ticket through an agent, the agent receives a commission from the cruise line, not from you. There may be surcharges on other agency services, however, with the recent airline caps restricting the commission an agent can make from booking an air ticket.

low to go through immigration:

Have your passport ready and in your hand.

Be sure you're in the correct line; signs often indicate certain lines are restricted to airline crews, nationals of that country or members of European Community nations only.

When you near the immigration officer, be sure to remain behind the taped or painted line on the floor until the person ahead of you has finished and left.

Answer any questions asked, but don't volunteer comments, and don't fidget while he's examining your passport.

How to go through customs:

Have ready any receipts for large purchases you may have made on the trip.

Fill out the requisite form honestly.

Be prepared to open any bags or suitcases if requested, but never hesitate or ask officer if he wants it opened, even when the man in front of you has had to open

Trip cancellation insurance:

This covers you if you have to cancel your cruise at the last minute, after the full has been paid and the cancellation penalties kick in, because of illness, death in family or business emergencies.

Travel agents usually recommend a client take this insurance; some of the more c tious even ask a client who refuses it to sign a form indicating they were offered insurance. Cruise lines, while not wanting to appear heartless, point out that wh an emergency of this sort may happen once in your lifetime, it happens to th every sailing.

Vaccinations and medications:

If you are going to exotic areas of the world, check with your doctor or pub health authorities about any medications or vaccinations recommended for travel to that region. Remember that if you eat and sleep only aboard the cruise ship y will not be taking the same risks as someone on a trek or a safari.

Port Taxes:

Those friendly tropical islands who love tourists also love slapping on huge p taxes, also sometimes called "head taxes," for visitors. The highest one we' encountered in North American waters is Bermuda's $60 a passenger.

Some sharp-eyed cruisers may note that the cruise line's port fees may actua exceed the total of the individual ports' actual taxes. The usual explanation for th is administrative costs, whatever that means.

Pre- and post-cruise packages:

Most cruise line brochures have add-on pre- or post-cruise packages for the cities embarkation and disembarkation. If you're interested in such a package, discuss with your travel agent to be sure the hotel being used is one you would like and th the price is less than you could get on your own. The upside of these packages is th they usually include transfers, which could save a lot of money in some cities.

INDEX

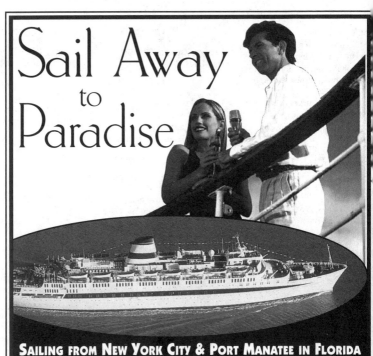

Order Your Guide to Travel and Adventure

Title	ISBN	Price
Fielding's Alaska Cruises and the Inside Passage	1-56952-068-2	$18.95
Fielding's The Amazon	1-56952-000-3	$16.95
Fielding's Asia's Top Dive Sites	1-56952-129-8	$19.95
Fielding's Australia	1-56952-097-6	$16.95
Fielding's Bahamas	1-56952-105-0	$16.95
Fielding's Baja California	1-56952-106-9	$18.95
Fielding's Bermuda	1-56952-107-7	$16.95
Fielding's Borneo	1-56952-026-7	$18.95
Fielding's Budget Europe	1-56952-084-4	$17.95
Fielding's Caribbean	1-56952-109-3	$18.95
Fielding's Caribbean Cruises	1-56952-126-3	$18.95
Fielding's Disney World and Orlando	1-56952-110-7	$18.95
Fielding's Diving Indonesia	1-56952-089-5	$19.95
Fielding's Eastern Caribbean	1-56952-120-4	$17.95
Fielding's England	1-56952-108-5	$17.95
Fielding's Europe	1-56952-087-9	$18.95
Fielding's European Cruises	1-56952-074-7	$18.95
Fielding's Far East	1-56952-111-5	$18.95
Fielding's France	1-56952-112-3	$18.95
Fielding's Freewheelin' USA	1-56952-125-5	$18.95
Fielding's Hawaii	1-56952-113-1	$18.95
Fielding's Italy	1-56952-116-6	$18.95
Fielding's Kenya	1-56952-038-0	$16.95
Fielding's Las Vegas Agenda	1-56952-075-5	$14.95
Fielding's London Agenda	1-56952-039-9	$14.95
Fielding's Los Angeles	1-56952-117-4	$16.95
Fielding's Malaysia & Singapore	1-56952-041-0	$16.95
Fielding's Mexico	1-56952-118-2	$18.95
Fielding's New Orleans Agenda	1-56952-122-0	$16.95
Fielding's New York Agenda	1-56952-124-7	$16.95
Fielding's New Zealand	1-56952-101-8	$16.95
Fielding's Paris Agenda	1-56952-045-3	$14.95
Fielding's Portugal	1-56952-102-6	$16.95
Fielding's Paradors, Pousadas and Charming Villages	1-56952-119-0	$18.95
Fielding's Rome Agenda	1-56952-077-1	$14.95
Fielding's San Diego Agenda	1-56952-088-7	$14.95
Fielding's Southeast Asia	1-56952-065-8	$18.95
Fielding's Southern Vietnam on 2 Wheels	1-56952-064-X	$15.95
Fielding's Spain	1-56952-127-1	$18.95
Fielding's Surfing Indonesia	1-56952-093-3	$19.95
Fielding's Sydney Agenda	1-56952-123-9	$16.95
Fielding's Thailand, Cambodia, Laos and Myanmar	1-56952-069-0	$18.95
Fielding's Vacation Places Rated	1-56952-062-3	$19.95
Fielding's Vietnam	1-56952-095-X	$17.95
Fielding's Western Caribbean	1-56952-121-2	$18.95
Fielding's The World's Most Dangerous Places	1-56952-104-2	$19.95
Fielding's Worldwide Cruises '97	1-56952-115-8	$19.95

To place an order: call toll-free 1-800-FW-2-GUIDE
(VISA, MasterCard and American Express accepted)
or send your check or money order to:
Fielding Worldwide, Inc., 308 S. Catalina Avenue, Redondo Beach, CA 90277
add $2.00 per book for shipping & handling (sorry, no COD's), allow 2–6 weeks for delivery

NEW FIELDINGWEAR!

Now that you own a Fielding travel guide, you have graduated from being a tourist to a full-fledged traveler! Celebrate your elevated position by proudly wearing one of these heavy-duty, all-cotton shirts, selected by our authors for their comfort and durability (and their ability to hide dirt). Choose from three styles—radical "World Tour," politically correct "Do the World Right," and elegant "All-Access."

Important note: Fielding authors have field-tested these shirts and found that they can be swapped for much more than their purchase price in free drinks at some of the world's hottest clubs and in-spots. They also make great gifts.

WORLD TOUR

Hit the hard road with a travel fashion statement for our times. Visit all 35 of Mr. D.P.'s favorite nasty spots (listed on the back), or just look like you're going to. This is the real McCoy, worn by mujahadeen, mercenaries, U.N. peacekeepers and the authors of Fielding's *The World's Most Dangerous Places.* Black, XL, heavy-duty 100% cotton. Made in the U.S.A. $18.00.

DO THE WORLD RIGHT

Start your next adventure wearing Fielding's politically correct "Do the World Right" shirt, complete with freaked-out red globe and blasting white type. A shirt that tells the world that within that high-mileage, overly educated body beats the heart of a true party animal. Only for adrenaline junkies, hard-core travelers and seekers of knowledge. Black, XL, heavy-duty 100% cotton. Made in the U.S.A. $18.00.

Name:

Address:

City:

State: Zip:

ALL-ACCESS

Strike terror into the snootiest maitre d', make concierges cringe, or just use this elegant shirt as the ultimate party invitation. The combination of the understated red Fielding logo embroidered on a jet-black golf shirt will get you into the snobbiest embassy party or jumping nightspot. An elegant casual shirt for those who travel in style and comfort. Black, XL or L, 100% preshrunk cotton, embroidered Fielding Travel Guide logo on front. Made in the U.S.A. $29.00.

Telephone:
Shirt Name:
Quantity:

For each shirt, add $4 shipping and handling. California residents add $1.50 sales tax. Allow 2 to 4 weeks for delivery.
Send check or money order with your order form to:

Fielding Worldwide, Inc.
308 South Catalina Ave.
Redondo Beach, CA 90277

Or
order your shirts by phone:
1-800-FW-2-GUIDE
Visa, MC, AMex accepted

Yesterday while you were

watching TV

working at your desk

sitting in traffic

cleaning your sink

a magnificent ship left port

to explore the oceans of your planet.

(Why weren't you on it?)

It's different

out here.

NORWEGIAN
CRUISE LINE

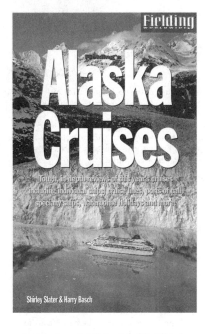

FIELDING'S CARIBBEAN

"A candid and fascinating look at the region."
—Washington Times

This annually updated handbook to the Caribbean is the ultimate escape-vacation guide to more than 40 islands. It contains everything the reader needs to know to plan a vacation—including choice hotels, ways to save money, and the best places to go for romance or adventure.

With 155 maps, 3-D tour guides and b/w photos.

- *Candid reviews:* More than 1500 star-rated listings of hotels and restaurants, along with 180 special-interest comparison charts.
- *Ideas for high adventure:* Including hiking to the summit of La Soufriere volcano, exploring coral reefs, taking a submarine ride, trekking through the rain forest, sailing to uninhabited islands, diving off a cliff and river rafting.
- *Island comparisons:* The best islands for singles or families, as well as for watersports, trekking or partying—or for doing absolutely nothing!
- *Tips on music and celebrations:* The best carnivals, jazz festivals, nightclubs and spots for local music.

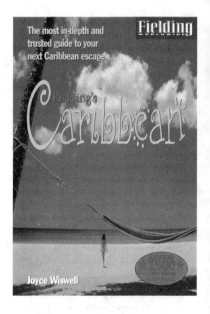

1024 pages, 5" x 7-1/4", 50 b/w photos, 155 maps, 3-D tour guides

September 1996

$18.95

UK £10.95 CAN $23.95 AUS $24.95

ISBN 1-56952-109-3

Replaces ISBN#1-56952-085-2

FIELDING'S CARIBBEAN CRUISES

Frank, in-depth reviews of every major ship that sails the Caribbean.

The most comprehensive guide to the ships that ply the Caribbean and all 35 ports of call. Written in a descriptive, entertaining style, it contains all the facts the reader needs to choose the right ship and the right destinations.

Filled with hundreds of helpful hints, loads of charts and tables, plus 43 maps, 150 b/w photos and 868 restaurant and attraction listings.

- *Comprehensive reviews:* Profiles of 87 ships, from luxury liners to chartered yachts and sailing vessels, including facilities, features and star-ratings.
- *Ship comparisons:* Which ships are best for singles, families, seniors, adventurers or honeymooners—plus theme cruises.
- *Essential info:* From how to reserve a cabin, book a table, pack the right stuff, to even avoid seasickness—plus how much to tip and safety measures at sea.
- *Ideas for things to do in the various ports of call:* Such as explore bustling Fort-de-France on Martinique and tour the colorful gabled houses in Willemstad.

976 pages, 5-3/8" x 8-3/8", 150 b/w photos, 43 maps
October 1996

$18.95

UK £10.95 CAN $23.95 AUS $24.95
ISBN 1-56952-126-3
Replaces ISBN#1-56952-070-4

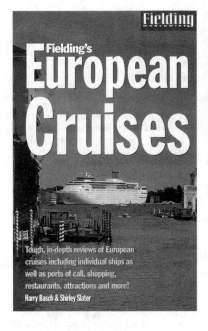

International Conversions

TEMPERATURE

To convert °F to °C, subtract 32 and divide by 1.8.

To convert °C to °F, multiply by 1.8 and add 32.

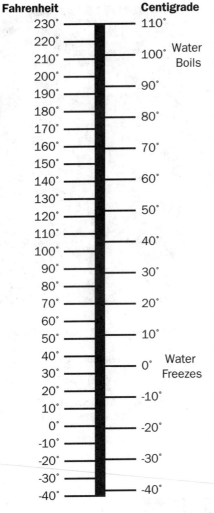

Fahrenheit / **Centigrade**

100° — Water Boils
0° — Water Freezes

WEIGHTS & MEASURES

LENGTH		
1 km	=	0.62 miles
1 mile	=	1.609 km
1 meter	=	1.2936 yards
1 meter	=	3.28 feet
1 yard	=	0.9144 meters
1 yard	=	3 feet
1 foot	=	30.48 centimeters
1 centimeter	=	0.39 inch
1 inch	=	2.54 centimeters

AREA		
1 square km	=	0.3861 square miles
1 square mile	=	2.590 square km
1 hectare	=	2.47 acres
1 acre	=	0.405 hectare

VOLUME		
1 cubic meter	=	1.307 cubic yards
1 cubic yard	=	0.765 cubic meter
1 cubic yard	=	27 cubic feet
1 cubic foot	=	0.028 cubic meter
1 cubic centimeter	=	0.061 cubic inch
1 cubic inch	=	16.387 cubic centimeters

CAPACITY		
1 gallon	=	3.785 liters
1 quart	=	0.94635 liters
1 liter	=	1.057 quarts
1 pint	=	473 milliliters
1 fluid ounce	=	29.573 milliliters

MASS and WEIGHT		
1 metric ton	=	1.102 short tons
1 metric ton	=	1000 kilograms
1 short ton	=	.90718 metric ton
1 long ton	=	1.016 metric tons
1 long ton	=	2240 pounds
1 pound	=	0.4536 kilograms
1 kilogram	=	2.2046 pounds
1 ounce	=	28.35 grams
1 gram	=	0.035 ounce
1 milligram	=	0.015 grain

cm 0 1 2 3 4 5 6 7 8 9 10

Inch 0 1 2 3 4